THE GUIDE OF THE PERPLEXED

THE GUIDE

OF THE

PERPLEXED

Moses Maimonides

Translated with an Introduction and Notes by

SHLOMO PINES

With an Introductory Essay by

LEO STRAUSS

THE

UNIVERSITY OF CHICAGO

PRESS

THE UNIVERSITY OF CHICAGO PRESS, CHICAGO AND LONDON
THE UNIVERSITY OF TORONTO PRESS, TORONTO 5, CANADA

© 1963 BY THE UNIVERSITY OF CHICAGO. PUBLISHED 1963

LIBRARY OF CONGRESS CATALOG CARD NUMBER: 62-18113

PUBLISHED WITH THE AID OF THE BOLLINGEN FOUNDATION

PRINTED IN GREAT BRITAIN

DESIGNED BY ANDOR BRAUN

SPONSORS

*

ACKNOWLEDGMENT

*

To Professor Ralph Lerner of the University of Chicago we wish to express our deepest thanks for the most valuable editorial task he has performed. He has contributed greatly to giving this translation an English style that reflects Maimonides' subtle prose. This contribution involved repeated recourse to both the Arabic and Hebrew versions of the *Guide* in order to verify the consistency and clarity of the translation. While we must absolve him of any responsibility for such defects as may still exist, we are very much obliged to Professor Lerner for his devoted labors, skill, patience, and wise understanding of the problems.

Shlomo Pines
Leo Strauss

PREFACE

*

EVERYONE connected with the production of this translation of Maimonides' *Guide of the Perplexed* has long felt that such a new translation was necessary. The legitimate demand that must be made of any translation is not satisfied by any of the existing modern language translations of the *Guide*. We rightly demand that a translation should remain as close as is practicable to the original, that within the limits of the possible it should give the reader an impression — both in general and in detail — resembling the impression offered by the original. In the present translation, pains have been taken to meet this demand. As far as was compatible with intelligibility, every Arabic technical term has been rendered by one and the same English term. Wherever the original is ambiguous or obscure, the translation has preserved or attempted to preserve that very ambiguity or obscurity. A special effort has been made to reproduce the artful interplay of Maimonides' Arabic text with his Hebrew and Aramaic quotations from the classic Jewish sources. Besides, considerable progress has been made, within the last generation, in the understanding of the *Guide*. These advances have, of course, been based on a close study of the original text, and as always in such cases, by virtue of these advances the existing translations prove now to be less adequate than they had appeared to be before. In other words, to the extent that earlier translators were not sufficiently sensitive to certain facets of the *Guide*, their translations failed to disclose those facets. A single example must suffice: where Maimonides speaks of "political," previous translators speak of "social"; where Maimonides says "city," they translate "state"; where Maimonides speaks of "political civic actions," they speak of "social conduct." A moment's reflection shows that an entirely different perspective is provided when the political is mentioned, rather than the social.

The present translation is based on the Arabic text established by S. Munk *Le Guide des Égarés*; 3 vols.; Paris, 1856–66) and edited with variant readings

Preface

by Issachar Joel (*Dalālat al-ḥaʾirīn;* Jerusalem: J. Junovitch, 5691 [1930/31]). Where the readings adopted by Munk and Joel have not been followed, this has been noted. The pagination of the Munk edition is indicated by thin vertical lines in the body of the text and by bracketed numerals in the running head. These numerals refer to those pages of the Arabic text whose beginnings are denoted by the first and last vertical lines occurring on the two facing pages. Italic type in the text has been reserved to indicate Maimonides' use of words that are clearly identifiable as being Hebrew or Aramaic. The division of the text into parts and chapters is Maimonides'. The Arabic text has no paragraphing, very little punctuation, and, of course, no capitalization; the translator is responsible for such features in this volume.

Shlomo Pines
Leo Strauss

CONTENTS

*

HOW TO BEGIN TO STUDY

The Guide of the Perplexed

*

IBELIEVE that it will not be amiss if I simply present the plan of the *Guide* as it has become clear to me in the course of about twenty-five years of frequently interrupted but never abandoned study. In the following scheme Roman (and Arabic) numerals at the beginning of a line indicate the sections (and subsections) of the *Guide* while the numbers given in parentheses indicate the Parts and the chapters of the book.

A. Views (I 1–III 24)

A′. Views regarding God and the angels (I 1–III 7)

I. Biblical terms applied to God (I 1–70)

א. Terms suggesting the corporeality of God (and the angels) (I 1–49)

1. The two most important passages of the Torah that seem to suggest that God is corporeal (I 1–7)

2. Terms designating place, change of place, the organs of human locomotion, etc. (I 8–28)

3. Terms designating wrath and consuming (or taking food) that if applied to divine things refer to idolatry on the one hand and to human knowledge on the other (I 29–36)

4. Terms designating parts and actions of animals (I 37–49)

ב. Terms suggesting multiplicity in God (I 50–70)

5. Given that God is absolutely one and incomparable, what is the meaning of the terms applied to God in nonfigurative speech? (I 50–60)

6. The names of God and the utterances of God (I 61–67)

The *Guide* consists then of seven sections or of thirty-eight subsections. Wherever feasible, each section is divided into seven subsections; the only section that does not permit of being divided into subsections is divided into seven chapters.

The simple statement of the plan of the *Guide* suffices to show that the book is sealed with many seals. At the end of its Introduction Maimonides describes the preceding passage as follows: "It is a key permitting one to enter places the gates to which were locked. When those gates are opened and those places are entered, the souls will find rest therein, the eyes will be delighted, and the bodies will be eased of their toil and of their labor." The *Guide* as a whole is not merely a key to a forest but is itself a forest, an enchanted forest, and hence also an enchanting forest: it is a delight to the eyes. For the tree of life is a delight to the eyes.

The enchanting character of the *Guide* does not appear immediately. At first glance the book appears merely to be strange and in particular to lack order and consistency. But progress in understanding it is a progress in becoming enchanted by it. Enchanting understanding is perhaps the highest form of edification. One begins to understand the *Guide* once one sees that it is not a philosophic book — a book written by a philosopher for philosophers — but a Jewish book: a book written by a Jew for Jews. Its first premise is the old Jewish premise that being a Jew and being a philosopher are two incompatible things. Philosophers are men who try to give an account of the whole by starting from what is always accessible to man as man; Maimonides starts from the acceptance of the Torah. A Jew may make use of philosophy and Maimonides makes the most ample use of it; but as a Jew he gives his assent where as a philosopher he would suspend his assent (cf. II 16).

Accordingly, the *Guide* is devoted to the Torah or more precisely to the true science of the Torah, of the Law. Its first purpose is to explain biblical terms and its second purpose is to explain biblical similes. The *Guide* is then devoted above all to biblical exegesis, although to biblical exegesis of a particular kind. That kind of exegesis is required because many biblical terms and all biblical similes have an apparent or outer and a hidden or inner meaning; the gravest errors as well as the most tormenting perplexities arise from men's understanding the Bible always according to its apparent or literal meaning. The *Guide* is then devoted to "the difficulties of the Law" or to "the secrets of the Law." The most important of those secrets are the Account of the Beginning (the beginning of the Bible) and the Account of the Chariot (Ezek. 1 and 10). The *Guide* is then devoted primarily and chiefly to the explanation of the Account of the Beginning and the Account of the Chariot.

Yet the Law whose secrets Maimonides intends to explain forbids that they be explained in public, or to the public; they may only be explained in private and only to such individuals as possess both theoretical and political wisdom as well as the capacity of both understanding and using allusive speech; for only "the chapter headings" of the secret teaching may be transmitted even to those who belong to the natural elite. Since every explanation given in writing, at any rate in a book, is a public explanation, Maimonides seems to be compelled by his intention to transgress the Law. There were other cases in which he was under such a compulsion. The Law also forbids one to study the books of idolaters on idolatry, for the first intention of the Law as a whole is to destroy every vestige of idolatry; and yet Maimonides, as he openly admits and even emphasizes, has studied all the available idolatrous books of this kind with the utmost thoroughness. Nor is this all. He goes so far as to encourage the reader of the *Guide* to study those books by himself (III 29–30, 32, 37; *Mishneh Torah*, H. ᶜAbodah Zarah II 2 and III 2). The Law also forbids one to speculate about the date of the coming of the Messiah, yet Maimonides presents such a speculation or at least its equivalent in order to comfort his contemporaries (*Epistle to Yemen*, 62, 16 ff., and 80, 17 ff. Halkin; cf. Halkin's Introduction, pp. xii–xiii; *M.T.*, H. Melakhim XII 2). Above all, the Law forbids one to seek for the reasons of the commandments, yet Maimonides devotes almost twenty-six chapters of the *Guide* to such seeking (III 26; cf. II 25). All these irregularities have one and the same justification. Maimonides transgresses the Law "for the sake of heaven," i.e., in order to uphold or to fulfill the Law (I Introd. and III Introd.). Still, in the most important case he does not, strictly speaking, transgress the Law, for his written explanation of the secrets of the Law is not a public but a secret explanation. The secrecy is achieved in three ways. First, every word of the *Guide* is chosen with exceeding care; since very few men are able or willing to read with exceeding care, most men will fail to perceive the secret teaching. Second, Maimonides deliberately contradicts himself, and if a man declares both that *a* is *b* and that *a* is not *b*, he cannot be said to declare anything. Lastly, the "chapter headings" of the secret teaching are not presented in an orderly fashion but are scattered throughout the book. This permits us to understand why the plan of the *Guide* is so obscure. Maimonides succeeds immediately in obscuring the plan by failing to divide the book explicitly into sections and subsections or by dividing it explicitly only into three Parts and each Part into chapters without supplying the Parts and the chapters with headings indicating the subject matter of the Parts or of the chapters.

The plan of the *Guide* is not entirely obscure. No one can reasonably doubt for instance that II 32–48, III 1–7, and III 25–50 form sections. The plan is most obscure at the beginning and it becomes clearer as one proceeds; generally speaking, it is clearer in the second half (II 13–end) than in the first half. The *Guide* is then not entirely devoted to secretly transmitting chapter headings of the secret teaching. This does not mean that the book is not in its entirety devoted to the true science of the Law. It means that the true science of the Law is partly public. This is not surprising, for the teaching of the Law itself is of necessity partly public. According to one statement, the core of the public teaching consists of the assertions that God is one, that He alone is to be worshipped, that He is incorporeal, that He is incomparable to any of His creatures and that He suffers from no defect and no passion (I 35). From other statements it would appear that the acceptance of the Law on every level of comprehension presupposes belief in God, in angels, and in prophecy (III 45) or that the basic beliefs are those in God's unity and in Creation

(II 13). In brief one may say that the public teaching of the Law in so far as it refers to beliefs or to "views," can be reduced to the thirteen "roots" (or dogmas) which Maimonides had put together in his Commentary on the Mishnah. That part of the true science of the Law which is devoted to the public teaching of the Law or which is itself public has the task of demonstrating the roots to the extent to which this is possible or of establishing the roots by means of speculation (III 51 and 54). Being speculative, that part of the true science of the Law is not exegetic; it is not necessarily in need of support by biblical or talmudic texts (cf. II 45 beginning). Accordingly, about 20 per cent of the chapters of the *Guide* contain no biblical quotations and about 9 per cent of them contain no Hebrew or Aramaic expressions whatever. It is not very difficult to see (especially on the basis of III 7 end, 23, and 28) that the *Guide* as devoted to speculation on the roots of the Law or to the public teaching consists of sections II–III and V–VI as indicated in our scheme and that the sequence of these sections is rational; but one cannot understand in this manner why the book is divided into three Parts, or what sections I, IV, and VII and most, not to say all, subsections mean. The teaching of the *Guide* is then neither entirely public or speculative nor is it entirely secret or exegetic. For this reason the plan of the *Guide* is neither entirely obscure nor entirely clear.

Yet the *Guide* is a single whole. What then is the bond uniting its exegetic and its speculative ingredients? One might imagine that while speculation demonstrates the roots of the Law, exegesis proves that those roots as demonstrated by speculation are in fact taught by the Law. But in that case the *Guide* would open with chapters devoted to speculation, yet the opposite is manifestly true. In addition, if the exegesis dealt with the same subject matter as that speculation which demonstrates the public teaching par excellence, namely, the roots of the Law, there would be no reason why the exegesis should be secret. Maimonides does say that the Account of the Beginning is the same as natural science and the Account of the Chariot is the same as divine science (i.e., the science of the in- corporeal beings or of God and the angels). This might lead one to think that the public teaching is identical with what the philosophers teach, while the secret teaching makes one understand the identity of the teaching of the philosophers with the secret teaching of the Law. One can safely say that this thought proves to be untenable on almost every level of one's comprehending the *Guide*: the nonidentity of the teaching of the philosophers as a whole and the thirteen roots of the Law as a whole is the first word and the last word of Maimonides. What he means by identifying the core of philosophy (natural science and divine science) with the highest secrets of the Law (the Account of the Beginning and the Account of the Chariot) and therewith by somehow identifying the subject matter of speculation with the subject matter of exegesis may be said to be the secret par excellence of the *Guide*.

Let us then retrace our steps. The *Guide* contains a public teaching and a secret teaching. The public teaching is addressed to every Jew including the vulgar; the secret teaching is addressed to the elite. The secret teaching is of no use to the vulgar and the elite does not need the *Guide* for being apprised of the public teaching. To the extent to which the *Guide* is a whole, or one work, it is addressed neither to the vulgar nor to the elite. To whom then is it addressed? How legitimate and important this question is appears from Maimonides' remark that the chief purpose of the *Guide* is to explain as far as possible the Account of the Beginning and the Account of the Chariot "with a view to him for whom (the book) has been composed" (III beginning). Maimonides answers our question both explicitly and implicitly. He answers it explicitly in two ways; he says on the one hand that the *Guide* is addressed to believing Jews who are perfect in their religion and in their character, have studied the sciences of the philosophers, and are perplexed by the literal meaning of the Law; he says on the other hand that the book is addressed to such perfect human beings as are Law students and perplexed. He answers our question more simply by dedicating the book to his disciple Joseph and by stating that it has been composed for Joseph and his like. Joseph had come to him "from the ends of the earth" and had studied under him for a while; the interruption of the oral instruction through Joseph's departure, which "God had decreed," induced Maimonides to write the *Guide* for Joseph and his like. In the Epistle Dedicatory addressed to Joseph, Maimonides extolls Joseph's virtues and indicates his limitation. Joseph had a passionate desire for things speculative and especially for mathematics. When he studied astronomy, mathematics, and logic under Maimonides, the teacher saw that Joseph had an excellent mind and a quick grasp; he thought him therefore fit to have revealed to him allusively the secrets of the books of the prophets and he began to make such revelations. This stimulated Joseph's interest in things divine as well as in an appraisal of the Kalām; his desire for knowledge about these subjects became so great that Maimonides was compelled to warn him unceasingly to proceed in an orderly manner. It appears that Joseph was inclined to proceed impatiently or unmethodically in his study and that this defect had not been cured when he left Maimonides. The most important consequence of Joseph's defect is the fact, brought out by Maimonides' silence, that Joseph turned to divine science without having studied natural science under Maimonides or before, although natural science necessarily precedes divine science in the order of study.

The impression derived from the Epistle Dedicatory is confirmed by the book itself. Maimonides frequently addresses the reader by using expressions like "know" or "you know already." Expressions of the latter kind indicate what the typical addressee knows and expressions of the former kind indicate what he does not know. One thus learns that Joseph has some knowledge of both the content and the character of divine science. He knows for example that divine science in contradistinction to mathematics and medicine requires an extreme of rectitude and moral perfection, and in particular of humility, but he apparently does not yet know how ascetic Judaism is in matters of sex (I 34, III 52). He had learned from Maimonides' "speech" that the orthodox "views" do not last in a man if he does not confirm them by the corresponding "actions" (II 31). It goes without saying that while his knowledge of the Jewish sources is extensive, it is not comparable in extent and thoroughness to Maimonides' (II 26, 33). At the beginning of the book he does not know that both according to the Jewish view and according to demonstration, angels have no bodies (I 43, 49) and he certainly does not know, strictly speaking, that God has no body (I 9). In this respect as well as in other respects his understanding necessarily progresses while he advances in his study of the *Guide* (cf. I 65 beginning). As for natural science, he has studied astronomy but is not aware of the conflict between the astronomical principles and the principles of natural science (II 24), because he has not studied natural science. He knows a number of things that are made clear in natural science, but this does not mean that he knows them through having studied natural science (cf. I 17, 28; III 10). From the ninety-first chapter (II 15) it appears that while he knows Aristotle's *Topics* and Fārābī's commentary on that work, he does not know the *Physics* and *On the Heaven* (cf. II 8). Nor will he acquire the science of nature as he acquires the science of God and the angels while he advances in the study of the *Guide*. For the *Guide*, which is addressed to a reader not conversant with natural science, does not itself transmit natural science (II 2). The following remark occurring in the twenty-sixth chapter is particularly revealing: "It has been demonstrated that everything moved undoubtedly possesses a magnitude and is divisible; and it will be demonstrated that God possesses no magnitude and hence possesses no motion." What "has been demonstrated" has been demonstrated in the *Physics* and is simply presupposed in the *Guide*; what "will be demonstrated" belongs to divine science and not to natural science; but that which "will be demonstrated" is built on what "has been demonstrated." The student of the *Guide* acquires knowledge of divine science but not of natural science. The author of the *Guide* in contradistinction to its addressee is thoroughly versed in natural science. Still, the addressee needs some awareness of the whole in order to be able to ascend from the whole to God, for there is no way to knowledge of God except through such ascent (I 71 toward the end); he acquires that awareness through a report of some kind (I 70) that Maimonides has inserted into the *Guide*. It is characteristic of that report that it does not contain a single mention of philosophy in general and of natural science in particular. The serious student cannot rest satisfied with that report; he must turn from it to natural science itself, which demonstrates what the report merely asserts. Maimonides cannot but leave it to his reader whether he will turn to genuine speculation or whether he will be satisfied with accepting the report on the authority of Maimonides and with building on that report theological conclusions. The addressee of the *Guide* is a man regarding whom it is still undecided whether he will become a genuine man of speculation or whether he will remain a follower of authority, if of Maimonides' authority (cf. I 72 end). He stands at the point of the road where speculation branches off from acceptance of authority.

Why did Maimonides choose an addressee of this description? What is the virtue of not being trained in natural science? We learn from the seventeenth chapter that natural science had already been treated as a secret doctrine by the pagan philosophers "upon whom the charge of corruption would not be laid if they exposed natural science clearly": all the more is the community of the Law-adherents obliged to treat natural science as a secret science. The reason why natural science is dangerous and is kept secret "with all kinds of artifices" is not that it undermines the Law — only the ignorant believe that (I 33), and Maimonides' whole life as well as the life of his successors refutes this suspicion. Yet it is also true that natural science has this corrupting effect on all men who are not perfect (cf. I 62). For natural science surely affects the understanding of the meaning of the Law, of the grounds on which it is to be obeyed and of the weight that is to be attached to its different parts. In a word, natural science upsets habits. By addressing a reader who is not conversant with natural science, Maimonides is compelled to proceed in a manner that does not upset habits or does so to the smallest possible degree. He acts as a moderate or conservative man.

But we must not forget that the *Guide* is written also for atypical addressees. In the first place, certain chapters of the *Guide* are explicitly said to be useful also for those who are simply beginners. Since the whole book is somehow accessible to the vulgar, it must have been written in such a way as not to be harmful to the vulgar (I Introd.; III 29). Besides, the book is also meant to be useful to such men of great intelligence as have been trained fully in all philosophic sciences and as are not in the habit of bowing to any authority — in other words, to men not inferior to Maimonides in their critical faculty. Readers of this kind will be unable to bow to Maimonides' authority; they will examine all his assertions, speculative or exegetic, with all reasonable severity; and they will derive great pleasure from all chapters of the *Guide* (I Introd.; I 55, 68 end, 73, tenth premise).

How much Maimonides' choice of his typical addressee affects the plan of his book will be seen by the judicious reader glancing at our scheme. It suffices to mention that no section or subsection of the *Guide* is devoted to the bodies that do not come into being and perish (cf. III 8 beginning, and I 11), i.e., to the heavenly bodies, which according to Maimonides possess life and knowledge, or to "the holy bodies," to use the bold expression used by him in his Code (*M.T.*, H. Yesodei ha-Torah IV 12). In other words, no section or subsection of the *Guide* is devoted to the Account of the Beginning in the manner in which a section is devoted to the Account of the Chariot. More important, Maimonides' choice of his typical addressee is the key to the whole plan of the *Guide*, to the apparent lack of order or to the obscurity of the plan. The plan of the *Guide* appears to be obscure only so long as one does not consider the kind of reader for which the book is written or so long as one seeks for an order agreeing with the essential order of subject matter. We recall the order of the sciences: logic precedes mathematics, mathematics precedes natural science, and natural science precedes divine science; and we recall that while Joseph was sufficiently trained in logic and mathematics, he is supposed to be introduced into divine science without having been trained properly in natural science. Maimonides must therefore seek for a substitute for natural science. He finds that substitute in the traditional Jewish beliefs and ultimately in the biblical texts correctly interpreted: the immediate preparation for divine science in the *Guide* is exegetic rather than speculative. Furthermore, Maimonides wishes to proceed in a manner that changes habits to the smallest possible degree. He himself tells us which habit is in particular need of being changed. After having reported the opinion of a pagan philosopher on the obstacles to speculation, he adds the remark that there exists now an obstacle that the ancient philosopher had not mentioned because it did not exist in his society: the habit of relying on revered "texts," i.e., on their literal meaning (I 31). It is for this reason that he opens his book with the explanation of biblical terms, i.e., with showing that their true meaning is not always their literal meaning. He cures the vicious habit in question by having recourse to another habit of his addressee. The addressee was accustomed not only to accept the literally understood biblical texts as true but also in many cases to understand biblical texts according to traditional interpretations that differed considerably from the literal meaning. Being accustomed to listen to authoritative interpretations of biblical texts, he is prepared to listen to Maimonides' interpretations as authoritative interpretations. The explanation of biblical terms that is given by Maimonides authoritatively is in the circumstances the natural substitute for natural science.

But which biblical terms deserve primary consideration? In other words, what is the initial theme of the *Guide*? The choice of the initial theme is dictated by the right answer to the question of which theme is the most urgent for the typical addressee and at the same time the least upsetting to him. The first theme of the

Guide is God's incorporeality. God's incorporeality is the third of the three most fundamental truths, the preceding ones being the existence of God and His unity. The existence of God and His unity were admitted as unquestionable by all Jews; all Jews as Jews know that God exists and that He is one, and they know this through the biblical revelation or the biblical miracles. One can say that because belief in the biblical revelation precedes speculation, and the discovery of the true meaning of revelation is the task of exegesis, exegesis precedes speculation. But regarding God's incorporeality there existed a certain confusion. The biblical texts suggest that God is corporeal and the interpretation of these texts is not a very easy task (II 25, 31, III 28). God's incorporeality is indeed a demonstrable truth but, to say nothing of others, the addressee of the *Guide* does not come into the possession of the demonstration until he has advanced into the Second Part (cf. I 1, 9, 18). The necessity to refute "corporealism" (the belief that God is corporeal) does not merely arise from the fact that corporealism is demonstrably untrue: corporealism is dangerous because it endangers the belief shared by all Jews in God's unity (I 35). On the other hand, by teaching that God is incorporeal, one does not do more than to give expression to what the talmudic Sages believed (I 46). However, the Jewish authority who had given the most consistent and the most popularly effective expression to the belief in God's incorporeality was Onqelos the Stranger, for the primary preoccupation of his translation of the Torah into Aramaic, which Joseph knew as a matter of course, was precisely to dispose of the corporealistic suggestions of the original (I 21, 27, 28, 36 end). Maimonides' innovation is then limited to his deviation from Onqelos' procedure: he does explicitly what Onqelos did implicitly; whereas Onqelos tacitly substituted noncorporealistic terms for the corporealistic terms occurring in the original, Maimonides explicitly discusses each of the terms in question by itself in an order that has no correspondence to the accidental sequence of their occurrence in the Bible. As a consequence, the discussion of corporealism in the *Guide* consists chiefly of a discussion of the various biblical terms suggesting corporealism, and, vice versa, the chief subject of what Maimonides declares to be the primary purpose of the *Guide*, namely, the explanation of biblical terms, is the explanation of biblical terms suggesting corporealism. This is not surprising. There are no biblical terms that suggest that God is not one, whereas there are many biblical terms that suggest that God is corporeal: the apparent difficulty created by the plural *Elohim* can be disposed of by a single sentence or by a single reference to Onqelos (I 2).

The chief reason why it is so urgent to establish the belief in God's incorporeality, however, is supplied by the fact that that belief is destructive of idolatry. It was of course universally known that idolatry is a very grave sin, nay, that the Law has, so to speak, no other purpose than to destroy idolatry (I 35, III 29 end).

xxii The Guide of the Perplexed

But this evil can be completely eradicated only if everyone is brought to know that God has no visible shape whatever or that He is incorporeal. Only if God is incorporeal is it absurd to make images of God and to worship such images. Only under this condition can it become manifest to everyone that the only image of God is man, living and thinking man, and that man acts as the image of God only through worshipping the invisible or hidden God alone. Not idolatry but the belief in God's corporeality is a fundamental sin. Hence the sin of idolatry is less grave than the sin of believing that God is corporeal (I 36). This being the case, it becomes indispensable that God's incorporeality be believed in by everyone whether or not he knows by demonstration that God is incorporeal. With regard to the majority of men it is sufficient and necessary that they believe in this truth on the basis of authority or tradition, i.e., on a basis that the first subsections of the *Guide* are meant to supply. The teaching of God's incorporeality by means of authoritative exegesis, i.e., the most public teaching of God's incorporeality, is indispensable for destroying the last relics of paganism: the immediate source of paganism is less the ignorance of God's unity than the ignorance of His radical incorporeality (cf. I 36 with *M.T.*, H. ᶜAbodah Zarah I 1).

It is necessary that we understand the character of the reasoning that Maimonides uses when he determines the initial theme of the *Guide*. We limit ourselves to a consideration of the second reason demanding the teaching of Incorporeality. While the belief in Unity leads immediately to the rejection of the worship of "other gods" but not to the rejection of the worship of images of the one God, the belief in Incorporeality leads immediately only to the rejection of the worship of images or of other bodies but not to the rejection of the worship of other gods: all gods may be incorporeal. Only if the belief in God's incorporeality is based on the belief in His unity, as Maimonides' argument indeed assumes, does the belief in God's incorporeality appear to be the necessary and sufficient ground for rejecting "forbidden worship" in every form, i.e., the worship of other gods as well as the worship of both natural things and artificial things. This would mean that the prohibition against idolatry in the widest sense is as much a dictate of reason as the belief in God's unity and incorporeality. Yet Maimonides indicates that only the theoretical truths pronounced in the Decalogue (God's existence and His unity), in contradistinction to the rest of the Decalogue, are rational. This is in agreement with his denying the existence of rational commandments or prohibitions as such (II 33; cf. I 54, II 31 beginning, III 28; *Eight Chapters* VI). Given the fact that Aristotle believed in God's unity and incorporeality and yet was an idolater (I 71, III 29), Maimonides' admiration for him would be incomprehensible if the rejection of idolatry were the simple consequence of that belief. According to Maimonides, the Law agrees with Aristotle in holding that the heavenly bodies are endowed with life and intelligence and that they are superior to man in dignity; one could say that he agrees with Aristotle in implying that those holy bodies deserve more than man to be called images of God. But unlike the philosophers he does not go so far as to call those bodies "divine bodies" (II 4–6; cf. Letter to Ibn Tibbon). The true ground of the rejection of "forbidden worship" is the belief in creation out of nothing, which implies that creation is an absolutely free act of God or that God alone is the complete good that is in no way increased by creation. But creation is according to Maimonides not demonstrable, whereas God's unity and incorporeality are demonstrable. The reasoning underlying the determination of the initial theme of the *Guide* can then be described as follows: it conceals the difference of cognitive status between the belief in God's unity and incorporeality on the one hand and the belief in creation on the other; it is in accordance with the opinion of the Kalām. In accordance with this, Maimonides brings his disagreement with the Kalām into the open only after he has concluded his thematic discussion of God's incorporeality; in that discussion he does not even mention the Kalām.

It is necessary that we understand as clearly as possible the situation in which Maimonides and his addressee find themselves at the beginning of the book, if not throughout the book. Maimonides knows that God is incorporeal; he knows this by a demonstration that is at least partly based on natural science. The addressee does not know that God is incorporeal; nor does he learn it yet from Maimonides: he accepts the fact that God's incorporeality is demonstrated, on Maimonides' authority. Both Maimonides and the addressee know that the Law is a source of knowledge of God; only the Law can establish God's incorporeality for the addressee in a manner that does not depend on Maimonides' authority. But both know that the literal meaning of the Law is not always its true meaning and that the literal meaning is certainly not the true meaning when it contradicts reason, for otherwise the Law could not be "your wisdom and your understanding in the sight of the nations" (Deut. 4:6). Both know in other words that exegesis does not simply precede speculation. Yet only Maimonides knows that the corporealistic expressions of the Law are against reason and must therefore be taken as figurative. The addressee does not know and cannot know that Maimonides' figurative interpretations of those expressions are true: Maimonides does not adduce arguments based on grammar. The addressee accepts Maimonides' interpretations just as he is in the habit of accepting the Aramaic translations as correct translations or interpretations. Maimonides enters the ranks of the traditional Jewish authorities: he simply tells the addressee what to believe regarding the meaning of the biblical terms. Maimonides introduces Reason in the guise of Authority. He takes on the garb of authority. He tells the addressee to believe in

God's incorporeality because, as he tells him, contrary to appearance, the Law does not teach corporeality, because, as he tells him, corporeality is a demonstrably wrong belief.

But we must not forget the most important atypical addressee, the reader who is critical and competent. He knows the demonstration of God's incorporeality and the problems connected with it as well as Maimonides does. Therefore the exegetic discussion of God's incorporeality which is presented in the first forty-nine chapters of the *Guide*, and which is pre-speculative and hence simply public as far as the typical addressee is concerned, is post-speculative and hence secret from the point of view of the critical and competent reader. The latter will examine Maimonides' explanations of biblical terms in the light of the principle that one cannot establish the meanings of a term if one does not consider the contexts in which they occur (II 29; cf. *Epistle to Yemen* 46, 7 ff.) or that while grammar is not a sufficient condition, it is surely the necessary condition of interpretation. For while the competent reader will appreciate the advantages attendant upon a coherent discussion of the biblical terms in question as distinguished from a translation of the Bible, he will realize that such a discussion may make one oblivious of the contexts in which the terms occur. He will also notice contradictions occurring in the *Guide*, remember always that they are intentional, and ponder over them.

The readers of the *Guide* were told at the beginning that the first purpose of the book is the explanation of biblical terms. They will then in no way be surprised to find that the book opens with the explanation of biblical terms in such a way that, roughly speaking, each chapter is devoted to the explanation of one or several biblical terms. They will soon become habituated to this procedure: they become engrossed by the subject matter, the What, and will not observe the How. The critical reader, however, will find many reasons for becoming amazed. To say nothing of other considerations, he will wonder why almost the only terms explained are those suggesting corporeality. It is perhaps not a matter of surprise that one chapter is devoted to the explanation of "place" and another to the explanation of "to dwell." But why is there no chapter devoted to "one," none to "merciful," none to "good," none to "intelligence," none to "eternity"? Why is there a chapter devoted to "grief" and none to "laughter"? Why is there a chapter devoted to "foot" and another to "wing" but none to "hand" nor to "arm"? Assuming that one has understood Maimonides' selection of terms, one still has to understand the order in which he discusses them. To what extent the explanation of terms is limited to terms suggesting corporeality, appears with particular clarity when one considers especially those chapters that are most visibly devoted to the explanation of terms, the lexicographic chapters. By a lexicographic chapter I understand a chapter that opens with the Hebrew term or terms to be explained in the chapter regardless of whether these terms precede the first sentence or form the beginning of the first sentence, and regardless of whether these terms are supplied with the Arabic article *al-* or not. The lexicographic chapter may be said to be the normal or typical chapter in the discussion of God's incorporeality (I 1–49); thirty out of the forty-nine chapters in question are lexicographic whereas in the whole rest of the book there occur at most two such chapters (I 66 and 70). All these thirty chapters occur in I 1–45: two thirds of the chapters in I 1–45 are lexicographic. Thus the question arises why nineteen chapters of the discussion of God's incorporeality — and just the nineteen chapters having both the subject matters and the places that they do — are not lexicographic. Why do ten of these thirty lexicographic chapters begin with Hebrew terms preceding the first sentence and twenty of them begin with Hebrew terms forming part of the first sentence? Thirteen of the terms in question are nouns, twelve are verbs and five are verbal nouns: why does Maimonides in some cases use the verbs and in other cases the verbal nouns? Within the chapters, generally speaking, he discusses the term that is the subject of the chapter in question, first in regard to the various meanings it has when it is not applied to God and then in regard to the various meanings it has when applied to God; he proves the existence of each of these meanings in most cases by quoting one or more biblical passages; those quotations are sometimes explicitly incomplete (ending in "and so on") and more frequently not; the quotations used to illustrate a particular meaning of a particular term do not always follow the biblical order; they are frequently introduced by "he said" but sometimes they are ascribed to individual biblical authors or speakers; in most cases he does not add to the name of the biblical author or speaker the formula "may he rest in peace," but in some cases he does; sometimes "the Hebrew language" or "the language" is referred to. In a book as carefuly worded as is the *Guide* according to Maimonides' emphatic declaration, all these varieties, and others that we forgo mentioning, deserve careful consideration. It goes without saying that there is not necessarily only one answer to each of the questions implied in each of these varieties; the same device — e.g., the distinction between lexicographic and nonlexicographic chapters or the tracing of a biblical quotation to an individual biblical author — may fulfill different functions in different contexts. In order to understand the *Guide*, one must be fully awake and as it were take nothing for granted. In order to become enabled to raise the proper questions, one does well to consider the possibility that there exists the typical chapter or else to construct the typical chapter, i.e., to find out which of the varieties indicated are most in accordance with the primary function of the chapters devoted to the explanation of biblical terms: only the other varieties are in need of a special reason.

The first chapter of the *Guide* is devoted to "image and likeness." The selection of these terms was necessitated by a single biblical passage: "And God said, Let us make man in our image, after our likeness. . . . So God created man in his image, in the image of God created he him, male and female created he them" (Gen. 1:26–27). The selection of these terms for explanation in the first chapter is due to the unique significance of the passage quoted. That passage suggests to the vulgar mind more strongly than any other biblical passage that God is corporeal in the crudest sense: God has the shape of a human being, has a face, lips, and hands, but is bigger and more resplendent than man since He does not consist of flesh and blood, and is therefore in need, not of food and drink, but of odors; His place is in Heaven from which He descends to the earth, especially to high mountains, in order to guide men and to find out what they do, and to which He ascends again with incredible swiftness; He is moved, as men are, by passions, especially by anger, jealousy, and hate, and thus makes men frightened and sad; His essence is Will rather than Intellect. (Cf. I 10, 20, 36–37, 39, 43, 46, 47, 68.) Maimonides tells his addressee that *selem* (the Hebrew term which is rendered by "image") does not mean, if not exactly in any case, but certainly in the present case, a visible shape; it means the natural form, the specific form, the essence of a being: "God created man in his image" means that God created man as a being endowed with intellect or that the divine intellect links itself with man. Similar considerations apply to the Hebrew term rendered by "likeness." The Hebrew term designating form in the sense of visible shape is *to'ar*, which is never applied to God. After having dispelled the confusion regarding "image" Maimonides says: "We have explained to thee the difference between *selem* and *to'ar* and we have explained the meaning of *selem*." He thus alludes to the twofold character of his explanation here as well as elsewhere: one explanation is given to "thee," i.e., to the typical addressee, and another is given to indeterminate readers; the latter explanation comes to sight only when one considers, among other things, the context of all biblical passages quoted. To mention only one example, the second of the three quotations illustrating the meaning of *to'ar* is "What form is he of?" (I Sam. 28:14). The quotation is taken from the account of King Saul's conversation with the witch of Endor, whom the king had asked to bring up to him the dead prophet Samuel; when the woman saw Samuel and became frightened and the king asked her what she saw, she said: "I saw gods (*elohim*) ascending out of the earth." The account continues as follows: "And he said unto her, What form is he of? And she said: an old man cometh up; and he is covered with a mantle." Maimonides himself tells us in the next chapter that *elohim* is an equivocal term that may mean angels and rulers of cities as well as God; but this does not explain why that term is also applied to the shades of the venerable departed — beings without flesh and blood — which frighten men either because those shades do not wish to be "disquieted," i.e., they wish to rest in peace, or for other reasons. To say nothing of other reasons, the rational beings inhabiting the lowest depth are in truth not men who have died, but all living men, the Adamites, i.e., the descendants of Adam, who lack Adam's pristine intellectuality (cf. I 2 with I 10). It looks as if Maimonides wished to draw our attention to the fact that the Bible contains idolatrous, pagan, or "Sabian" relics. If this suspicion should prove to be justified, we would have to assume that his fight against "forbidden worship" and hence against corporealism is more radical than one would be inclined to believe or that the recovery of Sabian relics in the Bible with the help of Sabian literature is one of the tasks of his secret teaching. However this may be, his interpretation of Genesis 1 : 26 seems to be contradicted by the fact that the Torah speaks shortly afterward of the divine prohibition addressed to Man against eating of the fruit of the tree of knowledge: if Man was created as an intellectual being and hence destined for the life of the intellect, his Creator could not well have forbidden him to strive for knowledge. In other words, the biblical account implies that man's intellectuality is not identical with man's being created in the image of God but is a consequence of his disobedience to God or of God's punishing him for that sin. As we are told in the second chapter, this objection was raised not by the addressee of the *Guide* but by another acquaintance of Maimonides, a nameless scientist of whom we do not even know whether he was of Jewish extraction and who was apparently not very temperate in regard to drink and to sex. (Compare the parallel in III 19.) Maimonides tells his addressee that he replied to his objector as follows: the knowledge that was forbidden to Man was the knowledge of "good and evil," i.e., of the noble and base, and the noble and base are objects not of the intellect but of opinion; strictly speaking they are not objects of knowledge at all. To mention only the most important example, in Man's perfect state, in which he was unaware of the noble and base, although he was aware of the naturally good and bad, i.e., of the pleasant and painful, he did not regard the uncovering of one's nakedness as disgraceful. After having thus disposed of the most powerful objection to his interpretation of Genesis 1 : 26, or after having thus taught that the intellectual life is beyond the noble and base, Maimonides turns to the second most important passage of the Torah that seems to suggest that God is corporeal. More precisely, he turns both to the terms applied in that passage to God and to kindred terms. The passage, which occurs in Numbers 12 : 8, reads as follows: "he (Moses) beholds the figure of the Lord." He devotes to this subject three chapters (I 3–5); in I 3 he discusses explicitly the three meanings of "figure" and in I 4 he discusses explicitly the three meanings of the three terms designating "beholding" or "seeing"; in one of the biblical passages partly quoted, the Lord is presented as having appeared to Abraham in the guise of three men who yet were one. Maimonides tells the addressee that the Hebrew terms designating "figure" and "beholding" (or its equivalents) mean, when they are applied to God, intellectual truth and intellectual grasp. The relation of I 5 to I 3–4 resembles the relation of I 2 and I 1. The view that man was created for the life of the intellect was contradicted by the apparent prohibition against acquiring knowledge. Similarly, "the prince of the philosophers" (i.e., Aristotle) apparently contradicts his view that man exists for the life of the intellect by apologizing for his engaging in the investigation of very obscure matters: Aristotle apologizes to his readers for his apparent temerity; in fact, he is prompted only by his desire to know the truth. This restatement of an Aristotelian utterance affords an easy transition to the Jewish view according to which Moses was rewarded with beholding the figure of the Lord because he had previously "hid his face; for he was afraid to look upon God" (Exod. 3:6). The pursuit of knowledge of God must be preceded by fear of looking upon God or, to use the expression that Aristotle had used in the passage in question (*On the Heaven* 291b 21 ff.) and that does not occur in Maimonides' summary, by sense of shame: the intellectual perfection is necessarily preceded by moral perfection—by one's having acquired the habit of doing the noble and avoiding the base—as well as by other preparations. Maimonides' emphasis here on moral perfection, especially on temperance, as a prerequisite of intellectual perfection is matched by his silence here on natural science as such a prerequisite. The weeding-out of corporealism proceeds *pari passu* with the watering of asceticism. Having arrived at this point, Maimonides does something strange: he abruptly turns to the explanation of the terms "man and woman" (I 6) and "to generate" (I 7). The strangeness, however, immediately disappears once one observes that I 6–7 are the first lexicographic chapters after I 1 and one remembers that I 2 is merely a corollary of I 1: the explanation of "man and woman" and of "to generate" forms part of the explanation of Genesis 1:26–27. There it is said that "in the image of God created (God man); male and female created he them." Literally understood, that saying might be thought to mean that man is the image of God because he is bisexual or that the Godhead contains a male and a female element that generate "children of God" and the like. Accordingly, the last word of I 7 is the same as the first word of I 1: "image." Maimonides does not discuss the implication which was stated, for it is one of the secrets of the Torah and we are only at the beginning of our training. The explanation of the key terms (or their equivalents) occurring in Genesis 1:26–27 surrounds then the explanation of the key terms (or their equivalents) occurring in Numbers 12:8. The discussion of the most important passages of the Torah regarding Incorporeality forms the fitting subject of the first subsection of the *Guide*. That subsection seems to be devoted to five unnconected groups of terms; closer inspection shows that it is devoted to two biblical passages: Maimonides seems to hesitate to sever the umbilical cord connecting his exegesis with Onqelos'.

At first glance the theme of the second subsection is much easier to recognize than that of the first. This seems to be due to the fact that that theme is not two or more biblical passages but biblical terms designating phenomena all of which belong essentially together: place as well as certain outstanding places, occupying place, changing place, and the organs for changing place. Nineteen of the twenty-one chapters of the second subsection are manifestly devoted to this theme. The discussion begins with "place" (I 8), turns to "throne" (I 9), a most exalted place that if ascribed to God designates not only the temple but also and above all the heaven, and then turns to "descending and ascending" (I 10). While this sequence is perfectly lucid, we are amazed to find that, whereas I 8 and 9 are lexicographic chapters, I 10 is not a lexicographic chapter. This irregularity can be provisionally explained as follows: when Maimonides treats thematically several verbs in one lexicographic chapter, those verbs are explicitly said to have the same or nearly the same meaning (I 16, 18); when he treats thematically verbs that primarily designate opposites but do not designate opposites if applied to God, he treats them in separate chapters (I 11, 12, 22, 23); but "descending" and "ascending" designate opposites both in their primary meaning and if applied to God: God's descending means both His revealing Himself and His punitive action, and His ascending means the cessation of His revelation or punitive action (cf. the silence on "returning" at the beginning of I 23). Maimonides indicates the unique character of the subject "descent and ascent" by treating it in a nonlexicographic chapter surrounded on the one side by four and on the other side by three lexicographic chapters. On the basis of "the vulgar imagination" God's natural state would be sitting on His throne and sitting is the opposite of rising. "Sitting" and "rising" (I 11 and 12) designate opposites but do not designate opposites if applied to God: although God's "sitting" refers to His unchangeability, His "rising" refers to His keeping His promises or threats, it being understood that His promises to Israel may very well be threats to Israel's enemies. A talmudic passage that confirms Maimonides' public explanation and in which "sitting" is mentioned together, not with "rising," but with "standing up" naturally leads to the discussion of "standing up" (I 13), which term, according to Maimonides, means if applied to God His unchangeability, an unchangeability not contradicted, as he indicates, by God's threats to destroy Israel.

Having arrived at this point, Maimonides interrupts his discussion of verbs or of other terms that refer to place and turns to the explanation of "man" (I 14). A similar interruption occurs shortly afterwards when he turns from "standing" and "rock" (I 15 and 16) to an explanation of the prohibition against the public teaching of natural science (I 17). Although these chapters are subtly interwoven with the chapters preceding and following them, at first glance they strikingly interrupt the continuity of the argument. By this irregularity our attention is drawn to a certain numerical symbolism that is of assistance to the serious reader of the *Guide*: 14 stands for man or the human things and 17 stands for nature. The connection between "nature" and "change of place" (or, more generally, motion), and therewith the connection between the theme of I 17 and the subsection to which that chapter belongs, has been indicated before. The connection between "14" and the context cannot become clear before we have reached a better understanding of the relation between nature and convention; at present it must suffice to say that I 7 deals with "to generate." Although I 26 obviously deals with terms referring to place, it also fulfills a numerological function: the immediate theme of that chapter is the universal principle governing the interpretation of the Torah ("the Torah speaks according to the language of human beings"); 26 is the numerical equivalent of the secret name of the Lord, the God of Israel; 26 may therefore also stand for His Torah. Incidentally, it may be remarked that 14 is the numerical equivalent of the Hebrew for "hand"; I 28 is devoted to "foot": no chapter of the *Guide* is devoted to "hand," the characteristically human organ, whereas Maimonides devotes a chapter, the central chapter of the fourth subsection, to "wing," the organ used for swift descent and ascent. In all these matters one can derive great help from studying Joseph Albo's *Roots*. Albo was a favorite companion living at the court of a great king.

Of the twenty-one chapters of the second subsection sixteen are lexicographic and five (I 10, 14, 17, 26, 27) are not. Of these sixteen chapters two begin with Hebrew terms supplied with the Arabic article (I 23 and 24). Thus only seven of the twenty-one chapters may be said to vary from the norm. In seven of the fourteen chapters beginning with a pure Hebrew term, that term precedes the first sentence and in the seven others the Hebrew term forms part of the first sentence. Seven of these chapters begin with a verb and seven with a noun or a verbal noun. It is one thing to observe these regularities and another thing to understand them. The distinction between the verbs and the verbal nouns is particularly striking, since lexicographic chapters beginning with verbal nouns occur only in our subsection. Furthermore, of the three lexicographic chapters of the first subsection, one opens with nouns preceding the first sentence, one with nouns forming part of the first sentence, and one with a verb preceding the first sentence; orderliness would seem to require that there be a chapter opening with a verb that forms part of the first sentence. One of the chapters of the second subsection (I 22) begins with a verb preceding the first sentence but the first sentence opens with the verbal noun (supplied with the Arabic article) of the same verb; there occurs no other case of this kind in the whole book. If we count this ambiguous chapter among the chapters beginning with a verbal noun forming part of the first sentence, we reach this conclusion: the second subsection contains four chapters beginning with verbs or verbal nouns preceding the first sentence and eight chapters beginning with verbs or verbal nouns forming part of the first sentence. Furthermore, the second subsection contains six chapters beginning with verbs and six chapters beginning with verbal nouns; of the latter six chapters three begin with pure verbal nouns and three begin with verbal nouns supplied with the Arabic article. The second subsection surpasses the first subsection in regularity especially if I 22 is properly subsumed. From all this we are led to regard it as possible that I 22 somehow holds the key to the mystery of the second subsection.

The first chapter of the second subsection (I 8) is devoted to "place," a term that in post-biblical Hebrew is used for designating God Himself. To our great amazement Maimonides is completely silent about this meaning of "place." His silence is all the more eloquent since he quotes in this very chapter post-biblical Hebrew expressions containing "place," since he admonishes the readers in this very chapter to consult regarding his explanation of any term not only "the books of prophecy" but also other "compilations of men of science" — Talmud and Midrash are such compilations — and since he had concluded the preceding chapter with a quotation from the Midrash. In the only other lexicographic chapter devoted to a term used for designating God Himself — in I 16, which is devoted to "rock" — he does not hesitate to say that that term is also used for designating God, for that meaning of "rock" is biblical. We see then how literally he meant his declaration that the first intention of the *Guide* is to explain terms occurring in "the books of prophecy," i.e., primarily in the Bible: he is primarily concerned with the theology of the Bible in contradistinction to post-biblical Jewish theology. He is alive to the question raised by the Karaites. As he puts it, not only does criticism of the talmudic Sages do no harm to them — it does not even do any harm to the critic or rather to the foundations of belief (I Introd., 5 end, 19 end, 46 end; cf. *Resurrection* 29, 10–30, 15 Finkel). This observation enables us to solve the difficulty presented by I 22.

I 18–21 opened with verbs; I 22 marks the transition from chapters opening with verbs to chapters opening with verbal nouns supplied with the Arabic article; I 23–24 open with verbal nouns supplied with the Arabic article. I 25 opens again with a verb. That verb is "to dwell." The transition made in I 22 and the procedure in I 23–24 make us expect that I 25 should open with the verbal noun "the dwelling," the *Shekhinah*, the post-biblical term particularly used for God's Indwelling on earth, but this expectation is disappointed. Maimonides makes all these preparations in order to let us see that he is anxious to avoid as a

2

chapter heading the term *Shekhinah*, which does not occur in the Bible in any sense, and to avoid the Hebrew term *Shekhinah* in its theological sense within the most appropriate chapter itself: when speaking there of the *Shekhinah* theologically, he uses the Arabic translation of *Shekhinah* but never that Hebrew term itself. He does use the Hebrew term *Shekhinah* in a theological meaning in a number of other chapters, but *Shekhinah* never becomes a theme of the *Guide*: there are no "chapters on the *Shekhinah*" as there are "chapters on providence" or "chapters on governance" (I 40 and 44). It should also be noted that the chapter devoted to "wing" does not contain a single reference to the *Shekhinah* (cf. particularly Maimonides' and Ibn Janāh's explanation of Isaiah 30:20 with the Targum *ad loc.*). In the chapter implicitly devoted to the *Shekhinah*, which is the central chapter of the part devoted to Incorporeality (I 1–49), Maimonides had mentioned the *Shekhinah* together with providence, but *Shekhinah* and providence are certainly not identical (cf. I 10 and 23). One should pay particular attention to the treatment of the *Shekhinah* in the chapters obviously devoted to providence strictly understood (III 17–18 and 22–23). With some exaggeration one may say that whereas the *Shekhinah* follows Israel, providence follows the intellect. In other words, it is characteristic of the *Guide* that in it *Shekhinah* as a theological theme is replaced by "providence," and "providence" in its turn to some extent by "governance," "governance" being as it were the translation of *Merkabah* ("Chariot"), as appears from I 70. Needless to say, it is not in vain that Maimonides uses the Arabic article at the beginning of I 23 and 24. He thus connects I 23 and 24 and the context of these chapters with the only other group of chapters all of which begin with a Hebrew term supplied with the Arabic article: III 36–49. That group of chapters deals with the individual biblical commandments, i.e., with their literal meaning rather than their extra-biblical interpretation, as is indicated in the chapter (III 41) that stands out from the rest of the group for more than one reason and that is devoted to the penal law. One reason why that chapter stands out is that it is the only chapter whose summary, in III 35, is adorned with a biblical quotation, III 35 being the chapter that serves as the immediate introduction to III 36–49. To repeat, the second subsection of the *Guide* draws our attention to the difference between the biblical and the post-biblical Jewish teaching or to the question raised by the Karaites. Maimonides, it need hardly be said, answered that question in favor of the Rabbanites, although not necessarily in their spirit. It suffices to remember that not only *Shekhinah* but also "providence" and "governance" are not biblical terms.

Like the first subsection, the second subsection is based on two biblical passages, although not as visibly and as clearly as the first. The passages are Exodus 33:20–23 and Isaiah 6. In the former passage the Lord says to Moses:

"Thou canst not see my face; for there shall no man see me, and live: . . . thou shalt see my back parts: but my face shall not be seen." Accordingly, Moses sees only the Lord's "glory pass by." In the latter passage Isaiah says: "I saw the Lord sitting upon a throne, high and lifted up. . . . Mine eyes have seen the king, the Lord of hosts." Isaiah does not speak, as Moses did, of "the figure of the Lord" or of "the image of God." Nor is it said of Isaiah, as it is said of Moses, Aaron, Nadab, Abihu, and seventy of the elders of Israel: "they saw the God of Israel: *and there was under his feet etc.* . . . And the nobles of the children of Israel . . . saw God, *and did eat and drink*" and thus suggested that the vision was imperfect (cf. I 5 with Albo's *Roots* III 17). We are thus induced to believe that Isaiah reached a higher stage in the knowledge of God than Moses or that Isaiah's vision marks a progress beyond Moses'. At first hearing, this belief is justly rejected as preposterous, not to say blasphemous: the denial of the supremacy of Moses' prophecy seems to lead to the denial of the ultimacy of Moses' Law, and therefore Maimonides does not tire of asserting the supremacy of Moses' prophecy. But the belief in the ultimacy of Moses' Law and even in the supremacy of Moses' prophecy in no way contradicts the belief in a certain superiority of Isaiah's speeches to Moses' speeches — to say nothing of the fact that Maimonides never denied that he deliberately contradicts himself. The following example may prove to be helpful. In his *Treatise on Resurrection*, Maimonides teaches that resurrection, one of the thirteen roots of the Law, is clearly taught within the Bible only in the book of Daniel, but certainly not in the Torah. He explains this apparently strange fact as follows: at the time when the Torah was given, all men, and hence also our ancestors, were Sabians, believing in the eternity of the world, for they believed that God is the spirit of the sphere, and denying the possibility of revelation and of miracles; hence a very long period of education and habituation was needed until our ancestors could be brought even to consider believing in that greatest of all miracles, the resurrection of the dead (26, 18–27, 15 and 31, 1–33, 14 Finkel). This does not necessarily mean that Moses himself did not know this root of the Law but he certainly did not teach it. At least in this respect the book of Daniel, of a late prophet of very low rank (II 45), marks a great progress beyond the Torah of Moses. All the easier is it to understand that Isaiah should have made some progress beyond Moses.

The reason why progress beyond the teaching of the Torah is possible or even necessary is twofold. In the first place, the Torah is the law par excellence. The supremacy of Moses' prophecy — the superiority of Moses' knowledge even to that of the Patriarchs — is connected with its being the only legislative prophecy (I 63, II 13, 39). But precisely because his prophecy culminates in the Law, it reflects the limitations of law. Law is more concerned with actions than with thoughts

(III 27–28; I Introd.). Mosaic theology reflects this orientation. According to the opinion of many of our contemporaries, Maimonides' theological doctrine proper is his doctrine of the divine attributes (I 50–60). In that subsection he quotes passages from the Torah only in that single chapter (I 54) in which he discusses the thirteen divine attributes revealed to Moses (Exod. 34:5–7); those attributes – all of them moral qualities – constitute the Mosaic theology; they express positively what in negative expression is called in the same context "God's back parts." Although God's goodness had been revealed to Moses in its entirety, the thirteen attributes articulate only that part of God's goodness which is relevant for the ruler of a city who is a prophet. Such a ruler must imitate the divine attributes of wrath and mercy not as passions – for the incorporeal God is above all passion – but because actions of mercy or wrath are appropriate in the circumstances, and he must imitate God's mercy and wrath in due proportion. The ruler of a city on the other hand must be more merciful than full of anger, for extreme punitiveness is required only because of the necessity, based on "human opinion," to exterminate the idolaters by fire and sword (I 54). Following another suggestion of Maimonides (I 61–63) one could say that the adequate statement of Mosaic theology is contained in the divine name YHVH – a name by which God revealed Himself for the first time to Moses as distinguished from the Patriarchs: "I appeared unto Abraham, unto Isaac, and unto Jacob, by the name of God Almighty, but by my name YHVH was I not known to them" (Exod. 6:3). Maimonides recognizes that this verse asserts or establishes the superiority of Moses' prophecy to that of the Patriarchs (II 35) but he does not explain that verse: he does not explain, at least not clearly, which theological verities other than the thirteen attributes were revealed to Moses but were unknown to the Patriarchs. Only this much may be said to emerge: Abraham was a man of speculation who instructed his subjects or followers rather than a prophet who convinced by miracles and ruled by means of promises and threats, and this is somehow connected with the fact that he called "on the name of YHVH, the God of the world" (Gen. 21:33) (I 63, II 13), i.e., the God of the trans-moral whole rather than the law-giving God. It is this Abrahamitic expression that opens each Part of the *Guide* as well as other writings of Maimonides. Considering all these things, one will find it wise to limit oneself to saying that the Mosaic theology par excellence is the doctrine of the thirteen moral attributes.

Second, the Mosaic legislation was contemporary with the yet unbroken and universal rule of Sabianism. Therefore the situation in the time of Moses was not different from the situation in the time of Abraham, who disagreed with all men, all men having the same Sabian religion or belonging to the same religious community. The innovation was naturally resisted, even with violence, although it was not a principle of Sabianism to exterminate unbelievers. Yet the Torah has only one purpose: to destroy Sabianism or idolatry. But the resistance by the Sabians proper was less important than the inner Sabianism of the early adherents of the Torah. It was primarily for this reason that Sabianism could be overcome only gradually: human nature does not permit the direct transition from one opposite to the other. To mention only the most obvious example, our ancestors had been habituated to sacrifice to natural or artificial creatures. The sacrificial laws of the Torah are a concession to that habit. Since the simple prohibition or cessation of sacrifices would have been as unintelligible or distasteful to our ancestors as the prohibition or cessation of prayer would be now, God provided that henceforth all sacrifices be transferred to Him and no longer be brought to any false gods or idols. The sacrificial laws constitute a step in the gradual transition, in the progress from Sabianism to pure worship, i.e., pure knowledge, of God (cf. I 54, 64); the sacrificial laws were necessary only "at that time." The Sabians believed that success in agriculture depends on worship of the heavenly bodies. In order to eradicate that belief, God teaches in the Torah that worship of the heavenly bodies leads to disaster in agriculture whereas worship of God leads to prosperity. For the reason given, the open depreciation of sacrifices as such occurs not yet in the Torah but in the prophets and in the Psalms. Conversely, the Torah is less explicit than the later documents regarding the duty of prayer (III 29, 30, 32, 35–37). No less important an adaptation to Sabian habits is the corporealism of the Bible. For Sabianism is a form of corporealism; according to the Sabians, the gods are the heavenly bodies or the heavenly bodies are the body of which God is the spirit (III 29). As for the Bible, Maimonides' teaching on this subject is not free from ambiguity. The first impression we receive from his teaching is that according to it the corporealistic understanding of the Bible is a mere misunderstanding. For instance, *ṣelem* simply does not mean visible shape but only natural form, and even if it should sometimes mean visible shape, the term must be considered to be homonymous, and it certainly does not mean visible shape but natural form in Genesis 1:26–27 (I 1; cf. I 49). In other cases, perhaps in most cases, the primary meaning of the term — say, "sitting" — is corporealistic but when it is applied to God, it is used in a derivative or metaphoric sense; in those cases the meaning of the text, the literal meaning, is metaphoric. Generally stated, the literal meaning of the Bible is not corporealistic. But there are also cases in which the literal meaning is corporealistic, for instance in the many cases in which the Bible speaks of God's anger (cf. I 29). One must go beyond this and say that generally speaking the literal meaning of the Bible is corporealistic because "the Torah speaks in accordance with the language of the children of Man," i.e., in accordance with "the imagination of the vulgar," and the vulgar mind does not admit, at least to begin with, the existence of any being that is not bodily; the Torah therefore describes God in corporealistic terms in order to indicate that He is (I 26, 47, 51 end). The Bible contains indeed innumerable passages directed against idolatry (I 36), but, as we have seen, idolatry is one thing and corporealism is another. The corporealistic meaning is not the only meaning, it is not the deepest meaning, it is not the true meaning, but it is as much intended as the true meaning; it is intended because of the need to educate and to guide the vulgar and, we may add, a vulgar that originally was altogether under the spell of Sabianism. What is true of the biblical similes is true also of the metaphoric biblical terms. According to the talmudic Sages, the outer of the similes is nothing while the inner is a pearl; according to King Solomon, who was "wiser than all men" (I Kings 5:11), the outer is like silver, i.e., it is useful for the ordering of human society, and the inner is like gold, i.e., it conveys true beliefs (I Introd.). Hence it is not without danger to the vulgar that one explains the similes or indicates the metaphoric character of expressions (I 33). For such biblical teachings as the assertions that God is angry, compassionate, or in other ways changeable, while not true, yet serve a political purpose or are necessary beliefs (III 28). A third possibility emerges through Maimonides' thematic discussion of providence. There he makes a distinction between the view of the Law regarding providence and the true view (III 17, 23). He could well have said that the true view is the secret teaching of the Law. Instead he says that the true view is conveyed through the book of Job, thus implying that the book of Job, a nonprophetic book whose characters are not Jews and that is composed by an unknown author (II 45; *Epistle to Yemen* 50, 19–52, 1 Halkin) marks a progress beyond the Torah and even beyond the prophets (cf. III 19). We recall that the simple co-ordination, taught by the Torah, of the worship of the Lord with agricultural and other prosperity was merely a restatement of the corresponding Sabian doctrine. As Maimonides indicates when explaining the account of the revelation on Mount Sinai, the beautiful consideration of the texts is the consideration of their outer meaning (II 36 end, 37). This remark occurs within the section on prophecy in which he makes for the first time an explicit distinction between the legal (or exegetic) and the speculative discussion of the same subject (cf. II 45 beginning). Accordingly, he speaks in his explanation of the Account of the Chariot, at any rate apparently, only of the literal meaning of this most secret text (III Introd.). Or to state the matter as succinctly as Maimonides does in the last chapter, the science of the Law is something essentially different, not only from the post-biblical or at any rate extra-biblical legal interpretation of the Law, but from wisdom, i.e., the demonstration of the views transmitted by the Law, as well.

Undoubtedly Maimonides contradicts himself regarding Moses' prophecy. He declares that he will not speak in the *Guide* explicitly or allusively about the characteristics of Moses' prophecy because or although he had spoken most explicitly about the differences between the prophecy of Moses and that of the other prophets in his more popular writings. And yet he teaches explicitly in the *Guide* that Moses' prophecy, in contradistinction to that of the other prophets, was entirely independent of the imagination or was purely intellectual (II 35, 36, 45 end). His refusal to speak of Moses' prophecy has indeed a partial justification. At least one whole subsection of the section on prophecy (II 41–44) is devoted to the prophecy of the prophets other than Moses, as is indicated by the frequent quotation in that subsection of this passage: "If there be a prophet among you, I the Lord will make myself known unto him in a vision, and will speak unto him in a dream"; for the Bible continues as follows: "My servant Moses is not so, who is faithful in all my house" (Num. 12:6–7). Still the assertion that Moses' prophecy was entirely independent of the imagination leads to a great difficulty if one considers the fact, pointed out by Maimonides in the same context (II 36; cf. II 47 beginning), that it is the imagination that brings forth similes and, we may add, metaphors, as well as the fact that the Torah abounds if not with similes, at any rate with metaphors. To mention only one example, Moses' saying that Eve was taken from one of Adam's ribs or that Woman was taken out of Man (Gen. 2:21–23) or derived from man reflects the fact that the word *ishah* (woman) is derived from the word *ish* (man) and such substitutions of the relation of words for the relation of things are the work of the imagination (cf. II 30 and 43; I 28; and *M.T.*, H. Yesodei ha-torah I). In order to understand the contradiction regarding Moses' prophecy, we must return once more to the beginning. Maimonides starts from accepting the Law as seen through the traditional Jewish interpretation. The Law thus understood is essentially different from "demonstration" (II 3), i.e., the views of the Law are not as such based on demonstration. Nor do they become evident through "religious experience" or through faith. For, according to Maimonides, there is no religious experience, i.e., specifically religious cognition; all cognition or true belief stems from the human intellect, sense perception, opinion, or tradition; the cognitive status even of the Ten Commandments was not affected by or during the revelation on Mount Sinai: some of these utterances are and always remained matters of "human speculation," while the others are and always remained matters of opinion or matters of tradition (I 51 beginning and II 33; *Letter on Astrology* §§ 4–5 Marx; and *Logic* chap. 8). As for faith, it is, according to Maimonides, only one of the moral virtues, which as such do not belong to man's ultimate perfection, the perfection of his intellect (III 53–54). The views of the Law are based on a kind of "speculative perception" that human speculation is unable to understand and that grasps the truth without the use of speculative premises or without reasoning; through this kind of perception peculiar to prophets, the prophet sees and hears nothing except God and angels (II 38, 36, 34). Some of the things perceived by prophets can be known with certainty also through demonstration. While for instruction in these things nonprophetic men are not absolutely in need of prophets, they depend entirely on prophets regarding those divine things that are not accessible to human speculation or demonstration. Yet the nonrational element in the prophetic speeches is to some extent imaginary, i.e., infra-rational. It is therefore a question how nonprophetic men can be certain of the supra-rational teaching of the prophets, i.e., of its truth. The general answer is that the supra-rational character of the prophetic speeches is confirmed by the supra-natural testimony of the miracles (II 25, III 29). In this way the authority of the Law as wholly independent of speculation is established wholly independently of speculation. Accordingly the understanding or exegesis of the Law can be wholly independent of speculation and in particular of natural science; and considering the higher dignity of revelation, exegesis will be of higher rank than natural science in particular; the explanations given by God Himself are infinitely superior to merely human explanations or traditions. This view easily leads to the strictest biblicism. "The difficulty of the Law" may be said to arise from the fact that the miracles do not merely confirm the truth of the belief in revelation but also presuppose the truth of that belief; only if one holds in advance the indemonstrable belief that the visible universe is not eternal can one believe that a given extraordinary event is a miracle (II 25). It is this difficulty that Maimonides provisionally solves by suggesting that Moses' prophecy is unique because it is wholly independent of the imagination, for if this suggestion is accepted, the difficulty caused by the presence of an infra-rational element in prophetic speeches does not arise. Yet if Moses' prophecy alone is wholly independent of the imagination, the Torah alone will be simply true, i.e., literally true, and this necessarily leads to extreme corporealism. Since corporealism is demonstrably wrong, we are compelled to admit that the Torah is not always literally true and hence, as matters stand, that the teaching of the other prophets may be superior in some points to that of Moses. The fundamental difficulty of how one can distinguish the supra-rational, which must be believed, from the infra-rational, which ought not to be believed, cannot be solved by recourse to the fact that we hear through the Bible, and in particular through the Torah, "God's book" par excellence (III 12), not human beings but God Himself. It is indeed true in a sense that God's speech gives the greatest certainty of His existence, and His declaring His attributes sets these attributes beyond doubt (cf. I 9 and 11, II 11), but God Himself cannot explain clearly the deepest secrets of the Torah to flesh and blood (I Introd., 31 beginning), He "speaks in accordance with the language of the children of man" (I 26), things that might have been made clear in the Torah are not made clear in it

(I 29), God makes use of ruses and of silence for only "a fool will reveal all his purpose and his will" (I 40; cf. III 32, 45 and 54) and, last but not least, as Maimonides explains in the *Guide*, God does not use speech in any sense (I 23) and this fact entails infinite consequences. One is therefore tempted to say that the infra-rational in the Bible is distinguished from the supra-rational by the fact that the former is impossible whereas the latter is possible: biblical utterances that contradict what has been demonstrated by natural science or by reason in any other form cannot be literally true but must have an inner meaning; on the other hand, one must not reject views the contrary of which has not been demonstrated, i.e., which are possible — for instance, creation out of nothing — lest one become thoroughly indecent (I 32, II 25). Yet this solution does not satisfy Maimonides. Whereas he had originally declared that the human faculty that distinguishes between the possible and the impossible is the intellect and not the imagination, he is compelled, especially in his chapters on providence, to question this verdict and to leave it open whether it is not rather the imagination that ought to have the last word (I 49, 73, III 15). He is therefore induced to say that the certainty of belief is one's awareness of the impossibility of the alternative or that the very existence of God is doubtful if it is not demonstrated or that man's intellect can understand what any intelligent being understands (I 50 and 51 beginning, 71, III 17). This is acceptable if the Account of the Beginning and the Account of the Chariot are indeed identical with natural science and divine science and if these sciences are demonstrative. But this enigmatic equation leaves obscure the place or the status of the fact of God's free creation of the world out of nothing: does this fact belong to the Account of the Beginning or to the Account of the Chariot or to both or to neither? (Cf. *Commentary on the Mishnah*, Hagigah II 1.) According to the *Guide*, the Account of the Chariot deals with God's governance of the world, in contradistinction not only to His providence (cf. I 44 on the one hand, and on the other I 40, where Maimonides refers to III 2 and not, as most commentators believe, to the chapters on providence, just as in III 2 he refers back to I 40), but also to His creation. By considering the relation of the Account of the Beginning and the Account of the Chariot, one is enabled also to answer completely the question that has led us to the present difficulty, the question concerning the order of rank between the Mosaic theophany and the Isaian theophany. The Account of the Beginning occurs in the Torah of Moses but the Account of the Chariot, which is identical with the divine science or the apprehension of God (I 34), occurs in the book of Ezekiel and in its highest form precisely in the sixth chapter of Isaiah (III 6; cf. also the quotations from the Torah on the one hand and from other biblical books on the other in III 54).

Once one has granted that there is an intra-biblical progress beyond the teaching of Moses, one will not be compelled to deny the possibility of a post-biblical progress of this description. The fact of such a progress can only be proven if there are characteristic differences between the Bible and the post-biblical authoritative books. We could not help referring for instance to Maimonides'tacit confrontation of the talmudic view according to which the outer of the similes is "nothing" and of Solomon's view according to which it is "silver," i.e., politically useful; taken by itself this confrontation suggests that Solomon appreciated the political to a higher degree than did the talmudic Sages. The differences in question are to some extent concealed, since the post-biblical view ordinarily appears in the guise of an explanation of a biblical text. Maimonides discusses this difficulty in regard to homiletic rather than legal explanations; he rejects both the opinion that these explanations are genuine explanations of biblical texts and the opinion that since they are not genuine explanations, they ought not to be taken seriously; in fact the talmudic Sages used a poetic or a charming device, playing as it were with the text of the Bible, in order to introduce moral lessons not found in the Bible (III 43). He indicates that he will not stress his critique of the talmudic Sages (III 14 end). Since the emphasis on serious differences between the Bible and the Talmud could appear in the eyes of the vulgar as a criticism of the talmudic Sages, he has spoken on this subject with considerable, although not extraordinary, restraint. Whenever he presents a view as a view of the Law, one must consider whether he supports his thesis at all by biblical passages, and if he does so, whether the support is sufficient according to his standards as distinguished from traditional Jewish standards. In other words, in studying a given chapter or group of chapters one must observe whether he uses therein any post-biblical Jewish quotations at all and what is the proportion in both number and weight of post-biblical to biblical quotations. In the first chapter explicitly dealing with providence (III 17), he speaks of an "addition" to the text of the Torah that occurs "in the discourse of the Sages"; as one would expect, he disapproves of this particular "addition." This statement is prepared by an immediately preceding cluster of talmudic quotations that are in manifest agreement with the teaching of the Torah and that strike us with particular force because of the almost complete absence of talmudic quotations after the end of III 10. In this twofold way he prepares his silence on the future life in his presentation of the Torah view on providence: the solution of the problem of providence by recourse to the future life is more characteristic of the post-biblical teaching than of the Bible. According to the talmudic Sages, "in the future life there is no eating, nor drinking" and this means that the future life is incorporeal (*M.T.*, H. Teshubah VIII 3). It follows that the Talmud is freer from corporealism than the Bible (I 46, 47, 49, 70, II 3). Accordingly certain talmudic thoughts resemble Platonic thoughts and are expressed with the help of terms of

Greek origin (II 6). Similarly it was Onqelos the Stranger who more than anyone else made corporealism inexcusable within Judaism and may well have thought that it would be improper to speak in Syriac (i.e., Aramaic), as distinguished from Hebrew, of God's perceiving an irrational animal (I 21, 27, 28, 36, 48; cf. II 33). The progress of incorporealism is accompanied by a progress of asceticism. To mention only one example, the Talmud is to say the least much clearer than the Bible about the fact that Abraham had never looked at his beautiful wife until sheer self-preservation compelled him to do so (III 8, 47, 49). There is a corresponding progress in gentleness (I 30 and 54). Finally, the Talmud is more explicit than the Bible regarding the value of the intellectual life and of learning for men in general and for prophets in particular (II 32, 33, 41, III 14, 25, 37, 54). But even the Talmud and Onqelos do not contain the last word regarding the fundamentals as Maimonides indicates by a number of remarks (I 21, 41, II 8–9, 26, 47, III 4–5, 14, 23). One example for each case must suffice. The talmudic Sages follow at least partly the opinion according to which the Law has no other ground than mere Will, whereas "we," says Maimonides, follow the opposite opinion (III 48). "We" is an ambiguous term. As Maimonides has indicated by as it were opening only two chapters (I 62 and 63) with "we," the most important meanings are "we Jews" and "Maimonides." As for Onqelos, he removes through his translation the corporealistic suggestions of the original but he does not make clear what incorporeal things the prophets perceived or what the meaning of a given simile is; this is in accordance with the fact that he translated for the vulgar; but Maimonides explains the similes and he is enabled to do so because of his knowledge of natural science (I 28). Progress beyond Onqelos and the Talmud became possible chiefly for two reasons. In the first place, the ever more deepened effect of the Torah on the Jewish people as well as the rise and political victory of Christianity and Islam have brought it about that the Sabian disease has completely disappeared (III 49, 29). Second, the fundamental verities regarding God are genuinely believed in by nonprophetic men only when they are believed in on the basis of demonstration, but this requires for its perfection that one possess the art of demonstration, and the art of demonstration was discovered by the wise men of Greece or the philosophers, or more precisely by Aristotle (II 15). Even Kalām, i.e., what one may call theology or more precisely the science of demonstrating or defending the roots of the Law, which is directly of Christian origin, owes its origin indirectly to the effect of philosophy on the Law. In spite of its defects, the Kalām is very far from being entirely worthless; and properly understood, as prior to Maimonides it was not, it is even indispensable for the defense of the Law. Kalām entered Judaism long after the talmudic period, in the Gaonic period (I 71, 73). All the more must the introduction of philosophy into Judaism be regarded as a great progress, if it is introduced in due subordination to the Law or in the proper manner (i.e., as Maimonides introduced it to begin with in his legal works). One must also consider the considerable scientific progress that was made by both Greeks and Muslims after Aristotle's time (II 4, 19). All this does not mean, however, that Maimonides regarded his age as the peak of wisdom. He never forgot the power of what one may call the inverted Sabianism that perpetuates corporealism through unqualified submission to the literal meaning of the Bible and thus even outdoes Sabianism proper (I 31); nor did he forget the disastrous effect of the exile (I 71, II 11): "If the belief in the existence of God were not as generally accepted as it is now in the religions [i.e., Judaism, Christianity, and Islam], the darkness of our times would even be greater than the darkness of the times of the sages of Babylon" (III 29). This is to say nothing of the fact that Sabianism proper was not completely eradicated and could be expected to have a future (cf. I 36). It goes without saying that Maimonides also never forgot the Messianic future, a future that may or may not be followed by the end of the world (cf. I 61 with II 27). In spite of this, one is entitled to say that Maimonides regarded the step that he took in the *Guide* as the ultimate step in the decisive respect, namely, in the overcoming of Sabianism. As he modestly put it, no Jew had written an extant book on the secrets of the Law "in these times of the exile" (I Introd.). At the beginning, the power of Sabianism was broken only in a limited part of the world through bloody wars and through concessions to Sabian habits; those concessions were retracted almost completely by the post-Mosaic prophets, by the Aramaic translators, and by the Talmud, to say nothing of the cessation through violence of the sacrificial service, and the conversion of many pagans, which was assisted by military victories, to Christianity or Islam. Now the time has come when even the vulgar must be taught most explicitly that God is incorporeal. Since the Bible suggests corporealism, the vulgar will thus become perplexed. The remedy for this perplexity is the allegoric explanation of the corporealistic utterances or terms that restores the faith in the truth of the Bible (I 35), i.e., precisely what Maimonides is doing in the *Guide*. But the progress in overcoming Sabianism was accompanied by an ever increasing oblivion of Sabianism and thus by an ever increasing inability to remove the last, as it were, fossilized concessions to Sabianism or relics of Sabianism. Maimonides marks a progress even beyond the post-Mosaic prophets in so far as he combines the open depreciation of the sacrifices with a justification of the sacrificial laws of the Torah, for his depreciation of the sacrifices does not as such mean a denial of the obligatory character of the sacrificial laws. He is the man who finally eradicates Sabianism, i.e., corporealism as the hidden premise of idolatry, through the knowledge of Sabianism recovered by him. He recovered that knowledge also through his study of Aristotle, who after all belonged to a Sabian society (II 23).

If the *Torah for the Perplexed* thus marks a progress beyond the Torah for the Unperplexed, Maimonides was compelled to draw the reader's attention at an early stage to the difference between the biblical and the post-biblical teaching. In that stage that difference alone was important. Hence to begin with he treats the Bible on the one hand and the post-biblical writings on the other as unities. Generally speaking, he introduces biblical passages by "he says" (or "his saying is") and talmudic passages by "they say" (or "their saying is"). He thus suggests that in the Bible we hear only a single speaker while in the Talmud we hear indeed many speakers who, however, all agree at least in the important respects. Yet in the first chapter of the *Guide* "he" who speaks is in fact first God, then the narrator, then God, and then "the poor one"; in the second chapter "he" who speaks is the narrator, the serpent, God, and so on; God "says" something and the narrator "makes clear and says." But the *Guide* as a whole constitutes an ascent from the common view, or an imitation of the common view, to a discerning view. Accordingly, Maimonides gradually brings out the differences concealed by the stereotyped, not to say ritual, expressions. For instance, in I 32 he introduces each of four biblical quotations by the expression "he indicated by his speech"; only in the last case does he give the name of the speaker, namely, David; the saying of David is somewhat more akin in spirit than the preceding three sayings (of Solomon) to a saying of the talmudic Sages quoted immediately afterward; the talmudic Sages had noted that Solomon contradicted his father David (I Introd. toward the end). In I 34 he introduces by the expression "they say" the saying of a talmudic Sage who tells what "I have seen." The unnamed "he" who, according to I 44, spoke as Jeremiah's providence was Nebuchadnezzar. In I 49 he quotes five biblical passages; in two cases he gives the names of the biblical authors, in one of the two cases adding "may he rest in peace" to the name. In I 70 he introduces a talmudic passage with the expression "They said," while he says at the end of the quotation, "This is literally what he said." Names of biblical teachers occur with unusual frequency in some chapters, the first of which is II 19 and the last of which is III 32. Near the beginning of II 29 Maimonides notes that every prophet had a diction peculiar to him and that this peculiarity was preserved in what God said to the individual prophet or through him. The prophet singled out for extensive discussion from this point of view is Isaiah; thereafter six of the other prophets are briefly discussed in a sequence that agrees with the sequence of their writings in the canon; only in the case of the prophet who occupies the central place (Joel) is the name of the prophet's father added to the name of the prophet. One must also not neglect the references to the difference between the Torah proper and the

Mishneh Torah, i.e., Deuteronomy (cf. II 34–35 and III 24). Maimonides' link with the Torah is, to begin with, an iron bond; it gradually becomes a fine thread. But however far what one may call his intellectualization may go, it always remains the intellectualization of the Torah.

Our desire to give the readers some hints for the better understanding of the second subsection compelled us to look beyond the immediate context. Returning to that context we observe that after Maimonides has concluded the second subsection, he again does something perplexing. The last chapter of the second subsection dealt with "foot"; that passage of the Torah on which the second subsection is based speaks emphatically of God's "face" and His "back"; nothing would have been simpler for Maimonides than to devote the third subsection to terms designating parts of the animate body or of the animal. Instead he devotes the fourth subsection to this subject; the first two chapters of the fourth subsection are devoted precisely to "face" and to "back" (I 37 and 38). The third subsection, which deals with an altogether different subject, thus seems to be out of place or to be a disconcerting insertion. Furthermore, the third subsection is the least exegetic or the most speculative among the subsections devoted to Incorporeality; six of its eight chapters are not lexicographic; five of them are in no obvious sense devoted to the explanation of biblical terms and do not contain a single quotation from the Torah; one of these chapters (I 31) is the first chapter of the *Guide* that does not contain a single Jewish (Hebrew or Aramaic) expression, and another (I 35) does not contain a single quotation of Jewish (biblical or talmudic) passages. One is tempted to believe that it would have been more in accordance with the spirit of the book if the most speculative among the subsections devoted to Incorporeality had formed the end of the part devoted to that subject. In order to understand these apparent irregularities, it is best to start from the consideration that, for the general reason indicated, Maimonides desired to divide each of the seven sections of the *Guide* into seven subsections and that for a more particular reason he decided to treat Unity in three subsections; hence Incorporeality had to be treated in four subsections. Furthermore, it was necessary to place almost all lexicographic chapters within the part treating Incorporeality or conversely it was necessary that the majority of chapters dealing with Incorporeality should be lexicographic. For the reasons given where they had to be given, it proved convenient that the majority of chapters of the first subsection should be nonlexicographic and the majority of chapters of the second subsection should be lexicographic. It is this proportion of the first two subsections that Maimonides decided to imitate in the last two subsections devoted to Incorporeality: the majority of chapters of the third subsection became nonlexicographic and the majority of chapters of the fourth subsection became lexicographic, but — for a reason to be indicated presently — in such a way that the third subsection is more predominantly nonlexicographic than the first, and the fourth subsection is more predominantly lexicographic than the second. It is reasonable to expect that the distribution of lexicographic and nonlexicographic chapters among the four subsections has some correspondence to the subject matter of those subsections. If one defines their subject matter by reference to the subject matter of their lexicographic chapters, one arrives at this result: the first subsection deals with the specific form, the sexual difference, and generating, while the third subsection deals with sorrow and eating; the second subsection deals chiefly with acts of local motion or rest, while the fourth subsection deals chiefly with the parts of the animate body and sense-perception. To understand this arrangement it suffices both to observe that the first quotation regarding sorrow is "in sorrow thou shalt bring forth children" (Gen. 3:16) and to read Maimonides' explanation (in I 46) of the relation that links the parts of the animal and its acts to the ends of preservation. Furthermore, it would be a great mistake to believe that the emphasis on sorrow and eating is weakened because these two themes are the only lexicographic themes of the subsection in which they are discussed. Finally, Maimonides used in the most appropriate manner the lexicographic chapters devoted to sorrow and to eating as an introduction to the first series of speculative chapters occurring in the *Guide* and thus brought it about that the third subsection (in contradistinction to the first and the second) ends with nonlexicographic chapters (I 31–36); he thus prepared a similar ending of the fourth subsection (I 46–49); this enabled him to indicate by the position of the next lexicographic chapter (I 70), which is the last lexicographic chapter, as clearly as possible the end of the first section or the fact that I 1–70 form the first section.

The term ʿaṣab, which we thought convenient in our context to render by "sorrow," as well as the term "eating," may refer to God's wrath with those who rebel against Him or to His enmity to them. Since His wrath is directed exclusively against idolatry and since His enemies are exclusively the idolaters (I 36), the two terms refer indirectly to idolatry. But "eating" is used also for the acquisition of knowledge. With a view to this second metaphoric meaning of "eating," Maimonides devotes to the subject of human knowledge the five speculative chapters immediately following the explanation of "eating" (I 30). In the last chapter of the subsection (I 36) he reconsiders the prohibition against idolatry on the basis of what had emerged in the five speculative chapters. The third subsection deals then with both idolatry and knowledge in such a way that the discussion of idolatry surrounds the discussion of knowledge. This arrangement affects the discussion of knowledge: Maimonides discusses knowledge with a view to its limitations, to the harm that may come from it and to the dangers attending it.

One can say that the first series of speculative chapters occurring in the *Guide* deals with forbidden knowledge (cf. particularly I 32) — forbidden to all or to most men — within the context of forbidden worship.

The third subsection throws light on the relation between the Bible and the Talmud. Since we have treated this subject before, we limit ourselves to the following remark. In the chapter dealing with "eating," Maimonides explicitly refuses to give an example of the use of the word in its primary meaning: the derivative meaning according to which the word designates the taking of non-corporeal food has become so widespread as to become as it were the primary meaning (cf. the quotation from Isa. 1:20 with Isa. 1:19). Regarding the meaning of "eating" as consuming or destroying, which he illustrates by four quotations from the Torah and two quotations from the prophets, he says that it occurs frequently, namely, in the Bible; regarding the meaning of "eating" as acquiring knowledge, which he illustrates by two quotations from Isaiah and two from the Proverbs, he says that it occurs frequently also in the discourse of the talmudic Sages and he proves this by two quotations. No talmudic quotation had illustrated the meanings of ᶜaṣab. The talmudic Sages compared the acquisition of knowledge of the divine things to the eating of honey and applied to that knowledge the saying of Solomon: "Hast thou found honey? Eat so much as is sufficient for thee, lest thou be filled therewith, and vomit it." They thus taught that in seeking knowledge one must not go beyond certain limits: one must not reflect on what is above, what is below, what was before, and what will be hereafter — which Maimonides takes to refer to "vain imaginings" (I 32): Maimonides, who explains what is meant by the fact that man has a natural desire for knowledge (I 34), warns not against the desire for comprehensive knowledge, but against seeming knowledge.

With regard to the fourth subsection, we must limit ourselves to the observation that it is the first subsection that lacks any reference to philosophy or philosophers. On the other hand the expression "in my opinion" (ᶜindī), which indicates the difference between Maimonides' opinion and traditional opinions, occurs about twice as frequently in the fourth subsection as in the first three subsections taken together. Another substitute is the references to grammarians in I 41 and 43 — references that ought to be contrasted with the parallels in I 8 and 10 — as well as the rather frequent references to the Arabic language. One grammarian is mentioned by name: Ibn Janāh, i.e., the Son of Wing who with the help of Arabic correctly interpreted the Hebrew term for "wing" as sometimes meaning "veil" and who may therefore be said to have uncovered "Wing." Another substitute is the reference (in I 42) to an Andalusian interpreter who, in agreement with Greek medicine, had explained as a natural event the apparent resurrection of the son of a widow by the prophet Elijah. Through his quotations from the Bible in the same chapter Maimonides refers among other things to a severe illness caused by the circumcision of adults as well as to the biblical treatment of leprosy. The chapter in question deals with the Hebrew term for "living"; that term is the only one occurring in the lexicographic chapters of this subsection that is not said to be homonymous; this silence is pregnant with grave implications regarding "the living God" (cf. I 30 and 41).

The last chapter of the fourth subsection is the only chapter of the *Guide* that opens with the expression "The angels." This chapter sets forth the assertion that the angels are incorporeal, i.e., it deals with the incorporeality of something of which there is a plurality. Maimonides thus makes clear that Incorporeality and not Unity is still the theme as it had been from the beginning. The next chapter opens the discussion of Unity. Incorporeality had presented itself as a consequence of Unity; Unity had been the presupposition, an unquestioned presupposition. Unity now becomes the theme. We are told at the beginning that Unity must be understood clearly, not, as it is understood by the Christians, to be compatible with God's trinity, or, more generally stated, with a multiplicity in God (I 50). In the fifth subsection Maimonides effects the transformation of the common, not to say traditional, understanding of Unity, which allowed a multiplicity of positive attributes describing God Himself, into such an understanding as is in accordance with the requirements of speculation. The fifth subsection is the first subsection of the *Guide* that may be said to be entirely speculative. Hence the discussion of Unity, in contradistinction to the discussion of Incorporeality, is characterized by a clear, if implicit, distinction between the speculative and the exegetic discussion of the subject. In the first four subsections there occurred only one chapter without any Jewish expression; in the fifth subsection five such chapters occur. In the first forty-nine chapters there occurred only nine chapters without any quotation from the Torah; in the eleven chapters of the fifth subsection ten such chapters occur. In spite of its speculative character the fifth subsection does not demonstrate that God is one; it continues the practice of the preceding subsections by presupposing that God is one (I 53, 58, 68). Yet from this presupposition it draws all conclusions and not merely the conclusion that God is incorporeal: if God is one, one in every possible respect, absolutely simple, there cannot be any positive attribute of God except attributes describing His actions.

Maimonides knows by demonstration that God is one. The addressee, being insufficiently trained in natural science (cf. I 55 with I 52), does not know Unity by demonstration but through the Jewish tradition and ultimately through the Bible. The most important biblical text is "Hear, O Israel, the Lord is our God, the Lord is one" (Deut. 6:4; cf. *M.T.*, H. Yesodei ha-Torah I 7). To our very great amazement, Maimonides does not quote this verse a single time in any of the chapters devoted to Unity. He quotes it a single time in the *Guide*, imitating the Torah, which, as he says, mentions the principle of Unity, namely, this verse, only once (*Resurrection* 20, 1–2). He quotes the verse in III 45, i.e., the 169th chapter, thus perhaps alluding to the thirteen divine attributes ("merciful, gracious . . .") proclaimed by God to Moses. Whatever else that silence may mean, it certainly indicates the gravity of the change effected by Maimonides in the understanding of Unity. The demonstrated teaching that positive attributes of God are impossible stems from the philosophers (I 59, III 20); it clearly contradicts the teaching of the Law in so far as the Law does not limit itself to teaching that the only true praise of God is silence but it also prescribes that we call God "great, mighty, and terrible" in our prayers. Hence the full doctrine of attributes may not be revealed to the vulgar (I 59) or is a secret teaching. But since that doctrine (which includes the provision that certain points that are made fully clear in the *Guide* are not to be divulged), is set forth with utmost explicitness and orderliness in that book, it is also an exoteric teaching (I 35), if a philosophic exoteric teaching.

As Maimonides indicates, the meaning of "the Lord is one" is primarily that there is no one or nothing similar or equal to Him and only derivatively that He is absolutely simple (cf. I 57 end with I 58). He develops the notion of God's incomparability, of there being no likeness whatsoever between Him and any other being on the basis of quotations from Isaiah and Jeremiah as distinguished from the Torah (cf. I 55 with I 54). He is silent here on Deuteronomy 4:35 ("the Lord he is God; there is none else beside him"), on a verse that he quotes in a kindred context in his Code (H. Yesodei ha-Torah I 4) and in different contexts in the *Guide* (II 33, III 32 and 51). Yet absolute dissimilarity or incomparability to everything else is characteristic of nothing as well as of God. What is meant by God's absolute dissimilarity or incomparability is His perfection: it is because He is of incomparable perfection that He is incomparable; it is because He is of unspeakable perfection that nothing positive can be said of Him in strict speech and that everything positive said of Him is in fact (if it does not indicate His actions rather than Himself) only the denial of some imperfection. The meaning of the doctrine of attributes is that God is the absolute perfect being, the complete and perfectly self-sufficient good, the being of absolute beauty or nobility (I 35, 53, 58, 59, 60 end, II 22). If this were not so, Maimonides' doctrine of attributes would be entirely negative and even subversive. For that doctrine culminates in the assertion that we grasp of God only that He is and not what He is in such a manner that every positive predication made of Him, including that He "is," has only the name in common with what we mean when we apply such predications to any being (I 56,

58, 59, 60). If we did not know that God is absolutely perfect, we would ascribe we know not what to what we do not know, in ascribing to Him "being," or we would ascribe nothing to nothing; we certainly would not know what we were talking about. What is true of "being" is true of "one," i.e., of the immediate presupposition of the whole argument of the first section of the *Guide*. Let no one say that Maimonides admits attributes of action as distinguished from the negative attributes; for, not to enter into the question whether this distinction is ultimately tenable (cf. I 59), through the attributes of action God is understood as the cause of certain effects, and it is difficult to see how "cause," if applied to God, can have more than the name in common with "cause" as an intelligible expression. But since we understand by God the absolutely perfect being, we mean the goodness of His creation or governance when we say that He is the "cause" of something (cf. I 46). By his doctrine of attributes Maimonides not only overcomes all possible anthropomorphisms, but also answers the question whether the different perfections that God is said to possess in the highest degree are compatible with one another or whether certain perfections known to us as human perfections — for instance, justice — can be understood to constitute in their absolute form divine perfection: God's perfection is an unfathomable abyss. Thus we understand why the doctrine in question in spite of its philosophic origin can be regarded as the indeed un-biblical but nevertheless appropriate expression of the biblical principle, namely, of the biblical teaching regarding the hidden God who created the world out of nothing, not in order to increase the good — for since He is the complete good, the good cannot be increased by His actions — but without any ground, in absolute freedom, and whose essence is therefore indicated by "Will" rather than by "Wisdom" (III 13).

From the speculative discussion of the divine attributes, which as positive predications about God Himself proved to be mere names, Maimonides turns in the second of the three subsections dealing with Unity to the purely exegetic discussion of the divine names; the exegetic discussion still deals with "the denial of attributes" (I 62 and 65 beginning). It seems that the audible holy names have taken the place of the visible holy images, and it is certain that "name" is connected with "honor" and everything related to honor. The difficulty is caused less by the multiplicity of divine names — for, as the prophet says, in the day of the Lord "the Lord shall be one and his name shall be one" (Zech. 14:9) — than by the fact that this most sacred name, the only divine name antedating creation (I 61), is communicated to men by God (Exod. 6:2-3) and not coined or created by human beings. Since God does not speak, Maimonides must therefore open the whole question of God's speaking, writing, and ceasing to speak or to act (I 65-67). Furthermore, the most sacred name, which is the only name indicating God's essence and which thus might be thought to lead us beyond the confines of human speculation, is certainly no longer intelligible, since we know very little of Hebrew today (I 61–62). Therefore in the last subsection devoted to Unity (I 68–70), which is the last subsection of the first section, Maimonides returns to speculation. It would be more accurate to say that he now turns to philosophy. In the three chapters in question he refers to philosophy, I believe, more frequently than in the whole discussion of Incorporeality (I 1–49) and certainly more frequently than in the speculative discussion of the attributes (I 50–60); in the exegetic discussion of the divine names (I 61–67), if I am not mistaken, he does not refer to philosophy at all. He now with the support of the philosophers takes up the subject that we cannot help calling the divine attribute of intellect as distinguished from the divine attribute of speech in particular (cf. I 65 beginning). We learn that in God the triad "intellect, intellecting, and the intellected" are one and the same thing in which there is no multiplicity, just as they are one in us when we actually think (I 68). Maimonides does not even allude here to the possibility that "intellect" when applied to God has only the name in common with "intellect" when applied to us. It may be true that God thinks only Himself so that His intellection is only self-intellection and is therefore one and simple in a way in which our intellection cannot be one and simple, but this does not contradict the univocity of "intellect" in its application to God and to us. Self-intellection is what we mean when we speak of God as "living" (cf. I 53). It follows that even "life" is not merely homonymous when applied to God and to us. It likewise follows that what is true of the intellect is not true of the will: the act of willing and the thing willed as willed are not the same as the act of thinking and the thing thought as thought are the same. The reader of the next chapter (I 69) may find this observation useful for understanding Maimonides' acceptance of the philosophic view according to which God is not only the efficient or moving and the final cause of the world but also the form of the world or, in the expression of the Jewish tradition, "the life of the worlds," which he says means "the life of the world."

This must suffice toward making clear the perplexing and upsetting character of Maimonides' teaching regarding Unity. The true state of things is somewhat obscured, to say nothing of other matters, by a certain kind of learning that some readers of the *Guide* can at all times be presumed to possess: the doctrine of attributes restates the Neoplatonic teaching, and Neoplatonism had affected Jewish thinkers long before Maimonides; those thinkers had already succeeded somehow in reconciling Neoplatonism with Judaism. But when different men do the same thing, it is not necessarily the same thing, and Maimonides surely did not do exactly the same thing as the pagan, Islamic, or Jewish Neoplatonists who preceded him. Every open minded and discerning reader must be struck by the difference between the hidden God of Maimonides' doctrine of attributes and the hidden God who spoke to the Patriarchs and to Moses or, to employ Maimonides' manner of expression, by the difference between the true understanding of God as it was possessed by the Patriarchs and by Moses and the understanding of God on the part of the uninitiated Jews. The result of his doctrine of the divine attributes is that the notion of God that gives life and light to the ordinary believers is not only inadequate or misleading but is the notion of something that simply does not exist—of a merely imaginary being, the theme of deceived and deceiving men (I 60). What is true of the ordinary believer is true at least to some extent of the addressee of the *Guide*. The destruction of the old foundation forces him to seek for a new foundation: he is now compelled to be passionately concerned with demonstration, with the demonstration not only of God's unity but of His very being in a sense of "being" that cannot be entirely homonymous. For now he knows that the being of God is doubtful as long as it is not established by demonstration (I 71). Now he has been brought to the point where he must make up his mind whether or not he will turn altogether to the way of demonstration. Maimonides shows him three ways of demonstrating God's being, unity, and incorporeality: the way of the Kalām, the way of the philosophers, and Maimonides' own way (I 71 end, 76 end, II 1 end). While Maimonides cannot simply accept the philosophers' way, he prefers it to that of the Kalām for the following reason. The Kalām begins, not from the world as we know it through our senses or from the fact that things have determinate natures, but from asserting that what the philosophers call the nature, say, of air is only custom and hence of no inherent necessity: everything could be entirely different from what it is. The Kalām cannot live without reference to what we know through our senses, for in contradistinction to simple belief whose first premise is the absolute will of God, it attempts to demonstrate that God is and hence it must start from the given, and at the same time it must deny the authoritative character of the given. The philosophers on the other hand start from what is given or manifest to the senses (I 71, 73). Maimonides turns first to the analysis and critique of the Kalām-demonstrations. He presents the premises of the Kalām (I 73) and then the Kalām demonstrations that are based on those premises (I 74–76). Maimonides' critique does not limit itself to the technical Kalām reasoning. For instance, the first proof of the createdness of the world and therewith of the being of the Creator assumes that the bodies that we see around us have come into being through an artificer and infers from this that the world as a whole is the work of an artificer. This proof, which does not make any use of the premises peculiar to the Kalām, is based on inability, or at any rate failure, to distinguish between the artificial and the natural. The second proof is based on the premise that no infinite whatever is possible; it therefore first traces men to a first man, Adam, who came out of dust, which in turn came out of water, and then traces water itself to unqualified nothing out of which water could not have been brought into being except by the act of the Creator (I 74; cf. *Logic* chaps. 7, 8, 11). It is not difficult to recognize in this proof elements of biblical origin. Since the Kalām premises as stated by Maimonides are necessary for the Kalām proofs (I 73 beginning and toward the end) and the Kalām proofs do not in all cases follow from those premises, those premises while necessary are not sufficient. After all, the Kalām selected its premises with a view to proving the roots of the Law: the premise of its premises is those roots. While the First Part ends with the critique of the Kalām, the Second Part opens with "The premises required for establishing the being of God and for demonstrating that He is not a body nor a force in a body and that He is one," i.e., with the premises established by the philosophers. Maimonides thus indicates that the seventy-six chapters of the First Part, which lead up to philosophy through a critique of the popular notions of God as well as of theology, are negative and pre-philosophic, whereas the one hundred and two chapters of the Second and Third Parts are positive or edifying. In other words, the First Part is chiefly devoted to biblical exegesis and to the Kalām, i.e., to the two trans-logical and trans-mathematical subjects mentioned even in the very Epistle Dedicatory.

The Kalām proves that God as the Creator is, is one, and is incorporeal by proving first that the world has been created; but it proves that premise only by dialectical or sophistical arguments. The philosophers prove that God is, is one, and is incorporeal by assuming that the world is eternal, but they cannot demonstrate that assumption. Hence both ways are defective. Maimonides' way consists in a combination of these two defective ways. For, he argues, "the world is eternal — the world is created" is a complete disjunction; since God's being, unity, and incorporeality necessarily follow from either of the only two possible assumptions, the basic verities have been demonstrated by this very fact (I 71, II 2). Yet the results from opposed premises cannot be simply identical. For instance, someone might have said prior to the Second World War that Germany would be prosperous regardless of whether she won or lost the war; if she won, her prosperity would follow immediately; if she lost, her prosperity would be assured by the United States of America who would need her as an ally against Soviet Russia; but the predictor would have abstracted from the difference between Germany as the greatest power which ruled tyrannically and was ruled tyrannically, and Germany as a second-rank power ruled democratically. The God whose being is proved on the assumption of eternity is the unmoved mover, thought that thinks only itself and that as such is the form or the life of the world. The God whose being is proved on the assumption of creation is the biblical God who is characterized by Will and whose knowledge has only the name in common with our knowledge. If we consider the situation as outlined by Maimonides, we see that what is demonstrated by his way is only what is common to the two different notions of God or what is neutral to the difference between God as pure Intellect and God as Will or what is beyond that difference or what has only the name in common with either Intellect or Will. But God thus understood is precisely God as presented in the doctrine of attributes: Maimonides' demonstration of God's being illumines retroactively his merely assertoric doctrine of attributes. God thus understood can be said to be more extra-mundane not only than the philosophers' God but even than the biblical God; this understanding of God lays the foundation for the most radical asceticism both theoretical and practical (III 51). In other words, both opposite assumptions lead indeed to God as the most perfect being; yet even the Sabians regard their god, i.e., the sphere and its stars, as the most perfect being (III 45); generally stated, everyone understands by God the most perfect being in the sense of the most perfect possible being; the doctrine of attributes understood in the light of its subsequent demonstration leads to God as the most perfect being whose perfection is characterized by the fact that in Him Intelligence and Will are indistinguishable because they are both identical with His essence (cf. I 69). Yet, since the world is of necessity either created or eternal, it becomes necessary to restore the distinction between Intellect and Will. Generally speaking, the *Guide* moves between the view that Intellect and Will are indistinguishable and the view that they must be distinguished (and hence that one must understand God as Intelligence rather than as Will) in accordance with the requirements of the different subjects under discussion (cf. II 25 and III 25). For instance, in his discussion of Omniscience — in the same context in which he reopens the question regarding the relative rank of imagination and intellect — Maimonides solves the difficulty caused by the apparent incompatibility of Omniscience and human freedom (III 17) by appealing to the identity of Intellect and Will, whereas in his discussion of the reasons for the biblical commandments he prefers the view that the commandments stem from God's intellect to the view that they stem from His will.

The reader of the *Guide* must consider with the proper care not only the outline of Maimonides' way but also all its windings. In doing this he must never forget that the demonstration of the basic verities and the discussion of that demonstration is immediately preceded by the discussion of Unity or that the discussion of Unity constitutes the transition from exegesis to speculation. If the world or more precisely the sphere is created, it is indeed self-evident that it was created by some agent but it does not necessarily follow that the creator is one, let alone absolutely simple, and that he is incorporeal. On the other hand, if the sphere is eternal, it follows, as Aristotle has shown, that God is and is incorporeal; but on this assumption the angels or separate intelligences, each of which is the mover of one of the many spheres, are as eternal as God (cf. I 71, II 2 and 6). It is therefore a question whether monotheism strictly understood is demonstrable. Maimonides does say that Unity and also Incorporeality follow from certain philosophic proofs that do not presuppose either the eternity of the world or its creation, but it is, to say the least, not quite clear whether the proofs in question do not in fact presuppose the eternity of the world (cf. II 2 with II 1). Besides, if there were such proofs, one is tempted to say that there is no need whatever for provisionally granting the eternity of the world in order to demonstrate God's being, unity, and incorporeality, yet Maimonides asserts most emphatically that there is such a need. None of these or similar difficulties is, however, by any means the most serious difficulty. For while the belief in God's unity, being, and incorporeality is required by the Law, that belief, being compatible with the belief in the eternity of the world, is compatible with the unqualified rejection of the Law: the Law stands or falls by the belief in the creation of the world. It is therefore incumbent on Maimonides to show that Aristotle or Aristotelianism is wrong in holding that the eternity of the world has been demonstrated: the eternity of the world which was the basis of the demonstration of God's being, unity, and incorporeality is a dubious assumption. Yet it is not sufficient to refute the claims of Aristotelianism in order to establish the possibility of creation as the Law understands creation, for if the world is not necessarily eternal it may still have been created out of eternal matter. Maimonides is then compelled to abandon or at any rate to refine the disjunction on which his original argument was based. The original disjunction (the world is either eternal or created) is incomplete at least to the extent that it blurs the difference between creation out of matter and creation out of nothing. It brings out the opposition between Aristotle and the Law but it conceals the intermediate possibility presented in Plato's *Timaeus*. Plato's version of the doctrine of eternity is not inimical to the Law, for while Aristotle's version excludes the possibility of any miracle, the Platonic version does not exclude all miracles as necessarily impossible. Maimonides does not say which miracles are excluded by the Platonic teaching. Two possible answers suggest themselves immediately. It is according to nature that what has come into being will perish; but according to the Law both Israel and the souls of the virtuous have come into being and will not perish; hence their eternity *a parte post* is a miracle, a miracle that is more in accordance with creation out of nothing than with creation out of eternal matter. Second, God's special providence for Israel, according to which Israel prospers if it obeys and is miserable if it disobeys, is a miracle not likely to be admitted by Plato, whose teaching on providence seems to have been identical with that presented in the Book of Job: providence follows naturally the intelligence of the individual human being. In accordance with his judgment on the relation between the Aristotelian doctrine and the doctrine of the Law, Maimonides proves by an extensive argument that the Aristotelian doctrine is not demonstrated and is in addition not probable. As for the Platonic doctrine, he explicitly refuses to pay any attention to it on the additional ground that it has not been demonstrated (II 13, 25–27, 29, III 18; *Yemen* 24, 7–10; *Resurrection* 33, 16–36, 17; *Letter on Astrology* §§ 19 ff. Marx). That ground is somewhat strange because according to Maimonides the Aristotelian and the biblical alternatives have not been demonstrated either. In his critique of the Aristotelian doctrine he makes use of the Kalām argument based on a premise that so defines the possible that it might be either the imaginable or the non-self-contradictory or that regarding which we cannot make any definite assertions because of our lack of knowledge; the premise in question excludes the view according to which the possible is what is capable of being or what is in accordance with the nature of the thing in question or with what possesses an available specific substratum (cf. I 75, II 14, III 15). The reader must find out what the premises of the preferred premise are, how Maimonides judges of those premises, and whether the argument based on the premise in question renders improbable not only the eternity of the visible universe but the eternity of matter as well. At any rate, being compelled to question the Aristotelian doctrine, Maimonides is compelled to question the adequacy of Aristotle's account of heaven. That questioning culminates in the assertions that Aristotle had indeed perfect knowledge of the sublunar things but hardly any knowledge of the things of heaven and ultimately that man as man has no such knowledge: man has knowledge only of the earth and the earthly things, i.e., of beings that are bodies or in bodies. In the words of the Psalmist (115:16): "The heavens, even the heavens, are the Lord's; but the earth hath he given to the children of Man." Accordingly, Maimonides suggests that the truth regarding providence, i.e., that theological truth which is of vital importance to human life, comes to sight by the observation of the sublunar phenomena alone. Even the proof of the First Mover of heaven, i.e., the philosophic proof of God's being, unity, and incorporeality, to say nothing of the being of the other separate intelligences, becomes a subject of perplexity (II 22, 24; cf. II 3, 19, III 23). And yet it was knowledge of heaven that was said to supply the best proof, not to say the only proof, of the being of God (II 18). Maimonides had said earlier that very little demonstration is possible regarding divine matters and much of it regarding natural matters (I 31). Now he seems to suggest that the only genuine science of beings is natural science or a part of it. It is obvious that one cannot leave it at this apparent suggestion. The least that one would have to add is that the strange remarks referred to occur within the context in which Maimonides questions Aristotle's account of heaven in the name of astronomy or, more precisely, in which he sets forth the conflict between philosophic cosmology and mathematical astronomy — that conflict which he calls "the true perplexity": the hypotheses on which astronomy rests cannot be true and yet they alone enable one to give an account of the heavenly phenomena in terms of circular and uniform motions. Astronomy shows the necessity of recurring for the purpose of calculation and prediction to what is possible in a philosophically inadmissible sense (II 24).

We have been compelled to put a greater emphasis on Maimonides' perplexities than on his certainties, and in particular on his vigorous and skillful defense of the Law, because the latter are more easily accessible than the former. Besides, what at first glance seems to be merely negative is negative only in the sense in which every liberation, being a liberation not only to something but also from something, contains a negative ingredient. So we may conclude with the words of Maimonides with which we began: The *Guide* is "a key permitting one to enter places the gates to which were locked. When those gates are opened and those places are entered, the souls will find rest therein, the bodies will be eased of their toil, and the eyes will be delighted."

Leo Strauss

TRANSLATOR'S INTRODUCTION

THE PHILOSOPHIC SOURCES OF
The Guide of the Perplexed

*

MAIMONIDES (1135–1204) wrote *The Guide of the Perplexed* in his mature age, after he had composed several works on the halakhah (notably *Mishneh Torah*) and also one treatise on logic, a juvenile effort, entitled *Sinā'at al-manṭiq*, "the art of logic," but better known under the Hebrew name *Milloth Ha-higgayon*. As far as the method of exposition is concerned, there is a striking difference between *Mishneh Torah* and the *Guide of the Perplexed*,[1] in which the earlier work is repeatedly referred to. In the *Mishneh Torah* Maimonides set out to produce order — a systematic, lucid, and authoritative legal code — out of the chaotic disorder of talmudic literature, and he succeeded most admirably in this undertaking. In the *Guide*, on the other hand, the systematic expositions of the Aristotelian philosophers are often dislocated and broken up; sometimes wholly unconnected subjects are brought together; in a word, order is turned into disorder. As Maimonides explains in his Introduction this was done for good and sufficient reasons and does not, by any means, indicate that he had lost his gift for lucid exposition. Indeed this gift is brilliantly displayed in certain passages of the *Guide*, for instance in the formulation of the premises of the Mutakallimūn (I 73) and of the premises of the philosophers (beginning of Part II).

The peculiar method used by Maimonides in composing his work is perhaps the main reason for the disconcerting impression it is apt to produce at first upon most of its readers. This impression was certainly aimed at by Maimonides. His book's impact depends upon it. However, the educated public of Maimonides'

1. See Leo Strauss, "The Literary Character of the Guide for the Perplexed," in *Essays on Maimonides; An Octocentennial Volume*, ed. S. W. Baron (New York, 1941), pp. 37–91.

times was better prepared than modern readers to grasp intentions hinted at in veiled language and doctrines deliberately obscured by an extremely unsystematic method of exposition, for the philosophic tradition upon which Maimonides drew was much easier of access in those days, as its study was included in a relatively widely used curriculum. The additional difficulties with which the present-day reader of this text is faced cannot accordingly be readily overcome. Nevertheless, after a few general remarks, indications, which may prove helpful, will be given concerning Maimonides' philosophic sources, his evaluation of them, and the way in which he utilizes them.

The Introduction to the *Guide* makes it clear that philosophic science may be dangerous; that the study of philosophy, or of its rudiments, may bring about that state of perplexity — due to an unresolved conflict between religious tradition and nonreligious knowledge — which gives the book its name; that strict precautions must be taken with a view to keeping the average reader, who is also an average man, in the dark concerning the philosophic solution propounded by Maimonides. Philosophy is thus regarded as a dangerous temptation and as a very potent one at that. From Maimonides' point of view the fascination it exercises can easily be accounted for. It is the fascination of truth. Maimonides was in a difficult predicament not so much because of the belief that he claims to hold that there can be no intellectually convincing answer to certain crucial questions, such as the temporal creation of the world, but because of his certainties; he knew, because his reason told him so, that for the greater part the Aristotelian doctrines were wholly true.

This does not merely mean that he regarded these doctrines as adequate for only a certain imperfect state of scientific knowledge. Historicism did not bedevil him as it does our contemporaries, at least not to the same extent. He recognized that sciences may progress and have done so in the past, but considered that some of them, for instance sublunar physics, were complete and perfect, being incapable of further progress except perhaps in details. He also considered that this was not merely a matter of personal opinion and would, no doubt, have held the modern question that concerns itself with what Maimonides really believed as nugatory or a red herring. The Introduction is avowedly to a large extent a study in the art of *suppressio veri* and *suggestio falsi*. But it is not his personal opinions that Maimonides primarily wishes to conceal from the insufficiently gifted or uneducated readers; he does not want to put them on the track of the secrets of the universe. And, conversely, his hints, his veiled language, and also the lucid expositions he sometimes inserts, are not meant in the first place to enable the sufficiently qualified readers to discover what were the beliefs sincerely held by Maimonides, but to give them an inkling of the true nature of things. This kind of knowledge was not Maimonides' personal discovery. He had no wish to be an innovator in either physics or metaphysics;[2] in fact he expressly disclaims any pretension to putting forward in the *Guide* an original philosophic doctrine.[3] This need not mean that no discoveries were any longer possible. He did, however, hold the conviction that, in regard to essentials the Aristotelian philosophy provides a system of knowledge, in part certainly true and in part more or less probable, that embodies the supreme achievements of the human intellect when geared to its highest form of activity.

This system is not accepted by Maimonides or by any other important philosopher on trust, but for good rational reasons. It is, however, accepted; which means that Aristotle's works, the commentaries on them, and the various interpretations of the Philosopher's opinions acquire considerable importance. There were many forms of Aristotelianism, and it may be a fruitful line of inquiry to try to define and, if necessary, to identify the philosophic influences that helped Maimonides to form the conceptions set forth in the *Guide* and, additionally, to indicate his own attitude to the various Peripatetic schools, which had incorporated many doctrines alien to Aristotle. The avowedly non-Aristotelian philosophic and kalām sources that Maimonides used when writing the *Guide* will also be investigated.

As we shall see later on, a considerable amount of information concerning Maimonides' sources and his way of using them is provided by the *Guide* itself. However we shall begin this investigation with another text of Maimonides, a letter written by him in Arabic to Samuel Ibn Tibbon, the translator of the *Guide* into Hebrew, which gives us invaluable indications regarding Maimonides' attitude toward earlier philosophers.

The letter has come down to us in several Hebrew versions, two of which have been edited by A. Marx in the *Jewish Quarterly Review* (see N.S. XXV, pp. 374 ff.; the relevant passages occur on pp. 378–80). Both versions have been utilized in the excerpts that are given here.

"The writings [literally: words] of Aristotle's teacher Plato are in parables and hard to understand. One can dispense with them, for the writings of Aristotle suffice, and we need not occupy [our attention] with the writings of earlier [philosophers]. Aristotle's intellect [represents] the extreme of human intellect, if we except those who have received divine inspiration."

"The works of Aristotle are the roots and foundations of all works on the sciences. But they cannot be understood except with the help of commentaries, those of Alexander of Aphrodisias, those of Themistius, and those of Averroes."

2. From a modern point of view he might, however, be held to have had new ideas on the philosophy of history.

3. See II 2. Evidently this does not mean that he wished to confine himself altogether to transcribing the philosophic opinions of his predecessors. On matters of detail, he sometimes sets forth opinions of his own.

"I tell you: as for works on logic, one should only study the writings of Abū Naṣr al-Fārābī. All his writings are faultlessly excellent. One ought to study and understand them. For he is a great man."

"Though the work of Avicenna may give rise to objections and are not as [good] as those of Abū Naṣr [al-Fārābī],[4] Abū Bakr[5] al-Ṣāʾigh [Ibn Bājja] was also a great philosopher, and all his writings are of a high standard."

Furthermore, Maimonides states his opinion (which has proved to be correct) that two works attributed to Aristotle, the *Book of the Apple* and the *Book of the Golden Palace*, are pseudepigraphs.

He advises against studying the commentaries on Aristotle of the Christian authors al-Ṭayyib, Yaḥyā Ibn ʿAdī, and Yaḥyā al-Biṭrīq. To read them would be a sheer waste of time.

He also states that he has no use for Abū Bakr al-Rāzī's *Book of Divine Science* and for Isaac Israeli's *Book of Definitions* and *Book of Elements*. He regards both authors as mere physicians (and no philosophers).

Isaac Israeli was a Jew. The only other Jewish philosopher named in this letter is Joseph Haṣṣadiq. Maimonides informs his correspondent that he has not read Haṣṣadiq's *Microcosm*, but was personally acquainted with the author and appreciated his learning. According to Maimonides, he adhered to the teaching of the Brethren of Purity, an observation implying criticism. For the authors of the philosophic encyclopedia entitled the *Epistles of the Brethren* were held in but slight esteem by the rigorous Aristotelian philosophers.

These evaluations may be taken as expressing the real opinion of Maimonides. At least, there is no reason for thinking otherwise. Furthermore, the evidence of the letter is sometimes corroborated by direct or oblique references occurring in the *Guide* to the philosophers mentioned in the letter or to their teaching. Conversely, the letter may sometimes help to interpret such references. In this way, the history of philosophy as conceived by Maimonides falls into focus.

This history is considered from a strictly Peripatetic point of view, which accepts unquestionably the supremacy of Aristotle. Indeed, Maimonides' description of the latter's intellectual powers calls to mind those of Maimonides' contemporary, Averroes. But Averroes' remarks are much more hyperbolic and put much greater emphasis on the uniqueness of Aristotle, on his overwhelming superiority over all philosophers — Plato included, whom Averroes sums up in even more disobliging fashion than does Maimonides. According to Averroes, the sciences

4. Another version of this passage reads: "Though the works of [Abū] ʿAlī Ibn Sīnā [Avicenna] manifest great accuracy and subtle study, they are not as [good] as the work of Abū Naṣr al-Fārābī.

5. The manuscript text has Abū Naṣr, a corruption that the peculiarities of the Arabic script render easily explicable.

of logic, physics, and metaphysics were brought by Aristotle to a state of supreme perfection.[6] Such affirmations of the unchallengeable pre-eminence of Aristotle over all other philosophers may be peculiar to the philosophic tradition of Spain and the Maghrib, a tradition in which Maimonides was brought up, as he sometimes, perhaps with a trace of intellectual arrogance, points out. The superiority of Aristotle over Plato was much less evident in the Moslem East.

There is no reason to doubt that Maimonides was acquainted with all the writings of Aristotle known in Moslem Spain, i.e., practically the whole *Corpus Aristotelicum* as we know it. Only one major work was lacking, Aristotle's *Politics*.[7] It is, moreover, abundantly clear that, from an early age, Maimonides had lived with these texts and that they formed a notable part of his intellectual makeup. Indubitably he sometimes drew upon them directly, rather than upon the commentaries and later accounts of the Peripatetic doctrine. This may, for instance, be the case in the exposition of the twenty-five philosophic premises at the beginning of Part II of the *Guide*. These facts give significance to his choice of the not very many explicit textual quotations from Aristotle that he makes in the *Guide*.

ARISTOTLE

If we abstract from a number of passages citing Aristotelian texts (such as the reference to the *Physics* in *Guide* III 10 and to the *Nicomachean Ethics* in III 43), which, in the main, appear merely to enounce a scientific proposition or to impart information without alluding to Aristotle's personal attitude toward his investigations and conclusions or to his moral evaluations, the following textual, but not always accurate, quotations may be considered.

In the first reference to Aristotle that occurs in the *Guide* (I 5) he is called the Chief of the Philosophers.[8] But the paraphrastic quotation from *De Caelo* that follows upon this honorific appellation has apologetic overtones. Aristotle bids the reader not to ascribe his engaging in (arduous) speculation to temerity, but to his eagerness to acquire, as far as human capacity permits, a correct view of things. Another quotation from this work of Aristotle (*Guide* II 14) refers to the universally held belief that the heaven is eternal. As Maimonides points out, Aristotle wishes

6. See S. Munk, *Mélanges de philosophie juive et arabe* (Paris, 1927), pp. 316 and 441.
7. Averroes states that it was unknown in Spain and the Maghrib, but believes that it was available in the Islamic East.
8. Moses, on the other hand, is designated in the *Guide* (I 54, III 12, and III 54) as the *Master of those who know*, an evidently higher rank. But in the contexts in which this appellation appears he is not — at least in an obvious way — opposed to Aristotle. The title might clearly have fitted the latter, to whom it is applied by Dante (*Divina Commedia*, *Inferno*, IV, 131), perhaps because of some recollection of the appellation used by Maimonides, which he might have encountered in a Latin translation of the *Guide*.

to strengthen his case by a recourse to the universal consensus. A third passage from *De Caelo*[9] quoted in the *Guide* (II 15) gives *inter alia* the Philosopher's reasons for citing the arguments of his opponents. If his own had been the only ones he set forth, they would have made a feebler impression upon the readers. One has to be equitable. This quotation is preceded in the same chapter by one from Aristotle's *Physics* (the same passage is also referred to in *Guide* II 13) asserting that, with the single exception of Plato, all natural philosophers who lived before Aristotle believed that motion is not subject to coming-to-be and passing-away, a statement interpreted by Maimonides as an appeal, with regard to a problem that reasoning was unable to solve, to the authority of the earlier philosophers. This interpretation appears to be corroborated by a quotation from the *Topics*, likewise figuring in *Guide* II 15, which, *prima facie*, in spite of al-Fārābī's different explanation, seems to indicate that in Aristotle's opinion no valid answer could be given to the question whether the world was eternal.

A further quotation from *De Caelo*, occurring in *Guide* II 19, gives a more extensive and more accurate version of the passage referred to in I 5 and is, accordingly, like the latter, more or less apologetic in tone. At least, this is the general opinion. The Philosopher admits that he tried to solve very difficult questions, but rejects the imputation of foolhardiness that might be directed against him on this account and claims that his attempts deserve admiration. Any plausible conclusion that he reaches ought to be greeted with joy.

A quotation from the *Physics* in *Guide* II 20 gives Aristotle's reasons for rejecting the opinion that the heavens have come into being spontaneously.

A quotation from the *Ethics*, which should also be mentioned with reference to Maimonides' indirect portrayal of Aristotle, is of a different nature. The *Guide* cites several times (II 36, 40; III 8, 49) a short sentence from the *Nicomachean Ethics* affirming the shamefulness of the sense of touch. This quotation is used to corroborate what appears to have been Maimonides' personal opinion; qua philosopher, though not qua teacher of the halakhah, he favored asceticism.

To go back to the quotations from the Aristotelian books on the natural sciences and from the *Topics*, many of them, a very considerable proportion of the total number—namely, all those referred to above, with the exception of the passage from the *Physics* occurring in *Guide* II 20 — fall into one pattern. They

9. Or rather from its Arabic version, in which the Greek text is somewhat altered. It may be noted that, if one abstracts from variations clearly due to errors of scribes, the quotations from *De Caelo* in *Guide* II 15 and 19 are practically identical with the corresponding passages of the Arabic translation of this work of Aristotle edited by A. Badawi (Cairo, 1961). The quotation in *Guide* II 15 figures on p. 196 of this edition and the quotation in *Guide* II 19 on pp. 269–70. The identity of the translator responsible for this version is not known for certain.

serve to build up an image of Aristotle regarded as an earnest seeker of truth tentatively propounding more or less plausible theories. As Maimonides twice points out in the *Guide*, once in II 19 with reference to the quotation from *De Caelo* and the second time in II 24, the science of mathematics was in an imperfect state in Aristotle's time (a fact that invalidates that philosopher's astronomical theories) and has progressed since then.[10]

The unassuming *persona* of Aristotle suggested by some of the quotations in the *Guide* is used by Maimonides to good effect in the fight he puts up against the overbearing claim of the Aristotelian system to contain the whole, or almost the whole, of truth knowable to man. I believe that to some extent this was shadow-boxing. The references to *De Caelo* in *Guide* I 5 and II 19 concern the theory of astronomy and of celestial physics, disciplines that orthodox Aristotelians had no reason to consider with complacency and self-satisfaction. Indeed the fact that the Ptolemaic system accepted by the majority of astronomers was incompatible with Aristotelian physics was a *skandalon* of science. A strictly orthodox Aristotelian like Averroes was as aware of this fact as Maimonides; though, contrary to the latter, he was not, as we shall see, prepared to believe that the true science of astronomy was beyond human ken, or that at least no theory concerning the celestial spheres could be held to be as certain as the science of terrestrial physics expounded by Aristotle. This does not, however, necessarily mean that the "order of nature" and a "conformity to the nature of existence," i.e., an intrinsic rationality that accounts for the possibility of a scientific explanation, do not subsist in the heavenly as well as the sublunar phenomena. The affirmation of such a rationality, which is a fundamental position of Maimonides as it enables him to reject the doctrines of the theologians of the kalām (see below), does not depend upon the existence of an adequate astronomical theory. These are two separate issues, though Maimonides may have sometimes deliberately confused them.

The quotations from *De Caelo* in II 14 and 15 as well as the quotation from the *Physics* and that from the *Topics* in the latter chapter involve the even graver question of the eternity or temporal creation of the world. Maimonides makes out quite a good case for this contention, suggested by these quotations, that in so far as the Aristotelian proof of the eternity of the world is dependent on physics it has not the force of a demonstration. Maimonides' own position on this issue may have depended on his conception of God. Of this more hereafter.

10. This observation was probably often made in Maimonides' times in Spain. For an animated debate was taking place in that country in consequence of the criticism directed by faithful Aristotelians against the partisans of the Ptolemaic system. On the incompatibility of this system with Aristotelian physics, see below.

ALEXANDER OF APHRODISIAS

The unified all-embracing system of physics and metaphysics that Maimonides knew and, to a large extent, adopted was in the last analysis based on the *Corpus Aristotelicum*. However, before the Arabic philosophers took over, it was largely Alexander of Aphrodisias who gave it the coherence that in several respects it had lacked, tying up many of its loose ends and propounding solutions to points that were left obscure. In his letter to Ibn Tibbon, Maimonides refers to him and to Themistius as being the two Greek commentators of Aristotle who ought to be consulted. In the *Guide*, however, he quotes Themistius only once (see I 71), and the sentence he cites is a mere echo of Aristotle, whereas there is considerable evidence to show that his personal point of view and his conception of Aristotelianism were decisively influenced by Alexander. Moreover it would seem that he was aware of this fact.

There are several explicit textual quotations from Alexander in the *Guide*, and they have considerable importance. In other passages his writings are, as far as we can judge, or as we may suppose, alluded to or drawn upon without his name being mentioned. There are also possibly some references to the works of this commentator that we are not in a position to identify, as Maimonides may have been acquainted with lost treatises of Alexander or treatises extant only in manuscript in an Arabic translation, and that have not yet been edited or studied.

The works of Alexander fall into two categories: commentaries on the *Corpus Aristotelicum*, and independent treatises. It may be taken as certain that Maimonides made extensive use of the commentaries. This may be inferred not only from the reference to them in the letter to Ibn Tibbon,[11] but also from the fact that the Spanish Aristotelians, whose philosophic education was probably similar to Maimonides', held the commentaries in high esteem: thus Ibn Bājja regards Alexander as the best of the commentators, and Averroes quotes extensively from his commentaries.

11. It is true that he also refers in this letter to the commentaries of his contemporary Averroes, which he apparently did not use when writing the *Guide* (see below); but the analogy does not apply, as Maimonides' only reason for not consulting the commentaries of Averroes was that they were not as yet available to him. It seems probable that, in his exposition of the "second philosophic speculation" in *Guide* II 1, Maimonides followed one of the commentaries of Alexander rather than the two Aristotelian texts, *Metaphysics* xii. 7, and *Physics* viii. 5, which deal with this speculation. Alexander's commentary, as quoted by Averroes, on the chapter of the *Metaphysics* has certain points in common with the text of the *Guide*. Unfortunately, his commentary on the *Physics* is lost. It may be noted that the speculation in question occurs also in Alexander's treatise *On the Principles of the All*, which is discussed below (pp. 257 f. of Badawi's edition; see below n. 15), but the text of his commentary on the *Metaphysics* seems to have a closer connection with the passage in *Guide* II 1.

Nevertheless it is a fact that Maimonides' textual quotations from Alexander are drawn not from his commentaries but from two of his treatises: the treatise *On Governance* (*Maqāla fi'l-tadbīr*), which appears to be identical with an as yet unpublished manuscript treatise of Alexander entitled *On Providence* (*Fi'l-ʿināya*), and the treatise *On the Principles of the All* (*Fī mabādīʾ al-kull*). The Greek originals of both treatises are lost.

The treatise *On Providence*, as I shall refer to it, this being the more usual title, affords an instructive illustration both of the capital importance of Alexander's writings for the formation of the medieval system of Peripatetic philosophy and of the way in which Maimonides utilized his sources. I shall deal with the second point first.

In III 17, Maimonides sets forth five opinions concerning providence: (1) the Epicurean; (2) the Aristotelian; (3) the Ashʿarite (i.e., that professed by a school of kalām that represents and already represented in Maimonides' times the official theology of Sunnite Islam); (4) the Muʿtazilite (professed by another kalām school); (5) that of Jewish law, from which Maimonides apparently differentiates his own opinion, likewise expounded in this chapter.

The first of these opinions are, as far as their doctrinal content is concerned, identical with opinions referred to in Alexander's treatise *On Providence*, as quoted by the tenth-century Jewish scholar Ibn Abī Saʿīd.[12] Two of these opinions, the Epicurean[13] and the Aristotelian, belong to the philosophers to whom they are attributed by Maimonides. However, with regard to the ascription of the third doctrine, which professes that God watches over all things, both the general and the particular, there is an interesting discrepancy. According to Alexander, this is Plato's view, whereas Maimonides attributes it to the Ashʿarites. Maimonides clearly adapted the statement of his source to the historical circumstances of his own times. It may be conjectured that he did not wish to confer philosophic respectability on the Ashʿarites by suggesting that their opinion was identical with Plato's. In this chapter of the *Guide*, Alexander is cited only in connection with the Aristotelian view, and there is no mention of the title of the treatise quoted. It may, however, be presumed that it is the treatise referred to in III 16 under the name *On Governance* (*Fi'l-tadbīr*) and that, as already stated, this work is identical with Alexander's treatise *On Providence* (*Fi'l-ʿināya*).

The sixteenth chapter sets forth various opinions concerning God's knowledge, a problem that, in Maimonides' view, is bound up with that of providence. One of these opinions, which is quoted from Alexander, closely parallels that ascribed

---

12. See S. Pines, "A Tenth Century Philosophical Correspondence," *Proceedings of the American Academy for Jewish Research*, XXIV (1955), 123 ff.
13. Which, according to Alexander, is also that of Democritus.

to the Ash'arites in the seventeenth chapter. For its partisans hold that God knows all things, nothing being hidden from Him. As stated by Maimonides with an explicit reference to Alexander, these partisans were "great men prior in time to Aristotle." A legitimate inference seems to be that Maimonides does not wish to mention in connection with this opinion (any more than in connection with the parallel opinion concerning providence) the name of Plato, which in all probability occurred in this context in Alexander's text.

In fine, Maimonides follows his source faithfully as long as this suits his book, but has no qualms about adapting and altering it when this may serve his intentions. A comparison of the treatise *On Providence* with the relevant chapters of the *Guide* exemplifies this method in a particularly clear way; but it may be supposed that Maimonides used it also with regard to other sources. These chapters also illustrate the influence Alexander had on Maimonides' views of Aristotelianism, which he tended to identify with philosophy *tout court*. It was both a direct influence and an indirect one — channeled through the writings of various Arabic philosophers.

There is no evidence to show that Aristotle put forward the view regarding providence ascribed to him by Alexander and Maimonides, i.e., the view that divine providence extends only to the celestial spheres up to the sphere of the Moon inclusively, but does not watch over the sublunar world. It is true that this opinion is inspired by Aristotle's way of thinking and is faithful to the spirit of his system. But Aristotle probably did not feel the need to take so clear a stand in the matter; in all probability, the doctrine in question was enunciated several centuries later by Alexander and other Peripatetics (some of whom may have preceded him), at a time when in the face of the pointed formulations of the Stoics concerning divine providence, the rival schools also had to state their position clearly.

The Peripatetic doctrine could be described as a halfway house between the Epicurean negation of teleology in nature and the Stoic proclamation of an all-embracing providence. But it differs from either of these schools in an essential point: it affirms the eternity of the cosmos and of the cosmic order, whose preservation may (it is a question of terminology) be attributed to divine providence. But as far as individual beings and individual events are concerned, it denies any intervention of providence. However, the Aristotelian doctrine was opposed to the Epicurean on yet another point. It considered that through intellectual activity some men, the happy few, may and should transcend the limitations of human nature, or at least of human nature as it is commonly conceived. As the *Nicomachean Ethics*, which was well known to Maimonides, puts it[14] (x. vii. 8. 1177b

14. The passages from the *Nicomachean Ethics* quoted here are translated by H. Rackham.

30 ff.): "If then the intellect is something divine in comparison with man, so is the life of the intellect divine in comparison with human life. Nor ought we to obey those who enjoin that a man should have man's thoughts and a mortal the thoughts of mortality, but we ought so far as possible to achieve immortality, and do all that man may to live in accordance with the highest thing in him." And again (x. viii. 13. 1179a28 ff.): "It seems likely that the man who pursues intellectual activity, and who cultivates his intellect and keeps that in the best condition, is also the man most beloved of the gods. For, if, as is generally believed, the gods exercise some supervision over human affairs, then it will be reasonable to suppose that they take pleasure in that part of man which is best and most akin to themselves, namely, the intellect, and that they recompense with their favors those men who esteem and honor this most, because these care for the things dear to themselves, and act rightly and nobly. Now it is clear that all these attributes belong most of all to the wise man. He therefore is most beloved by the gods; and if so, he is naturally most happy."

Whatever the correct interpretation of the reference to the gods may be, it is clear that Aristotle's position, as set forth in the second passage, foreshadows, and may account for, Maimonides' view that the human individual's share in divine providence is proportionate to his intellectual powers and that providence does not watch over the nonrational animals (see *Guide* III 17 and 51).

Thus Maimonides' opinion concerning providence appears to be a combination of the Aristotelian conception of the intellect with Alexander's version of what this commentator holds to be the Aristotelian view of providence. In other words, it is a combination of two Peripatetic doctrines.

Alexander's treatise *On the Principles of the All*, of which at least two Arabic versions, one of them published,[15] have been preserved, is in a way a much more important work than the treatise *On Providence*. For it seems to represent Alexander's most ambitious attempt to systematize Aristotle's physical as well as some of his metaphysical doctrines.

One of the two explicit quotations from this work occurring in the *Guide* mentions the title of the commentator's treatise; the other merely cites the name of Alexander. Neither of them refers to the doctrinal contents of the treatise. In the quotation referred to in the second place (see *Guide* I 31), Alexander enumerates the three causes of differences of opinion (to which, as the context makes it clear, erroneous doctrines are to be imputed; see Badawi's edition of Alexander's treatise, p. 276). These causes are: (1) lust for power, which prevents men from grasping the truth; (2) the fact that certain things are in themselves difficult to grasp; (3) the intellectual incapacity of certain men. Maimonides adds to this passage the

15. By A. Badawi, in *Arisṭū ʿindaʾl-ʿArab* (Cairo, 1947), pp. 253–77.

observation that "in our times" a fourth cause is operative, one that was not mentioned by Alexander because it did not exist at that time. The cause in question is constituted by habit and education, under the influence of which men cling to what they are accustomed to. In other words, Maimonides contrasts his own times, which he seems to have held to be dominated by superstition, to use Spinoza's term and that of the philosophers of Enlightenment, with Greek antiquity, in which the philosophers who aspired to know the true nature of things did not have to struggle against the dead hand of traditional belief. Maimonides was indubitably aware that the Greek philosophers lived in a pagan society, i.e., a society with religious beliefs and observances of its own, but apparently he chose not to mention this fact.[16]

The other explicit quotation from the *Principles of the All*, the one mentioning the title of this treatise, occurs in II 3. According to the *Guide*, Alexander states in this text that though the opinion of Aristotle regarding the causes of the motions of the spheres — i.e., the opinion from which he deduced the existence of separate intellects — are mere undemonstrated assertions, they are, of all the opinions put forward on the subject, those that give rise to the smallest number of doubts and that lend themselves best to being systematized.

This view is clearly in line with the image of Aristotle that, as has been shown, Maimonides appears to have tried to build up through his choice of quotations from the *Corpus Aristotelicum* — the first general impression being one of philosophers on the defensive. For one gathers that neither Aristotle nor Alexander was absolutely certain of the correctness of his system of physics. This is, of course, true. But their position has implications different from those indicated in the *Guide*, as a reference to Alexander's text will show. Maimonides certainly did not miss these implications, and I believe that he was in general agreement with these philosophers regarding the conclusions to be drawn.[17]

16. In III 29 and elsewhere, Maimonides speaks at length of the absurdly superstitious beliefs and observances that were prevalent in the pagan communities of the ancient East, designated by him as the Sabians. This point is of capital importance for his interpretation of history, as it explains and justifies Abraham's revolt against the traditions of his community and in addition throws light on Moses' intentions in promulgating the Law and accounts for many of its provisions. Maimonides does not, however, refer in that context to the pagan Greeks, though they, as well as the ancient Babylonians and various other communities, were designated as Sabians. However, in II 39, in fine, Maimonides puts "the nomoi of the Greeks" in the same category as "the ravings of the Sabians," but in the context this does not necessarily mean that he regards the first as being on a par with the second.

17. However, his awareness of the difficulties inherent in the philosophic explanation seems to have been sharper than that of the two Greek thinkers. And he had of course to take into account the challenge presented by the unscientific, but from a certain point of view irrefutable, view that God created the universe by an absolutely arbitary act of free will and that He sometimes intervenes with similar acts in the concatenation of causes and effects that constitutes the order of nature.

The two passages of Alexander's *Principles* that set forth the view referred to by Maimonides may be translated as follows (p. 253 of Badawi's edition): "I shall say: Things of this kind[18] are, in my opinion, best explained if one points out that the agreed upon principles are in accord with, and adhere to, the manifest, clearly apparent, and well-known phenomena.[19] For in this matter it is impossible to use the way of demonstration.[20] For demonstration must start with prior things and with the causes, whereas nothing is prior to the first principles; nor do they have a cause." (*Ibid.*, 276): "It is in this way that—[speaking] concisely and [referring] only to the principle[21]—the government of the universe is conducted, according to what we have taken over from the divine Aristotle. Everything that is in it preserves its peculiar nature and accomplishes[22] the functions that were given to this nature in particular within the eternity and order of the universe. This opinion is not only more than any other in accord with the divine government; it is also the one that more than any other is appropriate for speculation and that is verified because of its agreement with, and close relation to, the things visible to the cognizing [subject].[23] Everyone who philosophizes should, whatever the circumstances, use this opinion and prefer it to all others. For it is[24] the most correct of all the opinions that have been propounded concerning God, the Great and Sublime, and concerning the divine body.[25] It alone among the various opinions preserves the coherence and the order of the things that are produced because of this coherence and order. If it should occur to anyone that some [point] among those that we have set forth requires further and more subtle investigation, he should not, because of a slight difficulty that might become manifest, bring about a slackening of our vigilance and our effort [directed] toward defending this opinion in its totality. [He ought not to do this], even if [this opinion] is obnoxious and repugnant to him. On the contrary, we ought not only to stick to this opinion, but also to defend it. For of all the opinions that have been held concerning God, the Great and the Sublime, it is the one most appropriate to Him. The truth is that we seek to refute[26] all the opinions opposed to it and to correct, as far as we are able, their errors. [We shall do this] after having first stated that it is difficult to find a speculative opinion exempt from doubts."

18. Apparently: the principles of the physical world.   19. Literally: things.
20. Literally: the demonstrative speeches.
21. Literally: by the way of principle and concisely.   22. Literally: follows.
23. P. 276, l. 10, reading: *li'l-ᶜālim*. Perhaps the text should be emended to: *fi'l-ᶜālam*, "in the world."
24. P. 276, l. 11: Instead of *aw kānat*, I read: *idh kāna*.
25. I.e., the heavenly sphere.
26. P. 276, l. 17: *k.l.* makes no sense in the context. One could expect *radd* (refutation) or some other word having a similar meaning. My translation is based on this emendation.

This passage is followed in Alexander's treatise by the passage on the causes of differences of opinion quoted in the *Guide*. Evidently this portion of the work has been much pondered over by Maimonides.

The two texts that have been quoted give Alexander's views on the function and degree of verifiability of physical theories. The Peripatetic first principles cannot be demonstrated, as demonstration involves a recourse to some prior principle, but their use in scientific theory can be justified on the ground that they account for and correlate a great number of facts and observations. The model of the cosmos that Aristotelianism provides is more coherent and has more intrinsic verisimilitude than those proposed by the rival schools. There are, however, some discrepancies and consequently doubts. But before physics became mathematized, there was no reason, not even a purely theoretical reason, to hold that a single awkward fact should be allowed to topple to the ground a comprehensive, serviceable, and solidly established theory. In biology, up to quite recent times, Alexander's views on the way in which scientific theories may be verified would not have seemed very outdated. The method he recommends is not so very different from that applied by Charles Darwin in his two main works.

Alexander's conception of what a comprehensive and adequate physical theory should be and should accomplish is shared by Maimonides. In his opinion, such a theory should set forth the causes of the physical phenomena and disclose their natural order. Not all explanations are scientifically acceptable. For a natural order means one that is in accord with the "nature of existence." In fact, Maimonides' notion of a satisfactory physical theory seems to imply — at least according to some passages of the *Guide*[27] — that only the efficient causes should be taken into account in a scientific explanation of the natural phenomena.[28] This should not, of course, lead to an extremist position. One ought not to lose sight altogether of the teleological considerations. For otherwise, to take but one example, the cardinal assumption that none of the animal and vegetable species that have ever existed have died out and that all of them will be preserved from this fate to all eternity, would become quite indefensible. In other words, it may be assumed that the world is so arranged that the indefinite continuance of its existence in its present state is ensured. But it is the efficient causes that take care of this. In accordance

27. Cf., for instance, II 19: "All that he (i.e., Aristotle) has explained to us regarding what is beneath the sphere of the moon follows an order conforming to that which exists, an order whose causes are clear. One can say of it that it derives of necessity from the motion and the powers of the sphere." In other words, Maimonides finds Aristotle's views on the physics of the sublunar world satisfactory because they provide a mechanical explanation of the phenomena.

28. The Aristotelian scientific explanation of the universe is, of course, based in the last analysis on the existence of the Prime Mover, who is not an efficient cause. Here I am abstracting from this aspect of the doctrine.

with the logic of the Aristotelian system, nobody (except Nature itself, a very unclear concept), can be regarded as responsible for these characteristics of the world order. For the universe (or Nature) is a primary datum, which means that its working can be understood and described, but that it is, generally speaking, senseless to look beyond the things themselves for the final causes of their existence, or of their existence in one particular way.[29]

Of course, this does not mean that natural science should deny purposive action on the part of living beings. But such an action is a part of the natural order and does not determine the latter.

It is not Maimonides' contention that the Aristotelians set up an incorrect or objectionable ideal of what scientific theory ought to be. The objections that he proffers are of another kind, being concerned with the failure of the science of his time to conform to this ideal. As he points out, science as he knew it gave a satisfactory explanation of the processes of the sublunar world, but was quite inadequate in dealing with celestial physics. He is, of course, quite right. His contemporary, Averroes, knew this as well as he did. The Aristotelian celestial physics was in a sad confusion because some of its principles could not be reconciled with two essential devices of the on the whole dominant Ptolemaic system, namely, the eccentrics and the epicycles. One of the points upon which this conflict hinged may be summarized as follows: Aristotelian physics required that the center around which a body accomplishes a circular revolution should be stationary, whereas these two devices posited centers that were in motion. The epicycles and eccentrics were invented in order to provide a mathematical explanation for the astronomical observations. It was thus a case of mathematics, a science that was held at that time to include astronomy, against the as yet almost unmathematized physics. This was felt to be very awkward both by the physicists and by the mathematicians (but more by the first, whose concern was with things as they really are, than by the second); it was a frustrating state of affairs.

These difficulties seem to have come to a head in Spain in the twelfth century, perhaps because of the rigorous Aristotelianism of the philosophers of that country. The discrepancies between astronomical and physical theory did not,

29. Maimonides mentions in III 13 that Aristotle has shown that the plants exist for the sake of animals. In reading this chapter one has the impression that, though in this particular passage Maimonides pays lip service to Aristotle's teleological tendencies, they go much too far for him. Indeed, the general sense of the chapter seems to suggest that within the domain of the investigations of the natural sciences teleological explanations may be serviceable and valid only in so far as they concern the relation between the various parts of a living organism and also the relation between any and all of these parts and the functioning of the organism to which they belong taken as a whole. The notion that one species of living being may exist for the sake of another species was emphatically not in line with the tendency of Maimonides' thought. On the other hand, he apparently did believe in the harmony of Nature taken as a whole.

however, in spite of their gravity, shake the philosophers' confidence in Aristotle's and Alexander's conception of scientific theory; and for this purpose as well as for others, Maimonides may be included among the philosophers. The possibility suggested in II 24 of the *Guide*, that human science, because of the insufficiency of the available data, will never be able to work out a valid physical theory applicable to the heavenly spheres, does not mean that the latter are not determined by the order, or, to use a later term, by the laws, of nature.

Quite apart from these general considerations, Alexander's treatise *On the Principles of the All* may have influenced Maimonides' views on the subject with which this treatise is not concerned, namely, religious and political history. It is true that the evidence for this assertion may seem rather slender, being purely terminological. In fact it hinges on the use by Maimonides of a single word; but it is a key word.

The following sentence occurs in the treatise *On the Principles of the All* (p. 265, ll. 16 ff.): "For the fabric of this universe and the natural *grace* dealt out by the Creator in[30] the natural agreement and accord of its parts and in their being fashioned in [due] relation to the universe [as a whole] are such[31] that if you should conceive the thought that one of these parts should be considered as abolished [it would mean] that none of them could remain as it is."

The Arabic word translated as "grace" reads *lutf*. A very slight emendation would alter it into *talattuf*, a rarer word, which also makes sense, and perhaps even better sense. In that case the translation of the passage would read: "The wily graciousness," or "wily and gracious arrangements" used by the Creator, etc.[32] Now the noun *talattuf* and the corresponding verb *talattafa* occur altogether, in III 32, six times, in the different contexts; one of these calls to mind the text of Alexander that has just been quoted. There is a possibility that, in the copy of the treatise *On the Principles of the All* available to him, Maimonides may have read *talattuf* instead of *lutf*. But this is a secondary point; the probability that this chapter of the *Guide* was influenced by the treatise is very strong even without this assumption. As a matter of fact, Maimonides also uses the word *lutf* in this chapter (see below).

30. P. 265, l. 16: I read *fī mā* (instead of *fīh mā*).
31. Literally: are in such a state of order and accord.
32. "Wily graciousness" or "gracious ruse" being the terms used in the present translation of the *Guide* to render *talattuf*. My choice of the expression has been influenced by the fact that, in his Hebrew translation of the *Guide* Samuel Ibn Tibbon, who may have been influenced by the fact suggested in III 32 that some persons (not Maimonides himself) might impute to God the use of a stratagem (*ḥīla*), renders *talattuf* by ʿ*orma* ("cunning," "ruse"). Both this Hebrew word and the allusion to the notion of God's recurring to stratagems call to mind Hegel's expression: "the ruse of reason" – "List der Vernunft."

The relevant passages of III 32 read:

1. If you consider the divine actions — I mean to say the natural actions — the deity's wily graciousness [*talaṭṭuf*] and wisdom, as shown in the creation of living beings, in the gradation of the motions of the limbs, and the proximity of some of the latter to others, will through them become clear to you. Similarly His wisdom and wily graciousness [*talaṭṭuf*], as shown in the gradual succession of the various states of the whole individual, will become clear to you. The brain is an example of the gradation of the motions and the proximity of the limbs of an individual: for its front part is soft, very soft indeed, whereas its posterior part is more solid. . . . Similarly the deity made a wily and gracious arrangement [*talaṭṭafa*] with regard to all the individuals of the living beings that suck. For when born, such individuals are extremely soft and cannot feed on dry food. Accordingly breasts were prepared for them. . . .

2. Many things in our Law are due to something similar to this very governance on the part of Him who governs, may He be glorified and exalted. For a sudden transition from one opposite to another is impossible. And therefore man, according to his nature, is not capable of abandoning suddenly all to which he was accustomed. As therefore God sent *Moses our Master* to make out of us *a kingdom of priests and a holy nation* — through the knowledge of Him, may He be exalted. . .; and as at that time the way of life generally accepted and customary in the whole world and the universal service upon which we were brought up consisted in offering various species of living beings in the temples in which images were set up, in worshipping the latter, and in burning incense before them. . . His wisdom, may He be exalted, and His gracious ruse [*talaṭṭuf*], which is manifest in regard to all His creatures, did not require that He give us a Law prescribing the rejection, abandonment, and abolition of all these kinds of worship. . . . Therefore He, may He be exalted, suffered the above-mentioned kinds of worship to remain, but transferred them from created or imaginary and unreal things to His own name, may He be exalted, ordering us to practice them with regard to Him, may He be exalted. Thus He commanded us to build a temple for Him . . .; to bow down in worship before Him; and to burn incense before Him. And He forbade the performance of any of these actions with a view to someone else. . . . And because of their employment in the temple and the sacrifices in it, it was necessary to fix for them dues that would be sufficient for them; namely, the dues of the *Levites* and the *Priests*. Through this divine ruse [*talaṭṭuf*] it came about that the memory of *idolatry* was effaced and that the grandest and true foundation of our belief — namely, the existence and oneness of the deity — was firmly established, while at the same time the souls had no feeling of repugnance and were not repelled because of the abolition of modes of worship to which they were accustomed and than which no other mode of worship was known at that time.

I know that on thinking about this at first your soul will necessarily have a feeling of repugnance toward this notion and will feel aggrieved because of it; and you will ask me in your heart and say to me: How is it possible that none of the commandments, prohibitions, and great actions — which are very precisely set forth and prescribed for fixed seasons — should not be intended for its own sake, but for the sake of something else, as if this were a ruse invented for our benefit by God in order to achieve His first intention? . . . Hear then the reply to your question that will put an end to this sickness in your heart and reveal to you the true reality of that to which I have drawn your attention. It is to the effect that the text of the *Torah* tells a quite similar story, namely, in its dictum: *God led them not by the way of the land of the Philistines, although it was near, and so on. But God led the people about, by the way of the wilderness of the Red*

Sea. Just as God perplexed them in anticipation of what their bodies were naturally incapable of bearing — turning them away from the high road toward which they had been going, toward another road so that the first intention should be achieved — so did He in anticipation of what the soul is naturally incapable of receiving, prescribe laws that we have mentioned so that the first intention should be achieved, namely, the apprehension of Him, may He be exalted, and the rejection of *idolatry*. For just as it is not in the nature of man that, after having been brought up in slavish service occupied with clay, bricks, and similar things, he should all of a sudden wash off from his hands the dirt deriving from them and proceed immediately to fight against *the children of Anak*, so is it also not in his nature that, after having been brought up upon very many modes of worship and of customary practices, which the souls find so agreeable that they become as it were a primary notion, he should abandon them all of a sudden. And just as the deity used a gracious ruse [*talaṭṭafa*] in causing them to wander perplexedly in the desert until their souls became courageous — it being well known that life in the desert and lack of comforts for the body necessarily develop courage whereas the opposite circumstances necessarily develop cowardice — and until, moreover, people were born who were not accustomed to humiliation and servitude — all this having been brought about by *Moses our Master* by means of divine commandments. . . — so did this group of laws derive from a divine grace [*luṭf*], so that they should be left with the kind of practices to which they were accustomed and so that consequently the belief, which constitutes the first intention, should be validated in them.

These texts establish, first and foremost, the existence (within the limits defined above) of a teleological element in nature, a conception that, as the frequent use of the term *talaṭṭuf* suggests, is probably greatly indebted to Alexander's treatise *On the Principles of the All*; though Maimonides, in contradiction to this treatise, draws his examples from the living organisms (helped therein by Galen, whose book *On the Utility of the Parts of the Body* he quotes in this context). In the second place these texts show that this teleological conception of Alexander should not be restricted to natural phenomena. It ought to be extended to the domain of political and religious history, as it helps to explain the making of Israel and to account for major characteristics of the Torah. Just as Nature, or God working in Nature, makes shift with the available corporeal devices in order to form a viable organism, History, or God working in History, makes shift with available devices of a different kind in order to form a viable nation. In this latter case these devices included a forty years' sojourn in the desert intended to train the people in the military virtues.

The Mosaic commandments or some of them were likewise such devices. Not all of them are the best possible commandments in an absolute sense; some are the best that are possible in a particular historical situation; for the necessary break with the past would have been impracticable if, within limits, some form of continuity had not been preserved. Both in the domain of Nature and in that of History the devices to which Maimonides refers are attributed by him to God. But, as he states elsewhere (II 48), God works through intermediate causes.

Before we go on to the Islamic authors, Maimonides' attitude toward Greek philosophers not belonging (or not wholly belonging) to the Peripatetic tradition will be referred to. Some of these philosophers are not mentioned in the letter to Ibn Tibbon.

PLATO

First Plato. There is no doubt that in Maimonides' opinion, Plato, considered as a physicist and a metaphysician, rated much lower than Aristotle. The Arabic and Jewish so-called Aristotelian philosophers were concerned with sober truth demonstrable by the concordance of theory with the facts of the external world. In consequence, they tended to appreciate in scientific doctrines the discovery, through recourse to the sense data, of a permanent natural order. Aristotelian physics satisfied this exigency, whereas Plato's devalorization of the truth content of the sense data and his tendency to regard the current physical theories, his own included, as myths, did not. In the opinion of these medieval thinkers, the mythical mode of expression constituted, when used by a philosopher, a deliberate concealment of theoretical truth. Sometimes it was dictated by expediency. But a philosopher writing for philosophers had no need of these trappings. In his letter to Ibn Tibbon, Maimonides makes it very clear that, in view of the fact that Plato's works are full of parables, the serious student need not trouble to read them. As, however, Maimonides was fully aware that the reading public did not only consist of serious, fully qualified students, this remark does not, as we shall see below, give a complete idea of his evaluation of parables as a mode of exposition.

In the few passages of the *Guide* in which Plato is explicitly mentioned, the reference is to the *Timaeus* or to some paraphrase or doxographical summary of that dialogue, and in one passage (II 13) also a citation from the latter occurring in Aristotle's *Physics*. Only one of the Platonic physical or metaphysical doctrines is discussed in the *Guide* at some length, namely, the doctrine attributed to Plato according to which the world was created in time out of pre-existent matter (II 13 and 25–26). According to the second of these passages, the doctrine does not contradict religion. Maimonides, however, makes it clear that the doctrine does not interest him in the least. The intellectual choice with which he confronts his readers is that between an eternal and permanent world order with the workings of which divine intervention could never have interfered; and the absolutely free action of God's Will, which created the world out of nothing and can and does alter the natural order as it pleases. The Platonic doctrine was apt to confuse this clear-cut issue.

II 6 refers to a Platonic doctrine according to which God looks at the world of the intellects and thus causes the universe to emanate therefrom. This is in all probability a reference to some perhaps (though not necessarily) Neo-Platonic interpretation of the doctrine of the *Timaeus* (28A ff.) concerning the eternal model imitated by the Demiurge.

I 17 refers to Matter having been called a female by Plato and the philosophers who preceded him. With respect to Plato this is not quite accurate, as the Receptacle — a term that was sometimes interpreted as signifying Matter — is designated in the *Timaeus* (51A) as Mother. However, Maimonides may have followed some later Platonistic interpretation. This example is given by Maimonides to show that Plato, as well as the adherent of religious Law, uses veiled language.

Now the *Guide* itself is an example of the philosophic use of veiled language; and the need, the political necessity, to employ it constitutes one of the main themes of this work. It is a theme, moreover, that is bound up with others as, or even more, important: for instance, prophecy, the position and the function of the philosopher in human society, political doctrine in general. As Leo Strauss has shown,[33] Maimonides' views on these matters were in the last analysis determined by Plato's position, the principal direct impact being that of al-Fārābī and other Moslem philosophers who adapted Plato's doctrines to their own requirements.

No attempt can be made in the present Introduction to delimit and define the influence exercised by Plato on the *Guide* in this field, as it is too generalized, too diffuse, and often too indirect. It will, however, be referred to in the section dealing with al-Fārābī.

THE PYTHAGOREANS

The only reference to the Pythagoreans occurring in the *Guide* (II 8) refers to their doctrine of the harmony of the spheres, rejected by Aristotle and, in consequence, also by Maimonides.

EPICURUS

Epicurus' denial of providence was, as has been stated above, known to Maimonides from Alexander's treatise *On Providence* (see *Guide* III 17; cf. II 13). It might have been, but was not, recognized by him as presenting a serious challenge to Aristotelianism as well as to the orthodox religious attitude. Its weakness was that it was liable to be regarded as unscientific, science being based on the permanent existence of the cosmos. As far as the events of terrestrial life, at least those involving only individuals and not whole species, were concerned,

---

33. See *Philosophie und Gesetz* (Berlin, 1935); "Quelques remarques sur la science politique de Maïmonide et de Fārābī," *Revue des Études juives*, C (1936), 1–37; and in other studies.

the Aristotelians including Maimonides generally believed as much as the Epicureans in the working-out of the efficient causes (i.e., of blind chance or of necessity, two terms that in this context are equivalent). The fact that man's reason might help him to elude the dangers with which external necessity threatened him or to adopt an attitude that would alleviate or nullify the latter's impact was recognized, though with differences of formulation, by the Epicureans as well as by Maimonides and other Aristotelians.

In I 73, Maimonides contrasts on a point of detail the atomism of the Mutakallimūn with that of Epicurus, about which he must have had rather accurate information.

In I 73, the *Guide* refers to Euclid and to Apollonius of Perga's *Conic Sections*.

GALEN

Whereas Ptolemy, who is mentioned several times in the *Guide*, is quite rightly exclusively referred to as an astronomer, Galen is known to Maimonides not only as a physician but also as a philosopher. In the last chapter of his main medical work, entitled *The Medical Aphorisms of Moses* (in Arabic, *Fuṣūl Mūsā fi'l-ṭibb*; in Hebrew, *Pirqe Moshe*), Maimonides polemizes at length not only against some medical views of Galen but also against certain opinions of the latter on philosophic problems and on religion. As a matter of fact, the Greek physician had considerable influence, which might be designated as subversive, on the development of philosophic thought in the Arabic civilization. Much of the opposition to, or the sceptical attitude toward, Aristotle, was inspired by him. He did not accept Aristotle's theory of place and (a point that is perhaps more important in the context of the medieval debates) had doubts concerning the nature of time; the latter point is mentioned in the *Guide* (II 13; cf. I 73). He also took an agnostic attitude toward the problem of the immortality of the soul and that of the eternity of the world. The *Guide* does not refer to Galen's views with regard to the first point (which is understandable as this work does not contain an explicit discussion of the immortality of the soul), but it mentions (I 15) the disparaging remark to which al-Fārābī was provoked by Galen's view that the eternity of the world cannot be demonstrated. It is an interesting point that Maimonides does not attempt to defend Galen, although the latter's position was similar to the one ostensibly maintained in the *Guide*; and this despite the fact that, from the philosophic point of view, Galen could be regarded, in contradistinction to the Mutakallimūn, as a respectable ally.

III 12 quotes with approval a remark of Galen on the ineluctable limitations imposed on human beings by the fact that the material ingredients that are commingled at the moment of conception are of so inferior a kind. III 32 quotes from Galen an example illustrating the teleological element in the structure of living organisms. I 73 refers to Galen's remarks concerning the thinkers who believed that the senses deceive us.

PROCLUS

The *Guide* does not explicitly mention the sixth-century Neo-Platonist Proclus, who, in a work translated into Arabic, had made out a cogent case for the eternity of the world. It may be argued that the proofs for this thesis ascribed, in II 14 and 25, to philosophers later than Aristotle may derive from this treatise. But the resemblance between Proclus' proofs and those set forth by Maimonides does not extend to details. On the whole it seems more probable that Maimonides took over these proofs from some Moslem philosopher (it may have been al-Fārābī), who had reformulated Proclus' arguments while making use of them.

John Philoponus is mentioned in the *Guide* with reference to the origins of kalām and will be discussed in the present Introduction in that context.

AL-FĀRĀBĪ

After Aristotle, al-Fārābī is the philosopher whom, judging by the letter to Ibn Tibbon, Maimonides held in the highest esteem. In fact, the term that he applies to him may lend color to the suspicion that, as far as theoretical and political sciences were concerned, he was ready to follow al-Fārābī's lead in all points.

Be that as it may, it is clear that Maimonides was persuaded that the approach and the methods and style of exposition and formulation adopted by al-Fārābī in all matters impinging upon, or connected with, the sphere of organized religion constituted the most notable and authoritative of the responses made by philosophers to the challenge, the danger, and perhaps the opportunity presented by allegiance to a monotheistic religion. In other words, he felt that al-Fārābī had shown what attitude a philosopher ought to take in these latter times when, as Maimonides points out (I 31) a new cause of difference of opinion (and consequently of error) had been added to those enumerated by Alexander of Aphrodisias: namely, adherence to customary beliefs and to the notions inculcated by a tradition-ridden education.

The philosophic position with respect to the problem of the eternity of the world, the attitude that should be taken with regard to the apologetics of the Mutakallimūn, and, perhaps most important of all, the theory of prophecy as part of a political philosophy and of an anthropology going back in many essentials to Plato, were all set forth by al-Fārābī in a style and a mode of exposition that possibly influenced Maimonides as much as the doctrines themselves.

Al-Fārābī was not afraid of contradicting himself; perhaps he did it on purpose. At least, it is certain and was already pointed out by Arabic philosophers such as Ibn Ṭufayl that the doctrines of some of his treatises on such matters as the immortality of the soul are in radical opposition to opinions maintained by him in other treatises. This may of course be due to a change in his views. It is, however, more probable that the main reason for these apparent vacillations was that not all of these treatises were addressed to readers of the same kind.

This argues a certain degree of prudence. And yet in al-Fārābī's works, one often comes across outrageously unorthodox and startlingly plain-spoken statements, which presumably could be read by anyone who cared to do so. Al-Fārābī evidently believed that the very abstract and very precise style that he favored had the virtue of discouraging the curiosity of the uneducated and the semi-educated; he relied upon it to ward off danger from himself and from the community, which might be jeopardized by the indiscriminate dissemination of knowledge among people incapable of understanding what it all meant. On the whole, this belief seems to have been justified. This lesson of style was certainly not lost upon Maimonides. One observes accordingly that disconcertingly unorthodox statements, perhaps rendered innocuous by their abstract formulation, occur also in the *Guide* (for instance in I 68) though, probably, less often than in al-Fārābī's treatises. But then the *Guide* belongs to a very peculiar literary genre, of which it is the unique specimen. Its scope, its composition, and its purpose are quite different from those of any of al-Fārābī's works.

Four of al-Fārābī's treatises are explicitly mentioned in the *Guide*: (1) his commentary on Aristotle's *Physics*; (2) his commentary on the *Nicomachean Ethics*; (3) his treatise *On the Variable Substances*; (4) his treatise *On the Intellect*. Of these the first three have not been found and are perhaps totally lost.

The reference to the commentary on the *Physics* (II 19) presents no great interest outside the context of celestial physics with which it is concerned.

In contrast, the quotation from the commentary on the *Ethics* is of considerable significance; for it has a direct bearing on one of the main themes of the *Guide*, the theory of providence. This quotation reads as follows (III 18): "Those who have the capacity of making their soul pass from one moral quality to another are those of whom Plato has said that God's providence watches over them to a higher degree."

It seems clear that al-Fārābī maintained that the fact that human individuals progressed toward, or attained, perfection can be equated with providence watching over them.[34] This was Maimonides' own opinion, as he himself points in this context. In all probability, he took it over, with or without modifications, from al-Fārābī.

Al-Fārābī's commentary on the *Ethics* owes its wide notoriety to other passages. As Maimonides certainly knew, many of the most famous Spanish philosophers of the twelfth century were provoked into criticizing or explaining away certain uncompromising opinions expressed in this work. According to Ibn Ṭufayl,[35] al-Fārābī sets forth in this commentary the view that happiness exists in this life and this world and, after this assertion, makes a statement according to which "everything else that is spoken of is [nothing but] drivel and old wives' tales."

Ibn Bājja, for his part, in an as yet unpublished text[36] defends al-Fārābī against the charge that in this commentary he professed the opinion that there is no afterlife, that there is no happiness but political (*madanī*) happiness, that the only existence is that known to the senses, and that all assertions concerning a different kind of existence are old wives' tales.[37]

Averroes in his Great Commentary on *De anima* is concerned with a different, though related, complex of ideas expounded in this work of al-Fārābī.[38] These ideas, which Averroes regards as wholly unacceptable, are based upon the contention of Alexander of Aphrodisias that the hylic, i.e., the potential, intellect is a faculty subject to generation and corruption that subsists in the human individual. Al-Fārābī infers from this premise that this intellect is unable to cognize abstract forms, i.e., forms separate from matter. For an Aristotelian principle lays down that the intellect becomes identical with that which it cognizes, and such identity is inconceivable in the case of these forms and the lowly kind of intellect that is postulated by al-Fārābī. Hence, according to al-Fārābī, man cannot be united with the separate intellect or, to be more precise, with the Active Intellect. The Active Intellect functions with regard to man solely as an efficient cause and by no means as a form with which man can be invested.[39] Man's end is merely speculative perfection.[40] The last statement apparently means that man can have discursive science, but not that intuitive knowledge which, according to Greek and Arabic philosophers, is the highest form of knowledge.

34. Al-Fārābī apparently refers to moral perfection only, but he certainly had also (or rather first and foremost) in mind the perfection of the intellect.
35. Ibn Ṭufayl, *Hayy Ibn Yaqẓān*, ed. L. Gauthier (Beirut, 1936), p. 14.
36. See MS. Bodleian Library, Pococke 206, fol. 126b.
37. Cf. Plato *Gorgias* 527A5.
38. See Averroes, *Commentarium magnum in Aristotelis "De anima libros,"* ed. F. Stuart Crawford (Cambridge, Mass., 1953), p. 481.
39. *Ibid.*, pp. 485 and 502.
40. *Perfectio speculativa.* These two words are presumably a translation of the Arabic: *kamāl naẓarī.* Cf. al-Fārābī, *Falsafat Arisṭūṭālīs,* ed. M. Mahdi (Beirut, 1961), p. 131, l. 6.

This definition of man's end may seem to be a non sequitur. For it may be argued that it is a plausible conclusion from al-Fārābī's premises that the highest perfection possible to man is to be found in a life of practical action (Aristotle's *bios praktikos*) rather than in a life of thought (*bios theorētikos*). As the passage of Ibn Bājja referred to above shows, this was a view that rightly or wrongly was attributed to al-Fārābī, and certain passages in the latter's extant works suggest that this interpretation of his doctrine may not have been wholly baseless. However, Averroes' testimony seems to be opposed to it, and it is very unlikely that the relevant sentence is corrupt or mistranslated. Moreover, it seems implausible that in his commentary on the *Nicomachean Ethics* al-Fārābī should have categorically maintained the superiority of the practical life over the theoretical, an opinion that is wholly at variance with the system of values propounded in the work he is interpreting. He may, however, have steered a middle course.

It can be argued that these views of al-Fārābī, set forth in a work known to Maimonides, may legitimately be taken into account in an interpretation of the latter's philosophy. If this view is accepted, one should bear in mind (1) the high praise that Maimonides bestows on al-Fārābī, and (2) the fact that there is a certain likelihood that the doctrine of the *Guide* concerning Moses can be correctly interpreted as signifying that this prophet had attained the union with the Active Intellect that al-Fārābī, in one authoritative work, supposes to be impossible (see also below). In this connection it may be added that in all probability Maimonides adopted Alexander's and al-Fārābī's conception of the hylic intellect.

However, the matter also has another aspect. Not all the philosophers who accepted Alexander's views on the hylic intellect agreed with regard to the union with the Active Intellect. Averroes did not accept these views, but Ibn Bājja, the founder of the Aristotelian school of Moslem Spain, was by and large in accord with them, and yet, as we shall see, he strongly attacked al-Fārābī for his refusal to admit the possibility of man's conjunction with the Active Intellect. As the letter to Ibn Tibbon shows, Maimonides regarded Ibn Bājja as a genuine philosopher.

As a matter of fact not only Ibn Bājja contradicted al-Fārābī on this point. Al-Fārābī, who was famous for his inconsistencies, contradicted himself. In his treatise *On the Intellect*, which is repeatedly referred to in the *Guide*, he describes[41] the highest perfection that man can attain, the state in which he is supremely happy. In that state, which is the state of being endowed with the so-called acquired intellect, man is exceedingly close to the Active Intellect, and, at the same time, his activity is not transitive, it does not go beyond his own self. In fact, man, his act, and the fact that he is accomplishing an act are one and the same thing. In less recondite terminology this means that man has become an intellect

41. *Risāla fi'l-ʿaql*, ed. M. Bouyges (Beirut, 1938), pp. 31 f.

and that consequently (this being an essential quality of all intellects) he as subject is identical both with the act of intellection and with its object. In this state he can cognize without the help of the bodily organs.

Thus while al-Fārābī's commentary on the *Ethics* rules out the possibility of a human being attaining the state of supreme perfection that may have been attributed by Maimonides to Moses, one finds in al-Fārābī's treatise *On the Intellect* (and also in his treatise on *The Opinions of the People of the Virtuous City*, p. 58) a description of such a state. It should be remarked, however, that the author does not appear firmly to assert that this state can actually be achieved. The whole train of thought is put forward in a very tentative way (see p. 30, l. 8). Al-Fārābī does not suggest either explicitly or implicitly that he professed these views on the highest perfection of man. In fact the text of the treatise does not authorize a valid answer to the question. Nor does he affirm that Aristotle held that man's conjunction with the Active Intellect was attainable, though one may gather that this may be a possible, perhaps even probable, interpretation of the views of the Greek philosopher.[42] Al-Fārābī's various points of view as well as Ibn Bājja's position, which will be discussed below, have to be kept in mind in any attempt to assay Maimonides' views on the intellectual supremacy of Moses.

There is one explicit reference in the *Guide* (II 18 in the beginning) to al-Fārābī's treatise *On the Intellect*. The passage, which is quoted[43] (and which may be found in Bouyges' edition, p. 30, ll. 9–10) is concerned with the intermittence of the activity of the Active Intellect.

The somewhat later passage in the same chapter in which Maimonides expounds the opinion that this intermittence is due not to a quality inherent in the essence of the Active Intellect, but to the varying dispositions of the material substances that have to receive the forms emanating from the Active Intellect, and that in some cases are incapable of doing so, allude to a passage of the treatise *On the Intellect* (not mentioned by Maimonides in this connection). This passage occurs in the treatise in the same context (p. 33) as the one referred to first. There are some grounds for thinking that it was al-Fārābī's version of the doctrine, according to which forms emanating from the Active Intellect are received not only by the human mind but also by matter and the physical bodies, that was

42. It is an interesting fact that, although Averroes in his Great Commentary on *De anima* quotes several times al-Fārābī's treatise *On the Intellect* and even refers (p. 493) to the doctrine of the acquired intellect (*intellectus adeptus*) expounded in this treatise, he does not allude to the contradiction between this doctrine and al-Fārābī's views as stated in his commentary on the *Ethics*. As we have seen, Averroes repeatedly refers in the Commentary in question to these views.

43. The quotation is not quite accurate. Perhaps in making it, Maimonides relied on his memory.

taken over by Maimonides. This doctrine is of central importance in Maimonides' physics and psychology.

The philosophic thinking of Maimonides (as well as that of Averroes) is to a considerable extent determined by the necessity to face the challenge offered by Moslem and Jewish theologians known under the name of Mutakallimūn. In these polemics al-Fārābī was of great service because some of his works propounded definitions and descriptions of the purpose, attitude, and methods of the Muta-kallimūn that seemed to show that these opponents need not be taken too seriously by people interested in theoretical truth.

One of these definitions referred to in the *Guide* (I 73) as having been coined by al-Fārābī occurs in two passages of the treatise *On the Intellect* (pp. 7–8 and 11–12). The first of these reads:

"As for the intellect that the Mutakallimūn are always talking about, when they say about a thing, 'This is necessitated, or denied, or accepted, or not accepted by the intellect,' they mean thereby something that is universally accepted by the first [reflections] of the opinion of everybody. For they designate as intellect the first [reflections] of common opinion [professed] by everybody or by most people. This will become clear to you if you examine with regard to the use of this term, point by point, either their oral argumentation or their writings."

The second passage reads: "The Mutakallimūn believe that the intellect that they talk about among themselves is the intellect that is mentioned by Aristotle in the *Book of Demonstration*,[44] and they point this out. If, however, you examine the premises they make use of, you will find that all of these without exception derive from the first [reflections] of common opinion. Acordingly they point out one thing and make use of another."

As al-Fārābī points out in the same treatise (pp. 8–9), the intellect with which Aristotle is concerned in the *Book of Demonstration* is the psychic faculty that enables man to obtain certain knowledge of true general and necessary premises not by means of thought and reasoning but either because of his inborn disposition (i.e., a priori knowledge), or from his youth onwards, or without being aware in what way he acquired this knowledge. These premises constitute the principles of the speculative sciences. Al-Fārābī thus makes it clear that when the Muta-kallimūn claim that their doctrines are based on intellectual reasoning, they are from the philosophic point of view equivocating; the fact being that their premises are constituted by generally held opinions and not by first principles grounded on a priori intellectual certainty. What they call intellect (or reason) means simply immediate acceptance of such opinions. No true science can be developed on such flimsy foundations.

44. I.e., *The Posterior Analytics*.

In this demonstration of the unscientific position of the Mutakallimūn, al-Fārābī probably had in mind the Muʿtazilites who, self-proclaimed rationalists that they were, set great store by their use of the intellect. In al-Fārābī's time they wielded great influence. The situation had, however, radically shifted in the nearly three centuries between al-Fārābī and Maimonides. The Muʿtazilites were no longer an intellectual power to be reckoned with. But philosophy was challenged by another nonrationalist kalām school, the Ashʿarites, who in various parts of the Islamic world set about working out an official theology, building universities for their own brand of doctrine, and in some places. coercing those who disagreed. Moreover they had had, a generation or two before Maimonides' time, a redoubtable champion: al-Ghazālī.

In spite of the decline of the Muʿtazilites and the ascendancy of the Ashʿarites, Maimonides indubitably accepted in all essentials al-Fārābī's analysis of the intellectual inadequacy of kalām. His attitude on this point is not as anachronistic as it might seem; in spite of radical differences between the two schools, many fundamental Ashʿarite doctrines and notably their physical theories (if the term may be used in this context) were taken over with various changes from the Muʿtazilites. As far as these theories are concerned, Maimonides' quarrel with the Mutakallimūn is essentially caused by their denial of a permanent natural order, i.e., of a rational self-perpetuating cosmos explicable by science. As their tenth premise (*Guide* I 73) makes it clear, anything that is imaginable is in their opinion admissible by the intellect and can happen; e.g., the earth can turn into a revolving sphere. This implies that the apparent cosmic order is a haphazard or arbitrary arrangement. It is in the course of his discussion of this negation of the possibility of physical science conceived on Aristotelian lines that Maimonides, quite appropriately, cites al-Fārābī's opinion that the intellect of the Mutakallimūn was sometimes nothing but the first reflections of the common opinion, and sometimes, as the *Guide* adds (I 73), mere imagination. Thus Maimonides believes, as apparently did al-Fārābī, that because of their faulty epistemology and their incapacity to grasp what the philosophic intellect is and does, they cannot have access to science.

In his view of the Mutakallimūn, Maimonides was influenced not only by al-Fārābī's judgment on the conception of reason or intellect current among these theologians, but also by the earlier philosophers' definition of the purpose they had in mind in their theorizing. Both Maimonides and al-Fārābī consider that the Mutakullimūn are not engaged in a quest for the truth, but in a defense of religious belief and dogma, i.e., in apologetics. Al-Fārābī gives a very impressive description of their tactics in a treatise on the *Classification of the Sciences* (*Ihṣāʾ al-ʿulūm*), but there is no evidence to show that Maimonides used this treatise in the *Guide*.

On the other hand, a lost treatise of al-Fārābī entitled *The Changing Beings* (*al-Mawjūdāt al-mutaghayyira*), which is explicitly referred to in the *Guide* (I 74 in fine) appears to have been one of the main non-kalām sources from which Maimonides' knowledge and interpretation of the doctrines of the Mutakallimūn derive. This work seems to have been particularly well known in Moslem Spain, for Ibn Bājja[45] and Averroes[46] also quote it. Whereas Maimonides speaks of al-Fārābī's refuting in this work a kalām proof of the temporal creation of the world, the two other Spanish philosophers mention the attacks he directs therein against the Christian sixth-century Greek philosopher John Philoponus. It seems probable that al-Fārābī did not differentiate too sharply between the doctrine of John Philoponus, who believed in the temporal creation of the world,[47] and that of the Mutakallimūn, who held the same belief. Furthermore, the fact that in the treatise with which we are at present concerned al-Fārābī seems to have polemized, on account of this belief, both against the former and against the latter suggests that this treatise may have been the source of the brief sketch of the beginnings and development of kalām occurring in the *Guide* (I 71). In Maimonides' opinion as given there, the first origins of this school of thought may be found in the teachings of the pre-Islamic Christian theologians, both Syrians and Greeks, who endeavored to counter such opinions of the philosophers as were incompatible with religion. Al-Fārābī's treatise may well have contained the assertion put forward by Maimonides that the first Moslem Mutakallimūn took over the doctrine of John Philoponus.[48]

It seems certain that the main purpose of the work on *The Changing Beings* was to defend the doctrine of the eternity of the world. Evidence in favor of this view may be found not only in Maimonides' explicit reference to this work, but also, as has been partly indicated,[49] in the quotations from it found in Ibn Bājja's and in Averroes' commentaries. In view of these facts it may be regarded as more

45. See his Commentary on Aristotle's *Physics*, MS. Bodleian, Pococke 206, fol. 56a. On this Commentary, see below. Like Maimonides, Ibn Bājja refers to al-Fārābī's polemics against John Philoponus in the treatise in question.

46. See his Great Commentary on the *Physics* (Venice, 1530), Apud Iuntas, 154a, col. b. We learn from Averroes that al-Fārābī examined in this treatise the various kinds of changes (or transformations; *transmutatio*) that may be imagined to precede every change. Evidently this piece of information and others that go with it do not give an adequate idea of al-Fārābī's argumentation, but they do corroborate the evidence from other sources that al-Fārābī's main theme in the work in question was the eternity of the world.

47. And wrote a lengthy work to refute Proclus, who believed in the eternity of the world. John Philoponus' *De aeternitate mundi contra Proclum* was known to the Arabs, though they may not have possessed the complete text of the work.

48. And, according to Maimonides, also of Yaḥyā Ibn ᶜAdī. This is a chronological blunder; see below.

49. See n. 46.

than probable that when Maimonides refers (II 15) to al-Fārābī's being convinced that the eternity of the world can be demonstrated and that Aristotle could have no doubts about it, and, in the same context, to al-Fārābī's disparagement of Galen because the latter took an agnostic position in this matter, he had in mind this treatise of the Arabic philosopher.

None of the political writings of al-Fārābī (a loose term, but one that may be conveniently applied to *The Opinions of the People of the Virtuous City*, *The Political Regimes*, and other treatises) are explicitly cited in the *Guide*. It is quite evident, however, that they had a very strong influence on Maimonides. In fact, the latter's views on the nature and function of prophecy and on the two-fold purpose of the good city stem from al-Fārābī's conceptions. However, the divergencies between the political doctrines of the two are also very significant. They point to influences posterior to al-Fārābī by which Maimonides was affected[50] and also to a different conception of the perils inherent in the study and the propagation of philosophic knowledge. Al-Fārābī was, doubtless, less conscious than Maimonides of the danger that these pursuits represented for society at large. Accordingly none of his writings is as carefully designed as is the *Guide* to throw the unqualified readers and many qualified ones off the right track.

Charting these similarities and these differences would involve a detailed exposition of the whole of Maimonides' practical philosophy. In most cases, however, such an exact and extensive comparison would not result in the discovery of more or less certain, or at least very probable, sources of Maimonides (which is the philological task with which the present Introduction is mainly concerned). On the other hand, in view of the fact that the whole of Maimonides' political philosophy is set within the scheme of reference established by al-Fārābī, certain salient points exemplifying the latter philosopher's influence and its limits must be mentioned. Otherwise the over-all picture would become hopelessly lopsided.

Moreover, in order to get the right perspective one should go beyond al-Fārābī back to Plato, at least in order to give some slight indication of the specific category of the political themes with which Maimonides is concerned. For al-Fārābī's position and criteria are, as far as political philosophy is concerned, largely Platonic. Maimonides, who in this field was decisively influenced by al-Fārābī, was thus a Platonist at a second remove, but perhaps not aware, or not fully aware, of this fact.

The following point should also be noted: Whereas it is practically certain that

50. To take a case in point, al-Fārābī's opinion that philosophers are qua philosophers called upon, circumstances permitting, to play a central role in politics has no explicit counterpart in Maimonides' theory as expounded in the *Guide*, an omission that is certainly not due to chance. This conception may, however, have partly determined his practical activities and is hinted at in this work.

Maimonides had no access to Aristotle's work on politics and may not even have been aware of the book's existence, no such certainty exists with regard to al-Fārābī; it is possible that this work of Aristotle or at least excerpts from, or a paraphrase of, it may have been available to him. If this were so, it would mean that his adoption of Plato's political philosophy rather than Aristotle's was not solely determined by historical accident. Free choice on his part may not have been altogether absent in this matter, which was of crucial importance for the whole course of medieval Arabic and Jewish philosophy.

Some relevant points on which the Platonic and Aristotelian positions differ may be mentioned at this stage.

Aristotle takes the existence of human society for granted, much as he does the existence and the order of the cosmos. It is a primary datum accounted for by man's being a political animal, as are other animal species, i.e., by man's social instinct.[51] It is clear that this explanation is designed to bring home the superfluity of further inquiry rather than to indicate an efficient cause of human society that would, even if only ideally, be prior to it (a method that is employed, to cite but one instance, in the social theories that take as their starting point the isolated human being). Nor does Aristotle's political doctrine posit for the city an end that transcends society and man as a political animal. When Aristotle says that "while [the polis] came into existence for the sake of life, it exists for the sake of the good life" (*Politics* 1252b30; Rackham), he doubtless has in mind a good political life in a flourishing and civilized city, but not the highest way of life—this being the theoretical life,[52] i.e., that of the philosopher. The perfect philosopher, who has outgrown, as in Aristotle's view he can and should do, the need for intellectual companionship, belongs to the city only in so far as he has to provide for his physical

51. Cf. Aristotle *Politics* 1252b31–1253a29. 1253a30 reads: "He who first united people in such a partnership was the greatest of benefactors." Taken by itself this statement might be interpreted to mean that the human communities and cities are not natural products whose existence is determined by fundamental characteristics of the species but rather institutions that have to be invented by some outstanding individual. But such an interpretation is contradicted by the passage that precedes this statement.

52. In other words, the intellectual virtues are not the natural end of the ethical virtues, though practicing the latter may be an indispensable preparation for the acquisition of the former. This implies that the tenth book of the *Nicomachean Ethics,* or at least the portion in it that treats of the theoretical life and its superiority over the life of action, is not the natural conclusion of the preceding books: a break intervenes.

A different interpretation of the *Nicomachean Ethics* is, of course, possible and has often been put forward. It is a moot question. However, for our present purposes it is relevant to note that the relation between the ethical and the intellectual virtues that has been indicated above seems to be the one accepted by the medieval Jewish and Arabic philosophers. It is, for instance, implied in Maimonides' attitude toward ordinary morality and in his evaluation of the practical intellect as compared with the theoretical (see *Guide* I 2). The Platonistic political doctrine of the philosophers in question did not on these points interfere with their Aristotelianism.

necessities. Qua philosopher, he is self-sufficient. In fact, allowing for differences of vocabulary, Aristotle seems to have anticipated Epicurus' discovery that the life of the philosopher was a private life, with which civic activities had no intrinsic connection either in fact or in theory.

Plato's position is different. He does not regard the existence of the cities or of human societies in general as a primary datum or as the direct product of the social instincts and propensities of mankind. The starting point of his political doctrine as set forth in the *Republic* is from a certain point of view prior to the city (just as the starting point of the natural science of the *Timaeus* is prior to the cosmos). It is individual man and his material needs, the realm of Ananke. For it is economic necessity (*chreia*) that impels the human individual to form the embryo of a city (see *Republic* 369B5 ff.). On the other hand, beyond all existent cities, there is the ideal polis ruled by philosophers. Though the latter is a conception that may and probably will never be realized, its very notion implies that no actually existent regime can be regarded as an end in itself. On the part of the philosopher, the acceptance of this conception entails in a way a double allegiance; the point being that, contrary to Aristotle, philosophy even in its highest reaches cannot be held to be a purely private occupation. Man qua metaphysical animal is obligatorily tied up with man the political animal.

But this connection cannot be easily defined or circumscribed; for it has different aspects. The Platonic philosopher is called upon to be the ruler of the ideal city. But he also constitutes an apparent or real danger for the real city and is himself in danger in it.[53] It is an equivocal position. For evident reasons, the perils inherent in it for the philosopher were incalculably increased with the advent, or, in the case of Judaism, with the crystallization into a definitive pattern, of the monotheistic prophetic religions—tending as they do to evolve a hard-and-fast concept of orthodoxy.

Nevertheless in his *Attainment of Happiness* (*Taḥṣīl al-suʿāda*), al-Fārābī did not hesitate to adopt a very exposed position. He declared that it was the philosopher's duty to engage in politics, that, in fact, the four terms philosopher, king, legislator, and imām (religious and political leader) were synonymous.[54]

This is an extreme to which no counterpart can be found in the *Guide;* no political role being explicitly assigned in this work to the philosophers. However, certain injunctions to a life of action occurring in it may be interpreted to mean that the philosopher ought not to keep away from public affairs.[55]

53. Plato's dialogues make it clear that the sentence of death passed on Socrates was no accident. It was the natural conclusion of his life. Plato's political activities in Syracuse, as known from his *Letters*, may also be called to mind in this connection.
54. See, for instance, *Taḥṣīl al-saʿāda* (Hyderabad, 1345 A.H.), pp. 43 f.
55. See, for instance, *Guide* III 54. There is also the conception of Moses expounded in the *Guide*. It may be interpreted to mean that he was more a philosopher than a prophet.

The point may also be made that Maimonides through his own activities was an exemplar of the Platonic philosopher-statesman. And this refers not only to *Mishneh Torah*, which codifies the Jewish law and consequently constitutes an eminently political achievement, but also to the *Guide* itself, which, as its Introduction makes clear, is not comparable, either in its external and internal structure or in its objectives, to the exclusively theoretical, systemized treatises of the philosophers. To some degree at least, the purpose that Maimonides had in mind when writing the *Guide* may be fairly described as political. This purpose, which will be more fully considered later on, aimed both at the legitimation of prophetic religion from the philosophic point of view and of philosophy from the religious. This means that it entailed *inter alia* the acceptance by the philosophers of the fact that not they and their intellectual masters but the prophets were the most suitable legislators of the community. The philosophic justification that this position needed was provided by a theory that was elaborated by al-Fārābī[56] and that was integrally taken over by Maimonides except as far as his conception of Moses is concerned. This theory propounds the following theses:

The prophets have the same kind of theoretical knowledge as the philosophers. They are, among other things, also philosophers. However, in contradistinction to the philosophers, they have a highly developed imaginative faculty. This faculty was conceived as being intermediate between the senses and the intellect, and in that capacity it was regarded by al-Fārābī as not only receiving and sometimes transforming the sense data, but also as being open to an influx coming from the intellect. The imaginative faculty was accordingly supposed to transform intellectual concepts into sensible images and thus to enable men endowed with the appropriate gifts to have veridical dreams and, in the waking state, prophetic visions. In addition, this faculty gave the prophets the power to convey their message and thereby ensure the adhesion and obedience of the common people. Thus imagination appears as the political faculty par excellence.

The teaching of the prophets cannot set forth the philosophic truths in explicit language, for it is addressed to men who are naturally quite incapable of under-

56. In *The Opinions of the People of the Virtuous City* (*Arāʾ ahl al-madīna al-fāḍila*, ed. F. Dieterici [Leiden, 1895], pp. 47 ff.). In other works, for instance, in *Taḥṣīl al-saʿāda*, pp. 43 f., al-Fārābī does not seem to admit any difference between the right kind of the philosopher and the prophet. For Maimonides' theory of prophecy, see *Guide* II 36. It should be added that the relation between the prophetic powers and the imaginative faculty was no novel discovery of al-Fārābī. He merely perfected a theory that has a long history in Greek philosophy. A kindred conception occurs in a text of Isaac Israeli (see A. Altmann and S. M. Stern, *Isaac Israeli* [Oxford, 1958], pp. 135 ff.). For some of the problems connected with al-Fārābī's theory of prophecy, see also R. Walzer, *Greek into Arabic* (Oxford, 1962), pp. 206 ff. The first adequate recognition of the relation between al-Fārābī's and Maimonides' political theory is found in Leo Strauss' "Quelques Remarques" referred to above in n. 33.

standing these truths. It does, however, hint at them and must accordingly receive an allegorical interpretation. In fact, according to al-Fārābī, the various religions are a more or less close and accurate imitation or mimesis of philosophic truth.[57] This means of course that there is no essential difference between monotheistic prophetic religions, though they can be distinguished and evaluated according to the degree of their approximation to philosophic truth. This attitude toward the various religions could find a certain legitimation in the traditional Islamic doctrines. It was much harder to justify it from the Jewish point of view. We find accordingly an admittedly slight discrepancy between two consecutive chapters of the *Guide* II 39 and 40. In the first, Maimonides makes the categorical statement that there is only one divine law, namely, Judaism. On a cursory reading of II 40, one may get the impression that this statement is simply repeated there, but this may be an overhasty interpretation. For in this chapter Maimonides affirms that a religious law, which is not restricted to political and social arrangements but also attempts to propagate correct beliefs concerning God, the angels, and the world, is divine. It is clear from this chapter that Moses is the only legislator who received an authentic revelation of such a law and that the founders of other religions whose laws also inculcate more or less correct beliefs (Maimonides obviously has Muhammad in mind) are plagiarists. It is not as clear that the laws produced by these plagiarists are (except with regard to their origin) intrinsically and essentially inferior to Mosaic Law.

Al-Fārābī's doctrine of prophecy, taken over by Maimonides, was in its daring wide open to the attacks of the orthodox or would-be orthodox. This is particularly true with regard to the assertion made in the treatise on *The Opinions of the People of the Virtuous City* that the essential difference between the philosophers and the prophets is to be found in the fact that the latter, as opposed to the former, are endowed with a powerful imagination; i.e., a faculty that they have in common with unenlightened nonphilosophic politicians.[58] In his treatise referred to above, al-Fārābī briefly alludes to people endowed with an active imagination, but having no access to things of the intellect. Maimonides elaborates and amplifies this statement in the *Guide* (II 37 and 38). His analysis will be discussed in the section on Avicenna.

Both al-Fārābī and Maimonides maintain that the prophet who is a lawgiver and the founder of a community is superior qua philosopher to most philosophers. In his treatise on *The Opinions of the People of the Virtuous City*,[59] al-Fārābī affirms

57. The term "mimesis" calls to mind the Platonic and Aristotelian theories of poetry and art in general. And this is as it should be. There must clearly be a resemblance between the specific mode of utterance of the prophet and that of the poet — in so far as the two are held by the philosophers both to indicate and to conceal the ultimate truth.
58. *The Opinions of the People of the Virtuous City*, p. 52.   59. P. 52.

that the lawgiver achieves union with the Active Intellect (and thus perfect and complete cognition of all that can be intellectually cognized).[60] Al-Fārābī makes this assertion, though in his commentary on the *Ethics* he denies the possibility of such a union. But, as we have seen, he admits it in his treatise *On the Intellect*.[61] These contradictions may be due to an evolution in his thought. There is no absolute necessity, though there is a possibility, to impute them to the need in certain contexts to exalt the prophet-lawgiver in his philosophic capacity. Maimonides for his part does not explicitly state that Moses achieved this union, though this would have probably involved no inconsequence on his part, as he, according to the most probable interpretation of I 72, seems to have thought that this state could be attained by man. But this does not save him from being or appearing to be inconsistent, especially if his statements are compared to al-Fārābī's in the treatise on *The Opinions of the People of the Virtuous City*. Al-Fārābī does not deny in this treatise that the prophet-lawgiver and philosopher who achieves union with the Active Intellect pursues his legislative and political activity with the help of his powerful imaginative faculty,[62] whereas Maimonides declares (II 33; cf. II 45 in fine) that, unlike the other prophets, Moses in the exercise of his prophecy made no use of the imagination and that in his case prophetic inspiration did not overflow onto this inferior faculty—the proof being that he did not prophesy in figures and parables. This statement seems to be wholly incompatible with Maimonides' often expressed view that it is through the strength of his imaginative faculty that a statesman is enabled to play an outstanding political role.

Both al-Fārābī and Maimonides compare the function of the prophet who is a lawgiver in the city he founds to that of God in the universe. But this was a hackneyed comparison, having been used and abused by the Greek Pythagoreans or neo-Pythagoreans in the theory of kingship. But Maimonides gives it a new twist and fills it with new meaning by combining it with a doctrine concerning the imitation of God that may be all his own. This doctrine will be referred to below.

Al-Fārābī (at least in his published works) is much less clear than Maimonides about the inability of the common run of man to establish a viable city. The relevant doctrine of the *Guide* will likewise be discussed below.

On the other hand there seems to me to be an indubitable, though a limited,

---

60. See his treatise on *The Political Regimes* (*al-Siyāsāt al-madaniyya*) (Hyderabad, 1346 A.H.), p. 49.
61. It should be stated that in this treatise he describes this union without referring to the prophets.
62. It should, however, be noted that in another work, the treatise on *The Political Regimes*, al-Fārābī does not mention the part played by the imaginative faculty in prophetic revelation. On this point Maimonides adopted the conception set forth in the treatise on *The Opinions of the People of the Virtuous City*.

connection between al-Fārābī's admittedly very general views on the ideal virtuous city and Maimonides' notion of the Jewish community created by Moses and based on the Torah, which is assimilated by him to the ideal philosophic city.

A similarity between the two conceptions can be found not only in al-Fārābī's and Maimonides' description of the lawgiver of the city, but also in the fact that according to al-Fārābī the ideal city and according to Maimonides the Jewish community founded on the Torah assume the task of perfecting the intellects of their members and of guiding them toward philosophic truth. Those born to be philosophers are given the possibility to know the real nature of things, while the others are taught not the naked truth but the parables and metaphors by means of which the prophets render this truth accessible to the less gifted. As already stated, this is the mimesis of which al-Fārābī speaks. Maimonides sometimes applies to beliefs of this kind, instilled into people incapable of being philosophers, the term "true opinions" (III 27 and 28). It is in accord with the spirit of al-Fārābī's treatise on the virtuous city (p. 99) that Maimonides (II 40) lays down that the divine law, i.e., the Law of the Torah, inculcates correct opinions with regard to God and the angels.

There is, however, between al-Fārābī's conception and Maimonides' a marked shift of emphasis. In his known works al-Fārābī hardly alludes (or does not allude at all) to the practical, mundane tasks of the ideal city. He does not speak in this context (or, as far as I know, in any other) of the necessity and difficulties of overcoming by suitable devices the unsocial element existing in human nature, or of the historical contingencies that to a certain extent, one should have thought, must condition the emergent ideal city. These, however, are some of the main themes in Maimonides' analysis and justification of Judaism. It is a natural and readily explicable difference. Al-Fārābī's descriptions are in part generalized schemata for a nonexistent ideal city, which may be brought into being by revolutionary action. In depicting its structure, he is not bound by the servitudes of the past or the stubborn ill-conditioned facts of the present. Maimonides' task is incomparably more difficult. He has to give a philosophically valid proof that the commandments of Mosaic Law and the beliefs that, according to him, must be professed by every member of the Jewish community (or at least every member who is not a philosopher) qualify this community to be regarded as the ideal philosophic city. In order to fulfill this task he had quite obviously to fall back on anthropological and historical necessity. This is not meant as an allegation that he did not believe in the capital importance of these factors. I am persuaded that on this point his apologetics were in line with his genuine convictions. These questions will be discussed in greater detail in the next section, which deals with Maimonides' relation to Avicenna.

AVICENNA

Avicenna (d. 1036) is the only eminent philosopher considered as belonging to the Aristotelian school with regard to whom Maimonides, in his letter to Ibn Tibbon, expresses some reservations and even some distrust. From a certain point of view this attitude is quite understandable. On his own showing, Avicenna was no orthodox Peripatetic at all (he rather tends to overemphasize his freedom from this tradition). And he certainly put forward new views that explain, though they do not justify, the accusation leveled against him by Averroes that he tried to contaminate the philosophic doctrine with suitably modified ideas deriving in the last analysis from the kalām. This charge was characteristic for the rigoristic school of Spanish Aristotelianism, to which both Averroes and, albeit to a lesser extent, Maimonides belonged.

Nevertheless, Avicenna's fame and philosophic authority stood high even in Spain and the Maghrib, as is proven by the repeated references to him in *Ḥayy Ibn Yaqzān*, the philosophic novel of Maimonides' elder contemporary Ibn Ṭufayl.

Moreover, Avicenna's system, which teaches *inter alia* that the individual soul survives the death of the body and lives eternally, and which regards the mystical experience of the ṣūfis as a valid subject for philosophic investigation and attempts to utilize it in its theory of prophecy, is much more consonant with religious feeling — to use a modern, anachronistic, and perhaps irrelevant term — and doubtless also with religion *tout court* as conceived in the Middle Ages than the doctrine of the orthodox Aristotelians. If Maimonides had been the eclectic and the apologist he is sometimes thought to have been, and if his aim had been merely to devise some sort of a compromise between, and amalgam of, philosophy and a religion freed from the reproach of backwardness and obscurantism, Avicenna would have provided the perfect solution both because of his teaching and of his reputation. He might have been regarded as giving religion, or at least the varieties of religious experience, the hallmark of intellectual respectability. The fact that, regarding the crucial point in which religion and prophecy are involved, Maimonides did not follow Avicenna's lead (though he did so with respect to other questions), indicates the quality of his feeling about philosophic truth as he saw it. It shows that he was not interested in apologetics at any price, or even in apologetics at all, if the word means the cutting and pruning of philosophic theory so that it should accord with religious dogmas.

I do not, of course, wish to contradict Maimonides' express statements that he wanted to bring about in the mind of the various classes of his readers a conciliation between religion and philosophy. But it seems to me that he thought to achieve this result not through a doctrinal, consistent compromise, but through the use or

misuse of semantic interpretation, the recourse to a sometimes accurate and sometimes deliberately inaccurate style, through a technique of over- and under-
emphasis in some of his theoretical expositions, and, as he says himself, through
deliberate self-contradiction.

It may be asserted with a certain plausibility that Maimonides shows traces
of being contaminated by Avicennian doctrines in two fields: (1) metaphysics,
i.e., the doctrine of being and of God, and (2) the theory of prophecy. It may be
added that his recourse to Avicenna's metaphysical doctrines possibly exemplifies
some of the techniques of indirection mentioned above.

The metaphysical doctrines in question are concerned with the notions of
essence and existence, and of necessary and contingent. Avicenna contended (and,
because of this contention, was taken to task by Averroes and charged with intro-
ducing suitably modified kalām teaching into philosophy) that in all being, except
God, there is a duality consisting of essence and existence. The essences by themselves have, contrary to the Platonic ideas, no existence; they are neutral with
respect to being. With regard to them existence is an accident, which may or may
not supervene. Hence all beings except God are contingent, or, to use the medieval Arabic and Hebrew term, possible; God, in whom the difference between
essence and existence does not exist, is the only necessary being.

This doctrine, which is neither Aristotelian nor, as far as we know, found in
the genuine writings of al-Fārābī, is quite evidently referred to and taken over
by Maimonides in the beginning of II 57.

What are the implications of this deviation from the strict Aristotelian doctrine if one considers Maimonides' philosophic position as a whole? Prima facie
they seem to be considerable. For according to this view the existence of the
universe ceases to be the primary datum postulated by Aristotle, beyond which
one cannot and must not go; the cosmos is no longer taken for granted. Considered
by itself, it is an accident that might not have occurred. Should one add (for the
last phrase might seem unsatisfactory, attributing as it does the existence of the
universe to chance): that might not have occurred but for the will of God?

Avicenna leaves no loophole for such an interpretation, if it implies that God
might have chosen not to create a universe at all, or not this universe but a different
one. In fact, in his philosophic system the contingent character of the world merely
veils and disguises the essential necessity of the latter. For every contingent being
is only contingent if it is taken by itself, but is ineluctably necessary if it is considered in relation to the concatenation of causes and effects starting with the First
Cause, God, to which it owes its existence. In fact, Avicenna's system is strictly
deterministic. And this determinism extends to God and His activity. There is no
room in this philosophy for Leibnitz' conception of a God choosing among the

various possible worlds the one that is the best of all and bringing it into existence. The universe could not have been other than it is, there being no element of choice about God's causative function.

Thus Maimonides' adoption of Avicenna's distinction between essence and existence and the fact that, like Avicenna, he differentiates on the basis of this distinction between necessary and contingent being had either no bearing at all on his position in the question of God's freedom of will and of action — on which, according to the *Guide* the conflict between religion and philosophy hinges — or if he gave unqualified support to the Avicennian doctrine, should have impelled him to negate this freedom.[63]

It is more relevant from Maimonides' point of view to note that the terminology and notional framework of Avicenna's doctrine tended to emphasize God's remoteness from human conception. This is a cardinal point of Maimonides' theology; it is also one of the most frequently cited, but it may not have the meaning and the implications usually ascribed to it.

According to Maimonides' often expressed assertion, God should not be regarded as having any positive attributes pertaining to His essence and superadded to it; any positive attribute describing Him should be given a negative meaning (I 52, 53, 56, 57, 58). Thus His being characterized as wise or living merely signifies that He is not ignorant or dead, but has no reference at all to anything we can recognize as wisdom or life. This applies even to His existence, which beyond the homonymy has nothing in common with anything we conceive as existence (I 56). This is a radical doctrine and Maimonides obviously takes pains to place it in the foreground of his "divine science." Now this negative theology was no intrinsic or important part of the traditional Aristotelian system. It does not play any conspicuous part in al-Fārābī's doctrines. It does, however, in Avicenna's,[64] and this fact may, as I believe, justify my discussing the problems involved in this particular context. It seems probable that it was Avicenna who conferred upon negative theology the philosophic reputability that made it possible for Maimonides to introduce it as the apparently central part of his, i.e., the philosophic, doctrine of God; in fact he lays even greater stress upon it and uses more radical formulas than Avicenna. For that matter, it may be taken as pretty certain that in formulating his views on this point Maimonides also used texts belonging to authors who, from the Aristotelian point of view, were much less

---

63. It may be apposite to remark in this connection that in my opinion the commonly held view that Maimonides qua philosopher believed in the freedom of man's will and action is mistaken, if one accepts the current definitions of such freedom. See the preliminary observation made in S. Pines, "Abu'l-Barakāt's Poetics and Metaphysics," *Scripta Hierosolymitana*, VI, "Studies in Philosophy" (Jerusalem, 1960), Excursus, pp. 195–98.
64. See "Abu'l-Barakāt's Poetics and Metaphysics," pp. 163–65.

respectable than Avicenna; thus he may have utilized Neo-Platonic writings[65] or perhaps even the book on *The Duties of the Hearts* of the Jewish mystic Baḥya. He manages, however, to give his negative theology a very personal touch. By affirming the absolute transcendence of God, it proposes to man the cosmos as his highest and main study.

In this context Maimonides' insistence (I 59) on the value of the cognition of the various negative attributes should be mentioned. A similar approach may be found in mystical writings, but Maimonides is no mystic. His intention is not to recommend progressive detachment from the knowledge of all things that are not God, but to further that kind of knowledge by teaching people to avoid misplaced references to God's essence.

Moses, whose request to apprehend God's essence was refused because it was impossible to fulfil it, was granted another boon: he achieved knowledge of God's workings in the universe (I 54). These divine activities, taken in conjunction with the various descriptions and qualifications given to them by people judging them from the human point of view, represent God's attributes of action. On one hand knowledge of these attributes is the only positive knowledge concerning God possible to man. On the other hand this knowledge – if it is unadulterated by human moral judgment – can practically be equated with the grasp of the sequence and (natural) causes of the natural phenomena.

Thus Maimonides is quite consistent when, in a formula that forcibly calls to mind Spinoza,[66] he speaks of "divine," i.e., natural, actions (III 32). The study of nature and of the order of nature is the only way open to man to know something of God.

The import of these views may be realized more clearly if one considers the reinterpretation of biblical terms that Maimonides has in mind. His attributes of action are such terms as "Merciful" or "Revengeful" applied to God. According to Maimonides expressions of this kind originate in man's teleological anthropocentric interpretation of the inhuman, self-conserving, and self-perpetuating order of nature. Thus God is sometimes called "Merciful" because in accordance with that order the embryos of animals develop satisfactorily and parents have been endowed with the instinct to protect their children. Or He is called "Revengeful" because, again in accordance with the order of nature, storms, floods, earthquakes, and wars work destruction. One is again reminded of Spinoza's attacks on the ascription of a finalistic man-centered causality to Nature, or to call it by another name, to God.

65. Some of which had no doubt influenced Avicenna himself in his exposition of negative theology.
66. Whose expression, "God or Nature" (*Deus sive natura*), may have been, at least in part, suggested by this passage of the *Guide*.

Anticipating a little, I shall add that this interpretation of the attributes of action enables Maimonides to explain in a rather unusual way what the imitation of God required by the philosophers and by the Jewish tradition really means. Of this more hereafter. It may also be noted in this connection that the fact that the *Guide* is centered on a reinterpretation of the Bible and other religious Jewish texts leads Maimonides to stress what one may call the naturalistic aspect of his thought. In some respects he gives it a more striking, because more controversial, expression than the Arabic Aristotelian philosophers, with whom he is in essential agreement on these matters.

The discussion of Maimonides' negative theology can be fittingly followed by a reference to his conception of God's intellectual activity, not because the two are complementary, but because they appear to be contradictory. The second doctrine has in the last analysis its source in Aristotle and is expounded by all the Peripatetic philosophers, but its conjunction with radical negative theology is by no means usual and may not be attested at all before the advent of Avicenna's philosophy. Maimonides for his part gives this doctrine an interpretation that brings out, more than Avicenna's does, its incompatibility with negative theology.

The doctrine in question states (see I 68; cf. I 53) that God is engaged in intellectual cognition, and that He is both the subject and the object of cognition and the cognitive activity, three in one. This conception derives from Aristotle's *Metaphysics Λ*, and the philosophic proposition embodying it, which is quoted by Maimonides at the beginning of I 68, represents a stock formula used by practically all Aristotelian philosophers. In Aristotle's *Metaphysics* this conception ties up with the idea that God only cognizes Himself, because all other things are unworthy of being known by Him. If, in accordance with a probable intention of Aristotle, the last statement is interpreted as excluding God's cognition of the ideas or the universals, the content of God's cognition would be most strictly circumscribed.

Whatever Avicenna's position on this point may be (and the fact is that he apparently does not favor this exclusion), it is evident that the statement that God cognizes and the consequent assertions that He cognizes Himself or Himself and the forms or essences assimilated to Himself are positive statements and as such in contradiction with the spirit and tendency of negative theology. In the face of such statements any attempt to make out a case for God's cognition having nothing except homonymy in common with man's cognition may easily seem mere quibbling; and yet only such an attempt can satisfy negative theology. Avicenna tacitly leaves the question open,[67] for he does not make a comparison

67. See *The Book of the Healing of the Soul* (*Kitāb shifāʾ al-nafs*) (Teheran, lithographed), II, 586 ff. (The pages are not numbered.)

and indicate an essential similarity between God's knowledge and man's. Other Arabic philosophers do not, as far as I am aware, do this either. Maimonides, on the other hand, goes out of his way to point out the similarity. In order to drive this home he shows the relatedness of two Aristotelian doctrines, which, as far as I know, nobody beforehand had regarded as closely connected. Nevertheless, Maimonides may be said to make his point.

One of these doctrines, the one that in substance is set forth in *Metaphysics Λ*, proclaims that in God the subject, object, and act of intellectual cognition are identical. The other doctrine is expounded in Aristotle's *De anima*. It concerns intellectual activity in general, and first and foremost the human variety of that activity, and asserts that in intellectual cognition the subject is identical with the object. In order to illustrate this conception Maimonides uses (probably deliberately) a humble example: the intellect of a man who cognizes the separate form of a piece of wood is identical with this form and because such is its nature is also identical with the act of intellection. Thus, as Maimonides explicitly states, man's intellect manifests when actualized exactly the same kind of threefold identity as God's. Obviously this view goes counter to negative theology. It may be recalled in this connection that in his Introduction to the *Guide* Maimonides states that for reasons given by him he deliberately inserted into this work contradictory theses (one false and one correct). Is this an instance of this didactic method, and if so, which of the two doctrines represents Maimonides' real opinion? Prima facie either of them is admissible.

The example of the form of wood used by Maimonides does, however, make another point pretty clear. Though Maimonides does not explicitly say so, it follows from the analogy he draws between God's and man's intellectual activity that God's knowledge is not only confined to His own essence, if the latter is conceived as not including the forms that are also the objects of human science. However, if He does cognize the system of forms (and we may add, using a later term, of natural laws) subsisting in the universe, He must be held (in virtue of the Aristotelian thesis stressed by Maimonides) to be identical with these forms and laws, i.e., with the scientific system of the universe. This would make Him out to be something coming perilously close to Spinoza's attribute of thought (or to his "Intellect of God").

I should add that, while it is pretty clear that these are the evident consequences of Maimonides' view, it may be argued that he may have been guilty of that inconsistency of not having drawn these conclusions. In this particular case this point of view would amount to a grave and, in my opinion, very implausible accusation of muddle-headedness directed against Maimonides.

As far as political philosophy and the doctrines regarding prophecy and religious observances are concerned, there are several points in which Avicenna's influence on Maimonides may be discerned with some degree of precision. In other cases a general resemblance between the views of the two philosophers may be noted, but the similarity may not be so close as to demonstrate that Avicenna was the direct source of Maimonides. The relation between their views on the political and social function of prophecy is of the second kind.

Like Avicenna, Maimonides believed on the one hand that man is a social animal in the sense that he cannot live, or at least cannot have a satisfactory life, except within a political community. On the other hand, both of them are of the opinion (which may not have been held by al-Fārābī), that the common run of men, if left to themselves, are unfit by nature to establish such a community. However, the reasons they give for the second thesis are different. According to Avicenna[68] the inability of average men to create by their own unaided efforts a political society that would be viable is due to the fact that people if left to their own devices find it impossible to agree upon a common law valid for all, because everyone thinks that the things that accord with his own interests are right and that the things that are unfavorable to him are wrong. Consequently men are naturally hostile to one another. Only a prophet, i.e., a man endowed with certain faculties not found in the common run of people, can create a social bond between them and thus preserve them from the calamities and the destruction that wait upon the solitary.

Maimonides' position is essentially not very different, but he formulates it in another way (II 40). According to him the inability of men to constitute viable society is due to the great differences subsisting between the human individuals with respect to their character and moral qualities; to cite an example, some men are very cruel, while others are averse to hurting even an insect. Only a leader endowed with special gifts can weld people who present such an enormous range of differences (which is greater than any that can be found between the individuals of any other animal species) into one society and make them submit to a law binding on all.

According to both Avicenna and Maimonides the fact that such lawgivers appear is due to a teleological provision of nature (II 40). It is true that Avicenna attributes this device to primary providence, but in this context the two terms are interchangeable, as he makes clear by comparing the appearance of prophets and their legislative activities with such useful contrivances of nature as eyelashes and the concavity of the soles. There seems, however, to be a certain divergency, perhaps more apparent than real, between Avicenna's and Maimonides' view of these lawgivers. In his magnum opus, *The Book of the Healing of the Soul*, Avicenna

68. The relevant views of Avicenna referred to in this context may be found *ibid.*, pp. 646 ff.

appears to take it for granted that all such legislators are prophets, imposing upon their community a monotheistic religion. It is inconceivable that Avicenna, who was familiar with Greek philosophic and scientific literature and no doubt also with Arabic historical and geographical texts, did not know better than to extrapolate from Islamic and Jewish history and to suppose that all other legislations had a similar origin. From his point of view this statement must have been inaccurate (perhaps deliberately so), unless one supposes that, in the teeth of much of the evidence available to him, he believed that in every community there had existed a primitive monotheism instituted by a prophet.

Maimonides' position is much more understandable and much easier to defend. It is based on al-Fārābī's psychological analysis of prophecy, according to which prophets are characterized by an unusual vigor both of their intellectual and their imaginative faculties. In this connection Maimonides makes the point (II 37 and 38) that philosophers can be differentiated from the prophets by the fact that only their intellectual capacity, and not their imagination, is outstanding. Symmetry seems to require that there should be a third category of people, namely, those who do not have an extraordinary intellectual ability (and are, consequently, no philosophers), but have a strong imagination. In Maimonides' opinion these are the characteristics of those lawgivers who are no prophets and of politicians and also of sorcerers. In this way Maimonides propounds a definition of the nonphilosophic statesmen, a problem that exercised Plato in relation to such men as Themistocles, Pericles, and lesser politicians. Except for a brief passage of al-Fārābī referred to above, I know of no earlier text in which such an analysis occurs. Obviously it gives Maimonides the possibility — of which Avicenna in *The Book of the Healing of the Soul* deprives himself — to give an acceptable explanation for the origin of laws in "idolatrous" or "unreligious" communities not founded by prophets, the evident inference being that their founders were legislators lacking true philosophic insight.

It may be added that by establishing this category Maimonides laid himself wide open to attack. It was an easy point to make that there is no scriptural evidence whatever that the biblical prophets were philosophers, and Spinoza makes it.[69] He believes that the distinctive characteristic of these prophets, including Moses, was the force of their imagination; in other words he relegates them to the category of the nonphilosophic lawgivers and politicians with which he was familiar through his study of the *Guide*. This modification of the theory of the *Guide* by Spinoza is no doubt unfortunate from the point of view of a disciple of Maimonides, but it is also fairly natural. Any unprejudiced comparison of the doctrine with the facts was apt to suggest it. In passing, we may wonder whether

69. See *Tractatus theologico-politicus*, chaps. i and ii, and *passim*.

Maimonides and al-Fārābī permitted themselves to be aware of the lack of any historical evidence for the contention that the prophets were philosophers; but this is an unprofitable speculation. However, Maimonides fairly certainly knew that his (and al-Fārābī's) view that in all essentials the prophets only differed from the philosophers by having a more vigorous imagination was regarded as derogatory to the former.[70] This being the case, it is surely significant that he had so little use for Avicenna's attempt to elucidate the phenomenon of prophecy by assimilating it to the recorded experiences of the mystics – to whom as well as to the prophets he applied the term "gnostics" (ʿārifūn). These "gnostics" appeared to have a different and more impressive way of acceding to divine things than the philosophers, and it is possible that they can progress further than the latter.

It is at least probable that Maimonides had read texts setting forth this explanation of prophecy; indeed he may have borrowed several ideas and terms used by Avicenna in this connection; and yet he was not prepared to accept the doctrine as a whole, although it was put forward by an eminent philosopher and might have rendered his position much easier in the face of the attacks of the orthodox. No doubt the temper of his mind was against it. He was also schooled in a different philosophic tradition.

Avicenna's doctrine[71] that the prophet and men belonging to that category had natural faculties that enabled them to work so-called miracles does not seem to be referred to by Maimonides either. It was probably less objectionable from the Aristotelian point of view than the attempt to allow supreme validity to mystical experience, but it may have seemed to Maimonides dubious and, even worse, irrelevant. He may, however, have borrowed from Avicenna[72] the image of flashes of lightnings used in the Introduction to the *Guide* and usually interpreted as applying to the inspirations of prophecy. However, as we shall see, there are some grounds for thinking that in the passage in question he may have drawn also on another source. The image is frequent, and its significations can be very different.

Avicenna's influence can perhaps be recognized in another particular, namely, in Maimonides' statement that the prophets can reach knowledge of reality without having previously grasped the apparently necessary theoretical premises to this knowledge (II 38). Parallels to this view can be found in Avicenna's works.[73]

---

70. Ibn Ṭufayl, who was somewhat older than Maimonides, but can rate as the latter's contemporary, blames al-Fārābī for regarding philosophy as superior to religion (*Hayy Ibn Yaqzan*, p. 14).
71. See *Kitāb al-ishārāt wa'l-tanbīhāt*, ed. J. Forget (Leiden, 1892), pp. 208 f.
72. *K. al-ishārāt*, pp. 202 f. Ibn Ṭufayl draws upon this passage in *Hayy Ibn Yaqzan*, pp. 6 f.
73. See, for instance, Avicenna, *Risāla fı ithbāt al-nubuwwāt*, *Tisᶜ rasāʾil* (Cairo, 1908), pp. 122 f. Avicenna justifies this view on theoretical grounds.

In *The Book of the Healing of the Soul* Avicenna briefly refers to the prophets instituting prayers, religious feasts, sacrifices, and whatever else pertains to an established religion. But whatever similarities there may exist between this short passage and Maimonides' detailed explanations of the reasons for the various commandments are rather vague.

There is perhaps a better warrant for attributing to a direct or indirect influence of Avicenna the rather uncharacteristic passage in III 32 in which Maimonides, in order to bring home to the readers the historical reasons for various cultic commandments such as the prescriptions concerning sacrifices and to make it clear to them that the force of habit is quite as strong in their times as in those of Moses, envisages the (impossible) hypothesis that a prophet would call upon Maimonides' contemporaries to replace the prescribed religious offices, the fasts, and the prayers addressed to God in times of disaster by simple meditation. Maimonides implies (1) that no prophet could do this with any hope of success because of the fact that people cling to traditional customs, and (2) that, apart from such considerations, meditation regarded as a form of the worship of God is superior to verbal prayer. This is in the main the thesis of Avicenna in his *Treatise on Prayer*[74] — written, as he informs us, in less than half an hour — if we assimilate, as we legitimately may, Maimonides' meditation to Avicenna's spiritual prayer, which he opposes to the exoteric prayer prescribed by religious Law. Elsewhere Maimonides uses another expression that is even more reminiscent of Avicenna's views. He speaks of "rational worship," upon which man should be intent in solitude, and which consists in being close to God in truth and not through the impressions of the imagination (III 51).

The various points discussed above tend to show that at a certain level of philosophic thought Avicenna had considerable influence upon Maimonides; this is indicated by the latter's adoption of negative theology, of the distinction between essence and existence, and of various particulars of Avicenna's prophetology and theory of the worship of God. This influence, however (even when Avicennian theses were not taken over merely for the purposes of window-dressing), did not essentially modify Maimonides' fundamental position, which he inherited from al-Fārābī and the Spanish Aristotelian school. In fact, as has already been suggested, the importance of a comparison between his doctrines and Avicenna's is to be found partly in the fact that it permits us to gauge the steadfastness of Maimonides' (often tacit) rejection of philosophic beliefs that were much less obnoxious from the religious point of view than his own.

This applies *inter alia* to Avicenna's belief in the immortality of the individual souls, which Maimonides — like other Aristotelians — did not share qua philosopher.

74. *Risālat al-ṣalāt*, in *Jāmiᶜ al-badāʾiᶜ* (Cairo, 1917), pp. 2–14.

This negative attitude is quite evident. But apparently he did not regard this as a crucial problem for the relations between philosophy and religion. It is remarkable how little space — even if one counts the indirect references — he devotes to it in the *Guide*.

One of the passages in question appears to refer to Avicenna (I 74, seventh way); for it is pretty certain that he is the "modern philosopher" who is said by Maimonides to have tried to prove that the doctrine of the eternity of the world is not incompatible with belief in the afterlife of the individual soul. For, despite an unnamed adversary's argument, it is not impossible that an infinite number of immaterial souls should exist. This would have been impossible only if these souls were in a place and had a local position. The infinity of the number of the disembodied souls is a corollary of the Aristotelian assumption that mankind is as eternal as the world. Maimonides does not endorse this argument and makes it pretty clear that he rejects Avicenna's views on the afterlife of the soul and that he has a certain preference for Ibn Bājja's position. This is not fortuitous. As may be seen from the letter to Ibn Tibbon, Maimonides' attitude toward Ibn Bājja is not marked by the reticence that he shows toward Avicenna.

IBN BĀJJA

This is understandable. Ibn Bājja (d. 1138)[75] was the founder of the Spanish school of Aristotelian philosophy, to which Maimonides belonged and which derived from al-Fārābī rather than from Avicenna; and he could not be, or at least was not, accused of teaching a doctrinally too lax and pliant philosophy. He was, however, by no means a mere disciple but an innovator full of ideas that were heterodox, if they were considered from the point of view of Aristotle or, for that matter, of al-Fārābī. He was often criticized on this count by the faithful Aristotelian Averroes, who nevertheless respected him, as did Maimonides.

In rejecting Avicenna's view concerning the disembodied soul, Maimonides makes one of his few explicit references to Ibn Bājja. He credits this philosopher quite correctly[76] with having made clear that as far as only the pure intellect is concerned there are no individual differences. In other words, Aristotle qua intellect is identical with the other "happy ones"; they are not a multiplicity of beings, but "one." The intellect being regarded as the only portion of man that survives bodily death, this doctrine of Ibn Bājja means that, contrary to Avicenna, nothing individual remains after death.

75. In dealing with the relation between Ibn Bājja and Maimonides I have made some use of the as yet unpublished thesis of L. V. Berman, *Ibn Bājjah and Maimonides*, submitted in 1959 to the Hebrew University, Jerusalem.
76. See, for instance, *Risālat al-ittiṣāl*, ed. by A. F. al-Ahwani, in the volume containing his edition of Averroes' *Kitāb al-nafs* (Cairo, 1950), pp. 115 f.

As has already been stated, Maimonides seems to incline to this opinion of Ibn Bājja, yet he does not wholly commit himself, these being, according to him, "hidden matters" (I 74, seventh way).

It may be added that while the so-called Arabic and Jewish Aristotelian philosophers— with the sizable exception of al-Kindī, Avicenna, and their respective disciples— did not as a rule believe in individual afterlife, Ibn Bājja was perhaps the first to have formulated a clear and consistent philosophic position on this point. It was a position which Judah Hallevi,[77] who was by and large Ibn Bājja's contemporary, was acquainted with and which he rejected, but which was taken over with modifications due to a different conception of the intellect by Averroes and his Jewish disciples. As we have seen, the latter had a certain justification for believing that Maimonides sided with them, at least in so far as they accepted some fundamental ideas belonging to the original theory of Ibn Bājja.

Ibn Bājja's frequently expressed belief that union with the Active Intellect conceived as the last in the series of the ten separate intellects was possible to man pretty certainly influenced, at least to some extent, the views expounded by Maimonides concerning Moses. As we have seen, al-Fārābī, in spite of some texts that appeared to regard such a union as possible, was held by Averroes, on account of other quite equivocal texts, to consider it as an impossibility.

Ibn Bājja's impact on Maimonides' thought can occasionally be traced not only in his conceptions but also in his imagery, notably in the imagery used in a striking passage of the Introduction to the *Guide*.

Speaking of man's (generally limited) understanding of the secrets of the Torah, which are none other than the truths of physics and metaphysics, Maimonides states in this passage, which has already been referred to above, that some of us see lightning flashes in the dark night that encompasses us. Moses saw these flashes continuously, so that his night was turned as it were into day; others see during the whole of their life only a few flashes; others again only one. It is they who are referred to in Numbers 11:25: "And they prophesied, but they did so no more." There are also people who are not able to see lightning flashes, but who see in the darkness of the night some light coming from polished bodies such as certain stones. There exists of course also a category of men who see no light at all.

The interpretation of this text poses some problems. The most obvious solution would perhaps be to suppose that the people seeing the lightnings are the prophets conceived in Avicennian fashion as endowed with a faculty of intuitive intellection, which enables them to arrive at true and certain conclusions without

---

77. It is the philosophic position outlined in the philosopher's exposé in *Kuzari*, I 1. In the fifth book of the *Kuzari*, Judah Hallevi expounds and criticizes a different philosophic doctrine, that of Avicenna. But he seems to suggest in V 14 that if one accepts the Aristotelian premises, Ibn Bājja's conclusions might be the logical ones.

having to know the premises and the intermediate links of reasoning that lead up
to these conclusions. On this hypothesis the people who only see by the light
coming from polished bodies could be the philosophers. However, a passage
occurring in one of Ibn Bājja's works[78] lends color to a different interpretation
(which, however, may not be wholly incompatible with the first). Like Maimonides,
Ibn Bājja distinguishes three categories of men. There are those who resemble
nonpolished surfaces, or, to use, as Ibn Bājja does, a second simile, they resemble
people who see only such light as is reflected from bodies. Then there are those
who may be likened to a polished surface, or again to people seeing the sun in a
mirror. Finally there are the happy ones, such as Aristotle, who may be likened
to the sun itself, or, to use another simile employed by Ibn Bājja, may be said to
have a direct view of it.

In Ibn Bājja's doctrine these distinctions have the following meaning: the
men belonging to the first category lack any kind of theoretical knowledge; they
are the common run of people. After them come the men of science and the
theoretical thinkers who use only discursive reasoning and have as their starting
point the empirical data. It is that latter fact which is referred to in the statement
that they see only reflected light. The third category is that of the supreme philosophers who have achieved union with the Active Intellect and thereby an immediate, intuitive, and certain knowledge of all the systems of sciences.

The images used by Maimonides and Ibn Bājja with reference to the men
belonging to the second category being similar, it may be presumed that Maimonides too assigns this category to the men whose theoretical knowledge is
dependent on empirical data and discursive thought.

Pursuing this analogy, one may conclude—as I believe, correctly—that the
higher kind of men (in the passage of the *Guide*) who see lightning flashes should
be equated with those who have intuitive theoretical knowledge. At this point,
however, either the analogy fails us altogether or we are faced in Maimonides'
text with a fundamental ambiguity. To Ibn Bājja's mind, the men endowed with
intuitive knowledge are philosophers, Aristotle being a supreme exemplar. In
Maimonides' text on the other hand, Moses appears as the only man permanently
endowed with complete intuitive knowledge. This might mean that Moses, the
quality of whose prophecy has, as Maimonides states elsewhere, nothing in common
with that of the other prophets, is to be regarded as the supreme philosopher,
"the Master of those who know" as the *Guide* calls him in other passages. As has
already been stated, it is the appellation applied by Dante to Aristotle. However,
the use of the quotation from Numbers suggests (though in my opinion it does

78. *Risālat al-ittiṣāl*, pp. 115 f. On p. 114 Ibn Bājja introduces, evidently under Platonic
influence, a somewhat simplified version of the parable of the "cave."

not conclusively prove) that all men seeing the lightning flashes are prophets. This might mean that Maimonides confined intuitive knowledge to prophets, and this interpretation might be thought to be corroborated by Maimonides' stating, in conformity with Avicenna's views, that prophets are able to arrive at conclusions without knowing the logically necessary premises. However, if this were the correct explanation, Maimonides' failure clearly to affirm and bring out the difference in kind between the theoretical knowledge of the prophets (other than Moses) and that of the philosophers and the essential superiority of the former over the latter would be quite inexplicable.[79] Moreover the Aristotelian school professed, with very few exceptions[80] or none, belief both in the superiority of intuitive knowledge over the discursive (i.e., in the superiority of *nous* over *dianoia*, to use the Greek terms) and in the ability of the philosophers to attain intuitive knowledge. Both beliefs are especially in evidence in the Aristotelian school of Spain, first and foremost in the writings of Ibn Bājja. When Maimonides borrowed a part of his imagery from Ibn Bājja he must have been aware that all his readers who were more or less familiar with the main philosophic texts of his times would tend to identify the men seeing the lightning flashes with the highest type of philosopher and not, as the passage might suggest, with the prophets. It would seem that in this case as in many others Maimonides deliberately aimed at ambiguity.[81]

In pointed contrast to al-Fārābī, who considered that political activity was, if circumstances permitted it, a most essential duty of the philosopher, Ibn Bājja

79. In I 62 Maimonides refers in his interpretation of a talmudic passage to man's knowledge of the Active Intellect. He does not in any way suggest that such knowledge is confined to prophets. It should be noted that in a nonphilosophic work of Maimonides, namely, his *Commentary on the Mishnah, Sanhedrin* (see *Introduction to Pereq Ḥeleq*, sixth fundamental dogma of Judaism, ed. J. Holzer [Berlin, 1901], p. 23) the prophets are said to achieve union with the Active Intellect. The philosophers are not mentioned; in the context any reference to them would have been wholly out of place. It may be added that no certain conclusions as to Maimonides' point of view in the *Guide* can be drawn from his statements in this commentary.

80. Al-Fārābī — but not, in my opinion, Avicenna — might have been one (though he was not, at least if one accepts the evidence of the texts, a consistent one). In al-Fārābī's case it seems to me that at least sometimes he negated altogether the possibility of intuitive theoretical knowledge (other than knowledge of axiomatic truths). Avicenna, on the one hand, clearly believed in the possibility of such knowledge. On the other, it is highly improbable, in spite of his interest in, and exposition of, mystical experiences, that he intended to restrict this kind of knowledge to the mystics and the prophets.

81. *Guide* I 62 refers in the interpretation of a talmudic passage to the grasp of the Active Intellect by a human individual. In the context it is clear that this intellectual achievement is possible for men other than Moses (who is not mentioned in the passage). On the other hand, it is clear that if man is capable of grasping the Active Intellect, this degree was attained by Moses.

held[82] that under the unfavorable conditions prevailing in his time, conditions that were not likely to be changed for the better in any foreseeable future, there was no possibility of working for the creation of a philosophic city. It may be argued that this position merely implies a shift of emphasis away from politics and statesmanship rather than a doctrinal opposition to al-Fārābī. However, it transforms the whole temper of Ibn Bājja's philosophy. He advises the philosopher to choose solitude and loneliness as his lot in his own country; but he should commune in spirit with his fellow philosophers, those who lived before him and those who live like himself in isolation in various, sometimes distant countries. Ibn Bājja was able to adopt this view, because he believed that man's supreme goal was union with the Active Intellect, and that this union was not dependent upon living in the ideal philosophic city but could be achieved in solitude. Some remarks of Maimonides may echo the conception or the vocabulary used by Ibn Bājja when dealing with these problems; his recommendation of solitude with a view to rational meditation in III 51 may be a case in point. A more significant instance occurs in II 36, in a passage in which Maimonides speaks of the human individual apt to be a prophet. He describes him as a perfect solitary, who regards the common run of human beings as either domestic animals or beasts of prey. Such a superior person has only two wishes in his sometimes unavoidable dealings with the multitude of his inferiors: (1) to avoid being harmed by them, and (2) to make such use of them as his material necessities may oblige him to. This passage indubitably reflects both in terminology and in spirit Ibn Bājja's thought. On the other hand it does not, if it is taken by itself, give an adequate idea of the attitude of Maimonides.

Apart from the passage quoted above, Ibn Bājja is mentioned by name in three passages of the *Guide*. Two of these (II 9 and II 24) deal with his astronomical views. The second of these passages indicates that Ibn Bājja was one of the initiators of the revolt of the Spanish Aristotelians against the dominance of the Ptolemaic system. The third passage (III 29) quotes a statement of Ibn Bājja made in his commentary on Aristotle's *Physics*,[83] which refers to the conception that God is the spirit of a body constituted by the celestial sphere and the stars.

Chronologically Ibn Ṭufayl (d. 1185) comes between Ibn Bājja, who is mentioned by him in a cursory survey of Islamic philosophy, and Averroes, whom he

82. This view is one of the main themes of his *Tadbīr al-mutawaḥḥid* (*The Regime of the Solitary*) and accounts for the title of this work, edited, with a Spanish translation, by M. Asín Palacios (Madrid, 1946).

83. This commentary, which was believed to have been lost (see *inter alia* S. Munk's French translation of the *Guide* [Paris, 1866], III, 222, n. 3), was recognized by me as being one of the texts figuring in MS Pococke 206 of the Bodleian Library, which constitutes a collection of Ibn Bājja's work.

helped in the beginnings of his career. Ibn Ṭufayl seems to have been, if one considers his times and his country (i.e., the West of the Islamic world, which includes Spain and the Maghrib), a rather unusual sort of philosopher as he was preoccupied with the mystical or semimystical aspects of Avicenna's thought. There is no explicit reference to him or to his philosophy in the *Guide*, and there is no evidence to show that Maimonides was in any way influenced by Ibn Ṭufayl's philosophic tale *Ḥayy Ibn Yaqẓān*.

AVERROES

The relation between Maimonides and Averroes (d. 1198) presents much greater interest, though there is no conclusive proof that at the time of the writing of the *Guide* Maimonides was in any way influenced by Averroes' doctrines. His commendation of that philosopher's commentaries in the letter to Ibn Tibbon is of a later date; and in another[84] letter written to his disciple Joseph ben Judah, who is the addressee of the epistle with which the *Guide* opens, Maimonides states that he has just received these commentaries except the one on *De sensu et sensibili* but has not yet read them through. He adds a word of praise for their correctness. This letter was written at a time when he had completed some portions of the *Guide*.

It may of course be argued that this fact does not preclude the possibility that Averroes' views may have had some impact on the part of the *Guide* that had not as yet been written. For that matter Maimonides may have had cognizance of philosophic works of Averroes other than the commentaries before he began working on the *Guide*. But, as far as I can see, no clear evidence can be adduced for either of these suppositions.[85] On the other hand, there is an overwhelming presumption that when he was engaged in working on the *Guide* he had no knowledge of a distinctive doctrine of Averroes, namely, his conception of the nature and the unity of the intellect *in potentia*, set forth, for instance, in his great commentary on *De anima*.[86] It was this doctrine that provoked the attack of Thomas Aquinas against the Latin Averroists. It seems to me to be inconceivable that Maimonides should have failed (as is the case) to mention, or to make an allusion to, this doctrine in the *Guide* if he had been aware of it when writing that work.

Nevertheless a comparison between these two philosophers may be instructive, though it will unavoidably entail some repetition. In part such a comparison must be a study in contrast; for the ideas of the two as to what is prudent and

84. See Moses ben Maimon, *Epistulae*, fasc. 1, ed. D. H. Baneth (Jerusalem, 1946), p. 70.
85. Passages of the *Guide* that may indicate that Maimonides did have some knowledge of Averroes' views or terminology are discussed below.
86. See n. 38 above.

what not in philosophic politics and what is desirable in theological exposition seem to be radically different. On the other hand Maimonides and Averroes were by and large contemporaries; and until the former left the Maghrib for Egypt they had lived under the rule of the same intolerant Moslem sect, the so-called Almohads, who enforced a variety of kalām as the official theology. Moreover, the philosophic background of Maimonides and Averroes was identical, being common to all the Aristotelians of the Spanish school. They had a rather similar naturalistic hard-headedness, and a similar suspicion of many of Avicenna's Neo-Platonic proclivities and probably also of his tendency to regard mystical experience as revelatory of the supreme plane of being. The juxtaposition of Maimonides and Averroes in a letter addressed to the former by his disciple Joseph ben Judah has considerable justification.

In view of the common culture and of the (at least to some extent) similar milieu in which they had been brought up, it could be expected—and the facts prove these expectations to be correct—that, in spite of the difference in religion and, consequently, in the conduct of life and in the attitude toward, and the possibilities of, practical activity, many of the problems with which Averroes and Maimonides were concerned would be identical; they were the problems that arose or for some reason acquired actuality and urgency in the philosophic debate of twelfth-century Spain. However, the *Guide* was written not in Spain or in the Maghrib, but in Egypt, after Maimonides had lived for many years in that country. At that time Egypt does not seem to have been an intellectual center comparable to Spain, yet it was not wholly negligible from that point of view, and, even more important, it was relatively near to, and in close connection with, the countries farther east up to and including Persia, where an intense speculative activity was going on and new ground was being broken, for instance by Suhrawardī Maqtūl, who was executed in 1191 under the authority of Maimonides' patron Saladin. There is some reason to believe that the Jews of these Eastern countries participated to some extent in these intellectual activities. Under these circumstances Maimonides' philosophic views and interests could very well have become modified under the impact of the new intellectual influences he could have encountered in Egypt. Yet this is not the case as can be shown, *inter alia*, by a comparison between him and Averroes. When at a mature age he wrote the *Guide*, he was, in the domain of philosophy and philosophic theology, still almost exclusively involved with the problems with which he must have been familiar in his youth in Spain and the Maghrib.

One of the problems that had come to a head in Spain and was accorded in their different ways considerable importance by both Maimonides and Averroes is, as has already been mentioned, the problem of the relation between the theory of celestial physics and the dominant Ptolemaic system of astronomy. The difficulties to which, from the Aristotelian point of view, the Ptolemaic hypotheses of epicycles and eccentrics give rise have already been referred to.

It may have been Ibn Bājja who initiated this crisis of the sciences, which, as far as its acute phase goes, seems to have been confined to Moslem Spain and the Maghrib; or at least as the *Guide* (II 24) indicates he played a part in it by criticizing the use of the epicycles as incompatible with Aristotelian physics.[87] Ibn Ṭufayl seems to have been unable to accept either epicycles or eccentrics. Both are likewise reflected by Averroes,[88] who takes a very dim view of the astronomy of his own time, believes that a return to the forgotten astronomy of the pre-Aristotelian philosophers and of Aristotle himself was indicated, if only that doctrine could be reconstituted, and avows that in his youth he had the ambition, which he did not realize, to re-create that science and that in his old age he hopes that some young man will make this his task.

Maimonides' ostensible reaction to, and conclusions from, the discrepancy between physical and astronomical theory are quite different. He apparently wishes to utilize it in order to cast doubt on Aristotelian natural science. Yet obviously, like Averroes, and doubtless also Ibn Bājja, he attaches great importance to the point, not only because it provides him with a convenient weapon in his theological debate, but also because of the exigencies of scientific theory. Rather paradoxically, because all the Spanish Aristotelian philosophers concerned accepted unquestioningly the master's view of the radical difference between the heavens and the sublunar world, the aspiration for unified physical science (unified at least as far as method was concerned) was very much in evidence.

Maimonides' remarks in II 13 may be regarded as a case in point. Maimonides mentions there as a typical example of a satisfactory physical theory an explanation that holds at least in part the differences between the four sublunar elements to be a function of the distance of the natural places from the heavenly sphere. According to this view, matter situated near this sphere acquires because of this proximity the disposition needed for receiving the form of fire. And the same applies *mutatis mutandis* to the three other elements. Thus there is a unified (and therefore, from the methodological point of view, eminently acceptable) explanation of a great variety of sublunar phenomena; a fact that is used by Maimonides to point the contrast between the theory of terrestrial physics, which he regards

87. In II 9 Maimonides also mentions Ibn Bājja's opinion on the place of Venus and Mercury in the planetary system, but this point has no connection with the crisis of science referred to in the text. We know from a manuscript autobiographical letter addressed by Ibn Bājja to his friend Abū Jaᶜfar Yūsuf (MS. Pococke 206, Bodleian Library, fol. 118b) that the Spanish philosopher fancied himself as an astronomer.

88. In his Great Commentary on Aristotle's *Metaphysics*, ed. M. Bouyges (Beirut, 1948), III, 1163.

as true and proven, and Aristotle's largely unsatisfactory celestial physics, which held that, for no conceivable natural reason, the direction and the velocity of the motions of the various spheres differed. The conclusion apparently drawn by Maimonides is that we should be wary of accepting on the basis of this kind of physical theory such fundamental doctrines as the eternity of the world.

Does this mean that Maimonides was incurably skeptical about the possibility of working out a satisfactory comprehensive and unified physical theory in which the explanations of the celestial phenomena would be methodologically as valid as those of the sublunar phenomena? It is not easy to answer this question. Obviously, for his own purposes (at least for the purposes he had in mind in Part II)[89] Maimonides made capital out of the crisis of natural science due to the incompatibility of the Ptolemaic system with Aristotle's physics. He also pointed out quite correctly that it is much more difficult to obtain scientific data concerning the heavenly spheres than it is to obtain such data with regard to the sublunar world. It can even be maintained that the thoroughly skeptical position was, for the reasons he gave, the only consistent and logical one. Yet it seems to me that such agnosticism would stultify all that Maimonides set out to accomplish in the *Guide* and would also be quite irreconcilable with his general views, expressed in quite different contexts, on man's highest destination and man's knowledge.

At this point a few remarks on the role of physical theory as conceived in the Spanish philosophic school may be relevant. It was a very considerable role, a point of view that was in keeping with the spirit and early tradition of the Peripatetic school as exemplified by Aristotle himself and by Alexander of Aphrodisias. This evaluation of physical theory is in contrast with the opinion of the Greek Neo-Platonists, such as Proclus, in whose hierarchy of planes of being the corporeal world, which is the object of physics, occupies a lowly place, parallel to that of physical science regarded as inferior to metaphysics and mathematics.

For other reasons, this attitude of the Spanish philosophers, if we may call them so for the sake of convenience, differed from that of Avicenna. I do not of course wish to imply that Avicenna did not set great store by physical science: it was an indissoluble part of that complete system of knowledge which was philosophy. But there are degrees of interest. Avicenna introduced into that system his speculations concerning mystical experience and his investigation of self-awareness

89. It is not impossible that in this second part Maimonides gave a rather exaggerated expression to whatever qualms he may have had about the science of astronomy of his time. This overemphasis may be explained by his wishing to shake the confidence of a certain category of readers in the philosophic doctrine of the eternity of the world, a confidence that was certainly connected with belief in the trustworthiness of Greek science in general. In I 72, where he sums up the main points of physical science and astronomy, he seems to accept the Ptolemaic system and gives the reader no hint that he regards it as dubious.

and of the ego regarded as a central notion of psychology; and at least the second of these two lines of inquiry, neither of which is pursued either by Maimonides or by Averroes, seems to have been very much in the foreground of his thought. It is even more to the point that according to him,[90] the science of metaphysics or the "divine science" deals with several subjects. It is notably concerned with (1) knowledge of God and other incorporeal substances, and (2) knowledge of being and its various modes. This includes the knowledge of the difference between essence and existence and between necessary and contingent being, which, according to Avicenna, may without any recourse to natural science prove the existence of God.

In several important particulars the views of both Maimonides and Averroes on the status of physical theory and its relation with "divine science," i.e., metaphysics, stand in contrast to this attitude. They are similar, though by no means identical; some of the divergencies are due to the fact that, in contradistinction to Maimonides' general usage, Averroes did not hesitate to propound his own personal interpretation with regard to purely theoretical questions not connected with theological debates. Thus he considers[91] that the primary and main object of metaphysics is knowledge of the highest formal and final causes, i.e., in the final resort, of God (and the immaterial substances). Maimonides, on the other hand, in his early work on logic[92] — and there is no reason to think that he changed his position later on — states that the "divine science" has two main subjects: (1) God and the immaterial substances, and (2) general notions such as being.

He thus continues the tradition of Avicenna and also of al-Fārābī.[93] As we have seen, he also conforms to Avicenna's views on the relation between essence and existence. But he treats of this relation and, in general, of the second subject of metaphysics referred to above in so cursory a fashion that I believe we would not be far out in asserting that in fact, though not in theory, Averroes' definition would be adequate for the "divine science" as envisaged in the Guide.

Seen from this angle, metaphysics is closely connected with, and in a way

90. See the long discussion at the beginning of the section of *The Book of the Healing of the Soul* dealing with metaphysics, II, 2 ff. It may be added that, according to Avicenna, metaphysics is also concerned with the fundamental principles of each particular science; see S. Pines, Abstracta VI, *Revue des Études islamiques* (1938), pp. 51 f.

91. See Averroes, *Kitāb mā baᶜd al-ṭabīᶜa* (Hyderabad, 1365 A.H.), pp. 4 f. Averroes polemizes (p. 5) against Avicenna's contention that the conclusions of physical science concerning the existence of immaterial principles are superfluous in metaphysics. The fact that according to Averroes the primary object of this science is as stated, does not prevent him from taking into consideration the circumstance that in his *Metaphysics* Aristotle deals also with other subjects (see pp. 5 f.).

92. *Kitāb fi ṣināᶜat al-manṭiq*, better known under its Hebrew title *Millot-Hahhiggayon*, ed. and trans. by I. Efros (New York: American Academy for Jewish Research, 1938), p. 61 of the Hebrew Section and p. 63 of the English translation.

93. See S. Pines's paper (p. 51) referred to in n. 90.

based on, physics, which it prolongs. This seems to be exactly Maimonides' conception of the connection between the two sciences, repeatedly alluded to in the *Guide* — sometimes with reference to the Hebrew expression *The Account of the Beginning* (or "physics" in Maimonides' interpretation) and *The Account of the Chariot* (or "metaphysics"; see I 17). This accounts *inter alia* for Maimonides' believing in the necessity of keeping secret from unqualified people the greater part of physical science (see *ibid.*): it has too close a bearing on metaphysics, which is the dangerous science par excellence.

On these points Averroes takes a comparable line, though he is, doubtless, more consistent than Maimonides. His proof, taken over from Aristotle, of the existence of the Prime Mover has as its starting point and primary datum the existence and nature of motion, i.e., it presupposes physical phenomena. In other words, God, the principal object of metaphysics, can be proved to exist only by a reference to physics.

According to Avicenna's conception, such a reference, though legitimate, is not indispensable; for God's existence may be demonstrated without straying beyond the bounds of metaphysics by showing that contingent being necessarily presupposes Necessary Being, both of which are purely metaphysical notions.

As has already been stated, Maimonides, at the time he wrote the *Guide*, may not have been conversant with, or influenced by, Averroes' attempt to disqualify these Avicennian concepts in the name of the pure unadulterated Aristotelian doctrine. Accordingly he freely uses in one of his proofs of the existence of God (II 1, third method) the term Necessary Being. It is all the more noteworthy and, as I believe, indicative of the underlying tendencies of his thought that neither this proof nor any of the others propounded by him can be considered purely metaphysical. As opposed to the Avicennian proof referred to above, all of them presuppose the existence of motion or of change, i.e., the existence of the cosmos, and are in this respect in accord with Averroes (and with Aristotle himself). It is by no means disconcerting to compare these arguments with Maimonides' assertion in I 70 that the motion of the heavenly sphere is the strongest proof of the existence of God. No radical change of position is involved, perhaps no change at all.

It may be added that the use by Maimonides in II 1 of Avicennian terminology may be appropriate or not in the context but does not appear to involve self-contradiction.

On another point, however, on which Averroes is opposed to Avicenna, the position of the former is maintained in two passages of the *Guide* and the latter's position in one. The question is: should God be equated with, or differentiated from, the separate intellect that moves the Supreme Sphere?

By distinguishing God, the Necessary Being, from this intellect Avicenna negated His having any definite physical function in the cosmos, whereas Averroes by his identification of the two clearly assigns God such a function: He is the first of the separate intellects, the last of which is the Active Intellect. All of these intellects except the last are prime movers of heavenly spheres.

The three relevant passages of the *Guide* read:

(I 72): "In the same way there exists in being something that rules it as a whole and puts into motion its first principal part granting it the power of putting into motion, in virtue of which this part governs the things that are other than itself."

(II 1): "It is necessary that the mover of the first sphere . . . should not at all be a body or a force in a body. . . . Now this is the deity."

(II 4): "It cannot be true that the intellect that moves the highest sphere should be identical with the necessary of existence."

It may be noted that the Avicennian point of view, which Maimonides professes to hold in II 4, is in keeping with the critique of natural science, which is one of the main themes of the first half of Part II. On the other hand, the Averroistic conception of I 72 and II 1 befits the wholesale acceptance of the main current doctrines of philosophic natural science characteristic of I 72.

The points at issue involve much more than the minutiae of scholastic discussions; in fact they concern the relation of God and the cosmos and concurrently of metaphysics and physics.[94] Averroes' view, which, as we have seen, seems to be maintained likewise by Maimonides at least in two passages, places God squarely

---

94. It may be argued that the contradiction between the passages of the *Guide* quoted above may be attenuated by a reference to the last part of I 72. Maimonides states there that the parallel he draws in the first part of the chapter between the relation that exists between the human organism and man's rational soul, on the one hand, and that which exists between the universe and God on the other, is not rigorously accurate, the reason being that he did not wish to baffle the ill-prepared reader. It would have been more correct to compare God's relation to the cosmos to that of the acquired intellect to man's organism. This assertion of Maimonides need not, however, mean that in the final analysis there is no similarity between the point of view he professes in I 72 and Avicenna's thesis. In point of fact it is as a separate intellect that Avicenna's God is (qua final cause) the mover of the highest sphere. Rather disconcertingly Maimonides seems to imply elsewhere that God's relation to the world is comparable to that of a soul to the living organism it animates. For no one as familiar with Aristotle as were Maimonides' fellow philosophers could disregard the associations evoked in a passage of *Guide* I 58 *in fine*, in which the relation of God to the world is compared to that of a captain to his ship. The allusion to *De anima* ii. 1. 413a 8–9 must have been unmistakable: for in that much quoted passage Aristotle refers to the possibility that the relation of the soul to the body could be regarded as comparable to that of a navigator to his ship. The apparent implications of these and perhaps also other passages of the *Guide* are most curious, not only because the view that God should be considered as the soul of the world is at variance with the philosophic doctrine, but also because this was the belief of the Sabians, i.e., the Pagans. Maimonides decries them because of their holding this belief, as it proves deficiency of philosophic knowledge.

within the system of the cosmos as its "principal part," a term borrowed by Maimonides from al-Fārābī. The domains of metaphysics and physics are thus brought very close together (whereas, as has already been stated, if Avicenna were to jettison the Aristotelian heritage, which sometimes hampered his personal philosophy, his metaphysics could, if this were required, altogether dispense with physical science).

Two important chapters of the *Guide* relevant to this problem have already been discussed. They are I 68 and I 54. The first of these suggests—if we follow up Maimonides' hints to their logical conclusion—that God may be identical with the system of sciences, including physical science. If this is so, this may imply a higher valuation of natural science than any that may be found in Averroes' works.

I 54 deals with the interpretation of Moses' two requests, of which only one is fulfilled: he is vouchsafed knowledge of the operations of God in nature. Maimonides speaks in that connection of the attributes of action, i.e., of the application to God of such names as the "merciful," "revengeful," and so forth. As has already been stated, the use of these attributes is due to an anthropomorphic interpretation of natural or historical events regarded as beneficent or untoward. Quite evidently, the man who is granted knowledge of God, for instance Moses, must go beyond these anthropomorphic descriptions and grasp the workings of natural order. The chapter appears to indicate that the only positive knowledge of God possible to man consists of his understanding the natural phenomena.

Now if the conclusions that have been drawn from I 68 are correct, this knowledge of the system of nature may represent the essence of God. This might be the explanation of the rather enigmatic text in III 52 according to which God apprehends us by the same light by which we apprehend Him. This may mean that, in accordance with the Aristotelian assumption of the unity of the subject and object of intellection, God is identical with the system of the natural sciences, and that man too may to some degree achieve this identity.

Other texts in the *Guide* tie up with this line of thought, notably parts of the parable of the castle in III 51. This parable refers *inter alia* to a category of people who go around the ruler's house looking for a gate, which they do not find. Maimonides tells us at first that these are the talmudic scholars who follow the authorities, but have no knowledge of theoretical speculation. Immediately afterwards, however, he offers another interpretation, which, as it seems to me, rather completes than contradicts the first one:

"Know, my son, that as long as you are engaged in studying the mathematical sciences and the art of logic, you are one of those who walk around the house searching for its gate. . . . If, however, you have understood the natural things, you have entered the habitation and are walking in the antechambers. If, however, you have achieved perfection in the natural things and have understood the divine science, you have entered in the ruler's place *into the inner court* and are with him in one habitation. This is the rank of the men of science."

Thus knowledge of physics and metaphysics gives access to the castle, i.e., enables such men as are versed in these sciences to reach a state of nearness to God. It may be noted that apparently, at least as far as knowledge is concerned, no essential difference is supposed to exist between this state and that of the prophets. The latter are said to have a perfect knowledge of metaphysics and to direct all the activity of the intellect toward an examination of the existents with a view to drawing an inference from them to God and to understanding, as far as possible, His governance, i.e., with a view to obtaining the knowledge of natural phenomena granted to Moses (III 51).

I should add that the part of the parable referred to above seems to me to contain a key to Maimonides' intention (or one of his intentions) in writing the *Guide*. The fact is that the description of the people going round the house searching for a gate tallies exactly with that of Maimonides' pupil Joseph ben Judah, for whose benefit the *Guide* is supposed to have been written.[95] Like them he has knowledge of logic, mathematics, and Jewish law and tradition, but is ignorant of physics and metaphysics. If, as is stated and implied by Maimonides, the *Guide* was written for him and for people like him, its purpose must have been to give him and them access to the ruler's house; in other words, to turn them into complete philosophers having the requisite knowledge of physics and metaphysics.[96] The acquisition of this knowledge is, as we are told in another passage

95. Maimonides may have thought of him when using in the passage in III 51 the form of address: my son.

96. However, the *Guide* is quite evidently not a systematic presentation of philosophic doctrine. It is, in fact, in many ways the contrary of such an exposé. A reader endowed with all the qualities required by Maimonides could obtain from it no more than an inkling of physics and metaphysics. This was recognized by an early commentator on Maimonides, Shemtob Palquera, who in the *Book of the Seeker* (*Hammebaqqesh*) makes it clear that the study of the *Guide* is merely a preliminary to the systematic study of the philosophic sciences, and is borne out by the history of Jewish philosophy after Maimonides. We encounter the constant phenomenon that, while the *Guide* is used as the fundamental textbook, the actual doctrines discussed derive from Averroes, who serves as an indispensable supplement to the insufficient exposé of the *Guide*. If the *Guide* was intended to bring about by itself the required confirmation of philosophers *in potentia* into actual philosophers, it could not but fail in this task; whereas an adequate knowledge of philosophy could be acquired from the study of the works of Aristotle and his commentators and expositors. Evidently Maimonides could not be unaware of this fact. It may be supposed that in writing the *Guide* he intended to accomplish a twofold purpose: (1) to set his readers, at least those of them who had the necessary quality, upon the highroad leading toward philosophic knowledge; and (2) to prevent them from acquiring the indifference toward the specific form of Jewish law and tradition that could be considered the hallmark

of III 51, enjoined by religion. For the Torah commands us to love God, and love is proportionate to knowledge, it being impossible to love something one does not know.

The passage setting forth this idea is reminiscent of Avicenna's exposition of his conception of intellectual worship, but also of certain views of Averroes.

This last similarity may be partly explained by the fact that both Maimonides and Averroes were authorities on the religious law of their respective communities — it makes no odds in this connection that the former, as the author of *Mishneh Torah* and other halakhic works, was much more eminent in this respect than the latter, who was an accomplished qāḍī and wrote a number of legal treatises. They were rather exceptional in this respect; none of the outstanding Aristotelian philosophers who preceded them seem to have pursued this avocation. In contradistinction to their predecessors, they could not only discuss in an informed way the question whether the study of philosophy was permitted and, if this was the case, enjoined by Jewish or Islamic religious Law, but could also give an authoritative answer. The one given by Maimonides is, as we have seen, based on the commandment to love God. Averroes, for his part, had no difficulty in finding in the Koran suitable verses that could be interpreted as a divine command to study philosophy.[97]

Evidently both Maimonides' and Averroes' pronouncements on the religious duty of philosophizing were meant to normalize the philosopher's position in society, to show that he could be a regular and respectable member of the community. In the Islamic polity of the West this was at that time a much more difficult and, consequently, more needful task than it used to be, as Almohad rulers, whose subject Averroes was (and also Maimonides up to his departure for Egypt), had promulgated an official theology inspired by certain teaching of the kalām as well as an official policy of intolerance. As the attacks directed against Maimonides during his lifetime show, the Jewish notables of that period were

of the philosopher who, living as he does a theoretical life, is not concerned with the outward forms of legal and cultic observance or with popular religious beliefs. The second objective could only be legitimately achieved by according the political life a status it did not have in Ibn Bājja's philosophy, nor for that matter perhaps in Aristotle's. We shall see below what was Maimonides' theoretical justification for this evaluation. Maimonides' own activity perhaps illustrates the possibility of attaining both objectives and beyond them the practical and the theoretical goal for which they served as a preparation. But he was an exceptional person. It seems to me that none of his disciples and commentators had the same success in balancing the two objectives. In so far as they had a mind of their own, they were either out and out Aristotelians or Averroists in the Latin sense of the term, which has an antireligious connotation, or they were much more prepared than Maimonides to renounce scientific theory in favor of religious tradition.

97. See the translation of Averroes' "Decisive Treatise, Determining the Nature of the Connection between Religion and Philosophy," in G. F. Hourani's *Averroes: On the Harmony of Religion and Philosophy* (London, 1961), pp. 44 ff.

likewise very much aware of the danger of philosophy for religious belief. For that matter that danger was not minimized by either Maimonides or Averroes.

Hence the peculiar character of the religious commandment to study philosophy as envisaged by Maimonides and Averroes. In contradistinction to most other commandments, it was not addressed to all the members of the Jewish or Islamic religious community, but only to the few who were capable of grasping the philosophic doctrines. Those who were not were forbidden to have access to this kind of knowledge. The philosophers and would-be philosophers had moreover to be made aware that it was a part of the philosophic way of life to conform to, and uphold, the religious Law. We have noted that some passages of the *Guide* show traces of the influence of Ibn Bājja's conception of the philosopher as an isolated stranger in his own community. Theoretically this view need not conflict with those of Maimonides and Averroes; for the obligations imposed by the latter upon the philosopher to dissemble or at least to refrain from giving a public expression to his true opinions may be considered as leading to the philosopher's isolation.[98]

But owing to a change of emphasis, the prevailing attitude of these two authors appears to be wholly different. In the *Guide* and in the relevant writings of Averroes the solitude of the philosopher is much less in evidence than his faithful observance of the law of his religious community and the care he takes to avoid saying or doing anything that might dangerously weaken the hold of religious tradition upon the multitude.

Both of them posed the question of the necessity of teaching, and imposing upon, the common people obligatory religious beliefs, i.e., dogmas, which, without being philosophic, would not be compatible with simple, literal-minded, wholly unsophisticated faith.

The problem probably came to the fore because of the policy of the Almohads, who compelled all their subjects to profess an official theology. On this point the positions of Maimonides and Averroes differ. Maimonides had very strong convictions concerning the utility and even necessity of an official system of religious beliefs for the preservation of communal obedience to the law. What is more, he lived up to his convictions by formulating in his commentary on the Mishnah the thirteen principal dogmas of Judaism. Many of these dogmas run counter to philosophic truth. Nevertheless Maimonides did not accept the idea that

98. This attitude does not, at least as far as Averroes is concerned, interfere with the purely theoretical consideration of the possibility of desirable revolutionary changes in the constitution of society. In his *Paraphrase* of Plato's *Republic*, he regards it as not wholly impossible that, given a succession of enlightened rulers, the Moslem state of his time, i.e., the Almohad kingdom, could be transformed into Plato's ideal philosophic republic. There is no doubt that, in Averroes' opinion, such a development would have been most desirable. See S. Pines, "Notes on Averroes' Political Philosophy" (in Hebrew), ᶜ*Iyyun* (1957), pp. 68 f. and 76.

the common folk should be permitted to hold on to the primitive belief. In fact he chose to take a leaf out of the Almohads' book and to make the belief (imposed by these Moslem rulers upon all their subjects)[99] in the noncorporeality of God obligatory for all members of the Jewish community.[100] Evidently this dogma could not but modify the simple faith of the ordinary people. It could be regarded as impelling them to take a first step, fraught with peril for their like, on the slippery road of religious speculation; the risk being the loss of faith and of the habit of obedience to religious Law.

It was a risk about which Averroes felt very strongly. He took the position that the simple faith of the average nonphilosophical person should not be troubled; he should be left free to stick to his own unsophisticated beliefs even in such matters as the corporeality of God. This does not mean that Averroes attributed an intrinsic value to naïve faith. He had the same kind of attitude toward saintly simplicity as Maimonides. Both of them believed that mankind is essentially divided into philosophers and the multitude of nonphilosophers. But Averroes insists,[101] perhaps more vehemently than Maimonides has ever done, upon the harmfulness of the third, apparently intermediate, category of semi-intellectuals, identified with the Mutakallimūn,[102] who are incapable of grasping the philosophic truths, but raise in public all kinds of theological questions and trouble the acquiescent faith of the ordinary folk. The proclamation of such dogmas as the incorporeality of God was probably regarded by Averroes as one of the ways in which they disturb the peace of the community. At any rate he saw no reason to impose the profession of this dogma upon the ordinary people.[103] We should remember that Averroes had more urgent grounds than Maimonides to adopt a hostile attitude toward the Mutakallimūn, who were the official theologians of the Almohad kingdom and in that capacity a source of danger for the philosophers.

99. On the probable relation between this policy of the Almohads and Maimonides' views, see I. Heinemann, "Maimuni und die arabischen Einheitslehrer," *Monatsschrift für Geschichte und Wissenschaft des Judentums*, LXXIX (1935), 102–48.

100. The incorporeality of God is the third of the thirteen fundamental dogmas of Judaism formulated in Maimonides' *Commentary on the Mishnah, Sanhedrin, Introduction to Pereq Ḥeleq*, pp. 21 f.

101. On Averroes' attitude on this point, see L. Gauthier, *La théorie d'Ibn Rochd (Averroès) sur les rapports de la religion et de la philosophie* (Paris, 1909). See Averroes' al-Kashf ʿan manāhij al-adilla fī ʿaqāʾid al-milla, in *Falsafat Ibn Rushd* (Cairo, 1935), pp. 96 ff. It may be noted that Averroes speaks in the same context (p. 97) of the doubt and perplexity engendered in people belonging to this category (which is the category of the diseased, while both the men of knowledge and the common men are healthy), because of erroneous interpretations of scriptural texts. The term *hayra*, which has been translated as "perplexity," derives from the same root as the second word in the Arabic title of *The Guide of the Perplexed: Dalālat al-ḥāʾirīn*.

102. And the sufi mystics.

103. See *al-Kashf*, p. 91.

This prudent attitude of Averroes made him set considerable restrictions upon the allegorical interpretation of the scriptures. These restrictions are clearly inspired by political considerations, namely, the necessity not to undermine the religious foundations of society, but in his formulations he uses the legal concepts: lawful and prohibited. In one of his treatises dealing with the relation between religion and philosophy he makes the following promise:[104]

"From our account you have now become aware of the amount of error that occurs as a result of allegorical interpretation. It is our desire to have the chance to fulfill this aim with regard to all the statements of Scripture: i.e., to discuss which of them have to be interpreted allegorically and which not, and, when they have to be interpreted, to whom the interpretations should be given; I mean, (to deal thus) with every difficult passage in the Koran and the Traditions. . . ."

This project, which as far as is known was not carried out by Averroes, is much more cautious and limited in its scope than the program (whose conception and beginnings are recorded by Maimonides in his Introduction) of allegorical interpretation of the terms and parables found in the Bible and in later Jewish texts that is tackled with considerable daring in the *Guide*. Nevertheless there exists an unmistakeable similarity between the two undertakings. There is no reason to assume that Averroes influenced Maimonides on this point (or vice versa). In all probability, each of them had had this idea independently of the other. They were contemporaries, and the state of their world, whether Jewish or Islamic, and the climate of opinion apparently suggested these tasks.

It should be noted that the way in which Maimonides carried out his project in the *Guide* quite evidently signifies that this work is centered upon the proposition that the prophets were philosophers. What Maimonides really thought about this is anybody's guess. But quite apart from such unprofitable conjectures, the proposition in question may, in view of the fact that it is not supported by any evidence whatever, be legitimately qualified as a "noble fiction," in the Platonic sense of the word. The fact that in the period after Maimonides Aristotelian philosophy could become an integral part of the way of life of the Jewish elite, or a considerable portion of it, is largely due to the acceptance of this fiction.

The Platonic political theory, as adopted by the Arabic and Jewish Aristotelian philosophers, takes as its starting point the division of mankind into three categories: (1) the actual, or (2) the potential philosophers, and (3) the nonphilosophers. The relevance of this qualification is due to the fact that a specific character of political action, at least of political action on the part of the philosopher, is that it is a mode of dealing (1) with the potential philosophers, who have to be

104. The following passage occurs in Averroes' *al-Kashf*. The translation used here is taken from G. F. Hourani's *Averroes: On the Harmony of Religion and Philosophy* (p. 81).

recognized as such and turned into active philosophers, and (2) with the non-philosophers, who have to be kept in line, influenced for their own benefit and that of the philosophers, and, in the ideal case, ruled by the latter. Plato in many of his dialogues may be considered as applying himself to the first of these two tasks; and so did Maimonides in the *Guide*, whereas Aristotle and Averroes, who in most of their works relied to a much greater extent upon straightforward exposition and logical demonstration, have mainly in mind a reading public made up of actual philosophers, all the others being incapable of understanding their mode of reasoning.

In his great work, *Mishneh Torah*, which codifies the Jewish law and, in its first part, the *Book of Knowledge*, propounds a system of beliefs, Maimonides engaged, to the extent to which he considered it advisable, upon the second of the political tasks referred to above.

Maimonides did not only — contrary to, for instance, Ibn Bājja's practice and theory — undertake this kind of "political" activity; it also held a very high degree in his scale of values. This does not mean that he thought that a theoretical way of life was overappreciated by the philosophers. When all is said and done he, just like other Aristotelian philosophers, held this way of life to be the supreme achievement possible to man. But, perhaps rather paradoxically, in a way reminiscent of al-Fārābī,[105] he seems to have thought that this supreme attainment should be rounded off by being combined with practical activity. Accordingly he points to the example of the three Patriarchs and of Moses, who engaged in all kinds of mundane occupations. It is even more significant that he propounded a perhaps at least partly original theoretical legitimation for the activity of the legislator and the statesman by regarding it as a kind of imitation of God. (In this he possibly went beyond the Plato of the *Republic*, who required the philosopher to return to the "cave,"[106] but did not attempt to mitigate the regret that they must feel at being torn from the pure contemplation of the eternal truths and obliged to govern the polis.) As we already know, man's only positive knowledge of God consists, according to Maimonides, in his knowledge of the workings of nature or God, whose characteristic it is to ensure the preservation of the permanent features of the cosmic order. This includes *inter alia* the preservation of the various animal species and of mankind, but does not presuppose special care being taken of the average human (or of the animal) individual. It is because of this functioning of natural order that God is thought of as working judgment, righteousness, and loving-kindness.

105. Though the formulation is different, and though Maimonides may have had higher hopes than al-Fārābī as to what man can achieve in a theoretical life. See above.
106. Cf. Plato's *Republic*, 516C–517A, 519C, 520A.

As Maimonides points out in the last chapter of the *Guide* (III 54), man should endeavor to imitate Him in this respect. This statement has sometimes been interpreted as meaning that—in contradiction to the whole trend of his thought and to many definite assertions occurring in the *Guide* and even in the chapter in question—Maimonides at the end adopted the quasi-Kantian idea that the ordinary moral virtues and moral actions are of greater importance and value than the intellectual virtues and the theoretical way of life. It seems to me that a study of this last chapter and of the chapter preceding it (III 53 as well as of I 52) cannot but show that this explanation is completely false. As Maimonides explicitly states, man should imitate God in His attributes of action, i.e., as a reference to III 53 and I 52 proves, both in the bestowal of benefits and in bringing about calamities; the former and the latter are required for the preservation and functioning of the cosmic order.

A man engaged in the highest form of practical activity, that of the legislator and the statesman, should in his imitation of God be, according to the circumstances, either beneficent or cruel, not because he has the corresponding sentiments, but because these modes of action are necessary for his purpose, which consists in the creation and preservation of the highest possible type of community. In I 54 Maimonides adds the rider that, in point of fact, the ruler of a country should indulge more frequently in beneficent than in punitive action.

Such an imitation of God or of the order of nature is not only a moral imperative concerned with the present and the future. It may also be used to explain history, notably history made by men of a certain type, the great example being Moses.

We have seen that Maimonides has taken over from Alexander of Aphrodisias "wily graciousness" used with reference to the ingenious, sometimes apparently makeshift, contrivances with the help of which nature utilizes to the best effect the materials at hand and produces the self-perpetuating natural order, overcoming or bypassing the various impediments as well as the dangers that threaten the existence of every animal species. As has already been suggested, Moses' attitude toward, and use of, the historical circumstances in which he was placed was similar. In order to hammer into shape the religious and national community that he founded, he (or divine "wisdom" manifesting itself through his agency as well as through nature's) utilized various contrivances.

As far as legislation goes, Moses' task was twofold: (1) to institute laws and commandments different from, and better than, those that were in force at that time among the pagans of his part of the world; (2) to provide for certain continuity. Thus he could and did reform the religious laws dealing with sacrifices but he could not, in the face of the universal uses prevalent at that time, have abrogated sacrifices altogether.

By applying these considerations Maimonides accounts for a considerable portion of the Mosaic commandments. It may of course be argued that the notion of better commandments is not quite clear and unambiguous. However, at least once Maimonides introduces a more precise criterion: he asserts that the main purpose of the Mosaic legislation was to make the religious laws and cults less burdensome than they were among the pagans (III 47).

In this way Maimonides' defense of the law of the Torah does not (or does not altogether) rest upon the assumption that, absolutely speaking, it is the best conceivable law. His contention is that under the circumstances no better law could have been instituted (and that changing it would destroy the Jewish community). His apologetic purpose consequently involves him in a historical task, obliging him to give an account of ancient oriental paganism.

The Sabians

For this purpose he had at his disposal (III 29) the source he needed, the so-called *Nabatean Agriculture*, composed by Ibn Waḥshiyya in the tenth century, a work that purported to give an account of the religious tradition and practices of ancient Babylonia, the rebellion against which by Abraham marks the beginning of the distinctive Jewish faith. From the geographical point of view this was not the exact brand of paganism with which Moses was concerned, but by and large Maimonides seems to consider that those cults manifest the same general characteristics.

Now Ibn Waḥshiyya's claim to give an authentic description of the religion in which Abraham had been brought up, the so-called Sabianism, was false, but not implausible; in the nineteenth century it took in the competent orientalist Chwolsohn. There is no reason to think that Maimonides' regarding it as a genuine historical account is a piece of make-believe.

At all events this account, which he doubtless supplemented with the help of other sources mentioned by him in III 29, fitted in with his historical scheme. For it seemed to show that the paganism in question was essentially a hotchpotch of magical superstitions, the absurdity of the beliefs being paralleled by that of the religious rites and customs, described by Ibn Waḥshiyya as being practiced principally because they were supposed to be beneficial to agriculture.

Abraham's throwing off the yoke of superstitious belief and Moses' prohibition of magic clear the way for true scientific knowledge. If we can go by III 29, Maimonides also acquired, through reading Ibn Waḥshiyya, the conviction that in addition to the fact that the common people of the pagan society of the Sabians denied science because of their addiction to magic, this society produced no philosopher having a true conception of the universe.[107] At least by implication this is an important point in his indictment of the Sabians, the assumption being that in other societies religion renders possible the appearance of this exceptional type of man.

In Arabic usage the appellation Sabians came to be applicable to all pagans; in particular, it served to translate the term Hellenes used by Christian writers to designate the adherents of the paganism prevalent in the Roman Empire in the first centuries of the Christian era. No example of this linguistic usage occurs in the *Guide*, but in one passage the Greeks and the Sabians are bracketed together for derogatory mention (see above).

On the other hand, Maimonides makes it clear in a commentary on a passage of Alexander of Aphrodisias (see above) that he realized that the ancient Greek way of life was more favorable to the development of philosophy than the prophetic religions of his own time.[108] This is a significant admission, as the fostering of knowledge is one of the two main tasks of the Torah. It should be noted that Maimonides' objection to paganism is not due to the latter's supposedly polytheistic doctrines. He has no doubt at all that all communities (except, perhaps, the savages of Africa and of the Far North; cf. III 51) believe in the existence of a supreme God.[109] The Torah's condemnation is not directed against the theory, but against the practice, namely, the cultic worship accorded to the intermediaries that exist between God and man. Evidently such worship does not imply a false belief; it is nevertheless harmful for practical political reasons.

The Kalām

If closely examined, the attitude of Maimonides toward the kalām may appear quite as intentionally ambiguous as his attitude toward Aristotelian philosophy. Indeed, given the antithetical relation between the two systems of thought, this was perhaps inevitable. Even the fact that he does not hesitate clearly to express the respect he feels for philosophy and the intellectual contempt with which the theological efforts of the Mutakallimūn inspire him, does not, while giving a useful pointer, prima facie permit us to disregard the essential equivocality of the relevant data. For it may be held — indeed this is the ostensible position of the *Guide* itself

107. Abraham was born in that society, but was not of it.
108. It is true that he affirmed that these sciences flourished among the Jews of antiquity (I 71). We have no means of knowing whether in Maimonides' view this statement of a widespread opinion is to be taken at its face value. He does not enlarge upon it. In particular, he does not indicate in what way the study of the sciences was fostered in Jewish antiquity.
109. See *Guide* I 56: the images worshipped by the idolators are symbols of entities that are intermediaries between us and God.

— that Maimonides, while refuting certain extreme teachings of the Mutakallimūn, saw eye to eye with them on the most decisive point of all, namely, the temporal creation of the world.

At all events he took pains to let his great powers of systematic exposition have full play in his summing-up of the main principles of the kalām.

We do not know what kalām treatises he used in his exposition of these "premises." It is a pretty safe assumption that generally he drew upon the same sources as Averroes, who also attempted to formulate some of the first principles of the Mutakallimūn,[110] though his account of the doctrines is conceived on a much less ambitious scale than Maimonides'. The works utilized by the latter, or some of them, may not have been preserved. But even if they are, it might be a difficult task to prove that he had made use of them, as the composition and the style of the exposition concerning kalām bear the unmistakable stamp of his literary personality. This does not in any way mean that he falsifies his sources. His exposé of the "premises" of the Mutakallimūn is verifiably accurate in its details as well as its main points. Nevertheless the importance and the emphasis given in it to the various propositions may not have been quite the same as those accorded to them in the kalām treatises he knew.

It should also be noted that Maimonides' "premises" of the Mutakallimūn, as well as his "premises" of the philosophers, are mainly, or indeed exclusively, concerned with physical science, if, in accordance with the medieval classification, the concept of this science is extended so as to include the psychology of perception. But whereas the propositions of the philosophers expound and account for the order and the causality of the cosmos, the principles of the Mutakallimūn, such as their atomism, the assumption that everything that can be imagined can happen, and so on, are meant to prove that no causality and no permanent order exist in the world; all events are determined directly, without the intervention of intermediate causes, by the will of God, which is not bound by any law. In other words, there is no cosmos and there is no nature, these two Greek notions being replaced by the concept of congeries of atoms, with atomic accidents inherent in them being created in every instant by arbitrary acts of divine volition.

This is an exact presentation of the peculiarity of the doctrines of the Mutakallimūn as they appeared to the philosophers; but as far as the fundamental notions of kalām physics are concerned, this exposition is perhaps a more coherent and articulate one than those usually achieved by these theologians, and the absence of any concept of cosmic order and natural causality is probably more in evidence in this exposition than it generally was in the run-of-the-mill kalām treatises. From Maimonides' point of view this slight shift of emphasis in his otherwise

110. To be precise, of the Ashʿariyya, see *al-Kashf*, pp. 43 ff.

trustworthy account was, doubtless, justified, not only because, for didactic reasons, the opposition between the Aristotelian doctrine and that of the Mutakallimūn had to be made as pointed as possible, but also because of his conception of the origins and primary tasks of kalām. Maimonides unreservedly accepts al-Fārābī's view[111] that the unique function of kalām consists in the defense of religion, which means that it does not regard the grasp of theoretical truth as an end in itself. Maimonides' idea that the doctrine of the kalām was originally taken over by the Moslem Muʿtazilite or Ashʿarite theologians from Christian doctors, who wrote in Greek or in Syriac, may also derive from al-Fārābī. To a certain extent it seems to be historically correct, *inter alia* in its allusion to the influence of John Philoponus[112] (or John the Grammarian to give him his Arabic name; see I 71).

Thus this Christian commentator of Aristotle maintained — in accordance with the Peripatetic doctrine — that an actual infinite cannot exist, but drew from this proposition the un-Aristotelian inference that the world must have been created in time.[113] Both the proposition and the inference from it figure, quite correctly from the historical point of view, in Maimonides' exposition of the kalām doctrine (I 73 and I 74, fourth way); and the general idea may have been taken over from John Philoponus. But as the Mutakallimūn had to adapt these conceptions to the exigencies of their peculiar doctrine, the resemblance between their argumentation as given in the *Guide* and other texts and that of John Philoponus does not extend to particulars.[114]

The most outstanding Mutakallim of the period before Maimonides and perhaps of all time was al-Ghazālī, whose personality also had other facets: he was also a mystic and occasionally perhaps a philosopher; in fact he was accused by

111. Which does not seem to be wholly correct, especially with regard to the early period of Muʿtazilite kalām.

112. However al-Fārābī obviously could not have been guilty of the egregious anachronism committed by Maimonides, who regards not only John Philoponus (Yaḥyā al-Naḥwī in Arabic), but also al-Fārābī's younger contemporary, the Christian Arabic philosopher Yaḥyā Ibn ʿAdī, as one of the ancestors of the kalām (I 71). This error, which makes evident a glaring lacuna in his knowledge of the history of philosophy, may, in the last analysis, be due to the fact that Yaḥyā Ibn ʿAdī copied out excerpts from at least one work of John Philoponus, the latter's commentary on Aristotle's *Physics*. These excerpts are marked *Yaḥyā*, a name borne by both of them, which may have led to some confusion; see S.Pines, in *Isis*, No. 137 (1953), p. 250. Ibn Bājja makes as grave a mistake as Maimonides, as he amalgamates the names: Yaḥyā Ibn ʿAdī and Yaḥyā al-Naḥwī (John Philoponus), which produces Yaḥyā Ibn ʿAdī al-Naḥwī (see MS. Pococke 206, Bodleian Library, fol. 56a).

113. See John Philoponus, *De aeternitate mundi*, ed. H. Rabe (Leipzig, 1899), pp. 7 ff.

114. In a treatise by the Arabic tenth-century philosopher Abu'l-Khayr al-Ḥasan Ibn Suwār al-Baghdādī, a kalām proof for the temporal creation of the world is contrasted with, and declared inferior to, a proof set forth by John Philoponus. The treatise is edited by A. Badawi in *Neoplatonici apud Arabes* (Cairo, 1955), pp. 243–47.

Averroes of trying to be all things to all men. He exercised a dominant influence on the theology of the Almohads.

Al-Ghazālī, starting from kalām premises and often using stock kalām arguments, made a serious bid to challenge the intellectual supremacy of Aristotelian and more particularly Avicennian philosophy, to expose the inconsistency and inadequacy of this system of thought, and to make it clear which points of the doctrines of the philosophers were incompatible with Islam. He did this in a work entitled *Tahāfut al-falāsifa*, a title traditionally translated: *The Destruction of the Philosophers*, though "Incoherence of the Philosophers," preferred by S. Van den Bergh, would be more accurate. This work provoked Averroes into writing a lengthy refutation: *Tahāfut al-tahāfut*, *The Destruction of the Destruction*, or *Incoherence of the Incoherence*, which as well as al-Ghazālī's work had a considerable influence.

Al-Ghazālī differed from his predecessors among the Mutakallimūn by his thorough knowledge of Avicennian philosophy, of which he has written a lucid and very well-known exposition, *The Intentions of the Philosophers*, and by his recognition of the paramount importance of certain issues in the conflict between the kalām (or religion, as he saw it) and philosophy. In a way his lucidity is a match for Maimonides', though his point of view is entirely different. Hence the question whether Maimonides was acquainted with al-Ghazālī's *Tahāfut* presents considerable interest.

No absolutely certain answer can be given to it; however, the probabilities are that at the time of the writing of the *Guide* Maimonides had read the celebrated work. No philosopher who wished to keep abreast of the intellectual debate of this period could have afforded not to have done so; and such a lacuna in Maimonides' knowledge of Arabic theological literature would have been most uncharacteristic. We may accordingly entertain the supposition that the antithesis established by Maimonides between the God of religion who possesses a free will, in the exercise of which He is not bound to act in accordance with the order of nature, and the God of the Aristotelian philosophers, who is hamstrung by the immutability of this order, owes a great deal to al-Ghazālī.

This antithesis is indicated in a passage of the *Guide* that would not have been disowned by al-Ghazālī:

(II 22): "If, however, we believe that all this [i.e., the heavenly spheres and the universe in general] has been produced through the purpose of one who purposed, made, and particularized it — as His wisdom, which cannot be grasped, required — none of these questions affect us, whereas they do affect him who claims that all this has come about through necessity and not through the will of one who wills. This is an opinion that does not agree with the order of that which

5

exists, an opinion in favor of which no cause and no new persuasive proof have been brought forward. Withal very disgraceful conclusions would follow upon it. Namely, it would follow that the deity whom everyone who is intelligent recognizes to be perfect in every kind of perfection, could, as far as all the beings are concerned, produce nothing new in any of them; if He wished to lengthen a fly's wing or to shorten a worm's foot, He would not be able to do it."

In addition it may be noted that al-Ghazālī's conception of the nature of will is expressed in the following statement of the *Guide:*

(II 18): ". . . The true reality and the quiddity of will means: to will and not to will. . . . The fact that it [a being separate from matter] may wish one thing now and another thing tomorrow does not constitute a change in its essence and does not call for another cause."

The defense of this conception of the will, which is traditional in the kalām, is one of the main objects of al-Ghazālī's *Tahāfut.*

However, the probability that it is, at least in part, because of al-Ghazālī's apologetics that Maimonides realized the true issue between philosophy and religion, or religious Law, does not necessarily mean that in the final analysis he, like al-Ghazālī though for different reasons, chose religion. In *Guide* II 25 he states that he did make this choice, as he implies, by an act of will, seeing that human reason is not capable of demonstrating with regard to the crucial question of the eternity of the world the truth of either position.[115] As has already been indicated, Maimonides also does his best to make Aristotelianism appear vulnerable by picking holes in his physics, while the smoke screen of negative theology is supposed to put out of court any definitive statement about what God may not be — certain evident impossibilities excepted.

However, as has been suggested, negative theology may not hold up to close scrutiny: Maimonides makes it clear that God is an intellect, with which the human intellect has at least an analogy; and he also affirms (though, taken literally, this statement contradicts his doctrine of the divine attributes) that in God will follows wisdom (see II 18 and III 25). From al-Ghazālī's point of view the last statement is tantamount to a negation of the nature of will. Unless we suppose that Maimonides was, all unaware, floundering in a welter of inconsistencies and, quite inadvertently, contradicting himself on fundamental issues, it seems plausible to believe that, while for practical reasons, out of public spirit, Maimonides chose

115. It may be noted that, whereas in II 25 Maimonides makes the categorical assertion that belief in the eternity of the world destroys religion, he mentions in I 71 the possibility of asking whether prophecy can be true (or valid) if the world is eternal, but refrains from giving an answer, as the question should only be dealt with after prophecy has been studied. No definite conclusion can be drawn from this passage, but it tends to produce the impression that prophecy can be true (or valid) even if the world is eternal.

to aid and abet the faithful adherents of religion through the act of will referred to above, he belonged as far as his overriding intellectual convictions were concerned to the opposite camp.

Nevertheless he saw clearly (and correctly) that whereas the Aristotelian "divine science" could be accepted as far as its theory was concerned, Aristotelian physics was wide open to legitimate objections, some of which were even more fundamental than those concerned with the discrepancy between Peripatetic science and the Ptolemaic system. As has already been indicated, Aristotle grasps the world as a datum, as a given fact; contrary to such members of the Early Academy as Xenocrates, he did not try to derive every phenomenon in it from the first principles. Sometimes explicitly, and perhaps more often tacitly, he accepted apparently with equanimity the existence in the cosmos of a constituent element that was not amenable to such derivation, of something corresponding to Plato's "necessity" (the *ananke* of the *Timaeus*, 48A).

Maimonides attributes the existence of this residue of obdurate facts, which are irreducible to scientific explanation, to God's having willed them, which from the physical (though, as has been stated, not from the metaphysical) point of view is as satisfactory or as unsatisfactory an explanation as any other that reflects the inability of science to account for the universe being as it is. This explanation, moreover, has the advantage of being reassuring and politically useful.

For similar reasons Maimonides adapts for his own purposes the old kalām terms "Particularizer" (*mukhaṣṣiṣ*) and "particularization" (*takhṣīṣ*), which do not seem to have an equivalent in Greek philosophic vocabulary. As Maimonides (perhaps following the Mutakallim Abū'l-Maʿālī al-Juwaynī Imām al-Ḥaramayn[116] as well as al-Ghazālī) correctly states in his account of the fifth kalām "way" of demonstrating the temporal creation of the world (I 74), the use of these terms by the Mutakallimūn is due to their conviction that there is no intrinsic reason why anything, from the world as a whole downwards, should exist at all, or exist in the way it does and with such attributes as it has. The fact that things do exist and that they are endowed with one particular set of characteristics must consequently be due to the action of a "Particularizer" who willed them the way they are.

These views of the Mutakallimūn are bound up with the negation of nature and natural causality, i.e., of the realm of mediate causes. They are therefore quite unacceptable to Maimonides, who not only affirms the validity of these Aristotelian concepts, which he sometimes designates by the inclusive term,

116. To whom Averroes refers when speaking of particularization (see *al-Kashf*, p. 60, cf. p. 55). This concept is referred to in Imām al-Ḥaramayn's lengthy work, *al-Irshād*, edited and translated by J. D. Luciani (Paris, 1938), pp. 16 f. of the Arabic section, pp. 36 f. of the French section.

"nature of existence," but also believes that, with regard to the sublunar world, physical science can up to a certain point give a rational causal explanation of the phenomena. But there does not exist a physical theory giving a satisfactory account of the celestial spheres and their motions, let alone of the causes that led to their being arranged and to their moving as they do; these are matters that may be beyond human ken. This deficiency of man's knowledge necessitates, according to *Guide* II 19 (cf. II 21), the introduction of the notion of a "Particularizer," who in His wisdom arranged the celestial (and also the sublunar) world the way it is. This view, as stated in the passages referred to, seems to be based either on a belief in the existence of an irreducible element of irrationality in nature or on disbelief in man's ability to work out a correct all-comprehensive system of celestial physics. On the first supposition, Maimonides' view of God as the "Particularizer" approximates Whitehead's description of God as "the Principle of Concretion" and "the ground for concrete reality." "God is the ultimate limitation, and His existence is the ultimate irrationality." Even Whitehead's choice of terms occasionally calls to mind the kalām or Maimonides: "Some particular *how* is necessary, some particularization in the *what* of matter of fact is necessary."[117] According to him it is because of this necessity that metaphysics requires God.

However, quite evidently, this view of God as the source of the irrational element in nature does not square with Maimonides' conception of God as the supreme intellect. There are thus serious reasons for preferring the second interpretation of Maimonides' recourse to the notion of the "Particularizer." If this interpretation is accepted, this notion would only mean that man's unavoidable ignorance is put to a good and pious use.

This second interpretation conforms to Averroes' utilization of the term "Particularizer" in his *Incoherence of the Incoherence*. The possibility that Maimonides may have been acquainted with, and influenced by, this work when writing the *Guide* should be taken into account. The passage in question reads:[118]

"For the particularization which the philosophers infer is different from that which the Ashᶜarites intend, for the Ashᶜarites understand by 'particularization' the distinguishing of one thing either from a similar one or from an opposite one without this being determined by any wisdom in the thing itself which makes it necessary to particularize one of the two opposite things. The philosophers, on the

117. See A. N. Whitehead, *Science in the Modern World* (Penguin Books, 1938), pp. 203, 208, 207.
118. S. Van den Bergh's translation of Averroes' *Tahāfut al-tahāfut* (London, 1954), I, 248 f., has been used. But the terms "particularize" and "particularization" have been substituted for "differentiate" and "differentiation," used by Van den Bergh to render *khaṣṣaṣa* and *takhṣīṣ*. The passage that is quoted forms a part of Averroes' refutation of an argument occurring in al-Ghazālī's *Tahāfut* that makes use of the notion of "particularization."

other hand, understood here by the particularizing principle only that which is determined by the wisdom in the product itself, namely the final cause, for according to them there is no quantity or quality in any being that has not an end based on wisdom, an end which must either be a necessity in the nature of the act of this being or exist in it, based on the principle of superiority. For if, so the philosophers believe, there were in created things a quantity or quality not determined by wisdom, they would have attributed to the First Maker and Creator an attitude in relation to His work which may only be attributed to the artisans among His creatures, with the intention of blaming them."

AL-RĀZĪ

Maimonides does not cite the name of any Moslem Mutakallim.[119] In fact he only quotes in the *Guide* the name of one thinker of Moslem antecendents[120] of whom he clearly disapproves: Abū Bakr al-Rāzī (d. 923 or 925 or 932). According to Maimonides' letter to Ibn Tibbon, he was only a physician. In fact, he is one of the greatest names in the history of medieval medicine; but in thus curtly dismissing his claim to be a philosopher, Maimonides does him less than justice. He was no Aristotelian it is true, but a Platonist; at least that is what he called himself, apparently principally because of his physical doctrine, which conforms to a conception of Platonism found in the Arabic doxographical tradition. He was not interested in Plato's conceptions of the ideal city. More than that, he was the proponent of a thesis that might have seriously challenged al-Fārābī's and Maimonides' political and sociological Platonism. Al-Rāzī believed in the radical intellectual equality of men. However, the derogatory remark that Maimonides makes in the *Guide* (III 12) concerning al-Rāzī does not refer to these views. Maimonides takes al-Rāzī to task because of his affirmation that there is more evil in the world than there is good. This statement, which is not known to us from other sources—the work of Al-Rāzī quoted in the *Guide* not having come down to us—might seem to express the views of an ascetic. But this description does not apply to al-Rāzī. Indeed, whereas Maimonides (to be accurate the Maimonides of the *Guide*, but not of *Mishneh Torah*) appears to disapprove even of moderate bodily pleasure, al-Rāzī, while recommending temperance, is opposed to asceticism. Nevertheless the view that evil is dominant in the world is in keeping with al-Rāzī's teaching. For he believed that the existence of the world is an unfortunate accident brought about by the desire for conjunction with Matter conceived by the ignorant Soul—

119. He does name Yaḥyā Ibn ᶜAdī as one of the forerunners of the kalām, but as we have seen, this is a mistake on his part on two counts: chronologically Yaḥyā could not have been a forerunner of the kalām; he considered himself to be a good Aristotelian.
120. He cannot be called a Moslem, being violently opposed to all religions.

the Soul and Matter being two of the five Eternal Beings postulated by the gnostic doctrine he adopted. This conjunction will be dissolved, and the world come to an end, after the Soul has acquired the requisite knowledge. As against this doctrine, Maimonides, in spite of his view of matter as a hindrance to human perfection, considers, in common with all Aristotelians, that, taken as a whole, the world is essentially good. The evils found in it loom so large only because men tend to take a quite unjustifiable anthropocentric view. They shrink to their proper insignificant dimensions if one considers the universe as a whole, in which mankind has a very unimportant role (III 12).[121]

Maimonides also cites some Arabic scientists as distinct from the philosophers: al-Qabīsī (II 24), who wrote a book on the distances between the heavenly spheres; Jābir Ibn Aflaḥ (II 9), a twelfth-century Spanish astronomer who differed from Ptolemy with regard to the question whether Venus and Mercury are above or below the sun; Thābit Ibn Qurra (II 24, III 14), a famous astronomer and mathematician; the Banū Shākir (I 73), authors of a book concerning mechanical devices. Quite evidently he had a knowledge of scientific literature that would have been regarded as adequate in the philosophic circles of his time.

THE JEWISH AUTHORS

Maimonides' references, or allusions, to Jewish philosophic or kalām texts are exceedingly and rather surprisingly scanty. Maimonides' marked disinterest in this literature is in striking contrast to his attitude toward the Bible, the Talmud, the Midrashim, and kindred texts, which are quoted by him with great frequency, and also to his habit of citing Onqelos' Aramaic translation of the Torah, whose unsophisticated[122] avoidance of anthropomorphic expressions was apparently regarded by Maimonides as providing the unphilosophic majority with an acceptable mode of belief. No allusion to Isaac Israeli or Joseph Haṣṣadiq, the two Jewish philosophers mentioned in the letter to Ibn Tibbon, seems to occur in the *Guide*.

The only two passages that explicitly mention post-talmudic speculative opinions held among Jews refer to the Gaonim, i.e., the heads of certain talmudic academies in Iraq.

Saadia Gaon (d. 942) is perhaps one of those alluded to in a passage in I 71 referring to Gaonim (and Qaraites) who adopted Muʿtazilite ideas on the unity of God.

121. In III 25 Maimonides, speaking of the final end of the universe and rebutting the anthropomorphic illusions to which men are prone, states that the primary purpose is to bring into existence everything that is capable of existence. For being is a good. This is a formulation of the "principle of plenitude," whose history is traced in A. O. Lovejoy's *Great Chain of Being* (New York, 1960 ed.); a definition of this principle is to be found on p. 52.
122. At least unsophisticated by the standards of medieval Aristotelians.

According to III 17, certain Gaonim believed (likewise in accordance with Mu'tazilite ideas) that in the afterlife animals will receive a compensation for the sufferings they endure in this life.

There is some reason to presume that a passage of *Guide* I 46 may have been, at least in part, meant to serve as a sort of counterblast to a parable in the *Kuzari* of Judah Hallevi (d. about 1141), a book that Maimonides probably knew. Judah Hallevi's parable (*Kuzari* I 19–22) indicates that the fact that information has been received that justice and fair-dealing are practiced in India should not be considered as proof that the country is ruled by a just king, whereas the arrival of envoys bearing gifts sent by the king of India would prove the existence of that king. In other words, the existence of God should be proved not by a reference to cosmic order, but by the fact of divine intervention in the history of the people of Israel and by the mission of the prophets.

The parable used by Maimonides in I 46 resembles that of Judah Hallevi, though it is perhaps a little more elaborately worked out, but his conclusion is different. According to the *Guide* one may be persuaded in various ways that a certain country has a king: one may see him in person, or see the retinue surrounding him, or one may consider that he exists because things are done (for instance, buildings and bridges are built) upon his order. One may also infer his existence from the fact that a robust beggar does not attack and rob a wealthy moneychanger, even if the latter is physically quite weak. This signifies that, contrary to Judah Hallevi, Maimonides believes that the fact of cosmic order should be used to prove the existence of God.

Maimonides often does not explicitly mention the sources he utilized in his allegorical interpretation of biblical terms and expressions. It seems probable that for this purpose he made frequent use of Jewish philosophic texts.[123] However, the matter requires further study.

The fact that, relatively speaking, Maimonides had so little recourse to Jewish philosophic literature is significant. It implies *inter alia* that he had no use for a specific Jewish philosophic tradition. In spite of the convenient fiction, which he repeats, that the philosophic sciences flourished among the Jews of antiquity, he

123. It may be mentioned that Maimonides' remark in III 8 concerning the absence in the Hebrew language of terms connected with sexual acts may derive from a similar observation made by the eclectic philosopher and Hebrew poet Moses Ibn Ezra; see S. Pines, *Tarbiz* (January 1958), p. 218, n. 2. There is a marked similarity between Maimonides' analysis of the various meanings of the Hebrew word *Elohim* (I 2) and that of another Jewish philosopher of Spain, Abraham Ibn Da'ūd, born in 1110, twenty-five years before Maimonides; see his philosophic treatise *Emunah Ramah*, ed. S. Weil (Frankfurt am Main, 1852), p. 83 of the Hebrew text. In *Guide* I 43 Maimonides refers, concerning a point of the Hebrew language, to the eleventh-century grammarian Abū'l-Walīd Marwān Ibn Janāḥ.

evidently considered that philosophy transcended religious or national distinction. Qua philosopher he had the possibility to consider Judaism from the outside. From this vantage point he could discover the justification that, if one takes into account human nature and condition, can be adduced for accepting the obligations of a strict member of the Jewish community and could apprehend and try to eliminate or to mitigate the dangers inherent in philosophic truth and trace the task of the philosophers-statesmen, one of whom he was.

Shlomo Pines

THE FIRST PART

of

The Guide of the Perplexed

*

My knowledge goes forth to point out the way,

To pave straight its road.

Lo, everyone who goes astray in the field of Torah,

Come and follow its path.

The unclean and the fool shall not pass over it ;

It shall be called Way of Holiness.[1]

1. Cf. Isa. 35 : 8.

In the name of the Lord, God of the World [1]

[EPISTLE DEDICATORY]

My honored pupil *Rabbi Joseph*,[2] *may the Rock guard you, son of Rabbi Judah, may his repose be in Paradise.* When you came to me, having conceived the intention of journeying from the country farthest away in order to read texts under my guidance, I had a high opinion of you because of your strong desire for inquiry and because of what I had observed in your poems of your powerful longing for speculative matters. This was the case since your letters and compositions in rhymed prose came to me from Alexandria, before your grasp was put to the test. I said however: perhaps his longing is stronger than his grasp. When thereupon you read under my guidance texts dealing with the science of astronomy and prior to that texts dealing with mathematics, which is necessary as an introduction to astronomy, my joy in you increased because of the excellence of your mind and the quickness of your grasp. I saw that your longing for mathematics was great, and hence I let you train yourself in that science, knowing where you would end. When thereupon you read under my guidance texts dealing with the art of logic, my hopes fastened upon you, and I saw that you are one worthy to have the secrets of the prophetic books revealed to you so that you would consider in them that which perfect men ought to consider. Thereupon I began to let you see certain flashes and to give you certain indications. Then I saw that you demanded of me additional knowledge | and asked me to make clear to you certain things pertaining to divine matters, to inform you

---

1. Gen. 21 : 33. The correct sense of this Hebrew invocation is " God of Eternity." However, in current Hebrew the words mean " God of the World "; this seems to have been the meaning that Maimonides had in mind.
2. As Maimonides states in this Epistle, the *Guide* was written for the benefit of this disciple and for those like him. For this reason, some importance should be attached to the description, given in the text, of the intellectual attainment of Joseph, son of Judah.

of the intentions of the Mutakallimūn in this respect, and to let you know whether their methods were demonstrative and, if not, to what art they belonged. As I also saw, you had already acquired some smattering of this subject from people other than myself; you were perplexed, as stupefaction had come over you; your noble soul demanded of you to *find out acceptable words*.[3] Yet I did not cease dissuading you from this and enjoining upon you to approach matters in an orderly manner. My purpose in this was that the truth should be established in your mind according to the proper methods and that certainty should not come to you by accident. Whenever during your association with me a [biblical] *verse* or some text of the *Sages* was mentioned in which there was a pointer to some strange notion, I did not refrain from explaining it to you. Then when God decreed our separation and you betook yourself elsewhere, these meetings aroused in me a resolution that had slackened. Your absence moved me to compose this Treatise, which I have composed for you and for those like you, however few they are. I have set it down in dispersed chapters. All of them that are written down will reach you where you are, one after the other. Be in good health.

3. Eccles. 12 : 10.

[INTRODUCTION TO THE FIRST PART]

Cause me to know the way wherein I should walk,
For unto Thee have I lifted my soul.[1]

Unto you, O men, I call,
And my voice is to the sons of men.[2]

Incline thine ear, and hear the words of the wise,
And apply thy heart unto my knowledge.[3]

The first purpose of this Treatise is to explain the meanings of certain terms occurring in books of prophecy. Some of these terms are equivocal; hence the ignorant attribute to them only one or some of the meanings in which the term in question is used. Others are derivative terms; hence they attribute to them only the original meaning from which the other meaning is derived. Others | are amphibolous terms, so that at times they are believed to be univocal and at other times equivocal. It is not the purpose of this Treatise to make its totality understandable to the vulgar or to beginners in speculation, nor to teach those who have not engaged in any study other than the science of the Law — I mean the legalistic study of the Law. For the purpose of this Treatise and of all those like it is the science of Law in its true sense. Or rather its purpose is to give indications to a religious man for whom the validity of our Law has become established in his soul and has become actual in his belief — such a man being perfect in his religion and character, and having studied the sciences of the philosophers and come to know what they signify. The human intellect having drawn him on and led him to dwell within its province, he must have felt distressed by the externals of the Law and by the meanings of the above-mentioned equivocal, derivative, or amphibolous terms, as he continued to understand them by himself or was made to understand them by others. Hence he would remain in a state of perplexity and confusion as to whether he should follow his intellect, renounce what he knew concerning the terms in question, and consequently consider that he has renounced the foundations of the Law. Or he should hold fast to his understanding of these terms and not

1. Ps. 143:8.   2. Prov. 8:4.   3. Prov. 22:17.

let himself be drawn on together with his intellect, rather turning his back on it and moving away from it, while at the same time perceiving that he had brought loss to himself and harm to his religion. He would be left with those imaginary beliefs to which he owes his fear and difficulty and would not cease to suffer from heartache and great perplexity.

This Treatise also has a second purpose: namely, the explanation of very obscure parables occurring in the books of the prophets, but not explicitly identified there as such. Hence an ignorant or heedless individual might think that they possess only an external sense, but no internal one. However, even when one who truly possesses knowledge considers these parables and interprets them according to their external meaning, he too is overtaken by | great perplexity. But if we explain these parables to him or if we draw his attention to their being parables, he will take the right road and be delivered from this perplexity. That is why I have called this Treatise "The Guide of the Perplexed."

I do not say that this Treatise will remove all difficulties for those who understand it. I do, however, say that it will remove most of the difficulties, and those of the greatest moment. A sensible man thus should not demand of me or hope that when we mention a subject, we shall make a complete exposition of it, or that when we engage in the explanation of the meaning of one of the parables, we shall set forth exhaustively all that is expressed in that parable. An intelligent man would be unable to do so even by speaking directly to an interlocutor. How then could he put it down in writing without becoming a butt for every ignoramus who, thinking that he has the necessary knowledge, would let fly at him the shafts of his ignorance? We have already explained in our legal compilations some general propositions concerning this subject and have drawn attention to many themes. Thus we have mentioned there that the *Account of the Beginning*[4] is identical with natural science, and the *Account of the Chariot*[5] with divine science; and have explained the rabbinic saying: *The Account of the Chariot ought not to be taught even to one man, except if he be wise and able to understand by himself, in which case only the chapter headings may be transmitted to him.*[6] Hence you should not ask of me here anything beyond *the chapter headings.* And even those are not set down in order or arranged in coherent fashion in this Treatise, but rather are scattered and entangled with other subjects that are to be clarified. For my purpose is that the truths be glimpsed and

---

4. *maʿaseh bereshith*. Literally: *the Work of the Beginning.*
5. *maʿaseh merkabah*. Literally: *the Work of the Chariot.*
6. Babylonian Talmud (hereafter cited as B.T.), Ḥagigah, 11b, 13a.

then again be concealed, so as not to oppose that divine purpose which one cannot possibly oppose and which has concealed from the vulgar among the people those truths especially requisite for His apprehension. As He has said: *The secret of the Lord is with them that fear Him.*[7] Know that with regard to natural matters as well, | it is impossible to give a clear exposition when teaching some of their principles as they are. For you know the saying of [the Sages], *may their memory be blessed: The Account of the Beginning ought not to be taught in the presence of two men.*[8] Now if someone explained all those matters in a book, he in effect would be *teaching* them to thousands of men. Hence these matters too occur in parables in the books of prophecy. The *Sages, may their memory be blessed*, following the trail of these books, likewise have spoken of them in riddles and parables, for there is a close connection between these matters and the divine science, and they too are secrets of that divine science.

You should not think that these great *secrets* are fully and completely known to anyone among us. They are not. But sometimes truth flashes out to us so that we think that it is day, and then matter and habit in their various forms conceal it so that we find ourselves again in an obscure night, almost as we were at first. We are like someone in a very dark night over whom lightning flashes time and time again. Among us there is one[9] for whom the lightning flashes time and time again, so that he is always, as it were, in unceasing light. Thus night appears to him as day. That is the degree of the great one among the prophets, to whom it was said: *But as for thee, stand thou here by Me,*[10] and of whom it was said: *that the skin of his face sent forth beams, and so on.*[11] Among them there is one to whom the lightning flashes only once in the whole of his night; that is the rank of those of whom it is said: *they prophesied, but they did so no more.*[12] There are others between whose lightning flashes there are greater or shorter intervals. Thereafter comes he who does not attain a degree in which his darkness is illumined by any lightning flash. It is illumined, however, by a polished body or something of that kind, stones or something else that give light in the darkness of the night. And even this small light that shines over us is not always there, but flashes and is hidden again, as if it were the *flaming sword which turned every way.*[13] | It is in accord with these states that the degrees of the perfect vary. As for those who never even once see a light, but grope about in their night, of them it is said: *They know not, neither do*

7. Ps. 25:14.   8. B.T., Ḥagigah, 11b.   9. Or: there are those.
10. Deut. 5:28.   11. Exod. 34:29.   12. Num. 11:25.   13. Gen. 3:24.

they understand; They go about in darkness.[14] The truth, in spite of the strength of its manifestation, is entirely hidden from them, as is said of them: *And now men see not the light which is bright in the skies.*[15] They are the vulgar among the people. There is then no occasion to mention them here in this Treatise.

Know that whenever one of the perfect wishes to mention, either orally or in writing, something that he understands of these *secrets*, according to the degree of his perfection, he is unable to explain with complete clarity and coherence even the portion that he has apprehended, as he could do with the other sciences whose teaching is generally recognized. Rather there will befall him when teaching another that which he had undergone when learning himself. I mean to say that the subject matter will appear, flash, and then be hidden again, as though this were the nature of this subject matter, be there much or little of it. For this reason, all the Sages possessing knowledge of God the Lord,[16] knowers of the truth, when they aimed at teaching something of this subject matter, spoke of it only in parables and riddles. They even multiplied the parables and made them different in species and even in genus. In most cases the subject to be explained was placed in the beginning or in the middle or at the end of the parable; this happened where a parable appropriate for the intended subject from start to finish could not be found. Sometimes the subject intended to be taught to him who was to be instructed was divided — although it was one and the same subject — among many parables remote from one another. Even more obscure is the case of one and the same parable corresponding to several subjects, its beginning fitting one subject and its ending another. Sometimes the whole is a parable | referring to two cognate subjects within the particular species of science in question. The situation is such that the exposition of one who wishes to teach without recourse to parables and riddles is so obscure and brief as to make obscurity and brevity serve in place of parables and riddles. The men of knowledge and the sages[17] are drawn, as it were, toward this purpose by the divine will just as they are drawn by their natural circumstances. Do you not see the following fact? God, may His mention be exalted, wished[18] us to be perfected and the state of our societies to be improved by His laws regarding actions. Now this can come

14. Ps. 82:5.   15. Job 37:21.

16. In the context this appears to be the meaning of the two adjectives *al-ilāhī* and *al-rabbānī*; the literal meaning of the former is "divine"; the latter is derived from *rabb* signifying "the Lord."

17. *al-hukamā*. The term often designates the philosophers.

18. In the text: God . . . when He wished. The sentence that follows is anacoluthic.

about only after the adoption of intellectual beliefs, the first of which being His apprehension, may He be exalted, according to our capacity. This, in its turn, cannot come about except through divine science, and this divine science cannot become actual except after a study of natural science. This is so since natural science borders on divine science, and its study precedes that of divine science in time as has been made clear to whoever has engaged in speculation on these matters. Hence God, may He be exalted, caused His book to open with the *Account of the Beginning*, which, as we have made clear, is natural science. And because of the greatness and importance of the subject and because our capacity falls short of apprehending the greatest of subjects as it really is, we are told[19] about those profound matters — which divine wisdom has deemed necessary to convey to us — in parables and riddles and in very obscure words. As [the Sages], *may their memory be blessed*, have said: *It is impossible to tell mortals*[20] *of the power of the Account of the Beginning. For this reason Scripture tells you obscurely: In the beginning God created, and so on.*[21] They thus have drawn your attention to the fact that the above-mentioned subjects are *obscure*. You likewise know *Solomon's* saying: *That which was is far off, and exceeding deep; who can find it out?*[22] That which is said about all this is in equivocal terms so that the multitude might comprehend them in accord with the capacity of their understanding | and the weakness of their representation, whereas the perfect man, who is already informed, will comprehend them otherwise.

We had promised in the Commentary on the *Mishnah* that we would explain strange subjects in the "Book of Prophecy" and in the "Book of Correspondence" — the latter being a book in which we promised to explain all the difficult passages in the *Midrashim*[23] where the external sense manifestly contradicts the truth and departs from the intelligible. They are all parables. However, when, many years ago, we began these books and composed a part of them, our beginning to explain matters in this way did not commend itself to us. For we saw that if we should adhere to parables and to concealment of what ought to be concealed, we would not be deviating from the primary purpose. We would, as it were, have replaced one individual by another of the same species. If, on the other hand, we explained what ought to be explained, it would be unsuitable for the vulgar among the people. Now it was to the vulgar that we wanted to explain the import

19. *khūtibnā*. The Arabic word for rhetoric derives from the same verbal form of the root in question.
20. Literally: *flesh and blood.*   21. Cf. Midrash Sheni, Ketubim, Batei Midrashoth, IV.
22. Eccles. 7:24.   23. Maimonides uses here and subsequently the term *drashoth*.

of the *Midrashim* and the external meanings of prophecy. We also saw that if an ignoramus among the multitude of Rabbanites should engage in speculation on these *Midrashim*, he would find nothing difficult in them, inasmuch as a rash fool, devoid of any knowledge of the nature of being, does not find impossibilities hard to accept. If, however, a perfect man of virtue should engage in speculation on them, he cannot escape one of two courses: either he can take the speeches in question in their external sense and, in so doing, think ill of their author and regard him as an ignoramus — in this there is nothing that would upset the foundations of belief; or he can attribute to them an inner meaning, thereby extricating himself from his predicament and being able to think well of the author whether or not the inner meaning of the saying is clear to him. With regard to the meaning of prophecy, the exposition of its various degrees, and the elucidation of the parables occurring in the prophetic books, another manner of explanation is used in this Treatise. In view of these considerations, we have given up composing these two | books in the way in which they were begun. We have confined ourselves to mentioning briefly the foundations of belief and general truths, while dropping hints that approach a clear exposition, just as we have set them forth in the great legal compilation, *Mishneh Torah*.

My speech in the present Treatise is directed, as I have mentioned, to one who has philosophized[24] and has knowledge of the true sciences,[25] but believes at the same time in the matters pertaining to the Law and is perplexed as to their meaning because of the uncertain terms and the parables. We shall include in this Treatise some chapters in which there will be no mention of an equivocal term. Such a chapter will be preparatory for another, or it will hint at one of the meanings of an equivocal term that I might not wish to mention explicitly in that place, or it will explain one of the parables or hint at the fact that a certain story is a parable. Such a chapter may contain strange matters regarding which the contrary of the truth sometimes is believed, either because of the equivocality of the terms or because a parable is taken for the thing being represented or vice versa.

As I have mentioned parables, we shall make the following introductory remarks: Know that the key to the understanding of all that the prophets, peace be on them, have said, and to the knowledge of its truth, is an understanding of the parables, of their import, and of the meaning of the words

24. Or: has become a philosopher.
25. Translated in accordance with the Ibn Tibbon Hebrew translation, which supposes a very slight graphical alteration of the Arabic text as we have it. The Arabic text could be rendered: and really have knowledge of the sciences. But the sentence is awkward.

occurring in them. You know what God, may He be exalted, has said: *And by the ministry of the prophets have I used similitudes.*[26] And you know that He has said: *Put forth a riddle and speak a parable.*[27] You know too that because of the frequent use prophets make of parables, the prophet has said: *They say of me: Is he not a maker of parables?*[28] You know how *Solomon* began his book: *To understand a proverb, and a figure; The words of the wise, and their dark sayings.*[29] And it said in the *Midrash:* | *To what were the words of the Torah to be compared before the advent of Solomon? To a well the waters of which are at a great depth and cool, yet no man could drink of them. Now what did one clever man do? He joined cord with cord and rope with rope and drew them up and drank. Thus did Solomon say one parable after another and speak one word after another until he understood the meaning of the words of the Torah.*[30] That is literally what they say. I do not think that anyone possessing an unimpaired capacity imagines that the *words of the Torah* referred to here that one contrives to understand through understanding the meaning of parables are ordinances concerning the building of *tabernacles,* the *lulab,* and the *law of four trustees.* Rather what this text has in view here is, without any doubt, the understanding of obscure matters. About this it has been said: *Our Rabbis say: A man who loses a sela*[31] *or a pearl in his house can find the pearl by lighting a taper worth an issar.*[32] *In the same way this parable in itself is worth nothing, but by means of it you can understand the words of the Torah.*[33] This too is literally what they say. Now consider the explicit affirmation of [the Sages], *may their memory be blessed,* that the internal meaning of the *words of the Torah* is a *pearl* whereas the external meaning of all parables *is* worth *nothing,* and their comparison of the concealment of a subject by its parable's external meaning to a man who let drop a pearl in his house, which was dark and full of furniture. Now this pearl is there, but he does not see it and does not know where it is. It is as though it were no longer in his possession, as it is impossible for him to derive any benefit from it until, as has been mentioned, he lights a lamp — an act to which an understanding of the meaning of the parable corresponds. The Sage has said: *A word fitly spoken is like apples of gold in settings [maskiyyoth] of silver.*[34] Hear now an elucidation of the thought that he has set forth. The term *maskiyyoth* denotes filigree traceries; I mean to say traceries in which there are apertures with very small

26. Hos. 12:11.   27. Ezek. 17:2.   28. Ezek. 21:5.   29. Prov. 1:6.
30. Cf. Midrash on the Song of Songs, 1:1.   31. A silver coin.
32. A coin; ninety-six *issar* were worth a *sela*[c].
33. Cf. Midrash on the Song of Songs, 1:1.   34. Prov. 25:11.

eyelets, like the handiwork | of silversmiths. They are so called because a glance penetrates through them; for in the [Aramaic] *translation* of the Bible the Hebrew term *va-yashqeph* — meaning, he glanced — is translated *va-istekhe.*[35] The Sage accordingly said that a saying uttered with a view to two meanings is like an apple of gold overlaid with silver filigree-work having very small holes. Now see how marvellously this dictum describes a well-constructed parable. For he says that in a saying that has two meanings — he means an external and an internal one — the external meaning ought to be as beautiful as silver, while its internal meaning ought to be more beautiful than the external one, the former being in comparison to the latter as gold is to silver. Its external meaning also ought to contain in it something that indicates to someone considering it what is to be found in its internal meaning, as happens in the case of an apple of gold overlaid with silver filigree-work having very small holes. When looked at from a distance or with imperfect attention, it is deemed to be an apple of silver; but when a keen-sighted observer looks at it with full attention, its interior becomes clear to him and he knows that it is of gold. The parables of the prophets, peace be on them, are similar. Their external meaning contains wisdom that is useful in many respects, among which is the welfare of human societies,[36] as is shown by the external meaning of *Proverbs* and of similar sayings. Their internal meaning, on the other hand, contains wisdom that is useful for beliefs concerned with the truth as it is.

Know that the prophetic parables are of two kinds. In some of these parables each word has a meaning, while in others the parable as a whole indicates the whole of the intended meaning. In such a parable very many words are to be found, not every one of which adds something to the intended meaning. They serve rather to embellish the parable | and to render it more coherent or to conceal further the intended meaning; hence the speech proceeds in such a way as to accord with everything required by the parable's external meaning. Understand this well.

An example of the first kind of prophetic parable is the following text: *And behold a ladder set up on the earth, and so on.*[37] In this text, the word *ladder* indicates one subject; the words *set up on the earth* indicate a second subject; the words *and the top of it reached to heaven* indicate a third subject; the words *and behold the angels of God* indicate a fourth subject; the word

---

35. A verbal form deriving from the same root as the word *maskiyyoth*. Gen. 26:8.
36. Literally: the weal of the circumstances of the human societies.
37. Gen. 28:12–13. After the word *earth*, the verses read: *and the top of it reached to heaven; and behold the angels of God ascending and descending on it. And behold the Lord stood above it.*

ascending indicates a fifth subject; the words *and descending* indicate a sixth subject; and the words *And behold the Lord stood above it* indicate a seventh subject. Thus every word occurring in this parable refers to an additional subject in the complex of subjects represented by the parable as a whole.

An example of the second kind of prophetic parable is the following text: *For at the window of my house I looked forth through my lattice; And I beheld among the thoughtless ones, I discerned among the youths, A young man void of understanding, Passing through the street near her corner, And he went the way to her house; In the twilight, in the evening of the day, In the blackness of night and the darkness. And, behold, there met him a woman With the attire of a harlot, and wily of heart. She is riotous and rebellious, and so on.*[38] *Now she is in the streets, now in the broad places, and so on.*[39] *So she caught him, and so on.*[40] *Sacrifices of peace-offerings were due from me, and so on.*[41] *Therefore came I forth to meet thee, and so on.*[42] *I have decked with coverlets, and so on.*[43] *I have perfumed my bed, and so on.*[44] *Come, let us take our fill of love, and so on.*[45] *For my husband is not at home, and so on.*[46] *The bag of money, and so on.*[47] *With her much fair speech she causeth him to yield. With the blandishment of her lips she enticeth him away.*[48] The outcome of all this is a warning against the pursuit of bodily pleasures and desires. Accordingly he [Solomon] likens matter, which is the cause of all these bodily pleasures, to a *harlot* who is also a *married woman.* In fact | his entire book is based on this allegory. And we shall explain in various chapters of this Treatise his wisdom in likening matter *to a married harlot,* and we shall explain how[49] he concluded this book of his with a eulogy of the *woman* who is not a *harlot* but confines herself to attending to the welfare of her household and husband.[50] For all the hindrances keeping man from his ultimate perfection, every deficiency affecting him and every disobedience, come to him from his matter alone, as we shall explain in this Treatise. This is the proposition that can be understood from this parable

38. The omitted words are: *her feet abide not in her house.*
39. The omitted words are: *and lieth in wait at every corner.*
40. The omitted words are: *and kissed him, and with impudent face she said unto him.*
41. The omitted words are: *this day have I paid my vows.*
42. The omitted words are: *diligently to seek thy face, and I have found thee.*
43. The omitted words are: *my bed, with striped cloths of the yarn of Egypt.*
44. The omitted words are: *with myrrh, aloes and cinnamon.*
45. The omitted words are: *until the morning; let us solace ourselves with loves.*
46. The omitted words are: *he is gone a long journey.*
47. The omitted words are: *he has taken with him, and will come home at the full moon.*
48. Prov. 7:6–21.
49. A literal translation; perhaps the sense requires "why."
50. Literally: the state of her husband.

as a whole. I mean that man should not follow his bestial nature;[51] I mean his matter, for the proximate matter of man is identical with the proximate matter of the other living beings.[52] And as I have explained this to you and disclosed the secret of this parable, you should not hope [to find some signification corresponding to every subject occurring in the parable][53] so that you could say: what can be submitted for the words, *Sacrifices of peace-offerings were due from me; this day have I paid my vows?* What subject is indicated by the words, *I have decked my couch with coverlets?* And what subject is added to this general proposition by the words, *For my husband is not at home?* The same holds good for the other details in this *chapter*. For all of them only figure in the consistent development of the parable's external meaning, the circumstances described in it being of a kind typical for adulterers. Also the spoken words and other such details are of a kind typical of words spoken among adulterers. Understand this well from what I have said for it is a great and important principle with regard to matters that I wish to explain.

When, therefore, you find that in some chapter of this Treatise I have explained the meaning of a parable and have drawn your attention to the general proposition signified by it, you should not inquire into all the details occurring in the parable, nor should you wish to | find significations corresponding to them. For doing so would lead you into one of two ways: either into turning aside from the parable's intended subject, or into assuming an obligation to interpret things not susceptible of interpretation and that have not been inserted with a view to interpretation. The assumption of such an obligation would result in extravagant fantasies such as are entertained and written about in our time by most of the sects of the world, since each of these sects desires to find certain significations for words whose author in no wise had in mind the significations wished by them. Your purpose, rather, should always be to know, regarding most parables, the whole that was intended to be known. In some matters it will suffice you to gather from my remarks that a given story is a parable, even if we explain nothing more; for once you know it is a parable, it will immediately become clear to you what it is a parable of. My remarking that it is a parable will be like someone's removing a screen from between the eye and a visible thing.

51. Literally: his bestiality.   52. Or: the other animals.
53. The words enclosed in brackets appear in Ibn Tibbon's Hebrew translation, but not in the printed Arabic text. There is little doubt that in this case Ibn Tibbon's text is more correct.

INSTRUCTION WITH RESPECT TO THIS TREATISE

If you wish to grasp the totality of what this Treatise contains, so that nothing of it will escape you, then you must connect its chapters one with another; and when reading a given chapter, your intention must be not only to understand the totality of the subject of that chapter, but also to grasp each word that occurs in it in the course of the speech, even if that word does not belong to the intention of the chapter. For the diction of this Treatise has not been chosen at haphazard,[54] but with great exactness and exceeding precision, and with care to avoid failing to explain any obscure point. And nothing has been mentioned out of its place, save with a view to explaining some matter in its proper place. You therefore should not let your fantasies elaborate on what is said here, for that would hurt me and be of no use to yourself. You ought rather to learn everything | that ought to be learned and constantly study this Treatise. For it then will elucidate for you most of the obscurities of the Law that appear as difficult to every intelligent man. I adjure — by God, may He be exalted! — every reader of this Treatise of mine not to comment upon a single word of it and not to explain to another anything in it save that which has been explained and commented upon in the words of the famous Sages of our Law who preceded me. But whatever he understands from this Treatise of those things that have not been said by any of our famous Sages other than myself should not be explained to another; nor should he hasten to refute me, for that which he understood me to say might be contrary to my intention. He thus would harm me in return for my having wanted to benefit him and would *repay evil for good.*[55] All into whose hands it falls should consider it well; and if it slakes his thirst, though it be on only one point from among the many that are obscure,[56] he should thank God and be content with what he has understood. If, on the other hand, he finds nothing in this Treatise that might be of use to him in any respect, he should think of it as not having been composed at all. If anything in it, according to his way of thinking, appears to be in some way harmful, he should interpret it, even if in a far-fetched way, in order to *pass a favorable judgment.*[57] For as we are enjoined

54. Literally: the speech does not fall as it may happen.
55. Cf. Ps. 38:21.
56. Literally: though it were only in a certain matter from among the complex of what is difficult.
57. Cf. Mishnah, Aboth, I 6.

to act in this way toward our vulgar ones, all the more should this be so with respect to our erudite ones and Sages of our Law who are trying to help us to the truth as they apprehend it. I know that, among men generally, every beginner will derive benefit from some of the chapters of this Treatise, though he lacks even an inkling of what is involved in speculation. A perfect man, on the other hand, devoted to Law and, as I have mentioned, perplexed, will benefit from all its chapters. How greatly will he rejoice in them and how pleasant will it be to hear them! But those who are confused and whose brains have been polluted by false opinions and misleading ways deemed by them to be | true sciences, and who hold themselves to be men of speculation without having any knowledge of anything that can truly be called science,[58] those will flee from many of its chapters. Indeed, these chapters will be very difficult for them to bear because they cannot apprehend their meaning and also because they would be led to recognize the falseness of the counterfeit money in their hands—their treasure and fortune held ready for future calamities. God, may He be exalted, knows that I have never ceased to be exceedingly apprehensive about setting down those things that I wish to set down in this Treatise. For they are concealed things; none of them has been set down in any book—written in the religious community[59] in these times of *Exile*[60]—the books composed in these times being in our hands. How then can I now innovate and set them down? However, I have relied on two premises, the one being [the Sages'] saying in a similar case, *It is time to do something for the Lord, and so on;*[61] the second being their saying, *Let all thy acts be for the sake of Heaven.*[62] Upon these two premises have I relied when setting down what I have composed in some of the chapters of this Treatise.

To sum up: I am the man who when the concern pressed him and his way was straitened and he could find no other device by which to teach a demonstrated truth other than by giving satisfaction to a single virtuous man while displeasing ten thousand ignoramuses—I am he who prefers to address that single man by himself, and I do not heed the blame of those many creatures. For I claim to liberate that virtuous one from that into

58. In this phrase the same Arabic term is translated by two words: "knowledge" and "science."

59. Meaning the Jewish community.   60. The Hebrew word *galuth* is used.

61. The verse continues as follows: *for they have infringed Thy Law.* Ps. 119:126; cf. B.T., Berakhoth, 63.

62. Mishnah, Aboth, II 17.

which he has sunk, and I shall guide him in his perplexity until he becomes perfect and he finds rest.

INTRODUCTION

One of seven causes should account for the contradictory or contrary statements to be found in any book or compilation.

The first cause. The author | has collected the remarks of various people with differing opinions, but has omitted citing his authorities and has not attributed each remark to the one who said it. Contradictory or contrary statements can be found in such compilations because one of the two propositions is the opinion of one individual while the other proposition is the opinion of another individual.

The second cause. The author of a particular book has adopted a certain opinion that he later rejects; both his original and later[63] statements are retained in the book.

The third cause. Not all the statements in question are to be taken in their external sense; some are to be taken in their external sense, while some others are parables and hence have an inner content. Alternatively, two apparently contradictory propositions may both be parables and when taken in their external sense may contradict, or be contrary to, one another.

The fourth cause. There is a proviso that, because of a certain necessity, has not been explicitly stated in its proper place; or the two subjects may differ, but one of them has not been explained in its proper place, so that a contradiction appears to have been said, whereas there is no contradiction.

The fifth cause arises from the necessity of teaching and making someone understand. For there may be a certain obscure matter that is difficult to conceive. One has to mention it or to take it as a premise in explaining something that is easy to conceive and that by rights ought to be taught

63. Literally: his first and his second.

before the former, since one always begins with what is easier. The teacher, accordingly, will have to be lax and, using any means that occur to him or gross speculation, will try to make that first matter somehow understood. He will not undertake to state the matter as it truly is in exact terms, but rather will leave it so in accord with the listener's imagination that the latter will understand only what he now wants him to understand. Afterwards, in the appropriate place, that obscure matter is stated in exact terms and explained as it truly is.

The sixth cause. | The contradiction is concealed and becomes evident only after many premises. The greater the number of premises needed to make the contradiction evident, the more concealed it is. It thus may escape the author, who thinks there is no contradiction between his two original propositions. But if each proposition is considered separately — a true premise being joined to it and the necessary conclusion drawn — and this is done to every conclusion — a true premise being joined to it and the necessary conclusion drawn —, after many syllogisms the outcome of the matter will be that the two final conclusions are contradictory or contrary to each other. That is the kind of thing that escapes the attention of scholars who write books. If, however, the two original propositions are evidently contradictory, but the author has simply forgotten the first when writing down the second in another part[64] of his compilation, this is a very great weakness, and that man should not be reckoned among those whose speeches deserve consideration.

The seventh cause. In speaking about very obscure matters it is necessary to conceal some parts and to disclose others. Sometimes in the case of certain dicta this necessity requires that the discussion proceed on the basis of a certain premise, whereas in another place necessity requires that the discussion proceed on the basis of another premise contradicting the first one. In such cases the vulgar must in no way be aware of the contradiction; the author accordingly uses some device to conceal it by all means.

The contradictions that are to be found in the *Mishnah* and the *Baraithoth* are due to the first cause. Thus you will find that they constantly ask: *Does not the beginning* [*of the passage*] *constitute an objection against its end?* In such cases the answer is: *The beginning is the opinion of a certain rabbi and the end that of another rabbi.* You likewise will find that

64. Literally: place.

they say: *Rabbi [Judah ha-Nasi] agreed with the opinion of a certain rabbi in this one* | *matter and therefore cited it anonymously. In that other matter he agreed with the opinion of that other rabbi and therefore cited it anonymously.* You often will find them also saying: *Who is the author of this anonymous passage? Such and such rabbi. Who is the author of that passage of the Mishnah? Such and such rabbi.* Such cases are innumerable. The contradictions or divergences to be found in the *Talmud* are due to the first cause and to the second. Thus you find them constantly saying: *In this matter he agreed with this rabbi and in that with another rabbi.* They likewise say: *He agreed with him on one point and disagreed on another.* They also say: *[The two statements are made by] two Amoraim who disagree as to the opinion of a certain rabbi.* All contradictions of this kind are due to the first cause. Contradictions due to the second cause are referred to when they say: *Rab abandoned this opinion. Raba abandoned that opinion.* In such cases an inquiry is made as to which of the two statements is the later one. This is similar to their saying: *In the first recension [of the Talmud] by Rabbi Ashi, he said one thing, and in the second another.* That some passages in every prophetic book, when taken in their external sense, appear to contradict or to be contrary to one another is due to the third cause and to the fourth. And it was with this in view that this entire introduction was written. You already know how often [the Sages], *may their memory be blessed,* say: *One verse says this and another verse says that.* They straightway establish that there is an apparent contradiction. Thereupon they explain that a proviso is lacking in the statement of the subject or that the two texts have different subjects. Thus they say: *Solomon, is it not enough for you that your words contradict those of your father? They also contradict themselves, and so on.*[65] Cases of this are frequent in the sayings of the *Sages, may their memory be blessed;* however, most of the prophetic statements they refer to concern commandments or precepts regarding conduct. We, on the other hand, | propose to draw attention to *verses* that are apparently contradictory with regard to opinions and beliefs. Part of this will be explained in some of the chapters of this Treatise, for this subject too belongs to *the mysteries of the Torah.* Whether contradictions due to the seventh cause are to be found in the books of the prophets is a matter for speculative study and investigation. Statements about this should not be a matter of conjecture. As for the divergences occurring in the books of the philosophers, or rather of those who know the truth, they are due to the fifth cause. On

65. B.T., Shabbath, 30a.

the other hand, the contradictions occurring in most of the books of authors and commentators other than those we have mentioned are due to the sixth cause. Likewise in the *Midrashim* and the *Haggadah* there is to be found great contradiction due to this cause. That is why the Sages have said: *No questions should be asked about difficulties in the Haggadah*. There are also to be found therein contradictions due to the seventh cause. Divergences that are to be found in this Treatise are due to the fifth cause and the seventh. Know this, grasp its true meaning, and remember it very well so as not to become perplexed by some of its chapters.

And after these introductory remarks, I shall begin to mention the terms whose true meaning, as intended in every passage according to its context, must be indicated. This, then, will be a key permitting one to enter places the gates to which were locked. And when these gates are opened and these places are entered into, the souls will find rest therein, the eyes will be delighted, and the bodies will be eased of their toil and of their labor. |

Open ye the gates, that the righteous nation

that keepeth faithfulness may enter in[1]

CHAPTER 1

Image [ṣelem] and *likeness* [*demuth*]. People have thought that in the Hebrew language *image* denotes the shape and configuration of a thing. This supposition led them to the pure doctrine of the corporeality of God, on account of His saying: *Let us make man in our image, after our likeness.*[2] For they thought that God has a man's form, I mean his shape and configuration. The pure doctrine of the corporeality of God was a necessary consequence to be accepted by them. They accordingly believed in it and deemed that if they abandoned this belief, they would give the lie to the biblical text; that they would even make the deity to be nothing at all unless they thought that God was a body provided with a face and a hand, like them in shape and configuration. However, He is, in their view, bigger and more resplendent than they themselves, and the matter of which He is composed is not flesh and blood. As they see it, this is as far as one can go in establishing the separateness of God from other things. Now with respect to that which ought to be said in order to refute the doctrine of the corporeality of God and to establish His real unity — which can have no true reality unless one disproves His corporeality — you shall know the demonstration of all of this from this Treatise. However, here, in this chapter, only an indication is given with a view to elucidating the meaning of *image* and *likeness*.

Now I say that in the Hebrew language the proper term designating the form that is well known among the multitude, namely, that form which is the shape and configuration of a thing, is *to'ar*. Thus Scripture says: *beautiful in form [to'ar] | and beautiful in appearance;*[3] *What form [to'aro] is he of?;*[4] *As the form [to'ar] of the children of a king.*[5] This term is

1. Isa. 26:2.   2. Gen. 1:26.   3. Gen. 39:6.   4. I Sam. 28:14.   5. Judg. 8:18.

also applied to an artificial form; thus: *He marketh its form [yeta'arehu] with a line, and he marketh its form [yeta'arehu] with a compass.*[6] Those terms[7] are never applied to the deity, may He be exalted; far and remote may this thought be from us. The term *image*, on the other hand, is applied to the natural form, I mean to the notion in virtue of which a thing is constituted as a substance and becomes what it is. It is the true reality of the thing in so far as the latter is that particular being. In man that notion is that from which human apprehension derives. It is on account of this intellectual apprehension that it is said of man: *In the image of God created He him.*[8] For this reason also, it is said: *Thou contemnest their image.*[9] For *contempt* has for its object the soul, which is the specific form, not the shape and configuration of the parts of the body. I assert also that the reason why idols are called *images* lies in the fact that what was sought in them was the notion that was deemed to subsist in them, and not their shape and configuration. I assert similarly with regard to the scriptural expression: *images of your emerods.*[10] For what was intended by them was the notion of warding off the harm caused by the *emerods*, and not the shape of the *emerods.* If, however, there should be no doubt concerning the expressions *the images of your emerods* and *images* being used in order to denote shape and configuration, it would follow that *image* is an equivocal or amphibolous term applied to the specific form and also to the artificial form and to what is analogous to the two in the shapes and configurations of the natural bodies. That which was meant in the scriptural dictum, *let us make man in our image,*[11] was the specific form, which is intellectual apprehension, not the shape and configuration. We have explained to you the difference between *image* and *form*, and have explained the meaning of *image.*

As for the term *likeness [demuth]*, it is a noun derived from the verb *damoh [to be like]*, and it too signifies likeness in respect of a notion. For the scriptural dictum, *I am like a pelican in the wilderness,*[12] does not signify that its author | resembled the pelican with regard to its wings and feathers, but that his sadness was like that of the bird. In the same way in the verse, *Nor was any tree in the garden of God like unto it in beauty,*[13] the likeness is with respect to the notion of beauty. Similarly the verses, *Their venom is in the likeness of the venom of a serpent*[14] and *His likeness is that of a lion that*

6. Isa. 44:13.
7. The plural conforms to the Arabic text. However, as far as one can see, the sentence has in view only one term, namely, *to'ar.*
8. Gen. 1:27.   9. Ps. 73:20.   10. I Sam. 6:5.   11. Gen. 1:26.   12. Ps. 102:7.
13. Ezek. 31:8.   14. Ps. 58:5.

is eager to tear in pieces,[15] refer both of them to a likeness in respect of a notion and not with respect to a shape and a configuration. In the same way it is said, *the likeness of the throne, the likeness of a throne;*[16] the likeness referred to being in respect of elevation and sublimity, not in respect of a throne's square shape, its solidity, and the length of its legs, as wretched people think. A similar explanation should also be applied to the expression: *the likeness of the living creatures.*[17] Now man possesses as his proprium something in him that is very strange as it is not found in anything else that exists under the sphere of the moon, namely, intellectual apprehension. In the exercise of this, no sense, no part of the body, none of the extremities are used; and therefore this apprehension was likened unto the apprehension of the deity, which does not require an instrument, although in reality it is not like the latter apprehension, but only appears so to the first stirrings of opinion. It was because of this something, I mean because of the divine intellect conjoined with man, that it is said of the latter that he is *in the image of God and in His likeness*, not that God, may He be exalted, is a body and possesses a shape.

CHAPTER 2

Years ago a learned man propounded as a challenge to me a curious objection. It behooves us now to consider this objection and our reply invalidating it. However, before mentioning this objection and its invalidation, I shall make the following statement. Every Hebrew knew that the term *Elohim* is equivocal, designating the deity, the angels, and the rulers governing the cities. *Onqelos the Proselyte*, peace be on him, has made it clear, and | his clarification is correct, that in the dictum of Scripture, *And ye shall be as Elohim, knowing good and evil*,[1] the last sense is intended. For he has translated: *And ye shall be as rulers.*

After thus having set forth the equivocality of this term, we shall begin to expound the objection. This is what the objector said: It is manifest from the clear sense of the biblical text that the primary purpose with regard to man was that he should be, as the other animals are, devoid of intellect, of thought, and of the capacity to distinguish between good and evil. However, when he disobeyed, his disobedience procured him as its necessary

15. Ps. 17:12.   16. Ezek. 1:26.   17. Ezek. 1:13.
1. Gen. 3:5.

consequence the great perfection peculiar to man, namely, his being endowed with the capacity that exists in us to make this distinction. Now this capacity is the noblest of the characteristics[2] existing in us; it is in virtue of it that we are constituted as substances. Now it is a thing to be wondered at that man's punishment for his disobedience should consist in his being granted a perfection that he did not possess before, namely, the intellect. This is like the story told by somebody that a certain man from among the people disobeyed and committed great crimes, and in consequence was made to undergo a metamorphosis,[3] becoming a star in heaven. This was the intent and the meaning of the objection, though it was not textually as we have put it.

Hear now the intent of our reply. We said: O you who engage in theoretical speculation using the first notions that may occur to you and come to your mind and who consider withal that you understand a book that is the guide of the first and the last men while glancing through it as you would glance through a historical work or a piece of poetry — when, in some of your hours of leisure, you leave off drinking and copulating: collect yourself and reflect, for things are not as you thought following the first notion that occurred to you, but rather as is made clear through reflection upon the following speech.[4] For the intellect that God made overflow unto man and that is the latter's ultimate perfection, was that which *Adam* had been provided with before he disobeyed. It was because of this that it was said of him that he was created *in the image of God and in His likeness.* It was likewise on account of it that he was addressed by God and given commandments, as it says: *And the Lord | God commanded, and so on.*[5] For commandments are not given to beasts and beings devoid of intellect. Through the intellect one distinguishes between truth and falsehood, and that was found in [Adam] in its perfection and integrity. Fine and bad,[6] on the other hand, belong to the things generally accepted as known,[7] not to those cognized by the intellect. For one does not say: it is fine that heaven

---

2. *maʿānī.* The term has many meanings and often, as in this passage, cannot be satisfactorily translated.
3. The Arabic verb sometimes designates a particular kind of transmigration.
4. The word may also refer to the scriptural story, but the translation given in the text is somewhat more probable.
5. Gen. 2:16.
6. These two terms, rather than good and evil, have been chosen because the Arabic text does not use here the two most common terms (*al-khayr waʾl-sharr* employed earlier in this chapter) denoting the two notions in question, but rather has *al-ḥasan* and *al-qabīḥ.*
7. The expression, "the words (the things) generally accepted as known," render the Arabic term *al-mashhūrāt,* which is used as a translation of the Greek *endoxa.*

is spherical, and it is bad that the earth is flat; rather one says true and false with regard to these assertions. Similarly one expresses in our language the notions of truth and falsehood by means of the terms *emeth* and *sheqer*, and those of fine and bad by means of the terms *tov* and *ra*ᶜ.[8] Now man in virtue of his intellect knows *truth* from *falsehood*; and this holds good for all intelligible things. Accordingly when man was in his most perfect and excellent state, in accordance with his inborn disposition and possessed of his intellectual cognitions — because of which it is said of him: *Thou hast made him but little lower than Elohim*[9] — he had no faculty that was engaged in any way in the consideration of generally accepted things, and he did not apprehend them. So among these generally accepted things even that which is most manifestly bad, namely, uncovering the genitals, was not bad according to him, and he did not apprehend that it was bad. However, when he disobeyed and inclined toward his desires of the imagination and the pleasures of his corporeal senses — inasmuch as it is said: *that the tree was good for food and that it was a delight to the eyes*[10] — he was punished by being deprived of that intellectual apprehension. He therefore disobeyed the commandment that was imposed upon him on account of his intellect and, becoming endowed with the faculty of apprehending generally accepted things, he became absorbed in judging things to be bad or fine. Then he knew how great his loss was, what he had been deprived of, and upon what a state he had entered. Hence it is said: *And ye shall be like Elohim knowing good and evil;*[11] and not: *knowing the false and the true*, or *apprehending the false and the true*. With regard to what is of necessity, there is no *good* and *evil* at all, but only the *false* and the *true*. Reflect on the dictum: *And the eyes of them both were opened, and they knew that they were naked.*[12] It is not said: *And the eyes of them both were opened, | and they saw.* For what was seen previously was exactly that which was seen afterwards. There had been no membrane over the eye that was now removed, but rather he entered upon another state in which he considered as bad things that he had not seen in that light before. Know moreover that this expression, I mean, *to open*,[13] refers only to uncovering mental vision and in no respect is applied to the circumstance that the sense of sight has been newly acquired. Thus: *And God opened her eyes;*[14] *Then the eyes of the blind shall be opened;*[15] *Opening the ears, he heareth not*[16] — a verse that is analogous to its dictum, *That have eyes to see and see not.*[17] Now concerning

---

8. In Hebrew. 9. Ps. 8:6. 10. Gen. 3:6. 11. Gen. 3:5. 12. Gen. 3:7.
13. Used in the verse. 14. Gen. 21:19. 15. Isa. 35:5. 16. Isa. 42:20.
17. Ezek. 12:2.

6

its dictum with regard to *Adam — He changes his face and Thou sendest him forth*[18] — the interpretation and explanation of the verse are as follows: when the direction toward which man tended[19] changed, he was driven forth. For *panim*[20] is a term deriving from the verb *panoh* [*to turn*], since man turns his face toward the thing he wishes to take as his objective. The verse states accordingly that when man changed the direction toward which he tended and took as his objective the very thing a previous commandment had bidden him not to aim at, he was driven out of the *Garden of Eden*. This was the punishment corresponding to his disobedience; it was *measure for measure*. He had been given license to eat good things and to enjoy ease and tranquillity. When, however, as we have said, he became greedy, followed his pleasures and his imaginings, and ate what he had been forbidden to eat, he was deprived of everything and had to eat the meanest kinds of food, which he had not used as aliment before — and this only after toil and labor. As it says: *Thorns also and thistles shall it bring forth to thee, and so on; In the sweat of thy brow, and so on.*[21] And it explains and says: *And the Lord God sent him forth from the Garden of Eden, to till the ground.*[22] And God reduced him, with respect to his food and most of his circumstances, to the level of the beast. It says accordingly: *And thou shalt eat the grass of the field.*[23] And it also says in explanation of this story: *Adam,*[24] *unable to dwell in dignity, is like the beasts that speak not.*[25]

Praise be to the Master of the will whose aims and wisdom cannot be apprehended! |

CHAPTER 3

It is thought that in the Hebrew language the meanings of the words *figure* [*temunah*] and *shape* [*tabnith*] are identical. This is not the case. For *tabnith* is a term deriving from the verb *banoh* [*to build*], and it signifies the build and aspect of a thing; I mean to say its shape, for instance, its being a square, a circle, a triangle, or some other shape. Accordingly it

---

18. Job 14:20.
19. The Arabic word derives from a root from which the usual word for "face" is likewise derived.
20. The Hebrew word for "face."   21. Gen. 3:18–19.   22. Gen. 3:23.   23. Gen. 3:18.
24. Or: man.   25. Ps. 49:13.

says: *The shape of the tabernacle and the shape of all its vessels.*[1] And it says: *According to the shape which thou wast shown upon the mountain;*[2] *the shape of any bird;*[3] *the shape of a hand;*[4] *the shape of the porch.*[5] In all these passages the word means shape. For this reason the Hebrew language does not use this word[6] with reference to attributes that apply in any way to the deity.

As for the term *figure*, it is used amphibolously in three different senses. It is used to designate the form of a thing outside the mind that is apprehended by the senses, I mean the shape and configuration of the thing. Thus it says: *And make you a graven image, the figure of any, and so on;*[7] *For ye saw no figure.*[8] It is also used to designate the imaginary form of an individual object existing in the imagination after the object of which it is the form is no longer manifest to the senses.[9] Thus it says, *In thoughts from the visions of the night, and so on,*[10] the conclusion of the dictum being, *It stood still, but I could not discern the appearance thereof, a figure was before mine eyes.* He means: a fantasm of the imagination[11] that is before my eyes while in sleep. The term is also used to designate the true notion grasped by the intellect. It is with a view to this third meaning that the word *figure* is used with reference to God, may He be exalted. Thus it says: *And the figure of the Lord shall he look upon.*[12] The meaning and interpretation of this verse are: he grasps the truth of God. |

CHAPTER 4

Know that the three words *to see* [*ra'oh*], *to look at* [*habbit*], and *to vision* [*ḥazoh*] are applied to the sight of the eye and that all three of them are also used figuratively to denote the grasp of the intellect. As for the verb *to see*, this is generally admitted by the multitude. Thus it says: *And he saw, and behold a well in the field.*[1] This refers to the sight of the eye. But it also says: *Yea, my heart hath seen much of wisdom and knowledge;*[2] and this refers to intellectual apprehension. Every *mention of seeing*, when referring to God, may He be exalted, has this figurative meaning—as when

1. Exod. 25:9.   2. Exod. 25:40.   3. Deut. 4:17.   4. Ezek. 8:3.
5. I Chron. 28:11.   6. Literally: these words.   7. Deut. 4:25.   8. Deut. 4:15.
9. Literally: after its absence from the senses.   10. Job 4:13.
11. Literally: he means an imagination.   12. Num. 12:8.
1. Gen. 29:2.   2. Eccles. 1:16.

Scripture says: *I saw the Lord;*[3] *And the Lord became seen to him;*[4] *And God saw that it was good;*[5] *I beseech Thee, let me see Thy glory;*[6] *And they saw the God of Israel.*[7] All this refers to intellectual apprehension and in no way to the eye's seeing, as the eye can only apprehend a body, one that is placed in some direction and, in addition, with some of the accidents of the body, I mean the body's coloring, shape, and so forth. Similarly God, may He be exalted, does not apprehend by means of an instrument, as will be explained later.

In the same way the word *to look at* is applied to the act of turning the eye toward a thing. Thus: *Look not behind thee;*[8] *But his wife looked back from behind him;*[9] *And if one look unto the land.*[10] The word is also used figuratively to designate the mind's turning and directing itself to the contemplation of a thing until it grasps it. Thus it says: *He*[11] *hath not looked at iniquity in Jacob;*[12] for *iniquity* is not seen by the eye. Similarly it says: *And they looked after Moses;*[13] of which words the *Sages, may their memory be blessed*, have said[14] that they too have this figurative meaning, as they inform us that the Israelites watched his actions and words and scrutinized them. The word likewise has this meaning when it says: *Look now toward heaven;*[15] for this was in a *prophetic vision*. Every *mention of looking*, when referring | to God, may He be exalted, is in this figurative sense. Thus: *To look upon God;*[16] *And the figure of the Lord shall he look upon;*[17] *And Thou canst not look on mischief.*[18]

The word *to vision* is likewise used to designate the eye's seeing. Thus: *And let our eyes vision Zion.*[19] It has been applied figuratively to the apprehension of the heart. Thus: *Which he visioned concerning Judah and Jerusalem;*[20] *The word of the Lord came unto Abram in a vision.*[21] The word is used in the same figurative sense when it is said: *And they visioned God.*[22] Know this.

3. I Kings 22:19.   4. Gen. 18:1.   5. Gen. 1:10.   6. Exod. 33:18.
7. Exod. 24:10.   8. Gen. 19:17.   9. Gen. 19:26.   10. Isa. 5:30.
11. Apparently Maimonides, contrary to other opinions, considers that God is not the subject of this verse.
12. Num. 23:21.   13. Exod. 33:8.
14. Cf. Tanḥuma, Ki Tissa; Exodus Rabbah, LI; B.T., Qiddushin, 33b. Cf. B.T., Sanhedrin, 110a.
15. Gen. 15:5.   16. Exod. 3:6.   17. Num. 12:8.   18. Hab. 1:13.
19. Mic. 4:11.   20. Isa. 1:1.   21. Gen. 15:1.   22. Exod. 24:11.

CHAPTER 5

When the chief of the philosophers began to investigate very obscure matters and to attempt a proof concerning them, he excused himself by making a statement the meaning of which was as follows.[1] A student of his books should not, because of the subject of these researches, ascribe to him effrontery, temerity, and an excess of haste to speak of matters of which he had no knowledge; but rather he should ascribe to him the desire and the endeavor to acquire and achieve true beliefs to the extent to which this is in the power of man. In the same way we say that man should not hasten too much to accede to this great and sublime matter at the first try, without having made his soul undergo training in the sciences and the different kinds of knowledge, having truly improved his character, and having extinguished[2] the desires and cravings engendered in him by his imagination.[3] When, however, he has achieved and acquired knowledge of true and certain premises and has achieved knowledge of the rules of logic and inference and of the various ways of preserving himself from errors of the mind, he then should engage in the investigation of this subject. When doing this he should not make categoric affirmations in favor of the first opinion that occurs to him and should not, from the outset, strain and impel his thoughts toward the apprehension of the deity; he rather should feel awe and refrain and hold back until he gradually elevates himself. It is in this sense that it is said, | *And Moses hid his face, for he was afraid to look upon God;*[4] this being an additional meaning of the verse over and above its external meaning that indicates that he hid his face because of his being afraid to look upon the light manifesting itself — and not that the deity, who is greatly exalted above every deficiency, can be apprehended by the eyes. [Moses], peace be on him, was commended for this; and God, may He be exalted, let overflow upon him so much of His bounty and goodness that it became necessary to say of him: *And the figure of the Lord shall he look upon.*[5] The *Sages, may their memory be blessed,* have stated that this is a reward for his having at first *hidden his face so as not to look upon God.*[6]

1. Cf. Aristotle *De Caelo* ii.12.291b24 ff. Part of this passage may be translated as follows: ". . . one should say that which appears to be plausible, looking upon the readiness to do so as evidence of modesty rather than of temerity, provided that one rests content with but a little success in matters that cause us very great perplexity."
2. Literally: killed.   3. Literally: his imaginary desires and cravings.
4. Exod. 3:6.   5. Num. 12:8.
6. B.T., Berakhoth, 7a; Tanḥuma (Verona ed.), 23b.

The nobles of the children of Israel,[7] on the other hand, were overhasty, strained their thoughts, and achieved apprehension, but only an imperfect one. Hence it is said of them: *And they saw the God of Israel, and there was under His feet, and so on;*[8] and not merely: *And they saw the God of Israel.* For these words are solely intended to present a criticism of their act of seeing, not to describe the manner of their seeing. Thus they were solely blamed for the form that their apprehension took inasmuch as corporeality entered into it to some extent[9] — this being necessitated by their overhasty rushing forward before they had reached perfection. They deserved *to perish.* However, [Moses], peace be on him, interceded for them; and they were granted a reprieve until the time they were burnt at *Taberah,* whereas *Nadab* and *Abihu* were burnt in the *Tabernacle of the Congregation,* as is stated in a correct tradition.[10] This having happened to these men, it behooves us, all the more, as being inferior to them, and it behooves those who are inferior to us, to aim at and engage in perfecting our knowledge of preparatory matters and in achieving those premises that purify apprehension of its taint, which is error. It will then go forward to look upon the divine holy Presence. It is accordingly said: *And let the priests also, that come near to the Lord, sanctify themselves, lest the Lord break forth upon them.*[11] Accordingly *Solomon* has bidden the man who wishes to reach this rank to be most circumspect. He said | warningly in parabolic language: *Guard thy foot when thou goest to the house of God.*[12]

I shall now go back in order to complete what we began to explain, and I shall say: Because of the hindrances that were a stumbling block to *the nobles of the children of Israel* in their apprehension,[13] their actions too were troubled; because of the corruption of their apprehension, they inclined toward things of the body. Hence it says: *And they visioned God, and did eat and drink.*[14] As for the rest[15] of this passage — namely, from the words of Scripture: *And there was under His feet, as it were, a work of the whiteness of sapphire stone, and so on*[16] — it will be explained in some[17] of the chapters of this Treatise.

7. Exod. 24:11.   8. Exod. 24:10.

9. Literally: in which was included of corporeality that which was included.

10. Tanḥuma, Behaᶜalotkha; Leviticus Rabbah, XX.

11. Exod. 19:22.   12. Eccles. 4:17.

13. Literally: *The nobles of the children of Israel* with what happened to them in their apprehension [in the way] of stumbling-blocks.

14. Exod. 24:11.

15. *tamām.* From the linguistic point of view Ibn Tibbon's translation of *sof* (end) is quite correct. However, the passage that Maimonides is about to quote precedes, in the biblical text, that to which he has just referred.

16. Exod. 24:10.   17. Or: in one.

Our whole purpose was to show that whenever the words *seeing*, *vision*, and *looking* occur in this sense, intellectual apprehension is meant[18] and not the eye's sight, as God, may He be exalted, is not an existent that can be apprehended with the eyes. If, however, an individual of insufficient capacity should not wish to reach the rank to which we desire him to ascend and should he consider that all the words [figuring in the Bible] concerning this subject are indicative of sensual perception of created lights — be they angels or something else — why, there is no harm in his thinking this.

CHAPTER 6

Man [*'ish*] and *woman* [*'ishshah*] are terms that at first were given the meaning[1] of a human male and a human female.[2] Afterwards they were used figuratively to designate any male or female among the other species of living beings. Thus it says: *Of every clean beast thou shalt take to thee seven and seven, the man and his woman.*[3] It is as if it said *male* and *female*. Thereupon the term *woman* was used figuratively to designate any object apt for, and fashioned with a view to being in, conjunction with | some other object. Thus it says: *The five curtains should be coupled together, a woman to her sister.*[4] Hereby it has been made clear to you that the terms *sister* [*aḥoth*] and *brother* [*aḥ*] are likewise used equivocally with figurative meaning just as with *man* and *woman*.

18. Literally: that all *seeing*, *vision*, and *looking* that occur in this sense are intellectual apprehension.
1. Literally: were posited. The implication is that the meaning of words is conventional.
2. Literally: man and woman. This translation could not be adopted because the Hebrew terms with which Maimonides is concerned in this chapter have also been rendered by these words.
3. Gen. 7:2.   4. Exod. 26:3.

To *bear children* [*yalod*]. The notion understood by means of this word is well known. It is that of procreation. Thus: *And they have borne him children.*[1] Afterwards this word was used figuratively to designate the bringing to existence of natural things. Thus: *Before the mountains were brought forth.*[2] It was likewise used figuratively to designate, by analogy with procreation, the notion of earth bringing forth her vegetal produce. Thus: *And make it bring forth and bud.*[3] It was likewise used figuratively with reference to happenings occurring in time, as though they were things that were born. Thus: *Thou knowest not what a day may bring forth.*[4] It was likewise used figuratively with reference to happenings within thought and the opinions and doctrines that they entail. Thus it says: *And bore falsehood.*[5] It is a derivation from this meaning when it is said: *And they please themselves in the children*[6] *of strangers,*[7] that is, they are content with their opinions; or, as *Jonathan ben Uziel*, peace be on him, has put it in his interpretation of this verse: *They walk according to the laws of the gentiles.* In this sense whoever instructs an individual in some matter and teaches[8] him an opinion, has, as far as his being provided with this opinion is concerned, as it were engendered that individual. In this sense the prophets' disciples were called *sons of the prophets*, as we shall explain when treating the equivocality of the term *son*. In this figurative sense it is said of *Adam: And Adam lived a hundred and thirty years and begot*[9] [*a son*] *in his own likeness, after his image.*[10] It has already been explained to you what the meaning of *the image of Adam and his likeness* is. Now none of the children of [Adam] born before [Seth] had been endowed with true human form, which is | *the image of Adam and his likeness* referred to in the words: *the image of God and His likeness.* As for Seth, it was after [Adam] had instructed him and procured him understanding and after he had attained human

---

1. Deut. 21:15.   2. Ps. 90:2.   3. Isa. 55:10.   4. Prov. 27:1.   5. Ps. 7:15.
6. The word derives from the same Hebrew root as the verb dealt with in this chapter.
7. Isa. 2:6.
8. *afāda.* The original meaning of the word is "to be useful to." The fact that it acquired the secondary meaning "to teach," is indubitably due to its having been used as an equivalent of the Greek verb *ōphelein*, the original signification of which is identical with that of *afāda*. In late Greek philosophic texts it sometimes also has the meaning "to teach." In medieval texts the Hebrew *hoᶜil* sometimes also has this meaning, as it was used by the translators to render *afāda* in all its senses.
9. The Hebrew word derives from the root with which this chapter is concerned.
10. Gen. 5:3.

perfection that it was said of him: *And [Adam] begot [a son] in his own likeness, after his image.* You know that whoever is not endowed with this form, whose signification we have explained, is not a man, but an animal having the shape and configuration of man. Such a being, however, has a faculty to cause various kinds of harm and to produce evils that is not possessed by the other animals. For he applies the capacities for thought and perception, which were to prepare him to achieve a perfection that he has not achieved, to all kinds of machinations entailing evils and occasioning and engendering all kinds of harm. Accordingly, he is, as it were, a thing resembling man or imitating him. The children of *Adam* who preceded *Seth* were of this sort. The authors of the *Midrash* say accordingly:[11] *During the entire period of a hundred and thirty years, when Adam was under rebuke, he begot spirits;* they mean *devils.* When, however, He again accorded him His favor, he begot a son resembling him, I mean *in his own likeness, after his image.* Accordingly it says: *And Adam lived a hundred and thirty years and begot [a son] in his own likeness, after his image.*

CHAPTER 8

Place [*maqom*]. Originally this term was given the meaning of particular and general place. Subsequently, language extended its meaning and made it a term denoting an individual's rank and situation; I mean to say with reference to his perfection in some matter, so that it is said: *A certain man has a certain place* with regard to a certain matter. You know how often the people of our language use this meaning when they say: *Occupying the place of his ancestors; He occupied the place of his ancestors in wisdom or piety;* | or when they say: *The difference of opinion still subsists in its place,* which means, in its station. It is in this figurative manner that it is said: *Blessed be the glory of the Lord from His place,*[1] meaning, according to His rank and the greatness of His portion in existence. Similarly in every mention of *place* referring to God, the sole intention is to signify the rank of His existence, may He be exalted; there being nothing like or similar to that existence, as shall be demonstrated.

     Know with regard to every term whose equivocality we shall explain

11. B.T., ᶜErubin, 18b; cf. Genesis Rabbah, XX and XXIV.
 1. Ezek. 3:12.

to you in this Treatise that our purpose in such an explanation is not only to draw your attention to what we mention in that particular chapter. Rather do we open a gate and draw your attention to such meanings of that particular term as are useful for our purpose, not for the various purposes of whoever may speak the language of this or that people. As for you, you should consider the books of prophecy and other works composed by men of knowledge, reflect on all the terms used therein, and take every equivocal term in that one from among its various senses that is suitable in that particular passage. These our words are the key to this Treatise and to others; a case in point being the explanation we have given here of the meaning of the term *place* in the dictum of Scripture: *Blessed be the glory of the Lord from His place*. For you should know that this very meaning is that of the term *place* in its dictum: *Behold, there is a place by Me*.[2] In this verse the term signifies a rank in theoretical speculation and the contemplation of the intellect — not that of the eye; this being in addition to the meaning alluding to a local place that was to be found on that mountain on which the separation and the achievement of perfection came to pass.

CHAPTER 9

Throne [*kisse*]. Originally the meaning given to this word in the Hebrew language was that it was the term designating the throne.[1] As, however, | only people of high rank and great authority, such as kings, used to sit on a throne, and the throne became an existent thing indicative of the grandeur, the high rank, and the great dignity of him who was thought worthy of it, the *Sanctuary* was called a *throne*, because of its indicating the grandeur of Him who manifested Himself therein and let His light and glory descend upon it. Thus Scripture says: *Thou throne of glory, on high from the beginning,*[2] *and so on.*[3] On account of this sense, the heaven is called a *throne*, as indicating to those who have knowledge of them and reflect upon them the greatness of Him who caused them to exist and to move, and who governs this lower world by means of the overflow of their bounty. Accordingly it says: *Thus saith the Lord: The heaven is My throne, and so on.*[4]

2. Exod. 33:21.
1. Maimonides uses the Arabic term to render the Hebrew one.
2. Jer. 17:12.
3. The verse continues: *Thou place of our Sanctuary*.
4. Isa. 66:1.

That is, He says: the heaven indicates My existence, grandeur, and power, as a *throne* indicates the greatness of the individual who is considered worthy of it. That is the doctrine that those who investigate the truth ought to believe, whereas they ought not to believe that there is a body onto which the deity, may He be greatly exalted, raises Himself. For it will be demonstrated to you that He, may He be exalted, is not a body. How, therefore, could there be for Him a place and an abode situated above a body? The matter is just as we have pointed out: namely, every place, such as the *Sanctuary* or the heaven, distinguished by God and singled out to receive His light and splendour is called a *throne*. This term is given a wider meaning in the Hebrew language when it says: *For my hand upon the throne of the Lord.*[5] What is meant is the attribute of His greatness and sublimity; this ought not to be imagined as a thing outside His essence or as a created being from among the beings created by Him, so that He, may He be exalted, should appear to exist both without a *throne* and with a *throne*. That would be infidelity beyond any doubt. For it states explicitly: *Thou, O Lord, sittest for all eternity, Thy throne is from generation to generation*;[6] whereby it indicates that the throne is a thing inseparable from Him. Hence the term *throne* signifies, in this passage and in all those similar to it, His sublimity and greatness that do not constitute a thing existing outside His essence, as will be explained in some[7] of the chapters of this Treatise. |

CHAPTER 10

It already has been set forth that when we mention one of the equivocal terms in this Treatise, it is not our purpose to cite all the senses in which that particular term is used, for this is not a treatise on language. Of those senses we cite only such as we require for our purpose and no others. Of this sort are the terms *to descend* [*yarod*] and *to ascend* [*ᶜaloh*].

The two terms *descending* and *ascending* have been given in the Hebrew language the respective meaning of descent and ascent.[1] Accordingly when a body moves from a certain place to a lower place, it is said *to descend*; and

5. Exod. 17:16.   6. Lam. 5:19.   7. Or: in one.

1. It seemed preferable to use the same English words for the Hebrew terms and their Arabic equivalents.

when it moves from a certain place to a higher place than the place in which it was, it is said *to ascend*. Subsequently these two terms were used figuratively to denote sublimity and greatness; so that when an individual's rank was lowered, he was said *to have descended*; when, on the other hand, his rank became higher in respect of sublimity, he was said *to have ascended*. Thus God, may He be exalted, says: *The stranger that is in the midst of thee shall ascend above thee higher and higher, and thou shalt descend, and so on.*[2] The text also says: *The Lord thy God will set thee in ascendancy above all the nations of the earth.*[3] And it says: *And the Lord magnified Solomon in ascendancy.*[4] You know also how often the Sages use the expression: *With regard to what is holy, men may be made to ascend, but not to descend.*[5] Similarly the term [to descend] is also used to denote a lower state of speculation; when a man directs his thought toward a very mean object, he is said *to have descended*; and similarly when he directs his thought toward an exalted and sublime object, he is said *to have ascended*. Now we, the community of men,[6] are, in regard to place as well as degree of existence, in a most lowly position if we are compared to the all-encompassing heavenly sphere;[7] whereas He, may He be exalted, | is in respect of true existence, sublimity, and greatness in the very highest position — an elevation that is not a spatial one. And as He, may He be exalted, wished — as He did — to let some of us have knowledge deriving from Him and an overflow of prophetic inspiration, the alighting of the prophetic inspiration upon the prophet or the coming-down of the Indwelling[8] to a certain place was termed *descent*; whereas the removal of this prophetic state from a particular individual or the cessation of the Indwelling in a place was termed *ascent*. In every case in which you find the terms *descent* and *ascent* applied to the Creator, may He be exalted, this last meaning is intended. Another similar case is that of a calamity befalling a people or a terrestrial zone in accordance with His pre-eternal will. With regard to this the prophetic books begin by stating, before describing the affliction, that He visited the action of these people and after that made their punishment come down upon them. This notion too is expressed by means of the term *descent*; the reason being that man is too insignificant to have his actions visited and to be punished for them, were it not for the pre-eternal will. This has been made clear in the books of prophecy, where it is said: *What is*

2. Deut. 28:43.   3. Deut. 28:1.   4. I Chron. 29:25.
5. Cf., e.g., Mishnah, Sheqalim, VI 4.
6. Literally: Adamites. I.e., descendants of Adam.
7. I.e., the highest heavenly sphere.
8. *sakīna*, an Arabic word that is the equivalent of the Hebrew *shekhinah*.

man that thou art mindful of him, and the son of man that Thou shouldst visit him, and so on.[9] For this verse refers to this notion. It is for this reason that this is called *descent.* Thus Scripture says: *Come, let us descend, and there confound their language;*[10] *And the Lord descended to see;*[11] *I will descend now and see.*[12] In all these verses the notion is that of punishment befalling people of low condition. As for the first meaning—I mean that which refers to prophetic inspiration and to ennobling—it is frequent. Thus: *And I will descend and speak with thee;*[13] *And the Lord descended upon Mount Sinai;*[14] *The Lord will descend in the sight of all the people;*[15] *And God ascended from him;*[16] *And God ascended from Abraham.*[17] When, on the other hand, Scripture says, *And Moses ascended to God,*[18] the third meaning[19] of the term [to ascend] is meant; this, in addition to the fact that [Moses] *ascended to the top of the mountain* upon which the created light had descended. The verse does not mean that God, may He be exalted, | has a place up to which one may ascend or from which one may descend; He is exalted very high above the imaginings of the ignorant.

CHAPTER 11

Sitting [*yeshibah*]. The first meaning given to this term in our language was that of being seated. Thus: *Now Eli the priest sat upon a seat.*[1] But in view of the fact that a sitting individual is in a state of the most perfect stability and steadiness, this term is used figuratively to denote all steady, stable, and changeless states. Thus when promising *Jerusalem* permanence and stability while she is in possession of the highest of ranks, Scripture says: *She will rise and sit in her place.*[2] And it also says: *He maketh the barren woman to sit in her house;*[3] which means that He makes her firm and steady. In the latter sense it is said of God, may He be exalted: *Thou, O Lord, sittest for all eternity;*[4] *O Thou who sittest in the heaven;*[5] *He that sitteth in heaven.*[6] That is, the stable One who undergoes no manner of change, neither a change in His essence—as He has no modes[7] besides His essence

9. Ps. 8:5.   10. Gen. 11:7.   11. Gen. 11:5.   12. Gen. 18:21.   13. Num. 11:17.
14. Exod. 19:20.   15. Exod. 19:11.   16. Gen. 35:13.   17. Gen. 17:22.   18. Exod. 19:3.
19. Denoting the direction of thought to an exalted object.
1. I Sam. 1:9.   2. Zech. 14:10.   3. Ps. 113:9.   4. Lam. 5:19.   5. Ps. 123:1.   6. Ps. 2:4.
7. ḥāl. Modes were attributed to God by some of the latter Muᶜtazilites, notably by Abū Hishām (d. 933) and his followers.

with respect to which He might change — nor a change in His relation to what is other than Himself — since, as shall be explained later, there does not exist a relation with respect to which He could change. And herein His being wholly changeless in every respect achieves perfection, as He makes clear, saying: *For I the Lord change not*,[8] meaning that He undergoes no change at all. In this sense, the term *sitting* is applied to Him, may He be exalted, in the verses I have cited. In most of these passages this term is used with reference to heaven, as the latter is changeless and without diversity; I mean to say that the individuals existing in it do not change, as do the individuals constituted by the terrestrial things, which are subject to generation and corruption. | Similarly when a relation is ascribed equivocally to Him, may He be exalted, with respect to the various species of beings subject to generation and corruption, He is also said to be *sitting*. For these species are permanent, well ordered, endowed with a stable existence, such as is the existence of the individuals of heaven. Thus it says: *He that sitteth above the circle of the earth;*[9] that is, the permanent and stable One over and above the circling of the earth — he means its rotation, the reference being to the things generated in it in rotation. It also says: *The Lord sitteth at the flood*.[10] It means that when the state of the earth is changed and corrupted, there is no change in the relation of God, may He be exalted, to things; this relation remains the same — stable and permanent — whether the thing undergoes generation or corruption. For this relation subsists only with regard to the species of the various things subject to generation, not with regard to the individuals. Consider every *mention of sitting* applied to God, and you will discover that it is used in this sense.

CHAPTER 12

Rising [*qimah*] is an equivocal term. One of its meanings is to get up, which is the opposite of *sitting*. Thus: *He did not rise nor move for him*.[1] It also has a meaning denoting the stability and validity of a matter. Thus: *The Lord will let His promise rise;*[2] *The field of Ephron arose;*[3] *The house that is in the* [*walled*] *city shall arise;*[4] *And the kingdom of Israel shall*

8. Mal. 3:6.   9. Isa. 40:22.   10. Ps. 29:10.
1. Esther 5:9.   2. I Sam. 1:23. I.e., He will keep His promise.
3. Gen. 23:17. I.e., was made sure.   4. Lev. 25:30.

arise in thy hand.[5] All *mention of rising* applied to God, may He be exalted, has this meaning. Thus: *Now will I rise, saith the Lord.*[6] What He intends to say by this is: Now will I carry out My decree, My promise, and My menace. Thus also: *Thou wilt arise and have compassion upon Zion;*[7] that is, Thou wilt carry out what Thou hast promised as to having mercy upon her. As one who decides to do something marks his impulse to do it | by rising, so whoever has revolted over some matter is said to rise up. Thus: *That my son hath made my servant rise up against me.*[8] And the word taken in this sense is used figuratively to denote the execution of God's decree against a people who have deserved punishment entailing their destruction. Thus: *And I will rise against the house of Jeroboam;*[9] *But he will rise against the house of the evil-doers.*[10] His words, *Now will I rise,* may likewise have this meaning; and similarly the words: [*Thou*] *wilt arise and have compassion upon Zion;*[11] he means: *Thou wilt arise against her enemies.* Many biblical texts conform to this meaning,[12] for there is not to be found in them a rising-up and a sitting-down of God, may He be exalted. Accordingly [the Sages], peace be on them, have said: *In the upper world there is neither sitting nor standing;*[13] for *standing* sometimes occurs in the sense of *rising.*

CHAPTER 13

Standing [*ᶜamidah*] is an equivocal term. Sometimes it has the meaning: to rise and stand. Thus: *When he stood before Pharaoh;*[1] *Though Moses and Samuel stood;*[2] *And he stood by them.*[3] And sometimes it has the meaning: to abstain and desist. Thus: *Because they stood still and answered no more;*[4] *And she left off*[5] *bearing.*[6] Elsewhere it has the meaning: to be stable and durable. Thus: *That they may stand many days;*[7] *Then shalt thou be able to stand;*[8] *His taste stood in him,*[9] that is, it was stable, durable,

---

5. I Sam. 24:21. I.e., shall be established.
6. Ps. 12:6; Isa. 33:10.   7. Ps. 102:14.   8. I Sam. 22:8.   9. Amos 7:9.
10. Isa. 31:2.
11. Ps. 12:6; Isa. 33:10.
12. Literally: and from this meaning occur many texts.
13. B.T., Ḥagigah, 15a.
1. Gen. 41:46.   2. Jer. 15:1.   3. Gen. 18:8.   4. Job 32:16.
5. Literally: *stood.*   6. Gen. 29:35.   7. Jer. 32:14.
8. Exod. 18:23. I.e., to endure.   9. Jer. 48:11.

and unchanged; *His righteousness standeth for ever*[10] that is, it is permanent and enduring. Whenever the term *standing* occurs with reference to God, may He be exalted, it is used in the last sense. Thus: *And His feet shall stand in that day upon the Mount of Olives*,[11] that is, his intermediate causes, I mean His effects, shall be established. This shall be made clear when the equivocality of the term *foot* is mentioned. This meaning also occurs in the words of God, may He be exalted, [to Moses]: *But as for thee, stand thou here by Me;*[12] and in the verse: *I stood between the Lord and you.*[13] |

CHAPTER 14

The equivocality of the word *Adam*.[1] It is the name of *Adam the first man*, and is a derivative word; for, as the biblical text states, it is derived from the word *adamah*.[2] It is also the term designating the species. Thus: *My spirit shall not abide in man;*[3] *Who knoweth the spirit of the sons of man;*[4] *So that man hath no pre-eminence above a beast*.[5] It is also a term designating the multitude, I mean the generality as distinguished from the elite. Thus: *Both the sons of man and the sons of an [outstanding] individual*.[6] This third meaning is to be found in the following verses: *The sons of Elohim saw the daughters of man;*[7] *Nevertheless ye shall die as men*.[8]

CHAPTER 15

To *stand erect* [*naṣob* or *yaṣob*]. Though these two roots are different, their meaning, as you know, is identical in all their various forms. The term is equivocal. Sometimes it has the meaning of rising and being erect. Thus: *And his sister stood erect afar off;*[1] *The kings of the earth stood*

10. Ps. 111:3.   11. Zech. 14:4.   12. Deut. 5:28.   13. Deut. 5:5.
1. In Hebrew the word also means "man."   2. I.e., earth.
3. *Adam* in Hebrew. Gen. 6:3.   4. Eccles. 3:21.   5. Eccles. 3:19.   6. Ps. 49:3.
7. *Adam* in Hebrew. The expression, *the daughters of man*, signifies "belonging to the common people." It would seem therefore that the expression, *the sons of Elohim*, refers to the elite. Gen. 6:2.
8. Ps. 82:7.
1. Exod. 2:4.

erect;[2] *They came out and stood erect.*[3] The term has also another meaning: to be stable and permanent. Thus: *Thy word stands erect in heaven;*[4] this means that it is stable and constant. In all cases where this term occurs with reference to the Creator, it has this meaning. Thus: *And, behold, the Lord stood erect upon it,*[5] that is, was stably and constantly upon it — I mean upon the ladder, one end of which is in heaven, while the other end is upon the earth. Everyone who ascends does so climbing up this ladder,[6] so that he necessarily apprehends Him who is upon it,[7] as He is stably and permanently at the top of the ladder. It is clear that what I say here of Him conforms to the parable propounded. For *the angels of | God*[8] are the prophets with reference to whom it is clearly said: *And He sent an angel;*[9] *And an angel of the Lord came up from Gilgal to Bochim.*[10] How well put is the phrase *ascending and descending,*[11] in which *ascent* comes before *descent*. For after the *ascent* and the attaining of certain[12] rungs of the ladder that may be known comes the descent with whatever decree[13] the prophet has been informed of — with a view to governing and teaching the people of the earth. As we have made clear,[14] it is on this account that this is called *descent*. I shall now return to our purpose. *Stood erect upon it* signifies God's being stable, permanent, and constant, not the erect position of a body. The same meaning is *to* be found in the verse: *And thou shalt stand erect upon the rock.*[15] It has thus been made clear to you that as far as this purpose is concerned the terms *to stand erect* [naṣob] and *to stand* [ʿamod] have the same meaning. For Scripture also says: *Behold, I will stand before thee there upon the rock in Horeb.*[16]

2. Ps. 2:2.   3. Num. 16:27.   4. Ps. 119:89.   5. Gen. 28:13.
6. Literally: upon it climbs and ascends everyone who ascends.
7. The Arabic phrase might also be translated: so that he apprehends Him who is upon it necessarily. However, for syntactic and other reasons, the translation in the text is probably the correct one.
8. Seen by Jacob going up and down the ladder.
9. Num. 20:16.   10. Judg. 2:1.   11. Gen. 28:12.
12. The Arabic word *maʿlūma* may also be translated "which are known."
13. The word *amr* may also be translated "matter" or "thing."
14. Cf. above in chap. 10: "When a man directs his thought toward a very mean object, he is said *to have descended.*"
15. Exod. 33:21.
16. Exod. 17:6. This verse appears to state that God will stand.

Rock [*ṣur*] is an equivocal term. It is a term denoting a mountain. Thus: *And thou shalt smite the rock.*[1] It is also a term denoting a hard stone like flint. Thus: *Knives of rock.*[2] It is, further, a term denoting the quarry from which quarry-stones are hewn. Thus: *Look unto the rock whence ye were hewn.*[3] Subsequently, in derivation from the last meaning, the term was used figuratively to designate the root and principle of every thing. It is on this account that after saying: *Look unto the rock whence ye were hewn,* Scripture continues:[4] *Look unto Abraham your father, and so on,*[5] giving, as it were, an interpretation according to which the *rock* whence *ye were hewn* is *Abraham your father.* Tread therefore in his footsteps, adhere to his religion, and acquire his character, inasmuch as the nature of a quarry ought to be present in what is hewn from it. On account of the last meaning, God, may He be exalted, is designated as the *Rock,* as He is the principle | and the efficient cause of all things other than himself. Accordingly it is said: *The Rock, His work is perfect;*[6] *Of the Rock that begot thee thou wast unmindful;*[7] *Their Rock had given them over;*[8] *And there is no Rock like our God;*[9] *The Rock of Eternity.*[10] The verse *And thou shalt stand erect upon the rock*[11] means: Rely upon, and be firm in considering, God, may He be exalted, as the first principle. This is the entryway through which you shall come to Him, as we have made clear when speaking of His saying [to Moses]: *Behold, there is a place by Me.*[12]

CHAPTER 17

Do not think that only the divine science should be withheld from the multitude. This holds good also for the greater part of natural science. In fact we have repeatedly[1] set down for you our dictum: *The Account of the Beginning*[2] *ought not to be taught in the presence of two men.* This is

1. Exod. 17:6.   2. Josh. 5:2.   3. Isa. 51:1.   4. Literally: says.
5. Isa. 51:2.   6. Deut. 32:4.   7. Deut. 32:18.   8. Deut. 32:30.
9. I Sam. 2:2.   10. Isa. 26:4.   11. Exod. 33:21.
12. The verse continues: *and thou shalt stand erect upon the rock,* a passage just quoted by Maimonides.
1. Cf. I Introduction.   2. I.e., natural science.

not only the case with regard to people adhering to Law, but also with regard to the philosophers and learned men of the various communities[3] in ancient times. For they concealed what they said[4] about the first principles and presented it in riddles. Thus Plato and his predecessors designated Matter as the female and Form as the male. Now you know that the principles of the existents subject to generation and corruption are three: Matter, Form, and Particularized Privation, which is always conjoined with Matter. For, were it not for this conjunction with Privation, Matter would not receive Form. It is in this sense that Privation is to be considered as one of the principles. However, when a form is achieved, the particular privation in question, I mean the privation of the form that is achieved, disappears, and another privation is conjoined with matter; and this goes on for ever, as has been made clear in natural science. Now as even those upon whom the charge of corruption would not be laid in the event of clear exposition used terms figuratively and resorted to teaching in similes, | how much all the more is it incumbent upon us, the community of those adhering to Law, not to state explicitly a matter that is either remote from the understanding of the multitude or the truth of which as it appears to the imagination of these people is different from what is intended by us. Know this also.

CHAPTER 18

To *approach* [*qarob*], to *touch* [*nago^ca*], to *come near* [*nagosh*]. Those three terms, I mean *approaching*, *touching*, and *coming near*, sometimes signify to draw near and approach in space. Elsewhere they signify the union of cognition with what is cognized, which is, as it were, similar to the proximity of one body to another.

Examples of the first signification of *approaching*[1] — that is, approaching in space — are: *As he approached the camp;*[2] *And Pharaoh approached.*[3] The first signification of *touching* is the drawing near of one body to another. Thus: *And she caused it to touch his feet;*[4] *And he caused it to touch my mouth.*[5] The first signification of *coming near* is the act in which one

3. *milal.* The word means, in the first place, "religious communities"; but it also may have the secondary meaning of "national communities."
4. Literally: the speech.
1. Literally: as for the first meaning of *approaching*.
2. Exod. 32:19.   3. Exod. 14:10.   4. Exod. 4:25.   5. Isa. 6:7.

individual goes and moves toward another individual. Thus: *And Judah came near unto him.*[6]

The second signification of these three terms is union in[7] knowledge and drawing near through apprehension, not in[8] space. Thus Scripture, using the word *touching* in the sense of union in knowledge, says: *For her judgment toucheth heaven.*[9] As for *approaching*, it is said: *And the cause that is too hard for you, cause it to approach me.*[10] Scripture says, as it were, let me know it. The word is thus used to denote the act of letting somebody know a knowable thing. As for *coming near*, it is said: *And Abraham came near and said,*[11] while he was in a state of inspiration and prophetic trance, as shall be explained;[12] *Forasmuch as this people came near, and with their mouth and with their lips do honor Me.*[13]

Every *mention of approaching* and *coming near* that you find in the books of prophecy referring to a relation between God, may He be exalted, and a created being[14] | has this last meaning. For God, may He be exalted, is not a body, as shall be demonstrated to you in this Treatise. And accordingly He, may He be exalted, does not draw near to or approach a thing, nor does anything[15] draw near to or approach Him, may He be exalted, inasmuch as the abolition of corporeality entails that space be abolished;[16] so that there is no nearness and proximity, and no remoteness, no union and no separation, no contact and no succession. I do not think that you shall grow doubtful or perplexed because Scripture says: *The Lord is nigh unto all them that call upon Him;*[17] *They take delight in approaching unto God;*[18] *The nearness of God is my good.*[19] For in all these verses nearness through cognition,[20] I mean cognitive apprehension, is intended, not nearness in space.[21] The same applies to its dicta: *Nigh unto it;*[22] *Approach thou and hear;*[23] *And Moses alone shall come near unto the Lord, but they shall not come near.*[24] The verse is to be interpreted in this way, unless you wish to consider that the expression *shall come near*, used with reference to *Moses*, means that the latter shall approach the place on the mountain upon which

6. Gen. 44:18.   7. Literally: of.   8. Literally: of.   9. Jer. 51:9.
10. Deut. 1:17.   11. Gen. 18:23.   12. Cf. I 21, and II 41.   13. Isa. 29:13.
14. Literally: a created of the created ones.
15. Literally: a thing of the things.
16. Literally: Inasmuch as in virtue of the abolition of corporeality space is abolished.
17. Ps. 145:18.   18. Isa. 58:2.   19. Ps. 73:28.
20. Literally: nearness of cognition.
21. Literally: nearness of place.
22. Deut. 4:7. The complete verse is as follows: *For what nation is there so great who hath God so nigh unto it, as the Lord our God is in all things that we call upon Him for?*
23. Deut. 5:24. The verse continues: *all that the Lord our God shall say.*
24. Exod. 24:2.

the light, I mean *the glory of God*, has descended. For you are free to do so. You must, however, hold fast to the doctrinal principle[25] that there is no difference whether an individual is at the center of the earth, or, supposing that this were possible, in the highest part of the ninth heavenly sphere. For he is not farther off from God in the one case[26] and no nearer to Him in the other.[27] For nearness to Him, may He be exalted, consists in apprehending Him; and remoteness from Him is the lot of him who does not know Him.[28] And there are very many gradations in being near to or far away from Him in this respect. I shall explain the manner of these gradations in apprehension in one of the chapters of this Treatise. As for its dictum, *Touch the mountains that they may smoke*,[29] Scripture signifies thereby in parabolic language: let Thy decree come to them. It says in a similar way:[30] *And touch Thou him himself*,[31] meaning let Thy infliction come upon him. Consider in a similar way the term *touching* and all its derivatives in every passage in which they occur according to the context.[32] Sometimes the word is intended to signify the approach of one body to another, and sometimes union through[33] the cognition and apprehension of a certain thing. | For one who apprehends a thing that he did not apprehend before has, as it were, approached a thing that previously had been remote from him. Understand this.

CHAPTER 19

To fill [*malle*]. This is an equivocal term applied by people speaking the Hebrew language to a body's entering and filling up another body. Thus: *And she filled her pitcher*;[1] *An omerful for each.*[2] This usage is frequent.[3] The term is likewise applied to the coming to an end and completion of a measurable period of time. Thus: *And her days were fulfilled*;[4] *And forty days were fulfilled for him.*[5] The term is also employed to signify

25. Literally: root.　26. Literally: here.　27. Literally: there.
28. Literally: is for him that does not know Him.
29. Ps. 144:5.　30. Literally: just as it says.　31. Job 2:5.
32. Literally: according to it.　33. Literally: of.
1. Gen. 24:16.
2. Exod. 16:32–33. Maimonides' quotation does not conform exactly to the present biblical text.
3. Literally: and this is many.　4. Gen. 25:24.
5. Gen. 50:3.

the achievement of perfection in virtue and of the latter's ultimate end. Thus: *And full with the blessing of the Lord;*[6] *Them hath He filled with wisdom of heart;*[7] *He was filled with wisdom and understanding and skill.*[8] In this sense it is said: *The whole earth is full of His glory;*[9] the meaning of this verse being that the whole earth bears witness to His perfection, that is, indicates it. Similar is its dictum: *And the glory of the Lord filled the tabernacle.*[10] Every *mention of filling* that you will find referring to God is used in this sense, and not in the sense of there being a body filling a place. However, if you wish to consider that the *glory of the Lord* is the created light that is designated as *glory* in every passage and that *filled the tabernacle*, there is no harm in it.

CHAPTER 20

H*igh* [*ram*] is an equivocal term having the signification of being elevated in space and of being elevated in degree, I mean to say in exalted station, nobility, and great worth. Thus it says: *And the ark was lifted high above the earth.*[1] In this passage | the first sense of the term is employed. It also says: *I have placed on high one chosen*[2] *out of the people;*[3] *Forasmuch as I have placed thee on high from among*[4] *the dust;*[5] *Forasmuch as I have placed thee on high from among the people.*[6] In these verses the term in question has its second meaning. Every word derived from *heightening*[7] [*haramah*] has this second meaning when occurring with reference to God. Thus: *Be thou heightened, O God, above the heavens.*[8]

The term *to bear* [*naso*ʾ][9] has similarly the signification of elevation in space and of elevation in degree and abundance of good fortune. The

---

6. Deut. 33:23.   7. Exod. 35:35.   8. I Kings 7:14.   9. Isa. 6:3.
10. Exod. 40:34.
1. Gen. 7:17. The quotation is not quite exact. The text reads: *And the waters increased and bore up the ark and it was lifted high above the earth.*
2. Or: *a young man.*   3. Ps. 89:20.
4. The preposition preceding the words, *the dust*, is not correctly quoted by Maimonides, who replaces *min* by *mit-tokh*, a preposition occurring in the verse quoted by him immediately afterwards.
5. I Kings 16:2.   6. I Kings 14:7.
7. Literally: every word of *heightening*.   8. Ps. 57:6.
9. The adjective *nissa*, derivin gfrom this root, means " high," and a similar meaning is also to be found in certain verbal forms.

verse, *And they bore aloft their corn upon their asses*,[10] uses the word in its first sense. And similar instances are frequent in cases in which the word is used to signify carrying and transporting, for this implies lifting in space. The second meaning of the term is found in: *And his kingdom shall be borne aloft;*[11] *And He carried them and bore them;*[12] *Wherefore do you bear yourselves high.*[13] Every *mention of bearing* that occurs with reference to God, may He be exalted, has this latter meaning. Thus: *Bear Thee on high, Thou Judge of the earth;*[14] *Thus saith the High, [He that is] borne on high.*[15] In these passages, the word means elevation, exalted station, and great worth, not height in space. Perhaps my saying elevation in degree, exalted station, and great worth, creates a difficulty for you. For you may ask:[16] how can you consider that many notions are included in one meaning?[17] However, it shall be made clear to you that in the opinion of those who have perfect apprehension, there should not be many attributive qualifications predicated of God; and that all the numerous attributive qualifications indicating any exaltation of Him and of His great worth, power, perfection, bounty, and various other things, refer to one and the same notion. That notion is His essence and nothing outside this essence. Chapters on the names and attributes will reach you later. In this chapter my purpose is to show that the words: *The High, [He that is] borne on high*, do not have the meaning and signification of height in space, but of elevation[18] in degree.

CHAPTER 21

To *pass* [*ᶜabor*]. The first meaning of this term is that of passage[1] in Arabic; and the first instances of its being used as concerned with | the movements of living beings over a certain distance in a straight line. Thus: *And he passed over them;*[2] *Pass before the people.*[3] Such instances are numerous. Subsequently the word was used figuratively to signify the

---

10. Gen. 42:26.   11. Num. 24:7.   12. Isa. 63:9.   13. Num. 16:3.   14. Ps. 94:2.
15. Isa. 57:15.   16. Literally: say.
17. The word *maᶜānī*, translated as "notions," is the plural of the word *maᶜnā*, translated as "meaning." The sentence might be translated literally as follows: How can you make many meanings out of one meaning?
18. In Arabic the same word is used as that which has been translated "height."
1. An Arabic word deriving from the same root as the Hebrew word dealt with in this chapter.
2. Gen. 33:3.   3. Exod. 17:5.

propagation of sounds in the air. Thus: *And they caused a voice to pass throughout the camp;*[4] *Which I hear the Lord's people cause to pass.*[5] Afterwards the word was figuratively used to signify the descent of the light and of the Indwelling[6] seen by the prophets *in the vision of prophecy*. Thus it says: *And behold a smoking furnace and a flaming torch that passed between these pieces.*[7] This happened *in a vision of prophecy*. For it says at the beginning of the story: *And a deep sleep fell upon Abram, and so on.*[8] It is in conformity with this figurative use that it is said: *And I shall pass through the land of Egypt,*[9] and that the term is used in all similar instances. Sometimes the term is applied figuratively to a man who, in accomplishing a certain action, has fallen into excess and overpassed the bounds. Thus it says: *And as a man whom wine has caused to overpass [the limit].*[10] The term is also applied sometimes to one who has been caused to miss[11] one objective and thereupon aimed at another objective and at another goal. Thus: *He shot an arrow, causing it to pass by.*[12] In my opinion the dictum of Scripture, *And the Lord passed by before his face,*[13] conforms to this last figurative use; the possessive suffix in the third person attached to the Hebrew word *face* refers to God,[14] may He be exalted. The *Sages* have likewise considered that the *face*[15] mentioned in the verse is that of God, may He be exalted.[16] Though they have mentioned this opinion while setting forth *legends* that are out of place here, this affords some corroboration for our view. Accordingly, the third person of the possessive suffix figuring in the Hebrew word *His face* refers to *the Holy One, blessed be He.*[17] The explanation of this, according to what I think and to what occurs to me, is that *Moses*, peace be on him, demanded a certain apprehension — namely, that which in its dictum, *But My face shall not be seen,*[18] is named *the seeing of the face* — and was promised an apprehension inferior to that which he had demanded. It is this latter apprehension that is named *the seeing of the back* in its dictum: *And thou shalt see My back.*[19] We have already given a hint as to this meaning in *Mishneh Torah*.[20] Scripture accordingly says in this passage

4. Exod. 36:6.   5. I Sam. 2:24.
6. *sakīna* in Arabic, corresponding to *shekhinah* in Hebrew.
7. Gen. 15:17.   8. Gen. 15:12.   9. Exod. 12:12.   10. Jer. 23:9.
11. Or according to Ibn Tibbon's interpretation: who has missed. The Arabic also permits the interpretation: who has overpassed.
12. I Sam. 20:36.   13. Exod. 34:6.   14. And not to Moses.
15. Literally: this *His face*.
16. Cf. B.T., Rosh Hashanah, 17b.
17. Literally: *His face* is the third person of *the Holy One, blessed be He.* "His face" is expressed in Hebrew in one word.
18. Exod. 33:23.   19. Exod. 33:23.
20. Yesodei ha-Torah, I 10.

that God, may He be exalted, hid from him the apprehension called that *of the face* and made him pass over to something different; | I mean the knowledge of the acts ascribed to Him, may He be exalted, which, as we shall explain,[21] are deemed to be multiple attributes. When I say He hid from him, I intend to signify that this apprehension is hidden and inaccessible in its very nature. Moreover every perfect man — after his intellect has attained the cognition of whatever in its nature can be grasped — when longing for another apprehension beyond that which he has achieved, cannot but have his faculty of apprehension deceived or destroyed — as we shall explain in one of the chapters of this Treatise[22] — unless divine help attends him. As Scripture says: *And I will cover thee with My hand until I have passed.*[23] The [Aramaic] *translation*[24] of the Bible, when rendering this verse, does what it customarily does in similar cases.[25] For in every case in which it finds that a thing is ascribed to God to which the doctrine of corporeality or some concomitants of this doctrine are attached, it assumes that the nomen regens[26] has been omitted and considers that the ascription concerns something expressed by a term that is the nomen regens[27] of the genitive God and that has been omitted. Thus when Scripture says, *And, behold, the Lord stood erect upon it,*[28] it translates: *The glory of the Lord stood arrayed above it.* Again when Scripture says, *The Lord watch between me and thee,*[29] it translates: *The word of the Lord shall watch [between me and thee].* This occurs throughout the translation of [Onqelos],[30] peace be upon him. He does the same thing with regard to the dictum of Scripture, *And the Lord passed by before his face,*[31] which he translates: *The Lord caused his Indwelling*[32] *to pass before his face, and he called.*[33] Thus according to him it was indubitably a created thing that *passed by*; he considers that in the expression, *his face*, the possessive suffix in the third person refers to *Moses our Master*. The interpretation of *before his face* would accordingly be: in his presence, as when Scripture says: *So the present passed before his face.*[34] This too is an excellent interpretation that may be approved of. A

21. Cf. I 34.   22. Cf. I 32.   23. Exod. 33:22.   24. That of Onqelos.
25. Literally: went according to its habit in these matters.
26. The Arabic word is *muḍāf*, the primary sense of which is "adjunct." Accordingly it is implied that in grammatical analysis the word thus described is less important than the genitive to which it is an adjunct. The term "nomen regens" obviously implies the opposite.
27. Cf. preceding note.   28. Gen. 28:13.   29. Gen. 31:49.
30. Literally: his translation.   31. Exod. 34:6.   32. *shekhinah.*
33. The Hebrew word that may be translated, *and he called*, is omitted by Maimonides when he quotes the Hebrew text of Exod. 34:6, but occurs in the Aramaic translation of this passage as quoted by him.
34. Gen. 32:22.

corroboration of the interpretation of *Onqelos the Proselyte, may his memory be blessed*, may be found in the dictum of Scripture: *And it shall come to pass, while My glory passeth by.*[35] This verse makes it clear that what *passeth* is a thing related[36] to God, may He be exalted, not the essence[37] of God, may His name be sublime; and it is thus of this *glory* that Scripture says, *Until I have passed by*, and, *And the Lord passed by before his face*. If it is necessary to assume an omitted nomen regens, as is always done by *Onqelos* — for, in accord with the context, sometimes he takes | the omitted word to be *glory*, and sometimes he takes it to be *Indwelling*, and sometimes he takes it to be *word* — we, for our part too, take the nomen regens omitted here to be *voice*. The assumption accordingly would be that the verse should read: *And the voice of the Lord passed by before him and called*. We have already explained that the Hebrew language uses the word *passage* in a figurative sense with reference to *voice*. Thus: *And they caused a voice to pass throughout the camp.*[38] In the verse in question it would[39] be the *voice* that *called*. You should not consider it as improbable that a *call* is ascribed to a *voice*, for it is in these very words[40] that expression is given to the fact that God, may He be exalted, spoke to *Moses*. For it says: *Then he heard the voice speaking unto him.*[41] Just as in this latter verse *speech* is ascribed to the *voice*, a *call* is attributed to the *voice* in the verse we are discussing. Sometimes this, I mean the ascription of *speech*[42] and of a *call* to a *voice*, occurs quite explicitly. Thus it says: *A voice saith: Call. And he said: What shall I call?*[43] According to this assumption, the interpretation of our verse would thus be: a voice from God passed by in his presence and called: *Lord, Lord*. The repetition of the word *Lord* would be due to its being a call, for He, may He be exalted, would be the one who is called. It would be like saying: *Moses, Moses; Abraham, Abraham*. This too is a very fine interpretation.

You should not consider as blameworthy the fact that this profound subject, which is remote from our apprehension, should be subject to many different interpretations. For this does no harm with respect to that toward which we direct ourselves. And you are free to choose whatever belief you wish. You may believe that the great station attained by [Moses] was

---

35. Exod. 33:22.   36. Or: ascribed.
37. *dhātuh*. The term may be translated either as "God's essence" or as "God Himself."
38. Exod. 36:6.
39. According to this explanation.
40. This statement contains a minor inaccuracy. In one verse the two Hebrew words are *qol* and *va-yiqra*. In the other the words are *haq-qol medabber*. This is pointed out by Maimonides two sentences further on.
41. Num. 7:89.   42. *amirah*.   43. Isa. 40:6.

indubitably, in its entirety, *a vision of prophecy* and that he solely desired intellectual apprehensions—everything, namely, that which he had demanded, that which was denied to him, and that which he apprehended, being intellectual and admitting of no recourse to the senses, as we had interpreted in the first place. Or you may believe that there was, in addition to this intellectual apprehension, an apprehension due to the sense of sight, which, however, had for its object a created thing, through seeing which the perfection of intellectual apprehension might be achieved. This would be the interpretation of this passage by *Onqelos*,[44] unless one assumes that this ocular[45] apprehension also occurred in *the vision of prophecy*, | as is stated with regard to *Abraham: Behold a smoking furnace and a flaming torch that passed.*[46] Or again you may believe that there was in addition an apprehension due to the sense of hearing; that which *passed by before his face* being the *voice*, which is likewise indubitably a created thing. Choose whatever opinion you wish, inasmuch as our only purpose is that you should not believe that when Scripture says, in the verse we are discussing, *He passed by*, the phrase is analogous to *Pass before the people.*[47] For God, may He be honored and magnified, is not a body, and it is not permitted to ascribe motion to Him. It is therefore impossible that He should have been said *to pass by* if the word is used in the first meaning given to it in the Hebrew language.

CHAPTER 22

To come [*boʾ*]. In the Hebrew language the word *coming* has been given a meaning that refers to the coming of a living being, I mean his drawing near some place or some other individual. Thus: *Thy brother came with guile.*[1] The word has also been given a meaning that refers to a living being entering some place. Thus: *And Joseph came home;*[2] *When ye be come to the land.*[3] This term is also used figuratively to denote the coming about[4] of something that is not at all corporeal. Thus: *When thy words come to*

---

44. Literally: just as Onqelos interpreted this.
45. In Arabic an adjective derived from a word meaning "sight."
46. Gen. 15:17.
47. Exod. 17:5; in this passage Moses is ordered to pass.
 1. Gen. 27:35.   2. Gen. 43:26.   3. Exod. 12:25.
 4. *ḥulūl*. One of the primary senses of this word is "the act of descending."

pass we may do thee honor;[5] *From the things that shall come upon thee.*[6] It is, in consequence, applied figuratively even to certain privations.[7] Thus: *Yet trouble came;*[8] *And darkness came.*[9] Since the term had been thus figuratively applied to what is in no way a body, it was also figuratively applied to the Creator, may He be honored and magnified, either to the descent[10] of His decree or to that of His Indwelling. It is in view of this figurative use that it is said: *Lo, I come unto thee in a thick cloud;*[11] *For the Lord, the God of Israel, comes through it.*[12] All passages similar to these signify the descent of the Indwelling.[13] The verse, *And the Lord my God shall come, and all the holy ones with thee,*[14] signifies, on the other hand, the descent of God's decree or the realization of the promises made by Him through His prophets. This last notion is signified in | the dictum: *All the holy ones with thee.* Scripture says, as it were: *And the word of the Lord my God shall come through all the holy ones who are with thee;* the people of *Israel* being the one addressed.

CHAPTER 23

Going out [al-*yeṣiʾah*] is the contrary of *coming*. The term is used to denote the going-out of a body, which may be a living being or not, from a place in which it rested to another place. Thus: *They were gone out of the city;*[1] *If fire break out.*[2] The term is applied figuratively to the manifestation of things that are in no way a body. Thus: *The word went out of the king's mouth;*[3] *When this deed of the queen shall come abroad,*[4] meaning the propagation[5] of the matter; *For out of Zion shall go forth the law.*[6] Thus also: *The sun was risen*[7] *upon the earth;*[8] I refer to the manifestation of the light. Every *mention of going out* occurring in Scripture with reference to Him, may He be exalted, conforms to this figurative use. Thus: *For, behold, the Lord goeth out of His place,*[9] that is, His decree, which at present is hidden from us, will become manifest. I refer to the coming into being of

---

5. Judg. 13:17.   6. Isa. 47:13.
7. The term is used here in the technical Aristotelian sense.
8. Job 30:26.   9. Job 30:26.   10. *ḥulūl.* Cf. n. 4, this chap.   11. Exod. 19:9.
12. Ezek. 44:2.   13. *sakīnah.*   14. Zech. 14:5.
1. Gen. 44:4.   2. Exod. 22:5.   3. Esther 7:8.
4. Literally: *shall go out.* Esther 1:17.   5. *nufūdh.* The word also means "effect."
6. Isa. 2:3.   7. Literally: *gone out.*   8. Gen. 19:23.   9. Isa. 26:21.

something[10] after its not having existed, for everything that comes into being from God, may He be exalted, is attributed to His decree. Thus: *By the word of the Lord were the heavens made, and all the host of them by the breath of His mouth.*[11] In this verse God's acts are likened to those that proceed from kings, whose instrument in giving effect[12] to their will is speech. However, God, may He be exalted, does not require an instrument by means of which He could act, for His acts are accomplished exclusively by means of His will alone; neither is there any speech at all, as shall be made clear.[13] Inasmuch as the term *going out*, as we have made clear, was figuratively applied to the manifestation of an act of God[14] — for Scripture says: *For, behold, the Lord goeth out of His place*[15] — the term *returning* [*shibah*] is figuratively applied to the cessation of such an act likewise brought about in virtue of God's will. It says accordingly, *I will go and return to My place,*[16] the signification of which is that the *Indwelling* | that had been among us is removed. This removal is followed[17] by a privation of providence, as far as we are concerned.[18] As it says by way of a threat: *And I will hide My face from them, and they shall be devoured.*[19] For a privation of providence leaves one abandoned and a target to all that may happen and come about, so that his ill and weal come about according to chance. How terrible is this threat! It is to this that it refers in its dictum: *I will go and return to My place.*[20]

CHAPTER 24

Going [*al-halikhah*] too is one of the terms referring to some particular motions of living beings. Thus: *And Jacob went on his way.*[1] This usage is frequent. Sometimes this term is used figuratively to designate the extension of bodies more subtle than the bodies of living beings. Thus: *And the waters went and decreased;*[2] *And fire went down unto the earth.*[3]

---

10. Literally: of that which comes into being.　　11. Ps. 33:6.
12. *tanfīdh.* The verbal form derives from the same root as *nufūdh* (cf. n. 5, this chap.), also occurring in this chapter and translated "propagation."
13. Cf. I 65.
14. Literally: to the manifestation of an act of His acts.　　15. Isa. 26:21.　　16. Hos. 5:15.
17. According to the strict letter of the Arabic text, the Indwelling, rather than the removal, is followed by the privation of providence.
18. More or less literally: of providence among us.
19. Deut. 31:17.　　20. Cf. this chapter, above.
1. Gen. 32:2.　　2. Gen. 8:5. I.e., were gradually decreasing.　　3. Exod. 9:23.

Subsequently this term was used figuratively to designate the spread and the manifestation of a certain thing even if the latter were in no way corporeal. Thus it says: *The voice thereof shall go like a serpent.*[4] Similar is its dictum: *The voice of the Lord God going about in the garden.*[5] It is the *voice* that was said to be *going about*. Every *mention of going* that occurs with reference to God, may He be exalted, conforms to this figurative use. I mean that with respect to what is incorporeal, it is used figuratively to denote either the spread of a thing[6] or the withdrawal of providence, which, in the case of a living being, has its analogy in the latter's turning away from a thing through *going*. And just as the withdrawal of providence is referred to as *the hiding of the face* — as in its dictum: *As for Me, I will surely hide My face*[7] — it also is referred to as *going*, which has the meaning | to turn away from a thing. Thus Scripture says: *I will go and return to My place.*[8] As for its dictum, *And the anger of the Lord was kindled against them, and He went away,*[9] the two significations subsist together in the passage. I mean the signification of a withdrawal of providence referred to by means of the term "turning away," and the signification of a spread, diffusion, and manifestation of a thing. I mean to say that it was the *anger* that *went* and extended toward the two.[10] For this reason, [Miriam] *became leprous, as white as snow.*[11] The *term going* is also applied figuratively to living a good life,[12] without in any way moving a body. Thus it says: *And thou shalt go in His ways;*[13] *After the Lord your God shall ye go;*[14] *Come ye, and let us walk in the light of the Lord.*[15]

---

4. Jer. 46:22.   5. Gen. 3:8.
6. *amr*. The word also means "command." However, other passages in this chapter seem to indicate that in this case the word should be translated "thing" or "matter."
7. Deut. 31:18.   8. Hos. 5:15.   9. Num. 12:9.
10. Viz., Aaron and Miriam.   11. Num. 12:10.
12. *Li'l-sayr bi'l-sīra al-fāḍila*. Literally: to going (or walking) a good or virtuous life. The word *sīra*, meaning "life" or "the conduct of life," derives from the verb *sāra*, "to go" or "walk."
13. Deut. 28:9.   14. Deut. 13:5.   15. Isa. 2:5.

CHAPTER 25

Shakhon. It is known that the meaning of this verb is, to dwell. Thus: *And he was dwelling by the terebinths of Mamre;*[1] *And it came to pass, while Israel dwelt.*[2] This is well known and generally accepted. Now dwelling signifies a permanent stay in a place of one's abode. Accordingly, when a living being has his abode in a place, by which either a general or a particular place may be meant, it is said of him that he dwells in that place, even if he undoubtedly moves within it. This verb is also figuratively applied to things that are not living beings and in fact to everything that is permanent and is attached to another thing. Of all such things the *term dwelling* may be used, even in cases in which the thing to which they are attached is not a place and they themselves not living beings. Thus it says: *Let a cloud dwell upon it.*[3] For there is no doubt that a *cloud* is not a living being, nor a *day* in any way a body,[4] being a portion of time. It is on account of this latter figurative sense that the verb is applied figuratively to God, may He be exalted — I mean to the permanence of His Indwelling[5] or His providence in | whatever place they may subsist in permanent fashion or toward whatever matter providence may be permanently directed.[6] Thus it is said: *And the glory of the Lord dwelt;*[7] *And I will dwell among the children of Israel;*[8] *And the good will of Him that dwelt in the bush.*[9] In every case in which this occurs with reference to God, it is used in the sense of the permanence of His Indwelling — I mean His created light — in a place, or the permanence of providence with regard to a certain matter. Each passage should be understood according to its context.[10]

1. Gen. 14:13.   2. Gen. 35:22.   3. Job 3:5.
4. A reference to the passage in Job. Job wishes that the cloud should dwell upon a day (Job 3:5).
5. *sakīna.*
6. Literally: or every matter in which providence subsists permanently.
7. Exod. 24:16.   8. Exod. 29:45.   9. Deut. 33:16.
10. Literally: each place according to itself.

CHAPTER 26

You know their dictum that refers in inclusive fashion to all the kinds of interpretation connected with this subject, namely, their saying: *The Torah speaketh in the language of the sons of man.*[1] The meaning of this is that everything that all men are capable of understanding and representing to themselves at first thought has been ascribed to Him as necessarily belonging to God, may He be exalted. Hence attributes indicating corporeality have been predicated of Him in order to indicate that He, may He be exalted, exists, inasmuch as the multitude cannot at first conceive of any existence save that of a body alone; thus that which is neither a body nor existent in a body does not exist in their opinion. In a similar way one has ascribed to Him, may He be exalted, everything that in our opinion[2] is a perfection in order to indicate that He is perfect in every manner of perfection and that no deficiency whatever mars[3] Him. Thus none of the things apprehended by the multitude as a deficiency or a privation are predicated of Him. Hence it is not predicated of Him that He eats, drinks, sleeps, is ill, does an injustice, or that He has any similar characteristic. On the other hand, everything that the multitude consider a perfection is predicated of Him, even if it is only a perfection in relation to ourselves — for in relation to Him, may He be exalted, all things that we consider perfections are the very extreme of deficiency. However, | if people imagined that this human perfection was lacking in Him, may He be exalted, this would constitute, in their opinion, a deficiency in Him. Thus you know that motion belongs to the perfection of a living being and is necessary to such a being for its perfection. For just as it requires eating and drinking in order to replace what has been dissolved, it also requires motion in order to direct itself toward what agrees with it and to escape from what disagrees. There is, accordingly, no difference between, on the one hand, predicating eating and drinking of God, may He be exalted, and, on the other, predicating movement of Him. However, in accordance with *the language of the sons of man,* I mean the imagination of the multitude, eating and drinking are considered in their opinion as a deficiency with reference to God, whereas motion is not considered as a deficiency with reference to Him; and this notwithstanding the fact that only need obliges recourse to motion. It has

1. B.T., Yebamoth, 71a; B.T., Baba Meṣiᶜa, 31b.
2. Apparently that of men in general.
3. Literally: mingles with Him.

already been demonstrated that everything that is capable of motion is endowed with a magnitude that, without any doubt, can be divided. And it shall be demonstrated further on that He, may He be exalted, is not endowed with magnitude, and that in consequence motion does not pertain to Him, and that rest should not be predicated of Him either — for it can only be predicated of one who is characterized by the capacity for motion. All these terms indicative of various kinds of motions of living beings are predicated of God, may He be exalted, in the way that we have spoken of, just as life is predicated of Him. For motion is an accident attaching to living beings. There is no doubt that when corporeality is abolished, all these predicates are likewise abolished. I mean such terms as *to descend, to ascend, to go, to stand erect, to stand, to go round, to sit, to dwell, to go out, to come, to pass,* and all terms similar to these. To speak at length of this matter would be superfluous, were it not for the notions to which the minds of the multitude are accustomed. For this reason it behooves to explain the matter to those whose souls grasp at human perfection and, by dint of expatiating a little on the point in question just as we have done, to put an end to the fantasies that come to them from the age of infancy. |

CHAPTER 27

Onqelos the Proselyte was very perfect in the Hebrew and Syrian languages and directed his effort toward the abolition of the belief in God's corporeality. Hence he interprets in accordance with its meaning every attribute that Scripture predicates of God and that might lead toward the belief in corporeality. Thus whenever he encounters one of the terms indicative of one of the kinds of motion, he makes motion to mean the manifestation and appearance of a created light, I mean the *Indwelling* or the action of providence. Thus he renders, *The Lord will descend,*[1] by the words, *The Lord will manifest Himself; And the Lord descended,*[2] by the words, *And the Lord manifested Himself.* He does not translate: *And the Lord came down.* He also translates, *I will descend now and see,*[3] by, *I will manifest Myself now and see.* This occurs continually in his interpretation. However, he translates, *I will descend with thee into Egypt,*[4] by, *I will go*

1. Exod. 19:11.   2. Exod. 19:20.   3. Gen. 18:21.   4. Gen. 46:4.

7

down with thee to Egypt.[5] And this is a very marvellous story that indicates the perfection of this distinguished man as well as the fine quality of his interpretation and of his understanding of things as they really are. This translation also reveals to us an important matter regarding prophecy. For in the beginning of the story, Scripture says:[6] *And God spoke unto Israel in the visions of the night, and said, Jacob, Jacob, and so on. And He said, I am God, and so on. I will descend with thee into Egypt.* Now in view of the fact that the beginning of the passage includes the statement that this happened *in the visions of the night,*[7] Onqelos did not think that it would be unseemly to conform wholly to the text in his rendering of what was said *in the visions of the night.* This was the correct procedure. For this passage contains a relation of what was said and not a relation of a story of such as is to be found in the verse: *And the Lord descended upon Mount Sinai.*[8] For that is a relation of what took place within matters having existence. On this account [Onqelos] uses in connection with this the term "manifestation" and discards in his rendering everything indicative of the existence of motion.[9] On the other hand, he left in his translation the things of the imagination — I mean the retelling of what was said to him — as they are according to the text. This is a marvellous thing. Through this your attention will be drawn to the fact that there is | a great difference between that which is said to happen[10] *in a dream* or *in the visions of the night,* that which is said to happen *in a vision* and *apparition,*[11] and that of which it is said without qualification:[12] *And the word of the Lord came unto me, saying,* or, *And the Lord said unto me.* In my opinion it is also possible that *Onqelos* interpreted the word *God*[13] occurring here as signifying an angel, and that, on this account, he did not think it improper that he should have Him say: *I will go down with thee to Egypt.*[14] Do not think it unseemly that he should have believed that *God* means here an angel, though He says to him: *I am God, the God of thy father.*[15] For this is also said in the same terms by an angel. Do you not see that [Jacob] says: *And the angel of God said unto me in a dream: Jacob; and I said: Here am I;*[16] and that at the end of the relation of what he said to him you find the words: *I am the God of Bethel, where*

---

5. I.e., in this case Onqelos gives a literal translation of the Hebrew sentence.
6. Gen. 46:2–3.   7. Gen. 46:2.   8. Exod. 19:20.
9. Obviously motion in God is meant.   10. I.e., to Jacob.
11. Which are not said to have taken place in the night. The word *mahazeh*, translated in the text as *apparition*, means etymologically *vision*, as does the word *mar'eh* (translated in the text as *vision*).
12. Literally: absolutely.   13. *Elohim.*
14. Gen. 46:4 is meant; the text is quoted in Aramaic.
15. Gen. 46:3.   16. Gen. 31:11.

thou didst anoint a pillar, and where thou didst vow a vow unto Me.[17] Now there is no doubt that *Jacob* made a vow to God and not to the angel. However, this happens continually in the dicta of the prophets, I mean the retelling of things told to them by an angel in the name of God as if God had spoken to them. In all of them there is an omission of the nomen regens. It is as though he who addresses the prophet said: *I am the messenger of the God of thy father; I am the messenger of God who appeared to thee in Bethel,* or used similar formulae.

Concerning prophecy and its degrees and concerning the angels, a lengthy exposition will be made in accordance with the purpose of this Treatise.

CHAPTER 28

Foot [*regel*] is an equivocal term. It is a term denoting a foot.[1] Thus: *Foot for foot.*[2] It also occurs with the meaning of following. Thus: *Go thee out and all the people that are in thy feet*[3] — the meaning of which is, that follow thee. It is likewise used in the sense of causation. Thus: *And the Lord hath blessed thee for my foot*[4] — I being the cause, that is to say, for my sake. For when a thing | exists for the sake of some other thing, the latter is the cause of the former. This meaning is frequently employed. Thus: *For the foot of the cattle that goeth before me and for the foot of the children.*[5] Accordingly when Scripture says: *And His feet shall stand in that day upon the Mount of Olives,*[6] it signifies thereby the establishment of the things He has caused[7] — I mean of the wonders that will then become manifest at that place[8] and of which God, may He be exalted, is the cause, I mean the maker. This interpretation was adopted by *Jonathan ben Uziel,* peace be on him. He translates:[9] *And He will manifest Himself in His might on that day upon the Mount of Olives.* In a similar way he translates

17. Gen. 31:13.
1. I.e., the part of the body. Maimonides uses the Arabic word to explain the Hebrew term of which he treats.
2. Exod. 21:24.   3. Exod. 11:8.   4. Gen. 30:30.   5. Gen. 33:14.
6. Zech. 14:4.
7. Literally: the establishment of his causes. The word *sabab,* "cause," is sometimes used by Maimonides in the sense of "effect."
8. I.e., on the Mount of Olives.
9. Literally: said. Jonathan translated the Bible into Aramaic.

every part of the body having the function of grasping or moving by the terms *His might*, for all of them are intended to signify actions proceeding from God's will. Now as for its dictum: *And there was under his feet, as it were, a work of the whiteness of sapphire stone.*[10] The interpretation of *Onqelos* is, as you know, as follows. He considers that the third person suffix, "his,"[11] in the words *his feet* refers to God's *throne*; accordingly he translates: *And under the throne of His glory*. Understand this and admire how far *Onqelos* was from belief in the corporeality of God and from everything that leads to it even though it be by the longest way. For he does not say: *And under His throne*. For should the term *throne* have been referred to God in the sense that has been explained above, this would have entailed the consequence that He would have been conceived of as sitting upon a body and thus would have entailed the belief in corporeality. Accordingly [Onqelos] referred the term *throne* to *His glory*, I mean to the *Indwelling*,[12] which is a created light. Similarly he renders in his *translation* the verse: *For my hand upon the throne of the Lord*,[13] as: *From God whose Indwelling is on the throne of glory*. And in a similar way you find on the tongue of the whole nation the words: *the throne of glory*.

We have gone beyond the subject of the chapter in order to deal with a matter that will be made clear in other chapters. I shall now return to the subject of this chapter. As for the interpretation of *Onqelos*, you already know it. However, the final end of the matter[14] consists in the rejection of the doctrine of the corporeality of God. He does not explain to us what they apprehended[15] and what is intended by this parable. He acts in a similar way in all other passages; that is to say, he is not concerned with such significations, | but only with the rejection of the doctrine of the corporeality of God. For this rejection is a matter of demonstration and is necessary in belief.[16] Therefore he made a decision about it and translated accordingly. On the other hand the explanation of the meaning of parables is a suppositious matter, for their intention may be this or that. They are also most hidden matters, and it is not a part of the foundations of belief[17] to understand them, nor are they easily grasped by the multitude. Hence [Onqelos] did not concern himself with their signification.

As for us, it certainly is incumbent upon me in accordance with the purpose of this Treatise to interpret something of this parable. I shall

10. Exod. 24:10.   11. In Hebrew "his" is a third person possessive suffix.
12. *shekhinah*.   13. Exod. 17:16.
14. I.e., the end with a view to which Onqelos makes this translation.
15. I.e., Moses, Aaron, and the elders of Israel, mentioned in Exod. 24:9.
16. I.e., religious belief.   17. I.e., religious belief.

accordingly say that when it says, *under His feet*, it intends to signify: He being the cause and because of Him, as we have already explained. For what they apprehended[18] was the true reality of first matter, which derives from Him, may He be exalted, He being the cause of its existence. Consider its dictum: *As it were, a work of the whiteness of sapphire stone.* If the intended signification had been the color, it would have said: *As it were, the whiteness of sapphire stone.* The word *work* was added, because Matter, as you know, is always receptive and passive, if one considers its essence, and is not active except by accident. Form, on the other hand, is in its essence always active, as has been made clear in the books on natural science, and is passive only by accident. That is why Scripture applied to the first matter the expression: *as it were, a work.* As for the *whiteness of sapphire stone*, the expression is intended to signify transparency and not a white color. For the whiteness of a crystal[19] is not due to a white color, but solely to its transparency. And, as has been demonstrated in the books on natural science, transparency is not a color; for if it were a color, it would not let all the colors be seen behind it and would not receive all of them.[20] Now a transparent body receives all the colors in succession just because it lacks a color of its own. In this it resembles the first matter, which in respect of its true reality lacks all forms and on this account is capable of receiving all forms in succession. Accordingly | their apprehension[21] had as its object the first matter and the relation of the latter to God, inasmuch as it is the first among the things He has created that necessitates generation and corruption; and God is its creator ex nihilo.[22] A disquisition on this notion will come further on.[23] Know that you require such an interpretation even according to the interpretation of *Onqelos*, who translates: *And under the throne of His glory.* I mean to say that the first matter is also in true reality under the heaven that is called the *throne*. A pointer to this marvellous[24] interpretation was only given to me by a dictum of *Rabbi Eliezer ben Hyrqanos* that I came across. You will see it in one of the chapters of this Treatise.[25] The purpose of everyone endowed with intellect should be wholly directed to rejecting corporeality with respect to God, may He be exalted, and to considering all these apprehensions as intellectual, not sensory. Understand this and reflect on it.

18. I.e., Moses, Aaron, and the elders of Israel.
19. *billūr*. The use of this Arabic word may mean that Maimonides considered that the Hebrew word *sappir* (sapphire) meant "crystal."
20. I.e., receive its coloring from them.
21. That of Moses, Aaron, and the elders of Israel.
22. *mubdiʾuhā*. The Arabic word generally connotes a creator ex nihilo, but it is less explicit than this Latin-English expression.
23. Cf. II 26.   24. *gharīb*. The word generally means "strange."   25. Cf. II 26.

CHAPTER 29

*S*orrow [*ʿeṣeb*] is an equivocal term. It is a term denoting pain and aching: *In sorrow thou shalt bring forth children.*[1] It is also a term denoting anger: *And his father had not caused him to be sorry at any time,*[2] which means that he had not angered him. *For he was sorrowful for the sake of David;*[3] he was angry for his sake. The term also denotes contrariety and disobedience: *They rebelled and caused sorrow to His holy spirit;*[4] *And cause Him sorrow in the desert;*[5] *If there be in me any way of causing sorrow;*[6] *Every day they cause sorrow*[7] *to my words.*[8] In accordance with the second or third sense it is said: *He*[9] *sorrowed unto His heart,*[10] In accordance with the second sense, the interpretation of the verse would be that God was angry with them[11] because of their evil action. As for Scripture saying, *unto his heart*, it uses a similar expression in the story of *Noah,* namely: *And God said unto His heart.*[12] Hear its meaning. The matter with regard to which it is said of | a man that he *said in his heart* or *said unto his heart* is a matter to which that man does not give utterance and that he does not tell to somebody else. Similarly it is said of every matter willed by God of which He does not speak to a prophet at the time when He accomplished an act corresponding to His will in this regard: *God said unto His heart.* It is thus likened to the human matter in virtue of the continual use of the rule: *The Torah speaketh in the language of the sons of man.*[13] This is clear and manifest. Inasmuch as it is not made clear in the *Torah* with regard to the disobedience of *the generation of the flood* that an envoy of God was sent to them at that time, nor that prohibitions were imposed on them and that they were threatened with destruction, it is said of them that God was angry with them *in His heart.* Similarly in regard to His will that there should not be another *flood.* He did not say to a prophet at that time: Go and inform them of this. For this reason it is said: *unto His heart.* As for the interpretation of the passage, *He sorrowed unto His heart,* according to the third sense, its meaning[14] would be as follows: man went

---

1. Gen. 3:16.   2. I Kings 1:6.   3. I Sam. 20:34.
4. Isa. 63:10.   5. Ps. 78:40.   6. Ps. 139:24.
7. I.e., disobey.   8. Ps. 56:6.   9. God.   10. Gen. 6:6.
11. With Adam and Eve.   12. Gen. 8:21.
13. B.T., Yebamoth, 71a; B.T., Baba Meṣiʿa, 31b.
14. Literally: its interpretation. But the word used in Arabic is not the one occurring at the beginning of the sentence.

contrary to the will of God regarding him. For the term *heart* is also used
to designate the will, as we shall make clear when treating of the equivocality of the term *heart*.[15]

CHAPTER 30

To eat [*'akhol*]. The first meaning given to this word in the Hebrew
language signifies the taking of food by living beings. This does not
require an example. Subsequently the Hebrew language saw two
notions in the action of eating. One of them was the destruction and
disappearance of the thing eaten, I mean the corruption of its form that first
takes place. The other notion is that of the growth of the living being due
to the food he takes, the continuance of his life[1] due to it, and the duration
of the existence, as well as the good condition, of all the forces of his body,
likewise due to it. In accordance with | the one notion, the *term eating* is
figuratively applied to all destruction and undoing and, in general, to all
putting-off of a form. Thus: *And the land of your enemies shall eat you up;*[2]
A land that eateth up its inhabitants;[3] *Ye shall be eaten by the sword;*[4] *Shall
the sword eat;*[5] *And the fire of the Lord burnt among them, and ate them up
that were in the uttermost part of the camp.*[6] *He*[7] *is a fire that eateth,*[8] which
means that He destroys those who disobey Him as a fire destroys that which
is in its power. This use of the word is frequent. In accordance with the
last notion, the *term eating* is applied figuratively to knowledge, learning,
and, in general, the intellectual apprehensions through which the permanence[9] of the human form endures in the most perfect of states, just as
the body endures through food in the finest of its states. Thus: *Come ye,
buy and eat;*[10] *Hearken diligently unto Me, and eat ye that which is good;*[11]
It is not good to eat much honey;[12] *My son, eat thou honey, for it is good,
and the honeycomb is sweet to thy taste; so know thou wisdom to be unto thy
soul.*[13] This use is also frequent in the speech of the *Sages*, I mean the

15. Cf. I 38.
1. Literally: of his remaining. *baqā'* in Arabic.   2. Lev. 26:38.
3. Num. 13:32.   4. Isa. 1:20.   5. II Sam. 2:26.   6. Num. 11:1.
7. I.e., God.   8. Deut. 4:24.
9. Or: the remaining. In Arabic the same word is used as that referred to in n. 1, this
chap.
10. Isa. 55:1.   11. Isa. 55:2.   12. Prov. 25:27.   13. Prov. 24:13–14.

designation of knowledge as eating. Thus: *Come, eat fat meat at the house of Raba.*[14] They have also said: *All eating and drinking referred to in this book*[15] *signify wisdom exclusively,*[16] or, according to some copies, *the Torah.* Similarly they[17] often designate knowledge as water. Thus: *Ho, every one that thirsteth, come ye for water.*[18] Inasmuch as this use has become so frequent and widespread in the Hebrew language that it has become, as it were, the first meaning,[19] the words meaning hunger and thirst are likewise employed to designate lack of knowledge and of apprehension. Thus: *I will send a famine in the land, not a famine of bread nor a thirst for water, but of hearing the words of the Lord;*[20] *My soul thirsteth for God, for the living God.*[21] This use is frequent. *Jonathan ben Uziel,* peace be on him, translates[22] the verse, *With joy shall ye draw water out of the wells of salvation,*[23] by the words: *With joy shall you receive a new teaching from the chosen of the righteous.* Consider accordingly | that he interprets the word *water* as being the knowledge that will be received in those days. And he takes the Hebrew word for *wells*—*ma^cyene*—to be the equivalent of *me^ceyne ha^cedah*;[24] I mean thereby the notables[25] who are the men of knowledge. And he[26] says: *From the chosen of the righteous,* as *righteousness* is true *salvation.* See accordingly how he interprets every word in this *verse* with a view to the notion of knowledge and learning. Understand this.

14. B.T., Baba Bathra, 22a.   15. The Ecclesiast.
16. Midrash Qoheleth, 3:13. According to the present text of this Midrash, when the Ecclesiast speaks of eating, he refers solely to the Torah and to good works.
17. As the example in the following sentence shows, the third plural used in this passage refers to Scripture, and not or not only to the talmudic Sages.
18. Isa. 55:1.
19. The Arabic word used here signifies "conventional meaning."
20. Amos 8:11.   21. Ps. 42:3.   22. Into Aramaic.   23. Isa. 12:3.
24. Literally: *from the important people of the community.* The word *me^ceyne*—which, if the vocalization is not taken into account, is written in Hebrew in the same way as *ma^cyane* (sources)—means "from the eyes," "from the sources," and (as Maimonides interprets it) "from the notables." Num. 15:24.
25. *al-a^cyān.* This Arabic term derives from the same root as the Hebrew word in question (see preceding note) and has the same range of meanings.
26. Jonathan ben Uziel.

CHAPTER 31

K now that the human intellect has objects of apprehension that it is within its power and according to its nature to apprehend. On the other hand, in that which exists[1] there also are existents and matters that, according to its nature, it is not capable of apprehending in any way or through any cause;[2] the gates of their apprehension are shut before it. There are also in that which exists things of which the intellect may apprehend one state while not being cognizant of other states. The fact that it apprehends does not entail the conclusion that it can apprehend all things — just as the senses have apprehensions but it is not within their power to apprehend at whatever distance the objects of apprehension may happen to be. Similarly with regard to all other bodily faculties, for the fact that a man is able to carry two hundred-weights does not mean that he is able to carry ten. The difference in capacity existing between the individuals of the species[3] with regard to sensory apprehensions and all the other bodily faculties is manifest and clear to all men. However, it has a limit, inasmuch as these capacities[4] cannot attain to every distance however far away nor to every degree however great it may happen to be. The identical rule obtains with regard to human intellectual apprehensions. There are great differences in capacity between the individuals of the species. This also is manifest and very clear to the men of knowledge. It may thus happen that whereas one individual discovers a certain notion by himself through his speculation, another individual | is not able ever to understand that notion. Even if it were explained to him for a very long time by means of every sort of expression and parable, his mind would not penetrate to it in any way, but would turn back without understanding it. This difference in capacity is likewise not infinite, for man's intellect indubitably has a limit at which it stops. There are therefore things regarding which it has become clear to man that it is impossible to apprehend them. And he will not find that his soul longs for knowledge of them, inasmuch as he is aware of the

1. The Arabic word *wujūd*, which usually means "existence," is often used by Maimonides with the meaning "that which exists" or "the totality of that which exists." In the text to which this note refers, the word seems to have the latter meaning.
2. *sabab*. In Maimonides' peculiar use of the term it may also mean "effect."
3. The Arabic word *al-nawᶜ* (the species), most probably but not quite certainly, refers in this passage to only the human species.
4. Literally: and the matter. These words may refer to the capacities or to their difference. The meaning in any case remains practically identical.

impossibility of such knowledge and of there being no gate through which one might enter in order to attain it. Of this nature is our ignorance of the number of the stars of heaven and whether that number is even or odd, as well as our ignorance of the number of the species of living beings, minerals, plants, and other similar things.

On the other hand, there are things for the apprehension of which man will find that he has a great longing. The sway of the intellect endeavoring to seek for, and to investigate, their true reality exists at every time and in every group of men engaged in speculation. With regard to such things there is a multiplicity of opinions, disagreement arises between the men engaged in speculation, and doubts crop up; all this because the intellect is attached to an apprehension of these things, I mean to say because of its longing for them; and also because everyone thinks that he has found a way by means of which he will know the true reality of the matter. Now it is not within the power of the human intellect to give a demonstration of these matters. For in all things whose true reality is known through demonstration there is no tug of war and no refusal to accept a thing proven — unless indeed such refusal comes from an ignoramus who offers a resistance that is called resistance to demonstration.[5] Thus you can find groups of people who dispute the doctrine that the earth is spherical and that the sphere has a circular motion[6] and with regard to other matters of this kind. These folk do not enter into our purpose. The things about which there is this perplexity are very numerous in divine matters, few in | matters pertaining to natural science, and nonexistent in matters pertaining to mathematics.

Alexander of Aphrodisias[7] says that there are three causes of disagreement about things. One of them is love of domination and love of strife, both of which turn man aside from the apprehension of truth as it is. The second cause is the subtlety and the obscurity of the object of apprehension in itself and the difficulty of apprehending it. And the third cause is the ignorance

5. Literally: demonstrational resistance.
6. *wa-kawn al-falak mustadīran.* Ibn Tibbon translates: and that the sphere is round. The difference between his translation and that proposed above is due to the fact that the word *mustadīr* means both "round" and "turning about." In this case the latter meaning seems more appropriate.
7. Cf. Translator's Introduction on the influence of this Greek commentator of Aristotle on Maimonides. The passage quoted by Maimonides occurs in a work of Alexander on "The Principles of the All according to the opinion of Aristotle" ("Maqālah fi'l-qawl fī mabādi' al-kull ʿalā raʾy Arisṭāṭālīs al-faylasūf," ed. A. Badawi, in: *Arisṭū ʿinda'l-ʿArab* [Cairo, 1947], pp. 253–77). This treatise is preserved only in an Arabic translation. There are only slight differences between Maimonides' quotation and the text published by Badawi (*loc. cit.*, p. 276, ll. 18–21).

of him who apprehends and his inability to grasp things that it is possible to apprehend. That is what Alexander mentioned. However, in our times there is a fourth cause that he did not mention because it did not exist among them. It is habit and upbringing. For man has in his nature a love of, and an inclination for, that to which he is habituated. Thus you can see that the people of the desert — notwithstanding the disorderliness of their life, the lack of pleasures, and the scarcity of food — dislike the towns, do not hanker after their pleasures, and prefer the bad circumstances to which they are accustomed to good ones to which they are not accustomed. Their souls accordingly would find no repose in living in palaces, in wearing silk clothes, and in the enjoyment of baths, ointments, and perfumes. In a similar way, man has love for, and the wish to defend, opinions to which he is habituated and in which he has been brought up and has a feeling of repulsion for opinions other than those. For this reason also man is blind to the apprehension of the true realities and inclines toward the things to which he is habituated. This happened to the multitude with regard to the belief in His corporeality and many other metaphysical[8] subjects as we shall make clear. All this is due to people being habituated to, and brought up on, texts that it is an established usage to think highly of and to regard as true and whose external meaning is indicative of the corporeality of God and of other imaginings with no truth in them, for these have been set forth as parables and riddles. This is so for reasons | that I shall mention further on.

Do not think that what we have said with regard to the insufficiency of the human intellect and its having a limit at which it stops is a statement made in order to conform to Law.[9] For it is something that has already been said and truly grasped by the philosophers without their having concern for a particular doctrine or opinion. And it is a true thing that cannot be doubted except by an individual ignorant of what has already been demonstrated. We have put this chapter before others only with a view to its serving as an introduction to that which shall come after it.

8. Or: divine — which is the literal meaning of the Arabic term used.
9. Literally: a speech said according to [religious] Law.

CHAPTER 32

You[1] who study my Treatise, know that something similar to what happens to sensory apprehensions happens likewise to intellectual apprehensions in so far as they are attached to matter. For when you see with your eye, you apprehend something that is within the power of your sight to apprehend. If, however, your eyes are forced to do something they are reluctant to do — if they are made to gaze fixedly and are set the task of looking over a great distance, too great for you to see, or if you contemplate very minute writing[2] or a minute drawing[3] that is not within your power to apprehend — and if you force your eye, in spite of its reluctance, to find out the true reality of the thing, your eye shall not only be too weak to apprehend that which you are unable to apprehend, but also too weak to apprehend that which is within your power to apprehend. Your eye shall grow tired, and you shall not be able to apprehend what you could apprehend before having gazed fixedly and before having been given this task. A similar discovery is made by everyone engaging in the speculative study of some science with respect to his state of reflection.[4] For if he applies himself to reflection and sets himself a task demanding his entire attention,[5] he becomes dull and does not then understand even that which is within his scope to understand. | For the condition of all bodily faculties is, in this respect, one and the same. Something similar can happen to you with regard to intellectual apprehensions. For if you stay your progress because of a dubious point; if you do not deceive yourself into believing that there is a demonstration with regard to matters that have not been demonstrated; if you do not hasten to reject and categorically to pronounce false any assertions whose contradictories have not been demonstrated; if, finally, you do not aspire to apprehend that which you are unable to apprehend — you will have achieved human perfection and attained the rank of *Rabbi Aqiba*, peace be on him, who *entered in peace and went out in peace*[6] when engaged in the theoretical study of these metaphysical[7] matters. If, on the other hand, you aspire to apprehend things that are beyond your apprehension; or if you hasten to pronounce false, assertions the contradictories of which have not been demonstrated or that are possible, though very

1. In the singular.   2. *khaṭṭ*. The word also means "line."   3. Or: painting.
4. Reflection (*tafakkur*) is a bodily faculty.
5. *khāṭir*, a term which may signify impulsions and thoughts which occur to an individual.
6. B.T., Ḥagigah, 14b.   7. Literally: divine.

remotely so — you will have joined *Elisha Aḥer.*[8] That is, you will not only
not be perfect, but will be the most deficient among the deficient; and it
shall so fall out that you will be overcome by imaginings and by an inclination toward things defective, evil, and wicked — this resulting from the
intellect's being preoccupied and its light's being extinguished. In a similar
way, various species of delusive imaginings are produced in the sense of
sight when the visual spirit[9] is weakened, as in the case of sick people and
of such as persist in looking at brilliant or minute objects.

In this regard it is said: *Hast thou found honey? Eat so much as is
sufficient for thee, lest thou be filled therewith and vomit it.*[10] In a similar
way, the *Sages, may their memory be blessed,* used this verse as a parable
that they applied to *Elisha Aḥer.* How marvellous is this parable, inasmuch
as it likens knowledge to eating, a meaning about which we have spoken.[11]
It also mentions the most delicious of foods, namely, honey. Now, according
to its nature, honey, if eaten to excess, upsets the stomach and causes
vomiting. Accordingly Scripture says, as it were, that in spite of its sublimity, greatness, and what it has of perfection, the nature of the apprehen-
sion in question[12] — | if not made to stop at its proper limit and not
conducted with circumspection — may be perverted into a defect, just as the
eating of honey may. For whereas the individual eating in moderation is
nourished and takes pleasure in it, it all goes if there is too much of it.
Accordingly Scripture does not say, *Lest thou be filled therewith and loathe
it,* but rather says, *and vomit it.* This notion is also referred to in Scripture
in the dictum: *It is not good to eat much honey, and so on,*[13] as well as in the
dictum, *Neither make thyself overwise; why shouldst thou destroy thyself?*[14]
It likewise refers to this in the dictum: *Guard thy foot when thou goest to the
house of God, and so on.*[15] This is also referred to by *David* in the dictum:
*Neither do I exercise myself in things too great or in things too marvellous
for me.*[16] The Sages too intended to express this notion in their dictum: *Do
not inquire about things that are too marvellous for you; do not investigate
what is hidden from you; inquire into things that are permitted to you; you
have no business with marvels.*[17] This means that you should let your
intellect move about only within the domain of things that man is able to
grasp. For in regard to matters that it is not in the nature of man to grasp,

---

8. Literally: *Elisha the Other.*
9. A subtle corporeal substance supposed to transmit the images of objects seen by the eyes
    to the brain.
10. Prov. 25:16.   11. Literally: as we have said. Cf. I 30.
12. I.e., intellectual apprehension.   13. Prov. 25:27.   14. Eccles. 7:16.
15. Eccles. 4:17.   16. Ps. 131:1.   17. B.T., Ḥagigah, 13a.

it is, as we have made clear, very harmful to occupy oneself with them. This is what the Sages intended to signify by their dictum, *Whoever considers four things, and so on,*[18] completing the dictum by saying, *He who does not have regard for the honor of his Creator;* whereby they indicated what we have already made clear: namely, that man should not press forward to engage in speculative study of corrupt imaginings. When points appearing as dubious occur to him or the thing he seeks does not seem to him to be demonstrated, he should not deny and reject it, hastening to pronounce it false, but rather should persevere and thereby *have regard for the honor of his Creator.* He should refrain and hold back. This matter has already become clear. The intention of these texts set down by the prophets and the *Sages, may their memory be blessed,* is not, however, wholly to close the gate of speculation and to deprive the intellect of the apprehension of things that it is possible to apprehend — as is thought by the ignorant and neglectful, who | are pleased to regard their own deficiency and stupidity as perfection and wisdom, and the perfection and the knowledge of others as a deficiency and a defection from Law, and who thus *regard darkness as light and light as darkness.*[19] Their purpose, in its entirety, rather is to make it known that the intellects of human beings have a limit at which they stop.

Do not criticize the terms applied to the intellect in this chapter and others. For the purpose here is to guide toward the intended notion and not to investigate the truth of the essence of the intellect; for other chapters are devoted to a precise account of this subject.[20]

CHAPTER 33

Know that to begin with this science is very harmful, I mean the divine science. In the same way, it is also harmful to make clear the meaning of the parables of the prophets and to draw attention to the figurative senses of terms used in addressing people, figurative senses of which the books of prophecy are full. It behooves rather to educate the young and to give firmness to the deficient in capacity according to the measure of their

18. B.T., Ḥagigah, 11b. The entire passage reads: *Whoever considers four things does not deserve to have come into the world, [namely, he who considers] what is above, what is below, what is in front, and what is behind.*
19. Isa. 5:20.   20. Cf. I 68 and 72.

apprehension. Thus he who is seen to be perfect in mind and to be formed for that high rank—that is to say, demonstrative speculation and true intellectual inferences—should be elevated step by step, either by someone who directs his attention or by himself, until he achieves his perfection. If, however, he begins with the divine science, it will not be a mere confusion in his beliefs that will befall him, but rather absolute negation.[1] In my opinion an analogous case would be that of someone feeding a suckling with wheaten bread and meat and giving him wine to drink. He would undoubtedly kill him, not because these aliments are bad or unnatural for man, but because the child that receives them is too weak to digest them so as | to derive a benefit from them. Similarly these true opinions were not hidden, enclosed in riddles, and treated by all men of knowledge with all sorts of artifice through which they could teach them without expounding them explicitly, because of something bad being hidden in them,[2] or because they undermine the foundations of Law, as is thought by ignorant people who deem that they have attained a rank suitable for speculation. Rather have they been hidden because at the outset the intellect is incapable of receiving them; only flashes of them are made to appear so that the perfect man should know them. On this account they are called *secrets and mysteries of the Torah*, as we shall make clear. This is the cause of the fact that the *Torah speaketh in the language of the sons of man*, as we have made clear.[3] This is so because it[4] is presented in such a manner as to make it possible for the young, the women, and all the people to begin with it and to learn it. Now it is not within their power to understand these matters as they truly are. Hence they are confined to accepting tradition with regard to all sound opinions that are of such a sort that it is preferable that they should be pronounced true and with regard to all representations of this kind—and this in such a manner that the mind is led toward the existence of the objects of these opinions and representations but not toward grasping their essence as it truly is. When, however, a man grows perfect *and the mysteries of the Torah are communicated to him*[5] either by somebody else

---

1. The term *taʿṭīl* used by Maimonides may mean the emptying of the concept of God of all content, the denial of His having any action whatever, and so forth.
2. The Arabic text of Joel's edition (p. 48, l. 5) reads: *kawnihā fīhā*—which seems meaningless. On the other hand, Ibn Tibbon's translation seems to correspond to an Arabic text—*kawnin fīhā*—which makes better sense. In this case the English translation conforms to Ibn Tibbon's. The fact that the word *kawnihā* occurs in the same sentence a few words later may have caused *kawnin* to be miswritten *kawnihā*.
3. B.T., Yebamoth, 71a; B.T., Baba Meṣiʿa, 31b. Cf. I 26.
4. Namely, the Torah.   5. Cf. B.T., Ḥagigah, 13a.

or because he himself discovers them[6] — inasmuch as some of them draw his attention to others —, he attains a rank at which he pronounces the above-mentioned correct opinions to be true; and in order to arrive at this conclusion, he uses the veritable methods,[7] namely, demonstration in cases where demonstration is possible or strong arguments where this is possible. In this way he represents to himself these matters, which had appeared to him as imaginings and parables, in their truth and understands their essence. Accordingly the following speech of the Sages has been repeated to you several times in our speech:[8] *The Account of the Chariot ought not to be taught even to one man, except if he be wise and able to understand by himself*, in which case *only the chapter headings may be transmitted to him*.[9] On this account one ought not to begin to teach this subject to anyone unless it be according to his capacity and then only under these two conditions; one of them | being that the one who is to be taught is *wise*, I mean that he has achieved knowledge of the sciences from which the premises of speculation derive; and the other, that he be full of understanding, intelligent, sagacious by nature, that he divine a notion even if it is only very slightly suggested to him in a flash. This is the meaning of the dictum of the Sages: *able to understand by himself*.

I shall make clear to you the cause[10] that prevents the instruction of the multitude in the veritable methods of speculation and that prevents their being taught to begin to grasp the essences of things as they are. I shall also explain to you that it is requisite and necessary that this should not be otherwise than thus. These explanations shall be made in the chapter following upon the present one. I shall then say:

CHAPTER 34

The causes that prevent the commencement of instruction with divine science, the indication of things that ought to be indicated, and the presentation of this to the multitude, are five.

The first cause is the difficulty, subtlety, and obscurity of the matter

6. Literally: either from someone other than he or from himself.
7. Literally: he pronounces these correct opinions to be true in virtue of the veritable methods for pronouncing a thing true.
8. Cf. I Introduction.   9. B.T., Ḥagigah, 11b, 13a.
10. In fact there are several causes, as is explained in the following chapter.

in itself. Thus Scripture says: *That which was is far off and exceeding deep; who can find it out?*[1] And it is said: *But wisdom, where shall it be found?*[2] Now it is not fitting in teaching to begin with what is most difficult and obscure for the understanding. One of the parables generally known in our community is that likening knowledge to water. Now the Sages, peace be on them, explained several notions by means of this parable; one of them being that he who knows how to swim brings up pearls from the bottom of the sea, whereas he who does not know, drowns. For this reason, no one should expose himself to the risks of swimming except he who has been trained in learning to swim.

The second cause is the insufficiency of the minds of all men at their beginnings. For man is not granted his ultimate perfection at the outset; for perfection exists in him only potentially, and in his beginnings he | lacks this act. Accordingly it is said: *And man is born a wild ass.*[3] Nor is it necessarily obligatory in the case of every individual who is endowed with some thing in potency, that this thing should become actual. Sometimes it remains in its defective state either because of certain obstacles or because of paucity of training in what transforms that potentiality into actuality. Accordingly it is clearly said: *Not many are wise.*[4] The Sages too, *may their memory be blessed*, have said: *I saw the people who have attained a high rank,*[5] *and they were few.*[6] For the obstacles to perfection are very many, and the objects that distract from it abound. When should he be able to achieve the perfect preparation and the leisure required for training so that what subsists in a particular individual in potency should be transformed into actuality?

The third cause lies in the length of the preliminaries. For man has in his nature a desire to seek the ends;[7] and he often finds preliminaries tedious and refuses to engage in them. Know, however, that if an end could be achieved without the preliminaries that precede it, the latter would not be preliminaries, but pure distractions and futilities. Now if you would awaken a man—even though he were the dullest of all people—as one awakens a sleeping individual, and if you were to ask him whether he desired at that moment to have knowledge of the heavenly spheres,[8] namely, what their number is and what their configuration, and what is contained in them, and what the angels are, and how the world as a whole

---

1. Eccles. 7:24.   2. Job 28:12.   3. Job 11:12.   4. Job 32:9.
5. Literally: *I saw the sons of elevation.*
6. B.T., Sukkah, 42b; B.T., Sanhedrin, 43b.
7. Here in the sense of objects with a view to which an act may be accomplished.
8. Literally: of these heavens.

was created, and what its end is in view of the arrangement of its various parts with one another, and what the soul is, and how it is created in time[9] in the body, and whether the human soul can be separated from the body, and, if it can, in what manner and through what instrument and with what distinction in view, and if you put the same question to him with regard to other subjects of research of this kind, he would undoubtedly answer you in the affirmative. He would have a natural desire to know these things as they are in truth; but he would wish this desire to be allayed, and the knowledge of all this to be achieved by means of one or two words that you would say to him. If, however, you would lay upon him the obligation to abandon | his occupation for a week's time until he should understand all this, he would not do it, but would be satisfied with deceptive imaginings through which his soul would be set at ease. He would also dislike being told that there is a thing whose knowledge requires many premises and a long time for investigation. You know that these matters are mutually connected; there being nothing in what exists besides God, may He be exalted, and the totality of the things He has made. For this totality includes everything comprised in what exists except only Him. There is, moreover, no way to apprehend Him except it be through the things He has made; for they are indicative of His existence and of what ought to be believed about Him, I mean to say, of what should be affirmed and denied with regard to Him. It is therefore indispensable to consider all beings as they really are so that we may obtain for all the kinds of beings true and certain premises that would be useful to us in our researches pertaining to the divine science. How very many are the premises thus taken from the nature of numbers and the properties of geometrical figures from which we draw inferences concerning things that we should deny with respect to God, may He be exalted! And this denial is indicative to us of many notions. As for the matters pertaining to the astronomy of the spheres and to natural science, I do not consider that you should have any difficulty in grasping that those are matters necessary for the apprehension of the relation of the world to God's governance as this relation is in truth and not according to imaginings. There are also many speculative subjects that, although no premises can be obtained from them for the use of this science, nevertheless train the mind and procure it the habitus of drawing inferences and know-ledge of the truth in matters pertaining to its essence. They also put an end to the confusion in most of the minds of those engaged in speculation, a

9. ḥudūth, the Arabic term used, may mean "happening" or "taking place in time."

confusion mistaking things that are accidental for those that are essential;[10] hereby an end is also put to the perversion of opinions arising out of this confusion. All this is achieved in addition to the representation of these | subjects as they really are, even if they in no way belong to the divine science. These subjects are also not devoid of utility in other points, namely, with respect to matters that lead up to that science. Accordingly it is certainly necessary for whoever wishes to achieve human perfection to train himself at first in the art of logic, then in the mathematical sciences according to the proper order, then in the natural sciences, and after that in the divine science. We find many people whose mind stops short at one of these sciences; and sometimes even if their mind does not miss the mark, they are cut off by death while engaged in some preliminary study. Accordingly if we never in any way acquired an opinion through following traditional authority and were not correctly conducted toward something by means of parables, but were obliged to achieve a perfect representation by means of essential definitions and by pronouncing true only that which is meant to be pronounced true in virtue of a demonstration — which would be impossible except after the above-mentioned lengthy preliminary studies — this state of affairs would lead to all people dying without having known whether there is a deity for the world, or whether there is not, much less whether a proposition should be affirmed with regard to Him or a defect denied. Nobody would ever be saved from this perdition except *one of a city or two of a family*.[11] As for the few solitary individuals[12] that are *the remnant whom the Lord calls*,[13] the perfection, which constitutes the end to be aimed at, is realized for them only after the above-mentioned preliminary studies. *Solomon* has made it clear that the need for preliminary studies is a necessity and that it is impossible to attain true wisdom except after having been trained. For he says: *If the iron be blunt, and he do not whet the edge, then must he put to more strength; but even more preparation is needed for wisdom;*[14] and he also says: *Hear counsel and receive instruction, that thou mayest be wise in thy latter end.*[15] There is also a necessity of another kind for achieving knowledge of the preliminary studies. | It arises from the fact that when a man seeks to obtain knowledge quickly, many doubts occur to him, and he moreover quickly understands objections — I mean to say the destruction of a particular doctrine, this being similar to the demolition of a building. Now the establishment of doctrines as true and the solution of doubts can

10. Literally: that are of its essence. Namely, of the essence of the mind.
11. Jer. 3:14.   12. *al-āḥād*. Literally: ones or units.   13. Cf. Joel 3:5.
14. Eccles. 10:10   15. Prov. 19:20.

only be grounded upon many premises taken from these preliminary studies. One engaged in speculation without preliminary study is therefore comparable to someone who walked on his two feet in order to reach a certain place and, while on his way, fell into a deep well without having any device to get out of there before he perishes. It would have been better for him if he had foregone walking and had quietly remained in his own place. In *Proverbs*, *Solomon* describes at length the state of lazy people and their incapacity — all this being a parable for the incapacity to seek knowledge of the sciences. Thus speaking of the desire of someone desirous to achieve his ends, but making no effort to achieve knowledge of the preliminary studies leading up to these ends does nothing else but desire, he says: *The desire of the slothful killeth him; for his hands refuse to labor. He coveteth greedily all the day long; but the righteous giveth and spareth not.*[16] In these verses he says that the reason why the desire of the slothful kills him is to be found in the fact that he makes no effort and does not work with a view to that which would allay that desire; he has only an abundance of longing and nothing else, while he aspires to things for whose achievement he lacks the necessary instrument. It would be healthier for him if he renounced this desire. Consider now how the ending of the parable explains its beginning. For in his dictum, *But the righteous giveth and spareth not*, the word *righteous* is not antithetical to *slothful* except according to the explanation we have propounded. For [Solomon] says that the just one among men is he who gives everything its due; he means thereby that he gives all his time to seeking knowledge and spares no portion of his time for anything else. He says, as it were: *But the righteous gives his days to wisdom and is not sparing of them*; which corresponds to his saying: *Give not thy strength unto women.*[17] Now the majority | of the men of knowledge, I mean those generally known as men of knowledge, labor under this disease — I mean that which consists in seeking to achieve the ends and in speaking about them without having engaged in the studies preliminary to them. With some of them, their ignorance or their desire to have the first place goes so far as to cause them to disapprove of these preliminary studies, which they are incapable of grasping or are too lazy to seek to understand. Accordingly they wish to show that these studies are harmful or useless. However, when one reflects, the truth of the matter is clear and manifest.[18]

The fourth cause is to be found in the natural aptitudes. For it has been explained, or rather demonstrated, that the moral virtues are a prepara-

16. Prov. 21:25–26.   17. Prov. 31:3.
18. Literally: And the truth in contemplating is clear and manifest.

tion for the rational[19] virtues, it being impossible to achieve true, rational acts[20] — I mean perfect rationality — unless it be by a man thoroughly trained with respect to his morals and endowed with the qualities of tranquillity and quiet. There are, moreover, many people who have received from their first natural disposition a complexion of temperament[21] with which perfection is in no way compatible. Such is the case of one whose heart is naturally exceedingly hot; for he cannot refrain from anger, even if he subject his soul to very stringent training. This is also the case of one whose testicles have a hot and humid temperament and are of a strong constitution and in whom the seminal vessels abundantly generate semen. For it is unlikely that such a man, even if he subject his soul to the most severe training, should be chaste. Similarly you can find among people rash and reckless folk whose movements, being very agitated and disordered, indicate a corruption of the complexion and a poor quality of the temperament, of which it is impossible to give an account. Perfection can never be perceived in such people. And to make an effort for their benefit in this matter is pure ignorance on the part of him who makes the effort. For this science, as you know, is not like the science of medicine[22] or the science of geometry, and not everyone has the disposition required for it in the various respects we have mentioned. It is accordingly indubitable that preparatory moral training should be carried out before beginning with this science, so that man should be in a state of | extreme uprightness and perfection; *For the perverse is an abomination to the Lord, but His secret is with the righteous.*[23] For this reason the teaching of this science to the young is disapproved of. In fact it is impossible for them to absorb it because of the effervescence of their natures and of their minds being occupied with the flame of growth. When, however, this flame that gives rise to perplexity is extinguished, the young achieve tranquillity and quiet; and their hearts submit and yield with respect to their temperament. They then may call upon their souls to raise themselves up to this rank, which is that of the apprehension of Him, may He be exalted; I mean thereby the divine science that is designated as the *Account of the Chariot.* Accordingly Scripture says: *The Lord is nigh unto them that are of a broken heart.*[24] And it says: *I dwell in the high and holy place, with him also that is of a*

---

19. *nuṭqiyya.* The word from which this adjective derives means, like *logos* in Greek, both speech and reason.
20. *nuṭqiyyāt ḥaqīqiyya.* Literally: true rational things.
21. More or less literally: a temperamental disposition.
22. Literally: is not the science of medicine.
23. Prov. 3:32.   24. Ps. 34:19.

contrite and humble spirit, and so on.[25] For this reason they say in the *Talmud* with respect to the dictum of the [Sages of the Mishnah]: *The chapter headings may be transmitted to him; The chapter headings ought not to be transmitted except to a President of the Court, and one whose heart within him is full of care.*[26] The purpose of this is to signify obedience, submission, and great piety joined to knowledge. It is also said there: *The mysteries of the Torah may only be transmitted to a counsellor, wise in crafts, and endowed with understanding of whispering.*[27] Now these are matters that undoubtedly require a natural predisposition. Do you not know among various people one who is very feeble in point of opinion,[28] though he be the most understanding of men? Another, on the other hand, may have an unerring opinion and an excellent way of conducting affairs in political matters; such a one is called *counsellor.* However, someone of that sort might not understand an intelligible notion even though it were close to being one of the first intelligibles. He might be very stupid and lacking in ingenious devices. Thus it is said: *Wherefore is there a price in the hand of a fool to buy wisdom, seeing he hath no heart for it?*[29] Among men there is also found one who is naturally full of understanding and perspicacity and capable of giving concise and coherent expression to the most hidden notions. Such a one is called *endowed with understanding of whispering.* However, someone of this sort does not necessarily occupy himself with, and achieve knowledge of, the sciences. The one who actually has achieved knowledge of the sciences | is called *wise in crafts.* Of him the Sages say: *When he speaks, they all become deaf.*[30] Consider how, by means of a text of a book,[31] they laid down as conditions of the perfection of the individual, his being perfect in the varieties of political regimes as well as in the speculative sciences and withal his possessing natural perspicacity and understanding and the gift of finely expressing himself in communicating notions in flashes. If all this is realized in someone, then *the mysteries of the Torah may be transmitted to him.* It is likewise said there:[32] *Rabbi Yoḥanan said to Rabbi Elazar: Come, so that I should teach you the Account of the Chariot! Whereupon [Rabbi Elazar] said to him: I am not yet old;*[33] he means: I am not yet aged and up to now find in myself the effervescence of

25. Isa. 57:15.   26. B.T., Ḥagigah, 13a.   27. Or: incantation. B.T., Ḥagigah, 13a.
28. *raʾy*, a term which here is the equivalent of the Greek *doxa*.   29. Prov. 17:16.
30. A pun arising from the resemblance between two Hebrew words: *hershim* (deaf) and *harashim* (in crafts). B.T., Ḥagigah, 14a.
31. *kitāb.* This Arabic word may sometimes, and in this case does, denote a book which has authority.
32. I.e., in the same text.   33. B.T., Ḥagigah, 14a.

nature and the recklessness of adolescence. See accordingly how they posed age as a condition superadded to the above-mentioned excellencies. How then could one plunge into these studies together with all the multitude, *the women, and the children?*

The fifth cause is to be found in the fact that men are occupied with the necessities of the bodies, which are the first perfection; and more particularly if, in addition, they are occupied with taking care of a wife and of children; and even more especially if there is in them, superadded to that, a demand for the superfluities of life, which becomes an established habitus as a result of a bad conduct of life and bad customs. Things are so that if even a perfect man, as we have mentioned, were to occupy himself much with these necessary things and all the more if he were to occupy himself with unnecessary things, and if his desire for them should grow strong, he would find that his theoretical desires had grown weak and had been submerged. And his demand for them would slacken and become intermittent and inattentive. He accordingly would not grasp things that otherwise would have been within his power to grasp; or else he would grasp them with a confused apprehension, a mixture of apprehension and failure to apprehend.

In view of all these causes, these matters are only for a few solitary individuals[34] of a very special sort, not for the multitude. For this reason, they should be hidden from the beginner, and he should be prevented from taking them up, just as | a small baby is prevented from taking coarse foods and from lifting heavy weights.

CHAPTER 35

Do not think that all that we have laid down in the preceding chapters regarding the greatness and the hidden nature of the matter, the difficulty of apprehending it, and its having to be withheld from the multitude, refers also to the denial of the corporeality of God and to the denial of His being subject to affections.[1] It is not so. For just as it behooves to bring up children in the belief, and to proclaim to the multitude, that God, may He be magnified and honored, is one and that none but He ought

34. *āḥād.* Cf. n. 12, this chap.
1. Regarded as exclusively passive. The Arabic word used is a noun deriving from the passive form of the verb "to act."

to be worshipped, so it behooves that they should be made to accept on traditional authority the belief that God is not a body; and that there is absolutely no likeness in any respect whatever between Him and the things created by Him; that His existence has no likeness to theirs; nor His life to the life of those among them who are alive; nor again His knowledge to the knowledge of those among them who are endowed with knowledge. They should be made to accept the belief that the difference between Him and them is not merely a difference of more and less, but one concerning the species of existence. I mean to say that it should be established in everybody's mind that our knowledge of our power does not differ from His knowledge or His power in the latter being greater and stronger, the former less and weaker,[2] or in other similar respects, inasmuch as the strong and the weak are necessarily alike with respect to their species, and one definition comprehends both of them. Similarly any relation can subsist only between two things belonging to one species.[3] This likewise has been made clear in the natural sciences. Now everything that can be ascribed to God, may He be exalted, differs in every respect from our attributes, so that no definition can comprehend the one thing and the other. Similarly, as I shall make clear, the term "existence" | can only be applied equivocally to His existence and to that of things other than He. This measure of knowledge will suffice for children and the multitude to establish in their minds that there is a perfect being, who is neither a body nor a force in a body, and that He is the deity, that no sort of deficiency and therefore no affection whatever can attain Him. As for the discussion concerning attributes and the way they should be negated with regard to Him; and as for the meaning of the attributes that may be ascribed to Him, as well as the discussion concerning His creation of that which He created, the character of His governance of the world, the "how" of His providence with respect to what is other than He, the notion of His will, His apprehension, and His knowledge of all that He knows; and likewise as for the notion of prophecy and the "how" of its various degrees, and the notion of His names, though they are many, being indicative of one and the same thing — it should be considered that all these are obscure matters. In fact, they are truly *the mysteries of the Torah* and the *secrets* constantly mentioned in the books of the prophets and in the dicta of the *Sages, may their memory be blessed.* They are the matters that

2. Literally: that our knowledge and His knowledge or our power and His power do not differ by the more and the less and the stronger and the weaker.
3. The use of the word *naw*[c] (species) in this passage is not very precise. Maimonides obviously had in mind the more comprehensive categories as well, that is to say, the genera.

ought not to be spoken of except *in chapter headings*, as we have mentioned, and only with an individual such as has been described.

On the other hand, the negation of the doctrine of the corporeality of God and the denial of His having a likeness to created things and of His being subject to affections are matters that ought to be made clear and explained to everyone according to his capacity and ought to be inculcated in virtue of traditional authority upon children, women, stupid ones, and those of a defective natural disposition, just as they adopt the notion that God is one, that He is eternal, and that none but He should be worshipped. For there is no profession of unity[4] unless the doctrine of God's corporeality is denied. For a body cannot be one, but is composed of matter and form, which by definition are two; it also is divisible, subject to partition. When people have received this doctrine, are habituated to and educated and grown up in it, and subsequently become perplexed over the texts of the books of the prophets, the meaning of these books should be explained to them. They should be elevated | to the knowledge of the interpretation of these texts, and their attention should be drawn to the equivocality and figurative sense of the various terms — the exposition of which is contained in this Treatise — so that the correctness of their belief regarding the oneness of God and the affirmation of the truth of the books of the prophets should be safe. If, however, someone's mind fails to understand the interpretation of the texts and the possibility of an identity of terms going together with a difference in meaning, he should be told: The interpretation of this text is understood by the men of knowledge. You, however, know that God, may He be honored and magnified, is not a body or subject to affections. For affection is a change, and He, may He be exalted, is not touched by change. He is not like unto any thing of all those that are other than He, nor is He comprehended together with one of these things in any definition whatever. You know likewise that these dicta of the prophets are true and have an interpretation. In dealing with such a man, one should stop at this measure of knowledge. But it is not meet that belief in the corporeality of God or in His being provided with any concomitant of the bodies should be permitted to establish itself in anyone's mind any more than it is meet that belief should be established in the nonexistence of the deity, in the association[5] of other gods with Him, or in the worship of other than He.

4. Literally: no unification. *tawḥīd* (unification) is a term applied to the belief, or the profession of faith, in One God.
5. The usual Arabic term for polytheism is employed.

I shall explain to you, when speaking of the attributes, in what respect it is said that God is pleased with, or made angry and wrathful by, a certain thing. It is in this sense that it is said of certain individuals among men that God was pleased or angry with them or full of wrath. This notion is not the subject of this chapter — the subject being that which I am about to speak of.

Know that if you consider the whole of the *Torah* and all the books | of the prophets, you will find that the *expressions, wrath, anger*, and *jealousy*, are exclusively used with reference to *idolatry*. You will also find that the expressions, *enemy of God* or *adversary* or *hater*, are exclusively used to designate an *idolater*. Thus Scripture says: *And ye serve other gods, and so on, and the Lord's wrath will be kindled against you;*[1] *Lest the wrath of the Lord be kindled;*[2] *To provoke Him to anger through the work of your hands;*[3] *They have roused Me to jealousy with a no-god; they have provoked Me to anger with their vanities, and so on;*[4] *For a jealous God, and so on;*[5] *Why have they provoked Me to anger with their graven images;*[6] *Because of the anger provoked by His sons and His daughters;*[7] *For a fire is kindled in My wrath;*[8] *For He will take vengeance on His adversaries and repay His enemies;*[9] *And repayeth them that hate Him;*[10] *Until He hath driven out His enemies;*[11] *Which the Lord thy God hateth;*[12] *For every abomination to the Lord, which He hateth.*[13] Expressions of this kind are too numerous to be counted. However, if you trace them in all the books, you will find that it is as we have said.

Now the books of the prophets[14] only make this strong assertion because it concerns a false opinion attaching to Him, may He be exalted, I refer to *idolatrous worship*. For the deviation from truth of one who believes that Zayd is standing at a time when he is sitting, is not like the deviation of him who believes that fire is under the air or water under the earth or that the earth is flat and other things of a similar kind. And this second deviation

---

1. Deut. 11:16–17.   2. Deut. 6:15.   3. Deut. 31:29.   4. Deut. 32:21.
5. Deut. 6:15.   6. Jer. 8:19.   7. Deut. 32:19.   8. Deut. 32:22.
9. Nah. 1:2. The biblical text is somewhat altered in Maimonides' quotation of this verse. In the first half, *He* is substituted for *the Lord*. In the second half, the correct biblical text is: *and reserveth wrath for His enemies*, whereas Maimonides cites the verse as reading: *and will repay His enemies.*
10. Deut. 7:10.   11. Num. 32:21.   12. Deut. 16:22.   13. Deut. 12:31.
14. I.e., the books of the Bible.

from truth is not like the deviation of him who believes that the sun consists of fire or that the heavenly sphere forms a hemisphere and other things of a similar kind. Again this third deviation from truth is not like the deviation of him who believes that the angels eat and drink and other things of a similar kind. Finally this fourth deviation from truth is not like the deviation of him who believes that a thing other than God ought to be worshipped. For whenever ignorance and infidelity[15] bear upon a great thing, I mean to say upon someone whose rank in what exists is well established, they are of greater consequence than if they bear upon someone | who was of a lower rank. By infidelity, I mean belief about a thing that is different from what the thing really is. By ignorance, I mean ignorance of what it is possible to know. Accordingly the ignorance of him who does not know the measure of the cone of a cylinder or does not know that the sun is spherical is not like the ignorance of him who does not know whether a deity exists or whether there is no deity for the world. Nor is the infidelity[16] of him who thinks that the cone of a cylinder is half a cylinder or that the sun is a circle like the infidelity of him who thinks that there are more deities than one.

Now you know that whoever performs *idolatrous worship* does not do it on the assumption that there is no deity except the idol. In fact, no human being of the past has ever imagined on any day, and no human being of the future will ever imagine, that the form that he fashions either from cast metal or from stone and wood has created and governs the heavens and the earth. Rather is it worshipped in respect of its being an image of a thing that[17] is an intermediary between ourselves and God. Scripture makes this clear, saying: *Who would not fear Thee, O King of the nations, and so on.*[18] It also says: *And in every place incense is offered unto My name, and so on,*[19] whereby Scripture refers to what they regard as the First Cause. We have made this clear in our great compilation.[20] No one among the people of our

15. The word rendered by "infidelity" is *kufr*, a term whose usual meaning is approximately: disbelief in one or several principal religious dogmas. However, a few sentences farther on Maimonides explains that in his use of the word, *kufr* means an untrue belief about a thing. He does not indicate that the term in question is employed only in connection with beliefs related in some way to religion. Nevertheless, in view of the theological connotations of *kufr*, it seemed necessary to translate the word with a term deriving from the sphere of religious thought.

16. *kufr*. Cf. preceding note.

17. The Arabic pronoun translated by the relative pronoun "that" may refer either to "image" or to "thing." The second possibility is stylistically the more probable and is the one to which Ibn Tibbon's translation conforms.

18. Jer. 10:7.   19. Mal. 1:11.

20. Cf. *Mishneh Torah*, ᶜAbodah Zarah, I.

Law disputes this. However, in spite of the fact that those infidels[21] believe in the existence of the deity, their idolatrous worship entails their deserving destruction; for the reason that their infidelity bears upon a prerogative reserved to God alone, may He be exalted — I mean the prerogative of being worshipped and magnified — just as Scripture says: *And ye shall serve the Lord, and so on.*[22] This is so ordained in order that God's existence may be firmly established in the belief of the multitude. Now the idolaters thought that this prerogative belonged to that which was other than God; and this led to the disappearance of the belief in His existence, may He be exalted, from among the multitude. For the multitude grasp only the actions of worship, not their meanings or the true reality of the Being worshipped through them. Consequently the idolatrous worship of the infidels | entails their deserving destruction;[23] just as the text has it: *Thou shalt not save alive a soul.*[24] And it explains the reason for this, which is to put an end to this false opinion so that others should not be corrupted through it. As Scripture says: *That they teach you not to do, and so on.*[25] And it calls them *enemies, haters,* and *adversaries,* and says that he who does this *provokes* [God's] *jealousy, anger,* and *wrath.*

What then should be the state of him whose infidelity bears upon His essence, may He be exalted, and consists in believing Him to be different from what He really is? I mean to say that he does not believe that He exists; or believes that there are two gods, or that He is a body, or that he is subject to affections; or again that he ascribes to God some deficiency or other. Such a man is indubitably more blameworthy than *a worshipper of idols* who regards the latter as intermediaries or as having the power to *do good or ill.* Know accordingly, you who are that man, that when you believe in the doctrine of the corporeality of God or believe that one of the states of the body belongs to Him, you *provoke His jealousy and anger, kindle the fire of His wrath,* and are *a hater, an enemy,* and *an adversary* of God, much more so than *an idolater.* If, however, it should occur to you

---

21. *al-kāfirīn,* a participle deriving from the same root as *kufr.* Cf. n. 15, this chap.
22. Exod. 23:25.
23. Literally (as from twelve lines above): However, with these infidels believing in the existence of the deity, as their infidelity is attached to a right, which is to Him only, may He be exalted, I mean worship and magnification — just as it says: *And ye shall serve the Lord, and so on* — in order that His existence be firmly established in the belief of the multitude; and they thought that this right is to what is other than He. Accordingly this called for the privation of His existence, may He be exalted, from the belief of the multitude since the multitude apprehends only the actions of worship, not their meanings nor the true reality of the Worshipped through them. Accordingly this entailed their deserving destruction.
24. Deut. 20:16.   25. Deut. 20:18.

that one who believes in the corporeality of God should be excused because of his having been brought up in this doctrine or because of his ignorance and the shortcomings of his apprehension, you ought to hold a similar belief with regard to *an idolater*; for he only worships idols because of his ignorance or because of his upbringing: *They continue in the custom of their fathers.*[26] If, however, you should say that the external sense of the biblical text causes men to fall into this doubt, you ought to know that *an idolater* is similarly impelled to his idolatry by imaginings and defective representations. Accordingly there is no excuse for one who does not accept the authority of men who inquire into the truth and are engaged in speculation if he himself is incapable of engaging in such speculation. I do not consider as an infidel one who cannot demonstrate that the corporeality of God should be negated. But I do consider as an infidel one who does not believe in its negation; and this particularly in view of the existence of the interpretations of *Onqelos* and of *Jonathan | ben Uziel*, may peace be on both of them, who cause their readers to keep away as far as possible from the belief in the corporeality of God. This was the subject of this chapter.

CHAPTER 37

Face [*panim*] is an equivocal term, its equivocality being mostly with respect to its figurative use. It is the term designating the face of all living beings. Thus: *And all faces are turned into paleness;*[1] *Wherefore are your faces so sad.*[2] This use is frequent. It is also a term denoting anger. Thus: *And her face*[3] *was gone.*[4] The term is frequently used in this sense to denote the anger and wrath of God. Thus: *The face*[5] *of the Lord hath divided them;*[6] *The face*[7] *of the Lord is against them that do evil;*[8] *My face*[9] *shall go, and I will give thee rest;*[10] *Then I will set My face*[11] *against that man and his family.*[12] This use is frequent. It is also a term denoting the presence and station of an individual. Thus: *He settled in the face of all his brethen;*[13] *And in the face of all the people, I will be glorified*[14] — meaning, while they are present; *Surely he will blaspheme Thee to Thy face*[15] — meaning, while Thou art present and existent. In this sense it is said: *And*

26. B.T., Ḥullin, 13a.
1. Jer. 30:6.   2. Gen. 40:7.   3. I.e., the anger.   4. I Sam. 1:18.
5. I.e., the anger.   6. Lam. 4:16.   7. I.e., the anger.   8. Ps. 34:17.
9. I.e., My anger.   10. Exod. 33:14.   11. I.e., My anger.   12. Lev. 20:5.
13. Gen. 25:18.   14. Lev. 10:3.   15. Job 1:11.

the Lord spoke unto Moses face to face [16] — which means, as a presence to another presence without an intermediary, as is said: *Come, let us look one another in the face.* [17] Thus Scripture says: *The Lord spoke with you face to face.* [18] In another passage it explains, saying: *Ye heard the voice of words, but ye saw no figure, only a voice.* [19] Hence this kind of speaking and hearing are described as being *face to face.* Similarly the words, *And the Lord spoke unto Moses face to face,* describe His speaking as being in the form of an address. [20] Accordingly it is said: *Then he heard the voice speaking to him.* [21] It has accordingly been made clear to you that the hearing of a speech without the intermediary of an angel is described as being *face to face.* In this sense it is also said: *But My face shall not be seen,* [22] meaning that the true reality of My existence | as it veritably is cannot be grasped. *Face* is also an adverb of place that is rendered in Arabic by the words: "in front of thee" [23] or "in thy presence." [24] It is often used in this sense with regard to God, may He be exalted. Thus: *In the face* [25] *of the Lord.* [26] The biblical expression, *But My face shall not be seen,* [27] is understood in this sense in the interpretation of *Onqelos,* who translates: *And those in front of Me shall not be seen.* He indicates by this that there are likewise great created beings whom man cannot apprehend as they really are. These are the separate intellects. They have been thought to be in a relation to God as being constantly in front of Him and in His presence because of the power of the providence constantly watching over them. On the other hand, the things that in his opinion, I mean that of *Onqelos,* can be grasped in their true reality are such as are beneath the separate intellects with respect to their rank in that which exists. I mean things endowed with matter and form. Of them [Onqelos] has said: *And thou shalt see that which is behind Me.* [28] He means the beings from which I have, as it were, turned away, and upon which, speaking in parables, I have turned My back, because of their remoteness from the existence of God, may He be exalted. Further on you shall hear my interpretation of that which was demanded by *Moses our Master,* peace be on him. *Face* is also an adverb of time having the meaning: before or ancient. [29] Thus: *In the face in Israel;* [30] *In the face* [31] *Thou didst*

---

16. Exod. 33:11.   17. II Kings 14:8.   18. Deut. 5:4.   19. Deut. 4:12.
20. An address to Moses.   21. Num. 7:89.   22. Exod. 33:23.   23. *amāmaka.*
24. *bayna yadayka.* Literally: between your hands.   25. I.e., in front.
26. Gen. 18:22.   27. Exod. 33:23.   28. Ibid.; in Aramaic.
29. *qadīm.* In philosophic language the word means "eternal a parte ante," whereas its ordinary signification is "ancient."
30. Ruth 4:7. I.e., in the former time in Israel.
31. I.e., according to the explanation given in n. 29 above, either "of old" or "in the eternity a parte ante."

lay the foundation of the earth.[32] *Face* is also a term denoting protection and providence. Thus: *Thou shalt not bear the face of the poor;*[33] *And the honorable man;*[34] *Who does not bear the face.*[35] This use is frequent. In this sense it is also said: *The Lord bear His face*[36] *to thee and give thee peace,*[37] which refers to His making providence accompany us.

CHAPTER 38

Back [*ʾaḥor*] is an equivocal term. It is a term denoting the back.[1] Thus: *Over the back of the tabernacle;*[2] *The spear came out | at his back.*[3] Sometimes it is used as an adverb of time in the sense of: after. *Neither at the back of him*[4] *arose there any like him;*[5] *At the back of these things.*[6] This use is frequent. The term also occurs in the meaning of following and imitating the conduct of some individual with respect to the conduct of life. Thus: *Ye shall walk at the back of the Lord*[7] *your God;*[8] *They shall walk at the back of the Lord,*[9] which means following in obedience to Him and imitating His acts and conducting life in accordance with His conduct. Thus: *He walked at the back of a commandment.*[10] In this sense it is said: *And thou shalt see My back,*[11] which means that thou shalt apprehend what follows Me, has come to be like Me, and follows necessarily from My will— that is, all the things created by Me, as I shall explain in a chapter[12] of this Treatise.[13]

32. Ps. 102:26.   33. Lev. 19:15. I.e., thou shalt not respect the person of the poor.
34. Isa. 3:3. I.e., one who receives attention.   35. Deut. 10:17. I.e., show regard.
36. I.e., protect.   37. Num. 6:26.
 1. The Arabic word is used to render the Hebrew term under discussion.
 2. Exod. 26:12.   3. II Sam. 2:23.   4. I.e., after him.   5. II Kings 23:25.
 6. Gen. 15:1. I.e., after these things.   7. I.e., after the Lord.   8. Deut. 13:5.
 9. Hos. 11:10. I.e., after the Lord.   10. Hos. 5:11. I.e., after the commandment.
11. Exod. 33:23.   12. Or: in some of the chapters.   13. Cf. I 54.

CHAPTER 39

Heart [*leb*] is an equivocal term. It is a term denoting the heart,[1] I mean the part of the body in which resides the principle of life of every being endowed with a heart. Thus: *And thrust them in the heart of Absalom.*[2] And inasmuch as this part[3] is in the middle of the body, the term is used figuratively to designate the middle of every thing. Thus: *Unto the heart*[4] *of heaven;*[5] *The heart*[6] *of fire.*[7] It is also a term denoting thought. Thus: *Went not my heart,*[8] which means that thou wast present in my thought when this and that happened. In this sense it is said: *And that ye go not about after your own heart,*[9] which refers to your following your thoughts; and: *Whose heart turneth away this day,*[10] which means that his thought is discontinued. It is also a term signifying opinion. Thus: *All the rest of Israel were of one heart to make David king*[11] — that is, they were of one opinion. A similar meaning is to be found in the dictum: *But fools die for want of heart*[12] — which is intended to signify: through the deficiency of their opinion. And in the same way this meaning is to be found in the dictum: *My heart shall not turn away*[13] *so long as I live*[14] — the meaning of which is: my opinion shall not turn away from, and shall not let go of, this matter. For the beginning of this passage reads:[15] *My righteousness I hold fast and will not let it go; My heart shall not turn away | so long as I live.* In my opinion it is with reference to this meaning of *yeheraph*[16] that the expression *shiphhah neherephet le-ʾish*[17] [*a handmaid betrothed to a man*] is to be explained — [the term "neherephet"] being akin to an Arabic word, namely, "munharifa"[18] [turned away] — that is, one who turns from being possessed as a slave to being possessed as a wife. It [heart] is also a term

1. Here the Arabic word for "heart" is used.   2. II Sam. 18:14.
3. Literally: part of the body, or limb.   4. I.e., the middle.   5. Deut. 4:11.
6. I.e., midst. The Hebrew word *labba* occurring in this verse is usually interpreted as "flame."
7. Exod. 3:2.   8. II Kings 5:26.   9. Num. 15:39.   10. Deut. 29:17.
11. I Chron. 12:39.   12. Prov. 10:21.
13. The usual meaning of this Hebrew word is better rendered by the customary translation *shall not reproach* than by the one given in the text which accords with Maimonides' interpretation occurring in the next sentence. In giving this interpretation Maimonides uses the Arabic verb *inharafa* which appears to derive from the same root as the Hebrew word in question (*yeheraph*) and means "to turn away," "deviate."
14. Job 27:6.
15. Literally: for the first of this speech. Maimonides quotes the entire verse (Job 27:6) of which he has just quoted the second part.
16. Cf. n. 13, this chap.   17. Lev. 19:20.   18. Cf. n. 13, this chap.

denoting will. Thus: *And I will give you shepherds according to My heart*;[19]
Is thy heart right as my heart is?[20] — that is, is thy will like my will in
rectitude? Sometimes the word is figuratively applied with this meaning:
That shall do according to that which is in My heart and in My soul,[21] the
meaning of which is: he shall do according to My will; *And Mine eyes and
My heart shall be there perpetually*[22] — that is, My providence and My will.
It is also a term denoting the intellect. Thus: *But an empty man will act
with his heart,*[23] meaning that he will cognize with his intellect. And
similarly: *A wise man's heart is at his right hand*[24] — that is, his intellect is
directed toward the perfect things. This use is frequent. It is in this sense
— I mean that indicative of the intellect — that the term is applied figuratively to God in all the passages in question, save certain exceptional ones
where it sometimes is used to indicate the will. Every passage should therefore be understood according to its context.[25] In this way [heart] is applied
to the intellect in the verses: *And lay it to thy heart*;[26] *And none considereth
in his heart*;[27] and all the others that are similar. In the same way Scripture
says: *But the Lord hath not given you a heart to know,*[28] in a way analogous
to its saying: *Unto thee it was shown that thou mightest know.*[29] As for the
dictum of Scripture: *And thou shalt love the Lord thy God with all thy
heart*[30] — in my opinion its interpretation is: with all the forces of your
heart; I mean to say, with all the forces of the body, for the principle of all
of them derives from the heart. Accordingly the intended meaning is, as
we have explained in the Commentary on the *Mishnah*[31] and in *Mishneh
Torah,*[32] that you should make His apprehension the end of all your actions.

19. Jer. 3:15. . 20. II Kings 10:15.   21. I Sam. 2:35.   22. I Kings 9:3.
23. Job 11:12. The Hebrew text of the Bible has the verb *yelabbeb*, deriving from *leb*
(heart). In the English translation of the Bible, the verb in this verse is rendered: *will
get understanding.*
24. Eccles. 10:2.   25. Literally: every place according to itself.   26. Deut. 4:39.
27. Isa. 44:19.   28. Deut. 29:3.   29. Deut. 4:35.   30. Deut. 6:5.
31. Cf. *Eight Chapters (Shemonah Peraqim),* V. This is the introduction to Maimonides'
commentary on the tractate Aboth.
32. Cf. Yesodei ha-Torah, II 2; De°oth, III 2.

CHAPTER 40

A*ir* [*ruaḥ*][1] is an equivocal term. It is a term denoting air; I mean the element that is one of | the four elements. Thus: *And the air of God hovered.*[2] It is also a term denoting the blowing wind. Thus: *And the east air*[3] *brought the locusts;*[4] *West air.*[5] This use of the term is frequent. It is also a term denoting the animal spirit. Thus: *An air*[6] *that passeth away and cometh not again;*[7] *Wherein is the air*[8] *of life.*[9] It is also a term denoting the thing that remains of man after his death and that does not undergo passing-away.[10] Thus: *And the air*[11] *shall return unto God who gave it.*[12] It is also a term denoting the divine intellectual overflow that overflows to the prophets and in virtue of which they prophesy, as we shall explain to you when speaking of prophecy, in the way in which it is proper to mention it in this Treatise. Thus: *And I will take of the air*[13] *which is upon thee, and I will put it upon them;*[14] *And it came to pass that when the air rested upon them;*[15] *The air*[16] *of the Lord spoke by me.*[17] This use of the word is frequent. It is also a term denoting purpose and will. Thus: *A fool uttereth all his air,*[18] his purpose and will. Similarly in the verse: *And the air of Egypt shall be made empty within it, and I will make void the counsel thereof;*[19] it says that [Egypt's] purposes will be divided and its governance will be hidden. Similarly also in the verse: *Who hath comprehended the air of the Lord, or who is familiar with His counsel that he may tell us?*[20] Scripture says that he who knows the ordering of His will or apprehends His governance of that which exists as it really is, should teach us about it — as we shall explain in the chapters that will deal with His governance.[21] In all cases in which the term *air* is applied to God, it is used in the fifth sense;

1. The Hebrew word *ruaḥ* usually means "wind" or "spirit." Here it is rendered by "air" because according to Maimonides this is the primary meaning of the word.
2. Gen. 1:2   3. I.e., wind.
4. Exod. 10:13.   5. Exod. 10:19. I.e., wind.
6. I.e., animal spirit.   7. Ps. 78:39.
8. I.e., animal spirit.   9. Gen. 7:15.
10. Corruption (*fasād*): the antithesis of generation.
11. The usual translation is "spirit." Maimonides may mean that in this context the word signifies the intellect.
12. Eccles. 12:7.   13. The usual translation is "spirit."   14. Num. 11:17.
15. Num. 11:25. The usual translation is "spirit."
16. The usual translation is "spirit."
17. II Sam. 23:2.   18. Prov. 29:11.   19. Isa. 19:3.
20. Isa. 40:13.   21. Cf. III 2.

in some of them also in the last sense, which is that of will, as we have explained. Thus the term should be interpreted in every passage according to what is indicated in the context.[22]

CHAPTER 41

*S*oul [*nephesh*] is an equivocal term. It is a term denoting the animal soul common | to every sentient being. Thus: *Wherein there is a living soul.*[1] And it is also a term denoting blood. Thus: *Thou shalt not eat the soul*[2] *with the flesh.*[3] It is also a term denoting the rational soul, I mean the form of man. Thus: *As the Lord liveth that made us this soul.*[4] And it is a term denoting the thing that remains of man after death. Thus: *Yet the soul of my lord shall be bound in the bundle of life.*[5] It is also a term denoting the will. Thus: *To bind his princes according to his soul,*[6] which means: through his will. Similarly: *And deliver not Thou him unto the soul of his enemies,*[7] which means: Thou will not deliver him to their will. In my opinion this is similar to: *If it be according to your soul to bury my dead,*[8] which means: if it be according to your purpose and will. And similarly: *Though Moses and Samuel stood before Me, yet My soul could not be toward this people,*[9] the meaning which is that I have no will toward them—that is, I do not wish that they endure. In all cases in which the term *soul* is applied to Him, may He be exalted, it has the meaning of will, as has already been set forth by us[10] with regard to the dictum of Scripture: *That shall do according to that which is in My heart and in My soul*[11]—the meaning of which is: in My will and purpose. One should interpret according to this sense the verse: *And His soul was grieved in the misery of Israel,*[12] which means that His will refrained from rendering *Israel* miserable. This *verse* was not translated at all by *Jonathan ben Uziel,* for he took it as using the term [soul] in its first sense, thought that he had met with a case of affection being ascribed to God, and accordingly refrained from translating[13] it. However, if the

22. Literally: that speech. The translation given in the text seems to be more probable than one referring the words, "that speech," to the present chapter of *The Guide of the Perplexed.*
1. Gen. 1:30.   2. I.e., the blood.   3. Deut. 12:23.   4. Jer. 38:16.
5. I Sam. 25:29.   6. Ps. 105:22.   7. Ps. 41:3.   8. Gen. 23:8.
9. Jer. 15:1.   10. Cf. I 39.   11. I Sam. 2:35.   12. Judg. 10:16.
13. Literally: interpreting.

term is taken in its last sense, the interpretation of the verse is very clear. For it is preceded by the statement that the providence of God, may He be exalted, had abandoned them so that they were perishing; and they implored God for help, but He did not help them. However, when they had gone far in repentance and their wretchedness had increased and the enemy had dominated them, He took pity on them; and His will refrained from letting their misery and wretchedness continue. Know this accordingly, for it is strange. In the words of Scripture: *in the misery of Israel,*[14] "in" is used instead of *from.* | It is therefore as if he said: *from the misery of Israel.* Many instances of this use [of "in"] have been enumerated by the linguists. Thus: *And that which remaineth in*[15] *the flesh and in*[16] *the bread;*[17] *Remains in*[18] *the years;*[19] *In the stranger and in the native of the land.*[20] This use is frequent.

CHAPTER 42

L iving [ḥay] is a term denoting a being that grows and is sentient. Thus: *Every moving thing that liveth.*[1] It is also a term denoting recovery from a very severe illness. Thus: *And lived*[2] *from his illness;*[3] *In the camp till they lived.*[4] Similarly in the expression: *A living flesh.*[5] Similarly *death [maveth]* is a term denoting both death and severe illness. Thus: *And his heart died within him, and he became as a stone,*[6] which refers to the severity of his illness. On this account Scripture makes it clear with regard to *the son of the woman of Zarephath* — that *his sickness was so sore, that there was no breath left in him.*[7] For if it had said: *And he died,* it would have been possible to interpret this as meaning that it was a case of severe illness in which the sick individual was near death, as *Nabal* was, when he heard the news. Some[8] of the men of Andalusia[9] interpret the verse as meaning that his breath was suspended so that no breath at all could be perceived in him — as happens to people struck with apoplexy or with asphyxia deriving from the womb, so that it is not known if the one in question is dead or alive and the doubt remains a day or two. The term

14. Figuring in the verse under discussion.   15. Instead of: *from.*
16. Instead of: *from.*   17. Lev. 8:32.   18. Instead of: *from.*   19. Lev. 25:52.
20. Exod. 12:19. Instead of: *from the stranger and from the native of the land.*
 1. Gen. 9:3.   2. I.e., was recovered.   3. Isa. 38:9
 4. Josh. 5:8. I.e., was recovered.   5. Lev. 13:10. I.e., flesh grown healthy.
 6. I Sam. 25:37.   7. I Kings 17:17.   8. Or: one.   9. Or: of Spain (in general).

[living] is often used also in the sense of acquisition of knowledge. Thus: *So shall they be life unto thy soul;*[10] *For whoso findeth me findeth life;*[11] *For they are life unto those that find them.*[12] This use is frequent. In accordance with it, correct opinions are called *life* and false opinions *death*. God, may He be exalted, says accordingly: *See, I have set before thee this day life and good, and so on.*[13] He has thereby made it clear that *good* is *life* and that *evil* is *death* | and has explained these terms. I make a similar interpretation of His dictum, may He be exalted, *That ye may live,*[14] analogous to the traditional interpretation[15] of the dictum of Scripture: *That it may be well with thee, and so on.*[16] Because of this figurative sense being generally known in the Hebrew language, the Sages have said: *The righteous even in death are called living, [whereas] the wicked even in life are called dead.*[17] Know this.

CHAPTER 43

Wing [*kanaph*] is an equivocal term, and its equivocality is mostly due to its being used in a figurative sense. The first meaning given to it is that of a wing of the living beings that fly. Thus: *Any winged fowl that flieth in the heaven.*[1] Subsequently it was applied figuratively to the extremities and corners of garments. Thus: *Upon the four wings*[2] *of thy covering.*[3] Afterwards it was applied figuratively to the farthest ends and extremities of the habitable part of the earth, which are remote from the places where we live.[4] Thus: *That it might take hold of the wings*[5] *of the earth;*[6] *From the uttermost wing*[7] *of the earth have we heard songs.*[8] Ibn Janāḥ[9] says that the term also occurs with the signification of concealing, as it is akin to the Arabic, in which one may say, "kanaftu" a thing, meaning: I have concealed it. He accordingly interprets[10] the verse, *Yet shall not thy*

10. Prov. 3:22.   11. Prov. 8:35.   12. Prov. 4:22.
13. Deut. 30:15. The verse continues: *and death and evil.*   14. Deut. 5:30.
15. *tafsīr*, the word used here, may mean both "interpretation" and "translation."
16. Deut. 22:7. Cf. B.T., Qiddushin, 39, and the Aramaic translation of the verse attributed to Jonathan.
17. B.T., Berakhoth, 18a–b.
1. Deut. 4:17.   2. I.e., corners.   3. Deut. 22:12.   4. Literally: from our places.
5. I.e., ends.   6. Job 38:13.   7. I.e., end.   8. Isa. 24:16.
9. A grammarian and lexicographer of the eleventh century.
10. See *The Book of Hebrew Roots, by Abū'l-Walīd Marwān Ibn Janāḥ*, ed. Ad. Neubauer (Oxford, 1875), p. 325.

Teacher be winged[11] [*yikaneph*], as meaning: thy Enlightener shall not be concealed and hidden away from thee; and this is a good explanation.[12] In my opinion this meaning occurs also in the verse, *And he shall not uncover the wing of his father*,[13] which means that he shall not uncover that of his father which is concealed. Similarly the verse, *Spread therefore thy wings over thy handmaid*,[14] has to be interpreted in my opinion as meaning: spread that by which thou concealest over thy handmaid. In my opinion it is in this sense that *wing* is figuratively applied to the Creator, may He be exalted, and also to the angels. For according to our opinion the angels have no bodies, as I shall make clear.[15] Accordingly the interpretation of the dictum of Scripture, *Under whose wings thou art come to trust*,[16] should be: thou art come | to be hidden under that by which He conceals. Similarly in all cases in which *wing* occurs with reference to the angels, it signifies that which conceals. Will you not consider the dictum of Scripture: *With twain*[17] *he covered his face, and with twain he covered his feet?*[18] This means that the cause of his existence, I mean that of the angel, is most hidden and concealed, that cause being indicated by the expression *his face*. And similarly the things of which he, I mean the angel, is the cause — these being *his feet*, as we have made clear[19] when dealing with the equivocality of the word *foot* — are also hidden. For the acts of the intellects are hidden, and their effects become clear only after one has trained oneself. This is due to two causes, one of which should be referred to them and one to us.[20] I mean the weakness of our apprehension and the difficulty of apprehending, in its true reality, that which is separate from matter. As for the dictum of Scripture, *And with twain he did fly*,[21] I shall explain in a separate chapter[22] in what sense the motion of flying is attributed to the angels.

11. Isa. 30:20.   12. Or: translation. For *tafsīr*, see n. 15, preceding chap.
13. Deut. 23:1.   14. Ruth 3:9.   15. Cf. I 49.
16. Ruth 2:12. The complete verse reads: *The Lord recompense thy work and a full reward be given thee of the Lord God of Israel, under whose wings thou art come to trust.*
17. I.e., two wings.   18. Isa. 6:2.   19. Cf. I 28.
20. Literally: from their direction and from our direction.
21. Isa. 6:2.   22. Cf. I 49.

CHAPTER 44

Eye [*ᶜayin*] is an equivocal term. It is a term denoting a well[1] of water. Thus: *By an eye*[2] *of water in the wilderness.*[3] It is also a term denoting the seeing eye. Thus: *Eye for eye.*[4] It is further a term denoting providence.[5] Thus Scripture says with regard to *Jeremiah:*[6] *Take him and have*[7] *thy eyes on him;*[8] the meaning of which is: direct thy watchfulness to him. It is in the figurative sense that the term is used of God in every passage in question. Thus: *And Mine eyes and My heart shall be there perpetually,*[9] which means My providence and My purpose, as we have set forth before;[10] *The eyes of the Lord thy God are always upon it,*[11] which means that His providence is upon it; *Which are the eyes of the Lord that run to and fro,*[12] which means that His providence extends also to everything that is on earth, as shall be mentioned in the chapters dealing with providence that will come later on.[13] When, however, the word *seeing* or *beholding*, is joined with the word "eyes" — as for instance in the verses: *Open Thine two eyes . . . and see,*[14] and *His eyes behold*[15] — it is | intellectual apprehension that is meant in all these cases, and not sensory apprehension. For all sensation is, as you know, an affection and a state in which impressions are received, whereas He, may He be exalted, is active and not passive,[16] as I shall explain later on.

1. Maimonides here uses the Arabic word *ᶜayn*, which, like the Hebrew *ᶜayin*, means both an eye and a well of water.
2. I.e., well.   3. Gen. 16:7.   4. Exod. 21:24.
5. The term *ᶜināyah* used here also means "watchfulness."
6. The words are spoken by Nebuchadnezzar, king of the Chaldees, and are addressed to Nebuzaradan, who served him.
7. Literally: put.   8. Jer. 39:12.   9. I Kings 9:3.   10. Cf. I 39.   11 Deut. 11:12.
12. Zech. 4:10. The quotation as given by Maimonides is slightly inaccurate.
13. In Part III.
14. II Kings 19:16. The quotation as given by Maimonides is slightly inaccurate.
15. Ps. 11:4.
16. The word *munfaᶜil* used here in the Arabic text is a passive participle of the verb *faᶜala*: to do, to act. *infiᶜāl*, which is the verbal noun of *munfaᶜil*, has been rendered in this translation by the term "affection."

To hear [*shamoʿa*] is an equivocal word. It is used sometimes as having the meaning, to hear,[1] and sometimes as having the meaning, to accept. As for the meaning, to hear, it is found in the verses: *Neither let it be heard out of thy mouth;*[2] *And the report thereof was heard in Pharaoh's house.*[3] This use is frequent. Of a like frequency is use of *to hear* with the meaning, to accept. Thus: *And they heard*[4] *not Moses;*[5] *If they hear*[6] *and serve;*[7] *Shall we then hear*[8] *you?*[9] *And shall not hear*[10] *thy words.*[11] The word is also used in the sense of science and knowledge. Thus: *A nation whose tongue thou shalt not hear;*[12] the interpretation being, whose speech you shall not know. In all cases in which the word *hearing* occurs in relation to God and in which, according to the external meaning of the text, the word appears to be used in its first sense, it expresses the notion of apprehension, which pertains to the third sense. Thus: *And the Lord heard;*[13] *For that He hath heard your murmurings.*[14] In all these passages the apprehension of science is meant. If, however, according to the external meaning of the text, the word is used in its second sense, it expresses the notion that God, may He be exalted, responds, or does not respond, to the prayer of him who prays. Thus: *I will surely hear his cry;*[15] *I will hear, for I am gracious;*[16] *Incline Thine ear, O Lord, and hear;*[17] *But the Lord would not hear your voice, nor give ear unto you;*[18] *Yea, when ye make many prayers, I will not hear;*[19] *For I will not hear thee.*[20] This use is frequent. As for these figurative senses and similes, you will be given an explanation that will quench your thirst and clear your doubt. The meanings of all of them will be made manifest to you, so that no difficulty will remain in anything that is in them. |

1. Maimonides here uses the Arabic word.   2. Exod. 23:13.
3. Gen. 45:16.   4. I.e., accepted.   5. Exod. 6:9.   6. I.e., accept.
7. Job 36:11.   8. I.e., accept.   9. Neh. 13:27.   10. I.e., accept.
11. Josh. 1:18.   12. Deut. 28:49.   13. Num. 11:1.   14. Exod. 16:7.
15. Exod. 22:22.   16. Exod. 22:26.   17. II Kings 19:16.   18. Deut. 1:45.
19. Isa. 1:15.   20. Jer. 7:16.

CHAPTER 46

We have mentioned in one[1] of the chapters of this Treatise[2] that there is an immense difference between guidance leading to a knowledge of the existence of a thing and an investigation of the true reality of the essence and substance of that thing. The reason is that guidance leading to the knowledge of the existence of a thing can be had even if that should be through the accidents of the thing or through its acts or through a relation — which may be very remote from the thing — existing between the latter and things other than itself. For instance, if you wish to make known the ruler of a certain region of the earth to one of the people of that ruler's country, who does not know him, you can inform him about that ruler and draw his attention to the latter's existence in many different ways. One of them consists in your saying that the ruler is a tall individual who is white in color and gray-haired. Thus you would make him known through his accidents. You may also say that he is the one whom you see surrounded by a great company of people, who are riding or on foot, with drawn swords around him and banners raised above his head, while trumpets are sounded in front of him; or that he is the one residing in a castle, that is in a certain city of that region of the earth; or that he is the one who ordered this wall to be built or this bridge to be laid; or you may mention similar actions of his and similar relations of his to what is other than he. You may, however, indicate his existence through circumstances that are of a more hidden nature than those that have been mentioned. For instance, if someone asks you, Has this country a ruler? you shall answer him, Yes, undoubtedly. And if he asks you, What proof is there for this? you shall tell him, This proof is to be found in the fact that while this money-changer is, as you see, a weak and small man and this great amount of dinars is placed before him, this other big, strong, and poor individual is standing in front of him | and asking him to give him as alms a carob-grain and that the money-changer does not do this, but reprimands him and drives him off by means of words. For, but for his fear of the ruler, the poor man would have been quick to kill him or to drive him away and to take the wealth that is in his possession. Accordingly, this is a proof of the fact that this city has a king. Thus you would have proved the existence of the king through the fact

1. Or: in some.   2. Cf. I 33.

that matters in the city proceed in an orderly fashion,[3] the cause of which is the fear of the ruler and the anticipation of the punishment he metes out.

Now in all that we have said by way of parable there is nothing to give an indication of the ruler's essence and of the true reality of his substance in respect of his being a ruler. A similar thing has occurred with regard to the knowledge of God, may He be honored and magnified, given to the multitude in all the books of the prophets and also in the *Torah*. For necessity required that all of them be given guidance to the belief in the existence of God, may He be exalted, and in His possessing all the perfections. I mean to say guidance to the belief that He does not merely exist, as the earth and the heavens do, but that He is an existent who is living, possessed of knowledge and of power,[4] active, and having all the other characteristics that ought to be believed in with reference to His existence. This shall be made clear later on. The minds of the multitude were accordingly guided to the belief that He exists by imagining that he is corporeal,[5] and to the belief that He is living by imagining that He is capable of motion.[6] For the multitude perceive nothing other than bodies as having a firmly established existence and as being indubitably true, for anything that is not a body, but subsists in a body, is existent; but its existence is more deficient than that of a body, as it requires a body in order to exist. That, however, which is neither a body nor in a body is not an existent thing in any respect, according to man's initial representation, particularly from the point of view of the imagination. Similarly the multitude do not represent to themselves the notion of life as anything other than motion and consider that that which has no local motion due to its will is not alive, despite the fact that motion does not pertain to the substance of the living but is an accident attaching to it. Similarly apprehension, | as it is habitually known among us, comes about through the instrumentality of the senses, I mean to say through hearing and seeing. And similarly we do not know nor can we represent to ourselves how a notion can be transmitted from the soul of one individual who is among us to the soul of another individual except through the instrumentality of speech, which is a sound produced by the lips,[7] the tongue, and the other organs of speech. Accordingly, as our minds are likewise guided to the belief that God, may He be exalted, apprehends and that notions are communicated from Him to the prophets in order that

3. Literally: through the orderliness of the circumstances of the city.
4. Literally: knowing and being able.
5. Literally: by means of the imagination of corporeality.
6. Literally: by means of the imagination of motion.
7. More or less literally: cut by the lip.

they should communicate them to us, He is described to us as hearing and seeing; the meaning thereof being that He apprehends and knows the visible and audible things. He is also described to us as speaking; the meaning thereof being that notions are communicated from Him, may He be exalted, to the prophets. This is the meaning of prophecy. Later on this shall be made extremely clear. Again, as we have no intellectual cognition of our bringing somebody other than us to existence except through a direct act,[8] He is described as active. Similarly, in view of the fact that the multitude apprehend no living thing that is not endowed with a soul, He is also described to us as having a soul. And though the term "soul" is an equivocal one, as has been made clear,[9] the meaning is that He is living. Since with regard to us the apprehension can be made that all these acts are only performed by means of bodily organs, all these organs are figuratively ascribed to Him: those by means of which local motion takes place — I mean the feet and their soles; those by means of which hearing, seeing, and smelling come about — that is, the ear, the eye, and the nose; those by means of which speech and the matter[10] of speech are produced — that is, the mouth, the tongue, and the voice; finally, those by means of which he among us who acts carries out his actions — those organs are the hands, the fingers, the palm, and the arm.

To sum up all this: God, may He be exalted above every deficiency, has had bodily organs figuratively ascribed to Him in order that | His acts should be indicated by this means. And those particular acts are figuratively ascribed to Him in order to indicate a certain perfection, which is not identical with the particular act mentioned. For instance, an eye, an ear, a hand, a mouth, a tongue, have been figuratively ascribed to Him so that by this means, sight, hearing, action, and speech should be indicated. But sight and hearing have been figuratively ascribed to Him with a view to indicating apprehension in general. For this reason you will find that the Hebrew language substitutes the apprehension made by one sense for that made by another. Thus Scripture says: *See the word of the Lord;*[11] which is like *hear,* for the intended meaning is: apprehend the meaning of His speech. Similarly: *See the smell of my son;*[12] which is like saying, *Smell the smell of my son,* for the intended meaning refers to the apprehension

8. The word *mubāshara* used here also means "an act accomplished through contact" and "sexual intercourse."
9. Cf. I 41.
10. Maimonides uses the word *mādda,* meaning "matter" (*materia*). The expression "matter of speech" refers to sounds.
11. Jer. 2:31.   12. Gen. 27:27.

of his smell. In conformity with this it is said, *And all the people saw the sounds*,[13] although this station also constituted *a vision of prophecy*, as is well known and universally admitted in our community.[14] Action and speech are ascribed to God so that an overflow proceeding[15] from Him should thereby be indicated, as shall be made clear further on.[16] All bodily organs that you can find mentioned in all of the books of prophecy are either organs of local motion mentioned with a view to indicating life, or organs of sensation mentioned with a view to indicating apprehension, or organs of prehension mentioned with a view to indicating action, or organs of speech mentioned with a view to indicating the overflow of the intellects toward the prophets, as will be made clear. The guidance contained in all these figurative senses is intended to establish in us the belief that there is an existent who is living, is the agent[17] who produces everything other than He, and in addition apprehends His own act. When we shall begin to expound the negation of the attributes, we shall make clear[18] how all this is reducible to one notion, which is exclusively that of the essence of God, may He be exalted. For the purpose of the present chapter is solely to make clear the meaning of the bodily organs ascribed to God, may He be exalted above every deficiency, and to explain that | all of them are mentioned with a view to indicating the actions proper to these organs, which actions — according to us[19] — constitute a perfection. In this way we indicate that He is perfect in various manners of perfection, a circumstance to which the Sages draw our attention by saying: *The Torah speaketh in the language of the sons of man.*[19a]

The organs of local motion ascribed to Him, may He be exalted, are, for instance, those figuring in scriptural dicta such as these: *The stool of My feet;*[20] *And the place of the soles of My feet.*[21]

The organs of prehension ascribed to Him may be found in scriptural dicta such as these: *The hand of the Lord;*[22] *With the finger of God;*[23] *The work of Thy fingers;*[24] *And Thou hast laid Thine palm upon me;*[25] *And to whom hath the arm of the Lord been revealed?*[26] *Thy right hand, O Lord.*[27]

13. Exod. 20:15.
14. Literally: in the community. The word translated "community" is *millah*, which in Maimonides' time connoted primarily a religious community.
15. Literally: overflowing (as a participle).   16. Cf. II 12.
17. *fāᶜil*, a participle of the verb *faᶜala*, which may mean "to act," but which also has a transitive sense coming close to the verbs "to do" or even "to make."
18. Cf. I 53.
19. I.e., according to the human point of view.
19a. B.T., Yebamoth, 71a; B.T., Baba Meṣiᶜa, 31b.
20. Isa. 66:1.   21. Ezek. 43:7.   22. Exod. 9:3.   23. Exod. 31:18.
24. Ps. 8:4.   25. Ps. 139:5.   26. Isa. 53:1.   27. Exod. 15:6.

The organs of speech ascribed to Him may be found in the scriptural dicta such as these: *The mouth of the Lord has spoken;*[28] *And He would open His lips against thee;*[29] *The voice of the Lord is powerful;*[30] *And His tongue is as a devouring fire.*[31]

The organs of sensation ascribed to Him may be found in scriptural dicta such as these: *His eyes behold, His eyelids try, the children of men;*[32] *The eyes of the Lord that run to and fro;*[33] *Incline Thine ear, O Lord, and hear;*[34] *For ye have kindled a fire in My nostril.*[35]

Of the hidden parts of the body, only the heart is ascribed to Him because of its being an equivocal term. For it is also a term denoting the intellect; it is, moreover, the principle of life in living beings. For the dicta of Scripture, *My bowels are troubled for him,*[36] and, *The trouble of Thy bowels,*[37] are intended likewise to signify the heart, for bowel is a term used in a general and particular sense. In its particular sense, it is a term denoting the intestines; whereas in its general sense, it is a term denoting all the hidden parts of the body. It is accordingly also a term denoting the heart. A proof of this is to be found in the dictum, *And Thy Law is within my bowels,*[38] which is equivalent to its saying, *within my heart.* On this account it says in the *verse*: *My bowels are troubled,* and, *The trouble of Thy bowels.*[39] For the *expression trouble* is applied to the heart rather than to the other parts of the body. Thus: *My heart troubles me.*[40] Similarly a shoulder is not figuratively ascribed to Him because it is, according to what is generally known, an organ of transport, and also because the thing that is transported touches it. All the more are the organs of nutrition not figuratively ascribed to Him, for even | according to what first comes to mind, these are clearly deficient.

In truth, the status of all the organs is the same — all of them, both the apparent and the hidden, being organs required for the various actions of the soul. Some of them are organs required of necessity in order that the individual may last for a certain time. All the hidden parts of the body are of this nature. And some are organs required of necessity in order that the species should last. The organs of generation are of this nature. Some again are organs required in order that the individual be in a good state and that his actions be perfected. The feet, the hands, and the eyes are of this nature

---

28. Isa. 1:20.   29. Job 11:5.   30. Ps. 29:4.   31. Isa. 30:27.
32. Ps. 11:4.
33. Zech. 4:10. The quotation as given by Maimonides is slightly inaccurate.
34. II Kings 19:16.   35. Jer. 17:4.   36. Jer. 31:20.   37. Isa. 63:15.
38. Ps. 40:9.   39. Two verses quoted above are referred to here.
40. Jer. 4:19.

— all of them being required for the perfection of motion, work, and apprehension. Now the necessity of motion for living beings is due to its being required for the pursuit of what agrees with them and for the avoidance of what disagrees. The necessity of the senses, on the other hand, lies in their being required in order that what disagrees should be distinguished from what agrees with one.[41] Again the need of man for manufacturing work is due to its being required for the preparation of his food, his clothing, and his place of shelter. For this is bound up with his nature, I mean his needing to prepare what is suitable for him. Sometimes it is found that some animals possess a certain craft because of their need for that particular craft. Now I perceive no one who would doubt the fact that God, may He be exalted, has no need of a thing that would prolong His existence or improve His circumstances. Accordingly He has no organs; I mean to say by this that He is not a body and that His acts are performed through His essence and not through an organ. Now faculties[42] undoubtedly pertain to the class of organs. Accordingly He does not possess any faculty. Thereby I mean that there does not exist in Him anything other than His essence in virtue of which object He might act, know, or will. For the attributes are merely faculties[43] with regard to which the terminology, and nothing else, has been changed. However, this is not the subject of this chapter.

The Sages, *may their memory be blessed*, have made a comprehensive dictum rejecting everything that is suggested to the estimative faculty by any of the corporeal attributive qualifications mentioned by the prophets. This dictum will indicate to you that the doctrine of the corporeality of God did not ever occur even for a single day to the *Sages, may their memory be blessed*, and that this was not according to them a matter lending itself to imagination or to confusion. | For this reason you will find that in the whole of the *Talmud* and in all the *Midrashim*[44] they keep to the external sense of the dicta of the prophets . This is so because of their knowledge that this matter is safe from confusion[45] and that with regard to it no error is to be feared in any respect; all the dicta have to be considered as parables and as a guidance conducting the mind toward one being. And when the parable is of a consistent nature — as when God, may He be exalted, is

41. Literally: as for the necessity of the senses, it is for the knowledge of what disagrees from what agrees.
42. *quwwā*. The word also means "forces."
43. Cf. preceding note.   44. In the text: *Midrashoth*.
45. The Arabic text also permits this translation: In this matter confusion is safe. (In fact, if one solely considers the wording of the text, the latter translation seems to be more exact.)

likened to a king, who gives orders and prohibitions to, and punishes and rewards, the people of his country, and who has servants and executives who carry out his orders and do for him what he wishes to be done — they, I mean the *Sages*, likewise kept to this parable in every passage and spoke, in conformity with what the parable requires, of speech, of a favorable answer being given, or of a refusal with regard to a particular matter, and of other such actions of kings. In all this they felt themselves sure and safe in that there would not be confusion and difficulty with regard to this point. The comprehensive dictum to which we have alluded is their dictum in *Bereshith Rabbah*,[46] which reads: *Great is the power of the prophets; for they liken a form to its creator. For it is said: And upon the likeness of the throne was a likeness as the appearance of a man.*[47] They have thus made clear and manifest that all the forms apprehended by all the prophets in *the vision of prophecy* are created forms of which God is the Creator. And this is correct, for every imagined form is created. How admirable is their saying: *Great is the power*, as though to say they, peace be on them, considered this matter great. For they always speak in this way when they express their appreciation of the greatness of something said or done, but whose appearance is shocking. Thus they say:[48] *A certain rabbi performed the act [of ḥaliṣa[49]] with a slipper, alone and by night. Another rabbi said thereupon: How great is his strength to have done it alone.*[50] *How great is his strength* means *how great is his power*. They say, as it were: how great was the thing that the prophets were driven | to do when they indicated the essence of God, may He be exalted, by means of the created thing that He has created. Understand this thoroughly. They have thus made clear and manifest, as far as they themselves are concerned, that they were innocent of the belief in the corporeality of God; and furthermore, that all the shapes and figures that are seen *in the vision of prophecy* are created things. However, the prophets *likened a form to its creator*, as the Sages, *may their memory be blessed*, put it. If, however, after these things have been said, someone out of malice wishes to think ill of them, depreciating men who are not seen and about whom there is no clear indication at present,[51] his doing this will not harm them, *may their memory be blessed*.

46. Genesis Rabbah, XXVII.   47. Ezek. 1:26.   48. B.T., Yebamoth, 104a.

49. A rite by which a man renounces the obligation to marry his brother's widow and sets her free to marry somebody else.

50. The current editions of the Talmud have a slightly different text, the meaning of which is: *to have followed the minority.* This dictum is in Aramaic, whereas the one quoted from Genesis Rabbah is in Hebrew.

51. Or: men whom he has not seen and of whom he has at present no knowledge; or: men who did not see him and who have at present no knowledge.

We have mentioned several times[1] that the books of the prophets do not figuratively ascribe to God anything that the multitude imagine to be a deficiency or that one cannot represent to oneself as belonging to Him, may He be exalted, even if these things have the same status[2] as those that are figuratively ascribed to Him. For the things that are predicated of Him suggest to the estimative faculty certain perfections or can be imagined to be perfections with respect to Him. Accordingly, in view of this having been established, it behooves us to explain why hearing, sight, and the sense of smell are figuratively ascribed to Him, may He be exalted, whereas the sense of taste and that of touch are not.

Now the status of all five senses — with regard to the fact that He, may He be exalted, is high above them — is one and the same.[3] And all the senses are a deficiency from the standpoint of apprehension. This is so even with regard to a being that only apprehends by means of the senses, for the latter are passive, receptive of impressions, intermittent, and subject to pain, as are all the other organs. The meaning of our saying that He, may He be exalted, has sight is that He apprehends the visible things, and that of our saying that He has hearing is that He apprehends the audible things. He could similarly have had the sense of taste | and that of touch predicated of Him, and that could have been interpreted as meaning that He apprehends the things that are objects of the senses of taste and of touch. For the status of the apprehension of all of them is one and the same. If, however, the apprehension characteristic of one of the senses is denied Him, it would necessarily follow that the apprehensions characteristic of all of them[4] — I mean of all the five senses — should be denied Him. If, however, His having an apprehension characteristic of one of them — I mean an apprehension of what one of these senses apprehends — should be affirmed of Him, it would necessarily follow that He apprehends all the things apprehensible by the five senses.

Now we find that our books say, *And the Lord saw,*[5] *And the Lord heard,*[6] *And the Lord smelled,*[7] but they do not say, *And the Lord tasted,* nor do they say, *And the Lord touched.* The cause of this is to be found in

1. Cf. I 26 and 46.   2. Literally: law, or judgment.
3. Literally: and the law of [God's], may He be exalted, being elevated above the five senses is one.
4. Literally: all their five apprehensible [categories of objects of apprehension].
5. Cf. Gen. 6:5.   6. Cf. Num. 11:1.   7. Cf. Gen. 8:21.

the fact that it is firmly established in everyone's imagination that God does
not encounter bodies in the way one body encounters another, for people
do not even see it. Now these two senses, I mean the sense of taste and the
sense of touch, do not apprehend the things sensed by them before they are
in contact with them. On the other hand, the sense of sight, that of hearing,
and that of smell, can apprehend from a distance the qualities sensed by
them as well as the bodies that are the bearers of those qualities. It is, therefore, according to the imagination of the multitude, permitted to ascribe
them to God. In addition, the purpose and the intent in figuratively ascribing
to Him these senses are to indicate that He apprehends our actions. Now the
sense of hearing and that of sight suffice for this; I mean hereby that by
means of them everything that someone other than oneself does or says
can be apprehended. Thus the Sages have said, when setting forth their
admonitions by way of reproof and warning: *Know what is above thee, a
seeing eye and a hearing ear.*[8]

Now when you investigate the true reality, you shall see that the
status of all the senses is that of any one of them, and that from the same
standpoint from which it is negated that He has apprehensions involving
touch and taste, it should also be negated that He has sight, hearing, and
the sense of smell. For all of them are apprehensions of a corporeal nature,
affections, and changeable states. However, with regard to some of them,
it is apparent that they are deficiencies, whereas others are deemed | to be
perfections; just as it is manifest that to imagine is a deficiency, whereas
it is not manifest that to reflect and gradually to understand is likewise a
deficiency. Therefore *fancy*,[9] which word means imagination, is not
figuratively ascribed to Him, whereas *thought* [*maḥshabah*] and *comprehension* [*tebunah*], which words mean reflection and understanding, are
figuratively ascribed to Him. Thus it is said: *Which* [*the Lord*] *thought;*[10]
And with His comprehension He stretched out the heavens.[11] Accordingly, the
position with regard to the internal apprehensions is similar to that obtaining
with regard to the external sensory apprehensions; some of the former as
well as of the latter are figuratively ascribed to Him, while others are not.
All this is *according to the language of the sons of man.* For they predicate
of God what they deem to be a perfection in respect to Him and do not

8. Mishnah, Aboth, II 1.   9. *raʿyon*. This Hebrew word usually means "thought."
10. Jer. 49:20. The quotation as given by Maimonides is not accurate. The word equivalent
    to *the Lord* does not occur in the portion of the verse quoted in the text. However, this
    inaccuracy does not lead to an alteration of the meaning of the verse, nor does it entail
    the invalidation of the point that Maimonides makes.
11. Jer. 10:12.

predicate of Him that which is manifestly a deficiency. When, however, the true reality is investigated it will be found — as shall be demonstrated — that He has no essential attribute[12] existing in true reality, such as would be superadded to His essence.

CHAPTER 48

In all cases in which the notion of hearing occurs with reference to God, may He be exalted, you will find that *Onqelos the Proselyte* avoids the expression and has interpreted its meaning as signifying that the matter in question reached Him, may He be exalted, or that He apprehended it. Or if it occurs with regard to a prayer, he interprets its meaning as signifying that He accepted it or did not accept it. Thus when interpreting the words, *The Lord heard*, he always says, *It was heard before the Lord*. And with regard to prayer, he translates, *I will surely hear his cry*,[1] by the phrase, *I will surely accept*.[2] This happens continually in his interpretation, and he does not deviate from this usage in any place.

As for the expressions denoting sight that occur with reference to Him, may He be exalted, *Onqelos* varies with regard to them in a strange way, the purpose and intention of which are not clear to me. For in some place he interprets the words, *And the Lord saw*, by the words, *And the Lord beheld;* whereas in other passages he interprets these as follows: | *And it was revealed before the Lord*. Now the fact that in his interpretation he uses the words, *And the Lord beheld*, is a clear proof that the word *to behold* is equivocal in the Syriac[3] language, inasmuch as it indicates both the notion of an apprehension of the intellect and that of an apprehension of the senses. This being so, according to his opinion, would that I knew why in some cases he avoids the expression and interprets the Hebrew words as: *And it was revealed before the Lord*. When I examined the copies of this *translation* that I could find and withal what I had heard in the course of instruction, I discovered that in the cases in which the word *seeing* is found in conjunction

12. The word translated "attribute" derives from the same root as the verb translated "to predicate of."

1. Exod. 22:22.   2. In Aramaic.

3. *suryāniyya*. Syriac being a dialect of Aramaic, the Arabic word is applied by Maimonides and other writers also to the language of Onqelos, which is another dialect of Aramaic.

with wrongdoing or harming and committing an act of aggression, he interprets it as: *It was revealed before the Lord*. Thus there is no doubt that the
word *to behold* has in that language[4] the meaning: to apprehend and to
establish the thing apprehended as it is apprehended. Therefore when
seeing is mentioned in connection with wrongdoing, he did not say, *And
He beheld*, but, *And it was revealed before the Lord*. For I found that he
used the word *to behold* to interpret the term *seeing* in all the passages in
the whole of *Torah* in which the [Hebrew] word is used with reference to
God, except in the verses that I am about to cite to you. *Because the Lord
hath seen my affliction*,[5] translated by him: *Because my affliction was revealed
before the Lord. For I have seen all that Laban doeth unto thee*,[6] translated
by him: *For before me it is revealed;* although in this case the speaker is but
an angel, an apprehension indicative of his establishing the fact apprehended
by him cannot be ascribed to him because this fact consists in wrongdoing.
And God saw the children of Israel,[7] translated by him: *And the enslavement of the children of Israel was revealed before the Lord. I have surely
seen the affliction of My people*,[8] translated by him: *The enslavement of My
people was surely revealed before Me. And I have also seen the oppression*,[9]
translated by him: *And the oppression was also revealed before Me. And
that He had seen their affliction*,[10] translated by him: *For their enslavement
was revealed before Him. I have seen this people*,[11] translated by him: *This
people was revealed before me* — for the meaning of this verse is: I saw their
disobedience; just as in the verse, *And God saw the children of Israel*,[12] the
meaning is that He saw their misery. *And when the Lord saw [it]*, *He
abhorred [them]*,[13] translated by him: *And it was revealed before the Lord.
When He seeth that their power is gone*,[14] translated by him: *For it was
revealed before Him* — for this | too is a state when wrong was done to them
and when the enemy was dominant. All these passages are consistent and
take into account the verse: *And Thou canst not look on iniquity*.[15] Thus it is
on this account that [Onqelos] translates every reference to *enslavement* or
disobedience by: *It was revealed before Him*, or *It was revealed before Me*.

However, this excellent and lengthy explanation,[16] which is not subject to doubt, is spoilt for me by three passages that, if the analogy held
good,[17] ought to have been interpreted by him: *And it was revealed before
the Lord*. But in the copies of his translation we find that he translates:

4. I.e., Syriac or Aramaic.   5. Gen. 29:32. Maimonides' quotation is slightly inaccurate.
6. Gen. 31:12.   7. Exod. 2:25.   8. Exod. 3:7.   9. Exod. 3:9.
10. Exod. 4:31.   11. Exod. 32:9.   12. This verse is quoted earlier in this chapter.
13. Deut. 32:19.   14. Deut. 32:36.   15. Hab. 1:13.   16. Of Onqelos' method.
17. Literally: according to this analogy (or syllogism).

And the Lord beheld. These passages are: *And the Lord saw that the wickedness of man was great;*[18] *And God saw the earth and, behold, it was corrupt;*[19] *And the Lord saw that Leah was hated.*[20] The explanation that seems to me the most probable is that those are mistakes that have crept into the copies of the translation, for we do not have *Onqelos'* autograph of these passages; if we had, we should have said that perhaps[21] he had in mind some interpretation with regard to this. As for his interpreting the verse, *God will see for Himself the lamb,*[22] by the words, *The lamb is revealed before the Lord,* this is so either because this does not suggest to the estimative faculty that God, may He be exalted, will start to seek the lamb and to bring it into existence, or because from the standpoint of the [Syriac] language it was considered shocking that His apprehension should be connected with such an individual as an animal devoid of reason. As far as these passages are concerned,[23] a careful investigation should be made with a view to correcting the copies of the translation. If, however, the passages are found to have the text we cited, I do not know what purpose [Onqelos] had in translating them in this manner.[24]

CHAPTER 49

The angels too are not endowed with bodies, but are intellects separate from matter. However, they are the objects of an act,[1] and God has created them, as will be explained.[2] The Sages say in *Bereshith Rabbah:*[3] *The flaming sword which turns every way,*[4] *is called thus with reference to the verse: His ministers a flaming fire.*[5] [*The expression*], *which turns every way,* | *alludes to the fact that sometimes they turn into men, sometimes into women, sometimes into spirits, and sometimes into angels.* Through this dictum they have made it clear that the angels are not endowed with matter and

18. Gen. 6:5.   19. Gen. 6:12.   20. Gen. 29:31.
21. Literally: Onqelos' autograph in this so as to say that perhaps. . . .
22. Gen. 22:8.
23. Maimonides evidently has in mind the three passages in which Onqelos' translation does not eliminate the suggestion that God apprehends evil.
24. Literally: I do not know for him a purpose in this.
1. *mafᶜūlūna,* which is the past passive participle of the verb *faᶜala:* "to act" or "to do."
2. Cf. II 2 and 6.   3. Genesis Rabbah, XXI *in fine.*   4. Gen. 3:24.
5. Ps. 104:4. Literally: *The flaming of the sword which turns every way, upon the name His ministers a flaming fire.*

that outside the mind they have no fixed corporeal shape, but that all such shapes are only to be perceived in *the vision of prophecy* in consequence of the action of the imaginative capacity, as will be mentioned in connection with the notion of the true reality of prophecy. As for their dictum, *sometimes into women* — which implies that the prophets likewise sometimes see the angels *in the vision of the prophecy* in *the form of women* — it refers to the dictum of *Zechariah*, peace be on him: *And, behold, there came forth two women, and the wind was in their wings, and so on.*[6]

Now you already know that it is very difficult for man to apprehend, except after strenuous training, that which is pure of matter and absolutely devoid of corporeality. It is particularly difficult for one who does not differentiate between that which is cognized by the intellect and that which is imagined and who tends mostly toward imaginative apprehension alone. For such a one everything that is imagined exists or can exist, whereas that which does not enter within the net of imagination is in his opinion non-existent and incapable of existing. Accordingly, to individuals of this kind — and they form the majority of those engaged in speculation — the true reality of a notion never becomes known, nor does a difficulty ever become clear to them. Because of the difficulty of this matter, the books of the prophets likewise contain dicta whose external sense can be understood as signifying that the angels are corporeal, that they move, that they are in the form of men, that they are given orders by God, and that they carry out His orders and do what He wishes in virtue of His orders. All this is said so as to guide the mind to a knowledge of their existence and of their being alive and perfect, as we have explained with regard to God.[7]

However, if one would stop at this imagining with regard to the angels, their true reality and essence would be like the essence of God as it is conceived in the imagination of the multitude. For about God too, | statements are made from whose external sense it appears that He is a living, mobile[8] body, having the form of a man. Therefore the mind is guided toward a knowledge of the fact that the rank of the existence of the angels is below the rank of the deity through the admixture with their shape of something belonging to the shape of irrational animals, so that what is understood with regard to the existence of the Creator should be more perfect than what is understood with regard to their existence, just as man is more perfect than the irrational animals. However, an animal shape is attributed to them by attribution of wings only and in no other way. For flying cannot be represented to oneself without wings, just as walking cannot be represented to

6. Zech. 5:9.   7. Cf. I 46.   8. Or: moving.

oneself without legs. For the existence of these faculties cannot possibly be represented to oneself except in so far as they subsist in these substrata. The motion of flying has been chosen in order to point to the angels being living beings. For it is the most perfect and the noblest of the motions of the irrational animals, and man believes it to be a great perfection; so that he even wishes to fly in order that it might be easy for him to flee from all that harms him and that he might betake himself swiftly to whatever agrees with him, even if it be far off. Accordingly this motion is ascribed to the angels. Moreover, a bird appears and is hidden, approaches and moves far away, in very quick time; and all these are characteristics that, as shall be explained,[9] it behooves us to believe that the angels possess.

However, this which is deemed to be perfection, I mean the motion of flying, is not in any way ascribed to God, because it is a motion pertaining to an animal not endowed with reason. For you should not make a mistake with regard to the dictum, *And He rode upon a cherub, and did fly*,[10] for it is the *cherub* that *did fly*. And this parable is merely intended to indicate the swiftness of the coming to pass of that matter.[11] Similarly Scripture says: *Behold, the Lord rideth upon a swift cloud, and cometh unto Egypt*,[12] which refers to the swiftness of the descent upon them of the calamity referred to.

Nor should you be led into error by what you find especially in *Ezekiel* with regard to *the face of an ox* and *the face of a lion* and *the face of an eagle* and *the sole of the foot of a calf*.[13] For this has | another interpretation, which you will hear.[14] It is also merely a description of the *animals*. These intentions will be explained by means of hints sufficient to awaken the attention.

As for the motion of flying, it occurs in the texts in every passage, and it cannot be represented to oneself without a wing. Accordingly it was supposed that the angels had wings in order that guidance be given concerning the state of their existence, but not with a view to obtaining knowledge of the true reality of their essence. Know that everyone who accomplishes a very swift movement is described as flying so as to indicate the swiftness of the movement. Thus Scripture says: *As the eagle swoopeth down*.[15] For the eagle is swifter in his flight and swoop than any other bird; for this reason it is used in the parable. Know also that the two wings are the causes of flying. For this reason the number of wings seen in the prophetic vision corresponded to that of the causes of motion of a moving[16] thing. However, this is not the subject of this chapter.

9. Cf. II 42.   10. Ps. 18:11.   11. The word also means "command."   12. Isa. 19:1.
13. Ezek. 1:10 and 1:7.   14. Cf. III 1.   15. Deut. 28:49.   16. Or: mobile.

Know, thou who studiest this my Treatise, that belief is not the notion that is uttered, but the notion that is represented in the soul when it has been averred of it that it is in fact just as it has been represented. If you belong to those who are satisfied with expressing in speech the opinions that are correct or that you deem to be correct, without representing them to yourself and believing them, and still less without seeking certain knowledge regarding them, you take a very easy road. In accordance with this, you will find many stupid people holding to beliefs to which, in their representation, they do not attach any meaning whatever. If, however, you belong to those whose aspirations are directed toward ascending to that high rank which is the rank of speculation, and to gaining certain knowledge with regard to | God's being One by virtue of a true Oneness, so that no composition whatever is to be found in Him and no possibility of division in any way whatever — then you must know that He, may He be exalted, has in no way and in no mode any essential attribute, and that just as it is impossible that He should be a body, it is also impossible that He should possess an essential attribute. If, however, someone believes that He is one, but possesses a certain number of essential attributes, he says in his words that He is one, but believes Him in his thought to be many. This resembles what the Christians say: namely, that He is one but also three, and that the three are one. Similar to this is the assertion of him who says that He is one but possesses many attributes and that He and His attributes are one, while he denies at the same time His being corporeal and believes in His absolute simplicity; as if what we aimed at and investigated were what we should say and not what we should believe. For there is no belief except after a representation; belief is the affirmation that what has been represented is outside the mind just as it has been represented in the mind. If, together with this belief, one realizes that a belief different from it is in no way possible and that no starting point can be found in the mind for a rejection of this belief or for the supposition that a different belief is possible, there is certainty. When you shall have cast off desires and habits, shall have been endowed with understanding, and shall reflect on what I shall say in the following chapters, which shall treat of the negation of attributes, you shall necessarily achieve certain knowledge of it. Then you shall be one of those who represent to themselves *the unity of the Name* and not one of those who merely proclaim it with their mouth without representing to themselves that it has a meaning. With regard to men of this category, it is said: *Thou art near in their mouth, and far from their reins.*[1] But men ought rather to belong to the category of those who represent the truth[2] to themselves and apprehend it, even if they do not utter it, as | the virtuous are commanded to do — for they are told: *Commune with your own heart upon your bed, and be still. Selah.*[3]

CHAPTER 51

There are many things in existence that are clear and manifest: primary intelligibles and things perceived by the senses and, in addition, the things that come near to these in respect to their clarity. If man had been left as[1] he [naturally] is, he would not have needed a proof of them — for instance, for the existence of motion, the existence of man's ability to act, the manifestations of generation and corruption, the natures of the things that are apparent to the senses, like the hotness of fire, the coldness of water, and many other things of this kind. Yet since strange opinions have arisen due either to people who committed errors or to people who acted with some end in view, so that professing such opinion they ran counter to the nature of existence and denied a sensibly perceived thing or wished to suggest to the estimative faculty the existence of a nonexistent thing, the men of science have had to resort to proving those manifest things and to disproving the existence of things that are only thought to exist. Thus we find that Aristotle establishes the fact of motion, as it had been denied, and demonstrates the nonexistence of atoms, as their existence had been asserted.[2] To this category belongs the denial of essential attributes to God, may He be exalted. For that denial is a primary intelligible, inasmuch as an attribute is not the essence of the thing of which it is predicated, but is a certain mode of the essence and hence an accident. If, however, the attribute were the essence of the thing of which it is predicated, the attribute

1. Jer. 12:2.   2. The word may also mean "God."   3. Ps. 4:5.
1. In accordance with the readings of several MSS, I read *kamā* instead of *wa-mā*, figuring in the text of Joel's edition.
2. The word *athbata*, translated "asserted," is also used by Maimonides in this chapter and elsewhere to denote the fact that true opinions were proved to be such. In those cases it is translated "establish" or "establish the truth of."

would be either a tautology[3] — as if you were saying that man is man —
or the attribute would be a mere explanation of a term — as if you said that
man is a rational living being. For being a rational animal | is the essence
and true reality of man, and there does not exist in this case a third notion,
apart from those of animal and of rational, that constitutes man. For man
is the being of which life and rationality are predicated. Thus those
attributes[4] merely signify an explanation of a term and nothing else. It is
as if you said that the thing denoted by the term "man" is the thing
composed of life and rationality. It is then clear that an attribute may be
only one of two things. It is either the essence of the thing of which it is
predicated, in which case it is an explanation of a term. We, in this respect,
do not consider it impossible to predicate such an attribute of God, but do
consider it impossible in another respect, as shall be made clear.[5] Or the
attribute is different from the thing of which it is predicated, being a
notion superadded to that thing. This would lead to the conclusion that
that attribute is an accident belonging to that essence.

Now by denying the assertion that terms denoting accidents are
attributes of the Creator, one does not deny the notion of accident. For every
notion superadded to an essence is an adjunct to it and does not perfect its
essence, and this is the meaning of accident. This should be considered in
addition to the circumstances that there would be many eternal things if
there were many attributes. For there is no oneness at all except in believing
that there is one simple essence in which there is no complexity or multipli-
cation of notions, but one notion only; so that from whatever angle you
regard it and from whatever point of view you consider it, you will find that
it is one, not divided in any way and by any cause into two notions; and
you will not find therein any multiplicity either in the thing as it is outside
of the mind or as it is in the mind, as shall be demonstrated in this Treatise.[6]

In discussing this subject, some people engaged in speculation have
ended by saying that His attributes, may He be exalted, are neither His
essence nor a thing external to His essence. This is similar to what others
say, namely, that the modes — by which term they mean the universals —
are neither existent nor nonexistent, and, again similar to what others
say, that the atom | is not in a place, but occupies a locality, and that there
is no act of a man but that there may be an acquisition of an act by him.
These are things that are merely said; and accordingly they subsist only in

3. The Arabic word *tikrāran* means "several times."
4. In the singular in the Arabic. The attributes in question are life and rationality.
5. In the next chapter.   6. Cf. II 22.

words, not in the mind; all the more, they have no existence outside of the mind. But as you know and as everyone knows who does not deceive himself, these assertions are defended by means of many words and falsifying parables and are proved correct by shouting defamatory polemics and various complicated kinds of dialectic arguments and sophistries. Should, however, the man who proclaims these things and attempts to establish them in the ways indicated, reflect upon his belief, he would find nothing but confusion and incapacity. For he wants to make exist something that does not exist and to create a mean between two contraries that have no mean. Or is there a mean between that which exists and that which does not exist, or in the case of two things is there a mean between one of them being identical with the other or being something else? What forces him to this is, as we have said, the wish to preserve the conceptions of the imagination and the fact that all existent bodies are always represented to oneself as certain essences. Now every such essence is of necessity endowed with attributes, for we do not ever find an essence of a body that while existing is divested of everything and is without an attribute. This imagination being pursued, it was thought that He, may He be exalted, is similarly composed of various notions, namely, His essence and the notions that are superadded to His essence. Several groups of people pursued the likening of God to other beings and believed Him to be a body endowed with attributes. Another group raised themselves above this consequence and denied His being a body, but preserved the attributes. All this was rendered necessary by their keeping to the external sense of the revealed books as I shall make clear in later chapters that will deal with these notions.[7] |

CHAPTER 52

An attribute predicated of any thing, of which thing it is accordingly said that it is such and such, must necessarily belong to one of the following five groups:

The first group is characterized by the thing having its definition predicated of it — as when it is predicated of man that he is a rational living being. This attribute, which indicates the essence and true reality of a thing, is, as we have already made clear,[1] merely the explanation of a term and

7. Cf. I 53.
1. Cf. I 51.

nothing else. This kind of attribute should be denied to God according to everybody. For He, may He be exalted, has no causes anterior to Him that are the cause of His existence and by which, in consequence, He is defined. For this reason it is well known among all people engaged in speculation, who understand what they say, that God cannot be defined.

The second group is characterized by the thing having part of its definition predicated of it — as when it is predicated of man that he is a living being or a rational being. This attribute signifies an inseparable connection. For our saying, every man is rational, signifies that reason must be found in every being in whom humanity is found. This kind of attribute should be denied to God, may He be exalted, according to everybody. For if He has a part of an essence, His essence must be composite. The absurdity of divine attributes belonging to this group is like the absurdity recognized with regard to the first group.

The third group consists of attributes predicated of a thing that go beyond its true reality and its essence so that the attribute in question is not a thing through which the essence is perfected and constituted. Consequently that attribute is a certain quality with respect to the thing of which it is predicated. Now quality, considered one of the supreme genera,[2] is regarded as one | of the accidents. Thus if an attribute belonging to this group would subsist in Him, may He be exalted, He would be a substratum of accidents. This is sufficient to show how far from His true reality and essence this is, I mean the supposition that He is endowed with quality. It is, however, strange that those who proclaim the existence of attributes, deny with reference to Him, may He be exalted, the possibility of likening Him to something else and of qualifying Him. For what is the meaning of their saying that He may not be qualified unless it be that He is not endowed with quality? Now every attribute that is affirmed of a certain essence as pertaining to it essentially either constitutes the essence, in which case it is identical with the latter, or is a quality of that essence.

Now there are, as you know, four genera of qualities. I will accordingly give you examples in the way of attributes of every one of these genera, in order that the impossibility of the subsistence of attributes of this kind in God, may He be exalted, be made clear to you. The first example is as follows. You predicate of a man one of his speculative or moral habits or one of the dispositions subsisting in him qua an animate being, as when you say someone is a carpenter or chaste or ill. There is no difference between

2. Literally: and it is a supreme genus. By "supreme genus" is meant one of the Aristotelian categories.

your saying a carpenter or your saying a learned man or a sage,[3] all of these being dispositions subsisting in the soul. There is also no difference between your saying a chaste man and your saying a merciful man. For all arts, sciences, and settled moral characters are dispositions subsisting in the soul. All this is clear to whoever has occupied himself even to the slightest extent with the art of logic. The second example is as follows. You predicate of a thing a natural faculty that is in it or the absence of a natural faculty, as when you say soft or hard. And there is no difference between your saying soft and hard and your saying strong and weak, all these being natural dispositions. The third example is as follows. You predicate of a man a passive quality or an affection,[4] as when you say someone is irascible, irritable, timid, or merciful, | in cases in which this character is not firmly established. Your predicating a color, a taste, a smell, warmth, coldness, dryness, and humidity of a certain thing also belongs to this kind. The fourth example is as follows. You predicate of a thing that which pertains to it in respect of quantity considered as such, as when you say long, short, crooked, and straight and other similar things. Now when you consider all these attributes and what is akin to them, you will find that it is impossible to ascribe them to God. For He does not possess quantity so that there might pertain to Him a quality pertaining to quantity as such. Nor does He receive impressions and affections so that there might pertain to Him a quality belonging to the affections. Nor does He have dispositions so that there might be faculties and similar things pertaining to Him. Nor is He, may He be exalted, endowed with a soul, so that He might have a habitus pertaining to Him — such as clemency, modesty, and similar things — or have pertain to Him that which pertains to animate[5] beings as such — for instance, health and illness. It is accordingly clear to you that no attribute that may be brought under the supreme genus of quality can subsist in Him, may He be exalted.

With regard to those three groups of attributes — which are the attributes indicative of the essence or of a part of the essence or of a certain quality subsisting in the essence — it has already been made clear that they are impossible with reference to Him, may He be exalted, for all of them are indicative of composition, and the impossibility of composition in respect to the deity we shall make clear by demonstration.[6]

The fourth group of attributes is as follows. It is predicated of a thing

3. *ḥakīm*. The word often means "philosopher."
4. The Arabic term translated "passive" is an adjective derived from the term rendered by "affection."
5. I.e., beings having a soul.   6. Cf. II 1.

that it has a relation to something other than itself. For instance, it is related to a time or to a place or to another individual, as for instance when you predicate of Zayd that he is the father of a certain individual or the partner of a certain individual or an inhabitant of a certain place or one who was at a certain time. Now this kind of attribute does not necessarily entail either multiplicity or change in | the essence of the thing of which it is predicated. For the Zayd who is referred to may be the partner of Umar, the father of Bakr, the master of Khālid, a friend of Zayd, an inhabitant of such and such dwelling place, and one who was born in such and such a year. Those notions of relation are not the essence of the thing or something subsisting in its essence, as do the qualities. At first thought it seems that it is permissible to predicate of God, may He be exalted, attributes of this kind. However, when one knows true reality and achieves greater exactness in speculation, the fact that this is impossible becomes clear. There is no relation between God, may He be exalted, and time and place; and this is quite clear. For time is an accident attached to motion, when the notion of priority and posteriority is considered in the latter and when motion becomes numbered, as is made clear in the passages especially dealing with this subject. Motion, on the other hand, is one of the things attached to bodies, whereas God, may He be exalted, is not a body. Accordingly there is no relation between Him and time, and in the same way there is no relation between Him and place. The subject of investigation and speculation is therefore the question whether there is between Him, may He be exalted, and any of the substances created by Him a true relation of some kind so that this relation might be predicated of Him. It is clear at the first glance that there is no correlation between Him and the things created by Him. For one of the properties of two correlated things is the possibility of inverting the statement concerning them while preserving their respective relations.[7] Now He, may He be exalted, has a necessary existence while that which is other than He has a possible[8] existence, as we shall make clear.[9] There accordingly can be no correlation between them. As for the view that there is some relation between them, it is deemed correct, but this is not correct. For it is impossible to represent oneself that a relation subsists between the intellect and color although, according to our school, both of them are comprised by the same "existence." How then can a relation be represented between Him and what is other than He when there is no notion comprising in any respect both of the two, inasmuch as

7. More or less literally: inverting with equipoise.   8. Or: contingent.
9. Cf. II Introduction and II 1.

see 782/99

existence is, in our opinion, affirmed of Him, may He be exalted, and of what | is other than He merely by way of absolute equivocation. There is, in truth, no relation in any respect between Him and any of His creatures. For relation is always found between two things falling under the same — necessarily proximate — species, whereas there is no relation between the two things if they merely fall under the same genus. On this account one does not say that this red is more intense than this green or less or equally so, though both fall under the same genus, namely, color. If, however, two things fall under two different genera, there is no relation between them in any respect whatever, not even according to the inchoate notions of common opinion; this holds even for cases in which the two things[10] fall in the last resort under one higher genus. For instance, there is no relation between a hundred cubits and the heat that is in pepper inasmuch as the latter belongs to the genus quality and the former to the genus quantity. There is no relation either between knowledge and sweetness or between clemency and bitterness, though all of them fall under the supreme genus quality. How then could there subsist a relation between Him, may He be exalted, and any of the things created by Him, given the immense difference between them with regard to the true reality of their existence, than which there is no greater difference? If a relation subsisted between them, it would necessarily follow that the accident of relation must be attached to God. Even if it is not an accident with regard to His essence, may He be exalted, nevertheless it is, generally speaking, some sort of accident. There is accordingly no way of escape offering the possibility of affirming that He has an attribute, not even with regard to relation, if one has knowledge of true reality. However, relation is an attribute with regard to which it is more appropriate than with regard to the others that indulgence should be exercised if it is predicated of God. For it does not entail the positing of a multiplicity of eternal things or the positing of alteration taking place in His essence, may He be exalted, as a consequence of an alteration of the things related to Him.

The fifth group of the affirmative attributes is as follows. A thing has its action predicated of it. I do not intend to signify by the words, his action, the habitus of an art that belongs to him who is described — as when you say | a carpenter or a smith — inasmuch as this belongs to the species of quality, as we have mentioned. But I intend to signify by the words, his action, the action that he who is described has performed — as when you

10. Or: the two genera. The sense of the Arabic phrase admits of both interpretations.

say Zayd is the one who carpentered[11] this door, built that particular wall, or wove this garment. Now this kind of attribute is remote from the essence of the thing of which it is predicated. For this reason it is permitted that this kind should be predicated of God, may He be exalted, after you have — as shall be made clear[12] — come to know that the acts in question need not be carried out by means of differing notions subsisting within the essence of the agent, but that all His different acts, may He be exalted, are all of them carried out by means of His essence, and not, as we have made clear, by means of a superadded notion.

A summary of the contents of the present chapter would be as follows: He, may He be exalted, is one in all respects; no multiplicity should be posited in Him; there is no notion that is superadded to His essence; the numerous attributes possessing diverse notions that figure in the Scriptures[13] and that are indicative of Him, may He be exalted, are mentioned in reference to the multiplicity of His actions and not because of a multiplicity subsisting in His essence, and some of them, as we have made clear,[14] also with a view to indicating His perfection according to what we consider as perfection. As for the question whether it is possible that one simple essence in which no multiplicity is posited should perform diverse actions, the answer shall be made clear by means of examples.

CHAPTER 53

The reasons that led those who believe in the existence of attributes belonging to the Creator to this belief are akin to those that led those who believe in the doctrine of His corporeality to that belief. For he who believes in this doctrine was not led to | it by intellectual speculation; he merely followed the external sense of the texts of the Scriptures.[1] This is also the case with regard to the attributes. For inasmuch as the books of the prophets and the revealed books existed, which predicated attributive qualifications of Him, may He be exalted, these were taken in their literal sense; and He was believed to possess attributes. The people in question

---

11. The verb *najara* used in the Arabic text is akin to and perhaps derives from the word *najjār*, meaning "carpenter."
12. In the next chapter.   13. Literally: books.   14. Cf. I 26, 46, 47.
1. Literally: books.

have, as it were, divested God of corporeality but not of the modes of corporeality, namely, the accidents – I mean the aptitudes of the soul, all of which are qualities. For with regard to every attribute that the believer in attributes considers to be essential in respect to God, may He be exalted, you will find that the notion of it is that of a quality, even if these people do not state it clearly; for they in fact liken the attribute in question to what they meet with in the various states of all bodies endowed with an animal soul. Of all this it is said: *The Torah speaketh in the language of the sons of man.*[2] The purpose for which all these attributes are used is to predicate perfection of Him, but not the particular notion that is a perfection with respect to creatures possessing a soul. Most of these attributes are attributes pertaining to His diverse actions. Now there need not be a diversity in the notions subsisting in an agent because of the diversity of his various actions. Of this I shall give you an instance taken from things that are to be found with us – I mean an example of the fact that though an agent is one, diverse actions may proceed from him, even if he does not possess will and all the more if he acts through will. An instance of this is fire: it melts some things, makes others hard, cooks and burns, bleaches and blackens. Thus if some man would predicate of fire that it is that which bleaches and blackens, which burns and cooks, which makes hard and which melts, he would say the truth. Accordingly he who does not know the nature of fire thinks that there subsist in it six diverse notions, by means of one of which it blackens, whereas it bleaches by means of another, cooks by means of a third, | burns by means of a fourth, melts by means of a fifth, and makes hard by means of a sixth – all these actions being opposed to one another, for the meaning of any one of them is different from that of any other. However, he who knows the nature of fire, knows that it performs all these actions by virtue of one active quality, namely, heat. If, however, such a state of affairs exists with respect to a thing acting by virtue of its nature, it exists all the more with respect to one who acts through will, and again all the more with respect to Him, may He be exalted, who is above every attributive qualification. We have grasped with regard to Him relations having corresponding diverse notions – for the notion of knowledge is in us other than the notion of power, and the latter other than the notion of will. Yet how can we regard as a necessary consequence of this the subsistence in Him of diverse notions that are essential to Him, so that there would subsist in Him something by virtue of which He knows as well as something by virtue of which He wills and something by virtue

2. B.T., Yebamoth, 71a; B.T., Baba Meṣiʿa, 31b.

of which He has power, for this is the meaning of the attributes whose existence is asserted by the people in question? Some of them state this clearly, enumerating the notions that are superadded to the essence. Others belonging to them do not state this clearly; however it is quite clear in their belief, even if it is not expressed in comprehensible language. This is the case when some of them assert that He possesses power[3] because of His essence, possesses knowledge[4] because of His essence, is living because of His essence, possesses will[5] because of His essence.

I shall illustrate this by the example of the rational faculty subsisting in man. It is one faculty with regard to which no multiplicity is posited. Through it he acquires the sciences and the arts; through the same faculty he sews, carpenters, weaves, builds, has a knowledge of geometry,[6] and governs the city. Those very different actions, however, proceed from one simple faculty in which no multiplicity is posited. Now these actions are very different, and their number is almost infinite—I mean the number of the arts brought forth by the rational faculty. It accordingly should not be regarded as inadmissible in reference to God, may He be magnified and honored, that | the diverse actions proceed from one simple essence in which no multiplicity is posited and to which no notion is superadded. Every attribute that is found in the books of the deity, may He be exalted, is therefore an attribute of His action and not an attribute of His essence, or it is indicative of absolute perfection. There accordingly is not, as these people believe, an essence composed of diverse notions. For the fact that they do not use the term "composition" does not abolish the notion of composition with regard to the essence possessing attributes. However, there exists a point of doubt that led them to this doctrine. This is the one I am going to explain to you. For those who believe in attributes do not do so because of the multiplicity of His actions. Rather do they say: Yes, the One Essence performs diverse actions, but the attributes that are essential to Him, may He be exalted, do not belong to His actions. For it is not permissible to imagine that God has created His own essence. They differ with respect to those attributes that they call essential, I mean with regard to their number, inasmuch as all of them follow the text of some book. We shall mention that as to which all of them agree and consider to be cognized by the intellect and in which case there is no need to follow the text of the word of a prophet. There are four such attributes: living,

---

3. Literally: powerful.   4. Literally: knowing.   5. Literally: willing.
6. This is the usual meaning of *handasa* in medieval Arabic; however, the word may also signify "architecture." Possibly Maimonides had the second meaning in mind in this passage.

9

possessing power, possessing knowledge, possessing will.[7] They say that these are distinct notions and such perfections that it would be impossible for the deity to be deprived of any of them. It is not permissible to suppose that they belong to His actions. This is a summary of their opinion.

Now you know that the notion of knowledge in reference to Him, may He be exalted, is identical with the notion of life, for everyone who apprehends his own essence possesses both life and knowledge by virtue of the same thing. For we wished to signify by "knowledge" the apprehension of one's own essence. Now the essence that apprehends is undoubtedly the same as the essence that is apprehended. For in our opinion He is not composed of two things, | the thing that apprehends and another thing that does not apprehend, as man is composed of a soul that apprehends and of a body that does not apprehend. Accordingly, inasmuch as our saying "possessing knowledge" is intended to signify "he who apprehends his own essence," life and knowledge form in this case one notion. However, the people in question do not consider this notion but consider rather His apprehension of His creatures. Similarly, without any doubt, neither power nor will exists in, and belongs to, the Creator in respect to His own essence; for He does not exercise His power on His own essence, nor can it be predicated of Him that He wills His own essence. And nobody represents this to himself. Rather have these attributes been thought of in reference to the diverse relations that may obtain between God, may He be exalted, and the things created by Him. For He possesses the power to create what He created, and possesses the power to bring into being that which exists in the manner in which He has brought it into being, and also possesses the knowledge of what He has brought into being. Thus it has become clear to you that these attributes too are not to be considered in reference to His essence, but in reference to the things that are created. For this reason, we, the community of those who profess the Unity by virtue of a knowledge of the truth — just as we do not say that there is in His essence a superadded notion by virtue of which He has created the heavens, and another one by virtue of which He has created the elements, and a third one by virtue of which He has created the intellects — so we do not say that there is in Him a superadded notion by virtue of which He possesses power, and another by virtue of which He possesses will, and a third one by virtue of which He knows the things created by Him. His essence is, on the contrary, one and simple, having no notion that is superadded to it in any respect. This essence has created everything that it has created and knows it, but

7. Literally: powerful, knowing, willing.

absolutely not by virtue of a superadded notion. It makes no difference whether these diverse attributes correspond to His actions or to diverse relations between Him and the things produced by the actions, in conformity with what we have likewise explained[8] regarding the truth of relation and its being merely something that is in thought.[9] This is what ought | to be believed with regard to the attributes mentioned in the books of the prophets; or, as we shall make clear,[10] it may be believed with regard to some of them that they are attributes indicative of a perfection likened to our perfections, which are understood by us.

CHAPTER 54

Know that the master of those who know, *Moses our Master*, peace be on him, made two requests and received an answer to both of them. One request consisted in his asking Him, may He be exalted, to let him know His essence and true reality. The second request, which he put first, was that He should let him know His attributes. The answer to the two requests that He, may He be exalted, gave him consisted in His promising him to let him know all His attributes, making it known to him that they are His actions, and teaching him that His essence cannot be grasped as it really is. Yet He drew his attention to a subject of speculation through which he can apprehend to the furthest extent that is possible for man. For what has been apprehended by [Moses], peace be on him, has not been apprehended by anyone before him nor will it be apprehended by anyone after him.

His request regarding the knowledge of [God's] attributes is conveyed in his saying: *Show me now Thy ways, that I may know Thee, and so on.*[1] Consider the wondrous notions contained in this dictum. For his saying, *Show me now Thy ways, that I may know Thee*, indicates that God, may He be exalted, is known through His attributive qualifications; for when he would know the *ways*, he would know Him. Furthermore his saying, *That I may find grace in Thy sight*,[2] indicates that he who knows God *finds grace in His sight* and not he who merely fasts and prays, but everyone who has knowledge of Him. Accordingly those who know Him are those who are favored by Him and permitted to come near Him, whereas those

8. Cf. I 52.   9. Literally: its being deemed.   10. Cf. I 59.
1. Exod. 33:13.   2. Exod. 33:13.

who do not know Him are objects of His wrath and are kept far away from Him. For His favor and wrath, His nearness and remoteness, correspond to | the extent of a man's knowledge or ignorance. However, we have gone beyond the limits of the subject of this chapter. I shall accordingly return to the subject.

When [Moses] asked for knowledge of the attributes and asked for forgiveness for the nation, he was given a [favorable] answer with regard to their being forgiven. Then he asked for the apprehension of His essence, may He be exalted. This is what he means when he says, *Show me, I pray Thee, Thy glory;*[3] whereupon he received a [favorable] answer with regard to what he had asked for at first — namely, *Show me Thy ways.* For he was told: *I will make all My goodness pass before thee.*[4] In answer to his second demand, he was told: *Thou canst not see My face, and so on.*[5] This dictum — *All my goodness* — alludes to the display to him of all existing things of which it is said: *And God saw every thing that He had made, and, behold, it was very good.*[6] By their display, I mean that he will apprehend their nature and the way they are mutually connected so that he will know how He governs them in general and in detail. This notion is indicated when it says: *He is trusted in all My house;*[7] that is, he has grasped the existence of all My world with a true and firmly established understanding. For the opinions that are not correct are not firmly established. Accordingly the apprehension of these actions is an apprehension of His attributes, may He be exalted, with respect to which He is known. The proof of the assertion that the thing, the apprehension of which was promised to him, was the actions of God, may He be exalted, is the fact that what was made known to him were simply pure attributes of action: *merciful and gracious, long-suffering*[8]. It is then clear that the *ways* — for a knowledge of which he had asked and which, in consequence, were made known to him — are the actions proceeding from God, may He be exalted. The *Sages* call them *characteristics* and speak of the *thirteen characteristics.* This term, as they use it, is applied to moral qualities. Thus: *There are four characteristics among people who give charity; there are four characteristics among people who go to the house of learning.*[9] This expression | occurs frequently. The meaning here is not that He possesses moral qualities, but that He performs actions resembling the actions that in us proceed from moral qualities — I mean from aptitudes of the soul; the meaning is not that He, may He be exalted, possesses aptitudes of the soul. Scripture has restricted itself to mentioning only

3. Exod. 33:18.   4. Exod. 33:19.   5. Exod. 33:20.   6. Gen. 1:31.
7. Num. 12:7.   8. Exod. 34:6–7.   9. Mishnah, Aboth, V 13–14.

those *thirteen characteristics*, although [Moses] apprehended *all His good-ness* — I mean to say all His actions — because these are the actions proceeding from Him, may He be exalted, in respect of giving existence to the Adamites[10] and governing them. This was [Moses'] ultimate object in his demand, the conclusion of what he says being: *That I may know Thee, to the end that I may find grace in Thy sight and consider that this nation is Thy people*[11] — that is, a people for the government of which I need to perform actions that I must seek to make similar to Thy actions in governing them.

It thus has become clear to you that the *ways* and the *characteristics* are identical. They are the actions proceeding from God, may He be exalted, in reference to the world. Accordingly, whenever one of His actions is apprehended, the attribute from which this action proceeds is predicated of Him, may He be exalted, and the name deriving from that action is applied to Him. For instance, one apprehends the kindness[12] of His governance in the production of the embryos of living beings, the bringing of various faculties to existence in them and in those who rear them after birth — faculties that preserve them from destruction and annihilation and protect them against harm and are useful to them in all the doings that are necessary to them. Now actions of this kind proceed from us only after we feel a certain affection and compassion, and this is the meaning of mercy. God, may He be exalted, is said to be *merciful*, just as it is said, *Like as a father is merciful to his children,*[13] and it says, *And I will pity them, as a man pitieth his own son.*[14] It is not that He, may He be exalted, is affected and has compassion. But an action similar to that which proceeds from a father in respect to his child and that is attached to com-passion, pity, and an absolute passion, proceeds from Him, may He be exalted, in reference to His holy ones, not because of | a passion or a change. And just as when we give a thing to somebody who has no claim upon us, this is called *grace* in our language — as it says: *Grant them graciously*[15] — [so is the term applied to Him:] *Whom God hath graciously given;*[16] *Because God hath dealt graciously with me.*[17] Such instances are frequent. For He, may He be exalted, brings into existence and governs beings that have no claim upon Him with respect to being brought into existence and being governed. For this reason He is called *gracious*.

10. I.e., to men.   11. Exod. 33:13.
12. Literally: when the kindness. . . . In the Arabic text the sentence continues until "merciful" or even farther.
13. Ps. 103:13.   14. Mal. 3:17.   15. Judg. 21:22.   16. Gen. 33:5
17. Gen. 33:11.

Similarly we find among His actions that proceed with regard to the Adamites great calamities overtaking certain individuals and destroying them, or some universal event[18] annihilating whole tribes or even an entire region,[19] exterminating the children and the children of the children, leaving in existence neither the products of the soil nor the offspring of living beings — for instance, submergence of land, earthquakes, destructive storms, military expeditions of one people against others in order to exterminate the latter by the sword and to efface all traces of them. Many of these actions would proceed from one of us in reference to another only because of a violent anger or a great hatred or a desire for vengeance. With reference to these actions He is called *jealous and avenging and keeping anger and wrathful*,[20] meaning that actions similar to those that proceed from us from a certain aptitude of the soul — namely, jealousy, holding fast to vengeance, hatred, or anger — proceed from Him, may He be exalted, because of the deserts of those who are punished, and not because of any passion whatever, may He be exalted above every deficiency. Similarly all [His] actions are such as resemble the actions proceeding from the Adamites on account of passions and aptitudes of the soul, but they by no means proceed from Him, may He be exalted, on account of a notion superadded to His essence. It behooves the governor of a city, if he is a prophet, to acquire similarity to these attributes, so that these actions may proceed from him according to a determined measure and according to the deserts of the people who are affected by them and not merely because of his following a passion. He should not let loose the reins of anger nor let | passion gain mastery over him, for all passions are evil; but, on the contrary, he should guard against them as far as this lies within the capacity of man. Sometimes, with regard to some people, he should be *merciful and gracious*, not out of mere compassion and pity, but in accordance with what is fitting. Sometimes, with regard to some people, he should be *keeping anger and jealous and avenging* in accordance with their deserts, not out of mere anger; so he may order an individual to be burned without being angry and incensed with him and without hating him, because he perceives the deserts of that individual and considers the great benefit that many people will derive from the accomplishment of the action in question. Do you not see in the texts of the *Torah*, when it commanded the extermination of the *seven nations* and said *thou shalt save alive nothing that*

18. Literally: matter.
19. Or: an entire climate. I.e., one of the seven climates into which the earth was divided.
20. Cf. Nah. 1:2.

breatheth,[21] that it immediately follows this by saying: *That they teach you not to do after all their abominations, which they have done unto their gods and so ye sin against the Lord your God*?[22] Thus it says: do not think that this is hard-heartedness or desire for vengeance. It is rather an act required by human opinion, which considers that everyone who deviates from the ways of truth[23] should be put an end to and that all the obstacles impeding the achievement of the perfection that is the apprehension of Him, may He be exalted, should be interdicted. In spite of all this, it behooves that acts of mercy, forgiveness, pity, and commiseration should proceed from the governor of a city to a much greater extent than acts of retaliation. For the *thirteen characteristics* are all of them, with one exception, *characteristics of mercy* — the exception being: *visiting the iniquity of the fathers upon the children*.[24] For it says: *And that will by no means clear the guilty*.[25] The meaning is: and He will not utterly destroy — an interpretation deriving from the words: *And utterly destroyed, she shall sit upon the ground*.[26] Know that his speech — *visiting the iniquity of the fathers upon the children* — only applies to the sin of *idolatry* in particular and not to any other sin. A proof of this is His saying | in *the ten commandments: unto the third and fourth generation of them that hate Me*.[27] For only *an idolater* is called *hater: for every abomination to the Lord, which He hateth*.[28] He restricts Himself to the *fourth generation* only because the utmost of what man can see of his offspring is the *fourth generation*. Accordingly, when the people of an *idolatrous* city are killed, this means that an *idolatrous* old man and the offspring of the offspring of his offspring — that, is, the child of the fourth generation — are killed. Accordingly Scripture, as it were, predicated of Him that His commandments, may He be exalted, which undoubtedly are comprised in His actions, comprise the commandment to kill the offspring of *idolaters*, even if they are little children, together with the multitude[29] of their fathers and grandfathers. We find this commandment continuously in the *Torah* in all passages. Thus he commands with regard to the *city that has been led astray* to idolatry: *Destroy it utterly and all that is therein*[30] — all this being done with a view to blotting out traces that bring about necessarily great corruption, as we have made clear.

    We have gone beyond the subject of this chapter; however, we have made clear why Scripture, in enumerating His actions, has confined itself

---

21. Deut. 20:16.   22. Deut. 20:18.   23. *al-ḥaqq.* The word may also mean "God."
24. Exod. 34:7.   25. Exod. 34:7.   26. Isa. 3:26.   27. Exod. 20:5.   28. Deut. 12:31.
29. *fī ghumār* or *fī ghimār.* The latter reading may also have the meaning "in the calamity."
30. **Deut. 13:16.**

here to those mentioned above, and that those actions are needed for the governance of cities. For the utmost virtue of man is to become like unto Him, may He be exalted, as far as he is able; which means that we should make our actions like unto His, as the Sages made clear when interpreting the verse, *Ye shall be holy*.[31] They said: *He is gracious, so be you also gracious; He is merciful, so be you also merciful*.[32] The purpose of all this is to show that the attributes ascribed to Him are attributes of His actions and that they do not mean that He possesses qualities.[33]

CHAPTER 55

It has already been said before in a number of passages of this Treatise that | anything that entails corporeality ought of necessity to be negated in reference to Him and that all affections likewise should be negated in reference to Him. For all affections entail change, and moreover the agent who effects those affections is undoubtedly not identical with him who is acted upon [or affected]. Accordingly if He, may He be exalted, were subject to affection in any respect whatever, someone other than He would act upon Him and effect change in Him. Likewise all privation ought of necessity to be negated in reference to Him; it should be negated that He sometimes lacks a certain perfection, while that at other times it exists in Him. For if this should be supposed, He would be only potentially perfect. Now privation is necessarily attached to all potentiality, and everything that passes from potentiality to actuality cannot but require some other thing existing in actuality that causes the former to pass to actuality. For this reason, all His perfections must exist in actuality, and nothing may belong to Him that exists potentially in any respect whatever. One must likewise of necessity deny, with reference to Him, His being similar to any existing thing. Everyone has already been aware of this; clear statements are made in the books of the prophets negating the conception that He is like any thing. He says: *To whom then will ye liken Me, that I should be equal?*[1] He says: *To whom then will ye liken God? Or what likeness will ye compare unto Him?*[2] He says: *There is none like unto Thee, O Lord*.[3] This occurs frequently. The basis of the matter is that anything that leads to one of

31. Lev. 19:2.   32. Siphre to Deut. 10:12.   33. Literally: quality.
1. Isa. 40:25.   2. Isa. 40:18.   3. Jer. 10:6.

these four kinds of attributions ought of necessity to be negated in reference to Him by means of a clear demonstration; namely, anything that leads to attributing to Him corporeality, or that leads to attributing to Him affection and change, or that leads to attributing to Him, for example, a statement that He has not something in actuality and thereafter this occurs to Him in actuality, or that leads to attributing to Him a likeness to a thing among His creatures.

These are some of the useful teachings of natural science with regard to the knowledge of the deity. For he who has no knowledge of these sciences is not aware of the deficiency inherent in affections, and does not understand the meaning | of what is potential and of what is in actuality, and does not know that privation attaches necessarily to everything potential and that what is potential is more deficient than that which is in motion — because in the latter case potentiality is passing into actuality — while that which is in motion is in its turn deficient in comparison[4] to that for the sake of which it moves until it achieves actuality. And even if such a one[5] knows these things, he does not know them through their demonstrations. Accordingly he does not know the particular corollaries following necessarily from these universal primary propositions. For this reason he does not have at his disposal a demonstration of the existence of God or one of the necessity[6] of negating these kinds of attributions in reference to Him.

Having made this introduction, I will start upon another chapter in which I will make clear the absurdity of what is thought by those who believe that He has essential attributes. But that can be understood only by someone who already possesses knowledge of the art of logic and of the nature of being.

4. Literally: in its relation.
5. One who has not studied science.
6. *luzūm*. The word means here logical or scientific necessity.

Know that likeness is a certain relation between two things and that in cases where no relation can be supposed to exist between two things, no likeness between them can be represented to oneself. Similarly in all cases in which there is no likeness between two things, there is no relation between them. An example of this is that one does not say that this heat is like this color, or that this voice is like this sweetness. This is a matter that is clear in itself. Accordingly, in view of the fact that the relation between us and Him, may He be exalted, is considered as nonexistent — I mean the relation between Him and that which is other than He — it follows necessarily that likeness between Him and us should also be considered nonexistent.

Know also that any two things that fall under the same species[1] — I mean to say thereby that their essences | are the same — even if these things differ in regard to bigness and smallness or strength and feebleness or in other similar ways, are all of them necessarily alike even if they differ in this kind of way. An example of this is that a mustard grain and the sphere of the fixed stars are alike in having three dimensions; even though the latter is exceedingly big and the former exceedingly small, the notion of the existence of the dimensions in both of them is the same. Similarly wax melted in sunshine and the element of fire are alike in respect to heat; even though this heat is very intense in the latter and very feeble in the former, the notion of the appearance of this quality in both of them is the same.

Similarly it behooves those who believe that there are essential attributes that may be predicated of the Creator — namely, that He is existent, living, possessing power, knowing, and willing — to understand that these notions are not ascribed to Him and to us in the same sense. According to what they think, the difference between these attributes and ours lies in the former being greater, more perfect, more permanent, or more durable than ours, so that His existence is more durable than our existence, His life more permanent than our life, His power greater than our power, His knowledge more perfect than our knowledge, and His will more universal than our will. In this way both notions[2] would be, as they think, included in the same definition. However, the matter is not so in any respect. For the comparative is used only with regard to things in reference to which the

1. The word *naw*ᶜ (species) seems to be used here in a rather loose sense.
2. That of a divine attribute and that of a human one designated by the same term.

notion in question is used univocally. And if this is so, there is necessarily a likeness between the things in question. According to the opinion of those who consider that there are essential attributes, His | essential attributes, may He be exalted, in the existence of which they believe, must not be like the attributes of other beings and must not be comprised in the same definition, just as His essence, may He be exalted, is necessarily not like other essences. However, they do not act upon this opinion. Rather do they think that the divine and human attributes are comprised in the same definition, however clear it is to all those who understand the meaning of being alike that the term "existent" is predicated of Him, may He be exalted, and of everything that is other than He, in a purely equivocal sense. Similarly the terms "knowledge," "power," "will," and "life," as applied to Him, may He be exalted, and to all those possessing knowledge, power, will, and life, are purely equivocal, so that their meaning when they are predicated of Him is in no way like their meaning in other applications. Do not deem that they are used amphibolously. For when terms are used amphibolously they are predicated of two things between which there is a likeness in respect to some notion, which notion is an accident attached to both of them and not a constituent element of the essence of each one of them. Now the things attributed to Him, may He be exalted, are not accidents in the opinion of anyone among the men engaged in speculation, while, on the other hand, all the attributes belonging to us are accidents according to the opinion of the Mutakallimūn. Would that I knew accordingly whence the likeness could come so that the divine and the human attributes could be comprised in the same definition and be used in a univocal sense, as these people believe.

Accordingly this is a cogent demonstration that the meaning of the qualificative attributions ascribed to Him and the meaning of the attributions known to us have nothing in common in any respect or in any mode; these attributions have in common only the name and nothing else. This being so, you must not believe that there exist in Him notions superadded to His essence that are like the attributes that are superadded to our essence, because the name is common. The conception is of immense sublimity according to those who know. Keep it in memory and realize its true meaning so that it be ready to hand with a view to what we wish to make you understand. |

O n the attributes; more obscure than what preceded. It is known that existence is an accident attaching to what exists. For this reason it is something that is superadded to the quiddity of what exists. This is clear and necessary with regard to everything the existence of which has a cause. Hence its existence is something that is superadded to its quiddity.

As for that which has no cause for its existence, there is only God, may He be magnified and glorified, who is like that. For this is the meaning of our saying about Him, may He be exalted, that His existence is necessary. Accordingly, His existence is identical with His essence and His true reality, and His essence is His existence. Thus His essence does not have an accident attaching to it when it exists, in which case its existence would be a notion that is superadded to it. For His existence is necessary always; it is not something that may come suddenly to Him nor an accident that may attain Him. Consequently He exists, but not through an existence other than His essence; and similarly He lives, but not through life;[1] He is powerful, but not through power;[2] He knows, but not through knowledge.[3] For all these attributes refer back to one notion in which there is no idea of multiplicity, as will be made clear.

It is likewise necessary to know that oneness and multiplicity are accidents that attain an existent thing with regard to its being many or one. This is made clear in the "Metaphysics." Oneness is not identical with the thing that becomes one, just as number is not identical with the things that are numbered. For all these things[4] are accidents belonging to the genus "discrete quantity," which is attached to the existent things that have the disposition to receive accidents of this kind.

Now to ascribe to Him—whose existence is necessary, who is truly simple, to whom composition cannot attach in any way—the accident of oneness is just as absurd as to ascribe to Him the accident of multiplicity. | I mean to say that oneness is not a notion that is superadded to His essence, but that He is one not through oneness.

These subtle notions that very clearly elude the minds cannot be considered through the instrumentality of the customary words, which are the greatest among the causes leading unto error. For the bounds of expression in all languages are very narrow indeed, so that we cannot represent this

1. Other than His essence.   2. Other than His essence.   3. Other than His essence.
4. I.e., Oneness, number, etc.

notion to ourselves except through a certain looseness of expression. Thus when we wish to indicate that the deity is not many, the one who makes the statement cannot say anything but that He is one, even though "one" and "many" are some of the subdivisions of quantity. For this reason, we give the gist of the notion and give the mind the correct direction toward the true reality of the matter when we say, one but not through oneness, just as we say eternal in order to indicate that He has not come into being in time. For when we say eternal, we speak loosely, as is clear and manifest, since eternal can only be predicated of a thing to which time attaches. Now time is an accident of motion that is attached to a body. And eternal is likewise something correlated. For your saying eternal is said with reference to the accident of time, similar to your saying long and short with reference to that other accident, the line. For with regard to all the things to which the accident time is not attached, it cannot be truly predicated that they are eternal or that they come into being in time — just as it cannot be predicated of sweetness that it is either crooked or straight, and just as it cannot be predicated of sound that it is either salty or insipid. These things are not hidden from one who is trained to understand notions according to their true reality and has considered them with the apprehension that the intellect has of them and in the manner the latter has of stripping them [of accidents and matter], that is, has considered them not merely in the summary fashion of which words are indicative.

All passages that you find in the Scriptures[5] in which it is predicated of Him, may He be exalted, that He is *the First and the Last*[6] are analogous to those in which it is predicated of Him that He has an eye or an ear. The purpose of this is to indicate that He, may He be exalted, | is not subject to change and that no notion is produced in Him anew. It is not meant to indicate that God, may He be exalted, falls under time, so that there would be some analogy between Him and that which is other than He and is in time, so that He would be *the First and the Last*. All these words as applied to Him are *according to the language of the sons of man*. Similarly when we say *one*, the meaning is that He has no equal and not that the notion of oneness attaches to His essence.

5. Literally: books.   6. Cf., e.g., Isa. 44:6.

CHAPTER 58

More obscure than what preceded. Know that the description of God, may He be cherished and exalted, by means of negations is the correct description — a description that is not affected by an indulgence in facile language and does not imply any deficiency with respect to God in general or in any particular mode. On the other hand, if one describes Him by means of affirmations, one implies, as we have made clear, that He is associated with that which is not He and implies a deficiency in Him. I must make it clear to you in the first place how negations are in a certain respect attributes and how they differ from the affirmative attributes. After that I shall make it clear to you that we have no way of describing Him unless it be through negations and not otherwise.

I shall say accordingly that an attribute does not particularize any object of which it is predicated in such a way that it is not associated by virtue of that particular attribute with other things. On the contrary, the attribute is sometimes attributed to the object of which it is predicated in spite of the fact that the latter has it in common with other things and is not particularized through it. For instance, if you would see a man at some distance and if you would ask: What is this thing that is seen? and were told: This is a living being — this affirmation would indubitably be an attribute predicated of the thing seen though it does not particularize the latter, distinguishing it from everything else. However, a certain particularization is achieved through it; namely, it may be learnt from it that the thing seen is not a body belonging to | the species[1] of plants or to that of the minerals. Similarly if there were a man in this house and you knew that some body is in it without knowing what it is and would ask, saying: What is in this house? and the one who answered you would say: There is no mineral in it and no body of a plant — a certain particularization would be achieved and you would know that a living being is in the house though you would not know which animal. Thus the attributes of negation have in this respect something in common with the attributes of affirmation, for the former undoubtedly bring about some particularization even if the particularization due to them only exists in the exclusion of what has been

1. *naw*[c] means "species" and not "genus." At first blush the latter term would seem more suitable.

negated from the sum total of things that we had thought of as not being negated. Now as to the respect in which the attributes of negation differ from the attributes of affirmation: The attributes of affirmation, even if they do not particularize, indicate a part of the thing the knowledge of which is sought, that part being either a part of its substance or one of its accidents; whereas the attributes of negation do not give us knowledge in any respect whatever of the essence the knowledge of which is sought, unless this happens by accident as in the example we have given.

After this preface, I shall say that it has already been demonstrated that God, may He be honored and magnified, is existent of necessity and that there is no composition in Him, as we shall demonstrate, and that we are only able to apprehend the fact that He is and cannot apprehend His quiddity.[2] It is consequently impossible that He should have affirmative attributes. For he has no "That" outside of His "What," and hence an attribute cannot be indicative of one of the two; all the more His "What" is not compound so that an attribute cannot be indicative of its two parts; and all the more, He cannot have accidents so that an attribute cannot be indicative of them. Accordingly He cannot have an affirmative attribute in any respect.

As for the negative attributes, they are those that must be used in order to conduct the mind toward that which must be believed with regard to Him, may He be exalted, for no | notion of multiplicity can attach to Him in any respect on account of them; and, moreover, they conduct the mind toward the utmost reach that man may attain in the apprehension of Him, may He be exalted. For instance, it has been demonstrated to us that it is necessary that something exists other than those essences apprehended by means of the senses and whose knowledge is encompassed by means of the intellect. Of this thing we say that it exists, the meaning being that its nonexistence is impossible. We apprehend further that this being is not like the being of the elements, for example, which are dead bodies. We say accordingly that this being is living, the meaning being that He, may He be exalted, is not dead. We apprehend further that this being is not like the being of the heaven, which is a living body. We say accordingly that He is not a body. We apprehend further that this being is not like the being of the intellect, which is neither a body nor dead, but is caused. We say accordingly that He, may He be exalted, is eternal, the meaning being that

2. The statements regarding God are considered in this sentence as already demonstrated and as to be demonstrated later. This inconsistency, which may of course be explained away, cannot but strike the reader of this sentence.

He has no cause that has brought Him into existence. We apprehend further that the existence of this being, which is its essence, suffices not only for His being existent, but also for many other existents flowing from it, and that this overflow — unlike that of heat from fire and unlike the proceeding of light from the sun — is an overflow that, as we shall make clear, constantly procures for those existents duration and order by means of wisely contrived[3] governance. Accordingly we say of Him, because of these notions, that He is powerful and knowing and willing. The intention in ascribing these attributes to Him is to signify that He is neither powerless nor ignorant nor inattentive nor negligent. Now the meaning of our saying that He is not powerless is to signify that His existence suffices for the bringing into existence of things other than He. The meaning of our saying that He is not ignorant is to signify that He apprehends — that is, is living, for every apprehending thing is living. And the meaning of our saying that He is not inattentive or negligent is to signify that all the existent things in question proceed from their cause according to a certain order | and governance — not in a neglected way so as to be generated as chance would have it, but rather as all the things are generated that a willing being governs by means of purpose and will. We apprehend further that no other thing is like that being. Accordingly our saying that He is one signifies the denial of multiplicity.

It has thus become clear to you that every attribute that we predicate of Him is an attribute of action or, if the attribute is intended for the apprehension of His essence and not of His action, it signifies the negation of the privation of the attribute in question. Moreover, even those negations are not used with reference to or applied to Him, may He be exalted, except from the following point of view, which you know: one sometimes denies with reference to a thing something that cannot fittingly exist in it. Thus we say of a wall that it is not endowed with sight. Now you who read this Treatise with speculative intent know that whereas this heaven is a moving body of which we have measured the cubits and inches and in regard to which we have moreover achieved knowledge of the dimension of certain of its parts and of most of its movements, our intellects are quite incapable of apprehending its quiddity. And this, in spite of our knowing that it has of necessity matter and form, for its matter is not like that which is in us. For this reason we are unable to predicate of it any attributes

---

3. *muḥkam* may only mean "well-arranged." However, Maimonides probably wished the reader to remember the fact that the Arabic term derives from a root from which the word *ḥikma* (wisdom) and other words having a similar meaning also derive.

except in terms whose meaning is not completely understood, but not by means of affirmations that are completely understood. Accordingly we say that the heavens are neither light nor heavy nor acted upon and consequently not receptive to external impressions, that they have no taste and no smell; and we make other negations of this kind. All this is due to our ignorance with regard to that matter.

What then should be the state of our intellects when they aspire to apprehend Him who is without matter and is simple to the utmost degree of simplicity, Him whose existence is necessary, Him who has no cause and to whom no notion attaches that is superadded to His essence, which is perfect — the meaning of its perfection being, as we have made clear, that all deficiencies are negated with respect to it — | we who only apprehend the fact that He is? There is accordingly an existent whom none of the existent things that He has brought into existence resembles, and who has nothing in common with them in any respect; in reference to whom there is no multiplicity or incapacity to bring into existence things other than He; whose relation to the world is that of a captain to his ship. Even this is not the true relation and a correct likeness, for this likeness has been used in order to lead the mind toward the view that He, may He be exalted, governs the existent things, the meaning of this being that He procures their existence and watches over their order as it ought to be watched over. This notion will be made clear more completely than it is here.

Glory then to Him who is such that when the intellects contemplate His essence, their apprehension turns into incapacity; and when they contemplate the proceeding of His actions from His will, their knowledge turns into ignorance; and when the tongues aspire to magnify Him by means of attributive qualifications, all eloquence turns into weariness and incapacity!

CHAPTER 59

Someone may ask and say: If there is no device leading to the apprehension of the true reality of His essence and if demonstration proves that it can only be apprehended that He exists and that it is impossible, as has been demonstrated, to ascribe to Him affirmative attributes, in what respect can there be superiority or inferiority between those who apprehend Him? If, however, there is none, *Moses our Master* and *Solomon* did not apprehend anything different from what a single individual among the pupils apprehends, and there can be no increase in this knowledge.

Now it is generally accepted by the men of the Law, nay even by the philosophers, that there exist numerous differences of degree in this respect. Know, therefore, that this is indeed so and that the differences of degree between those who apprehend are very great indeed. For the thing of which | attributes are predicated becomes more particularized with every increase in attributes that are predicated of it, and he who predicates these attributes accordingly comes nearer to the apprehension of the true reality of the thing in question. In a similar way, you come nearer to the apprehension of Him, may He be exalted, with every increase in the negations regarding Him; and you come nearer to that apprehension than he who does not negate with regard to Him that which, according to what has been demonstrated to you, must be negated. For this reason a man sometimes labors for many years in order to understand some science and to gain true knowledge of its premises so that he should have certainty with regard to this science, whereas the only conclusion from this science in its entirety consists in our negating with reference to God some notion of which it has been learnt by means of a demonstration that it cannot possibly be ascribed to God. To someone else who falls short in his knowledge of speculation, this demonstration will not be clear; and he will consider it doubtful whether or not this notion exists with reference to God. Again another one belonging to those who are struck with intellectual blindness ascribes to Him that notion which has been demonstrated should rather be negated with reference to Him. For instance, I shall demonstrate that He is not a body, whereas another man will doubt and not know whether or not He is a body, and a third one will categorically decide that He is a body and will seek to approach[1] God by means of this belief. How great is the difference between the three individuals! The first is undoubtedly nearer to God, while the second is far away from Him, and the third still farther away. Similarly if we may suppose a fourth one to whom the impossibility of affections in Him, may He be exalted, has become clear by demonstration — whereas this was not the case with regard to the first one who denied His corporeality — this fourth individual would undoubtedly be nearer to God than the first. And so on always; so that if an individual exists to whom it has been made clear by demonstration that many things, whose existence with reference to Him or whose proceeding from Him we hold possible, are, on the contrary, impossible with reference to Him, may He be exalted

1. Literally: meet.

— and this applies of course all the more if we believe that these things are necessarily attached to Him — that individual will undoubtedly be more perfect than we.

It has accordingly become manifest to you that in every case in which the demonstration that a certain thing should be negated with reference to Him becomes clear to you, you become more perfect, | and that in every case in which you affirm of Him an additional thing, you become one who likens Him to other things and you get further away from the knowledge of His true reality. It is from this point of view that one ought to come nearer to an apprehension of Him by means of investigation and research: namely, in order that one should know the impossibility of everything that is impossible with reference to Him — not in order that one should make an affirmation ascribing to Him a thing as being a notion superadded to His essence or because the notion in question is held to be a perfection with reference to Him, since one finds it a perfection with reference to us. For all perfections are habitus, and not every habitus can exist in every being possessing habitus. Know that when you make an affirmation ascribing another thing to Him, you become more remote from Him in two respects: one of them is that everything you affirm is a perfection only with reference to us, and the other is that He does not possess a thing other than His essence, which, as we have made clear, is identical with His perfections.

As everyone is aware that it is not possible, except through negation, to achieve an apprehension of that which is in our power to apprehend and that, on the other hand, negation does not give knowledge in any respect of the true reality of the thing with regard to which the particular matter in question has been negated — all men, those of the past and those of the future, affirm clearly that God, may He be exalted, cannot be apprehended by the intellects, and that none but He Himself can apprehend what He is, and that apprehension of Him consists in the inability to attain the ultimate term in apprehending Him. Thus all the philosophers say: We are dazzled by His beauty, and He is hidden from us because of the intensity with which He becomes manifest, just as the sun is hidden to eyes that are too weak to apprehend it. This has been expatiated upon in words that it would serve no useful purpose to repeat here. The most apt phrase concerning this subject is the dictum occurring in the *Psalms, Silence is praise to Thee*,[2] which interpreted signifies: silence with regard to You is praise. This is a most perfectly put phrase regarding this matter. For of whatever we say intending to magnify and exalt, on the one hand we find that it can have

2. Ps. 65:2.

some application to Him, may He be exalted, and on the other we perceive |
in it some deficiency. Accordingly, silence and limiting oneself to the
apprehensions of the intellects are more appropriate — just as the perfect
ones have enjoined when they said: *Commune with your own heart upon
your bed, and be still. Selah.*[3]

You also know their famous dictum — would that all dicta were like it.
I shall quote it to you textually, even though it is well remembered,[4] so as
to draw your attention to the various significations it expresses. They have
said:[5] *Someone who came into the presence of Rabbi Ḥaninah said* [*in
prayer*]: *God the Great, the Valiant, the Terrible, the Mighty, the Strong,
the Tremendous, the Powerful. Thereupon* [*Rabbi Ḥaninah*] *said to him:
Have you finished all the praises of your Master? Even as regards the first
three epithets* [*used by you*] *we could not have uttered them if Moses our
Master had not pronounced them in the Law*[6] *and if the men of the Great
Synagogue had not* [*subsequently*] *come and established* [*their use*] *in prayer.
And you come and say all this. What does this resemble? It is as if a mortal
king who had millions of gold pieces were praised for possessing silver.
Would this not be an offense to him?* Here ends the dictum of this perfect
one. Consider in the first place his reluctance and unwillingness to multiply
the affirmative attributes. Consider also that he has stated clearly that if
we were left only to our intellects we should never have mentioned these
attributes or stated a thing appertaining to them. Yet the necessity to
address men in such terms as would make them achieve some representation — in accordance with the dictum of the Sages: *The Torah speaks in the
language of the sons of man*[7] — obliged resort to predicating of God their own
perfections when speaking to them. It must then be our purpose to draw a
line at using these expressions and not to apply them to Him except only in
reading the *Torah*. However, as[8] the *men of the Great Synagogue*, who were
prophets, appeared in their turn and inserted the mention of these attributes in the prayer, it is our purpose to pronounce only these attributes when
saying our prayers. According to the spirit, this dictum makes it clear that,
as it happened, two necessary obligations determined our naming these attri-
butes in | our prayers: one of them is that they occur in the *Torah*, and the
other is that the prophets in question used them in the prayer they composed. Accordingly, we should not have mentioned these attributes at all

3. Ps. 4:5.
4. Well remembered, or well preserved. Ibn Tibbon translates: well known.
5. B.T., Berakhoth, 33b.   6. Cf. Deut. 10:17.
7. B.T., Yebamoth, 71a; B.T., Baba Meṣiʿa, 31b.   8. Literally: when.

but for the first necessary obligation; and but for the second necessity, we should not have taken them out of their context and should not have had recourse to them in our prayers.[9] As you continue to consider the attributes, it will become clear to you from this statement that we are not permitted in our prayers to use and to cite all the attributes ascribed to God in the books of the prophets. For [Rabbi Ḥaninah] not only says:[10] *If Moses our Master had not pronounced them, we could not have uttered them*, but poses a second condition: *And if the men of the Great Synagogue had not [subsequently] come and established [their use] in prayer* — whereupon we are permitted to use them in our prayers.

Thus what we do is not like what is done by the truly ignorant who spoke at great length and spent great efforts on prayers that they composed and on sermons that they compiled and through which they, in their opinion, came nearer to God. In these prayers and sermons they predicate of God qualificative attributions that, if predicated of a human individual, would designate a deficiency in him. For they do not understand those sublime notions that are too strange for the intellects of the vulgar and accordingly took God, may He be magnified and glorified, for an object of study for their tongues; they predicated attributes of Him and addressed Him in all the terms that they thought permitted and expatiated at such length in this way that in their thoughts they made Him move on account of an affection. They did this especially when they found the text of a prophet's speech regarding these terms. Thereupon they had full license to bring forward texts that ought to be interpreted in every respect, and to take them according to their external meaning, to derive from them inferences and secondary conclusions, and to found upon them various kinds of discourses. This kind of license is frequently taken by poets and preachers or such as think that what they speak is poetry, so that the utterances of some of them constitute an absolute denial of faith, while other utterances contain such rubbish and such perverse imaginings | as to make men laugh when they hear them, on account of the nature of these utterances, and to make them weep when they consider that these utterances are applied to God, may He be magnified and glorified. If I were not unwilling to set out the deficiencies of those who make these utterances, I should have quoted to you something of the latter in order that you should give heed to the points in which they may be impugned. However, the deficiencies in these utterances are most manifest to him who understands. It also behooves you to consider and say that in view of the fact that *speaking ill* and *defamation*

9. Literally: prayer.   10. B.T., Berakhoth, 33b.

are acts of great disobedience, how much all the more so is the loosening of the tongue with regard to God, may He be exalted, and the predicating of Him qualificative attributions above which He is exalted. But I shall not say that this is an act of disobedience, but rather that it constitutes *unintended obloquy and vituperation* on the part of the multitude who listen to these utterances and on the part of the ignoramus who pronounces them. As for him who apprehends the deficiency of those speeches and yet uses those speeches, he belongs in my opinion to the category of people of whom it is said, *And the children of Israel did impute things that were not right unto the Lord their God,*[11] and is said elsewhere, *And to utter error against the Lord.*[12] Accordingly if you are one *who has regard for the honor of his Creator,*[13] you ought not to listen in any way to these utterances, let alone give expression to them and still less make up others like them. For you know the extent of the sin of him who *makes vituperative utterances against what is above.*[14] You accordingly ought not to set forth in any respect the attributes of God in an affirmative way — with a view, as you think, to magnifying Him — and ought not to go beyond that which has been inserted in the prayers and *benedictions* by the *men of the Great Synagogue.* For this is sufficient from the point of view of necessity; in fact, as *Rabbi Ḥaninah* said, it is amply sufficient. But regarding the other attributes that occur in the books of the prophets and are recited during the perusal of these books, it is believed, as we have made clear, that they are attributes of action or that they indicate the negation of their nonexistence in God. This notion concerning them also should not be divulged to the vulgar. For this kind of | speculation is more suitable for the elite who consider that the magnification of God does not consist in their saying improper things but in their understanding properly.

Hereupon I shall return to completing the indications concerning the dictum of *Rabbi Ḥaninah* and to giving it correct interpretation. He does not say, for example: *What does this resemble? It is as if a mortal king*[15] *who had millions of gold pieces were praised for possessing one hundred pieces.* For this example would have indicated that the perfections of Him, may He be exalted, while more perfect than the perfections that are ascribed to Him, still belong to the same species as the latter. As we have demonstrated, this is not so. But the wisdom manifest in this parable lies in his saying: *gold pieces and were praised for possessing silver.* He says this in

11. II Kings 17:9.   12. Isa. 32:6.   13. Or: *Owner.*
14. Cf. B.T., Sukkah, 23; B.T., Taᶜanith, 25.
15. Literally: *a king who is flesh and blood.*

order to indicate that in God, may He be exalted, there is nothing belonging
to the same species as the attributes that are regarded by us as perfections,
but that all these attributes are deficiencies with regard to God, just as he
made clear in this parable when he said: *Would this not be an offense to Him?*
I have then already made it known to you that everything in these attributes that you regard as a perfection is a deficiency with regard to Him,
may He be exalted, as it belongs to a species to which the things that are
with us belong. *Solomon*, peace be on him, has rightly directed us with
regard to this subject, in words that should be sufficient for us, when he
said: *For God is in heaven and thou upon the earth; therefore let thy words
be few.*[16]

CHAPTER 60

I wish to tell you in this chapter parables by means of which you will be
able to add to your representation of the necessity to multiply His attributes by means of negations and also to add to your shrinking from the
belief in positive attributes regarding Him, may He be exalted.

Assume that a man has acquired true knowledge regarding the exis-
tence of a ship, but does not know | to what it is that this term is applied:
namely, whether it is applied to a substance or to an accident. Then it
became clear to some other individual that a ship is not an accident; afterwards it became clear to yet another individual that it is not a mineral;
then it became clear to someone else that it is not a living being; then it
became clear to someone else that it is not a plant forming a continuum
with the earth; then it became clear to someone else that it is not one body
naturally forming a continuum; then it became clear to someone else that
it does not possess a simple shape as do tables and doors; then it became clear
to someone else that it is not a sphere, and to another individual that it is
not conical, and to yet another individual that it is not spherical and not
possessed of equal sides, and to someone else again that it is not solid all
through. Now it is clear that the last individual has nearly achieved, by
means of these negative attributes, the representation of the ship as it is.
He has, as it were, attained equality with one who has represented the ship
as being a body consisting of timber, a body that is hollow, oblong, and

16. Eccles. 5:1.

composed of a number of pieces of timber; that is, he has attained equality with one who has represented the ship by means of affirmative attributes. As for those whom we have cited in the parable as being prior to him, every one of them is more remote from representing the ship to himself than the one who comes after him; thus the first one figuring in our parable knows nothing but the bare term alone. Accordingly the negative attributes make you come nearer in a similar way to the cognition and apprehension of God, may He be exalted. Desire then wholeheartedly that you should know by demonstration some additional thing to be negated, but do not desire to negate merely in words. For on every occasion on which it becomes clear to you by means of a demonstration that a thing whose existence is thought to pertain to Him, may He be exalted, should rather be negated with reference to Him, you undoubtedly come nearer to Him by one degree. In this respect there are people who are very near to Him, whereas others are extremely far away from Him — not that there is in this matter a local nearness so that one may come nearer or get farther away from Him, as is thought by those whose | mental eyes are blind. Understand this well and know it and rejoice therein. For the way has become clear to you by walking in which you may come near to Him, may He be exalted. Walk accordingly therein if you so wish.

On the other hand, the predication of affirmative attributes of Him, may He be exalted, is very dangerous. For it has been already demonstrated that anything that we think of as a perfection — even if it existed as pertaining to Him — in accordance with the opinion of those who believe in the attributes, nevertheless would not belong to the species of perfection that we think of,[1] save only by equivocation, just as we have made clear.[2] Accordingly you must of necessity go over to the notion of negation. For if you say that, with one knowledge and with this changeless knowledge that has no multiplicity in it, He knows the multiple and changeable things that are constantly being renewed without any renewal of knowledge in Him, and that His knowledge of a thing before it has come into being and after it has acquired reality as existent and after it has ceased to exist is one and the same knowledge in which there is no change, you have clearly stated that He knows with a knowledge that is not like our knowledge. Similarly it follows necessarily that He exists, but not according to the notion of that existence which is in us. Consequently you resort to negations. Accordingly you have not arrived at a knowledge of the true reality of an essential attribute, but you have arrived at multiplicity. For you believe

1. Or: that we think perfection.   2. Cf. I 56.

that He is a certain essence possessing unknown attributes. Now with regard to the attributes that, as you deem, should be affirmed with reference to Him, if you deny that they have a likeness to the attributes known to us, it follows that they do not belong to the same species as the latter. Accordingly the matter of affirmation of attributes has, as it were, withdrawn from you; for if you say God, may He be exalted, is a certain substratum bearing certain things as adjuncts[3] and that this substratum is not like these adjuncts, the utmost of our apprehension would be, on the basis of this belief, polytheism[4] and nothing else. For every substratum bearing things is undoubtedly, | according to its definition, a duality,[5] even if it be one in its existence. For the notion of the substratum is different from that of the adjunct borne by it. Now the demonstration of the impossibility of composition in Him, may He be exalted, and, to go even further, the demonstration of His absolute simplicity, which is extreme and ultimate,[6] will be made clear to you in certain chapters of this Treatise.

I shall not say that he who affirms that God, may He be exalted, has positive attributes either falls short of apprehending Him or is an associator or has an apprehension of Him that is different from what He really is, but I shall say that he has abolished his belief in the existence of the deity without being aware of it. To make this clear: he who falls short of the apprehension of the true reality of some matter is one who apprehends part of it and is ignorant of another part — for instance, someone who apprehends in the notion of man the necessary concomitants of animality and does not apprehend in it the necessary concomitants of rationality. Now there is no multiplicity in the true reality of the existence of God, may He be exalted, so that one thing pertaining to Him might be understood while another remains unknown. In a similar way an associator with reference to a certain thing is one who represents to himself the true reality of a certain essence as this essence veritably is and affirms of another essence that its true reality is like that of the first essence. Now in the opinion of those who think that the attributes in question exist, these attributes are not the essence of the deity, but rather notions superadded to the essence. Furthermore, one who has an apprehension of a thing that is different from what that thing really is, must yet necessarily apprehend something of it as it really is. However, I shall not say of him who represents to himself that taste is a quantity, that his representation of the thing is different from what the latter really is;

3. A more literal translation would be: upon which certain borne things are superposed.
4. Literally: associationism.   5. Literally: is undoubtedly two.
6. Literally: in the uttermost extremity.

rather I shall say that he is ignorant of the being of taste and does not know to what the term applies. This is a very subtle speculation; understand it.

In accordance with this elucidation you shall know that he is incapable of apprehending the deity and is far removed from knowledge of Him who has no clear understanding of the necessity of negating with respect to God a notion negated by someone else on the basis of a demonstration. And, as we have made clear in the beginning of this chapter, the fewer | negations there are on his part, the more his apprehension falls short.

As for one who affirms an attribute of Him without knowing a thing about it except the mere term, it may be considered that the object to which he imagines the term applies is a nonexistent notion—an invention that is false; for he has, as it were, applied this term to a notion lacking existence, as nothing in existence is like that notion. An example is that of a man who has heard the term elephant and knows that it is an animal and demands to know its shape and true reality. Thereupon one who is himself mistaken or who misleads others tells him that it is an animal possessing one leg and three wings, inhabiting the depths of the sea, having a transparent body and a broad face like that of man in its form and shape, talking like a man, and sometimes flying in the air, while at other times swimming like a fish. I will not say that this representation of the elephant differs from what the latter really is, nor that the man in question falls short in his apprehension of the elephant. But I shall say that the thing that he has imagined as having these attributes[7] is merely an invention and is false and that there is nothing in existence like that, but that it is a thing lacking existence to which a term signifying an existent thing has been applied—a thing like "anqā mughrib"[8] or a centaur and other imaginary forms of this kind to which a term simple[9] or compound, signifying some existent thing, has been applied. In the present case the matter is similar and of the same kind.[10] For God, may His praise be magnified, is an existent whose existence has been demonstrated to be necessary. And, as I shall demonstrate,[11] from His being the necessarily existent there necessarily follows His absolute simplicity.

As for thinking that this simple essence—whose existence, as has been said, is necessary—is endowed with attributes and with other notions accompanying it: the thing thus imagined cannot, as has been demonstrated, be existent in any respect. Accordingly, if we say that | this essence, which

7. Literally: this attribute.   8. A fabulous bird.
9. Literally: one. Ibn Tibbon translates: simple.
10. Literally: equal.   11. Cf. II 1.

for the sake of example shall be called deity, is an essence in which subsist many notions that are predicated of it, we apply this term[12] to absolute nonexistence. Consider accordingly how great is the danger in affirming with reference to Him [positive] attributes. Accordingly it behooves us to believe with regard to the attributes figuring in the revealed books or the books of the prophets that all of them are mentioned only to direct the mind toward nothing but His perfection, may He be exalted, or that they are attributes referring to actions proceeding from Him, as we have made clear.

CHAPTER 61

All the names of God, may He be exalted, that are to be found in any of the books derive from actions. There is nothing secret in this matter. The only exception is one name: namely, *Yod, He, Vav, He.* This is the name of God, may He be exalted, that has been originated without any derivation, and for this reason it is called the *articulated name.* This means that this name gives a clear unequivocal indication of His essence, may He be exalted. On the other hand, all the other great names give their indication in an equivocal way, being derived from terms signifying actions the like of which, as we have made clear,[1] exist as our own actions. Even the name that is uttered instead of *Yod, He, Vav, He,* is derived from a term signifying lordship: *The man, the lord [ʾadoni] of the land, spoke.*[2] The difference between your saying ʾ*Adoni* — with an "I" vocalization of the *nun* — and your saying [ʾAdonai — with] an *A* vocalization of the *nun* — is analogous to the difference between your saying *Sarri,* which means my chief, and your saying *Sarai, the wife of Abram.*[3] For these words [those having a termination "ai"] are emphatic and of a general character applicable also to other beings. Thus it has been said to an angel: ʾ*Adonai* [*my lord*], *pass not away, I pray thee.*[4]

I have explained | this to you especially with regard to ʾ*Adonai* [which is uttered instead of Y.H.V.H.] because it is the most particularized of the commonly known names of [God], may He be exalted; for in the case of all the others, such as the *Judge,* the *Just,* the *Gracious,* the *Merciful,* and *Elohim,* it is manifest that they are used in a general way as well as

12. Literally: these terms. The term in question appears to be God.
1. Cf. I 54.   2. Gen. 42:30.   3. Gen. 12:17.   4. Gen. 18:3.

that they are derived. As for the *name* that, if pronounced, is composed of *Yod, He, Vav,* and *He,* no commonly accepted derivation of it is known and none other than He has a part in it. There can be no doubt about the fact that this great name, which as you know is not pronounced except in the *Sanctuary* by the *sanctified Priests of the Lord* and only in *the benediction of the Priests* and by *the High Priest* upon *the day of fasting*, is indicative of a notion with reference to which there is no association between God, may He be exalted, and what is other than He. Perhaps it indicates the notion of a necessary existence,[5] according to the [Hebrew] language, of which we today know only a very scant portion and also with regard to its pronunciation. Generally speaking, the greatness of this name and the prohibition against pronouncing it are due to its being indicative of the essence of Him, may He be exalted, in such a way that none of the created things is associated with Him in this indication. As the Sages, *may their memory be blessed,* have said of it: *My name that is peculiar to Me.*

As for the other names, all of them, because of their being derived, indicate attributes; that is, not an essence alone, but an essence possessing attributes. For this reason they produce in one's fantasy the conception of multiplicity; I mean to say that they produce in one's fantasy the thought that the attributes exist, and that there is an essence and a notion superadded to this essence. For the indications of all derivative terms are such that they indicate a notion and a substratum that is not clearly stated and with which the notion in question is connected. However, as it has been demonstrated that God, may He be exalted, is not a substratum with which some notions are connected, it is known that the derived names are to be understood either with reference to the relation of a certain action to Him or with reference to directing the mind toward His perfection. For this reason | *Rabbi Ḥaninah* would have shrunk from the dictum of Scripture, *the Great, the Valiant, and the Terrible,* were it not for the two necessary obligations mentioned by him. He would have done so because these names produce in one's fantasy the thought of essential attributes; I mean the thought that these names refer to perfections existing in Him. And when the names deriving from the actions pertaining to Him, may He be exalted, were multiplied, they produced in the fantasy of some men the thought that He has many attributes, just as there is a multiplicity of actions from which these names derive. Hence Scripture promises that an apprehension that will put an end to this delusion will come to men. Thus it says: *In that day shall the Lord be one, and His name one;*[6] which means that in the same way

5. Literally: the notion of a necessity of existence.   6. Zech. 14:9.

as He is one, He will be invoked at that time by one name only, by that which is indicative only of the essence and which is not derivative. In the *Chapters of Rabbi Eliezer* they have said: *Before the world was created, there were only the Holy One, blessed be He, and His name.*[7] Consider now how this dictim states clearly that all the derivative names have come into being after the world has come into being. This is correct, for all these names have been laid down[8] so as to correspond to the actions existing in the world. However, if you envisage His essence as it is when divested and stripped of all actions, He no longer has a derived name in any respect whatever, but only one original name that indicates His essence. In fact we have no nonderivative *name* except the one in question, namely, *Yod, He, Vav, He,* which is *the articulated name* simply.

Do not think anything other than this and do not let occur to your mind the vain imaginings of the writers of charms[9] or what names you may hear from them or may find in their stupid books, names that they have invented, which are not indicative of any notion whatsoever, but which they call the *names* and of which they think that they necessitate *holiness and purity* and work miracles. All these are stories that it is not seemly for a perfect man to listen to, | much less to believe. None is called *the articulated name* except the name *having four letters* that is written but not read in accordance with the sounds written down. For the Sages have stated clearly in *Sifre*: *Thus shall ye bless the children of Israel.*[10] Thus: [*that is*], *in these words; Thus:* [*that is*], *using the articulated name.* It is also said there: *In the Temple,* [*the name is pronounced*] *as it is written,* [*whereas*] *in* [*the rest of*] *the country the name used to replace it* [*is pronounced instead*]. And in the *Talmud* it is said:[11] *Thus means with the articulated name. And if you ask: With the articulated name or with the name used to replace it? this may be learnt from the words: And they shall put My name*[12] — *that is, My name that is peculiar to Me.* Thus it has become clear to you that *the articulated name* is the *name having four letters* and that it alone is indicative of the essence without associating any other notion with it. For this reason the Sages have said of it that it is the name *that is peculiar to Me.* Now I shall make clear to you what has incited men to the beliefs with regard to the

7. Chapters of Rabbi Eliezer, III.
8. *wuḍicat.* The terms implied that the names in question were invented and assigned the generally accepted meanings they have.
9. *qamicot;* i.e., holy names, etc., written on a piece of parchment or on paper and used as protective charms.
10. Num. 6:23, and the Sifre on this verse.   11. B.T., Sota, 38a.   12. Num. 6:27.

names, and I will make clear to you the root of this question, and I will strip it of its covering so that nothing doubtful remains, unless you wish to lead yourself astray with reference to a chapter coming after this.

CHAPTER 62

We have received a commandment with regard to the *benediction of Priests* in which *the name of the Lord* figures *as it is written.* This name is *the articulated name.* Now not everybody knew how this name was to be pronounced and how every one of its letters should be vocalized and which of the letters, if any, should be redoubled. Accordingly the men of knowledge have transmitted this, I mean the mode of pronouncing it, but they did not teach it to anyone except *once a week to a worthy scholar.*[1] I believe | that the dictum, *The sages transmit the name having four letters once a week to their sons and their pupils,*[2] refers not only to their teaching the mode of pronouncing this name but also to their making known the notion because of which this name has been originated without any derivation. Accordingly there also would be in this notion a divine secret.

Furthermore, though they used[3] a name having twelve letters, that name was in *sanctity* inferior to the *name having four letters.* In my opinion the most probable supposition is that the name that had twelve letters was not one name but two or three, the sum of the letters of which came to twelve. This name was uttered in all the cases in which the *name having four letters* occurred in the *reading* of Scripture, just as we utter today in the same cases the letters *aleph* and *daleth.* Now this *name* also, namely, that *having twelve letters,* is undoubtedly indicative of a notion more particularly pertaining to God than is the case with regard to what is indicated by *aleph* and *daleth.* But this name was not prohibited and withheld from any of the men of knowledge; on the contrary, everybody who sought to learn this name was taught it. This was not the case with regard to *the name having four letters.* For no one of those knowing it taught it to anyone except *once a week to his son and his pupil.* In consequence, blameworthy people started learning *the name having twelve letters,* and through this corrupted beliefs. This happens whenever anyone who is not a perfect man comes to know that something

1. B.T., Qiddushin, 71a.   2. B.T., Qiddushin, 71a.
3. Literally: a name was with them.

is not as he had imagined it to be in the first place. The Sages therefore made a secret of this *name* likewise, and taught it only to the *discreet among the Priests* that they might use it in giving their benediction to the people in the *Sanctuary*, as they had ceased mentioning *the articulated name* in the *Sanctuary* because of the corruption of the people. They say: *After the death of Simon the Just, his brethren the Priests stopped using the name in giving their benediction;*[4] in giving their benediction they used *the name* | *having twelve letters.* They also say: *At first the name having twelve letters was transmitted to everyone.* [*However*] *when libertines became numerous, it was transmitted only to the discreet among the Priests; and the discreet among the Priests uttered it* [*in such fashion*] *that it should be inaudible in the* [*singing of*] *melodies by their brethren the* [*other*] *Priests. Rabbi Tarphon says: Once I ascended the dais after the father of* [*my*] *mother, listened to an* [*officiating*] *Priest, and heard that he uttered* [*the name in question in such fashion*] *that it should be inaudible in the* [*singing of*] *melodies by his brethren the* [*other*] *Priests.*[5] They also had a *name having forty-two letters.* Now it is known to everyone capable of mental representation that it is in no way possible that forty-two letters should form one word; these were certainly several words, the number of the letters of which amounted to forty-two. There is no doubt that these words were necessarily indicative of several notions and that these notions came near to a representation of the essence of Him, may He be exalted, in the way we have stated.

These words that had numerous letters were called *name* only because of their being indicative of one notion only, like the other names originated without any derivation. And these words were numerous only with a view to making the notion in question understood. For sometimes many words are used in order to make a single notion understood. Understand this accordingly, and know that that which was taught were the notions indicated by these names and not merely the pronunciation, devoid of all representation, of the letters. The term *articulated name* is never applied to the *name having twelve letters* or to the *name having forty-two letters.* For *the articulated name* is *the name that is peculiar to Him,* as we have made clear, whereas the two others necessarily taught some sort of divine science. The fact that it taught science is proved by | the following dictum on this subject: *The name having forty-two letters is holy and sanctified and is only transmitted to one who is discreet, has reached the middle of his life, is not prone to anger or to drunkenness, does not arouse criticism by his way of life, and speaks agreeably with people. And he who knows it is heedful*

4. Cf. B.T., Yoma, 39b; B.T., Menaḥoth, 109b.   5. B.T., Qiddushin, 71a.

thereof and observes it in purity, is beloved on high and popular below. He is feared by the people, his learning is preserved by him, and he inherits the two worlds, this world and the next.[6] This is literally what the *Talmud* says. How very remote is the way in which this saying is usually understood from the intention of its speaker. For most people think that it deals solely with the pronunciation of letters, and it is not taken into consideration that these letters may have a meaning, so that great things may be acquired through them and that for this reason there is needed the moral preparation and the multiple forming of dispositions that were mentioned. It is clear then that all this is solely instruction in divine notions belonging to the totality of notions that, as we have elucidated, are *mysteries of the Torah.* It has been made clear in the books that have been composed concerning divine science that it is impossible to forget this science; I mean thereby the apprehension of the active intellect; this is the meaning of the dictum of the Sage: *his learning is preserved by him.* When wicked and ignorant people found these texts, they had great scope for lying statements in that they would put together any letters they liked and would say: this is a *name* that has efficacy and the power to operate if it is written down or uttered in a particular way. Thereupon these lies invented by the first wicked and ignorant man were written down, and these writings transmitted to good, pious, and foolish men who lack the scales by means of which they could know the true from the false. These people accordingly made a secret of these writings, and the latter were found in the belongings left behind them, so that they were thought to be correct. To sum it up: | *A fool believes everything.*[7]

We have gone beyond our noble subject and our subtle speculation, turning to speculation designed to invalidate vain imaginings the lack of validity of which is manifest to every beginner in speculation. However the necessity that made us mention the *names* and their meaning and the opinion concerning them that is generally accepted by the vulgar has led us to do so. I shall now return to my subject.

We have already pointed out that all the names of God, may He be exalted, are derived except *the articulated name.* It behooves us to speak of this name, which is *I am that I am,*[8] in a separate chapter as it includes the subtle notion with which we are dealing, I mean the negation of attributes.

6. B.T., Qiddushin, 71a.　　7. Prov. 14:15.　　8. Exod. 3:14.

CHAPTER 63

We shall begin with an introductory remark. We shall say regarding the saying of [Moses], peace be on him — *And they shall say to me, What is His name? What shall I say unto them?*[1] — why was this question necessarily attached to the matter under discussion so that [Moses] demanded to know how he should answer it? As for his saying, *But, behold, they will not believe me, nor hearken unto my voice; for they will say: the Lord hath not appeared unto thee,*[2] it is very clear that everyone who lays claim to prophecy should be spoken to in this way until he brings proof. Furthermore if the matter concerned, as it may appear, merely a name to be pronounced, there are only two possibilities: namely, that [the Children of] *Israel* already knew this name or that they had never heard it. If it was known to them, [Moses'] telling it would be no argument in his favor,[3] for his knowledge of it would be like their knowledge. If, on the other hand, this name had not been heard among them, what would be the proof of this being the name | of God, supposing that the knowledge of His name were a proof? Besides, after He, may He be exalted, had made known this name to him, He told him: *Go, and gather the elders of Israel together. And they shall hearken to your voice.*[4] There came the answer of [Moses], peace be on him: *But, behold, they will not believe me, nor hearken unto my voice.*[5] Yet this answer was preceded by His dictum, may He be exalted: *And they shall hearken to your voice;* and it is followed by Him, may He be exalted, saying to [Moses]: *What is that in thy hand? And he said: A rod.*[6] What you should know so that this whole difficulty should be made clear to you is that which I shall tell you.

You know that in those times the teachings of the Sabians were generally accepted and that all except a few men were *idolaters.* I mean by this that they believed in spirits, that they believed that those spirits can be made to descend among men, and that they made talismans. At those times everyone who claimed to be listened to either claimed, like *Abraham,* that speculation and reasoning had come to him indicating to him that the world as a whole has a deity, or else he claimed that the spirit of a star or an angel or something similar had descended upon him. Yet that an individual should make a claim to prophecy on the ground that God had spoken to him and had sent him on a mission was a thing never heard of prior to

1. Exod. 3:13.   2. Exod. 4:1.   3. *ḥujja.* Literally: proof.
4. Exod. 3:16 and 18.   5. Exod. 4:1.   6. Exod. 4:2.

10

Moses our Master. You should not be led into error on this point by what
is said in Scripture with regard to the *Patriarchs*, with reference to whom
it is mentioned that God spoke and manifested Himself to them. For you
do not find in their cases the kind of prophecy that would have made them
call upon people or guide correctly others than themselves, that is, the kind
of prophecy that would have made *Abraham* or *Isaac* or *Jacob* or those who
preceded them say to people: "God told me: You should act or not act in a
certain way"; or: "He has sent me to you." This had never happened
before. The Patriarchs were addressed in regard to their private affairs only;
I mean only in regard to their perfection, their right guidance concerning
their actions, and the good tidings for them concerning the position their
descendants would attain. They had addressed a call to people by means of
speculation and instruction, as is made clear, in our opinion, | in the passage:
And the soul[s] that they had gotten in Harran.[7]

Accordingly when God, may He be held sublime and magnified,
revealed Himself to *Moses our Master* and ordered him to address a call to
people and to convey to them his prophetic mission, [Moses] said: the first
thing that they will ask of me is that I should make them acquire true
knowledge that there exists a god with reference to the world; after that
I shall make the claim that He has sent me. For at that time all the people
except a few were not aware of the existence of the deity, and the utmost
limits of their speculation did not transcend the sphere, its faculties, and
its actions, for they did not separate themselves from things perceived by
the senses and had not attained intellectual perfection. Accordingly God
made known to [Moses] the knowledge that he was to convey to them and
through which they would acquire a true notion of the existence of God,
this knowledge being: *I am that I am.*[8] This is a name deriving from the
verb *to be* [*hayah*], which signifies existence, for *hayah* indicates the
notion: he was. And in Hebrew, there is no difference between your saying:
he was, and he existed. The whole secret consists in the repetition in a
predicative position of the very word indicative of existence. For the word
that [in the phrase "I am that I am"] requires the mention of an attribute
immediately connected with it. For it is a deficient word requiring a connection with something else; it has the same meaning as alladhī and allatī,
the male and female relative pronouns in Arabic. Accordingly the first word
is *I am* considered as a term to which a predicate is attached; the second
word that is predicated of the first is also *I am*, that is, identical with the
first. Accordingly Scripture makes, as it were, a clear statement that the

7. Gen. 12:5.   8. Exod. 3:14.

subject is identical with the predicate. This makes it clear that He is existent not through existence. This notion may be summarized and interpreted in the following way: the existent that is the existent, or the necessarily existent. This is what demonstration necessarily leads to: namely, to the view that there is a necessarily existent thing that has never been, or ever will be, nonexistent. I shall make clear the demonstration of this thesis.

Accordingly when He, may He be exalted, had made known to [Moses] the proofs[9] that would establish His existence among their[10] men of knowledge — this may be inferred from the words that follow: *Go, and gather the elders | of Israel together*[11] — and had promised him that they would understand what I have transmitted and would accept it — this is signified by His words: *And they shall hearken to your voice*[12] — [Moses], peace be on him, posed another question saying: once they have accepted by means of these intellectual demonstrations the view that there is an existent deity, what shall be my proof that this existent deity has sent me? Thereupon he was granted the miracle. Thus it has been made clear that the meaning of his saying, *What is His name?* means only: who is He who you think has sent you? He said, *What is His name?* only with a view to magnifying and exalting [God] in address. He says as it were: no one is ignorant of Your essence and true reality; if, however, I am asked about Your name, what is the meaning indicated by that name? He only thought that it would be a reprehensible thing to say in speaking that there are those who are ignorant of that existent and consequently made out that they were ignorant of His name only and not of that which is signified by that name.

The name *Yah* refers similarly to the notion of the eternity of existence, whereas *Shaddai* derives from the word *day*, meaning a sufficiency. Thus: *For the stuff they had was sufficient* [*dayam*].[13] The letter *shin* [occurring at the beginning of Shaddai] has the meaning *who*, as in *shekbar*.[14] Accordingly the meaning [of Shaddai] is *He who is sufficient*; the intention here being to signify that He does not need other than Himself with reference to the existence of that which He has brought into existence or with reference to prolonging the latter's existence, but that His existence, may He be exalted, suffices for that. Similarly the name *Hassin* derives from the

9. A being endowed with intellect cannot but accept the truth of a demonstration. A proof (*dalīl*) does not have this irrefragable character.

10. In the context probably the men of knowledge among the Children of Israel are meant.

11. Exod. 3:16.   12. Exod. 3:18.

13. Exod. 36:7.   14. Eccles. 4:2.

notion of power; thus: *And he was strong [ḥason] as the oaks.*[15] Similarly
the name *Rock [ṣur]* applied to Him is equivocal, as we have made clear.[16]
Accordingly it has become clear to you that all names are derived or are
used equivocally, as *Rock* and others similar to it. He, may He be exalted,
has no *name* that is not derivative except the *name having four letters,*
which is *the articulated name.* This name is not indicative of an attribute
but of simple existence and nothing else. Now absolute existence implies[17]
that He shall always be, I mean He who is necessarily existent. Understand
the point at which this discourse has finally arrived. |

CHAPTER 64

K now that the *name Y.H.V.H.*[1] sometimes is intended to signify the name
exclusively, as in his saying: *Thou shalt not take the name of the Lord
thy God in vain;*[2] *And he that blasphemeth the name of the Lord.*[3] This
occurs innumerable times. The term is sometimes intended to signify the
essence and true reality of Him, may He be exalted, as for instance: *And
they shall say to me: What is His name?*[4] The term is sometimes intended
to signify His commandment, may He be exalted, so that when we say *the
name of Y.H.V.H.*[5] it is as if we said *the word of Y.H.V.H.*[6] or *the speech of
Y.H.V.H.,*[7] as when Scripture says, *for My name is within him,*[8] which
means *My word is within him* or *My speech is within him.* The meaning is
that he[9] is an instrument of My will and volition. I shall make this statement clear when speaking of the equivocality of *angel.*[10] Similarly *the glory
of Y.H.V.H.*[11] is sometimes intended to signify the created light that God
causes to descend in a particular place in order to confer honor upon it in
a miraculous way: *And the glory of Y.H.V.H. abode upon Mount Sinai,
and [the cloud] covered it, and so on;*[12] *And the glory of Y.H.V.H. filled the
tabernacle.*[13] The expression is sometimes intended to signify His essence
and true reality, may He be exalted, as when he says, *Show me, I pray
Thee, Thy glory,*[14] and was answered: *For man shall not see Me and live.*[15]

---

15. Amos 2:9.   16. Cf. I 16.   17. Literally: includes.
1. In the text "Y.Y." is substituted for "Y.H.V.H."   2. Exod. 20:7.
3. Lev. 24:16.   4. Exod. 3:13.   5. "Y.Y." in the text.   6. "Y.Y." in the text.
7. "Y.Y." in the text.   8. Exod. 23:21.   9. Or: it. I.e., God's word or speech.
10. Cf. II 6 and 32.   11. "Y.Y." in the text.   12. Exod. 24:16.   13. Exod. 40:34.
14. Exod. 33:18.   15. Exod. 33:20.

This answer indicates that the *glory* that is spoken of here is His essence, and that [Moses'] saying *Thy glory* is by way of honoring Him, in the same way as we have made clear[16] with regard to his saying: *And they shall say to me: What is His name? Glory* is sometimes intended to signify the honoring of Him, may He be exalted, by all men. In fact all that is other than God, may He be exalted, honors Him. For the true way of honoring Him consists in apprehending His greatness.[17] Thus everybody who apprehends His greatness and His perfection, honors Him according to the extent of his apprehension. Man in particular honors Him by speeches so that he indicates thereby that which he has apprehended by his intellect and communicates it to others. Those beings that have no apprehension, as for instance the minerals, | also as it were honor God through the fact that by their very nature they are indicative of the power and wisdom of Him who brought them into existence. For this induces him who considers them to honor God, either by means of articulate utterance or without it if speech is not permitted him. The Hebrew language gives itself latitude in that it applies to this notion the *term saying*. Accordingly it is said of that which is devoid of apprehension that it praises God. Thus Scripture says: *All my bones shall say, Lord, who is like unto Thee;*[18] whereby it conveys that the bones necessitate this belief, as though they put it into speech, for they too make this known. It is in view of this notion being named *glory* that it is said, *The whole earth is full of His glory,*[19] this being equivalent to the dictum, *And the earth is full of His praise,*[20] for praise is called *glory*. Thus it is said: *Give glory to the Lord your God;*[21] and it is said: *And in His temple all say: Glory.*[22] This occurs frequently. Understand then likewise the equivocality with reference to *glory* and interpret the latter in every passage in accordance with the context. You shall thus be saved from great difficulty.

16. In the preceding chapter.
17. The word *ta'zīm*, translated by "honoring," and the word *izma*, translated by "greatness," derive from the same root.
18. Ps. 35:10.   19. Isa. 6:3.   20. Hab. 3:3.   21. Jer. 13:16.   22. Ps. 29:9.

I do not consider that — after having attained this degree and having gained the true knowledge that He, may He be exalted, exists not by virtue of an existence and is one not by virtue of a oneness — you require that the denial of the attribute of speech with reference to Him be explained to you. This is the case particularly in view of the general consensus of our community on the *Torah* being created. This is meant to signify that His speech that is ascribed to Him is created. It was ascribed to Him only because the words heard by *Moses* were created and brought into being by God, just as He has created all the things that He has created and brought into being. Later prophecy will be treated of at length. | The intention here is to indicate that predicating speech of Him is similar to predicating of Him all the actions resembling ours. Thus the minds of people are rightly guided toward the view that there is a divine science apprehended by the prophets in consequence of God's speaking to them and telling it to them so that we should know that the notions transmitted by them from God to us are not, as shall be made clear, mere products of their thought and insight. But this subject has already been mentioned by us.

The purpose of this chapter is to set forth that the words *speaking* and *saying* are equivocal, applied both to utterance by the tongue — as when it says, *Moses spoke;*[1] *And Pharaoh said*[2] — and to notions represented by the intellect without being uttered — as when it says, *Then said I in my heart;*[3] *Then I spoke in my heart;*[4] *And thy heart shall speak;*[5] *My heart said unto thee;*[6] *And Esau said in his heart.*[7] This meaning is frequent. The terms in question are also used to denote wishing, as in the verse, *He thought*[8] *to have slain David.*[9] It is as if it said he wished to slay him, that is, gave his mind to it. Thus: *Thinkest thou*[10] *to kill me;*[11] the interpretation and meaning of it are: do you want to kill me? And also in the verse: *But all the congregation wanted*[12] *to stone them with stones.*[13] This meaning likewise is frequent.

Now in all cases in which the words *saying* and *speaking* are applied to God, they are used in one of the two latter meanings. I mean to say that they are used to denote either will and volition or a notion that has been grasped by the understanding having come from God, in which case it is

1. Exod. 19:19.   2. Exod. 5:5.   3. Eccles. 2:15.   4. Eccles. 2:15.
5. Prov. 23:33.   6. Ps. 27:8.   7. Gen. 27:41.   8. Literally: *said.*
9. II Sam. 21:16.   10. Literally: *sayest thou.*   11. Exod. 2:14.
12. Literally: *said.*   13. Num. 14:10.

indifferent whether it has become known by means of a created voice or through one of the ways of prophecy, which we shall make clear. The terms in question never signify that He, may He be exalted, spoke using the sounds of letters and a voice, nor that He, may He be exalted, possesses a soul into which notions are impressed so that there would subsist in His essence a notion superadded to that essence. For these notions are attached to and related to Him in the same way as all other actions. As regards volition and will being denoted by the words *saying* and *speaking* | — this, as we have made clear, is one of the meanings because of which these words are equivocal. In this case too they are used by way of likening Him to us. For as we have pointed out above,[14] man cannot understand at first how, where there is a will that a thing should be done, that thing should be done by the mere will alone. In fact, if one thinks of it in a superficial way,[15] there is no doubt that he who wills either does the thing the existence of which he wills, or commands somebody else to do it. For this reason the term "command" is figuratively used of God with reference to the coming to be of that which He has willed. Thus it is said that He commanded that this should come to be. The words are used accordingly by way of likening His actions to ours, in addition to their being used, as we have made clear, to indicate the meaning: he wished. In all cases in which *He said, He said*, occurs in the *Account of the Beginning*,[16] it means He willed or wanted. This has already been said by an individual[17] other than we and is very well known. The demonstration of this, I mean that His *sayings* [at the creation of the world] were volitions only and not speeches, lies in the fact that speech may only be addressed to an existent that receives the command in question. Thus the dictum of Scripture, *By the word of the Lord were the heavens made*,[18] is analogous to its dictum, *And all the host of them by the breath of His mouth*, in the same verse. For the terms *His word* and *His saying* are used figuratively in the same way as the terms *His mouth* and *the breath of His mouth*, the intention being to signify that the heavens have come to exist through His purpose and will. No one among our renowned men of knowledge is ignorant of this. I do not need to make clear that the words *saying* and *speaking* have an identical meaning

14. Cf. I 46.
15. The Arabic expression, *fī bādi° al-ra°y*, is frequently used by the philosophers. Literally it means "in the beginning of opinion."
16. *ma°aseh bereshith*. As Maimonides states in his Introduction, this expression may mean "physics."
17. Or: individuals. 18. Ps. 33:6.

in the Hebrew language, as is shown by the verse: *For it hath heard all the sayings of the Lord which He spoke.*[19]

CHAPTER 66

A*nd the tables were the work of God.*[1] He intends to signify by this that this existence was natural | and not artificial, for all natural things are called *the work of the Lord: These saw the works of the Lord.*[2] Accordingly after he has mentioned all natural things, such as plants, animals, winds, rains, and others of the same kind, he says: *How manifold are Thy works, O Lord!*[3] He went even further than this ascription in saying: *The cedars of Lebanon which He hath planted.*[4] It is because the existence of the cedars is natural and not artificial that he says that God has planted them. Similarly when it says[5] *the writing of God,*[6] it has already made clear in what way the writing may be ascribed to God by its saying[7] *written with the finger of God.*[8] Its saying *with the finger of God* is analogous to its saying, with reference to the heavens, *the work of Thy fingers.*[9] For Scripture has made clear with regard to the heavens that they have been made by *saying: By the word of the Lord were the heavens made.*[10] It has then become clear to you that, with regard to the coming into being of a thing, the texts figuratively use the *terms saying* and *speaking* and that it is one and the same thing of which it is said that it was *made by speech* and of which it is said that it is the *work of a finger.* Similarly the dictum *written with the finger of God* is equivalent to its saying *by the word of God.* Furthermore, the expression *by the word of God* would, if Scripture had used it, be equivalent to its saying *written by the will of God,* I mean by His will and volition.[11] As for *Onqelos,* with reference to this matter he puts forward a strange interpretation, for he translates: *written with a finger belonging to the Lord.* For he makes out that *finger* is a certain thing related to God and interprets the *finger of the Lord* in an analogous way to

19. Josh. 24:27.
1. Exod. 32:16.   2. Ps. 107:24.   3. Ps. 104:24.   4. Ps. 104:16.
5. With reference to the Tables of the Law.   6. Exod. 32:16.
7. With reference to the Tables of the Law.   8. Exod. 31:18.
9. Ps. 8:4.   10. Ps. 33:6.
11. This clause is intended to explain the Hebrew word for "will," which Maimonides has just used.

the mountain of the Lord, the rod of the Lord. He intends to signify by this that the finger is a created instrument that has cut into the tables through the will of God. I do not know what has led him to make this interpretation. For it would have been more plausible to translate *written by the word of the Lord*, just as the Scripture says: *By the word of the Lord were the heavens made.* Do you think that the existence of writing on the tables is any stranger than the existence of stars in the spheres? For just as the stars came into being through the First Will and not through an instrument, so this inscribed writing came into being through the First Will and not through an instrument. You already know | the text of the *Mishnah*[12] about *ten things created in the twilight*,[13] among which were *the writing and the inscription.* This proves that there was a general consensus among the multitude that the *writing on the tables* was like all the other *work in the beginning*, as we have made clear in the Commentary on the *Mishnah*.

CHAPTER 67

As the term *to say* [*ʾamirah*] is figuratively used for the will in regard to everything that has been created in the *six days of the beginning*—with reference to which it is said: *He said, He said*—the term *to rest* [*shebithah*] is derivatively used with reference to the Sabbath as there was no creation on that day. It is accordingly said: *And He rested on the seventh day.*[1] For refraining from speech is likewise called *rest.* Thus it is said: *So these three men ceased*[2] *to answer Job.*[3] Similarly the *term to repose* [*niḥah*] occurs in the sense of refraining from speech. Thus it says: *They spoke to Nabal according to all those words in the name of David and reposed*[4] [*yanuḥu*]; the meaning of which in my opinion is: "and then refrained from speech until they heard the answer." For in the preceding verses there is no mention of their being tired in any way, so that even if they were tired, the term *reposed* would be quite extraneous to the story. Scripture merely relates that they brought out that speech with its effort at graciousness and then were silent; that is, they did not add any other uttered notion to that speech, or any act, that would necessitate his reply to them to be such as

12. Mishnah, Aboth, V 6.
13. Of the sixth day of the days in which the world was created.
 1. Gen. 2:2.   2. Literally: *rested.*   3. Job. 32:1.   4. I Sam. 25:9.

he gave. For the purpose of the story is to give an account of [Nabal's] blameworthiness and to make clear that it was extreme.

In this sense it is likewise said: *And He reposed [va-yanah] the seventh day*.[5] However, the *Sages* and the other commentators have made | out that the signification of the verb derives from that of rest and that it is a transitive verb. Accordingly the *Sages, may their memory be blessed*, have said: *He let His world repose on the seventh day*,[6] meaning that creation ceased on that day. It is also possible that [the verb va-yanah, meaning He reposed] is one of those verbs the first or the third radicals of which are weak. If this were so, it would mean: He established existence, or He made the latter endure as it was on the seventh day. Thus Scripture would say that on every day of the preceding six, events occurred that did not correspond to the established nature that exists at present in the whole of existence, whereas on the seventh day the state of things became lasting and established just as it is at present. This assertion made by us is not refuted by observation that the conjugation of the verb in question is not like that of the verbs the first or third radicals of which are weak. For sometimes conjugations are irregular and may be found not to correspond to other analogous examples. This occurs more particularly in the case of these weak verbs. The doing-away with the notion in question, which gives rise to vain imagining, should not be negated because of the rules of conjugation obtaining in the [Hebrew] language, for we know that today we have no complete understanding of the science of our language and that in all languages rules merely conform to the majority of cases. On the other hand, we find in the case of this root that that verb too whose second radical is weak has sometimes the meaning: to set, to establish. Thus the dictum: *And she shall be set [va-hunihah] there*.[7] And similarly: *And she suffered neither the birds of the air to be established*[8] *on them*[9]. In my opinion the verb has this meaning also in the verse: *That I might be established*[10] *in the day of trouble*.[11] As for the verb *vayyinaphash*,[12] it is a passive form deriving from the word *nephesh [soul]*. Now we have already made clear[13] the equivocality of the term *soul* and have explained that it may have the meaning of purpose and volition. Accordingly it means that His purpose was perfected and all His will realized.

5. Exod. 20:11.   6. Genesis Rabbah, X *in fine*.   7. Zech. 5:11.
8. Literally: *rest (la-nuah)*.   9. II Sam. 21:10.   10. Literally: *rest*.   11. Hab. 3:16.
12. Generally translated "to rest." The verb figures in the following verse: *For in six days the Lord made heaven and earth, and on the seventh day He ceased from work and rested* (Exod. 31:17).
13. Cf. I 41.

CHAPTER 68

You already know that the following dictum | of the philosophers with reference to God, may He be exalted, is generally admitted: the dictum being that He is the intellect as well as the intellectually cognizing subject and the intellectually cognized object, and that those three notions form in Him, may He be exalted, one single notion in which there is no multiplicity.[1] We have mentioned this likewise in our great compilation,[2] since this, as we have made clear there, is one of the foundations of our Law; I mean the fact that He is one only and that no other thing can be added to Him, I mean to say that there is no external thing other than He. For this reason it is said, *by the Lord the living*, and not, *by the life of the Lord*. For His life is not something other than His essence, as we have made clear when speaking of the negation of attributes. However, there is no doubt that anyone who has not studied the books that have been composed concerning the intellect has not grasped the essence of the intellect, has not acquired knowledge of its quiddity, and has no understanding of it other than one that resembles his understanding of the notions of blackness and whiteness, has great difficulty in understanding this notion. In fact our saying that He is the intellectual cognition[3] as well as the intellectually cognizing subject and the intellectually cognized object will appear to him as if we had said that whiteness, that which has become white, and that which whitens, are one and the same thing. How many ignoramuses there are who hasten to refute us by means of this and similar examples, and how many pretending to knowledge there are who have great difficulties with regard to this and who hold that the minds cannot attain the knowledge that it is correct that this matter should be necessarily true. Yet this notion is a matter of demonstration and is quite clear, as the theologizing[4] philosophers have explained. Here I shall make clear to you that which they have demonstrated.

Know that before a man intellectually cognizes a thing, he is potentially the intellectually cognizing subject. Now if he has intellectually cognized a thing (it is as if you said that if a man has intellectually cognized this piece

1. On this dictum, cf. Translator's Introduction.
2. Cf. *Mishneh Torah*, Yesodei ha-Torah, I.
3. ʿaql. The term also means "intellect."
4. al-mutaʾallihūn. This participle sometimes refers to those who become divine (for instance by union with, or imitation of, God). In this context, however, Maimonides seems to have in mind the philosophers interested in the divine science.

of wood to which one can point, has stripped its form from its matter, and has represented to himself the pure form — this being the action of the intellect), at that time the man would become one who has intellectual cognition in actu. Intellect realized in actu is the pure abstract form, | which is in his mind, of the piece of wood. For intellect is nothing but the thing that is intellectually cognized. Accordingly it has become clear to you that the thing that is intellectually cognized is the abstract form of the piece of wood, that this form is identical with the intellect realized in actu, and that these are not two things — intellect and the intellectually cognized form of the piece of wood. For the intellect in actu is nothing but that which has been intellectually cognized; and the thing by means of which the form of wood was intellectually cognized and made abstract, that thing being the intellectually cognizing subject, is also indubitably identical with the intellect realized in actu. For in the case of every intellect, its act is identical in essence; for intellect in actu is not one thing and its act another thing; for the true reality and the quiddity of the intellect[5] is apprehension. You should not then think that the intellect in actu is a certain thing existing by itself apart from apprehension and that apprehension is something else subsisting in that intellect. For the very being and true reality of the intellect is apprehension. Whenever, therefore, you assume that an intellect exists in actu, that intellect is identical with the apprehension of what has been intellectually cognized. This is most clear to whoever has attempted this kind of speculation. Accordingly it is clear that the act of the intellect, which is its apprehension, is the true reality and the essence of the intellect. Consequently the thing by means of which the form of that piece of wood was abstracted and apprehended, which thing is the intellect,[6] is also the intellectually cognizing subject. For it is that very intellect that abstracted the form and apprehended it, this being its act because of which it is said to be an intellectually cognizing subject. Now its act is identical with its essence. Accordingly that which has been assumed to be an intellect in actu has nothing belonging to it except the form of the piece of wood. Accordingly it is clear that whenever intellect exists in actu, it is identical with the intellectually cognized thing. And it has become clear that the act of every intellect, which act consists in its being intellectually cognizing, is identical with the essence of that intellect. Consequently the intellect,[7] the intellectually cognizing subject, and the intellectually cognized object

5. In this passage this translation seems to be more appropriate than "intellectual cognition." It is, however, impossible to separate the two senses.
6. Or: intellectual cognition.   7. Or: the intellectual cognition

are always one and the same thing in the case of everything that is cognized
in actu. |

If, however, potential cognition is assumed, they — that is, the intellect
in potentia and the potentially cognizable object — are necessarily two things.
It is as if you said the hylic intellect subsisting in Zayd is a potential intellect,
and similarly this piece of wood is in potentia an intellectually cognized
object. Indubitably these are two things. When thereupon the intellect
becomes actual and the form of the piece of wood is realized as intellectually
cognized, then the intellectually cognized form is identical with the intellect — that very intellect, which is an intellect in actu, being the one by
means of which the form was abstracted and intellectually cognized. For
everything that has an existing act exists in actu. Thus every intellect in
potentia and potentially cognizable objects are two things. Moreover,
everything that is in potentia must undoubtedly have a substratum sup-
porting this potentiality, such a substratum as, for instance, man. Thus
there are three things: the man who supports that potentiality and who is
the intellectually cognizing subject in potentia; the potentiality that is the
intellect in potentia; and the thing apt to be intellectually cognized, which
is the potentially cognizable object. In the example in question, this would
be as if you said: man, hylic intellect, and the form of the piece of wood —
these being three separate notions. When, however, the intellect is realized
in actu, the three notions become one. Accordingly you will never find in
that case that intellect is one thing and the intellectually cognized object
another thing, unless they are regarded as being in potentia.

Now when it is demonstrated that God, may He be held precious and
magnified, is an intellect in actu and that there is absolutely no potentiality
in Him — as is clear and shall be demonstrated — so that He is not by way
of sometimes apprehending and sometimes not apprehending[8] but is always
an intellect in actu, it follows necessarily that He and the thing apprehended
are one thing, which is His essence. Moreover, the act of apprehension
owing to which He is said to be an intellectually cognizing subject is in
itself the intellect, which is His essence. Accordingly He is always the intellect as well as the intellectually cognizing subject and the intellectually
cognized object. It is accordingly also clear | that the numerical unity of the
intellect, the intellectually cognizing subject, and the intellectually cognized
object, does not hold good with reference to the Creator only, but also with
reference to every intellect. Thus in us too, the intellectually cognizing

8. Cf. Aristotle *Metaphysics* xii.7.1072b14 ff.; *De Anima* iii.5.430a10 ff. Cf. Translator's
    Introduction.

subject, the intellect, and the intellectually cognized object, are one and the same thing wherever we have an intellect in actu. We, however, pass intellectually from potentiality to actuality only from time to time. And the separate intellect too, I mean the active intellect, sometimes gets an impediment that hinders its act — even if this impediment does not proceed from this intellect's essence, but is extraneous to it — being a certain motion happening to it by accident.

We do not intend at present to explain this, our intention being to affirm that that which pertains solely to Him, may He be exalted, and which is specific to Him is His being constantly an intellect in actu and that there is no impediment either proceeding from His essence or from another that might hinder His apprehending. Accordingly it follows necessarily because of this that He is always and constantly an intellectually cognizing subject, an intellect, and an intellectually cognized object. Thus His essence is the intellectually cognizing subject, the intellectually cognized object, and the intellect, as is also necessarily the case with regard to every intellect in actu. We have repeated this notion several times in this chapter because the minds of men are very much strangers to this way of representing the thing to oneself. I do not consider that you might confuse intellectual representation with imagination and with the reception of an image of a sense object by the imaginative faculty, as this Treatise has been composed only for the benefit of those who have philosophized and have acquired knowledge of what has become clear with reference to the soul and all its faculties.

CHAPTER 69

The philosophers, as you know, designate God, may He be exalted, as | the first cause and the first ground.[1] On the other hand, those who are generally known as Mutakallimūn avoid these designations very deliberately and designate Him as the maker[2] and think that there is a great difference between our saying cause and ground and our saying maker. For they say that if we say that He is a cause, the existence of that which is caused follows necessarily, and that this leads to the doctrine of the

1. The text has *al-ᶜilla al-ūlā* and *al-sabab al-awwal*. In this context the expressions are synonymous, both of them meaning "the first cause."
2. The act of making (*fiᶜl*) is the same as the "act" spoken of in the preceding chapter.

eternity of the world and of the world necessarily following from God. If, however, we say that He is the maker, it does not necessarily follow that that which is made exists together with Him. For the maker sometimes precedes the act of making. But they only consider a maker as preceding the act of making. Now this is the assertion of people who do not make a distinction between what is in potentia and what is in actu.

But you know that, regarding this subject, there is no difference between your saying a cause and your saying a maker. For if you regard the cause as being likewise in potentia, it precedes its effect in time. If, on the other hand, it is a cause in actu, its effect exists necessarily in virtue of the existence of the cause as a cause in actu. Similarly if you regard a maker as a maker in actu, the existence of that which is made by him follows necessarily. For before he builds a house, a builder is not a builder in actu, but a builder in potentia; just as the matter of a particular house, before it is built, is matter in a state of potentiality. However, when a builder builds, he is a builder in actu, and then the existence of a built thing follows necessarily. Thus we have gained nothing by preferring the term "maker" to the term "cause and ground." The whole purpose here is to show the equivalence of those two terms. For just as we designate Him as a maker — even if that which is made by Him be nonexistent — because there is no impediment hindering Him from accomplishing the act of making whenever He wills to, we are also permitted to designate Him in very | same sense as a cause and a ground — though that which is caused be nonexistent.

In fact the philosophers were induced to designate Him, may He be exalted, as a cause and not as a maker, not because of their generally known opinion with regard to the eternity of the world, but because of other notions of which I will give you a summary account. In natural science, it has been made clear that there are causes for everything that has a cause; that they are four: namely, matter, form, the efficient cause, and the end; and that some of them are proximate causes and others remote ones. Every cause belonging to one of these four is designated as cause and ground. Now one of the opinions of the philosophers, an opinion with which I do not disagree, is that God, may He be held precious and magnified, is the efficient cause, that He is the form, and that He is the end. Thus it is for this reason that they say that He, may He be exalted, is a cause and a ground, in order to comprise these three causes — that is, the fact that God is the efficient cause[3] of the world, its form, and its end.

3. *fāᶜil*, the Arabic term translated here as "efficient cause," has been rendered above by the word "maker."

My purpose in this chapter is to make it clear to you in what respect it is said of Him, may He be exalted, that He is the efficient cause, that He is the form of the world, and that He is its end. You should not busy your mind at this place with the subject of the temporal creation of the world by Him or of its necessarily proceeding from Him, as is the opinion of the philosophers, for there will come subsequently a long discussion of that problem appropriate to the subject. The subject here, on the other hand, is God's being the efficient cause[4] of the partial actions occurring in the world, just as He is the efficient cause of the world as a whole.

I shall accordingly say: It has been made clear in natural science that for every one of the four kinds of causes one also needs to seek a cause. Accordingly, with reference to every generated thing, there are to be found four causes proximate to it, and there are to be found causes for these causes and causes for the causes of the latter until one arrives at the first causes. For instance this effected thing has a certain N as its efficient cause, | and this efficient cause in its turn has an efficient cause; and this continues until the first mover is attained, who is in true reality the efficient cause of all these intermediaries. For if the letter Alif is moved by the letter Bā, and the latter is moved by the letter Jīm, which is moved by the Dāl, moved in its turn by the letter Hā, this process cannot go on endlessly. Thus we have to stop for instance at the letter Hā. And there is accordingly no doubt that the letter Hā is the mover of Alif, of Bā, of Jīm, and of Dāl. And it is truly said with reference to the motion of Alif that it is due to an action of Hā. In this way every action that occurs in Being is referred to God, as we shall make clear, even if it is worked by one of the proximate efficient causes; God, considered as efficient cause, is then the remotest one.[5]

Similarly we find, when attentively investigating the natural forms subject to generation and corruption, that they are inevitably preceded by another form that gives that particular matter the disposition required for the reception of that particular form; that second form is in its turn preceded by another form until we finally come to the ultimate form that is necessary for the existence of the intermediate forms, while the latter are the cause of the proximate form. This ultimate form for all that exists[6] is God, may He be exalted. You should not think that our saying of Him that He is the ultimate form of the whole world refers to the ultimate form of which Aristotle says in the "Metaphysics" that it is not subject to generation and

4. *fāᶜil.* Cf. preceding note.   5. Literally: the remotest cause.
6. Literally: in all existence.

corruption; the form mentioned there is a natural one and is not a separate intellect. For our saying of Him, may He be exalted, that He is the ultimate form of the world does not denote that there is an analogy between Him and the form endowed with matter in its being a form to that particular matter,[7] so that | He, may He be exalted, would be a form to a body. It was not said with reference to this point of view. One should rather consider that just as every existent thing endowed with a form is what it is in virtue of its form — in fact its being passes away and is abolished when its form passes away — there subsists the very same relation between the deity and the totality of the remote principles of existence. For the universe[8] exists in virtue of the existence of the Creator, and the latter continually endows it with permanence in virtue of the thing that is spoken of as overflow — as we shall make clear in one[9] of the chapters of this Treatise.[10] Accordingly if the nonexistence of the Creator were supposed, all that exists would likewise be nonexistent; and the essence of its remote causes, of its ultimate effects, and of that which is between these, would be abolished. God has therefore, with reference to the world, the status of a form with regard to a thing possessing a form, in virtue of which it is that which it is: a thing the true reality and essence of which are established by that form. Such is the relation of the deity to the world. In this respect it is said of Him that He is the ultimate form and the form of forms; that is, He is that upon which the existence and stability of every form in the world ultimately reposes and by which they are constituted, just as the things endowed with forms are constituted by their forms. Because of this notion, God is called in our language the *Living of the worlds*, meaning that He is the life of the world, as shall be made clear.[11]

Matters are similar with regard to every end, for when a thing has an end you should seek the end of that end. You say, as it were, for instance that a throne has wood as its matter, a carpenter as its efficient cause, squareness of a particular shape as its form, and to be sat upon as its end. You should consequently ask: what is the end of sitting upon the throne? Thereupon it will be said that it consists in the lifting up, and the being elevated above the earth, of the sitter upon the chair. Thereupon you will ask again, saying: what is the end of being lifted up above | the earth? Thereupon you will receive the answer that it consists in the magnification

---

7. Literally: Our saying that He is the ultimate form of the world is not in the image of the being of the form endowed with matter as a form to that matter.
8. *al-kull* (the all). The word has a less definite connotation than "universe."
9. The word *baᶜḍ* may also mean "several."
10. Cf. II 12.   11. Cf. I 72.

of the sitter in the eyes of those who see him. Thereupon you will ask: what is the end of his being great in the opinion of those who see him? Thereupon you will receive the answer that it consists in his being feared and regarded with awe. Thereupon you will ask, saying: what is the end of his being feared? Thereupon you will receive the answer that it consists in his orders being obeyed. Thereupon you will demand: what is the end of his orders being obeyed? Thereupon you will receive the answer that it consists in the prevention of harm being done by some people to others. Thereupon you will further demand to know the end of this. Thereupon you will receive the answer that it consists in the permanence of their existence in an orderly fashion. This should be done with regard to every end occurring in time until one finally arrives at His mere will,[12] may He be exalted — according to a certain opinion, as shall be made clear so that ultimately the answer will be: God willed it so; or — according to the opinion of others, as I shall make clear — one finally arrives at the decision of His wisdom so that ultimately the answer will be: His wisdom decided it so. Thus according to these two opinions the order of all ends is ultimately due to His will and wisdom, as to which it has been made clear, according to our opinion, that they are identical with His essence: His will and His volition or His wisdom not being things extraneous to His essence. I mean to say that they are not something other than His essence. Consequently He, may He be exalted, is the ultimate end of everything; and the end of the universe[13] is similarly a seeking to be like unto His perfection as far as is in its capacity. This, as shall be made clear,[14] is the meaning of His will, which is His essence. In virtue of this it is said of Him that He is the end of the ends. Thus I have made clear to you in what respect it is said of Him, may He be exalted, that He is an efficient cause, a form, and an end. For this reason the philosophers designated Him as a cause and not only as a maker.[15]

Know, however, that in some people[16] from among the Mutakallimūn engaged in speculation, ignorance and presumption reached such a degree that finally they[17] said that if the nonexistence of the Creator were assumed, the nonexistence of the thing that the Creator has brought into existence — they mean[18] the world — would not follow necessarily. For it does not necessarily follow that | that which has been effected passes away when the

12. Literally: until the matter finally attains His mere will.
13. Literally: the all. Cf. n. 8, this chap.   14. Cf. III 13.
15. The word also means "efficient cause." Cf. n. 3, this chap.
16. Or: in one individual.   17. Or: he.   18. Or: he means.

maker[19] has passed away after having effected[20] it. Now that which they have mentioned would be correct if He were only the maker[21] and if the thing that He effected had no need of Him for its permanence to be lasting, as in the case of the carpenter upon whose death the chest does not pass away for he does not continually endow it with permanence. Now as He, may He be exalted, is also the form of the world, as we have made clear, and as He continually endows the latter with permanence and constant existence, it would be impossible that He who continually endows with permanence should disappear and that which is continually endowed by Him and which has no permanence except in virtue of this endowment should remain. This is the measure of the vain imagining necessitated by the opinion that He is only a maker[22] and not an end or a form.

CHAPTER 70

To ride [*rakhob*]. This word is equivocal. The first instance in which it is used means man's riding in the usual manner on beasts: *He was riding upon his she-ass*.[1] Afterwards it is used figuratively to designate domination over a thing, for a rider dominates over and rules that which he rides. Thus the dictum: *He made him ride on the heights of the earth;*[2] *I will make thee to ride upon the heights of the earth*[3] — meaning that you shall dominate the heights of the earth; *I will make Ephraim ride*[4] — that is I shall make him dominate and rule. In this sense it is said of God, may He be exalted: *The rider of the heavens is helping you;*[5] the interpretation of which is: He who dominates the heavens. Similarly: *The rider in the araboth;*[6] meaning: He who dominates the highest heaven encompassing the universe.[7]

The textual words of the *Sages, may their memory be blessed,* which are repeated in every relevant passage,[8] assert that there are *seven heavens* and that *araboth* is | the highest encompassing the universe. Do not think it blameworthy that according to their reckoning there were *seven heavens,*

19. Or: the efficient cause.   20. Or: made.   21. Or: the efficient cause.
22. Or: an efficient cause.
  1. Num. 22:22.   2. Deut. 32:13.   3. Isa. 58:14.   4. Hos. 10:11.
  5. Deut. 33:26.   6. Ps. 68:5. The usual meaning of ʿ*araboth* is "desert," "plains."
  7. Literally: the all.   8. Cf. B.T., Ḥagigah, 12b.

whereas there are more than that. For sometimes, as is clear to those engaged in speculation on this subject and as I shall make clear further on,[9] a sphere is counted as one though there be several heavens contained in it. What is intended here is to call attention to the fact that they constantly indicate that *araboth* is the highest part of the universe. It is with reference to *araboth* that it says: *The rider of the heavens [shamayim] is helping you.* Compare the text of *Ḥagigah;*[10] they say: *[As to] araboth, the high and sublime One resides upon it. For it is said: Extol the rider in the araboth. How do we know that [araboth] are also called heavens [shamayim]? [Because] it is written in this passage: the rider in the araboth, while in another [passage] it is written: the rider of the heavens.* Thus it is clear that the term refers solely to one heaven: that which encompasses the universe. About that heaven you will hear some information. Consider their saying: *resides upon it.* They did not say: *resides in it.* For if they had said, *resides in it,* this expression would have necessitated the attribution to Him of a place or the notion that He is a force subsisting in a certain place. In such fashion do the sects of the Sabians imagine that God is the spirit of heaven.[11] Thus by saying, *resides upon it,* they have shown that He, may He be exalted, is separate from the heaven and is not a force in it. Know that the expression, *the rider of the heavens,* is figuratively used of Him, may He be exalted, for the sake of a strange and wondrous likeness. For the rider is more excellent than that upon which he rides, yet cannot be called more excellent except through a certain impropriety of language, for the rider does not belong to the same species as that which is ridden by him. Moreover the rider is he who makes the beast of burden move and go where he wishes; for it is an instrument for him that he uses as he wishes, being at the same time free from any dependence on it and not attached to it, but on the contrary external to it. Similarly the deity, may His name be held sublime, is the mover of the highest heaven, by whose motion everything that is in motion within this heaven[12] is moved; at the same time, He, may He be exalted, is separate from this heaven and not a force subsisting within it. Accordingly the Sages interpreting | His speech, may He be exalted, *The eternal God is a dwelling place,*[13] say in *Bereshith Rabbah:*[14]

9. Cf. II 4.   10. B.T., Ḥagigah, 12b.

11. *al-falak* (the heavenly sphere). Because of Maimonides' use of *kurra*, which means "sphere" as well, *falak* is translated in this chapter by "heaven." But the translation "heavenly sphere" used elsewhere is perhaps more appropriate.

12. All the universe encompassed by the highest heaven may be considered as being within this sphere.

13. Deut. 33:27.   14. Genesis Rabbah, LXVIII.

He is *the dwelling place of His world,* [*whereas*] *His world is not His dwelling place.* And they follow this by saying: *The horse is subsidiary to the rider,* [*whereas*] *the rider is not subsidiary to the horse. In this sense it is written: That Thou dost ride upon Thy horses.*[15] This is literally what they say. Consider it, and it shall become clear to you how they explained His relation, may He be exalted, to heaven: that it is His instrument by means of which He governs that which is existent. For whenever you find that according to the *Sages, may their memory be blessed,* there exists one thing in one particular heaven[16] and another thing in another, the meaning of the passage is not that in that particular heaven there are to be found bodies other than that heaven, but that the forces generating the particular thing in question and safeguarding its order come from that heaven. A proof of what I have said to you is their saying: *Araboth—that in which* [*exist*] *righteousness, right-dealing, justice, the treasures of life, the treasures of peace, the treasures of blessing, the soul of the righteous ones, the souls and the spirits that shall be created in the future, and the dew by means of which the Holy One, blessed be He, will revive the dead.*[17] Now it is clear that not one of all the things that they have enumerated here is a body and therefore to be located in a place. For the *dew* is not the dew denoted by the word in its external meaning. Consider that they said in this passage: *that in which*—I mean to say that the things mentioned are in *araboth*—and they did not say that the things are *upon* it. Thus they have, as it were, given the information that these things existent in the world only exist because they proceed from forces coming from the *araboth* of God, may He be exalted, who caused [the araboth] to be their first origin and who situated them in it. To these things belong *the treasures of life.* In fact it is correct and the absolute truth to say that every life existing in a living being only proceeds from that life,[18] as I shall subsequently[19] mention.

Reflect also that they enumerated in the list *the soul of the righteous ones, and the souls and the spirits that shall be created in the future.* How sublime | is this notion to him who has understood it! For the *souls* that remain after death are not the *soul* that comes into being in man at the time he is generated. For that which comes into being at the time a man is

---

15. Hab. 3:8.
16. In this context *samā* seems to be a synonym of *falak*, translated in this chapter by "heaven." Cf. n. 11, this chap. Maimonides probably uses the word *samā* in this passage because of its kinship with the Hebrew word *shamayim,* employed in the texts to which he alludes.
17. B.T., Ḥagigah, 12b.
18. The life to which the expression *treasures of life* alludes.   19. Cf. I 72, II 10.

generated[20] is merely a faculty consisting in preparedness, whereas the thing that after death is separate from matter is the thing that has become actual and not the *soul* that also comes into being; the latter is identical with the spirit that comes into being. Because of this the Sages have numbered the *souls and spirits* among the things that come into being. What is separate is, on the contrary, one thing only. We have already made clear the equivocality of the term *spirit*.[21] We have likewise made clear, in the last portion of the *Book of Knowledge*,[22] the equivocality regarding these terms.

Consider accordingly that these strange but correct notions attained by the speculation of the most sublime of those who have philosophized are found scattered in the *Midrashim*. When a man who has knowledge, but is not equitable, studies these texts, he laughs at them at the beginning of his study because he sees that their external meanings diverge so widely from the true realities of existence. The cause of all of this is, as we have told several times, the enigmatic presentation of these things, which is due to the fact that they are too strange to be understood by the vulgar.

I shall return to the remainder of what I have started out to explain. I shall then say that [the Sages], *may their memory be blessed*, tried by means of the texts of the scriptural verses to furnish proof that the things enumerated by them were found in *araboth*, saying: [*As for*] *righteousness and justice, as it is written: Righteousness and justice are the foundation of Thy throne.*[23] They similarly furnished proof that those things, which they enumerated as standing in relation to God, may He be exalted, are with Him. Understand this. They said in the *Chapters of Rabbi Eliezer:*[24] *The Holy One, blessed be He, has created seven firmaments; and of all them, He chose as throne of glory for His kingship only araboth. For it is said: Extol the rider in the araboth.*[25] This is literally what he says. Understand it likewise. Know that a set of beasts that are ridden upon is called *chariot*.[26] This occurs in frequent | repetition: *And Joseph made ready his chariot;*[27] *in the second chariot;*[28] *Pharaoh's chariots.*[29] A proof that this term is applied to a number of beasts is found in the dictum: *And a chariot came up and went out of Egypt for six hundred shekels of silver, and a horse for a hundred and fifty.*[30] This is a proof that the term *chariot* is applied to four

---

20. The words translated in this passage by "come into being" and "be generated" are two different forms of the same Arabic verb.
21. Cf. I 40.
22. A section of the *Mishneh Torah*. Cf. *Mishneh Torah*, Yesodei ha-Torah, IV.
23. Ps. 89:15.   24. Chapters of Rabbi Eliezer, XVIII.   25. Ps. 68:5.
26. This is the usual meaning of the Hebrew word *merkabah* cited by Maimonides.
27. Gen. 46:29.   28. Gen. 41:43.   29. Exod. 15:4.   30. I Kings 10:29.

horses. With regard to this I say that since it is said, in accordance with what is said in Scripture, that *the throne of glory* was borne by *four animals*, the *Sages, may their memory be blessed,* called it a *chariot*; they thus likened it to a *chariot* that is made up of four individuals.[31] This is the limit to which the speech advances in this chapter. There is no doubt that there are many other intimations with reference to this subject. However, the purpose of this chapter, toward which the argument was repeatedly brought back, is that the dictum, *The rider of the heavens,*[32] signifies: He who makes the encompassing heaven revolve and who moves it in virtue of His power and His will. A similar interpretation should be given to the rest of the *verse: and in His excellency*[33] *on the skies,* meaning that *in virtue of His excellency* He makes the *skies* revolve — bringing out the first of them, which is *araboth,* as we made clear in our discussion of the word *riding* and explained the remainder of it in our discussion of the word *excellency.* For all the heavens move as parts in virtue of the movement of the highest heaven, that is, the diurnal movement. And this great power of His is that which moves the whole. Because of this Scripture calls it: *excellency.* This notion should always be present in your mind with regard to new matters about which I shall speak. For it is the greatest proof through which one can know the existence of the deity — I mean the revolution of the heaven — as I shall demonstrate. Understand this. |

CHAPTER 71

Know that the many sciences devoted to establishing the truth regarding these matters that have existed in our religious community have perished because of the length of the time that has passed, because of our being dominated by the pagan nations, and because, as we have made clear,[1] it is not permitted to divulge these matters to all people. For the only thing it is permitted to divulge to all people are the texts of the books. You already know that even the legalistic science of law was not put down in writing in the olden times because of the precept,[2] which is widely

31. I.e., four horses.   32. Deut. 33:26.
33. The usual meaning of the Hebrew word is "pride."
1. Cf. I 34.
2. Literally: matter, thing. This translation seems to be more in harmony with Maimonides' use of the Arabic word than the meaning "command," which is also denoted by *amr.*

known in the nation: *Words that I have communicated to you orally, you are not allowed to put down in writing.*[3] This precept shows extreme wisdom with regard to[4] the Law. For it was meant to prevent what has ultimately come about in this respect: I mean the multiplicity of opinions, the variety of schools, the confusions occurring in the expression of what is put down in writing, the negligence that accompanies what is written down, the divisions of the people, who are separated into sects, and the production of confusion with regard to actions. All these matters should be within the authority of *the Great Court of Law*, as we have made clear in our juridical compilations[5] and as the text of the *Torah* shows.[6] Now if there was insistence that the legalistic science of law should not, in view of the harm that would be caused by such a procedure, be perpetuated in a written compilation accessible to all the people, all the more could none of the *mysteries of the Torah* have been set down in writing and be made accessible to the people. On the contrary they were transmitted by a few men belonging to the elite to a few of the same kind, just as I made clear to you[7] from their saying: *The mysteries of the Torah may only be transmitted to a counsellor, wise in crafts, and so on.*[8] This was the cause that necessitated the disappearance | of these great roots of knowledge from the nation. For you will not find with regard to them anything except slight indications and pointers occurring in the *Talmud* and the *Midrashim*. These are, as it were, a few grains belonging to the core, which are overlaid by many layers of rind, so that people were occupied with these layers of rind and thought that beneath them there was no core whatever.

As for that scanty bit of argument[9] regarding the notion of the unity of God and regarding what depends on this notion, which you will find in the writings of some *Gaonim* and in those of the Qaraites, it should be noted that the subject matter of this argument was taken over by them from the Mutakallimūn of Islam and that this bit is very scanty indeed if compared to what Islam has compiled on this subject. Also it has so happened that Islam first began to take this road owing to a certain sect, namely, the Muᶜtazila,[10] from whom our coreligionists[11] took over certain things

3. B.T., Gittin, 60b.   4. Or: on the part of.
5. Cf. *Mishneh Torah*, Introduction.   6. Cf. Deut. 17:8–12.
7. Cf. I 34.   8. B.T., Ḥagigah, 14a.
9. Or: of kalām. The word "argument" is used here to translate *kalām*.
10. A Moslem sect whose beginnings go back to the eighth century. The earliest comprehensive and rationalized system of Moslem theology was worked out by the Muᶜtazilites.
11. Literally: companions.

walking upon the road the Muʿtazila had taken. After a certain time another sect arose in Islam, namely, the Ashʿariyya,[12] among whom other opinions arose. You will not find any of these latter opinions among our coreligionists. This was not because they preferred the first opinion[13] to the second, but because it so happened that they had taken over and adopted the first opinion and considered it a matter proven by demonstration.

As for the Andalusians[14] among the people of our nation, all of them cling to the affirmations of the philosophers and incline to their opinions, in so far as these do not ruin the foundation of the Law. You will not find them in any way taking the paths of the Mutakallimūn. In many things concerning the scanty matter of which the later ones among them had knowledge,[15] they have therefore approximately the same doctrine that we set forth in this Treatise.

Know also that all the statements that the men of Islam — both the Muʿtazila and the Ashʿariyya — have made concerning these notions are all of them opinions | founded upon premises that are taken over from the books of the Greeks and the Syrians who wished to disagree with the opinions of the philosophers and to reject their statements. The reason for this was that: inasmuch as the Christian community came to include those communities,[16] the Christian preaching being what it is known to be, and inasmuch as the opinions of the philosophers were widely accepted in those communities in which philosophy had first risen, and inasmuch as kings rose who protected religion — the learned of those periods from among the Greeks and the Syrians saw that those preachings are greatly and clearly opposed to the philosophic opinions. Thus there arose among them this science of kalām. They started to establish premises that would be useful to them with regard to their belief and to refute those opinions that ruined the foundations of their Law. When thereupon the community of Islam arrived and the books of the philosophers were transmitted to it, then were also transmitted to it those refutations composed against the books of the philosophers. Thus they found the kalām[17] of John Philoponus,[18] of Ibn

12. The disciples of Abu'l-Ḥasan ʿAlī al-Ashʿarī (d. 940) who propounded the principles of the doctrine that by and large was adopted as the official theology of Sunnite Islam.

13. That of the Muʿtazila.   14. Or: the Spaniards.

15. Literally: the scanty matters found among the later ones of them. This apparently refers to the passages of the Talmud and the Midrashim that, as Maimonides states in the beginning of this chapter, belong to the old esoteric tradition.

16. I.e., the Greeks and the Syrians.   17. Or: the argumentation.

18. In Arabic, Yaḥyā al-Naḥwī; i.e., John the Grammarian, a translation of a Greek cognomen of this philosopher.

ᶜAdī,[19] and of others with regard to these notions, held on to it, and were victorious in their own opinion in a great task that they sought to accomplish. They also selected from among the opinions of the earlier philosophers everything that the one who selected considered useful for him, even if the later philosophers had already demonstrated the falseness of these opinions — as for instance that affirming the existence of atoms and the vacuum. And they considered that these were conceptions common to all and premises that everyone who accepts a Law is obliged to admit. Afterwards the kalām became wider in scope, and these people descended to other strange roads that had never been taken by the Mutakallimūn from among the Greeks and others, for these were near to the philosophers. Then there arose in Islam assertions of the Law that were particular to the members of that community and that | they necessarily had need to defend. Furthermore, differences of opinion between them with regard to these questions made their appearance, so that every sect among them established premises useful to it in the defense of its opinions. There is no doubt that there are things that are common to all three of us, I mean the Jews, the Christians, and the Moslems: namely, the affirmation of the temporal creation of the world, the validity of which entails the validity of miracles and other things of that kind. As for the other matters that these two communities took the trouble to treat and were engrossed in — for instance, the study of the notion of trinity into which the Christians plunged and the study of the kalām into which certain sects of the Moslems plunged — so that they found it requisite to establish premises and to establish, by means of these premises that they had chosen, the conceptions into the study of which they had plunged and the notions that are peculiar to each of the two communities, having been established in it: these are things that we do not require in any respect whatever.

To sum up: all the first Mutakallimūn from among the Greeks who had adopted Christianity and from among the Moslems did not conform in their premises to the appearance of that which exists, but considered how being ought to be in order that it should furnish a proof for the correctness of a particular opinion, or at least should not refute it. And when such a fantasy held good, they assumed that what exists corresponds to that form and started to argue in order to establish the truth of the assertions from which are taken the premises that show the correctness of their doctrine or that at least do not refute it. This is the way of the men of intellect who

19. This is an anachronism, for Yaḥya Ibn ᶜAdī — a Christian (monophysitic) theologian and an Aristotelian philosopher — died in 974, more than two centuries after the beginning of the Muᶜtazilite kalām. Cf. Translator's Introduction.

first used this method, put it down in books, and claimed that speculation alone impelled them to do so and that they did not seek thereby to protect a doctrine or a preconceived opinion. Men of later periods who study these books know nothing about all this and consequently find in | these ancient books a vigorous argumentation and a powerful endeavor to establish the truth of a certain thing or to refute a certain thing and think thereupon that its establishment or its refutation is in no way required for these foundations of the Law that are required. They believe accordingly that their predecessors did what they did only in order to confuse the opinions of the philosophers and to make them doubt of what they regarded as a demonstration. Those who say this are not aware, and do not know, that matters are not as they thought, but that their predecessors toiled to establish the truth of what they desired to establish as true and to refute what they desired to refute because of the harm that would come if this were not done — even if it were after a hundred propositions — to an opinion whose recognition as correct was desired by them. These ancient Mutakallimūn[20] did away with the disease starting with its root.

To sum up: I shall say to you that the matter is as Themistius puts it: that which exists does not conform to the various opinions, but rather the correct opinions conform to that which exists.

When I studied the books of these Mutakallimūn, as far as I had the opportunity — and I have likewise studied the books of the philosophers, as far as my capacity went — I found that the method of all of the Mutakallimūn was one and the same in kind, though the subdivisions differed from one another. For the foundation of everything is that no consideration is due to how that which exists is, for it is merely a custom; and from the point of view of the intellect, it could well be different. Furthermore, in many places they follow the imagination and call it intellect. Thus when they propound the premises that we will let you hear, they found by their demonstrations the [affirmative] judgment that the world is created in time. And when it is thus established that the world is created in time, it is likewise undoubtedly established that it has a maker | who has created it in time. Then they adduced arguments in favor of the inference that this maker is one; whereupon, basing themselves upon his being one, that he is not a body. This is the way of every Mutakallim from among the Moslems in anything concerning this subject. Thus also do those belonging to our community who imitate them and follow their ways. While the ways in which they adduce the arguments in favor of the inference as to, and

20. Literally: most ancient of the Mutakallimūn.

propound the premises with regard to, the establishment of the temporal creation of the world or to the refutation of its pre-eternity, differ from one another, the universal thesis of all of them consists in the first place in the affirmation of the temporal creation of the world. And by means of its temporal creation, it is established as true that the deity exists.

Now when I considered this method of thought, my soul felt a very strong aversion to it, and had every right to do so. For every argument deemed to be a demonstration of the temporal creation of the world is accompanied by doubts and is not a cogent demonstration except among those who do not know the difference between demonstration, dialectics, and sophistic argument. As for those who know these arts,[21] it is clear and evident to them that there are doubts with regard to all these proofs and that premises that have not been demonstrated have been used in them. The utmost power of one who adheres to a Law[22] and who has acquired knowledge of true reality consists, in my opinion, in his refuting the proofs of the philosophers bearing on the eternity of the world. How sublime a thing it is when the ability is there to do it! And everyone who engages in speculation, who is perceptive, and who has acquired true knowledge of reality and does not deceive himself, knows that with regard to this question — namely the eternity of the world or its temporal creation — no cogent demonstration can be reached and that it is a point before which the intellect stops. Later we shall speak about this at length. At present it will be enough for you to know with regard to this question that the philosophers of the various epochs disagree with respect to it for the last three thousand years up to this our time, as we can find in their works and the reports concerning them.

Now if this is the state of this question, how | can we take the doctrine of the temporal creation of the world as a premise upon which we found the existence of the deity? For in that case the existence of the deity would be doubtful. One would have to say that if the world were created in time, there would be a deity; and if it were eternal, there would be no deity in existence. Things either would be like that or we would claim that we have a demonstration of the creation of the world in time and we would use the sword[23] to prove it so that we should claim to know God by means of a demonstration. All this is remote from truth. For according to me the correct way, which is the method of demonstration about which there can be no doubt, is to establish the existence and the oneness of the deity and the

21. Apparently the arts of demonstration and argument.
22. Or: to the [Jewish] Law.   23. Literally: smite with the sword.

negation of corporeality through the methods of the philosophers, which methods are founded upon the doctrine of the eternity of the world. This is not because I believe in the eternity of the world or because I concede this point to the philosophers; but because it is through this method that the demonstration becomes valid and perfect certainty is obtained with regard to those three things: I mean the existence of the deity, His oneness, and His not being a body — and all this without making a judgment upon the world's being eternal or created in time. Thereupon, when these three great and sublime problems have been validated for us through a correct demonstration, we shall return to the question of the creation of the world in time and we shall enounce with regard to it all the argumentation that is possible.

If you are one of those who are persuaded by what the Mutakallimūn say, and if you believe that the demonstration with regard to the creation of the world in time is correct, bravo for you. If, however, it is not demonstrated in your opinion, and if you take over from the prophets, through obeying their authority, the doctrine that it was created in time, there is no harm in that. And you should not ask how prophecy can be true if the world is eternal, before you have heard our discourse concerning prophecy; however, at present we are not dealing with this notion. You ought to know that the premises that are established by those concerned with the roots, | I mean among the Mutakallimūn, with a view to affirming the creation of the world in time, imply — in a measure that you will hear defined — an *upsetting of the world* and a *change in the order established at the time of creation.* For I shall certainly set forth their premises and their way of drawing inferences.

As to this my method, it is as I shall describe to you in a general way now. Namely, I shall say: the world cannot but be either eternal or created in time. If it is created in time, it undoubtedly has a creator who created it in time. For it is a first intelligible that what has appeared at a certain moment in time has not created itself in time and that its creator is other than itself. Accordingly the creator who created the world in time is the deity. If, however, the world is eternal, it follows necessarily because of this and that proof that there is an existent other than all the bodies to be found in the world; an existent who is not a body and not a force in a body and who is one, permanent, and sempiternal; who has no cause and whose becoming subject to change is impossible. Accordingly he is a deity. Thus it has become manifest to you that the proofs for the existence and the oneness of the deity and of His not being a body ought to be procured from the starting point afforded by the supposition of the eternity of the world, for in this way the demonstration will be perfect, both if the world is eternal and if it is created in time. For this reason you will always find that whenever, in what I have written in the books of jurisprudence, I happen to mention the foundations and start upon establishing the existence of the deity, I establish it by discourses that adopt the way of the doctrine of the eternity of the world. The reason is not that I believe in the eternity of the world, but that I wish to establish in our belief the existence of God, may He be exalted, through a demonstrative method as to which there is no disagreement in any respect. Thus we shall not cause the true opinion, which is of immense importance, to be supported by a foundation that everyone can shake and wish to destroy, while other men think that it has never been constructed. This method is particularly justified in view of the fact that these philosophic proofs concerning the three problems in question are derived | from the nature of existence that can be perceived and that is not denied except with a view to safeguarding certain opinions.

The proofs of the Mutakallimūn, on the other hand, are derived from premises that run counter to the nature of existence that is perceived so that they resort to the affirmation that nothing has a nature in any respect. In this Treatise, when speaking of the creation of the world in time, I shall devote for your benefit a chapter explaining to you some proof for the creation of the world in time. For I reach the goal that every Mutakallim desires, without abolishing the nature of existence and without disagreeing with Aristotle with regard to any point he has demonstrated. For whereas the proof, with the aid of which some Mutakallimūn prove by inference the creation of the world in time and which is their most powerful proof, is not consolidated for them until they abolish the nature of all existence and disagree with everything that the philosophers have made clear, I reach a similar proof without running counter to the nature of existence and without having recourse to violating that which is perceived by the senses. I saw fit to mention to you the general premises of the Mutakallimūn by means of which they establish the creation of the world in time, the existence of the deity, His oneness, and the rejection of His corporeality; and I shall show you their way in this and shall make clear to you what follows necessarily from each of those premises. After that I shall mention to you the proximate premises of the philosophers regarding this and I shall show you their way.

Do not, however, demand from me in this Treatise that I should establish the correctness of those philosophic premises that I shall formulate for your benefit. For doing this constitutes the greater part of the natural and the divine science. Likewise you should not desire that I should let you hear in this Treatise the argumentation of the Mutakallimūn that is intended to establish the correctness of their premises. For | their lives passed away in this argumentation, and the lives of those who will come after them will likewise pass away in this, and their books have grown numerous. For every one of their premises, with few exceptions, is contradicted by what is perceived of the nature of that which exists, so that doubts come up with regard to them. Accordingly, the Mutakallimūn resort to compilations and disputations in order to establish this and that particular premise and to dispel the doubts coming with regard to it and to ward off that which is perceived and runs counter to the premise if there is no possibility of a stratagem with a view to getting around this. As for the philosophic premises that I shall formulate for your benefit with a view to a demonstration regarding the three problems in question — I mean the existence and oneness of the deity and the refutation of the doctrine of His corporeality — most of them are premises regarding which you achieve certainty as soon as you first hear them and understand their meaning. However, some of them refer you to the passages in which their demonstration occurs in the books concerning natural science or metaphysics. Accordingly you should have the intention of looking up the relevant passage and thus establishing the correctness of what may be required to have its correctness established.

I have already let you know that there exists nothing except God, may He be exalted, and this existent world and that there is no possible inference proving His existence, may He be exalted, except those deriving from this existent taken as a whole and from its details. Accordingly it necessarily behooves one to consider this existent as it is and to derive premises from what is perceived of its nature. For this reason it follows that you should know its perceptible form and nature, and then it will be possible to make an inference from it with regard to what is other than it. For this reason I judged that in the first place it behooves me to set down a chapter in which I would explain to you that which exists as a whole by informing you of what is demonstrated and is indubitably correct. After that I shall set down for your benefit other chapters in which I shall mention the premises of the Mutakallimūn and shall make clear their methods by means of which they elucidate the four problems in question. After that I shall set down for your benefit other chapters in which I shall make clear to you | the premises of the philosophers and their methods of inference with regard to these problems. After that I shall summarize for your benefit the method that I shall adopt, as I have already informed you, with regard to these four problems.

CHAPTER 72

Know that this whole of being is one individual and nothing else. I mean to say that the sphere of the outermost heaven with everything that is within it is undoubtedly one individual having in respect of individuality the rank of Zayd and Umar. The differences between its substances, I mean the substances of this sphere with everything that is within it, are like unto the differences between the limbs of a man, for instance. Thus just as Zayd, for instance, is one individual and is at the same time composed of various parts of the body such as the flesh and the bones and of various mixtures and of several spirits,[1] the sphere in question as a whole is composed of the heavens, the four elements, and what is compounded of the latter. In that sphere there is absolutely no vacuum; it is solid and filled up. Its center is the sphere of the earth, while water encompasses the earth, air encompasses the water, fire encompasses the air, and the fifth body encompasses the fire. There are many spheres, one contained within the other, with no hollows between them and no vacuum in any way whatever. For they are perfectly spherical and cling to each other, all of them moving in a circular uniform motion in no part of which there is acceleration or deceleration. I mean to say that none of these spheres moves more quickly at some times and more slowly at others. On the contrary, every one of them follows its nature | in its velocity and the direction of its motion. However some of these spheres have a more rapid motion than others; the most rapid of all being the motion of the heaven encompassing the universe. This heaven is endowed with the diurnal motion and moves all the other heavens simultaneously with itself, as a part is moved in a whole, for all these heavens are parts of it.

These heavens have different centers. The center of some of them is identical with the center of the world, while the center of others is eccentric to the center of the world. Some of them move perpetually in a motion proper to them from the east to the west, while others move perpetually from the west to the east. Every star in these heavens is a part of the heavens

1. The animal spirits are meant.

in which it is fixed in its place and has no motion proper to it. It is seen as being in motion only because of the motion of the body of which it is a part. The matter of this fifth body as a whole, which is endowed with circular motion, is not like the matter of the bodies composed of the four elements that are contained within it.

It is not possible in any respect or in any fashion that the number of the spheres encompassing the world should be less than eighteen. It is, however, possible that their number should be greater than eighteen. This is a matter of speculation. It is also a matter of speculation whether there are epicycles, that is, spheres that do not encompass the world.[2]

In the interior of the nethermost sphere, which is near us, there is one kind of matter that differs from the matter of the fifth body and receives four primary forms. Through these four forms, earth, water, air, and fire come into being. Every one of these four elements has a natural place proper to it and is not found elsewhere if left to its nature. These four elements are inanimate bodies in which there is no life and no perception, | and they do not move of their own accord, but are at rest in their natural places. If, however, one of them is made by violence to leave its natural place, it moves, when the agent exerting violence has ceased to act, so as to return to its natural place. For there subsists in it a principle that makes it move in order to return to its place in a straight line. There is, however, no principle in it that would make it to be at rest[3] or that would make it move in other than a straight line. The motions in a straight line, which are found to belong to these four elements when they move in order to return to their places, are two: a motion toward the encompassing sphere, which motion belongs to fire and to air, and a motion toward the center of the world, which belongs to water and to earth. Every body belonging to these four elements comes to rest when it reaches its natural place.

As for the bodies that move in circles, they are animate, endowed with a soul that makes them move. And there is in time no principle at all that would make them to be at rest. No change attains them, except with regard to position, as they move in a circle. As regards the question whether they

2. On the astronomical problems referred to, cf. Translator's Introduction.
3. The principle to which Maimonides refers is closely connected with what medieval philosophy designates as the natural inclination of the elements, i.e., the heaviness of earth and water and the lightness of fire and air. In their natural places the elements have no natural inclination, according to Avicenna. If, however, a portion of one of them has been displaced, it tends to move downward, if it is heavy, or upward, if it is light. In this passage Maimonides apparently wishes to assert, among other things, that a displaced portion of an element does not have a principle of rest, but has the impulse to move toward its natural place.

have an intellect by means of which they make mental representations: this does not become clear except after subtle speculation.

Inasmuch as the fifth body as a whole is engaged perpetually in a circular motion, it thus engenders forced motion in the elements because of which they leave their places. I have in view fire and air, which are pushing toward the water. All of them penetrate toward the body of the earth, in the valleys. In consequence a mixture of the elements comes about. Afterwards they start to move in order to return to their places; and because of this, portions of the earth in their turn are made to leave their places as they accompany the water, the air, and the fire. In all this, the elements exert influence upon one another and are influenced by one another. Accordingly changes occur in the mixture so that, in the first place, | the various species of vapors come into being from it, then the various species of minerals, then all the species of plants, then many species of living beings in accordance with what is determined by the composition[4] of the mixture. Everything that is subject to generation and corruption is generated from the elements and, being corrupted, passes away into them. The elements likewise are generated from one another and, being corrupted, pass away into one another; for the matter of the all is one; and the existence of matter without form is impossible and, on the other hand, no natural form subject to generation and corruption exists without matter. Thus the state of things with regard to the generation and corruption of the elements and with regard to the generation of everything that is generated of them and is corrupted so as again to be changed into them, comes back in a circle similar to the circular movement of heaven; so that the movement of this matter endowed with forms is, in respect to the succession of the forms subsisting in it, like the movement of heaven in respect to the "where," every part of heaven returning repeatedly to the selfsame positions.

And just as in the body of man there are ruling parts and ruled parts requiring for their continued existence the governance of the ruling part governing them, so are there in the world as a whole ruling parts — namely, the fifth encompassing body — and ruled parts requiring a governor — they are the elements and what is composed of them. And just as the ruling part, which is the heart, is always in motion and is the principle of every motion to be found in the body, whereas the other parts of the body are ruled by the heart, which in virtue of its motion sends toward them the forces they require for their functions; so heaven in virtue of its motion exerts governance over the other parts of the world and sends to every generated thing

4. Or: temperament.

the forces that subsist in the latter. Accordingly, every motion existing in the world has as its first principle the motion of heaven, and every soul existing in the beings endowed with souls that are in the world | has as its principle the soul of heaven.

Know that, as has been made clear, the forces that come from heaven to this world are four: [1] the force that necessitates the mixture and composition — there is no doubt that this force suffices to engender the minerals; [2] the force that gives to every plant a vegetal soul; [3] the force that gives to every animal an animal soul; [4] the force that gives to every rational being a rational faculty.⁵ All this takes place through the intermediary of the illumination and the darkness [on earth] resulting from the light in heaven and from heaven's motion round the earth [which is the cause of the succession of days and nights]. And just as an individual would die and his motions and forces would be abolished if the heart were to come to rest even for an instant, so the death of the world as a whole and the abolition of everything within it would result if the heavens were to come to rest. And just as a living being lives as a whole in virtue of the motion of its heart, even if there subsist in it parts of the body that are at rest and not sentient — as for instance bones, cartilage, and others; so is this whole being one individual that lives in virtue of the movement of heaven, which has with regard to it the rank that the heart has with regard to the beings endowed with hearts — and this even though there are in the world many inanimate bodies that are at rest.

Accordingly it behooves you to represent to yourself in this fashion the whole of this sphere as one living individual in motion and possessing a soul. For this way of representing the matter to oneself is most necessary or most useful for the demonstration that the deity is one, as shall be made clear. By means of this representation it will also be made clear that the One has created one being. For just as it is impossible that the limbs of a man should exist separately while being truly the part of a man — I mean to say that the liver should exist separately or the heart should exist separately or the flesh should exist separately — so is it impossible that the parts of the world should exist, in this permanent existence | with which our discourse is concerned, without one another in such a way that light would exist without the earth or the earth without the heaven⁶ or the heaven without the earth. And just as in this human individual there is a force that connects

5. Or: force.
6. The Arabic term *samāʾ* is used here, and not the term *falak*, which in other passages of this chapter has been translated by "heaven."

the parts of his body one with the other, that governs them, provides every
part of the body with what is needed for the safeguard of its well-being, and
wards off from it that which harms — namely, the force of which the
physicians have clearly spoken and which they have designated as the force
governing the body of living beings and have frequently named "nature";
so there subsists in the world as a whole a force that connects its portions
one with the other, safeguards its various species from perishing, safeguards
also the individuals belonging to its species for the time for which it is
possible to safeguard them, and also safeguards some of the individuals of
the world.[7] As to this force, there is speculation whether or not it subsists
through the intermediary of heaven. Furthermore, in the body of a human
individual there are things that are intended: the purpose of some of them —
for instance, that of the organs of nutrition — being the continued existence
of the individual; that of others — for instance, that of the organs of pro-
creation — the continued existence of the species; while that of others
again — of the hands and the eyes for instance — is related to the needs to
which he is compelled in his nutrition and suchlike matters and other
things that are not intended for themselves but are connected with, and
consequent upon, the composition of the parts of the body, that particular
composition being necessary for the achievement of the form in question as
it is, so that it should carry out the intended actions. Accordingly, the fact
that certain things are intended has as a consequence other things, as for
instance the hair and the color of the body, because of the necessity inherent
in matter. For this reason the state of these latter things does not follow an
orderly arrangement; some of them are frequently lacking, and the differences between the various individuals with respect to their superiority or
inferiority in these things are very great, which is not the case with regard
to the parts of the body. For you do not find an individual who has a liver |
that is ten times as big as the liver of another individual, but you do find a
man lacking a beard or hair on certain parts of his body or who has a beard
that is ten or twenty times as big as the beard of another individual. In fact
this occurs in the majority of cases belonging to this category; I mean
differences due to superiority or inferiority as regards hair or color. Now
similarly in being as a whole, there are species whose generation is intended,
stable, and subsisting according to an orderly arrangement, and between
which there are only small differences to the extent of an accident that may
have befallen that particular species with regard to its quality and quantity;
and there are species that are not intended, but are consequent upon the

7. Probably such individuals as the heavenly bodies are meant.

nature of universal generation and corruption — for instance, the various species of worms that are engendered from dung and the various species of living beings that are engendered in fruit when it is putrefying and those that are engendered from the putrefaction of moistures and the worms engendered in the intestines and other things of that kind. Generally speaking, it seems to me that every living being that has not the faculty of procreating its like belongs to this group, and for this reason you will not find that they keep to an orderly arrangement even though they cannot but exist, just as is the case for different colors and for different species of hair in human individuals.

And just as in man there are bodies constituting species, the individuals of which are stable as the fundamental parts of the body, and other bodies having continued existence in this species, not in the individual; so are there in being as a whole stable bodies having continued existence as individuals, namely, the fifth body in all its parts, and bodies having continued existence as a species, such as the elements and what is composed of them.

And just as the forces of man that necessitate his generation and continued existence for the time in which he continues to exist are identical with those necessitating his corruption and passing-away, so are the causes of generation in the whole world of generation and corruption identical with those of corruption. To take an example: | if it were possible that the four faculties that are to be found in the body of every being that nourishes itself — namely, the attractive faculty, the retentive faculty, the digestive faculty, and the repellent faculty — be like the intellectual faculties and not act except as is proper, in the time in which it is proper, and in the measure in which it is proper, man would be preserved from many very great afflictions and from a number of diseases. However, as this is impossible and these faculties carry out natural activities without reflection and discernment and do not apprehend in any respect the activities they carry out, it follows necessarily that grave disease and affliction occur because of them, even though these faculties are at the same time the instrument through which living beings are produced and have a continued existence during the time in which they have it.

This can be made clear as follows. If, to take an example, the attractive faculty would draw to the human body only things that are suitable in every respect and only to the extent needed, man would be preserved from many diseases and afflictions. But as this is not so, and it draws to the body any matter that happens to belong to the genus it attracts even if that matter diverges slightly from the norm in its quantity and quality, it follows necessarily that it draws to the body matter that is warmer or colder, coarser or finer, than is needed, or more of it than is needed. Consequently the veins are plugged up with this matter, sclerosis and putrefaction occur, the quality of the humors is corrupted and their quantity changed; whereupon diseases appear such as scab, itch, and warts, or great afflictions such as cancerous growths, elephantiasis, and canker, so that the form of one or several parts of the body is corrupted.

This is the case also with regard to the other four faculties in question. And this is also the case with regard to all that exists as a whole. For the thing that necessitates the generation of what is generated and the permanence of its existence | for some time is the mixing of the elements through the heavenly forces that move them and pervade them. And this is the very cause of the occurrence of causes of damage in that which exists — such as torrents, harmful rains, snow, hail, tempestuous winds, thunder, lightning, and the putrefaction of the air — or of the occurrence of causes that are very destructive and may bring about the annihilation of one or several lands or of a whole geographical zone — such causes are the sinking of land, earthquakes, hurricanes, and water overflowing from the seas and the depths.

Know that it was not because of all that we have mentioned in comparing the world as a whole to a human individual that it has been said about man that he is a small world. For this whole comparison can be consistently applied to every individual animal that has perfect limbs; but you never hear that one of the ancients[8] has said that an ass or a horse is a small world. This has been said only about man. This is because of that which is a proprium of man only, namely, the rational faculty — I mean the intellect, which is the hylic intellect; something that is not to be found in any of the species of living beings other than man. This can be explained as follows. None of the individual animals requires for its continued existence reflection, perspicacity, and governance of conduct. For it goes about and runs in accordance with its nature, eating what it finds from among the things suitable to it, inhabiting any place to which it has happened to come, and copulating with any female it finds during its heat, if it has a period of heat. Consequently the individual remains in existence during the time in which it exists,[9] and the existence of the species continues; such an individual does not require in any respect another individual belonging to its species to help and sustain it by making for it things | that it does not make

8. Literally: first.   9. Literally: remains in existence.

itself. As for man, and only man, let us suppose the case of an individual belonging to the human species that existed alone, had lost the governance of its conduct, and had become like the beasts. Such an individual would perish immediately; he could not last even one day except by accident — I mean if he should happen to find something he might feed on. For the foods through which he exists require the application of some art and a lengthy management that cannot be made perfect except through thought and perspicacity, as well as with the help of many tools and many individuals, every one of whom devotes himself to one single occupation. For this reason one is needed who would rule them and hold them together so that their society would be orderly and have continued existence in order that the various individuals should help one another. Similarly the precautions against heat in the hot season and against cold in the cold season and the finding of protection against the rains, the snow, and the blowing of winds, require arrangements for many preparations, none of which can be perfected except through thought and perspicacity. Because of this one finds in man the rational faculty in virtue of which he thinks, exerts his perspicacity, works, and prepares by means of various arts his food, his habitation, and his clothing. Through it he rules all the parts of his body in such a way that the ruling part acts in the way it does and the ruled part is governed the way it is ruled. Because of this a human individual who, according to a supposition you might make, would be deprived of this faculty and left only with the animal faculties, would perish and be destroyed immediately. This faculty is very noble indeed, being the noblest of the faculties of the living beings. It is also very secret, and its true reality cannot be understood at the first attempt of common opinion, as one can understand the other natural faculties.

In the same way there exists in being something that rules it as a whole and puts into motion its first principal part[10] granting it the power of putting into motion, in virtue of which this part governs the things that are other than itself. | And if one supposed that this thing had passed into nothingness, it would have to be supposed that the existence of this sphere as a whole, that of its principal and that of its subordinate parts, had also passed into nothingness. For it is in virtue of this thing that the existence of the sphere and of every part of it endures. This thing is the deity, may its name be exalted. It is only with a view to this that it is said of man alone that he is a small world, inasmuch as there subsists in him a certain principle that governs the whole of him. And because of this, God, may He be

10. The Arabic term used here has been translated elsewhere "part of the body."

exalted, is called in our language the life of the world. Thus it is said: *And swore by the living of the world.*[11]

Know that in this comparison that we have established between the world as a whole and a human individual, there is a discrepancy with respect to what we have mentioned only with regard to three points. The first is this. The ruling part of every living being possessing a heart is profited by the ruled parts; the profit deriving from the latter accrues to it so as to be useful to it. There is nothing like this in the universal being. For to no being, the governance of which overflows or confers a force, does any profit accrue in any respect from that which is ruled by it. For its giving the gifts it gives is like the giving of gifts on the parts of a generous and superior man who does it because of the nobility of his nature and the excellence of his disposition, not because of a hope for a reward: this is to become like to the deity, may His name be exalted.

The second point is this. The heart of every living being possessing a heart is in its middle; thus the other ruled parts surround it so that the utility deriving from them should extend to it wholly in that it is protected and safeguarded by them in such a way that harm coming from outside cannot rapidly reach it. Now in the world as a whole, the position is inverse. Its nobler part surrounds its inferior part, for the former is secure against receiving an influence from what is other than itself. And even if it were capable of receiving such an influence, it would not find outside itself another body that could influence it. Accordingly, this part occasions an overflow into what is inside it, whereas no influence reaches it in any respect nor any force deriving from | bodies other than itself. With regard to this point there is also a certain similarity. For in the living being, a part is less noble than other parts to the extent to which it is far off from the ruling part, whereas other parts are nearer to the latter. The position in the world as a whole is the same. For whenever the bodies are near the center, they grow dimmer and their substance coarser, and their motion becomes more difficult, while their light and transparency disappear because of their distance from the noble, luminous, transparent, moving, subtle, and simple body—I mean heaven. On the other hand, whenever bodies are near the latter, they acquire some of these characteristics because of their proximity to it and achieve a certain superiority over what is lower than they.

The third point is this. The rational faculty is a faculty subsisting in a body and is not separable from it, whereas God, may He be exalted, is not a faculty subsisting in the body of the world, but is separate from all parts of

11. Dan. 12:7.

the world. For the governance and the providence of Him, may He be exalted, accompany the world as a whole in such a way that the manner and true reality of this accompaniment are hidden from us; the faculties of human beings are inadequate to understand this. On the one hand, there is a demonstration of His separateness, may He be exalted, from the world and of His being free from it; and on the other hand, there is a demonstration that the influence of His governance and providence[12] in every part of the world, however small and contemptible, exists. May He whose perfection has dazzled us be glorified!

Know that it behooved us to compare the relation obtaining between God, may He be exalted, and the world to that obtaining between the acquired intellect and man; this intellect is not a faculty in the body but is truly separate from the organic body and overflows toward it. We should have compared, on the other hand, the rational faculty to the intellects of the heavens, which are in bodies. However, the case of the intellects of the heavens, that of the existence of separate intellects, and that of the representation of the acquired intellect, which is also separate, are matters open to speculation | and research. The proofs with regard to them are well hidden though correct; many doubts arise with regard to them; the critic may well find in them objects for his criticism and the caviller objects for his cavilling. We have preferred that at first you should represent to yourself that which exists in clear form. As far as this form is concerned, no one could be unaware of any point we have mentioned by way of simple[13] assertion unless he belongs to one of two kinds of individuals: that which is ignorant of matters that are clear — just as one who is not a geometrician is unaware of mathematical matters that have been demonstrated — or that which prefers to hold fast to a certain opinion that the individual in question had adopted previously so that he deceives himself. On the other hand, he who wishes to engage in true speculation should study until the correctness of everything we have narrated becomes clear to him. He then will know that this is the form of this permanent existent whose existence is beyond doubt and dispute. If he wishes to accept this as true from one to whom all the demonstrations of the demonstrated points are known, let him accept it in this way and build on it syllogisms and proofs. If, however, he prefers not to rely on authority — not even with regard to these first principles — he should study, and in due course of time it will become clear to him that

12. I read *wa-ᶜināyatihi* instead of *ᶜināyatihi* (Joel ed., p. 134, l. 3).
13. *mursal*, a term that sometimes means "absolute." Maimonides means to say that in this chapter his exposé was not accompanied by proofs.

matters are just as they have been stated. *Lo this, we have searched it, so it is, hear it, and know thou it.*[14]

After this simplifying presentation, I shall begin to mention what we have promised to mention and to explain.

CHAPTER 73

The common premises laid down by the Mutakallimūn, in spite of the diversity of their opinions and the multiplicity of their methods, that are necessary with a view to establishing what they wish to establish with regard to the four problems in question, are twelve in number. I shall mention them to you and afterwards I shall explain to you the meaning of each of these premises and what necessarily follows from it.[1] |

The first premise: establishing the existence of atoms.[2] The second premise: the existence of a vacuum. The third premise: time is composed of instants.[3] The fourth premise: that substance[4] cannot be exempt from a certain number of accidents. The fifth premise: that the accidents that I shall describe subsist in the atom, which cannot be exempt from them. The sixth premise: that an accident does not endure for two units of time. The seventh premise: that the status of the habitus is that of their privation and that the former and the latter are all of them existent accidents requiring an efficient cause. The eighth premise: that nothing except substances and accidents subsist in all that exists — they mean to say, in all the created things — and that natural form is likewise an accident. The ninth premise: that accidents do not support one another.[5] The tenth premise: that the possibility of a thing should not be considered in establishing a correspondence between that which exists and mental representation. The eleventh premise: that with regard to the impossibility of the infinite, there is no difference between the latter's existing in actu, in potentia, or by accident; I mean to say that there is no difference between the simultaneous existence

14. Job 5:27.
1. On Maimonides' exposition of the views of the Mutakallimūn, cf. Translator's Introduction.
2. The term used can also mean "separate substance."   3. Literally: "now's."
4. The term can also mean "atom." However, comparison with Maimonides' exposition of this premise farther on in this chapter shows that the translation "substance" seems indicated.
5. This means that an accident cannot inhere in another accident.

of those infinite things, or their being supposed to be made up of what exists and of what has ceased to exist, which is infinity by accident. They say that all these kinds of infinity are impossible. The twelfth premise consists in their saying that the senses commit mistakes and that many of the objects of their apprehension elude them and for this reason their judgment should not be appealed to and they should not be regarded in absolute fashion as principles of demonstration. After having thus enumerated these common premises, I shall start to explain their meanings and to explain what necessarily follows from every one of them.|

THE FIRST PREMISE

Its meaning is that they thought that the world as a whole — I mean to say every body in it — is composed of very small particles that, because of their subtlety, are not subject to division. The individual particle does not possess quantity in any respect. However, when several are aggregated, their aggregate possesses quantity and has thus become a body. If two particles are aggregated together, then according to the statements of some of them, every particle has in that case become a body, so that there are two bodies. All these particles are alike and similar to one another, there being no difference between them in any respect whatever. And, as they say, it is impossible that a body should exist in any respect except it be composed of these particles, which are alike in such a way that they are adjacent to one another. In this way, according to them, generation consists in aggregation, and corruption in separation. They do not, however, call this process corruption, but say that there are the following generations: aggregation and separation, motion and rest. They also say that these particles are not restricted in their existence,[6] as was believed by Epicurus and others who affirmed the existence of such particles; for they say that God, may He be exalted, creates these substances constantly whenever He wishes, and that their annihilation is likewise possible. Further on, I shall let you hear their opinions regarding the annihilation of substance.

THE SECOND PREMISE

The assertion concerning the vacuum. The men concerned with the roots [the Mutakallimūn] believe likewise that vacuum exists and that it is a certain space[7] or spaces in which there is nothing at all, being accordingly

6. Perhaps in point of numbers. Ibn Tibbon's translation of the phrase could be rendered: do not exist from of old.

7. When used by philosophers, the word *bu‘d* often means "dimension."

empty of all bodies, devoid of all substance. This premise is necessary for them because of their belief in the first premise. For if the world were full of the particles in question, how | can a thing in motion move? It would also be impossible to represent to oneself that bodies can penetrate one another. Now there can be no aggregation and no separation of these particles except through their motions. Accordingly they must of necessity resort to the affirmation of vacuum so that it should be possible for these particles to aggregate and to separate and so that it should be possible for a moving thing to move in this vacuum in which there is no body and none of these substances.[8]

THE THIRD PREMISE

This is their saying that time is composed of instants, by which they mean that there are many units of time that, because of the shortness of their duration, are not divisible. This premise is also necessary for them because of the first premise. For they undoubtedly had seen Aristotle's demonstrations, by means of which he has demonstrated that distance, time, and locomotion are all three of them equal as far as existence is concerned. I mean to say that their relation to one another is the same and that when one of them is divided the other two are likewise divided and in the same proportion. Accordingly they knew necessarily that if time were continuous and infinitely divisible, it would follow of necessity that the particles that they had supposed to be indivisible would also be divisible. Similarly if distance were supposed to be continuous, it would follow of necessity that the instant that had been supposed to be indivisible would be divisible — just as Aristotle had made it clear in the "Akroasis." Therefore they supposed that distance is not continuous, but composed of parts at which divisibility comes to an end, and that likewise the division of time ends with the instants that are not divisible. For example, an hour | consists of sixty minutes, a minute of sixty seconds, and a second of sixty thirds. And thus this division of time ends up accordingly with parts constituting, for instance, tenths or something even briefer, which cannot in any respect be separated in their turn into parts and are not subject to division, just as extension is not subject to it. Consequently, time becomes endowed with position and order. In fact they have no knowledge at all of the true reality of time. And this is only appropriate with regard to them; for seeing that the cleverest philosophers were confused by the question of time and that some of them did not understand its notion — so that Galen could say that

8. Here the word denotes "atoms."

it is a divine thing, the true reality of which cannot be perceived — this applies all the more to those who pay no attention to the nature of any thing.

Hear now what they were compelled to admit as a necessary consequence of these three premises and what they therefore believed. They said that motion is the passage of an atom belonging to these particles from one atom to another that is contiguous to it. It follows that no movement can be more rapid than another movement. In accordance with this assumption, they said that when you see that two things in motion traverse two different distances in the same time, the cause of this phenomenon does not lie in the greater rapidity of the motion of the body traversing the longer distance; but the cause of this lies in the motion that we call slower being interrupted by a greater number of units of rest than is the case with regard to the motion we call more rapid, which is interrupted by fewer units of rest. And when the example of an arrow shot from a strong bow was alleged as an objection against them, they said that the motions of the arrow were also interrupted by units of rest. In fact your thinking that a certain object is moving in continuous motion is due to an error of the senses, for many of the objects of the perception of the senses elude the latter, as they lay down in the twelfth premise. In consequence, it was said to them: Have you seen a millstone making | a complete revolution? Has not the part that is at its circumference traversed the distance represented by the bigger[9] circle in the same time in which the part near the center has traversed the distance represented by the smaller[10] circle? Accordingly the motion of the circumference is more rapid than the motion of the inner circle. And there is no opportunity for you to assert that the motion of the latter part is interrupted by a greater number of units of rest as the whole body is one and continuous, I mean the body of the millstone. Their answer to this objection is that the various portions of the millstone become separated from one another in the course of its revolution and that the units of rest that interrupt the motion of all the revolving portions that are near the center are more numerous than the units of rest that interrupt the the motion of the parts that are farther off from the center. Thereupon it was said to them: How then do we perceive the millstone as one body that cannot be broken up even by hammers? One must accordingly assume that when it turns round, it splits into pieces; and when it comes to rest, it is welded up and becomes as it was before. How is it that one does not perceive its portions as separated from one another? Thereupon, in order to reply to

9. Literally: big.   10. Literally: small.

this, they had recourse to the same twelfth premise, which states that one should not take into account the apprehensions of the senses, but rather the testimony of the intellect.

You should not think that the doctrines I have explained to you are the most abhorrent of the corollaries necessarily following from those three premises, for the doctrine that necessarily follows from the belief in the existence of a vacuum is even stranger and more abhorrent. Furthermore, the doctrine that I have mentioned to you with regard to motion is not more abhorrent than the assertion going with this view that the diagonal of a square is equal to one of its sides, so that some of them say that the square is a nonexistent thing. To sum up: By virtue of the first premise all geometrical demonstrations become invalid, and they belong to either one or the other of two categories. Some of them are absolutely invalid, as for instance those referring to the properties of incommensurability and commensurability of lines and planes and the existence | of rational and irrational lines and all that are included in the tenth book of Euclid and those that resemble them. As for the others, the demonstrations proving them are not cogent, as when we say we want to divide a line into two equal halves. For in the case in which the number of its atoms[11] is odd, the division of the line into two equal parts is impossible according to their assumption. Know, moreover, that the Banū Shākir have composed the famous "Book of Ingenious Devices," which includes one hundred odd ingenious devices, all of them demonstrated and carried into effect. But if vacuum had existed, not one of them would have been valid, and many of the contrivances to make water flow would not have existed. In spite of this, the lives [of the Mutakallimūn] have been spent in argumentation with a view to establishing the validity of these premises and others resembling them. I shall now return to the explanation of the meaning of their remaining premises that were mentioned.

THE FOURTH PREMISE

This is their saying that the accidents exist, and that they are something superadded to the something that is the substance, and that no body is exempt from one of them. If this premise did not mean more than this, it would be a correct, clear, evident premise, and give rise to no doubt and no difficulty. However, they say that in every substance in which there does not subsist the accident of life, there necessarily subsists the accident of

---

11. It is to be borne in mind throughout this chapter that the same Arabic term is being translated variously as "atom(s)" or "substance(s)."

death, for the recipient cannot but receive one of two contraries. They say: similarly it has a color, a taste, motion or rest, aggregation or separation. And if the accident of life subsists in it, there cannot but subsist in it other genera of accidents such as knowledge or ignorance, or will or its contrary, | or power or powerlessness, or apprehension or one of its contraries. To sum up: there must necessarily subsist in it all the accidents that may subsist in a living being or one of their contraries.

THE FIFTH PREMISE

This is their saying that these accidents subsist in the atom and that it cannot be exempt from them. The explanation and the meaning of this premise are as follows. They say that every atom of the atoms that God creates is provided with accidents from which it cannot be exempt; such accidents, for example, as color, smell, motion or rest, but not quantity — since these atoms do not possess quantity. For in accordance with their opinion, they do not call quantity an accident and do not understand that quantity includes the notion of accidentality. In virtue of this premise, they hold with regard to all accidents subsisting in a body that it should not be said that one of them is a proprium of that body as a whole; for the accident in question subsists, according to them, in every atom of the atoms of which that body is composed. For instance, in the case of this piece of snow, the whiteness does not subsist only in the entire whole; rather every single atom of the atoms of the snow is white, and it is because of this that whiteness subsists in their aggregate. In a similar way they say of a body in motion that every atom of its atoms is in motion and that because of this it is in motion as a whole. Similarly life subsists, according to them, in every single part of the living body, and also the senses; every atom is a whole endowed with sensation, being according to them endowed with sensation. | For life, the senses, intellect, and knowledge are, according to them, accidents just as blackness and whiteness are, as we shall make clear on the basis of their doctrines. As regards the soul, they disagree; the opinion of most of them[12] is that it is an accident subsisting in one atom that belongs to the whole consisting of the atoms of which man, for example, is composed. This whole is designated as being endowed with a soul because of the fact that that atom subsists in it. Some of them, however, affirm that the soul is a body composed of subtle atoms and that these atoms are doubtless provided with a certain accident, which is their proprium and in virtue of which they become a soul. They affirm that these atoms are mixed with the

12. Literally: most of their assertions.

atoms of the organic body. Accordingly they are not exempt from the belief that the thing that is the soul is an accident. As for the intellect, I consider that they are unanimous in thinking that it is an accident subsisting in an atom belonging to an intellectually cognizing whole. As regards knowledge, there is perplexity among them over whether it is an accident subsisting in every atom belonging to the whole endowed with knowledge, or an accident subsisting in one atom only. Both affirmations entail abhorrent conclusions. It has been objected against them that we find that most minerals and stones have a very intense color, but when they are pulverized this color disappears. Thus when we pulverize the intensely green emerald, it turns into white dust — which is proof that the accident in question resides in the whole and not in every particle included in that whole. It is even more manifest that parts cut off from a living being are not alive — which is proof that this entity[13] is constituted by the whole and not by each of the parts included in that whole. In answer to this, they say that the accident in question has no continued existence, but is always created anew, as I shall explain on the basis of their opinion as formulated in the next premise. |

THE SIXTH PREMISE

It consists in their assertion that an accident does not last during two units of time. The meaning of this premise is as follows. They think that God, may He be glorified and magnified, creates an atom and creates together with it, at one and the same time, any accident He wills as an accident subsisting in the atom. For it may not be predicated of Him, may He be exalted, that He has the power to create an atom without an accident, for this is impossible. Now the true reality of an accident and its notion consist in its not enduring or lasting during two units of time, by which they mean: two instants. While this accident is being created, it disappears, having no continued existence. Whereupon God creates another accident of the same species, which accident disappears in its turn; whereupon He creates a third one belonging to the same species, and so on always in the same way in the period during which God wishes the species of that accident to last. If, however, He, may He be exalted, wishes to create in the atom another species of accident, He does so. If, however, He refrains from the act of creation and does not create an accident, the atom in question becomes nonexistent. This is the opinion of some of them — namely, of those who are the majority — this being the creation of accidents, which

13. Namely, life.

they affirm. However, some of them belonging to the Mu'tazila assert that some accidents last for a certain time, whereas others do not last during two units of time. As to this, they have no rule to which to refer so as to be able to say: this particular species of accidents lasts and that other does not. What led them to this opinion is that it is not to be said that there is a nature in any respect whatever and that the nature of one particular body may require that this and that accident be attached to that body. Quite the contrary, they wish to say that God, may He be exalted, created the accidents in question now, without the intermediary of nature — without any other thing. But if this is asserted, it follows according to them necessarily that | that accident in question does not last; for if you should say that it lasts for some time and then becomes nonexistent, it becomes necessary to inquire what thing has caused it to become nonexistent. If you should say thereupon that God, if He wills, causes it to become nonexistent, this answer would not be valid according to their opinion. For an agent does not act to bring about nonexistence, since nonexistence does not require an agent. On the contrary, the nonexistence of an act comes about when the agent refrains from acting. This is valid in a certain respect. For this reason, accordingly, their assertions led them — as they wished that there be no nature necessitating the existence or the nonexistence of a thing — to the point of affirming the creation of successive accidents. According to some of them, when God wishes to cause the nonexistence of a substance, He does not create an accident in it, in consequence whereof the substance becomes nonexistent. Others affirm that if God should wish the world to be annihilated, He would create in it the accident of passing-away — an accident that would be without a substratum. Thereupon this accident of passing-away would be opposed to the existence of the world. In accordance with this premise, they assert that when we, as we think, dye a garment red, it is not we who are by any means the dyers; God rather creates the color in question in the garment when the latter is in juxtaposition with the red dye, which we consider to have gone over to the garment. They say that this is not the case, but that God has instituted a habit according to which, for example, black color does not appear except when a garment is juxtaposed with indigo. However, this blackness, which God creates when an object about to turn black is juxtaposed with blackness, does not last, but disappears instantly, and another blackness is created. God has also instituted the habit of not creating, after the disappearance of blackness, redness or yellowness, but a blackness similar to the one before. In conformity with this assumption, they have drawn the corollary that the things we know

now | are not identical with the contents of the knowledge known by us yesterday; for that knowledge has become nonexistent, and another knowledge similar to it has been created. They maintain that this is so, because knowledge is an accident. Similarly it necessarily behooves those who believe that the soul is an accident to consider that, to take an example, one hundred thousand souls are created every minute for the requirements of every being endowed with a soul. For as you know, time, according to them, is composed of indivisible instants. In conformity with this premise, they assert that when a man moves a pen, it is not the man who moves it; for the motion occurring in the pen is an accident created by God in the pen. Similarly the motion of the hand, which we think of as moving the pen, is an accident created by God in the moving hand. Only, God has instituted the habit that the motion of the hand is concomitant[14] with the motion of the pen, without the hand exercising in any respect an influence on, or being causative in regard to, the motion of the pen. For they maintain that an accident does not go beyond its substratum. There is unanimity among them with regard to their belief that a white garment that has been put into a vat full of indigo and has become dyed, has not been blackened by the indigo, blackness being an accident that is inherent in the body that is the indigo and that does not go beyond it so as to affect something else. According to them, there is no body at all endowed with the power of action. On the other hand, the ultimate agent is God; and it is He who, in view of the fact that He has instituted such a habit, has created the blackness in the body that is the garment when the latter was juxtaposed with indigo.

To sum up: it should not be said in any respect that this is the cause of that. This is the opinion of the multitude [of the Mutakallimūn]. One[15] of them, however, maintained the doctrine of causality and in consequence was regarded as abhorrent by them. As for the actions of man, they are in disagreement about them. The doctrine of the majority and in particular that of the multitude of the Ashᶜariyya is that when the pen is put into motion, God creates four accidents, no one of which is a cause of any other — all of them being concomitant | in regard to their existence, not otherwise. The first accident is my will to put the pen into motion; the second accident, my power to put it into motion; the third accident, human motion itself — I mean the motion of the hand; the fourth accident, the motion of the pen.

14. The Arabic term *qārana* is used; it also occurs in an earlier passage in this chapter adducing the example of the dyeing of a garment. In that passage the term is translated by the verb "juxtapose" or its derivatives.
15. The word may also denote several individuals.

For they think that when a man wills a thing and, as he thinks, does it, his will is created for him, his power to do that which he wills is created for him, and his act is created for him. For he does not act in virtue of the power created in him, and the power has no influence on the action. On the other hand, the Muʿtazila maintain that man acts in virtue of the power created in him; and one of the Ashʿariyya says that this created power has a certain influence on, and connection with, the act. But they regard this as abhorrent. As all of them think, the created will and the created power and — in the opinion of some of them — also the created act, are accidents that do not last, God constantly creating in that way motion after motion in the pen in question as long as the pen is in motion. Thereafter, when it comes to rest, it does so only after He has created in it a unit of rest. And He does not cease to create in it one unit of rest after another as long as the pen is at rest. Accordingly God creates at every one of the instants — I mean the separate units of time — an accident in every individual among the beings, whether that individual be an angel, a heavenly sphere, or something else. This He does constantly at every moment of time. They maintain that this is the true faith in God's activity; and in their opinion, he who does not believe that God acts in this way denies the fact that God acts. With regard to beliefs of this kind, it has been said in my opinion and in that of everybody endowed with an intellect: *Or as one mocketh | a man, do ye so mock him*[16] — this being in truth the very essence of *mockery*.

THE SEVENTH PREMISE

It consists in their belief that privations of habitus are things that exist in a body, being superadded to its substance, and are accordingly also existent accidents. In consequence they are always being created, and whenever one of them disappears, another is created. The explanation is as follows. They do not hold that rest is the privation of motion, that death is the privation of life, and that blindness is the privation of sight; in fact they do not believe this with regard to any privations of habitus similar to those mentioned. For according to them, the status[17] of motion and rest is the same as that of heat and cold. For just as heat and cold are accidents existing in the hot and cold substrata, motion is an accident created in the moving body, and rest an accident which God creates in the body that is at rest, which accident likewise does not last for two units of time, as has been set forth before in the preceding premise. According to them, God has created

16. Job 13:9.   17. Literally: judgment.

a unit of rest in every particle of the body that is at rest and, as long as it is at rest, creates another unit of rest every time a unit of it becomes non-existent. The position is completely analogous, according to them, with regard to knowledge and ignorance. According to them, the latter exists and is an accident. In consequence, a unit of ignorance continually disappears and another is created as long as a particular ignorant individual continues to be ignorant in anything. The position is also completely analogous with regard to life and death. For both of these are, according to them, accidents, and they clearly assert that a unit of life disappears and another is created as long as a particular living being is alive. Then, when God wills its death, He creates in it the accident of death following upon the disappearance of the accident of life, which | does not last two units of time. All this they assert clearly. Now according to this assumption, it clearly follows that the accident of death, which God creates, likewise becomes nonexistent after a moment of time, so that God creates another unit of death. But for that, death would not last. However, as one unit of life is created after another, one unit of death is created after another. Would that I knew till when God creates the accident of death in a dead individual; does He do so as long as that individual's external form endures, or as long as one of that individual's atoms endures? For, according to what they wish, God creates the accident of death in every single atom of the atoms of the individual in question. Now we find molars of dead individuals that are thousands of years old. Accordingly this is a proof that God has not annihilated that substance. In consequence, He should be creating in it the accident of death all through these thousands of years, creating a unit of death as soon as another unit of it disappears. This is the doctrine of the multitude of them. However one Muʿtazilite says that certain privations of habitus are not existent things. He does not, however, say this consistently with regard to every privation. Thus he does not say that darkness is the privation of light, that rest is the privation of motion. In fact he regards some of the privations as existent and some others as being merely a privation of habitus, just as it suits him with respect to his belief. They did a similar thing with regard to the continued existence of accidents. For according to them, some of the accidents last for some time, whereas others do not last for two units of time. For the purpose of all of them is to suppose an existent universe,[18] the nature of which fits in with our opinions and teachings.

18. Literally: an existence. The meaning is: all that which is existent.

THE EIGHTH PREMISE

It consists in their assertion that there exists nothing except substances and accidents and that the natural forms | are likewise accidents. The explanation of this premise is as follows. According to them, all bodies are composed of atoms resembling one another, as we have made clear when setting out the first of their premises. These atoms differ from one another only with regard to accidents and in nothing else. Thus according to them, animality, humanity, sensation, and rationality are all accidents having the same status as whiteness, blackness, bitterness, and sweetness, so that the difference existing between an individual belonging to one species and an individual belonging to another is like the difference between individuals belonging to the same species. In consequence, the body of heaven, even the body of the angels, or even the body of [God's] throne, as it is imagined in fantasy, and the body of any insect you like from among the insects of the earth or of any plant you like, are, according to them, of one substance, differing only with regard to accidents and in nothing else. And the substances of which the universe is composed are the atoms.

THE NINTH PREMISE

It consists in their assertion that accidents do not serve as a substratum for one another. According to them, it may not be said that one accident has as its substratum another, which latter has as its substratum a substance. In their opinion all accidents, in the first place and in the same way, have substance as a substratum.[19] They avoid the opposing doctrine because it has as its necessary consequence that an ultimate accident may not subsist in a substance unless a primary accident precedes it in subsisting in it. They do not wish to admit this in the case of certain accidents, desiring to create the possibility that certain accidents may subsist in any substance that they may happen to encounter without any need for another accident previously providing the substance with a proprium. This is in accordance with their view that all accidents provide a proprium. Furthermore, from | another angle it may be seen that the substratum to which an accident may attach itself[20] has to be stable and has to endure for a certain time. However, as an accident, according to them, does not last for two units of time — I mean for two instants — how can it be possible according to this hypothesis that it should serve as a substratum for something other than itself?

19. Literally: are borne in a primary bearing on substance.
20. Literally: upon which that which is borne is borne.

THE TENTH PREMISE

It consists in the affirmation of admissibility that they mention. This is the main proposition of the science of kalām. Listen to its meaning. They are of the opinion that everything that may be imagined is an admissible notion for the intellect. For instance, it is admissible from the point of view of intellect that it should come about that the sphere of the earth should turn into a heaven endowed with circular motion and that the heaven should turn into the sphere of the earth. Or to take another example, it is admissible that the sphere of fire should move toward the center of the earth and that the sphere of the earth should move toward the encompassing heaven. For as they say, according to intellectual admissibility, one place is not more appropriate for one particular body than another place. They also say with regard to all things that are existent and perceptible that supposing anything among them should be bigger than it is or smaller or different from what it is in shape or place — should a human individual, for instance, have the size of a big mountain having many summits overtopping the air, or should there exist an elephant having the size of a flea, or a flea having the size of an elephant — all such differences would be admissible from the point of view of the intellect. The whole world is involved in this method of admissibility as they practice it. For whatever thing of this kind they assume, they are able to say: it is admissible that it should be so, and it is possible that it should be otherwise; and it is not more appropriate that one particular thing should be so than that it should be otherwise. And they say this without paying attention to the correspondence or lack of correspondence of that which exists to their assumptions. For they say of the existent things — provided with | known forms and determinate sizes and necessarily accompanying modes that are unchangeable and immutable — that their being as they are is merely in virtue of the continuance of a habit. In the same way it is the habit of a sultan not to pass through the market places of the city except on horseback, and he has never been seen doing it in a way other than this. However, it is not held impossible by the intellect that he should walk on foot in the city; rather is it undoubtedly possible, and it is admissible that this should occur. They say that the fact that earth moves toward the center and fire upwards or the fact that fire burns and water cools is in a similar way due to the continuance of a habit. It is, in consequence, not impossible from the point of view of the intellect that this habit should undergo a change so that fire should cool and move downwards, while still being fire, and so that similarly water should warm and move upwards, while still being water. The whole edifice[21] is founded on this assumption. At the same time they are unanimous in holding that the coming-together of two contraries in the same substratum[22] and at the same instant is impossible, cannot be true, and cannot be admitted by the intellect. They further assert that it is impossible and cannot be admitted by the intellect that a substance should exist without there being any accident in it; or, as some of them say, it is also impossible and cannot be admitted by the intellect that an accident should exist without being in a substratum. Similarly they say that it cannot be true that a substance should be transformed into an accident or an accident into a substance or that a body should compenetrate another body; they acknowledge that these are impossibilities from the point of view of the intellect. Now it is a true assertion that none of the things that they consider as impossible can be mentally represented to oneself in any way whatever, whereas the things they call possible can be. Yet the philosophers say that when you call a thing "impossible," it is because it cannot be imagined, and when you call a thing "possible," it is because it can be imagined. Thus what is possible according to you is possible only from the point of view of the imagination and not from that of the intellect. Accordingly in this premise you consider that which is necessary, admissible, or impossible, sometimes | with the imagination and not with the intellect and sometimes with the first suggestions of common opinion — just as Abū Naṣr[23] has noted when speaking of the notion to which the Mutakallimūn apply the term "intellect." Thus it has already been made clear that that which can be imagined is, according to them, something possible, whether something existent corresponds to it or not. On the other hand, everything that cannot be imagined is impossible. Now this premise cannot be true except in virtue of the nine premises previously mentioned. Undoubtedly it was because of it that they had recourse to expounding these nine premises before it. The explanation of this is in accordance with what I shall set forth to you while I reveal to you the secrets of these matters in the form of a dispute taking place between a Mutakallim and a philosopher.

The Mutakallim said to the philosopher: Why is it that we find this body, which is iron, is endowed with extreme hardness and strength, while

---

21. Literally: matter.   22. Or: in the same place.
23. Abū Naṣr Muḥammad al-Fārābī (d. 950) is meant. This philosopher's principal treatises and his influence on Maimonides are referred to in the Translator's Introduction. The passage alluded to in the text occurs in al-Fārābī's *Risāla fi'l-ʿAql* (*Epistle on the Intellect*), ed. M. Bouyges (Beirut, 1938), pp. 11–12.

being black; whereas that other body, which is cream, is endowed with extreme softness and looseness, while being white?

The philosopher replied to him: Every natural body has two species of accidents: those that are attached to it in respect to its matter, such as those making man healthy and ill; and those that are attached to it in respect to its form, such as man's feeling of wonder and his laughing. Now the various kinds of matter found in bodies that are in the stage of ultimate composition differ greatly because of the forms, which particularize these various kinds of matter, so that the substance of iron becomes different from that of cream and so that each of these substances has attached to it the differing accidents that you see. Thus strength subsisting in the one substance and softness subsisting in the other are accidents that follow from the difference of their forms, and blackness and whiteness are accidents that follow from the difference of their ultimate matter.

Thereupon the Mutakallim controverted this entire reply by means of the premises of his doctrine as I shall set forth to you. In effect he said: There does not exist at all, contrary to what you think, any form constituting a substance so that a variety of substances is thereby brought about. | On the contrary, everything that you consider as a form is an accident — as we have made clear from their assertion in the eighth premise. Then he said: There is no difference between the substance of iron and the substance of cream, the whole being composed of atoms similar to one another — as we have made clear from their opinions set forth in the first premise, from which, as we have explained, the second and the third follow necessarily. Similarly the twelfth premise is required for establishing the existence of atoms. Furthermore, it is not true, in the opinion of a Mutakallim, that there are certain accidents that particularize a substance so that because of them it is disposed and prepared to receive other secondary accidents. For in his opinion, one accident cannot serve as a substratum for another — as we have made clear in the ninth premise — and moreover, an accident has no continued existence — as we have made clear in the sixth premise. Then when, according to the Mutakallim, everything he wishes with regard to his premises is established as true, the resultant conclusion is that the substances of the iron and the cream are the same substances,[24] substances similar to one another in every respect. Each of these substances has the same relation with any accident,[25] one particular substance not being more appropriate for one particular accident than another. And just as one atom

24. Literally: one substance.   25. Literally: with every accident.

is not more fitted to move than to be at rest, so one particular atom is not more appropriate for the reception of the accident of life, the accident of the intellect, the accident of sense, than any other atom. The greater or smaller number of the atoms does not in this point constitute a significant addition to the final result, as an accident subsists in every atom — as we have made clear on the basis of their assertion in the fifth premise. Accordingly it follows necessarily from all these premises that man is not more fitted to cognize intellectually than a beetle. And thus the admissibility of which [the Mutakallimūn] speak in the present premise follows necessarily. In fact it was with a view to this premise | that the whole endeavor was made, because this premise is more firm than any other thing for establishing everything that there is a wish to establish, as shall be made clear.

A CALL UPON THE READER'S ATTENTION

Know, thou who studiest this Treatise: if you are of those who know the soul and its powers and have acquired true knowledge of everything as it really is, you already know that imagination exists in most living beings. As for the perfect animal, I mean the one endowed with a heart, the existence of imagination in it is clear. Accordingly, man is not distinguished by having imagination; and the act of imagination is not the act of the intellect but rather its contrary. For the intellect divides the composite things and differentiates their parts and makes abstractions of them, represents them to itself in their true reality and with their causes, and apprehends from one thing very many notions, which differ for the intellect just as two human individuals differ in regard to their existence for the imagination. It is by means of the intellect that the universal is differentiated from the individual, and no demonstration is true except by means of universals. It is also through the intellect that essential predicates are discerned from accidental ones. None of these acts belongs to the imagination. For the imagination apprehends only that which is individual and composite as a whole, as it is apprehended by the senses; or compounds things that in their existence are separate, combining one with another; the whole[26] being a body or a force of the body. Thus someone using his imagination imagines a human individual having a horse's head and wings and so on. This is what is called a thing invented and false, for nothing existent corresponds to it at all. In its apprehension, imagination is in no way able to hold itself aloof from matter, even if it turns a form into the

26. Resulting from this activity.

extreme of abstraction. For this reason there can be no critical examination in the imagination.

Hear what | the mathematical sciences have taught us and how capital are the premises we have obtained from them. Know that there are things that a man, if he considers them with his imagination, is unable to represent to himself in any respect, but finds that it is as impossible to imagine them as it is impossible for two contraries to agree; and that afterwards the existence of the thing that is impossible to imagine is established by demonstration as true, and existence manifests it as real. Thus if you imagine a big sphere of any size you like, even if it be the size of the encompassing heaven; imagine further a diameter passing through the center of the sphere; and thereupon imagine the two human individuals standing upon the two extremities of the diameter so that their feet are put in a straight line with respect to the diameter, so that their feet and the diameter form one and the same straight line — then one of two possibilities must be true: either the diameter is parallel to the horizon or it is not. Now if it is parallel, both individuals should fall. If it is not parallel, one of them — namely the lower one — should fall, while the other is firmly placed. It is in that way that imagination would apprehend the matter. Now it has been demonstrated that the earth is spherical in form and that portions of the inhabited part of it lie at both extremities of its diameter. Thus the head of every individual from among the inhabitants of the two extremities is near heaven while his feet are near the feet of another individual who is opposite him. It is thus impossible in every way that either of them would fall. This cannot even be represented to oneself; for one of them is not placed above and the other below, but each of them is both above and below in relation to the other. Similarly it has been made clear in the second book of the "Conic Sections"[27] that two lines, between which there is a certain distance at the outset, may go forth in such a way that the farther they go, this distance diminishes and they come nearer to one another, but without it ever being possible for them to meet even if they are drawn forth to infinity and even though they come nearer to one another the farther they go. This cannot be | imagined and can in no way enter within the net of the imagination. Of these two lines, one is straight and the other curved, as has been made clear there in the above-mentioned work.

Accordingly it has been demonstrated that something that the imagination cannot imagine or apprehend and that is impossible from its point of

27. Maimonides refers to the *Conic Sections* of the Greek mathematician Apollonius; Book II, theorem xiii.

view, can exist. It has similarly been demonstrated that something the imagination considers as necessary is impossible — namely, that God, may He be exalted, should be a body or a force in a body. For according to the imagination, there are no existents[28] except bodies[28] or things[28] in bodies.[28]

Accordingly it is clear that there is something else by means of which that which is necessary, that which is admissible, and that which is impossible, can be discerned, something that is not the imagination. How excellent is this speculation and how great its utility for him who wishes to awaken from this dormancy, I mean the state of following the imagination! Do not think that the Mutakallimūn are not aware of anything concerning this point. On the contrary, they are aware of it to a certain extent; they know it and call that which may be imagined while being at the same time impossible — as for instance God's being a body — a fantasy and a vain imagining. And often do they clearly state that fantasies are false. For this reason they have recourse to the nine premises we have mentioned, so as to be able to establish with their help the truth of this tenth premise — which asserts the admissibility of those imaginings that they wanted to be declared admissible — in order to maintain the similarity of the atoms to one another and the equality of the accidents with respect to "accidentality," as we have made clear.

Consider, thou who art engaged in speculation, and perceive that a method of profound speculation has arisen. For with regard to particular mental representations, one individual claims that they are intellectual representations, whereas another affirms that they are imaginative representations. We wish consequently to find something that would enable us to distinguish the things cognized intellectually from those imagined. For if the philosopher says, as he does: That which exists[29] is my witness and by means of it we discern the necessary, the possible, and the impossible; the adherent of the Law says to him: The dispute between us is with regard to this point. For we claim[30] that that which exists | was made[31] in virtue of will and was not a necessary consequence. Now if it was made in this fashion, it is admissible that it should be made in a different way, unless intellectual representation decides, as you think it decides, that something different from what exists at present is not admissible. This is the chapter of admissibility. And about that I have something to say, which you will

28. In the singular in the Arabic text.   29. Or: existence.
30. The text suggests that a literal translation may be: we claim, as far as I am concerned.
31. The verb used generally means "done" or "acted."

learn[32] in various passages of this Treatise. It is not something one hastens to reject in its entirety with nonchalance.

THE ELEVENTH PREMISE

This is their saying that the existence of that which is infinite in any mode whatever is impossible. The explanation of this is as follows. The impossibility of the existence of an infinite magnitude has already been demonstrated, or the existence of magnitudes infinite in number — even if each of them is of finite magnitude — provided that those magnitudes infinite in number are supposed to coexist in time. Similarly the existence of an infinite number of causes is impossible — I mean to say that a thing should be the cause of something, that this thing should have a cause[33] in its turn, that that cause should again have a cause, and so forth to infinity, so that an infinite number of numerable[34] things should exist in actu; and it is indifferent whether these be bodies or things separate from matter, provided only that some of them are the causes of others. It is this natural and essential orderly arrangement with regard to which it has been demonstrated that the infinite is impossible in it. But as for what is infinite in potentia or accidentally, the existence of such an infinite has, in some cases, been demonstrated: thus it has been demonstrated that the division of magnitudes to infinity is possible in potentia, and likewise the division of time to infinity. Another case is an object of speculation: namely, the existence of what is infinite by way of succession. This is what is called the infinite by accident. And it consists in a thing coming to exist after the passing-away | of another thing, the latter's coming to exist after the passing-away of a third thing, and so forth to infinity. About this there is an extremely profound speculation. Thus he who claims to have demonstrated the eternity of the world says that time is not finite, and nothing absurd follows necessarily for him therefrom. For as soon as a portion of time is actualized, another portion passes away. Similarly the succession of accidents, which attach themselves to matter, goes on, in his opinion, to infinity, without an absurdity necessarily following for him from this assertion. For the accidents do not all exist simultaneously, but in succession; and the impossibility of this has not been demonstrated. As for the Mutakallimūn, there is no difference, in their opinion, between saying that a certain infinite magnitude exists and saying that bodies and time are liable to be divided to infinity. There likewise is no difference, in their opinion, between asserting the simultaneous existence of things infinite in number, arranged,

32. Literally: hear.   33. Literally: another cause.   34. Or: numbered.

[at the same time] in orderly fashion — your saying this, for instance, as it were, about the human individuals existing at present — or your asserting that things infinite in number came into existence, but passed away one after the other. It is as if you said: Zayd is the son of Umar, Umar is the son of Khālid, Khālid is the son of Bakr, and so forth to infinity. This position is likewise absurd according to them, just as the first was. Thus these four divisions of the infinite are equivalent according to them. Some of them wish, in a way that I shall explain to you in the present Treatise, to establish the correctness of the last of these divisions — I mean to say, they wish to make clear its impossibility. Others say that this impossibility is self-evident for the intellect through the spontaneous perception of the mind and that it does not require demonstration. Now if it is a clear absurdity that things infinite in number should exist successively, even though those of them that exist at present are finite in number, the eternity of the world can be considered | through the spontaneous perception of the mind as absurd. And there is no need in any respect for any other premise. However, this is not the place for the investigation of this subject.

THE TWELFTH PREMISE

This is their saying that the senses do not always procure certain knowledge. For the Mutakallimūn have been suspicious with regard to the apprehension of the senses on two counts. One of them arises from the fact that, as they say, the senses miss many of the objects of their sensations either because of the subtlety of the body of the object of apprehension — as they mention with regard to the atoms and what pertains to them, as we have made clear — or because of the distance of the objects of apprehension from the apprehending subject. Thus a man does not see, hear, and smell at a distance extending to several parasangs, and it is impossible to apprehend the motion of the heaven. The second count arises from their saying that the senses can be mistaken with regard to the object of their apprehension. Thus a man, when he is far off, sees a big thing as small; a small thing as big, if it is in water; and a crooked thing as straight, if part of it is in water and part of it outside. Similarly someone suffering from jaundice sees things as yellow, and one whose tongue is steeped with yellow bile tastes sweet things as bitter. They enumerate many things of that kind. They say: for this reason the senses should not be trusted to the extent of adopting them as the principles of demonstration. Do not think that agreement of the Mutakallimūn in affirming this premise is gratuitous. That would be similar to the belief[35] of the majority of the later Mutakallimūn that the wish of their predecessors to establish the existence of the indivisible particle did not correspond to a need. In fact, all their assertions that we have set forth in the foregoing passages are necessary; and if one premise were to be destroyed, the whole purpose would be destroyed. Indeed this | last of the premises is most necessary. For whenever we apprehend with our senses things controverting their assumptions, they are able to say: no attention should be paid to the senses as the matter — which, as they think, has been proven by the testimony of the intellect — is demonstrated. This is the case with regard to their claim that continuous motion is interrupted by units of rest, with regard to their other claim that the millstone undergoes a division when revolving, and with regard to still another claim of theirs that the whiteness of this garment has become nonexistent at this instant and that this whiteness is another whiteness. These are assertions that run counter to what can be seen. There are furthermore many things necessarily following from the existence of vacuum, all of which are contradicted by the senses. Consequently the answer to all this is, when this answer is possible, that the particular thing one is concerned with has been missed by the senses. In other cases, the answer is given that it is one of the errors of the senses. You already know that all these are ancient opinions, which had been held by the Sophists. About the latter, Galen, in his book "On the Natural Faculties,"[36] states that they taxed the senses with lying and relates everything that you already know.[37]

   After having prefaced these premises, I shall begin to make clear their methods with regard to the four above-mentioned problems.

35. Literally: thinking.
36. The passage referred to occurs in Book I, chap. ii. It reads (in A. J. Brock's translation): "The Sophists, however, while allowing that bread in turning into blood becomes changed as regards sight, taste, and touch, will not agree that this change occurs in reality. Thus some of them hold that all such phenomena are tricks and illusions of our senses; the senses, they say, are affected now in one way, now in another, whereas the underlying substance does not admit of any of these changes to which the names are given."
37. Literally: as Galen states in his book "On the Natural Faculties" about them who taxed the senses with lying and relates everything that you already know.

CHAPTER 74

In this chapter I shall include for your benefit a narration of the proofs of the Mutakallimūn showing that the world is created in time. Do not demand of me that I set them forth in their terminology and at such length as they do. However I shall inform you of what every one of them intends and of the method he uses in order to adduce proof establishing the creation of the world in time | or refuting its eternity. I shall draw your attention with brevity to the premises used by the author of each method. When you shall read their lengthy books and famous works, you shall not find in them in any respect, in the proofs they adduce with regard to the subject in question, a single notion in addition to what you will understand from my exposition here. However, you shall find a lengthier exposition and resplendent and fine diction. Sometimes they use rhymed prose and symmetrical words and choose eloquent language. Sometimes also, they make their diction obscure intending to astonish the listener and to strike terror into the student. In their works you shall likewise very often find reiteration of notions, formulations of doubts and — as they think — their solution, and polemics against those who disagree with them.

THE FIRST METHOD

Some[1] of them think that any single happening occurring in time may be adduced as proof that the world has been created in time. You say, as it were: the individual Zayd has been a drop of sperm and has thereupon passed from one state to another until he has reached his perfection. It is impossible that it was he who changed himself and made himself pass from one state to another. There accordingly must be in his case someone outside him who changes him. Thus it has been made clear that he requires an artificer who has constructed his frame and has made him pass from one state to another. The same inference applies to a palm tree and other things. The same inference, he says, applies to the world as a whole. Thus you see that he believes that whatever rule may be found with regard to one particular body must necessarily be applied to every body.

THE SECOND METHOD

They say likewise that the fact that a procreative individual is created in time | demonstrates that the whole world has been created in time. The

1. Or: one.

explanation of this is as follows. Once upon a time this Zayd was not here; then he is. Accordingly if he is, it is impossible in every respect that he should not derive from his father Umar. Now his father Umar is likewise produced in time. Accordingly if his father is, it is impossible that he, Umar, should not be generated from Zayd's grandfather Khālid. But Zayd's grandfather Khālid is also produced in time. Thus this goes on to infinity. However, they have assumed, as we have made clear in the eleventh of their premises, that the existence of an infinity of this kind is impossible. Similarly if I should ultimately come to a first individual having no father — that is, *Adam* — there would necessarily arise the question: from what was this *Adam* generated? Accordingly you would say, to take an example: from dust. Thereupon it would necessarily be asked: from what was that dust generated? To take an example, the answer would be given: from water. Thereupon it would be asked: from what was this water generated? They say that this series of questions and answers might undoubtedly either go on to infinity, which is absurd, or would ultimately stop at the existence of one thing — an existence that would come to pass after pure nothingness — and that this latter solution is the true one and that questioning ceases when it has arrived at this ultimate term. Accordingly this constitutes, as they say, a demonstration of the world's having come into existence after pure and absolute nothingness.

THE THIRD METHOD

They say that the substances[2] of the world cannot in any respect be anything but aggregated or separated. And sometimes certain substances are aggregated, whereas others are separated. It is accordingly clear and manifest that in respect of the essence of the atoms, neither aggregation nor separation was necessarily in them to the exclusion of the other possibility. For if their essence and nature would only require their being separated, they would never aggregate. Similarly if their essence and true reality would | only require their being aggregated, they would never be separated. And therefore separation is not more fit for them than aggregation, nor is aggregation more appropriate to them than separation. Thus the fact that some of them are aggregated, while others are separated, and still others undergo modifications of their state, being sometimes aggregated and sometimes separated, is a proof that they, I mean the substances, require someone who aggregates those that are aggregated and separates those that are separated. Thus this is, as they say, as proof of the world's being created

2. Cf. n. 11 of the preceding chapter.

in time. It is already clear to you that the author of this method has used the first of their premises and all that necessarily follows from it.

THE FOURTH METHOD

They say: the world in its entirety is composed of substances and accidents. Now no substance can be exempt from one or several accidents. And all accidents are produced in time. Accordingly it follows necessarily that the substance that serves as a substratum for them is also produced in time. For everything that is conjoined with accidents and cannot be exempt from them is produced in time. Accordingly the world in its entirety is produced in time. If, however, someone says: perhaps substance is not produced in time, whereas accidents are conjoined successively — one following the other to infinity — with the atoms; they say: it would necessarily follow that there is an infinite number of things produced in time. Now this they have assumed to be absurd. This is, according to them, the most intelligent and the best of the methods in question, so that many think it is a demonstration. Now in this method three premises are assumed, which are required for an object that cannot be hidden from those engaged in speculation. One of these premises is that anything that is infinite through succession is impossible. The second | is that all accidents come into being in time. Now our adversary who maintains the eternity of the world contradicts us with regard to one accident — namely, circular movement. For Aristotle considers that circular movement is not subject to generation and corruption. Because of this, the thing that is endowed with this motion is, in his opinion, not subject to generation and corruption. It is accordingly useless for us to establish the coming-into-being in time of the other accidents with regard to whose coming-into-being in time our adversary does not contradict us, maintaining that they succeed one another in rotation supervening on something that is not produced in time. Similarly he maintains with respect to the above-mentioned accident alone, that is, the circular movement — I mean the movement of the heavenly sphere — that it is not produced in time and that it does not belong to any of the species of the accidents produced in time. Accordingly this accident is the only one that has to be investigated and the production of which in time has to be made clear. The third of the premises assumed by the author of this method is that there is no sensible being except substances and accidents, I mean to say the atoms and such of their accidents as he believes in. But if the body is composed of matter and form, as our adversary has demonstrated, it ought to be demonstrated that the first matter and the first form are subject to generation

12

and corruption. If this is done, the demonstration of the coming-into-being of the world in time will be true.

THE FIFTH METHOD

This is the method of particularization. And it is a method to which they accord very great preference. Its principle refers back to what I have made clear to you in regard to the tenth of their premises. For [the Mutakallim] directs his thought to the world as a whole or to any part of it he likes and says: it is admissible that this should be endowed with | the shape, size, and accidents it has and that it should be in the time and place in which it exists; and it is also admissible that it should be bigger or smaller, endowed with another shape or with those other accidents, or that it should exist prior to or after the time in which it exists or in another place than that in which it is found. Accordingly its particularization in respect of a certain shape or a certain size or place or accident and a particular time and therewithal the admissibility of all this being different, is a proof of the existence of someone who particularizes, who has freedom of choice, and who has willed one of two admissible possibilities. Now the fact that the world as a whole or any part of it requires someone who particularizes is a proof of its being created in time. For there is no difference between your saying someone who particularizes or who makes or who creates or who brings into existence or who creates in time or who purposes the universe — all these terms being intended to signify one single notion. They ramify this method into very many subdivisions of a general or a particular nature. Thus they say: the earth's being under the water is not more appropriate than its being above the water. Who therefore has particularized that place for it? And the sun's being circular is not more appropriate than its being square or triangular, as all shapes bear the same relation to the bodies endowed with shapes. Who therefore has particularized the sun in respect of the shape it has? They consider in a similar way all the particulars[3] of the world as a whole, so that when they see flowers of different colors they marvel, and this proof becomes even firmer for them. They say: this is the same earth and the same water; wherefore is this flower yellow and that one red? Can this be except through the agency of someone who particularizes? And this someone who particularizes is the deity. Thus the world as a whole requires someone to particularize it as a whole and each of its parts by means

3. The Arabic word *juzʾiyyāt* used here derives from another root than the word translated as "particularization."

of one of the various admissible possibilities.[4] All this follows necessarily if the tenth premise is assumed as true. | Moreover some who believe in the eternity of the world do not contradict us with regard to particularization, as we shall make clear. To sum up: this is to my mind a most excellent method. I have, with regard to it, an opinion which you shall hear.

THE SIXTH METHOD

One of the later ones thought that he had come upon a most excellent method superior to all the methods known before. This method is concerned with the preponderance given to existence over nonexistence. He said: according to everyone, the world is possible in respect of existence; for if its existence were necessary, it would be the deity. Now we only engage in discussion with those who, on the one hand, affirm the existence of the deity and, on the other, maintain the eternity of the world. Now that which is possible is that of which it is possible that it should exist and it is equally possible that it should not exist, existence not being more appropriate to it than nonexistence. Now the fact that this thing, which is possible in respect of existence, exists in spite of the equal validity of its status as an existent[5] and of its status as a nonexistent[6] proves that there is someone who gives preponderence to its existence over its nonexistence. This is a very persuasive method and is a ramification of the method of particularization of which we have just now spoken. The author of this method has merely replaced the expression "someone who particularizes" by the expression "someone who gives preponderance," and replaced the states of an existent by the very existence of an existent.[7] He has led us into error or made an error himself with regard to the meaning of the statement: the world is possible in respect of its existence. For our adversary who believes in the eternity of the world, when he says that the world is possible in respect of existence, uses the term "possible," as we shall make clear, in another sense than that in which it is used by the Mutakallim. Furthermore, the assertion of the author of this method that the world requires someone who should give preponderance to its existence over its nonexistence is a subject of very pronounced vain fantasy. For there can be giving of preponderance and

4. In accord with some MSS, I read *jāʾizāt* and not *juzʾiyyāt*, the latter being the reading adopted by Munk, who follows certain other MSS. This second reading agrees with the Hebrew translations of Ibn Tibbon and Alḥarizi. *juzʾiyyāt* means "particulars."
5. Literally: of existence.　　6. Literally: of nonexistence.
7. Whereas according to the Fifth Method, someone who particularizes determines the states of the existents, the Sixth Method maintains that their existence or nonexistence requires someone who gives preponderance.

particularization only with respect to a particular existent that is equally receptive of two contraries or of two different things. Accordingly it can be said of it that inasmuch as | we have found it in a certain state and not in another, there is proof of the existence of an artificer possessing purpose. It is as if you said that this copper is not more suitable for the reception of the form of a pitcher than of the form of a lamp. In consequence, when we find it as a lamp or a pitcher, we know with necessity that someone who particularizes and who has a purpose purposed one of those two admissible things. Consequently it is clear that the copper exists and that two admissible things brought in relation with it are nonexistent in it before he who gives preponderance has given it. On the other hand, this notion cannot be represented in any respect of an existent thing as to which there is disagreement whether its existence, as it is, has had no limit in the past and will have no limit in the future or whether it has come to existence after nonexistence. The question — who has given the preponderance to its existence over its nonexistence? — can be asked only after it has been recognized that this existent has come to existence after nonexistence. For this is the subject concerning which there is disagreement. Now if we consider its existence and nonexistence only from the mental point of view, we come back to the identical tenth premise. For it is concerned with the consideration of imaginations and vain fantasies, not with that of existents and intellectually cognized things. For the adversary who believes in the eternity of the world is of the opinion that our imagining its nonexistence is similar to our imagining any impossible thing whatever that occurs to the imagination. The purpose is not to demolish their assertions. I have merely made it clear to you that this method — which was thought to be different from the preceding one — is not correct, for its status is identical with that of what preceded as far as the assumption of the well-known admissibility is concerned.

THE SEVENTH METHOD

One[8] of the creationists maintains that the creation of the world in time is established by what the philosophers say regarding the permanent existence of the souls. He says: if | the world is eternal, the number of the men who died in the limitless past is infinite. There would therefore be an infinite number of souls existing simultaneously. Now this is a thing of which it has been indubitably demonstrated that it is false — I mean the simultaneous existence of an infinite number of numerable things. Now

8. Or: some.

this is a wondrous method, for it makes clear a hidden matter by something even more hidden. To this, the proverb well known among the Syrians may truthfully be applied: *Your guarantee needs another guarantee*. It is as if he already possessed a demonstration of the permanence of the souls and as if he knew in what form they last and what thing it is that lasts, so that he could make use thereof for drawing inferences. Now if his intention was to force doubt upon the adversary who believes in the eternity of the world and at the same time in the permanence of the souls, this consequence would follow necessarily if the adversary would concede to him who tried to arouse the doubt that the imaginings that that individual entertains about his[9] [to wit, the adversary's] speech concerning the continued existence of the souls were well-founded. Now some of the later philosophers have resolved this doubt by saying that the souls endowed with continued existence were not bodies so that they would have place and position; and that in regard to their existence, infinity in number would be impossible for them. Now you know that regarding the things separate from matter — I mean those that are neither bodies nor forces in bodies, but intellects — there can be no thought of multiplicity of any mode whatever, except that some of them are the causes of the existence of others and that thus there is a difference among them since one is the cause and the other the effect. However, what remains of Zayd is neither the cause nor the effect of what remains of Umar. Consequently all are one in number, as Abū Bakr Ibn al-Ṣā'igh[10] and others who were drawn into speaking of these obscure matters have made clear.[11] To sum up: | premises by which other points are to be explained should not be taken over from such hidden matters, which the mind is incapable of representing to itself.

Know that whoever wishes to establish as true the coming-into-being of the world in time or to prove false its eternity by means of these methods of the kalām must necessarily use one of these two premises or both of them: these premises being the tenth, whereby I mean the doctrine of mental admissibility with a view to establishing someone who particularizes; or the eleventh premise, according to which the infinite by succession is impossible. They establish the correctness of this latter premise in various ways. One

---

9. Or: in his.
10. Abū Bakr Ibn al-Ṣā'igh Ibn Bājja (the Avempace of the Latins; d. 1138), was the founder of the Peripatetic philosophic school of Moslem Spain. His works, one of which is entitled the *Regimen of the Solitary* (*Tadbīr al-Mutawaḥḥid*), seem to have been well known to Maimonides.
11. Ibn Bājja's doctrine of the Unity of the Intellect accordingly seems to be accepted by Maimonides. Cf. Translator's Introduction.

of them consists in that he who adduces the proof directs his attention to one of the species whose individuals are subject to generation and corruption. Furthermore, he directs his attention in his mind to a time in the past. Now from the belief that the world is eternal, it follows necessarily that all the individuals of that particular species going back from a given time in the past to the preceding time are infinite in number. And similarly, all the individuals of that same species from a date posterior by one thousand years, for example, to the preceding time are likewise infinite in number. Now the latter group of individuals is greater than the former by the number of those who were born during the thousand years. Accordingly they conclude from this consideration — necessarily, as they believe — that an infinite may be greater in number than another infinite. They do the same thing also with regard to the revolutions of the heavenly sphere, from which they conclude — necessarily, as they believe — that an infinite number of revolutions may be greater than another infinite number of revolutions. They also compare the number of revolutions of one heavenly sphere with that of another and slower one, both of which numbers are infinite. They do the same also with regard to all accidents produced in time. For they count their nonexistent individuals[12] and act in imagination as if they were existent and as if they had some beginning, and thereupon they add to | the objects of fantasy or subtract from them. All these are matters of fantasy, not of existence. Abū Naṣr al-Fārābī has demolished[13] the premise in question and has laid bare what belongs to fantasy in all its various details. You will find a clear limpid exposition of his argument if you study without partisanship in his well-known book, "The Changing Beings."[14]

The foregoing are the principal methods of the Mutakallimūn in establishing the coming-into-being of the world in time. Now when, by means of these proofs, it was established to their mind that the world was produced in time, it followed of necessity that it has an artificer who has produced it in time with a purpose and by the use of will and freedom of choice. Thereupon they made clear that He is one by means of methods that we shall explain to you in the next chapter.

12. Apparently the individuals of the accidents.   13. Literally: has brained the premise.
14. This treatise has not been found. On al-Fārābī, cf. Translator's Introduction.

CHAPTER 75

I shall explain to you likewise in this chapter the proofs of the belief in unity according to the opinion of the Mutakallimūn. They say that that which is indicated by what exists as being its maker and its bringer into existence is one. Their principal methods in establishing oneness are two: the method referring to reciprocal hindering, and the method of differing from one another.

THE FIRST METHOD

Namely, the method referring to reciprocal hindering is the one preferred by the multitude [of Mutakallimūn]. Its meaning is this: he says that if the world had two gods, it would necessarily follow that a substance, which cannot be exempt from one of two contraries, could either be deprived of both contraries — which is impossible — or that two contraries could be conjoined in it at | the same time and in the same substratum — which is likewise impossible. For instance, one god wishes at present to warm one or more substances, whereas the other wishes to cool them. This would have one of two consequences: [1] They would be neither warm nor cold because the two actions hinder each other; and that is impossible, for every body must receive one of these two contraries. Or [2] the body in question would be at the same time both warm and cold. Similarly if one of the two gods would wish to move a particular body, it would be admissible that the other would wish to set it at rest. Accordingly it would necessarily follow that it would be neither in motion nor at rest, or that it would be at the same time both in motion and at rest. This kind of argumentation meant to lead to a proof is founded on the doctrine of the atoms, which is the first of their premises, and on the premise concerning the creation of accidents and on the premise according to which the privations of habitus are existent things requiring an agent to bring them into existence. For if someone should maintain that the lower matter, in which there is — according to the opinion of the philosophers — a succession of generation and corruption, is not the higher matter (I mean the substrata of the heavenly spheres), which assumption has been demonstrated; and if, furthermore, someone should affirm — according to the belief of the dualists — that there exist two gods, one of whom governs the lower matter, there being no connection between his activity and the heavenly spheres, while the other governs the spheres, there being no connection between his activity and hyle: this opinion would in no way necessitate reciprocal hindering. If, however, someone would maintain that this view implies a deficiency in each of the two gods, as either of them would not be able to act freely upon the things upon which the other acts freely, he could be given the answer: this is not a deficiency in either of them if it is impossible for him to exert an action upon the thing with which his activity has no connection. Nor is it a deficiency for an artificer to have no power over what is impossible for him, just as in our opinion — that of the community of believers in unity — it is no deficiency | in the One that He does not conjoin contraries in one substratum, and His power is not affected by this and by other similar impossibilities. As [the Mutakallimūn] became aware of the weakness of this method, in spite of their having some incentive to choose it, they adopted another method.

THE SECOND METHOD

They say: if there were two gods it would be necessary that one notion apply to both, while another notion would apply only to one and not to the other; this second notion would account for the difference between the two gods. Now this is a philosophic and demonstrative method, if it is followed step by step and if its premises are made clear. I shall make them clear when speaking of the opinions of the philosophers regarding this subject. However, this method too may not be applied in the doctrines of any of those who believe in the divine attributes. For according to him, the Eternal, may He be exalted, has several different notions subsisting in Him. The notion of knowledge is, in his opinion, different from that of power, and that of power is, in his opinion, different from that of will. And withal it would not be impossible[1] that either of the two gods should possess several notions, some of which he would have in common with the other god, while differing from the latter through possession of others.

THE THIRD METHOD

There is a further method that is in need of one of the premises of the partisans of this method. For some of them, namely, the ancients among them, believe that God wills by a will that is not something superadded to the essence of the creator, but is a will that does not subsist in a substratum. And in accordance with | this premise, which we have made clear, or rather in accordance with the conception of it, which you shall see, they maintained that there is one will that does not subsist in a substratum and cannot

1. Ibn Tibbon adds: according to that opinion.

belong to two beings. For as they say, there cannot be a single cause that necessarily effects two statuses for two different essences. As I have let you know, this amounts to the explanation of something hidden by something even more hidden. For the will they refer to cannot be represented to oneself. According to some of them it is an impossibility. As for the others who hold to this opinion, doubts in unlimited numbers arise regarding it. And yet they have recourse to it as being a proof of unity.

THE FOURTH METHOD

They say: the existence of an act necessarily indicates an agent and does not indicate to us a number of agents. Again there is no difference between the affirmations that the deity is two or three or twenty or any other number that might occur. This is clear and manifest. If, however, you say that this proof does not prove the impossibility of multiplicity in the deity, but merely proves an ignorance of the number of the deities — it being possible that there is only one and it being possible that there are many — he would complete his demonstration by saying: there is no possibility in respect of the being of God, for it is necessary. Accordingly, the possibility of a multiplicity of gods is shown to be false. This is the way in which this prover fashioned his proof. The error in this is most clear. For in the being of Him, may He be exalted, there resides no possibility, whereas possibility resides in our knowledge of it. For what is possible in respect of knowledge is not yet possible in respect of being. Perhaps just as the Christians think that He is three, and it is not so, we think that He is one, and the matter is not so. This is clear to whoever has trained himself in the knowledge of the necessary proceeding of conclusions from their premises. |

THE FIFTH METHOD

One of the later ones thought that he had found a demonstrative method for the belief in unity, namely, the method starting from need. The explanation of it is as follows. He says: if one is sufficient for making the beings, a second one is superfluous and not required. If, however, being cannot be perfected and brought into orderly arrangement except by the two of them in conjunction, then incapacity is attached to each of them, as each of them needs the other and is in consequence not self-sufficient. Now this is merely a ramification of the method concerning reciprocal hindering. This way of arguing with a view to a proof may be criticized by means of the statement that not everyone who does not do that which it is not within his substance to do is called incapable. For we do not call a human individual weak because he cannot move one thousand hundred-weights, and we do not attribute to God, may He be exalted, incapacity because He is unable to corporify His essence or to create someone like Him or to create a square whose diagonal is equal to its side. And similarly we should not say that he is incapable because he does not create alone, for it is a necessity of their being that they should be two. This is not need but a necessity, anything different from which is an impossibility. For just as we do not say that God, may He be cherished and magnified, is incapable because He is not able — according to their opinion — to bring a body into existence other-wise than through creating atoms and aggregating them by means of accidents that He creates in them; and just as we do not call this need and incapacity because anything different from it is impossible: so the associa-tionist, for his part, maintains that it is impossible the one should act alone; this is not an incapacity in either of the two, for it belongs to their necessary being that they should be two.

One of [the Mutakallimūn] was so wearied by those tricks that he affirmed that the belief in unity was accepted in virtue of the Law. The Mutakallimūn considered this statement as very disgraceful | and despised him who made it. As for me, I am of the opinion that he among them who had made this statement was a man of a most rightly directed mind, averse to the acceptance of sophistries. Accordingly, as he did not hear in their speeches anything that was in truth a demonstration and found that his soul was not at peace with what they considered a demonstration, he said that the belief in unity was a thing accepted from the Law. For these groups of people did not leave being with any permanent nature so that arguments could be adduced from it with a view to correct proof, nor did they leave the intellect with a sound, inborn disposition by means of which correct conclusions could be drawn. All this was done on purpose so that we could assume that there is an existent of such a kind that by means of it we could demonstrate what cannot be demonstrated. Accordingly the necessary consequence was that we failed to demonstrate what can be demonstrated. No complaint can be made except to God and to the equitable among the men of intellect.

CHAPTER 76

Concerning the refutation of the doctrine of corporeality according to the doctrine of the Mutakallimūn. The methods and the argumentations of the Mutakallimūn purporting to refute the doctrine of corporeality are very feeble, even feebler than their proofs in favor of the belief in unity. For the refutation of the corporeality [of God] is, in their opinion, as it were a ramification necessarily deriving from the root of the belief in unity. They say: the body is not one. Now whoever refutes the doctrine of corporeality because a body is necessarily composed of matter and form and thus is compound — while, on the other hand, it is clear that there can be no composition in the essence of the deity — is, in my opinion, no Mutakallim. | For this proof is not founded on the roots of the Mutakallimūn, but is a correct demonstration founded on the belief in matter and form and on the representation of their notion. And this is a philosophic doctrine, which I shall mention and make clear when speaking of the demonstrations of the philosophers regarding this. In this chapter our purpose is only to mention the proofs, according to their premises and argumentations, of the Mutakallimūn concerning the refutation of corporeality.

THE FIRST METHOD

They say: if the deity is a body, there are only two possibilities with regard to the notion and true reality of divinity. Either it is constituted by all the substances[1] of that body, I mean to say every atom of them, or else it is constituted by only one substance from among the substances of that body. Now if it were constituted by one atom, what would be the utility of the rest of these particles? The existence of that body would have no meaning. If, however, every single particle[2] of that body were required for its constitution, there would be many deities and not one deity. But they have already made clear that he is one. If you consider this proof, you will find that it is built on the first and fifth of their premises.—[But what] if they were told that the body of the deity is not composed of indivisible particles? I mean to say that it is not composed of substances resembling those that, as all of you say, He creates, but is one continuous body not admitting division except in fantasy; and fantasies should not be considered. For you imagine in a similar way that the body of heaven admits of being divided

1. Cf. n. 11, chap. 73 above.   2. I.e., atom.

and split up, whereas the philosopher | maintains that this possibility of division is only due to the action of imagination and of an inference from what is manifest — that is, the bodies existing in our world — to what is hidden.

THE SECOND METHOD

Which is grand in their opinion, refers to the impossibility of resemblance. For He does not resemble any of His creatures. Now if He were a body, He would resemble bodies. They expatiate at great length on this theme and say: if we were to say that He is a body that is not like bodies, you would thereby contradict yourself. For every body is like every other body in respect of corporeality. For bodies only differ from one another in other respects; they mean by the accidents. According to them, it would moreover follow [from the corporeality of God] that He has created something like Him. This proof may be invalidated in two ways. One of them consists in someone's saying: I do not concede the denial of resemblance. What demonstration have you that it is not admissible that God should in any way resemble a thing He has created — by God! — unless you rely in this point, I mean in the denial of God's in any way resembling a created thing, upon the text of a prophetic book? In that case the denial of corporeality would be a doctrine accepted on the authority of a tradition, and not an intellectually cognized doctrine. If you say that if He resembles a thing created by Him, He has created a thing like Him, the disputant says: that thing would not be like Him in all aspects. I do not deny that there are in the deity a multiplicity of notions, so that He offers several aspects. For a believer in corporeality does not shrink from this conclusion. Another way of objecting, which is more arduous, is as follows. It is established and considered correct, among those who have philosophized and have plunged into the doctrines of philosophers, that it is | in a purely equivocal sense that the term "body" is applied both to the heavenly spheres and to the hylic bodies here.[3] For matter here[4] is not identical with matter there,[5] and the forms here[6] are not identical with the form there;[7] but the terms "matter" and "form" are likewise applied equivocally to what is here as well as to the heavenly spheres. And although the heavenly sphere undoubtedly possesses dimensions, the dimensions in themselves are not a body; but a body is a thing composed of matter and form. Now if this is said with regard to the heavenly spheres, the partisan of the doctrine of

3. Literally: these material bodies.   4. Literally: this matter.
5. Literally: that matter.   6. Literally: these forms.   7. Literally: those forms.

corporeality can all the more say it of the deity. Accordingly he would say: the deity is a body possessing dimensions; but His essence, true reality, and substance do not resemble anything that is in the bodies of the created things; and the term "body" is applied to Him and to these bodies in an equivocal sense, just as in the opinion of those who have reached true knowledge of reality, the term "being" is applied to Him and to them in an equivocal sense. The proclaimer of the doctrine of corporeality does not concede that all bodies are composed of particles[8] resembling each other. On the contrary, he says that God is the creator of all these bodies and that they differ in respect of their substance and true reality. And just as he holds that the body of dung is not identical with the body of the sphere of the sun, so he says that the body of created light—I mean the *Indwelling*—is not identical with the body of the heavenly spheres and of the stars; and that the body of the *Indwelling* or the created *Pillar of Cloud* is not identical with the body of the deity, may it be exalted, in his opinion. On the contrary, he says that this body is the perfect and noble essence, which was never composed or changed and which cannot possibly be changed. In this way the being of this body becomes permanently necessary. And by its act[9] it makes everything that is other than itself in accordance with its will and volition. Would that I knew how this feeble opinion can be controverted by means of these wondrous methods of theirs, which I have already let you know. |

THE THIRD METHOD

is this. They say: if the deity were a body, it would be finite, which is correct. If, however, it were finite, it would have a certain magnitude and a certain permanent shape, which is likewise a correct necessary consequence. Then they say: it is admissible that the deity qua body could have been of a bigger or a smaller size or of a different shape than any life or shape whatever. Accordingly its being particularized to a certain size and shape requires something that particularized it. I have heard them greatly praise this proof. It is, however, feebler than all the foregoing proofs, for it is built upon the tenth premise, with regard to which we have already made clear to what extent it is subject to doubts when applied as to the other beings, if it is assumed that they might exist in a way different from their nature. All the more do these doubts arise with regard to the deity. There is no difference between this proof and their assertion concerning the preponderance given to the existence of the world over its nonexistence;

8. I.e., atoms.   9. Literally: acts.

according to that assertion, the existence of the world proves the existence of an agent who has given preponderance to its existence over its nonexistence since it is equally possible that the world should, and that it should not, exist. If now the question should be posed to them why this does not apply to the deity, may it be exalted — and it should be said that inasmuch as it is an existent it follows necessarily that it must have a factor giving preponderance to its existence over its nonexistence — then he undoubtedly would answer by saying that this would lead to an infinite series and hence that the series must doubtlessly end with the necessarily existent in which there is no possibility[10] and who therefore does not require something that would bring him into existence. Now the selfsame answer would necessarily follow in respect of shape and size. For it may be said of all the shapes and sizes whose existence is possible[11] — in the sense that a particular shape or size has not existed and has then come into existence — | that any particular size could have been bigger or smaller than it is in fact, and a shape could have been different; hence there is necessarily a need for something that particularizes. However, the shape and size of the deity, may it be exalted above all deficiency and likening, have not been — so the partisan of the doctrine of corporeality says — nonexistent, and thereafter at a certain time have come into existence so that they would need a factor that particularizes. On the contrary, its essence with its size and shape is necessarily existent. Thus it does not need a factor that particularizes, [nor one that gives preponderance][12] to existence over nonexistence, as there is no possibility of nonexistence in it. Similarly it will not need a factor that particularizes its shape and size since their existence as they are is necessary.

Consider, therefore, you who are engaged in speculation, if you give the preference to the quest for the truth and cast aside passion, blind following of authority, and obeisance to what you are accustomed to hold great. Your soul should not be led into error by the circumstances of these men engaged in speculation, neither by what has happened to them nor by what has come from them. For they are like one who flees from torrid heat into fire. For they have abolished the nature of being and have altered the original disposition of the heavens and the earth by thinking that by means of those premises, it would be demonstrated that the world was created in time. In consequence whereof, they have not demonstrated the creation of the world in time and have destroyed for us the demonstrations of the

---

10. Or: contingency.   11. Or: contingent.
12. The words in brackets are missing in all but one of the MSS collated in Joel's edition of the Arabic text.

existence and oneness of the deity and of the negation of His corporeality. For the demonstrations, by means of which all this can be made clear, can only be taken from the permanent nature of what exists, a nature that can be seen and apprehended by the senses and the intellect.

Now as we have finished setting forth the end at which their discourse arrives, we shall start upon a presentation of the philosophic premises and of their demonstrations proving the existence and the oneness of the deity and the impossibility of its being a body; whereby we shall grant them for their benefit that the world is eternal, though we do not believe in it. After that I shall show you our own method, that to which correct speculation has conducted us in respect of the perfecting of the demonstration | regarding the three problems in question. After that I shall return and plunge together with the philosophers into the consideration of their assertion concerning the eternity of the world

with the help of the Almighty [Shaddai].

*

This First Part

OF THE GUIDE OF THE PERPLEXED

HAS BEEN COMPLETED

THE SECOND PART

of

The Guide of the Perplexed

*

In the name of the Lord, God of the World[1]

[INTRODUCTION TO THE SECOND PART]

The premises[2] needed for establishing the existence of the deity, may He be exalted, and for the demonstration that He is neither a body nor a force in a body and that He, may His name be sublime, is one, are twenty-five — all of which are demonstrated without there being a doubt as to any point concerning them. For Aristotle and the Peripatetics after him have come forward with a demonstration for every one of them. There is one premise that we will grant them, for through it the objects of our quest will be demonstrated, as I shall make clear; this premise is the eternity of the world.

1] The first premise: The existence of any infinite magnitude is impossible.

2] The second premise: The existence of magnitudes of which the number is infinite is impossible — that is, if they exist together.[3]

3] The third premise: The existence of causes and effects of which the number is infinite is impossible, even if they are not endowed with magnitude. For instance, the assumption that one particular intellect, for example, has as its cause a second intellect, and that the cause of this second intellect is a third one, and that of the third a fourth, and so on to infinity, | is likewise clearly impossible.

4] The fourth premise: Change exists in four categories: it exists in the category of substance, the changes occurring in a substance being generation and corruption. It exists in the category of quantity, namely, as growth and decrease. It exists in the category of quality, namely, as alteration. It exists in the category of place, namely, as the motion of translation. It is this change in the category of place that is more especially called motion.

1. Gen. 21:33. Cf. above, Epistle Dedicatory, n. 1.
2. No example prior to Maimonides of a list of twenty-five or twenty-six "premises" seems to be known.
3. Or: simultaneously.

5] The fifth premise: Every motion is a change and transition from potentiality to actuality.

6] The sixth premise: Of motions, some are essential and some accidental, some are violent and some are motions of a part — this being a species of accidental motion. Now essential motion is, for example, the translation of a body from one place to another. Accidental motion is, for example, when a blackness existing in this particular body is said to be translated from one place to another. Violent motion is, for example, the motion of a stone upwards through the action of something constraining it to that. Motion of a part is, for example, the motion of a nail in a ship; for when the ship is in motion, we say that the nail is likewise in motion. Similarly when any compound is in motion as a whole, its parts are likewise said to be in motion.

7] The seventh premise: Everything changeable is divisible. Hence everything movable is divisible and is necessarily a body. But everything that is indivisible is not movable; hence it will not be a body at all.

8] The eighth premise: Everything that is moved owing to accident must of necessity come to rest, inasmuch as its motion is not in virtue of its essence. Hence it cannnot be moved forever in that accidental motion.

9] | The ninth premise: Every body that moves another body moves the latter only through being itself in motion when moving the other body.

10] The tenth premise: Everything that is said to be in a body is divided into two classes: either it subsists through the body, as do the accidents, or the body subsists through it, as in the case of the natural form. Both classes are to be considered as a force in the body.

11] The eleventh premise: Some of the things that subsist through body are sometimes divided through the division of the body and hence are divisible according to accident, as for instance the colors and the other forces that are distributed through the whole of the body. In a like manner some of the things that constitute a body are not divisible in any way, as for instance the soul and the intellect.

12] The twelfth premise: Every force that is found distributed through a body is finite because the body is finite.

13] The thirteenth premise: It is impossible that one of the species of motion be continuous, except local motion, and of this only that which is circular.

14] The fourteenth premise: Local motion is the primary and the first by nature among all motions; for generation and corruption are preceded by alteration, and alteration is preceded by the approach of that which alters to that which is to be altered; and there is no growth and diminution except when they are preceded by generation and corruption.

15] The fifteenth premise: Time is an accident consequent upon motion and is necessarily attached to it. Neither of them exists without the other. Motion does not exist except in time, and time cannot be conceived by the intellect except together with motion. And all that with regard to which no motion can be found, does not fall under time.

16] The sixteenth premise: In whatsoever is not a body, | multiplicity cannot be cognized by the intellect, unless the thing in question is a force in a body, for then the multiplicity of the individual forces would subsist in virtue of the multiplicity of the matters or substances in which these forces are to be found.[4] Hence no multiplicity at all can be cognized by the intellect in the separate things, which are neither a body nor a force in a body, except when they are causes and effects.

17] The seventeenth premise: Everything that is in motion has of necessity a mover; and the mover either may be outside the moved object, as in the case of a stone moved by a hand, or the mover may be in the body in motion, as in the case of the body of a living being, for the latter is composed of a mover and of that which is moved. It is for this reason that when a living being dies and the mover—namely, the soul—is lacking from it, that which is moved—namely, the organic body—remains at the moment in its former state, except that it is not moved with that motion. However, inasmuch as the mover that exists in that which is moved is hidden and does not appear to the senses, it is thought of living

4. Literally: of their matters and substrata.

beings that they are in motion without having a mover. Everything moved that has a mover within itself is said to be moved by itself — the meaning being that the force moving that which, in the object moved, is moving according to essence, exists in the whole of that object.

18] The eighteenth premise: Everything that passes from potentiality to actuality has something other than itself that causes it to pass, and this cause is of necessity outside that thing. For if that cause were that thing and there were no obstacle to prevent this passage, the thing would not have been for a certain time in potentia but would have always been in actu. If, however, the cause of the passage from potentiality to actuality subsisted in the thing, and if there was at the same time an obstacle to it, which was subsequently removed, there is no doubt that the factor that put an end to the obstacle is the one that caused that potentiality to pass into actuality. Understand this.

19] The nineteenth premise: Everything that has a cause for its existence is only possible with regard to existence in respect to its own essence. For it exists if its causes are present. If, however, they are not present, or if they become nonexistent, or if their relation | that entails the existence of the thing in question has changed, that thing does not exist.

20] The twentieth premise: Everything that is necessarily existent in respect to its own essence has no cause for its existence in any way whatever or under any condition.

21] The twenty-first premise: Everything that is composed of two notions has necessarily that composition as the cause of its existence as it really is, and consequently is not necessarily existent in respect to its own essence, for it exists in virtue of the existence of its two parts and of their composition.

22] The twenty-second premise: Every body is necessarily composed of two things and is necessarily accompanied by accidents. The two things constituting it are its matter and its form; and the accidents accompanying it are quantity, shape, and position.

23] The twenty-third premise: It is possible for whatsoever is in potentia and in whose essence there is a certain possibility, not to exist in actu at a certain time.

24] The twenty-fourth premise: Whatsoever is something in potentia is necessarily endowed with matter, for possibility is always in matter.

25] The twenty-fifth premise: The principles of an individual compound substance are matter and form. And there is no doubt about the necessity of there being an agent, I mean to say a mover that moves the substratum so as to predispose it to receive the form. That is the proximate mover, which predisposes the matter of a certain individual. At this point it is necessary to engage in speculation with regard to motion, the mover, and the moved. However, with regard to all this, everything that it was necessary to explain has already been explained. The text of the words of Aristotle is: Matter does not move itself.[5] This therefore is the capital premise calling for an inquiry concerning the existence of the Prime Mover. |

Of the twenty-five premises that I have put before you in the form of a preface, some become manifest with very little reflection and are demonstrative premises and first intelligibles or notions approaching the latter, as may be seen in the epitome we have made of their orderly exposition. Others require a number of demonstrations and premises leading up to them. However, all of them have been given demonstrations as to which no doubt is possible. With regard to some of them, this has been done in the Book of "Akroasis"[6] and its commentaries; with regard to others, in the Book of "Metaphysics" and its commentary. I have already made it known to you that the purpose of this Treatise is not to transcribe the books of the philosophers and to explain the most remote of the premises, but to mention the proximate premises that are required for our purpose.

I shall add to the premises mentioned before, one further premise that affirms as necessary the eternity of the world. Aristotle deemed it to be correct and the most fitting to be believed. We shall grant him this premise by way of a hypothesis[7] in order that the clarification of that which we intended to make clear should be achieved. This premise, which among them

5. *Metaphysics* xii.6.1071b29–30. The quotation is accurate.
6. Aristotle's *Physics* is meant.
7. I read *taqdīr* instead of the word *taqrīr* found in the Arabic text. Graphically this emendation is very slight. It is in conformity with Ibn Tibbon's Hebrew translation.

is the twenty-sixth, [consists in Aristotle's statement] that time and move-ment are eternal, perpetual, existing in actu.[8] Hence it follows of necessity, in his opinion, that there is a body, moving with an eternal movement, existing in actu; and this is the fifth body. For this reason, he says that the heaven is not subject to generation and corruption. For according to him, movement is not subject to generation and corruption; for he says that every movement is necessarily preceded by another movement either of the same species as itself or of other species, and that what is thought with regard to living beings — namely, that their local movement is not preceded at all by another movement — is not correct. For the cause of their movement after rest goes back finally to things calling for this local movement; these things being either an alteration | of temperament necessitating a desire to seek what agrees with the living being or to flee from what disagrees with it, or an imagination, or an opinion occurring to it. Accordingly, any one of these three factors sets the living being in motion, and every one of them is necessitated by other movements. Similarly he says that in the case of everything that comes about in time, the possibility of its coming-about precedes in time its coming-about. From this there follow necessarily several points liable to validate his premise.[9] According to this premise, a finite moving object moves upon a finite distance an infinite number of times, going back over the same distance in a circle. Now this is impossible except in circular movement, as is demonstrated in the thirteenth of these premises. According to this premise, that which is infinite must necessarily exist as a succession and not simultaneously.[10]

This is the premise that Aristotle constantly wishes to establish as true. Now to me it seems that he does not affirm categorically that the arguments he puts forward in its favor constitute a demonstration. The premise in question[11] is rather, in his opinion, the most fitting and the most probable. However, his followers and the commentators of his books claim that the premise is necessary and not merely possible and that it has already been demonstrated. On the other hand, every Mutakallim desires to establish that it is impossible. They say that there can be no mental representation of the coming-about in succession of an infinite number of things occurring in time. The strength of their argument is that

8. Cf. *Physics* viii.1.251b20 ff.; *Metaphysics* xii.6.1071b5 ff.
9. Concerning the eternity of movement.   10. Or: together.
11. The Arabic pronoun for which the words, "the premise in question," are substituted in this translation, may alternatively refer to "the arguments" mentioned in the preceding sentence. This was Ibn Tibbon's opinion. However, the sentences that follow appear to prove the correctness of the translation propounded in the text.

it constitutes, in their opinion, a first intelligible. But to me it seems that the premise in question is possible — that is, neither necessary, as is affirmed by the commentators of the writings of Aristotle, nor impossible, as is claimed by the Mutakallimūn. It is not the purpose now to explain the arguments of Aristotle, or to raise our doubts concerning him, or to explain my opinion concerning the creation of the world in time. But the purpose at this point is to circumscribe the premises that we need for our | three problems; after first having set forth these premises and having agreed to take them as granted, I shall set out explaining what necessarily follows from them.

CHAPTER 1

It follows necessarily from the twenty-fifth premise that there is a mover, which has moved the matter of that which is subject to generation and corruption so that it received form. If now it is asked: what moved this proximate mover? — it follows of necessity that there exists for it another mover either of its own species or of a different species; for motion exists in four categories,[1] and sometimes these different kinds of change are called motion in a general way, as we have mentioned in the fourth premise. Now this does not go to infinity, as we have mentioned in the third premise. For we have found that every movement goes back, in the last resort, to the movement of the fifth body, and no further. It is from this movement that every mover and predisposer in the whole lower world proceeds and derives. Now the sphere moves with a movement of translation, and this is prior to all other movements, as has been mentioned in the fourteenth premise. Similarly every movement of translation goes back, in the last resort, to the movement of the sphere. It is as if you say: this stone, which was in motion, was moved by a staff; the staff was moved by a hand; the hand by tendons; the tendons by muscles; the muscles by nerves; the nerves by natural heat; and the natural heat by the form that subsists therein, this form being undoubtedly the first mover. What obliges this mover to move could be an opinion, for instance an opinion that the stone should be brought by the blow of the staff | to a hole[2] in order to stop it, so that blowing wind should not enter thereby toward the man who had this opinion.[3] Now the mover of this wind and the factor causing it to blow is the movement of the sphere. In a similar way you will find that every cause of generation and corruption goes back, in the last resort, to the movement of the sphere. Now when, in the last resort, we have gone back to this sphere, which is in motion, it follows necessarily that it must have a mover, according to what has been set forth before in the seventeenth premise. Now the mover cannot but be either in the moved or outside it, for this is a necessary division. Now if the mover is outside the sphere, it cannot but be either a body or not a body; in which latter case it should not be said to be outside the sphere, but separate from it, for what is not a

1. Literally: in the four categories. I.e., those enumerated in the fourth premise.
2. Or: a window.
3. Literally: to him (or: to it). It is practically certain that the man who moved the stone is referred to in the Arabic pronominal suffix.

body is not said to be outside a body except through an extension of the meaning of the expression. If, however, its mover is in it—I mean the mover of the sphere—it cannot but be either that the mover is a force distributed in the whole of the body of the sphere and divisible through the latter's being divided—as heat in fire—or that it is a force in the sphere that is not divisible—as are the soul and the intellect—just as has been expounded before the tenth premise. There is, accordingly, no doubt as to the mover of the sphere being one of these four: either another body outside it, or separate from it,[4] or a force distributed in it, or an indivisible force.

Now the first supposition—namely, that the mover of the sphere is another body outside the sphere—is absurd, as I shall point out. For if it is a body, it must—as has been set forth in the ninth premise—be in motion when moving another body. Now in that case, this sixth body[5] likewise must be in motion when moving another body. Accordingly it would necessarily follow that it is moved by a seventh body. This in its turn must be supposed to be in motion. Accordingly it would follow necessarily that an infinite number of bodies must exist and that only in that case is the sphere in motion. Now this is absurd, | as has been set forth before in the second premise.

The third possibility—namely, that the mover of the sphere is a force distributed in the latter—is likewise absurd, as I shall point out. For the sphere is a body and in consequence necessarily finite, as has been set forth before in the first premise. In consequence its force must be finite, as has been set forth in the twelfth premise. Hence this force must be divisible if the sphere is divided, as has been set forth in the eleventh premise. Hence it cannot move something for an infinite time, as we have supposed that it does in the twenty-sixth premise.

As for the fourth possibility—namely, that the mover of the sphere is an indivisible force subsisting in the sphere, as for example man's soul does in man—it is likewise absurd that this mover alone should be the cause for this perpetual motion, even if it is indivisible. The explanation of this lies in the fact that if this mover is the first mover of the sphere, it also must be in motion according to accident, as has been mentioned in the sixth premise.

I shall add here the explanation that follows. When, for example, the

---

4. In this case the mover is supposed to be an immaterial entity.
5. The sphere being considered as the fifth body, Maimonides calls its mover, should that turn out to be a body, the sixth body.

soul of a man, which is his form, moves him to go up from the house to an upper chamber, it is the body that is in motion according to essence, the soul being the first mover according to essence. However, the soul is in motion according to accident, for through the transporting of the body from the house to the upper chamber, the soul, which was in the house, was transported and came to be in the upper chamber. Now if the action of moving exerted by the soul would come to rest, that which was moved by it, namely, the body, also would come to rest. But then through the fact that the body would come to rest, the accidental motion, which had come to the soul, would be abolished. Now, everything that is moved according to accident must of necessity come to rest, as has been mentioned in the eighth premise. When, however, it comes to rest, that which is moved by it likewise comes to rest. It follows accordingly of necessity that the first mover in question | necessarily must have another cause subsisting outside the whole, which is composed of a mover and of a moved. When this cause, which is the beginning of movement, is present, the first mover, which subsists in this whole, moves that in it which may be moved. When, however, it is not present, that which may be moved in the whole is at rest.[6] For this reason the bodies of animals are not perpetually in motion, even though there is in every one of them an indivisible first mover. For their mover does not move them perpetually according to essence, for the factors that incite it to cause to move are matters outside it: either quest for what agrees with that particular animal, or flight from what disagrees with it, or again an imagination or a representation in the case of those animals that have representations.[7] When acted upon by these factors, the mover causes movement. When doing this, it itself is moved accidentally. And accordingly there is no doubt about its coming to rest at a certain time, as we have mentioned. If, however, the mover of the sphere were in it in this manner, it would not be able to be in motion eternally.

Accordingly, if the motion in question is perpetual and eternal, as is stated by our adversary — and this is possible, as has been mentioned in the thirteenth premise — it follows necessarily, according to this opinion,[8] that the first cause of the movement of the sphere conforms to the second

6. This appears to be the probable meaning of the phrase. However, if one keeps to the letter of the text, it would seem that that which is at rest in the circumstances under discussion is "the mover" rather than "that which may be moved." There are certain considerations that seem to favor the latter interpretation.
7. In the singular in Arabic. In the context the Arabic word may mean the faculty of representation.
8. Namely, the opinion that regards the movement of the sphere as eternal.

possibility; I mean to say that it is separate from the sphere according to what is required by the above division.[9] It accordingly has been demonstrated that it is necessary that the mover of the first sphere, if the movement of the latter is regarded as eternal and perpetual, should not at all be a body or a force in a body; in this way the mover of this sphere would have no movement, either according to essence or to accident, and would not be subject to division or to change, as has been mentioned in the seventh and the fifth of the premises. Now this is the deity, may His name be sublime; I am referring to the first cause moving the sphere. And it is absurd that there should be two or more of them because it is absurd that there should be multiplicity in the separate things, which are not bodies, except when | one of them is a cause and the other an effect, as has been mentioned in the sixteenth premise. It has also been made clear that this first cause does not fall under time because it is impossible that there should be movement with regard to it, as has been mentioned in the fifteenth premise. Accordingly this speculation has led by means of a demonstration to the knowledge that it is impossible that the sphere should move itself in an eternal motion; that the first cause to which its being set in motion is due, is not a body or a force in a body; and that this first cause is one and unchangeable because its existence is not conjoined with time. These are the three problems with regard to which the most excellent among the philosophers gave demonstrations.

A second speculation made by them. Aristotle propounded, by way of introduction, a premise that runs as follows: Supposing that there exists a thing composed of two things and that one of these two things exists separately outside this compound thing, it follows necessarily that the other thing also must exist outside the compound thing.[10] For if the existence of these two things had required that they exist only together, as do matter and natural form, one of them would not have existed in any way without the other. Accordingly, the fact that one of them exists separately is a proof for the absence of an obligatory mutual connection. Consequently the second thing, which enters into the compound thing, must necessarily exist separately. The following example for this may be adduced: if oxymel exists and honey likewise exists by itself, it follows necessarily that vinegar must exist by itself. After having explained this premise, he says: We find that many things are composed of a mover and a moved.

9. The one posing four prima facie possible hypotheses regarding the nature of the mover of the sphere.
10. I.e., the second element entering into the makeup of the compound thing.

He means to say thereby that these things move other things, and, when moving the latter, are themselves moved by other things. This is manifest with regard to all the things that have an intermediate status as far as causing to move is concerned. Now we find that there exists a thing that is moved and does not at all cause to move; this is the last of the moved things. It follows accordingly that there must exist a mover that is not moved at all; this is the first mover.[11] And inasmuch as no | motion is possible in it, it is not divisible and not a body, and it does not fall under time, as has become clear in the preceding demonstration.

A third philosophic speculation about this subject is taken over from Aristotle's argumentation, even though he sets it forth with a view to another purpose. This is how the argument is ordered. There is no doubt that there are existent things. These are the existent things that are apprehended by the senses. Now there are only three possible alternatives,[12] this being a necessary division: namely, either no existents are subject to generation and corruption, or all of them are subject to generation and corruption, or some of them are subject to generation and corruption whereas others are not. Now the first alternative is clearly absurd, for we perceive many existents that are subject to generation and corruption. The second alternative is likewise absurd, the explanation of this being as follows: if every existent falls under generation and corruption, then all the existents and every one of them have a possibility of undergoing corruption. Now it is indubitable, as you know, that what is possible with regard to a species must necessarily come about. Thus it follows necessarily that they, I mean all existents, will necessarily undergo corruption. Now if all of them have undergone corruption, it would be impossible that anything exists, for there would remain no one who would bring anything into existence. Hence it follows necessarily that there would be no existent thing at all. Now we perceive things that are existent. In fact we ourselves are existent. Hence it follows necessarily, according to this speculation that if there are, as we perceive, existents subject to generation and corruption, there must be a certain existent that is not subject to generation and corruption. Now in this existent that is not subject to generation and corruption, there is no possibility of corruption at all; rather, its existence is necessary, not possible. He also says that, with reference to this existent's

11. In this passage, Maimonides appears to be referring to one of Alexander of Aphrodisias' commentaries rather than to Aristotle himself. Cf. Translator's Introduction.
12. Literally: And the matter is not free from three divisions.

being necessary of existence, there are two possibilities: this may be either in respect to its own essence or in respect to the cause of this existent. In the latter case, | its existence and nonexistence are possible in respect to its own essence, but necessary in respect to its cause. Thus its cause would be necessary of existence, as has been mentioned in the nineteenth premise. Now it has been demonstrated that, of necessity, there can be no doubt that there is an existent that is necessary of existence in respect to its own essence. For without it, there would be no existent at all, neither one that is subject to generation and corruption, nor one that is not subject to them — if there is a thing that exists in this manner, as Aristotle states; I mean to say a thing that is not subject to generation and corruption because of its being an effect caused by a cause that is necessary of existence. This is a demonstration concerning which there can be no doubt, no refutation, and no dispute, except on the part of one who is ignorant of the method of demonstration. After this we shall say that it follows necessarily that the existence of everything that is necessary of existence with respect to its own essence can have no cause, as has been set forth in the twentieth premise; and that in anything that is necessary of existence there cannot be a multiplicity of notions, as has been mentioned in the twenty-first premise. Hence it follows necessarily that, as has been set forth in the twenty-second premise, it is not a body or a force in a body. It thus has been demonstrated in this speculation that there is an existent that is necessary of existence and is so necessarily with respect to its own essence, and that this existent has no cause for its existence and has no composition in itself, and for this reason is neither a body nor a force in a body. It is he who is the deity, may His name be sublime. Similarly it can be easily demonstrated that it is impossible that necessity of existence in respect to essence should exist in two beings. For the species, necessity of existence, is a notion that would be superadded to the essence of each one of these two supposed beings. Accordingly, none of them would be necessary of existence in virtue only of itself, but it would be necessary of existence in virtue of the notion representing the species — necessity of existence — a species subsisting both in that particular being and in another one. Now it has been made clear in a number of ways that no duality at all, nor | the existence of an equal or of a contrary, can be true with reference to the necessary of existence. The cause of all this is the latter's absolute [13] simplicity and absolute [13] perfection — leaving no residue outside its essence that pertains to the species, the necessary of existence — as well as the nonexistence in any way of a primary or

13. Literally: pure.

secondary cause[14] for it. Accordingly, nothing at all can be associated with the necessary of existence.

The fourth speculation, likewise philosophic. It is well known that we constantly see things that are in potentia and pass into actuality. Now everything that passes from potentiality into actuality has something outside itself that causes it to pass, as has been mentioned in the eighteenth premise. It is also clear that this something, which in one particular case causes to pass from potentiality to actuality, had been a cause of this passage in potentia and then only became such a cause in actu. Now the reason for its having been in potentia might lie either in an obstacle subsisting in its own right or in a relation — which had been absent before — between it and the thing it is to cause to pass from potentiality to actuality. When this relation is realized, it actually causes the thing to pass from potentiality to actuality. Now these two explanations necessarily require something that causes to pass from potentiality to actuality or a factor that puts an end to a hindrance. And the same thing must necessarily be said of the second something that causes to pass from potentiality to actuality or of the second factor that puts an end to a hindrance. And this series of causes or factors cannot continue to infinity. There is no doubt that, in the last resort, one must come to something that causes the passage from potentiality to actuality, that is perpetually existent in one and the same state, and in which there is no potentiality at all. I mean to say that in it, in its essence, there is nothing in potentia. For if there were possibility[15] in its essence, the thing in question would at some time become nonexistent, as has been mentioned in the twenty-third premise. It is further impossible that the thing in question should be endowed with matter; rather is it separate from matter, as has been mentioned in the twenty-fourth premise. Now the being that is separate from matter, in which there is no possibility whatever, but that exists in virtue of its essence, is the deity. And it has already been made clear that He is not a body and that He is one, as has been mentioned in the sixteenth premise.

All these are demonstrative methods of proving the existence of one deity, who is neither a body nor a force in a body, while believing at the same time in the eternity | of the world.

There is also a demonstrative method of refuting the belief in the

14. *al-ᶜilla wa'l-sabab*. These two terms are often synonymous, both of them meaning "cause." Sometimes, however, each may have a distinctive shade of meaning; in that case *sabab* tends to mean secondary cause.
15. In the sense of potentiality.

13

corporeality of [God] and of establishing [God's] unity. For if there were two deities it would follow necessarily that they must have one separately conceivable thing in which they participate, this being the thing in virtue of which each one of them merits being called a deity. They also must necessarily have another separately conceivable thing in virtue of which their separation came about and they became two. Now in virtue of the fact that in each of them there must be a separately conceivable thing other than the one subsisting in the other deity, each one of them must be composed of two separately conceivable things. Accordingly, as has been explained in the nineteenth premise, none of them can be a first cause or necessary of existence in respect to its own essence, but each of them must have several causes. If, however, the separately conceivable thing causing the separation between them exists in only one of them, the one in which the two separately conceivable things[16] exist, is not according to his essence, existent of necessity.

Another method with regard to the belief in unity. It has already been established as true by means of a demonstration that all that exists is like one individual whose parts are bound up with each other, and that the forces of the sphere pervade this lowly matter and fashion it. At the same time it is impossible — and this has already been established as true — that one deity should be exclusively concerned with one part of what exists, and the other deity[17] with another part; for one part is bound up with the other. According to the division of possibilities, the only hypotheses that remain open are that one deity acts during a certain time and the other during another time, or that both of them always act together so that no act is perfect unless it has been carried out by both of them together. Now the supposition that one of them acts during a certain time and the other during another time is absurd from several points of view. For if it were possible that during the time | in which one of them acts the other should act also, what could be the cause necessitating that one of them acts during that time whereas the other remains inactive? If, however, it were impossible for one of them to act during the time in which the other acts, there consequently must be another cause that necessitates that at a given time it is possible for one of them to act whereas for the other it is impossible. For there is no differentiation in time as a whole; and the substratum for the action[18] is one, and its parts are bound up with one another, as we have

16. Namely, necessity of existence and the separately conceivable thing causing separation between the two hypothetical deities.
17. Assumed to exist ex hypothesi.
18. To be accomplished by the two deities whose existence is supposed.

made clear. Furthermore, according to this supposition, each one of them would fall under time inasmuch as his work would be tied up with time. Furthermore, each one of them, at the time of his action, would have to pass from potentiality to actuality, and, in consequence, each one of them would need something that would cause him to pass from potentiality to actuality. Furthermore, possibility would subsist in the essence of each of them. If, however, they were supposed always to make together everything that is in existence, so that one of them would not act without the other, that also would be absurd, as I shall set forth. For in the case of any complex composed of parts, which cannot cause a certain act to become perfect except through the co-operation of each one of its parts, none of these parts is an agent in respect to its own essence or the first cause of the act; that first cause is the coming-together of the parts of the complex. Now it has been demonstrated that it is a necessary conclusion that what is necessary of existence can have no cause. Moreover the coming-together of the parts of the complex represents a certain act, which requires another agent, namely, one who causes the parts of the complex to come together. Now if the agent who causes the parts of the complex to come together — without which the act cannot become perfect — is one, he is indubitably the deity. If, however, this agent who causes the parts of this complex to come together is another complex, the same conclusions follow necessarily with regard to this second complex as with regard to the first. Thus there can be no doubt about ultimately reaching One who is the cause of the existence of this existent, which is one,[19] whatever the manner of this may have been: whether through creating it in time after it had been nonexistent, or because it proceeds necessarily from this One. | It has thus become clear, also according to this method, that the fact that all that exists is one, indicates to us that He who caused it to exist is one.

Another method of refuting the belief in the corporeality [of God]. As has been mentioned in the twenty-second premise, every body is a compound. Now there can be no doubt that every compound requires an agent, which is the cause of the subsistence of its form in its matter. Now it is most clear that every body is divisible and has dimensions. Accordingly, it is indubitably something to which accidents must be attached. Hence a body cannot be one, both because of its divisibility and because of its being a compound — I mean to say, because of its being two as far as statement is concerned. For every body is a certain body only because of some separately conceivable thing subsisting in it that is superadded to the fact of its being a

19. I.e., the cause of the universe.

body. In consequence, every body is necessarily provided with two separately conceivable things. Now it has been demonstrated that in the necessary of existence there is no composition in any way at all.

After having first set forth these demonstrations, I shall start to give an epitome of that method which is emphatically ours, as we have promised.

CHAPTER 2

The fifth body, namely, the sphere, cannot but be either subject to generation and corruption — in which case movement would likewise be subject to generation and corruption — or, as the adversary says, not be subject to generation and corruption. If the sphere is subject to generation and corruption, it is the deity, may His name be sublime, who brought it into existence after its having been nonexistent. This is a first intelligible, for everything that exists after having been nonexistent must have of necessity someone who has brought into existence — it being absurd that it should bring itself into existence. If, however, the sphere has not ceased and will not cease thus to be moved in a perpetual and eternal movement, it follows necessarily from the premises that have been set forth before that | the mover that causes it to move in this eternal movement is not a body or a force in a body; it is in fact the deity, may His name be sublime. Thus it has become clear to you that the existence of the deity, may He be exalted — who is the necessary of existence that has no cause and in whose existence in respect to His essence there is no possibility — is proved by cogent and certain demonstrations, regardless of whether the world has come into being in time after having been nonexistent or whether it has not come into being in time after having been nonexistent. Similarly, demonstrations prove that He is one and not a body, as we have set forth before. For the demonstration that He is one and not a body is valid, regardless of whether the world has come into being in time after having been nonexistent or not — as we have made clear by means of the third philosophic method and when refuting the belief in His corporeality and when establishing His oneness by means of philosophic methods.

Now I think it fit that I should complete the exposition of the opinions of the philosophers, that I should explain their proofs concerning the existence of separate intellects, and that I should explain the concordance of this opinion with the foundations of our Law—I refer to what the Law teaches concerning the existence of angels. I accordingly shall complete this purpose. After that I shall go back, as I have promised, to arguing with a view to proving that the world has come into existence in time. For our strongest proofs for this are valid and can be made clear only after one knows that the separate intellects exist and after one knows how proofs for their existence may be adduced. Now before all that, it is obligatory to set forth a preface, which is like a lamp illuminating the hidden features of the whole of this Treatise, both of those of its chapters that come before and of those that come after. This preface is as follows.

PREFACE

Know that my purpose in this Treatise of mine was not to compose something on natural science, or to make an epitome of notions pertaining to the divine science according to some doctrines, or to demonstrate what has been demonstrated in them.[1] Nor was my purpose in this Treatise | to give a summary and epitomized description of the disposition of the spheres, or to make known their number. For the books composed concerning these matters are adequate. If, however, they should turn out not to be adequate with regard to some subject, that which I shall say concerning that subject will not be superior to everything else that has been said about it. My purpose in this Treatise, as I have informed you in its introduction is only to elucidate the difficult points of the Law and to make manifest the true realities of its hidden meanings, which the multitude cannot be made to understand because of these matters being too high for it. Hence if you perceive that I speak about the establishment of the existence of the separate intellects and about their number, or about the number of the spheres and the causes of their motions, or about investigating the true reality of the notion of matter and form, or about the notion of divine overflow and about other such notions, you ought not to think and it ought not to occur to you that I intended only to investigate the true reality of that particular philosophic notion. For these notions have been expounded in many books, and the correctness of most of them has been demonstrated. I only intend to mention matters, the understanding of which may elucidate some difficulty of the Law; in fact, many knots will be unraveled through the knowledge of a notion of which I give an epitome. Now you know

---

1. Literally: from them. The pronoun may refer back either to the two sciences mentioned in the text or to "some doctrines."

already from the introduction of this my Treatise that it hinges on the explanation of what can be understood in the *Account of the Beginning* and the *Account of the Chariot* and the clearing-up of the difficulties attaching to prophecy and to the knowledge of the deity. Accordingly in whatever chapter you find me discoursing with a view to explaining a matter already demonstrated in natural science, or a matter demonstrated in divine science, or an opinion that has been shown to be the one fittest to be believed in, or a matter attaching to what has been explained in mathematics — know that that particular matter necessarily must be a key to the understanding of something to be found in the books of prophecy, | I mean to say of some of their parables and secrets. The reason why I mentioned, explained, and elucidated that matter would be found in the knowledge it procures us of the *Account of the Chariot* or of the *Account of the Beginning* or would be found in an explanation that it furnishes of some root regarding the notion of prophecy or would be found in the explanation of some root regarding the belief in a true opinion belonging to the beliefs of Law.

After having first set forth this preface, I shall go back to completing the exposition upon which we had started.

CHAPTER 3

Know that though the opinions held by Aristotle regarding the causes of the motion of the spheres — from which opinions he deduced the existence of separate intellects — are simple assertions for which no demonstration has been made, yet they are, of all the opinions put forward on this subject, those that are exposed to the smallest number of doubts and those that are the most suitable for being put into a coherent order, just as Alexander says in "The Principles of the All."[1] These sayings also are in harmony with many sayings of the Law and more particularly, with what is explained in the generally known *Midrashim*,[2] about whose having been composed by the *Sages* there is no doubt, as I shall explain. I therefore shall set forth his[3] opinions and his proofs, so that I may cull from them what agrees with the Law and corresponds to the sayings of the *Sages, may their memory be blessed.*

1. Cf. I 31, n. 7. Maimonides possibly refers to two passages of this work, one occurring at its beginning and the other near the end. Cf. Translator's Introduction.
2. In the text: *Midrashoth.*   3. I.e., Aristotle's.

CHAPTER 4

That the sphere is endowed with a soul is clear upon reflection. However, he who hears this may deem this a matter that is difficult to grasp or | may regard it as impossible because of his imagining that when we say, "endowed with a soul," the soul referred to is like the soul of a man, or an ass and a bull. Now this is not the meaning of that dictum. This meaning is rather that the local motion of the sphere is a proof of there indubitably being in it a principle in virtue of which it is moved. And this principle is undoubtedly and incontestably a soul. This may be explained as follows. It is absurd that the circular motion of the sphere should be similar to the rectilinear motion of the stone downwards or to the motion of the fire upwards, so that the principle of that motion[1] would be a nature and not a soul. For what is moved in natural motion is only moved by the principle subsisting in it, when the object to be moved is not in its place, and it is moved in order that it may seek to come to its place. However, when the object in question reaches its place, it comes to rest. The sphere, on the other hand, is moved in its own place in a circular motion. Now it does not follow from the fact that the sphere is likewise endowed with a soul that it should be in motion in such a way. For every being endowed with a soul moves because of a certain nature or because of a mental representation. I mean here by the expression "nature," the seeking to attain what agrees with one and the flight from what disagrees. Now it makes no difference whether the mover, in this, of the being endowed with a soul is outside that being — as in the case of an animal fleeing from the heat of the sun or betaking itself when it is thirsty to a place where there is water — or whether that mover is an imagination — for an animal is moved also through imagining what disagrees and agrees with it. Now the sphere is not set in motion with a view to fleeing from what disagrees with it or with a view to seeking to attain what agrees with it. For it moves away from the point toward which it had moved, and it moves toward every point from which it had moved away. Furthermore if the motion of the sphere were because of this,[2] it would follow necessarily that the sphere, at some time, must reach the point toward which it was moved and come to rest. For if it was moved in order to seek to attain something or in order to flee from something, and

1. I.e., the motion of the sphere.
2. I.e., if it was intended either to attain what agrees with the sphere or to avoid what disagrees with it.

it must be considered that this end can never be achieved—then consequently a motion of this kind would be in vain. In consequence this circular motion | can only come about in virtue of a certain mental representation, which determines the sphere's moving in that particular way. Now there is no mental representation without an intellect. In consequence the sphere must be endowed with an intellect. Again, not everyone who has an intellect with which he represents a certain notion to himself and who has a soul in virtue of which he is able to move, moves while representing something to himself. For mental representation alone does not necessitate motion, as has been explained in the first philosophy and as is clear. For you can find with regard to your own self that you may represent many notions to yourself and be capable of moving toward them, and yet not move toward them in any way before a desire for the notion you had represented to yourself is necessarily produced in you. Thereupon you move in order to obtain[3] what you had represented to yourself. Accordingly it likewise is clear that the soul, in virtue of which there is the motion, and the intellect, by which the object is represented to oneself, are not both of them together sufficient to account for the coming-about of such a motion until desire for the notion represented is conjoined with them. Furthermore, it follows necessarily from this that the sphere has a desire for that which it represents to itself and which is the beloved object: namely, the deity, may His name be exalted. He[4] says that it is in this manner that the deity causes the sphere to move, I mean to say through the fact that the sphere desires to come to be like that which it apprehends, which is the notion represented—a notion that is most exceedingly simple, in which there is no change and no coming-about of a new state, and from which good always overflows. This[5] is impossible for the sphere qua a body unless its activity be a circular motion and nothing else. For this is the final perfection of what is possible for a body to have as its perpetual activity. For it is the simplest of motions that a body may have; and no change occurs because of it in the essence of the body or in the overflow of good[6] effects resulting necessarily from the motion of the body.

When all this became clear to Aristotle, he started to reflect again and found that it may be proved | by demonstration that the spheres are many and that the motion of one particular sphere differs from that of

3. Or: to realize.   4. I.e., Aristotle.
5. I.e., the endeavour to achieve likeness to God.
6. The Arabic equivalent of the word "good" is employed in this passage as a noun and in the plural.

another in regard to swiftness or slowness as well as the direction of movement, although circular motion was common to all of them. According to
physical speculation, he was compelled to believe that the notion represented
to itself by one particular sphere, in consequence of which notion it accomplishes the movement[7] swiftly in one day, is not the notion represented to
itself by another sphere, which accomplishes one movement in thirty years.
Accordingly he affirmed categorically that there exist separate intellects
whose number is equal to that of the spheres, that every sphere desires
the intellect that is its principle and is the mover causing it to move according
to the movement proper to it, and that that intellect is the mover of that
sphere. Neither Aristotle nor anyone else has affirmed categorically that the
number of the intellects is ten or one hundred; but he stated that their
number was equal to that of the spheres. As it was thought in his time
that there are fifty spheres, Aristotle stated that, if that were so, there were
fifty separate intellects. For in his time there was little knowledge of
mathematics, and this science had not been brought to perfection. It
accordingly was thought that every motion requires a separate sphere.
For they did not know that many apparent movements may result from the
inclination of one sphere. Thus you might speak of the motion of a star
with respect to longitude and declination and also of its apparent motion in
the circle of the horizon as far as the places of its rising and setting are
concerned. However, this is not our subject, and we shall now go back to
that with which we were dealing.

With regard to the opinion of the later philosophers that there are
ten separate intellects, it may be explained by the fact that they counted
the globes in which there are stars as well as the all-encompassing sphere,
although in some of these globes there are several spheres. The globes are
nine according to their reckoning; namely, the one that encompasses the
universe, the sphere of the fixed stars, and the spheres of the seven | plan-
ets.[8] The tenth intellect is the Active Intellect, whose existence is indicated
by the facts that our intellects pass from potentiality to actuality and that
the forms of the existents that are subject to generation and corruption
are actualized after they have been in their matter only in potentia.
Now everything that passes from potentiality to actuality must have necessarily something that causes it to pass and that is outside it. And this cause
must belong to the species of that which it causes to pass from potentiality
to actuality. For a carpenter does not build a storehouse qua a maker,
but because there subsists in his mind the form of the storehouse. For it

7. I.e. one revolution.   8. Literally: seven stars.

is the form of the storehouse subsisting in the mind of the carpenter that caused the form of the storehouse to pass into actuality and to be realized in timber. In this way the giver of a form is indubitably a separate form, and that which brings intellect into existence is an intellect, namely, the Active Intellect. Thus the relation of the Active Intellect to the elements[9] and that which is composed of them is similar to the relation obtaining between every separate intellect particularly related to a sphere and that sphere. Furthermore the relation of the intellect in actu existing in us, which derives from an overflow of the Active Intellect and through which we apprehend the Active Intellect, is similar to that of the intellect of every sphere that exists in the latter, deriving its being in it from the overflow of a separate intellect — an intellect through which the sphere apprehends the separate intellect, makes a mental representation of the latter, desires to become like it, and in consequence moves.[10]

In this connection [Aristotle] deals further with a matter that has already been demonstrated, namely, that God, may He be magnified and held sublime, does not do things in a direct fashion. Thus He burns by means of a fire, and this fire is moved by means of the motion of the sphere, and the sphere in its turn is moved by means of a separate intellect. For the intellects are the angels, which are near to Him, by means of whom the spheres are moved. And as by reason of their being separate from matter, no multiplicity due to | a difference between their essences is at all possible with regard to them because they are not bodies, it follows necessarily that the deity, may He be exalted, has — according to him[11] — brought into existence the first intellect, who is the mover of the first sphere in the way that we have explained. Again the intellect that causes the second sphere to move has as its cause and principle the first intellect, and so on, so that the intellect that causes the sphere that is contiguous with us to move is the cause and principle of the Active Intellect. With the latter the separate intellects come to an end, just as bodies begin similarly with the highest sphere and come to an end with the elements and what is composed of them. It cannot be true that the intellect that moves the highest

9. The four elements found in the world of generation and corruption are meant.
10. The text does not make clear what is the second term of the relation of which the first term is either the intellect in actu existing in man or the one existing in each heavenly sphere. It seems probable, however, that Maimonides had in mind the relation between the human intellect in actu and the Active Intellect, on the one hand, and the relation between the intellect in actu of each sphere and the separate intellect on which that sphere depends, on the other.
11. I.e., according to Aristotle.

sphere should be identical with the necessary of existence. For it has in common with the other intellects one separately conceivable thing, namely, that represented by the act of causing bodies to move. Now every intellect is distinguished from any other intellect with respect to one separately conceivable thing. In consequence each one of the ten intellects is endowed with two separately conceivable things. Accordingly there can be no doubt that all of them have one first cause. This is the assertion and the opinion of Aristotle; and his proofs for this, in so far as they are probable, are set forth in the works of his followers. All his disquisition may be summed up as follows: All spheres are living bodies, endowed with a soul and an intellect, having a mental representation and an apprehension of the deity and also a mental representation of their own first principles. In that which exists,[12] there are separate intellects that are in no way a body. All of them overflow from God, may He be exalted, and they are the intermediaries between God and all these bodies.

I now shall explain to you in the following chapters what in our Law corresponds to these opinions and what in it differs from them. |

CHAPTER 5

As for the assertion that the spheres are living and rational, I mean to say endowed with apprehension, it is true and certain also from the point of view of the Law; they are not dead bodies similar to fire and earth — as is thought by the ignorant — but they are — as the philosophers say — living beings who obey their Lord and praise Him and extol Him greatly. Thus Scripture says: *The heavens tell of the glory of God, and so on.*[1] How very remote from mental representation of the truth are those who think that this is language appropriate to the state of the speaker. For the *terms speaking and telling*[2] are applied together in Hebrew only to a being endowed with intellect. The manifest proof of the fact that Scripture describes their state according to their essence — I mean to say the state of the spheres — not the state according to which people consider them, is the dictum:[3] *There is no speech, there are no words, neither is their voice*

---

12. Literally: in existence.
1. Ps. 19:2. The verse continues: *and the firmament speaketh of His handiwork.*
2. The verb "to speak" occurs in the second part of the verse; cf. preceding note.
3. Occurring in the same Psalm as the verse quoted earlier in this chapter.

heard.[4] It thus makes it clear and manifest that it describes the essence of the spheres as praising God and making known His wonders without speech of lip and tongue. And this is correct. For he who praises through speech only makes known what he has represented to himself. Now this very representation is the true praise, whereas the words concerning it are meant to instruct someone else or to make it clear concerning oneself that one has had the apprehension in question. Thus it says, *Commune with your own heart upon your bed, and be still, Selah,*[5] as we have explained.[6] This is a proof based on the Law that may be denied only by one who is ignorant or obstinate. As for the opinion of the *Sages* concerning this, I do not think that it requires to be explained or proved. Consider the way they arranged *the blessing of the moon*, as well as what is repeatedly stated in the prayers and the texts of the *Midrashim*[7] regarding the dicta: *And the host of heaven | worshippeth Thee,*[8] and: *When the morning stars sang together, and all the sons of God shouted for joy.*[9] Similar dicta occur frequently in what they say. Thus they say in *Bereshith Rabbah*[10] with regard to the dictum of Him, may He be exalted,[11] *And the earth was tohu*[12] *and bohu:*[13] [*It was*] *mourning* [*toha*][14] *and crying* [*boha*][14] — which means that it, I mean the earth, cried woe and howled[15] because of her evil lot. *It said, I and they were created together* — which means the earth and the heavens. [*Yet*] *those above are alive and those below dead.* They also have said explicitly that the heavens are living bodies and not dead ones like the elements. Thus it has become clear to you that what Aristotle said likewise with regard to the sphere being endowed with apprehension and mental representation corresponds to the dicta of our prophets and of the bearers of our Law, who are the *Sages, may their memory be blessed.*

Know that there is a consensus of all the philosophers to the effect that the governance of this lower world is perfected by means of the forces overflowing to it from the sphere, as we have mentioned,[16] and that the spheres apprehend and know that which they govern. This also is expounded in the letter of the *Torah*, which says:[17] *Which the Lord thy God hath*

---

4. Ps. 19:4.   5. Ps. 4:5.   6. Cf. I 50 and 64.   7. In the text: *Midrashoth.*
8. Neh. 9:6. Cf. B.T., Sanhedrin, 91b.   9. Job 38:7. Cf. B.T., Ḥullin, 91b.
10. Genesis Rabbah, II.   11. Gen. 1:2.
12. In the English Bible this word is translated: *without form.*
13. In the English Bible this word is translated: *void.*
14. An Aramaic word.   15. Or: writhed in pain.   16. Cf. I 72.
17. Deut. 4:19. The verse begins as follows: *And lest thou lift up thine eyes unto heaven, and when thou seest the sun and the moon and the stars, even all the host of heaven, thou be drawn away and worship them and serve them.* The words quoted by Maimonides follow.

allotted unto all the peoples, which means that He made the spheres intermediaries for the governance of the created beings and not with a view to
their being worshipped. It says clearly: *And to rule over the day and over
the night, and to divide, and so on.*[18] Now the meaning of *ruling* is domination
through governance; and this is a supplementary notion added to that of
light and darkness, which is the proximate cause of generation and corruption. For the meaning of light and darkness is referred to in the words:
And to divide the light from the darkness.[19] Now it is absurd to assume that
he who governs something should not know that thing which he governs,
provided that the true reality of governance, as the word is applied here,
is known. We shall speak at length about this subject elsewhere. |

CHAPTER 6

The fact that angels exist does not require that a proof deriving from the
Law be brought forward. For the *Torah* has stated this in a number of
passages. Now you should know that *Elohim* is a term applied to judges.
Thus: *The cause of both parties shall come before Elohim.*[1] For this reason
this word is applied figuratively to the angels and to the deity because of
His being a judge of the angels. Hence it says: *For the Lord your Elohim*[2] —
this being addressed to the whole of mankind; after which it says:[3] *He is the
Elohim of the Elohim* — which means, the deity of the angels — *and the
Lord of lords* — that is, the Master of the spheres and the stars, which are
the *lords* of everybody other than themselves. This is the meaning of the
verse, and not that the *Elohim and the lords*[4] belong to the human species;
for they are too lowly for that. This is so particularly in view of the fact that
the dictum, *your Elohim*, includes the whole human species, the rulers as
well as the ruled. Nor can the meaning[5] be either that He, may He be
exalted, is the master of everything that is believed to be divine — even if
it is fashioned of stone and wood. For there is no glorification and no magnification in the affirmation that the deity is the master of stone, timber,

18. Gen. 1:18. The verse refers to the sun and the moon.   19. Gen. 1:18.
  1. Exod. 22:8. *Elohim* in this verse means "judges." This is also the interpretation found
    in the English Bible's translation of this passage.
  2. Deut. 10:17.   3. In the same verse.   4. Referred to therein.
  5. Of the expression, *Elohim of the Elohim*, and perhaps also of that other expression,
    the Lord of lords.

and of a piece of cast metal. What is meant is that He, may He be exalted, is the Judge of the judges, I mean to say of the angels, and the Master of the spheres. Now a chapter making it clear for us that the angels are not bodies occurs previously in this Treatise.[6] This is also what Aristotle says. But there is a difference in the terms; for he speaks of separate intellects, and we speak of *angels*.

As for his saying that these separate intellects are also intermediaries | between God, may He be exalted, and the existents; and that it is through their intermediation that the spheres are in motion, which motion is the cause of the generation of the things subject to generation: this too is the textual teaching of all the books. For you never find therein that an act was performed by God otherwise than *through an angel*. Now you already know that the meaning of *angel* is messenger. Accordingly everyone who carries out an order is an *angel*; so that the movements of animals, even when these beings are not rational, are stated in the text of the Scripture to have been accomplished *through an angel*, if the motion was produced in accordance with the intention of the deity, who put a force in the living being that moved him according to that motion. Thus it says: *My God hath sent His angel, and hath shut the lions' mouths, and they have not hurt me.*[7] The movements of *Balaam's she-ass* are all of them brought about *through an angel*. Even the elements are in their turn called *angels*. Thus: *Who makest winds His angels, the flaming fire His ministers.*[8] It will be explained to you that *angel* is said of a messenger[9] from among men; Thus: *And Jacob sent angels.*[10] It is also said of a prophet; thus: *And the angel of the Lord came up from Gilgal to Bochim;*[11] *And He sent an angel, and brought us forth from Egypt.*[12] It is furthermore said of the separate intellects that appear to the prophets *in the vision of prophecy*. In addition it is said of the animal forces, as we shall explain later on.

Now our discourse here shall deal only with the *angels*, who are separate intellects. For our Law does not deny the fact that He, may He be exalted, governs that which exists here through the intermediation of the *angels*. Thus there is the text of the *Sages* with reference to the dictum of the *Torah: Let us make man in our image,*[13] and its dictum: *Come, let us go down,*[14] which dicta are *in the plural*. They said: *The Holy One, blessed be He, as it were, does nothing without contemplating*[15] *the host*

6. Cf. I 49.   7. Dan. 6:23.   8. Ps. 104:4.
9. *rasūl*. The word also means "prophet"; i.e., an envoy of God.
10. Gen. 32:4.   11. Judg. 2:1.   12. Num. 20:16.   13. Gen. 1:26.
14. Gen. 11:7. The verse continues: *and there confound their language.*
15. Literally: *before He has contemplated.*

[*pamalya*] *above.*[16] Marvel[17] at their saying *contemplating*, for Plato uses literally the same expression, saying that God looks at the world of the intellects | and that in consequence that which exists overflows from Him. In certain other passages, they similarly make the absolute assertion: *The Holy One, blessed be He, does nothing without consulting*[18] *the host* [*pamalya*] *above.*[19] The word *pamalya* means, in the Greek language, army. In *Bereshith Rabbah*[20] and in *Midrash Qoheleth*,[21] it is likewise said in reference to the dictum: *What they have already made.*[22] *It is not said: He has made, but: they have made.* [*That is,*] *He, as it were, and His tribunal have decided regarding each of your limbs and have put it in its position; for it is said: He hath made thee and established thee.*[23] In *Bereshith Rabbah*, they have likewise said: *Wherever it is said: And the Lord, He and His tribunal* [*are meant*].[24]

In all these texts the intention is not, as is thought by the ignorant, to assert that there is speech on the part of [God], may He be exalted, or deliberation or sight or consultation and recourse for help to the opinion of someone else. For how could the Creator seek help from that which He has created? Rather do all these texts state plainly that all this — including the various parts of that which exists and even the creation of the limbs of animals as they are — has been brought about through the intermediation of angels. For all forces are angels. How great is the blindness of ignorance and how harmful! If you told a man who is one of those who deem themselves *the Sages of Israel* that the deity sends an angel, who enters the womb of a woman and forms the fetus there, he would be pleased with this assertion and would accept it and would regard it as a manifestation of greatness and power on the part of the deity, and also of His wisdom, may He be exalted. Nevertheless he would also believe at the same time that the *angel* is a body formed of burning fire and that his size is equal to that of a third part of the whole world. He would regard all this as possible with respect to God. But if you tell him that God has placed in the sperm a formative force shaping the limbs and giving them their configuration

---

16. The Hebrew *pamalya*, deriving in the last analysis from the Latin *familia*, means servants or courtiers surrounding a dignitary. The translation "host" is intended to conform to Maimonides' explanation of *pamalya* as meaning an army. The origin of this quotation is unknown. Cf. n. 19 below for the source of a similar dictum.

17. Or: I marvel.   18. Literally: *before He has consulted.*

19. B.T., Sanhedrin, 38b; Jerusalem Talmud (hereafter cited J.T.), Sanhedrin, I.

20. Genesis Rabbah, XII.   21. Midrash Qoheleth, 2:12.

22. Eccles. 2:12. The entire verse reads: *And I turned myself to behold wisdom, and madness and folly; for what can the man make that cometh after the king? what they have already made.*

23. Deut. 32:6.   24. Genesis Rabbah, LI.

and that this force is the *angel*, or that all the forms derive from the act of the Active Intellect and that the latter is the *angel* and the *prince of the world* constantly mentioned by the *Sages*, | the man would shrink from this opinion. For he does not understand the notion of the true greatness and power that consists in the bringing into existence of forces active in a thing, forces that cannot be apprehended by any sense. The *Sages, may their memory be blessed*, have stated explicitly for the benefit of him who is a *Sage* that every force appertaining to the bodily forces is an *angel* — all the more, the forces distributed in the world — and that every force has only one particular activity proper to it and not two activities. For it is said in *Bereshith Rabbah: It has been learnt: one angel does not perform two missions, nor do two angels perform one mission.*[25] Now this is the characteristic of all forces. A circumstance that should confirm in your opinion the assertion that individual natural and psychic forces are called *angels* is their dictum figuring in a number of passages and deriving originally from *Bereshith Rabbah: Every day the Holy One, blessed be He, creates a group of angels; they sing before Him, and go away.*[26] When this dictum was criticized by a recourse to another dictum indicating that the angels are permanent — and in fact it has been explained several times that the angels are *living and existing permanently* — the answer is given that some of them are permanent and others liable to perish. And such is the truth of the matter. For the individual forces are being constantly generated and corrupted, whereas the species to which these forces belong are permanent and do not become defective. In the source referred to,[27] it is said with reference to the story of *Judah and Tamar: Rabbi Yoḥanan said: [Judah] wanted to pass by, but the Holy One, blessed be He, caused the angel put in charge of lust* — he means to say: the force of orgasm — *to present himself to him*. Thus this force too is called by him an *angel*. And thus you will find that they constantly speak of: *an angel put in charge of this or that*. For every force charged by God, may He be exalted, with some business is *an angel put in charge of that thing*. Accordingly, *Midrash Qoheleth* has the following text: *When man sleeps, his soul speaks to the angel,* | *and the angel to the cherub.*[28] Thereby they have stated plainly to him who understands and cognizes intellectually that the imaginative faculty[29]

25. Genesis Rabbah, L.
26. Genesis Rabbah, LXXVIII. Cf. also (Ekhah Rabbathi) Midrash on Lamentations, 3:23; and B.T., Ḥagigah, 14a.
27. Genesis Rabbah, LXXXV.   28. Midrash Qoheleth, 10:20.
29. The Arabic text has the word *quwwah*, which in other passages of the present chapter has been translated "force."

is likewise called an *angel* and that the intellect is called a *cherub*. How beautiful must this appear to him who knows, and how distasteful to the ignorant!

We have already spoken of the fact that every form in which an *angel* is seen, exists *in the vision of prophecy*. You will find that there are prophets who see the *angels* as if they were human individuals. Thus it is said: *And, lo, three men.*[30] Others from among them see [an angel] as if he were a man causing terror and amazement. Thus it is said: *And his countenance was like the countenance of the angel of God, very terrible.*[31] Again others from among them see [an angel] as fire. Thus: *And the angel of the Lord appeared unto him in the heart of fire.*[32] There[33] it is said: *To Abraham whose power was great,*[34] *they appeared in the likeness of men; to Lot whose power was weak,*[35] *they appeared in the likeness of angels.* This is a great prophetic secret. However, the discussion of prophecy will occur later on when it is proper. There[36] it is further said: *Before they accomplish their mission, they are called men; when they have accomplished it, they are endued with the angelic state.* Consider how clear it is in every respect that the notion of an *angel* is that of a certain act, and that every *vision of an angel* occurs only *in a vision of prophecy* and according to the state of him who apprehends.

There is then nothing in what Aristotle for his part has said about this subject that is not in agreement with the Law. However, a point on which he disagrees with us in all this is constituted by his belief that all these things are eternal and that they proceed necessarily from Him, may He be exalted, in that way. For we ourselves believe that all this has been created, and that God has created the separate intellects and has put in the sphere the force of desire toward them, and that it was He who created the intellects and the spheres and put in them the governing forces. As to this we do disagree with him. Later on you shall hear his opinion and the opinion of the true Law regarding the world's having been produced in time. |

30. Gen. 18:2.   31. Judg. 13:6.   32. Gen. 3:2.
33. I.e., in Genesis Rabbah, L.   34. Literally: *beautiful.*   35. Literally: *bad.*
36. I.e., in Genesis Rabbah, L. The passage, as quoted by Maimonides, differs slightly from the one found in the text of Genesis Rabbah known to us.

CHAPTER 7

We have explained the equivocality of the term *angel* and that it includes the intellects, the spheres, and the elements, inasmuch as all of them carry out orders.[1] Do not think, however, that the spheres or the intellects have the same rank as the other[2] corporeal forces, which are a thing of nature and do not apprehend their acts.[3] For the spheres and the intellects apprehend their acts, choose freely, and govern, but in a way that is not like free choice and our governance, which deal wholly with things that are produced anew. The *Torah* has by its letter expressed several notions that drew our attention to this. Thus the *angel* says to *Lot: For I cannot do anything, and so on;*[4] and again in order to deliver him, he says to him: *Behold, I have accepted thee concerning this thing also.*[5] Scripture also says: *Take heed of him, and hearken unto his voice; Be not rebellious against him; for he will not pardon your transgression; for My name is in him.*[6] All this indicates to you that they[7] apprehend their acts and have will and free choice with regard to the governance committed to them, just as we have will with regard to that which from the foundation of our existence has been committed to us and given over to our power. Only we sometimes do things that are more defective than other things, and our governance and our action are preceded by privations; whereas the intellects and the spheres are not like that, but always do that which is good, and only that which is good is with them, as we shall explain in several chapters; and all that they have exists always in perfection and in actu since they have come into existence. |

1. In the singular in the text.
2. Or: all the (*sāʾir*). In classical Arabic the word means "the other" or "all the other." However, in later Arabic it may mean "all."
3. In the singular in the text.
4. Gen. 19:22.   5. Gen. 19:21.   6. Exod. 23:21.
7. I.e., the spheres and the intellects.

One of the ancient opinions that are[1] widespread among the philosophers and the general run of people consists in the belief that the motion of the spheres produces very fearful and mighty sounds. Their proof for this belief consisted in their saying that when the small bodies that are with us move with a rapid motion, a great clatter and a disturbing boom are heard to proceed from them. In consequence this should be all the more the case with respect to the bodies of the sun, the moon , and the stars, having regard to their size and velocity. The entire sect of Pythagoras believes that these bodies emit pleasant sounds having — though mighty — the same proporttion to each other as that obtaining in musical melodies. And it was their task to give the reasons why we do not hear these fearful and mighty sounds. This opinion also is generally known in our religious community. Do you not see that the *Sages* describe the might of the sound produced by the sun when it every day proceeds on its way in the sphere?[2] The same affirmation with regard to the whole necessarily follows.

Aristotle, however, does not accept this[3] and makes it clear that the heavenly bodies produce no sound. You will find this statement in his book "On the Heaven"; from the passage there you will understand this. You should not find it blameworthy that the opinion of Aristotle disagrees with that of the *Sages, may their memory be blessed,* as to this point. For this opinion, I mean to say the one according to which the heavenly bodies produce sounds, is consequent upon the belief in *a fixed sphere and in stars that return.*[4] You know, on the other hand, that in these astronomical matters they preferred the opinion of *the sages of the nations of the world* to their own. For they explicitly say: *The sages of the nations of the world have vanquished.*[5] And this is correct. For everyone who argues in speculative matters does this according to the conclusions to which he was led by his speculation. Hence the conclusion whose demonstration is correct is believed. |

1. Or: were.   2. Cf. B.T., Yoma, 20b; Genesis Rabbah, VI.
3. Cf. *De Caelo* ii.9.290b12 ff.   4. B.T., Pesaḥim, 94b.   5. Cf. B.T., Pesaḥim, 94b.

We have already made it clear to you that in Aristotle's time the number of the spheres had not been accurately established and that those who in our time count nine spheres, only count as one a globe that includes several spheres, as is clear to whoever has studied the science of astronomy. For this reason you also should not regard as blameworthy this dictum of some[1] of the *Sages, may their memory be blessed:*[2] *There are two firmaments; for it is said: Behold, unto the Lord thy God belongeth the heaven, and the heaven of heavens.*[3] For he who says this counts the whole globe of the stars — I mean the spheres in which there are stars — as one globe, and again counts the globe of the all-encompassing sphere in which there is no star as the second globe. Consequently, he says: *There are two firmaments.*

Now I shall first set forth for your benefit a preface needed for the purpose that I have in view in this chapter. This preface is as follows. Know that regarding the spheres of Venus and Mercury there exists a difference of opinion among the early mathematicians about whether they are above the sun or below the sun.[4] For there is no demonstration proving to us what the position of these two spheres[5] is. The doctrine of all the ancients was that the spheres of Venus and Mercury are above the sun. Know this and keep it entirely present in your mind. Then Ptolemy came and decided in favor of the opinion that they were both below the sun, saying that the greatest likeness to a natural order would be manifested in the sun's being in the middle with three planets[6] above and three below. Then came latter-day groups of people in Andalusia[7] who became very proficient in mathematics and explained, conforming to Ptolemy's premises, that Venus and Mercury were above the sun. In fact, | Ibn Aflaḥ of Sevilla,[8] whose son I have met, has written a celebrated book about this. Thereupon the excellent philosopher Abū Bakr Ibn al-Ṣaʾigh,[9] under the guidance of one of whose pupils I have read texts, reflected on this notion and showed various ways of argumentation — transcribed by us from him — by means of

1. Or: one.   2. B.T., Ḥagigah, 12b.   3. Deut. 10:14.
4. On the theories concerned, cf. Translator's Introduction.
5. Maimonides does not use here and in the following sentence the usual astronomical term *falak* occurring in the preceding sentence, but the term *kurra* which likewise signifies "sphere" or "globe." Sometimes the term *kurra*, as used by Maimonides, comprehends several spheres.
6. Literally: stars.   7. Or: Spain. The Arabic word is *Andalus.*
8. Jābir Ibn Aflaḥ, an astonomer of the twelfth century, is meant.
9. Cf. I 74, n. 10.

which the opinion that Venus and Mercury are above the sun may be shown to be improbable. However, the argument set forth by Abū Bakr is one ✓ purporting to show that this opinion is improbable, not one purporting to disprove in entirely. Whether this matter be so or not, all the early mathematicians put Venus and Mercury above the sun. For this reason they counted five spheres:[10] namely, the sphere of the moon, which undoubtedly is contiguous with us; that of the sun, which is necessarily above it; that of the five planets; that of the fixed stars; and the all-encompassing sphere[11] in which there are no stars. Accordingly, the number of informed spheres,[12] I mean to say the spheres with forms, in which there are stars — for as is generally known from their books, the ancients called the stars forms — is four; namely, the sphere of the fixed stars, that of the five planets, that of the sun, and that of the moon; while above all of them there is one empty sphere[13] in which there is no star.

Now this number is for me a very important basis for a notion that has occurred to me and that I have not seen explicitly stated by any philosopher. I found, however, in the dicta of the philosophers and the discourse of the *Sages* indications that drew my attention to it. I shall accordingly mention them and explain the notion in the following chapter. |

CHAPTER 10

It is known and generally recognized in all the books of the philosophers speaking of governance that the governance of this lower world — I mean the world of generation and corruption — is said to be brought about through the forces overflowing from the spheres.[1] We have mentioned this several times, and you will find likewise that the *Sages* say:[2] *There is not a single herb below that has not a "mazzal"[3] in the firmament that beats upon it and tells it to grow. For it is said: Knowest thou the ordinances of*

---

10. *kurra.* Cf. n. 5, this chap.   11. *falak.* Cf. n. 5, this chap.
12. *kurra.*   13. *falak.*
1. The Arabic sentence is grammatically incorrect. It may be interpreted as saying that what is generally known is not the governance of this lower world, etc., but that all philosophers say these things about it.
2. Genesis Rabbah, X.
3. The most frequent meaning of this Hebrew word is "a constellation in the zodiac"; but as Maimonides points out in the next sentence, it may also mean "star."

the heavens? Canst thou establish the dominion thereof in the earth?[4] Now they also call a *star: mazzal.* You will find this clearly in the beginning of *Bereshith Rabbah* in the same passage. For they say: *There is a "mazzal" that completes its motion in thirty days, and there is a "mazzal" that completes its motion in thirty years.*[5] By means of this dictum[6] they have made it clear that even individuals subject to generation have forces of the stars that are specially assigned to them. And though all the forces of the sphere pervade all the existents, yet there also exists a force specially assigned to a certain species — as is the case with regard to the forces of a single body — inasmuch as all that exists is, as we have mentioned, a single individual.

The philosophers have likewise mentioned that the moon has an additional force specially assigned to the element of water. The proof for this consists in the increase of the seas and the rivers due to the increase of the moon and in their decrease due to the latter's decrease, as well as in the fact that the flow of the seas comes with the advance of the moon and its ebb with its retrogression — I mean to say with its ascending and descending in the several quarters of the sphere, as is clear and manifest to whoever has observed this. As | for the fact that the rays of the sun set in motion the element of fire, it is very manifest, as you may see from the fact that heat going together with the sun interpenetrates that which exists and that cold becomes preponderant when the sun gets farther from a place on the earth or is hidden in relation to it. This is too clear to be dwelt upon at length. In consequence, when I knew this, it occurred to me that while the four spheres[7] having stars have forces that overflow from them as a whole toward all the things subject to generation — these spheres being the causes of the latter — each sphere is also specially assigned to one of the four elements, the sphere being the principle from which the forces of that particular element exclusively derive and that in virtue of its motion causes the element to move in the motion of generation.[8] Thus the sphere of the moon moves the water, the sphere of the sun the fire, while the sphere of the other planets moves the air. It is because of the multiplicity of the motions of these planets[9] — their differences, their retrogressions, their direct progressions, and their stations — that the shapes of the air, its differences, and its rapid contractions and expansions are multiple. The

---

4. Job 38:33.   5. Genesis Rabbah, X.
6. The reference is to the first passage from Genesis Rabbah quoted in this chapter.
7. *kurra* is used, and not the more usual astronomical term *falak;* cf. preceding chap., n. 5.
8. According to Aristotelian terminology, the process of generation is a motion.
9. Or: of this sphere. Literally: of their motions.

sphere of the fixed stars moves the earth. Perhaps the earth is so sluggish in moving to receive the action being brought to bear upon it and in undergoing combinations because of the slowness of the fixed stars in their motion. [The Sages] gave an indication of the fixed stars' being specially assigned to the earth in their saying that the number of the species of plants is the same as the number of the individual stars belonging to the totality of stars.

It is likewise possible that the arrangement of the universe should be as follows. The spheres are four; the elements moved by the spheres are four; and the forces proceeding from the spheres into that which exists in general are four, as we have made clear. Similarly the causes of every motion belonging to the sphere are four: namely, the shape of the sphere — I mean to say its sphericity;[10] its soul; and its intellect through which it has conceptions, as we have explained; and the | separate intellect, which is its beloved. Understand this well. The explanation of this is as follows. Were the shape of the sphere not that particular shape, it would not be at all possible for it to be moved in a circular continuous motion. For a continuity of a motion combined with a return to the same places is only possible in circular motion. For in the case of rectilinear motion, the motion is not continuous even if the moving object should return and cross the same distance several times. For between two motions in opposite directions there is an interval of rest, as has been demonstrated in the appropriate place. Accordingly it is clear that for the continuity of a motion in which there are returns over the same distance it is necessary that the moving object should move in a circular motion. Now only an object endowed with a soul has motion. Accordingly the existence of the soul follows necessarily. There must also indubitably be something inciting to motion, namely, a conceiving and a desire for that which has been conceived, as we have mentioned. This can only come about there through an intellect, for it cannot consist in the avoidance of what disagrees with one or the seeking of what agrees with one. Thus there must indubitably be a certain being of which a conception is made and for which there is desire, as we have explained.

There are thus four causes of the motion of the sphere and four sorts of general forces proceeding from it toward us. These are, as we have explained, the force causing the generation of the minerals, the force of the vegetative soul, the force of the animal soul, and the force of the rational soul. Now if you consider the activities of these forces, you will find that

10. The Arabic term for "sphere" used in this sentence is *falak*. The term for "sphericity" derives from another root and is *kurriyya*. Cf. preceding chap., n. 5.

they are of two species. For they cause either the generation of all that is generated or the preservation of what is generated — I mean to say the preservation of its species in a permanent way and the preservation of its individuals for a certain duration. This is the meaning of "nature," which is said to be wise, having governance, caring for the bringing into existence of animals by means of an art similar to that of a craftsman, and also caring for their preservation and permanence through the bringing into existence of formative forces, which are the cause of the existence of living beings, and | nutritive forces, which are the cause of their lasting for whatever duration is possible. What is intended hereby is the divine decree[11] from which these two activities derive through the intermediary of the sphere.

This number four is wondrous and should be an object of reflection. They said in *Midrash Rabbi Tanḥuma:*[12] *How many steps were in the ladder? Four* — which refers to the dictum: *And behold a ladder set up on the earth.*[13] And in all the *Midrashim*[14] it is mentioned and repeated that *there are four camps of angels.*[15] However, in some manuscripts I have seen the text: *How many steps were in the ladder? Seven.* But all the manuscripts and all the *Midrashim*[16] agree that *the angels of God,* whom [Jacob] saw *ascending and descending* were only four and not any other number — *two ascending and two descending* — and that the four gathered together upon one step of the *ladder,* all four being in one row — namely, the two who *ascend* and the two who *descend.* They even learned from this that the breadth of the *ladder* seen *in the vision of prophecy* was equal to the dimension of the world plus one third. For the breadth of one *angel in the vision of prophecy* is equal to the dimension of one third of the world according to the dictum: *And his body was like tarshish.*[17] Accordingly the breadth of the four is equal to that of the world plus one third. In his parables, *Zechariah* — when describing that *there came out four chariots from between the two mountains, and the mountains were mountains of brass*[18] — says in interpretation of this: *these are the four airs*[19] *of the heavens which go forth after presenting themselves before the Lord of all*

---

11. Or: the divine thing.
12. The passage does not occur in the text of Midrash Tanḥuma known to us. Cf. Yalqut Reubeni, Malʾakh, 99.
13. Gen. 28:12.   14. In the text: *Midrashoth.*
15. Cf. Chapters of Rabbi Eliezer, IV; Numbers Rabbah, II.
16. In the text: *Midrashoth.*   17. Dan. 10:6.   18. Zech. 6:1.
19. *ruḥoth.* According to Maimonides, the word *ruaḥ* has as its primary signification "air." Ordinarily it is translated "wind" or "spirit."

the earth.[20] They are accordingly the cause of everything that comes to pass in time. In regard to his mentioning *brass* and likewise the dictum *burnished brass,*[21] perceive in them a certain equivocality. You shall hear an indication regarding this. As for their dictum that an *angel* is equal in breadth to a third of the world — namely, their dictum in *Bereshith Rabbah,* which reads textually: *That the angel is the third part of the world*[22] — it is | very clear. And we have explained it in our great compilation on the legalistic study of the Law.[23] For all created things are divided into three parts: the separate intellects, which are the *angels*; the second, the bodies of the spheres; the third, first matter — I mean the bodies subject to constant change, which are beneath the sphere.

In this way will he who wants to understand the prophetic riddles understand them. And he will awaken from the sleep of negligence, be saved from the sea of ignorance, and rise up toward the high ones. He, however, who is pleased to swim in the seas of his ignorance and *comes down lower and lower,*[24] has no need to weary his body and his heart. When he ceases moving, he goes down to what is lowest in nature. Understand all that has been mentioned and reflect on it.

CHAPTER 11

Know with regard to the astronomical matters mentioned that if an exclusively mathematical-minded man reads and understands them, he will think that they form a cogent demonstration that the form and number of the spheres is as stated. Now things are not like this, and this is not what is sought in the science of astronomy. Some of these matters are indeed founded on the demonstration that they are that way. Thus it has been demonstrated that the path of the sun is inclined against the equator. About this there is no doubt. But there has been no demonstration whether the sun has an eccentric sphere or an epicycle. Now the master of astronomy does not mind this, for the object of that science is to suppose as a hypothesis an arrangement[1] that renders it possible for the motion of the star to be

20. Zech. 6:5.   21. Ezek. 1:7.   22. Genesis Rabbah, X.
23. Cf. *Mishneh Torah,* Yesodei ha-Torah, II 3.   24. An allusion to Deut. 28:43.
  1. *hayʾa.* Literally: shape. The word also means "astronomy" and is used in this sense by Maimonides in the present chapter.

uniform[2] and circular with no acceleration or deceleration or change in it and to have | the inferences necessarily following from the assumption of that motion agree with what is observed. At the same time the astronomer seeks, as much as possible, to diminish motions and the number of the spheres. For if we assume, for instance, that we suppose as a hypothesis an arrangement by means of which the observations regarding the motions of one particular star can be accounted for through the assumption of three spheres,[3] and another arrangement by means of which the same observations are accounted for through the assumption of four spheres,[4] it is preferable for us to rely on the arrangement postulating the lesser number of motions. For this reason we have chosen in the case of the sun the hypothesis of eccentricity, as Ptolemy mentions, rather than that of an epicycle. In accordance with this purpose and in view of the fact that we have apprehended that the motions of all the fixed stars constitute one immutable motion in which the relative positions of these stars do not change, we are confident that all of them are situated in one sphere. Now it is not impossible that every fixed star is situated in a sphere of its own, while the motions of these stars are one and the same — all of these spheres being situated on the same poles. In that case the number of the intellects would be equal to that of the stars, as is said: *Is there any number of His armies?*[5] — he means because of their multiplicity. For the intellects, the heavenly bodies, and all forces are all together *His armies*. However, there is no doubt that their species may be numbered.

Thus even on this hypothesis, our ordering of the universe in which we counted the sphere[6] of the fixed stars as one sphere[7] — just as we have counted the five spheres[8] of the planets, in spite of the multiplicity of their spheres,[9] as one sphere[10] — would not be disarranged. For, as you have understood, our purpose is to count all the forces that we have apprehended in a general way in that which exists without troubling to give a precise account of the true reality of the intellects and the spheres. For the whole intended purpose is to show that the existents that are below the Creator, may He be exalted, | are divided into three parts: one of them being constituted by the separate intellects; the second, by the bodies of the

2. Literally: one.
3. Literally: with which the seen of the motions of this star is true in virtue of three spheres.
4. Literally: with which the selfsame is true in virtue of four spheres.
5. Job 25:3.   6. The word used is *falak*. Cf. II 9, n. 5.
7. The word used is *kurra*. Cf. II 9, n. 5.
8. *falak*.   9. *falak*.   10. *kurra*.

spheres, which bodies are substrata to permanent forms in such a way that a form subsisting in them does not go over from one substratum to another and that a substratum is immutable in its essence; and the third, by the bodies subject to generation and corruption, which have one matter in common. It is further to show that governance overflows from the deity, may He be exalted, to the intellects according to their rank; that from the benefits received by the intellects, good things and lights overflow to the bodies of the spheres; and that from the spheres — because of the greatness of the benefits they have received from their principles — forces and good things overflow to this body subject to generation and corruption.

Know that in the case of every being that causes a certain good thing to overflow from it according to this order of rank, the existence, the purpose, and the end of the being conferring the benefits, do not consist in conferring the benefits on the recipient. For pure absurdity necessarily would follow from this assumption. For the end is nobler than the things that subsist for the sake of the end. It would, however, necessarily follow from the above-mentioned assumption that the existence of what is the highest, the most perfect, and the most noble, is for the sake of what is inferior. No one who is intelligent can imagine this. The matter is rather as I shall describe it. In effect a thing that is perfect in some kind of perfection sometimes possesses this perfection within such limits that it perfects the thing itself; perfection does not, however, pass over from it to something else. Sometimes its perfection is within such limits that a residue of perfection is left over from it for something else. It is as if you said, by way of example, that there is an individual who has wealth sufficing only for his own necessities, no residue being left over from it from which someone else might receive a benefit; and that there is another individual who has enough wealth for a residue to be left over from it sufficient for the enrichment of many people, so that this one may give a measure of it to another individual through which | this second would also become rich, while a residue is left over from it that suffices for the enrichment of a third individual. The case of being is similar. For the overflow coming from Him, may He be exalted, for the bringing into being of separate intellects overflows likewise from these intellects, so that one of them brings another one into being and this continues up to the Active Intellect. With the latter, the bringing into being of separate intellects comes to an end.

Moreover a certain other act of bringing into being overflows from every separate intellect until the spheres come to an end with the sphere of the moon. After it there is the body subject to generation and corruption, I mean the first matter and what is composed of it. Furthermore, forces from every sphere enter the elements until their overflow is completed with the completion of generation and corruption.

We have already explained that all these views do not contradict anything said by our prophets and the sustainers of our Law. For our community[11] is a community that is full of knowledge and is perfect, as He, may He be exalted, has made clear through the intermediary of the Master who made us perfect, saying: *Surely, this great community is a wise and understanding people.*[12] However, when the wicked from among the ignorant[13] communities ruined our good qualities, destroyed our words of wisdom and our compilations, and caused our men of knowledge to perish, so that we again became ignorant, as we had been threatened because of our sins—for it says: *And the wisdom of their wise men shall perish, and the understanding of their prudent men shall be hid;*[14] when, furthermore, we mingled with these communities and their opinions were taken over by us, as were their morals and actions—for just as it says regarding the similarity of actions: *They mingled themselves with the communities and learned their works,*[15] it says with regard to the adoption by us of the opinions of the ignorant: *And they please themselves in the children of strangers,*[16] which is translated[17] by *Jonathan ben Uziel,* peace be on him: *And they walk according to the laws of the gentiles;* when, in consequence of all this, we grew up accustomed to the opinions of the ignorant, these philosophic views appeared to be, as it were, foreign to our Law, just as they are foreign to the opinions of the ignorant. | However, matters are not like this.

As the overflow from the deity and from the intellects has been mentioned repeatedly in our discourse, we must explain to you its true reality, I mean that of the subject that is designated as overflow. After that I shall start upon the discourse concerning the world's being produced in time.

---

11. *milla.* The word also means "nation."   12. Deut. 4:6.

13. *jāhiliyya.* The word derives from the verb *jahila* (to be ignorant), and is applied ordinarily to the pre-Islamic Arabs because of their paganism. Certainly Maimonides did not wish to suppress this shade of meaning when speaking a little further on of the Jews of his day having become *jāhiliyya.* However, the biblical verse that follows refers to their ignorance, and for this reason the translation "ignorant" was chosen, even though it does not render an essential element of the meaning. It should be borne in mind that whenever the term "ignorant" appears in this paragraph, it corresponds to *jāhiliyya* in the Arabic text.

14. Isa. 29:14.   15. Ps. 106:35.   16. Isa. 2:6.   17. Into Aramaic.

CHAPTER 12

It is clear that everything produced in time has of necessity an efficient cause that causes it to be produced after not having been existent. This proximate agent must either be a body or not a body. A body, however, does not act through being a body; rather does it accomplish a particular act through being a particular body. I mean through its form. I shall speak about this in what shall come after.

This proximate agent, which produces in time the thing that is produced in time, may itself also be produced in time. This, however, cannot go on to infinity. For of necessity there is no doubt for us that, if there is a thing produced in time, we finally must come to something eternal and not produced in time that has caused that thing to be produced in time. Accordingly the question remains why it has produced the thing at one particular moment and not before, as it itself was existent before. Now of necessity there can be no doubt that the impossibility that the act produced in time could come about before it was produced is due either to the absence of a certain relation between the agent and the object of the action — if the agent is a body — or to the absence of the requisite preparation of matter — if the agent is not a body. All these preliminary remarks are in accordance with what in natural speculation is established as an obligatory doctrine, without any attention being given at present to the question of the eternity of the world or its being produced in time. For that is not the subject of the present chapter.

It has been made clear in natural science that every | body that acts in some manner upon another body does this only through encountering it or through encountering something that encounters it, if this agent acts through intermediaries. For instance, this particular body, which at present has grown hot, was heated either because a body of fire had encountered it or because fire had heated the air and the air surrounding that particular body had heated it; thus the proximate agent that has heated that particular body is the hot air. Even a magnet exerts an attraction upon iron at a distance through a force, spreading out from it in the air, which encounters the iron. For this reason this particular fire does not exert an attraction at every distance, whatever that may be, but only at a distance in which the air between it and the thing heated undergoes a change through the instrumentality of the force of the fire. If, however, the air heated by that fire[1] stops short and does not reach a candle, the latter is not melted by the heat. This is the case also with regard to what attracts. Now something that was not hot and then grew hot must necessarily be provided with a cause produced in time that caused it to be heated. This might be either a fire produced in time or one that had been at a certain distance from that particular object. In that case that distance was subsequently changed; and consequently a relation between the fire and the heated object, which had been nonexistent, was produced in time. Similarly we shall find that the causes of everything that, within that which exists, is produced in time is the mixture of the elements, which are bodies acting upon one another and acted upon by one another. I mean to say that the cause of the production of that which is produced in time is the nearness of a body to a body or the remoteness of a body from a body. As for the things produced in time that we find are not consequent upon the mixture of the elements, namely all the forms, they also must indubitably have an agent — I mean the giver of the form, which giver is not a body. For the agent that produces the form is another form, which is not in matter, as | has been explained in various passages in which this explanation was appropriate. We also have drawn attention to the proof for this in what has preceded.[2] This also can be made clear to you through the fact that every mixture of elements is capable of receiving an increase and a decrease and is produced gradually, whereas the forms are not like this, for they are not produced gradually. Accordingly there is no motion in them. They invariably are produced or pass away in no time. Accordingly they do not come about through the action of the mixture, but the mixture only prepares matter for the reception of the form, whereas the agent that produces the form is a thing that is not capable of being divided, for that which is produced by its act belongs to the same species as itself. Hence it is clear that the agent that produces a form — I mean to say its giver — must of necessity be a form, namely, one that is separate. Now it is absurd that any preference accorded by this agent, which is not a body, should be due to a certain relation.[3] For it is not a body and accordingly cannot draw near or recede or have a body draw near to or recede from it, for there is no relation of distance between a body and that which is not a body. Accordingly the cause of the nonexistence of a particular action[4] is the nonexistence of the preparation of that particular matter to receive the action of the separate

1. Literally: the heat of the air from that fire.   2. Cf. II 4.
3. A relation between the agent and what it acts upon is meant.
4. An action of the above-mentioned agent is meant.

agent. Accordingly it has become clear that the action of bodies upon one another, in respect of their forms, necessitates the preparation of the various kinds of matter with a view to the reception of the act of that which is not a body, these acts being the forms. Considering that the effects produced by the separate intellect are clear and manifest in that which exists — being everything that is produced anew, but does not result solely from the mixture of elements itself — it is necessarily known that this agent does not act either through immediate contact or at some particular distance, for it is not a body. Hence the action of the separate intellect is always designated as an overflow, being likened to a source of water that overflows in all directions and does not have one particular direction from which it draws while giving its bounty to others. For it springs forth from all directions and | constantly irrigates all the directions nearby and afar. Similarly the intellect in question may not be reached by a force coming from a certain direction and from a certain distance; nor does the force of that intellect reach that which is other than itself from one particular direction, at one particular distance, or at one particular time rather than another. For its action is constant as long as something has been prepared so that it is receptive of the permanently existing action, which has been interpreted as an overflow. Similarly with regard to the Creator, may His name be sublime; inasmuch as it had been demonstrated that He is not a body and had been established that the universe is an act of His and that He is its efficient cause — as we have explained and shall explain — it has been said that the world derives from the overflow of God and that He has caused to overflow to it everything in it that is produced in time. In the same way it is said that He caused His knowledge to overflow to the prophets. The meaning of all this is that these actions are the action of one who is not a body. And it is His action that is called overflow.

This term, I mean "overflow," is sometimes also applied in Hebrew to God, may He be exalted, with a view to likening Him to an overflowing spring of water, as we have mentioned. For nothing is more fitting as a simile to the action of one that is separate from matter than this expression, I mean "overflow." For we are not capable of finding the true reality of a term that would correspond to the true reality of the notion. For the mental representation of the action of one who is separate from matter is very difficult, in a way similar to the difficulty of the mental representation of the existence of one who is separate from matter. For just as the imagination cannot represent to itself an existent other than a body or a force in a body, the imagination cannot represent to itself an action taking place otherwise than through the immediate contact of an agent or at a certain distance and from one particular direction. Accordingly when it was established as true among some belonging to the multitude that the deity is not a body or that He does not draw near to that which He does,[5] they imagined that He gives commands to the angels and that they accomplish the actions in question through immediate contact and the drawing near of one body to another, as | we do with regard to what we act upon. They also imagined that the angels were bodies. Some[6] of them believe that He, may He be exalted, gives a command to a particular thing by means of speech similar to our speech — I mean through the instrumentality of letters and sounds — and that in consequence that thing is affected. All this follows imagination, which is also in true reality the *evil impulse*. For every deficiency of reason or character is due to the action of the imagination or consequent upon its action.

This, however, is not the object of this chapter, for its purpose is to understand the notion of overflow used with regard to God and the intellects, I mean to say the angels, because of their not being bodies. It also is said with regard to the forces of the spheres that they overflow toward that which exists. Thus the overflow of the sphere is spoken of, though its actions proceed from a body. Hence the stars act at some particular distances; I refer to their nearness to or remoteness from the center or their relation to one another.[7] From there astrology[8] comes in.

As for our remark that the books of the prophets likewise apply figuratively the notion of overflow to the action of the deity, a case in point is the dictum, *They have forsaken Me, the fountain of living waters*[9] — which refers to the overflow of life, that is, of being, which is life without any doubt. Similarly the dictum, *For with Thee is the fountain of life*,[10] signifies the overflow of being. In the same way the remaining portion of this verse, *In Thy light do we see light*, has the selfsame meaning — namely, that through the overflow of the intellect that has overflowed from Thee, we intellectually cognize, and consequently we receive correct guidance, we draw inferences, and we apprehend the intellect. Understand this. |

5. Or: "makes," or "acts."   6. Or: one.   7. I.e., with regard to position in space.
8. Literally: the judgments of the stars.   9. Jer. 2:13.   10. Ps. 36:10.

CHAPTER 13

There are three opinions of human beings, namely, of all those who believe that there is an existent deity, with regard to the eternity of the world or its production in time.

The first opinion, which is the opinion of all who believe in the Law of *Moses our Master, peace be on him,* is that the world as a whole — I mean to say, every existent other than God, may He be exalted — was brought into existence by God after having been purely and absolutely nonexistent, and that God, may He be exalted, had existed alone, and nothing else — neither an angel nor a sphere nor what subsists within the sphere. Afterwards, through His will and His volition, He brought into existence out of nothing all the beings as they are, time itself being one of the created things. For time is consequent upon motion, and motion is an accident in what is moved. Furthermore, what is moved — that is, that upon the motion of which time is consequent — is itself created in time and came to be after not having been. Accordingly one's saying: God "was" before He created the world — where the word "was" is indicative of time — and similarly all the thoughts that are carried along in the mind regarding the infinite duration of His existence before the creation of the world, are all of them due to a supposition regarding time or to an imagining of time and not due to the true reality of time. For time is indubitably an accident. According to us it is one of the created accidents, as are blackness and whiteness. And though it does not belong to the species[1] of quality, it is nevertheless, generally stated, an accident necessarily following upon motion, as is made clear to whoever has understood the discourse of Aristotle on the elucidation of time and on the true reality of its existence.

We shall expound here a notion | that, though it does not belong to the purpose that we pursue, is useful with regard to it. This notion is as follows. What caused the nature of time to be hidden from the majority of the men of knowledge so that that notion perplexed them — like Galen[2] and others — and made them wonder whether or not time had a true reality in that which exists, is the fact that time is an accident subsisting in an accident. For the accidents that have a primary existence in bodies, as for instance colors and tastes, can be understood at the outset and a mental representation can be had of their notions. But the nature of the accidents

---

1. *nawᶜ* in Arabic. One would have expected a term signifying genus or category.
2. Galen's views on time are known from various quotations.

14

whose substrata are other accidents, as for instance the glint of a color and the curve and circularity of a line, is most hidden — more particularly if, in addition, the accident that serves as a substratum has no permanent state, but passes from one state to another. For in consequence the matter becomes even more hidden. In time both characteristics are conjoined. For it is an accident concomitant with motion, the latter being an accident in that which is moved. Moreover, motion has not the status of blackness and whiteness, which constitute a permanent state. For the true reality and substance of motion consist in its not remaining in the same state even for the duration of the twinkling of an eye. This accordingly is what has rendered it necessary for the nature of time to be hidden. The purpose however is that, according to us, time is a created and generated thing as are the other accidents and the substances serving as substrata to these accidents. Hence God's bringing the world into existence does not have a temporal beginning, for time is one of the created things. Consider this matter thoroughly. For thus you will not be necessarily attached to objections from which there is no escape for him who does not know it. For if you affirm as true the existence of time prior to the world, you are necessarily bound to believe in the eternity [of the world]. For time is an accident which necessarily must have a substratum. Accordingly it follows necessarily that there existed some thing prior to the existence of this world existing now. But this notion must be avoided.

This | is one of the opinions.[3] And it is undoubtedly a basis of the Law of *Moses our Master*, peace be on him. And it is second to the basis that is the belief in the unity [of God]. Nothing other than this should come to your mind. It was *Abraham our Father, peace be on him*, who began to proclaim in public this opinion to which speculation had led him. For this reason, he made his proclamation *in the Name of the Lord, God of the world;*[4] he had also explicitly stated this opinion in saying: *Maker of heaven and earth.*[5]

The second opinion is that of all the philosophers of whom we have heard reports and whose discourses we have seen. They say that it is absurd that God would bring a thing into existence out of nothing. Furthermore,

3. I.e., one of the three opinions mentioned above concerning the eternity a parte ante of the world or its production in time.

4. Gen. 21:33. This is the invocation with which Maimonides begins each of the three parts of *The Guide of the Perplexed*. As has been stated in the notes, the correct translation is "God of Eternity." However, in current Hebrew the word ᶜolam (eternity) very often means "world." This is clearly the signification that Maimonides has in mind here.

5. Gen. 14. 22.

according to them, it is likewise not possible that a thing should pass away into nothing; I mean to say that it is not possible that a certain being, endowed with matter and form, should be generated out of the absolute nonexistence of that matter, or that it should pass away into the absolute nonexistence of that matter. To predicate of God that He is able to do this is, according to them, like predicating of Him that He is able to bring together two contraries in one instant of time, or that He is able to create something that is like Himself, may He be exalted, or to make Himself corporeal, or to create a square whose diagonal is equal to its side, and similar impossibilities. What may be understood from their discourse is that they say that just as His not bringing impossible things into existence does not argue a lack of power on His part — since what is impossible has a firmly established nature that is not produced by an agent and that consequently cannot be changed — it likewise is not due to lack of power on His part that He is not able to bring into existence a thing out of nothing, for this belongs to the class of all the impossible things. Hence they believe that there exists a certain matter that is eternal as the deity is eternal; and that He does not exist without it, nor does it exist without Him. They do not believe that it has the same rank in what exists as He, may He be exalted, but that He is the cause of its existence; and that it has the same relation toward Him as, for instance, clay has toward a potter | or iron toward a smith; and that He creates in it whatever He wishes. Thus He sometimes forms out of it a heaven and an earth, and sometimes He forms out of it something else. The people holding this opinion believe that the heaven too is subject to generation and passing-away, but that it is not generated out of nothing and does not pass away into nothing. For it is generated and passes away just as the individuals that are animals are generated from existent matter and pass away into existent matter. The generation and passing-away of the heaven is thus similar to that of all the other existents that are below it.

The people belonging to this sect are in their turn divided into several sects. But it is useless to mention their various sects and opinions in this Treatise. However, the universal principle held by this sect is identical with what I have told you. This is also the belief of Plato. For you will find that Aristotle in the "Akroasis"[6] relates of him that he, I mean Plato, believed that the heaven is subject to generation and passing-away. And you likewise will find his doctrine plainly set forth in his book to Timaeus.[7] But he does not believe what we believe, as is thought by him who does not examine

6. Cf. *Physics* viii.1.251b17 ff.
7. On the Arabic interpretation of Plato's *Timaeus*, cf. Translator's Introduction.

opinions and is not precise in speculation; he [the interpreter] imagines that our opinion and his [Plato's] opinion are identical. But this is not so. For as for us, we believe that the heaven was generated out of nothing after a state of absolute nonexistence, whereas he believes that it has come into existence and has been generated from some other thing. This then is the second opinion.

The third opinion is that of Aristotle, his followers, and the commentators of his books. He asserts what also is asserted by the people belonging to the sect that has just been mentioned, namely, that something endowed with matter can by no means be brought into existence out of that which has no matter. He goes beyond this by saying that the heaven is in no way subject to generation and passing-away. His opinion on this point may be summed up as follows. He thinks that this being as a whole, such as it is, has never ceased to be and will never do so; | that the permanent thing not subject to generation and passing-away, namely, the heaven, likewise does not cease to be; that time and motion are perpetual and everlasting and not subject to generation and passing-away; and also that the thing subject to generation and passing-away, namely, that which is beneath the sphere of the moon, does not cease to be. I mean to say that its first matter is not subject in its essence to generation and passing-away, but that various forms succeed each other in it in such a way that it divests itself of one form and assumes another. He thinks furthermore that this whole higher and lower order cannot be corrupted and abolished, that no innovation can take place in it that is not according to its nature, and that no occurrence that deviates from what is analogous to it can happen in it in any way. He asserts — though he does not do so textually, but this is what his opinion comes to — that in his opinion it would be an impossibility that will should change in God or a new volition arise in Him; and that all that exists has been brought into existence, in the state in which it is at present, by God through His volition; but that it was not produced after having been in a state of nonexistence. He thinks that just as it is impossible that the deity should become nonexistent or that His essence should undergo a change, it is impossible that a volition should undergo a change in Him or a new will arise in Him. Accordingly it follows necessarily that this being as a whole has never ceased to be as it is at present and will be as it is in the future eternity.[8]

This is a summary and the truth of these opinions. They are the opinions of those according to whom the existence of the deity for this world

8. Or: the future time.

has been demonstrated. Those who have no knowledge of the existence of the deity, may He be held sublime and honored, but think that things are subject to generation and passing-away through conjunction and separation due to chance and that there is no one who governs and orders being, are Epicurus, his following, and those like him, as is related by Alexander.[9] It is useless for us to mention these sects. | For the existence of the deity has already been demonstrated, and there can be no utility in our mentioning the opinions of groups of people who built their doctrine upon a foundation the reverse of which has been demonstrated as true. Similarly it is useless for us to wish to prove as true the assertion of the people holding the second opinion, I mean that according to which the heaven is subject to generation and passing-away. For they believe in eternity; and there is, in our opinion, no difference between those who believe that heaven must of necessity be generated from a thing and pass away into a thing or the belief of Aristotle who believed that it is not subject to generation and corruption. For the purpose of every follower of the Law of *Moses and Abraham our Father* or of those who go the way of these two is to believe that there is nothing eternal in any way at all existing simultaneously with God; to believe also that the bringing into existence of a being out of nonexistence is for the deity not an impossiblity, but rather an obligation, as is deemed likewise by some[10] of the men of speculation.

After we have expounded those opinions, I shall begin to explain and summarize the proofs of Aristotle in favor of his opinion and the motive that incited him to adopt it.

CHAPTER 14

I do not need to repeat in every chapter that I compiled this Treatise for your benefit only because of my knowledge of your achievements. I do not need to set forth in every passage the text of the discourse of the philosophers, but only their intentions. I shall not write at length, but only draw your attention to the methods that they aim at, as I did for you regarding the opinions of the Mutakallimūn. I shall pay no attention to anyone who besides Aristotle has engaged in speculative discourse, for it is his opinions that ought to be considered. And if there are good grounds for refuting him or raising doubt with regard to these opinions as to some point on which

9. On this reference to Alexander of Aphrodisias, cf. Translator's Introduction. 10. Or: one.

we make a refutation or | raise doubts, these grounds will be even firmer and stronger with respect to all the others who disagreed with the fundamental principles of the Law.

I say then that Aristotle asserts that motion is not subject to generation and passing-away — he means motion in the absolute sense. For he says that if a motion is produced in time, it should be considered that everything that is produced in time is preceded by a certain motion, namely, that consisting in its passage to actuality and its being produced after it had been nonexistent. Consequently a motion exists, namely, the motion by means of which the latter motion was brought into being. Consequently the first motion must of necessity be eternal or else the series will go on to infinity. Likewise in conformity with this principle, he asserts furthermore that time is not subject to generation and passing-away. For time is consequent upon, and attached to, motion, and there is no motion except in time; and again time cannot be intellectually conceived except through motion, as has been demonstrated. This is a method of his by means of which the eternity of the world is necessarily inferred.

A second method of his: He asserts that the first matter, which is common to the four elements, is not subject to generation and passing-away. For if the first matter were subject to generation, it would have to have a matter out of which it would be generated. And it necessarily would follow that the generated matter would have to be endowed with form, for the latter is the true reality of generation. But we have assumed that the matter in question was matter not endowed with form. Now such matter necessarily must not be generated from some thing. It is consequently eternal and not liable to be destroyed. These considerations too render obligatory the eternity of this world.

A third method of his: He asserts that the matter of the heaven as a whole has no contraries, for circular motion has no contrary, as has been made clear; and there are contraries only in rectilinear motion, as has been demonstrated. He asserts further that in everything that passes away, the cause of its passing-away consists in there being contraries in it. Accordingly as there are no contraries in the sphere, it is not subject to passing-away. | Now what is not subject to passing-away is likewise not subject to generation. He thus stated several propositions in an absolute manner and explained them. These propositions are:

Everything that is subject to generation is subject to passing-away.
Everything that is subject to passing-away is subject to generation.

Everything that has not been generated will not pass away.

Everything that will not pass away has not been generated.

This too is a method that renders obligatory the eternity of the world, which he wishes to establish.

    A fourth method: He asserts that with respect to everything that is produced in time, the possibility of its being produced precedes in time the production of the thing itself. And similarly with respect to everything that changes, the possibility of its changing precedes in time the change itself. From this premise he made a necessary inference as to the perpetuity of circular motion, its having no end and no beginning. His later followers in their turn made it clear by means of this premise that the world was eternal. They said: Before the world came into being, its production in time must have been either possible or necessary or impossible. Now if it was necessary, the world could not have been nonexistent. If its production in time was impossible, it could not be true that it ever would exist. And if it was possible, what was the substratum for this possibility? For there indubitably must be an existent thing that is the substratum of this possibility and in virtue of which it is said of the thing that it is possible. This is a very power-ful method for establishing the eternity of the world. However, an intelli-gent man from among the later Mutakallimūn thought that he had solved this difficulty. He said: Possibility resides in the agent and not in the thing that is the object of action. This, however, is no reply, for there are two possibilities. For with respect to everything produced in time, the possibility of its being produced precedes in time the thing itself. And similarly in the agent that produced it, there is the possibility to pro-duce that which it has produced before it has done so. These are indubit-ably two possibilities: a possibility in the matter to become that particular thing, and a possibility in the agent to produce that particular thing. These are the most important of the methods followed by Aristotle in | establishing the eternity of the world by starting from the world itself.

    There also are methods set forth by those who came after him, methods that they derived from his philosophy and by which they established the eternity of the world by starting from the deity, may His name be sublime.

    One of them is as follows. They say that if God, may His name be sublime, has produced the world in time after its having been nonexistent, God must have been an agent in potentia before He had created the world; and after He had created it, He became an agent in actu. God had therefore passed over from potentiality to actuality. Consequently there had been in Him, may He be exalted, a certain possibility and there indubitably must have been in His case something that caused Him to pass over from potentiality into actuality. This also is a great difficulty. Every intelligent man ought to reflect concerning its solution and the disclosing of its secret.

Another method. They say: An agent acts at one time and does not act at another only because of the impediments or incentives that may supervene upon him or in him. For the impediments may render necessary the nonaccomplishment of a certain action that the agent wishes to accomplish, and on the other hand the incentives may render necessary a certain wish that the agent did not have before. Now as the Creator, may His name be sublime, has no incentives necessitating the alteration of a will, nor hindrances or impediments that supervene and cease to exist, there is no reason in respect of which He should act at one time and not act at another; but on the contrary His action exists, just as His permanence does, permanently in actu.

Another method. They say: His acts, may He be exalted, are most perfect; there is nothing in them that is a defect; there is nothing in them that is without an object or is supererogatory. This is the notion always reiterated by Aristotle,[1] who says that nature is wise and does not do anything without an object and that it does everything in the most perfect possible way. They say accordingly: It follows from this that the existent in question[2] is the most perfect existent that is and that it does not serve an end beyond it. | Consequently it is necessary that it should perpetually exist, for His wisdom is perpetual, as is His essence; or rather His essence is His wisdom, which has required the existence of this existent.

All the arguments of the believers in the eternity of the world that you may encounter are ramifications of these methods and stem from one of them.

They also say in order to prove that the opposed doctrines are disgraceful: How could the deity, may He be honored and sublime, be idle and not do a thing in any respect whatever or cause a happening to take place in the course of the perdurable pre-eternity, so that whereas He did not do a thing throughout the duration of His existence — which is eternal and unending — He inaugurated that which exists when yesterday came? For if you were to say, for instance, that God created many worlds before this one — their number being that of the mustard seeds required to fill

1. Cf., e.g., *De Caelo* i.4.271a33; *De partibus animalium* iv.13.695b18.
2. I.e., the world.

the globe of the ultimate sphere — and that each of these worlds has remained in existence a number of years equal to that of the mustard seeds
required to fill it, this, in respect to its status compared to His infinite
existence, may He be exalted, would have been as if you were to say that
God created the world yesterday. For as soon as we affirm the inauguration
of that which exists after nonexistence, there is no difference between
one's positing that this happened hundreds of thousands of years since or
at a very recent time. Accordingly this is also a way by means of which
those who believe in the eternity of the world prove the incongruity of the
opposed doctrines.

They also argue through drawing an inference from what was universally admitted in the past among all nations. For this necessitates that
this belief is natural and not conventional and that for this reason there
was a general consensus regarding it. Thus Aristotle says:[3] All men
explicitly affirm the perpetuity and permanence of the heavens. And
when they became aware that they were not subject to coming-about and
passing-away, they asserted that they were the dwelling-place of God,
may He be exalted, and of the spiritual beings — he means to say, of the
angels. They attributed the heavens to Him in order to indicate their
perpetuity. He also sets forth other points of this | kind concerning this
subject in order to buttress the opinion, which according to him speculation
has shown to be true, by means of universally admitted beliefs.

CHAPTER 15

My purpose in this chapter is to make it clear that Aristotle possesses
no demonstration for the world being eternal, as he understands this.
Moreover he is not mistaken with regard to this. I mean to say that he himself knows that he possesses no demonstration with regard to this point,
and that the arguments and the proofs that he sets forth are merely such as
occur to the mind and to which the soul inclines. Alexander[1] thinks that
they involve a lesser number of doubts. However, Aristotle cannot be

3. Cf. *De Caelo* i.3.270b5 ff. In Guthrie's translation, the passage reads as follows: "All
   men have a conception of gods, and all assign the highest place to the divine, both
   barbarians and Hellenes, as many as believe in gods, supposing, obviously, that immortal
   is closely linked with immortal. It could not, they think, be otherwise."
1. Of Aphrodisias.

supposed to have believed that these statements were demonstrations, for it was Aristotle who taught mankind the methods, the rules, and the conditions of demonstration.

What led me to speak of this is the fact that the latter-day followers of Aristotle believe that Aristotle has demonstrated the eternity of the world. Most of the people who believe themselves to philosophize follow Aristotle as an authority in this question and think that everything that he has mentioned constitutes a cogent demonstration as to which there can be no doubt. They regard it as disgraceful to disagree with him or to suppose that some concealed point or some false imagining in one of the issues has remained hidden from him. For this reason I thought that it was indicated to challenge them with regard to their opinion and to explain to them that Aristotle himself did not claim to have a demonstration in this question. Thus he says in the "Akroasis": All the physicists preceding us believe that motion is not subject to generation and passing-away, except Plato, who believes that motion is subject to generation and passing-away, and | the heaven too according to him is subject to generation and passing-away.[2] This is literally what he says. Now it is certain that if there had been cogent demonstrations with regard to this question, Aristotle would not have needed to buttress his opinion by means of the fact that the physicists who preceded him had the same belief as he. Nor would he have needed to make all the assertions he makes in that passage concerning the vilification of those[3] who disagree with him and the worthlessness of their[4] opinion. For when something has been demonstrated, the correctness of the matter is not increased and certainty regarding it is not strengthened by the consensus of all men of knowledge with regard to it. Nor could its correctness be diminished and certainty regarding it be weakened even if all the people on earth disagreed with it. You will find likewise that Aristotle in "The Heaven and the World," when embarking upon the explanation that the heavens are not subject to generation and passing-away, states:[5] Now after

---

2. *Physics* viii.1.251b15 ff. The quotation is not exact.   3. Or in the singular.
4. Or in the singular.
5. *De Caelo* i.10.279b4 ff. The two passages quoted by Maimonides read as follows in Guthrie's translation: "Having established so much, let us next decide whether [the world] has been from all time or has had a beginning, and whether it is indestructible or destructible. But first let us run over the theories of others, since to expound one theory is to raise the difficulties involved in its contrary. At the same time also the arguments which are to follow will inspire more confidence if the pleas of those who dispute them have been heard first. It will not look so much as if we are procuring judgment by default. And indeed it is arbiters, not litigants who are wanted for the obtaining of an adequate recognition of the truth." The Arabic translation of *De Caelo* can be shown to be accountable for the differences between Maimonides' quotations and the Greek text. Cf. Translator's Introduction.

this we wish also to investigate the heavens. We shall accordingly say: Do you regard them as generated from some thing, or not; are they liable to pass away or can they not at all pass away? After assuming this question to have been posed, he desired to mention the arguments of those who assert the heavens to be generated, and accordingly continues literally as follows. He says: If we do this,[6] our words will be more acceptable for, and more worthy of approval by, those who proceed correctly in speculation, and more particularly if they have first heard the arguments of those who disagree with us. For if, without mentioning the arguments of those who disagree with us, we only mention our opinion and our arguments, these[7] would appear too weak to be accepted by the listeners. It behooves him who wishes to judge according to the truth not to be hostile to those who disagree with him, but to be friendly to, and equitable toward, them — meting out the same measure in granting that their arguments were correct as he would with regard to his own arguments. This is literally the discourse of the man.

Consequently, O community of people who are engaged in speculation, after this introduction, can any blame remain attached to that man, and can anyone think after reading these words | that he had found a demonstration with regard to this question? For can anyone, much less Aristotle, imagine that the readiness to accept a thing that is demonstrated would be feebler if the arguments of those who disagree with it were not heard first? Moreover, there is the fact that he stated[8] that this doctrine[9] was an opinion and that his proofs[10] in favor of it were mere arguments.

Can Aristotle have been ignorant of the difference between mere arguments and demonstrations, as well as between opinions, which when thought about may be accepted to a greater or lesser extent, and things of demonstration? Furthermore, does one need in demonstration that rhetorical statement, which he has made by way of introduction, that one should be equitable toward the adversary in order to strengthen one's opinion? No; rather his whole purpose is to make it clear that his opinion is more correct than the opinions of those who disagree with him — that is, those who claim that philosophic speculation leads to the belief that the heavens are subject to generation and passing-away, but that they have never been

6. I.e., set forth the arguments of those who believe in the generation of the heavens.
7. Or: our opinion. 8. In the passage just quoted.
9. That of the eternity of the world.
10. Maimonides refers to the term *ḥujaj* used in the Aristotelian passage just quoted. This term does not necessarily imply an absence of cogent demonstration. It only does so if it is opposed, as it is by Maimonides, to the term *burhān* (demonstration).

nonexistent, or that they have been generated but will not pass away, and whatever other of these opinions he mentions. Now this is indubitably correct. For his opinion is nearer to correctness than the opinions of those who disagree with him in so far as inferences are made from the nature of what exists. However, we do not think so,[11] as I shall make clear. But passions get the better of all sects, even of the philosophers. Consequently the latter wish to establish as a fact that Aristotle produced a demonstration with regard to this question. Perhaps, according to their opinion, Aristotle produced a demonstration with regard to this question without being aware of having done so, so that attention was called to this only after him. As for me, I have no doubt that the opinions mentioned by Aristotle with regard to these subjects — I mean such opinions as that concerning the eternity of the world and that concerning the cause of the difference of the motions of the spheres and the ordered arrangement of the intelligences — are none of them provided with a demonstration. And Aristotle never at any time had the fantasy that what he said in this connection constituted a demonstration. On the contrary, he thought, as he says, that the gates of the ways to inferential reasoning | on these matters are closed before us and that we have at our disposition no principle pertaining to them from which to start to draw inferences. You know the text of his words, which reads as follows:[12] As for the matters concerning which we have no argument or that are too great in our opinion, it is difficult for us to say: Why is this so? For instance, when we say: Is the world eternal or not? This is literally what he says. However, you know Abū Naṣr [al-Fārābī's] interpretation of this example,[13] what he made clear with regard to it, as well as the fact that he considered disgraceful the notion that Aristotle could have doubted of the eternity of the world. He had an extreme contempt for Galen because of the latter's saying that this was an obscure question with regard to which no demonstration is known. As Abū Naṣr holds, it is clear and manifest, being proved by demonstration, that the heavens are eternal whereas that which is within them is subject to generation and passing-away.

To sum up: Nothing in the methods that we have set forth in this chapter is capable either of establishing an opinion as correct or of proving it false or of arousing doubts with regard to it. And we have advanced the

11. The meaning may be either that Maimonides does not agree with Aristotle's doctrine regarding the eternity of the world or that he does not think that in this matter "inferences from the nature of what exists" should be used as demonstrative proofs.
12. *Topica* i.11.104b15 ff. The quotation is by and large accurate.
13. The passage of al-Fārābī to which reference is made has not yet been identified.

things we have only because we know that the majority of those who consider themselves as perspicacious, even though they have no under-standing of anything in the sciences, decide simply that the world is eternal through acceptance of the authority of men celebrated for their science who affirm its eternity, whereas they reject the discourse of all the prophets, because their discourse[14] does not use the method of scientific instruction, but that of imparting reports coming from God. Only a few favored by the intellect have been guided aright through this second method. As for what we desire in regard to the subject of the creation of the world according to the opinion of our Law, I shall speak of it in chapters that will follow. |

CHAPTER 16

This is a chapter in which I shall explain to you what I believe with regard to this question. After that I shall give proofs for what we desire to maintain. I say then with regard to all that is affirmed by those Mutakal-limūn who think that they have demonstrated the newness of the world, that I approve of nothing in those proofs and that I do not deceive myself by designating methods productive of errors as demonstrations. If a man claims that he sets out to demonstrate a certain point by means of sophisti-cal arguments, he does not, in my opinion, strengthen assent to the point he intends to prove, but rather weakens it and opens the way for attacks against it. For when it becomes clear that those proofs are not valid, the soul weakens in its assent to what is being proved. It is preferable that a point for which there is no demonstration remain a problem or that one of the two contradictory propositions simply be accepted. I have already set forth for your benefit the methods of the Mutakallimūn in establishing the newness of the world, and I have drawn your attention to the points with regard to which they may be attacked. Similarly all that Aristotle and his followers have set forth in the way of proof of the eternity of the world does not constitute in my opinion a cogent demonstration, but rather arguments subject to grave doubts, as you shall hear. What I myself desire to make clear is that the world's being created in time, according to the opinion of our Law—an opinion that I have already explained—is not

14. I.e., the prophets' discourse.

impossible and that all those philosophic proofs from which it seems that the matter is different from what we have stated, all those arguments have a certain point through which they may be invalidated and the inference drawn from them against us shown to be incorrect. Now inasmuch as this is true in my opinion and inasmuch as this | question — I mean to say that of the eternity of the world or its creation in time — becomes an open question, it should in my opinion be accepted without proof because of prophecy, which explains things to which it is not in the power of speculation to accede. For as we shall make clear, prophecy is not set at nought even in the opinion of those[1] who believe in the eternity of the world.

After I have made it clear that what we maintain is possible, I shall begin to make it prevail[2] likewise, by means of speculative proof, over any other affirmations; I refer to my making prevail the assertion of creation in time over the assertion of eternity. I shall make it clear that just as a certain disgrace attaches to us because of the belief in the creation in time, an even greater disgrace attaches to the belief in eternity. I shall now start to bring into being a method that shall render void the proofs of all those who prove by inference the eternity of the world.

CHAPTER 17

In the case of everything produced in time, which is generated after not having existed — even in those cases in which the matter of the thing was already existent and in the course of the production of the thing had merely put off one and put on another form — the nature of that particular thing after it has been produced in time, has attained its final state, and achieved stability, is different from its nature when it is being generated and is beginning to pass from potentiality to actuality. It is also different from the nature the thing had before it had moved so as to pass from potentiality to actuality. For example, the nature of the feminine seed, which is the blood in the blood vessels, is different from the nature of this seed as it exists in the state of pregnancy after it has encountered the masculine sperm and has begun to move toward the transition from potentiality to actuality. And even at the latter period, its nature is different from the nature of an animal that, after having been born, achieves perfection.

1. Or: of him.   2. Literally: that it outweighs.

No inference can be drawn in any respect from the nature of a thing after it has been generated, has attained its final state, and has achieved stability | in its most perfect state, to the state of that thing while it moved toward being generated. Nor can an inference be drawn from the state of the thing when it moves toward being generated to its state before it begins to move thus. Whenever you err in this and draw an inference from the nature of a thing that has achieved actuality to its nature when it was only in potentia, grave doubts are aroused in you. Moreover, things that must exist become impossible in your opinion, and on the other hand things that are impossible become necessary in your opinion. Assume, according to an example we have made, that a man of a most perfect natural disposition was born and that his mother died after she had suckled him for several months. And the man,[1] alone in an isolated island, took upon himself the entire upbringing of him who was born, until he grew up, became intelligent, and acquired knowledge. Now this child had never seen a woman or a female of one of the species of the other animals. Accordingly he puts a question, saying to a man who is with him: How did we come to exist, and in what way were we generated? Thereupon the man to whom the question was put replied: Every individual among us was generated in the belly of an individual belonging like us to our species, an individual who is female and has such and such a form. Every individual among us was — being small in body — within the belly, was moved and fed there, and grew up little by little — being alive — until it reached such and such limit in size. Thereupon an opening was opened up for him in the lower part of the body, from which he issued and came forth. Thereupon he does not cease growing until he becomes such as you see that we are. Now the orphaned child must of necessity put the question: Did every individual among us — when he was little, contained within a belly, but alive and moving and growing — did he eat, drink, breathe through the mouth and nose, produce excrements? He is answered: No. Thereupon he indubitably will hasten to set this down as a lie and will produce a demonstration that all these true statements are impossible, drawing inferences from | perfect beings that have achieved stability. He will say: If any individual among us were deprived of breath for the fraction of an hour, he would die and his movements would cease. How then can one conceive that an individual among us could be for months within a thick vessel surrounding him, which is within a body, and yet be alive and in motion? If one of us were to swallow a sparrow,

1. According to Ibn Tibbon, the father is meant. However, several Arabic manuscripts have "men," in the plural. This reading is adopted by Ibn Falquera and by Alḥarizi.

that sparrow would die immediately upon entering the stomach, and all the more the underbelly. Every individual among us would undoubtedly perish within a few days if he did not eat food with his mouth and drink water; how then can an individual remain alive for months without eating and drinking? Every individual among us, if he had taken food and had not given off excrements, would die in very great pain within a few days; how then could the individual in question remain for months without giving off excrements? If the belly of one of us were perforated, he would die after some days; how then can it be supposed that the navel of the fetus in question was open? How is it that he does not open his eyes, put out his palms, stretch his feet, while all the parts of his body are whole and have no defect as you thought? Similarly all the analogies[2] will be carried on in order to show that it is in no respect possible that man should be generated in that manner.

Consider this example and reflect upon it, you who are engaged in speculation, and you shall find that this is exactly our position with regard to Aristotle. For we, the community of the followers of *Moses our Master and Abraham our Father*, may peace be on them, believe that the world was generated in such and such manner and came to be in a certain state from another state and was created in a certain state, which came after another state. Aristotle, on the other hand, begins to contradict us and to bring forward against us proofs based on the nature of what exists, a nature that has attained stability, is perfect, and has achieved actuality. As for us, we declare against him that this nature, after it has achieved stability and perfection, does not resemble in anything the state it was in while in the state of being generated, and that it | was brought into existence from absolute nonexistence.[3] Now what argument from among all that he advances holds good against us? For these arguments necessarily concern only those[4] who claim that the stable nature of that which exists, gives an indication of its having been created in time. I have already made it known to you that I do not claim this.

Now I shall go back and set forth for your benefit the principles of his methods and shall show you that nothing in them of necessity concerns us in any respect, since we contend that God brought the world as a whole into existence after nonexistence[5] and formed it until it has achieved perfection as you see it. He said that the first matter is subject to neither

2. In the singular in Arabic. Or: the syllogism.
3. Other possible translations are "privation" and "nothingness."
4. Or in the singular.   5. Cf. n. 3, this chap.

generation nor passing-away and began to draw inferences in favor of this thesis from the things subject to generation and passing-away and to make clear that it was impossible that the first matter was generated. And this is correct. For we do not maintain that the first matter is generated as man is generated from the seed or that it passes away as man passes away into dust. But we maintain that God has brought it into existence from nothing and that after being brought into existence, it was as it is now — I mean everything is generated from it, and everything generated from it passes away into it; it does not exist devoid of form; generation and corruption terminate in it; it is not subject to generation as are the things generated from it, nor to passing-away as are the things that pass away into it, but is created from nothing.[6] And its Creator may, if He wishes to do so, render it entirely and absolutely nonexistent. We likewise say the same thing of motion. For he has inferred from the nature of motion that motion is not subject to generation and passing-away. And this is correct. For we maintain that after motion has come into existence with the nature characteristic of it when it has become stable, one cannot imagine that it should come into being as a whole and perish as a whole, as partial motions come into being and perish. This analogy[7] holds good with regard to everything that is attached | to the nature of motion. Similarly the assertion that circular motion has no beginning is correct. For after the spherical body endowed with circular motion has been brought into being, one cannot conceive that its motion should have a beginning. We shall make a similar assertion with regard to the possibility that must of necessity precede everything that is generated. For this is only necessary in regard to this being that is stabilized — in this being everything that is generated, is generated from some being. But in the case of a thing created from nothing, neither the senses nor the intellect point to something that must be preceded by its possibility. We make a similar assertion with regard to the thesis that there are no contraries in heaven. That thesis is correct. However, we have not claimed that the heavens have been generated as the horse and palm tree are. Nor have we claimed that their being composite renders necessary their passing-away as is the case with plants and animals because of the contraries that subsist in them.

The essential point is, as we have mentioned, that a being's state of perfection and completion furnishes no indication of the state of that being

6. The verb *abdaᶜa* (to create), of which Maimonides uses a participle, often connotes creation from nothing.
7. Or: "syllogism," and by extension "reasoning."

preceding its perfection. It involves no disgracefulness for us if someone says that the heavens were generated before the earth or the earth before the heavens or that the heavens have existed without stars or that a particular species of animals has existed without another species being in existence. For all this applies to the state of this universe when it was being generated. Similarly in the case of animals when they are being generated, the heart exists before the testicles — a circumstance that may be ocularly perceived — and the veins before the bones; and this is so in spite of the fact that after the animal has achieved perfection, no part of its body can exist in it if any part of all the others, without which the individual cannot possibly endure, does not exist.

All these assertions are needed if the text of Scripture is taken in its external sense, even though it must not be so taken, as shall be explained[8] when we shall speak of it at length. | You ought to memorize this notion. For it is a great wall that I have built around the Law, a wall that surrounds it warding off the stones of all those who project these missiles against it.

However, should Aristotle, I mean to say he who adopts his opinion, argue against us by saying: If this existent[9] provides no indication for us, how do you know that it is generated and that there has existed another nature that has generated it — we should say: This is not obligatory for us in view of what we wish to maintain. For at present we do not wish to establish as true that the world is created in time. But what we wish to establish is the possibility of its being created in time. Now this contention cannot be proved to be impossible by inferences drawn from the nature of what exists, which we do not set at nought. When the possibility of this contention has been established, as we have made clear, we shall go back and we shall make prevail the opinion asserting creation in time.

In this question[10] no way remains open to him except to show the impossibility for the world having been created in time, not by starting from the nature of being, but by starting from the judgments of the intellect with regard to the deity: these being the three methods that I have mentioned to you before.[11] By means of these methods they[12] wish to prove the eternity of the world, taking the deity as their starting point. I shall accordingly show you, in a following chapter, how doubts can be cast on these methods so that no proof whatever can be established as correct by means of them.

8. Cf. II 30.   9. I.e., the world.   10. Literally: "door," or "chapter."
11. Cf. II 14, methods 5, 6, and 7.   12. I.e., the Aristotelian philosophers.

The first method they mention is the one through which, in their opinion, we are obliged to admit that the deity passed from potentiality to actuality inasmuch as He acted at a certain time and did not act at another time.

The way to destroy this doubt is most clear. For this conclusion necessarily follows only with regard to everything composed | of matter, which is endowed with possibility, and of form. When such a body acts in virtue of its form after not having acted, there was indubitably in it a thing that was in potentia and afterwards made the transition into actuality. Accordingly it undoubtedly must have undergone the action of something causing it to make this transition. For this premise has been demonstrated only with regard to things endowed with matter. On the other hand, that which is not a body and is not endowed with matter, has in its essence no possibility in any respect whatever. Thus all that it has is always in actu. Accordingly with regard to it, their contention does not necessarily follow; and it is not impossible with regard to it that it acts at a certain time and does not act at another time. For in a being separate from matter, this does not imply change or a passage from potentiality to actuality.

A proof of this is provided by the Active Intellect as it is conceived by Aristotle and his followers. For the Active Intellect, on the one hand, is separate from matter; and, on the other, it acts at a certain time and does not act at another time, as Abū Naṣr [al-Fārābī] has explained in his treatise "On the Intellect." For there he has set down a statement that runs literally as follows. He says:[1] It is clear that the Active Intellect does not always act; rather it acts at a certain time and does not act at another time. This is literally what he says, and it is clearly true. But even if this is so, it cannot be said that the Active Intellect undergoes change or that it was acting potentially and became actual, because it did at a certain time what it did not do before. For there is no relation between bodies and that which is not body and no resemblance in any respect either at the time of their acting or at the time of their abstention from acting. In fact the acts of forms endowed with matter and the acts of a separate being are both called "act" only by equivocation. Hence it does not follow that if a separate being does not accomplish at a certain time the

1. This quotation, which is accurate (or nearly so), occurs in Bouyges' edition at p. 32, ll. 9–10. See above, I 73, n. 23.

act that it accomplishes later on, it has passed from potentiality to actuality, as we find it to follow in the case of forms endowed with matter. Perhaps, however, someone may think that this speech contains something misleading. For if the | Active Intellect necessarily acts at a certain time and does not act at another time, this does not result from a certain cause subsisting in its essence, but from the disposition of the portions of matter. For its action is perpetual with regard to all things properly disposed. Hence if there is an obstacle to this action, this results from a material disposition [2] and not from the Intellect in itself. He who thinks thus should know that our purpose is not to give information as to the cause for which God, may He be exalted, has acted at a certain time and has not acted at another time. We did not pursue this example to a conclusion; we did not say that just as the Active Intellect acts at a certain time and does not act at another time, though it be separate from matter, so God, may He be exalted, can do the same. We have not said this nor drawn this conclusion. If we had done this, it would indeed have been misleading. But the conclusion that we have drawn — and this conclusion is correct — is that though the Active Intellect, which is not a body or a force in a body, acts at one time but does not perform "the same action" at another time — whatever the cause of this may be — it is not said of it that it has passed from potentiality to actuality nor that there subsists possibility in its essence nor that it needs something causing it to make the transition from potentiality to actuality. Thus we are relieved from this great doubt that has been raised against us by him who affirms the eternity of the world. For as for us, we believe that He, may He be exalted, is neither a body nor a force in a body; and hence it does not follow that He changes if He acts after not having acted.

The second method is the one in which eternity is shown to be necessary because there do not subsist for Him, may He be exalted, any incentives, supervening accidents, and impediments. It is difficult to resolve this doubt, and the solution is subtle. Hear it.

Know that every agent endowed with will, who performs his acts for the sake of something, must of necessity act at a certain time | and not act at another time because of impediments or supervening accidents. To take an example: a man, for instance, may wish to have a house but does not build it because of impediments — if the building materials are not at hand or if they, though being at hand, have not been prepared for receiving the form because of the absence of tools. Sometimes, too, both the materials and the tools are at hand, but the man does not build because he does not

---

2. The disposition of the body upon which the Active Intellect exerts an action.

wish to build since he can dispense with a shelter. If, however, accidents like heat or cold supervene, he is compelled to seek a shelter, whereupon he will wish to build. It has thus become clear that supervening accidents may change the will and that impediments may oppose the will in such a way that it is not executed. All this, however, only occurs when acts are in the service of something that is external to the essence of the will. If, however, the act has no purpose whatever except to be consequent upon will, that will has no need of incentives. And the one who wills is not obliged, even if there are no impediments, to act always. For there is no external end for the sake of which he acts and that would render it necessary to act whenever there are no impediments preventing the attainment of the end. For in the case envisaged, the act is consequent upon the will alone.

Somebody might object: All this is correct, but does not the supposition that one[3] wishes at one time and does not wish at another time imply in itself a change? We shall reply to him: No, for the true reality and the quiddity of will means: to will and not to will. If the will in question belongs to a material being, so that some external end is sought thereby, then the will is subject to change because of impediments and supervening accidents. But as for a being separate from matter, its will, which does not exist in any respect for the sake of some other thing, is not subject to change. The fact that it may wish one thing now and another thing tomorrow does not constitute a change in its essence | and does not call for another cause; just as the fact that it acts at one time and does not act at another does not constitute a change, as we have explained. It shall be explained later on that it is only by equivocation that our will and that of a being separate from matter are both designated as "will," for there is no likeness between the two wills. Thus this objection has likewise been invalidated and it has been made clear that no incongruity necessarily follows for us in consequence of this method. As you know this was what we desired to achieve.

The third method: It is the one in which they argue the eternity of the world to be necessary because everything, with regard to which Wisdom decides that it should come forth, comes forth at the very moment of the decision. For His wisdom is eternal as is His essence, and in consequence that which necessarily proceeds from it is likewise eternal. This is a very feeble way of going on to an obligatory conclusion. For in the same way as we do not know what was His wisdom in making it necessary that the spheres should be nine — neither more nor less — and the number of the stars equal to what it is — neither more nor less — and that they should be neither

3. Or: God.

bigger nor smaller than they are, we do not know what was His wisdom in bringing into existence the universe at a recent period after its not having existed. The universe is consequent upon His perpetual and immutable wisdom. But we are completely ignorant of the rule of that wisdom and of the decision made by it. For, in our opinion, volition too is consequent upon wisdom; all these being one and the same thing — I mean His essence and His wisdom — for we do not believe in attributes. You shall hear much about this notion, when we shall speak of providence.[4] By looking at the matter in this way, this disgracefulness is thus abolished.

As for Aristotle's remark that the nations were agreed in past time that the angels dwell in heaven and that the deity is in heaven — something similar occurs in the external meaning of the scriptural texts — this does not serve as an indication of the eternity of the heavens, as he wishes to consider it. But this has been said because it serves as an indication that | the heaven proves to us the existence of the separate intellects, who are the spiritual beings and the angels, and the heaven proves to us the existence of the deity, who is its mover and its governor, as we shall explain. We shall make it clear that there is no proof indicating to us the existence of the Maker, according to our opinion, like the indication deriving from the heaven.[5] The latter also proves, as we have mentioned, according to the opinion of the philosophers, the existence of the Mover of the heaven and His not being either a body or a force subsisting in a body.

After having explained to you that our contention is possible and not — as is thought by him who affirms the eternity of the world — an impossibility, I shall return in the chapters that will follow, to explaining that our opinion can be shown, by means of speculation, to outweigh the other in the scales and to making manifest the disgraceful consequences necessarily deriving from his opinion.[6]

CHAPTER 19

It is clear to you from the doctrine of Aristotle, as well as from that of everyone who affirms the eternity of the world, that in his view that which exists has proceeded from the Creator in virtue of a necessity; that He,

4. Cf. Translator's Introduction.
5. The meaning seems to be that the proof in question is the most convincing of all.
6. The opinion of those who believe in the eternity a parte ante of the world is meant.

may He be exalted, is a cause and this world an effect and it was necessary that this should be so. Just as one does not ask with regard to Him, may He be exalted, why He exists or how He exists thus — I mean to say as One and incorporeal — so it may not be asked with regard to the world as a whole why it exists or how it exists thus. For all this, both the cause and the effect, exist thus necessarily, and nonexistence is not possible with regard to them in any respect nor their changing from the way they exist. Hence it follows necessarily from this opinion that of necessity everything must remain permanently as it is according to its nature and that nothing can change as far as its nature is concerned. For according to this opinion, it is impossible that a thing from among the existents should change as far as its nature is concerned. | Accordingly no thing has come into being in virtue of the purpose of One possessing purpose who chose freely and willed that all things should be as they are. For if they had come into being in virtue of the purpose of One possessing purpose, they would not have existed thus before they were purposed.

Now as for us, the matter is clear in our opinion: namely, that all things exist in virtue of a purpose and not of necessity, and that He who purposed them may change them and conceive another purpose, though not absolutely any purpose whatever. For the nature of impossibility is stable and cannot be abolished, as we shall make clear.

My purpose in this chapter is to explain to you, by means of arguments that come close to being a demonstration, that what exists indicates to us of necessity that it exists in virtue of the purpose of One who purposed; and to do this without having to take upon myself what the Mutakallimūn have undertaken — to abolish the nature of that which exists and to adopt atomism, the opinion according to which accidents are perpetually being created, and all their principles, which I have explained to you and which they only wished to use as an introduction in order to establish the method of particularization. Do not think that they have also said what I shall say. On the other hand, there is no doubt that they wished what I wish. They have also mentioned the same things that I shall mention and observed in them particularization. But in their opinion there is no difference between plants particularized through being red rather than white or through being sweet rather than bitter or between the heavens being particularized through having the shape they have instead of having been made square or triangular. They have established particularization by means of their premises, which you already know. I, on the other hand, shall establish particularization regarding the things with respect to which it ought to be established by means of philosophic premises derived from the nature of that which exists.

I shall explain this method after first setting forth this premise: In every case in which things differing in any way from one another possess a common matter, there must of necessity be a cause other than, and different from, | the common matter — a cause that rendered it necessary that some of the things have a certain attribute, whereas some others have a different one. Or there may be several causes according to the number of the things differing from one another. This premise is unanimously agreed to both by those who believe in the eternity of the world and by those who believe in its having come into being in time. After having set forth this premise, I shall begin to explain what I wanted to explain by means of questions and answers concerning Aristotle's opinion.

We put a question to Aristotle, saying to him: You have demonstrated to us that the matter of everything that is beneath the sphere of the moon is one and common to everything. What then is the cause of the differences between the individals of every species?

Then he gives us an answer to this, saying: The cause of the differences lies in the changes in the mixture of the compounds composed of this matter. For this common matter has in the first place received four forms, two qualities being consequent to each of these forms. In virtue of these four qualities, matter[1] was transformed into elements for that which is composed of it. For these elements[2] were first mixed through the action of the motion of the sphere and then they combined. Consequently, the differences in the compounds representing a mixture of the elements came about through the differing measures of the warm, the cold, the humid, and the dry. For in virtue of these various combinations, various dispositions to receive various forms come about in the compounds. Again through these forms, the compounds become disposed to receive other forms. And this continues constantly in this manner. Again the matter of the specific form, which is one, has great latitude with regard to quantity and quality, and the individuals of the species differ in a way corresponding to this latitude, as has been elucidated in the natural science. All this is correct and clear to whoever treats his own soul equitably and does not deceive it.

Thereupon we | again put a question to Aristotle, saying to him: Since

1. In the context it seems more likely that "matter" is the subject of this sentence rather than "the four forms." From the syntactical point of view there is nothing to choose between these two constructions.
2. In this case the subject seems to be "elements" rather than "matter."

the mixture of the elements is the cause of the various matters being predisposed to receive the various forms, what is it that prepared this first matter so that a part of it receives the form of fire and part of it the form of earth and that which is intermediate between these two parts is prepared to receive the forms of water and of air, while at the same time the matter of the universe is one and common to all things? Why is the matter of earth more fitted for the form of earth and the matter of fire for the form of fire?

Thereupon Aristotle gave an answer to this, saying: This has been made necessary by the differences between the various places, for these differences have made it necessary for this one matter to have various dispositions. For the part that is near the encompassing sphere, was endowed by the latter with an impress of subtlety and swiftness of motion and nearness to the nature of the sphere. Consequently it received, in virtue of this disposition, the form of fire. And the more distant matter is from the encompassing sphere in the direction of the center of the earth,[3] the thicker and denser and less luminous it becomes, so that it becomes earth. The same cause obtains with regard to water and air. Thus this is necessary; for it is absurd that the matter in question should not be in a place, or that the encompassing sphere should be the center of the earth,[4] and the center of the earth[4] the encompassing sphere. This has been made necessary by particularization of matter by means of various forms; I mean by this the disposition to receive various forms.

Thereupon we put a question to him, saying: Is the matter of the encompassing sphere — I mean to say the heavens — the same as the matter of the elements?

He said: No. That[5] is another matter and those are other forms. And the term "body," applied to the bodies that are with us and to the heavenly bodies, is equivocal, as has been explained by latter-day thinkers. All this has been demonstrated.

From here on listen, you who are engaged in the study of this my Treatise, to what I shall say. You already know Aristotle's demonstration that from the difference of acts | the difference of forms may be inferred. Consequently, inasmuch as the motions of the four elements are rectilinear and the motion of the sphere is circular, it is known that the matter of these elements is not the matter of the sphere. And this is correct according to natural speculation. And as you have also found that the elements whose motions are rectilinear differ from one another with regard to direction —

3. Or: of the world.   4. Or: of the world.
5. I.e., the matter of the heavenly spheres.

some of them moving upwards and the others downwards — and as it has likewise been found that in considering those that move in the same direction one is the more rapid and the other the slower, it is known that the elements differ with regard to their forms. And thereby it is known that there are four elements. If one has recourse to this very kind of inference, it also follows necessarily that the matter of all the heavenly spheres is one, as all of them have circular motion, and that the form of every sphere is different from that of every other sphere, as one moves from the East to the West and another from the West to the East and as they also differ in their rapidity or slowness.

Accordingly the following question should be put to him,[6] and it should be said to him: Inasmuch as the matter in question is common to all the heavenly spheres and, on the other hand, since every substratum in them has been particularized so as to receive a certain form other than the forms received by the others, who is it that has particularized these sub-strata and has predisposed them to receive various forms? Is there beyond the sphere something else to which this particularization can be attributed except God, may He be cherished and exalted?

Here I shall call your attention to the depth of Aristotle's penetration and to his extraordinary apprehension and to the extent to which this objection undoubtedly pressed hard upon him so that he wished to escape from it by recourse to means in which the nature of that which exists did not help him. Even though he does not mention this objection, it appears from what he says that he wished to bring order for our benefit into the being of the spheres, as he has brought order for us into the existence of that which is beneath the sphere. He wished to do this in order that | the whole should exist in virtue of natural necessity and not in virtue of the purpose of one who purposes according to his will whatever it be and the particularization of one who particularizes in whatever way he likes. Now this task has not been accomplished by him, nor will it ever be accomplished. For he wished to give a cause for the fact that the sphere moves from the East and not from the West; and he wished to give a cause for the fact that some of them are swift of motion and others slow and that this is necessary because of the order of their position with regard to the highest sphere. He also wished to give a cause for the fact that every star[7] from among the seven has a number of spheres, while this great number of fixed stars is to be found in one sphere. He wished to assign causes for all this so that these things would be ordered for us in a natural order that is

6. I.e., to Aristotle.   7. I.e., planet.

due to necessity. However, he has accomplished none of these undertakings. As a matter of fact, all that he has explained to us regarding what is beneath the sphere of the moon follows an order conforming to that which exists, an order whose causes are clear. One can say of it that it derives of necessity from the motion and the powers of the sphere. On the other hand, one can say of all that he has stated with regard to matters pertaining to the sphere, that he has assigned no clear cause with regard to this, and that the matter, as he sets it out, does not follow an order for which necessity can be claimed. For we see that in the case of some spheres, the swifter of motion is above the slower; that in the case of others, the slower of motion is above the swifter; and that, again in another case, the motions of the spheres are of equal velocity though one be above the other. There are also other very grave matters if regarded from the point of view that these things are as they are in virtue of necessity. I shall deal with these points in a special chapter of this Treatise.[8]

To sum up: It was undoubtedly when Aristotle realized the feebleness of what he said in setting forth and expounding the ground and the causes[9] of these things, that he prefaced his starting upon these investigations with a statement | that runs literally as follows: Now we desire to make a sufficient inquiry into two questions. For it is obligatory for us to inquire into them and to speak concerning them according to the capacity of our intellects, our knowledge, and our opinion. However, no one ought to attribute this undertaking to overboldness and temerity on our part, but rather should our desire and ardor for philosophy be admired. When, therefore, we seek out noble and important questions and are able to propound for them — though it be only to some small extent—a well-founded solution, it behooves the hearer to feel great joy and jubilation.[10] This is literally what he says. It has thus become clear to you that he was indubitably aware of the feebleness of those assertions; and all the more so since the

8. Cf. II 24.
9. Maimonides uses the word *taʿlīl* (which is related to *ʿilla*) as well as the term *sabab* (in the plural). Both *ʿilla* and *sabab* signify "cause" and are often synonymous. However, *sabab* sometimes means "intermediate cause," and Maimonides may have used it here in this sense in contradistinction to *ʿilla*. It is, however, equally possible that Maimonides' reference to both terms in this passage does not indicate an intention to differentiate them.
10. *De Caelo* ii.12.291b24. ff. The translation is rather free. In Guthrie's translation the passage reads: "There are two difficulties which might naturally be felt, and we must do our best to give the most plausible solution, looking upon a readiness to do so as evidence of modesty rather than of rashness, if the seeker, out of thirst for philosophy, rests content with but a little enlightenment in matters where we are surrounded by such unfathomable obscurities." Cf. Translator's Introduction.

science of mathematics had not been perfected in his time and since the motions of the sphere were not known in his time to the extent to which we know them today. It appears to me that his assertion in the "Metaphysics"[11] that a separate intellect should be supposed for every sphere is also made with a view to the notion in question: namely, in order that there should be there something that would particularize every sphere by means of some motion with which it would be endowed. We shall explain later on that he gains nothing by this. With regard to his saying in the text that I have set out for you, "according to the capacity of our intellects, our knowledge, and our opinion": I shall explain to you the meaning of this, a meaning that I have not seen set forth by any of the commentators. When saying "our opinion," he has in mind the point of view of necessity that is represented by the affirmation of the eternity of the world. When saying "our knowledge," he has in mind the clear and generally accepted point that each of those things[12] certainly has a cause and ground and that it is not a thing that happens by chance. When saying "our intellects," he has in mind our incapacity to assign causes for things of such perfection and accomplishment. But he | deemed that to a small extent these might be assigned, and he did this. For his statement regarding the rapidity of the universal motion and the slowness of the sphere of the fixed stars because of its opposite direction has recourse to a strange and bizarre cause. Similarly he says that as the distance of a sphere from the eighth sphere is greater, its motion is more rapid. However, this is not consistently so, as I have made clear to you.[13] There is something even more striking: namely, that there are spheres beneath the eighth that move from the East to the West. These consequently must be more rapid than what is beneath them and likewise moves from the East to the West, even though the rapidity of the motion of the latter spheres moving from the East is near to that of the motion of the ninth sphere. However, as I have let you know, the science of astronomy was not in his[14] time what it is today.

Know that on the basis of our opinion, that is, the opinion of the community of those who affirm the production of the world in time, all this becomes easy and is consistent with our principles. For we say that there is a being that has particularized, just as it willed, every sphere in regard to its motion and rapidity; but we do not know in what respect there is wisdom in making these things exist in this fashion. Now if Aristotle had been

11. Cf. *Metaphysics* xii.8.1074a15 ff.
12. I.e., the heavenly spheres and things pertaining to them.
13. Earlier in this chapter.   14. I.e., Aristotle's.

able—as he thought—to give us the cause for the differences between the motions of the spheres so that these should be in accordance with the order of the positions of the spheres with regard to one another, this would have been extraordinary. In that case the cause of particularization would have been constituted by the differences between the motions of the spheres, just as the cause of the differences between the elements lies in their various positions between the encompassing sphere and the center of the earth.[15] However, things are not ordered thus, as I have explained to you.

A fact that makes even more clear than what has been said about the existence of particularization in the sphere, and with regard to which no one would be able to find a cause particularizing it other than the purpose of one who purposes, is the existence of the stars. For the fact that a sphere is always in motion and a star | is always fixed proves that the matter of the stars is not the matter of the spheres. In fact Abū Naṣr [al-Fārābī] in his glosses on the "Akroasis,"[16] has made a statement of which the literal text is as follows. He said: There is a difference between a sphere and the stars, for a sphere is transparent whereas the stars are not transparent. The cause for this lies in the fact that there is a difference between the two matters and the two forms. But this difference is small. This is literally the text of his statement. I, however, do not say "small," but say that they are very different. For I do not infer this from the fact of transparency but from the motions. Accordingly it has become clear to me that there are three kinds of matter and three kinds of forms: the bodies that are always by themselves at rest—these are the bodies of the stars; the bodies that are always in motion—these are the bodies of the spheres; the bodies that are sometimes in motion and sometimes at rest—these are the elements. Would that I knew what made the two kinds of matter,[17] between which there is either an extreme difference—this is what it appears to be to me—or a small difference—as is stated by Abū Naṣr [al-Fārābī]—and who has provided the kinds of matter in question with the dispositions necessary for this union.

To sum up: It would be a strange thing that there should be two different bodies, one of which, being fixed in, but not mixed with, the other, should be localized in the latter in a particular place and attached to this second body; and that this should come about without its having been produced through the purpose of one who purposed it. And it is even stranger that there should exist the numerous stars that are in the eighth

15. Or: of the world.   16. I.e., Aristotle's *Physics*.
17. I.e., the matter of the spheres and the matter of the stars.

sphere, all of which are globes, some of them small and some big, one star being here and another at a cubit's distance according to what seems to the eye, or ten stars being crowded and assembled together while there may be a very great stretch in which nothing is to be found. What is the cause that has particularized one stretch in such a way that ten stars should be found in it and has particularized another stretch in such a way that no star should be found in it? Again the body of the whole sphere is one simple body in which there are no differences. What accordingly can be the cause for the fact that a certain part of the sphere should be | more fitted to receive the particular star found in it than another part? All this and everything that is of this sort would be very unlikely or rather would come near to being impossible if it should be believed that all this proceeded obligatorily and of necessity from the deity, as is the opinion of Aristotle. If, however, it is believed that all this came about in virtue of the purpose of one who purposed who made this thus, that opinion would not be accompanied by a feeling of astonishment and would not be at all unlikely. And there would remain no other point to be investigated except if you were to say: What is the cause for this having been purposed? What is known may be epitomized as follows: All this has been produced for an object that we do not know and is not an aimless and fortuitous act. In fact you know that the veins and nerves of any individual dog or ass have not happened fortuitously, nor are their measures fortuitous. Neither is it by chance that one vein is thick and another thin, that one nerve has many ramifications and another is not thus ramified, that one descends straight down and another is bent. All this is as it is with a view to useful effects whose necessity is known. How then can one who uses his intellect imagine that the positions, measures, and numbers of the stars and the motions of their various spheres are without an object or fortuitous? There is no doubt that all of these things are necessary according to the purpose of one who purposes. On the other hand, the supposition that all these things have been ordered in virtue of necessity and not in virtue of a purpose is very remote indeed from being conceivable. To my mind there is no proof of purpose stronger than the one founded upon the differences between the motions of the spheres and upon the fact that the stars are fixed in the spheres. For this reason you will find that all the prophets used the stars and the spheres as proofs for the diety's existing necessarily. Thus in the traditional story of *Abraham*, there occurs the tale, | which is generally known, about his contemplation of the stars. Again *Isaiah*, calling attention to the conclusions to be drawn from the stars, says: *Lift up your eyes on high, and see: who hath created these?*

and so on.[18] *Jeremiah* says similarly: *He made the heavens.*[19] *Abraham* says: *The Lord, the God of the heavens.*[20] And the chief of the prophets says: *Who rideth upon the heaven,*[21] an expression we have explained.[22] This is the correct proof, which is not exposed to doubt. The explanation thereof is as follows: With regard to all the differences in the things beneath the sphere and even though the matter subsisting in these things is one, as we have explained, you can make out that they were particularized through the powers of the sphere and through the various positions of matter with regard to the sphere, just as Aristotle has taught us. But who is the one who particularized the differences that are found in the spheres and the stars unless it be God, may He be exalted? If, however, someone says that the separate intellects did it, he gains nothing by saying this. The explanation of this is as follows: The intellects are not bodies, which they would have to be in order to have a local position in relation to the sphere. Why then should one particular sphere move in its motion induced by desire toward its separate intellect in an eastern direction, and another in a western? Do you consider that one particular intellect is to be found in an eastern direction and another in a western? Then there is the fact that one sphere is relatively slower, while another is more rapid; and this, as you know, does not correspond to the relations obtaining between the distances of the various spheres from each other. Thus, of necessity, one cannot avoid saying that the nature and substance of that particular sphere require that its motion be in a certain direction and with a certain velocity and that a necessary concomitant of its desire for a certain notion should manifest itself in this manner.[23] And this is what Aristotle says and explicitly states.

We have accordingly come back to the point we were dealing with at first. Accordingly we shall say: If the matter of all the spheres is one and the same, in virtue of what thing has any sphere been so particularized as to receive a nature other than the nature of any other sphere? How then is there to be found in that sphere a certain desire, different from the desire of that other sphere, that | obliges one to move in this direction and the other to move in another direction? There must of necessity be something

18. Isa. 40:26.
19. These words do not occur in Jeremiah. Cf., however, Jer. 32:17, 10:12, and 51:15.
20. Gen. 24:7.   21. Deut. 33:26.   22. Cf. I 70.
23. This translation seems to me to render more faithfully the construction of the Arabic sentence than the renderings of Ibn Tibbon and Munk. The latter's translation would read in English as follows: " . . . and that the result of its desire should be such a thing obtained in this manner."

that particularizes. This examination has thus conducted us to the investigation of two problems, one of which may be stated as follows: Is it of necessity obligatory or not, considering the existence of these differences, that these should be due to the purpose of one who purposed and not due to necessity? The second problem may be stated as follows: Supposing that all this is due to the purpose of one who purposed and who particularized the spheres in this way, is it obligatory that this should have been produced after its having been nonexistent, or is it not obligatory so that He who particularizes has never ceased doing this? This second opinion has also been affirmed by some[24] of those who believe in the eternity of the world. In the following chapters I shall begin to treat of these two problems, and I shall explain what is necessary to explain concerning them.

CHAPTER 20

Aristotle demonstrates regarding all natural things that they do not come about by chance — his demonstration being, as he has stated it: the fortuitous things do not occur either always or in the majority of cases;[1] the natural things, however, occur either always or in the majority of cases. Thus the heavens and all that is in them remain always in certain states that do not change, as we have explained, either in their essences or through change of place. As for the natural things that are beneath the sphere of the moon, some of them occur always and others in the majority of cases. Instances of what occurs always are the heating action of fire and the falling-down of a stone, while instances of what occurs in the majority of cases are the shapes and acts of the individuals of every species. All this is clear. Now if the particular things of the world are not due to chance, how can the whole of it be due to chance? This is a demonstration | proving that these beings are not due to chance. Here is the text of the statement of Aristotle in his refutation of those of his predecessors who believed that this world has happened to come about by chance and spontaneously, without a cause. He says:[2] Other people have thought that the cause of these heavens and all these worlds is to be sought in their spontaneity. They say that the

24. Or: one.
1. Cf. *Physics* ii.5.196b10 ff.
2. *Physics* ii.4.196a25 ff. The translation is by and large accurate.

revolution and the motion that has differentiated and constituted all things[3] according to this order were due to their spontaneity. Now this is a point that arouses strong astonishment; I mean the fact that they say concerning animals and plants that they do not come about and are not produced by chance, but have a cause, which is either nature or intellect or some other similar thing — for not any haphazard thing is generated from every seed or sperm, but from this particular seed there comes into being an olive tree and from that sperm a human being — and that at the same time they say of the heavens and of the bodies that alone are divine among all the visible bodies, that they have come into being spontaneously and that they have no cause at all such as is possessed by the animals and the plants. This is the text of his statement. Then he starts to explain in a more lengthy passage the falsity of these imaginings.

Accordingly it is clear to you that Aristotle believes and demonstrates that none of these beings are through chance. Now what contradicts their having come into being[4] through chance is their having come into being[5] essentially — I mean their having a cause that renders it necessary for them to come into being in this particular fashion. It is because of this cause that they exist in the way they do. This is what has been demonstrated, and this is what Aristotle believes. But it is not clear to me that Aristotle believes that, because these beings have not come into being spontaneously, it follows necessarily that they have come into being in virtue of the purpose of one who purposed and the will of one who willed. For | to me a combination between existing in virtue of necessity and being produced in time in virtue of a purpose and a will — a combination uniting these two — comes near to a combination of two contraries. For the meaning of necessity, as Aristotle believes it, is that everything among the beings, which is not an artifact, cannot but have a cause necessitating that particular thing — a cause that has brought it into being as it is — and that this cause has a second cause and this second cause similarly a third one, until finally a first cause is reached from which everything is necessarily derived. This is so because of the impossibility of an infinite series of causes. However, he does not believe withal that the necessity in virtue of which the existence of the world is derived from the Creator — I mean to say from the First Cause — is like the necessity in virtue of which shadow is derived from a body or heat from fire or light from the sun, as those say of him who do not understand what he said. Rather does he believe that this necessity is somewhat like the necessity of the derivation of an intellectum from an intellect, for the

3. Or: the universe.   4. Or: their being.   5. Or: their being.

15

intellect is the agent[6] of the intellectum in respect of its being an intellectum. For this First Cause — though it is according to him an intellect of the highest and most perfect rank of being so that he says that it wills what is necessarily derived from it and rejoices and takes pleasure in it — cannot will anything contrary to this.[7] Now this is not called purpose, and the notion of purpose is not included in it. For a man may will to have two eyes and two hands, and rejoice in having them and take pleasure in it and cannot will anything contrary to this. However, that individual does not have two eyes and two hands because of a purpose on his part and because of his having particularized this shape and these actions. For the notions of purpose and of particularization only apply to a nonexistent thing for which it is possible to exist just as it was purposed and particularized and for which it also is possible not to exist in this fashion. I do not know whether | the discourse and speech of Aristotle that these things must necessarily have a cause was understood by certain latter-day men to refer to purpose and particularization, or whether they disagree with him on this and choose the opinion affirming purpose and particularization, deeming that it does not contradict the eternity of the world.

After what we have explained, I shall begin to treat of the opinion of these latter-day men.

CHAPTER 21

Know that among the latter-day philosophers who affirm the eternity of the world there are some[1] who maintain that God, may He be exalted, is the Agent[2] of the world, who chose that it should exist, purposed it, and particularized it so that it should be as it actually is. They think, however, that it is impossible that this should have happened at one particular time rather than at another; according to them the world has always been and will always be like this. They say: What compels us to conceive of an agent[3] as unable to effect a thing unless the agent precedes the act in time is the fact that this necessarily happens to us when we effect something. This is so because in every agent of whom this may be

6. I.e., the efficient cause.   7. I.e., to what is drived from it.
1. The Arabic word may also refer to a single philosopher.
2. Or: Maker. The Arabic term used is applied to the efficient cause.
3. Cf. preceding note.

predicated, there is a certain privation; accordingly he is at first an agent in potentia and, when he acts, he passes into actuality. But the deity, may He be exalted, in whom there is no privation and nothing at all in potentia, does not precede His act, for He has always been an agent in actu. And just as there is a difference — and what a difference! — between His essence and ours, so is there a difference between the relation linking His act and Himself and the relation linking our act and ourselves. They draw the same analogy[4] with regard to particularization and will. For there is no difference between your saying, when treating of this matter: an agent, one who wills, one who purposes, one who chooses freely, or one who particularizes. And they say | it is also impossible that His act or His will should change, as we have explained.[5]

It has already become clear to you, who are engaged in the study of this my Treatise, that these people have altered the term "necessity," but have let its meaning remain. Perhaps they intended to choose a more beautiful expression or to get rid of one that is shocking. For the meaning of the assertion, as maintained by Aristotle, that this being proceeds necessarily from its cause and is perpetual in virtue of the latter's perpetuity — that cause being the deity — is identical with the meaning of their assertion that the world derives from the act of the deity or exists in virtue of His purpose, will, free choice, and particularization, but that it has always been and will always be as it is — just as the sunrise is indubitably the agent of the day, though neither of them precedes the other in point of time. But this is not the meaning of purpose, as we propose to conceive it. For we wish to signify by the term that it — I mean the world — does not necessarily proceed from Him, may He be exalted, as an effect necessarily proceeds from its cause without being able to be separated from it or to change unless its cause or one of its modes also changes. Now if you understand the meaning of the term in this way, it is already known that it is absurd to say that the world necessarily proceeds from the being of the deity as an effect proceeds from its cause, and it is further known that the world has come about through an act of the deity or through His particularization.

Accordingly the matter is reduced to this, and the discussion finally leads us to an inquiry concerning the diversity existing in the heavens, with regard to which it has been demonstrated that it must necessarily have a cause. The inquiry concerns the question whether this cause is the ground of

4. The Arabic word also means "syllogism" and is sometimes used in the sense of "reasoning."
5. Cf. II 13.

this diversity, the latter having necessarily proceeded from the existence of this cause, or whether this cause is the agent that has brought about this diversity and has particularized it in the way in which we, the followers of *Moses our Master*, believe. We shall speak of this after we have first set forth a preface by which we shall explain to you the meaning of the necessity maintained by Aristotle so that you should conceive it. Thereupon | I shall begin to explain to you, with the help of speculation and philosophic proofs devoid of falsification, my preference in favor of the opinion according to which the world has been produced in time.

When he[6] says that the first intellect necessarily proceeds from God, the second from the first, and the third from the second, and also when he holds that the spheres necessarily proceed from the intellects, and when he sets forth the famous order that you know from various passages in his writings — that order of which we have already expounded a part here[7] — it is clear that he does not wish to signify thereby that first a certain thing was, and then, later, the thing necessarily proceeding from the first thing was produced in time. For he does not say that any of these was produced in time. By the term "necessity," he merely means to signify causality; it is as if he said the first intellect is the cause of the existence of the second intellect, the second of the third, and so on till the last of them. The same applies to the discourse concerning the spheres and the first matter; according to him, none of these things precedes in time, or exists without, any of these other things. It is, to take an example, as if someone said that roughness, smoothness, hardness, softness, thickness, and absorbency, necessarily derive from the first qualities. For no one doubts that these qualities — I mean heat, cold, humidity, and dryness — produce roughness, smoothness, hardness, softness, thickness, absorbency, and other similar qualities. Accordingly they necessarily derive from the four first qualities, even though it is impossible that a body should exist endowed with the four first qualities and devoid of the secondary ones. It is in an exactly analogous way that Aristotle says, concerning that which exists in general, that in it this particular thing necessarily proceeds from that and so forth till the series ends with the First Cause, as he himself says, or the first intellect or however you may wish to call it. All of us aim at one and the same principle. But | he holds, as I have recounted to you, that everything that is other than it necessarily proceeds from it. We affirm that all these things have been made by Him in virtue of a purpose and a will directed toward this particular being, which did not exist and now became an

6. I.e., the Aristotelian philosopher.   7. Cf. II 4.

existent in virtue of His will, may He be exalted. Now I shall begin to set forth in the following chapters my proofs and my preference in favor of the world's having been produced in time according to our opinion.

CHAPTER 22

A proposition universally agreed upon, accepted by Aristotle and by all those who have philosophized, reads as follows: It is impossible that anything but a single simple thing should proceed from a simple thing. If the thing is composite, there may proceed from it several things according to the number of simple things of which the compound is composed. Thus, for instance, what proceeds from fire, in which two qualities — heat and dryness — have combined is the action of heating by means of its heat and that of drying by means of its dryness. Similarly in the case of a thing composed of matter and form, certain things proceed from it in respect to its matter and certain other things in respect to its form, if it is of multiple composition. In accordance with this proposition, Aristotle says that what first proceeded from God was constituted by a single simple intellect only.

A second proposition: Any thing at random does not proceed from any other thing at random, but there subsists necessarily a certain conformity between the cause and its effect. Even in the case of accidents, one accident at random does not proceed from any other accident at random, as would be the case if, for instance, a quantity would proceed from a quality, or a quality from a quantity. Similarly form does not proceed from matter nor matter from form. |

A third proposition: Every agent, acting in virtue of purpose and will and not in virtue of its nature, accomplishes many different acts.

A fourth proposition: A whole composed of various juxtaposed substances may more appropriately be termed a composition than a whole composed of various substances that have combined with one another. For instance, a bone, flesh, a vein, a nerve, are simpler than the whole of a hand or that of a foot composed of nerves, flesh, veins, and bones. This is too clear to require additional discourse.

After having set forth these premises, I say: With regard to Aristotle's statement that the first intellect is the cause of the second, the second of the third, and so on — even if there were thousands of degrees, the last intellect would indubitably still be simple. How then can the composition have come to exist, the composition existing — as Aristotle believes — in the beings in virtue of necessity? We shall concede to him all that he says concerning a composition of various notions coming about in the intellects, as their intellecta are multiple, when the intellects get farther away from the First Cause. But even if we grant him this guess and conjecture, how can the intellects be a cause for the procession of the spheres from them? And what relation can there be between matter and that which being separate has no matter at all? And supposing that we concede that the cause of every sphere is, in the fashion stated, an intellect — inasmuch as there subsists composition in the intellect, which intellectually cognizes itself and what is other than itself, so that it is as it were composed of two things, from one of which another and lower intellect proceeds, whereas a sphere proceeds from the other — he should still be asked: How does a sphere proceed from the one simple thing from which it proceeds? | A sphere is composed of two kinds of matter and two forms: the matter and the form of the sphere itself and the matter and the form of the star fixed in the sphere. Now if this comes about in virtue of a procession, we cannot but require for this compound a composite cause, the procession of the body of the sphere being occasioned by one of its parts and that of the body of the star by the other. This would be so if the matter of the stars were all of it one and the same. However, the substance of the bright stars may be a certain substance and that of the dim ones may be another substance. It is also known that every body is composed of its matter and its form.

Accordingly it has become clear to you that these things do not conform to the conception of necessity that he sets forth. Similarly the diversity of the motions of the spheres does not agree with the order of their arrangement one beneath the other, in such a way that necessity could be claimed in this field. We have already mentioned this.[1] There is, furthermore, another point that ruins everything that has been established with regard to natural things if the state of the heavens is considered. For if the matter of all the spheres is one and the same, why is it not necessary for the form of one particular sphere to be transferred to the matter of another, in accord with what happens beneath the sphere of the moon because of the aptitude of matter? And why is one particular form permanently in one particular matter although the matter of all is common? Unless — by God! — someone asserts that the matter of every sphere is other than that of the others.

1. Cf. II 19.

In that case the form of the motion of the spheres would not be indicative of their matter. This would be the ruin of all principles. Furthermore, if the matter of all the stars is one and the same, whereby are their individuals differentiated — is it by their forms or by accidents? In either case it would be necessary that the forms or accidents in question should be transferred one after the other to each of the stars, in order that | the aptitude of matter not be set at nought. Hereby it has become clear to you that when we say the matter of the spheres or the matter of the stars, these expressions contain none of the meaning of that matter here, this being a case of the equivocal use of terms; and that every being from among the bodies of the spheres has an existence that is proper to it and that it does not have in common with anything other than itself. How then could it happen that the spheres have in common their circular motion and the stars their fixity?

If, however, we believe that all this has been produced through the purpose of one who purposed, made, and particularized it — as His wisdom, which cannot be grasped, required — none of these questions affect us, whereas they do affect him who claims that all this has come about through necessity and not through the will of one who wills. This is an opinion that does not agree with the order of that which exists, an opinion in favor of which no cause and no new persuasive proof have been brought forward. Withal very disgraceful conclusions would follow upon it. Namely, it would follow that the deity, whom everyone who is intelligent recognizes to be perfect in every kind of perfection, could, as far as all the beings are concerned, produce nothing new in any of them; if He wished to lengthen a fly's wing or to shorten a worm's foot, He would not be able to do it. But Aristotle will say that He would not wish it and that it is impossible for Him to will something different from what is; that it would not add to His perfection but would perhaps from a certain point of view be a deficiency. I shall sum up for your benefit, and though I know that many men imbued with a partisan spirit shall tax me because of this statement either with having but little comprehension of their argument or with deliberately deviating from it, yet shall I not, because of that, refrain from saying what I in my inadequacy have apprehended and understood. Accordingly this summing-up will be as follows:

Everything that Aristotle has said about all that exists from beneath ✓ the sphere of the moon to the center of the earth is indubitably correct, and no one | will deviate from it unless he does not understand it or unless he has preconceived opinions that he wishes to defend or that lead him to a denial of a thing that is manifest. On the other hand, everything that

Aristotle expounds with regard to the sphere of the moon and that which is above it is, except for certain things, something analogous to guessing and conjecturing. All the more does this apply to what he says about the order of the intellects and to some of the opinions regarding the divine that he believes; for the latter contain grave incongruities and perversities that manifestly and clearly appear as such to all the nations,[2] that propagate evil, and that he cannot demonstrate.

Do not criticize me for having set out the doubts that attach to his opinion. You may say: Can doubts disprove an opinion or establish its contrary as true? Surely this is not so. However, we shall treat this philosopher as his followers have enjoined us to treat him. For Alexander has explained that in every case in which no demonstration is possible, the two contrary opinions with regard to the matter in question should be posited as hypotheses, and it should be seen what doubts attach to each of them: the one to which fewer doubts attach should be believed. Alexander says[3] that things are thus[4] with respect to all the opinions regarding the divine that Aristotle sets forth and regarding which no demonstration is possible. For everyone who has come after Aristotle says that what Aristotle stated about them arouses fewer doubts than whatever else might be said about them. We have acted in this way when it was to our mind established as true that, regarding the question whether the heavens are generated or eternal, neither of the two contrary opinions could be demonstrated. For we have explained the doubts attaching to each of the opinions and have shown to you that the opinion favoring the eternity of the world is the one that raises more doubts and is more harmful for the belief that ought to be held with regard to the deity. | And this, in addition to the fact that the world's being produced in time is the opinion of *Abraham our Father* and our prophet *Moses*, may peace be on both of them.

As we have mentioned that opinions should be examined by means of the doubts they arouse, I see fit to explain to you something with regard to that.

2. Or: to all the religious communities.
3. On this quotation from Alexander of Aphrodisias, cf. Translator's Introduction.
4. Or: that he conducts things thus.

K now that when one compares the doubts attaching to a certain opinion with those attaching to the contrary opinion and has to decide which of them arouses fewer doubts, one should not take into account the number of the doubts but rather consider how great is their incongruity and what is their disagreement with what exists. Sometimes a single doubt is more powerful than a thousand other doubts. Furthermore this comparison can be correctly made only by someone for whom the two contraries are equal. But whoever prefers one of the two opinions because of his upbringing or for some advantage, is blind to the truth. While one who entertains an unfounded predilection cannot make himself oppose a matter susceptible of demonstration, in matters like those under discussion such an opposition is often possible. Sometimes, if you wish it, you can rid yourself of an unfounded predilection, free yourself of what is habitual, rely solely on speculation, and prefer the opinion that you ought to prefer. However, to do this you must fulfill several conditions. The first of them is that you should know how good your mind is and that your inborn disposition is sound. This becomes clear to you through training in all the mathematical sciences and through grasp of the rules of logic. The second condition is to have knowledge of the natural sciences and to apprehend their truth so that you should know your doubts in their true reality. The third condition concerns your morals. For | whenever a man finds himself inclining — and to our mind it makes no difference if this happens because of his natural disposition or because of an acquired characteristic — toward lusts and pleasures or preferring anger and fury, giving the upper hand to his irascible faculty and letting go its reins, he shall be at fault and stumble wherever he goes. For he shall seek opinions that will help him in that toward which his nature inclines. I have drawn your attention to this in order that you should not be deceived. For someone may some day lead you into vain imaginings through setting forth a doubt concerning the creation of the world in time, and you may be very quick to let yourself be deceived. For in this opinion is contained the destruction of the foundation of the Law and a presumptuous assertion with regard to the deity. Be therefore always suspicious in your mind as to this point and accept the authority of the two prophets[1] who are the pillars of the well-being of the human species with

1. I.e., Abraham and Moses.

regard to its beliefs and its associations. Do not turn away from the opinion according to which the world is new, except because of a demonstration. Now such a demonstration does not exist in nature.

Furthermore, the student of this Treatise should not engage in criticism because of my using this rhetorical mode of speech in order to support the affirmation of the newness of the world. For Aristotle, the prince of the philosophers, in his main writings has likewise used rhetorical speeches in support of his opinion that the world is eternal. In such cases it may truly be said: *Shall not our perfect Torah be* [*worth as much*] *as their frivolous talk?*[2] If he refers in support of his opinion to the ravings of the Sabians, how can we but refer in support of our opinion to the words of *Moses* and *Abraham* and to everything that follows therefrom?

I have promised you a chapter in which I shall expound to you the grave doubts that would affect whoever thinks that man has acquired knowledge as to the arrangement of the motions of the sphere and as to their being natural things going on according to the law of necessity, things whose order and arrangement are clear. I shall now explain this to you. |

CHAPTER 24

You know of astronomical matters what you have read under my guidance and understood from the contents of the "Almagest." But there was not enough time to begin another speculative study with you. What you know already is that as far as the action of ordering the motions and making the course of the stars conform to what is seen is concerned, everything depends on two principles: either that of the epicycles or that of the eccentric spheres or on both of them. Now I shall draw your attention to the fact that both those principles are entirely outside the bounds of reasoning[1] and opposed to all that has been made clear in natural science. In the first place, if one affirms as true the existence of an epicycle revolving round a certain sphere, positing at the same time that that revolution is not around the center of the sphere carrying the epicycles — and this has been supposed with regard to the moon and to the five planets — it follows necessarily that there

2. B.T., Baba Bathra, 116a; Megillath Taᶜanith, V.
1. The Arabic word used is *qiyās*; it means "syllogism" (and in a broader sense, "reasoning") or "analogy."

is rolling, that is, that the epicycle rolls and changes its place completely. Now this is the impossibility that was to be avoided, namely, the assumption that there should be something in the heavens that changes its place. For this reason Abū Bakr Ibn al-Ṣāʾigh[2] states in his extant discourse on astronomy that the existence of epicycles is impossible. He points out the necessary inference already mentioned. In addition to this impossibility necessarily following from the assumption of the existence of epicycles, he sets forth there other impossibilities that also follow from that assumption. I shall explain them to you now.

The revolution of the epicycles is not around the center of the world. Now it is a fundamental principle of this world that there are three motions: a motion from the midmost point of the world, a motion toward that point, and a motion around that point. But if | an epicycle existed, its motion would be neither from that point nor toward it nor around it.

Furthermore, it is one of the preliminary assumptions of Aristotle in natural science that there must necessarily be some immobile thing around which circular motion takes place. Hence it is necessary that the earth should be immobile. Now if epicycles exist, theirs would be a circular motion that would not revolve round an immobile thing. I have heard that Abū Bakr has stated that he had invented an astronomical system in which no epicycles figured, but only eccentric circles. However, I have not heard this from his pupils. And even if this were truly accomplished by him, he would not gain much thereby. For eccentricity also necessitates going outside the limits posed by the principles established by Aristotle, those principles to which nothing can be added. It was by me that attention was drawn to this point. In the case of eccentricity, we likewise find that the circular motion of the spheres does not take place around the midmost point of the world, but around an imaginary point that is other than the center of the world. Accordingly, that motion is likewise not a motion taking place around an immobile thing. If, however, someone having no knowledge of astronomy thinks that eccentricity with respect to these imaginary points may be considered — when these points are situated inside[3] the sphere of the moon, as they appear to be at the outset — as equivalent to motion round the midmost point of the world, we would agree to concede this to him if that motion took place round a point in the zone of fire or of air, though in that

2. I.e., Ibn Bājja. Cf. I 74, n. 10. The work to which the text refers is not known at present. On the philosophic criticism of the Ptolemaic system, cf. Translator's Introduction.

3. I.e., beneath.

case that motion would not be around an immobile thing. We will, however, make it clear to him that the measures of eccentricity have been demonstrated in the "Almagest" according to what is assumed there. And the latter-day scientists have given a correct demonstration, regarding which there is no doubt, of how great the measure of these eccentricities is compared with half the diameter of the earth, just as they have set forth all the other distances and dimensions. It has consequently become clear that the eccentric point around which the sun revolves | must of necessity be outside the concavity of the sphere of the moon and beneath the convexity of the sphere of Mercury. Similarly the point around which Mars revolves, I mean to say the center of its eccentric sphere, is outside the concavity of the sphere of Mercury and beneath the convexity of the sphere of Venus. Again the center of the eccentric sphere of Jupiter is at the same distance — I mean between the sphere of Mercury and Venus. As for Saturn, the center of its eccentric sphere is between the spheres of Mars and Jupiter. See now how all these things are remote from natural speculation! All this will become clear to you if you consider the distances and dimensions, known to you, of every sphere and star, as well as the evaluation of all of them by means of half the diameter of the earth so that everything is calculated according to one and the same proportion and the eccentricity of every sphere is not evaluated in relation to the sphere itself.

Even more incongruous and dubious is the fact that in all cases in which one of two spheres is inside the other and adheres to it on every side, while the centers of the two are different, the smaller sphere can move inside the bigger one without the latter being in motion, whereas the bigger sphere cannot move upon any axis whatever without the smaller one being in motion. For whenever the bigger sphere moves, it necessarily, by means of its movement, sets the smaller one in motion, except in the case in which its motion is on axis passing through the two centers. From this demonstrative premise and from the demonstrated fact that vacuum does not exist and from the assumptions regarding eccentricity, it follows necessarily that when the higher sphere is in motion it must move the sphere beneath it with the same motion and around its own center. Now we do not find that this is so. We find rather that neither of the two spheres, the containing and the contained, is set in motion by the movement of the other nor does it move around the other's center or poles, | but that each of them has its own particular motion. Hence necessity obliges the belief that between every two spheres there are bodies other than those of the spheres. Now if this be so, how many obscure points remain? Where will you suppose the centers of those bodies existing between every two spheres to be? And those bodies should likewise have their own particular motion. Thābit[4] has explained this in a treatise of his and has demonstrated what we have said, namely, that there must be the body of a sphere between every two spheres. All this I did not explain to you when you read under my guidance, for fear of confusing you with regard to that which it was my purpose to make you understand.

As for the inclination and deviation that are spoken of regarding the latitude of Venus and Mercury, I have explained to you by word of mouth and I have shown you that it is impossible to conceive their existence in those bodies. For the rest Ptolemy has said explicitly, as you have seen, that one was unable to do this, stating literally: No one should think that these principles and those similar to them may only be put into effect with difficulty, if his reason for doing this be that he regards that which we have set forth as he would regard things obtained by artifice and the subtlety of art and which may only be realized with difficulty. For human matters should not be compared to those that are divine.[5] This is, as you know, the text of his statement. I have indicated to you the passages from which the true reality of everything I have mentioned to you becomes manifest, except for what I have told you regarding the examination of where the points lie that are the centers of the eccentric circles. For I have never come across anybody who has paid attention to this. However this shall become clear to you through the knowledge of the measure of the diameter of every sphere and what the distance is between the two centers as compared with half the diameter of the earth, according to what has been demonstrated by al-Qabīṣī[6] in the "Epistle Concerning the Distances." If you examine those distances, | the truth of the point to which I have drawn your attention will become clear to you.

Consider now how great these difficulties are. If what Aristotle has stated with regard to natural science is true, there are no epicycles or eccentric circles and everything revolves round the center of the earth. But in that case how can the various motions of the stars come about? Is it in any way possible that motion should be on the one hand circular, uniform, and perfect, and that on the other hand the things that are observable should be observed in consequence of it, unless this be accounted

4. Thābit Ibn Qurra, a well-known mathematician, astronomer, philosopher, and translator, who belonged to the pagan community of Ḥarrān. He died in 900.
5. *Almagest* xiii.2.
6. A tenth-century astronomer.

for by making use of one of the two principles[7] or of both of them? This consideration is all the stronger because of the fact that if one accepts everything stated by Ptolemy concerning the epicycle of the moon and its deviation toward a point outside the center of the world and also outside the center of the eccentric circle, it will be found that what is calculated on the hypothesis of the two principles is not at fault by even a minute. The truth of this is attested by the correctness of the calculations — always made on the basis of these principles — concerning the eclipses and the exact determination of their times as well as of the moment when it begins to be dark and of the length of time of the darkness. Furthermore, how can one conceive the retrogradation of a star, together with its other motions, without assuming the existence of an epicycle? On the other hand, how can one imagine a rolling motion in the heavens or a motion around a center that is not immobile? This is the true perplexity.

However, I have already explained to you by word of mouth that all this does not affect the astronomer. For his purpose is not to tell us in which way the spheres truly are, but to posit an astronomical system in which it would be possible for the motions to be circular and uniform and to correspond to what is apprehended through sight, regardless of whether or not things are thus in fact. You know already that in speaking of natural science, Abū Bakr Ibn al-Ṣāʾigh[8] expresses a doubt whether Aristotle knew about the eccentricity of the sun and passed over it in silence — treating of what necessarily follows from the sun's inclination, inasmuch as the effect of eccentricity is not distinguishable from | that of inclination— or whether he was not aware of eccentricity. Now the truth is that he was not aware of it and had never heard about it, for in his time mathematics had not been brought to perfection. If, however, he had heard about it, he would have violently rejected it; and if it were to his mind established as true, he would have become most perplexed about all his assumptions on the subject. I shall repeat here what I have said before.[9] All that Aristotle states about that which is beneath the sphere of the moon is in accordance with reasoning;[10] these are things that have a known cause, that follow one upon the other, and concerning which it is clear and manifest at what points wisdom and natural providence are effective. However, regarding all that is in the heavens, man grasps nothing but a small measure of what is mathematical; and you know what is in it. I shall accordingly say in the manner of poetical preciousness: *The heavens are the heavens of the Lord,*

7. I.e., of the epicycles and the eccentric circles. 8. I.e., Ibn Bājja. Cf. n. 2, this chap.
9. Cf. II 22.   10. *qiyās*; cf. n. 1, this chap.

but the earth hath He given to the sons of man.[11] I mean thereby that the deity alone fully knows the true reality, the nature, the substance, the form, the motions, and the causes of the heavens. But He has enabled man to have knowledge of what is beneath the heavens, for that is his world and his dwelling-place in which he has been placed and of which he himself is a part. This is the truth. For it is impossible for us to accede to the points starting from which conclusions may be drawn about the heavens; for the latter are too far away from us and too high in place and in rank. And even the general conclusion that may be drawn from them, namely, that they prove the existence of their Mover, is a matter the knowledge of which cannot be reached by human intellects.[12] And to fatigue the minds with notions that cannot be grasped by them and for the grasp of which they have no instrument, is a defect in one's inborn disposition or some sort of temptation. Let us then stop at a point that is within our capacity, and let us give over the things that cannot be grasped by reasoning[13] to him who was reached by the mighty divine overflow so that it could be fittingly said of him: *With him do I speak mouth to mouth.*[14] That is | the end of what I have to say about this question. It is possible that someone else may find a demonstration by means of which the true reality of what is obscure for me will become clear to him. The extreme predilection that I have for investigating the truth is evidenced by the fact that I have explicitly stated and reported my perplexity regarding these matters as well as by the fact that I have not heard nor do I know a demonstration as to anything concerning them.

CHAPTER 25

Know that our shunning the affirmation of the eternity of the world is not due to a text figuring in the *Torah* according to which the world has been produced in time. For the texts indicating that the world has been produced in time are not more numerous than those indicating that the deity is a body. Nor are the gates of figurative interpretation shut in our faces

---

11. Ps. 115:16.
12. In Ibn Tibbon's translation the passage has a different meaning: "The general proof from them is that they indicate the existence of their Mover, but the knowledge of other matters concerning them cannot be reached by human intellects."
13. *qiyās.*   14. Num. 12:8.

or impossible of access to us regarding the subject of the creation of the world in time. For we could interpret them as figurative, as we have done when denying His corporeality. Perhaps this would even be much easier to do: we should be very well able to give a figurative interpretation of those texts and to affirm as true the eternity of the world, just as we have given a figurative interpretation of those other texts and have denied that He, may He be exalted, is a body.

Two causes are responsible for our not doing this or believing it. One of them is as follows. That the deity is not a body has been demonstrated; from this it follows necessarily that everything that in its external meaning disagrees with this demonstration must be interpreted figuratively, for it is known that such texts are of necessity fit for figurative interpretation. However, the eternity of the world has not been demonstrated. Consequently in this case the texts ought not to be rejected and figuratively interpreted in order to make prevail an opinion whose contrary can be made to prevail by means of various sorts of arguments. This is one cause.

The second cause is as follows. Our belief that the deity is not | a body destroys for us none of the foundations of the Law and does not give the lie to the claims of any prophet. The only objection to it is constituted by the fact that the ignorant think that this belief is contrary to the text; yet it is not contrary to it, as we have explained, but is intended by the text. On the other hand, the belief in eternity the way Aristotle sees it — that is, the belief according to which the world exists in virtue of necessity, that no nature changes at all, and that the customary course of events cannot be modified with regard to anything — destroys the Law in its principle, necessarily gives the lie to every miracle, and reduces to inanity all the hopes and threats that the Law has held out, unless — by God! — one interprets the miracles figuratively also, as was done by the Islamic internalists;[1] this, however, would result in some sort of crazy imaginings.

If, however, one believed in eternity according to the second opinion we have explained[2] — which is the opinion of Plato — according to which the heavens too are subject to generation and corruption, this opinion would not destroy the foundations of the Law and would be followed not by the lie being given to miracles, but by their becoming admissible. It would also be possible to interpret figuratively the texts in accordance with this opinion.

1. *ahl al-bāṭin.* In Arabic *bāṭin* may mean "the internal sense." The Ismāʿīlī and similar sects are often designated as *ahl al-bāṭin.* An allegorical interpretation of the Qurʾān was part of their faith.
2. Cf. II 13.

And many obscure passages[3] can be found in the texts of the *Torah* and others with which this opinion could be connected or rather by means of which it could be proved. However, no necessity could impel us to do this unless this opinion were demonstrated. In view of the fact that it has not been demonstrated, we shall not favor this opinion, nor shall we at all heed that other opinion, but rather shall take the texts according to their external sense and shall say: The Law has given us knowledge of a matter the grasp of which is not within our power, and the miracle attests to the correctness of our claims.

Know that with a belief in the creation of the world in time, all the miracles become possible and the Law becomes possible, and all questions that may be asked on this subject, vanish. Thus it might be said: Why did God give prophetic revelation to this one and not to that? Why did | God give this Law to this particular nation, and why did He not legislate to the others? Why did He legislate at this particular time, and why did He not legislate before it or after? Why did He impose these commandments and these prohibitions? Why did He privilege the prophet with the miracles mentioned in relation to him and not with some others? What was God's aim in giving this Law? Why did He not, if such was His purpose,[4] put the accomplishment of the commandments and the nontransgression of the prohibitions into our nature? If this were said, the answer to all these questions would be that it would be said: He wanted it this way; or His wisdom required it this way. And just as He brought the world into existence, having the form it has, when He wanted to, without our knowing His will with regard to this or in what respect there was wisdom in His particularizing the forms of the world and the time of its creation — in the same way we do not know His will or the exigency of His wisdom that caused all the matters, about which questions have been posed above, to be particularized. If, however, someone says that the world is as it is in virtue of necessity, it would be a necessary obligation to ask all those questions; and there would be no way out of them except through a recourse to unseemly answers in which there would be combined the giving the lie to, and the annulment of, all the external meanings of the Law with regard to which no intelligent man has any doubt that they are to be taken in their

3. It seems gramatically more correct to interpret the Arabic word "sh.b.h." as being *shubah*, the plural of *shubha*, "an obscure passage," rather than as *shibh*, a singular meaning "analogy." Ibn Tibbon's translation and that of Munk, which conforms to it, seem to be based on the second interpretation.

4. I.e., if He wished us to accomplish the commandments and not to transgress the prohibitions.

external meanings. It is then because of this that this opinion is shunned[5] and that the lives of virtuous men have been and will be spent in investigating this question. For if creation in time were demonstrated — if only as Plato understands creation — all the overhasty[6] claims made to us on this point by the philosophers would become void. In the same way, if the philosophers would succeed in demonstrating eternity as Aristotle understands it, the Law as a whole would become void, and a shift to other opinions would take place. I have thus explained to you that everything is bound up with this problem. Know this. |

CHAPTER 26

I have seen a statement of *Rabbi Eliezer the Great*, figuring in the celebrated *Chapters*[1] known as *Chapters of Rabbi Eliezer*, which is the strangest statement I have seen made by one who follows the Law of *Moses our Master*. Hear the text of the statement he made. He says:[2] *Wherefrom were the heavens created? From the light of His garment. He took some of it, stretched it like a cloth, and thus they were extending continually, as it is said: Who coverest Thyself with light as with a garment. Who stretchest out the heavens like a curtain.*[3] *Wherefrom was the earth created? From the snow under the throne of His glory. He took some of it and threw it, as it is said: For He saith to the snow, Be thou earth.*[4] This is the text of the statement made there. Would that I knew what that *Sage* believed. Did he believe that it is impossible that something should come into being out of nothing and that there must necessarily be matter out of which that which is generated is produced? Did he for this reason seek to find *wherefrom were created* the heavens and the earth? However, whatever results from this answer, he ought to be asked: *Wherefrom was the light of His garment created? Wherefrom was the snow under the throne of glory created? Wherefrom was the throne of glory itself created?* If, however, he wished to signify by *the light of His garment* an uncreated thing and similarly by the *throne of glory* something uncreated, this would be a great incongruity. For he would have admitted thereby the eternity of the world, if only as it is

5. I.e., the affirmation of the eternity of the world a parte ante.   6. Or: incoherent.
1. *Peraqim* in Hebrew.   2. Chapters of Rabbi Eliezer, III.
3. Ps. 104:2.   4. Job 37:6.

conceived according to Plato's opinion. As for the *throne of glory* belonging to the created things, the *Sages* state this expressly, but in a strange manner. For they say that it was created before the creation of the world.[5] But the scriptural texts, in connection with it, do not refer in any way to creation, with the exception of *David's* statement: *The Lord | hath established His throne in the heavens,*[6] which statement admits very well of figurative interpretation. However, the throne's eternity a parte post is expressly stated: *Thou, O Lord, sittest for all eternity, Thy throne is from generation to generation.*[7] Now if *Rabbi Eliezer* believed in the eternity a parte ante of the *throne*, the latter must have been an attribute of God, and not a created body. But how is it possible for a thing to be generated from an attribute? Strangest of all is his saying: *the light of His garment.* All in all, this statement will confuse very much indeed the belief of a learned man who adheres to the Law. No persuasive figurative interpretation with regard to it has become clear to me. I have only mentioned it to you in order that you should make no mistake about it. However, its author has in any case rendered us a great service by making it quite clear that the matter of the heavens is other than that of the earth and that they are two altogether distinct matters. One of them is attributed to Him, may He be exalted, because of its sublimity and high rank, and this is *the light of His garment;* the other matter is remote from His light and splendor, may He be exalted, and this is the lowly matter that the author of the statement makes out to derive *from the snow under the throne of glory.* This has made me interpret figuratively the passage of the *Torah, And there was under his feet, as it were, a work of the whiteness of sapphire stone,*[8] as meaning that they apprehended in this *prophetic vision* the true reality of the inferior first matter. For *Onqelos* makes out, as I have explained to you,[9] that *his feet* refers to the *throne.* And this clearly indicates that the whiteness, which is under the *throne*, is the terrestrial matter. Thus *Rabbi Eliezer* repeated the very same thing and made it clear — I mean the fact that there are two matters, a high and an inferior one, and that the matter of the universe is not one. This is a great mystery, and do not think disdainfully of the fact that the greatest *Sages of Israel* have made a clear statement about it. For it is one of the mysteries of being and a *mystery among the mysteries of the Torah.*

They say in *Bereshith Rabbah: Rabbi Eliezer says: The creation of everything that is in the heavens derives from the heavens, and the creation*

5 Cf. Genesis Rabbah, I; B.T., Pesaḥim, 54a; B.T., Nedarim, 39b.
6. Ps. 103:19.   7. Lam. 5:19.   8. Exod. 24:10.   9. Cf. I 28.

of everything that is | in the earth derives from the earth.[10] Consider how this *Sage* has made it clear to you that the matter of everything that is on earth — I mean to say, of everything that is beneath the sphere of the moon — is one common matter, and that the matter of all the heavens and of what is in them is another matter and not the same as the one just mentioned. In *his Chapters*, [Rabbi Eliezer] clearly states this one additional subtlety. I mean to say the sublimity of that matter and its nearness to Him and the defectiveness of the other and also the place where it is located. Know this.

CHAPTER 27

I have already made it clear to you that the belief in the production of the world is necessarily the foundation of the entire Law. However, the belief in its passing-away after it has come into being and been generated is not, in our opinion, in any respect a foundation of the Law, and none of our beliefs would be hurt through the belief in its permanent duration. Perhaps you will say: Has it not been demonstrated that everything that comes into being passes away?; if then the world is generated it will pass away. Know then that this need not apply to us. For we do not assert that it has been generated according to the rule applying to the generation of the natural things that follow a natural order. For what is generated in accordance with the course of nature[1] must of necessity pass away in accordance with the course of nature. For just as its nature had required that at first it should not exist in this particular way whereas after that it has come to exist in that way, it necessarily also requires that it should not exist in that way forever. For it is established as true that this mode of existence is not permanently attached to it by its nature. However, in view of our claim, based on the Law, that things exist and perish according to His will, may He be exalted, and not in virtue of necessity, | it is not necessary for us to profess in consequence of that opinion that when He, may He be exalted, brings into existence a thing that had not existed, He must necessarily cause this existent to pass away. Rather does the matter inevitably depend on His will: if He wills, He causes the thing to pass away; and if He wills, He

10. Genesis Rabbah, X; cf. B.T., Yoma, 54b.
1. Literally: the natural course.

causes it to last; or it depends on what is required by His wisdom. It is accordingly possible that He should cause it to last for ever and ever and to endure as He Himself, may He be exalted, endures.

You know that while the *Sages* state explicitly that the *throne of glory* has been created, they never say that it will become nonexistent. No *prophet* and no *Sage* has ever been heard to say that the *throne of glory* will pass away or become nonexistent. Rather does the text of Scripture state that it will last forever. The same applies to the souls of the virtuous; for according to our opinion, they are created, but will never become non-existent. According to certain opinions of those who follow the literal sense of the *Midrashim*,[2] their bodies[3] will also be in a state of perpetual felicity for ever and ever — an opinion resembling that of those whose belief as to the inhabitants of Paradise is generally known.

To sum up: Speculation obliges us to affirm that the passing-away of the world need not necessarily follow. Thus it only remains to examine this question in the light of the information imparted by the prophets and the *Sages*. Have they given information that this world will without any doubt pass away, or have they not? Most of the vulgar among us believe that such information has been given and that all this world will pass away. However, I shall explain to you that this is not so, but that there are many texts that signify that it will last forever. All the passages from whose external sense it appears that the world will pass away, are most manifestly parables, as I shall explain. If, however, one of the externalists refuses to admit this and says that he must necessarily believe in the passing-away of the world, he should not be dealt with illiberally. However, he needs to be informed that the world's passing-away does not necessarily follow from the fact of its having been created in time, but that he believes in this, as he thinks, by way of accepting the veracity of the one who stated | that parable, which he takes in its external sense. From the point of view of the Law, there is no harm in this in any respect whatever.

2. In the text: *Midrashoth*.   3. Or: corpses.

Many of the adherents of our Law have thought that *Solomon*, peace be on him, believed in the eternity of the world. It is amazing that it should be imagined that a man belonging to the adherents of the Law of *Moses our Master* believed in the eternity of the world. If, however, someone deems—may God protect us!—that in this he abandoned the opinions of the Law, how was it that all the prophets and the *Sages* accepted this from him and did not attack him on this point or blame him after his death, as had to be done in connection with the *alien women* and on other counts? This vain imagining was occasioned by the statement of the *Sages, may their memory be blessed; [People] wanted to suppress the book of Ecclesiastes because its words incline to those of the heretics.*[1] This is undoubtedly so; I mean to say, in this book, taken in its external sense, there are passages that incline to opinions foreign to those of the Law and that need a figurative interpretation. However, the affirmation of the eternity of the world does not belong to them. There is no text in it indicating this, and no text whatever is to be found in it that states explicitly that the world is eternal a parte ante. However, some texts in it indicate that it is eternal a parte post, which is true. When people saw texts indicating that the world is eternal a parte post, they thought that he [Solomon] believed that the world was not created in time. This is not so.

The text in the book regarding the eternity a parte post of the world reads: *And the earth abideth for ever [leᶜolam].*[2] But those who were not aware of this subtlety resorted to the explanation: during the time predetermined for it. And they explain similarly His words, may He be exalted, *Yet all the days of the earth,*[3] as referring to the | predetermined length of its life. Would that I knew what is said with regard to *David's* words: *Who didst establish the earth upon its foundations, that it should not be moved for ever and ever [ᶜolam vaᶜed].*[4] For if the words, *ᶜolam vaᶜed,*[5] do not point to eternity a parte post, this would mean that the deity has a certain duration. For the scriptural text says with reference to His eternity a parte post, may He be exalted: *The Lord shall reign for ever and ever [le ᶜolam vaᶜed].*[6] You know that the word *ᶜolam* does not signify eternity a parte post unless it be conjoined with the word *ᶜad*, which may come

1. Leviticus Rabbah, XXVIII; Midrash Qoheleth, 1:3. 2. Eccles. 1:4.
3. Gen. 8:22. 4. Ps. 104:5. 5. Meaning "for ever and ever."
6. Exod. 15:18.

either after it — as in the scriptural expression: *ᶜolam vaᶜed* — or before it — as in the scriptural expression: *ᶜad ᶜolam*. Consequently *Solomon's* statement:[7] *abideth for ever* [*le ᶜolam*], means less than *David's* statement:[8] *that it should not be moved for ever and ever* [*ᶜolam vaᶜed*].[9] *David*, peace be on him, likewise makes clear and manifest the eternity a parte post of the heavens and the permanence in an immutable state of their statutes and of all that is in them. For he says: *Praise ye the Lord from the heavens, and so on. For He commanded and they were created. He hath established them for ever and ever; He hath made a statute, which shall not be transgressed.*[10] He means by this that the statutes, which He has laid down, will never be changed. For the word *statute* alludes to the *statutes of heaven and earth,*[11] which have been mentioned previously. However, he makes it clear that they are created, saying: *For He commanded, and they were created.* And *Jeremiah*, peace be on him, says: *Who giveth the sun for a light by day, and the statutes of the moon and of the stars for a light by night, and so on. If these statutes depart from before Me, saith the Lord, then the seed of Israel also shall cease from being a nation.*[12] Thus he has likewise clearly stated that they — I mean these statutes — even though created, shall not *depart.*

Thus if this matter is pursued, this doctrine will be found not only in *Solomon's* words. On the other hand, *Solomon* himself has likewise stated that these works of the deity — I mean the world and what is in it — even though they are made, are permanently established according to their nature for ever. For he says: *That whatsoever God doeth, it shall be for ever; nothing can be added to it, nor any thing taken from it.*[13] Thus he imparts in | this *verse* the information that the world is a work of the deity and that it is eternal a parte post. He also states the cause of its being eternal a parte post; namely, in his words: *nothing can be added to it, nor any thing taken from it.* For this is the cause of its *being for ever.* It is as if he said that the thing that is changed, is changed because of a deficiency in it that should be made good or because of some excess that is not needed and should be got rid of. Now the works of the deity are most perfect, and with regard to them there is no possibility of an excess or a deficiency. Accordingly they are of necessity permanently established as they are, for there is no possibility of something calling for a change in them. He has also, as it were, stated an end for what

---

7. See above in this chapter.　　8. See above in this chapter.

9. Solomon's statment is less strong than David's because he uses the expression *leᶜolam* to signify "perpetual duration," and not the expression *ᶜolam vaᶜed* employed by David.

10. Ps. 148:1, 5, 6.　　11. Jer. 33:25.　　12. Jer. 31:34–35.　　13. Eccles. 3:14.

has come to exist or given an excuse for what changes, saying in the final part of the *verse*: *And God hath so made it, that they should fear before Him*[14] — he refers to the production in time of miracles. In saying after that, *That which hath been is now, and that which is to be hath already been; and God seeketh that which is pursued,*[15] the author states that He, may He be exalted, desires that that which exists should continue and that its various parts should be consecutive to one another. As for his mention of the perfection of the acts of the deity and of its being impossible to add or to take away from them, the Master of those who know had already clearly stated this, saying: *The Rock, His work is perfect.*[16] He means that all His works — I mean to say His creatures — are most perfect, that no deficiency at all is commingled with them, that there is no superfluity in them and nothing that is not needed. Similarly all that is being accomplished for and by the created things is absolute justice and follows from the requirement of wisdom, as shall be made clear in some of the chapters of this Treatise. |

CHAPTER 29

Know that if one does not understand the language of a human being whom one hears speaking, one indubitably knows that he speaks, but without knowing what he intends to say. Something of even graver import may occur: sometimes one may hear in someone else's speech words that in the language of the speaker indicate a certain meaning, and by accident that word indicates in the language of the hearer the contrary of what the speaker intended. Thus the hearer will think that the signification that the word has for the speaker is the same as its signification for him. For instance if an Arab hears a Hebrew man saying ʾ*aba* [*he wishes*], the Arab will think that he speaks of an individual who was reluctant with regard to some matter and refused [ʾ*abā*] it.[1] However, the Hebrew only wished to convey that the individual was pleased with the matter and wished it. This is similar to what happens to the multitude with regard to the speech of the prophets, excepting certain portions that they do not understand at all. As it says: *the vision of all this is become unto you as the words of a book that*

14. Eccles. 3:14.   15. Eccles. 3:15.   16. Deut. 32:4.
1. The two words have the same radicals. In Hebrew ʾ*aba* means "to wish"; in Arabic ʾ*abā* means "to be reluctant" and "to refuse."

is sealed.[2] With regard to other portions, they understand what is the contrary of, or contradictory to, the true meaning. As it says: *And ye have perverted the words of the living God.*[3] Know that every prophet has a kind of speech peculiar to him, which is, as it were, the language of that individual, which the prophetic revelation peculiar to him causes him to speak to those who understand him.

After this preface, you ought to know that in the speech of *Isaiah*, peace be on him, it very frequently occurs — whereas in the speech of other prophets it rarely occurs — that when he speaks of the fall of a dynasty or the destruction of a great religious community,[4] he uses such expressions as: the stars have fallen, the heavens were rolled up, the sun was blackened, the earth was devastated and quaked, and many similar | figurative expressions. This is similar to what is said by the Arabs with regard to someone whom a great misfortune has befallen: his heavens were cast upside down upon his earth. In the same way when he describes the prosperity of a dynasty and the renewal of happiness, he calls them: an increase of the light of the sun and the moon, a renewal of the heavens and a renewal of the earth, and so forth; just as when describing the destruction of an individual or a religious community or a city, they ascribe to God in relation to the latter the states of anger and extreme wrath; and when describing the prosperity of a people, they ascribe to God the states of joy and gladness. Accordingly they say about states of anger with regard to men or communities: *He went forth* and *He went down* and *He roared* and *He thundered* and *He gave forth His voice*, and many other similar expressions; they say likewise: *He ordered* and *He said* and *He acted* and *He did*, and so on, as I shall set forth. Similarly when a prophet gives information as to the destruction of the people of a certain locality, he sometimes substitutes for the people of that locality, the whole human species. Thus *Isaiah*, peace be on him, says: *And the Lord will remove man far away;*[5] he refers to the destruction of *Israel*. And *Zephaniah* says on this subject: *And I will cut off man from off the face of the earth. And I will stretch out My hand upon Judah.*[6] Know this also.

After having interpreted this language to you in a general way, I shall show you the correctness of this interpretation and the demonstration thereof. When God had given *Isaiah*, peace be on him, prophetic inspiration regarding the fall of the *Babylonian* dynasty, the destruction of *Sennacherib* and of *Nebuchadnezzar* who rose up after him, and the end of his kingdom; and when that prophet began to describe the disaster that

2. Isa. 29:11.   3. Jer. 23:36.   4. Or: nation.   5. Isa. 6:12.   6. Zeph. 1:3-4.

befell them at the end of their reigns, their defeats, and the misfortunes that came upon them and were such misfortunes as come upon all the defeated who flee the victory of the sword — he said: *For the stars of heaven and the constellations thereof shall not give their light; the sun shall be darkened in his going forth, and the moon shall not cause her light to shine.*[7] And he also said in the course of the same description: *Therefore I will make the heavens to tremble, and the earth shall be shaken out of her place, in the wrath of* | *the Lord of hosts, and in the day of His fierce anger.*[8] I do not think that there has been anyone in whom ignorance, blindness, and the inclination to adhere to the external sense of figurative expressions and of rhetorical speeches, have reached such a point that he thought that the stars of the heavens and the light of the sun and of the moon have been changed when the kingdom of Babylon came to an end, or that the earth was removed from its center,[9] as was stated. All of this is merely a description of the state of someone put to flight; for without any doubt, he sees all light as black, finds everything that is sweet bitter, and imagines that the earth has narrowed for him and that the heavens are closed[10] over him. Similarly when he began to describe the state of extreme humiliation and servitude to which *Israel* would be reduced throughout the time of *the wicked Sennacherib* — when he would capture *all the fortified cities of Judah,*[11] take the people captive, and put them to flight, and when various calamities would befall them in quick succession at his hands and the whole *land of Israel* perish through him, he said: *Terror, and the pit, and the trap, are upon thee, O inhabitant of the earth.*[12] *And it shall come to pass, that he who fleeth from the noise of the terror shall fall into the pit; and he that cometh out of the midst of the pit shall be taken in the trap; for the windows on high are opened, and the foundations of the earth do shake. The earth is broken, broken down, the earth is crumbled in pieces, the earth trembleth and tottereth. The earth reeleth to and fro like a drunkard, and so on.*[13] At the conclusion of this passage, when he began to describe what God would do to *Sennacherib*, the destruction of his proud kingdom before *Jerusalem*, and the shame that God would cause him to suffer there, he said, speaking in parables: *Then the moon shall be confounded, and the sun ashamed; for the Lord of hosts will reign, and so on.*[14] *Jonathan ben Uziel,* peace be on him, has given a very good interpretation of this passage,

7. Isa. 13:10.   8. Isa. 13:13.   9. Or: its position.
10. Or, according to the translation of Ibn Tibbon, who may have had a somewhat different Arabic text: are upset.
11. Isa. 36:1.   12. Or: *the land.*   13. Isa. 24:17–20.   14. Isa. 24:23.

saying that when that which was going to come to pass before *Jerusalem* would happen to *Sennacherib*, the idolaters would know that that was a divine act and would be astonished and confused. For he, may peace be on him, says:[15] | *They who worship the moon will be ashamed, and they who bow down to the sun will be humbled, for the Kingdom of God will be revealed, and so on.*

Again when he began to describe how great shall be the stable security of *Israel* after the destruction of *Sennacherib*, as well as the fertility and cultivation of their lands and the good fortune of their dynasty brought about by *Hezekiah*, he said, speaking in parables, that the light of the sun and of the moon would increase. For whereas, as has been mentioned, with reference to someone put to flight, the light of the sun and of the moon goes out and becomes darkness, their light increases according to him who is victorious. For you will always find that when a great misfortune befalls a man, his eyes are darkened and the light of his sight is not clear, because the visual spirit is disturbed by the superfluity of vapors and also because it is weak and there is not much of it in consequence of the greatness of the sorrow and the contraction of the soul. On the contrary, when there is joy, when the soul expands outwards and the spirit is clear, man sees as it were that the light is stronger than it was. He says: *For, O people that dwellest in Zion at Jerusalem, thou shalt weep no more, and so on.*[16] The conclusion of the passage is: *Moreover the light of the moon shall be as the light of the sun, and the light of the sun shall be sevenfold, as the light of the seven days, in the day that the Lord bindeth up the bruise of His people, and healeth the stroke of their wound.*[17] He refers to their being raised from the fall *caused by the wicked Sennacherib.* As for his words, *as the light of seven days,* the commentators have said that he means thereby the multiplicity of light, for the Hebrews denote multiplicity by the number seven. However, it occurs to me that he refers to *the seven days of the dedication of the Temple,* which took place in the days of *Solomon.* For the religious community[18] had never had such good fortune, happiness, and general joy, as in those days. He says accordingly that their good fortune and happiness will be then as it was in those seven days. | When he described the destruction of *wicked Edom,* which oppressed *Israel,* he said: *Their slain also shall be cast out, and the stench of their carcasses shall come up, and the mountains shall be melted with their blood. And all the host of heaven shall moulder away, and the heavens shall be rolled together as a scroll; and all their host shall fall down,*

15. In the Aramaic translation attributed to him.   16. Isa. 30:19.
17. Isa. 30:26.   18. Or: nation.

as a leaf falleth off from the vine, and as a falling fig from the fig tree. For my sword hath drunk its fill in heaven; behold, it shall come down upon Edom, and so on.[19] Consider, you who are able to see, whether there is anything in these texts that is obscure or leads one to imagine that he describes a future state of the heavens, whether this description is anything but a parable signifying the end of their dynasty, the withdrawal of God's protection from them, ill luck befalling them, and the shrinking-away of the position of their great dignitaries — all this being due to happen within a very short time and with very little effort. It is as if he said that individuals who were like the stars because of their fixed position, their high rank, and their remoteness from the change, would fall down within a very short time, *as a leaf falleth off from the vine, and so on.* This is too clear even to be mentioned in a Treatise like this. Nor then should it be expatiated upon. But necessity requires this; for the common people and even some of those who are supposed to belong to the elite use this *verse* as a proof, without considering what comes before it and after it and without paying attention to the context in which it occurs; as if it contained information given to us in the *Torah* about the end of the heavens, just as there is given to us in it information about their coming to be.

Again when *Isaiah* began to give *Israel* the good tidings about the destruction of *Sennacherib* and of all the nations and the kings that were with him, as is well known, and the victory that would be won over them with the help of God and no one else, he said to them, speaking in parables: See how those heavens are rent, this earth worn out, and how those who live on it die away, while you are succored. It is as if he said that those who have extended over the whole earth and who were thought to be as firmly established as the heavens, speaking hyperbolically, would quickly perish and disappear like smoke, | while their visible monuments, which were as firmly established as the earth, would crumble like a worn-out garment. In the beginning of the passage he says: *For the Lord hath comforted Zion; He hath comforted all her waste places, and so on. Attend unto Me, O My people, and so on. My righteousness is near, My salvation is gone forth, and so on. Lift up your eyes to the heavens, and look upon the earth beneath; for the heavens shall vanish away like smoke, and the earth shall wax old like a garment, and they that dwell therein shall die in like manner; But My salvation shall be for ever, and My righteousness shall not be abolished.*[20]

With regard to the return of the *king of Israel*, his stability, and his

19. Isa. 34:3-5.   20. Isa. 51:3-6.

permanence, he says that God will produce anew the heavens and the earth. For in his speech he frequently refers to the reign of a king as if it were a world existing especially for the king, I mean to say a heaven and an earth. Accordingly when he begins *the consolations*, saying: *I, even I, am He that comforteth you*,[21] and what immediately follows — he goes on to say: *And I have put My words in thy mouth, and have covered thee in the shadow of My hand, that I may plant the heavens, and lay the foundations of the earth, and say unto Zion: Thou art My people.*[22]

With regard to the permanence of the possession by *Israel* of kingly rule and to the latter's departure from the great and celebrated potentates, he says: *For the mountains shall depart, and so on*,[23] With regard to the permanence of the *King* that is the *Messiah* and to *Israel*'s kingdom not being destroyed after that, he says: *Thy sun shall no more go down, and so on*.[24] After that *Isaiah* goes on in his speech consistently using those figurative expressions, for they appear thus to him who understands the meaning of those speeches. Thus describing the state of *Exile* and its various particularities and thereupon the restoration of the kingdom and the disappearance of all those sorrows, he says, speaking in parables: I shall create another heaven and another earth; and those that are now will be forgotten and their traces effaced. Then he explains this in continuity, saying: When I have said "I shall create," I meant thereby that I shall produce for you, instead of those sorrows and hardships, a state of constant joy and gladness so that the | former sorrows will not be remembered. Listen to the arrangement of the notions and the mutual connection of the *verses* indicating these notions: how in the first beginning of this passage, he says: *I will make mention of the loving-kindnesses of the Lord and the praises of the Lord, and so on*.[25] Then he described, in the first place, the bounties that He, may He be exalted, bestows upon us, saying: *And He bore them and carried them all the days of old, and so on*,[26] and what immediately follows. Then he describes our disobedience, saying: *But they rebelled and grieved His holy spirit*,[27] and what immediately follows. Then he describes the enemy obtaining dominion over us, saying: *Our adversaries have trodden down Thy sanctuary; we were ever*,[28] and what immediately follows. Then he intercedes for us, saying: *Be not wroth very sore, O Lord*,[29] and what immediately follows. Then he sets forth how we have deserved the great misfortunes that have befallen us, because of our

21. Isa. 51:12.   22. Isa. 51:16.   23. Isa. 54:10.   24. Isa. 60:20.
25. Isa. 63:7.   26. Isa. 63:9.   27. Isa. 63:10.   28. Isa. 63:18–19.
29. Isa. 64:8.

having received a call to truth and having not responded; he says: *I offered Myself to be sought of them that asked not for Me, and so on.*[30] Then he promises pardon and pity, saying: *Thus saith the Lord, As when new wine is found in the cluster, and so on,*[31] and what immediately follows. Then he threatens with punishment those who have wronged us, saying: *Behold, My servants shall eat, but ye shall be hungry, and so on.*[32] Then he follows this by stating that the beliefs of this religious community shall be the right ones, that it will be a blessing on the earth, and that it will forget all the various above-mentioned vicissitudes. This is the text of what he says: *And He shall call His servants by another name; so that he who blesseth himself in the earth shall bless himself by the God of truth; and he that sweareth in the earth shall swear by the God of truth, because the former troubles are forgotten, and because they are hid from Mine eyes. For, behold, I create new heavens and a new earth; and the former things shall not be remembered, nor come into mind. But be ye glad and rejoice for ever in that which I create; for, behold, I create Jerusalem a rejoicing, and her people a joy. And I will rejoice in Jerusalem, and so on.*[33]

Accordingly the whole matter has become clear and manifest to you. For after saying, *For, behold, I create | new heavens and a new earth,* he immediately explains this by saying: *For, behold, I create Jerusalem a rejoicing, and her people a joy.* After this preamble, he says: Just as those states of faith and of joy in that faith which I promised you to create, will always be permanently established—for the faith in God and the joy in that faith are states that cannot cease or ever be altered in all those who have attained them—and therefore he says:[34] Just as this state of faith and of joy in it, as to which I promised that it will extend over the earth, will be firmly established and permanent, so will your progeny and your name endure. That is his statement which follows: *For as the new heavens and the new earth, which I will make, shall remain before Me, saith the Lord, so shall your seed and your name remain.*[35] For it sometimes happens that the *seed* remains while the *name* does not. Thus you can find many peoples that are indubitably the seed of *Persia* or *Greece,* but are not known by a special name, being absorbed in another religious community.[36] This, to my mind, is likewise an indication of the eternity of the Law because of which we have a special *name.*

Inasmuch as these figurative expressions occur often in *Isaiah,* I have

30. Isa. 65:1.   31. Isa. 65:8.   32. Isa. 65:13.   33. Isa. 65:15–19.
34. After an anacoluthon, Maimonides repeats most of the sentence.
35. Isa. 66:22.   36. Or: nation.

examined all of them. However, they also occur sometimes in the speech of others. Thus *Jeremiah*, when describing the destruction of *Jerusalem* caused *by the sins of our forefathers*, says: *I beheld the earth, and, lo, it was waste and void, and so on.*[37] *Ezekiel*, describing the ruin of the kingdom of Egypt and the destruction of *Pharaoh* at the hands of *Nebuchadnezzar*, says: *And when I shall extinguish thee, I will cover the heaven, and make the stars thereof black; I will cover the sun with a cloud, and the moon shall not give her light. All the bright lights of heaven will I make black over thee, and set darkness upon thy land, saith the Lord God.*[38] *Joel, son of Pethuel*, speaking | of the multitude of locusts that came in his days, says: *Before them the earth quaketh, the heavens tremble; the sun and the moon are become black, and the stars withdraw their shining.*[39] *Amos*, describing the destruction of *Samaria*, says: *That I will cause the sun to go down at noon, and I will darken the earth in the clear day; and I will turn your feasts, and so on.*[40] *Micah*, referring to the ruin of *Samaria*, constantly uses the well-known rhetorical expressions: *For, behold, the Lord cometh forth out of His place, and will come down, and tread upon the high places of the earth. And the mountains shall be molten, and so on.*[41] *Haggai*, referring to the fall of the kingdom of the Persians and the Medes, says: *And I will shake the heavens, and the earth, and the sea, and the dry land; and I will shake all nations.*[42] When, during *Joab's* expedition against *Edom*, [Scripture] begins to describe the weakness and lowly state of the religious community[43] as it was before and their being vanquished and put to flight, and intercedes for their victory now, it says: *Thou hast made the earth to shake, thou hast cleft it: heal the branches thereof; for it tottereth.*[44] In order to signify that we should have no fear when the nations are destroyed and perish, inasmuch as we put our trust in His help, may He be exalted, and not in our fighting and our strength—being, as it says, *a people saved by the Lord*[45]—it says: *Therefore we will not fear, though the earth do change, and though the mountains be moved into the heart of the seas.*[46] In the description of the drowning of the Egyptians, the following occurs: *The waters saw Thee; they were in pain; the depths also trembled. The voice of Thy thunder was in the whirlpool, and so on; the earth trembled and shook.*[47] *Was the Lord displeased with the rivers, and so on.*[48] *Smoke arose up in His nostrils, and so on.*[49] Similarly in the *Song of Deborah*: *The earth trembled, and so*

37. Jer. 4:23.   38. Ezek. 32:7–8.   39. Joel 2:10.   40. Amos 8:9–10.
41. Mic. 1:3–4.   42. Hag. 2:6–7.   43. Or: nation.   44. Ps. 60:4.
45. Deut. 33:29.   46. Ps. 46:3.   47. Ps. 77:17 and 19.
48. Hab. 3:8.   49. Ps. 18:9.

on.[50] There occur many passages of this kind. Draw an analogy from what has been mentioned to what has not.

As for the passage in *Joel: And I will show wonders in the heavens and in the earth, blood, and fire, and pillars of smoke. The sun shall be turned into darkness, and the moon into blood, before the great and terrible day of the Lord come. And it shall come to pass, that whosoever | shall call on the name of the Lord shall be delivered; for in Mount Zion and in Jerusalem shall be deliverance, and so on.*[51] According to me the most probable interpretation is that he describes the destruction of *Sennacherib* before *Jerusalem*. If, however, you do not wish to accept this, it may be held to be a description of the destruction of *Gog* before *Jerusalem in the days of the King Messiah*, though the only things mentioned in this passage are great slaughter, the burning of the fires, and the eclipse of the two luminaries. Perhaps you will say: How can the day of the destruction of *Sennacherib* be called *the great and terrible day of the Lord* according to our interpretation? Know therefore that every day in which a great victory or a great disaster comes to pass is called *the great and terrible day of the Lord.* Thus *Joel* said of the day when the locusts come upon them: *For great is the day of the Lord and very terrible; and who can abide it?*[52]

The notion toward which we are driving has already been made clear; namely, that the passing-away of this world, a change of the state in which it is, or a thing's changing its nature and with that the permanence of this change, are not affirmed in any prophetic text or in any statement of the *Sages* either. For when the latter say, *The world lasts six thousand years, and one thousand years it is a waste,*[53] they do not have in mind total extinction of being. For his expression, *and one thousand years it is a waste,* indicates that time remains. Besides, it is the saying of an *individual* that corresponds to a certain manner of thinking. On the other hand, you constantly find as the opinion of all *Sages* and as a foundation on which every one among *the Sages of the Mishnah and the Sages of the Talmud* bases his proofs, his saying: *There is nothing new under the sun,*[54] and the view that nothing new will be produced in any respect or from any cause whatever. Even he who takes *new heavens and a new earth* to mean what people think it means, says: *Even the heavens and the earth that will be created in the future are already created and subsist, for it is said: they subsist before me. It is not said: they will subsist, but: they subsist.*[55] And he quotes in proof his saying:

---

50. Judg. 5:4.   51. Joel 3:3-5.   52. Joel 2:11.
53. B.T., Rosh Hashanah, 31a; B.T., Sanhedrin, 97a.   54. Eccles. 1:9.
55. Genesis Rabbah, I. The text known to us differs considerably from Maimonides' quotation.

There is nothing new under the sun. Do not | think that this is in contradiction
to what I have explained. For it is possible that he means that the nature
that will necessitate in time the states of existence that have been promised,
is created since the *six days of the Beginning.* And this is true.

I have said that a thing does not change its nature in such a way that
the change is permanent merely in order to be cautious with regard to the
miracles. For although the rod was turned into a serpent, the water into
blood, and the pure and noble hand became white[56] without a natural
cause that necessitated this, these and similar things were not permanent
and did not become another nature. But as they, *may their memory be
blessed,* say: *The world goes its customary way.*[57] This is my opinion, and
this is what ought to be believed. The *Sages, may their memory be blessed,*
have made a very strange statement about miracles, the text of which you
will find in *Bereshith Rabbah* and in *Midrash Qoheleth.* This notion consists
in their holding the view that miracles too are something that is, in a certain
respect, in nature. They say that when God created that which exists and
stamped upon it the existing natures, He put it into these natures that all
the miracles that occurred would be produced in them at the time when they
occurred. According to this opinion, the sign of a prophet consists in God's
making known to him the time when he must make his proclamation,
and thereupon a certain thing is effected according to what was put into its
nature when first it received its particular impress. If this statement is
as you will see it,[58] it indicates the superiority of the man who made it and
the fact that he found it extremely difficult to admit that a nature may
change after the *Work of the Beginning*[59] or that another volition may
supervene after that nature has been established in a definite way. For
instance, he seems to consider that it was put into the nature of water to be
continuous and always to flow from above downwards except at | the time
of the drowning of the Egyptians; it was a particularity of that water to
become divided. I have drawn your attention to the spirit of that passage
and to the fact that all this serves to avoid having to admit the coming-into-
being of something new. It is said in the passage:[60] *Rabbi Jonathan said:
The Holy One, blessed be He, has posed conditions to the sea: [to wit,] that
it should divide before Israel. That is [the meaning of the words]: And the
sea returned to its strength when the morning appeared.*[61] *Rabbi Jeremiah,*

56. I.e., leprous.　　57. B.T., ᶜAbodah Zarah, 54b.
58. Scil., when you look up this text.
59. The expression used by Maimonides has been translated elsewhere as "Account of the
　　Beginning."
60. Genesis Rabbah, V.　　61. Exod. 14:27.
16

son of Elazar, said: The Holy One, blessed be He, has posed conditions not only to the sea, but to all that has been created in the six days of the Beginning. That is [the meaning of the words]: I, even My hands have stretched out the heavens, and all their hosts have I commanded.[62] *I have commanded the sea to divide; the fire not to harm Hananiah, Mishael, and Azariah; the lions not to harm Daniel; and the fish to spit out Jonah.* All the other miracles can be explained in an analogous manner.

The matter has now become clear to you and the doctrine epitomized. Namely, we agree with Aristotle with regard to one half of his opinion and we believe that what exists is eternal a parte post and will last forever with that nature which He, may He be exalted, has willed; that nothing in it will be changed in any respect unless it be in some particular of it miraculously — although He, may He be exalted, has the power to change the whole of it, or to annihilate it, or to annihilate any nature in it that He wills. However, that which exists has had a beginning, and at first nothing at all existed except God. His wisdom required that He should bring creation into existence at the time when He did do it, and that what He has brought into existence should not be annihilated nor any of its natures changed except in certain particulars that He willed to change; about some of these we know, whereas about others that will be changed in the future we do not know. This is our opinion and the basis of our Law. Aristotle, on the other hand, thinks that just as the world is eternal a parte post and will not pass away, it is also eternal a parte ante and has not been produced. Now we have already said and explained that this doctrine can be arranged in a coherent way only through a recourse to the law of necessity and that necessity contains | a presumptuous assertion with regard to the deity, as we have explained.

As the exposition has finally reached this point, we shall now put in a chapter that shall likewise give several indications as to texts concerned with the *Account of the Beginning.* For the first purpose of this Treatise is to explain what can be explained of the *Account of the Beginning* and of the *Account of the Chariot.* We shall put in this chapter after we have first set forth two preambles of general import. One of these is as follows: Not everything mentioned in the *Torah* concerning the *Account of the Beginning* is to be taken in its external sense as the vulgar imagine. For if the matter were such, the men of knowledge would not have been chary[63]

62. Isa. 45:12.
63. With the medieval Hebrew translators and with Munk, I read *danna* instead of *zanna*, which figures in the manuscripts.

of divulging knowledge with regard to it, and the *Sages* would not have expatiated on its being kept secret and on preventing the talk about it in the presence of the vulgar. For the external sense of these texts leads either to a grave corruption of the imagination and to giving vent to evil opinions with regard to the deity, or to an absolute denial of the action of the deity and to disbelief in the foundations of the Law. The correct thing to do is to refrain, if one lacks all knowledge of the sciences, from considering these texts merely with the imagination. One should not act like the wretched *preachers* and commentators who think that a knowledge of the interpretation of words is science and in whose opinion wordiness and length of speech add to perfection. On the other hand it is obligatory to consider them with what is truly the intellect after one has acquired perfection in the demonstrative sciences and knowledge of the secrets of the prophets. However, as I have explained several times in our Commentary on the *Mishnah*,[64] none of those who know something of it should divulge it. And they say explicitly: *As from the beginning of the book up to here, the glory of God* [*requires*] *to conceal the thing.*[65] They say it at the end of what is said concerning the *sixth day* [of the Beginning]. Thus what we have said has become clear. However, inasmuch as the divine commandment necessarily obliges everyone who has obtained a certain | perfection to let it overflow toward others — as we shall make clear in the chapters on prophecy that follow — every man endowed with knowledge who has come to possess an understanding of something pertaining to these secrets, either through his own speculation or through being conducted toward this by a guide, must indubitably say something. It is, however, forbidden to be explicit about it. He must accordingly make the secret appear in flashes. Many such flashes, indications, and pointers occur in the sayings of some of the *Sages, may their memory be blessed,* but these sayings are mixed up with the sayings of others and with sayings of another kind. For this reason you will find that with regard to these *mysteries*, I always mention the single saying on which the matter is based, while I leave the rest to those whom it befits that this should be left to them.

The second preamble: As we have said, the prophets use in their speeches equivocal words and words that are not intended to mean what they indicate according to their first signification, the word being mentioned because of its derivation. For instance, the words *maqqel shaqed* [*a rod of an almond tree*][66] are used because from this indication one may go on to

64. E.g., in the commentary on Ḥagigah, II, 1.
65. Genesis Rabbah, IX *ab init*. The allusion is to Prov. 25:2.   66. Jer. 1:11.

the words that follow: *Shoqed 'ani, and so on* [*I watch over*],[67] as we shall explain in the chapters on prophecy.[68] With regard to the same principle, in a reference to the *Chariot* there occurs the word *hashmal*,[69] as they have explained, and also *regel 'egel* [*the foot of a calf*][70] and *nehoshet qalal* [*burnished brass*].[71] In a similar way, *Zechariah* says:[72] *And the mountains were mountains of nehoshet* [*brass*].[73] The same applies to other words.

After these two preambles I shall give the chapter that we have promised.

CHAPTER 30

Know that there is a difference between "the first" and "the principle." Namely, a principle exists in the thing whose principle it is or simultaneously with it, even if it does not | precede it in time. Thus it is said that the heart is the principle of the living being, and the element the principle of that of which it is the element. "First" is also sometimes used in this sense. Sometimes, however, "the first" is applied solely to what is prior in time even when that which is prior in time is not the cause of what is posterior to it. Thus it may be said that the first one who lived in that house was so and so and after him so and so. It may not, however, be said [in a case like this] that so and so is the principle of so and so. The word indicative of "the first" in our language is *tehillah* [*beginning*]: Thus: *The beginning of* [*tehillat*] *the word of the Lord to Hosea*.[1] That indicative of "the principle" is *reshith*. For it derives from *rosh* [*head*], which in view of its position is the principle[2] of the living beings.

67. Jer. 1:12. The word *shaqed* (almond tree) is supposed by the medieval commentators to derive from the root *shaqod* (to hasten), because it blossoms more quickly than other trees.

68. Cf. II 43.

69. Ezek. 1:4. There are various medieval explanations of the word *hashmal*, a hapax legomenon applied to the divine chariot. According to one explanation, it signifies *hayot esh memalelot* (fiery talking animals). According to another, it derives from *hashoh* (to be silent) and *malol* (to speak). According to a third explanation, it derives from *hāsh* (to hasten) and *mūl* (to cut, to stop).

70. Ezek. 1:7. The word *'egel* (calf) contains an allusion to the root *'agol* (to be round).

71. Ezek. 1:7. According to the commentators of the *Guide*, the word *nehoshet* (brass) alludes to the word *hashata* (corruption, i.e., incorruptible), and to the word *qal* (light, swift).

72. Zech. 6:1.   73. Another reference to this passage of Zechariah is found in II 10.

  1. Hos. 1:2.   2. Meaning here "the beginning."

Now the world has not been created in a temporal beginning,[3] as we have explained, for time belongs to the created things. For this reason it says: *In the beginning* [*bereshith*].[4] For the "be"[5] has the meaning of "in." The true translation of this *verse*[6] is: In the origin[7] God created what is high and what is low. This is the translation that fits in with creation in time. On the other hand the statement, which you find formulated by some of the *Sages*, that affirms that time existed before the creation of the world is very difficult. For that is the opinion of Aristotle, which I have explained to you: he holds that time cannot be conceived to have a beginning, which is incongruous. Those who made this statement were conducted to it by their finding in Scripture the terms: *one day*,[8] *a second day*.[9] He who made this statement understood these terms according to their external sense and as follows: Inasmuch as a rotating sphere and a sun did not yet exist, whereby was *the first day* measured? They express their opinion in the following text: *The first day — Rabbi Judah, son of Rabbi Simon, said: Hence* [*we learn*] *that there existed before that an order of time. Rabbi Abahu said: Hence* [*we learn*] *that the Holy One, may His name be blessed, used to create worlds and to destroy them* [*again*].[10] | This second opinion is even more incongruous than the first. Consider what was the difficulty for these two [Sages]. It was the notion that time existed prior to the existence of this sun. The solution of what seemed obscure to both of them will soon become clear to you; unless — by God! — those two meant to say that *the order of time* necessarily exists eternally a parte ante. That, however, is the belief in the eternity a parte ante of the world, and all who adhere to the Law should reject it. This passage is to my mind only the counterpart of the passage in which *Rabbi Eliezer* says, *Wherefrom were the heavens created?*[11] To sum up: you should not, in considering these points, take into account the statements made by this or that one. I have already made it known to you that the foundation of the whole Law is the view that God has brought the world into being out of nothing without there having been a temporal

---

3. The word *mabda²* is used, which has been translated "principle" but which cannot be so translated here.

4. Gen. 1:1. It is the first word of the Bible.

5. In the word *bereshith*, the *be* signifies a preposition meaning "in."

6. I.e., Gen. 1:1.

7. In this sentence Maimonides does not use the word *mabda²* (principle), but the word *bad²a*, which derives from the same root.

8. Gen. 1:5.   9. Gen. 1:8.   10. Genesis Rabbah, III.

11. Chapters of Rabbi Eliezer, III. Cf. II 26.

beginning.[12] For time is created, being consequent upon the motion of the sphere, which is created.

Among the things you ought to know is the fact that the *Sages* have explicitly stated in a number of passages that the word *eth*[13] figuring in his words,[14] *eth hash-shamayim ve-eth ha-aretz* [*the heaven and the earth*],[15] has in that verse the meaning: with. They mean by this that He created together with the heavens all that is in heaven and together with the earth all that is in the earth. You already know that they make it clear that the heaven and the earth were created together because He says: *I call unto them, they stand up together.*[16] Accordingly everything was created simultaneously; then gradually all things became differentiated. They have compared this to what happens when an agricultural laborer sows various kinds of grain in the soil at the same moment. Some of them sprout within a day, others within two days, others again within three days, though everything was sowed at the same hour. It is according to this opinion, which is indubitably correct, that the doubt that impelled *Rabbi Judah, son of Rabbi Simon*, to say what he said, may be resolved. It was difficult for him to understand whereby *the first day and the second and the third day* were measured. There is an explicit statement on this point | made by the *Sages, may their memory be blessed*, in *Bereshith Rabbah*. With reference to the *light* said in the *Torah*[17] *to have been created on the first day*, they make literally the following statement: *Those are the luminaries that have been created on the first day, but that He did not suspend until the fourth day.*[18] Thus a clear explanation as to this point has been made.

Among the things you ought to know is that *earth* is an equivocal term used in a general and a particular sense. In a general sense it is applied to all that is beneath the sphere of the moon, I mean the four elements. In a particular sense it is applied to one element, the last among them, namely, earth. A proof of this is his saying: *And the earth was unformed and void, and the darkness was upon the face of the deep; and the spirit of God, and so on.*[19] Thus sometimes all the elements are called

12. *mabda²*. Cf. n. 3, this chap. As to the connotations of the word "principle," see the beginning of this chapter.
13. A preposition signifying the object of a sentence. It also has the meaning "with."
14. Gen. 1:1.
15. The whole verse is: *In the beginning God created the heaven and the earth.*
16. Isa. 48:13. Cf. B.T., Ḥagigah, 12a; Genesis Rabbah, I *in fine*.
17. In Gen. 1:3.
18. The passage that follows is not to be found in Genesis Rabbah; it occurs in B.T., Ḥagigah, 12a.
19. Gen. 1:2.

earth. Afterwards he says: *And God called the dry land Earth.*[20] That also is a great secret; namely, wherever you find him saying, *God named something thus,* he does this in order to differentiate between the particular notion envisaged and the other notion equally signified by the term. For this reason I have interpreted to you the *verse*[21] as follows: In the origin God created what is high and what is low. Hence the *earth* mentioned in the first place is what is low — I mean to say the four elements — whereas the earth of which it is said, *And God called the dry land Earth,* is the element earth alone. This is now clear.

Among the things you ought to know is that the four elements are the first to be mentioned after the heaven. For, as we have said, the term *earth* mentioned in the first place applies to them. For he mentions *earth, water, spirit,*[22] and *darkness.* Now *darkness* is the elemental fire; do not think anything else. He says: *And thou didst hear His words out of the midst of the fire;*[23] and he says: *When ye heard the voice out of the midst of the darkness.*[24] And it also says: *All darkness is laid up for His treasures; a fire not blown [by man] shall consume him.*[25] The elemental fire was designated by this term, because it is not | luminous, but only transparent. For if the elemental fire had been luminous, we should have seen at night the whole atmosphere in flame like fire. The elements are mentioned according to their natural position; namely, first the earth, then the water that is above it, then the air that adheres to the water, then the fire that is above the air. For in view of the specification of the air as being *over the face of the waters,*[26] *darkness* that is *upon the face of the deep*[27] is indubitably above the *spirit.*[28] It was impelled to use the expression, *the spirit of God,*[29] in order to designate the air in view of the fact that the latter is supposed to be in motion, I mean to say *merahepheth [moving],* and that the motion of the wind is always ascribed to God. Thus: *And there went forth a wind from the Lord;*[30] *Thou didst blow with Thy wind;*[31] *And the Lord turned a west wind.*[32] This occurs frequently. In view of the fact that the term *darkness* [*hoshekh*], as employed in the first place,[33] which designates the element,[34] differs in its meaning from the term *darkness* [*hoshekh*], as employed afterwards in the signification of obscurity, it begins to explain and to differentiate, saying: *And the darkness [hoshekh] He called Night,*[35] as we have explained. Consequently this is now clear.

20. Gen. 1:10.   21. I.e., Gen. 1:1. See above in this chapter.
22. I.e., the element of air.   23. Deut. 4:36.   24. Deut. 5:20.   25. Job 20:26.
26. Cf. Gen. 1:2.   27. Ibid.   28. Ibid. Maimonides identifies the *spirit* with the air.
29. Ibid.   30. Num. 11:31.   31. Exod. 15:10.   32. Exod. 10:19.
33. In Gen. 1:2.   34. I.e., fire.   35. Gen. 1:5.

Among the things you ought to know is that the words, *And He divided between the waters, and so on*,[36] do not refer merely to a division in place in which one part is located above and one below, while both have the same nature. The correct interpretation of these words is that He made a natural division between both of them — I mean with regard to their form — making one part, that which He first calls water, into one particular thing by means of the natural form with which He invested it, and bestowing upon the other part a different form, that latter part being water proper. Hence it says: *And the gathering of the waters He called Seas.*[37] In this way it makes it clear to you that first *water* of which it is said, *over the face of the waters*,[38] is not the water that is in the *seas*, but that part of the water situated above the air was differentiated by means of a certain form, whereas another part is this water here. Thus the phrase, *And He divided between the waters which were under the firmament, and so on*,[39] is analogous to the phrase, *And God divided between the light and the darkness*,[40] in which the division is in respect of a certain form. The *firmament* itself | was produced from water; as [the Sages] say: *The middle group congealed.*[41] The words, *And God called the firmament Heaven*,[42] is intended, according to what I have explained to you, to make clear that the term is equivocal and that the *heaven* mentioned in the first place, in the words *the heaven and the earth*,[43] is not what is generally named *heaven*. It has rendered this signification even more certain by the use of the words, *In the face of the firmament of heaven*,[44] whereby it meant to make clear that the *firmament* is not the *heaven*. Because of this equivocality of the terms, the true *heaven* is sometimes likewise called *firmament*, just as the true *firmament* is called *heaven*. Thus it says: *And God set them in the firmament of the heaven.*[45] In these words there is likewise a clear indication of what has already been demonstrated, namely, of the fact that all the stars as well as the sun and the moon are situated within the sphere — as there is no vacuum in the world — and that they are not located upon the surface of a sphere, as the vulgar imagine. This appears from his saying: *in the firmament of the heaven*, and not: *upon the firmament of the heaven*. Thus it has become clear that there was a certain common matter, which it names *water*. Afterwards it was divided into three forms; a part of it turned into one thing, namely, the *seas*; another part of it turned into another thing, namely, the *firmament*; a third part turned into a thing that is above the *firmament*.

36. Gen. 1:7.   37. Gen. 1:10.   38. Gen. 1:2.   39. Gen. 1:7.
40. Gen. 1:4.   41. Genesis Rabbah, IV.   42. Gen. 1:8.   43. Gen. 1:1.
44. Gen. 1:20.   45. Gen. 1:17.

The latter is entirely beyond the earth.[46] With regard to that subject, He chose a different method of approach leading to extraordinary secrets. With regard to the fact that that which is above the *firmament* is called water in name only and that it is not the specific water known to us, a statement setting this forth has also been made by the *Sages, may their memory be blessed.* They made it in the following passage:[47] *Four entered the Paradise, and so on. Rabbi Aqiba said to them: When you come to the stones of pure marble, do not say, Water, Water, for it is written: He that speaketh falsehood shall not be established before mine eyes.*[48] Reflect, if you are one of those who reflect, to what extent he has made clear and revealed the whole matter in this statement, provided that you consider it well, | understand all that has been demonstrated in the "Meteorologica,"[49] and examine everything that people have said about every point mentioned in that work.

Among the things you ought to know and have your attention aroused to is the reason why it is not said regarding the work of the second day *that it was good.* You already know what the *Sages, may their memory be blessed,* have said about this according to the method of *nonliteral interpretation.*[50] The best statement of this kind they have made about this is their saying that this was so *because the work of the water had not been terminated.*[51] To my mind also the reason in question is very clear. For whenever it mentions a thing among those that exist, having been produced in time and subsisting in durable, perpetual, and permanent fashion, it says with reference to it *that it was good.* But there is something hidden, as you will see, with regard to the *firmament* and the thing above it, which is called *water.* For if the matter is considered according to its external meaning and with a recourse only to superficial speculation, it does not exist at all. For between us and the lowest heaven, there exists no body except the elements, and there is no water above the air. This judgment applies all the more if someone imagines that this *firmament* and what is above it are above the heaven. In that case the thing would be even more impossible and remote from apprehension. If, on the other hand, the matter is considered according to its inner meaning and to what was truly intended, it is most hidden. For in that case it was necessary for it to be one of the concealed secrets so that the vulgar should not know it. How then could it be proper

---

46. This translation appears to make better sense than the more literal rendering: All this is outside the earth.
47. B.T., Ḥagigah, 14b.   48. Ps. 101:7.   49. I.e., Aristotle's work bearing this title.
50. The Hebrew word *derash*, which is used here, is often employed in contradistinction to *peshat*, which means literal interpretation.
51. Genesis Rabbah, IV.

to say of such a matter *that it was good?* For the meaning of the words, *that it was good,* is that the thing in question is of externally visible and manifest utility for the existence and permanence of that which exists. But in a matter whose meaning is hidden and that, understood in its external meaning, does not exist in such a way as to appear useful, what utility externally visible to the people at large could there be so that the words, *that it was good,* could be said with reference to it? I cannot help adding for you the following explanation: The thing in question, though it represents a very great part of the existents, | does not constitute the purposed end for the permanence of that which exists; and therefore the words, *that it was good,* could not be said with reference to it. This could rather occur with reference to a compelling necessity that the earth be uncovered. Understand this.

Among the things you ought to know is that the *Sages* have made it clear[52] that God only made grass and trees grow from the earth after He had caused rain to fall upon them, and that its saying, *And there went up a mist from the earth, and so on,*[53] is a description of the first state of matters obtaining before the command: *Let the earth put forth grass.*[54] For this reason *Onqelos* translates: *And there had gone up a mist from the earth.*[55] This is also clear from the [scriptural] text itself because of its saying: *And no shrub of the field was yet in the earth.*[56] This is clear by now.

You who are engaged in speculation, know that, after the forces of the sphere, the first of the causes producing generation and passing-away are light and darkness — because of the heat and the cold consequent upon them. The elements intermix in consequence of the motion of the sphere, and their combinations vary because of light and darkness. The first combination that is produced by them is constituted by two exhalations, which are the first causes of all the meteorological phenomena among which rain figures. They are also the causes of the minerals and, after them, of the composition of the plants and, after those, of that of the living beings; the final composition being that of man. Darkness is the nature of the existence of the whole lower world, light supervening in it. It should be sufficient for you to know that when there is no light, the state of matters remains permanent. The [scriptural] text about the *Account of the Beginning* goes exactly in this order, leaving out nothing.

Among the things you ought to know is their saying: *All the works of the Beginning were created according to their [perfect] stature, [perfect]*

---

52. Genesis Rabbah, XIII *ab init.*   53. Gen. 2:6.   54. Gen. 1:11.
55. Gen. 2:6. In Aramaic.   56. Gen. 2:5.

reason, and [perfect] beauty [le-ṣibyonam].[57] He means that everything that
was created, was created according to the perfection of quantity, the per-
fection of form, and with the most beautiful accidents. This is | expressed
in the word *le-ṣibyonam [according to their beauty]*, which derives from the
word *ṣebi [beauty]* as used, for instance, in the phrase: *which is the ṣebi
[beauty] of all lands.*[58] Know this, too, for it is a great principle, which has
been established as true and has become clear.

Among the things on which you ought to reflect carefully is the fact
that it mentions the creation of *man* in the *six days of the Beginning* and
says: *Male and female created He them.*[59] It then concludes its account of
the creation, saying: *And the heaven and the earth were finished, and all
the host of them.*[60] Then it makes a new start regarding the creation of
Eve from *Adam*, and mentions *the tree of life* and *the tree of knowledge*
and the tale of the *serpent* and all that story; and it makes out that all this
happened after *Adam* had been placed in the *Garden of Eden*. Now all the
Sages, may their memory be blessed, are unanimous in thinking that all
this story occurred on Friday and that nothing was changed in any respect
after the *six days of the Beginning*. For this reason, none of these things
should be judged incongruous; for, as we have said, up till then no permanently established nature had come about. Withal they have mentioned
things that I will let you hear, having gleaned them in their various places,
and I shall give you pointers to certain things, just as they, *may their
memory be blessed*, have given us pointers. Know that those things that I
shall mention to you from the dicta of the *Sages* are sayings that are of
utmost perfection; their allegorical interpretation was clear to those to
whom they were addressed, and they are unambiguous. Hence I will not
go too far in interpreting them, and I will not set forth their meaning at
length.[61] For I will not be *one who divulges a secret*. However, it will suffice
for someone like you if I mention them in a certain order and by means of
slight indications. One of these dicta is their saying[62] that *Adam and Eve*
were created together, having their backs joined, and that this being was
divided and one half of it, namely, *Eve*, taken and brought up to [Adam].
The expression, *one of his ribs*,[63] means according to them one of his sides.
They quote as proof the expression, *a rib of the tabernacle*,[64] which [the
Aramaic version] translates: *a side of the tabernacle*. In accordance with this,

57. B.T., Rosh Hashanah, 11a; B.T., Ḥullin, 6oa.   58. Ezek. 20:6.
59. Gen. 1:27.   6o. Gen. 2:1.   61. Or: plainly.
62. Cf. Genesis Rabbah, VIII; cf. B.T., ʿErubin, 18a.   63. Gen. 2:21.
64. This occurs, e.g., in Exod. 26:20.

they say that ["of his ribs"] means: *of his sides.*[65] Understand in what way it has been explained that they | were two in a certain respect and that they were also one; as it says: *bone of my bones, and flesh of my flesh.*[66] This has received additional confirmation through the fact that it says that both of them have the same name: for she is called *'ishshah* [*woman*], *because she was taken out of 'ish* [*man*].[67] It also confirms their union by saying: *And shall cleave unto his wife, and they shall be one flesh.*[68] How great is the ignorance of him who does not understand that all this is necessary with a view to a certain notion. This then has become clear.

Among the things you ought to know is the following explanation, which they give in the *Midrash.* They mention[69] that the *Serpent* had a rider, that it was of the size of a camel, that it was the rider who led *Eve* astray, and that the rider was *Sammael.* They apply this name to *Satan.* Thus you will find that they say in a number of passages that *Satan* wanted to tempt *Abraham our Father* not to agree to offer *Isaac* as a sacrifice, and that he also wanted to tempt *Isaac* not to obey his father. And with reference to that story, I mean to say the *binding* [of Isaac], they say likewise: *Sammael came to our Father Abraham and told him: What, old man! have you lost your senses, and so on.*[70] Thus it has become clear to you that *Sammael* is *Satan.* This name is used with a view to a certain signification, just as the name *serpent* [*nahash*] is used with a view to a certain signification. When they speak of its coming to deceive *Eve,* they say: *Sammael was riding upon it; and the Holy One, blessed be He, was laughing at both the camel and its rider.*

Among the things you ought to know and have your attention aroused to is the fact that the *Serpent* had in no respect direct relations with *Adam* and that it did not speak to him, and that such a conversation and relation only took place between him and *Eve;* it was through the intermediation of *Eve* that *Adam* was harmed and that the *Serpent* destroyed him. Extreme enmity only comes to be realized between the *Serpent* and *Eve* and *its seed and hers.* On the other hand *her seed* is indubitably the *seed of Adam.* Even more strange is the tie between the *Serpent* and *Eve,* I mean between *its seed and hers,* a tie that is in *the head and the heel;*[71] she being victorious over it *through the head* | and it over her *through the heel.* This also is clear.

Among the amazing dicta whose external meaning is exceedingly

65. Those of Adam at the time of the creation of Eve.   66. Gen. 2:23.
67. Gen. 2:23.   68. Gen. 2:24.   69. Chapters of Rabbi Eliezer, XIII.
70. Genesis Rabbah, LVI.
71. Cf. Gen. 3:15. *And I will put enmity between thee and the woman, and between thy seed and her seed; he shall bruise thy head, and thou shalt bruise his heel.*

incongruous, but in which — when you obtain a true understanding of the chapters of this Treatise — you will admire the wisdom of the parables and their correspondence to what exists, is their statement: *When the Serpent came to Eve, it cast pollution into her. The pollution of [the sons of] Israel, who had been present at Mount Sinai, has come to an end. [As for] the pollution of the nations who had not been present at Mount Sinai, their pollution has not come to an end.*[72] This too you should follow up in your thought.

Among the things you ought to know is their dictum: *[The size of] the tree of life [corresponds] to a walk of five hundred years, and all the waters of the Beginning spring up from beneath it.*[73] They make it clear there that this measure is meant to apply to the thickness of its body and not to the dimension of its boughs. They say: *The object of this saying is not its body, but its trunk, [whose size corresponds] to a walk of five hundred years.* The interpretation of *its trunk* is: the thickness of its upright timber. They added this supplementary remark in order to complete the explanation and exposition of the meaning. This then is clear.

Among the things you ought also to know is their dictum: *As for the tree of knowledge, the Holy One, blessed be He, has never revealed that tree to man and will never reveal it.*[74] This is correct inasmuch as the nature of what exists requires it.

Among the things you ought to know is their dictum:[75] *And the Lord God took the man*[76] — [that is,] *raised him* — and *put him into the garden of Eden*[77] — [that is,] *He gave him rest.* Thus they do not make out that this text means that He took him away from one place and put him in another, but that He raised the rank of his existence among the existents that come into being and pass away and established him in a certain state.

Among the things you ought also to know and have your attention aroused to is the manifestation of wisdom constituted by the facts that the two children of *Adam* were called *Cain* and *Abel*; that it was *Cain* who slew *Abel in the field*;[78] that both of them perished, though the aggressor had a respite; | and that only *Seth* was vouchsafed a true existence: *For God hath appointed [shath]*[79] *me another seed.*[80] This has already been shown to be correct.[81]

Among the things you ought to know and have your attention aroused to is the dictum: *And the man gave names, and so on.*[82] It informs us

72. B.T., Shabbath, 146a; B.T., Yebamoth, 103b.
73. Genesis Rabbah, XV; J.T., Berakhoth, XI.   74. Genesis Rabbah, XV *in fine*.
75. Genesis Rabbah, XVI.   76. Gen. 2:15.   77. Gen. 2:15.   78. Gen. 4:8.
79. The verb from which the name *Sheth* (i.e., Seth) is said to derive.
80. Gen. 4:25.   81. Cf. I 7.   82. Gen. 2:20.

that languages are conventional and not natural, as has sometimes been thought.

Among the things you ought to reflect upon are the four words that occur with reference to the relation between the heaven and God. These words are *baro²* [*to create*] and *ᶜassoh* [*to make*] and *qanoh* [*to acquire, possess*] and *El* [*God*]. It says: *God* [*Elohim*] *created* [*bara²*] *the heaven and the earth.*[83] And it says: *In the day that the Lord God made* [*ᶜassoth*] *earth and heaven.*[84] It says also: *Possessor* [*qoneh*] *of heaven and earth.*[85] And it says:[86] *God* [*El*] *of the World.*[87] And: *The God* [*Elohe*] *of the heaven, and the God* [*Elohe*] *of the earth.*[88] Regarding the dicta: *which Thou hast established* [*konanta*];[89] *hath spread out* [*tipphah*] *the heavens;*[90] *Who stretchest out the heavens,*[91] the terms used therein are included in the verb *to make* [*ᶜassoh*]. As for the word *yeṣirah* [*forming*], it does not occur in this sense; for it seems to me that *yeṣirah* is only applied to shaping and forming a configuration or to one of the other accidents, for shape and configuration are also accidents. For this reason it says: *Who formeth* [*yoṣer*] *the light*[92] — for light is an accident — and: *That formeth* [*yoṣer*] *the mountains*[93] — that is, who shapes them. Similarly: *And the Lord God formed* [*va-yiṣer*], *and so on.*[94] However, with regard to the existence proper to the whole of the world, which is constituted by the heaven and the earth, the term *baro²* [*create*] is used. For according to us it signifies bringing into existence out of non-existence. It also says *ᶜassoh* [*to make*], which is applied to the specific forms that were given to them[95] — I mean their natures. With reference to them, it says *qanoh* [*acquire, possess*], because He, may He be exalted, has dominion over them just as a master has over his slaves. For this reason He is also called *the Lord* [*²adon*] *of all the earth*[96] and *the Lord* [*ha-²adon*].[97] However, as there is no *Lord* [*²adon*] without there being something *possessed* [*qinyan*][98] by Him, and this tends toward the road of the belief in the eternity of a certain matter, the terms *baro²* [*create*] and *ᶜassoh* [*make*] are used with reference to them.[99] As for the expressions, *the God* [*Elohe*] *of the heaven* and also *God of the World* [*El ᶜolam*],[100] they are used with

---

83. Gen. 1:1.   84. Gen. 2:4.   85. Gen. 14:19 and 22.   86. Gen. 21:33.
87. In the biblical context, "God of Eternity" is the correct translation of the Hebrew phrase *El ᶜolam*. However, the word *ᶜolam* also means "world," "universe"; and Maimonides evidently (see below) means to interpret the biblical phrase in this sense.
88. Gen. 24:3.   89. Ps. 8:4.   90. Isa. 48:13.   91. Ps. 104:2.
92. Isa. 45:7.   93. Amos 4:13.   94. Gen. 2:7 and 19.
95. This pronoun probably refers to the heaven and the earth.
96. Josh. 3:11 and 13.   97. Exod. 23:17; 34:23.
98. A noun deriving from the verb *qanoh* mentioned earlier in this paragraph.
99. This pronoun probably refers to the heaven and the earth.
100. Cf. n. 87, this chap.

respect to His perfection, may He be exalted, and theirs. He is *Elohim*—
that is, | He who governs—and they are those governed by Him, not in the
sense of domination—for that is the meaning of *qoneh* [*possessor*]—but
with respect to His rank, may He be exalted, in being and in relation to
theirs. For He is the deity and not they—I mean heaven. Know this.

The sum of observations given here, together with what has been
stated before and what will be stated after with regard to this subject, is
sufficient considering the purpose of this Treatise and considering him who
studies it.

CHAPTER 31

Perhaps it has already become clear to you what is the cause of the Law's
establishing the Sabbath so firmly and ordaining *death by stoning* for
breaking it. The Master of the prophets has put people to death because of it.
It comes third after the existence of the deity and the denial of dualism.
For the prohibition of the worship of anything except Him only aims at the
affirmation of the belief in His unity. You know from what I have said that
opinions do not last unless they are accompanied by actions that strengthen
them, make them generally known, and perpetuate them among the
multitude. For this reason we are ordered by the Law to exalt this day, in
order that the principle of the creation of the world in time be established
and universally known in the world[1] through the fact that all people refrain
from working on one and the same day. If it is asked: What is the cause of
this?, the answer is: *For in six days the Lord made.*[2]

For this commandment two different causes are given, corresponding
to two different effects. In the first *Decalogue*, the cause for exalting
the Sabbath is stated as follows: *For in six days the Lord made, and so on.*
In *Deuteronomy*,[3] on the other hand, it is said:[4] *And thou shalt remember
that thou wast a slave in Egypt.*[5] *Therefore the Lord thy God commanded
thee to keep the sabbath day.* This is correct. For the effect, according to the

1. Literally: in existence.   2. Exod. 20:11.
3. Maimonides here designates the book of Deuteronomy by the term *Mishneh Torah*.
4. Deut. 5:15.
5. The biblical text has: *in the land of Egypt.* This alteration may be due to Maimonides'
having had in mind, in addition to the verse referred to, Deut. 16:12 and 24:18.

first statement, is to regard | that day as noble and exalted. As it says: *Wherefore the Lord blessed the sabbath day, and hallowed it.*[6] This is the effect consequent upon the cause stated in the words: *For in six days, and so on.* However, the order given us by the Law with regard to it and the commandment ordaining us in particular to keep it are an effect consequent upon the cause that we had been *slaves in Egypt* where we did not work according to our free choice and when we wished and where we had not the power to refrain from working. Therefore we have been commanded inactivity and rest so that we should conjoin the two things: the belief in a true opinion — namely, the creation of the world in time, which, at the first go and with the slightest of speculations, shows that the deity exists — and the memory of the benefit God bestowed upon us by giving us rest *from under the burdens of the Egyptians.*[7] Accordingly the Sabbath is, as it were, of universal benefit, both with reference to a true speculative opinion and to the well-being of the state of the body.

CHAPTER 32

The opinions of people concerning prophecy are like their opinions concerning the eternity of the world or its creation in time. I mean by this that just as the people to whose mind the existence of the deity is firmly established, have, as we have set forth, three opinions concerning the eternity of the world or its creation in time, so are there also three opinions concerning prophecy. I shall not pay attention to the opinion of Epicurus, for he does not believe in the existence of a deity and all the more does he not believe in prophecy. I only aim to set forth the opinions of those who believe in the deity.

The first opinion — that of the multitude of those among the Pagans who considered prophecy as true and also believed by some of the common people professing our Law — is that God, may He be exalted, chooses whom He wishes from among men, turns him into a prophet, and sends him with a mission. According to them it makes no difference whether this individual is a man of knowledge or | ignorant, aged or young. However, they also posit as a condition his having a certain goodness and sound morality. For up to now people have not gone so far as to say that God sometimes

6. Exod. 20:11.   7. Exod. 6:7.

turns a wicked man into a prophet unless He has first, according to this opinion, turned him into a good man.

The second opinion is that of the philosophers. It affirms that prophecy is a certain perfection in the naure of man. This perfection is not achieved in any individual from among men except after a training that makes that which exists in the potentiality of the species pass into actuality, provided an obstacle due to temperament or to some external cause does not hinder this, as is the case with regard to every perfection whose existence is possible in a certain species. For the existence of that perfection in its extreme and ultimate form in every individual of that species is not possible. It must, however, exist necessarily in at least one particular individual; if, in order to be achieved, this perfection requires something that actualizes it, that something necessarily exists. According to this opinion it is not possible that an ignoramus should turn into a prophet; nor can a man not be a prophet on a certain evening and be a prophet on the following morning, as though he had made some find. Things are rather as follows: When, in the case of a superior individual who is perfect with respect to his rational and moral qualities, his imaginative faculty is in its most perfect state and when he has been prepared in the way that you will hear, he will necessarily become a prophet, inasmuch as this is a perfection that belongs to us by nature. According to this opinion it is not possible that an individual should be fit for prophecy and prepared for it and not become a prophet, except to the extent to which it is possible that an individual having a healthy temperament should be nourished with excellent food, without sound blood and similar things being generated from that food.

The third opinion is the opinion of our Law and the foundation of our doctrine. It is identical with | the philosophic opinion except in one thing. For we believe that it may happen that one who is fit for prophecy and prepared for it should not become a prophet, namely, on account of the divine will. To my mind this is like all the miracles and takes the same course as they. For it is a natural thing that everyone who according to his natural disposition is fit for prophecy and who has been trained in his education and study should become a prophet. He who is prevented from it is like him who has been prevented, like *Jeroboam*,[1] from moving his hand, or, like the *King of Aram's* army going to seek out *Elisha*,[2] from seeing. As for its being fundamental with us that the prophet must possess preparation and perfection in the moral and rational qualities, it is indubitably the opinion expressed in their dictum: *Prophecy only rests upon a wise, strong,*

1. I Kings 13:4.   2. II Kings 6:18.

and rich man.[3] We have explained this in our Commentary on the *Mishnah*[4] and in our great compilation,[5] and we have set forth that the *disciples*[6] *of the prophets* were always engaged in preparation. As for the fact that one who prepares is sometimes prevented from becoming a prophet, you may know it from the history of *Baruch, son of Neriah.* For he followed *Jeremiah,* who trained, taught, and prepared him. And he set himself the goal of becoming a prophet, but was prevented; as he says: *I am weary with my groaning, and I find no rest.*[7] Thereupon he was told through *Jeremiah: Thus shalt thou say unto him: Thus saith the Lord, and so on. And seekest thou great things for thyself? Seek them not.*[8] It is possible to say that this is a clear statement that prophecy is too *great a thing* for *Baruch.* Similarly it may be said, as we shall explain,[9] that in the passage, *Yea, her prophets find no vision from the Lord,*[10] this was the case because they were in *Exile.* However, we shall find many texts, some of them scriptural and some of them dicta of the *Sages,* all of which maintain this fundamental principle that God turns whom He wills, whenever He wills it, into a prophet — but only someone perfect and superior to the utmost degree. But with regard to one of the ignorant among the common people, | this is not possible according to us — I mean, that He should turn one of them into a prophet — except as it is possible that He should turn an ass or a frog into a prophet. It is our fundamental principle that there must be training and perfection, whereupon the possibility arises to which the power of the deity becomes attached. You should not be led astray by His saying: *Before I formed thee in the belly I knew thee, and before thou camest forth from the womb I sanctified thee.*[11] For this is the state of every prophet: he must have a natural preparedness in his original natural disposition, as shall be explained. As for his saying, *For I am young* [*na\u1ebdar*],[12] you know that in the Hebrew language *Joseph the righteous* was called *young* [*na\u1ebdar*][13] though he was thirty years old, and that *Joshua* was called *young* [*na\u1ebdar*] though he was near his sixtieth year. For it says with reference to the time of *the doings* concerning the calf: *But his servant Joshua, son of Nun, a young man, departed not, and so on.*[14] Now *Moses our Master* was at that time eighty-one years old, and his whole life lasted one hundred and twenty years. *Joshua* lived after him fourteen years, and the life of *Joshua* lasted one hundred and ten years.

---

3. B.T., Shabbath, 92a; B.T., Nedarim, 38a.
4. Cf. Introduction to Seder Zeraᶜim.
5. Cf. *Mishneh Torah*, Yesodei ha-Torah, VII.
6. Literally: *sons.*   7. Jer. 45:3.   8. Jer. 45:4-5.   9. Cf. II 36.
10. Lam. 2:9.   11. Jer. 1:5.   12. Jer. 1:6.   13. Gen. 41:12.
14. Exod. 33:11.

Accordingly it is clear that *Joshua* was at that time at least fifty-seven years
old, and was nevertheless called *young* [*na͏ᶜar*]. Again you should not be
led astray by His dictum figuring in the promises: *I will pour out My spirit
upon all flesh, and your sons and your daughters shall prophesy;*[15] for He
interprets this and lets us know what kind of prophecy is meant, for He
says: *Your old men shall dream dreams, your young men shall see visions.*[16]
For everyone who communicates knowledge as to something secret,
whether this be with the help of soothsaying and divination or with the
help of a veridical dream, is likewise called a *prophet.* For this reason
prophets of Baal and *prophets of Asherah* are called *prophets.* Do you not see
that He, may He be exalted, says: *If there arise among you a prophet or a
dreamer of dreams?*[17] As for the *Gathering at Mount Sinai,* though through
a miracle all the people saw the great fire and heard the frightening and
terrifying voices, | only those who were fit for it achieved the rank of
prophecy, and even those in various degrees. Do you not see that He
says: *Come up unto the Lord, thou and Aaron, Nadab and Abihu, and
seventy of the elders of Israel.*[18] He, peace be upon him, had the highest
rank, as He said: *And Moses alone shall come near unto the Lord; but they
shall not come near.*[19] *Aaron* was below him; *Nadab and Abihu* below
Aaron; the *seventy elders* below *Nadab and Abihu;* and the other people
below the latter according to their degrees of perfection. A text of the
Sages, may their memory be blessed, reads: *Moses is an enclosure apart,
and Aaron an enclosure apart.*[20]

As we have come to speak of the *Gathering at Mount Sinai,* we shall
give indications, in a separate chapter, concerning what becomes clear
regarding that *Gathering* as it was, from the scriptural texts, if they are
well examined, and from the dicta of the *Sages.*

CHAPTER 33

It is clear to me that at the *Gathering at Mount Sinai,* not everything that
reached *Moses* also reached all *Israel.* Speech was addressed to *Moses* alone;
for this reason, in the whole *Decalogue* the second person singular is used,

15. Joel 3:1.   16. Joel 3:1.   17. Deut. 13:2.   18. Exod. 24:1.
19. Exod. 24:2.   20. Mekhilta, commentary on Exod. 19:24.

and he, peace be on him, went to the foot of the mountain and communicated to the people what he had heard. The text of the *Torah* reads: *I stood between the Lord and you at that time to declare unto you the word of the Lord.*[1] It also says: *Moses spoke, and God answered him by a voice.*[2] And it is explicitly said in the *Mekhilta*[3] that he repeated to them each and every *commandment* as he heard it. Again a text of the *Torah* reads: *That the people may hear when I speak with thee, and so on.*[4] This is a proof that it was he who was spoken to and that they heard the great voice, but not the articulations of speech. About hearing | this great voice, it says: *When ye heard the voice.*[5] And it also says: *Ye heard the voice of words, but ye saw no figure; only a voice.*[6] It does not say: *ye heard the words.* Thus every time when their hearing words is mentioned, it is their hearing the *voice* that is meant, *Moses* being the one who heard words and reported them to them. This is the external meaning of the text of the *Torah* and of most of the dicta of the *Sages, may their memory be blessed.* However, they also have a dictum formulated in several passages of the *Midrashim*[7] and also figuring in the *Talmud.* This is their dictum:[8] *They heard "I"*[9] *and "Thou shalt have"*[10] *from the mouth of the Force.*[11] They mean that these words reached them just as they reached *Moses our Master* and that it was not *Moses our Master* who communicated them to them. For these two principles, I mean the existence of the deity and His being one, are knowable by human speculation alone. Now with regard to everything that can be known by demonstration, the status of the prophet and that of everyone else who knows it are equal; there is no superiority of one over the other. Thus these two principles are not known through prophecy alone. The text of the *Torah* says: *Unto thee it was shown, and so on.*[12] As for the other *commandments,* they belong to the class of generally accepted opinions and those adopted in virtue of tradition, not to the class of the intellecta.

Taking into consideration whatever else they have said about this, the texts and the dicta of the *Sages* permit considering as admissible that all *Israel* only heard at that *Gathering* one *voice* one single time — the *voice* through which *Moses* and all *Israel* apprehended *I*[13] and *Thou shalt not,*[14] which commandments *Moses* made them hear again as spoken in his own

---

1. Deut. 5:5.   2. Exod. 19:19.   3. Mekhilta, commentary on Exod. 20:1.
4. Exod. 19:9.   5. Deut. 5:20.   6. Deut. 4:12.   7. In the text: *Midrashoth.*
8. B.T., Makkoth, 24a; Midrash on the Song of Songs, 1:2.
9. I.e., the First Commandment.   10. I.e., the Second Commandment.
11. The Hebrew word *geburah,* here translated "force," sometimes designates the deity.
12. Deut. 4:35.   13. I.e., the First Commandment.
14. I.e., the Second Commandment.

speech with an articulation of the letters that were heard. The *Sages* said this, quoting in support of this assertion the dictum: *God hath spoken once, twice have I heard this.*[15] And they made it clear at the beginning of *Midrash Ḥazith*[16] that they had not heard another | *voice* coming from Him, may He be exalted. Thus too a text of the *Torah: A great voice, and He added no more.*[17] It was after they had heard that first *voice* that they, as is mentioned, were terrified of the thing and felt a great fear, and that they, as is reported, said: *And ye said, Behold the Lord* [*our God*] *hath shown us, and so on. Now therefore why should we die, and so on. Go thou near and hear, and so on.*[18] Thereupon he, who was greater than anyone born of man, went forward a second time, received the rest of the *commandments* one after the other, descended to the foot of the mountain, and made them hear these commandments in the midst of that great gathering. Meanwhile they were seeing the fires and hearing the voices, I mean those voices that are said to be *voices and lightnings,*[19] like thunder and *the loud voice of the trumpet.* All that you find mentioned about hearing many *voices* — as for instance the dictum: *And all the people saw the voices, and so on*[20] — refers only to *the voice of the trumpet,* the thunderings, and the like. As for *the voice of the Lord,* I mean the created voice from which the *speech* [of God] was understood, they heard it once only, according to what the text of the *Torah* states and according to what the *Sages* make clear in the passage to which I drew your attention. This was *the voice on hearing which their soul went out of them,*[21] and through which *the first two commandments* were apprehended. Know that with regard to that *voice* too, their rank was not equal to the rank of *Moses our Master.* I shall draw your attention to this secret, and I shall let you know that this is a matter that is transmitted by tradition in the religious community[22] and that is known to its men of knowledge. Thus in all the passages in which you will find, *And the Lord spoke* [*va-yedabber*] *to Moses saying, Onqelos* translates: *And the Lord spoke* [*u-mallel*]. Thus: *And God spoke* [*va-yedabber*] *all* [*these*] *words,*[23] is translated: *And the Lord spoke* [*u-mallel*] *all* [*these*] *words.* On the other hand, the words of *Israel* to *Moses: But let not God speak* [*yedabber*] *with us,*[24] he translates: [*Speech*] *should not be spoken* [*yitmallel*] *with us on the part of the Lord.* Thus he, peace be on him, has made clear to you the proposition that we have set forth in detail. | You know that, as has

---

15. Ps. 62:12.   16. Midrash on the Song of Songs, 1:2.   17. Deut. 5:19.
18. Deut. 5:21–24.   19. Exod. 19:16.   20. Exod. 20:15.
21. Midrash on the Song of Songs, 5:6.
22. Or: nation.   23. Exod. 20:1.   24. Exod. 20:16.

been made clear,[25] *Onqelos* received these wondrous and sublime notions that he transmits *from the mouth of Rabbi Eliezer and Rabbi Joshua* who are the *Sages of Israel* par excellence. Know this and remember it. For it is impossible to expound the *Gathering at Mount Sinai* to a greater extent than they spoke about it, for it is one of the *mysteries of the Torah.* The true reality of that apprehension and its modality are quite hidden from us, for nothing like it happened before and will not happen after. Know this.

CHAPTER 34

Regarding the text that is in the *Torah*, namely, His saying, *Behold, I will send an angel before thee, and so on*[1] — the meaning of that text is the one explained in *Deuteronomy*,[2] namely, that God said to *Moses* at the *Gathering at Mount Sinai: I will raise them up a prophet, and so on.* A proof for this is His saying concerning this *angel: Take heed of him, and hearken unto his voice, and so on.*[3] Now there is no doubt that this injunction is addressed only to the multitude. An *angel*, however, does not manifest himself to the multitude and does not give them orders and prohibitions; consequently they could not be ordered not to disobey him. Accordingly, the meaning of this dictum is that He, may He be exalted, gave them knowledge that there would be a prophet among them to whom an *angel* would come who would speak to him and give him orders and prohibitions. Thus God forbade us to disobey that *angel* whose words the prophet would transmit to us. It makes that clear in *Deuteronomy*,[4] saying: *Unto him ye shall hearken.* And it also says: *And it shall come to pass, that whosoever shall not hearken unto My words which he shall speak in My name, and so on*[5] — this being the explanation of the dictum: *For My name is in him.*[6] | All this merely taught them this: this great gathering that you saw — I mean to say, the *Gathering at Mount Sinai* — will not be a thing subsisting

25. Literally: as they have made clear.
1. Exod. 23:20.
2. Deut. 18:18. Maimonides here designates the book of Deuteronomy by the term *Mishneh Torah.*
3. Exod. 23:21.
4. Deut. 18:15. Maimonides here designates the book of Deuteronomy by the term *Mishneh Torah.*
5. Deut. 18:19.   6. Exod. 23:21.

permanently with you, and in the future there will not be anything like it; and there will not permanently be *fire* and a *cloud*, such as those that are now *always on the tabernacle*.[7] However, an *angel* whom I shall send to your prophets will conquer the country for you, will smooth out the land before you, and will let you know what you should do. He will let you know what you should approach and what you ought to avoid. Thereby the fundamental principle was given, which I have never ceased explaining, namely, that to every prophet except *Moses our Master* prophetic revelation comes through an *angel*. Know this.

CHAPTER 35

I have already explained to all the four differences by which the prophecy of *Moses our Master* is distinguished from the prophecy of the other prophets, and I have proved it and made it manifest in the Commentary on the *Mishnah*[1] and in *Mishneh Torah*.[2] Accordingly there is no need to repeat it; moreover it does not enter into the purpose of this Treatise. I will let you know that everything I say on prophecy in the chapters of this Treatise refers only to the form of prophecy of all the prophets who were before *Moses* and who will come after him. As for the prophecy of *Moses our Master*, I shall not touch upon it in these chapters with even a single word, either in explicit fashion or in a flash. For to my mind the term *prophet* used with reference to *Moses* and to the others is amphibolous. The same applies, in my opinion, to his miracles and to the miracles of others, for his miracles | do not belong to the class of the miracles of the other prophets. The proof taken from the Law as to his prophecy being different from that of all who came before him is constituted by His saying: *And I appeared unto Abraham, and so on, but by My name, the Lord, I made Me not known to them*.[3] Thus it informs us that his[4] apprehension was not like that of the *Patriarchs*, but greater — nor, all the more, like that of others who came before. As for the difference between his prophecy and that of all those who came after, it is stated by way of communicating information in the dictum: *And there hath not arisen a prophet since in*

7. Cf. Exod. 40:38; Num. 9:15 and 16.
1. Cf. Commentary on Sanhedrin X (Pereq Ḥeleq), Introduction, seventh article of faith.
2. Yesodei ha-Torah, VII 6. 3. Exod. 6:3. 4. I.e., Moses'.

Israel like unto Moses, whom the Lord knew face to face.[5] Thus it has been made clear that his apprehension is different from that of all those who came after him in *Israel* — which is *a kingdom of priests and a holy nation,*[6] *and in whose midst is the Lord*[7] — and, all the more, from the apprehension of all those who came in other religious communities.[8]

✓   As for the difference between his miracles in general and those of every prophet in general, it should be said that all the miracles worked by the prophets or for them were made known to a few people only. Thus, for instance, the signs of *Elijah* and *Elisha*: Do you see that the *King of Israel* inquired about them, asking *Gehazi* to communicate to him information about them? For he says: *Tell me, I pray thee, all the great things that Elisha hath done. And it came to pass, as he was telling, and so on. And Gehazi said: My lord, O king, this is the woman, and this is her son, whom Elisha restored to life.*[9] The same holds good for the signs of all the prophets except *Moses our Master.* For that reason Scripture makes it clear, likewise by way of information with reference to him, that no prophet will ever arise who will work signs both before those who are favorably and those who are unfavorably disposed toward him, as was done by *Moses.* This is the meaning of the dictum: *And there hath not arisen a prophet since, and so on, in all the signs and wonders, and so on, in the sight of all Israel.*[10] For here it establishes a connection and a tie between the two notions, namely, that there will not arise either someone who will have an apprehension similar to his or one who will perform actions similar to his. | Thereupon it makes it clear that these signs were worked in front of *Pharaoh, all his servants, and all his land* — who were unfavorably disposed to him — and also in the presence of *all Israel* — who followed him: *in the sight of all Israel.* This was a thing that had not happened to any prophet before him. Prior to that,[11] there occurred this truthful announcement that it will not happen to anyone else. You should not be led astray by what is said with regard to the light of the sun standing still for *Joshua* for certain hours — namely, *And he said in the sight of Israel*[12] — for it does not say *all Israel*, as is said with reference to *Moses.* Similarly *Elijah* on *Mount Carmel* performed his actions before a small number of men.[13] I said "certain hours," because it appears to me that the words *kayyom tamim [about a whole day]*[14] mean: as the longest day that may happen. For *tamim* means perfect. It is as if it said that the day of *Gibeon*

5. Deut. 34:10.   6. Exod. 19:6.   7. Num. 16:3.   8. Or: nations.
9. II Kings 8:4–5.   10. Deut. 34:10–12.   11. I.e., Deut. 34:10.
12. Josh. 10:12.   13. Cf. I Kings 18:19–39.   14. Josh. 10:13.

was for them as the longest of the days of the summer that may occur there.

After the prophecy and the miracles of *Moses* have, in accordance with my injunction, been set apart in your mind — seeing that the extraordinary character of his apprehension is similar to the extraordinary character of his actions — and after you have come to believe that his is a rank that we are incapable of grasping in its true reality, you shall hear what I say in all these chapters about prophecy and about the degree of the prophets in respect of prophecy — all these degrees being after this degree [of Moses]. This was the purpose of this chapter.

CHAPTER 36

Know that the true reality and quiddity of prophecy consist in its being an overflow overflowing from God, may He be cherished and honored, through the intermediation of the Active Intellect, toward the rational faculty in the first place and thereafter toward the imaginative faculty. This is the highest degree of man and the ultimate term of perfection that | can exist for his species; and this state is the ultimate term of perfection for the imaginative faculty. This is something that cannot by any means exist in every man. And it is not something that may be attained solely through perfection in the speculative sciences and through improvement of moral habits, even if all of them have become as fine and good as can be. There still is needed in addition the highest possible degree of perfection of the imaginative faculty in respect of its original natural disposition. Now you know that the perfection of the bodily faculties, to which the imaginative faculty belongs, is consequent upon the best possible temperament, the best possible size, and the purest possible matter, of the part of the body that is the substratum for the faculty in question. It is not a thing whose lack could be made good or whose deficiency could be remedied in any way by means of a regimen. For with regard to a part of the body whose temperament was bad in the original natural disposition, the utmost that the corrective regimen can achieve is to keep it in some sort of health; it cannot restore it to its best possible condition. If, however, its defect derives from its size, position, or substance, I mean the substance of the matter from which it is generated, there is no device that can help. You know all this; it is therefore useless to explain it at length.

You know, too, the actions of the imaginative faculty that are in its nature, such as retaining things perceived by the senses, combining these things, and imitating them. And you know that its greatest and noblest action takes place only when the senses rest and do not perform their actions. It is then that a certain overflow overflows to this faculty according to its disposition, and it is the cause of the veridical dreams. This same overflow is the cause of the prophecy. There is only a difference in degree, not in kind. You know that [the Sages] have said time and again: *A dream is the sixtieth part of prophecy.*[1] | No proportion, however, can be established between two things differing in their species. One is not allowed to say, for instance, that the perfection of a man is a certain number of times greater than the perfection of a horse. They reiterated this point in *Bereshith Rabbah*, saying: *Dream is the unripe fruit [nobeleth] of prophecy.*[2] This is an extraordinary comparison. For *unripe fruit [nobeleth]* is the individual *fruit* itself, but one that has fallen before it was perfect and before it had matured. Similarly the action of the imaginative faculty in the state of sleep is also its action in the state of prophecy; there is, however, a deficiency in it and it does not reach its ultimate term. Why should we teach you by means of the dicta of [the Sages], *may their memory be blessed*, and leave aside the texts of the *Torah? If there be a prophet among you, I the Lord do make Myself known unto him in a vision, I do speak with him in a dream.*[3] Thus He, may He be exalted, has informed us of the true reality and quiddity of prophecy and has let us know that it is a perfection that comes in a *dream* or in a *vision [marʾeh]*. The word *marʾeh [vision]* derives from the verb *raʾoh [to see]*. This signifies that the imaginative faculty achieves so great a perfection of action that it sees the thing as if it were outside, and that the thing whose origin is due to it appears to have come to it by the way of external sensation. In these two groups, I mean *vision* and *dream*, all the degrees of prophecy are included, as shall be explained. It is known that a matter that occupies a man greatly — he being bent upon it and desirous of it — while he is awake and while his senses function, is the one with regard to which the imaginative faculty acts while he is asleep when receiving an overflow of the intellect corresponding to its disposition.[4] It would be superfluous to quote examples of this and to expatiate on it as this is a manifest matter that everyone knows. It is similar to the

1. B.T., Berakhoth, 57b.　　2. Genesis Rabbah, XVII and XLIV.
3. Num. 12:6.　　4. I.e., the disposition of the imagination.

apprehension of the senses with regard to which no one whose natural disposition is healthy disagrees.

After these preliminary propositions, you should know[5] that the case to be taken into consideration | is that of a human individual the substance of whose brain at the origin of his natural disposition is extremely well proportioned because of the purity of its matter and of the particular temperament of each of its [that is, the brain's] parts and because of its size and position, and is not affected by hindrances due to temperament, which derive from another part of the body. Thereupon that individual would obtain knowledge and wisdom[6] until he passes from potentiality to actuality and acquires a perfect and accomplished human intellect and pure and well-tempered[7] human moral habits. Then all his desires will be directed to acquiring the science of the secrets of what exists and knowledge of its causes. His thought will always go toward noble matters, and he will be interested only in the knowledge of the deity and in reflection on His works and on what ought to be believed with regard to that. By then, he will have detached his thought from, and abolished his desire for, bestial things—I mean the preference for the pleasures of eating, drinking, sexual intercourse, and, in general, of the sense of touch, with regard to which Aristotle gave a clear explanation in the "Ethics," saying that this sense is a disgrace to us.[8] How fine is what he said, and how true it is that it is a disgrace! For we have it in so far as we are animals like the other beasts, and nothing that belongs to the notion of humanity pertains to it. As for the other sensual pleasures—those, for instance, that derive from the sense of smell, from hearing, and from seeing—there may be found in them sometimes, though they are corporeal, pleasure for man as man, as Aristotle has explained. We have been led to speak of things that are not to the purpose, but there was need for it. For most of the thoughts of those who are outstanding among the men of knowledge are preoccupied with the pleasures of this sense,[9] are desirous of them. And then they wonder how it is that they do not become prophets, if prophecy is something natural. It is | likewise necessary for the thought of that individual should be

5. Literally: You should know that if an individual. . . . These words begin a long period that is grammatically rather incoherent.
6. Or: science and philosophy.   7. I.e., observing the golden mean.
8. Cf. *Nicomachean Ethics* iii.10.1118b2 ff. The passage referring to the sense of touch reads as follows in Rackham's translation: "Hence the sense to which profligacy is related is the most universal of the senses; and there appears to be good ground for the disrepute in which it is held, because it belongs to us not as human beings but as animals."
9. I.e., the sense of touch.

detached from the spurious kinds of rulership and that his desire for them should be abolished — I mean the wish to dominate or to be held great by the common people and to obtain from them honor and obedience for its own sake. He should rather regard all people according to their various states with respect to which they are indubitably either like domestic animals or like beasts of prey. If the perfect man who lives in solitude thinks of them at all, he does so only with a view to saving himself from the harm that may be caused by those among them who are harmful if he happens to associate with them, or to obtaining an advantage that may be obtained from them if he is forced to it by some of his needs. Now[10] there is no doubt that whenever — in an individual of this description — his imaginative faculty, which is as perfect as possible, acts and receives from the intellect an overflow corresponding to his[11] speculative perfection, this individual will only apprehend divine and most extraordinary matters, will see only God and His angels, and will only be aware and achieve knowledge of matters that constitute true opinions and general directives for the well-being of men in their relations with one another. It is known that with regard to these three aims set forth by us — namely, the perfection of the rational faculty through study, the perfection of the imaginative faculty through natural disposition, and the perfection of moral habit through the turning-away of thought from all bodily pleasures and the putting an end to the desire for the various kinds of ignorant and evil glorification — there are among those who are perfect very many differences in rank; and on the differences in rank with regard to these aims there depend the differences in rank that subsist between the degrees of all the prophets.

You know that every bodily faculty | sometimes grows tired, is weakened, and is troubled, and at other times is in a healthy state. Now the imaginative faculty is indubitably a bodily faculty. Accordingly you will find that the prophecy of the prophets ceases when they are sad or angry, or in a mood similar to one of these two. You know their saying that *prophecy does not descend [during a mood of] sadness or of languor;*[12] that prophetic revelation did not come to *Jacob our Father* during the time of his mourning because of the fact that his imaginative faculty was preoccupied with the loss of *Joseph*;[13] and that prophetic revelation did not come to *Moses*, peace be on him, after the disastrous incident of the *spies* and until the whole *generation of the desert* perished, in the way that revelation used to

10. This is the conclusion of the period whose beginning is indicated above, n. 5.
11. Or: the intellect's.   12. B.T., Shabbath, 30b.
13. Chapters of Rabbi Eliezer, XXXVIII.

come before,[14] because — seeing the enormity of their crime — he suffered greatly because of this matter. This was so even though the imaginative faculty did not enter into his prophecy, peace be on him, as the intellect overflowed toward him without its intermediation. For, as we have mentioned several times, he did not prophesy like the other prophets by means of parables. This will be made clear later on, for it is not the purpose of this chapter. Similarly you will find that several prophets prophesied during a certain time and that afterwards prophecy was taken from them and could not be permanent because of an accident that had supervened. This is indubitably the essential and proximate cause of the fact that prophecy was taken away during the time of the *Exile.* For what *languor* or *sadness* can befall a man in any state that would be stronger than that due to his being a thrall slave in bondage to the ignorant[15] who commit great sins and in whom the privation of true reason is united to the perfection of the lusts of the beasts? *And there shall be no might in thine hand.*[16] This was with what we have been threatened. And this was what it meant by saying: *They shall run to and fro to seek the word of the Lord, and shall not find it.*[17] And it also says: *Her king and her princes are among the nations, the Law is no more; yea, her prophets find no vision from the Lord.*[18] This is true, and the cause thereof is clear. For the instrument has ceased to function. This also will be the cause for prophecy being restored | to us in its habitual form, as has been promised *in the days of the Messiah, may he be revealed soon.*

CHAPTER 37

It is fitting that your attention be aroused to the nature of that which exists in the divine overflow coming toward us, through which we have intellectual cognition and through which there is a difference of rank between our intellects. For sometimes something comes from it to a certain individual, the measure of that something being such that it renders him perfect, but has no other effect. Sometimes, on the other hand, the measure

14. B.T., Taᶜanith, 3ob.
15. *jāhiliyya,* which is the word used in the text, derives from the verb *jahila* (to be ignorant), and designated Pagans and idolaters, especially those of pre-Islamic Arabia. Maimonides may have had this meaning in mind.
16. Deut. 28:32.   17. Amos 8:12.   18. Lam. 2:9.

of what comes to the individual overflows from rendering him perfect toward rendering others perfect. This is what happens to all beings: some of them achieve perfection to an extent that enables them to govern others, whereas others achieve perfection only in a measure that allows them to be governed by others, as we have explained.

After this, you should know that the case in which the intellectual overflow overflows only toward the rational faculty and does not overflow at all toward the imaginative faculty — either because of the scantiness of what overflows or because of some deficiency existing in the imaginative faculty in its natural disposition, a deficiency that makes it impossible for it to receive the overflow of the intellect — is characteristic of the class of men of science engaged in speculation. If, on the other hand, this overflow reaches both faculties — I mean both the rational and the imaginative — as we and others among the philosophers have explained, and if the imaginative faculty is in a state of ultimate perfection owing to its natural disposition, this is characteristic of the class of prophets. If again the overflow only reaches the imaginative faculty, the defect of the rational faculty deriving either from its original natural disposition or from insufficiency of training, this is characteristic of the class of those who govern cities, | while being the legislators, the soothsayers, the augurs, and the dreamers of veridical dreams. All those who do extraordinary things by means of strange devices and secret arts and withal are not men of science belong likewise to this third class. You ought to obtain knowledge of the true reality, which is that some people belonging to this third class have — even while they are awake — extraordinary imaginings, dreams, and amazed states, which are like the *vision of prophecy* so that they think about themselves that they are prophets. And they are very much pleased with what they apprehend in these imaginings and think that they acquired sciences without instruction; and they bring great confusion into speculative matters of great import, true notions being strangely mixed up in their minds with imaginary ones. All this is due to the imaginative faculty, to the weakness of the rational faculty, and to its not having obtained anything — I mean thereby that it has not passed into actuality.

It is known that in each of these three classes there are very many differences of degree and that each of the first two classes is divided into two parts, as we have explained. For the measure of the overflow that comes to each of these two is either such as only to render the individual who receives it perfect and to have no other effect, or such that from that individual's perfection there is something left over that suffices to make others perfect. With regard to the first class — that of the men of science — the measure of the overflow that reaches the rational faculty of the individual is sometimes such that it makes him into a man who inquires and is endowed with understanding, who knows and discerns, but is not moved to teach others or to compose works, neither finding in himself a desire for this nor having the ability to do it. And sometimes the measure of the overflow is such that it moves him of necessity to compose works and to teach. The same holds good for the second class. Sometimes the prophetic revelation that comes to a prophet only renders him perfect and has no other effect. And sometimes the prophetic revelation that comes to him | compels him to address a call to the people, teach them, and let his own perfection overflow toward them.

It has already become clear to you that, were it not for this additional perfection, sciences would not be set forth in books and prophets would not call upon the people to obtain knowledge of the truth. For a man endowed with knowledge does not set anything down for himself in order to teach himself what he already knows. But the nature of that intellect is such that it always overflows and is transmitted from one who receives that overflow to another one who receives it after him until it reaches an individual beyond whom this overflow cannot go and whom it merely renders perfect, as we have set out in a parable in one of the chapters of this Treatise.[1] The nature of this matter makes it necessary for someone to whom this additional measure of overflow has come, to address a call to people, regardless of whether that call is listened to or not, and even if he as a result thereof is harmed in his body. We even find that prophets addressed a call to people until they were killed — this divine overflow moving them and by no means letting them rest and be quiet, even if they met with great misfortunes. For this reason you will find that *Jeremiah*, peace be on him, explicitly stated that because of the contempt he met with at the hand of the disobedient and unbelieving people who lived in his time, he wished to conceal his prophecy and not to address to them a call to the truth, which they rejected, but he was not able to do it. He says: *Because the word of the Lord is made a reproach unto me, and a derision, all the day. And if I say: I will not make mention of him, nor speak anymore in His name; then there is in my heart as it were a burning fire shut up in my bones, and I weary myself to hold it in, but cannot.*[2] This is also the meaning of the words of the other prophet: *The Lord God hath spoken, who shall not prophesy?*[3] Know this. |

1. Cf. II 11.   2. Jer. 20:8–9.   3. Amos 3:8.

CHAPTER 38

Know that in every man there is necessarily the faculty of courage. Were this not so, he would not be moved in his thought to ward off that which harms him. Among the faculties of the soul, this faculty is to my mind similar to the faculty of repulsion among the natural faculties. This faculty of courage varies in strength and weakness, as do other faculties, so that you may find among people some who will advance upon a lion, while others flee from a mouse. You will find someone who will advance against an army and fight it, and will find another who will tremble and fear if a woman shouts at him. There also must necessarily exist a temperamental preparation in the original natural disposition, which may increase through the passage of that which is potential into actuality—a passage effected in consequence of an effort made with a view to it and in accordance with a certain opinion. It may also diminish through a deficiency of exercise and in accordance with a certain opinion. The abundance or the weakness of this faculty in the young is made clear to you from their infancy.

Similarly the faculty of divination exists in all people, but varies in degree. It exists especially with regard to things with which a man is greatly concerned and about which his thought turns. Thus you will find in your soul that so and so spoke or acted in such and such a manner in such and such an episode,[1] and the thing is really so. You will find among people a man whose conjecturing and divination are very strong and habitually hit the mark, so that he hardly imagines that a thing comes to pass without its happening wholly or in part as he imagined it. The causes of this are many—they are various anterior, posterior, and present circumstances. But | in virtue of the strength of this divination, the mind goes over all these premises and draws from them conclusions in the shortest time, so that it is thought to happen in no time at all. In virtue of this faculty, certain people give warnings concerning great future events.

These two faculties must necessarily be very strong in prophets, I mean the faculty of courage and that of divination. And when the intellect overflows toward them, these two faculties become very greatly strengthened so that this may finally reach the point you know: namely, the lone individual, having only his staff, went boldly to the great king in order to save a religious community[2] from the burden of slavery, and had no fear or dread,

1. Literally: story.   2. Or: a nation.

because it was said to him: *I will be with thee.*[3] This too is a state that varies in them,[4] but it is indispensable for them. Thus it was said to *Jeremiah: Be not afraid and so on. Be not dismayed at them, and so on. For, behold, I have made thee this day a fortified city, and so on.*[5] And it was said to *Ezekiel: Be not afraid of them or of their words.*[6] Similarly you will find all of them, peace be on them, to be endowed with great courage. Also, because of the abundance of the faculty of divination in them, they give information regarding future events in the shortest time. This faculty likewise varies in them as you know.

Know that the true prophets indubitably grasp speculative matters; by means of his speculation alone, man is unable to grasp the causes from which what a prophet has come to know necessarily follows. This has a counterpart in their giving information regarding matters with respect to which man, using only common conjecture and divination, is unable to give information. For the very overflow that affects the imaginative faculty — with a result of rendering it perfect so that its act brings about its giving information about what will happen and its apprehending those future events as if they were things that had been perceived by the senses and had reached the imaginative faculty from the senses | — is also the overflow that renders perfect the act of the rational faculty, so that its act brings about its knowing things that are real in their existence, and it achieves this apprehension as if it had apprehended it by starting from speculative premises. This is the truth that is believed by whoever chooses to be equitable toward himself. For all things bear witness to one another and indicate one another. This should be even more fitting for the rational faculty. For the overflow of the Active Intellect goes in its true reality only to it [that is, to the rational faculty], causing it to pass from potentiality to actuality. It is from the rational faculty that that overflow comes to the imaginative faculty. How then can the imaginative faculty be perfected in so great a measure as to apprehend what does not come to it from the senses, without the rational faculty being affected in a similar way so as to apprehend without having apprehended by way of premises, inference, and reflection?

This is the true reality of the notion of prophecy, and these are the opinions that are peculiar to the prophetic teaching. In my exposition I have put in the proviso that it refers to true prophets only. This was in order to exclude from it the people belonging to the third class, who have no rational conceptions at all and no knowledge, but only imaginings and whims.

3. Exod. 3:12.   4. I.e., in the prophets.   5. Jer. 1:8, 17, 18.   6. Ezek. 2:6.
17

Perhaps they — I mean what these people apprehend — are merely opinions that they once had had and of which traces have remained impressed upon their imaginings together with everything else that subsists in their imaginative faculty. Accordingly when they void and annul many of their imaginings, the traces of these opinions remain alone and become apparent to them; whereupon they think that these are things that have unexpectedly occurred to them and have come from outside. To my mind they may be compared to a man who had with him in his house thousands of individual animals. Then all of them except one individual, which was one of those that were there, went out of that house. When the man remained alone with that individual, | he thought that it had just now entered the house and joined him, wheras that was not the case, that individual being the one among that multitude that did not go out. This is one of the points that lead astray and cause perdition. How many among those who have aspired to obtain discernment have perished through this! Hence you will find that certain groups of people establish the truth of their opinions with the help of dreams that they have seen, thinking that what they have seen in sleep is something else than the opinion that they believe in or that they had heard while awake. Therefore one ought not to pay attention to one whose rational faculty has not become perfect and who has not attained the ultimate term of speculative perfection. For only one who achieves speculative perfection is able to apprehend other objects of knowledge when there is an overflow of the divine intellect toward him. It is he who is in true reality a prophet. This is explicitly stated: *And the prophet [possesseth] a heart of wisdom.*[7] It says here that one who is a prophet in true reality has *a heart of wisdom*. This too ought to be known.

CHAPTER 39

After we have spoken of the quiddity of prophecy, have made known its true reality, and have made it clear that the prophecy of *Moses our Master* is different from that of the others, we shall say that the call to the Law followed necessarily from that apprehension alone.[1] For nothing similar to the call addressed to us by *Moses our Master* has been made

7. Ps. 90:12.
1. I.e., that of Moses.

before him by any one of those we know who lived in the time between *Adam* and him; nor was a call similar to that one made by one of our prophets after him. Correspondingly it is a fundamental principle of our Law that there will never be another Law. Hence, according to our opinion, there never has been a Law and there never will be a Law except the one that is | the Law of *Moses our Master*. The explanation of this, according to ✓ what is literally stated in the prophetic books and is found in the tradition, is as follows. Not one of the prophets — such as the *Patriarchs, Shem, Eber, Noah, Methuselah,* and *Enoch* — who came before *Moses our Master*, has ever said to a class of people: God has sent me to you and has commanded me to say to you such and such things; He has forbidden you to do such and such things and has commanded you to do such and such things. This is a thing that is not attested to by any text of the *Torah* and that does not figure in any true tradition. These men only received prophetic relevation from God according to what we have set forth.[2] He who received a great overflow, as for instance *Abraham*, assembled the people and called them by the way of teaching and instruction to adhere to the truth that he had grasped. Thus *Abraham* taught the people and explained to them by means of speculative proofs that the world has but one deity, that He has created all the things that are other then Himself, and that none of the forms[3] and no created thing in general ought to be worshipped. This is what he instructed the people in, attracting them by means of eloquent[4] speeches and by means of the benefits[5] he conferred upon them. But he never said: God has sent me to you and has given me commandments and prohibitions. Even when the commandment of circumcision was laid upon him, his sons, and those who belonged to him, he circumcised them alone and did not use the form of a prophetic call to exhort the people to do this. Do you not see the text of the *Torah* referring to him that reads: *For I have known him, and so on.*[6] Thus it is made clear that he acted only through injunction. *Isaac, Jacob, Levi, Kohat,* and *Amram* also addressed their call to the people in this way. You will find likewise that the *Sages* say with reference to the prophets who came before him: *the court of justice of Eber, the court of justice of Methuselah, the school of Methuselah.*[7] For

2. Cf. I 63.   3. I.e., the forms of the stars, etc.   4. Literally: beautiful.

5. The word translated as "benefits" derives from the same verbal root as the word referred to in the preceding note.

6. Gen. 18:19. The verse continues: *to the end that he may command his sons and his house after him, that they may keep the way of the Lord, to do righteousness and judgment.*

7. Genesis Rabbah, XLIII.

all of them, peace be on them, were prophets who taught the people through being instructors, teachers, | and guides, but did not say: *The Lord said to me: Speak to the sons of so and so.* Things were like that before *Moses our Master.* As for *Moses,* you know what was said to him, what he said, and what all the people said to him: *This day we have seen that God doth speak, and so on.*[8] As for the prophets from among us who came after *Moses our Master,* you know the text of all their stories and the fact that their function was that of preachers who called upon the people to obey the Law of *Moses,* threatened those who rejected it, and held out promises to those who were firm in observing it. We likewise believe that things will always be this way. As it says: *It is not in heaven, and so on;*[9] *for us and for our children for ever.*[10] And that is as it ought to be; for when a thing is as perfect as it is possible to be within its species, it is impossible that within that species there should be found another thing that does not fall short of that perfection either because of excess or deficiency. Thus in comparison with a temperament whose composition is of the greatest equibalance possible in the species in question, all other temperaments are not composed in accordance with this equibalance because of either deficiency or excess. Things are similar with regard to this Law, as is clear from its equibalance. For it says: *Just statutes and judgments;*[11] now you know that the meaning of *just* is equibalanced. For these are manners of worship in which there is no burden and excess — such as monastic life and pilgrimage and similar things — nor a deficiency necessarily leading to greed and being engrossed in the indulgence of appetites, so that in consequence the perfection of man is diminished with respect to his moral habits and to his speculation — this being the case with regard to all the other nomoi of the religious communities[12] of the past. When we shall speak in this Treatise about the reasons accounting for the commandments,[13] their equibalance and wisdom will be made clear to you in so far as this is necessary. For this reason it is said with reference to them: *The Law of the Lord is perfect.*[14] As for those who deem that its burdens are grievous, heavy, and difficult to bear — all of this is due to an error in considering them. I shall explain later on | how easy they are in true reality according to the opinion of the perfect. For this reason it says: *What doth the Lord thy God require of thee, and so on.*[15] And it says: *Have I been a wilderness unto Israel, and so on.*[16] However, all this refers to the virtuous, whereas

8. Deut. 5:21.   9. Deut. 30:12.   10. Deut. 29:28.   11. Deut. 4:8.
12. Or: nations.   13. I.e., the commandments promulgated by Moses.
14. Ps. 19:8.   15. Deut. 10:12.   16. Jer. 2:31.

in the opinion of those who are unjust, violent,[17] and tyrannical, the existence of a judge who renders tyranny impossible is a most harmful and grievous thing. As for the greedy and the vile, the most grievous thing in their opinion is that which hinders their abandoning themselves to debauchery and punishes those who indulge in it. Similarly everyone who is deficient in any respect considers that a hindrance in the way of the vice that he prefers because of his moral corruption is a great burden. Accordingly the facility or difficulty of the Law should not be estimated with reference to the passions of all the wicked, vile, morally corrupt men, but should be considered with reference to the man who is perfect among the people. For it is the aim of this Law that everyone should be such a man. Only that Law is called by us divine Law, whereas the other political regimens — such as the nomoi of the Greeks and the ravings of the Sabians and of others — are due, as I have explained several times, to the action of groups of rulers who were not prophets.

CHAPTER 40

It has been explained with utmost clarity that man is political by nature and that it is his nature to live in society. He is not like the other animals for which society is not a necessity. Because of the manifold composition of this species[1] — for, as you know, it is the last one to have been composed — there are many differences between the individuals belonging to it, so that you can hardly find two individuals who are in any accord with respect to | one of the species of moral habits, except in a way similar to that in which their visible forms may be in accord with one another. The cause of this is the difference of the mixtures,[2] owing to which the various kinds of matter differ, and also the accidents consequent to the form in question. For every natural form has certain accidents proper and consequent to it, those accidents being other than those that are consequent to matter. Nothing like this great difference between the various individuals is found among the other species of animals, in which the difference between individuals belonging to the same species is small, man being in this respect an

17. *ghaḍab* (anger) in Joel's edition seems to be a misprint; the correct reading is *ghaṣb* (violence).

1. I.e., the human species.   2. Or: temperaments.

exception. For you may find among us two individuals who seem, with regard to every moral habit, to belong to two different species. Thus you may find in an individual cruelty that reaches a point at which he kills the youngest of his sons in his great anger, whereas another individual is full of pity at the killing of a bug or any other insect, his soul being too tender for this. The same holds good for most accidents.

Now as the nature of the human species requires that there be those differences among the individuals belonging to it and as in addition society is a necessity for this nature, it is by no means possible that his society should be perfected except — and this is necessarily so — through a ruler who gauges the actions of the individuals, perfecting that which is deficient and reducing that which is excessive, and who prescribes actions and moral habits that all of them must always practice in the same way, so that the natural diversity is hidden through the multiple points of conventional accord and so that the community becomes well ordered. Therefore I say that the Law, although it is not natural, enters into what is natural. It is a part of the wisdom of the deity with regard to the permanence of this species of which He has willed the existence, that He put it into its nature that individuals belonging to it should have the faculty of ruling. Among them there is the one to whom the regimen mentioned has been revealed by prophecy directly; he is the prophet or the bringer of the nomos. Among them there are also those who have the faculty to compel people to accomplish, observe, | and actualize that which has been established by those two.[3] They are a sovereign who adopts the nomos in question, and someone claiming to be a prophet who adopts the Law of the prophet — either the whole of it or a portion. His adopting a portion and abandoning another portion may be due either to this being easier for him or to his wishing out of jealousy to make people fancy that those matters came to him through a prophetic revelation and that with regard to them he does not follow somebody else. For among the people there are men who admire a certain perfection, take pleasure in it, have a passion for it, and wish that people should imagine that this perfection belongs to them, though they know that they possess no perfection. Thus you see that there are many who lay a claim to, and give out as their own, the poetry of someone else. This has also been done with regard to certain works of men of science and to particular points of many sciences. For an envious and lazy individual sometimes comes upon a thing invented by somebody else and claims that it

3. I.e., the prophet and the bringer of the nomos.

was he who invented it. This has also happened with regard to the prophetic perfection. For we find people who laid a claim to prophecy and said things with regard to which there had never been at any time a prophetic revelation coming from God; thus, for instance, *Zedekiah, son of Chenaanah.*[4] And we find other people who laid a claim to prophecy and said things that God has indubitably said — I mean things that had come through a prophetic revelation, but a prophetic revelation addressed to other people; thus, for instance, *Hananiah, son of Azzur.*[5] Accordingly these men give out as their own the prophetic revelation in question and adorn themselves with it. The knowledge and discernment of all this are very clear. I shall explain this to you in order that the matter should not be obscure to you and so that you should have a criterion by means of which you will be able to distinguish between the regimens of nomoi that have been laid down, the regimens of the divine Law, and the regimens of those who took over something from the dicta of the prophets, raised a claim to it, and give it out as their own.

Concerning the nomoi with respect to which those who have laid them down have stated clearly that these are nomoi that they have laid down by following their own thoughts, there is no need to adduce proofs for this, for with its being recognized by the adversary, no further evidence is needed. Accordingly I only want to give you knowledge concerning the regimens | with regard to which the claim is made that they are prophetic; some of them are truly prophetic — I mean divine — while others are nomoi,[6] and others again are plagiarisms.

Accordingly if you find a Law the whole end of which and the whole purpose of the chief thereof, who determined the actions required by it, are directed exclusively toward the ordering of the city[7] and of its circumstances and the abolition in it of injustice and oppression; and if in that Law attention is not at all directed toward speculative matters, no heed is given to the perfecting of the rational faculty, and no regard is accorded to opinions being correct or faulty — the whole purpose of that Law being, on the contrary, the arrangement, in whatever way this may be brought about, of the circumstances of people in their relations with one another and provision for their obtaining, in accordance with the opinion of that chief, a certain something deemed to be happiness — you must know that

4. Cf. I Kings 22:11 and 24.   5. Cf. Jer. 28:1 ff.
6. I.e., composed of man-made laws.   7. *madína*, i.e., *polis*.

that Law is a nomos[8] and that the man who laid it down belongs, as we have mentioned, to the third class, I mean to say to those who are perfect only in their imaginative faculty.

If, on the other hand, you find a Law all of whose ordinances are due to attention being paid, as was stated before, to the soundness of the circumstances pertaining to the body and also to the soundness of belief — a Law that takes pains to inculcate correct opinions with regard to God, may He be exalted in the first place, and with regard to the angels, and that desires to make man wise, to give him understanding, and to awaken his attention, so that he should know the whole of that which exists in its true form — you must know that this guidance comes from Him, may He be exalted, and that this Law is divine.

It remains for you to know whether he who lays claim to such a guidance is a perfect man to whom a prophetic revelation of that guidance has been vouchsafed, or whether he is an individual who lays claim to these dicta, having plagiarized them. The way of putting this to a test is to consider the perfection of that individual, carefully to examine his actions, and to study his way of life. The strongest of the indications you should pay attention to is constituted by his renunciation of, and contempt for, the bodily pleasures, for this is the first of the degrees of the people of science and, all the more, of the prophets. In particular this holds good with regard to the sense | that is a disgrace to us — as Aristotle has set forth[9] — and especially in what belongs to it with regard to the foulness of copulation. For this reason God has stigmatized through it everyone who lays a claim to prophecy, so that the truth should be made clear to those who seek it and they should not go astray and fall into error. Do you not see how *Zedekiah, son of Maaseiah, and Ahab, son of Kolaiah*, claimed prophecy, were followed by the people, and give forth dicta deriving from a revelation that had come to others; and how they were plunged into the vileness of the pleasure of sexual intercourse so that they fornicated with the wives of their companions and followers so that God made them notorious, just as He disgraced others, and *the King of Babylon* burned them. As *Jeremiah* has set forth, saying: *And of them shall be taken up a curse by all the exiles of Judah that are in Babylon, saying: The Lord make thee like Zedekiah and like Ahab, whom the King of Babylon roasted in the fire; because they have*

8. The expression used is *sharī͑a nāmūsiyya*; literally: nomic Law. *nāmūsiyya* derives from *nāmūs*, which is the Arabic form of the Greek word *nomos*. It signifies in the context a law promulgated by a legislator who was not a prophet.

9. Cf. above, II 36, n. 8.

wrought vile deeds in Israel, and have committed adultery with their neigh-
bors' wives, and have spoken words in My name falsely, which I commanded
them not; but I am He that knoweth and am witness, saith the Lord.[10]
Understand this intention.

CHAPTER 41

I do not need to explain what a *dream* is. As for a *vision* — as in: *I do make Myself known unto him in a vision*[1] — it is that which is called a *vision of prophecy* and is likewise called the *hand of the Lord*[2] and *sight* [*maḥazeh*].[3] It is a fearful terrifying state, which comes to a prophet when he is awake, as is made clear regarding *Daniel* in his saying: *And I saw this great vision, and there remained no strength in me; for my comeliness was turned in me into corruption, and I retained no strength.*[4] And he says: *And I was in a deep sleep on my face, with my face toward the ground.*[5] | The speech of the *angel* to him and his setting him upright, all this happened *in a vision of prophecy.* In a state such as this the senses too cease to function, and the overflow in question comes to the rational faculty and overflows from it to the imaginative faculty so that the latter becomes perfect and performs its function. Prophetic revelation begins sometimes *with a vision of prophecy.* Thereupon the terror and the strong affection consequent upon the perfection of the action of the imaginative faculty become intensified and then prophetic revelation comes, as is recounted of *Abraham.* For with regard to the beginning of that prophetic revelation, it is said: *The word of the Lord came unto Abram in a vision.*[6] And with regard to its termination: *And a deep sleep fell upon Abram, and so on.*[7] After that: *And He said unto Abram, and so on.*[8]

Know with regard to all the prophets, concerning whom it is mentioned[9] that prophetic revelation has come to them, that some ascribe it to an *angel* while others ascribe it to God, though indubitably it was produced

---

10. Jer. 29:22–23.
1. Num. 12:6.   2. Cf. II Kings 3:15; Ezek. 1:3; 3:22; 37:1; 40:1.
3. Cf. Gen. 15:1; Num. 24:4 and 16. The word *sight* renders *maḥazeh; vision* is used to translate *marᶜeh.*
4. Dan. 10:8.   5. Dan. 10:9.
6. Gen. 15:1. The word translated as *vision* in this verse is *maḥazeh.*
7. Gen. 15:12.   8. Gen. 15:13.   9. Or: who have mentioned.

through the agency of an *angel*. The *Sages, may their memory be blessed*, have expressed this by saying: *And the Lord said unto her*[10] — *through the agency of an angel*.[11] Know again that in the case of everyone about whom exists a scriptural text that an *angel* talked to him or that speech came to him from God, this did not occur in any other way than *in a dream* or *in a vision of prophecy*.

Information about the speech that comes to the prophets, according to the expression used in the prophetic books, occurs in four forms. In the first form the prophet explicitly states that the speech addressed to him came from the *angel in a dream* or *in a vision*. In the second form the prophet only mentions the speech addressed to him by the *angel*, but does not explicitly state that this happened *in a dream* or *in a vision* because he relies upon the fact that it is known that there is no prophetic revelation except in these two manners: *I do make Myself known unto him in a vision, I do speak with him in a dream*.[12] In the third form the prophet does not mention an *angel* at all, but attributes the words | of God as having been spoken by Him to him; yet he explicitly states that the speech in question came to him *in a vision* or *in a dream*. In the fourth form the prophet simply says that God talked to him or told him: Act thus! or Do thus! or Speak thus! without making an explicit statement as to an *angel* or a *dream*, because he relies upon the fact that it is known and established as a principle that no prophecy and no prophetic revelation come in any other way except *in a dream* or *in a vision* and through the agency of an *angel*.

According to the first form, there are such dicta as: *And the angel of God said unto me in the dream*;[13] *And God spoke unto Israel in the visions of the night*;[14] *And God came unto Balaam*;[15] *And God said unto Balaam*.[16] According to the second form, there are such dicta as: *And God said unto Jacob: Arise, go up to Bethel*;[17] *And God said unto him: Thy name is Jacob*;[18] *And the angel of the Lord called unto him out of heaven*;[19] *And the angel of the Lord called unto Abraham a second time, and so on*;[20] *And God said unto Noah*;[21] *And God spoke unto Noah*.[22] According to the third form, there are such dicta as: *The word of the Lord came unto Abram in a vision, and so on*.[23] According to the fourth form, there are such dicta as: *Now the Lord said unto Abram*;[24] *And the Lord said unto Jacob:*

10. Gen. 25:23.   11. Genesis Rabbah, LXIII.   12. Num. 12:6.
13. Gen. 31:11.   14. Gen. 46:2.   15. Num. 22:9.   16. Num. 22:12.
17. Gen. 35:1.   18. Gen. 35:10.   19. Gen. 22:11.   20. Gen. 22:15.
21. Gen. 6:13.   22. Gen. 8:15.   23. Gen. 15:1, Cf. n. 6, this chap.
24. Gen. 12:1.

Return unto the land of thy fathers;[25] *And the Lord said unto Joshua ;*[26] *And the Lord said unto Gideon.*[27] The dicta of most of [the prophets] are similar: *The Lord said unto me ;*[28] *And the word of the Lord came unto me ;*[29] *And the word of the Lord came;*[30] *And, behold, the word of the Lord came to him ;*[31] *The word of the Lord came expressly ;*[32] *The beginning of the word of the Lord to Hosea ;*[33] *The hand of the Lord was upon me.*[34] This manner of expression is very frequent.

All the dicta that are formulated according to one of these forms are prophecies, and those who utter them are prophets. However in the cases when it is said, *God came to so and so in a dream of the night,* there is no prophecy at all nor is the individual in question a prophet. | For this way of speech signifies that an intimation came to that individual from God. In addition it makes it clear to us[35] that this intimation came to pass in a dream. For just as God causes a motion of the individual in question with a view to another individual's being saved or his perishing, He also causes — by means of the vision of a dream — the creation in time of things that He wishes to be so created. For we do not doubt that *Laban the Aramean was a perfectly impious man,* and moreover an *idolater.* As for *Abimelech,* though he was a righteous man in comparison with his people, yet *Abraham our Father* said of his land and kingdom: *Surely the fear of God is not in this place.*[36] In spite of this, this is what is said of both of them — I mean *Laban* and *Abimelech: But God came to Abimelech in a dream of the night,*[37] and similarly with regard to *Laban: In a dream of the night.*[38] Know this and consider the difference between the dictum [of Scripture], *God came,* and its dictum, *God spoke;* as well as that between its dictum, *In a dream of the night,* and its dictum, *In the visions of the night.* Thus it is said of Jacob: *And God spoke unto Israel in the visions of the night;*[39] whereas it is said of *Laban* and *Abimelech: But God came, and so on, in a dream of the night.*[40] Accordingly the latter expression is rendered by *Onqelos: A word came from the Lord;* and he does not say with reference to these two individuals: *The Lord revealed himself.* Know that it is sometimes said: *And the Lord spoke to so and so* — although that *so and so* was not a prophet[41] and prophetic revelation had never come to him, but he was merely told

25. Gen. 31:3.   26. Josh. 3:7.   27. Judg. 7:2.   28. Isa. 8:1.
29. Ezek. 24:1.   30. II Sam. 24:11; I Kings 18:1.   31. I Kings 19:9.
32. Ezek. 1:3.   33. Hos. 1:2.   34. Ezek. 37:1; 40:1.
35. Or: it is made clear to us.   36. Gen. 20:11.   37. Gen. 20:3.
38. Gen. 31:24.   39. Gen. 46:2.   40. Gen. 20:3; 31:24.
41. Translated according to the reading of a manuscript given in Joel's critical apparatus, p. 484. The reading given in the text and corroborated by Ibn Tibbon's translation does not seem to make sense.

the things in question by a prophet. Thus the text says: *And she went to inquire of the Lord;*[42] but [the Sages] say in explanation: *To the school of Eber.*[43] And that school gave her an answer; and it is with reference to the same event that it is said: *And the Lord said unto her.*[44] And even though it has been said that the expression, *And the Lord said unto her*, means that this was done *through the agency of an angel,* this should be interpreted as signifying that *Eber* was the *angel*; for a prophet is sometimes called *angel*, as we shall make clear. Or else this explanation alludes to the *angel* who came to *Eber* with the prophecy in question; or it is intended to make explicit that whenever words are | unqualifiedly[45] ascribed to God, they came, as we have explained in the case of the other prophets, through the agency of an *angel*.

CHAPTER 42

We have explained that wherever it is mentioned that an *angel* was seen or had spoken, this has happened only *in a vision of prophecy* or *in a dream* whether this is explicitly stated or not, as has been said before. Know this and understand it thoroughly. And there is no difference between a statement in which the prophet literally affirms from the first that he saw the *angel* and a statement according to whose external sense the prophet at first thought that a human individual had appeared to him, whereas at the end it became clear to him that it was an *angel*. For inasmuch as you find in the course of the event that he who was seen and had spoken was an angel, you ought to know and to establish as true that the event was from the first *a vision of prophecy* or *a dream of prophecy*. For in *a vision of prophecy* or *a dream of prophecy*, the prophet sometimes sees God speaking to him, as we shall explain, and sometimes an angel speaking to him; sometimes he hears somebody speaking to him without seeing an individual who is speaking, and again sometimes he sees a human individual who is speaking, and again sometimes he sees a human individual who speaks to him, and afterwards it becomes clear to him that he who spoke was an *angel*. Thus in this kind of prophecy, the prophet mentions[1] that he saw a man who acted or spoke and that afterwards he knew that he was an *angel*.

42. Gen. 25:22.   43. Genesis Rabbah, LXIII.   44. Gen. 25:23.
45. Literally: absolutely.
 1. Or: it is mentioned.

One of the *Sages, may their memory be blessed,* in fact a great man among those of them who were great, arrived at this capital principle. It was *Rabbi Ḥiyya the Great,* when speaking of the text of the *Torah: And the Lord appeared unto him by the terebinths of Mamre, and so on.*[2] For after he had first propounded the proposition that God manifested Himself to him,[3] he began to explain what the form of this manifestation was; and he said that at first he saw *three men* and ran; | whereupon they spoke and were spoken to. He who propounded this allegoric interpretation says of *Abraham's* dictum — *And he said: My lord, if I now have found favor in thy sight, pass not away, I pray thee, from thy servant*[4] — that it too is a description of what he said in a *vision of prophecy* to one of them; he[5] says in fact: *He said it to the greatest among them.*[6] Understand this story too, for it is one of the secrets. I say likewise also of the story about *Jacob* in regard to its saying, *And there wrestled a man with him,*[7] that it is in conformity with the form of prophetic revelation, inasmuch as it is finally made clear that he who was there was an *angel.* This is quite similar to the story concerning *Abraham,* in which it at first informs us in a general way, *And the Lord appeared unto him, and so on,* and then begins to explain in what way this happened. It is similar with regard to *Jacob.* At first it says: *And the angels of God met him.*[8] Then it begins to explain what happened before *they met him,* and says that he sent messengers and acted and did this and that. Then *Jacob was left alone, and so on.*[9] And these[10] are *the angels of God* of whom it has been said at first: *And the angels of God met him.* All the wrestling and the conversation in question happened *in a vision of prophecy.* And likewise the whole story of *Balaam on the way*[11] and of the *she-ass* speaking; all this happened *in a vision of prophecy,* as it is finally made clear that an *angel of the Lord* spoke to him.[12] Similarly I shall say with regard to what *Joshua* said when *he lifted up his eyes and looked, and, behold, there stood a man over against him,*[13] that this happened *in a vision of prophecy,* as it is finally made clear that the man was *captain of the host of the Lord.*[14] With regard to the dictum: *And the angel of the Lord came up from Gilgal, and so on;*[15] *And it came to pass, when the angel of the Lord spoke these words unto all the children of Israel*[16] — the *Sages* have already literally stated that the *angel of the Lord* mentioned here was

2. Gen. 18:1.   3. To Abraham.   4. Gen. 18:3.   5. Rabbi Ḥiyya.
6. Genesis Rabbah, XLVIII.   7. Gen. 32:25.   8. Gen. 32:2.   9. Gen. 32:25.
10. The reference is to the second part of the verse that has just been quoted: *and there wrestled a man with him until the breaking of the day.*
11. Cf. Num. 22:22.   12. To Balaam.   13. Josh. 5:13.   14. Josh. 5:14.
15. Judg. 2:1.   16. Judg. 2:4.

Phinehas. They said: *This was Phinehas who, when the Indwelling descends upon him, resembles an angel of the Lord.*[17] We have already explained that the term *angel* is equivocal and that a prophet may likewise be called an *angel,* as | is said in the text: *And sent an angel, and brought us forth out of Egypt.*[18] It also says: *Then spoke Haggai the Lord's angel in the Lord's message.*[19] And it says: *But they mocked the angels of God.*[20] As for what *Daniel* says: *Even the man Gabriel, whom I had seen in the vision at the beginning, being caused to fly swiftly, approached close to me about the time of the evening offering*[21] — all this happened *in a vision of prophecy.* It should by no means occur to your thought that an *angel* can be seen or that the speech of an *angel* can be heard except *in a vision of prophecy* or *in a dream of prophecy,* according to what is stated as a principle: *I do make Myself known unto him in a vision, I do speak with him in a dream.*[22] You can draw inferences from what I have mentioned as to what remains of the things that I have not mentioned.

From what we have set forth before regarding the necessity of preparation for prophecy and from what we have mentioned regarding the equivocality of the term *angel,* you should know that *Hagar the Egyptian* was not a prophetess[23] and that *Manoah and his wife* were no prophets.[24] For the words that they heard or that occurred to their mind were similar to the *voices,*[25] which the *Sages* constantly mention. This is a state that accompanies an individual who is not prepared for prophecy. It is only the equivocality of the term that occasions errors as to this — this being the principle that removes most of the difficulties found in the *Torah.* Consider the dictum, *And the angel of the Lord found her*[26] *by a fountain of water, and so on,*[27] together with the use of a similar expression about *Joseph: And a certain man found him, and, behold, he was wandering in the field.*[28] With regard to this man, all the *Midrashim*[29] state literally that he was an *angel.*

17. Cf. Leviticus Rabbah, I.   18. Num. 20:16.   19. Hag. 1:13.
20. II Chron. 36:16.   21. Dan. 9:21.   22. Num. 12:6.
23. Cf. Gen. 16:7; 21:17.   24. Cf. Judg. 13:3 and 11.
25. *bath qōl.* Literally: *the daughter of a voice.*   26. Hagar.
27. Gen. 16:7.   28. Gen. 37:15.   29. In the text: *Midrashoth.*

We have already explained in our compilations[1] that prophets sometimes prophesy in parables. For sometimes a prophet sees a thing under the aspect of a parable, | the meaning of that parable being sometimes interpreted to him in that very same *vision of prophecy* — just as a man may see a dream and imagine in that dream that he has already awakened and that he has related the dream to somebody else and has interpreted its meaning to him, all this taking place in a dream. This is what they call *a dream solved in a dream*.[2] Again there are dreams whose meaning becomes known after one awakens. Similarly there are parables of the prophets whose meaning is interpreted *in a vision of prophecy*, as is made clear with regard to *Zechariah*, when he says, after having first set forth the parables: *And the angel that spoke with me returned, and waked me, as a man that is wakened out of his sleep, and he said unto me: What seest thou?, and so on*,[3] and then interpreted the parable for him; and as is made clear with regard to *Daniel* in the dictum: *Daniel had a dream and visions of his head upon his bed*.[4] Thereupon it sets forth all the parables and mentions his being anxious because he did not know their interpretation until he asked the *angel* who in that very *vision* made known to him their interpretation. And that is what he says: *I came near unto one of them that stood by, and asked him the truth concerning all this. So he told me, and made me know the interpretation of the things*.[5] It calls the whole story a *vision* [*ḥazon*] after having mentioned that [Daniel] *had a dream*; this in view of the fact that, as has been mentioned, an *angel* interpreted the dream to him in a *dream of prophecy*. This is made known in the dictum that comes afterwards: *A vision* [*ḥazon*] *appeared unto me, even unto Daniel, after that which appeared unto me at the first*.[6] This is manifest; for *ḥazon* derives from *ḥazoh* [*to perceive*], and *marʾeh* [*vision*] derives from *raʾoh* [*to see*], and *ḥazoh* and *raʾoh* have the same meaning. There is no difference between one's saying *in a marʾeh* [*vision*], *in a maḥazeh* [*sight*], or *in a ḥazon*.[7] And there is no third way other than the two stated expressly in the *Torah*: *I do make Myself known unto him in a vision, I do speak with him in a dream*.[8] However, there are degrees in regard to this, as shall be explained.[9] Among the parables of the prophets there are | many whose meaning is not

1. Cf. *Mishneh Torah*, Yesodei ha-Torah, VII 3.   2. B.T., Berakhoth, 55b.
3. Zech. 4:1–2.   4. Dan. 7:1.   5. Dan. 7:16.   6. Dan. 8:1.
7. The nouns *maḥazeh* and *ḥazon* both derive from the verb *ḥazoh* (to perceive).
8. Num. 12:6.   9. Cf. II 45.

interpreted in a *vision of prophecy*, but whose purpose is known by the prophet after he awakens; thus, for instance, the parable of the *staves* that *Zechariah* took *in a vision of prophecy*.[10]

Know that just as the prophets see things whose purpose it is to constitute a parable — as for instance *Zechariah's lamps*[11] and the *horses* and the *mountains*,[12] *Ezekiel's scroll*,[13] *the wall made by a plumbline* that was seen by *Amos*,[14] the *beasts* seen by *Daniel*,[15] and *the seething pot* that was seen by *Jeremiah*,[16] and other similar parables whose purpose it is to imitate certain notions — they[17] also see things whose purpose it is to point to what is called to the attention by the term designating the thing seen because of that term's derivation or because of an equivocality of terms. In that case the action of the imaginative faculty consists in occasioning the appearance of a thing designated by an equivocal term, through one of whose meanings another one can be indicated. This too is one of the kinds of the making of parables. For instance the intention in the dictum of *Jeremiah* concerning *maqqel shaqed* [*a rod of almond tree*] is an indication based on the equivocality of the term *shaqed* [*almond*]. Scripture accordingly proceeds to say: *Ki shoqed 'ani, and so on* [*For I watch over*].[18] Thus in this case the intention of the parable did not concern the notion of rod or that of almond. Similarly *Amos* saw *klub qayiṣ* [*a basket of summer fruit*],[19] so that he should infer from it the end of the period. It accordingly says: *Ba' haq-qeṣ* [*The end is come*].[20]

Stranger[21] than this is the intimation aroused through the use of a certain term whose letters are identical with those of another term; solely the order of the letters is changed; and between the two terms there is in no way an etymological connection[22] or a community of meaning.[23] You will find an example in the parables of *Zechariah*, when, *in a vision of prophecy*, he takes two staves in order to shepherd cattle, naming one of them *grace* [*no'am*] and the other *ravagers* [*ḥoblim*].[24] The intention

10. Zech. 11:7 ff.   11. Zech. 4:2.   12. Zech. 6:1–7.   13. Ezek. 2:9.
14. Amos 7:7.   15. Dan. 7 and 8.   16. Jer. 1:13.   17. I.e., the prophets.
18. Jer. 1:11–12. The word *shaqed* (almond tree) has the same radical as the verb *shaqod*, which is translated in this verse as "to watch over."
19. Amos 8:2.
20. Amos 8:2. The inference can be made because of the similarity of the words *qayiṣ* (summer) and *qeṣ* (end).
21. Or: more wonderful.
22. Literally: even if there is no etymological derivation between the two terms.
23. *ishtirāk ma'nā*. One would expect "equivocality of the terms" (*ishtirāk fi'l-asmā'*).
24. Zech. 11:7. The translation *grace* and *ravagers* seems to conform to Maimonides' interpretation, which follows immediately. In the English Bible, the two words are translated "Graciousness" and "Binders."

of this parable was to show that in its beginnings the religious community[25] subsisted in the *grace of the Lord*, who was the one who led | and consolidated it, and that it rejoiced and took pleasure in obedience to God, while God was pleased with it and loved it; just as it says: *Thou hast avouched the Lord this day, and so on. And the Lord hath avouched thee this day, and so on.*[26] *Moses* was the one who governed and directed this community at that time, and after him some of the prophets. Afterwards the state of this community came to such a pass that obedience to God became repugnant to it and that it became repugnant to God. Accordingly He set up *hoblim* [*ravagers*] like *Jeroboam* and *Manasseh* as its chiefs. This is to be understood according to the etymological derivation of the word; for *hoblim* derives from the expression, *mehabblim keramim* [*that spoil the vineyards*].[27] In addition the prophet inferred therefrom,[28] I mean from the term *hoblim*, their repugnance for the Law and the repugnance of God for them. However, this meaning can only be derived from *hoblim* through changing the order of the "ha," the "ba," and the "lam."[29] Now it says, within the context of this parable, to signify the notion of repugnance and disgust: *And My soul became impatient of them, and their soul also loathed* [*bohalah*] *Me*.[30] Accordingly it changed the order of *habol*[31] and transformed it into *bahol*.[32] Through this method very strange things appear, which are likewise *secrets*, as in its dictum with regard to the *Chariot*:[33] *brass* and *burnished* and *foot* and *calf* and *lightning*, and in other passages. If you carefully examine each passage in your mind, they will become clear to you — after your attention has been aroused — from the gist of what has been set forth here.

25. *milla*. Or: nation.   26. Deut. 26:17–18.   27. Song of Songs 2:15.
28. Or: it may be inferred therefrom.
29. I.e., *h*, *b*, and *l*. Maimonides uses the Arabic names of the letters even though the word is a Hebrew one.
30. Zech. 11:8.
31. The verb from which the form *hoblim* (ravagers) derives.
32. The verb from which the form *bohalah* (loathed) derives.   33. Ezek. 1.

Prophecy occurs only *in a vision* or *in a dream*, as we have already explained several times. Accordingly we shall not perpetually repeat this. We shall say now that when a prophet prophesies, he sometimes sees a parable, as we have explained several times. Sometimes he sees God, may He be exalted, in a *vision of prophecy*, speaking to him. Thus | *Isaiah* says: *And I heard the voice of the Lord, saying: Whom shall I send, and who will go for us?*[1] Sometimes he hears an angel speaking to him and he sees him. This occurs very frequently. Thus he says: *And the angel of God said unto me, and so on;*[2] *And he said unto me: Knowest thou not what these are? And the angel that spoke with me answered, and so on;*[3] *Then I heard a holy one speaking.*[4] This occurs innumerable times. Sometimes the prophet sees a human individual who speaks to him. Thus he says in [the book of] *Ezekiel: And, behold, there was a man, whose appearance was like the appearance of brass, and so on. And the man said unto me: Son of man, and so on.*[5] He says this after he has said beforehand: *The hand of the Lord was upon me.*[6] Sometimes the prophet does not see any form at all, but only hears, in a *vision of prophecy*, speech in which he is called. Thus *Daniel* says: *And I heard the voice of a man between [the banks of] Ulai.*[7] *Eliphaz* says: *There was silence, and I heard a voice saying.*[8] And *Ezekiel* also says, *And I heard Him that spoke unto me,*[9] for that which he apprehended *in the vision of prophecy* was not He who spoke to him. First he sets forth in detail the wondrous and strange story of that which he explicitly affirms to have apprehended. Thereupon he starts to explain the purpose and the form of the prophetic revelation, and says: *And I heard Him that spoke unto me.*

After we have set forth as a preface this classification, which is attested by the texts, I say that sometimes the prophet imagines the speech heard by him *in the vision of prophecy* to be extemely loud, just as a man may dream that he hears loud thunder or sees an earthquake or a hurricane. Such dreams are frequent. Sometimes he apprehends[10] the speech he hears *in the vision of prophecy* as familiar and well-known speech, so that nothing in it strikes him as strange. This may become clear to you from the story of

1. Isa. 6:8.   2. Gen. 31:11.
3. Zech. 4:5. Maimonides transposes the order of this verse.
4. Dan. 8:13.   5. Ezek. 40:3-4.   6. Ezek. 40:1.   7. Dan. 8:16.
8. Job 4:16.   9. Ezek. 2:2.   10. Literally: hears.

Samuel the prophet who, when God, may He be exalted, called to him while he was in a state | of prophetic revelation, thought time and again — three times in all — that *Eli the Priest* had summoned him.[11] Scripture then explains the cause of this, saying that he was obliged to act so and to think that it was *Eli* who called him because he did not know then that the speech of God to the prophets takes place in this form, this secret not having as yet been revealed to him. Accordingly in order to account for the cause of this, it says: *Now Samuel did not yet know the Lord, neither was the word of the Lord yet revealed unto him.*[12] It means that he did not know and that it had not been revealed to him that *the word of the Lord* comes in this way. The dictum, *did not yet know the Lord,* means that he had had no previous prophecy. For it is said of him who becomes a prophet: *I do make Myself known unto him in a vision.*[13] Thus the interpretation of the *verse* with respect to its meaning is as follows: Before that time *Samuel* had not become a prophet; neither did he know that such was the form of prophecy. Know this.

CHAPTER 45

After the preceding explanation of the true reality of prophecy according to the requirements of speculation combined with the explanation supplied by our Law, it behooves me to mention to you the degrees of prophecy according to these two sources. Now not everybody who is found in one of the degrees, which I call degrees of prophecy, is a prophet. For the first and second degree are steppingstones toward prophecy, and someone who has attained one of them is not to be considered as a prophet belonging to the class of prophets discussed in the preceding chapters. And even though he may sometimes be called a prophet, this term is applied to him in a general sort of way, because he is very close to the prophets. You should not be misled with regard to those degrees by the fact that sometimes you find in | the prophets' books that a prophetic revelation came to a prophet in the form characteristic of a certain degree and withal it is made clear with regard to the very same prophet that a prophetic revelation also came to him under a form characteristic of another degree. For with regard to the degrees I shall mention, it sometimes happens that some[1] of the prophetic

11. Cf. I Sam. 3:4–8. 12. I Sam. 3:7. 13. Num. 12:6.
1. Or: one.

revelation of one particular prophet comes to him according to a form characteristic of a certain degree, whereas another prophetic revelation, which comes to him at another time, corresponds to a degree inferior to that of the first prophetic revelation. For just as a prophet may not prophesy continuously the whole of his life, but prophesies at a certain moment and is abandoned by prophecy at many other moments, so may he also prophesy at a certain moment in a form characteristic of a high degree, and at another moment in a form characteristic of an inferior degree. Sometimes perhaps he achieves this high degree only once in his life and then is deprived of it and perhaps remains fixed in the inferior degree until the cessation of his prophesying. For there is no doubt that the prophesying of all[2] the prophets comes to an end before their death, either shortly or a long time before. This is made clear with regard to *Jeremiah* by the dictum, *At the termination of the word of the Lord by the mouth of Jeremiah*,[3] and with regard to *David* by the dictum: *Now these are the last words of David*.[4] From this one must draw an inference to all the prophets. After having made and propounded this introduction, I shall begin to set forth the degrees that have been alluded to, and shall accordingly make the following statement.

THE FIRST DEGREE

The first of the degrees of prophecy consists in the fact that an individual receives[5] a divine help that moves and activates him to a great, righteous, and important action — such as the deliverance of a community of virtuous people from a community of wicked people, or the deliverance of a virtuous and great man, or the conferring of benefits[6] on numerous people. The individual in question finds in himself something | that moves and incites him to the action, and that is called *the spirit of the Lord*. And it is said of the individual who was in such a state that *the spirit of the Lord came upon him*,[7] or that *the spirit of the Lord clothed him*,[8] or that *the spirit of the Lord rested upon him*,[9] or that *the Lord was with him*;[10] or other similar expressions are applied to him. This is the grade of all the *judges of Israel* of whom it is said in general that: *And when the Lord raised them up judges, then the Lord was with the judge, and delivered*

2. Or: the rest of the prophets.   3. Ezra 1:1.   4. II Sam. 23:1.
5. More or less literally: is accompanied by.   6. Literally: making good overflow.
7. Cf. Judg. 14:6 and 19; I Sam. 10:6; 16:13.
8. Cf. Judg. 6:34; I Chron. 12:19; II Chron. 24:20.
9. Cf. Num. 11:25–26; Isa. 11:2.   10. Cf. Judg. 2:18; I Sam. 3:19; 18:12.

them.[11] This is also the grade of all the virtuous *Messiahs*[12] of *Israel*. This is made clear especially with regard to some *judges* and *kings: Then the spirit of the Lord came upon Jephthah.*[13] And it is said of *Samson: And the spirit of the Lord came upon him.*[14] And it is said: *And the spirit of God came upon Saul when he heard [those] tidings.*[15] Similarly it is said of *Amasai* when *the Holy Spirit* moved him to help *David: Then the spirit clothed Amasai who was chief of the captains: Thine are we, David, and on thy side, thou son of Jesse; peace, and so on.*[16] Know that such a force did not abandon *Moses our Master* from the moment he reached a man's estate. It was because of this that he was moved to slay the *Egyptian* and to reprove the one who was in the wrong among the two men that struggled.[17] The strength of this force in him shows in the fact that when — after having been filled with fear and having fled — he came to *Midian* as a stranger full of fear and saw some wrong that was done, he could not refrain from putting an end to it and was incapable of patience with regard to it, as it says: *But Moses stood up and helped them.*[18] *David* likewise possessed[19] such a force after *being anointed with the oil of anointment.* Accordingly the text says: *And the spirit of the Lord came upon David from that day forward.*[20] And it was for this reason that he attacked the *lion,* the *bear,* and the *Philistine.* Such a *spirit of the Lord* by no means caused one of these to speak of anything; rather its object was to move the one strengthened[21] by it to a certain action: not to any | chance action, but to an action that succors a wronged one — whether it be one great man or a community — or to an action that leads to that result. And just as not everyone who has seen a veridical dream is a prophet, not everyone who has received [divine] help[22] in some chance matter — such as the acquisition of property or the achievement of an end that concerns him alone — can be said to have been accompanied by *the spirit of the Lord,* or to have *the Lord with him,* or to have done what he has done *through the Holy Spirit.* We only say this about one who has performed a good action of capital import or an action that leads to that result; as, for instance, *the success of Joseph in the house of the Egyptian,*[23] which was, as is clear, the first cause for great things that occurred afterwards.

11. Judg. 2:18.   12. Or: *anointed*   13. Judg. 11:29.   14. Judg. 14:19.
15. I Sam. 11:6.   16. I Chron. 12:19.   17. Cf. Exod. 2:11–13.
18. Exod. 2:17.   19. Literally: was accompanied by.   20. I Sam. 16:13.
21. *al-muʾayyad.* The term is habitually applied to one who has received divine inspiration and help.
22. More or less literally: who has been accompanied by help.
23. Cf. Gen. 39:2.

THE SECOND DEGREE

It consists in the fact that an individual finds that a certain thing has descended upon him and that another[24] force has come upon him and has made him speak; so that he talks in wise sayings, in words of praise, in useful admonitory dicta, or concerning governmental or divine matters — and all this while he is awake and his senses function as usual. Such an individual is said to *speak through the Holy Spirit*. It is through this kind of *Holy Spirit* that *David* composed *Psalms*, and *Solomon Proverbs* and *Ecclesiastes* and *Song of Songs*. *Daniel* and *Job* and *Chronicles* and all the other *Writings*[25] have likewise been composed through this kind of *Holy Spirit*. For this reason people call them *Writings*, meaning thereby that they are *written through the Holy Spirit*. [The Sages] have stated explicitly that *the scroll of Esther was spoken through the Holy Spirit*.[26] It is of this kind of *Holy Spirit* that *David* has said: *The spirit of the Lord spoke by me, and His word was upon my tongue;*[27] he meant that it caused him to speak the words in question. | It was to this group that the *seventy elders* belonged, of whom it is said: *And it came to pass, that, when the spirit rested upon them, they prophesied, but they did so no more.*[28] *Eldad* and *Medad* and every *High Priest who was questioned through the Urim and Thummim* also belong to this group; I mean to say that as [the Sages] have mentioned: *The Indwelling rests upon him, and he speaks through the Holy Spirit.*[29] *Yahaziel, son of Zechariah*, likewise belongs to this group, as it is he of whom it is said in *Chronicles: The spirit of the Lord came upon him in the midst of the congregation; and he said: Hearken ye, all Judah, and ye inhabitants of Jerusalem, and thou king Jehoshaphat. Thus saith the Lord unto you, and so on.*[30] So does *Zechariah, son of Jehoiada the priest*, belong to this group, for it is said of him: *And the spirit of God clothed Zechariah, son of Jehoiada the priest; and he stood above the people, and said unto them; Thus saith God.*[31] Similarly, *Azariah, son of Oded*, of whom it is said: *And the spirit of God came upon Azariah, son of Oded; and he went out to meet Asa, and so on.*[32] The same applies to all those of whom something similar is said. Know too that *Balaam*, when he was righteous, also belonged to this kind. This is the meaning that it intends to convey in the dictum:

24. I.e., as it seems, a force different from the one discussed by Maimonides when speaking of the first degree of prophecy.
25. The Hebrew Bible is divided into the *Torah* or Pentateuch, the *Prophets*, and the *Writings* or Hagiographa (*Ketubim*).
26. B.T., Megillah, 7a.   27. II Sam. 23:2.   28. Num. 11:25.
29. B.T., Yoma, 73b.   30. II Chron. 20:14–15.   31. II Chron. 24:20.
32. II Chron. 15:1–2.

And the Lord put a word in Balaam's mouth.[33] It is as if it said that *he spoke through the Holy Spirit.* It is for this reason that [Balaam] says of himself, *who heareth the words of God.*[34] One of the things to which we must draw attention is that *David* and *Solomon* and *Daniel* belong to this group and not to that of *Isaiah* and *Jeremiah* and *Nathan the prophet* and *Ahijah the Shilonite* and men similar to them. For they — I mean *David* and *Solomon* and *Daniel* — spoke and said what they said *through the Holy Spirit.* As for *David's* dictum, *The God of Israel said, the Rock of Israel spoke to me,*[35] it means that [God] gave him a promise through the instrumentality of a prophet, either through *Nathan* or somebody else; as in the case when it is said:[36] *And the Lord said unto her;*[37] and as in the case when it is said: *Wherefore the Lord said | unto Solomon: Forasmuch as this is done of thee, and thou hast not kept My covenant*[38] — a dictum that indubitably gives expression to an announcement of future ill[39] made through the instrumentality of the prophet *Ahijah the Shilonite* or somebody else. Similarly the dictum concerning *Solomon: In Gibeon the Lord appeared to Solomon in a dream by night; and God said, and so on,*[40] is not pure prophecy like the one mentioned in the verse: *The word of the Lord came unto Abram in a vision, saying,*[41] or like the one mentioned in the verse: *And God spoke unto Israel in the visions of the night,*[42] or like the prophecies of *Isaiah* and *Jeremiah.* For even if prophetic revelation came to each of the latter *in a dream,* every one of them was informed through that same prophetic revelation that this was a prophecy and that prophetic revelation had come to him; whereas in this story about *Solomon* it says at the end: *And Solomon awoke, and, behold, it was a dream;*[43] and similarly in the second story it says: *The Lord appeared to Solomon the second time, as he had appeared unto him at Gibeon;*[44] this makes it clear that it was a *dream.* This grade is below the one of which it is said: *I do speak with him in a dream.*[45] For those who prophesy *in a dream,* by no means call this state a *dream* after prophecy has come to them *in a dream,* but state decidedly that it was a prophetic revelation. Thus *Jacob our Father;* for after he had awakened from his *prophetic dream,* he did not say that it was a *dream,* but stated decidedly: *Surely the Lord is in this place, and so on.*[46] And he also said: *God Almighty appeared unto me at Luz in the land of Canaan;*[47] he thus decided that that was a prophetic revelation. Whereas with regard to

---

33. Num. 23:5.   34. Num. 24:4.   35. II Sam. 23:3.   36. Gen. 25:23.
37. To Rebekah.   38. I Kings 11:11.
39. The literal meaning of the word used is "a promise of ill."   40. I Kings 3:5.
41. Gen. 15:1.   42. Gen. 46:2.   43. I Kings 3:15.   44. I Kings 9:2.
45. Num. 12:6.   46. Gen. 28:16.   47. Gen. 48:3.

Solomon, it says: *And Solomon awoke, and, behold, it was a dream*. Similarly you will find that *Daniel* applies to them the expression "dreams," even though he saw an angel in those dreams and heard words spoken in them. He calls them dreams even after he has received knowledge through them. Thus it says: *Then was the secret revealed unto Daniel in a vision of the night*.[48] It also says: *Then he wrote the dream, and so on;*[49] *I saw in my vision by night, and so on;*[50] *And the visions of | my head affrighted me*.[51] And he says: *And I was appalled at the vision, but understood it not*.[52] There is no doubt that this grade is below the grade of those of whom it is said: *I do speak with him in a dream*.[53] For this reason the nation[54] has reached a consensus to put the *book of Daniel* among the *Writings*,[55] and not among the *Prophets*. For this reason I called your attention to the fact that in the kind of prophecy that came to *Daniel* and *Solomon*, they did not discover in their souls — even though they saw *an angel in a dream* — that this was a pure prophecy, but rather that this was a *dream* communicating the true reality of certain matters. This is characteristic of the group of people who speak *through the Holy Spirit*. This is the second degree. Similarly, when arranging the *Holy Scriptures*, they[56] made no difference between *Proverbs* and *Ecclesiastes* and *Daniel* and *Psalms*, on one hand, and the *Scroll of Ruth* or the *Scroll of Esther* on the other; *all of them have been written through the Holy Spirit*. Also all these are called, in a general way, prophets.

THE THIRD DEGREE

This is the first of the degrees of those who say, *The word of the Lord came to me*, or who use expressions having a similar sense. This class tends to be represented through a prophet's seeing[57] a parable *in a dream* according to all the conditions set forth before with regard to the true reality of prophecy. And it is in the *dream of prophecy* itself that the meaning of the parable — what was intended thereby — is made manifest to the prophet, as for instance in most of the parables of *Zechariah*.[58]

THE FOURTH DEGREE

consists in the prophet's hearing articulate and clear speech *in the dream*

48. Dan. 2:19.   49. Dan. 7:1.   50. Dan. 7:2.   51. Dan. 7:15.
52. Dan. 8:27.   53. Num. 12:6.   54. Or: religious community.
55. Cf. n. 25, this chap.   56. The ones who did this.
57. Literally: What from the expressions tended toward this meaning is that the prophet sees. . . .
58. Cf. II 43.

of prophecy, but without seeing the speaker; as has happened to *Samuel* in the first prophetic revelation that came to him, as we have explained with regard to him.[59] |

THE FIFTH DEGREE

This consists in the prophet's being addressed by a *man in a dream*, as it says in one of *Ezekiel's* prophecies: *And the man said unto me: Son of man, and so on.*[60]

THE SIXTH DEGREE

consists in the prophet's being addressed by an *angel in a dream.* This is the state of the majority of the *prophets*. Thus it says: *And the angel of God said unto me in the dream, and so on.*[61]

THE SEVENTH DEGREE

consists in the fact that in the *dream of prophecy* the prophet sees, as it were, that He, may He be exalted, addresses him. Thus *Isaiah* says: *I saw the Lord, and so on.*[62] *And He said,*[63] *Whom shall I send, and so on.*[64] Thus *Micaiah, son of Imla,* says: *I saw the Lord, and so on.*[65]

THE EIGHTH DEGREE

consists in the fact that a prophetic revelation comes to the prophet *in a vision of prophecy* and that he sees parables, as *Abraham in the vision between the pieces;*[66] for these parables came *in a vision* during the day, as has been set forth.[67]

THE NINTH DEGREE

consists in the prophet's hearing speech *in a vision*, as is said with regard to *Abraham: And, behold, the word of the Lord came unto him, saying, This shall not be thine heir.*[68] |

59. Cf. II 44.　　60. Ezek. 40:4.　　61. Gen. 31:11.
62. Isa. 6:1. The quotation is not quite accurate. The verb has a different tense in the Bible than the one used in Maimonides' quotation.
63. The verbal form used by Maimonides is not the one occurring in the biblical text.
64. Isa. 6:8.　　65. I Kings 22:19; II Chron. 18:18.　　66. Cf. Gen. 15:9–10.
67. Cf. II 41.　　68. Gen. 15:4.

THE TENTH DEGREE

consists in the prophet's seeing a *man* who addresses him *in a vision of prophecy*, as *Abraham* again by the *terebinths of Mamre* and as *Joshua* in *Jericho*.[69]

THE ELEVENTH DEGREE

consists in the prophet's seeing an *angel* who addresses him *in a vision*, as *Abraham at the time of the binding*.[70] In my opinion this is the highest of the degrees of the prophets whose states are attested by the prophetic books, after the perfection of the rational faculties of the individual, considered as necessary[71] by speculation, has been established, and provided one exempts *Moses our Master*. With regard to the question whether it is possible that a prophet would also see *in a vision of prophecy* that God, as it were, addressed him — this, in my opinion, is improbable, for the power of the act of the imagination does not reach this point. And we have not found this state in the other prophets.[72] For this reason it is clearly said in the *Torah: I do make Myself known unto him* [*elav ethvada*] *in a vision, I do speak with him in a dream*.[73] Thus it assigns *speech* to *dreams* only, assigning to *visions* the union and overflow of the intellect, this being signified by the words: *elav ethvada*. For ["*ethvada*"] is a reflexive form[74] of the verb *yadoᶜa* [*to know*]. Thus it is not explicitly stated that speech coming from God can be heard in a *vision*.

Inasmuch as I found scriptural texts attesting that prophets heard speech — it having been made clear that this was *in a vision* — I said by way of conjecture that it is possible that the speech that is heard *in a dream* and the like of which may not occur *in a vision*, is that regarding which it is imagined by the prophet that God addresses him; all this is said in following the external sense of the verse. One could also say that every *vision* in which you find the prophet hearing speech was in its beginning | a *vision*, but ended in a state of submersion[75] and became a *dream*, as we have explained with regard to the dictum: *And a deep sleep fell upon Abram*.[76] [The Sages] have said: *This is the deep sleep of prophecy*.[77] All

69. Cf. II 42.   70. Of Isaac with a view to sacrificing him; cf. Gen. 22.
71. Rather than "obtained," which is Munk's interpretation.
72. I.e., with the exception of Moses. However, the text can also be translated: in any of the prophets.
73. Num. 12:6.
74. In the text: *iftiᶜāl*, which is a reflexive form of Arabic verbs.   75. In sleep.
76. Gen. 15:12.   77. Genesis Rabbah, XVII and XLIV.

speech that is heard, whatever the way may be in which it is heard, is heard only *in a dream;* as the text has it: *I do speak with him in a dream.*[78] On the other hand, in a *vision of prophecy* only parables or intellectual unifications[79] are apprehended that give actual cognition of scientific matters similar to those, knowledge of which is obtained through speculation, as we have explained. This is the meaning of its dictum: *I do make Myself known unto him in a vision.*[80] Consequently, according to this last allegoric interpretation, there are eight degrees of prophecy; the highest and most perfect among them being the one in which the prophet prophesies ✓ *in a vision*—taking this in a general way—even though, as has been mentioned, he is merely addressed by a *man.* Perhaps you will proffer an objection to me, saying: You have counted among the degrees of prophecy the degree in which the prophet hears speech coming from God who addresses him, as in the cases of *Isaiah* and *Micaiah.* How can this be in view of the fact that our principle states that all prophets hear speech only through the intermediary of an *angel,* the sole exception being *Moses our Master,* of whom it is said: *With him do I speak mouth to mouth.*[81] Know then that this is in fact so, and that in these cases the intermediary is the imaginative faculty. For a prophet can hear only *in a dream of prophecy* that God has spoken to him. *Moses our Master,* on the other hand, heard Him *from above the ark-cover, from between the two cherubim,*[82] without action on the part of the imaginative faculty. We have already set forth in *Mishneh Torah* the peculiarities of this prophecy and have interpreted the meaning of the passages: *Mouth to mouth;*[83] *As a man speaketh unto his friend;*[84] and of other passages.[85] Understand this from there; and there will be no need to repeat what has already been said. |

CHAPTER 46

From a single individual an inference can be drawn concerning all individuals of the species, and it can be known that this particular form is that of all the individuals of the species. What I want to say by this is that from

78. Num. 12:6.
79. I.e., the union of the Active Intellect with the intellect of the prophet.
80. Num. 12:6.   81. Num. 12:8.   82. Exod. 25:22.   83. Num. 12:8.
84. Exod. 33:11.   85. Cf. *Mishneh Torah,* Yesodei ha-Torah, VII 6.

a single form of the communications of the prophets, an inference can be drawn to all the communications belonging to that species.

After this introduction you should know that just as a man sees while sleeping that he has made a journey to a certain country, has married there, has stayed there for a certain time, that a son was born to him there, that he called him by a certain name, and that this son's circumstances and state were such and such; so in the case of prophetic parables seen or enacted *in a vision of prophecy*, when the parable requires a certain action, when things are done by the prophet, when intervals of time are mentioned within the parable between the various actions and the transportation from one place to another, this takes place only *in a vision of prophecy*, they are not real actions, actions that exist for the external senses. Some of them are set forth in the books of prophecy without qualification.[1] For since it is known that all these things occur *in a vision of prophecy*, Scripture in the recounting of all details of the parable may dispense with reiterating that they happened *in a vision of prophecy*. Similarly a prophet may say, *And the Lord said unto me*,[2] without having the need to state explicitly that this happened *in a dream*. Therefore the multitude think that these actions, transportations, questions, and answers, occurred all of them in a state in which they could have been perceived by the senses, not in *a vision of prophecy*. As to this I shall cite you an example | about which no one can have fanciful notions, and I shall add to it some other examples belonging to the same species. And from these examples you will be able to draw an inference regarding those that I shall not mention.

An example that is clear and about which no one can have fanciful notions is the dictum of *Ezekiel*: *I sat in my house, and the elders of Judah sat before me, and so on. And a spirit lifted me up between the earth and the heaven, and brought me in the visions of God to Jerusalem*.[3] Similarly when he says, *Then I arose, and went forth into the plain*,[4] this also only happened *in the visions of God*. Just as when it is said of *Abraham: And He brought him forth abroad*,[5] this occurred *in a sight*.[6] In a similar way when he says, *And set me down in the midst of the valley*,[7] this only happened *in the visions of God*. With regard to the *vision* in which *Ezekiel* was brought

1. Literally: absolutely. Maimonides means to say that sometimes Scripture does not expressly state with regard to various details that they formed part of a vision.
2. Cf. Jer. 1:7, 9, 12, 14; Ezek. 44:2; Zech. 11:13.   3. Ezek. 8:1 and 3.
4. Ezek. 3:23.   5. Gen. 15:5.
6. Cf. Gen. 15:1. The word translated here as *sight* is *maḥazeh*. Unless otherwise noted, wherever *vision* occurs in this chapter, *marʾeh* is the Hebrew term used.
7. Ezek. 37:1.

into *Jerusalem*, he makes a dictum of which the text is as follows: *And when I looked, behold a hole in the wall. Then said He unto me: Son of man, dig now in the wall; and when I had digged in the wall, behold a door, and so on.*[8] And just as he saw *in the visions of God* that he was ordered to dig in the wall in order to enter and see what was being done there and that he dug—*in the visions of God*, as has been mentioned—and entered through the hole and saw that which he saw—all that *in a vision of prophecy*. So was his saying to him: *Thou also . . . take thee a tile, and so on. Moreover lie thou upon thy left side, and so on.*[9] *Take thou also unto thee wheat and barley, and so on;* as well as his saying to him: *And cause it*[10] *to pass upon thy head and upon thy beard*[11]—seen, all of it, *in a vision of prophecy* in which he saw that he carried out the actions he was ordered to carry out. God is too exalted than that He should turn His prophets into a laughing-stock and a mockery for fools by ordering them to carry out crazy actions. And this in addition to ordering them to commit acts of disobedience; for [Ezekiel] was a *Priest*, and *every side of beard or of hair he cut made him guilty of transgressing two prohibitions*. But all this happened merely *in a vision of prophecy*. In the same way when He says, *Like as My servant Isaiah hath walked naked and barefoot*,[12] | this only happened *in the visions of God*. Only those weak in syllogistic reasoning fancy with regard to all this that the prophet tells that he was ordered to do certain things and hence did them. For instance he tells that he was ordered, while he was in *Babylon*, to dig in the wall that is on *the mountain of the temple*, and thereupon he recounts that he actually dug in it; for he says: *And when I had digged in the wall*.[13] However, he had already made it clear that this was *in the visions of God*. Similarly it is said of *Abraham: The word of the Lord came unto Abram in a sight, saying*.[14] And it is said in this same *vision of prophecy: And He brought him forth abroad, and said: Look now toward heaven, and count the stars*.[15] It is therefore clear that it was in a *vision of prophecy* that he saw that he was brought out from the place he was in so that he should see the heavens and that afterwards it was said to him: *And count the stars*; and this is recounted in the way you see. I shall say the same thing regarding the order given to *Jeremiah* to hide the *girdle* in the *Euphrates*.[16] Thereupon he hid it and then, after a long time, going to fetch it, found that it had rotted away and was spoilt. All those happenings are parables *in a vision of prophecy*. For *Jeremiah* did not go out of the

8. Ezek. 8:7–8.   9. Ezek. 4:1, 4, 9.   10. I.e., a barber's razor.   11. Ezek. 5:1.
12. Isa. 20:3.   13. Ezek. 8:8.   14. Gen. 15:1.   15. Gen. 15:5.
16. Cf. Jer. 13:4–7.

Land of Israel to *Babylon* and did not see the *Euphrates*. The position is similar with regard to the words addressed to *Hosea: Take unto thee a wife of harlotry and children of harlotry*.[17] All this story concerning the birth of the children and their having been named so and so happened in its entirety *in a vision of prophecy*. For after it has been stated expressly that these were parables, there remains no room for obscurity as to any of these things having a real existence except according to what has been said of us: *And the vision*[18] *of all is become unto you as the words of a book, and so on*.[19] It likewise seems to me that the story concerning *Gideon* with regard to the *fleece* and other things[20] only occurred in the *vision*. I will not call it unqualifiedly a *vision of prophecy*. For *Gideon* did not reach the rank of the prophets; so how could he have reached the rank of one who works miracles? His highest achievement is that of having been included *among the judges of Israel* | and [the Sages] have even numbered him,[21] as we have made clear,[22] as being *among the inconsequential people of the world*. All this only happened *in a dream* similar to the *dream of Laban and of Abimelech* that we have mentioned.[23] Similarly what *Zechariah* says: *So I fed the flock of slaughter, verily the poor of the flock. And I took unto me two staves*,[24] and the whole tale till its ending about the wages asked for gently, his taking the wages, the number of the drachmas, and their being cast in the *house of the founder*,[25] was all of it seen in a *vision of prophecy*; he was ordered to do it and so he did it either in a *vision of prophecy* or *in a dream of prophecy*. This is a thing that can only be doubted or not known by him who confuses the possible things with the impossible ones.

From what I have mentioned you may draw an inference to what I have not mentioned, for all these things pertain to the same species and to the same method. All have occurred in a *vision of prophecy*. And everything that is said concerning such a *vision* — for instance that he[26] acted in it or heard or went out or went in or spoke or was spoken to or stood or sat down or went up or went down or made a journey or asked a question or was asked — all of it happens in a *vision of prophecy*. And even if such actions should have had a long duration and should have been attached to certain

17. Hos. 1:2.
18. The noun *ḥazuth*, used here, is derived from the same verb as *ḥazon* and *maḥazeh*.
19. Isa. 29:11. The verse continues: *that is sealed*.
20. Cf. Judg. 6:21 and 37.
21. B.T., Rosh Hashanah, 25a–b.
22. Cf. II 41 and 45 (section on the first degree of prophecy). Maimonides does not refer in those chapters to the dictum in disparagement of Gideon that is quoted here.
23. Cf. II 41.   24. Zech. 11:7.   25. Cf. Zech. 11:12–13.
26. I.e., the individual who had the vision.

times, to individuals that are indicated, and to places, you should — as soon as it has become clear to you that the action in question is a parable — have certain knowledge that it occurred *in a vision of prophecy*.

CHAPTER 47

Undoubtedly it has become clear and manifest that the greater part of the prophecies of the prophets proceeds by means of parables; for that is the action of the instrument for this,[1] I mean the imagination. Something should likewise be known about figurative uses | and hyperboles, for they sometimes occur in the text of the prophetic books. And if the words are understood according to their precise meaning and it is not known that they constitute a hyperbole or an exaggeration, or if they are understood according to their first conventional meaning and it is not known that they are used figuratively, incongruities arise. [The Sages] have given an explanation by saying, *The Torah speaks in exaggerated language*[2] — that is, hyperbole — and have used as a proof the dictum: *Cities great and walled up to heaven.*[3] And this is correct. The dictum, *For a bird of heaven shall carry the voice,*[4] belongs to the class of hyperbole. In a similar way it is said: *Whose height was like the height of the cedars, and so on.*[5] This kind of language occurs frequently in the dicta of all the prophets — I mean things said in a hyperbolical and exaggerated, not a precise and exact, way.

However, what the *Torah* literally states about *Og* does not belong to this group: *Behold, his bedstead was a bedstead* [*'eres*] *of iron, and so on.*[6] For *'eres* is a bed: *Also our bed* [*'arsenu*] *is verdant.*[7] Now a man's bed is not exactly his size, for it is not a garment, which one puts on. The bed is rather always bigger than the individual who sleeps on it. And the usual and well-known thing is for it to be longer than the individual by a third of his length. If the length of the bed in question came to nine cubits, the length of him who slept on it must, according to the usual proportion of beds, have come to six cubits or a little more. And its dictum, *after the cubit of a man,*[8] means according to the cubit of an individual from among ourselves —

1. I.e., for prophecy.   2. B.T., Ḥullin, 90a; B.T., Tamid, 2a.
3. Deut. 1:28.   4. Eccles. 10:20.   5. Amos 2:9.
6. Deut. 3:11.   7. Song of Songs 1:16.   8. Deut. 3:11.

I mean to say from among the rest of men—and not according to the cubit of *Og*. For all individuals have mostly proportionate members; accordingly it says that the length of *Og* was twice that of other men or a little more. This is doubtless anomalous for the individuals of the species, but is by no means impossible. | As for the precise statements made by the texts of the *Torah* regarding the length of life of certain individuals, I say that only that individual who is mentioned lived so long a life, whereas the other men lived lives that had the natural and usual duration. The anomaly in the individual in question may be due either to numerous causes attaching to his nutrition and his regimen or is due to a miracle and follows the laws thereof. It is not possible to say of this anything else.

Similarly one ought to examine carefully the things said in a figurative way. Some of them are clear and manifest and do not seem obscure to anybody. Thus, for instance, its dictum: *The mountains and hills shall break forth before you singing, and all the trees of the field shall clap their hands.*[9] This is clearly figurative language. And similarly its dictum: *Yea, the cypresses rejoice at thee, and so on.*[10] Jonathan ben Uziel translated this as follows: *Also the rulers rejoiced in thee, those rich in property.* Thus he set the passage down as a parable, like the passage: *Curd of kine and milk of sheep, and so on.*[11] This figurative use of language is exceedingly frequent in the books of prophecy. With regard to some of them the multitude are aware that the expressions are figurative, whereas with regard to others they think that they are not figurative. For no one doubts with respect to its dictum, *The Lord shall open unto thee His [good] treasure, and so on,*[12] that this is figurative and that God has no *treasure* in which there is *rain*. Similarly when it says, *And opened the doors of heaven, and caused manna to rain upon them,*[13] no one thinks that there are in heaven a gate and *doors*. For this is said as a simile, which is a species of figurative language. It is likewise in this way that one ought to understand its dicta: *The heavens were opened;*[14] *And if not, blot me, I pray Thee, out of Thy book which Thou hast written;*[15] *I will blot him out of My book;*[16] *Let them be blotted out of the book of the living.*[17] All these expressions are used as similes; | and they do not mean that there exists a *book* belonging to Him, may He be exalted, in which He writes and from which He blots out, as is thought by the multitude because of their not being aware of the use of figurative language in the passages in question.

9. Isa. 55:12.   10. Isa. 14:8.   11. Deut. 32:14.
12. Deut. 28:12. The verse continues: *the heaven to give the rain of thy land in its season.*
13. Ps. 78:23–24.   14. Ezek. 1:1.   15. Exod. 32:32.   16. Exod. 32:33.
17. Ps. 69:29.

All these expressions belong to the same class. Take, therefore, what I have not mentioned in the manner that I have mentioned in this chapter, and distinguish and differentiate between the various matters by means of your intellect. Then you will know clearly[18] what has been said by way of a parable, what has been said figuratively, what has been said by way of a hyperbole, and what has been said exactly according to the first conventional meaning. Then all the prophecies will become clear and manifest to you. And then only intelligible beliefs will remain with you, beliefs that are well ordered[19] and that are pleasing to God. For only truth pleases Him, may He be exalted, and only that which is false angers Him. Your opinions and thoughts should not become confused so that you believe in incorrect opinions that are very remote from the truth and you regard them as Law. For the Laws are absolute truth if they are understood in the way they ought to be. Accordingly it says: *Thy testimonies are righteous for ever, and so on;*[20] and: *I the Lord speak righteousness.*[21] Through these considerations you will be delivered from imagining beings that God has not brought into being and from evil thoughts, some of which may perhaps lead to infidelity[22] and to a belief that there may be a defect in God — such as modes of corporeality, attributes, and passions — as we have set forth.[23] Or again you may think[24] that these dicta of the prophets are false. The whole fault that incites to this is neglect of that to which we have drawn attention. These too are notions pertaining to the *mysteries of the Torah.* And though we have only spoken summarily about them, it is easy, after what has been set forth before, to know the details of these matters. |

CHAPTER 48

It is very clear that everything that is produced in time must necessarily have a proximate cause, which has produced it. In its turn that cause has a cause and so forth till finally one comes to the First Cause of all things, I mean God's will and free choice. For this reason all those intermediate causes are sometimes omitted in the dicta of the prophets, and an individual

18. Literally: It will be clear to you.   19. Literally: that go according to an order.
20. Ps. 119:144.   21. Isa. 45:19.
22. *kufr*; i.e., disbelief in fundamental religious dogma.   23. Cf. I 44 *et seq.*
24. I.e., if you are not guided by the considerations set forth above.

act produced in time is ascribed to God, it being said that He, may He be exalted, has done it. All this is known. We and other men from among those who study true reality have spoken about it, and this is the opinion of all the people adhering to our Law.

After this introduction, listen to what I shall explain in this chapter and consider it with particular attention, with an attention exceeding the attention with which you consider the other chapters of this Treatise. This is the matter that I shall make clear to you. Know that all proximate causes through which is produced in time that which is produced in time, regardless of whether these causes are essential and natural, or voluntary, or accidental and fortuitous — I mean by the voluntary cause of that particular thing produced in time, the free choice of a man — and even if the cause consists in the volition of an animal other than man: that all these causes are ascribed in the books of the prophets to God, may He be exalted. And according to their manner of expressing themselves, it is said of such and such an act that God did it or commanded it or said it. For all these things the *expressions to say, to speak, to command, to call,* | and *to send* are used. This is the notion to which I wished to draw attention in this chapter. For inasmuch as the deity is, as has been established, He who arouses a particular volition in the irrational animal[1] and who has necessitated this particular free choice in the rational animal[2] and who has made the natural things pursue their course — chance being but an excess of what is natural, as has been made clear, and its largest part partakes of nature, free choice, and volition — it follows necessarily from all this that it may be said with regard to what proceeds necessarily from these causes that God has commanded that something should be done in such and such a way or that He has said: Let this be thus. I shall cite for you examples of all these cases; draw an analogy to all those I have not mentioned.

Speaking of natural things, which always follow their course, such as the melting of the snow when the air becomes warm and waves being stirred up to a certain extent in the sea when the wind blows, it says: *He sendeth forth His word, and melteth them;*[3] *For He commanded, and raised the stormy wind, which lifted up the waves thereof.*[4] About the falling of rain, it says: *I will also command the clouds that they rain no rain upon it, and so on.*[5]

When speaking of things the cause of which lies with human free choice — such as the war waged by a ruling people upon another people or an

1. I.e., the animals other than man.   2. I.e., man.   3. Ps. 147:18.
4. Ps. 107:25.   5. Isa. 5:6.

individual's setting out to harm another individual, even if he only insults him — it says, for instance when treating of the tyranny of *the wicked Nebuchadnezzar* and his armies:[6] *I have commanded My consecrated ones, yea I have called My mighty ones for Mine anger.*[7] And it also says: *I will send him against a hypocritical nation.*[8] Dealing with the story of *Shimei, son of Gera*, it says: *Because the Lord hath said unto him, Curse David.*[9] With regard to the deliverance of *Joseph the righteous* from prison, it says: *He sent a king and loosed him.*[10] With reference to the victory of the *Persians* and the *Medes* over the *Kasdim*, it says: *And I will send unto Babylon scatterers who shall scatter her.*[11] In the story of *Elijah, peace be on him*, when | for his benefit God caused a woman to feed him, he is told: *Behold, I have commanded a widowed woman there to sustain thee.*[12] And *Joseph the righteous* says: *It was not you that sent me hither, but God.*[13]

When speaking of things the cause of which lies with the volition of animals and their being set in motion by their animal impulses, it says: *And the Lord spoke unto the fish.*[14] This means that it was God who aroused in it that particular volition, not that He turned the fish into a prophet and sent it a prophetic revelation. In a similar way it is said of the locusts that came in the days of *Joel, son of Pethuel: For he is mighty that executeth His word.*[15] Again in a similar way it is said of the fact that wild beasts gained mastery over the *land of Edom* after it had been devastated in the days of *Sennacherib: And He hath cast the lot for them, and His hand hath divided it unto them by line.*[16] Though the *expressions to say, to command,* and *to send*, are not used there, yet its meaning is clearly analogous. Compare analogically all other dicta having the same pattern.

Likewise when speaking of accidental things due to pure chance, it says in the story of *Rebekah: And let her be thy master's son's wife, as the Lord hath spoken.*[17] In the story of *David and Jonathan*, it says: *Go, for the Lord hath sent thee away.*[18] And in the story of *Joseph*, it says: *And God sent me before you.*[19]

Accordingly it has become clear to you that in order to designate the shaping of the causes in whatever way they are shaped, whether they are causes by essence or by accident or by free choice or by volition, these

---

6. As Munk remarks, following Ibn Kaspi, this reference is not correct; for the verse of Isaiah quoted immediately after it seems to refer to the army of the Medes setting out to conquer Babylon.

7. Isa. 13:3.   8. Isa. 10:6.   9. II Sam. 16:10.   10. Ps. 105:20.

11. Jer. 51:2.   12. I Kings 17:9.   13. Gen. 45:8. Joseph says this to his brothers.

14. Jonah 2:11.   15. Joel 2:11.   16. Isa. 34:17.

17. Gen. 24:51. The choice of Rebekah as Isaac's wife was due to chance.

18. I Sam. 20:22. David's going away was due to chance.   19. Gen. 45:7.

five terms are used — namely, *to command, to say, to speak, to send, to call.*
Know this and reflect upon it regarding every passage in the way that fits it.
Then many incongruities will disappear, and the true reality of the matter
will become clear to you in the passage in question, which could be fancied
to be remote from the truth.

This is the end to which my discussion of prophecy, | its parables, and
its expressions, has finally led me; and that is the sum of what I shall tell
you regarding this subject in this Treatise. We shall go on to other subjects

with the help of the Almighty [Shaddai].

*

This Second Part

OF THE GUIDE OF THE PERPLEXED

HAS BEEN COMPLETED

THE THIRD PART

of

The Guide of the Perplexed

*

In the name of the Lord, God of the World[1]

INTRODUCTION

We have already made it clear several times that the chief aim of this Treatise is to explain what can be explained of the *Account of the Beginning* and the *Account of the Chariot*, with a view to him for whom this Treatise has been composed. We have already made it clear that these matters belong to *the mysteries of the Torah*, and you know that [the Sages], *may their memory be blessed*, blame those who divulge *the mysteries of the Torah*. They, *may their memory be blessed*, have already made it clear that the reward of him who conceals *the mysteries of the Torah*, which are clear and manifest to the men of speculation, is very great. At the conclusion of *Pesaḥim*, when speaking of the signification of the dictum[2] — *For her gain shall be for them that dwell before the Lord, to eat their fill, and limekhasse athiq*[3] — they say: *For him who covers the things revealed by the Ancient of Days, namely, the mysteries of the Torah.*[4] Understand the extent of that toward which they give guidance, if you are of those that understand. They have already made it clear how secret the *Account of the Chariot* was and how foreign to the mind of the multitude. And it has been made clear that even that portion of it that becomes clear to him who has been given access to the understanding of it, is subject to a legal prohibition against its being taught and explained except orally to one man having certain stated qualities, and even to that one only the *chapter headings* may be mentioned. This | is the reason why the knowledge of this matter has ceased to exist in the entire religious community, so that nothing great or small remains of it. And it had to happen like this, for this knowledge was only transmitted from one chief[5] to another and has never been set down in writing. If this is so, what stratagem can I use to draw attention toward that which may have appeared to me as indubitably clear, manifest, and evident in my opinion, according to what I have understood in these matters? On the other hand, if I had omitted setting down something of that which has appeared to me as clear,

---

1. Gen. 21:33. Cf. above, Epistle Dedicatory, n. 1.   2. Isa. 23:18.
3. Translated in the English Bible: *for stately clothing*. The meaning of these two words is not clear. They may signify: *in order to have luxurious garments*. Taken literally, however, they may mean: *for him who covers the Ancient*. The latter seems to be the interpretation adopted in the talmudic passage quoted in the text.
4. B.T., Pesaḥim, 119a.
5. *ṣadr*. The Arabic word means both "breast" and "chief" or "principal."

so that that knowledge would perish when I perish, as is inevitable, I should have considered that conduct as extremely cowardly with regard to you and everyone who is perplexed. It would have been, as it were, robbing one who deserves the truth of the truth, or begrudging an heir his inheritance. And both those traits are blameworthy. On the other hand, as has been stated before, an explicit exposition of this knowledge is denied by a legal prohibition, in addition to that which is imposed by judgment.[6] In addition to this there is the fact that in that which has occurred to me with regard to these matters, I followed conjecture and supposition; no divine revelation has come to me to teach me that the intention in the matter in question was such and such, nor did I receive what I believe in these matters from a teacher. But the texts of the prophetic books and the dicta of the *Sages*, together with the speculative premises that I possess, showed me that things are indubitably so and so. Yet it is possible that they are different and that something else is intended. Now rightly guided reflection and divine aid in this matter have moved me to a position, which I shall describe. Namely, I shall interpret to you that which was said by *Ezekiel the prophet*, peace be on him, in such a way that anyone who heard that interpretation would think that I do not say anything over and beyond what is indicated by the text, but that it is as if I translated words from one language to another or summarized the meaning of the external sense of the speech. On the other hand, if that interpretation is examined with a perfect care by him for whom this Treatise is composed and who has understood | all its chapters — every chapter in its turn — the whole matter, which has become clear and manifest to me, will become clear to him so that nothing in it will remain hidden from him. This is the ultimate term that it is possible to attain in combining utility[7] for everyone with abstention from explicit statements in teaching anything about this subject — as is obligatory.[8]

After this introduction has preceded, apply your mind to the chapters that will follow concerning this great, noble, and sublime subject, which is *a stake upon which everything hangs and a pillar upon which everything is supported.*[9]

6. *raʾy*. Literally: opinion.   7. Or: teaching.
8. Syntactically it is not clear in the Arabic text whether the words rendered "as is obligatory" refer to "in combining" or to "abstention." The sense of the sentence is not affected.
9. The Hebrew does not seem to be an exact quotation. The first part of the phrase (up through "everything hangs") has a parallel in J.T., Berakhoth, IV, 19a; the second part, in the Bible, Judg. 16:26.

CHAPTER 1

It is known that there are men the form of whose faces resembles that of one of the other animals, so that one may see an individual whose face resembles that of a lion and another individual whose face resembles that of an ox and so forth. It is according to the shapes that tend to have a likeness to those of animals that people are nicknamed. Thus his saying: *The face of an ox and the face of a lion and the face of an eagle;*[1] all of them merely indicate *the face of a man* that tends to have a likeness to forms belonging to these species. Two proofs indicate this to you. One of them is his saying with regard to the *living creatures* in general: *And this was their appearance; they had the likeness of a man.*[2] Thereafter he describes every *living creature* among them as having *the face of a man and the face of an eagle and the face of a lion and the face of an ox.* The second proof is his explanation in the second *Chariot*, which he set forth in order to explain things left obscure in the first *Chariot*. He says in the second *Chariot:* | *And every one had four faces: the first face was the face of the cherub, and the second face was the face of a man, and the third the face of a lion, and the fourth the face of an eagle.*[3] Thus he explicitly indicates that what he had called *the face of an ox* is *the face of the cherub.* Now *cherub* designates a human being of tender age. With regard to the two remaining faces, the analogy likewise applies. Also he has omitted in this passage *the face of an ox* in order to draw attention to a certain derivation of words, as we have indicated in a flash.[4] It is impossible to say: Perhaps this was an apprehension of other forms. For he says at the end of this second description: *This is the living creature that I saw under the God of Israel by the river of Khebar.*[5] Thus that which we have begun to make clear has already become clear.

CHAPTER 2

He[1] states that he saw four *living creatures* and that every *living creature* among them had four faces, four wings, and two hands. As a whole, the form of each creature was that of a man; as he says: *They had the likeness of a man.*[2] He also states that their two hands were likewise the hands of a man,

---

1. Ezek. 1:10.   2. Ezek. 1:5.   3. Ezek. 10:14.   4. Cf. II 43.   5. Ezek. 10:20.
1. Ezekiel.   2. Ezek. 1:5.

it being known that a man's hands are indubitably formed as they are in order to be engaged in the arts of craftsmanship. Then he states that their feet are straight; he means that they have no articulations. This is the meaning of his dictum, *straight feet*,[3] according to its external sense. [The Sages] have likewise said: *And their feet were straight feet — this teaches [us] that above,*[4] *there is no sitting.*[5] Understand this also. Then he states that the soles of their two feet, which are instruments for walking, are not like the feet of a man, whereas their hands | are like the hands of a man. For the feet were round, *Like the sole of a calf's [ᶜegel] foot.*[6] Then he states that there is no interval and no space between those four *living creatures*, each of them adhering to the other; he says, *Coupled together, a woman to her sister.*[7] Then he states that though they adhered to one another, their faces and their wings were separated above; he says: *And their faces and their wings were separated above.*[8] Consider his saying *above*. For only the bodies adhered to one another, whereas their faces and their wings were separated, but only from above. That is why he says: *And their faces and their wings were separated above.* Then he states that they were brilliant *like the color of burnished brass.*[9] Then he states that they also gave light; he says: *Their appearance was like coals of fire.*[10] This is all that he says concerning the form of the *living creatures*, I mean their shape, their substance, their forms, their wings, their hands, and their feet.

Then he began to describe the manner of the motions of these *living creatures*. Regarding these he states that which you will hear. He says that in the motions of the *living creatures*, there was no turning, no deviation, and no curve, but only one motion. For he says: *They turned not when they went.*[11] Then he states that each of the *living creatures* went in the direction toward which its face was turned. For he says: *Each goes in the direction of its face.*[12] Thus he makes it clear that each *living creature* went only in the direction that was contiguous to its face. Would only that I knew to which face, for they had many faces. However, to sum up, the four did not all of them go in one direction. For if it had been so, he would not have assigned to each of them a separate motion, saying: *Each goes in the direction of its face.* Then he states that the form of the motion of these *living creatures* was running and that it was likewise by running that they retraced their way.

---

3. Ezek. 1:7.　　4. I.e., in the upper world.　　5. Genesis Rabbah, LXV.
6. Ezek. 1:7. The word ᶜegel (calf) has the same radicals as the verb and adjective ᶜagol (to be round, round). Maimonides implies that the word used in this verse has, or contains an allusion to, this meaning.
7. Ezek. 1:9.　　8. Ezek. 1:11.　　9. Ezek. 1:7.　　10. Ezek. 1:13.
11. Ezek. 1:12.　　12. Ezek. 1:9.

For he says: *And the living creatures ran and returned [raṣo va-shob].*[13] For *raṣo* is the infinitive of the verb *raṣ* [to run] and *shob* is the infinitive of the verb | *shab* [to return]. He did not use the verbs *halokh* [to go] and *bo* [to come], but said that their motion consisted in running and retracing their way. And he made it clear in an image, saying: *As the appearance of a flash of lightning [bazaq].*[14] For *bazaq* is another word for *baraq* [lightning]. Accordingly he says that it is like *lightning [baraq]*, whose motion appears to be the swiftest of motions and which stretches out rapidly and at a rush from a certain place and then with the same rapidity contracts and returns time after time to the place whence it moved. *Jonathan ben Uziel*, peace be on him, interpreted the words *raṣo va-shob* as follows: *They went round the world and returned [as] one creature and rapid as the appearance of lightning.* Then he[15] states that the motion takes place, not because of the direction toward which the *living creature* moves in this motion of running and retracing one's way, but because of something else, I mean the divine purpose. Accordingly he says that it is in the direction toward which the *living creature* should move according to the divine purpose that it accomplishes this rapid movement, which is a *running and returning [raṣo va-shobh].* For he says concerning the *living creatures: Whither the air [ruaḥ] will be [yihyeh] they will go; they turned not when they went.*[16] *Ruaḥ* here does not mean wind, but purpose, as we have made clear when speaking of the equivocality of *ruaḥ.*[17] He says accordingly that the *living creature* runs in the direction in which it is the divine purpose that the *living creature* run. *Jonathan ben Uziel*, peace be on him, has already interpreted this too in a similar way, saying: *They went wherever the will was that they should go, and they did not turn when going.* Now inasmuch as his saying reads, *Whither the air will be they will go*, and consequently its outer meaning signifies that sometimes God will wish in the future that the *living creature* should go in a certain direction and then it would take that direction and sometimes again He will wish that it should go in another direction different from the first and it would go accordingly; he[18] goes back to the passage and explains this obscure point, | letting us know that this is not so and that *yihyeh [will be]* has here the meaning *hayah [has been]*, as is often the case in Hebrew. Thus the direction in which God wished the *living creature* to go had been determined; the *living creature* takes the direction that God had wished it to take; and the will[19] is constant regarding this direction. In order to explain this matter and to complete what he has to say about it, he says in

13. Ezek. 1:14.   14. Ezek. 1:14.   15. I.e., the prophet.
16. Ezek. 1:12.   17. Cf. I 40.   18. I.e., the prophet.   19. Of God.

another *verse: Whithersoever the air*[20] *will go, they will go thither, as the air*[20] *to go.*[21] Understand this wondrous explanation. This too belongs to his description of the form of the motion of the four *living creatures*, which comes after the description of their shapes.

Then he started upon another description, saying that he had seen a single body beneath the *living creatures* and adhering to them. This body was joined to the earth and also formed four bodies and likewise had four faces. He does not ascribe to it any form at all, neither a man's form nor another form pertaining to living beings, but states that they were great, terrible, and fearful bodies without ascribing to them any shape at all. He states that all their bodies were *eyes.*[22] They are those that he calls *wheels* [*ophannim*], saying: *And I saw the living creatures, and, behold, one wheel upon the earth by the living creatures, with his four faces.*[23] Accordingly he has made it clear that it was a single body whose one extremity was *by the living creatures* while the other was on the earth, and that this *wheel* had four faces. He says: *The appearance of the wheels and their work was like unto the color of a beryl; and they four had one likeness.*[24] Thus after having spoken of one *wheel*, he goes on to speak of *four*. Accordingly he makes it quite clear that the four *faces* that the *wheel* has are the four *wheels*. Then he states that the shape of the four *wheels* is one and the same, for he says: *And the four had one likeness.* Then he explains with regard to these *wheels* that they | were encased one within the other, for he says: *And their appearance and their work was as it were a wheel within* [*be-tokh*] *a wheel.*[25] This is an expression that is not used with regard to the *living creatures*; for he does not use with regard to the *living creatures* the word *tokh* [*within*]. Rather do they adhere to each other; as he says: *Coupled together, a woman to her sister.*[26] As for the *wheels*, he states that they were encased one within the other, *as it were a wheel within a wheel.* As for the whole body of the *wheels* of which he says that it was *full of eyes* [*einayim*],[27] it is possible that he meant that they were really full of eyes; but it is also possible that he meant that they had many colors, as in the passage: *And the color thereof* [*ve-ʿeino*] *as the color of* [*ke-ʿein*] *bdellium.*[28] It is likewise possible that he meant that they were likenesses, just as we find that the ancient masters of the language say, *Ke-ʿein she-ganab, ke-ʿein she-gazal*,[29] meaning: Like

20. *ruaḥ*. According to Maimonides' explanation: *the purpose.*   21. Ezek. 1:20.
22. Cf. Ezek. 1:18.   23. Ezek. 1:15.
24. Ezek. 1:16.   25. Ezek. 1:16.   26. Ezek. 1:9.   27. Cf. Ezek. 1:18.
28. Num. 11:7. In this passage, the word *ʿayin*, which usually means "eye," signifies "color."
29. Cf. B.T., Baba Qamma, 65a and 66. The word *ke-ʿein*, in which the word *ʿayin* (eye) is included, means in this passage: *like unto.*

unto what one has stolen, like unto what one has robbed. [The word "ʿeinayim" may also mean] various states and attributes, as in its dictum:[30] *It may be that the Lord will look be-ʿeini*[31] — he means, [on] my state. This is what he describes with regard to the form of the *wheels*.

As for the motion of the *wheels*, he again says that there was in their motion no curve, no turning, and no deviation; there were only straight motions that did not vary. This is his saying: *When they went, they went upon their four sides; they turned not when they went.*[32] Then he states that these four *wheels* do not move essentially, as do the *living creatures*; for they have no essential motion at all, moving only when moved by something other than themselves. He insistently repeats this notion and reaffirms it several times. And he makes out that the movers[33] of the *wheels* are none other than the *living creatures*, so that, to use an image, the relation of a *wheel* to a *living creature* could be likened to what happens when one ties an inanimate body to the hands and the feet of a living being: every time the living being moves, the piece of timber or the stone tied to a limb of that living being moves likewise. Accordingly he says: *And when the living creatures went, | the wheels went by them; and when the living creatures were lifted up from the earth, the wheels were lifted up.*[34] And he also says: *And the wheels were lifted up facing them.*[35] And he explains the cause of this, saying: *For the air of the living creature was in the wheels.*[36] He repeats this notion in order to confirm it and to make it understood, saying: *When those went, these went; and when those stood, these stood; and when those were lifted up from the earth, the wheels were lifted up facing them; for the air of the living creature was in the wheels.*[37]

Accordingly the order of these motions is as follows: The *living creatures* moved in whatever direction it was the divine purpose that the *living creatures* should move, and by the motion of the *living creatures* the *wheels* were moved, following the former through being bound to them. For the *wheels* do not of their own accord move the *living creatures*. And he sets forth the order of that grade, saying: *Whithersoever the air will go, they will go thither, as the air to go; and the wheels were lifted up facing them; for the air of the living creature was in the wheels.*[38] I have already made known to you the translation of *Jonathan ben Uziel*, peace be on him: *Wherever the will was that they should go, and so on.*

When he had finished the description of the *living creatures*, of their

30. II Sam. 16:12.   31. I.e., in my ʿayin.   32. Ezek. 1:17.
33. In the singular in Arabic.   34. Ezek. 1:19.   35. Ezek. 1:20.
36. Ezek. 1:20.   37. Ezek. 1:21.   38. Ezek. 1:20.

forms, and of their motions, and had mentioned the *wheels* that are beneath the *living creatures*, their being bound to the latter and moved with their motion, he starts to set forth a third apprehension that he had and goes back to another description concerning that which is above the *living creatures*. He says that above the four *living creatures*, there is a *firmament;* upon the *firmament, the likeness of a throne;*[39] and upon the *throne, a likeness as the appearance of a man.*[40] This is the whole of the description he has made of what he has first apprehended *by the river of Khebar.* |

CHAPTER 3

After *Ezekiel*, peace be on him, had set forth the description of the *Chariot* as given in the beginning of the book, the selfsame apprehension returned to him a second time when, *in a vision of prophecy*, he was borne *to Jerusalem*. Thereupon he explained to us things that at first had not been explained. Thus for our benefit he replaced the word *living creatures* by the word *cherubim*, making it known to us that the *living creatures* that were mentioned at first are also angels — I mean, the *cherubim*. He says: *And when the cherubim went, the wheels went beside them; and when the cherubim lifted up their wings to mount up from the earth, the same wheels also turned not from beside them.*[1] Thus he confirms the fact that, as we have mentioned, the two motions were bound together. Then he says: *This is the living creature that I saw under the God of Israel by the river of Khebar; and I knew that they were the cherubim.*[2] Accordingly he repeats the description of the selfsame forms and the selfsame motions and makes it clear that the *living creatures* are the *cherubim* and the *cherubim* are the *living creatures*. Thereupon he explains in this second description another notion, namely, the notion that the *wheels* [*ophannim*] are the *galgallim*[3] [*spheres*]; he says:[4] *As for the wheels* [*ophannim*], *they were called in my hearing: Hagalgal.*[5] Then he explains a third notion regarding the *wheels* [*ophannim*],

---

39. Ezek. 1:22.   40. Ezek. 1:26.
 1. Ezek. 10:16.   2. Ezek. 10:20.
 3. The word *galgallim*, meaning "wheels" (like the word *ophannim*), has in later Hebrew the signification of "heavenly spheres."
 4. Ezek. 10:13.
 5. In the English Bible, this word is translated: *the wheelwork*. Maimonides takes it to refer to the heavenly spheres.

saying with reference to them: *But to the place whither the head looked they followed it; they turned not as they went.*[6] Thus he states explicitly that the compulsory motion of the *wheels* followed *to the place whither the head looked.* That is to say, as he has explained, it followed *whither the air will be.*[7] Then he adds a fourth notion regarding the *wheels;* he says: *And the wheels were full of eyes round about, even the wheels that they four had.*[8] | He did not mention this notion at first. Then he says in this last apprehension with regard to the *wheels: their flesh and their backs and their hands and their wings.*[9] At first he had not mentioned that the wheels had *flesh* or *hands* or *wings,* but only that they were bodies. Finally, however, he goes so far as to say that they have flesh, hands, and wings; but he does not ascribe to them any form whatever. In this second apprehension he also explains that every *wheel* is related to a *cherub,* saying: *One wheel beside one cherub, and another wheel beside another cherub.*[10] He also explains there that the four *living creatures* are *one living creature* because of the adherence of all of them to one another; for he says: *This is the living creature that I saw under the God of Israel by the river of Khebar.*[11] Similarly he calls the *wheels, One wheel upon the earth,*[12] in spite of there being, as he also mentions, *four wheels;* and this because of their being joined to one another and of their having[13] all *four one likeness.*[14] These are the explanations, regarding the forms of the *living creatures* and the *wheels,* that are added for our benefit in this second apprehension.

CHAPTER 4

It behooves us to draw your attention to a certain thought adopted by *Jonathan ben Uziel,* peace be on him. When he saw the explicit statement,[1] *As for the wheels [ophannim], they were called in my hearing: Hagalgal [the sphere],*[2] he categorically decided that the *wheels [ophannim]* are the heavens. Accordingly he translated in every case *ophan [wheel]* by *galgala [sphere]*[3] and *ophannim [wheels]* by *galgalaya [spheres].* I have no doubt that to his mind, peace be on him, this interpretation was corroborated | by the dictum of *Ezekiel,* peace be on him, regarding the

6. Ezek. 10:11.   7. Cf. Ezek. 1:2. Cf. preceding chapter.   8. Ezek. 10:12.
9. Ezek. 10:12.   10. Ezek. 10:9.   11. Ezek. 10:20.   12. Ezek. 1:15.
13. Literally: being all of them.   14. Ezek. 1:16.
1. Ezek. 10:13.   2. Cf. preceding chap., n. 3.   3. Cf. preceding chap., n. 3.

wheels [*ophannim*] that they were *like unto the color of a beryl*,[4] a color that is that attributed to the heavens, as is generally known. However, when he found the text, *Now as I beheld the living creatures, behold one wheel upon the earth*,[5] which indubitably indicates that the *wheels* are *upon the earth*, this appeared to him to constitute a difficulty with regard to this interpretation. Accordingly he went further in his interpretation, interpreting [the word] *earth* in this passage as referring to the surface of heaven, which is an *earth* with respect to what is above it. Accordingly he translated: *One wheel upon the earth beneath the height of heaven*. Understand this interpretation as it is in reality. It seems to me that he was led to this interpretation by his belief, peace be on him, that *galgal* is a term designating in the first place the heavens. It seems, however, to me that the matter is as follows. The [Hebrew] term for rolling is *galgel*. Thus: *And roll thee down* [*ve-gilgaltikha*] *from the rocks*;[6] *And rolled* [*va-yagel*] *the stone*.[7] For this reason it is said, *And like a rolling thing* [*u-khe-galgal*] *before the whirlwind*,[8] because of its rolling. For this reason too the cranium is called *gulgoleth*, because of its being nearly round. Because every sphere rolls rapidly, every spherical thing was called *galgal*. Hence the heavens were called *galgallim* because of their being round – I mean, because of their being spherical. Accordingly [the Sages] say [with reference to fate]: *it is a revolving galgal* [*sphere*].[9] For the selfsame reason they likewise call a pulley *galgal*. Accordingly [Ezekiel's] dictum – *As for the wheels* [*ophannim*], *they were called in my hearing: Hagalgal*[10] – makes their shape known to us. For he does not ascribe to them any shape or form except by saying that they are *galgallim*.

With regard to his saying about them, *like unto beryl*,[11] he interprets this also in the second description, saying with regard to the *wheels* [*ophannim*]: *And the appearance of the wheels was as the color of a beryl stone*.[12] *Jonathan ben Uziel*, peace be on him, translated this: *like unto a precious stone*. Now you know already that *Onqelos* used this very expression to translate: *As it were, a work of the whiteness of sapphire stone*;[13] he says: *As the work of a precious stone*. There is consequently no difference | between its saying, *As the color of a beryl stone*, and its saying, *As it were, a work of the whiteness of sapphire stone*. Understand this.

You must not find it incongruous that, having mentioned the interpretation of *Jonathan ben Uziel*, peace be on him, I propounded a different interpretation. You will find that many among the *Sages*, and even among

4. Ezek. 1:16.   5. Ezek. 1:15.   6. Jer. 51:25.   7. Gen. 29:10.
8. Isa. 17:13.   9. B.T., Shabbath, 151b.   10. Ezek. 10:13.
11. Cf. Ezek. 1:16.   12. Ezek. 10:9.   13. Exod. 24:10.

the commentators, differ from his interpretation with regard to certain words and many notions that are set forth by the *prophets*. How could this not be with regard to these obscure matters? Moreover I do not oblige you to decide in favor of my interpretation.[14] Understand the whole of his interpretation from that to which I have drawn your attention, and understand my interpretation. God knows in which of the two interpretations there is a correspondence to what has been intended.

CHAPTER 5

Among the things to which your attention ought to be directed is his[1] expression: *visions of God*.[2] He does not say *vision*, in the singular, but *visions*, because there were many apprehensions differing in species; I mean to say three apprehensions, that of the *wheels*, that of the *living creatures*, and that of the *man*, who is above the *living creatures*. With regard to every apprehension he says: *And I saw*. Thus with reference to the apprehension of the *living creatures* he says: *And I saw, and, behold, a whirlwind, and so on*;[3] with reference to the apprehension of the *wheels* he says: *And I saw the living creatures, and, behold, one wheel upon the earth*;[4] and with reference to the *man*, who in degree is above the *living creatures*, he says: *And I saw as the color of ḥashmal*,[5] *and so on, from the appearance of his loins, and so on*.[6] In the description of the *Chariot*, he only repeats the word *I saw* these three times. The *Sages of the Mishnah* have already explained this matter; in fact it is they who drew my attention to it. For they said that it is permissible to teach the first two apprehensions only, I mean | the apprehension of the *living creatures* and that of the *wheels*; whereas only *the chapter headings* may be taught with regard to the third apprehension, that of the *ḥashmal* and of what is connected with it. However, *our holy Rabbi*[7] believes that all three apprehensions are called the *Account of the Chariot* and that with respect to none of them may anything other than *the chapter headings* be taught. Their text with regard to this is as follows: *Till where [is it permissible to teach] the Account of the Chariot? Rabbi Meir says: Till the last*

14. Or, according to certain manuscripts: of one interpretation.
1. I.e., Ezekiel's.   2. Ezek. 1:1.   3. Ezek. 1:4.   4. Ezek. 1:15.
5. Several explanations of this Hebrew word are set forth below in III 7.
6. Ezek. 1:27.   7. I.e., Rabbi Judah, compiler of the Mishnah.

"*And I saw.*"[8] *Rabbi Isaac says: Till [the word]* "*ḥashmal.*" *From [the first]* "*And I saw*"[9] *till [the word]* "*ḥashmal,*" *[it is permissible] to teach; from there on the chapter headings are transmitted to [the disciple]. Some say: from [the first]* "*And I saw*" *till [the word]* "*ḥashmal,*" *the chapter headings are transmitted to him; from there on, [he may be taught] if he is a wise man, understanding in virtue of his own intelligence; and [he may] not, if [he is] not [that].*[10] It has thus become clear to you from their texts that there were various apprehensions to which attention is drawn by the expression: *And I saw, And I saw, And I saw*; that these signified different degrees; and that the last apprehension, that referred to in the words: *And I saw as the color of ḥashmal*[11] — I mean the apprehension of the form of the divided man of which it is said: *From the appearance of his loins and upward, and from the appearance of his loins and downward*[12] — is the ultimate perception and the highest of all. There is also a difference of opinion among the *Sages* about whether it is permissible for it to be alluded to in any way through teaching — I mean to say *through the transmission of the chapter headings* — or whether it is not permissible in any way that an allusion be made to the teaching of this third apprehension, though it be only *through the chapter headings*; but he who is a *wise man will understand in virtue of his own intelligence*. Similarly there is also, as you see, a difference of opinion among the *Sages* with regard to the first two apprehensions likewise — I mean those concerning the *living creatures* and the *wheels* — about whether it is permissible to teach explicitly the notions concerning them, or whether this is only permitted to be done through allusions and enigmas *through the chapter headings*.

You ought also to have your attention directed to the order of these | three apprehensions. Thus he[13] has put first the apprehension of the *living creatures*, for they come first because of their nobility and of their causality — according to what he says: *For the air of the living creature was in the wheels*[14] — and because of other things too. After the *wheels* comes the third apprehension, which is higher in degree than that of the *living creatures*, as is clear. The reason for this lies in the fact that the first two apprehensions necessarily precede the third apprehension in the order of knowledge, the latter being inferred with the help of the other two.

8. Ezek. 1:27.   9. Ezek. 1:4.   10. B.T., Ḥagigah, 13a.   11. Ezek. 1:27.
12. Ezek. 1:27.   13. I.e., Ezekiel.   14. Ezek. 1:20.

CHAPTER 6

Know that the great and sublime notion that *Ezekiel*, peace be on him — being moved by the prophetic motive force that incited him to let us know this began to teach us in describing the *Chariot* is the very notion that *Isaiah*, peace be on him, let us know summarily without having the need to go into these details. For he says: *And I saw the Lord sitting upon a throne high and lifted up, and his train filled the temple. The seraphim stood, and so on.*[1] The *Sages* have explained all this to us and have called our attention to this subject. They said that the apprehension grasped by *Ezekiel* was identical with that grasped by *Isaiah*. They made about it a comparison with two men who saw the ruler while the latter was riding: one of them belonged to the settled population and the other to the desert nomads. Because the former knew that city people know in what state the ruler rides, he did not describe that state, but said only: I saw the ruler. The latter, however, wishing to describe this to the desert nomads, | who have no knowledge at all regarding the state in which the ruler rides, described to them in detail this state and the characteristic of the ruler's troops, his servants, and those who execute his orders. An intimation of this scope is of very great utility. I refer to their dictum in *Ḥagigah*: *All that was seen by Ezekiel was [likewise] seen by Isaiah. Isaiah is like unto a city man who saw the king; whereas Ezekiel is like unto a villager who saw the king.*[2] It is possible that this text was interpreted by its author in accordance with what I have said at the beginning [of the chapter]: namely, that the contemporaries of *Isaiah* had no need of his expounding those details to them, it being sufficient for them that he said: *And I saw the Lord, and so on;* whereas *the people of the Exile* required these details. It is also possible that the author of this remark believed that *Isaiah* was more perfect than *Ezekiel*, and that the apprehension that amazed *Ezekiel* and was regarded by him as terrible was known by *Isaiah* through a knowledge the exposition of which did not require extraordinary language, the subject being well known to those who are perfect.

1. Isa. 6:1–2.   2. B.T., Ḥagigah, 13b.

CHAPTER 7

To the whole of things requiring investigation belongs the tying of the apprehension of the *Chariot* to a year, a month, and a day, and also to a place. This is something the significance of which ought to be sought. It should not be thought that this is a matter without significance. To the things that ought to be considered, for it is the key[1] to the whole, belongs his saying: *The heavens were opened.*[2] This is something that frequently occurs in the speech of the prophets — I mean the use of the figurative expressions of the opening and also of the opening of gates: *Open ye the gates;*[3] *And He opened the doors of heaven;*[4] *Yea, lift up the openings of the world;*[5] *Open to me | the gates of righteousness.*[6] This occurs frequently.

Among the things to which your attention ought to be directed belongs the fact that though this whole description[7] is based indubitably *on a vision of prophecy* — for as he says: *And the hand of the Lord was there upon him*[8] — there is between various parts of this description a very great difference in expression. For when he speaks of the *living creatures*, he says, *The likeness of four living creatures*, and does not only say, *Four living creatures.*[9] Similarly he says: *And the likeness of the firmament was upon the heads of the living creature;*[10] and: *The likeness of a throne, as the appearance of a sapphire stone;*[11] and: *The likeness as the appearance of a man.*[12] With regard to all this he uses the expression: *likeness*. With regard to the *wheels*, however, he by no means says concerning them, *the likeness of a wheel* or *the likeness of wheels*, but makes absolute statements regarding what they really are in a form expressive of that which really exists. Be not misled by his saying, *And the four had one likeness*,[13] for this dictum is not ordered in the same way and has not the signification referred to. In the last apprehension he corroborates and explains this notion. He mentions the *firmament* in an absolute manner, beginning as he does with it and setting forth the details concerning it; he says: *Then I saw, and, behold, in the firmament that was above the head of the cherubim, there appeared over them as it were a sapphire stone, as the appearance of the likeness of a throne.*[14] Thus he speaks

---

1. The Arabic and the Hebrew words for "key" derive from the same verbal root, which means in both languages, "to open."
2. Ezek. 1:1. 3. Isa. 26:2. 4. Ps. 78:23.
5. Ps. 24:9. In the English Bible this is translated: *Yea, lift them up, ye everlasting doors.*
6. Ps. 118:19. 7. That of Ezekiel. 8. Ezek. 1:3. 9. Ezek. 1:5.
10. Ezek. 1:22. 11. Ezek. 1:26. 12. Ezek. 1:26. 13. Ezek. 1:16.
14. Ezek. 10:1.

in this passage about the *firmament* in an absolute manner and does not say *the likeness of the firmament* as was the case when he spoke of it in connection with *the heads of the likeness of the living creatures.* As for the *throne* he says, *There appeared over them the likeness of a throne,* this being a proof that the apprehension of the *firmament* came first and that afterwards *there appeared to him over it the likeness of a throne.* Understand this.

Among the things to which your attention ought to be directed belongs the fact that in the first apprehension he states that the *living creatures* had both wings and the *hands of a man;* whereas in the second apprehension in which he explains that the *living creatures* are *cherubim,* he apprehended in the first place | only their wings, the *hands of a man* appearing in them afterwards in the course of his apprehension; for he says: *And there appeared in the cherubim the shape [tabnith] of a man's hand under their wings.*[15] His saying *shape [tabnith]* is analogous to his saying *likeness [demuth].* And the place of this[16] is *under their wings.* Understand this.

Consider also how he makes an explicit statement in his dictum, *And the wheels were facing them,*[17] though he does not ascribe a form to them.

He also says: *And the appearance of the rainbow that is in the cloud in the day of rain, so was the appearance of the brightness round about. This was the appearance of the likeness of the glory of the Lord.*[18] The matter, the true reality, and the essence of the *rainbow* that is described are known. This is the most extraordinary comparison possible, as far as parables and similitudes are concerned; and it is indubitably due to a prophetic force. Understand this.

Among the things to which your attention should be drawn belongs his dividing *the likeness of the man that was on the throne;* the upper part of the likeness being *as the color of ḥashmal* and the lower *as the appearance of fire.*[19] They[20] have explained[21] that the word *ḥashmal* is composed of two notions, *ḥash* and *mal;* this means, of the notion of rapidity, indicated by *ḥash,* and of that of cutting, indicated by *mal,* the intention being to combine through a simile two separate notions regarding two sides, above and below. They also give us a second hint, saying that the word derives from the notions of speech and silence, saying that *they*[22] sometimes *ḥashoth [are silent]* and sometimes *memalleloth [speak].* They ascribe the meaning "silence" [to "ḥash"] from the verse: *heḥesheiti [I have been silent] for a long time;*[23] there is thus an allusion to two notions through the indication of speech

15. Ezek. 10:8.   16. I.e., of *the shape of a man's hand.*   17. Ezek. 10:19.
18. Ezek. 1:28.   19. Cf. Ezek. 1:27 and 8:2.   20. I.e., the talmudic Sages.
21. B.T., Ḥagigah, 13a–b.   22. I.e., the *ḥashmallim.*   23. Isa. 42:14.

without a sound. There is no doubt that their dictum, *they sometimes are silent [ḥashoth] and sometimes speak [memalleloth],* refers to a created thing. See accordingly how they have made it quite clear to us that *the likeness of a man that was on the throne* and that was divided, is not a parable referring to Him, who is exalted above all composition, but to a created thing. Accordingly the *prophet* himself says: *This was the appearance of the likeness of the glory of the Lord.*[24] Now *the glory of the Lord* is not the *Lord*, as we have made clear several times. Accordingly everything | to which the parables contained in these apprehensions refer is only *the glory of the Lord*, I mean to say the *Chariot*, not the *Rider*, as He, may He be exalted, may not be presented in a likeness in a parable. Understand this.

We have thus given you also in this chapter such *chapter headings* that if you combine[25] the *headings* there will emerge from them a whole that is useful with regard to this theme. If you consider all that we have said in the chapters of this Treatise up to this chapter, the greater part or the entirety of the subject in question, except for a few slight details and repetitious speech, whose meaning remains hidden, will become clear to you. Perhaps upon thorough consideration, this too will be revealed, and nothing of this will remain hidden. Do not hope that, after this chapter, you will hear from me even a single word about this subject, be it as an explicit statement or in a flashlike allusion. For everything that it is possible to say about this has been said; I have even plunged deep into this with temerity. We shall accordingly start upon other subjects from among those that, I hope, I shall explain in this Treatise.

CHAPTER 8

All bodies subject to generation and corruption are attained by corruption only because of their matter; with regard to form and with respect to the latter's essence, they are not attained by corruption, but are permanent. Do you not see that all the specific forms are perpetual and permanent? Corruption attains the form only by accident, I mean because of its being joined to matter. The nature and the true reality of matter are such that it never |

24. Ezek. 1:28.
25. Or, according to certain manuscripts and to Ibn Tibbon's translation: if you complete them.

ceases to be joined to privation; hence no form remains constantly in it, for it perpetually puts off one form and puts on another. How extraordinary is what *Solomon* said in his wisdom when likening matter *to a married harlot*,[1] for matter is in no way found without form and is consequently always like *a married woman* who is never separated from a *man* and is never *free*.[2] However, notwithstanding her being *a married woman*, she never ceases to seek for another man to substitute for her husband, and she deceives and draws him on in every way until he obtains from her what her husband used to obtain. This is the state of matter. For whatever form is found in it, does but prepare it to receive another form. And it does not cease to move with a view to putting off that form that actually is in it and to obtaining another form; and the selfsame state obtains after that other form has been obtained in actu. It has then become clear that all passing-away and corruption or deficiency are due solely to matter. Thus in the case of a man, for instance, it is clear that the deformity of his form, the fact that his limbs do not conform to their nature, and also the weakness, the cessation, or the troubling of all his functions — no matter whether all this be inherent in his natural constitution from its beginning or be only a supervening accident — that all this is consequent upon his corrupt matter and not upon his form. Similarly every living being dies and becomes ill solely because of its matter and not because of its form. All man's acts of disobedience and sins are consequent upon his matter and not upon his form, whereas all his virtues are consequent upon his form. For example, man's apprehension of his Creator, his mental representation of every intelligible, his control of his desire and his anger, his thought on what ought to be preferred[3] and what avoided, are all of them consequent upon his form. On the other hand, | his eating and drinking and copulation and his passionate desire for these things, as well as his anger and all bad habits found in him, are all of them consequent upon his matter. Inasmuch as it is clear that this is so, and as according to what has been laid down by divine wisdom it is impossible for matter to exist without form and for any of the forms in question to exist without matter, and as consequently it was necessary that man's very noble form, which, as we have explained,[4] is the *image of God and His likeness*, should be bound to earthy, turbid, and dark matter, which calls down upon man

1. Cf. Prov. 6:26.   2. Cf. above, I Introduction and 17.

3. I read *yuʾthar*, in accord with one manuscript and the translation of Ibn Tibbon (and probably also that of Alḥarizi), rather than *yuʾtā*, the variant suggested by other manuscripts. The latter variant could be translated: ought to be brought forward. Cf. Joel's ed., p. 310, l. 17.

4. Cf. I 1.

every imperfection and corruption; He granted it — I mean the human form — power, dominion, rule, and control over matter, in order that it subjugate it, quell its impulses, and bring it[5] back to the best and most harmonious state that is possible.

In this respect the ranks of the Adamites differ. Among men, there are individuals who aspire always to prefer that which is most noble and to seek a state of perpetual permanence according to what is required by their noble form. They only reflect on the mental representation of an intelligible, on the grasp of a true opinion regarding everything, and on union with the divine intellect, which lets overflow toward them that through which that form exists. Whenever the impulses of matter impel such an individual toward the dirt and the generally admitted shame inherent in matter, he feels pain because of his entanglement, is ashamed and abashed because of what he has gone through, and desires to diminish this shame with all his power and to be preserved from it in every way. This is like the case of a man with whom the ruler had become angry; he ordered him accordingly, with a view to humiliating him, to transport dung from one place to another. Such a man will endeavor with all his power to be hidden at the time when he is humiliated in this manner; possibly he will transport a small quantity to a nearby place, so that perhaps his hands or clothes will not be dirtied and no one | else will see him. Free men would act in this manner. A slave, however, would rejoice in this and would not consider that he has been subjected to a great hardship. He would throw himself with his whole body into this dung and filth, soil his face and hands, and carry the dung in public, laughing the while and rejoicing and clapping his hands. The state of the various classes of people is similar. As we have said, there are among men individuals to whose mind all the impulses of matter are shameful and ugly things, deficiencies imposed by necessity; particularly so the sense of touch, which, as Aristotle has stated, is a shame for us, and because of which we wish to eat, to drink, and to copulate.[6] Consequently one's recourse to these things should be reduced to the extent to which this is possible; one should do them in secret, should feel sorrowful because one does them, and not have them spoken of and discoursed about; no gathering should be held with a view to these things. A man should be in control of all these impulses, restrict his efforts in relation to them, and admit only that which is indispensable. He should take as his end that which is the end of man qua man: namely, solely the mental representation of the intelligibles, the most certain and the noblest of which being the apprehension, in as far

5. Or: them.   6. Cf. II 36, n. 8.

as this is possible, of the deity, of the angels, and of His other works. These individuals are those who are permanently with God. They are those to whom it has been said: *Ye are gods, and all of you children of the Most High.*[7] This is what is required of man; I mean to say that this is his end. As far as the others are concerned — those who are separated from God by a veil, being the multitude of the ignorant[8] — the opposite is true: They refrain from all thought and perception about any intelligible thing and take as their end the sense that is our greatest shame, I mean the sense of touch. Accordingly they have no thought and no perception except only in relation to eating and copulation, as has been stated clearly with regard to these | wretched people wholly given over to eating, drinking, and copulating. It says: *But these also have erred through wine, and through strong drink are out of the way, and so on;*[9] and it says: *For all tables are full of filthy vomit, so that there is no place.*[10] It also says: *And women rule over him;*[11] this being contrary to what was required of them in the beginning of the creation: *And thy desire shall be to thy husband, and he shall rule over thee.*[12] It also describes the violence of their desire; it says: *Every one neigheth after his neighbor's wife;*[13] and also: *For they are all adulterers, and so on.*[14] For this reason *Solomon* has devoted the whole of *Proverbs* to warnings against fornication and intoxicating drink. For those who are the objects of divine wrath and who are remote from God are plunged deeply into these two vices. Of them it is said: *For they are not the Lord's;*[15] and also: *Cast them out of My sight, and let them go forth.*[16]

As for [Solomon's] dictum, *A woman of virtue who can find?,*[17] and this whole parable, it is clear. For if it so happens that the matter of a man is excellent, and suitable, neither dominating him nor corrupting his constitution, that matter is a divine gift. To sum up: it is easy, as we have mentioned, to control suitable matter. If it is unsuitable, it is not impossible for someone trained to quell it. For this reason *Solomon* — both he and others — inculcated all these exhortations. Also the commandments and prohibitions of the Law are only intended to quell all the impulses of matter. It behooves him who prefers to be a human being in truth, not a beast having the shape and configuration of a human being, to endeavor to diminish all

---

7. Ps. 82:6.
8. Possibly the translation, "pagans," should be preferred. The word *al-jāhiliyya*, used here by Maimonides, means etymologically "the ignorant." However, in ordinary Islamic terminology, it is applied to the pre-Islamic pagans of Arabia.
9. Isa. 28:7.   10. Isa. 28:8.   11. Isa. 3:12.   12. Gen. 3:16.
13. Jer. 5:8.   14. Jer. 9:1.   15. Jer. 5:10.   16. Jer. 15:1.   17. Prov. 31:10

the impulses of matter—such as eating, drinking, copulation, anger, and all the habits consequent upon desire and anger—to be ashamed of them, and to set for them limits in his soul. With regard to what is indispensable, like eating and drinking, he must confine himself to what is most useful and to what corresponds to the need for nourishment, not to | pleasure. He must also reduce speech about, and gatherings for, such matters. You know how [the Sages] disliked *meals that are not [partaken of] with a view to a commandment*[18] and that the virtuous like *Phinehas ben Yair* never ate in somebody else's house—*our holy Rabbi*[19] wished him to eat at his house, but he did not do it.[20] What is true of eating applies to drinking, as far as their purpose is concerned. As for gatherings with a view to drinking intoxicants, you should regard them as more shameful than gatherings of naked people with uncovered private parts who excrete in daylight[21] sitting together. The explanation of this is as follows: Excreting is a necessary thing that man cannot refrain from by any device whatever, whereas being drunk is an act committed by a bad man in virtue of his free choice. The disapproval of the uncovering of the private parts is a generally accepted opinion, not a thing cognized by the intellect, whereas the corruption of the intellect and of the body is shunned by the intellect. For this reason one who prefers to be a human being ought to shun it and not to speak of it. With regard to copulation, I need not add anything to what I have said in my Commentary on *Aboth*[22] about the aversion in which it is held by what occurs in our wise and pure Law, and about the prohibition against mentioning it or against making it in any way or for any reason a subject of conversation. You know the dictum of [the Sages][23] that *Elisha*, peace be on him, was called a *Saint* only because he never thought about these matters, so that he never had a venereal dream. And you know their dictum concerning *Jacob*, peace be on him, that *he had never had a seminal emission before [engendering] Reuben.*[24] All these are things traditionally transmitted in the religious community in order to make its members acquire human habits. You know what they say: *Thoughts about sin are worse than the sin.*[25] In order to explain this, I have a very extraordinary interpretation, which is as follows: A man committing an act of disobedience does it only, as I have made clear, because of the accidents consequent upon his matter; | I mean to say that he commits an act of disobedience through his bestiality. But thought is one of the

18. B.T., Pesaḥim, 49a.   19. I.e., Rabbi Judah.
20. Cf. B.T., Ḥullin, 7a–b.   21. Literally: by day.
22. Cf. *Commentary on the Mishnah*, Aboth, I 5.
23. Cf. Leviticus Rabbah, XXIV; B.T., Berakhoth, 10b.
24. Genesis Rabbah, XCVIII and XCIX.   25. B.T., Yoma, 29a.

properties of a human being that are consequent upon his form. Consequently if he gives his thought a free scope in respect to disobedience, he commits an act of disobedience through the nobler of his two parts. Now the sin of him who does an injustice through making an ignorant slave serve him is not like the sin of him who makes a free man who is excellent serve him. For the human form and the properties consequent upon it ought only to be employed with a view to what befits it, namely, union with what is the highest, and not with a view to descending to the lowest degree.

You know the severe prohibition that obtains among us against *obscene language*.[26] This also is necessary. For speaking with the tongue is one of the properties of a human being and a benefit that is granted to him and by which he is distinguished. As it says: *Who hath made man's mouth?*[27] And the *prophet* says: *The Lord God hath given me the tongue of them that are taught*.[28] Now this benefit granted us with a view to perfection in order that we learn and teach should not be used with a view to the greatest deficiency and utter disgrace, so that one says what the ignorant and sinful *Gentiles* say in their songs and their stories, suitable for them but not for those to whom it has been said: *And ye shall be unto Me a kingdom of priests, and a holy nation.*[29] And whoever has applied his thought or his speech to some of the stories concerning that sense which is a disgrace to us, so that he thought more about drink or copulation than is needful or recited songs about these matters, has made use of the benefit granted to him, applying and utilizing it to commit an act of disobedience with regard to Him who has granted the benefit and to transgress His orders. He is like those of whom it is said: *And I multiplied unto her silver and gold, which they used for Baal*.[30] I can also give the reason why this our language[31] is called *the Holy Language*. It should not be thought that this is, | on our part, an empty appellation[32] or a mistake; in fact it is indicative of true reality. For in this holy language no word at all has been laid down in order to designate either the male or the female organ of copulation, nor are there words designating the act itself that brings about generation, the sperm, the urine, or the excrements. No word at all designating, according to its first meaning, any of these things has been laid down in the Hebrew language, they being signified by terms used in a figurative sense and by allusions. It was intended thereby to indicate that these things ought not to be mentioned and consequently that no terms designating them should be coined. For these are things about which one

---

26. Cf., e.g., B.T., Kethuboth, 8b; B.T., Shabbath, 33a.   27. Exod. 4:11.
28. Isa. 50:4.   29. Exod. 19:6.   30. Hos. 2:10.   31. I.e., Hebrew.
32. *laghw*. Certain manuscripts have *ghuluww*, a word that may be translated "exaggeration." Ibn Tibbon's translation agrees with the latter version.

ought to be silent; however, when necessity impels mentioning them, a device should be found to do it by means of expressions deriving from other words, just as the most diligent endeavor should be made to be hidden when necessity impels doing these things. The male organ they have called *gid* [*sinew*], which is used because of the likeness; for they have said: *And thy neck is an iron sinew.*[33] They have also called it *shaphkha* [*instrument for pouring-out*][34] because of its function. The female organ has been called *qebatha* [*her stomach*],[35] *qeba* being the term designating the stomach. As for *rehem* [*vulva*] it is the term designating the part of the entrails in which the fetus is formed. The term designating excrements is *so'a*, deriving from *yaso'* [*to go out*]. The term designating urine is *meme raglayim* [*waters of the feet*]. The term designating sperm is *shikhbath zera*ᶜ [*layer of seed*]. The act itself that brings about generation has no name at all, the following expressions signifying it: *yishkab* [*he lies*], *yib*ᶜ*al* [*he marries*], *yiqah* [*he takes*], *yegalleh* ᶜ*ervah* [*he uncovers the nakedness*], and no others. The verb *yishgal* should not lead you into error so that you think that it is the term designating this action, for *shegal* is merely the term designating a female slave prepared for copulation. Thus: *At thy right hand doth stand the female slave.*[36] And its saying, *yishgalenah*,[37] in the text that is written,[38] means he shall take her as a slave girl for this purpose.

In the greater part of the chapter we have turned aside from the purpose of the Treatise | to deal with moral and also religious matters. However, though these matters do not wholly belong to the purpose of the Treatise, the order of the discourse has led to that.

CHAPTER 9

Matter is a strong veil preventing the apprehension of that which is separate from matter as it truly is. It does this even if it is the noblest and purest matter, I mean to say even if it is the matter of the heavenly spheres. All the more is this true for the dark and turbid matter that is ours. Hence whenever our intellect aspires to apprehend the deity or one of the

33. Isa. 48:4.   34. Deut. 23:2.   35. Num. 25:8.
36. Ps. 45:10.   37. Deut. 28:30.
38. In contradistinction to the rectification set down below the page and read when the text is recited. According to this rectification, the word should be read *yishkabenah* (he shall lie with her).

intellects,[1] there subsists this great veil interposed between the two. This is alluded to in all the books of the prophets; namely, that we are separated by a veil from God and that He is hidden from us by a heavy cloud, or by darkness or by a mist or by an enveloping cloud, and similar allusions to our incapacity to apprehend Him because of matter. This is the intention of its saying: *Clouds and darkness are round about Him;*[2] that intimates the fact that the obstacle consists in the tenebrous character of our substance, and not in His, may He be exalted, being a body surrounded by mist or an enveloping cloud or a heavy cloud, which prevents His being seen, as the external sense of the parable would indicate. Moreover this parable has been repeated, for it says: *He made darkness His hiding place.*[3] Similarly when it speaks of His manifestation, may He be exalted, *in a thick cloud*[4] and in *darkness, cloud, and thick darkness,*[5] it is also only in order that the notion in question be inferred from this manner of speech. For everything that is apprehended in *a vision of prophecy* is only a parable for some notion. And though that great assembly was greater than any *vision of prophecy* and beyond any analogy, it also indicated a | notion;[6] I refer to His manifestation, may He be exalted, *in a thick cloud.* For it draws attention to the fact that the apprehension of His true reality is impossible for us because of the dark matter that encompasses us and not Him, may He be exalted; for He, may He be exalted, is not a body. It is, moreover, well known and generally accepted in the religious community that the day of the *Gathering at Mount Sinai* was a day of clouds, of mist, and of a light rain. He says: *Lord, when Thou didst go forth out of Seᶜir, when Thou didst march out of the field of Edom, the earth trembled, the heavens also dropped, yea, the clouds dropped water.*[7] This is also what is intended in its dictum: *darkness, cloud, and thick darkness,* and not that He, may He be exalted, was encompassed by *darkness*; for near Him, may He be exalted, there is no darkness, but[8] perpetual, dazzling light the overflow of which illumines all that is dark — in accordance with what is said in the prophetic parables: *And the earth did shine with His glory.*[9]

1. I.e., one of the separate intellects.   2. Ps. 97:2.   3. Ps. 18:12.
4. Exod. 19:9.   5. Deut. 4:11.   6. Literally: it was not without a notion.
7. Judg. 5:4.   8. Or: unless it be.   9. Ezek. 43:2.

Those Mutakallimūn, as I have made known to you, do not imagine nonbeing[1] other than absolute nonbeing; but they do not consider the privations[2] of all the habitus as privations. For they think that every privation and the corresponding habitus — as, for instance, blindness and sight, death and life — have the status of two contraries, like the warm and the cold. For this reason they say in absolute parlance that nonbeing does not need an agent, for only an act calls necessarily for an agent. This is correct from a certain point of view. Though they say that nonbeing does not need an agent, they say, according to their principle, that God makes blind, makes deaf, and causes that which moves to rest. | For these privations are to their mind existent things. It behooves us to let you know our opinion about this, according to what is required by philosophic speculation. Now you know already that what removes an impediment of motion is, from a certain point of view, the mover. Thus in the case of one who removes a pillar from under a piece of wood, whereupon the latter falls down because of its natural weight, we say that he who moved the pillar moved the piece of wood; this is stated in the "Akroasis."[3] In the same way we say of one who removes a certain habitus that he produces the corresponding privation, though that privation is not an existent thing. Just as we say of him who puts out a lamp in the night that he has brought about darkness, we say of one who has destroyed sight that he has made blindness, even though darkness and blindness are privations and do not need an agent. In accord with this interpretation, the dictum of *Isaiah* — *who forms the light and creates darkness, who makes peace and creates evil*[4] — has become clear. For *darkness* and *evil* are privations. Consider that he does not say, *who makes darkness* and *who makes evil,* for these are not existent things with which the word *making* could be connected. With regard to these two things, he simply uses the expression *who creates.* For this word has a connection with nonbeing[5] in the Hebrew language. Thus it says: *In the beginning God created, and so on;*[6] namely, out of nonbeing. And the relation between privation[7] and the act of an agent is according to the manner that we have stated. It is in this way likewise that you should understand its dictum: *Who hath set man's mouth? Or*

1. *ᶜadam.* The term means both "nonbeing" and "privation."
2. *aᶜdām,* the plural of the word translated above as "nonbeing."
3. Cf. Aristotle *Physics* viii.4.255b24 ff.   4. Isa. 45:7.   5. Or: privation.
6. Gen. 1:1.   7. Or: nonbeing.

who setteth the dumb or deaf, or the seeing or the blind?[8] However, another
interpretation of this dictum is possible; namely, it can be said: who is he that
created man as a being endowed with speech, or who creates him as a being
lacking speech? In the latter case what would be meant would be the bring-
ing into existence of matter that is not capable of receiving | a certain habitus
whatever that habitus may be. For he who brings into existence a certain
kind of matter that is incapable of receiving a certain habitus may be said to
have made the privation in question; just as one who is able to save an
individual from perishing and refrains from saving him may be said to have
killed him. It has thus become clear to you that, according to every opinion,
the act of an agent can in no way be connected with a privation; the agent
can only be said to have produced the privation by accident, as we have
explained. On the other hand, that which is produced by an essential act of
the agent[9] is necessarily a thing that exists whoever the agent may be, for
his act can only be connected with an existent thing.

After this preamble, you should recall that which has been demonstrated
with regard to the fact that evils are only evils in relation to something; and
that everything that is an evil with reference to one particular existent, that
evil is the privation of this thing or of one of the states suitable for it. For
this reason the following proposition may be enunciated in an absolute manner: all evils are privations. With respect to a man, for instance, his death is
an evil, since death is his nonbeing.[10] Similarly his illness, his poverty, or his
ignorance are evils with regard to him, and all of them are privations of
habitus. If you pursue all the particular cases falling under the above-
mentioned general proposition, you will find that it is never at fault[11] except
in the opinion of one who does not distinguish between privation and
habitus and between two contraries or one who does not know the natures of
all things — one, for instance, who does not know that health is in general
a certain equilibrium belonging to the domain of relation and that the privation of this relation generally constitutes illness. With regard to every
living thing, death is the privation of form. Similarly with regard to everything that is destroyed among the other existents, its destruction is nothing
but the privation of its form.

After these premises, | it will be known with certainty that it may in no
way be said of God, may He be cherished and magnified, that He produces

---

8. Exod. 4:11.   9. Literally: that which the agent does by essence.
10. Or: his privation [of existence]. In this particular instance, the difference between the
     two meanings of the Arabic word ᶜ*adam* (cf. n. 1, this chap.) may be of no great im-
     portance for the signification of Maimonides' phrase.
11. Literally: never lies.

evil in an essential act; I mean that He, may He be exalted, has a primary intention to produce evil. This cannot be correct. Rather all His acts, may He be exalted, are an absolute[12] good; for He only produces[13] being, and all being is a good. On the other hand, all the evils are privations with which an act is only connected in the way we have explained: namely, through the fact that God has brought matter into existence provided with the nature it has — namely, a nature that consists in matter always being a concomitant of privation, as is known. Hence it is the cause of all passing-away and of all evil. For this reason all the things that were not provided by God with this matter are not subject to passing-away and to being attained by any of the evils. Accordingly the true reality of the act of God in its entirety is the good, for the good is being. For this reason the book that has illumined the darkness of the world has enunciated literally the following statement: *And God saw everything that He had made, and, behold, it was very good.*[14] Even the existence of this inferior matter, whose manner of being it is to be a concomitant of privation entailing death and all evils, all this is also *good* in view of the perpetuity of generation and the permanence of being through succession. For this reason *Rabbi Meir* interpreted the words: *And, behold, it was very* [*me'od*] *good — and, behold, death* [*maveth*] *was good,*[15] according to the notion to which we have drawn attention.

Remember what I have told you in this chapter and understand it. Then everything the prophets and the *Sages* have said will become clear to you regarding the good being in its entirety an essential act of the deity. *Bereshith Rabbah* says literally: *Nothing that is evil descends from above.*[16] |

CHAPTER 11

These great evils that come about between the human individuals who inflict them upon one another because of purposes, desires, opinions, and beliefs, are all of them likewise consequent upon privation. For all of them derive from ignorance, I mean from a privation of knowledge. Just as a blind man, because of absence of sight, does not cease stumbling, being wounded, and also wounding others, because he has nobody to guide him on his way, the various sects of men — every individual according to the extent

---

12. Literally: pure.   13. Literally: does (or: acts).   14. Gen. 1:31.
15. Genesis Rabbah, IX.   16. Genesis Rabbah, LI.

of his ignorance — does to himself and to others great evils from which individuals of the species suffer. If there were knowledge, whose relation to the human form is like that of the faculty of sight to the eye, they would refrain from doing any harm to themselves and to others. For through cognition of the truth, enmity and hatred are removed and the inflicting of harm by people on one another is abolished. It holds out this promise, saying: *And the wolf shall dwell with the lamb, and the leopard shall lie down with the kid, and so on. And the cow and the bear shall feed, and so on. And the sucking child shall play, and so on.*[1] Then it gives the reason for this, saying that the cause of the abolition of these enmities, these discords, and these tyrannies, will be the knowledge that men will then have concerning the true reality of the deity. For it says: *They shall not hurt nor destroy in all My holy mountain; for the earth shall be full of the knowledge of the Lord, as the waters cover the sea.*[2] Know this. |

CHAPTER 12

Often it occurs to the imagination of the multitude that there are more evils in the world than there are good things. As a consequence, this thought is contained in many sermons and poems of all the religious communities,[1] which say that it is surprising if good exists in the temporal, whereas the evils of the temporal are numerous and constant. This error is not found only among the multitude, but also among those who deem that they know something.[2]

Rāzī[3] has written a famous book, which he has entitled "Divine Things." He filled it with the enormity of his ravings and his ignorant notions. Among them there is a notion that he has thought up, namely, that there is more evil than good in what exists; if you compare man's well-being and his pleasures in the time span of his well-being with the pains, the heavy sufferings, the infirmities, the paralytic afflictions, the wretchedness, the

1. Isa. 11:6–8.   2. Isa. 11:9.
1. Or: nations.   2. Or: an individual who deems that he knows something.
3. Maimonides refers here to Abū Bakr Muḥammad Ibn Zakariyyā al-Rāzī, who died sometime between 923 and 932. Rāzī (the Rhazes of the Latins) was a famous physician and a philosopher who attacked religion based on prophetic revelation. Only fragments of the book mentioned by Maimonides have come down to us. Cf. Translator's Introduction.

19

sorrows, and the calamities that befall him, you find that his existence — he means the existence of man — is a punishment and a great evil inflicted upon him. He began to establish this opinion by inductively examining these misfortunes, so as to oppose all that is thought by the adherents of the truth regarding the beneficence and manifest munificence of the deity and regarding His being, may He be exalted, the absolute good and regarding all that proceeds from Him being indubitably an absolute good. The reason for this whole mistake lies in the fact that this ignoramus and those like him among the multitude consider that which exists only with reference to a human individual. Every ignoramus imagines that all that exists exists with a view to his individual sake; it is as if there were nothing that exists except him. And if something happens to him that is contrary to what he wishes, he makes the trenchant judgment that | all that exists is an evil. However, if man considered and represented to himself that which exists and knew the smallness of his part in it, the truth would become clear and manifest to him. For this extensive raving entertained by men with regard to the multitude of evils in the world is not said by them to hold good with regard to the angels or with regard to the spheres and the stars or with regard to the elements and the minerals and the plants composed of them or with regard to the various species of animals, but their whole thought only goes out to some individuals belonging to the human species. If someone has eaten bad food and consequently was stricken with leprosy, they are astonished how this great ill has befallen him and how this great evil exists. They are also astonished when one who frequently copulates is stricken blind, and they think it a marvelous thing[4] the calamity of blindness that has befallen such a man and other such calamities.

Now the true way of considering this is that all the existent individuals of the human species and, all the more, those of the other species of the animals are things of no value at all in comparison with the whole that exists and endures. It has made this clear, saying: *Man is like unto vanity, and so on.*[5] *Man, that is a worm; and the son of man, that is a maggot.*[6] *How much less in them that dwell in houses of clay, and so on.*[7] *Behold, the nations are as a drop of a bucket, and so on.*[8] There are also all the other passages figuring in the texts of the books of the prophets concerning this sublime and grave subject, which is most useful in giving man knowledge of his true value, so that he should not make the mistake of thinking that what

4. More or less literally: they think it great.   5. Ps. 144:4.   6. Job 25:6.
7. Job 4:19.   8. Isa. 40:15.

exists is in existence only for the sake of him as an individual. According to us, on the other hand, what exists is in existence because of the will of its Creator; and among the things that are in existence, the species of man is the least in comparison to the superior existents — I refer to the spheres and the stars. As far as comparison with the angels is concerned, there is in true reality no relation[9] between man and them. Man is merely the most noble among the things that are subject to generation, namely, in this our | nether world; I mean to say that he is the noblest thing that is composed of the elements. Withal his existence is for him a great good and a benefit on the part of God because of the properties with which He has singled him out and perfected him. The greater part of the evils that befall its individuals are due to the latter, I mean the deficient individuals of the human species. It is because of our own deficiencies that we lament and we call for aid. We suffer because of evils that we have produced ourselves of our free will; but we attribute them to God, may He be exalted above this; just as He explains in His book, saying: *Is corruption His? No; His children's is the blemish, and so on.*[10] *Solomon* too has explained this, saying: *The foolishness of man perverteth his way; and his heart fretteth against the Lord.*[11] The explanation of this lies in the fact that all the evils that befall man fall under one of three species.

The first species of evil is that which befalls man because of the nature of coming-to-be and passing-away, I mean to say because of his being endowed with matter. Because of this, infirmities and paralytic afflictions befall some individuals either in consequence of their original natural disposition, or they supervene because of changes occurring in the elements, such as corruption of the air or a fire from heaven and a landslide. We have already explained that divine wisdom has made it obligatory that there should be no coming-to-be except through passing-away. Were it not for the passing-away of the individuals, the coming-to-be relating to the species would not continue. Thus that pure beneficence, that munificence, that activity causing good to overflow, are made clear. He who wishes to be endowed with flesh and bones and at the same time not be subject to impressions and not to be attained by any of the concomitants of matter merely wishes, without being aware of it, to combine two contraries, namely, to be subject to impressions and not to be subject to them. For if he were not liable to receive impressions, he would not have been generated, and what exists of him would have been one single individual and not a multitude of individuals belonging

9. Or: proportion.   10. Deut. 32:5.   11. Prov. 19:3.

to one species.[12] Galen has put it well in the third of the book of "Utilities,"[13] saying: Do not set | your mind on the vain thought that it is possible that out of menstrual blood and sperm there should be generated a living being that does not die, is not subject to pain, is in perpetual motion, or is as brilliant as the sun. This dictum of Galen draws attention to one particular case falling under a general proposition. That proposition is as follows: Everything that is capable of being generated from any matter whatever, is generated in the most perfect way in which it is possible to be generated out of that specific matter; the deficiency attaining the individuals of the species corresponds to the deficiency of the particular matter of the individual. Now the ultimate term and the most perfect thing that may be generated out of blood and sperm is the human species with its well-known nature consisting in man's being a living, rational,[14] and mortal being. Thus this species of evils must necessarily exist. Withal you will find that the evils of this kind that befall men are very few and occur only seldom. For you will find cities, existing for thousands of years, that have never been flooded or burned. Also thousands of people are born in perfect health whereas the birth of an infirm human being is an anomaly, or at least — if someone objects to the word anomaly and does not use it — such an individual is very rare; for they do not form a hundredth or even a thousandth part of those born in good health.

The evils of the second kind are those that men inflict upon one another, such as tyrannical domination of some of them over others. These evils are more numerous than those belonging to the first kind, and the reasons for that are numerous and well known. The evils in question also come from us. However, the wronged man has no device against them. At the same time, there is no city existing anywhere in the whole world in which evil of this kind is in any way widespread and predominant[15] among the inhabitants of that city; but its existence is also rare — in the cases, for instance, when one individual surprises | another individual and kills him or robs him by night. This kind of evil becomes common, reaching many people, only in the course of great wars; and such events too do not form the majority of occurrences upon the earth taken as a whole.

12. As Munk has seen, Maimonides here wishes to express the thought that if man were not subject to impressions and were not generated, there would be only a single individual in the human species. This is the case with the heavenly spheres; the body and soul of each of them constitute one individual, the sole one of its species.
13. I.e., *De usu partium humani corporis*. The passage quoted is to be found in Book III, chap. 10 (ed. Kuhn, III, 238). The translation is accurate.
14. Or: capable of speech.
15. More or less literally: belongs to the majority of what happens.

The evils of the third kind are those that are inflicted upon any individual among us by his own action; this is what happens in the majority of cases, and these evils are much more numerous than those of the second kind. All men lament over evils of this kind; and it is only seldom that you find one who is not guilty of having brought them upon himself. He who is reached by them deserves truly to be blamed. To him one may say what has been said: *This hath been to you of your own doing.*[16] It has also been said: *He doeth it that would destroy his own soul.*[17] *Solomon* has said about evils of this kind: *The foolishness of man perverteth his way, and so on.*[18] He also has explained with reference to evils of this kind that they are done by man to himself; his dictum being: *Behold, this only have I found, that God made man upright; but they have sought out many thoughts;*[19] these thoughts are those that have been vanquished by these evils. About this kind it has also been said: *For affliction cometh not forth from the dust, neither doth trouble spring out of the ground.*[20] Immediately afterwards it is explained that this sort of evil is brought into existence by man, for it is said: *For man is born unto trouble, and so on.*[21] This kind is consequent upon all vices, I mean concupiscence for eating, drinking, and copulation, and doing these things with excess in regard to quantity or irregularly or when the quality of the foodstuffs is bad. For this is the cause of all corporeal and psychical diseases and ailments. With regard to the diseases of the body, this is manifest. With regard to the diseases of the soul due to this evil regimen, they arise in two ways: | In the first place, through the alteration necessarily affecting the soul in consequence of the alteration of the body, the soul being a corporeal faculty — it having already been said that the moral qualities of the soul are consequent upon the temperament of the body. And in the second place, because of the fact that the soul becomes familiarized with, and accustomed to, unnecessary things and consequently acquires the habit of desiring things that are unnecessary either for the preservation of the individual or for the preservation of the species; and this desire is something infinite. For whereas all necessary things are restricted and limited, that which is superfluous is unlimited. If, for instance, your desire is directed to having silver plate, it would be better if it were of gold; some have crystal plate; and perhaps plate is procured that is made out of emeralds and rubies, whenever these stones are to be found. Thus every ignoramus who thinks worthless thoughts is always sad and despondent because he is not able to achieve the luxury attained by someone else. In most cases such a man exposes himself to great

16. Mal. 1:9. The words *to you* do not occur in this verse of the Bible.   17. Prov. 6:32.
18. Prov. 19:3.   19. Eccles. 7:29.   20. Job 5:6.   21. Job 5:7.

dangers, such as arise in sea voyages and the service of kings; his aim therein being to obtain these unnecessary luxuries. When, however, he is stricken by misfortunes in these courses he has pursued, he complains about God's decree and predestination and begins to put the blame on the temporal and to be astonished at the latter's injustice in not helping him to obtain great wealth, which would permit him to procure a great deal of wine so as always to be drunk and a number of concubines adorned with gold and precious stones of various kinds so as to move him to copulate more than he is able so as to experience pleasure — as if the end of existence consisted merely in the pleasure of such an ignoble man. The error of the multitude has arrived at the point where they impute to the Creator deficiency of power because of His having produced that which exists and endowed it with a nature entailing, | according to their imagination, these great evils; inasmuch as this nature does not help every vicious man to achieve the satisfaction of his vice so that his corrupt soul should reach the term of its demand, which, according to what we have explained, has no limit. On the other hand, men of excellence and knowledge have grasped and understood the wisdom manifested in that which exists, as *David* has set forth, saying: *All the paths of the Lord are mercy and truth unto such as keep His covenant and His testimonies.*[22] By this he says that those who keep to the nature of that which exists, keep the commandments of the Law, and know the ends of both, apprehend clearly the excellency and the true reality of the whole. For this reason they take as their end that for which they were intended as men, namely, apprehension. And because of the necessity of the body, they seek what is necessary for it, *bread to eat, and raiment to put on,*[23] without any luxury. If one restricts oneself to what is necessary, this is the easiest of things and may be obtained with a very small effort. Whatever in it that is seen as difficult and hard for us is due to the following reason: when one endeavors to seek what is unnecessary, it becomes difficult to find even what is necessary. For the more frequently hopes cling to the superfluous, the more onerous does the matter become; forces and revenues are spent for what is unnecessary and that which is necessary is not found. You ought to consider the circumstances in which we are placed with regard to its being found.[24] For the more a thing is necessary for a living being, the more often it may be found and the cheaper it is. On the other hand, the less necessary it is, the less often it is found and it is very expensive. Thus, for instance, the necessary for man is air, water, and food. But air is the most necessary, for

22. Ps. 25:10.   23. Gen. 28:20.
24. The expression translated "being found" also means "existence."

nobody can be without it for a moment without perishing. As for water, one can remain without it for a day or two. Accordingly air is indubitably easier to find and cheaper than water. | Water is more necessary than food, for certain people may remain, if they drink and do not eat, for four or five days without food. Accordingly in every city you find water more frequently and at a cheaper price than food. Things are similar with regard to food-stuffs; those that are most necessary are easier to find at a given place and cheaper than the unnecessary. Regarding musk, amber, rubies, and emeralds, I do not think that anyone of sound intellect can believe that man has strong need for them unless it be for medical treatment; and even in such cases, they and other similar things can be replaced by numerous herbs and earths.

This is a manifestation of the beneficence and munificence of God, may He be exalted, shown even with regard to this weak living creature. Regarding manifestations of His justice, may He be exalted, and of the equality established by Him between them, they are very evident. For within the domain of natural generation and corruption, there is no case in which an individual animal belonging to any species whatever of animals is distinguished from another individual of the same species by having a special faculty possessed only by him or by having an additional part of the body. For all natural, psychic, and animal faculties and all the parts that are found in one particular individual are also found, as far as essence is concerned, in another — even though there be accidentally a deficiency because of something that has supervened and that is not according to nature. But this is rare, as we have made clear. There in no way exists a relation of superiority and inferiority between individuals conforming to the course of nature except that which follows necessarily from the differences in the disposition of the various kinds of matter; this being necessary on account of the nature of the matter of the particular species and not specially intended for one individual rather than another. As for the fact that one individual possesses many sachets and clothes adorned with gold whereas another lacks these superfluities of life, there is no injustice and no inequity in this. | He who has obtained these luxuries has not gained thereby an increment in his substance. He has only obtained a false imagining or a plaything. And he who lacks the superfluities of life is not necessarily deficient. *And he that gathered much had nothing over, and he that gathered little had no lack; they gathered every man according to his eating.*[25] This is what happens for the most part at

25. Exod. 16:18.

every time and at every place. And, as we have made clear, no attention should be paid to anomalies.

Through the two considerations that have been set forth, His beneficence, may He be exalted, with regard to His creatures will become clear to you, in that He brings into existence what is necessary according to its order of importance and in that He makes individuals of the same species equal at their creation. With a view to this true consideration, the Master of those who know[26] says: *For all His ways are judgment.*[27] And *David* says: *All the paths of the Lord are mercy and truth, and so on,*[28] as we have made clear. *David* also says explicitly: *The Lord is good to all; and His tender mercies are over all His works.*[29] For His bringing us into existence is absolutely the great good, as we have made clear, and the creation of the governing faculty in the living beings is an indication of His mercifulness with regard to them, as we have made clear.

CHAPTER 13

Often the minds of perfect men have grown perplexed over the question of what is the final end of that which exists. Now I will explain that in all schools this question is abolished. I say then that in the case of every agent who acts with a purpose, the thing he has done must necessarily have some end with a view to which it has been done. According to philosophic speculation, this is clear and is not in need of demonstration. It is also clear that a thing that has been done in this way with a purpose must have been produced in time after | not having existed. Among the things that are clear also belongs the fact, and this fact universally admitted, that He whose existence is necessary, who has never and will never be nonexistent, does not need an agent, as we have already made clear.[1] And as He has not been made,[2] no question as to the final end arises with reference to Him. For this reason, one does not ask: What is the final end of the existence of the Creator, may He be exalted?; for He is not a created thing. Through these premises it has become clear that a final end can only be sought with regard to all things produced in time that have been made through the purpose of an intelligent being. I mean to say that with regard to that which has its begin-

26. I.e., Moses.   27. Deut. 32:4.   28. Ps. 25:10.   29. Ps. 145:9.
 1. Cf. II Introduction, 20th premise.   2. By an agent.

ning in an intellect,[3] one necessarily must seek to find out what its final cause is. On the other hand, one must not, as we have said, seek the final end of what has not been produced in time. After this preamble, you should know that the final end of all that exists ought not to be sought — neither according to our opinion who assert that the world has been produced in time nor according to the opinion of Aristotle who holds that the world is eternal. For according to his opinion as to the eternity of the world, no ultimate end should be sought for any part of the world. For according to his opinion, it is not permitted to ask: What is the final end of the existence of the heavens, and why have they such and such dimensions and such and such numbers? or: Why is matter as it is? or: What is the final end of this particular species of animals or of plants? For all things derive, according to him, from an eternal necessity that has never ceased and will never cease. Though natural science seeks to find out the final end of every natural being, that end is not the ultimate end of which we treat in this chapter. For it is manifest, according to natural science, that every natural existent must necessarily have a final end; but that final cause, which is the noblest among the four causes, is hidden as far as the majority of species are concerned. Aristotle constantly states in an explicit way that nature does nothing | in vain, meaning thereby that every natural act has a certain final end. Aristotle also states in express terms that the plants have been created for the sake of the animals.[4] Similarly he explains with regard to certain beings that some exist for the sake of others; he does this in particular with regard to the limbs of animals.[5]

Know that the existence of this final end in natural things has of necessity led the philosophers to a belief in a principle other than nature; namely, the one that Aristotle calls the intellectual or divine principle, that being the one that makes one thing for the sake of another. Know too that to the mind of an equitable man, one of the strongest proofs for the production of the world in time is the fact, demonstrated with reference to natural beings, that every one of these has a certain final end, some of them existing for the sake of others; for this is a proof of purpose on the part of a being possessing purpose. And purpose can only be conceived with reference to the production in time of something so produced.

I shall return to the subject of this chapter, namely, to the discussion of final end. I say then: Aristotle has made it clear that in natural things the

3. More or less literally: that which has an intellectual beginning (or: principle).
4. Cf. Aristotle *Politics* i.8.1256b16; *Plants* i.2.817b25.
5. Cf. Aristotle *De partibus animalium* i.5.645b14.

agent,[6] the form, and the final end, are one and the same thing; I mean to say that they are one and the same thing in species. For, to take an example, the form of Zayd is the agent producing the form of the individual ʿUmar, who is his son; the thing it does is to give to ʿUmar's matter a form pertaining to its species, the final end of ʿUmar consisting in his having a human form. According to him, this is the case with regard to all individuals belonging to natural species, which are in need of reproduction; for in these, the three causes[7] belong to one species. However, all of this refers but to the first finality.[8] Regarding the ultimate finality of every species, all those who discourse on nature deem that it is indispensable, but that it is very difficult to know; all the more is this so of the finality of what exists as a whole. What appears to result from the discourse of Aristotle is that, | according to him, the ultimate finality of these species consists in the permanence of coming-to-be and passing-away, which is[9] indispensable for the continuance of coming-to-be in this inferior matter, since it is impossible that the individuals composed out of it should endure. Still, the end that can be generated, I mean the most perfect thing that is possible, is generated from it. For the ultimate purpose consists in bringing about perfection. And it is manifest that the most perfect thing, whose existence out of this matter is possible, is man; he is the last and the most perfect of these compounds. Accordingly even if it is said that all sublunar beings exist for his sake,[10] that would be true from this point of view; I mean because the movement of changeable things exists for the sake of coming-to-be in order that what is as perfect as it is possible to be should come about. Aristotle ought not to be asked concerning the finality of man's existence, seeing that he holds the doctrine affirming the eternity of the world. For, according to him, the first finality for every individual produced in time consists in the perfection of the form of the species. Consequently every individual in whom the acts necessarily deriving from that form are perfected, has achieved its finality perfectly and completely. The ultimate finality of the species is the permanence of this form through the continuance of generation and corruption so that there should always be a new process of generation in which the greatest possible perfection is sought. It is accordingly clear that, according to the doctrine of eternity, the question of ultimate finality for being as a whole does not arise.

On the other hand, it is sometimes thought that, according to our opinion and our doctrine of the production in time of the world as a whole

6. I.e., the efficient cause.   7. I.e., the efficient, formal, and final causes.
8. *ghāya.* This word has been translated "final end" in the preceding part of this chapter.
9. According to Ibn Tibbon's version: which are.   10. I.e., for man's sake.

after nonexistence, this question is obligatory — I mean that it is obligatory to seek out the finality of all that exists. It is likewise thought that the finality of all that exists is solely the existence of the human species so that it should worship God, and that all that has been made has been made for it alone so that even the heavenly spheres only revolve in order to be useful to it and to bring into existence | that which is necessary for it. Some passages in the books of the prophets, if taken according to their external sense, give strong support to this thought. Thus: *He formed it to be inhabited;*[11] *If My covenant had not been with day and night, I would not have appointed the statutes of heaven and earth;*[12] *And spreadeth them out as a tent to dwell in.*[13] Now if the spheres exist for the sake of man, all the more is this the case for all the species of animals and of plants. However, if this opinion is carefully examined, as opinions ought to be carefully examined by intelligent men, the flaw in it becomes clear. This result is achieved through posing to him who believes this opinion the following question: The final end being the existence of man, is the Creator able to bring him into existence without all these preliminaries, or was it possible for him to be brought into existence only after they were carried out? If someone answers that this is possible and that, for instance, God was able to bring man into existence without there being a heaven, the following question may be posed. What is the utility for him[14] of all these things, which are in themselves not the final end, but exist for the sake of a thing that could have existed without all of them? Even if the universe[15] exists for the sake of man, and the final end of man is, as has been said, to worship God, a question remains to be asked regarding the final end of his worship. For He, may He be exalted, would not acquire greater perfection if He were worshipped by all that He has created and were truly apprehended by them, nor would He be attained by a deficiency if nothing whatever existed except Him. If the answer is given that this is not with a view to His perfection, but to our perfection, for that is the most excellent thing for us — namely, our perfection — the same question follows necessarily: namely, what is the final end of our existence with that perfection? Necessarily and obligatorily the

11. Isa. 45:18.

12. Jer. 33:25. This explanation of the verse, which Maimonides evidently had in mind, is suggested in B.T., Pesaḥim, 68b, and is referred to in Rashi's commentary; however, the latter remarks that it does not fit in with the rest of the passage. The probable translation of the quoted portion of the verse is that given in the English Bible: *If My covenant be not with day and night, if I have not appointed the ordinances of heaven and earth.*

13. Isa. 40:22.   14. Probably God is referred to here.   15. Literally: the all.

argument must end with the answer being given that the final end is: God has wished it so, or: His wisdom has required this to be so. And this is the correct answer. Accordingly you will find that the *Sages of Israel* have inserted into the text of their prayers:[16] *Thou hast set man apart from the beginning and acknowledged him | that he should stand before Thee. Yet who shall say unto Thee, What dost Thou? and if he be righteous, what boon is this to Thee?* Thus they have explicitly stated that there does not exist a final end, but only the Will alone.[17] Now this being so and, in addition, given the belief in the production of the world in time — thus making it indispensable for us to say that what exists, its causes, and its effects, could be different from what they are — an incongruity follows necessarily with reference to the existence of everything brought into existence except man. It follows, namely, that all the beings in question have been brought into existence without any final end at all, inasmuch as the only purposed final end, namely, man, could have existed without all of them.

For this reason, to my mind, the correct view according to the beliefs of the Law — a view that corresponds likewise to the speculative views — is as follows: It should not be believed that all the beings exist for the sake of the existence of man. On the contrary, all the other beings too have been intended for their own sakes and not for the sake of something else. Thus even according to our view holding that the world has been produced in time, the quest for the final end of all the species of beings collapses. For we say that in virtue of His will He has brought into existence all the parts of the world, some of which have been intended for their own sakes, whereas others have been intended for the sake of some other thing that is intended for its own sake. Just as He has willed that the human species should come to exist, He also has willed that the spheres and their stars should come to exist; and He also has willed that the angels should come to exist. In respect to every being He intended that being itself; and whenever the existence of some thing was impossible unless it was preceded by some other thing, He first brought that thing into existence — as in the case of the senses, which precede reason.

This view too has been expressed in the prophetic books. Thus it says: *The Lord hath made everything lamaᶜanehu [for His sake or for its sake],*[18] where the third person[19] may refer to the complement.[20] If, however, it refers to the subject, the interpretation of the word[21] would be: for the sake

16. The following passage is in the prayer called *Neᶜilah*, recited on the Day of Atonement.
17. Or: except the Will alone.   18. Prov. 16:4.   19. I.e., *His* or *its*.
20. I.e., to *everything*.   21. Of *lamaᶜanehu*.

of His essence, may He be exalted—that is, | for the sake of His will, as the latter is His essence, according to what has been made clear in this Treatise.[22] We have already explained that His essence is also called *His glory*, as in its saying: *Show me, I pray Thee, Thy glory*.[23] Thus his saying here, *The Lord hath made everything lamacanehu [for His sake]*, would be like saying: *Everyone that is called by My name, and whom I have created for My glory, I have formed him, yea, I have made him*.[24] It says that everything whose making is ascribed to Me,[25] has been made by Me solely because of My will. The expression, *I have formed him, yea, I have made him*, refers to what I have explained to you, namely, to the fact that there are beings whose existence is only possible after that of something else. Thus He might say: I have created that first thing, as for instance matter, which must indispensably have come prior to everything material. Then I made in that thing which came first or after it that which I intended to bring into existence, without there being anything[26] except will alone.

If you consider that book which guides all those who seek guidance toward what is correct and therefore is called *Torah*,[27] the notion that we have in view will become manifest to you from the commencement of the *Account of the Beginning*[28] till the end. For with reference to none of them[29] is the statement made in any way that it exists for the sake of some other thing. He only says that He brought every part of the world into existence and that its existence conformed to its purpose. This is the meaning of his saying: *And God saw that it was good [tob]*.[30] For you know what we have explained with regard to their saying: *The Torah speaketh in the language of the sons of man*.[31] And *good [tob]* is an expression applied by us to what conforms to our purpose. About the whole,[32] it says: *And God saw everything that He had made, and, behold, it was very good [tob meʾod]*.[33] For the production in time of everything that was produced conformed to its purpose, and nothing went wrong. And that is the meaning of the expression: *very [meʾod]*; for sometimes a thing is *good* and conforms for a time to our purpose, whereas afterwards the goal is missed. Accordingly it gives the information that all the things made, conformed to | His intention and purpose

---

22. Cf. I 53.   23. Exod. 33:18. Cf. I 64.   24. Isa. 43:7.
25. Certain manuscripts have a text that may be translated: everything that may be ascribed to My action. Ibn Tibbon's translation conforms to the one given in this note.
26. In the way of finality.
27. The word derives from the verb *horoth* (to show the way).
28. I.e., the story of the Creation.   29. I.e., of the things created.   30. Cf. Gen. 1.
31. B.T., Yebamoth, 71a; B.T., Baba Meṣiʿa, 31b. Cf. I 26.
32. The whole work of Creation.   33. Gen. 1:31.

and that they continued without ceasing to correspond to what was intended with regard to them. Be not misled by its saying with regard to the stars, *To give light upon the earth, and to rule over the day and over the night,*[34] so that you think that it means: in order that they should do this.[35] It is merely information about their nature, which He willed to create thus — I mean to say, giving light and ruling. Similarly it says of *man, And have dominion over the fish of the sea, and so on,*[36] which dictum does not mean that man was created for the sake of this, but merely gives information about man's nature with which He, may He be exalted, has stamped him. As for its saying with regard to the plants[37] — namely, that they are given over to the Adamites and the other animals — Aristotle[38] and others have made explicit statements about this; and it is manifest that plants were brought into existence only for the sake of the animals, for these must of necessity be nourished. However, this does not apply to the stars; I mean to say that they do not exist for our sake and so that good should come to us from them. For, as we have made clear, its dictum, *to give light and to rule,* merely gives information about the utility of what comes from them and overflows toward that which is below, according to what I have made clear to you concerning the nature of the constant overflow of the good from one thing toward another. As far as what is reached by the good that is always coming is concerned, it may seem that what receives the benefit is the final end of the thing that caused its good and its liberality to overflow toward it. Thus an individual from among the people of a city might think that the final end of the ruler consists in safeguarding his[39] house at night against robbers. And this is true from a certain point of view. For since his house is safeguarded and this benefit comes to him because of the ruler, the matter looks as if the final end of the ruler were the safeguarding of the house of that individual. We must interpret in this sense every text whose external sense we find indicates that something sublime has been made for the sake of something inferior to it; this text means that this act follows necessarily from the nature of the sublime.

Thus we are obliged | to believe that all that exists was intended by Him, may He be exalted, according to His volition. And we shall seek for it no cause or other final end whatever. Just as we do not seek for the end of His existence, may He be exalted, so do we not seek for the final end of His

34. Gen. 1:17–18.
35. I.e., that the stars were created in order to give light upon the earth, and to rule over the day and over the night.
36. Gen. 1:28.   37. Cf. Gen. 1:29.   38. Cf. above in this chapter.
39. I.e., the individual's.

volition, according to which all that has been and will be produced in time comes into being as it is. Hence be not misled in your soul to think that the spheres and the angels have been brought into existence for our sake. For it has explained to us what we are worth: *Behold, the nations are as a drop of a bucket.*[40] Consider accordingly your substance and that of the spheres, the stars, and the separate intellects; then the truth will become manifest to you, and you will know that man and nothing else is the most perfect and the most noble thing that has been generated from this [inferior] matter; but that if his being is compared to that of the spheres and all the more to that of the separate beings, it is very, very contemptible. Accordingly it says: *Behold, He putteth no trust in His servants, and His angels He chargeth with deficiency [tahalah]. How much less in them that dwell in houses of clay, whose foundation is in the dust!*[41] Know that *His servants* that are referred to in this *verse* do not belong at all to the human species; this is proven by its saying: *How much less in them that dwell in houses of clay whose foundation is in the dust!* But *His servants* mentioned in this *verse* are the angels. Similarly also, *His angels* referred to in this *verse* are indubitably the spheres. The same notion is made clear and repeated by *Eliphaz* himself in different terms and in another text, saying: *Behold, He putteth no trust in His holy ones; yea, the heavens are not clean in His sight. How much less one that is abominable and impure, man [ish] who drinketh iniquity [ʿavlah] like water!*[42]

Thus it is made clear that *His holy ones* are identical with *His servants* and that they do not belong to the human species. *His angels,* which are referred to in this *verse,* are the *heavens.* And the word *deficiency [tahalah]* means the same thing as *are not clean in His sight.* I refer to their being endowed with matter. And though they have | the purest and most luminous matter, it is — if compared to the separate intellects — obscure, dark, and not clear. As for its saying regarding the angels, *Behold, He putteth no trust in His servants,* it means that they have no trustworthy existence. For, according to our opinion, they are made; according to the opinion of those who profess the doctrine of the eternity of the world, they are caused. And their part in existence is not trustworthy or fixed if compared with Him, may He be exalted, the absolutely necessary being. The words, *How much less one that is abominable and impure,* correspond to the words, *How much less in them that dwell in houses of clay.* It is as if it said: *How much less one that is*

40. Isa. 40:15.   41. Job 4:18–19.   42. Job 15:15–16.

abominable and impure, the human being [*ha-adam*] with whom obliquity[43] is mingled, spread, as it is, through all his members. I mean to say that privation is his concomitant. *ʿAvlah* means iniquity: *In the land of upright-ness will he deal iniquitously* [*yeʿavvel*].[44] Its saying *ish* [*man*][45] is like its saying *adam* [*human being*]; for sometimes the human species is called *ish* [*man*]: *He that smiteth a man* [*ish*], *so that he dieth.*[46]

This is what one ought to believe. For when man knows his own soul, makes no mistakes with regard to it, and understands every being according to what it is, he becomes calm and his thoughts are not troubled by seeking a final end for what has not that final end; or by seeking any final end for what has no final end except its own existence, which depends on the divine will — if you prefer you can also say: on the divine wisdom.

CHAPTER 14

What man ought also to consider in order to know what his own soul is worth and to make no mistake regarding this point, is what has been made clear concerning the dimensions of the spheres and of the stars and the measures of the distances separating us from them. For | the measures of all the distances with reference to half the diameter of the earth having been made clear and the dimensions of the diameter of the earth and con-sequently those of its half diameter being known, all the distances are known. Accordingly it has been demonstrated that the distance between the center of the earth and the highest part of the sphere of Saturn is one that could be covered in approximately eight thousand and seven hundred years of three hundred sixty-five days each, if each day a distance is covered of forty of our legal miles, of which each has two thousand of the cubits used for working purposes. Consider this great and terrifying distance. It conforms to what is said: *Is not God in the height of heaven? and behold the topmost of the stars, how high they are!*[1] This means: can you not draw from the height of heaven a conclusion as to the remoteness of the apprehension of the deity? For if we are at such an extreme remoteness from that body,

---

43. "Obliquity" is the literal translation of the Arabic term used by Maimonides. Obviously the figurative meaning "moral iniquity" is intended.
44. Isa. 26:10.   45. Cf. Job. 15:16.   46. Exod. 21:12.
1. Job 22:12.

which in point of place is so far away from us, so that its substance and most of its actions are hidden from us, this applies all the more to the apprehension of its maker, who is not a body. This great distance that has been demonstrated is only a minimum. It is not possible that the distance between the center of the earth and the concavity of the sphere of the fixed stars should be less than that measure, but it is possible that it be many times greater. For the thickness of the bodies of the spheres has only been demonstrated with respect to its minimum possible dimensions, as is made clear in the Epistles concerning distances. Similarly it is impossible to determine exactly the thickness of the bodies that, according to Thābit,[2] reasoning forces us to admit between every two spheres. For in these bodies there are no stars from which an inference can be drawn. As for the sphere of the fixed stars, its minimum thickness is equal to the distance that can be covered in | four years. This is known from the measure of some[3] of its stars, the body of each of these stars being ninety-odd times as great as that of the terrestrial globe. It is, however, possible that the thickness of their body[4] is even greater. As for the ninth sphere, which causes the universe[5] to accomplish the diurnal motion, its dimension is not known at all; for no star is to be found in it, and consequently we have no device enabling us to know its size. Consider how vast are the dimensions and how great the number of these corporeal beings. If the whole of the earth would not constitute even the smallest part of the sphere of the fixed stars, what is the relation of the human species to all these created things, and how can one of us imagine that they exist for his sake and because of him and that they are instruments for his benefit?

This is the state of things when the bodies are compared. How then would things look if you consider the existence of the intellects? Sometimes doubts are expressed concerning the opinion of the philosophers in this matter. It is said: If we claimed that the final end of the spheres consists in the governance of, for instance, a human, individual or of several individuals this would be impossible according to philosophic speculation. However inasmuch as we think that their final end consists in the governance of the human species, there is no absurdity in thinking that the final end of these great individual bodies is the existence of the individuals of the various

2. Thābit Ibn Qurrah. Cf. II 24, n. 4.

3. According to certain manuscripts: of the distance. This is a reading adopted by Ibn Tibbon, Alḥarizi, and Ibn Falquera.

4. Literally: its body. It seems more probable that the body of the stars, and not, as Munk would have it, the body of the sphere, is meant.

5. Literally: the all.

species, the number of which individuals cannot — according to their doctrine — ever have an end. This would resemble the case of the artisan who
has iron tools weighing one hundred-weight in order to manufacture a
small needle weighing one grain. If this were done for the sake of one
needle, this would have been bad management from the point of view of a
certain speculation, even though not in an absolute sense. But in view of the
fact that with the help of these heavy tools he manufactures one needle after
another | and thus several hundred-weights of needles, the making of these
tools is in all respects an act of wisdom and of good management. Similarly
the final end of the spheres consists in the continuance of coming-to-be and
passing-away; and the final end of coming-to-be and passing-away consists,
as has already been said, in the existence of the human species. We can find
texts and traditions that support this imagining.

However, the philosopher will resolve the doubt by saying: If the
difference between the bodies of the spheres and the individuals belonging
to the species subject to generation and corruption had only consisted in their
respective bigness and smallness, this objection would be possible. However,
seeing the difference there is between them concerning the nobleness of
substance, it would have been most disgraceful if what is nobler served as
an instrument for the existence of what is most base and vile.

To sum up: This doubt may be called upon to help us in our belief
concerning the production of the world in time, which notion was my main
object in this chapter. Besides there is the fact that I have always heard from
all those who had some smattering of the science of astronomy, that what the
Sages, may their memory be blessed, have said regarding distances[6] was
exaggerated. For they have clearly stated that the thickness of every sphere
equals a distance that can be covered in five hundred years and that the
distance between every two spheres can only be covered in five hundred
years.[7] There are seven spheres in all;[8] consequently the distance of the
seventh sphere, I mean its convex part, from the center of the earth can
only be covered in seven thousand years. Whoever hears this must imagine
that in these words there is great exaggeration and that the distance does
not reach this measure. However, from what has been demonstrated with
regard to distances, it has become clear to you that the distance between the
center of the earth and the lower part of the sphere of Saturn, which is the
seventh sphere, can only be covered in approximately seven thousand and
twenty-four years. As for the distance mentioned by us, which can only be

6. I.e., the astronomical distances.   7. Cf. J.T., Berakhoth, 1a.
8. According to the talmudic Sages.

covered in eight thousand seven hundred years, it | goes up to the concavity of the eighth sphere. When you find that [the Sages] say that between every two spheres there is such and such a distance, this refers to the thickness of the body found between the spheres and does not mean that there is a vacuum there.

Do not ask of me to show that everything they have said concerning astronomical matters conforms to the way things really are. For at that time mathematics were imperfect. They did not speak about this as transmitters of dicta of the prophets, but rather because in those times they were men of knowledge in these fields or because they had heard these dicta from the men of knowledge who lived in those times. Because of this I will not say with regard to dicta of theirs, which, as we find, corresponds to the truth, that they are incorrect or have been said fortuitously. For whenever it is possible to interpret the words of an individual in such a manner that they conform to a being whose existence has been demonstrated, this is the conduct that is most fitting and most suitable for an equitable man of excellent nature.

CHAPTER 15

The impossible has a stable nature, one whose stability is constant and is not made by a maker; it is impossible to change it in any way. Hence the power over the maker of the impossible is not attributed to the deity. This is a point about which none of the men of speculation differs in any way. And none but those who do not understand the intelligibles, is ignorant of this. The point about which there is difference of opinion among all the men of speculation concerns a certain species of imaginable things, with regard to which one[1] of the men of speculation says that they belong to the class of impossible things regarding which that power to change them cannot be attributed to the deity, whereas another says that | it belongs to the class of possible things depending on the power of the deity to be brought into existence when He wills. Thus, for example, the coming together of contraries at the same instant and at the same place and the transmutation of substances, I mean the transformation of a substance into an accident and of an accident into a substance, or the existence of a corporeal substance without

1. Or: some.

there being an accident in it — all of these things belong to the class of the impossible according to all men of speculation. Likewise that God should bring into existence someone like Himself, or should annihilate Himself, or should become a body, or should change — all of these things belong to the class of the impossible; and the power to do any of these things cannot be attributed to God. Regarding the question whether He is able to bring into existence an accident that exists alone, not in a substance, a group among the men of speculation, namely, the Muʿtazila, have imagined this and held that it was possible, whereas others have asserted that it was impossible. It is true that those who assert that an accident may exist without a substratum are not led to this affirmation by speculation alone, but wished to safeguard thereby certain doctrines[2] of the Law that are violently rebutted by speculation; thus the assertion in question was a way out for them. Similarly the bringing into being of a corporeal thing out of no matter whatever, belongs — according to us — to the class of the possible, and to the class of the impossible — according to the philosophers. The philosophers say similarly that to bring into being a square whose diagonal is equal to one of its sides or a corporeal angle encompassed by four plane right angles and other similar things belong all of them to the class of the impossible; and some of those who are ignorant of mathematics and, concerning these matters, know only the words by themselves and do not conceive their notion, think that they are possible.

Would that I knew whether this gate is open and licit, so that everyone can claim and assert with regard to any notion whatever that he conceives: This is possible; whereas someone else says: No, this is impossible because of the nature of the matter. Or is there something that shuts and blocks this gate so that | a man can assert decisively that such and such a thing is impossible because of its nature? Should this be verified and examined with the help of the imaginative faculty or with the intellect? And by what can one differentiate between that which is imagined and that which is cognized by the intellect? For an individual sometimes disagrees with someone else or with himself with regard to a thing that in his opinion is possible, so that he asserts that by its nature it is possible; whereas the objector says: This assertion that it is possible is the work of the imagination and not due to consideration by the intellect. Is there accordingly something that permits differentiation between the imaginative faculty and the intellect? And is that thing something altogether outside both the intellect and the imagination, or is it by the intellect itself that one distinguishes between that which is

2. Literally: matters.

cognized by the intellect and that which is imagined? All these are points for investigation, which may lead very far. However, this is not the object of this chapter.

It has then become clear that, according to every opinion and school, there are impossible things whose existence cannot be admitted. Power to bring them about cannot be ascribed to the deity. The fact that He does not change them signifies neither inability nor deficiency of power on His part. Accordingly they are necessarily as they are and are not due to the act of an agent. It has then become clear that the point with regard to which there is disagreement concerns the things that could be supposed to belong to either of the two classes — whether they belong to the class of the possible or to the class of the impossible. Learn this.

CHAPTER 16

An aberrant opinion is professed by the philosophers concerning God, may He be exalted, with respect to His knowledge of what is other than He; and it is a very great aberration, and they have stumbled in such a way that neither they nor those who follow them with regard to this opinion can find absolution. I shall let you hear the difficulties through which they were plunged into aberrant opinion. | I shall also let you hear the opinion of our Law about this and our opposition to them in regard to their evil and incongruous opinions concerning God's knowledge.

That which in the first place was mainly responsible for plunging them into, and impelling them toward, this opinion is what appears at first sight to be a lack of order in the circumstances of the human individuals and the fact that among the Adamites some excellent individuals are in a sorry and grievous plight whereas some wicked individuals are in good and pleasurable circumstances. This impelled them to formulate the division that you will now hear. They said: One of two things must be true: God either knows nothing about these individual circumstances and does not comprehend them, or He knows and apprehends them. This is a necessary division. Thereupon they said: If He apprehends and knows them, one of three things must be true: either He orders them, settling them according to the best, the most perfect, and the most accomplished order; or He is incapable of establishing order in them and has no power over them; or again He knows and is able to establish excellent order and governance, but neglects to do it in consequence of His disdain and contempt or in consequence of His jealousy — just as we find among human beings a man who is able to procure a benefit for another individual and who is aware of the latter's need to obtain this benefit from him, but who out of his ill-nature, his wickedness, and his jealousy, begrudges him this benefit and hence does not procure it. This division is likewise necessary and correct. I mean to say that everyone who knows a certain matter must necessarily either exercise care in the governance of what he knows, or neglect it — as a man, for instance, neglects the governance of the cats in his house or of even more contemptible beings; | again sometimes he who exercises care with regard to some matter may be incapable of governing it, though willing to do so. After they had established this division, they decided categorically that two of the three cases — one of which must necessarily be valid with regard to everyone that knows — are impossible with respect to God, may He be exalted; namely, the case in which He would have no power or the case in which He would have power, but not care for the things He knew. For this would create in Him evil or incapacity, and He is exalted above these two things. Thus in the whole division only the following cases remain: either He knows nothing at all of these circumstances, or He knows them and establishes in them the most excellent order. But we at any rate find that they are without order, do not observe analogies, and have no continuity such as they ought to have. Consequently this is a proof that He does not know these circumstances in any way or through any cause whatever. This is what has plunged them at first into this very aberrant opinion. You will find that all that I have summarized for you concerning their divisions and the point I made calling attention to the fact that this is where they erred are clearly set forth in Alexander of Aphrodisias' treatise "On Governance."[1]

See and marvel how they plunged into something worse than that which they tried to avoid and how they were ignorant of a matter to which they were constantly drawing our attention and that they were always explaining to us. As for their plunging into something worse than that which they tried to avoid, it consisted in the fact that in trying to avoid imputing negligence to God, they decided that He is ignorant and that everything that is in this lowly world is hidden from Him, and He does not apprehend it. As for their being ignorant of that to which they were constantly drawing our attention, it consists in their considering what exists from the point of

---

1. *Fi'l-tadbīr*. On this treatise of Alexander of Aphrodisias and its use by Maimonides, cf. Translator's Introduction.

view of the circumstances of human individuals. But the evils befalling the latter derive from them or from the necessity of the nature of matter, as [the philosophers] always say and make clear. We have already made clear what was necessary regarding this.[2] After having established this foundation that destroys every good foundation and deforms the beauty | of every correct opinion, they tried to eliminate its disgracefulness through thinking that the knowledge of these things is impossible for the deity for various reasons. One of them is as follows: Particular things are apprehended by means of the senses only and not by the intellect; but God does not apprehend by means of a sense. Another one is as follows: Particular things are infinite, whereas knowledge consists in comprehending;[3] but what is infinite cannot be comprehended through knowledge. Again another one is as follows: The knowledge of things being produced in time, which are indubitably particular, would necessitate some change in Him; for it involves a renewal of knowledge after knowledge. Because we, the community of those who adhere to Law, claim that He had known them before they came about, they charge us with two disgraceful opinions: first, that science can be attached to pure nonbeing; and second, that the knowledge of a thing being in potentia and of its being in actu is one and the same thing. Their thoughts were sometimes opposed to one another: some[4] of them said that He knows only the species and not the individuals; whereas others[5] said that He knows nothing at all outside Himself, so that, according to this opinion, there is no multiplicity of cognitions there. There are also some philosophers who believe, as we do, that He, may He be exalted, knows ✓ everything and that nothing secret is at all hidden from Him. These are great men,[6] prior in time to Aristotle, who are also mentioned by Alexander in that treatise. But he rejects their opinion, saying that it is principally refuted by the fact that we see that good men are attained by evils and evil men obtain the good things.

To sum up: It has become clear to you that all of them, if they had found that the circumstances of the human individuals are well ordered — according to what appears as order to the multitude — would not at all have plunged into all this speculation and would not have grown confused.[7] What first impelled them toward this speculation was the fact that they considered

2. Cf. III 12.
3. The two senses of this word seem more or less to approximate the two senses of the word *iḥaṭa* used by Maimonides, which means both "to understand" and "to embrace," "to surround."
4. Or: one.   5. Or: another.   6. Of the philosophers.
7. Or: would not have been overhasty.

the circumstances of people, | of the wicked and the good, and that in their opinion these matters were not well ordered; as was said by those among us who were ignorant: *The way of the Lord is not well ordered.*[8]

After I have explained that the discussion concerning knowledge[9] and that concerning providence are connected, I shall begin to explain the opinions of those engaged in speculation concerning providence. After that I shall begin to resolve the doubts expressed with regard to the deity's knowledge of particular things.

CHAPTER 17

The opinions of people about providence are five in all.[1] And all of them are ancient; I mean that they are opinions that have been heard at the time of the prophets, since the true Law has appeared that has illumined all this darkness.

The first opinion is the profession of those that consider that there is no providence at all with regard to anything whatever in all that exists; that everything in it, the heavens and the things other than they, has happened by chance and in accordance with the way things were predisposed; and that there is no one who orders, governs, or is concerned with anything. This is the opinion of Epicurus. He also professes that there are atoms, and holds that they mingle according to chance and that what is generated out of them, is generated by chance. Those in *Israel* who were unbelievers also professed this opinion; they are those of whom it is said: *They have belied the Lord, and said: It is not He.*[2] Aristotle has demonstrated that this opinion is inadmissible; that it cannot be true that all things should have been generated by chance; and that, on the contrary, there is someone who orders and governs them. In what precedes we have already mentioned something of this.[3]

The second opinion is the opinion of those who hold that providence watches over certain things and that these exist through the governance | and the ordering of one who governs and orders, whereas other things are left to chance. This is the opinion of Aristotle. I will sum up for your benefit

8. Ezek. 33:17.   9. I.e., God's knowledge.
1. On Maimonides' sources for this chapter, cf. Translator's Introduction.
2. Jer. 5:12.   3. Cf. II 20.

his opinion on providence. He holds that God, may He be exalted, takes care of the spheres and of what is in them and that for this reason their individuals remain permanently as they are. Alexander has formulated this, saying that in Aristotle's opinion God's providence ends at the sphere of the moon. This is a branch deriving from his root doctrine concerning the eternity of the world, for he believes that providence corresponds to the nature of what exists. Accordingly with regard to the spheres, whose individuals are permanent, and what is in them, providence regarding them means that they remain permanent in a changeless state. But just as the existence of other things — whose individuals have not, but whose species have, an enduring existence — derives necessarily from theirs, there is likewise an overflow from the providence in question, which overflow necessitates the durability and permanence of the species, though the durability of the latter's individuals be impossible. However, the individuals of every species are also not neglected in every respect. For in all portions of this matter that have been purified to the point of receiving the form of growth, there are placed faculties that preserve them for a certain time through attracting toward them that which agrees with them and through repelling that which is not useful for them. Again in those portions of the matter in question that have been purified to a greater extent so that they received the form of sensation, there are placed other faculties, which preserve and safeguard them, as well as another capacity: namely, that of moving so as to direct themselves toward that which agrees with them and so as to flee from that which disagrees. Furthermore every individual has been given that which the species he belongs to needs. Finally such portions of the matter in question that have been purified to the point of receiving the form of the intellect have been given another faculty through which every one of them, according to the perfection of the individual in question, governs, thinks, and reflects on what may render possible the durability of himself as an individual and the preservation of his species. As for the other motions[4] that occur in all | individuals of a species, they occur by chance and do not, according to Aristotle, come about through the governance or ordering of one who governs or orders. For instance, if a hurricane or a wind of less than hurricane force should blow, it would indubitably bring some leaves of this particular tree to fall, break a branch of another tree, topple a stone from a certain fence, raise up the dust so that it covers a certain plant and causes its destruction, and agitate great waves in the water so that a ship that is there would founder and so that all the people that are on board, or at least some

4. Or: all the motions.

of them, would be drowned. Consequently, according to him,[5] there is no difference between the fall of the leaf and the fall of the stone, on the one hand, or the drowning of the excellent and superior men that were on board the ship, on the other. Similarly he does not differentiate between an ox that defecates upon a host of ants so that they die, or a building whose foundations are shaken upon all the people at their prayers who are found in it so that they die. And there is no difference, according to him, between a cat coming across a mouse and devouring it or a spider devouring a fly, on the one hand, or a ravenous lion meeting a prophet and devouring him, on the other. To sum up, the basis of his opinion is as follows: Everything that, according to what he saw, subsisted continuously without any corruption or change of proceeding at all — as, for instance, the states of the spheres — or that observed a certain orderly course, only deviating from it in anomalous cases — as, for instance, the natural things — was said by him to subsist through governance; I mean to say that divine providence accompanied it.[6] On the other hand, all that, according to what he saw, does not subsist continuously or adhere to a certain order — as, for instance, the circumstances of the individuals of every species of plants, animals, and man — are said by him to exist by chance and not through the governance of one who governs; he means thereby that they are not accompanied by divine providence, and he also holds that it is impossible that providence should accompany these circumstances. This is consequent upon his opinion concerning the eternity of the world | and the impossibility of that which exists being in any respect different from what it is. Those who, deviating from our Law, believed in this opinion were those who said: *The Lord hath forsaken the earth.*[7]

The third opinion is opposed to this second opinion, being the opinion of those who hold that in all that exists there is nothing either among universal or particular things that is in any respect due to chance, for everything comes about through will, purpose, and governance. Now it is clear that everything that is governed is also known.[8] This is the opinion of the Islamic sect, the Ashᶜariyya.[9] Great incongruities are bound up with this opinion, and those who hold it are burdened with them and obliged to accept them. Thus they agree with Aristotle regarding the equality that he establishes between the fall of a leaf and the death of a human individual. They say: This is so; but the wind does not blow by chance, for God sets it in

5. I.e., Aristotle.   6. According to Aristotle's opinion.   7. Ezek. 9:9.
8. Or: that everyone that governs also knows.
9. On this sect, cf. Translator's Introduction.

motion; and it is not the wind that causes the leaves to fall, for every leaf falls through an ordinance and a decree of God; and it is He who causes them to fall now in this particular place; it is not possible that the time of their falling should be postponed or retarded; nor is it possible that they should fall in another place than this, for all this has been everlastingly decreed. In consequence of this opinion, they are obliged to think that every motion and rest of animals has been decreed and that man has in no way the ability to do or not to do a thing. It is likewise a consequence of this opinion that the nature of the possible is abolished regarding these matters, so that all things are either necessary or impossible. They were accordingly obliged to accept this and said that the matters that we designate as possible — such as Zayd's standing up and ʿUmar's coming — are only possible with reference to us, but that there is nothing whatever possible in them with reference to Him, may He be exalted; rather | they are either necessary or impossible. It also follows necessarily from this opinion that what the Laws entail is quite useless; for man for whose benefit every Law has come, has not the ability to do anything either to fulfill what he has been commanded or to avoid what he has been forbidden. In fact this sect says that He, may He be exalted, willed this: to send messengers, to command, to forbid, to threaten, to give hope, and to instill fear, even though we do not have the ability to do anything of our own accord; it is permissible that He should impose upon us impossible things; and it is likewise permissible that, having obeyed His order, we should be punished; and that, having transgressed it, we should be rewarded. It also necessarily follows from this opinion that His actions, may He be exalted, have no final end. They bear the burden of all these incongruities for the sake of the integrity of this opinion. They go so far as to hold that if we see an individual who was born blind or a leper, although we are unable to say that he might have deserved this because of a previous sin of his, we should say: He has willed this. And if we see that an excellent man who was devoted to God's worship has been killed through torture, we should say: He has willed this. And in this there is no injustice, for according to them, it is permissible for God to punish one who has not sinned and to reward a sinner with benefits. Their dicta on these matters are well known.

The fourth opinion is the opinion of those who hold that man has the ability to act of his own accord; it is for this reason that, according to them, the commandments, prohibitions, rewards, and punishments figuring in the Law are well ordered. They hold that all the actions of God are consequent upon wisdom, that injustice is not permissible for Him, and that He does not punish a man who does good. The Mu°tazila[10] also hold this opinion though, according to them, the ability of man to act of his own accord is not absolute. They also believe that He, may He be exalted, has knowledge of the falling of this particular leaf and of the creeping of this particular ant, and that His providence watches over all the beings. | Incongruities and contradictions follow necessarily also from this opinion. As for the incongruity, it is as follows. If some human individual is born with an infirmity without having sinned, they say: This is consequent upon His wisdom, and it is better for this individual to be thus than to be sound in body; we do not know in what this benefit consists, but this has not happened as a punishment for him, but as a benefit. And they have a similar answer with regard to the case in which an excellent man perishes, saying that this happens in order that his reward in the other world should become greater. Finally discussion with these reached a point at which they were asked: Why is He just toward man and not just to what is other than man? because of what sin has this particular animal been killed? Whereupon they assumed the burden of the following disgraceful answer: This is better for it,[11] so that God should compensate it in the other world. Even when a flea and a louse are killed, it is necessary that they have a compensation for them from God. They say in the same way that if this mouse, which has not sinned, is devoured by a cat or a hawk, His wisdom has required this with regard to the mouse and that the latter will receive compensation in the other world for what has happened to it.

To my mind no one among the partisans of these three opinions concerning providence should be blamed, for every one of them was impelled by strong necessity to say what he did. Aristotle followed what is manifest[12] in the nature of that which exists. The Ash°ariyya tried to avoid having to ascribe to Him, may He be exalted, ignorance with regard to anything, for it is not seemly to say that He knows this particular thing and is ignorant of that other particular thing. Thus the incongruities referred to were necessarily attached to, and borne by, them. The Mu°tazila also tried to avoid having to ascribe to Him, may He be exalted, injustice and wrongdoing. Moreover it was not fitting in their opinion to go against the inborn disposition by saying that there is no injustice in inflicting pain on one who has not sinned. Nor was it fitting in their opinion that all the prophets should have been sent and the Law revealed for no | intelligible purpose. Accordingly they too were burdened with incongruities referred to above,

10. On this sect, cf. Translator's Introduction.
11. I.e., for the animal.   12. *ẓāhir*, a word also used to signify "external."

and self-contradiction necessarily attached to them. For they believe both that He, may He be exalted, knows everything and that man has the ability to act; and this leads, as the slightest reflection should make clear, to self-contradiction.

The fifth opinion is our opinion, I mean the opinion of our Law. I shall let you know about it what has been literally stated in the books of our prophets and is believed by the multitude of our scholars; I shall also inform you of what is believed by some[13] of our latter-day scholars; and I shall also let you know what I myself believe about this. I say then: It is a fundamental principle of the Law of *Moses our Master*, peace be on him, and of all those who follow it that man has an absolute ability to act; I mean to say that in virtue of his nature, his choice, and his will, he may do everything that it is within the capacity of man to do, and this without there being created for his benefit in any way any newly produced thing. Similarly all the species of animals move in virtue of their own will. And He has willed it so; I mean to say that it comes from His eternal volition in the eternity a parte ante that all animals should move in virtue of their will and that man should have the ability to do whatever he wills or chooses among the things concerning which he has the ability to act. This is a fundamental principle about which — praise be to God! — no disagreement has ever been heard within our religious community. It is likewise one of the fundamental principles of the Law of *Moses our Master* that it is in no way possible that He, may He be exalted, should be unjust, and that all the calamities that befall men and the good things that come to men, be it a single individual or a group, are all of them determined according to the deserts of the men concerned through equitable judgment in which there is no injustice whatever. Thus if some individual were wounded in the hand by a thorn, which he would take out immediately, this would be a punishment for him, and if he received | the slightest pleasure, this would be a reward for him — all this being according to his deserts. Thus He, may He be exalted, says: *For all His ways are judgment, and so on.*[14] But we are ignorant of the various modes of deserts.

I have summed up these opinions for you as follows: All the various circumstances of the individuals among the Adamites are considered by Aristotle as due to pure chance, by the Ashᶜarite as consequent on will alone,[15] by the Muᶜtazila as consequent on wisdom,[16] and by us as consequent on the individual's deserts, according to his actions. For this reason the

13. Or: one.   14. Deut. 32:4.   15. I.e., the divine will.
16. I.e., the divine wisdom.

Ashᶜarite considers it as permissible that God should punish[17] an excellent and good man in this world and make him subsist eternally in that fire which is said to be in the other world. One merely says: He willed it so. The Muᶜtazila consider that this is injustice; and that one that has been punished, be it even an ant, as I have mentioned to you, receives a compensation; and that the fact that the being in question was punished in order to receive a compensation is consequent on His wisdom. As for us, we believe that all the human circumstances are according to the deserts, that He is exalted above injustice, and that among us only those deserving punishment are punished. This is what is stated literally in the *Torah of Moses our Master*, namely, that everything is consequent upon the deserts; and the multitude of our scholars also speak in accordance with this opinion. For you will find them saying explicitly: *There is no death without sin, and no sufferings without transgression.*[18] And they also say: *A man is measured with the measure he uses himself;*[19] this is the text of the *Mishnah*. And in every passage they state clearly that for Him, may He be exalted, justice is necessary and obligatory; namely, that an obedient individual receives compensation for all the pious and righteous actions he has accomplished, even if he was not ordered by a prophet to do them, and that he is punished for all evil acts committed by him, even if he was not forbidden by a prophet to do them; this being forbidden | by the inborn disposition — I refer to the prohibition against wrongdoing and injustice. Thus they say: *The Holy One, blessed be He, does not withhold from any creature that which it has deserved.*[20] They also say: *Everyone that says that the Holy One, blessed be He, is indulgent [in forgiving] should have his bowels torn. Rather is He long-suffering, but He exacts what is due to Him.*[21] And: *He who does [a thing] having been commanded [to do it] does not resemble him who does [it] without having been commanded.*[22] Thus they have made it clear that even he who has not been charged with a commandment *is given his reward*. All their discourse consistently conforms to this principle. However, in the discourse of the *Sages*, there occurs something additional over and above what is to be found in the text of the *Torah*, namely, the dictum of some of them regarding the

17. Unjustly, according to human judgment.   18. B.T., Shabbath, 55a.
19. Mishnah, Sota, I 7.
20. B.T., Baba Qamma, 38b; B.T., Pesaḥim, 118a.
21. Genesis Rabbah, LXVII; B.T., Baba Qamma, 50a.
22. B.T., Qiddushin, 31a; B.T., Baba Qamma, 87a; B.T., ᶜAbodah Zarah, 3a. The talmudic text that has come down to us differs somewhat from Maimonides' quotation. It may be translated: *He who has been commanded [to do a thing] and does [it] is greater than he who does without having been commanded.*

sufferings of love.[23] For according to this opinion, sometimes misfortunes befall an individual not because of his having sinned before, but in order that his reward should be greater. This is also the teaching of the Muʿtazila. But there is no text in the *Torah* expressing this notion. For you should not be led into error by what is said about *putting to trial*, as when *God put Abraham to a trial*,[24] and as when it says: *And He afflicted thee, and suffered thee to hunger, and so on*.[25] You shall hear the discourse about this later on.[26] Our Law is exclusively concerned with the circumstances of human individuals; and in ancient times the story of this compensation accorded to animals has never been heard in our religious community;[27] nor was it ever mentioned by one of the *Sages*. But some[28] of the later-day *Gaonim, may their memory be blessed*, have heard it from the Muʿtazila and have approved of it and believed it.

As for my own belief with regard to this fundamental principle, I mean divine providence, it is as I shall set it forth to you. In this belief that I shall set forth, I am not relying upon the conclusion to which demonstration has led me, but upon what has clearly appeared as the intention of the book of God and of the books of our prophets. This opinion, which I believe, is less disgraceful than the preceding opinions and nearer than they to intellectual reasoning. For I for one believe that | in this lowly world — I mean that which is beneath the sphere of the moon — divine providence watches only over the individuals belonging to the human species and that in this species alone all the circumstances of the individuals and the good and evil that befall them are consequent upon the deserts, just as it says: *For all His ways are judgment*.[29] But regarding all the other animals and, all the more, the plants and other things, my opinion is that of Aristotle. For I do not by any means believe that this particular leaf has fallen because of a providence watching over it; nor that this spider has devoured this fly because God has now decreed and willed something concerning individuals; nor that the spittle spat by Zayd has moved till it came down in one particular place upon a gnat and killed it by a divine decree and judgment; nor that when this fish snatched this worm from the face of the water, this happened in virtue of a divine volition concerning individuals. For all this is in my opinion due to pure chance, just as Aristotle holds. According to me, as I consider the matter, divine providence is consequent upon the divine overflow; and the species

23. B.T., Berakhoth, 5a.   24. Gen. 22:1.   25. Deut. 8:3.   26. Cf. III 24.
27. *milla*.   28. Or: one.   29. Deut. 32:4.

with which this intellectual overflow is united, so that it became endowed with intellect and so that everything that is disclosed to a being endowed with the intellect was disclosed to it, is the one accompanied by divine providence, which appraises[30] all its actions[31] from the point of view of reward and punishment. If, as he[32] states, the foundering of a ship and the drowning of those who were in it and the falling-down of a roof upon those who were in the house, are due to pure chance, the fact that the people in the ship went on board and that the people in the house were sitting in it is, according to our opinion, not due to chance, but to divine will in accordance with the deserts of those people as determined in His judgments, the rule of which cannot be attained by our intellects.

I was impelled to adopt this | belief by the fact that I never found in the book of a prophet a text mentioning that God has a providence watching over one of the animal individuals, but only over a human individual. The prophets are even sometimes astonished because providence watches over human individuals — man being too insignificant for providence to watch over him — and all the more, over the other animals. Thus it says: *What is man, that Thou takest knowledge of him, and so on.*[33] *What is man, that Thou art mindful of him, and so on.*[34] Sometimes, however, there are clear texts concerning providence watching over all the human individuals and exercising a surveillance over all their actions. Thus: *He that fashioneth the hearts of them all, that considereth all their works.*[35] It says: *For Thine eyes are open upon all the ways of the sons of man, to give every one according to his ways.*[36] It is also said: *For His eyes are upon the ways of man, and He seeth all his goings.*[37] The *Torah* too sometimes makes explicit statements concerning providence watching over human individuals and exercising a surveillance over their actions. Thus it says: *Nevertheless in the day when I visit, I will visit their sin upon them.*[38] And: *Whosoever hath sinned against Me, him will I blot out of My book.*[39] And: *That same soul will I destroy.*[40] And: *I will even set My face against that soul.*[41] Such statements occur frequently. And all the stories figuring [in Scripture] concerning *Abraham* and *Isaac* and *Jacob* are an absolute proof of there being an individual providence. As for the other individuals of animals, the position with regard to them is indubitably as Aristotle sees it. For this reason killing them and

---

30. *qaddarat.* The word also means "determines"; it is possible that it was this latter sense that Maimonides had in view in this passage.
31. I.e., those of the individuals belonging to this species.
32. Aristotle.   33. Ps. 144:3.   34. Ps. 8:5.
35. Ps. 33:15.   36. Jer. 32:19.   37. Job 34:21.   38. Exod. 32:34.
39. Exod. 32:33.   40. Lev. 23:30.   41. Lev. 20:6.

employing them usefully, as we wish, has been permitted and even enjoined. A proof that there is no providence watching over the animals other than man, except the kind of providence mentioned by Aristotle, may be found in the dictum of the prophet when he saw *Nebuchadnezzar's* tyranny and his great massacres of people. For the prophet says: O Lord, it is as if men were neglected and abandoned like fishes and insects of the earth; he indicates by this dictum that these species are neglected. For this is what he says: *And makest man as the fishes of the sea, as the creeping things, that have no | ruler over them. They take up all of them with the angle, and so on.*[42] Thereupon,[43] however, the prophet explains that this is not so; that what happened was not due to neglect and the withdrawal of providence, but was a punishment for those men because they deserved what befell them. For he says: *O Lord, thou hast ordained them for judgment, and Thou, O Rock, hast established them for correction.*[44]

Do not think that this opinion may be refuted in opposition to me by means of its dicta: *He giveth to the beast his food, and so on;*[45] *The young lions roar after their prey, and so on;*[46] *Thou openest Thy hand, and satisfiest every living thing with favor;*[47] and also by means of the dictum of the *Sages: He is seated and feeds all things from the horns of buffaloes to the eggs of lice.*[48] You will find many such texts; but there is nothing in them that disproves this opinion of mine. For all these texts refer to providence watching over the species and not to individual providence. It is as if they described His bounty, may He be exalted, which prepares for every species the food necessary for it and the matter for its subsistence. This is clear and manifest. Aristotle likewise holds that this kind of providence is necessary and exists. Alexander[49] too mentions this concerning Aristotle, namely, the preparation of the existence of the food required by every species for its individuals. Were it not for this, the species would indubitably perish. This is clear upon the slightest consideration. As for their dictum: [*To avoid causing*] *suffering to animals is* [*an injunction to be found*] *in the Torah*[50] — in which they refer to its dictum: *Wherefore hast thou smitten thine she-ass*[51] — it is set down with a view to perfecting us so that we should not acquire moral habits of cruelty and should not inflict pain gratuitously without any utility, but that we should intend to be kind and merciful even with a chance animal individual,

---

42. Hab. 1:14–15.
43. Actually Maimonides here refers to verses preceding those he has just quoted.
44. Hab. 1:12.   45. Ps. 147:9.
46. Ps. 104:21. The verse continues: *and seek their food from God.*   47. Ps. 145:16.
48. B.T., Shabbath, 107b; B.T., ʿAbodah Zarah, 3b.
49. Of Aphrodisias.   50. B.T., Baba Meṣiʿa, 32b. Cf. B.T., Shabbath, 154b.
51. Num. 22:32.

except in case of need — *Because thy soul desireth to eat flesh*[52] — for we must not kill out of cruelty or for sport. It does not follow for me that by virtue of this opinion, one may pose to me the following question, namely: Why does He watch over the human individuals, and does not watch in the same way over the individuals | belonging to the other species of animals? For he who propounds this question ought to ask himself: Why did He give intellect to man and not to the other species of animals? The answer to this last question is: He willed it so; or, His wisdom has required this to be so; or, nature has required this to be so — all according to which of the three preceding opinions one adopts. Now the selfsame answers may be given to the first question.

Grasp my opinion up to its last implications. I do not believe that anything is hidden from Him, may He be exalted, nor do I attribute to Him a lack of power. But I believe that providence is consequent upon the intellect and attached to it. For providence can only come from an intelligent being, from One who is an intellect perfect with a supreme perfection, than which there is no higher. Accordingly everyone with whom something of this overflow is united, will be reached by providence to the extent to which he is reached by the intellect. This is the opinion that to my mind corresponds to the intelligible and to the texts of the Law. As for the three preceding opinions, they either are excessive or they fall short. Those that are excessive lead to an absolute confusion and to contesting the intelligible and to opposing what is perceived by the senses; whereas the others that greatly fall short entail most vicious beliefs concerning the deity, as well as the ruin of order in human existence and the obliteration of all good qualities of man, both the moral and the rational. I am referring to the opinion of those who abolish providence with respect to human individuals, putting the latter on a par with the individuals of the other species of animals.

CHAPTER 18

After what I have stated before about providence singling out the human species | alone among all the species of animals, I say that it is known that no species exists outside the mind, but that the species and the other universals are, as you know, mental notions and that every existent outside the mind is an individual or a group of individuals. This being known, it is

52. Deut. 12:20.

also known that the divine overflow that exists united to the human species, I mean the human intellect, is merely what exists as individual intellects — that is, what has overflowed toward Zayd, ʿUmar, Khalid, and Bakr. Now if this is so, it follows necessarily according to what I have mentioned in the preceding chapter that when any human individual has obtained, because of the disposition of his matter and his training, a greater portion of this overflow than others, providence will of necessity watch more carefully over him than over others — if, that is to say, providence is, as I have mentioned, consequent upon the intellect. Accordingly divine providence does not watch in an equal manner over all the individuals of the human species, but providence is graded as their human perfection is graded. In accordance with this speculation it follows necessarily that His providence, may He be exalted, that watches over the prophets is very great and proportionate to their degree in prophecy and that His providence that watches over excellent and righteous men is proportionate to their excellence and righteousness. For it is this measure of the overflow of the divine intellect that makes the prophets speak, guides the actions of righteous men, and perfects the knowledge of excellent men with regard to what they know. As for the ignorant and disobedient, their state is despicable proportionately to their lack of this overflow, and they have been relegated to the rank of the individuals of all the other species of animals: *He is like the beasts that speak not.*[1] For this reason it is a light thing to kill them, and has been even enjoined because of its utility. This matter is one of the fundamental principles of the Law, which is built upon it, I mean to say upon the principle that providence watches over | each human individual in the manner proper to him.

Consider in what way the texts [of Scripture] speak of providence watching over the details of the circumstances of the *Patriarchs* in their various activities and even in their acquisition of property, and what they were promised in consequence of providence accompanying them. It was said to *Abraham: I am thy shield.*[2] And to *Isaac: And I will be with thee, and will bless thee.*[3] And to *Jacob: And, behold, I am with thee, and will keep thee whithersoever thou goest.*[4] And to the Master of the prophets: *Certainly I will be with thee.*[5] And to *Joshua: As I was with Moses, so I will be with thee.*[6] All these are explicit affirmations of providence watching over them according to the measure of their perfection. With regard to providence watching over excellent men and neglecting the ignorant, it is said: *He will keep the*

1. Ps. 49:13 and 21.   2. Gen. 15:1.   3. Gen. 26:3.   4. Gen. 28:15.
5. Exod. 3:12.   6. Josh. 1:5.

feet of His holy ones, but the wicked shall be put to silence in darkness; for not by strength shall man prevail.[7] It says thereby that the fact that some individuals are preserved from calamities, whereas those befall others, is due not to their bodily forces and their natural dispositions—this being the meaning of the dictum, *For not by strength shall man prevail*—but to their perfection and deficiency, I mean their nearness to, or remoteness from, God. For this reason, those who are near to Him are exceedingly well protected: *He will keep the feet of His holy ones;* whereas those who are far from Him are given over to whatever may happen to befall them. For there is nothing to protect them against whatever may occur; for they are like one walking in darkness, whose destruction is assured. With regard to providence watching over the excellent ones, it is also said: *He keepeth all his bones, and so on;*[8] *The eyes of the Lord are toward the righteous, and so on;*[9] *He shall call upon Me, and I will answer him, and so on.*[10] The texts that occur with regard to this notion are so numerous that they cannot be counted; I refer to the notion of providence watching over human individuals according to the measure of their perfection and excellence. The philosophers too mention this notion. Abū Naṣr [al-Fārābī] says in the Introduction to his Commentary on Aristotle's "Nicomachean [Ethics]":[11] | Those who have the capacity of making their soul pass from one moral quality to another are those of whom Plato has said that God's providence watches over them to a higher degree.

Consider how this kind of consideration has conducted us to the knowledge of the correctness of what all the prophets, may peace be on them, have said concerning individual providence watching over each individual in particular according to the measure of his perfection, and how this consideration follows necessarily from the point of view of speculation, provided that, as we have mentioned, providence is consequent upon the intellect. It would not be proper for us to say that providence watches over the species and not the individuals, as is the well-known opinion of some philosophic schools. For outside the mind nothing exists except the individuals; it is to these individuals that the divine intellect is united. Consequently providence watches only over these individuals. Consider this chapter as it ought to be considered; for through it all the fundamental principles of the Law will become safe for you and conformable for you to speculative philosophic opinions; disgraceful views will be abolished; and the form of providence, as it is, will become clear to you.

7. I Sam. 2:9.   8. Ps. 34:21.   9. Ps. 34:16.
10. Ps. 91:15.   11. This commentary seems to be lost.

After we have mentioned the opinion of people engaged in speculation concerning providence and the manner in which God governs the world, I shall also sum up for you the opinion of the people of our religious community concerning knowledge[12] and a discourse of mine about this.

CHAPTER 19

No doubt it is a primary notion that all good things must exist in God and that with regard to Him all deficiencies must be denied. It is almost a primary notion that ignorance with regard to anything whatever is a deficiency and that He, may He be exalted, is ignorant of nothing. However what incited, as I have mentioned to you, some[1] of the people of speculation | to have the temerity to say, He knows thus and not otherwise, was what they imagined as to the lack of order in the circumstances of the human individuals. Yet most of these circumstances are not merely natural, but also consequent upon the fact that man is endowed with the ability to act and with reflection. The prophets have already mentioned that the ignorant infer that the deity has no knowledge of our actions merely from the fact that they see wicked people living in prosperity and abundance. For this impels the excellent man to think that his inclination toward the good and the hardships due to the opposition of others that he endures because of that, are useless. Thereupon the prophet has mentioned that he had let his thought wander freely with regard to this subject until it had become clear to him that things should be considered as they are in their final outcome and not in their beginnings. This is how he describes the order of all these thoughts. He says: *And they say: How doth God know? And is there knowledge in the Most High? Behold, such are the wicked; and they that are always at ease increase riches. Surely in vain have I cleansed my heart, and washed my hands in innocency.*[2] Then he says: *And when I pondered how I might know this, it was wearisome in mine eyes; until I entered into the sanctuary of God, and considered their end. Surely in slippery places, and so on.*[3] *How are they a desolation in a moment, and so on.*[4] These same thoughts are mentioned by

12. I.e., divine knowledge.
1. Or: one.   2. Ps. 73:11–13.
3. The whole phrase reads: *Surely Thou settest them in slippery places.*
4. Ps. 73:16–19.

Malachi, who says: *Your words have been all too strong against Me, saith the Lord, and so on. Ye have said, It is vain to serve God; and what profit is it that we have kept His charge, and that we have walked mournfully because of the Lord of hosts? And now we call the wicked happy, and so on. Then they that feared the Lord spoke, and so on. Then shall ye again discern, and so on.*[5] *David* too has made clear that that opinion[6] was well known in his time and has made clear its necessary consequences, namely, the wronging and unjust treatment of men by one another. And he began to argue with a view to destroying that opinion and to making it known that He, may He be exalted, knows all this. | He says: *They slay the widow and the stranger, and murder the fatherless. And they say: The Lord will not see, neither will the God of Jacob give heed. Consider ye brutish among the people; and ye fools, when will ye be wise? He that planted the ear, shall He not hear? He that formed the eye, shall He not see?*[7]

I shall now explain to you the meaning of this argument after I have mentioned to you the way in which those who are overhasty in their interpretations of the prophets' discourse, misunderstand this discourse. Several years ago some distinguished individuals of our religious community, who were physicians, told me that they wondered at this dictum of *David*. They said: According to his way of reasoning, it would follow necessarily that the Creator of the mouth eats and the Creator of the lung shouts and the same would hold for all the other members. Reflect now, you who study this Treatise of mine, how far they were from a correct understanding of this argument, and hear its true meaning: In the case of everyone who makes any instrument, it is clear that unless he had a conception of the work to be done with that instrument, he would be unable to make it. For instance, unless a smith had a conception and an understanding of the meaning of sewing, he would not make a needle in that form which alone permits performing the act of sewing. The same applies to the other instruments. When, therefore, some of the philosophers thought that God does not apprehend these individual things because they are apprehended by the senses, whereas He, may He be exalted, does not apprehend with a sense but through an intellectual apprehension, he[8] argued against them by starting from the existence of the senses, saying: If the meaning of the apprehension of the sense of sight is hidden from Him and He does not know it, how did

5. Mal. 3:13–18.
6. I.e., the opinion that God has no knowledge of what happens in relation to human individuals.
7. Ps. 94:6–9.   8. I.e., David.

He bring into existence this instrument, which is disposed for visual apprehension? Do you hold that it could have happened by chance that a certain clear humor should be produced, and outside it another similar humor, and again outside it a certain membrane | in which a hole happened to be bored, and in front of that hole a clear and hard membrane? To sum up: Can someone endowed with intelligence conceive that the humors, membranes, and nerves of the eye — which, as is known, are so well arranged and all of which have as their purpose the final end of this act of seeing — have come about fortuitously? Certainly not. But as every physician and every philosopher has set forth, this is brought about of necessity through a purpose of nature. Now according to the general consensus of philosophers, nature is not endowed with intellect and the capacity for governance. Rather does this craftsmanlike governance proceed, according to the opinion of the philosophers, from an intellectual principle; and, according to us, it is the act of an intelligent being who impressed all the faculties in question into all the things in which a natural faculty exists. If, however, that intellect does not apprehend or know the matter in question, how — according to that opinion — can he have brought into existence, or how can there have proceeded from him, a nature tending toward a purpose of which he has no knowledge? Accordingly it is with truth that he[9] called them *brutish* and *fools*. Thereupon he begins to make clear that this is a deficiency in our apprehension; that God, may He be honored and magnified, who has given us the intellect with which we apprehend — and because of our incapacity to apprehend His true reality, may He be exalted, there arise in us these great doubts — knows, may He be exalted, this our deficiency; and that no attention should be directed to the rash reflections necessarily proceeding from this our inadequate thought.[10] He[11] says: *He that teacheth man knowledge; the Lord knoweth the thoughts of man, that they are vanity.*[12]

The whole of my aim in this chapter was to make it clear that this speculation is very ancient; I refer to the notion that God lacks apprehension, which has occurred to the ignorant in view of the fact that the circumstances of the human individuals, which by their nature are contingent, are not well ordered. Thus it says: *And the Children of Israel did impute things that were not | right unto the Lord.*[13] And it is said in the *Midrash: What did*

---

9. I.e., David.

10. According to certain manuscripts and Alḥarizi's Hebrew translation, the last part of this sentence could be rendered: and that their inadequate thought pays no attention to the rash reflections it has of necessity brought about.

11. I.e., David.   12. Ps. 94:10–11.   13. II Kings 17:9.

they say? They said: This column neither sees nor hears nor speaks.[14] They[15] wished to refer by this to their[16] imagining that God does not apprehend these circumstances and that no command or prohibition from Him reaches the prophets. The cause of all this and, according to them, the proof of it, are to be found in the fact that the circumstances of the human individuals do not take a course that is in accordance with what, as every one of us considers, ought to happen. Accordingly when they saw that things were not as they wished, they said: *The Lord seeth us not.*[17] *Zephaniah* says concerning these: [*Those*] *that say in their heart: The Lord will not do good, neither will He do evil.*[18]

As for what should be said concerning His knowledge, may He be exalted, of all things, I shall inform you of my opinion concerning this after I have made known to you the matters about which there is general consensus and that no one endowed with intellect can contradict in any point.

CHAPTER 20

A matter concerning which there is a general consensus is that it is not true that new knowledge should come to Him, may He be exalted, so that He would know now what He did not know before. And it is not true, even according to the opinion of those who believe in the attributes,[1] that He should have many and numerous insights. After this has been demonstrated, we, the community of those who adhere to a Law, say that He knows with one single knowledge the many and numerous things. For as far as He, may He be exalted, is concerned, insights do not differ because of the difference of the things known, as is the case in respect to us. Similarly we say that He has known all the things that are produced anew before they have come about and that He has known them perpetually. | For this reason no new knowledge comes to Him in any way. For, seeing that He knows that a certain man is now nonexistent, but will exist at a certain time, will go on existing for such and such a duration, and will then again become nonexistent, there will be for Him no additional knowledge when that individual comes into existence as He had known beforehand. Nothing was

14. The Midrash is unknown.   15. The authors of the Midrash.
16. The Children of Israel are meant.   17. Ezek. 8:12.   18. Zeph. 1:12.
1. I.e., the divine attributes.

produced thereby[2] that was unknown to Him. On the contrary, something was produced of which it had been perpetually known that it would be produced in the way it came into existence. Thus it follows necessarily from this belief that knowledge may have as its object nonexistent things and may embrace the infinite. And this is indeed our belief. For we say that it is not impossible that His knowledge should have as its object the nonexistent things about whose being brought into existence He knew beforehand and that He is able to bring into existence. On the other hand, that which is never brought into existence is, with reference to His knowledge, an absolutely nonexistent thing,[3] which is not an object for His knowledge, as that which is nonexistent for us is not an object for our knowledge.

As for knowledge of the infinite, there is a difficulty about it. Some of the people of speculation came to profess the opinion that knowledge[4] has for its object the species, but, in a certain sense, extends to all the individuals of the species. This is the opinion of all those who adhere to a Law in view of what is required by the necessities of speculation. The philosophers, however, affirm decidedly that His knowledge may not have for its object a nonexistent thing and that no knowledge may embrace that infinite; consequently, as no new knowledge may come to Him, it is impossible that He should know anything of the things that are produced anew. Accordingly He only knows the permanent immutable thing. Another doubt, however, arose in some[5] of them, and they said: Even if He should know only the permanent things, He would have many insights. For if the things known become many, the insights regarding them become many. For to everything known there is a knowledge that is special for it. Consequently | He only knows His own essence.[6]

What I myself say is that all these difficulties to which all of them are subject have as their cause the fact that they established a relation between our knowledge and His, may He be exalted; for every sect considers the things that are impossible for our knowledge and consequently thinks that this also holds necessarily with regard to His knowledge or else that the thing is obscure for it. The philosophers ought to be blamed more strongly than anyone else with regard to this question. For they were those who have demonstrated that there is no multiplicity in His essence,[7] may He be exalted, and that He has no attribute beyond His essence; but that, on the contrary, His knowledge is His essence, and His essence His knowledge. As

2. Through that individual's coming into existence.   3. Or: absolute nonexistence.
4. I.e., divine knowledge.   5. Or: one.   6. Or: self.   7. Or: self.

we have explained, they were those who have demonstrated that our
intellects are incapable of apprehending the true reality of His essence as it
really is. How then can they think that they can apprehend His knowledge, seeing that His knowledge is not a thing that is outside of His
essence? For the selfsame incapacity that prevents our intellects from apprehending His essence also prevents them from apprehending His knowledge
of things as they are. For this knowledge is not of the same species as ours so
that we can draw an analogy with regard to it, but a totally different thing.
And just as there is a necessarily existent essence from which — according to
their opinion — every existent derives of necessity, or that — according to our
opinion — produces all the things that are other than itself after they have
been nonexistent — so do we say that this essence apprehends all that is other
than itself; that in all the things that exist,[8] nothing whatever is hidden
from it; and that between our knowledge and His knowledge there is nothing in common, as there is nothing in common between our essence and
His essence. With regard to this point, only the equivocality of the term
"knowledge" occasions the error; for there is a community only in the terms,
whereas in the true reality of the things there is a difference. It is from this
that incongruities follow necessarily, as we imagine that things that obligatorily pertain to our knowledge pertain also to His knowledge.

One of the things that have become clear to me by the texts of the
Torah is that His knowledge, may He be exalted, that a certain possible[9]
thing | will come into existence, does not in any way make that possible
thing quit the nature of the possible. On the contrary, the nature of the
possible remains with it; and knowledge concerning what possible things
will be produced,[10] does not entail one of the two possibilities becoming
necessary. This is also one of the fundamental principles of the Law of *Moses*,
a principle concerning which there is neither doubt nor a contestation. If
this were not so, it would not have said: *Then thou shalt make a parapet for
thy roof*,[11] and likewise: *Lest he die in the battle, and another man take her*.[12]
Similarly the whole of religious legislation, the commandments, and the
prohibitions, goes back to this principle: namely, that His knowledge concerning what will happen does not make this possible thing quit its nature.
However, this constitutes a great difficulty for the apprehension of our
inadequate intellects.

Consider in how many ways His knowledge differs from ours, according
to the opinion of all those who adhere to a Law. In the first place, His

8. Or: that He (or: it) have brought into existence.　9. I.e., contingent.
10. Or: what will be produced from the possible.　11. Deut. 22:8.　12. Deut. 20:7.

knowledge, while being one, corresponds to many known things belonging to various species. In the second place, it may have as its object something that does not exist. In the third place, it may have as its object something that is infinite. In the fourth place, His knowledge undergoes no changes in its apprehension of things produced in time. And yet it might seem that the knowledge that a thing will exist is not identical with the knowledge that it already exists; for there is in the latter case a certain surplus, namely, the fact that what had been in potentia became actual. In the fifth place, it is in accordance with the opinion of our Law that God's knowledge, may He be exalted, does not bring about the actualization of one of the two possibilities even though He, may He be exalted, knows perfectly how one of them will come about. Accordingly, would that I knew in what way, according to the opinion of those who believe that knowledge is a superadded attribute,[13] our knowledge resembles His and whether there is here something other than a mere community in the terms. According to our opinion — that is, the opinion of people who say that His knowledge is not something super-added to His essence — it is truly necessary that His knowledge should differ from ours | in substance, just as the substance of the heavens differs from the substance of the earth. The prophets have explicitly stated this, saying: *For My thoughts are not your thoughts, neither are your ways My ways, saith the Lord. For as the heavens are higher than the earth, so are My ways higher than your ways, and My thoughts than your thoughts.*[14]

To sum up the notion that I have stated in résumé: Just as we do not apprehend the true reality of His essence, but know withal that His exist-ence is the most perfect of existences and not commingled in any way with any deficiency or change or being acted upon, so although we do not know the true reality of His knowledge because it is His essence, we do know that He does not apprehend at certain times while being ignorant at others. I mean to say that no new knowledge comes to Him in any way; that His knowledge is neither multiple nor finite; that nothing among all the beings is hidden from Him; and that His knowledge of them does not abolish their natures, for the possible remains as it was with the nature of possibility. All the con-tradictions that may appear in the union of these assertions are due to their being considered in relation to our knowledge, which has only its name in common with His knowledge. Similarly the word "purpose" is used equivocally when applied to what is purposed by us and to what is said to be His purpose, may He be exalted. Similarly the word "providence" is used

13. I.e., an attribute superadded to God's essence.   14. Isa. 55:8–9.

equivocally when applied to what we are provident about and to that of which it is said that He, may He be exalted, is provident with regard to it. It is accordingly true that the meaning of knowledge, the meaning of purpose, and the meaning of providence, when ascribed to us, are different from the meanings of these terms when ascribed to Him. When, therefore, the two providences or knowledges or purposes are taken to have one and the same meaning, the above-mentioned difficulties and doubts arise. When, on the other hand, it is known that everything that is ascribed to us is different from everything ascribed to Him, truth becomes manifest. The differences between the things ascribed | to Him and those ascribed to us have been explicitly stated, as have been mentioned above, in its dictum: *Neither are your ways My ways.*

CHAPTER 21

A great disparity subsists between the knowledge an artificer has of the thing he has made and the knowledge someone else has of the artifact in question. For if the artifact was made in a way conforming to the knowledge of its artificer, the artificer only made it through following his own knowledge. With regard to the other one who looks at that artifact, comprehending it with his knowledge, his knowledge follows the artifact. Thus, for instance, the artificer who made this box in which weights are moved by the flow of water so as to indicate the hours of the day or the night that have passed, apprehends and knows all the quantity of water that must flow in it, the changes in the position of the flow, all the threads that are drawn, and all the balls that come down. And he knows these motions not because he looks at the motions that take place now. The converse is true, for the motions that take place now only come about because they conform to his knowledge. However, this does not hold in the case of someone who looks at this instrument. For whenever the onlooker sees a movement, he obtains new knowledge. And by not ceasing to look on and gradually to obtain increase of new knowledge, he acquires in this way a knowledge of the whole of the instrument. However, if you suppose that the motions of this instrument are infinite, the onlooker could never contain them in his knowledge. In addition, the onlooker is incapable of knowing any | of these motions before they take place, for he only knows whatever he knows on the basis of what takes place. Such is the case with regard to that which exists[1] taken as a whole in its relation to our knowledge and His knowledge, may He be exalted. For we know all that we know only through looking at the beings; ✓ therefore our knowledge does not grasp the future or the infinite. Our insights are renewed and multiplied according to the things from which we acquire the knowledge of them. He, may He be exalted, is not like that. I mean that His knowledge of things is not derived from them, so that there is multiplicity and renewal of knowledge. On the contrary, the things in question follow upon His knowledge, which preceded and established them as they are: either as the existence of what is separate from matter; or as the existence of a permanent individual endowed with matter; or as the existence of what is endowed with matter and has changing individuals, but follows on an incorruptible and immutable order. Hence, with regard to Him, may He be exalted, there is no multiplicity of insights and renewal and change of knowledge. For through knowing the true reality of His own immutable essence, He also knows the totality of what necessarily derives from all His acts. For us to desire to have an intellectual cognition of the way this comes about is as if we desired that we be He and our apprehension be His apprehension. He who studies true reality equitably ought accordingly to believe that nothing is hidden in any way from Him, may He be exalted, but that, on the contrary, everything is revealed to His knowledge, which is His essence, and that it is impossible for us to know in any way this kind of apprehension. If we knew how it comes about, we would have an intellect in virtue of which an apprehension of this kind might be had. This, however, is a thing that in what exists[2] belongs only to Him, may He be exalted, and it is His essence. Understand this then. For I say that this is something most extraordinary and a true opinion; if it is carefully studied, no mistake or distortion will be found in it, nor will | incongruities be attached to it; and no deficiency is ascribed through it to God. No demonstration at all can be obtained with regard to these great and sublime notions, either for our opinion—that of the community of those who adhere to a Law—or for the opinion of the philosophers, even if one considers all the differences among the latter with regard to this question. And with regard to all problems with reference to which there is no demonstration, the method used by us with regard to this question—I mean the question of the deity's knowledge of what is other than He—ought to be followed. Understand this.

1. Literally: existence.   2. Literally: existence.

The story of *Job*, which is extraordinary and marvellous, belongs to the kind of things we are discussing now. I mean to say that it is a parable intended to set forth the opinions of people concerning providence. You know the explicit statement of some of [the Sages]: *Job has not existed and was not created, but was a parable.*[1] Those, on the other hand, who believe that he *has existed and was created* and that the story has happened, do not know at what time and in what place he lived. For some of the *Sages* say that he lived *in the days of the Patriarchs,* whereas others say that he lived *in the days of Moses;* again others say that he lived *in the days of David;* again others say that he was one of *those who came back from Babylon.* This confirms the opinions of those who say that *he has not existed and was not created.* To sum up: *whether he has existed or not,* with regard to cases[2] like his, which always exist, all reflecting people become perplexed; and in consequence such things as I have already mentioned to you are said about God's knowledge and His providence. I refer to the assertion that a righteous and perfect man, who was just in his actions and is most careful to avoid sins, was stricken — without his having committed a sin entailing this — by great and consecutive calamities with respect to | his fortune, his children, and his body. Now according to both opinions, the one that considers that *he has existed* and the one that considers that *he has not,* the prologue — I mean the discourse of *Satan,* that of God addressed to *Satan,* and the giving-over [of Job to Satan] — is indubitably, in the view of everyone endowed with intellect, a parable. However, it is not a parable like all others, but one to which extraordinary notions *and things that are the mystery of the universe*[3] are attached. Through it great enigmas are solved, and truths than which none is higher become clear. I shall mention to you what it is possible to mention, and I shall mention to you the words of the *Sages* that have drawn my attention to everything that I understand in this great parable.

The first thing that you will consider is its dictum, *There was a man in the land of Uṣ,*[4] in which figures the equivocal word *Uṣ*. It is the name of an individual: *Uṣ his first-born;*[5] and also the imperative of a verb meaning to reflect and meditate: *Uṣu ᶜeṣah [take counsel together].*[6] It is as if [Scripture]

1. B.T., Baba Bathra, 15a.
2. Or, according to certain manuscripts: stories like his.
3. The expression quoted occurs in B.T., Ḥagigah, 13a, but refers there to Ezekiel's vision.
4. Job 1:1.   5. Gen. 22:21.   6. Isa. 8:10.

said to you: Meditate and reflect on this parable, grasp its meaning, and see what the true opinion is. Then it mentions that *the sons of God* came *to present themselves before the Lord* and that *Satan* came in the midst of their crowd and multitude. For it does not say, *The sons of God and Satan came to present themselves before the Lord*, which would have meant that all of them were there because of an identical relation, but says: *The sons of God came to present themselves before the Lord, and Satan came also among them*.[7] This form of speech is only used with regard to one who has come without having been for his own sake the object of an intention or having been sought for his own sake, but came in the midst of those who came when those whose presence was the object of an intention presented themselves. Then it mentions that this *Satan* roamed and went all over the earth. Thus there is no relationship whatever between him and the upper world, in which there is no road for him. This is the meaning of its saying: *From going to and fro in the earth, and from walking up and down in it*.[8] Thus his going to and fro and his roaming take place on the earth. |

Then it mentions that this righteous and perfect man was delivered into the hands of this *Satan* and that all the calamities that befell him with respect to his fortune, his children, and his body, were caused by *Satan*. After having made this supposition it begins to set down speeches of people engaged in speculation with regard to this occurrence. Thus it mentions a certain opinion and ascribes it to *Job*, and ascribes other opinions to his friends. I shall make them clearly known to you; I am referring to those opinions about which there has been a conflict of thoughts and that are concerned with a story the cause of the whole of which was *Satan*; though all of them, *Job* and his friends, thought that God had done it Himself and not through the intermediary of *Satan*. The most marvellous and extraordinary thing about this story is the fact that knowledge is not attributed in it to *Job*. He is not said to be a *wise* or a *comprehending* or an *intelligent* man. Only moral virtue and righteousness in action are ascribed to him. For if he had been *wise*, his situation would not have been obscure for him, as will become clear.

Then it graduates his misfortunes according to the various circumstances of people. For some people are not frightened by the loss of their fortune and hold it a small thing, but are horrified by the death of their children and die because of their grief. Others support with patience and without terror even the loss of their children, but no one endowed with sensation can support pain patiently. Now all men, I mean the vulgar, glorify

7. Job 1:6; 2:1.   8. Job 1:7; 2:2.

God with their tongues and attribute to Him justice and beneficence when they are happy and prosperous or even when they are in a state of endurable suffering. However, when the misfortunes mentioned in *Job* befall them, some of them become unbelievers and believe that there is little order in all that exists at the time when they lose their fortune; others hold to the belief in justice and order in spite even of their having been stricken by the loss of their fortune, but | do not keep patient if tried by the loss of their children. Others again are patient and keep an untroubled belief even when they lose their children, but none of them supports patiently the pain of the body without complaining and repining either with the tongue or in the heart.

The dictum [of Scripture] referring to *the sons of God* says in the two passages: *To present themselves before the Lord.*[9] *Satan*, however, though he came among their crowd and multitude a first and a second time, is not said in the first passage *to present himself*. In the second passage, however, it says: *And Satan came also among them to present himself before the Lord.*[10] Understand this notion and consider how extraordinary it is, and see how these notions came to me through something similar to prophetic revelation. For the meaning of the words, *to present themselves before the Lord*, is that they exist as subject to His order in what He wills. Thus *Zechariah*, with reference to the *four chariots that go forth*,[11] says: *And the angel answered and said unto me: These are the four airs of the heavens, which go forth after presenting themselves before the Lord of all the earth.*[12] It is consequently manifest that the status of *the sons of God* and that of *Satan* in what exists are not identical. For *the sons of God* are more permanent and lasting, while [Satan] also has a certain portion, below them in what exists.

Furthermore one of the marvels of this parable consists in the fact that when it mentions that *Satan* roams especially[13] over the earth and accomplishes certain actions, it also makes clear that he is forbidden to gain dominion over the soul, that he has been given dominion over all terrestrial things, but that he is kept away by a barrier from the soul. This is the meaning of its saying: *Only spare his soul.*[14] I have already explained to you[15] that in our language the term *soul* is equivocal and that it is applied to the thing that remains of man after death; this is the thing over which *Satan* has no dominion.

After what I have mentioned, | hear the useful dictum of the *Sages* to whom the term *Sages* may truthfully be applied; it clarifies all that is obscure, reveals all that is concealed, and renders manifest most of the

9. Job 1:6; 2:1.   10. Job 2:1.   11. Zech. 6:1.   12. Zech. 6:5.
13. Or: only.   14. Job 2:6.   15. Cf. I 41.

mysteries of the Torah. It is their dictum in the *Talmud: Rabbi Simon ben Laqish said: Satan, the evil inclination, and the angel of death are one and the same.*[16] Thus he makes clear all that we have mentioned in a way that is not obscure for one who is endowed with understanding. It has thus become clear to you that these three terms designate one and the same notion and that all the actions attributed to each of these three are only the action of one and the same thing. This is also expressed literally by the ancient *Sages of the Mishnah,* who said: *This is taught: he descends and leads astray,* [then] *he ascends and accuses,* [then] *he takes permission and takes the soul.*[17] It is thus clear to you that what *David* saw *in a vision of prophecy* at the time of the plague, *having his drawn sword in his hand stretched out over Jerusalem,*[18] was only shown to him in order to indicate a certain notion. That same notion is also expressed *in the vision of prophecy* referring to the disobedience of the sons of *Joshua the high priest: And Satan standing at his right hand to accuse him.*[19] Thereupon it is made clear in the following dictum how far [Satan] is from Him, may He be exalted: *The Lord rebuke thee, O Satan, yea, the Lord that hath chosen Jerusalem rebuke thee.*[20] It was he who was seen also by *Balaam on the way in a vision of prophecy,* when he says to him:[21] *Behold, I am come forth for an adversary* [*satan*]. Know that the word *satan* derives from [the verb "satah," to turn away, figuring for instance in the verse]: *Steh* [*turn away*] *from it and pass on;*[22] I mean to say that it derives from the notion of turning-away and going-away. For it is he[23] who indubitably turns people away from the ways of truth and makes them perish in the ways of error. The same notion is expressed in the dictum: *For the inclination of man's heart is evil from his youth.*[24] You know how well known this notion is in | our Law, I mean the notion of *good inclination and evil inclination;* and you know their dictum: *With both your inclinations.*[25] They also say that *the evil inclination* is produced in the human individual at his birth: *Sin coucheth at the door;*[26] as the *Torah* states literally: *From his youth.*[27] On the other hand, *good inclination* is only found

---

16. B.T., Baba Bathra, 16a.   17. B.T., Baba Bathra, 16a.   18. I Chron. 21:16.

19. Zech. 3:1. According to B.T., Sanhedrin, 91a, the verse refers to the sin committed by the sons of Joshua in taking non-Jewish women for wives.

20. Zech. 3:2.   21. To Balaam. Num. 22:32.   22. Prov. 4:15.

23. I.e., Satan.   24. Gen. 8:21.

25. Mishnah, Berakhoth, IX 5. The Mishnah passage interprets *thy heart* in Deut. 6:5 (*And thou shalt love the Lord thy God with all thy heart*), as referring both to the good and the evil inclination.   26. Gen. 4:7.

27. Gen. 8:21. The whole biblical phrase may be translated (if one renders *yeṣer* by "inclination"): *For the inclination of man's heart is evil from his youth.*

in man when his intellect is perfected.[28] That is why [the Sages] say[29] that in the parable that deals with the body of the human individual and the difference of its faculties and that figures in [Scripture's] dictum, *There was a little city, and few men within it, and so on,*[30] the evil inclination is called a *great king* and good inclination is called a *poor wise child.*[31] All these things are dealt with in well-known texts set down by [the Sages], *may their memory be blessed.* Now as they have explained to us that *the evil inclination is Satan,* who indubitably is an *angel* — I mean that he too is called an *angel* inasmuch as he is found in the crowd of *the sons of God* — good inclination must consequently also be truly an *angel.* Consequently that well-known opinion figuring in the sayings of the *Sages,*[32] *may their memory be blessed,* according to which every man is accompanied by *two angels,* one to his right and the other to his left, identifies these two with *good inclination* and *evil inclination.* In the *Gemara Shabbath,* they, *may their memory be blessed,* say clearly with regard to these *two angels* that *one is good and the other evil.*[33] See how many marvels are revealed to us by this dictum and how many incorrect imaginings it abolishes.

As I see it now, I have analyzed and explained the story of *Job* up to its ultimate end and conclusion. I want, however, to explain to you the opinion ascribed to *Job* and the opinion ascribed to each of his friends, using proofs that I gleaned from the discourse of each of them. You should not, however, pay attention to the other dicta rendered necessary by the order of the discourse, as I explained to you in the beginning of this Treatise.[34] |

CHAPTER 23

If it is supposed that the story of *Job* happened, the first thing that occurred was a matter on which there was general agreement between the five, I mean *Job* and his friends, namely, that everything that had befallen *Job* was known to Him, may He be exalted, and that God had caused these misfortunes to befall him. All of them were also agreed that injustice was not permitted to Him and wrongdoing not to be ascribed to Him. You will find these

---

28. Cf. Midrash Qoheleth, 9:14; B.T., Sanhedrin, 91b; Genesis Rabbah, XXXIV.
29. Cf. B.T., Nedarim, 32b.   30. Eccles. 9:14.
31. A great king is mentioned in Eccles. 9:14. Eccles. 9:15 speaks of a poor wise man. A poor wise child is mentioned in Eccles. 4:13.
32. Cf. B.T., Ḥagigah, 16a. Cf. B.T., Berakhoth, 60b, and Rashi's commentary.
33. B.T., Shabbath, 119b.   34. Cf. I Introduction.

notions frequently also in the discourse of *Job*. If now you consider the discourse of the five in the course of their conversation, you may almost think[1] that whatever one of them says is said also by all the others, so that the same notions are repeated and overlap. They are interrupted by *Job's* description of the sufferings and misfortunes that had befallen him in spite of his outstanding righteousness and by the description of his justice, the nobleness of his character, and the goodness of his actions. Similarly they are interrupted in the discourse of his friends by exhortations to patience, words of consolation, appeals to him to be amicable, and advice that he ought to be silent and not give rein to his speech like an individual quarreling with another individual; he should rather submit to God's judgments and be silent. He, on the other hand, says that the violence of the sufferings makes it impossible to be patient and firm and to say what one ought to. All his friends are also agreed that everyone who does good obtains a reward and that everyone who does evil is punished; and that if you see a disobedient man who is fortunate, in the end this state of affairs will be transformed into its contrary, for he will perish and misfortunes will befall him, his sons, and his offspring. If, however, you see an obedient man in misery, his fracture will certainly be remedied. You will find this notion repeated in the discourses of *Eliphaz*, *Bildad*, and *Zophar*, all three being agreed on this opinion. This, however, is not the purpose of | this story as a whole; for this purpose is rather to show the peculiarity of each of them and to make known each one's opinion concerning this story: namely, that the greatest and heaviest misfortunes befall the most perfect individual, who was the most unblemished of them in righteousness. *Job's* opinion on this is that this happening proves that the righteous man and the wicked are regarded as equal by Him, may He be exalted, because of His contempt for the human species and abandonment of it. This is what he says in all his speeches: *It is all one — therefore I say: He destroyeth the innocent and the wicked. If the flood*[2] *slay suddenly, He will mock at the calamity of the guiltless.*[3] He says thus that if a torrent comes suddenly killing all those it meets and sweeping them away, He laughs at the calamity of the innocent. Thereupon he confirms this opinion in his dictum: *One dieth in his full strength, being wholly at ease and quiet. His pails are full of milk, and so on. And another dieth in bitterness of soul, and hath never tasted of good. They lie down alike in the dust, and the worm covereth them.*[4] He also begins to cite as proof the good fortune and

1. Literally: find.
2. Maimonides apparently thus interprets the Hebrew word *shot*, which in this context probably means "scourge."
3. Job 9:22–23.   4. Job 21:23–26.

prosperity of the wicked, treating at great length of this subject. He says: *Even when I remember I am affrighted, and horror taketh hold on my flesh. Wherefore do the wicked live, become old, yea, wax mighty in power? Their seed is established in their sight, and so on.*[5] Having described this perfect prosperity, he begins to say to his interlocutors: Even supposing matters are as you think and the children of the prosperous unbeliever perish after he is no more and their traces vanish, in what way is that prosperous man harmed by what happens to his family after he is no more? He says: *For what pleasure hath he in his house after him, when the number of his months is determined?*[6] Thereupon he begins to make clear that there is no hope after death, and that nothing remains but neglect.[7] Accordingly he begins to wonder how it is that He has not neglected in the origin the work of the generation and the creation of the human individual and neglects to govern him. He says accordingly:[8] *Hast Thou not poured me out as milk,* | *and curdled me like cheese? and so on.*[9] This is one of the opinions believed in concerning providence. You know the dictum of the *Sages* that this opinion of *Job's* is most unsound. They say:[10] *May there be dust upon Job's mouth.* And they say: *Job wanted to upset the plate.* And they say: *Job denied the resurrection of the dead.* They also say of him: *He began to blaspheme.* With regard to His[11] saying, may He be exalted, to *Eliphaz: For ye have not spoken of Me the thing that is right, as My servant Job hath*[12] — the *Sages*, in order to find an excuse for it, say, *A man is not to be blamed for* [*what he does when*] *suffering,*[13] meaning that he was excused because of his great sufferings. However, this kind of speech does not accord with the parable.[14] The cause of this[15] is as we shall now explain to you. [Job] had given up his opinion, which was most mistaken, and had demonstrated that he had been mistaken therein. This view was such as arises at the first reflection and in the beginning thereof, especially in the case of one whom misfortunes have befallen, while he knows of himself that he had not sinned — which is not denied by anyone. For this reason this opinion is ascribed to *Job*. However, the latter said all that he did say as long as he had no true knowledge and knew the deity only because of his acceptance of authority, just as the multitude adhering to a Law know it. But when he knew God with a certain knowledge, he admitted that true happiness, which is the knowledge of the deity, is guaranteed to all who know Him and that a human being cannot be

5. Job 21:6–8.   6. Job 21:21.   7. On the part of God.
8. This refers to the formation of the fetus.   9. Job 10:10.
10. B.T., Baba Bathra, 16a.   11. I.e., God's.   12. Job 42:7.
13. B.T., Baba Bathra, 16b.   14. Literally: is not of the sort of the parable.
15. Of God's words to Eliphaz.

troubled in it by any of all the misfortunes in question. While he had known God only through the traditional stories and not by the way of speculation, *Job* had imagined that the things thought to be happiness,[16] such as health, wealth, and children, are the ultimate goal. For this reason he fell into such perplexity and said such things as he did. | This is the meaning of his dictum: *I had heard of Thee by the hearing of the ear; but now mine eye seeth Thee; wherefore I abhor myself and repent of dust and ashes.*[17] This dictum may be supposed to mean, *Wherefore I abhor all that I used to desire and repent of my being in dust and ashes* — this being the position that he was supposed to be in: *And he sat among the ashes.*[18] It is because of this final discourse indicative of correct apprehension that it is said of him after this: *For ye have not spoken of Me the thing that is right, as My servant Job hath.*[19]

The opinion of *Eliphaz* concerning this event is also one of the opinions professed concerning providence. For he says that everything that befell *Job* was deserved by him, for he had committed sins because of which he served these misfortunes. This is what he says to *Job: Is not thy wickedness great? and are not thine iniquities without end?*[20] Then he began to tell *Job*: The righteousness of your actions and your excellent way of life upon which you relied do not entail your being perfect before God so that you should not be punished: *Behold, He putteth no trust in His servants, and His angels He chargeth with folly; how much less in them that dwell in houses of clay, whose foundation is in the dust.*[21] *Eliphaz* does not cease turning around this notion; I mean to say that he believes that everything that befalls a man is deserved, but that the deficiencies for which we deserve punishment and the way in which we deserve to be punished because of them are hidden from our perception.

The opinion of *Bildad the Shuhite* on this question consists in the belief in compensation. For he says to *Job*: If you are innocent and have not sinned, the reason for these great events is to make great your reward. You will receive the finest of compensations. All this is good for you, so that the good that you will obtain in the end be increased. This is | what he says to *Job: If thou art pure and upright, surely now He will awake for thee, and make the habitation of thy righteousness prosperous. And though thy beginning was small, yet thy end should greatly increase.*[22] You know already how well known this opinion on the subject of providence is, and we have already made it clear.

The opinion of *Zophar the Naamathite* is the one that considers that

16. Literally: the thought happinesses.   17. Job 42:5–6.   18. Job 2:8.
19. Job 42:7.   20. Job 22:5.   21. Job 4:18–19.   22. Job 8:6–7.

everything follows from the will[23] alone; no reason whatever should be sought for His actions, and the question should not be posed:[24] Why did He do this and why did He not do that? For this reason the point of view of justice or a requirement of wisdom should not be sought in whatever the deity does, for His greatness and true reality entail His doing what He wills. But we are incapable of penetrating the secrets of His wisdom, which necessitates His doing what He wills without there being another reason. This is what he says to *Job*:[25] *That God would speak, and open His lips against thee; and that He would tell thee the secrets of wisdom, that they may teach thee doubly.*[26] *Canst thou by searching find out God? Canst thou find out the Almighty unto perfection?*

✓   Know then and consider how the story, which has perplexed people, is composed and called upon them to adopt the various opinions that we have analyzed above concerning God's providence regarding the created things. All that is required by the classification[27] is mentioned and ascribed to one of the men famous at that time because of virtue and knowledge. That would have to be said if this is a parable. Or they might have expressed these opinions in true reality if this is a story that has happened. The opinion attributed to *Job* is in keeping with the opinion of Aristotle; the opinion of *Eliphaz* is in keeping with the opinion of our Law; the opinion of *Bildad* is in keeping with the doctrine of the Muᶜtazila; the opinion of *Zophar* is in keeping with the doctrine of the Ashᶜariyya. These were the ancient opinions concerning providence.

Thereupon another opinion supervenes, namely, the one attributed to *Elihu*. Hence he is considered by them[28] as superior.[29] For it is mentioned that he was the youngest among them in point of age and the most perfect among them in knowledge. He started to reprove *Job* and to tax him with ignorance | because of his having manifested his self-esteem and because of his not being able to understand how misfortunes could have befallen him though he performed good deeds. For he had expatiated at length on the goodness of his actions. He also described the opinions of [Job's] three friends on providence as senile drivel; and made extraordinary speeches that are full of enigmas, in such a way that if someone considers his discourse, he wonders

23. Of God.   24. Literally: it should not be said.   25. Job 11:5–7.
26. The following words are omitted: *Know therefore that God exacteth of thee less than thine iniquity deserveth.*
27. Of the opinions.   28. By Job and his three friends.
29. Or, according to manuscript variants: He is considered superior to them; or: He is distinguished from them.

and thinks that he[30] does not in any respect make an addition to what was said by *Eliphaz*, *Bildad*, and *Zophar*, but merely repeats in different terms and with amplifications the notions contained in their speeches. For he does not go beyond blaming *Job*, ascribing the attribute of justice to God, describing His wonders in the universe, and stating that He, may He be exalted, does not care either for the obedience of those who obey or for the disobedience of those who disobey. Now all these notions had been expressed by his companions. However, when you consider the matter, the additional notion that he introduced will become clear to you; this notion is the one that is intended;[31] it had not occurred before to one of the others. Together with that notion, however, he says all they have said, just as each of all the others — namely, *Job and his three friends* — repeats, as I have mentioned to you, the notion expressed by another among them. This is done in order to hide the notion that is peculiar to the opinion of each individual, so that at first it occurs to the multitude that all the interlocuters are agreed upon the selfsame opinion; however, this is not so. The notion added by *Elihu* and not mentioned by one of them is that which he expresses parabolically when he speaks of the intercession of an angel. For he says that it is an attested and well-known thing that when a man is ill to the point of death and when he is despaired of, if an angel intercedes for him — regardless of what angel — his intercession is accepted and he is raised from his fall. This invalid is accordingly saved and restored to the best of states. However, this does not continue always, there being no continuous intercession | going on forever, for it only takes place two or three times. He says: *If there be for him an angel, an intercessor, and so on.*[32] And, having described the various states of the convalescent and his joy at returning to the perfection of health, he says: *Lo, all these things doth God work, twice, yea thrice, with a man.*[33] This notion is made clear by *Elihu* alone. He also makes an addition — prior to speaking of this notion — by beginning to describe the how of prophecy in his dictum: *For God speaketh once, yea twice, yet [man] perceiveth it not. In a dream, in a vision of the night, when deep sleep falleth upon men.*[34] Thereupon he begins to confirm this opinion and to make clear its method by describing many natural circumstances, such as his describing thunder, lightning, rain, and the blowing of the winds. He combines this with many subjects belonging to the circumstances of animals — I mean an outbreak of pestilence referred to in his dictum, *In a moment they die, even at midnight, and so on;*[35] the occurrence of great wars referred to in his dictum, *He breaketh in pieces*

30. I.e., Elihu.   31. By the author of the book.   32. Job 33:23.
33. Job 33:29.   34. Job 33:14–15.   35. Job 34:20.

mighty men without number, and setteth others in their stead;[36] and many other such circumstances.

Similarly you will find that in the prophetic revelation that came to *Job*[37] and through which his error in everything that he had imagined became clear to him, there is no going beyond the description of natural matters — namely, description of the elements or description of the meteorological phenomena or description of the natures of the various species of animals, but of nothing else. For what is mentioned therein in the way of a description of the *firmaments* and the *heavens*[38] and *Orion* and *the Pleiades*[39] occur because of their influence upon the atmosphere; for He draws his[40] attention only to what is beneath the sphere of the moon. *Elihu* too derives his warnings from various species of animals. For he says:[41] *He teacheth us from the beasts of the earth, and maketh us wise from the fowls of heaven.*[42] In this speech[43] He dwells at the greatest length on a description of *Leviathan,* who is a combination of corporeal properties divided between the animals that walk, swim, and fly. | The purpose of all these things is to show that our intellects do not reach the point of apprehending how these natural things that exist in the world of generation and corruption are produced in time and of conceiving how the existence of the natural force within them has originated them. They[44] are not things that resemble what we make. How then can we wish that His governance of, and providence for, them, may He be exalted, should resemble our governance of, and providence for, the things we do govern and provide for? Rather is it obligatory to stop at this point and to believe that nothing is hidden from Him, may He be exalted. As *Elihu* here says: *For His eyes are upon the ways of man, and He seeth all his goings. There is no darkness, nor shadow of death, where the workers of iniquity may hide themselves.*[45] But the notion of His providence is not the same as the notion of our providence; nor is the notion of His governance of the things created by Him the same as the notion of our governance of that which we govern. The two notions are not comprised in one definition, contrary to what is thought by all those who are confused, and there is nothing in common between the two except the name alone. In the same way, our act does not resemble His act; and the two are not comprised in one and

36. Job 34:24.   37. Cf. Job 38–42.   38. Cf. Job 38:37.   39. Cf. Job 38:31.
40. I.e., Job's.   41. Job 35:11.
42. This seems to be, by and large, the meaning of the verse as understood by Maimonides. However, the translation figuring in the English translation of the Bible may be more correct. It reads: *Who teacheth us more than the beasts of the earth, and maketh us wiser than the fowls of heaven.*
43. Of God.   44. Or: it (i.e., the natural force).   45. Job 34:21–22.

the same definition. Just as natural acts differ from those of craftsmanship, so do the divine governance of, the divine providence for, and the divine purpose with regard to, those natural matters differ from our human governance of, providence for, and purpose with regard to, the things we govern, we provide for, and we purpose. This is the object of the *Book of Job* as a whole; I refer to the establishing of this foundation for the belief and the drawing attention to the inference to be drawn from natural matters, so that you should not fall into error and seek to affirm in your imagination that His knowledge is like our knowledge or that His purpose and His providence and His governance are like our purpose and our providence and our governance. If man knows this, every misfortune will be borne lightly by him. | And misfortunes will not add to his doubts regarding the deity and whether He does or does not know and whether He exercises providence or manifests neglect, but will, on the contrary, add to his love, as is said in the conclusion of the prophetic revelation in question: *Wherefore I abhor myself, and repent of dust and ashes.*[46] As [the Sages], *may their memory be blessed,* have said: *Those who do out of love and are joyful in sufferings.*[47] If you meditate upon everything I have told you with the attention that ought to be practiced in meditating upon this Treatise and if you consider this *Book of Job,* its meaning will become clear to you; and you will find that I have summed up all its notions, nothing being left aside except such matters as figure there because of the arrangement of the discourse and the continuation of the parables, according to what I have explained to you several times in this Treatise.

CHAPTER 24

The subject of *trial* is also very difficult; it is one of the greatest difficulties of the Law. The *Torah* mentions it in six passages, as I shall make clear to you in this chapter. What is generally accepted among people regarding the subject of *trial* is this: God sends down calamities upon an individual, without their having been preceded by a sin, in order that his reward be increased. However, this principle is not at all mentioned in the *Torah* in an

---

46. Job 42:6. This is Maimonides' interpretation of the verse, whose latter part is translated in the English Bible: *and repent, seeing I am dust and ashes.*
47. B.T., Shabbath, 88b.

explicit text. And there is in the *Torah* only one passage among the six whose external meaning suggests such a notion; I shall explain its meaning. The principle of the Law that runs counter to this opinion, is that contained in His dictum, may He be exalted: *A God of faithfulness and without iniquity.*[1] Nor do all the *Sages* profess this opinion of the multitude, for they say sometimes: *There is no death without sin and no sufferings without transgression.*[2] And this is the opinion | that ought to be believed by every adherent of the Law who is endowed with intellect, for he should not ascribe injustice to God, may He be exalted above this, so that he believes that Zayd is innocent of sin and is perfect and that he does not deserve what befell him. However, the external meaning of the *trials* mentioned in the *Torah* in the passages in question is that they took place in order to test and to receive information so that one could know the degree of faith or the degree of obedience of the individual or nation in question. And this is the great difficulty, especially in the story of the *binding*,[3] which was known only to God and to the two individuals involved, to one of whom[4] it was said: *For now I know that thou fearest God.*[5] It is the same with regard to its dictum: *For the Lord your God tries you out, to know whether ye do love the Lord, and so on.*[6] And also with regard to its dictum: *To know what was in thy heart, and so on.*[7] Now I will resolve all these difficulties for you.

Know that the aim and meaning of all the *trials* mentioned in the *Torah* is to let people know what they ought to do or what they must believe. Accordingly the notion of a *trial* consists as it were in a certain act being done, the purpose being not the accomplishment of that particular act, but the latter's being a model to be imitated and followed. Thus the interpretation of its dictum — *To know whether ye do love*[8] — is not: in order that God should know that, for He already knew it; but the meaning resembles that of its dictum — *To know that I am the Lord that doth sanctify you*[9] — the meaning of which is: in order that the religious communities should know. In the same manner [Scripture] says:[10] If a man claiming prophecy arise and if you see his suggestions tend to make one believe in the truth of his claim, know that God wished to make known hereby to the religious communities the extent of your certitude with regard to His Law, may He be exalted, and your apprehension of its[11] true reality; and also to make known that you do not let yourselves be deceived by the deceptions of a deceiver and

1. Deut. 32:4.   2. B.T., Shabbath, 55a.   3. I.e., of the sacrifice of Isaac.
4. Literally: to him (i.e., to Abraham).   5. Gen. 22:12.   6. Deut. 13:4.
7. Deut. 8:2.   8. Deut. 13:4.   9. Exod. 31:13.   10. Cf. Deut. 13:2 ff.
11. Or: His.

that your faith in God cannot be disturbed. | This will be a support for every-one who seeks the truth, for he will seek out the beliefs that are so firm that when one has them one pays no attention to the man who tries to compete through working a miracle. For this man issues a call to believe in impossible things, whereas a competition as to miracles is only useful[12] when something possible is claimed, as we have made clear in *Mishneh Torah*.[13]

After it has been made clear that the meaning of *to know* here is: in order that people should know, the same can be said with regard to its dictum concerning *manna: That He might afflict thee, to try thee out, to know what was in thy heart, whether thou wouldest keep His commandments, or no.*[14] The meaning of this is: in order that the religious communities should know this and that it should be generally accepted throughout the world that those who wholly devote themselves to His service, may He be exalted, are provided by Him with food in an unthought-of way. The same notion is expressed when *manna* is spoken of on the occasion when it first came down: *That I may try them out, whether they will walk in My Torah, or no;*[15] which means: in order that everyone should consider this and should see whether being devoted to His service is useful and sufficient or not sufficient. As for what is said [in Scripture] for the third time again concerning *manna* — namely, *Who fed thee in the wilderness with manna, which thy fathers knew not, that He might afflict thee, and that He might try thee out [nasotekha], to do thee good at thy latter end*[16] — it may suggest that God sometimes makes an individual suffer in order that his reward be greater. But this is not the truth of the matter. For this dictum has one of two meanings: One of them is the notion concerning *manna* repeatedly expressed in the first and second dictum, namely: in order that it should be known whether being devoted to God does or does not suffice as far as food is concerned and gives relief from fatigue and weariness. Or *nasotekha [try thee out]* may mean: to accustom thee, this being an interpretation that can refer to its dictum: *is not accus-tomed [nisstah] to set the sole of her foot, and so on.*[17] It is as if it said that He, may He be exalted, has first accustomed you to misery in the desert in order to make your well-being greater when once you came into the land.[18] And this is true, for to pass from weariness to rest is more pleasant than to be constantly at rest. And it is known that | but for their misery and weariness in the desert, they would not have been able to conquer the land and to fight. The *Torah* literally states this: *For God said: Lest peradventure the people repent when they see war, and they return to Egypt. But God led the people*

---

12. Or: instructive.   13. Cf. Yesodei ha-Torah, VIII.   14. Deut. 8:2.
15. Exod. 16:4.   16. Deut. 8:16.   17. Deut. 28:56.   18. I.e., into Palestine.

about, by the way of the wilderness of the Red Sea.[19] For prosperity does away with courage, whereas a hard life and fatigue necessarily produce courage — this being the *good* that, according to the story in question, will come *at their latter end.*[20]

As for its dictum, *For God is come to try you out,*[21] it expresses the same notion as the one stated in *Deuteronomy*[22] concerning a man claiming *to prophesy in the name of an idol: For the Lord your God tries you out,*[23] the meaning of which we have made clear. He told them similarly here at the *Gathering at Mount Sinai:* Be not afraid; this great gathering that you have seen has taken place only in order that you acquire certitude through sight, so that if, in order to make publicly known the extent of your faith, *the Lord your God tried you out with a false prophet* who would call upon you to demolish what you have heard, you should remain firm and keep your feet from stumbling. For if I had come to you as a prophet,[24] as you had thought,[25] and I had said to you what had been said to me without your hearing it for yourselves, it would have been possible for you to fancy that what is told by another[26] is true even if that other had come to you with something contradicting what has been made known to you; this is what could have happened if you had not heard it at this gathering.

As for the story of *Abraham* at the *binding,*[27] it contains two great notions that are fundamental principles of the Law. One of these notions consists in our being informed of the limit of *love* for God, may He be exalted, and *fear* of Him — that is, up to what limit they must reach. For in in this story he was ordered to do something that bears no comparison either with sacrifice of property or with sacrifice of life. In truth it is the most extraordinary thing that could happen in the world, such a thing that one would not imagine that human nature was capable of it. Here there | is a sterile man having an exceeding desire for a son, possessed of great property and commanding respect, and having the wish that his progeny should become a religious community. When a son comes to him after his having lost hope, how great will be his attachment to him and love for him! However, because of his fear of Him, who should be exalted, and because of his

19. Exod. 13:17–18.   20. Deut. 8:16.   21. Exod. 20:17.
22. The term used here by Maimonides is *Mishneh Torah,* which is both an alternate name of the fifth book of the Pentateuch and the title of Maimonides' legal compilation. Cf. II 31, n. 3, and II 34, n. 2 and 4.
23. Deut. 13:4.
24. *rasūl.* Etymologically the word means "envoy." In Moslem theology it is often applied to such prophets as are also lawgivers (in contradistinction to other prophets).
25. Cf. Exod. 20:16.   26. Literally: what is in the hand of another.
27. Of Isaac.

love to carry out His command, he holds this beloved son as little, gives up all his hopes regarding him, and hastens to slaughter him after a journey of days. For if he had chosen to do this immediately, as soon as the order came to him, it would have been an act of stupefaction and disturbance in the absence of exhaustive reflection. But his doing it days after the command had come to him shows that the act sprang from thought, correct understanding, consideration of the truth of His command, may He be exalted, love of Him, and fear of Him. No other circumstance should be put forward, nor should one opt for the notion that he was in a state of passion. For *Abraham our Father* did not hasten to slaughter *Isaac* because he was afraid that God would kill him or make him poor, but solely because of what is incumbent upon the Adamites — namely, to love Him and fear Him, may He be exalted — and not, as we have explained in several passages, for any hope of a reward or for fear of punishment. Accordingly the *angel* said to him : *For now I know that thou fearest God:*[28] meaning that through the act because of which the term *fearing God* is applied to you, all the Adamites will know what the limits of *the fear of the Lord* are. Know that this notion is corroborated and explained in the *Torah*, in which it is mentioned that the final end of the whole of the *Torah*, including its commandments, prohibitions, promises, and narratives, is one thing only — namely, fear of Him, may He be exalted. This is referred to in its dictum : *If thou wilt not take care to observe all the words of this Law that are written in this book, that thou mayest fear this glorious and awful Name, and so on.*[29] This is one of the two notions aimed at | in the *binding*.[30]

The second notion consists in making known to us the fact that the prophets consider as true that which comes to them from God in a prophetic revelation. For it should not be thought that what they hear or what appears to them in a parable is not certain or is commingled with illusion just because it comes about *in a dream and in a vision*, as we have made clear, and through the intermediary of the imaginative faculty. Accordingly [Scripture] wished to make it known to us that all that is seen by a prophet in *a vision of prophecy* is, in the opinion of the prophet, a certain truth, that the prophet has no doubts in any way concerning anything in it, and that in his opinion its status is the same as that of all existent things that are apprehended through the senses or through the intellect. A proof for this is the fact that [Abraham] hastened to slaughter, as he had been commanded, *his son, his only son, whom he loved,*[31] even though this command came to him *in a dream* or *in a vision*. For if a dream of prophecy had been obscure for the

28. Gen. 22:12.   29. Deut. 28:58.   30. Of Isaac.   31. Cf. Gen. 22:2.

prophets, or if they had doubts or incertitude concerning what they apprehended *in a vision of prophecy*, they would not have hastened to do that
which is repugnant to nature, and [Abraham's] soul would not have con-
sented to accomplish an act of so great an importance if there had been *a
doubt* about it.

In truth it was fitting that this story, I mean the *binding*, should come
to pass through the hand of *Abraham* and in regard to someone like *Isaac*.
For *Abraham our Father* was the first to make known the belief in Unity,
to establish prophecy, and to perpetuate this opinion and draw people to it.
It says: *For I have known him, to the end that he may command his children
and his household after him, that they may keep the way of the Lord, to do
righteousness and judgment.*[32] Thus just as they followed his correct and useful opinions, namely, those that were heard from him, so ought one to follow the opinions deriving from his actions and especially from this action
through which he validated the fundamental principle affirming the truth
of prophecy and made known to us the ultimate end toward which *the fear
and love of God* may reach.

It is in this way that | the meaning of *trials* should be understood.
And it should not be believed that God, may He be exalted, wants to test
and try out a thing in order to know that which He did not know before.
How greatly is He exalted above that which is imagined by ignorant fools in
their evil thoughts! Know this.

CHAPTER 25

The actions are divided with regard to their ends into four classes: futile
actions, frivolous actions, vain actions, or good and excellent actions.
The action that is called vain is that by which its agent aims at some end and
that end is not achieved, its achievement being hindered by obstacles. You
can often hear people saying: "I tired myself in vain," on an occasion when
he tired himself in seeking an individual without finding him, or when he
tired himself in the course of a journey without obtaining a profit in trade.
It is also said: "Our effort with this sick man was vain," when health is not
obtained. The same holds for all actions in which ends are sought, and those
ends are not achieved. A futile action is that action by which no end is

32. Gen. 18:19.

aimed at at all, as when some people play with their hands while thinking and as the actions of the negligent and the inattentive. A frivolous action is that action by which a low end is aimed at; I mean to say that something unnecessary and not very useful is aimed at therein, as when one dances not for exercise or as when one does things in order to make people laugh about those things. Such actions are indubitably called frivolous, but they differ according to the purposes | and the perfection of the agents. For there are many things that are necessary or very useful according to some people, whereas according to others they are not at all needed; as is the case with regard to the different kinds of bodily exercise, which are necessary for the preservation of health according to the prescriptions of those who know the art of medicine, and as is the case with regard to writing, which is very useful according to the men of knowledge. Thus those who accomplish acts exercising their body in the wish to be healthy, engaging in ball games, wrestling, boxing, and suspension of breathing, or those who engage in actions that are done with a view to writing, as for instance the cutting of reed pens and the making of paper, are in the opinion of the ignorant engaged in frivolous actions, whereas they are not frivolous according to the learned. The good and excellent action is that accomplished by an agent aiming at a noble end, I mean one that is necessary or useful, and achieves that end. This is a division against which, as it seems to me, no objection can be made at any point. For one who accomplishes a certain action in all cases either aims or does not aim thereby at some end. Again an end aimed at is in all cases either noble or low, and is either achieved or not. And this is what is necessarily required by the division.

After having explained this, I shall say: A man endowed with intellect is incapable of saying that any action of God is vain, futile, or frivolous. According to our opinion — that is, that of all of us who follow the Law of *Moses our Master* — all His actions are good and excellent. He says: *And God saw every thing that He had made, and, behold, it was very good.*[1] Consequently everything that He, may He be exalted, has done for the sake of a thing is necessary for the existence of the thing aimed at or is very useful. For instance, the nourishment of a living being is necessary for its preservation, and the existence of its two eyes | is very useful for its preservation. In fact nourishment is exclusively intended to preserve the living being alive for a certain time, and the senses are exclusively intended with a view to the utility of the sensorial apprehensions for the living being. The philosophic opinion is similar, holding as it does that in all natural things

1. Gen. 1:31.

there is nothing that may be described as futile; I mean to say that everything that is not artificial consists in actions through which some end is sought, regardless of whether we do or do not know that end.

As for that sect among the people of speculation that holds that God does not do a thing because of another and that there are no causes and no effects, but that all His actions correspond to His will so that one should not seek an end for them or say: Why did He do this? as He does what He wills, and as this[2] is not consequent upon wisdom — the actions of God are considered by these people as falling under the class of the futile or held to be even inferior to futile actions. For someone performing a futile action does not aim at an end and is careless of what he does; whereas God, according to these people, knows and intends what He does, but does it without any end whatsoever or without any utility.

That anything among His actions, may He be exalted, should be frivolous is impossible, as is manifest as soon as one thinks of it. No attention should be paid to the ravings of those who deem that the ape was created in order that man should laugh at it. What led to all this was ignorance of the nature of coming-to-be and passing-away and neglect of the fundamental principle: namely, that the entire purpose consists in bringing into existence the way you see it everything whose existence is possible; for His wisdom did not require in any way that it should be otherwise; for this is impossible, since matters take their course in accordance with what His wisdom requires.

As for those who say that no end is intended in any of the acts of God, they were led | to this by necessity, namely, by considering the totality of what exists in accordance with their opinion. For they say: What is the end of the existence of the world as a whole? Hence they assert of necessity what everyone asserts who maintains that the world was created in time: He willed it so, there being no other cause. Thereupon they proceed to apply this assertion to all the particular things in the world. They go so far as not to concede that the hole in the uvea and the transparency of the cornea exist for the sake of letting the visual spirit pass so that it might apprehend, and do not even regard this at all as a cause of sight. According to them it was not for the sake of sight that this membrane was perforated and the one above it made transparent, but He willed it so, even though sight would be possible if things were otherwise. We have some texts whose external sense might be fancied to suggest this meaning at the first glance. For instance his saying: *Whatsoever the Lord willed, that hath He done, and so on;*[3] and for instance

2. I.e., God's actions.   3. Ps. 135:6.

his saying: *And what His soul desireth, even that He doeth;*[4] and for instance his saying: *And who may say unto him, What doest thou?*[5] The meaning of these texts and of others of the same kind is that the things willed by God ✓ are necessarily accomplished, there being no obstacle to hinder the carrying-out of His volition; but that He, may He be exalted, wills only what is possible, and not everything that is possible, but only that which is required by His wisdom to be such. Similarly no obstacle intervenes between Him, may He be exalted, and the exceedingly excellent action that He wishes to accomplish, and nothing can hinder it. This is the opinion of all those that adhere to the Law and also the opinion of the philosophers, and it is also our own opinion. For while we believe that the world has been produced in time, none of our scholars and none of our men of knowledge believe that this came about through the will and nothing else. For they say that His wisdom, may He be exalted — the apprehension of which is beyond us — obligatorily necessitated the existence of this world as a whole at the moment when it came into existence, and that | the selfsame immutable wisdom necessitated nonexistence before the world came into existence. You will find this notion frequently repeated by the *Sages* when they interpret the verse:[6] *He hath made every thing beautiful in its time.*[7] All this was meant to avoid that which should be avoided: namely, the thought that the agent[8] may accomplish an act whereby he does not aim at any end at all. Such is the belief of the multitude of the men of knowledge in our Law, and this was explicitly stated by our prophets: namely, that the particulars of natural acts are all well arranged and ordered and bound up with one another, all of them being causes and effects; and that none of them is futile or frivolous or vain, being acts of perfect wisdom, as it says: *How manifold are Thy works, O Lord! In wisdom hast Thou made them all.*[9] And it is said: *And all His works are done in faithfulness.*[10] And it is said: *The Lord by wisdom founded the earth, and so on.*[11] This opinion occurs frequently; and the opposite ought not to be believed. Philosophic speculation similarly requires that there should not be anything futile, frivolous, or vain in all the acts of nature, and all the more in the nature of the spheres, for they are better arranged and ordered because of the nobility of their matter.

Know that the majority of the false imaginings that call forth perplexity in the quest for the end of the existence of the world as a whole or the end of every part of it have as their root an error of man about himself and his

4. Job 23:13.   5. Eccles. 8:4.   6. Eccles. 3:11.
7. Cf. Genesis Rabbah, IX; Midrash Qoheleth, 3:11.   8. I.e., in this context, God.
9. Ps. 104:24.   10. Ps. 33:4.   11. Prov. 3:19.

imagining that all that exists exists because of himself alone, as well as ignorance of the nature of inferior matter and ignorance of what is primarily intended — namely, the bringing into being of everything whose existence is possible, existence being indubitably a good. It is because of this error and of the ignorance of these two notions that the doubts and the perplexity arise, so that some of God's actions are imagined to be frivolous, others futile, and others vain. Know that those who | put up with this incongruity so that His acts, may He be exalted, became in their opinion like futile acts that aim at no end at all, abhorred making His acts consequent upon wisdom in order that this should not pass into the assertion maintaining the eternity of the world; accordingly they shut the door upon this opinion. However, I have already made known to you the opinion of our Law about this and the fact that this opinion ought to be believed. For there is no incongruity in our saying that the existence and nonexistence of all these acts are consequent upon His wisdom, may He be exalted; we, however, are ignorant of many of the ways in which wisdom is found in His works. It is upon this opinion that the whole of *the Torah of Moses our Master* is founded; it opens with it: *And God saw every thing that He had made, and, behold, it was very good;*[12] and it concludes with it: *The Rock, His work is perfect, and so on.*[13] Know this. If you consider this opinion and the philosophic opinion, reflecting upon all the preceding chapters in this Treatise that are connected with this notion, you will not find any difference between them regarding any of the particulars of everything that exists.[14] You will find no difference other than that which we have explained: namely, that they regard the world as eternal and we regard it as produced in time. Understand this.

CHAPTER 26

Just as there is disagreement among the men of speculation among the adherents of Law whether His works, may He be exalted, are consequent upon wisdom or upon the will alone without being intended toward any end at all, there is also the same disagreement among them regarding our Laws, which He has given to us. Thus there are people who do not seek for them | any cause at all, saying that all Laws are consequent upon the will alone. There are also people who say that every commandment and prohibition in

12. Gen. 1:31.   13. Deut. 32:4.   14. Literally: of existence.

these Laws is consequent upon wisdom and aims at some end, and that all
Laws have causes and were given in view of some utility. It is, however, the
doctrine of all of us — both of the multitude and of the elite — that all the
Laws have a cause, though we ignore the causes for some of them and we do
not know the manner in which they conform to wisdom. With regard to this
the texts of the Book are clear: *righteous statutes [ḥuqqim] and judgments;*[1]
The judgments of the Lord are true, they are righteous altogether.[2]

About the statutes designated as *ḥuqqim*[3] — for instance those concerning the *mingled stuff, meat in milk,* and *the sending of the goat*[4] — [the Sages],
may their memory be blessed, make literally the following statement: *Things
which I have prescribed for you, about which you have not the permission to
think, which are criticized by Satan and refuted by the Gentiles.*[5] They are
not believed by the multitude of the *Sages* to be things for which there is no
cause at all and for which one must not seek an end. For this would lead,
according to what we have explained, to their being considered as frivolous
actions. On the contrary, the multitude of the *Sages* believe that there   ✓
indubitably is a cause for them — I mean to say a useful end — but that it is
hidden from us either because of the incapacity of our intellects or the
deficiency of our knowledge. Consequently there is, in their opinion, a cause
for all the *commandments;* I mean to say that any particular commandment
or prohibition has a useful end. In the case of some of them, it is clear to us
in what way they are useful — as in the case of the prohibition of killing and
stealing. In the case of others, their utility is not clear — as in the case of the
interdiction of the *first products*[6] [of trees] and of [sowing] *the vineyard with
diverse seeds.*[7] Those commandments whose utility is clear to the multitude
are called *mishpatim [judgments],* and those whose utility is not clear to the
multitude are called *ḥuqqim [statutes].* They[8] always say with regard to the
verse: *For it is no vain thing*[9] — *And if it is vain, it is because of you;*[10] mean-
ing that this legislation is not | a vain matter without a useful end and that
if it seems to you that this is the case with regard to some of the *commandments,* the deficiency resides in your apprehension. You already know the
tradition that is widespread among us according to which the causes for all
the *commandments,* with the exception of that concerning the *red heifer,*

1. Deut. 4:8.   2. Ps. 19:10.
3. This Hebrew term is sometimes interpreted as designating those religious laws that have
   no (or no obvious) explanation in terms of human reason. Cf. below in this chapter.
4. Cf. Deut. 22:11; Exod. 23:19; Lev. 16:10 and 21.   5. B.T., Yoma, 67b.
6. Literally: *foreskin.* Cf. Lev. 19:23.   7. Cf. Deut. 22:9.
8. I.e., the talmudic Sages.   9. Deut. 32:47.
10. J.T., Peʾah, I; J.T., Kethuboth, VIII.

were known to *Solomon;*[11] and also their dictum[12] that God hid the causes for the *commandments* in order that they should not be held in little esteem, as happened to *Solomon* with regard to the three *commandments* whose causes are made clear.[13]

All their dicta proceed according to this principle, and the texts of the [scriptural] books indicate it. However, I found in *Bereshith Rabbah* a text of the *Sages, may their memory be blessed,* from which it appears when one first reflects on it that some of the *commandments* have no other cause than merely to prescribe a law, without there having been in view in them any other end or any real utility. This is their dictum in that passage:[14] *What does it matter to the Holy One, blessed be He, that animals are slaughtered by cutting their neck in front or in the back? Say therefore that the commandments were only given in order to purify the people. For it is said: The word of the Lord is purified.*[15] Though this dictum is very strange and has no parallel in their other dicta, I have interpreted it, as you will hear, in such a manner that we shall not abandon the views of all their dicta and we shall not disagree with a universally agreed upon principle, namely, that one should seek in all the Laws an end that is useful in regard to being: *For it is no vain thing.*[16] He says: *I said not unto the seed of Jacob: Seek ye Me for nothing; I the Lord speak righteousness, I declare things that are right.*[17]

What everyone endowed with a sound intellect ought to believe on this subject is what I shall set forth to you: The generalities of the *commandments* necessarily have a cause and have been given because of a certain utility; their details are that in regard to which it was said of the commandments that they were given merely for the sake of commanding something. | For instance the killing of animals because of the necessity of having good food is manifestly useful, as we shall make clear.[18] But the prescription that they should be killed through having the upper and not the lower part of their throat cut, and having their esophagus and windpipe severed at one particular place is, like other prescriptions of the same kind, imposed with a view *to purifying the people.* The same thing is made clear to you through their example: *Slaughtered by cutting their neck in front or in the back.* I have mentioned this example to you merely because one finds in their text, *may their memory be blessed: Slaughtered by cutting their neck in front or in the back.* However, if one studies the truth of the matter, one finds it to be as follows: As necessity occasions the eating of animals, the

11. Cf. Midrash Qoheleth, 7:23.   12. Cf. B.T., Sanhedrin, 21b.
13. Cf. Deut. 17:16–17.   14. Genesis Rabbah, XLIV *ab init.*   15. Ps. 18:31.
16. Deut. 32:47.   17. Isa. 45:19.   18. Cf. III 48.

commandment was intended to bring about the easiest death in an easy manner. For beheading would only be possible with the help of a sword or something similar, whereas a throat can be cut with anything. In order that death should come about more easily, the condition was imposed that the knife should be sharp. The true reality of particulars of commandments is illustrated by the sacrifices. The offering of sacrifices has in itself a great and manifest utility, as I shall make clear.[19] But no cause will ever be found for the fact that one particular sacrifice consists in a *lamb* and another in a *ram* and that the number of the victims should be one particular number. Accordingly, in my opinion, all those who occupy themselves with finding causes for something of these particulars are stricken with a prolonged madness in the course of which they do not put an end to an incongruity, but rather increase the number of incongruities. Those who imagine that a cause may be found for suchlike things are as far from truth as those who imagine that the generalities of a *commandment* are not designed with a view to some real utility.

Know that wisdom rendered it necessary — or, if you will, say that necessity occasioned — that there should be particulars for which no cause can be found; it was, as it were, impossible in regard to the Law that there should be nothing of this class in it. In such a case the impossibility is due to the circumstances that when you ask why a *lamb* should be prescribed and not a *ram*, the same question would have to be asked if a *ram* had been prescribed | instead of a *lamb*. But one particular species had necessarily to be chosen. The same holds for your asking why *seven lambs* and not *eight* have been prescribed. For a similar question would have been put if *eight* or *ten* or *twenty* had been prescribed. However, one particular number had necessarily to be chosen. This resembles the nature of the possible, for it is certain that one of the possibilities will come to pass. And no question should be put why one particular possibility and not another comes to pass, for a similar question would become necessary if another possibility instead of this particular one had come to pass. Know this notion and grasp it. The constant statements of [the Sages] to the effect that there are causes for all the commandments, as well as the opinion that the causes were known to *Solomon*, have in view the utility of a given *commandment* in a general way, not an examination of its particulars.

This being so, I have seen fit to divide the *six hundred and thirteen commandments* into a number of classes, every one of which comprises a number of *commandments* belonging to one kind or akin in meaning. I shall inform

19. Cf. III 46.

you of the cause of every one of these classes, and I shall show their utility about which there can be no doubt and to which there can be no objection. Then I shall return to each of the *commandments* comprised in the class in question and I shall explain to you the cause of it, so that only very few *commandments* will remain whose cause has not been clear to me up to now. Some of the particulars of, and conditions for, some of the *commandments* have also become clear to me, and it is possible to give their causes. You will hear all this. However, I shall not be able to clarify to you all this giving of causes before I set before you, as a preliminary, a number of chapters in which I will include premises that are useful as an introduction for the purpose I have in mind. These are the chapters with which I will begin now. |

CHAPTER 27

The Law as a whole aims at two things: the welfare of the soul and the welfare of the body. As for the welfare of the soul, it consists in the multitude's acquiring correct opinions corresponding to their respective capacity. Therefore some of them [namely, the opinions] are set forth explicitly and some of them are set forth in parables. For it is not within the nature of the common multitude that its capacity should suffice for apprehending that subject matter as it is. As for the welfare of the body, it comes about by the improvement of their ways of living one with another. This is achieved through two things. One of them is the abolition of their wronging each other. This is tantamount to every individual among the people not being permitted to act according to his will and up to the limits of his power, but being forced to do that which is useful to the whole. The second thing consists in the acquisition by every human individual of moral qualities that are useful for life in society so that the affairs of the city may be ordered. Know that as between these two aims, one is indubitably greater in nobility, namely, the welfare of the soul — I mean the procuring of correct opinions — while the second aim — I mean the welfare of the body — is prior in nature and time. The latter aim consists in the governance of the city and the well-being of the states of all its people according to their capacity. This second aim is the more certain one, and it is the one regarding which every effort has been made precisely to expound it and all its particulars. For the first aim can only be achieved after achieving this second one. For it has already been demonstrated that man has two perfections: a first perfection, which is the perfection of the body, and an ultimate perfection, which is the perfection of the soul. The first perfection | consists in being healthy and in the very best bodily state, and this is only possible through his finding the things necessary for him whenever he seeks them. These are his food and all the other things needed for the governance of his body, such as a shelter, bathing, and so forth. This cannot be achieved in any way by one isolated individual. For an individual can only attain all this through a political association, it being already known that man is political by nature. His ultimate perfection is to become rational in actu, I mean to have an intellect in actu; this would consist in his knowing everything concerning all the beings that it is within the capacity of man to know in accordance with his ultimate perfection. It is clear that to this ultimate perfection there do not belong either actions or moral qualities and that it consists only of opinions toward which speculation has led and that investigation has rendered compulsory. It is also clear that this noble and ultimate perfection can only be achieved after the first perfection has been achieved. For a man cannot represent to himself an intelligible even when taught to understand it and all the more cannot become aware of it of his own accord, if he is in pain or is very hungry or is thirsty or is hot or is very cold. But once the first perfection has been achieved it is possible to achieve the ultimate, which is indubitably more noble and is the only cause of permanent preservation.

The true Law then, which as we have already made clear[1] is unique — namely, the Law of *Moses our Master* — has come to bring us both perfections, I mean the welfare of the states of people in their relations with one another through the abolition of reciprocal wrongdoing and through the acquisition of a noble and excellent character. In this way the preservation of the population of the country and their permanent existence in the same order become possible, so that | every one of them achieves his first perfection; I mean also the soundness of the beliefs and the giving of correct opinions through which ultimate perfection is achieved. The letter of the *Torah* speaks of both perfections and informs us that the end of this Law in its entirety is the achievement of these two perfections. For He, may He be exalted, says: *And the Lord commanded us to do all these statutes* [*huqqim*], *to fear the Lord our God, for our good always, that He might preserve us alive, as it is at this day.*[2] Here He puts the ultimate perfection first because of its nobility; for, as we have explained, it is the ultimate end. It is referred to in the dictum: *For our good always.* You know already what [the Sages],

1. Cf. II 39.   2. Deut. 6:24.

may their memory be blessed, have said interpreting His dictum, may He be exalted: *That it may be well with thee, and that thou mayest prolong thy days.*[3] They said: *That it may be well with thee in a world in which everything is well and that thou mayest prolong thy days in a world the whole of which is long.*[4] Similarly the intention of His dictum here, *For our good always*, is this same notion: I mean the attainment of *a world in which everything is well and [the whole of which is] long.* And this is perpetual preservation. On the other hand, His dictum, *That He might preserve us alive, as it is at this day*, refers to the first and corporeal preservation, which lasts for a certain duration and which can only be well ordered through political association, as we have explained.

CHAPTER 28

Among the things to which your attention ought to be directed is that you should know that in regard to the correct opinions through which the ultimate perfection may be obtained, the Law has communicated only their end and made a call to believe in them in a summary way — that is, to believe in the existence of the deity, may He be exalted, His unity, His knowledge, His power, His will, and His eternity. All these points are ultimate ends, which can be made clear | in detail and through definitions only after one knows many opinions. In the same way the Law also makes a call to adopt certain beliefs, belief in which is necessary for the sake of political welfare. Such, for instance, is our belief that He, may He be exalted, is violently angry with those who disobey Him and that it is therefore necessary to fear Him and to dread Him and to take care not to disobey. With regard to all the other correct opinions concerning the whole of being — opinions that constitute the numerous kinds of all the theoretical sciences through which the opinions forming the ultimate end are validated — the Law, albeit it does not make a call to direct attention toward them in detail as it does with regard to [the opinions forming ultimate ends], does do this in summary fashion by saying: *To love the Lord.*[1] You know how this is confirmed in the dictum regarding *love: With all thy heart, and with all thy soul, and with all thy might.*[2] We have already explained in *Mishneh Torah*[3] that this *love* becomes valid only through the apprehension of the whole of being as it is

3. Deut. 22:7.   4. B.T., Qiddushin, 39b; B.T., Ḥullin, 142a.
1. Deut. 11:13 and 22; 19:9; 30:6, 16, and 20.
2. Deut. 6:5.   3. Cf. Yesodei ha-Torah, II 2 f.

and through the consideration of His wisdom as it is manifested in it. We have also mentioned there the fact that the *Sages, may their memory be blessed,* call attention to this notion.

What results from what we have now stated as a premise regarding this subject is that whenever a *commandment*, be it a prescription or a prohibition, requires abolishing reciprocal wrongdoing, or urging to a noble moral quality leading to a good social relationship, or communicating a correct opinion that ought to be believed either on account of itself or because it is necessary for the abolition of reciprocal wrongdoing or for the acquisition of a noble moral quality, such a *commandment* has a clear cause and is of a manifest utility. No question concerning the end need be posed with regard to such *commandments*. For no one was ever so perplexed for a day as to ask why we were commanded by the Law that God is one, or why we were forbidden | to kill and to steal, or why we were forbidden to exercise vengeance and retaliation, or why we were ordered to love each other. The matters about which people are perplexed and opinions disagree — so that some say that there is no utility in them at all except the fact of mere command, whereas others say that there is a utility in them that is hidden from us — are the *commandments* from whose external meaning it does not appear that they are useful according to one of the three notions we have mentioned: I mean to say that they neither communicate an opinion nor inculcate a noble quality nor abolish reciprocal wrongdoing. Apparently these *commandments* are not related to the welfare of the soul, as they do not communicate a belief, or to the welfare of the body, as they do not communicate rules useful for the governance of the city or for the governance of the household. Such, for instance, are the prohibitions of the *mingled stuff*, of the *mingling* [of diverse species], and of *meat in milk*,[4] and the commandment *concerning the covering of blood, the heifer whose neck was broken,* and the *firstling of an ass*,[5] and others of the same kind. However, you will hear my explanation for all of them and my exposition of the correct and demonstrated causes for them all with the sole exception — as I have mentioned to you — of details and particular *commandments*. I shall explain that all these and others of the same kind are indubitably related to one of the three notions referred to — either to the welfare of a belief or to the welfare of the conditions of the city, which is achieved through two things: abolition of reciprocal wrongdoing and acquisition of excellent characters.

Sum up what we have said concerning beliefs as follows: In some cases

4. Cf. Deut. 22:11; Lev. 19:19; Exod. 23:19.
5. Cf. Lev. 17:13; Deut. 21:1–9; Exod. 13:13.

a *commandment* communicates a correct belief, which is the one and only thing aimed at — as, for instance, the belief in the unity and eternity of the deity and in His not being a body. In other cases the belief is necessary for the abolition of reciprocal wrongdoing or for the acquisition of a noble moral quality — as, for instance, the belief that He, may He be exalted, has a violent anger against those who do injustice, according to what is said: *And My wrath shall wax hot, and I will kill, and so on,*[6] and as the belief that He, may He be exalted, | responds instantaneously to the prayer of someone wronged or deceived: *And it shall come to pass, when he crieth unto Me, that I will hear; for I am gracious.*[7]

CHAPTER 29

It is well known that *Abraham our Father*, peace be on him, was brought up in the religious community of the Sabians,[1] whose doctrine it is that there is no deity but the stars. When I shall have made known to you in this chapter their books, translated into Arabic, which are in our hands today, and their ancient chronicles and I shall have revealed to you through them their doctrine and histories, it will become clear to you from this that they explicitly asserted that the stars are the deity and that the sun is the greatest deity. They also said that the rest of the seven stars[2] are deities, but that the two luminaries[3] are the greatest of them. You will find that they explicitly say that the sun governs the upper and the lower world. They say it in these very terms. And you will find that they mention in those books and those chronicles the story of *Abraham our Father*, and they say literally what follows: When Ibrahīm, who was brought up in Kūthā, disagreed with the community and asserted that there was an agent other than the sun, various arguments were brought forward against him. In these arguments they[4] set forth the clear and manifest activities of the sun in what exists. Thereupon he, they mean *Abraham*, told them: You are right; it is like an axe in the hands of a carpenter. Then they mention a part of his

---

6. Exod. 22:23.   7. Exod. 22:26.
1. The term "Sabians," as used by Maimonides, designates the pagans.
2. Including the sun and the moon. Another possible translation is: all the seven stars.
3. The sun and the moon.   4. I.e., the Sabians who were Abraham's contemporaries.

argumentation, peace be on him, against them. At the conclusion of the story they mention that the king put *Abraham our Father*, may peace be upon him, into prison, and that, being in prison, he persevered | for days and days in arguing against them. Thereupon the king became afraid that he would ruin his[5] polity and turn the people away from their religions and banished him toward Syria after having confiscated all his property. This is what they relate. You will find this story set forth in this manner in "The Nabatean Agriculture."[6] They do not mention what is related in our true traditions, and the prophetic revelation that came to him. For they tax him with lying because of his disagreeing with their corrupt opinion. I have no doubt that in view of the fact that he, may peace be upon him, disagreed with the doctrine of all men, these erring men reviled, blamed, and belittled him. Accordingly, because he bore this for the sake of God, may He be exalted, and preferred truth to his reputation, he was told: *And I will bless them that bless thee, and him that curseth thee will I curse; and in thee shall all the families of the earth be blessed.*[7] And in point of fact his activity has resulted, as we see today, in the consensus of the greater part of the population of the earth in glorifying him and considering themselves as blessed through his memory, so that even those who do not belong to his progeny pretend to descend from him. No one is antagonistic to him or ignorant of his greatness except the remnants of this religious community that has perished, remnants that survive in the extremities of the earth, as for instance the infidels among the Turks in the extreme North and the Hindus in the extreme South. These are the remnants of the religious community of the Sabians, for this was a religious community that extended over the whole earth.

The utmost attained by the speculation of those who philosophized in those times consisted in imagining that God was the spirit of the sphere and that the sphere and the stars are a body of which the deity, may He be exalted, is its spirit. Abū Bakr Ibn al-Ṣāʾigh[8] has mentioned this in the commentary on the "Akroasis."[9] Therefore all the Sabians believed in the eternity of the world, since in their opinion heaven is the deity.

They deem *Adam* to have been an individual born of male | and female like the other human individuals, but they glorify him and say that he was a prophet, the envoy[10] of the moon, who called people to worship the moon, and that there are compilations of his on the cultivation of the soil. Similarly the Sabians say that *Noah* was a cultivator of the soil and that he did not

5. I.e., the king's.   6. A supposedly ancient Sabian book. Cf. this chapter below.
7. Gen. 12:3.   8. Ibn Bājja. Cf. I 74, n. 10.   9. I.e., Aristotle's *Physics*.
10. Or: prophetic lawgiver.

approve of the worship of idols. Therefore you will find that all the Sabians blame *Noah* and say that he never worshipped an idol. They also mention in their books that he was beaten and put into prison because of his worshipping God, and tell various other tales about him. They deem that *Seth* disagreed with the opinion of his father *Adam* concerning the worship of the moon, and tell most ridiculous lies that show a great deficiency of intellect, their being more remote from philosophy than any other men and their being extremely ignorant. Of *Adam* they say that when he left the clime of the sun, which is in the vicinity of India, and came to the clime of Babylon, he brought with him marvellous things: among them a golden tree that grew and had leaves and branches, also a stone tree, and a green leaf of a tree that fire could not burn. And he spoke of a tree, of a man's stature in height, that could given shelter to ten thousand men. He also brought with him two leaves in each of which two individuals could be wrapped. They also tell fables about other marvels. It is to be wondered at that people who think that the world is eternal should at the same time believe in these things that are impossible in nature for those who have knowledge of the speculation on nature. Their purpose in mentioning *Adam* and everything they ascribe to him is to fortify their doctrine concerning the eternity of the world so that it should follow that the stars and the sphere are the deity.

However, when *the pillar of the world*[11] grew up and it became clear to him that there is a separate deity that is neither a body nor a force in a body and that all the stars | and the spheres were made by Him, and he understood that the fables upon which he was brought up were absurd, he began to refute their doctrine and to show up their opinions as false; he publicly manifested his disagreement with them and called *in the name of the Lord, God of the world*[12] — both the existence of the deity and the creation of the world in time by that deity being comprised in that call.

In conformity with these opinions, the Sabians set up statues for the planets,[13] golden statues for the sun and silver ones for the moon, and distributed the minerals and the climes between the planets, saying that one particular planet was the deity of one particular clime. And they built temples, set up the statues in them, and thought that the forces of the planets overflowed toward these statues and that consequently these statues talked, had understanding, gave prophetic revelation to people — I mean, the statues — and made known to people what was useful to them. Similarly they

11. I.e., Abraham.   12. Gen. 21:33. Cf. II 13, n. 4.
13. *kawākib*. Literally: stars. In the following lines this Arabic term is rendered several times as "planets."

said of the trees, which were assigned to the various planets, that when one particular tree was set apart for one particular planet, planted with a view to the latter, and a certain treatment was applied to it and with it, the spirit of that planet overflowed toward that tree, gave prophetic revelation to people, and spoke to them in sleep. You will find all this set forth literally in their books, to which I shall draw your attention. These were *the prophets of Baal and the prophets of Asherah* that are mentioned in our texts; among them these opinions became so firm that they *they forsook the Lord*[14] and called: *O Baal, answer us.*[15] All this came about because of these opinions being generally accepted, ignorance being widespread and the world then often being given to raving concerning imaginings of this kind. Accordingly such opinions developed among them that some of them became *soothsayers, enchanters, sorcerers, charmers, consulters with familiar spirits, wizards, and necromancers.*[16] We have already made it clear in our great compilation, | *Mishneh Torah,*[17] that *Abraham our Father* began to refute these opinions by means of arguments and feeble preaching, conciliating people and drawing them to obedience by means of benefits. Then the Master of the prophets[18] received prophetic inspiration; thereupon he perfected the purpose in that he commanded killing these people, wiping out their traces, and tearing out their roots: *Ye shall break down their altars, and so on,*[19] and forbade following those ways of theirs in anything: *And ye shall not walk in the customs [huqqoth] of the nation, and so on.*[20] You know from texts of the *Torah* figuring in a number of passages that the first intention of the Law as a whole is to put an end to *idolatry,* to wipe out its traces and all that is bound up with it, even its memory as well as all that leads to any of its works — as, for instance, *familar spirits* and a *wizard* and *making to pass through fire, a diviner, a soothsayer, an enchanter, a sorcerer, a charmer, and a necromancer* — and to warn against doing anything at all similar to their works and, all the more, against repeating the latter. It is explicitly stated in the text of the *Torah* that everything that was regarded by them as worship of their gods and as a way of coming near to them, is hateful and odious to God. This is stated in His saying: *For every abomination to the Lord, which He hateth, have they done unto their gods.*[21] You will find that in their books, about which I shall give you information, they mention that under certain circumstances they offer to the sun, their highest deity, seven beetles, seven mice, and seven bats. This alone is sufficient to arouse

14. Cf. Isa. 1:4.   15. I Kings 18:26.   16. Cf. Deut. 18:10–11.
17. Cf. ʿAbodah Zarah, I 3.   18. I.e., Moses.
19. Judg. 2:2. Cf. Exod. 34:13; Deut. 7:5.   20. Lev. 20:23.   21. Deut. 12:31.

disgust in human nature. Consequently all the *commandments* that are concerned with the prohibition against *idolatry* and everything that is connected with it or leads toward it or may be ascribed to it, are of manifest utility, for all of them are meant to bring about deliverance from these unhealthy opinions that turn one's attention away from all that is useful with regard to the two perfections toward the crazy notions | in which our fathers and forefathers were brought up: *Your fathers dwelt of old time on the other side of the river, even Terah, the father of Abraham and the father of Nachor; and they served other gods.*[22] It is about these notions that the truthful prophets have said:[23] *For they walked after vain things that do not profit.* How great then is the utility of every *commandment* that delivers us from this great error and brings us back to the correct belief: namely, that there is a deity who is the Creator of all this; that it is He who ought to be worshipped and loved and feared and not the things that are deemed to be gods; and that to come near to this true deity and to obtain His good will, nothing is required that is fraught with any hardship whatever, the only things needed being *love of Him and fear of Him* and nothing else. For these two are, as we shall explain, the end of divine worship: *And now, Israel, what doth the Lord thy God require of thee, and so on.*[24] We shall exhaust this subject in the sequel.

I shall now return to my purpose and say that the meaning of many of the laws became clear to me and their causes became known to me through my study of the doctrines, opinions, practices, and cult of the Sabians, as you will hear when I explain the reasons for the *commandments* that are considered to be without cause. I shall mention to you the books from which all that I know about the doctrines and opinions of the Sabians will become clear to you so that you will know for certain that what I say about the reasons for these laws is correct.

The most important book about this subject is "The Nabatean Agriculture" translated by Ibn Waḥshiyya.[25] In a future chapter I shall let you know why the Sabians treated their doctrines and agriculture in the same work. This book is filled with the ravings of the *idolaters* and with notions to which the souls of the vulgar incline and by which they are captivated — I mean the actions | of talismans, practices with a view to causing spirits to descend, demons, and ghouls living in deserts. In this book are also included

22. Josh. 24:2.
23. The following quotation amalgamates two passages: I Sam 12:21, and Jer. 2:8.
24. Deut. 10:12.
25. Abū Bakr Aḥmad Ibn ʿAlī Ibn Waḥshiyya seems to have been the author of this work, which he passed off as a translation from the Chaldean. The work appeared in 904.

extraordinary ravings laughed at by the intelligent, which are thought to depreciate the manifest miracles through which the people of the earth know that there is a deity governing the people of the earth; as it says: *That thou mayest know that the earth is the Lord's;*[26] and: *That I am the Lord in the midst of the earth.*[27] Accordingly it is related there about *Adam, the first* man, that he recounts in his book that in India there is a tree whose branches, if taken and thrown on the earth, move, crawling as snakes do; and also that there is another tree there whose root has a human form; this root may be heard to growl and to emit isolated words. He also narrates that if a man take a leaf of an herb, whose description is given, and puts it against his breast,[28] he becomes hidden from people and is not seen wherever he comes in or goes out. If this herb is used in fumigations under the open sky, people hear a sound and fearsome voices in the atmosphere while the smoke rises. There are many such fables in the book, told in the course of setting forth information about marvels in plants and the properties of agriculture; in this way the miracles are criticized and the suggestion made that they are worked by means of tricks. In one of the fables figuring in that book, it is mentioned that an althea bush, which was one of the *asheroth*[29] that they used, as I have let you know, remained for twelve thousand years in *Nineveh*; that it quarreled with a mandragora because of the latter's wanting to take its place; that the individual who used to receive prophetic revelation from that tree was deprived of that revelation for a while. After that interval of time, it informed him by such a revelation | that it had been preoccupied with the quarrel with the mandragora and ordered him to write to the Chaldeans asking them to judge between them and to pronounce which of them — the althea or the mandragora — was better for, and more frequently utilized in, their magic. This is a long fable, from which, if you examine it, you may draw inferences concerning the intellect and the sciences of the people of those times. Such were the *Sages of Babylon* that are referred to in those dark times. For these were the religious beliefs upon which they were brought up. If the belief in the existence of the deity were not generally accepted at present to such an extent in the religious communities, our days in these times would be even darker than that epoch. However, their darkness is of different kinds. I am, however, returning to our subject.

In that book it is related that an individual from among the *prophets of idolatry,* named *Tammuz,* called upon a king to worship the seven

26. Exod. 9:29.　　27. Exod. 8:18.　　28. Or: in his pocket.
29. A biblical Hebrew word that Maimonides applies to trees that have been consecrated to gods.

planets[30] and the twelve signs of the Zodiac. Thereupon that king killed him in an abominable manner. It is narrated that on the night of his death all the statues from the various countries of the earth assembled in the temple in Babylon, near the great golden statue, which was the statue of the sun. This statue was suspended between heaven and earth. And it came to a stop in the middle of the temple, while all the other statues surrounded it. Then it began to eulogize *Tammuz* and to relate what had happened to him, and all the statues wept and lamented during the whole of the night. In the morning, however, the statues flew away and returned to their temples in the various countries of the earth. And this became an enduring traditional custom to lament and weep over *Tammuz* on the first day of the month of *Tammuz*. The women weep over him and eulogize him. Consider then and understand and see what were the opinions of the people in those times. For this | story of *Tammuz* is very ancient among the Sabians. And from this book you will understand most of the ravings, practices, and festivals of the Sabians.

As for the story they tell about *Adam* and the *serpent and the tree of the knowledge of good and evil*, a story that also alludes to unusual clothing, take great care not to be confused in your intellect in such a way as to have the notion that what they say is a thing that has ever happened to *Adam* or to somebody else. For it is by no means a story concerning something real. With very little reflection it will become clear to you that all that they set forth in this fable is absurd and that it is a story that they put out after the promulgation of the *Torah*. For when the *Torah* had become generally known among the religious communities[31] and they[32] had heard the external meaning of the *Account of the Beginning*, taking the whole of it according to its external meaning, they concocted this story in order that inexperienced people should listen to it and be so deceived as to think that the world is eternal and that the story described in the *Torah* happened the way they tell it. Even though a man like you does not have to have his attention drawn to this point — as you have already acquired such sciences as will prevent your mind from becoming attached to the fables of the Sabians and the ravings of the Chasdeans and Chaldeans who are devoid of all science that is truly a science — I have warned against this in order to safeguard others, for the multitude frequently incline to regarding fables as the truth.

Among these books there is also the book of al-Ustumākhus that is ascribed to Aristotle,[33] but he cannot have written it; also books concerning

30. Literally: stars.   31. Or: nations.   32. I.e., the Sabians.
33. This pseudo-Aristotelian work exists in manuscript.

talismans like the book of Tumtum, the book al Sarb, and the Book of the
Degrees of the Sphere and the Forms Appearing in Each of These Degrees;
also a book concerning talismans that is likewise attributed to Aristotle, a
book | ascribed to Hermes, and the book written by Isḥāq al-Ṣābi on the
defense of the religious community of the Sabians, and the big book of this
same author concerning the laws of the Sabians, the details of their religion,
their festivals, their sacrifices, their prayers, and other matters belonging to
their religion. All the books that I have mentioned to you are *books of
idolatry* that have been translated into Arabic. But there is no doubt that
they are but a very small part of this literature if compared to the writings
that have not been translated and are not even extant, but have perished and
been lost in the course of the years. However, the books extant among us today contain an exposition of the greatest part of the opinions and the practices of the Sabians; some of the latter are generally known at present in the
world. I mean the building of temples, the setting-up in them of images
made of cast metal and stone, the building of altars and the offering-up upon
them of either animal sacrifices or various kinds of food, the institution of
festivals, the gatherings for prayer and for various kinds of worship in those
temples in which they locate highly venerated places that are called by them
the temple of the intellectual forms, as well as the setting-up of images *upon
the high mountains, and so on*,[34] the veneration of those *asheroth*,[35] the setting-up of *monumental stones*, and other matters of which you will learn in
the books to which I have drawn your attention. The knowledge of these
opinions and practices is a very important chapter in the exposition of the
reasons for the *commandments*. For the foundation of the whole of our Law
and the pivot around which it turns, consists in the effacement of these
opinions from the minds and of these monuments from existence. With
respect to their effacement from the minds, it says: *Lest your heart be
deceived, and so on*;[36] *Whose heart turneth away this day, and so on*;[37] and
with respect to their effacement from existence, it says: *Ye shall break down
their altars . . . and hew down their groves, and so on*;[38] *And destroy their
name out of that place.*[39] | These two purposes are reiterated in a number of
passages. For this is the first intention extending over the whole of the Law,
as is made known to us by [the Sages], *may their memory be blessed*, in their
transmitted commentary on His dictum, may He be exalted: *Even all that
the Lord hath commanded you by the hand of Moses.*[40] For they say:

34. Deut. 12:2.   35. Cf. n. 29, this chap.   36. Deut. 11:16.
37. Deut. 29:17.   38. Deut. 7:5.   39. Deut. 12:3.   40. Num. 15:23.

Herefrom you may learn that everyone who professes idolatry, disbelieves in the Torah in its entirety; whereas he who disbelieves in idolatry, professes the Torah in its entirety.[41] Cognize this.

CHAPTER 30

When you consider these ancient and unhealthy opinions, it will become clear to you that among all men it was an accepted view that through the worship of stars the earth becomes populated and the soil fertile. Their men of knowledge, as well as the ascetics and the men of piety among them, preached this to the people and taught them that agriculture, on which the existence of man depends, can only be perfected and succeed according to wish if you worship the sun and the stars; if you anger them through disobedience, the land will become barren and devastated. In their books they say that Jupiter had been angry with the wildernesses and the deserts and that they therefore lacked water and lacked trees and were inhabited by ghouls. They had a very great esteem for the peasants and the cultivators of the soil because of their being engaged in cultivating the earth, an occupation that conforms to the will of the stars and pleases them. The reason why the *idolators* had a great esteem for oxen was the utility of the latter in agriculture. They even said that it was not permitted to kill them because force was joined in them | to handiness for man in agriculture; the oxen only acted thus and submitted to man in spite of their force because the gods were pleased with their work in agriculture. Inasmuch as these opinions were generally accepted, [the idolaters] connected *idolatry* with agriculture, the latter being necessary for the subsistence of man and of most animals. Accordingly *the priests of idolatry* preached to the people during their assemblies in the temples and fortified in their minds the notion that through the practices of this cult, rains would fall, the trees would bear fruit, and the land would become fertile and populous. Consider what they say in "The Nabatean Agriculture"[1] in the passage on the vineyard; you will find there the following text of the Sabians: All the ancient sages have said and the prophets have commanded and prescribed to play on musical

41. Siphre to Num. 15:23; B.T., Horayoth, 8a; B.T., Qiddushin, 40a. The subject is dealt with by Maimonides in *Mishneh Torah*, ᶜAbodah Zarah, II 4.

1. This work is referred to in the preceding chapter.

instruments before the statues during festivals. They said — and they were truthful — that the gods were pleased with this and accorded the best reward to those who acted thus. They multiplied the promises concerning this — promising, that is, a prolongation of life, a warding-off of calamities, the disappearance of infirmities, the fertility of the sowing, and the thriving of the fruits. The text of the Sabians continues up to here.

Now inasmuch as these notions were generally accepted so that they were regarded as certain, and as God, may He be exalted, wished in His pity for us to efface this error from our minds and to take away fatigue from our bodies through the abolition of these tiring and useless practices and to give us Laws through the instrumentality of *Moses our Master*, the latter informed us in His name, may He be exalted, that if the stars and the planets were worshipped, their worship would be a cause for the rain ceasing to fall, for the land being devastated | and producing nothing, for the fruit of the trees falling off, for misfortunes attending circumstances, for infirmities befalling the bodies, and for a shortening of lives. These are the intentions of *the words of the covenant, which the Lord made, and so on.*[2] You will find that this intention is reiterated in the whole of the *Torah:* I mean that it is a necessary consequence of the worship of the stars that rains will cease to fall, that the land will be devastated, that circumstances will become bad, that the bodies will suffer from diseases, and that lives will be short; whereas a necessary consequence of the abandonment of their worship and the adoption of the worship of God will be rainfall, the fertility of the land, good circumstances, health of the body, and length of life. This is the contrary of what was preached by the *idolaters* to the people in order that they worship idols. For the foundation of the Law consists in putting an end to this opinion and effacing its traces, as we have explained.

CHAPTER 31

There is a group of human beings who consider it a grievous thing that causes should be given for any law; what would please them most is that the intellect would not find a meaning for the commandments and prohibitions. What compels them to feel thus is a sickness that they find in their souls, a sickness to which they are unable to give utterance and of

2. Deut. 28:69. The quotation is not exact.

which they cannot furnish a satisfactory account. For they think that if those laws were useful in this existence and had been given to us for this or that reason, it would be as if they derived from the reflection and the understanding of some intelligent being. If, however, there is a thing for which the intellect could not find any meaning at all and that does not lead to something useful, it indubitably derives from God; for the reflection of man would not lead to such a thing. It is as if, | according to these people of weak intellects, man were more perfect than his Maker; for man speaks and acts in a manner that leads to some intended end, whereas the deity does not act thus, but commands us to do things that are not useful to us and forbids us to do things that are not harmful to us. But He is far exalted above this; the contrary is the case — the whole purpose consisting in what is useful for us, as we have explained[1] on the basis of its dictum: *For our good always, that He might preserve us alive, as it is at this day*.[2] And it says: *Which shall hear all these statutes [ḥuqqim] and say: Surely this great community is a wise and understanding people*.[3] Thus it states explicitly that even all the *statutes [ḥuqqim]*[4] will show to all the nations that they have been given with *wisdom and understanding*. Now if there is a thing for which no reason is known and that does not either procure something useful or ward off something harmful, why should one say of one who believes in it or practices it that he is *wise and understanding* and of great worth? And why should the religious communities think it a wonder? Rather things are indubitably as we have mentioned: every *commandment* from among these *six hundred and thirteen commandments* exists either with a view to communicating a correct opinion, or to putting an end to an unhealthy opinion, or to communicating a rule of justice, or to warding off an injustice, or to endowing men with a noble moral quality, or to warning them against an evil moral quality. Thus all [the commandments] are bound up with three things: opinions, moral qualities, and political civic actions. We do not count speeches as one of these things since the speeches that the Law enjoins or forbids belong in part to the class of civic actions, and in part are meant to cause opinions, and in part are meant to cause moral qualities. Therefore we have limited ourselves here, in giving reasons for every law, to these three classes. |

1. Cf. III 27.   2. Deut. 6:24.   3. Deut. 4:6.   4. Cf. III 26, n. 3.

CHAPTER 32

If you consider the divine actions — I mean to say the natural actions — the deity's wily graciousness and wisdom, as shown in the creation of living beings, in the gradation of the motions of the limbs, and the proximity of some of the latter to others, will through them[1] become clear to you. Similarly His wisdom and wily graciousness, as shown in the gradual succession of the various states of the whole individual, will become clear to you. The brain is an example of the gradation of the motions and the proximity of the limbs of an individual: for its front part is soft, very soft indeed, whereas its posterior part is more solid. The spinal marrow is even more solid and becomes more and more solid as it stretches on. The nerves are organs of sensation and of motion. Accordingly the nerves required only for apprehension by the senses or for motion that presents but little difficulty, like the motions of the eyelids and of the jaws, proceed from the brain, whereas the motions required for moving the limbs proceed from the spinal marrow. As, however, it is impossible for a nerve, in view of its softness — even for a nerve proceeding from the spinal marrow — to move an articulation, the matter was wilily and graciously arranged as follows: the nerves are ramified into fibers, and the latter, having been filled with flesh, become muscles. Thereupon the nerve, having overpassed the extremity of the muscle, having become more solid, and having been commingled with fragments of ligaments, becomes a tendon. The tendon joins and adheres to the bone; and thereupon, because of this gradation, the nerve is capable of moving a limb. I mentioned only this one example to you because it is the most obvious of the wonders explained in the treatise "On the Utilities of the Parts of the Body,"[2] all of which wonders are clear, manifest, and well known to those who consider them with a penetrating mind. Similarly the deity made a wily and gracious arrangement | with regard to all the individuals of the living beings that suck.[3] For when born, such individuals are extremely soft and cannot feed on dry food. Accordingly breasts were prepared for them so that they should produce milk with a view to their receiving humid food, which is similar to the composition of their bodies, until their limbs gradually and little by little become dry and solid.

Many things in our Law are due to something similar to this very governance on the part of Him who governs, may He be glorified and

1. I.e., through the above-mentioned actions.
2. Cf. Galen *De usu partium humani corporis* i.17; ii.3.   3. I.e., the mammals.

exalted. For a sudden transition from one opposite to another is impossible. And therefore man, according to his nature, is not capable of abandoning suddenly all to which he was accustomed. As therefore God sent *Moses our Master* to make out of us *a kingdom of priests and a holy nation*[4] — through the knowledge of Him, may He be exalted, accordingly to what He has explained, saying: *Unto thee it was shown that thou mightest know, and so on;*[5] *Know this day, and lay it to thy heart, and so on*[6] — so that we should devote ourselves to His worship according to what He said: *And to serve Him with all your heart,*[7] and: *And ye shall serve the Lord your God,*[8] and: *And Him shall ye serve;*[9] and as at that time the way of life generally accepted and customary in the whole world and the universal service upon which we were brought up consisted in offering various species of living beings in the temples in which images were set up, in worshipping the latter, and in burning incense before them — the pious ones and the ascetics being at that time, as we have explained, the people who were devoted to the service of the temples consecrated to the stars — : His wisdom, may He be exalted, and His gracious ruse, which is manifest in regard to all His creatures, did not require that He give us a Law prescribing the rejection, abandonment, and abolition of all these kinds of worship. For one could not then conceive the acceptance of [such a Law], considering the nature of man, which always likes that | to which it is accustomed. At that time this would have been similar to the appearance of a prophet in these times who, calling upon the people to worship God, would say: "God has given you a Law forbidding you to pray to Him, to fast, to call upon Him for help in misfortune. Your worship should consist solely in meditation without any works at all." Therefore He, may He be exalted, suffered the above-mentioned kinds of worship to remain, but transferred them from created or imaginary and unreal things to His own name, may He be exalted, commanding us to practice them with regard to Him, may He be exalted. Thus He commanded us to build a temple for Him: *And let them make Me a Sanctuary;*[10] to have an altar for His name: *An altar of earth thou shalt make unto Me;*[11] to have the sacrifice offered up to Him: *When any man of you bringeth an offering unto the Lord;*[12] to bow down in worship before Him; and to burn incense before Him. And He forbade the performance of any of these actions with a view to someone else: *He that sacrificeth unto the gods shall be utterly*

4. Exod. 19:6.　　5. Deut. 4:35.　　6. Deut. 4:39.　　7. Deut. 11:13.
8. Exod. 23:25.　　9. Deut. 13:5.　　10. Exod. 25:8.
11. Exod. 20:24 (v. 21 in some translations).　　12. Lev. 1:2.

destroyed, and so on;[13] *For thou shalt bow down to no other god.*[14] And he singled out *Priests* for the service of the *Sanctuary*, saying: *That they may minister unto Me in the priest's office.*[15] And because of their employment in the temple[16] and the sacrifices in it, it was necessary to fix for them dues that would be sufficient for them; namely, the dues of the *Levites* and the *Priests*. Through this divine ruse it came about that the memory of *idolatry* was effaced and that the grandest and true foundation of our belief — namely, the existence and oneness of the deity — was firmly established, while at the same time the souls had no feeling of repugnance and were not repelled because of the abolition of modes of worship to which they were accustomed and than which no other mode of worship was known at that time.

I know that on thinking about this at first your soul will necessarily have a feeling of repugnance toward this notion and will feel aggrieved because of it; and you will ask me in your heart and say to me: How is it possible that none of the commandments, prohibitions, and great actions — which are very precisely set forth and prescribed for fixed seasons — should be intended for its own sake, but for the sake of something else, as if this were a ruse | invented for our benefit by God in order to achieve His first intention? What was there to prevent Him, may He be exalted, from giving us a Law in accordance with His first intention[17] and from procuring us the capacity to accept this? In this way there would have been no need for the things that you consider to be due to a second intention. Hear then the reply to your question that will put an end to this sickness in your heart and reveal to you the true reality of that to which I have drawn your attention. It is to the effect that the text of the *Torah* tells a quite similar story, namely, in its dictum: *God led them not by the way of the land of the Philistines, although it was near, and so on. But God led the people about, by the way of the wilderness of the Red Sea.*[18] Just as God perplexed them in anticipation of what their bodies were naturally incapable of bearing — turning them away from the high road toward which they had been going, toward another road so that the first intention should be achieved — so did He in anticipation of what the soul is naturally incapable of receiving, prescribe the laws that we have mentioned so that the first intention should be achieved, namely, the apprehension of Him, may He be exalted, and the rejection of *idolatry*. For just as it is not in the nature of man that, after having been

13. Exod. 22:19. The entire verse reads: *He that sacrificeth unto the gods, save unto the Lord only, shall be utterly destroyed.*
14. Exod. 34:14.   15. Exod. 28:41.   16. Literally: house.
17. Or: from revealing His first intention.   18. Exod. 13:17–18.

brought up in slavish service occupied with clay, bricks, and similar things, he should all of a sudden wash off from his hands the dirt deriving from them and proceed immediately to fight against *the children of Anak*,[19] so is it also not in his nature that, after having been brought up upon very many modes of worship and of customary practices, which the souls find so agreeable that they become as it were a primary notion,[20] he should abandon them all of a sudden. And just as the deity used a gracious ruse in causing them to wander perplexedly in the desert until their souls became courageous—it being well known that life in the desert and lack of comforts for the body necessarily develop courage whereas the opposite circumstances necessarily develop cowardice—and until, moreover, people were born who were not | accustomed to humiliation and servitude—all this having been brought about by[21] *Moses our Master* by means of divine commandments: *At the commandment of the Lord they encamped, and at the commandment of the Lord they journeyed, at the commandment of the Lord by the hand of Moses*[22]—so did this group of laws derive from a divine grace, so that they should be left with the kind of practices to which they were accustomed and so that consequently the belief, which constitutes the first intention, should be validated[23] in them.

As for your question: What was there to prevent God from giving us a Law in accordance with His first intention[24] and from procuring us the capacity to accept this?—you lay yourself open to an inference from this second question. For one may say to you: What was there to prevent God from making them march *by the way of the land of the Philistines* and procuring them the capacity to engage in wars so that there should be no need for this roundabout way with *the pillar of cloud by day and the pillar of fire by night?*[25] Also you lay yourself open to a third question as an inference, a question regarding the reason for the detailing of promises and threats with regard to the whole Law. One may say to you: Inasmuch as God's first intention and His will are that we should believe in this Law and that we should perform the actions prescribed by it, why did He not procure us the capacity always to accept this intention and to act in accordance with it, instead of using a ruse with regard to us, declaring that He will procure us benefits if we obey Him and will take vengeance on us if we disobey Him and performing in deed all these acts of benefiting and all these acts of vengeance? For this too is a ruse used by Him with regard to us in order to

19. Cf. Num. 13:28. 20. Or: intelligible. 21. Or: through the instrumentality of.
22. Num. 9:23. 23. *yaṣuḥḥu*, the word used, may mean "to be correct" or "to be in a good state," "to be valid."
24. Or: from revealing to us His first intention. 25. Exod. 13:22.

achieve His first intention with respect to us. What was there to prevent Him from causing the inclination to accomplish the acts of obedience willed by Him and to avoid the acts of disobedience abhorred by Him, to be a natural disposition fixed in us?

There is one and the same general answer to all these three questions and to all the others that belong to the same class: Though all miracles change the nature of some individual being, | God does not change at all the nature of human individuals by means of miracles. Because of this great principle it says: *O that they had such an heart as this, and so on.*[26] It is because of this that there are commandments and prohibitions, rewards and punishments. We have already explained this fundamental principle by giving its proofs in a number of passages in our compilations. We do not say this because we believe that the changing of the nature of any human individual is difficult for Him, may He be exalted. Rather is it possible and fully within capacity.[27] But according to the foundations of the Law, of the Torah, He has never willed to do it, nor shall He ever will it. For if it were His will that the nature of any human individual should be changed because of what He, may He be exalted, wills from that individual, sending of prophets and all giving of a Law would have been useless.

I return to my subject and I say that, as this kind of worship — I mean the *sacrifices* — pertain to a second intention, whereas invocation, prayer, and similar practices and modes of worship come closer to the first intention and are necessary for its achievement, a great difference has been made[28] between the two kinds. For one kind of worship — I mean the offering of sacrifices — even though it was done in His name, may He be exalted, was not prescribed to us in the way it existed at first; I mean to say in such a way that sacrifices could be offered in every place and at every time. Nor could a temple be set up in any fortuitous place, nor could any fortuitous man offer the sacrifice: *Whosoever would, he consecrated him.*[29] On the contrary, He forbade all this and established one single house [as the temple], *Unto the place which the Lord shall chose,*[30] so that sacrifices should not be offered elsewhere: *That thou offer not thy burnt-offerings in every place that thou seest.*[31] Also only the offspring of one particular family can be *Priest[s].* All this was intended to restrict this kind of worship, so that only the portion of it should subsist | whose abolition is not required by His wisdom. On the other hand, invocation and prayers are made in every place and by anyone

26. Deut. 5:26.   27. I.e., the capacity of God.
28. Or: He has made a great difference.   29. I Kings 13:33.   30. Deut. 12:26.
31. Deut. 12:13.

whoever he may be. This also applies to the *fringes*,[32] the *doorposts*,[33] and the *phylacteries*[34] and other similar modes of worship. Because of the notion I have revealed to you, people are frequently blamed in the books of the prophets because of their zeal for sacrifices, and it is explained to them that they are not the object of a purpose sought for its own sake and that God can dispense with them. Thus *Samuel* says: *Hath the Lord as great delight in burnt-offerings and sacrifices, as in hearkening to the voice of the Lord? and so on.*[35] And *Isaiah* says: *To what purpose is the multitude of your sacrifices unto Me? saith the Lord, and so on.*[36] And *Jeremiah* says: *For I spoke not unto your fathers, nor commanded them in the day that I brought them out of the land of Egypt, concerning burnt-offerings or sacrifices; but this thing commanded I them, saying: Hearken unto My voice, and I will be your God, and ye shall be My people.*[37] This dictum has been regarded as difficult by everyone whose words I have seen or heard. They say: How can *Jeremiah* say of God that He has given us no injunctions *concerning burnt-offerings and sacrifices*, seeing that the greater part of the *commandments* are concerned with these things? However, the purpose of the dictum is as I have explained to you. For he says that the first intention consists only in your apprehending Me and not worshipping someone other than Me: *And I will be your God, and ye shall be My people*. Those laws concerning sacrifices and repairing to the temple were given only for the sake of the realization of this fundamental principle. It is for the sake of that principle that I transferred these modes of worship to My name, so that the trace of *idolatry* be effaced and the fundamental principle of My unity be established. You, however, came and abolished this end, while holding fast to what has been done for its sake. For you have doubted of My existence: *They have belied the Lord, and said: It is not He.*[38] And you have committed *idolatry: And burn incense unto Baal,* | *and walk after other gods . . . and come . . . unto the house, and so on.*[39] And still you continue to repair to *the temple of the Lord*, offering sacrifices, which are things that have not been intended in the first intention.

I have another way of interpreting this *verse*; it too leads to the very same purpose that we have mentioned. It has been made clear both in the [scriptural] text and in the tradition that in the first legislation given to us there was nothing at all *concerning burnt-offerings and sacrifices*. You ought

32. Cf. Num. 15:38.   33. Cf. Deut. 6:9; 11:20.
34. Cf. Exod. 13:9 and 16; Deut. 6:8; 11:18.   35. I Sam. 15:22.   36. Isa. 1:11.
37. Jer. 7:22–23.   38. Jer. 5:12.
39. Jer. 7:9–10. The quotation is not quite exact.

not to occupy your mind with *the passover of Egypt*[40] for the reason for this is clear and evident, as we shall set forth.[41] Moreover this happened in *the land of Egypt*, whereas the laws referred to in the *verse* in question are those that have been given to us after *the exodus from Egypt*. For this reason he[42] makes the following restriction in that *verse: In the day that I brought them out of the land of Egypt*. For the first *command* given after *the exodus from Egypt* was the one given to us in *Marah*, namely, His saying to us there: *If thou wilt diligently hearken to the voice of the Lord thy God, and so on.*[43] *There He made for them a statute and a judgment, and so on.*[44] And the correct tradition says: *The Sabbath and the civil laws were prescribed at Marah.*[45] Accordingly the *statute* referred to is the *Sabbath*, and the *judgment* consists in the *civil laws*, that is, in the abolition of mutual wrongdoing. And this is, as we have explained, the first intention: I mean the belief in correct opinions, namely, in the creation of the world in time. For you already know that the foundation of the law addressed to us concerning the Sabbath is its contribution in fortifying this principle, as we have explained in this Treatise.[46] Besides the correctness of the beliefs, the intention[47] also included the abolition of mutual wrongdoing among men. Accordingly it is already clear to you that in the first legislation there was nothing at all *concerning burnt-offerings and sacrifices*, for, as we have mentioned, these belong to the second intention. The very notion | expressed by *Jeremiah* is also set forth in *Psalms* by way of blame to the whole religious community[48] because of its being at that time ignorant of the first intention and not distinguishing between it and the second intention. [The Psalmist] says: *Hear, O My people, and I will speak; O Israel, and I will testify against thee: God, thy God, am I. I will not reprove thee for thy sacrifices and thy burnt-offerings, to have been continually before Me. I will take no bullock out of thy house, nor he-goats out of thy fold.*[49] Whenever this notion is repeated, this is what is aimed at thereby. Understand this thoroughly and reflect upon it.

40. Cf. Exod. 12:21 and 26–27, according to which the killing of a lamb in sacrifice was already prescribed in Egypt.
41. Cf. III 46.   42. I.e., Jeremiah.   43. Exod. 15:26.   44. Exod. 15:25.
45. B.T., Shabbath, 87b; B.T., Sanhedrin, 56b.   46. Cf. II 31.
47. The first intention is meant.   48. Or: nation.   49. Ps. 50:7–9.

To the totality of purposes of the perfect Law there belong the abandonment, depreciation, and restraint of desires in so far as possible, so that these should be satisfied only in so far as this is necessary. You know already that most of the lusts and licentiousness of the multitude consist in an appetite for eating, drinking, and sexual intercourse. This is what destroys man's last perfection, what harms him also in his first perfection,[1] and what corrupts most of the circumstances of the citizens and of the people engaged in domestic governance. For when only the desires are followed, as is done by the ignorant,[2] the longing for speculation is abolished, the body is corrupted, and the man to whom this happens perishes before this is required by his natural term of life; thus cares and sorrows multiply, mutual envy, hatred, and strife aiming at taking away what the other has, multiply. All this is brought about by the fact that the ignoramus regards pleasure alone as the end to be sought for its own sake. Therefore God, may His name be held sublime, employed a gracious ruse through giving us certain laws | that destroy this end and turn thought away from it in every way. He forbids everything that leads to lusts and to mere pleasure. This is an important purpose of this Law. Do you not see how the texts of the *Torah* command to kill him who manifestly has an excessive longing for the pleasure of eating and drinking? For he is *the stubborn and rebellious son*,[3] to whom its following dictum applies: *He is a glutton and a drunkard*.[4] He commands stoning and cutting him off speedily before the matter becomes serious and before he brings about the destruction of many and ruins by the violence of his lust the circumstances of righteous men.

Similarly to the totality of intentions of the Law there belong gentleness and docility; man should not be hard and rough, but responsive, obedient, acquiescent, and docile. You know already His commandment, may He be exalted: *Circumcise therefore the foreskin of your heart, and be no more stiffnecked*.[5] *Be silent, and hearken, O Israel*.[6] *If ye be willing and obedient*.[7] With regard to docility in accepting what ought to be accepted, it is said: *And we will hear it, and do it*.[8] By way of a parable, it is said about this: *Draw me, we will run after thee*.[9]

1. As to these two perfections, cf. III 27.   2. *jāhiliyya*. Cf. III 8, n. 8.
3. Deut. 21:18.   4. Deut. 21:20.   5. Deut. 10:16.   6. Deut. 27:9.
7. Isa. 1:19.   8. Deut. 5:24.
9. Song of Songs 1:4. In the Midrash to this verse, it is interpreted as referring to the obedience promised by Israel to God at the time of the revelation at Mount Sinai.

Similarly one of the intentions of the Law is purity and sanctification; I mean by this renouncing and avoiding sexual intercourse and causing it to be as infrequent as possible, as I shall make clear.[10] Thus when He, may He be exalted, commanded the religious community[11] to be sanctified with a view to receiving the *Torah*, and He said: *And sanctify them today and tomorrow*[12] — He said: *Come not near a woman.*[13] Consequently He states clearly that *sanctity* consists in renouncing sexual intercourse, just as He also states explicitly that the giving-up of the drinking of wine constitutes *sanctity*, in what He says about the *Nazarite: He shall be saintly.*[14] A text of *Siphra* reads: *Sanctify yourselves therefore, and be ye holy*[15] — *This concerns santification by the commandments*. And just as the Law designates obedience to these commandments as *sanctity* and *purity*, it also designates transgression of these commandments and the perpetration of evil actions as *impurity*, | as I shall make clear.

Cleaning garments, washing the body, and removal of dirt also constitute one of the purposes of this Law. But this comes after the purification of the actions and the purification of the heart from polluting opinions and polluting moral qualities. For to confine oneself to cleaning the outward appearance through washing and cleaning the garment, while having at the same time a lust for various pleasures and unbridled license in eating and sexual intercourse, merits the utmost blame. *Isaiah* says about this: *They that sanctify themselves and purify themselves to go unto the gardens behind one in the midst, eating the flesh of swine, and so on.*[16] He says: They purify themselves and sanctify themselves in the open and public places; and afterwards, when they are alone in their rooms and in the interior of their houses, they are engaged in acts of disobedience — that is, in their unbridled license in eating forbidden food: *the swine and the detestable thing and the mouse.*[17] Perhaps he refers by means of the words, *behind one in the midst*, to engaging in solitude in forbidden sexual intercourse. To sum up the dictum: Their outward appearances are clean and universally known as unsullied and pure, whereas innerly they are engaged in the pursuit of their desires and the pleasures of their bodies. But this is not the purpose of the Law, for the first purpose is to restrain desire — the purification of the outer coming after the purification of the inner. *Solomon* has drawn attention to those who rely upon washing the body and cleaning the garments, whereas their actions are

10. Cf. III 49.   11. Or: nation.   12. Exod. 19:10.   13. Exod. 19:15.
14. Num. 6:5.
15. Lev. 11:44. The following words are from the Siphra to this verse.
16. Isa. 66:17.   17. Isa. 66:17.

impure and their moral qualities evil. For he says: *There is a generation that are pure in their own eyes, and yet are not washed from their filthiness. There is a generation, O how lofty are their eyes! and their eyelids are lifted up.*[18]

If then you consider likewise these intentions we have mentioned in this chapter, the reasons for many laws will become clear to you; those reasons were unknown before these intentions were known, as I shall explain when recommencing. |

CHAPTER 34

Among the things that you likewise ought to know is the fact that the Law does not pay attention to the isolated. The Law was not given with a view to things that are rare. For in everything that it wishes to bring about, be it an opinion or a moral habit or a useful work, it is directed only toward the things that occur in the majority of cases and pays no attention to what happens rarely or to the damage occurring to the unique human being because of this way of determination and because of the legal character of the governance. For the Law is a divine thing; and it is your business to reflect on the natural things in which the general utility, which is included in them, nonetheless necessarily produces damages to individuals, as is clear from our discourse and the discourse of others. In view of this consideration also, you will not wonder at the fact that the purpose of the Law is not perfectly achieved in every individual and that, on the contrary, it necessarily follows that there should exist individuals whom this governance of the Law does not make perfect. For not everything that derives necessarily from the natural specific forms is actualized in every individual. Indeed, all things proceed from one deity and one agent and *have been given from one shepherd.*[1] The contrary of this is impossible, and we have already explained[2] that the impossible has a stable nature that never changes. In view of this consideration, it also will not be possible that the laws be dependent on changes in the circumstances of the individuals and of the times, as is the case with regard to medical treatment, which is particularized for every individual in conformity with his present temperament. On the contrary,

18. Prov. 30:12–13.

1. Eccles. 12:11.   2. Cf. III 15.

governance of the Law ought to be absolute and universal, including every-
one, | even if it is suitable only for certain individuals and not suitable for
others; for if it were made to fit individuals, the whole would be corrupted
and *you would make out of it something that varies.*[3] For this reason, matters
that are primarily intended in the Law ought not to be dependent on time
or place; but the decrees ought to be absolute and universal, according to
what He, may He be exalted, says: *As for the congregation, there shall be
one statute [huqqah] for you.*[4] However, only the universal interests, those
of the majority, are considered in them, as we have explained.

After I have set forth these premises, I shall begin to explain what I
have intended to explain.

CHAPTER 35

With a view to this purpose, I have divided all the *commandments* into
fourteen classes.

The first class comprises the *commandments* that are fundamental
opinions. They are those that we have enumerated in *Laws of the Foundations of the Torah [Hilkhoth Yesodei ha-Torah].*[1] *Repentance* and *fasts* also
belong, as I shall explain, to this class. With respect to inculcating opinions
that are correct and that are useful for belief in the Law, one should not say,
what is their utility? as we have explained.

The second class comprises the *commandments* concerned with the
prohibition of *idolatry*. They are those that we have enumerated in *Laws
concerning Idolatry [Hilkhoth ʿAbodah Zarah].* Know that the prohibitions
regarding *garments of diverse sorts, first products*[2] [of trees], and [sowing] *the
vineyard with diverse seeds,*[3] also belong to this class, as shall be explained.
The reason for this class is also well known. For all of them are meant to
validate the true opinions and to make the multitude cling to them through-
out | the ages.

The third class comprises the *commandments* concerned with improve-
ment of the moral qualities. They are those that we have enumerated in
Laws concerning Opinions [Hilkhoth Deʿoth]. It is well known that through

3. Cf. e.g., B.T., Shabbath, 35b; B.T., Ḥullin, 9a.   4. Num. 15:15.
1. This and the other titles referred to in this chapter are parts of Maimonides' legal compilation, *Mishneh Torah.*
2. Literally: *foreskin.*   3. Cf. III 26.

fine moral qualities human association and society are perfected, which is necessary for the good order of human circumstances.

The fourth class comprises the *commandments* concerned with giving alms, lending, bestowal of gifts, and matters that are connected with this — as for instance *estimations* and *anathemas*,[4] the ordinances concerning *loans* and *slaves*, and all the *commandments* that we have enumerated in the *Book of Seeds* [*Sepher Zeraᶜim*] with the exception of those treating of the *mingling* [of diverse species] and the *first products* [of trees]. The reason for all these is manifest, for they are equally useful in turn to all men. For one who is rich today will be poor tomorrow, or his descendants will be poor; whereas one who is poor today will be rich tomorrow, or his son will be rich.

The fifth class comprises the *commandments* concerned with prohibiting wrongdoing and aggression. They are those included in our compilation in the *Book of Torts* [*Sepher Neziqin*]. The utility of this class is manifest.

The sixth class comprises the *commandments* concerned with punishments, as for instance *laws concerning thieves and robbers and laws concerning false witnesses* — in fact most of the matters we have enumerated in the *Book of Judges* [*Sepher Shophetim*]. The utility of this is clear and manifest, for if a criminal is not punished, injurious acts will not be abolished in any way and none of those who design aggression will be deterred. No one is as weak-minded as those who deem that the abolition of punishments would be merciful on men. On the contrary, this would be cruelty itself on them as well as the ruin of the order of the city. On the contrary, mercy is to be found in His command, may He be exalted: *Judges and officers shalt thou make thee in all thy gates.*[5]

The seventh class comprises the laws of property concerned with the mutual transactions | of people, such as loans, hire for wages, deposits, buying, selling, and other things of this kind. Inheritance also belongs to this group. These are the *commandments* that we have enumerated in the *Book of Acquisition and Judgments* [*Sepher Qinyan ve-Mishpatim*]. The utility of this class is clear and manifest. For these property associations are necessary for people in every city, and it is indispensable that rules of justice should be given with a view to these transactions and that these transactions be regulated in a useful manner.

The eighth class comprises the *commandments* concerning the days in which work is forbidden,[6] I mean *Sabbaths and festivals*. Scripture has

4. I.e., vows that can be redeemed and those that cannot.
5. Deut. 16:18.   6. Literally: the forbidden days.

explained the reason of each of these days and has mentioned the cause for each of them, which may consist either in the intention to inculcate a certain opinion or to procure a rest for the body or in both these things, as we shall explain later on.

The ninth class comprises all the other practices of worship prescribed to everybody,[7] such as prayer and *recitation of Shema^c* and the other things we have enumerated in the *Book of Love* [*Sepher Ahabah*] with the exception of *circumcision*. The utility of this class is manifest, for it is wholly composed of works that fortify opinions concerning the love of the deity and what ought to be believed about Him and ascribed to Him.

The tenth class comprises the *commandments* concerned with the *Sanctuary* and its utensils and servants. These are the *commandments* that we have enumerated in a portion of the *Book of Divine Worship* [*Sepher Abodah*]. We have already set forth in the foregoing[8] the utility of this class of commandments.

The eleventh class comprises the *commandments* concerned with the *sacrifices*. These are the majority of the *commandments* that we have enumerated in the *Book of Divine Worship* and the *Book of Sacrifices* [*Sepher Qorbanoth*]. We have already set forth in the foregoing[9] the utility of the legislation with regard to the sacrifices in general and the necessity for it in those | times.

The twelfth class comprises the *commandments* concerned with things *unclean and clean*. The purpose of all of them is in general to make people avoid entering the *Sanctuary*, so that it should be considered as great by the soul and feared and venerated, as I shall explain.

The thirteenth class comprises the *commandments* concerned with the prohibition of certain foods and what is connected therewith. These are the *commandments* that we have enumerated in the *Laws concerning Forbidden Foods* [*Hilkhoth Ma'akholoth Asuroth*]. The [commandments concerning] *vows* and the state of the *Nazarites* belong to this class. The purpose of all this is, as we have explained in the Commentary on the *Mishnah* in the introduction to *Aboth*,[10] to put an end to the lusts and licentiousness manifested in seeking what is most pleasurable and to taking the desire for food and drink as an end.

The fourteenth class comprises the *commandments* concerned with the prohibition of certain sexual unions. They are those that we have enumerated in the *Book of Women* [*Sepher Nashim*] and in *Laws concerning*

---

7. I.e., not only to the Priests and the Levites.   8. Cf. III 32.
9. Cf. III 32.   10. Cf. Maimonides' *Eight Chapters*, IV *in fine*.

22

Prohibited Sexual Relations [*Hilkhoth Issurei Bi'ah*]. *The interbreeding of beasts* belongs to this class. The purpose of this too is to bring about a decrease of sexual intercourse and to diminish the desire for mating as far as possible, so that it should not be taken as an end, as is done by the ignorant,[11] according to what we have explained in the Commentary on the *Tractate Aboth*.[12] *Circumcision* also belongs to this class.

It is known that all the *commandments* are divided into two groups: *transgressions between man and his fellow man and transgressions between man and God*.[13] Among the classes we have differentiated and enumerated, the fifth, sixth, seventh, and a portion of the third, belong to the group devoted to the relation *between man and his fellow man*, while all the other classes deal with the relation *between man and God*. For every *commandment*, whether it be a prescription or a prohibition, whose purpose it is to bring about the achievement | of a certain moral quality or of an opinion or the rightness of actions, which only concerns the individual himself and his becoming more perfect, is called by them[14] [a commandment dealing with the relation] *between man and God*, even though in reality it sometimes may affect relations *between man and his fellow man*. But this happens only after many intermediate steps and through comprehensive considerations, and it does not lead from the beginning to harming a fellow man. Understand this.

After I have made known the reasons for these classes of commandments, I shall return to examining the *commandments* belonging to each class, namely, those of which it may be fancied that they have no utility or that they constitute a decree that cannot be comprehended by the intellect in any way. And I shall explain the reasons for them and in what respect they are useful, making an exception only for those few whose purpose I have not grasped up to this time.

11. Or: the pagan.   12. Cf. *Eight Chapters*, IV *in fine*.
13. Cf. B.T., Yoma, 85b. The Hebrew word signifying "God" in this context is *maqom*. Hitherto it has been translated literally as "place."
14. I.e., by the talmudic Sages.

CHAPTER 36

The *commandments* comprised in the first class, which are the opinions that we have enumerated in *Laws of the Foundations of the Torah*, have all of them a manifest cause. If you consider them one by one, you discover the correctness of this opinion and its being a demonstrable matter. Similarly all the encouragement to learning and teaching and the fortifying assurances with regard to them figuring therein, are of manifest utility; for if knowledge is not achieved, no right action and no correct opinion can be achieved. There is also a manifest utility in honoring the bearers of the Law; for if a great veneration is not accorded to them in the souls, their voice will not be listened to when they give guidance regarding opinions and actions. Within this *commandment* — I mean its dictum, *Thou shalt rise up before the hoary head*[1] — is also included the injunction to be invested with the moral quality of modesty.[2]

To this class also belongs the commandment addressed to us | to swear in His name and the prohibition addressed to us against breaking one's oath and swearing in vain.[3] All this has a manifest reason; for it is intended to glorify Him, may He be exalted. Accordingly these are actions necessitating a belief in His greatness.

In the same way the commandment given to us to call upon Him, may He be exalted, in every calamity — I mean its dictum, *Then ye shall sound an alarm with the trumpets*[4] — likewise belongs to this class. For it is an action through which the correct opinion is firmly established that He, may He be exalted, apprehends our situations and that it depends upon Him to improve them, if we obey, and to make them ruinous, if we disobey; we should not believe that such things are fortuitous and happen by chance. This is the meaning of its dictum,[5] *And if ye walk with Me in the way of chance*,[6] by which it means: If you consider that the calamities with which I cause you to be stricken are to be borne as a mere chance, I shall add for you unto this supposed chance its most grievous and cruel portion. This is the

1. Lev. 19:32.
2. Cf. B.T., Qiddushin, 32b (and Maimonides' *Mishneh Torah*, Talmud Torah, VI 9), where this verse is interpreted as enjoining a modest and humble attitude toward the aged, even if they are pagans.
3. Cf. Deut. 6:13; 10:20; Lev. 19:12; Exod. 20:7.
4. Num. 10:9.   5. Lev. 26:21.
6. Maimonides evidently considers, as do the commentators Ibn Ezra and David Qimḥi, that the word *qeri* (translated here: *in the way of chance*) derives from the same root as the word *miqreh* (chance).

meaning of its dictum:[7] [*And if ye*] *walk with Me in the way of chance*,[8] *then I will walk with you in the way of a furious chance*.[8] For their belief that this is chance contributes to necessitating their persistence in their corrupt opinions and unrighteous actions, so that they do not turn away from them; thus it says: *Thou hast stricken them, but they were not affected*.[9] For this reason we have been commanded to invoke Him, may He be exalted, and to turn rapidly toward Him and call out to Him in every misfortune.

It is manifest that *repentance* also belongs to this class, I mean to the opinions without the belief in which the existence of individuals professing a Law cannot be well ordered. For an individual cannot but sin and err, either through ignorance — by professing an opinion or a moral quality that is not preferable in truth — or else because he is overcome by desire or anger. If then the individual believed that this fracture can never be remedied, he would persist in his error and sometimes perhaps disobey even more because of the fact that no stratagem remains at his disposal. | If, however, he believes in repentance, he can correct himself and return to a better and more perfect state than the one he was in before he sinned. For this reason there are many actions that are meant to establish this correct and very useful opinion, I mean the *confessions*,[10] the *sacrifices* in expiation of negligence and also of certain sins committed intentionally, and the *fasts*. The general characteristic of repentance from any sin consists in one's being divested of it. And this is the purpose of this opinion. Thus the utility of all these things is become manifest.

CHAPTER 37

The *commandments* comprised in the second class are all those *commandments* that we have enumerated in *Laws concerning Idolatry*. It is manifest that all of them have in view deliverance from the errors of *idolatry* and from other incorrect opinions that may accompany *idolatry*, such as belief in *soothsayers, enchanters, sorcerers, charmers*,[1] and others belonging to the same group. When you will have read all the books I have mentioned to you, it will become clear to you that the magic of which you hear consists in actions that used to be performed by the Sabians, the

7. Lev. 26:27–28.   8. *qeri*. Cf. n. 6, this chap.   9. Jer. 5:3
10. Cf. Lev. 5:5; 16:21.
1. Cf. Deut. 37:10–11.

Chasdeans, and the Chaldeans; most of them were also found among the Egyptians and the Canaanites. They caused others to fancy or fancied themselves that these actions had marvellous and extraordinary effects on beings, whether these be a single individual or the population of a city. However, reasoning cannot judge nor can the intellect cognize as true that these actions performed by magicians can necessitate anything whatever — as, for instance, when they seek to gather definite plants at a definite time or | when a certain quantity of one thing and a certain quantity of another is taken. This is a very vast field; I, however, shall reduce — for your benefit — the practices involved to three kinds. The first one consists of those concerning one of the beings, which may be either a plant or an animal or a mineral; the second consists of those concerning the determination of the time at which these practices are performed; the third consists of human actions such as dancing, clapping hands, shouting, laughing, jumping with one leg, lying down upon the earth, burning something, fumigating with a definite fume, or uttering a speech understandable or not. These are the various species of the practices of the magicians.

Furthermore there are magical operations that can be accomplished only with the help of all these practices. For instance they say: This or that quantity of the leaves of a certain plant shall be taken while the moon is under a certain sign of the Zodiac in the East or in one of the other cardinal points; also a definite quantity shall be taken from the horns or the excrements or the hair or the blood of a certain animal while the sun is, for example, in the middle of the sky or at some other determined place; furthermore, a certain mineral or several minerals shall be taken and cast while a certain sign is in the ascendant and the stars in a certain position; then you shall speak and say these and these things and shall fumigate the cast-metal form with these leaves and similar things — whereupon a certain thing will come about. Furthermore, there are magical operations that, as they deem, may be accomplished with the help of only one of these kinds of practices. With regard to most of these magical practices, they pose the condition that those who perform them should necessarily be women. Thus you will find that they set forth with regard to the discovery of water that ten virgins must put on ornaments and red clothes and dance and crawl, | going in turn forward and backward, and point to the sun, and perform the rest of this long operation until, as they think the water goes forth. In the same way they mention that if four women lie down upon their backs, raise their legs, holding them apart, and say and do certain things while in this disgraceful posture, hail will cease falling down upon that place. And they recount many such fables and ravings. And you will never find them posing some condition other than that they should be performed by women. In all magical operations it is indispensable that the stars should be observed. I mean, they deem that a certain plant should be assigned to the portion of a certain star; similarly they assign every animal and every mineral to a star. They likewise deem that the operations performed by the magicians are various species of worship offered to a certain star, which, being pleased with that operation or speech or fumigation, does for us what we wish.

After these premises, which you will find valid upon reading such books of theirs as are at present in our hands and as I have let you know, hear my discourse: Inasmuch as the intent of the whole Law and the pole around which it revolves is to put an end to *idolatry*, to efface its traces, and to bring about a state of affairs in which it would not be imagined that any star harms or helps in anything pertaining to the circumstances of human individuals — this in view of the fact that such an opinion leads to star worship — it follows necessarily that all magicians must be killed. For a magician is indubitably an *idolater*, even though he goes in special and strange ways that are different from the ways in which the vulgar worship these divinities. And inasmuch as in all these practices the condition is posed that for the greater part they should be performed by women, it says: | *Thou shalt not suffer a sorceress to live.*[2] And as people naturally feel pity when women are to be killed, it also states specifically with regard to *idolatry*: *Man or woman,*[3] and again reiterates: *Even the man or the woman*[4] — an expression that is not used with regard to *profanation of the Sabbath* and other things. The reason for this is to be found in the fact that naturally women often inspire pity. Inasmuch as the magicians deemed that their magic was effective, that by means of these practices they drove away harmful animals like lions, serpents, and so forth, from the villages; and they also deemed that by means of their magic they warded off various sorts of damage from plants — thus you will find that they had practices that, as they deemed, could prevent hail from falling, and that they deemed that certain practices of theirs killed the worms in the vineyards so that the latter were not destroyed (the destruction of the worms in the vineyards by means of these *Amorite usages,*[5] mentioned in "The Nabatean Agriculture," being expounded at length by them, I mean by the Sabians); that furthermore they deemed that they knew practices that could prevent the leaves and fruits of plants from falling — because of these things that at that time were

2. Exod. 22:17.   3. Deut. 17:2.   4. Deut. 17:5.
5. Literally: *Amorite ways,* an expression designating pagan usages.

generally known, it is stated among other things in *the words of the covenant*[6] that it is because of *idolatry* and of the magical practices by means of which you think that these kinds of harm can be kept away from you that these calamities will befall you. It says: *And I will send the beasts of the field among you, which shall rob you of your children.*[7] And: *And the teeth of beasts will I send upon them, with the venom of crawling things of the dust.*[8] And: *The fruit of thy land shall the locust consume.*[9] And: *Thou shalt plant vineyards and dress them, but thou shalt neither drink of the wine, nor gather the grapes; for the worm shall eat them.*[10] And: *Thou shalt have olive trees throughout all thy borders, but thou shalt not anoint thyself with the oil, for thine olives shall drop off.*[11] To sum up the matter: Having in view all the devices used by the *idolaters* to perpetuate | their cult through suggesting to people that thereby certain kinds of harm may be warded off and certain kinds of benefits obtained, it is included in *the words of the covenant* that through their cult these kinds of benefits are lost and these kinds of damage come about. Thus it has already become clear to you, you who engage in speculation, what Scripture intended in these particulars of the *curses* and the *blessings* contained in *the words of the convenant*, singling out them rather than the others for statement. Know likewise the extent of the great utility of this.

In order to keep people away from all magical practices, it has been prohibited to observe any of their usages,[12] even those attaching to agricultural and pastoral activities and other activities of this kind. I mean all that is said to be useful, but is not required by speculation concerning nature, and takes its course, in their opinion, in accordance with occult properties. This is the meaning of its dictum: *And ye shall not walk in the customs [huqqoth] of the nation,*[13] these being those that are called by [the Sages], *may their memory be blessed, Amorite usages.* For they are branches of magical practices, inasmuch as they are things not required by reasoning concerning nature and lead to magical practices that of necessity seek support in astrological notions. Accordingly the matter is turned into a glorification and a worship of the stars. They say explicitly: *All that pertains to medicine does not pertain to the Amorite usages.*[14] They mean by this that all that is required by speculation concerning nature is permitted, whereas other practices are forbidden. It is for this reason that, after it has been said, *A tree which lets its fruits drop is loaded with stones and marked with red chalk,*

6. Cf. Deut. 28:69.　　7. Lev. 26:22.　　8. Deut. 32:24.　　9. Deut. 28:42.
10. Deut. 28:39.　　11. Deut. 28:40.　　12. I.e., of the usages of the idolaters.
13. Lev. 20:23.　　14. B.T., Shabbath, 67a.

this practice is criticized, and it is said: *Why is it loaded with stones? It is with a view to diminishing its sap. But [why] should it be marked with red chalk? and so on.* It is thus made clear that it could be forbidden, *as pertaining to Amorite usages*, to mark it with red chalk or to do similar things that are not required by reasoning. They similarly say with reference to *a fetus of consecrated animals, which should be buried:* | *It is not [allowed] to hang it upon a tree or to bury it at a crossroad with reference to Amorite usages.*[15] From this conclude by analogy. You must not consider as a difficulty certain things that they have permitted, as for instance *the nail of one who is crucified and a fox's tooth.*[16] For in those times these things were considered to derive from experience and accordingly *pertained to medicine* and entered into the same class as the hanging of a peony upon an epileptic and the giving of a dog's excrements in cases of the swelling of the throat and fumigation with vinegar and marcasite in cases of hard swellings of the tendons. For it is allowed to use all remedies similar to these that experience has shown to be valid even if reasoning does not require them. For they *pertain to medicine* and their efficacy may be ranged together with the purgative action of aperient medicines. O you who are engaged in speculation, grasp fully and remember the marvellous observations contained in my speech! *For they shall be an ornament of grace unto thy head, and chains about thy neck.*[17]

We have already explained in our great compilation[18] that the shaving of *the corner of the head and of the corner of the beard* has been forbidden[19] because it was a usage of *idolatrous priests.* This is also the reason for the prohibition of *mingled stuff,*[20] for this too was a usage of these *priests,* as they put together in their garments vegetal and animal substances bearing at the same time a seal made out of some mineral; you will find this set forth literally in their books.

This is also the reason for its dictum: *A woman shall not wear man's armor,*[21] *neither shall a man put on a woman's garment.*[22] You will find in the book of Tumtum[23] the commandment that a man should put on a woman's dyed garment when standing before [the planet] Venus and that a woman should put on a cuirass and arms when standing before Mars. In my opinion there is also another reason for this, namely, that

---

15. B.T., Ḥullin, 77a.   16. B.T., Shabbath, 67a.   17. Prov. 1:9.
18. Cf. *Mishneh Torah,* ʿAbodah Zarah, XII 7.   19. Cf. Lev. 19:27.
20. Cf. Deut. 22:11.
21. Maimonides, in accordance with various Jewish sources, considers that the word *keli* (vessel) signifies "armor" in this verse.
22. Deut. 22:5.   23. Cf. III 29.

such a practice arouses desires and necessarily brings about various kinds of debauchery.

As for the prohibition to profit from *idolatry*, the reason for it is most manifest. For | sometimes idols are taken in order to be broken, but are preserved and become a *snare* for him who has taken them. Even if they have been broken and melted down or sold to a *Gentile*, it is forbidden to draw profit from the price obtained for them. The reason for this is that the multitude often believe that accidental matters are essential causes. Thus, for instance, you will find that most people say that since they dwell in one particular house or since they have bought one particular beast of burden or tool, they have become rich and their fortune has increased, these things having been a blessing for them. Accordingly it might happen that a certain individual would have success in his commerce or increase his fortune because of the price obtained for the idols. He would then think that this price was the reason for this and that the blessing deriving from the image he had sold necessitated this result. He accordingly would believe things concerning this image to which the whole wish of the Law runs counter, as becomes clear from all the texts of the *Torah*. This is also the selfsame reason why it is forbidden[24] to draw profit from *ornaments covering an object of worship* and from *offerings to the idols*[25] and from the instruments of [idolatry] so that we should be preserved from this thought. For at that time their belief in such things was strong; it was believed that they caused to live or to die, that all good and evil came from them—I mean, from the stars. Therefore the Law made sure of putting an end to this opinion by means of covenants, attestation, strong oaths, and the *curses* quoted above, and it warned against taking anything and profiting by anything belonging to the idols. And He, may He be exalted, informed us that if anything that was a portion of the price obtained for them was mingled with the fortune of a certain man, it would bring about the loss and the ruin of that fortune. This is the meaning of its dictum: *And thou shalt not bring an abomination into thine house, and be accursed like unto it, and so on.*[26] All the more should it not be believed that there is a blessing in these things. If then you study carefully one by one all the *commandments* dealing with *idolatry*, you will find that the reason for them is manifest and consists in putting an end to these | corrupt opinions and turning people to another direction far away from them.

Among the things to which we shall draw attention belongs the following point: Those that set up these false opinions, which have no root or any

24. Cf. B.T., ʿAbodah Zarah, 51b.   25. Literally: *idolatry*.   26. Deut. 7:26.

utility, in order to fortify belief in them, use the device of spreading among the people the opinion that a certain calamity will befall those who do not perform an action perpetuating this belief. Now this may happen by accident some day to a certain individual, and consequently he will seek to perform the action in question and to follow that belief. Now it is known that it is the nature of men in general to be most afraid and most wary of losing their property and their children. Therefore the worshippers of fire spread abroad the opinion in those times that the children of everyone who would not *make his son or his daughter to pass through the fire*[27] would die. And there is no doubt that because of this absurd belief everybody hastened to perform this action because of the strong pity and apprehension felt with regard to children and because of the trifling character of the action and its ease, for it simply consisted in making them pass through fire. This was more particularly so because care for little children is generally entrusted to women, and it is well known how quickly they are affected and, speaking generally, how feeble are their intellects. Therefore the Law is strongly opposed to this action, an opposition that is affirmed in such terms as are not used with regard to other kinds of *idolatrous* practices: *To render unclean My Sanctuary, and to profane My holy name.*[28] Thereupon the truthful one[29] makes known in the name of God, may He be exalted, and says: Whereas you perform this action so that the children stay alive because of it, God will cause him who performs it to perish and will exterminate his descendants: he says: *Then I will set My face against that man and against his family, and so on.*[30] Know that traces of this action subsist up to now as a consequence of its having been generally accepted in the world. | You will see that midwives take small children in their swaddling clothes, throw a fumigant having a disagreeable odor upon the fire, and move the children over this fume above the fire. This is indubitably a sort of *passage through the fire*, which it is illicit to perform. Consider how perfidious was he who originated this opinion and how he perpetuated it through this imagining, so that its trace was not effaced though the Law has opposed it for thousands of years.

The *idolaters* have acted in a similar way with regard to property. They have made the ordinance that one tree, namely, the *asherah*,[31] should be consecrated to the object of their worship and that its fruits should be taken, part of them serving as an offering while the rest should be eaten in an *idolatrous temple*, as they have explained in the laws concerning the *asherah*.

27 Cf. Deut. 18:10.   28. Lev. 20:3.   29. I.e., Moses.   30. Lev. 20:5.
31. Cf. III 29, n. 29.

They have also prescribed that the first fruits of every tree whose fruits are edible should be used in the same manner, I mean that a portion of them should serve as an offering while the rest should be eaten in an *idolatrous temple*. They have also spread abroad the opinion that if the first fruits of any tree whatever were not treated in this manner, the tree in question would wither or its fruits would drop or its produce would be small or some calamity would befall it; just as they have spread abroad the opinion that every child that was not passed through fire would die. Inasmuch as men were afraid for their property, they likewise hastened to perform these practices. Accordingly the Law opposed this opinion, and He, may He be exalted, commanded that everything produced in the course of three years [32] by a tree whose fruits are edible should be burnt. [33] For some trees bear fruit after one year, others bear their first fruits after two years, and others again after three. This is what happens in the majority of cases when trees are planted in one of the three generally accepted ways, namely: *planting, layering, and grafting*. [34] No attention is paid to him who sows a kernel or a pip. For the Law ties up the commandments | with the majority of cases only, and the first produce of *planting* appears in the *Land of Israel* after a maximum delay of three years. Accordingly He, may He be exalted, has given us a pledge that because of the destruction and loss of the first fruits, the produce of the tree will increase. He says: *That it may yield unto you the increase thereof.* [35] And He has commanded to eat the *fourth-year fruit of planting before the Lord* [36] as a substitute for eating the *first products* [37] [of trees] in an *idolatrous temple*, as we have explained.

The ancient *idolaters* also mention in "The Nabatean Agriculture" that they let certain things mentioned by them putrefy, looking out in this connection for the sun's entering into a certain sign of the Zodiac, and performing many magical operations. They thought that this thing should be prepared by everybody and that whenever one planted a tree bearing edible fruit, one should scatter around it or at its very place a portion of the thing that has been made to putrefy, in order that the tree should grow more quickly and that it should bear fruit in a way contrary to what is usual, within the shortest possible period. They mentioned that this is a wondrous method that is of the same character as the talismans and that it is the most

---

32. I.e., of its first three years.
33. The biblical text (Lev. 19:23) does not command that these fruits be burnt. They are commanded to be destroyed in B.T., Pesaḥim, 22b, and B.T., Baba Qamma, 101a. Cf. Mishnah, Temurah, VII 5.
34. Cf. Mishnah, Shebiʿith, II 6.   35. Lev. 19:25.
36. Cf. Lev. 19:24; Mishnah, Maʿaser Sheni, V 4.   37. Literally: *foreskin*. Cf. Lev. 19:23.

wondrous of the methods of magic in regard to increase in rapidity in the production of the fruit of all trees that produce fruit. We have already explained to you and made known to you that the Law eschews all these magical operations. Therefore the Law forbids all that is grown by trees bearing edible fruit within the period of three years from the day they were planted. Accordingly there is no need, contrary to what they thought, to increase their rapidity in producing fruit. After three years, however, the produce of most of the trees in Syria bearing edible fruit attains its perfect state according to the course of nature, and there is no object in resorting to the generally known magical operation that was employed by them. Understand this wondrous thing too.

One of the opinions generally known in those times and perpetuated by the Sabians was expressed by their statement concerning the grafting of a tree of one species onto another tree. They said that if this is done | when a certain star is in the ascendant and if certain fumigations are made and certain invocations pronounced at the time of the grafting, that which is produced by the graft will be a thing that, as they believe, will be very useful. The clearest point concerning these things is the one mentioned in the beginning of the "Agriculture"[38] concerning the grafting of the olive tree onto the citron tree. In my opinion it must indubitably be true that the *book of medicaments* that *was suppressed by Hezekiah*[39] belonged to this group. They also mention that when one species is grafted upon another, the bough that is meant to be grafted ought to be held in the hand of a beautiful girl[40] and of a man who has come into her in a disgraceful manner that they describe and that the woman must graft the bough upon the tree while the two are performing this act. There is no doubt that this was generally adopted and that no one remained that acted otherwise, especially in view of the fact that in this custom pleasure of sexual intercourse is joined to the desire for the benefits in question. Therefore the *mingling* [of diverse species], I mean *the grafting of one tree upon another*, is forbidden, so that we shall keep far away from the causes of *idolatry* and from the *abominations* of their unnatural kinds of sexual intercourse. It is with reference to *the grafting of a tree* that it has been forbidden to join together any two species of *seeds*, even if only putting one near the other. If you examine what is transmitted in the legal science concerning this *commandment*, you will find that *the grafting of a tree should in all places be punished with whipping according to the Torah*,[41] for it is at the origin of the prohibition; whereas

38. I.e., "The Nabatean Agriculture."   39. B.T., Berakhoth, 10b; B.T., Pesaḥim, 56a.
40. Or: slave girl.   41. B.T., Qiddushin, 39a.

the *mingling of diverse seeds*, I mean their being put one near the other, is only forbidden in the *Land of Israel*.

They also state explicitly in the "Agriculture"[42] that it was their custom to sow barley and grapes together, for they thought that a vineyard could only prosper through this practice. Consequently the Law has forbidden the [sowing of] *a vineyard with diverse seeds* and has commanded burning all such things.[43] For all *the customs [ḥuqqoth] of the nations* that were thought to have occult properties were prohibited, even if | they did not at all smack of *idolatry*; just as we have explained with reference to their dictum: *It is not [allowed] to hang it upon a tree, and so on*.[44] All these, I mean *their customs [ḥuqqotehem]*, which are called *Amorite usages*,[45] have been forbidden because of their leading to *idolatry*. If you consider their customs in agriculture, you will find that in certain kinds of agriculture they turn toward the stars, in others toward the two luminaries.[46] Often they fix the time for sowing when certain constellations are in ascendant, making fumigations; and he who plants or sows goes about in a circle. Some of them consider that he should go about in a circle five times with a view to the five planets.[47] Others consider that he should go about in a circle seven times with a view to the five planets and two luminaries. And they deem that in all this there are occult properties that are very useful for agriculture, in order that they might bind people to the worship of the stars. Consequently all these *customs [ḥuqqoth] of the nations* have been forbidden in a general way, and it says: *And ye shall not walk in the customs [ḥuqqoth] of the nation, and so on*.[48] That among them which was more generally accepted and widespread or that which contained an explicit reference to some kind of *idolatry* was the object of various particular prohibitions—for instance, those regarding the *first products* [of trees], the *mingling* [of diverse species], the [sowing of] *a vineyard with diverse seeds*. I wonder at the dictum of *Rabbi Josiah*, considered as a *legal decision*, concerning [the sowing of] *a vineyard with diverse seeds*, according to which one has committed no transgression *unless one sows together, in one throw of the hand, wheat, barley, and pips of grapes*.[49] Doubtless he had learned that this custom had its origin in the *Amorite usages*.

42. I.e., "The Nabatean Agriculture."
43. Cf. Deut. 22:9; Mishnah, Kilʾaim, VIII 1; B.T., Qiddushin, 39a.
44. Mishnah, Ḥullin, IV 7. Cf. n. 15, this chap.   45. Cf. n. 5, this chap.
46. I.e., the sun and the moon.
47. Literally: scintillating stars. In this passage the sun and the moon are obviously not included among the five planets referred to.
48. Lev. 20:23.
49. B.T., Berakhoth, 22a; B.T., Qiddushin, 39a; B.T., Ḥullin 82b and 136b.

Thus it has been made clear to you, so that there can be no doubt about it, that *mingled stuff*, the *first products* [of trees], and the *mingling* [of diverse species] were forbidden because of *idolatry*, and that *their customs* [*ḥuqqotehem*], which have been referred to, were forbidden because they lead to *idolatry*, as we have explained. |

CHAPTER 38

The *commandments* comprised in the third class are those that we have enumerated in *Laws concerning Opinions*. The utility of all of them is clear and evident, for all concern moral qualities in virtue of which the association among people is in good condition. This is so manifest that I need not expatiate upon it. Know that certain *commandments* also contain prescriptions that are intended to lead to the acquisition of a useful moral quality, even if they prescribe certain actions that are deemed to be merely *decreed by Scripture*[1] and not to have a purpose. We will explain them one by one in their proper places. As for those that we have enumerated in *Laws concerning Opinions*, they are all explicitly stated to have as their purpose the acquisition of the noble moral qualities in question.

CHAPTER 39

The *commandments* comprised in the fourth class are those included in the *Book of Seeds* of our compilation, with the exception of those dealing with the *mingling* [of diverse species]; also the *law* concerning *estimations and anathemas*[1] and also the *commandments* that we have enumerated in *Laws concerning the Lender and the Borrower* and those that we have enumerated in *Laws concerning Slaves*. If you consider all these *commandments* one by one, you will find that they are manifestly useful through instilling pity for the weak and the wretched, giving strength in various

1. According to this view, no reason can be found for these prescriptions. Maimonides opposes this view.
1. Cf. III 35, n. 4.

ways to the poor, | and inciting us not to press hard upon those in straits and not to afflict the hearts of individuals who are in a weak position.

As for *gifts to the poor*, their meaning is manifest. The reason for the *offerings*[2] and the *tithes* is similarly manifest: *Because he hath no portion nor inheritance with thee.*[3] You know the reason for this: so that this *tribe* as a whole should be devoted exclusively to the divine service and to knowing the Law and should not be engaged in tilling and harvesting, but should be concerned exclusively with God; as it says: *They shall teach Jacob Thine judgments, and Israel Thy Torah.*[4] You will find that the text of the *Torah* speaks in several passages of *the Levite and the stranger and the orphan and the widow*; for it always considers [the Levite] as one of the *poor* in view of the fact that he has no property.

As for the *second tithe*, it is commanded that it should be spent exclusively on food in *Jerusalem.*[5] For this leads of necessity to giving some of it in alms; for as it could only be employed on nourishment, it was easy for a man to have others have it little by little. Thus it necessarily brought about a gathering in one place, so that brotherhood and love among the people were greatly strengthened.[6]

As for the *fourth-year fruit of planting*,[7] even though — because of its connection with the prescriptions concerning the *first products*[8] — it smacks, as we have mentioned, of *idolatry*, it falls into the same class as the prescriptions concerning the *offering*,[9] the *cake of dough*,[10] the *first fruits*,[11] *and the first of the fleece*;[12] for all first produces have been assigned to God so that the moral quality of generosity be strengthened and the appetite for eating and for acquisition be weakened. The *Priest's* receiving *the shoulder, the two jaws, and the stomach*[13] has the same meaning; for *jaws* are a primary part of the body of the animal, and *the shoulder* is the right shoulder and is also the first part that has branched off from the body, and the *stomach* is the first of all the intestines.

As for the *reading* on the occasion of the offering of *first fruits*,[14] it also is conducive to the moral quality of humility, for it is carried out by him who carries the basket *on his shoulders.*[15] It contains an acknowledgment

---

2. Destined for the Priests.   3. Deut. 14:29. The verse refers to the Levites.
4. Deut. 33:10.
5. Cf. Deut. 14:22–29; 26:12–13. Cf. Mishnah, Maʿaser Sheni, I–III.
6. Or: A gathering in one place necessarily leads to love and brotherhood among the people being greatly strengthened.
7. Cf. III 37, n. 33 and 36.   8. Literally: *foreskin*.
9. To the Priests. Cf. Deut. 18:4.   10. Cf. Num. 15:20.
11. Cf. Exod. 23:19; 34:26; Deut. 26:2.   12. Cf. Deut. 18:4.
13. Cf. Deut. 18:3.   14. Cf. Deut. 26:3–10.   15. Cf. Mishnah, Bikkurim, III 4.

of | God's beneficence and bountifulness, so that man should know that it is a part of the divine worship that man should remember states of distress at a time when he prospers. This purpose is frequently affirmed in the *Torah*: *And thou shalt remember that thou wast a servant, and so on.*[16] For there was a fear of the moral qualities that are generally acquired by all those who are brought up in prosperity — I mean conceit, vanity, and neglect of the correct opinions: *Lest when thou hast eaten and art satisfied, and houses, and so on.*[17] And it says: *But Jeshurun waxed fat, and kicked, and so on.*[18] It is because of this apprehension that the commandment has been given to carry out a *reading* every year before Him, may He be exalted, and in presence of His Indwelling, on the occasion of the offering of *first fruits.* You also know already that the *Torah* insists upon the *plagues*, which befell the Egyptians, being always remembered: *That thou mayest remember the day when thou camest forth, and so on.*[19] And it says: *And that thou mayest tell in the ears of thy son, and so on.*[20] And this was fittingly arranged, for these are the stories that show the truth of prophecy and of reward and punishment. Now in the case of every *commandment* leading to a mention of some miracle or to a perpetuation of this belief, the utility of the *commandment* is obvious.

It states explicitly with reference to [the redemption of] *the human firstborn* and [the sacrifice of] *the animal firstborn: And it came to pass, when Pharaoh would hardly let us go, and so on; therefore I sacrificed to the Lord, and so on.*[21] The reason why this is particularized with regard to *oxen, small cattle, and asses*[22] is most manifest. For these are domestic animals that are raised and are to be found in most places, more particularly in Syria, and even more particularly among [the people of] *Israel*; all of us being shepherds from fathers and grandfathers: *Thy servants were*[23] *shepherds, and so on.*[24] But horses and camels are in most cases not to be found in the possession of shepherds, nor are they found in all places. Consider the raid against *Midian:*[25] you will not find on that occasion any animals other than *oxen, small cattle, and asses.* For the species of asses was necessary to all men and especially | to those engaged in agricultural work: *And I have oxen and asses;*[26] but camels and horses are in most cases found only in the possession of few men and only in some places.

16. Deut. 5:15; 16:12.
17. Deut. 8:12. The sentence is continued in v. 14: *then thy heart be lifted up and thou forget the Lord thy God. . . .*
18. Deut. 32:15.   19. Deut. 16:3.   20. Exod. 10:2.   21. Exod. 13:15.
22. Cf. Num. 18:17; Exod. 13:13.
23. The Hebrew word for "were" (*hayu*) has been inserted in the verse by Maimonides; or, at least, it figures in the majority of the manuscripts and in Ibn Tibbon's translation.
24. Gen. 47:3.   25. Cf. Num. 31.   26. Gen. 32:6.

As for the prescription concerning *the breaking of the neck of the firstling of an ass*,[27] this is due to its leading necessarily to the firstling's being redeemed. Therefore it has been said: *The commandment that it be redeemed is prior to the commandment that its neck be broken.*[28]

With regard to all the *commandments* that we have enumerated in *Laws concerning the Sabbatical Year and the Jubilee*, some of them are meant to lead to pity and help for all men — as the text has it: *That the poor of thy people may eat; and what they leave the beasts of the field shall eat, and so on*[29] — and are meant to make the earth more fertile and stronger through letting it lie fallow. Others are meant to lead to benevolence toward slaves and poor people; I refer to *remission of debts and freeing of slaves*. Others consider what is useful from a permanent point of view in providing for a living, through turning the whole land into an inalienable possession that cannot be sold in absolute fashion: *And the land shall not be sold in perpetuity;*[30] consequently a man's property remains, as far as the landed property itself is concerned, reserved for him and his children, and he can only exploit its produce. Thus we have given reasons for everything that is included in the *Book of Seeds* figuring in our compilation with the exception of *the interbreeding of beasts*,[31] the reason for which will be explained later on.[32]

All the *commandments* that we have enumerated in *Laws concerning Estimations and Anathemas* likewise deal with charitable donations. Some of these go to the *Priests*, others for *repairing the Temple*. Through all this, likewise, the moral quality of generosity is acquired, and the result achieved that man holds property in slight esteem where God is concerned, and is not miserly. For most of the evils that arise among people in the cities are due only to a furious desire for possessions and for increasing them and to the passion of acquisition.

Similarly if you consider one by one all the *commandments* that we have enumerated in *Laws concerning the Lender and the Borrower*, you will find that all are imbued with benevolence, pity, | and kindness for the weak; they forbid depriving anyone of a utility necessary for his nourishment; I mean: *No man shall take the nether or the upper millstone to pledge.*[33]

Similarly all the *commandments* that we have enumerated in *Laws concerning Slaves* are all of them imbued with pity and benevolence for the weak. Thus great pity is manifested in the prescription according to which a *Canaanite slave* is set free if he has been deprived of a limb, so that slavery should not be conjoined in his case with mutilation. This applies even if

27. Cf. Exod. 13:13.   28. Mishnah, Bekhoroth, I 7.   29. Exod. 23:11.
30. Lev. 25:23.   31. Cf. Lev. 19:19.   32. Cf. III 49.   33. Deut. 24:6.

he has only been made to lose a tooth, and all the more in the case of other parts of the body. It is also not permitted, as we have explained in *Mishneh Torah*,[34] to strike him except with a whip or a stick or similar things. And, even so, if the master strikes him so hard that he dies, he is punished with death on his account, as all other men would be.

The *commandment* given in His saying, *Thou shalt not deliver unto his master a slave*,[35] besides manifesting pity, contains a great utility — namely, it makes us acquire this noble moral quality [that is, pity]; namely, it makes us protect and defend those who seek our protection and not deliver them over to those from whom they have fled. It is not even enough to protect those who seek your protection, for you are under another obligation toward him: you must consider his interests, be beneficent toward him, and not pain his heart by speech. This is the meaning of His dictum, may He be exalted: *He shall dwell with thee, in the midst of thee, . . . within one of thy gates, where it liketh him best; thou shalt not wrong him*.[36] If this law is imposed upon us with regard to the least of men and the lowest in degree, namely, the slave, how must you act when a man of great worth seeks your protection! What an obligation must you have with regard to him!

On the contrary, the wrongdoer and the worker of injustice should not be protected when he seeks our protection and should not be pitied, nor should his rightful punishment be abolished in any way, even if he seeks the protection of the greatest individual and the one having the highest rank. This is the meaning of its dictum: *Thou shalt take him from Mine altar, that he may die*.[37] Thus the man referred to seeks the protection of God, may He be exalted, and holds fast to a thing attached to His name; | in spite of that, however, He does not protect him, but orders him to be delivered over to him who has the right to inflict punishment on him and from whom he has fled. All the more if the man in question has sought the protection of a human individual: the latter ought not to protect or to pity him, for pity for wrongdoers and evil men is tantamount to cruelty with regard to all creatures. These are indubitably the moderate moral qualities that form a part of the *righteous statutes [huqqim] and judgments*.[38] These are not moral qualities pertaining to the Pagans[39] who considered pride and partisanship with regard to any chance individual, irrespective of his being the wrongdoer or the wronged, as praiseworthy virtues, as is generally known from their stories and poems. Accordingly every *commandment* that belongs to this class has a manifest reason and an evident utility.

34. Cf. Roṣeaḥ, XI 14.   35. Deut. 23:16.   36. Deut. 23:17.   37. Exod. 21:14.
38. Deut. 4:8. Cf. III 26.   39. Or: ignorant.

The *commandments* comprised in the fifth class are those that we have enumerated in the *Book of Torts*. All of them are concerned with putting an end to acts of injustice and with the prevention of acts causing damage. In order that great care should be taken to avoid causing damage, man is held responsible for every act causing damage deriving from his possessions or caused by an act of his, if only it was possible for him to be cautious and take care not to cause damage. Therefore we are held responsible for damage deriving from our beasts, so that we should keep watch over them; and also for damage from *fire*[1] and from a *pit*,[2] for these two belong to the works of man, and he can keep watch over them and take precautions with regard to them, so that no harm is occasioned by them. These laws contain considerations of justice to which I will draw attention. Thus one *is free from responsibility* [for the damage caused by] *a tooth or a foot*[3] *in a public place*.[4] For this is a matter with regard to which it is impossible | to take precautions, and also damage is seldom caused in this way. Moreover he who puts a thing *in a public place* is at fault toward himself and exposes his property to destruction. Accordingly one *is only responsible for* [damage caused by] *a tooth or a foot in the field of the injured party*.[5]

On the other hand, damage caused by a *horn* and similar things regarding which precautions can be taken in all places and with respect to which those who walk *in public places* cannot take care, the law applicable to it — I mean the *horn* — is one and the same in all places. There is, however, a distinction that is made between an animal that is *docile* and one about which its owner *has been warned*. If the act is exceptional, the owner is held responsible only for *half the damage*; if, however, the animal that causes the damage continually does similar things and is known for this, the owner is held responsible for *the whole of the damage*.[6]

The price of a slave is generally fixed at half the price at which a free man is generally estimated; for you will find that the *estimations of men* amount at the utmost to *sixty shekels*,[7] whereas *the money paid for a slave* amounts to *thirty shekels of silver*.[8] The fact that the *beast* that kills a man is

1. Cf. Exod. 22:5.   2. Cf. Exod. 21:33.   3. Of an animal.
4. Cf. B.T., Baba Qamma, 14a and 19b.   5. Cf. B.T., Baba Qamma, 14a and 19b.
6. Cf. Exod. 21:35–36; B.T., Baba Qamma, 26a.
7. Cf. Lev. 27:3. But the sum mentioned there is fifty shekels, which is also the sum mentioned by Maimonides himself in *Mishneh Torah*, ᶜArakhin, I 3.
8. Exod. 21:32.

killed,[9] is not to be regarded as a punishment for it — an absurd opinion that the heretics[10] impute to us — but is a punishment for its owner. For this reason it is forbidden to use its flesh, so that its owner should take great care in watching over it and should know that if it kills a child or an adult, a free man or a slave, he will obligatorily lose its price; and if he *has been warned* about it, he must pay *compensation* over and above the loss of its price. This is also the reason for killing *a beast with which a human being has lain,*[11] so that its owner should watch over and take care of it, just as he takes care of his own family, in order that he should not lose it. For men are as solicitous for their property as for their own selves; some of them even prefer their property to themselves. However, in most cases they hold both in equal esteem: *And take us for slaves, and take our asses.*[12]

This class also comprises the prescription to kill | the *pursuer.*[13] This law — I mean the prescription to kill him who wishes to accomplish an act of disobedience before he performs it — is only applicable to two kinds of acts: *If one pursues his fellow man in order to kill him, and if one pursues someone in order to expose the latter's nakedness.* For these are acts of wrongdoing that cannot be repaired once they have been accomplished. As for the other *transgressions* that are punished with *death by order of a court of law,* such as *idolatry* and the profanation of the *Sabbath,* they do not constitute an act of wrongdoing with regard to someone else, but concern only thoughts; and therefore the transgressor is not killed because of his wish, but only if he commits the transgression.

It is already known that *coveting* is prohibited because it leads to *desire,* and *desire* is prohibited because it leads to *robbery;* it is thus that [the Sages], *may their memory be blessed,* have explained it.

The situation with regard to the commandment *to return a lost thing*[14] is clear, for while this is an excellent moral quality from the point of view of good relations, it is also useful because there is reciprocity. For if you do not return a thing lost by somebody else, the thing lost by you will not be returned, just as your son will not honor you if you do not honor your father. There are many other examples of this.

The commandment that *one who kills a man unawares shall go into exile*[15] is imposed with a view to calming the soul of the *revenger of blood,*

9. Cf. Exod. 21:28–29.
10. *al-Khawārij,* the term used by Maimonides, often designates the Qaraites, when used in rabbinical texts.
11. Cf. Lev. 20:15–16.   12. Gen. 43:18.   13. Cf. Mishnah, Sanhedrin, VIII 7.
14. Cf. Deut. 22:1–3.
15. Cf. Exod. 21:13; Num. 35:11–28; Deut. 4:41–43; 19:2–10; Josh. 20.

so that he should not see the man by means of whom the misfortune has happened. And his return[16] is made to depend upon the death of the individual who, for the whole of *Israel*, is the greatest and most beloved of human beings. For thereby the soul of the victim of misfortune whose kinsman has been killed will have been calmed. For it is human nature that one who has been stricken by misfortune finds consolation in the fact that someone else has been stricken by a similar misfortune or by one that is greater. And among the misfortunes constituted by the death of individuals, none to our mind is greater than that constituted by the death of a *High Priest*.

As for the commandment regarding *the breaking of the neck of a heifer*,[17] its utility is manifest. For the responsibility for it is incumbent upon *the city that is nearest unto the slain*, and in most cases the killer is one of its inhabitants. According to what is stated in the interpretation, the elders of that city shall call | upon God to bear witness that they were not remiss in repairing and watching over the roads and protecting all the wayfarers. His having been killed in spite of this is not due to our having neglected the general interests. Furthermore, we do not know who killed him. Then necessarily in most cases there will be many stories and discussions among the people because of the investigation, the going-forth of the elders, the measurements, and the fact that the heifer is brought there. Thus, because of the matter being universally known, the killer could perhaps be recognized. For he who knows the killer, has heard about him, or has been led to him by certain conjunctures, will say: Such and such a one is the killer. Now when some individual, be it only a *woman* or a *female slave*, says: Such and such has killed him, *the neck of the heifer is not broken*.[18] For it is established that if the killer were known[19] and silence were kept about him while they called upon God to bear witness that they do not know the killer, there would be in this great foolhardiness and a great sin. Accordingly even a woman will tell about him if she knows. As soon as he is known, a useful purpose will be achieved. For even if the *court* does not sentence him to death, the ruler will kill him; for he may kill on the grounds of a presumption. And if the ruler does not kill him, the *revenger of blood* will do it; for he will use stratagems in order to take him by surprise and kill him. Accordingly it is clear that the utility of the commandment concerning *the breaking of the neck of a heifer* is to be found in the fact that in this way the killer becomes generally known. This notion is corroborated by the fact that the place in which *the heifer has her neck broken, should not ever be*

16. That of the killer.   17. Cf. Deut. 21:1–8.   18. Cf. Mishnah, Sota, IX 6.
19. Even though it be to only one individual.

tilled or sown.[20] Consequently the owner of that land will use all stratagems and investigate in order that the killer be known and that thus *the heifer will not have her neck broken* and that consequently his land will not be prohibited to him *forever.* |

CHAPTER 41

The *commandments* comprised in the sixth class are concerned with punishments; and their utility, speaking generally, is well known, and we have already mentioned it. Hear then the particulars concerning this and a judgment concerning every strange case figuring in them.

The punishment meted out to anyone who has done wrong to somebody else consists in general in his being given exactly the same treatment that he has given to somebody else. If he has injured the latter's body, he shall be injured in his body, and if he has injured him in his property, he shall be injured in his property. The owner of the property may be indulgent and forgive. To a murderer alone, however, because of the greatness of his wrongdoing, no indulgence shall be shown at all and no blood money shall be accepted from him: *And the land cannot be cleansed of the blood that is shed therein, but by the blood of him that shed it.*[1] Hence even if the victim[2] remains alive for an hour or for several days, speaks, and is in full possession of his mind and says: Let him who murdered me be dismissed; I have forgiven and pardoned him — this cannot be accepted from him. For necessarily there must be a soul for a soul — the young and the old, the slaves and the free, the men of knowledge and the ignorant, being considered as equal. For among the crimes of man there is none greater than this.

And he who has deprived someone of a member, shall be deprived of a similar member: *As he hath maimed a man, so shall it be rendered unto him.*[3] You should not engage in cogitation concerning the fact that in such a case we punish by imposing a fine. For at present my purpose is to give reasons for the [biblical] texts and not for the pronouncements of the legal science.[4] Withal I have an opinion concerning this provision of legal science, which should only be expressed by word of mouth. A fine was imposed in

---

20. Cf. Deut. 21:4.
1. Num. 35:33.   2. Literally: the slain.   3. Lev. 24:20.
4. This is the usual meaning of *fiqh*, the Arabic word used here. Maimonides applies it in this passage and elsewhere to the talmudic legal code.

the case of wounds in requital of which exactly similar wounds could not be inflicted: *Only he shall pay for the loss of his time, and shall cause him to be throughly healed.*[5]

He who has caused damage to property shall have inflicted upon him damage to his property up to exactly the same amount: *Whom | the judges shall condemn, he shall pay double unto his neighbor*[6] — that is, the thing taken by him and an equal amount taken from the property of the thief.

Know that the more frequent the kind of crime is and the easier it is to commit, the greater the penalty for it must be, so that one should refrain from it. On the other hand, the penalty for a thing that happens seldom is lighter. Therefore the fine imposed on him who steals sheep is double the fine imposed for the theft of other *transportable* objects, I refer to *fourfold reparation,*[7] the condition being that he has let them go out of his possession by selling them or has slaughtered them. For they have always been stolen in the majority of cases because they were in the fields where they cannot be watched over the way it is possible to watch over things that are in towns. And therefore those who steal them generally make haste to sell them so that they should not be recognized while being in their possession, or to slaughter them so that they should disappear. Hence the penalty for such cases of theft as are in the majority is greater. The fine imposed for the theft of an ox is even greater by the value of the thing stolen,[8] for it is easier to steal them. For sheep graze together, so that the shepherd can see all of them, and in most cases it is only by night that they can be stolen. Oxen, on the other hand, graze far apart from one another, as is mentioned in the "Agriculture," so that the shepherd cannot watch over them, and accordingly they are more often stolen.

Similarly the *law concerning false witnesses*[9] is that the thing that they wished to be done unto another shall be done unto them: if they wished the one they bore witness against to be killed, they shall be killed; if they wished him to be flogged, they shall be flogged: and if they wished him to be fined, they shall have a similar fine imposed on them. In all this the intention is to make the penalty equal to the crime, and this too is a meaning of the expression: *righteous judgments.*[10]

The fact that a *robber* does not have to pay something additional as a

---

5. Exod. 21:19.   6. Exod. 22:8.   7. Cf. Exod. 21:37; II Sam. 12:6.
8. More or less literally: by the amount of one. Cf. Exod. 21:37; five oxen must be paid for one that has been stolen.
9. Cf. Deut. 19:19.
10. Cf. Deut. 4:8. Cf. the interpretation of this expression that appears in III 26.

fine — for the *fifth part* is merely paid in *expiation* of a false oath[11] — is due to the rare occurrence | of robbery. For the calamity of stealing is more frequent than robbery; for a theft is possible in all places, whereas robbery in towns can only be carried out with difficulty. Furthermore, both things that are in the open and those that have been hidden away and safeguarded with care can be stolen, whereas only things that are in the open and exposed to being perceived can be robbed; so that a man can safeguard himself and take precautions against a robber, making preparations against him, but cannot do this with regard to a thief. Moreover the robber is known, so that he can be summoned and so that one can try to make him give back that which he has taken, whereas the thief is not known. For all these reasons the *thief*, but not the *robber*, is sentenced to pay a *fine*.

Introduction. Know that whether a penalty is great and most grievous or small and easy to bear depends on four things being taken into consideration. The first is the greatness of the crime: for actions from which great harm results entail a heavy penalty, whereas actions from which only small and slight harm results entail but a light penalty. The second is the frequency of the occurrence of the crime: for a crime that occurs rather often ought to be prevented by means of a heavy penalty, whereas a slight penalty suffices to prevent one that is rare in view of its rarity. The third is the strength of incitement: for a man can be made to give up a thing toward which he is incited — either because desire draws him strongly toward it or because of the strength of habit or because of his feeling great hardship when refraining from it — only by fear of a heavy penalty. The fourth is the ease with which the action can be committed in secret and concealment, so that the others are unaware of it: for the deterrent for this can only be the fear of a great and heavy penalty.

After this | introduction has been made, you should know that classification of punishments, according to the text of the *Torah*, comprises four degrees: [1] that which entails *death by order of a court of law*; [2] that which entails *being cut off* — that is, being whipped, the crime being believed withal to be a great one; [3] that which entails being whipped, but the crime is not believed to be a great one, but a mere *transgression*, or entails *death at the hands of God*;[12] [4] that in which there is only a prohibition the transgression of which does not even entail flogging. To this degree belong all *transgressions in which there is no action*[13] — except vain *oaths*, because of the belief one ought to hold as to glorifying Him, may He be

---

11. Cf. Lev. 5:24.   12. Literally: *Heaven.*
13. Cf. B.T., Makkoth, 16a; B.T., Shebu°oth, 21a; B.T., Temurah, 3a.

exalted; the *substitution* of an animal for one previously chosen for sacrifice, in order that this should not result in *sacrifices* consecrated to Him, may He be exalted, being held in light esteem; and *cursing one's fellow man in the name* [of God], for in the opinion of the multitude the injury resulting from curses is greater than that which may befall the body. All *transgressions*[14] other than these *in which there is no action* can only result in little damage, and it is also impossible to take care not to commit them, for they consist in words only. If their perpetrators were punished, people would have their backs flogged all the time. Moreover a *warning* with regard to them cannot be conceived.

There is also wisdom in the number of the strokes, for it is determinate with regard to the maximum and indeterminate with regard to the individuals. For an individual may receive only such flogging as he can bear, but the maximum number of strokes is forty, even if he can bear one hundred.

You will find there is no obligation for a [sentence of] *death* [to be pronounced] *by a court of law* with reference to prohibited foods, for in this there is no great harm, and people are not strongly attracted to them as they are by the pleasure of sexual intercourse. The penalty of *being cut off* is entailed by the eating of certain foods, blood[15] for instance, for they had a great desire at that time to eat of it because of a certain kind of *idolatrous cult*, as is explained in the book of Tumtum. Much stress is therefore laid upon this. | The penalty of *being cut off* is also entailed by the eating of fat[16] because people take pleasure in it; also it is especially used for *sacrifice* in order to glorify it, as shall be explained. Similarly the penalty of *being cut off* is entailed by the partaking of *leavened bread during Passover and of food on the day of fasting*[17] because of the hardship imposed by this kind of abstention and because of the belief to which these actions lead. For these are actions that fortify opinions that are foundations of the Law, I mean *the exodus from Egypt* and its miracles and the belief in *repentance: For on this day shall atonement be made, and so on.*[18] The penalty of *being cut off* is also entailed by the eating of the *remainder* [of a sacrifice] or of a *profaned* [sacrifice] or of something *holy while one was unclean*,[19] just as it is entailed by the eating of fat; the purpose being the glorification of the *sacrifice*, as will be explained later on.

14. Comprised in the class in question.　　15. Cf., e.g., Lev. 7:26–27.
16. More precisely, of certain fats. Cf. Lev. 7:23–25.
17. Cf. Exod. 12:15; Lev. 23:29.
18. Lev. 16:30.
19. Cf. Lev. 7:16–21; 19:5–8.

As for *death by order of a court of law*, you will find that this sentence is only brought on in grave cases: that is, either in the case of the corruption of belief or in that of a very great crime. I refer to *idolatry, adulterous or incestuous sexual intercourse, and the shedding of blood* and all that leads to these crimes as well as in the cases of the profanation of the *Sabbath*,[20] as the latter fortifies the belief in the creation of the world; of a false claim of prophecy; of a *rebellious elder*,[21] because of the great harm that results in these cases; of *him that smiteth his father and his mother and curseth his father and his mother*,[22] because of the great impudence of the thing and its destroying the good order of the household, which is the first part of the city. As for a *stubborn and rebellious son*,[23] he must be put to death because of what he will become, for necessarily he will murder later on. *He that stealeth a man*[24] must likewise be punished in this manner, for he exposes him to death. Also *he that comes breaking in*,[25] for he too is prepared to kill, as [the Sages], *may their memory be blessed*, have explained.[26] These three, I mean a *stubborn and rebellious son, he that stealeth a man and selleth him, and he that comes breaking in*, will become shedders of blood. You will not find that *death by order of a court of law* is prescribed except in the case of these great crimes. Not all *incestuous and adulterous sexual intercourse* is punished by *death by order of a court of law*; only such as is easy to engage in or is most shameful or has the strongest attraction. | That which is not of this kind is merely punished by *cutting off*. Nor are all species of *idolatry* punished by *death by order of a court of law*, but only the fundamental ones, such as calling the people to worship idols, *prophesying in their name, making* [children] *to pass through fire*, [consulting] *familiar spirits*, and being a *wizard* and a *sorcerer*.

It is clear that as there must be punishments, it is indispensable to have judges distributed in every town. There must be testimony of witnesses, and a ruler who is feared and held in awe and who uses all sorts of deterrents and fortifies the authority of the judges and in his turn draws strength from them. Thus the reasons for all the *commandments* that we have enumerated in the *Book of Judges* have been explained. It behooves us now, in conformity with the purpose of this Treatise, to call attention to some that figure there, among them to those concerning a *rebellious elder*. I shall say: Inasmuch as God, may He be exalted, knew that the commandments of this

20. Cf. Exod. 31:13–15.
21. Cf. Deut. 18:20; 17:12. Cf. Mishnah, Sanhedrin, XI 1–2.
22. Exod. 21:15 and 17. Cf. also Lev. 20:9.   23. Cf. Deut. 21:18–21.
24. Cf. Exod. 21:16; Deut. 24:7.   25. Cf. Exod. 22:1.
26. Cf. Mishnah, Sanhedrin, VIII 6.

Law will need in every time and place — as far as some of them are concerned — to be added to or subtracted from according to the diversity of
places, happenings, and conjunctures of circumstances, He forbade adding
to them or subtracting from them, saying: *Thou shalt not add thereto, nor
diminish from it.*[27] For this might have led to the corruption of the rules of
the Law and to the belief that the latter did not come from God. Withal He
permitted the men of knowledge of every period, I refer to the *Great Court
of Law*, to take precautions with a view to consolidating the ordinances of
the Law by means of regulations in which they innovate with a view to
repairing fissures, and to perpetuate these precautionary measures according
to what has been said by [the Sages]: *Build a hedge for the Torah.*[28]
Similarly they were permitted in certain circumstances or with a view to
certain events to abolish certain actions prescribed by the Law or to permit
some of the things forbidden by it; but these measures may not be perpetuated, as we have explained in the Introduction to the Commentary on the
Mishnah in speaking of *temporary decisions*. Through this kind of govern-
ance | the Law remains one, and one is governed in every time and with a
view to every happening in accordance with that happening. If, however,
every man of knowledge had been permitted to engage in this speculation
concerning particulars, the people would have perished because of the
multiplicity of the differences of opinion and the subdivisions of doctrines.
Consequently He, may He be exalted, has forbidden all the men of knowledge with the single exception of the *Great Court of Law* to undertake this,
and has those who disagree with [this Court] killed. For if it could be
opposed by everyone who engages in speculation, the intended purpose
would be annulled and the usefulness of these regulations abolished.

Know that with regard to the perpetration of things forbidden by the
Law there are four categories: the first being that of the *compelled transgressor*; the second that of the *inadvertent transgressor*; the third that of the
deliberate transgressor; the fourth that of *him who transgresses in a high-
handed manner.*[29]

As for the *compelled transgressor*, it is stated textually that he should
not be punished and that no sin whatever lies upon him. For He, may He be
exalted, says: *But unto the damsel thou shalt do nothing; there is in the damsel
no sin worthy of death.*[30]

As for the *inadvertent transgressor*, he sins, for if he had made efforts
to be firm and cautious there would have been no *inadvertence* on his part.
But he is not to be punished in any way, though he *needs atonement* and

27. Deut. 13:1.   28. Mishnah, Aboth, I 1.   29. Cf. Num. 15:30.   30. Deut. 22:26.

hence must *bring a sacrifice*. In this case the *Torah* distinguishes between *a private individual, a king, a High Priest*,[31] and a man qualified to give decisions on points of the Law. From this we learn that everyone who accomplishes an action or gives a decision on a point of the Law in accordance with a doctrine established by his own efforts, belongs, if he is not the *Great Court of Law* or the *High Priest*, to the class of *deliberate transgressors* and is not regarded as being among the *inadvertent transgressors*. Therefore a *rebellious elder* is killed even though he has acted and given decisions on points of the Law in accordance with a doctrine established by his own efforts. The *Great Court of Law*, however, have the right to establish a doctrine by their own effort. Accordingly if they are mistaken, they are held to have been so *inadvertently*; as He, may He be exalted, says: *And if the whole congregation of Israel shall err, and so on*.[32] Because of this fundamental principle [the Sages], *may their memory be blessed*, say: *An inadvertent mistake in doctrine is considered as a deliberate transgression*,[33] meaning that one who, while being deficient in doctrine, gives decisions on points of the Law and acts in accordance with this deficiency is regarded as a *deliberate transgressor*. | For the status of one who eats a piece of fat from the kidneys thinking that it is fat from the rump is not like the status of one who eats fat from the kidneys knowing what it is, but without knowing that it is one of the forbidden fats. For the latter, though he may offer an atoning sacrifice is *close to being a deliberate transgressor*; and he is this merely by acting in this manner. But one who gives decisions on points of the Law in accordance with his ignorance is indubitably a *deliberate transgressor*; for the text [of the Law] excuses a mistake in a decision on a point of the Law in the case of the *Great Court of Law* only.[34]

As for the *deliberate transgressor*, he must undergo the punishment prescribed by the text, namely, either *death by order of a court of law* or a *flogging* or *blows* [in punishment] *for insubordination in the case of transgressions not punishable by flogging* or a fine. As for those *transgressions* in the case of which *inadvertence* and *deliberation* are considered to have an equal status, this is done because they occur often and with ease, being committed by means of words and not of deeds; I refer to *the oath concerning testimony*[35] and *the oath concerning deposit*.[36] Similarly sexual intercourse

---

31. Cf. Lev. 4:27–28, 22, and 3.   32. Lev. 4:13.   33. Cf. Mishnah, Aboth, IV 13.
34. The sentence may also be translated: For a mistaken text in a decision concerning a point of the Law is only excused in the case of the *Great Court of Law*.
35. I.e., the oath sworn by those summoned as witnesses by which they attest that they know nothing. Cf. Lev. 5:1; Mishnah, Shebuᶜoth, IV 2–3; B.T., Shebuᶜoth, 31b.
36. Cf. Lev. 5:21; Mishnah, Shebuᶜoth, V 1. In this case an individual swears that he has not received that which has been entrusted to his keeping.

with a *bondmaid that is betrothed to a man*[37] is regarded as a light matter because it occurs often, inasmuch as she abandons herself because of her being neither completely a slave nor completely free, nor does she belong completely to a husband — as tradition has it when explaining this *commandment.*[38]

As for *him who transgresses in a high-handed manner*, he is a *deliberate transgressor* who acts with impudence and audacity and makes his transgression known in public. Accordingly such a one does not transgress merely because of desire or because, on account of his evil character, he wishes to obtain things that are forbidden by the Law, but in order to oppose and combat the Law. Therefore it says of him: *He reviles the Lord.*[39] He must indubitably be killed. Whoever acts in this manner does so only because of an opinion formed by him, in virtue of which he is opposed to the Law. Because of this the traditional interpretation[40] states: *The Scripture speaks about idolatry;*[41] for the latter is the opinion opposed to the foundation of the Law. For | a star cannot ever be worshipped except by one who believes that it is eternal a parte ante, as we have explained several times in our compilations. To my mind, the same applies in the case of every transgression in which the wish to ruin and oppose the Law manifests itself. To my mind, if an individual belonging to *Israel* would eat *meat with milk* or would *wear* [a garment of] *mingled stuff* or *round the corners of his head* because he holds these prescriptions in slight esteem in view of an opinion of his that makes it evident that he does not believe in the truth of this legislation, he would in my opinion *revile the Lord* and ought to be put to death as an infidel and not in order to punish him for his transgression — just *as the inhabitants of a town led astray* are put to death as infidels and not in order to punish them for their transgressions; therefore their property is burnt and does not belong to their heirs, as in the case of *the others sentenced to death by a court of law.* I shall say the same about every community of *Israelites* who decide unanimously to transgress any *commandment* whatever and *act highhandedly* — all of them shall be put to death. You may know this from the story of *the sons of Reuben and the sons of Gad*, about whom it is said: *And the whole congregation decided to go up to war against them.*[42] Then it was made clear to them in the *warning* that they had committed an act of infidelity through agreeing unanimously to perpetrate this *transgression*

37. Cf. Lev. 19:20–21; Mishnah, Kerithoth, II 2; B.T., Kerithoth, 9a.
38. Cf. Mishnah, Kerithoth, II 5; B.T., Kerithoth, 11a.   39. Num. 15:30.
40. Of the verse that has just been quoted.   41. Cf. B.T., Kerithoth, 7b.
42. Josh. 22:12. The quotation, as given by Maimonides, is not quite accurate.

and had thereby apostatized from religion as a whole. This is the meaning of what they[43] said to them: *To turn away this day from following the Lord.*[44] They,[45] on the other hand, replied: *If it be in rebellion, and so on.*[46] Grasp these principles also with regard to penalties.

The *Book of Judges* includes also the commandment to destroy *the seed of* ᶜ*Amaleq*, for one particular tribe or nation[47] ought to be punished, just as one particular individual is punished, so that all tribes should be deterred and should not co-operate in doing evil. For they will say: Lest be done to us what was done to the sons of such and such a man.[48] Thus even if there should grow up among them a wicked corrupt man who does not care about the wickedness of his soul and does not think of the wickedness of his action, he will not find | a helper of his own tribe to help him in the wicked things whose realization he desires. Accordingly it was commanded that ᶜ*Amaleq*, who hastened to use the sword, should be exterminated by the sword. On the other hand, ᶜ*Ammon* and *Moab*, who acted in a vile manner and caused harm by means of a stratagem, were punished only by the prohibition against becoming related to them through marriage, by being considered worthless, and by their friendship being shunned. All these matters belong to the divine estimation of penalties, so that these should not be too great or too small, as He, may He be exalted, has made it clear: *According to his wickedness.*[49]

This *book*[50] also includes the commandment *to prepare a* [secluded] *place and a paddle.*[51] For one of the purposes of this Law consists, as I have made known to you, in cleanliness and avoidance of excrements and of dirt and in man's not being like the beasts. And this *commandment* also fortifies, by means of the actions it enjoins, the certainty of the combatants that the *Indwelling* has descended among them — as is explained in the reason given for it: *For the Lord thy God walketh in the midst of thy camp.*[52] It has also included another notion, saying: *That He see no unclean thing in thee, and turn away from thee,*[53] this being against that which, as is well known, is widespread among soldiers in a camp after they have stayed for a long time away from their homes. Accordingly He, may He be exalted, has commanded us to perform actions that make call to mind that the *Indwelling* has descended among us so that we should be preserved from those actions, and has said: *Therefore shall thy camp be holy; that He see no unclean thing*

43. The Children of Israel.   44. Josh. 22:16.   45. The sons of Reuben and of Gad.
46. Josh. 22:22.   47. Or: religious community.
48. I.e., to the tribe that was punished.   49. Deut. 25:2.
50. I.e., the Book of Judges of Maimonides' *Mishneh Torah,* or Deuteronomy.
51. Cf. Deut. 23:13–14.   52. Deut. 23:15.   53. Deut. 23:15.

in thee, and so on.[54] He has even commanded that a man *who has polluted himself by night* should go out of the camp *until the sun sets; and afterward he may come into the camp.*[55] Accordingly everyone should have in his mind that the camp is *like a Sanctuary of the Lord* and not like the camps of the *Gentiles* destined only to destroy and to do wrong and to harm the others and to rob them of their property. On the contrary, our purpose is to make people apt to obey God and to introduce order | into their circumstances. I have already made it known to you that I shall give reasons for the [biblical] text according to its external meaning.

This *book*[56] also includes the *law concerning the beautiful* [captive] *woman.*[57] You know their dictum: [*Here*] *the Torah only speaks in consideration of concupiscence.*[58] Nevertheless this *commandment* includes an exhortation to noble moral qualities, which excellent men must acquire in a way I shall indicate. For though *his concupiscence overcomes him* and patience is impossible for him, he must obligatorily bring her to a hidden place; as it says: *Home to thine house.*[59] And as [the Sages] have explained, he is not permitted *to do her violence during the war.*[60] And he is not allowed sexual intercourse with her for the second time before her grief has calmed down and her sorrow has been quieted. And she should not be forbidden to grieve, to be disheveled, and to weep; as the text says: *And she shall bewail her father and her mother, and so on.*[61] For those who grieve find solace in weeping and in arousing their sorrow until their bodily forces are too tired to bear this affection of the soul; just as those who rejoice find solace in all kinds of play. Therefore the Law has had pity on her[62] and gave her the possibility to do so until she is weary of weeping and of grieving. You know that he can have sexual intercourse with her *while she is still a Gentile.* She may also, for thirty days in public, profess her religion, even *in an idolatrous cult,* and may not during that period be taken to task because of a belief. Withal if he does not succeed afterwards to convert her to the statutes of the Law, she may not be sold or treated as a slave. For the Law safeguards her inviolability on account of her having shown herself naked in sexual intercourse, even if this has happened through a certain act of disobedience—I refer to her having then been a *Gentile*—and says

54. Deut. 23:15.
55. Cf. Deut. 23:11–12; Lev. 15:16. The Hebrew phrase following the semicolon appears in Lev. 14:8 and Num. 19:7. However, these two passages do not refer to the case mentioned here by Maimonides.
56. I.e., the Book of Judges of Maimonides' *Mishneh Torah*, or Deuteronomy.
57. Cf. Deut. 21:10–14.   58. B.T., Qiddushin, 21b.   59. Deut. 21:12.
60. Cf. B.T., Qiddushin, 22a.   61. Deut. 21:13.   62. I.e., on the captive woman.

withal: *Thou shalt not make merchandise of her, because thou hast humbled her.*[63] Accordingly it has become clear that this *commandment* contains encouragement to a noble moral quality. The reasons for all the *commandments* contained in this *book*[64] have accordingly become clear. |

CHAPTER 42

The *commandments* comprised in the seventh class are the laws concerning property; they are those that we have enumerated in a portion of the *Book of Judgments* and in a portion of the *Book of Acquisition.* All of them have an evident reason. For they consist in an estimation of the laws of justice with regard to the transactions that of necessity occur between people and see to it that these do not deviate from a course of mutual help useful for both parties, lest one of them should aim at increasing his share in the whole and at being the gainer in all respects.

First and foremost there should be no swindling in buying and selling, and only the usual and habitually recognized profits should be sought.[1] Conditions have been laid down under which the contract becomes valid, and swindling, even if it consists in mere words, has been forbidden, as is well known.

Then there is the *law of four trustees.*[2] It is manifest in what way it is just and equitable. For the *trustee* who keeps a deposit *gratuitously* and derives no advantage whatever from this business and merely exercises charity is *not responsible for anything,* and every accident that may happen is borne by the purse of the owner of the property. A *borrower* who has all the advantage, whereas the owner of the property exercises charity with regard to him, is *responsible for everything,* and all accidents that may happen are paid for out of the purse of the *borrower.* As for him who takes charge of a deposit in *consideration of a salary* and *the lessor,* each one of them, I mean *the trustee* and *the owner of the property,* participates in the advantage; therefore damages from accidents are divided between them. Those that are due to lack of care in keeping watch are paid for out of the purse of the *trustee* as when the thing is *stolen* or *lost,* for | the fact of *theft*

63. Deut. 21:14.
64. I.e., the Book of Judges of Maimonides' *Mishneh Torah,* or Deuteronomy.
  1. Cf. Lev. 25:14–17.   2. Cf. Exod. 22:6–14.

or *loss* shows that he had neglected measures of great prudence and exceeding precautions. On the other hand, damages from such accidents as can be prevented by no device — as when the beast that has been lent is *crippled* or *carried off* or *died*, that is, when *circumstances are beyond one's control* — are borne by the purse of the owner of the property.

Then exceeding kindness is shown to the hired man because of his poverty, and it has been commanded that he receive his wages promptly and that he should in no way be cheated out of his due; I mean that he should be recompensed according to the value of his service.[3] It is a matter of pity for him that he or even a beast must not be prevented from eating some of the food on which they work, according to the statutes of this Law.[4]

The statutes concerning property also comprise inheritance. Herein is involved an excellent moral quality, I mean that a man should not withhold a good thing from one deserving it. Accordingly when he is going to die, he should not begrudge his heir and squander his property. On the contrary, he should leave it to him who among all the people deserves it most, namely, to his next of kin: *Unto his kinsman that is next to him of his family.*[5] As is well known, it is explained that this is first of all the child, then the brother, then the paternal uncle.[6] And he should grant perference to the eldest of his children because his love for him came first, and he should not follow his inclination: *He may not make the son of the beloved [wife] the first-born, and so on.*[7] This most just Law safeguards and fortifies[8] this moral quality — I refer to taking care of relatives and protecting them. You know what the prophet says: *But he that is cruel afflicts his own kinsman;*[9] and the text of the *Torah* when speaking of alms: *Unto thy brother, to thy poor, and so on.*[10] And the *Sages, may their memory be blessed,* praise very much the character of the individual *who causes his relatives to be close to him and who marries his sister's daughter.*[11]

The *Torah* has taught us that one must go exceedingly far indeed in the exercise of this moral quality. Namely, man ought to take care of his relative and grant very strong preference to the bond of the womb. Even if his relative should do him an injustice and a wrong and | should be extremely corrupt, he must nevertheless regard his kinsman with a protective eye. He, may He be exalted, says: *Thou shalt not abhor an Edomite, for he is thy brother.*[12] Similarly everyone of whom you have had need some day,

3. Cf. Lev. 19:13; Deut. 24:14–15.   4. Cf. Deut. 23:25.   5. Num. 27:11.
6. Cf. Num. 27:8–10.   7. Deut. 21:16.
8. Or: is fortified by. Or, according to another reading: perpetuates.
9. Prov. 11:17.   10. Deut. 15:11.   11. B.T., Yebamoth, 62b.
12. Deut. 23:8.

23

everyone who was useful to you and whom you found in a time of stress, even if afterwards he treated you ill, ought necessarily to have merit attaching to him because of the past. He, may He be exalted, says: *Thou shalt not abhor an Egyptian, because thou wast a stranger in his land.*[13] And it is generally known how greatly *the Egyptians vexed us*[14] afterwards.

See then how many noble moral qualities we learn from these commandments. The two last mentioned do not belong to this seventh class. But speaking of the care to be taken of relatives in inheritance, we went on to mention *the Egyptian and the Edomite.*

CHAPTER 43

The *commandments* comprised in the eighth class are the *commandments* that we have enumerated in the *Book of Times.*[1] The [biblical] text gives the reasons for all of them except a few.

With regard to the Sabbath, the reason for it is too well known to have need of being explained, for it is known how great a rest it procures. Because of it the seventh part of the life of every individual consists in pleasure and repose from the fatigue and weariness from which there is no escape either for the young or for the old. At the same time it perpetuates throughout the periods of time an opinion whose value is very great, namely, the assertion that the world has been produced in time.

The *fast* [of the Day] *of Atonement* has also an evident reason consisting in establishing the notion of *repentance.* It is the day on which the Master of the prophets descended with the *second Tables* [of the Law] and brought them the good news that their | great sin was forgiven. This day became forever a day of repentance exclusively consecrated to divine service. Therefore one must abstain on it from all corporeal pleasure and from all effort with a view to what is useful to the body — I mean from work in various crafts — and confine oneself to *confessions* — I mean to confessing one's sins and to turning away from them.

The *festivals* are all for rejoicings and pleasurable gatherings, which in most cases are indispensable for man; they are also useful in the establishment of friendship, which must exist among people living in political societies. There is a particular reason for every one of these days.

13. Deut. 23:8.   14. Cf. Num. 20:15.
1. Or: *Seasons.*

The account of *Passover* is generally known. It lasts for seven days, for the period of seven days is a mean between the natural day and the lunar month. You know already that this period plays a great role in natural matters. It does so likewise in matters pertaining to the Law. For the Law always tends to assimilate itself to nature, perfecting the natural matters in a certain respect. For nature is not endowed with thought and understanding, whereas the Law is the determining ruling and the governance of the deity, who grants the intellect to all its possessers. This, however, is not the purpose of this chapter. We shall accordingly return to the matter with which we are dealing at present.

The [Festival of] *Weeks* is the day of the *giving of the Torah*. In order to glorify and exalt that day, the days are counted from the first of the festivals up to it, as is done by one who waits for the coming of the human being he loves best and counts the days and the hours. This is the reason for *the counting of the ʿOmer*[2] from the day when they left Egypt till the day of the *giving of the Torah*, which was the purpose and the end of their leaving: *And brought you unto Myself.*[3] This great gathering only lasted one day; accordingly | it is commemorated every year during one day only. If, however, the eating of *unleavened bread* would only last for one day, we would not take notice of it and its meaning would not be made clear. For man often eats one kind of food for two or three days. Accordingly the meaning of [the eating of unleavened bread] only becomes clear and the account with which it is connected only becomes generally known through its being eaten for a complete period.

New Year lasts similarly for one day. For it is a day of repentance in which the attention of the people is called to their negligence. Therefore the *shophar* [*horn*] is blown on it, as we have explained in *Mishneh Torah.*[4] It is, as it were, a preparation for, and introduction to, *the Day of the Fast* [of Atonement]. Accordingly it is generally accepted in the tradition of the religious community[5] that *the ten days from New Year to the Day of Atonement* should be observed.

The [Festival of] *Tabernacles*, which aims at rejoicing and gladness, lasts for seven days, so that its meaning be generally known. The reason for its taking place in the season in question is explained in the *Torah: When thou gatherest in thy labors out of the field;*[6] this refers to the season of leisure when one rests from necessary labors. In the ninth book of the

---

2. The sheaf of the wave-offering; cf. Lev. 23:15.   3. Exod. 19:4.
4. Cf. Teshubah, III 4.   5. Or: the nation.   6. Exod. 23:16.

"Ethics,"[7] Aristotle states that this was the general practice of the religious communities in ancient times. He says literally: The ancient sacrifices and gatherings used to take place after the harvesting of the fruit. They were, as it were, offerings given because of leisure. This is literally what he says. In addition, it is possible to live in the *tabernacle* during that season, there being no great heat nor an uncomfortable rain. Both these festivals, I mean *Tabernacles* and *Passover*, inculcate both an opinion and a moral quality. In the case of *Passover*, the opinion consists in the commemoration of the *miracles of Egypt* and in the perpetuation of their memory throughout the periods of time. In the case of *Tabernacles*, the opinion consists in the perpetuation of the memory of the *miracles* of the *desert* throughout the periods of time. As for the moral quality, it consists in man's always remembering the days | of stress in the days of prosperity, so that his gratitude to God should become great and so that he should achieve humility and submission. Accordingly *unleavened bread* and *bitter herbs* must be eaten on *Passover* in commemoration of what happened to us. Similarly one must leave the houses[8] and dwell in tabernacles, as is done by the wretched inhabitants of deserts and wastelands, in order that the fact be commemorated that such was our state in ancient times: *That I made the children of Israel dwell in tabernacles, and so on.*[9] From this we went over to dwell in richly ornamented houses in the best and most fertile place on earth, thanks to the benefaction of God and His promises to our fathers, inasmuch as they were perfect people in their opinions and in their moral character — I mean *Abraham, Isaac, and Jacob.* For this too is one of the pivots of the Law, I mean the belief that every benefit that will be or has been granted is *due to the merit of the Fathers,* since *they kept the way of the Lord to do justice and judgment.*[10]

One's going over from *Tabernacles* to a second festival, I mean to the *Eighth Day of Assembly,* can be accounted for by the consideration that in this way one can complete such rejoicings as are impossible in *tabernacles* but only possible in spacious dwellings and in buildings.

As for the *four species that constitute a lulab,*[11] the *Sages, may their memory be blessed,* have set forth some reason for this in the manner of *Midrashim*[12] whose method is well known by all those who understand

---

7. In fact, the passage occurs in Book VIII (1160a25–28) of the *Nicomachean Ethics.*
8. During the Feast of Tabernacles.   9. Lev. 23:43.   10. Cf. Gen. 18:19.
11. In this passage the Hebrew word apparently means any bunch composed of four plants. The four species alluded to are the branches of the palm tree, the citron, the myrtle, and the willows of the brook.
12. Here and in the following passages, the term *Midrashim* is substituted for the word *derashoth* used by Maimonides.

their discourses. For these [namely, the Midrashim] have, in their opinion, the status of poetical conceits; they are not meant to bring out the meaning of the text in question. Accordingly, with regard to the *Midrashim*, people are divided into two classes: A class that imagines that [the Sages] have said these things in order to explain the meaning of the text in question, and a class that holds [the Midrashim] in slight esteem and holds them up to ridicule, since it is clear and manifest that this is not the meaning of the [biblical] text in question. The first class strives and fights with a view to proving, as they deem, the correctness of the *Midrashim* and to defending them, | and think that this is the true meaning of the [biblical] text and that the *Midrashim* have the same status as the traditional legal decisions. But neither of the two groups understands that [the Midrashim] have the character of poetical conceits whose meaning is not obscure for someone endowed with understanding. At that time this method was generally known and used by everybody, just as the poets use poetical expressions. Thus [the Sages], *may their memory be blessed*, say: *Bar Qappara teaches:* [*In the verse —*] *And thou shalt have a paddle* [*yathed*] *upon azenekha* [*thy weapon*][13] *— do not read azenekha, but aznekha* [*thy ear*]. *This teaches us that whenever a man hears a reprehensible thing, he should put his finger into his ear.*[14] Would that I knew whether, in the opinion of these ignoramuses, this *Tannaite* believed this to be the interpretation of this text, that such was the purpose of this *commandment*, that *yathed* [*paddle*] means a finger, and that *azenekha* [*thy weapon*] refers to the two ears. I do not think that anyone of sound intellect will be of this opinion. But this is a most witty poetical conceit by means of which he instills a noble moral quality, which is in accordance with the fact that just as it is forbidden to tell them, so is it forbidden to listen to obscene things; and he props it up through a reference to a [biblical] text, as is done in poetical compositions. Similarly all the passages in the *Midrashim* enjoining, *Do not read thus, but thus*, have this meaning. I have deviated from the subject, but this is a useful observation that may be needed by everyone endowed with intellect among those who profess the Law and are Rabbanites.[15] I will return to the order of our discourse. What seems to me regarding the *four species that constitute a lulab*[16] is that they are indicative of the joy and gladness [felt by the Children of Israel] when they left the *desert* — which was *no place of seed, or of figs, or of vines, or of pomegranates; neither was there any water to drink*[17] — for places in which there

13. Deut. 23:14.   14. B.T., Kethuboth, 15a.
15. This term is probably used in contradistinction to the term Qaraites.
16. Cf. n. 11, this chap.   17. Num. 20:5.

were fruit-bearing trees and rivers. For the purpose of commemoration, the finest fruit of these places was taken and the one that was most fragrant, as well as their finest leaves and finest verdure, I mean *the willows of the brook*. Three things are found in common in these *four species*. | The first one is that at that time they were plentiful in the *Land of Israel* so that everyone could procure them. The second one is that they are beautiful to look at and full of freshness; and some of them, namely, the *citron* and the *myrtle*, have an excellent fragrance, while the *branches of the palm tree* and the *willow* have neither a good nor an offensive smell. The third one is that they keep fresh for seven days, which is not the case with peaches, pomegranates, asparagus, pears, and the like.

CHAPTER 44

The *commandments* comprised in the ninth class are the *commandments* that we have enumerated in the *Book of Love*. All of them have manifest reasons and evident causes. I mean that the end of these actions pertaining to divine service is the constant commemoration of God, the love of Him and the fear of Him, the obligatory observance of the *commandments* in general, and the bringing-about of such belief concerning Him, may He be exalted, as is necessary for everyone professing the Law. Those commandments are: prayer, the *recital of Shema*,[1] the *blessing of food*[2] and what is connected with it, the *blessing of the Priests*,[3] *phylacteries*,[4] the *inscription on the posts of the houses and on the gates*,[5] acquiring a *book of the Torah* and reading in it at certain times.[6] All these are actions that bring about useful opinions. This is clear and manifest and does not require another discourse, for that would be nothing but repetition.

1. I.e., the recital of the passage (Deut. 6:4 ff.) that begins: *Shema Yisrael* (Hear, O Israel).
2. I.e., the recital of grace. Cf. Deut. 8:10.   3. Cf. Num. 6:23–26.
4. Cf. Exod. 13:9 and 16; Deut. 6:8; 11:18.   5. *mezuzah*. Cf. Deut. 6:9; 11:20.
6. According to rabbinic tradition, this last commandment may be deduced from Deut. 31:19. Cf. Maimonides' *Mishneh Torah*, Sepher Torah, VII 1.

The *commandments* comprised in the tenth class are those that | we have enumerated in *Laws concerning the Chosen Temple*, *Laws concerning the Utensils of the Sanctuary and Those Who Work in It*, and *Laws concerning Entry into the Sanctuary*. We have already made known in a general way the utility of this class of commandments.

It is known that *idolaters* sought to build their temples and to set up their idols in the highest places they could find there: *Upon the high mountains.*[1] Therefore *Abraham our Father* singled out *Mount Moriah*, because of its being the highest mountain there, proclaimed upon it the unity [of God], and determined and defined the direction toward which one would turn in prayer, fixing it exactly in the West. For *the Holy of Holies* is in the West. This is the meaning of the dictum of [the Sages]: *The Indwelling is in the West.*[2] They, *may their memory be blessed*, have made clear in the *Gemara* of the Tractate *Yoma*[3] that *Abraham our Father* fixed the direction toward which one should turn in prayer, I mean *the Temple of the Holy of Holies*. In my opinion, the reason for this is as follows: Inasmuch as at that time the opinion generally accepted in the world was to the effect that the sun should be worshipped and that it is the deity, there is no doubt that all men turned when praying toward the East. Therefore *Abraham our Father* turned, when praying on *Mount Moriah* — I mean in the *Sanctuary* — toward the West, so as to turn his back upon the sun. Do you not see what [the Children of] *Israel* did when they apostasized, became infidels, and returned to those ancient pernicious views? *Their backs were toward the temple of the Lord, and their faces toward the East; and they worshipped the sun toward the East.*[4] Understand this strange thing. In my opinion there is also no doubt that the place singled out by *Abraham* in virtue of prophetic inspiration was known to *Moses our Master* and to many others. For *Abraham* had recommended to them that that place should be a house of worship, just as the translator[5] sets forth when he says:[6] *Abraham worshipped and prayed in that place and said before the Lord: Here will worship the generations, and so on.* The fact that this place is not stated explicitly

---

1. Deut. 12:2.   2. B.T., Baba Bathra, 25a.
3. No explicit passage to this effect has been found in this tractate of the Babylonian Talmud. Maimonides may be referring to pages 28b and 54b where certain passages may be interpreted in the way suggested in the text.
4. Ezek. 8:16.   5. I.e., Onqelos.   6. In his Aramaic paraphrase of Gen. 22:14.

when mentioned in the *Torah* | and not designated, but only hinted at by means of the words, *Which the Lord shall choose, and so on*,[7] is due in my opinion to three wise considerations. The first is, lest nations[8] should hold fast to the place and fight for it with great violence, knowing as they do that this place is the final purpose of the Law on earth. The second is, lest those who then owned the place ravage and devastate it to the limit of their power. The third, and it is the strongest, lest every *tribe* should demand that this place be *within its allotted portion* and should seek to conquer it, which would lead to conflict and sedition, such as happened with regard to the *priesthood*. Therefore the command was given that the *Chosen Temple* should only be built after the *elevation of a King*, so that only one would be qualified to give commands and quarrels would cease, as we have explained in the *Book of Judges*.[9]

It is known that these people[10] built temples for the stars and that in that temple an idol whose worship was agreed upon was set up, I mean an idol assigned to a certain star or to a portion of a Sphere. Consequently we were commanded to build a temple for Him, may He be exalted, and place in it the *ark* within which were the *two Tables* containing the words *I* [am the Lord] and *Thou shalt not have.*

It is known that the fundamental principle of belief in prophecy precedes the belief in the Law. For if there is no prophet, there can be no Law. The prophet receives prophetic revelation only through the intermediary of the *angel.* Thus: *And the angel of the Lord called;*[11] *And the angel of the Lord said unto her.*[12] This occurs innumerable times. Even in the case of *Moses our Master*, his prophetic mission is inaugurated *through an angel: And there appeared unto him an angel of the Lord in the heart of fire.*[13] Consequently it has been made clear that that belief in the existence of angels precedes the belief in prophecy, and the belief in prophecy precedes the belief in the Law.

As the Sabians were ignorant of the existence of the deity, may He be exalted and glorified, and thought that | the Sphere with its stars is the being that is eternal and to which nonbeing can never come, and that forces flow over from the Sphere toward idols and certain trees — I mean the *asheroth* — they thought that the idols and the trees give prophetic revelation to the prophets, speak to them in the course of such a revelation, and make known to them what is useful and what is harmful, according to their

7. Cf. e.g., Deut. 16:6.   8. The pagan peoples are meant.
9. Cf. *Mishneh Torah*, Melakhim, I 1–2.   10. I.e., the idolaters.
11. Gen. 22:15.   12. Gen. 16:9, 10, and 11.
13. Exod. 3:2. The verse's word order is altered somewhat by Maimonides.

doctrines that we have explained to you with reference to *the prophets of Baal and the prophets of Asherah.*[14] Thereupon when the truth became clear to the men of knowledge and it became known by demonstration that there is a being that is neither a body nor a force in a body, who is the true deity, and that He is one; and that there are also other beings that are separate from matter and are not bodies, being toward whom His being, may He be exalted, overflows — namely, the angels, as we have explained;[15] and that all these beings are beyond the Sphere and its stars; — it became known with certainty that true prophetic revelation is given to the prophets by the angels, not by the idols and the *asheroth.* Thus it has become clear through what we have stated before that the belief in the existence of angels is consequent upon the belief in the existence of the deity and that thereby prophecy and the Law are established as valid. In order to fortify belief in this fundamental principle, He, may He be exalted, has commanded that the image of *two angels* be made over the *ark,* so that the belief of the multitude in the existence of angels be consolidated; this correct opinion, coming in the second place after the belief in the existence of the deity, constituting the originative principle of belief in prophecy and the Law and refuting *idolatry,* as we have explained. If there had been one image, I mean the image of *one cherub,* this might have been misleading. For it might have been thought that this was the image of the deity who was to be worshipped — such things[16] being done by the *idolaters* — or that there was only one individual angel, a belief that would have led to a certain dualism.[17] As, however, *two cherubim* were made and the explicit statement enounced: *The Lord is our God, the Lord is one,*[18] the validity | of the opinion affirming the existence of angels was established and also the fact that they are many. Thus measures were taken against the error that they are the deity — the deity being one and having created this multiplicity.

Thereupon a *candlestick* was placed in front of it[19] in order to glorify and honor the Temple. For the Temple, which was always illumined by lamps and separated by means of a veil [from the Holy of Holies], made a great impression upon the soul. You know to what extent the Law fortifies the belief in the greatness of the *Sanctuary* and the awe felt for it, so that on seeing it, man should be affected by a sentiment of submission and servitude. It says: *And ye shall fear My Sanctuary,*[20] an injunction that He has

14. Cf. III 29.   15. Cf. I 49 and II 6.
16. I.e., the worship of an image because of its being the image of the deity.
17. The two deities being God and one angel.   18. Deut. 6:4.
19. Apparently in front of the ark.   20. Lev. 19:30.

coupled with the precept *to keep the Sabbath* in order to strengthen *fear of the Sanctuary*.

The need for *the altar for incense* and *the altar for burnt-offering* and for their utensils is manifest.

As for the *table* and the bread that was always to be upon it,[21] I do not know the reason for this and I have not found up to now something to which I might ascribe this practice.

As for the prohibition against hewing the stones of the *altar*,[22] you know the reason [the Sages] have given for this in their dictum: *It is not fitting for that which shortens [human life] to be lifted up against that which prolongs it.*[23] This is excellent in the manner of the *Midrashim*,[24] as we have mentioned. However, the reason for this is manifest, for the *idolaters* used to build altars with hewn stones. Accordingly assimilation to them was prohibited, and in order to avoid this assimilation to them it was commanded that the *altar* be of earth. It says: *An altar of earth thou shalt make unto Me.*[25] If, however, it was indispensable to make it with stones, the latter must have their natural form and not be hewn. Similarly it is forbidden to set up a *figured stone* and to plant a tree *beside the altar*.[26] In all this there is one and the same purpose, namely, that we should not worship God in the form of the particular cults[27] practiced by them with regard to the objects of their worship; and this is the meaning of the prohibition in general. It says: *How | did these nations serve their gods? even so will I do likewise.*[28] The meaning is that one must not act in this way with regard to God for the reason that it states: *For every abomination to the Lord which He hateth, have they done unto their gods, and so on.*[29]

You know likewise how widespread was the worship of *Pe^cor* in those times, and that it consisted in the uncovering of the nakedness.[30] Therefore it commands the *Priests* to make themselves breeches *to cover the flesh of their nakedness*[31] during the *divine service*. Nevertheless they were commanded not to go up to the *altar* by steps: *That thy nakedness be not uncovered thereon.*[32]

As for the duty constantly *to keep watch* over the *Sanctuary* and to go around it, this was commanded in order to glorify and honor it, so that the ignorant, the unclean, and those who are in a disheveled state should not

21. Cf. Exod. 25:23–30.   22. Cf. Exod. 20:22; Deut. 27:5.
23. Mishnah, Middoth, III 4.   24. In the text: *derashoth*.
25. Exod. 20:24 (v. 21 in some translations).   26. Cf. Lev. 26:1; Deut. 16:21.
27. The cults were particular because they did not have in view the universal deity.
28. Deut. 12:30.   29. Deut. 12:31.   30. Cf. Num. 25:3.   31. Exod. 28:42.
32. Exod. 20:26 (v. 23 in some translations).

rush up to it, as shall be explained. For one of the things that necessarily resulted in an exaltation and glorification of the *Sanctuary*, bringing about in us *fear* of it, was the prohibition against drunken, unclean, and disheveled individuals — I mean *those with unkempt hair and torn garments* — entering it, together with the commandment that everyone *engaged in the divine service shall sanctify his hands and his feet*.

Also in order to exalt the Temple, the rank of its servants was exalted, the *Priests* and *Levites* were singled out, and the *Priests* wore the most splendid, finest, and most beautiful garments: *Holy garments . . . for splendor and for beauty*.[33] And it was commanded that *someone who has a blemish* should not be employed in the *divine service*; not only one who is afflicted with an infirmity, but also those afflicted with deformities *are disqualified from being Priests*,[34] as is explained in the regulations of legal science dealing with this *commandment*.[35] For to the multitude an individual is not rendered great by his true form,[36] but by the perfection of his limbs and the beauty of his clothes; and what is aimed at is that the Temple and its servants should be regarded as great by all.

As for the *son of Levi*, he did not sacrifice and was not imagined as imploring forgiveness for sin, as is stated with regard to the *Priests*:[37] *And he shall make atonement for him; And he shall make atonement for her*. But the purpose of the *Levite* consisted in *singing* only; he | is *disqualified* [only] *because of* [his] *voice*. For the purpose of *singing* too is to bring about an affection of the soul by means of the words in question; and the soul can only be affected by means of pleasing melodies with, in addition, the accompaniment of musical instruments, as was always the case in the *Sanctuary*. Even the *Priests* who were *fit* [for the divine service] and who sojourned in the *Sanctuary* were forbidden to sit down in it, to enter into the Temple at every moment, and ever to enter *the Holy of Holies*, except the *High Priest* who entered it on the *Day of Atonement* — four times, not more. All this was to exalt the *Sanctuary*.

Inasmuch as many beasts were slaughtered daily in that holy place, the flesh cut into pieces, and the intestines burnt[38] and washed, there is no doubt that if it had been left in that state its smell would have been like that of a slaughterhouse. Therefore it was commanded in regard to it that *incense be burnt* there twice daily *in the morning and in the afternoon* in order to improve its smell and the smell of the clothes of all who served

33. Exod. 28:2.   34. Cf. Lev. 21:16–21.   35. Cf. Mishnah, Bekhoroth, VII.
36. I.e., the rational soul or the intellect.   37. Lev. 4:26; 12:8.
38. Cf. Lev. 1:6–9

there. You know their dictum: *The odor of the incense was smelt even in Jericho.*[39] This also preserved *fear of the Sanctuary.* For if it had not had a pleasant smell, and all the more if the contrary were the case, the result would have been the opposite of glorification. For the soul is greatly solaced and attracted by pleasant smells and shrinks from stench and avoids it.

As for the *anointing oil,*[40] it has two useful functions: it gives a pleasant smell to whatever is anointed with it, and induces the belief that the anointed object is great, sanctified, and distinguished beyond other things of the same species, regardless of whether the thing is a human individual or a garment or a vessel. All this redounds to *fear of the Sanctuary,* which is a cause of *fear of the Lord.* For when one came there the soul was affected, so that hard hearts were softened and touched. | For the deity *with far-away counsels*[41] devised this gracious ruse in order that they be softened and become submissive when they came to the Temple, so that they accept God's guiding commands and fear Him, as is explained to us in the text of the *Torah: And thou shalt eat before the Lord thy God, in the place which He shall choose to cause His name to dwell there, the tithe of thy corn, of thy wine, and of thine oil, and the firstlings of thy herd and of thy flock; that thou mayest learn to fear the Lord thy God always.*[42] Thus the intended purpose of all these actions, whatever they may be, has become clear to you.

The reason for the prohibition against imitating the *anointing oil* and the *incense* is most clear. This was forbidden in order that this odor be smelt only there, so that it should produce a stronger affection in them, and also in order that it should not be thought that whoever was anointed with this oil or one similar to it was singled out thereby, a thought that would have produced ruin and sedition.

The fact that the *ark* had to be carried on the shoulder and not in a wagon[43] is clearly due to the intention to exalt it. Its shape ought not to be damaged, not even by moving the *staves* from the *rings.* Similarly the shape of the *ephod* and of the *breastplate* ought not to be damaged, not even by moving one from the other.[44] It was also commanded that the making of the *garments* [of the Priests] be wholly woven, not divided and cut, so that the shape of the woven object be not spoilt.

It was likewise forbidden for one individual among the servants of the *Sanctuary* to take over the function of another.[45] For slackness and negligence in all things occur when various functions are entrusted to a group

39. Mishnah, Tamid, III 8.   40. Cf. Exod. 30:22–23.   41. Isa. 25:1.
42. Deut. 14:23.   43. Cf. Num. 4:1–15; I Chron. 15:15.   44. Cf. Exod. 28:28.
45. Cf. Num. 4:19 and 49.

of people, and every individual has not his own particular work assigned to him. It is also clear that the gradation with regard to the various places[46] — in consequence of which different laws are prescribed with respect to *the Temple Mount*, to the *place between the two walls*, to the *Hall of Women*, to the *Hall*, and to *the Holy of Holies* — were all | intended to bring about additional glorification and to instill *a greater fear* into the heart of all those who came to the Temple.

We have thus set forth the reasons for all details belonging to this class.

CHAPTER 46

The *commandments* comprised in the eleventh class are those that we have enumerated in the remainder of the *Book of Divine Worship* and in the *Book of Sacrifices*. We have already set forth their utility in summary fashion. Now we shall begin to give the reasons, as we have apprehended them, for the single commandments. We shall accordingly say that the *Torah*, according to the interpretation of *Onqelos*, states literally that the Egyptians used to worship the sign of Aries and that they therefore forbade the slaughter of sheep and abominated shepherds. For it says: *Lo, if we shall sacrifice the abomination of the Egyptians;*[1] and it says: *For every shepherd is an abomination unto the Egyptians.*[2] Similarly certain sects of the Sabians worshipped the jinn and believed that they assumed the outward forms of goats and therefore called the jinn *goats*. This teaching was very widespread in the days of *Moses our Master: And they shall no more offer their sacrifices unto the goats [se*c*irim], and so on.*[3] Hence these sects also used to prohibit the eating of goats. As for the slaughter of oxen, nearly the majority of the *idolaters* abominated it, as all of them held this species in very great esteem. Hence you will find that up to our time the Indians do not slaughter oxen, even in countries where other species of animals are slaughtered. Thus it was in order to efface the traces of these incorrect opinions that we have been ordered by the Law to offer in sacrifices only these three species | of quadrupeds: *Ye shall bring your offering of oxen and of small cattle.*[4] In this way an action considered by them as an extreme act

---

46. Cf. Mishnah, Kelim, I 8–9.
  1. Exod. 8:22. The verse continues: *will they not stone us?*   2. Gen. 46:34.
  3. Lev. 17:7.   4. Lev. 1:2.

of disobedience was the one through which one came near to God and sought forgiveness for one's sins. Thus wrong opinions, which are diseases of the human soul, are cured by their contrary found at the other extreme.

With a view to the same purpose we have been commanded to slaughter *the paschal lamb* and to sprinkle with its blood *in Egypt* the gates from outside, so that we should manifest our rejection of these opinions, proclaim what is contrary to them, and bring forth the belief that the act, which they deemed to be a cause of destruction, saves from destruction: *And the Lord will pass over the door, and will not suffer the destroyer to come in unto your houses to smite.*[5] This is in recompense of their manifestation of obedience and their having put an end to the absurd things done by the *idolaters*. This is the reason for the choice of only these three species for sacrifice, over and beyond the fact that these are also domestic species that are numerous, not as is the case in the cults of the *idolaters* who sacrifice lions, bears, and other wild animals, as is mentioned in the book of Tumtum.[6]

As most people are not able to offer a *beast* in sacrifice, it was commanded that birds too should be offered up in sacrifice; namely, those among them that are most frequent in Syria and are the most excellent and the easiest to catch, namely, *turtledoves and young pigeons.* He who is not able to offer up in sacrifice even a bird, must offer bread baked in one of the various manners known at that time: either *baked in an oven* or *baked in a pan* or *baked in a frying-pan.* If baking was difficult for someone, he could offer flour.[7] All this was addressed to those who wished to offer sacrifices.

Then [Scripture] explains to us that in regard to this kind of divine service, I mean | sacrifices, no sin whatever will fall upon us if we do not perform it at all. For it says: *But if thou shalt forbear to vow, it shall be no sin in thee.*[8]

Inasmuch as the *idolaters* offered only leavened bread and made many offerings of sweet things and seasoned their sacrifices with honey, as is generally recognized in the books that I have mentioned to you, and thus no salt was to be found in any of their offerings, He, may He be exalted, forbade offering up *any leaven or any honey*[9] and commanded that salt always be offered: *With all thine offerings thou shalt offer salt.*[10]

He commanded that all the offerings be *perfect* in the most excellent condition, in order that the *sacrifice* should not come to be held in little

5. Exod. 12:23.   6. This book has been mentioned in III 29, 37, and 41.
7. Cf. Lev. 2:1–11.   8. Deut. 23:23.   9. Lev. 2:11.   10. Lev. 2:13.

esteem and that what was offered to His name, may He be exalted, be not despised. As it says: *Offer it now unto thy governor; will he be pleased with thee or will he accept thee?*[11]

For this reason it is also forbidden to sacrifice an animal that is not yet seven days old, for it is deficient among those of its kind and is considered disgusting, for it resembles an abortion.

This is also the reason for the prohibition against offering up *the hire of a harlot or the price of a dog*,[12] because both are considered vile.

This is also the reason for sacrificing the old of the turtledoves and the young of the pigeons, these being the best among them, for no pleasure can be taken in the old pigeons.

This is also the reason for the fact that *oblations* had to be mingled with oil and be of flour, for this is what is most perfect and most pleasant. Frankincense was chosen because of the good odor of its fumes in places filled with the odor of burnt flesh.

In order that the *sacrifice* be held in great esteem and that it not be regarded as repugnant and disgusting, it was commanded that the *burnt-offering* be flayed and its intestines and extremities washed, even though they were entirely burnt. You will find that this was a purpose that was always held in view and observed by [Scripture]: *In that ye say: The table of the Lord is polluted, and the fruit thereof, even the food thereof, is contemptible.*[13]

This is │ also the reason that the *sacrifice* may not be eaten by an *uncircumcised* or *unclean* man, or if it is polluted, or *past its proper time*, or when the intention concerning it is perverted;[14] and that it should be eaten in a special place. The *burnt-offering*, which is entirely consecrated to God, should not be eaten at all. What is offered because of a sin—that is, the *sin-offering* and the *guilt-offering*—should be eaten in the *court* [of the Sanctuary] only on the day of the slaughter and on the following night. The *peace-offerings*, which are of lower dignity and of *lesser sanctity*, may be eaten in the whole of *Jerusalem*, but only in it, and also on the morrow of the day of the sacrifice, but not afterwards, for after that they are spoilt and corrupted.

Again that the *sacrifice* and everything that is consecrated to His name, may He be exalted, be held in great esteem, the prescription was given us that *everyone who has procured pleasure for himself from the Sanctuary, is guilty* and needs an *expiatory sacrifice* to be made for him and must pay

11. Mal. 1:8.   12. Deut. 23:19.   13. Mal. 1:12.   14. Cf. Lev. 7:16–21.

one fifth[15] over and above what he has taken even if he has *transgressed inadvertently*.

It is likewise not permitted to *employ consecrated animals in work* or to *shear them;* all this in order that the *sacrifice* be held in great esteem. The law concerning the *exchange* of animals was prescribed as a precautionary measure; for if it were permitted to substitute a good animal for a poor one, poor ones would have been substituted for the good ones and would have been said to be the better ones. Accordingly as to this point the rule was laid down: *It and the exchange thereof shall be holy.*[16]

With regard to our having been given the command that whoever wishes to redeem a thing from among those *consecrated by him must add one fifth,*[17] the reason thereof is manifest; for *man is close to himself.*[18] Consequently it is always his nature to be niggardly with his property; accordingly he will not inquire with care regarding the price of the *consecrated* thing and will not take great pains to present it to others so that its true price be established. Consequently recourse had to be had against him by means of the addition, so that the consecrated thing could be sold to another at its true value. All this is prescribed in order that what has been named as consecrated to God and whereby one may come near Him should not be held in little esteem.

The reason for the burning of the *Priest's oblation* is as follows: Every *Priest* could offer his sacrifice with his own hands. Accordingly if he had brought an *oblation* and eaten it himself, | it would have been tantamount to his not having offered anything at all. For only *frankincense* and a *handful* of flour were offered upon the altar from *the oblation of one private individual.*[19] If then, not content with the smallness of this *sacrifice,* he who brought it had also eaten it, no act of worship at all would have been manifested. Hence the oblation is burnt.

The particular rules concerning the *paschal lamb,* namely, that it should only be eaten *roasted by fire and in one house, neither shall ye break a bone thereof,*[20] have all a manifest reason. For just as unleavened bread is due to haste, roasting the lamb is also due to haste. For there was then no time to cook various kinds of dishes and to prepare various sorts of food. Even delay in order to break its bones and to extract what is in it was forbidden. For the gist of all this has already been mentioned, namely, in its dictum: *And ye shall eat it in haste.*[21] Now haste does not admit of the delay

---

15. Cf. Lev. 5:15–16.   16. Lev. 27:10 and 33.
17. Cf. Lev. 27:13, 15, 19, 27, and 31. One fifth of the value is meant.
18. Cf., e.g., B.T., Sanhedrin, 10a.   19. Cf. Lev. 2:2.   20. Exod. 12:8 and 46.
21. Exod. 12:11.

required for breaking the bones or for lending parts of them from one house to another and for waiting for the return of the messenger. All these are actions indicative of laxity and sluggishness, whereas the purpose was to make a show of haste and hurry, lest someone delay and come too late to leave [Egypt] with the multitude of the people, whereupon he would be exposed to harm and to being set upon by surprise. These circumstances were then perpetuated in order to commemorate the matter as it really was. As it says: *And thou shalt keep this statute* [*ḥuqqah*] *in its season from year to year.*[22] The rule that [a paschal lamb] *is only eaten by those who were counted* [*with a view to partaking*] *of it,*[23] has been laid down in order to make sure that it is acquired and that no one relies in this matter upon a relative, a friend, or someone he chances to meet, but that he should take care of it from the beginning. The prohibition against *uncircumcised men* partaking of it[24] has been explained by the *Sages, may their memory be blessed,* for they said[25] that during their long stay in Egypt [the Children of Israel], with a view to assimilating themselves to the Egyptians, had omitted observing the *commandment of circumcision.* When thereupon the *paschal lamb* was prescribed by the Law and the condition was posed that it should only be sacrificed by someone after | *he himself, his sons, and the members of his household had been circumcised* — for only then *could he come near and keep it*[26] — all of them were circumcised; and *the blood of circumcision* mingled with *the blood of the paschal lamb* because of the great number of men who had just undergone circumcision, as [the Sages] have mentioned. It is referred to in the dictum [of Scripture]: *Wallowing in thy blood*[27] — *the blood of the paschal lamb and the blood of circumcision.*

Know that the Sabians held that blood was most unclean, but in spite of this used to eat of it, deeming that it was the food of the devils and that, consequently, whoever ate it fraternized with the jinn so that they came to him and let him know future events — according to what the multitude imagine concerning the jinn. There were, however, people there who considered it a hard thing to eat of blood, this being a thing abhorrent to the nature of man. Accordingly they used to slaughter an animal, collect its blood in a vessel or in a ditch, and eat the flesh of this slaughtered animal close by its blood. In doing this they imagined that the jinn partook of this blood, this being their food, whereas they themselves ate the flesh. In this way fraternization was achieved, because all ate at the same table and in one and the same gathering. Consequently, as they deemed, these jinn would

22. Exod. 13:10.　　23. Mishnah, Zebaḥim, V 8.　　24. Cf. Exod. 12:48.
25. Cf. Exodus Rabbah, XIX.　　26. Exod. 12:48.　　27. Ezek. 16:6.

come to them in dreams, inform them of secret things, and be useful to them. All these were opinions that were in those times followed, favored, and generally accepted; the multitude did not doubt of their truth. Thereupon the Law, which is perfect in the opinion of those who know it, began to put an end to these inveterate diseases.[28] Consequently it prohibited the eating of blood, putting the same emphasis on this prohibition as on the prohibition against *idolatry*. For He, may He be exalted, says, *I will set My face against that soul that eateth blood, and so on*,[29] just as He has said with regard to *him who gives of his seed to Moloch:*[30] *I will even set My face against that soul, and so on.*[31] No such text occurs regarding a third *commandment* other than the prohibition of *idolatry* and of *eating of blood*. This is so because | the eating of blood led to a certain kind of *idolatry*, namely, to the worship of the jinn. [Scripture] pronounced blood to be pure and turned it into a means of purification for those who come near it: *And sprinkle it upon Aaron, and upon his garments, and so on; and he and his garments shall be hallowed.*[32] It also commands the sprinkling of blood upon the *altar* and causes the whole act of worship to consist in pouring it out there, not in gathering it together: *And I have given it to you upon the altar to make atonement.*[33] There it was poured out according to what it says: *And all the [remaining] blood shall he pour out;*[34] and it says: *And the blood of thy sacrifices shall be poured out upon the altar of the Lord thy God.*[35] And it commands pouring the blood of every beast that is slaughtered, even if it was not offered up in *sacrifice*; it says: *Thou shalt pour it out upon the earth as water.*[36] Thereupon it forbids gathering around the blood and eating there, saying: *You shall not eat round the blood.*[37] When they continued in their disobedience and in following the generally accepted usage in which they had been brought up of fraternizing with the jinn through eating around the blood, He, may He be exalted, commanded that no *meat of desire*[38] be eaten at all *in the desert*, but that all be offered up as *peace-offerings*. It is clear to us that the reason for this is that the blood should be poured out upon the altar and that people should not gather around it. Accordingly it says: *To the end that the children of Israel may bring, and so on. And they shall no more offer their sacrifices unto the devils [seᶜirim], and so on.*[39] But the matter of *wild beasts* and of *birds* still remained to be

28. This translation seems preferable to the one proposed in Munk's translation: "The perfect Law undertook to put an end to these rooted diseases among those who recognize it."
29. Lev. 17:10.   30. Cf. Lev. 20:4–6.   31. Lev. 20:6.   32. Exod. 29:21.
33. Lev. 17:11.   34. Lev. 4:18.   35. Deut. 12:27.   36. Deut. 12:16 and 24.
37. Lev. 19:26.
38. I.e., meat that was not consecrated and that was eaten when one wished.
39. Lev. 17:5 and 7.

settled, for *wild beasts* may not be *sacrificed* at all and *birds* may not be offered as *peace-offerings*. Consequently He, may He be exalted, commanded that when any of the *wild beasts* or *birds* whose flesh it is permitted to eat has been slaughtered, its blood should be covered up with dust[40] so that people should not gather to eat around it. Thus the aim was achieved and the purpose realized: namely, *to break the brotherhood*[41] between those truly possessed[42] and their jinn. Know that the epoch of this belief was close to the time of *Moses our Master*, that it had a great following, and that people were led astray by it. You will find that this is literally stated in the song *Haʾazinu: They sacrificed unto devils, which are not | God, to gods which they have not known, and so on.*[43] The *Sages* have explained the meaning of its dictum, *which are not God*, in that they said that they not only persisted in worshipping existent things but even imaginary ones. This is the text of *Siphre: It is not enough that they worship the sun, the moon, and the constellations, they even worship their babuʾa.*[44] The word *babuʾa* means shadow. I shall now return to what we are discussing.

Know that the *meat of desire* was only forbidden *in the desert*. For it was one of the generally accepted opinions that the jinn lived in deserts and held converse and appeared there, but did not appear in cities and cultivated places; so that whenever a townsman wished to do something in the ways of this insanity, he had to go from the city to the desert and to isolated places. Therefore the *meat of desire* became permitted after the entry into the land [of Canaan]. Also because indubitably the strength of that malady had diminished, and the number of followers of those opinions had become less. Also because it was very difficult and nearly impossible that all those who wished to eat the *meat of a* [domestic] *beast* should go to *Jerusalem*. For these reasons the *meat of desire* was only forbidden *in the desert*.

Know that the greater the sin that had been committed, the more defective was the species from which the sacrifice offered up for it was taken. Therefore only a *she-goat* is offered up for an act of *idolatry* committed *inadvertently,*[45] and *other sins of a private individual* require a *ewe-lamb* or a *she-goat*. For a female is in all species more defective than the male, and there is no sin greater than *idolatry*, and no kind more defective

40. Cf. Lev. 17:13.   41. Cf. Zech. 11:14.
42. *al-majānīn.* In ordinary Arabic usage the word means "madmen"; but it has the same root as the word *jinn* (demons) and originally designated "those possessed by jinn."
43. Deut. 32:17. Moses' song figuring in Deut. 32 begins with the word *haʾazinu* (give ear).
44. The passage of Siphre discussing the scriptural verse quoted above. In our edition the passage is somewhat different, and the word *babuʾa* does not occur in it.
45. Cf. Num. 15:27.

than a *she-goat*. Because of the king's distinguished rank, the *sacrifice* required for *his inadvertent transgression* is a *he-goat*. As for the *High Priest and congregation*,[46] *their inadvertent transgressions* do not consist merely in actions, but also in legal decisions. Hence they had the distinction that the *sacrifices* required of *them* were *bullocks*,[47] and in cases of *idolatry*, *he-goats*.[48]

Inasmuch as the sins for which a *guilt-offering* was brought | were less important than those for which a *sin-offering* was required, the *sacrifice* offered up in a *guilt-offering* was a *ram* or a *young male lamb*;[49] thus both the species and the sex have distinction, the sacrifice being a male sheep. Do you not see that the sex of the *burnt-offering*, which is entirely consecrated to God, has distinction, for it may only be male.[50] For the same reason the *oblation of a sinner* and the *oblation of an unfaithful wife*, which latter is also due to her being suspected of having committed a *sin*, are deprived of ornamental additions and of good odors; it was forbidden to offer *oil and frankincense* with them. This ornamental addition was taken away from them because those who brought these offerings were not good nor were they fine in their actions; accordingly when they made a motion toward repentance, they were, as it were, told: Because of the disgraceful character of your actions, your sacrifice will be of a most defective condition. As the action of the *unfaithful wife* is more disgraceful than that committed by the *inadvertent transgressor*, her sacrifice was of a most defective matter, namely, *barley flour*.[51] These particulars have thus been set forth in a consistent way; they are wonderfully meaningful.

The *Sages* have already mentioned that the reason for the *offering on the eighth day of consecration being a calf, a young bullock for a sin-offering*,[52] was that it constituted an *atonement for the action of the [golden] calf*, and similarly that *the Day of Atonement's sin-offering being a young bullock for a sin-offering*[53] constituted an *atonement for the action of the [golden] calf*. In accordance with the notion that they have mentioned, it seems to me that the reason for the fact that all the *sin-offerings, both of private individuals and of the congregation, are he-goats [seᶜirim]* — I refer to *the he-goats [offered on the occasion of the festivals] of pilgrimage, on the New-Moons, on the Day of Atonement, and [for the sin] of idolatry* — is that the reason, in my opinion, was that their greatest act of disobedience consisted at that time in sacrificing to the *seᶜirim*;[54] as the text states: *And they shall no more*

46. Here the Sanhedrin is meant.   47. Cf. Lev. 4:4 and 14.   48. Cf. Num. 15:24.
49. Cf. Lev. 5:15, 18, and 25; 14:12–13; 19:21–22; Num. 6:12.
50. Cf. Lev. 1:3 and 10.   51. Cf. Num. 5:15.   52. Lev. 9:2.   53. Cf. Lev. 16:3.
54. The word denotes both "he-goats" and "devils."

offer their sacrifices to the se^cirim after whom they have gone a whoring.[55]
However the *Sages, may their memory be blessed,* consider that the reason
for which the *congregation is* constantly *atoned for by means of se^cirim* is
that the whole *congregation of Israel* committed their first act of dis-
obedience with the help of a *kid* [*se^cir*] *of goats.* They refer | to the sale of
Joseph the righteous, in whose story it is said: *And they killed a kid of goats,
and so on.*[56] Do not regard this reason as feeble. For the end of all these
actions is to establish firmly in the soul of every disobedient individual the
constant need for remembering and making mention of his sin — as it is
said: *And my sin is ever before me*[57] — and that he, his descendants, and the
descendants of his descendants, must seek forgiveness for the sin by an act
of obedience belonging to the same species as the act of disobedience. I mean
by this that if the act of disobedience was in connection with property, he
must expend his property in the act of obedience. If the act of disobedience
consists in corporeal pleasures, he must weary and afflict his body by means
of fasting and awakening at night. If the act of disobedience pertains to
morals, he must practice the contrary moral habit in opposition to it, as we
have explained in *Laws concerning Opinions*[58] and elsewhere. If the act of
disobedience consists in a speculation — I mean by this that if he believes in
an opinion that is not sound because of his incapacity and his slackness in
inquiry and in devoting himself to speculation — he must counter this by
suppressing his reflection and preventing it from reflecting about anything
pertaining to the things of this world, but direct it exclusively to the
intelligible and to an exact study of what ought to be believed. This
approximates its dictum: *And my heart hath been secretly enticed, but my
hand touched my mouth;*[59] this is a simile for withdrawal and abstention
with regard to something obscure, as we have explained in the beginning
of this Treatise. This was done, as you will see, in the case of *Aaron;* for
when he went astray in *the action of the* [*golden*] *calf,* it was prescribed that
he and those of his descendants who would replace him, should sacrifice a
bullock and a calf.[60] When the act of disobedience concerned a *kid* [*se^cir*] *of
goats,* the act of obedience also concerned a *kid of goats.* When these notions
are consolidated in the soul, this leads without any doubt necessarily to one's
taking a grave view of the act of disobedience and to an avoidance of it, so
that the individual in question will not, by stumbling into it, be in need of
a long and unpleasant quest for forgiveness, which sometimes may not | be

55. Lev. 17:7.   56. Gen. 37:31.   57. Ps. 51:5.
58. Cf. *Mishneh Torah,* De^coth, II 2.   59. Job 31:27.   60. Cf. Lev. 9:2; 16:3.

achieved. Accordingly he will avoid and flee from the act of disobedience from the outset. This is of most manifest utility. Grasp also this intention.

I see fit to call your attention here to a very strange matter, though its external meaning does not pertain to the purpose of the Treatise. This concerns the fact that only the *he-goat* [*se^c^ir*] offered on *the New-Moon as a sin-offering* is called in [Scripture] *a sin-offering unto the Lord*.[61] None of the *he-goats* offered on any of the [*festivals*] *of pilgrimage* or in the other *sin-offerings* are called thus. The reason for this is, in my opinion, most manifest; namely, that the *sacrifices* offered by the *congregation* at certain periods, I refer to the *additional* [*sacrifices*], were all of them *burnt-offerings*; and a *kid of goats* was brought on each of those days as a *sin-offering* and eaten. Now the *burnt-offerings* were burnt in their entirety, and therefore they are explicitly designated as *an offering made by fire unto the Lord;*[62] whereas it is never said, *a sin-offering unto the Lord* or *a peace-offering unto the Lord*, for these were eaten. It was not even permissible that the *sin-offerings* that were burnt[63] be called *an offering made by fire unto the Lord;* the reason for this I shall explain in this chapter. Consequently one cannot therefore conceive that the *he-goats* referred to above should be called *sin-offerings unto the Lord*, for they were eaten and not burnt in their entirety. As, however, it was apprehended that the *he-goat* offered on *the New-Moon* could be imagined to be a sacrifice to the moon, such as was offered by the Copts[64] of Egypt at the beginning of the months, it was explicitly stated that this goat was consecrated to God and not to the moon. This apprehension was not felt with regard to the *he-goats* offered on *the* [*festivals*] *of pilgrimage* and on other occasions because these days were not beginnings of months and had no natural sign to distinguish them, but were instituted by the Law through an imposed convention. The beginnings of the lunar months, on the other hand, were not instituted through a convention imposed by the Law; but the religious communities used to sacrifice on those days to the moon, just as they sacrificed to the sun when it rose and when it entered | certain degrees of the ecliptic, as is universally admitted in the books in question.[65] For this reason an anomalous expression is used with regard to the *he-goat* referred to above; it is said of it that it is to be offered *unto the Lord*, so that the fancies bound up with those hearts[66] suffering from inveterate disease be put to an end. Know then this marvellous thing too.

61. Num. 28:15.   62. Num. 28:19; 29:13 and 36.   63. Cf., e.g., Lev. 4:12 and 21.
64. Or: Egyptians. *Qubṭ.*   65. The books of the Sabians.
66. Those of the Children of Israel.

Know that all *sin-offerings* that are believed to serve in seeking forgiveness for great sins or for one great sin, such as the *sin-offering for ignorance* and others of the same kind, are burnt in their entirety *outside the camp* and not upon the *altar*; for only the *burnt-offering* and similar things may be burnt upon the *altar*. Hence it is called *the altar of the burnt-offering*,[67] for the smell of the meat of the *burnt-offering* is *a sweet odor*, and similarly all *memorials* are *a sweet odor*. And indubitably this is so, for these sacrifices were performed with a view to putting an end to *idolatrous* opinions, as we have explained. As for the burning of these *sin-offerings*, its purpose was to signify that the trace of the sin in question was wiped out and had disappeared just as the body that had been burnt had disappeared, and that no trace remained of that action just as no trace remained of the *sin-offering*, which was destroyed by having been burnt. Consequently its burning could not offer *a sweet odor unto the Lord*,[68] but the contrary; I mean that there was detestable and abhorrent smoke. It was therefore burnt in its entirety *outside the camp*. Do you not see what is said of *the oblation of an unfaithful wife: An oblation of memorial, bringing iniquity to remembrance?*[69] By no means is it described as a pleasing thing.

Inasmuch as the *he-goat that was sent forth* into the wilderness served wholly to atone for great sins, so that there was no *sin-offering of the congregation* that served as atonement in as great a measure as that goat, which was as it were the bearer of all the sins, it was not to receive at all such treatment as being slaughtered or burnt or sacrificed, but had to be removed to as great a distance as possible and sent forth unto *a land that is cut off*,[70] I mean one that was separated from habitation. No one has any doubt that sins are not | bodies that may be transported from the back of one individual to that of another. But all these actions are parables serving to bring forth a form in the soul so that a passion toward repentance should result: We have freed ourselves from all our previous actions, cast them behind our backs, and removed them to an extreme distance.

As for the offering of wine, I am up to now perplexed with regard to it: How could He have commanded to offer it, since the *idolaters* offered it? No reason for this has occurred to me. Someone else gave the following reason: For the desire, which is located in the liver, the most excellent thing is meat; for the animal faculty, which is located in the heart, the most excellent thing is wine; similarly the faculty located in the brain—that is,

67. Cf. e.g., Exod. 30:28.
68. Certain portions of the sacrifices and the offerings are called thus; cf., e.g., Lev. 2:9.
69. Num. 5:15.   70. Lev. 16:22.

the psychic faculty—takes pleasure in songs accompanied by instruments. Therefore every faculty offers to God the thing most cherished by it. Accordingly offerings consist in meat, wine, and sound—I mean *song*.

The reason for the utility of pilgrimage is well known. For such a gathering results in a renewal of the Law, this being a consequence of people being affected by it and of the fraternity that comes about among them because of it. This applies especially to the *commandment to assemble* [the people], whose reason is manifest: *That they may hear, and so on*.[71] *The money for the second tithe* was meant to be spent there,[72] as we have explained;[73] also the *fourth-year fruit of planting*[74] and the *tithe of the cattle*. There were accordingly there the meat of the *tithe*, the wine of the *fourth-year fruit of planting* and the *silver for the second tithe*. Consequently there was much food there, for it was not lawful to sell a part of this or to set it aside from one period to the next. But as He, may He be exalted, has said: *Year in year, and so on;*[75] hence of necessity it had to be used in giving alms. Now giving alms in the course of festivals is insisted upon. It says: *And thou shalt rejoice in thy festival, thou and thy son | and thy daughter, and so on, and the stranger and the fatherless and the widow.*[76]

We have now dealt with the single commandments belonging to this class and with many of their particulars.

CHAPTER 47

The *commandments* comprised in the twelfth class are those that we have enumerated in the *Book of Cleanness*. Even though we have already summarily mentioned their utility, we shall give additional explanations and we shall set forth the reasons for this class of commandments, as is proper. After that I will give the reasons for the various particular commandments—those of them whose reasons have become clear to me. I shall then say that this Law of God, which was prescribed to *Moses our Master*, to whom in consequence it is ascribed, came to facilitate the actions of worship and to lighten the burden. All the things in it that you may perhaps imagine to involve unpleasantness or a heavy burden appear so to you only because you do not know the usages and teachings that existed in those days.

71. Deut. 31:12.   72. Cf. Deut. 14:25–26.   73. Cf. III 39.   74. Cf. III 37.
75. Deut. 14:22. The quotation is not exact.   76. Deut. 16:14.

It behooves you to compare a rite in which for reasons of divine worship a man burns his child with one in which he burns a young pigeon. The *Torah* states literally: *For even their sons and their daughters do they burn in the fire to their gods.*[1] This was the worship they rendered to their gods. What corresponds to this in our worship is the burning of a young pigeon or even of a handful of flour. In view of this our religious community[2] was rebuked when in a state of apostasy, and was told: *O My people, what have I done unto thee? and wherein have I wearied thee? Testify against Me.*[3] It is also said concerning this subject: *Have I been a wilderness unto Israel? or a land of thick darkness? Wherefore say My people, we roam at large, and so on;*[4] he means, what unpleasant burden was imposed upon them by | this Law so that they turned away from it? He, may He be exalted, also addresses us, saying: *What iniquity have your fathers found in Me, that they are gone far from Me, and so on.*[5] All these texts have one purpose.

This is a premise of great importance that must not be lost from your mind. After having stated it, I shall say: We have already explained that the whole intention with regard to *the Sanctuary* was to affect those that came to it with a feeling of awe and of fear; as it says: *Ye shall fear My Sanctuary.*[6] Now if one is continually in contact with a venerable object, the impression received from it in the soul diminishes and the feeling it provokes becomes slight. The *Sages, may their memory be blessed,* have already drawn attention to this notion, saying that it is not desirable that the *Sanctuary* should be entered at every moment, and in support quoted its dictum: *Let thy foot be seldom in thy neighbor's house, lest he be sated with thee, and hate thee.*[7] This being the intention, He, may He be exalted, forbade the *unclean* to enter the *Sanctuary* in spite of there being many species of *uncleanness,* so that one could — but for a few exceptions — scarcely find a clean individual. For even if one were preserved from touching a *carcass* of a beast, one might not be preserved from touching one of the *eight creeping animals,*[8] which often fall into dwellings and into food and drink and upon which a man often stumbles in walking. And if one were preserved from that, one might not be preserved from contact with a *menstruating woman* or *a woman or a man having a running issue* or a *leper* or *their bed.*[9] And if one were preserved from that, one might not be preserved from *sexual intercourse with one's wife* or from *nocturnal pollution.*[10] And even if one were cleansed from these kinds of *uncleanness,* one would

1. Deut. 12:31.   2. Or: nation.   3. Mic. 6:3.   4. Jer. 2:31.
5. Jer. 2:5.   6. Lev. 19:30.   7. Prov. 25:17.   8. Cf. Lev. 11:29–30.
9. Cf. Lev. 15; 13:45–46.   10. Cf. Lev. 15:16–18; Deut. 23:11–12.

not be allowed to enter the *Sanctuary* till *after sunset.*[11] Nor was one allowed to enter the *Sanctuary* at night, as is made clear in *Middoth* and *Tamid;*[12] and on that night in most cases the man in question would have intercourse with his wife or one of the other courses of *uncleanness* would befall him, and he would find himself on the following day in the same position as on the day before. Thus all of this was | a reason for keeping away from the *Sanctuary* and for not entering it at every moment. You know already what [the Sages] literally say: *Even a clean man may not enter the Hall for the purpose of performing divine service before having immersed himself [in water].*[13] In consequence of such actions, *fear* will continue and an impression leading to the humility that was aimed at will be produced. To the extent that a certain kind of *uncleanness* was more frequent, purification from it was more difficult and was achieved at a later moment. Being under the same roof as dead bodies, more especially those of relatives and neighbors, is more frequent than any other kind of *uncleanness.* Accordingly one is purified from it only by means of the *ashes of a [red] heifer*, though these are very rare, and after seven days.[14] *Running issue* and *menstruation* are more frequent than contact with an *unclean individual;* hence these require *seven days* for purification,[15] and whoever approached someone who was unclean requires one day.[16] The purification of *a man or a woman having running issue* and of a *woman after childbirth* was only completed by means of a *sacrifice*, for such cases are rarer than *menstruation.* Also, all these things are disgusting — I mean *a menstruating woman, a man or a woman having running issue, a leper, a corpse, a carcass* of a beast, *a creeping animal*, and *issue of semen.* Accordingly many purposes are achieved by means of these laws. One of them is to keep men away from disgusting things. The second is to safeguard the *Sanctuary.* The third is to protect what is generally accepted and customary, for, as you will hear presently, unpleasant things were imposed on the Sabians in cases of uncleanness. The fourth is to ease unpleasant restrictions and to order things in such a manner that questions of *uncleanness* and *cleanness* should not prevent a man from engaging in any of his occupations; for this matter of *uncleanness* and *cleanness* concerns only *the Holy Place* and *holy things*, nothing else: *She shall touch no holy thing, nor come into the Sanctuary.*[17] As for the rest, there is no sin if one remains *unclean* as long as one wishes and eats, as one wishes, *ordinary* food that has become *unclean.* It is generally

11. Cf., e.g., Lev. 22:6–7.   12. Tractates of the Mishnah.
13. Mishnah, Yoma, III 3.   14. Cf. Num. 19.   15. Cf. Lev. 15:13, 19, and 28.
16. Cf. Lev. 15:5–11, 21–23, and 27.   17. Lev. 12:4.

known that according to the usages observed up to | our times by the Sabians in the lands of the East, I refer to the remnants of the Magians,[18] the *menstruating woman* remains isolated in her house; the places upon which she treads are burnt; whoever speaks with her becomes unclean; and if a wind that blows passes over a menstruating woman and a clean individual, the latter becomes unclean. See how great the difference is between this and our dictum: *All the various kinds of work that a wife does for her husband, are also done by a menstruating woman for her husband, except for washing his face, and so on.*[19] It is only forbidden to have intercourse with her in the days in which she is unclean and defiled. Another generally known usage of the Sabians that continues to our time is to regard as unclean everything that is separated from the body — that is, hair or nails or blood. Therefore every barber is unclean, in their opinion, because he touches blood and hair; and everyone who shaves must immerse in running water. They have many burdensome usages of this kind, whereas as for us we only claim that something is *unclean* or *clean* with regard to *holy things* and to the *Sanctuary*.

As for His dictum, may He be exalted, *Sanctify yourselves therefore, and be ye holy, for I am holy,*[20] it does not apply at all to *uncleanness* and *cleanness. Siphra* states literally: *This concerns sanctification by the commandments;* they also say of His dictum, *Ye shall be holy,*[21] that *this concerns sanctification by the commandments.* For this reason, transgression of the *commandments* is also called *uncleanness.* This expression is used with regard to the mothers and roots of the *commandments,* namely, [the commandments concerning] *idolatry, incest,* and *shedding of blood.* With regard to *idolatry* it says: *Because he hath given of his seed unto Molech to render unclean My Sanctuary.*[22] And with regard to *incest* it says: *Do not make yourself unclean with all these things, and so on.*[23] And with regard to *shedding of blood* it says: *You shall not make unclean the land, and so on.*[24] It therefore has become clear that the term *uncleanness* is used equivocally in three different senses: It is used of disobedience and of transgression of commandments concerning action or opinion; it is used of dirt and filth, | *Her uncleanness is in her skirts;*[25] and it is used according to these fancied notions, I refer to touching or carrying certain things or to being under the same roof with certain things. With reference to this last sense, we say: *The words of the Torah are not subject to becoming unclean.*[26] Similarly the

18. I.e., the Zoroastrians.   19. B.T., Kethuboth, 4b and 61a.
20. Lev. 11:44. The Siphra is to this verse.   21. Lev. 19:2. The Siphra is to this verse.
22. Lev. 20:3.   23. Lev. 18:24.
24. Num. 35:34. Maimonides' quotation is not exact.   25. Lam. 1:9.
26. Cf. B.T., Berakhoth, 22a.

term *holiness* is used equivocally in three senses opposed to those three senses.

In view of the fact that purification from the *uncleanness* caused by a *corpse* could only be achieved after seven days and also after *the ashes of a [red] heifer* have been found, and since the *Priests* were always in need of entering the *Sanctuary* for the purpose of sacrificing, every *Priest* in particular was forbidden to expose himself to being made *unclean by a corpse* unless it were a case of strong necessity in which it would be difficult for nature to avoid this; I refer to avoiding contact with one's parents, children, and brothers.[27] And as there was great need that the *High Priest* should be constantly *in the Sanctuary* — according to its dictum: *And it*[28] *shall always be upon his forehead*[29] — he was absolutely forbidden to expose himself to the *uncleanness of a corpse*, even of those of relatives. Do you not see that this prohibition does not extend to women? It is said: *The sons of Aaron*,[30] and *not: the daughters of Aaron*, women not being needed in sacrifice.

As it cannot be avoided that sometimes an individual may be negligent and may enter the *Sanctuary* while he is *unclean* or eat *holy things* while he is *unclean*, or else he may even do it *deliberately* — for the majority of *wicked people* commit grave acts of disobedience *deliberately* — *sacrifices* were commanded that would *atone for the uncleanness of the Sanctuary and its holy things*. These sacrifices were of various kinds, some of them intended to atone for *deliberate transgressions* and others for those committed *inadvertently*. These are *the he-goats of [the festivals of] pilgrimage, the he-goats of the New-Moons, and the he-goat that was sent forth*,[31] as has been explained in its place. These things were commanded so that the *deliberate transgressor* should not think that he has not committed a great sin in *rendering the Sanctuary of the Lord unclean;* but on the other hand he will know that his sin *has been atoned for by means of the he-goat.* For it says: *That they die not in their uncleanness;*[32] and it also says: | *And Aaron shall bear the iniquity committed in the holy things, and so on.*[33] This notion is often repeated.

As for the *uncleanness of leprosy*, we have already explained its meaning. The *Sages, may their memory be blessed,* have also explained it. They have made known to us that the established principle in regard to it is that it is a punishment for *slander*[34] and that at first this change appears in the walls.[35] If the man repents, the purpose has been achieved. If,

---

27. Cf. Lev. 21:2.   28. I.e., a plate of pure gold.   29. Exod. 28:38.
30. Cf. Lev. 21:1.   31. Cf. Lev. 16:16. Cf. III 46.   32. Lev. 15:31.
33. Exod. 28:38.   34. Cf., e.g., B.T., ⁣ᶜArakhin, 16b.   35. Cf. Lev. 14:34–48.

however, he continues in his disobedience, the change extends to his bed and his house furniture. If he still persists in his disobedience, it passes over to his clothing, then to his body. This is a miracle that was perpetuated in the religious community like that of the *waters of the woman suspected of adultery*.[36] The utility of this belief is manifest, there being also the fact that leprosy is contagious and that, almost by nature, all men find it disgusting. The reason why purification from it was effected by means of *cedar wood, hyssop, scarlet thread, and two birds*,[37] is given in the *Midrashim*;[38] but it does not fit in with our purpose, and up to now I do not know the reason for any of these things; nor why *cedar wood, hyssop, and scarlet thread* were used in the ceremony of the *red heifer* nor why *a bunch of hyssop* was used for the sprinkling of the blood of the *paschal lamb*. I cannot find any reason whereby I could account for these species having been singled out.

The reason why the *red heifer* is called a *sin-offering* is that through it the purification of the individual *rendered unclean by a corpse* is made perfect so that afterwards he may enter the *Sanctuary*. The meaning of this is that in the cases in which individuals were defiled by a *corpse*, they would have been forbidden *ever* to enter the *Sanctuary* and to eat *holy things* unless there had been this *heifer*, which carried away this *sin*. This is similar to the *plate* [worn by the High Priest on his forehead], which *brings expiation for uncleanness*, and similar to *the goats that are burnt*.[39] For this reason *one who engaged in* [*the sacrifice of*] *the* [*red*] *heifer and in* [*that of*] *the goats that are burnt, rendered the garments unclean*.[40] Similarly one who approached *the he-goat | that was sent forth* became unclean[41] — according to what is believed — because of the great sins that it carried away.

We have thus given the reasons, as they appear to us, for those commandments included in this class whose reasons we know.

36. Cf. Num. 5:11–31.   37. Cf. Lev. 14:4 and 51.
38. In the text: *Midrashoth*. Cf. Leviticus Rabbah, XVI.
39. Cf. Lev. 16:27; Num. 15:24.
40. Mishnah, Zebaḥim, XII 5. Cf. Num. 19:8, 10, 21, and 22; Lev. 16:28.
41. Cf. Lev. 16:26.

CHAPTER 48

The *commandments* comprised in the thirteenth class are those that we have enumerated in *Laws concerning Forbidden Foods*, in *Laws concerning Slaughtering* and in *Laws concerning Vows and Nazaritism*. We have already given, in this Treatise[1] and in the Commentary on *Aboth*,[2] an exhaustive and eloquent exposition of the utility of this class. We shall add to the clarity of this explanation by examining closely the single *commandments* included therein.

I say, then, that to eat any of the various kinds of food that the Law has forbidden us is blameworthy. Among all those forbidden to us, only pork and fat may be imagined not to be harmful. But this is not so, for pork is more humid than is proper and contains much superfluous matter. The major reason why the Law abhors it is its being very dirty and feeding on dirty things. You know to what extent the Law insists upon the need to remove filth out of sight, even in the field and in a military camp,[3] and all the more within cities. Now if swine were used for food, market places and even houses would have been dirtier than *latrines*, as may be seen at present in the country of the Franks.[4] You know the dictum of [the Sages], *may their memory be blessed: The mouth of a swine is like walking excrement.*[5]

The fat of the intestines, too, makes us full, spoils the digestion, and produces cold and thick blood. | It is more suitable to burn it. Blood, on the one hand, and carcasses of beasts that have died, on the other, are also difficult to digest and constitute a harmful[6] nourishment. It is well known that a beast that is *terephah*[7] *is close to being a carcass.*

With reference to the signs marking a permitted animal—that is, chewing the cud and divided hoofs in the case of beasts, and fins and scales in the case of fish[8]—know that their existence is not in itself a reason for animals being permitted nor their absence a reason for animals being prohibited; they are merely signs by means of which the praised species may be discerned from the blamed species.

The reason why *the sinew of the thigh vein* is prohibited, is given in the [scriptural] text.[9]

The reason for the prohibition against eating *a limb [cut off] a living*

1. Cf. III 35.　　2. A tractate of the Mishnah.　　3. Cf. Deut. 23:13–15. Cf. III 41.
4. I.e., of the western Europeans.　　5. B.T., Berakhoth, 25a.　　6. Literally: bad.
7. I.e., an animal that is diseased or wounded.
8. Cf. Lev. 11:3, 9, and 10; Deut. 14:6 and 9.　　9. Cf. Gen. 32:33.

animal[10] is because this would make one acquire the habit of cruelty. Such things were done in those times by the kings of the *Gentiles*; this was also an action used in *idolatry* — I mean to cut off a certain limb from a beast and to eat it.

As for the prohibition against eating *meat [boiled] in milk*,[11] it is in my opinion not improbable that — in addition to this being undoubtedly very gross food and very filling — *idolatry* had something to do with it. Perhaps such food was eaten at one of the ceremonies of their cult or at one of their festivals. A confirmation of this may, in my opinion, be found in the fact that the prohibition against eating *meat [boiled] in milk*, when it is mentioned for the first two times,[12] occurs near the commandment concerning pilgrimage: *Three times in the year, and so on*.[13] It is as if it said: When you go on pilgrimage and enter *the house of the Lord your God*, do not cook there in the way they used to do. According to me this is the most probable[14] view regarding the reason for this prohibition; but I have not seen this set down in any of the books of the Sabians that I have read.

The commandment concerning the slaughtering of animals is necessary. For the natural food of man consists only of the plants deriving from the seeds growing in the earth and of the flesh of animals, the most excellent kinds of meat being those that are | permitted to us. No physician is ignorant of this. Now since the necessity to have good food requires that animals be killed, the aim was to kill them in the easiest manner, and it was forbidden to torment them through killing them in a reprehensible manner by piercing the lower part of their throat or by cutting off one of their members, just as we have explained.

It is likewise forbidden to slaughter *it and its young on the same day*,[15] this being a precautionary measure in order to avoid slaughtering the young animal in front of its mother. For in these cases animals feel very great pain, there being no difference regarding this pain between man and the other animals. For the love and the tenderness of a mother for her child is not consequent upon reason, but upon the activity of the imaginative faculty, which is found in most animals just as it is found in man. This law applies in particular to *ox* and *lamb*, because these are the domestic animals that we are allowed to eat and that in most cases it is usual to eat; in their case the mother can be differentiated from her young.

10. Cf. Gen. 9:4; Deut. 12:23; B.T., Sanhedrin, 57a; B.T., Ḥullin, 101b.
11. Cf. Exod. 23:19; 34:26; Deut. 14:21. Cf. Onqelos' translation of these passages.
12. Cf. Exod. 23:19; 34:26.   13. Exod. 23:17; 34:23.
14. Literally: the strongest.   15. Cf. Lev. 22:28.

This is also the reason for the commandment *to let* [*the mother*] *go from the nest.*[16] For in general the eggs over which the bird has sat and the young that need their mother are not fit to be eaten. If then the mother is let go and escapes of her own accord, she will not be pained by seeing that the young are taken away. In most cases this will lead to people leaving everything alone, for what may be taken is in most cases not fit to be eaten. If the Law takes into consideration these pains of the soul in the case of beast and birds, what will be the case with regard to the individuals of the human species as a whole? You must not allege as an objection against me the dictum of [the Sages], *may their memory be blessed:*[17] *He who says: Thy mercy extendeth to young birds, and so on.*[18] For this is one of the two opinions mentioned by us[19] — I mean the opinion of those who think that there is no reason for the Law except only the will [of God] — but as for us, | we follow only the second opinion.

We have already drawn attention to the fact that the *Torah* itself set for the reason for *the covering of blood* and that this commandment applies in particular to *clean wild beasts and clean birds.*[20]

Besides the ordinances given to us concerning the prohibition of forbidden food, ordinances have also been prescribed to us with regard to the *vows* by which we impose *prohibitions* on ourselves.[21] Whenever a man says: This bread or this meat is forbidden to me, it is forbidden to him to eat it — all this being training with a view to achieving temperance and to restraining the appetite for eating and drinking. They say: *Vows are a fence for abstinence.*[22] As women are prone to anger, being easily affected and having weak souls, there would have been grave troubles, quarrels, and disorder in the house, if their oaths had been under their control. For a certain kind of food would have been permitted for the husband and forbidden for the wife and another kind would have been forbidden for the daughter and permitted for the mother. Therefore the matter, with everything pertaining to it, is given into the charge of the master of the house. Do you not see that a woman who is governed by herself and not dependent upon the control of the master of the house, has with regard to *vows* the same status as men? — I refer to a woman who has no husband and no father or has arrived at the age of puberty, I mean one that is *of age.*[23]

The reason for *nazaritism* is most manifest; it consists in bringing about abstinence from drinking wine, which has caused the ruin of the

16. Cf. Deut. 22:6–7.   17. Mishnah, Berakhoth, V 3.
18. Such an individual is blamed in the Mishnah.   19. Cf. III 26 and 31.
20. Cf. III 46.   21. Cf. Num. 30:3–17.   22. Mishnah, Aboth, III 13.
23. According to B.T., Nedarim, 70a–b, the age referred to is twelve years and six months.

ancients and the moderns: *Many, yea, a mighty host have been slain by it;*[24] *But these also have erred through wine, and so on.*[25] The prohibition you see against eating *anything that cometh of the grape vine*[26] results from the law regarding *nazaritism*, being an additional measure made with a view to the avoidance of wine, so that people should content themselves with no more of it than is necessary. For whoever avoids it is called *holy* and is put in the same rank as a *High Priest* as far as *holiness* is concerned, | so that, like the latter, he may not render himself *unclean* through contact with a corpse, even that of *his father or his mother.*[27] All this high esteem is given to him because he abstains from drink.

CHAPTER 49

The *commandments* included in the fourteenth class are those that we have enumerated in the *Book of Women* and in *Laws on Prohibited Sexual Relations*. The *interbreeding of beasts*[1] and *the commandment of circumcision* also belong to this class. The purpose of this class of commandments has already been reported.[2] Now I shall begin to explain the particulars.

I say then: It is well known that friends are something that is necessary for man throughout his whole life. Aristotle has already set this forth in the ninth book of the "Ethics."[3] For in a state of health and happiness, a man takes pleasure in their familiar relationship with him; in adversity he has recourse to them; and in his old age, when his body is grown weak, he seeks their help. The same things may be found to a much greater extent in the relationship with one's children and also in the relationship with one's relatives. For fraternal sentiments and mutual love and mutual help can be found in their perfect form only among those who are related by their ancestry. Accordingly a single tribe that is united through a common ancestor — even if he is remote — because of this, love one another, help one

24. Cf. Prov. 7:26.   25. Isa. 28:7.   26. Judg. 13:14. Cf. Num. 6:4.
27. Cf. Num. 6:7.
 1. No part of the *Mishneh Torah* is called "Interbreeding of Beasts." The subject is treated by Maimonides in the "Book of Seeds" (*Zeraᶜim*), "Laws concerning Interbreeding" (*Kilᵓaim*).
 2. Cf. III 35.
 3. In fact, the passage occurs in Book VIII (1155a3 ff.) of the *Nicomachean Ethics.*

another, and have pity on one another; and the attainment of these things is the greatest purpose of the Law. Hence *harlots* are prohibited,[4] because through them lines of ancestry are destroyed. For a child born of them is a stranger to the people; no one knows to what family group he belongs, and no one in his family group knows him; and this is the worst of conditions for him and for his father. Another important consideration comes in as a reason | for the prohibition of *harlots*. This is the prevention of an intense lust for sexual intercourse and for constant preoccupation with it. For lust is increased through the change of the individuals that are *harlots*, for man is not stirred in the same way by an individual to whom he has been continuously accustomed as by individuals who are constantly renewed and who differ in shapes and manners. In the prohibition of *harlots* there is a very great utility — namely, the prevention of evils; for if *harlots* were permitted, a number of men might happen to betake themselves at one and the same time to one woman; they would inevitably quarrel and in most cases they would kill one another or kill the woman, this being — as is well known — a thing that constantly happens: *And they assemble themselves in troops at a prostitute's house.*[5] In order to prevent these great evils and to bring about this common utility — namely, knowledge of the lines of ancestry — *harlots* and *male prostitutes* are prohibited and there is no way to engage in permitted sexual intercourse other than through singling out a woman for oneself and marrying her in public. For if it sufficed merely to single her out, most men would bring a *harlot* to their house for a certain time, having made an agreement with her about this, and say that she is a wife. Therefore a binding ceremony and a certain act have been prescribed signifying that the woman is allotted to the man; this is the *betrothal*. Then when the act is made in public, it is the ceremony of *marriage: And Boaz took ten men, and so on.*[6] Sometimes the union of the two may be discordant and matters in their household not in good order. Consequently divorce is permitted. However, if a divorce could become valid merely by means of the utterance of words or through the man's turning the woman out of his house, the woman might watch for some negligence on the part of her husband and then go out and claim to be divorced. Or if some individual had fornicated with her, she and the adulterer might claim that she had been divorced beforehand. Therefore the Law has given to us the ordinance that a divorce can only be made valid by means of a writ attesting it: *And he shall write her a bill of divorcement, and so on.*[7]

As accusations[8] of adultery | and imaginings concerned with it are very

4. Cf. Deut. 23:18.   5. Jer. 5:7.   6. Ruth 4:2.   7. Deut. 24:1.   8. Or: suspicions.

frequent with regard to women, the Law has given us ordinances concerning the *woman who is suspected of adultery*.[9] These ordinances oblige every married woman to take extreme care in her behavior and to have recourse to the greatest precautions, lest the heart of her husband be incensed on her account. For she anticipates with apprehension the horror of the *waters of the woman suspected of adultery*. If she is pure and has safeguarded herself, most men would give everything they possess in order to be liberated from having to make her undergo this procedure; they would even prefer death to this great shame, which consists in uncovering the woman's head, undoing her hair, tearing her garments so that the heart is exposed, and making her go round throughout the whole *Sanctuary* in the presence of the public, both men and women, and in the presence of the *Great Court of Law*.[10] Through these apprehensions, grave evils have been cut short that would have destroyed the order of a certain number of households.

As every *girl* who is a *virgin* is set for marriage with the first man that happens along, her seducer is only obliged to marry her; for he is the one who is most suitable for her, and this indubitably makes better repair for the flaw in her than her marrying another man. If, however, she or her father does not wish this, the seducer must pay a dowry.[11] There is additional punishment for a *man who has raped* a girl: *He may not put her away all his days*.[12]

As for the reason for the *levirate*, it is literally stated [in Scripture] that this was an ancient custom that obtained before the *giving of the Torah*[13] and that was perpetuated by the Law.[14] As for the ceremony of *taking off the shoe*,[15] the reason for it is to be found in the fact that the actions of which it is composed were considered shameful, according to the customs of those times, and that on account of this the brother-in-law might perhaps wish to avoid this shame and consequently to *marry his brother's widow*. This is made manifest in the text of the *Torah: So shall it be done unto the man, and so on. And his name shall be called in Israel, and so on*.[16]

From the story of *Judah*[17] a noble moral habit and equity in conduct may be learnt; this appears from [Judah's] words: *Let her take it, lest we be put to shame; behold, I sent | this kid*.[18] The interpretation of this is as follows: Before the *giving of the Torah* sexual intercourse with a *harlot* was regarded in the same way as sexual intercourse with one's wife is regarded

9. Cf. Num. 5:11–31. Cf. III 47.   10. Cf. Num. 5:18.   11. Cf. Exod. 22:16.
12. Deut. 22:29.   13. Cf. Gen. 38:8.   14. Cf. Deut. 25:5–6.
15. Cf. Deut. 25:7–10.   16. Deut. 25:9–10.
17. The story of Judah and Tamar; cf. Gen. 38.   18. Gen. 38:23.

after the *giving of the Torah.* I mean to say that it was a permitted act that did not by any means arouse repugnance. The payment of the hire that was agreed upon to a *harlot* was in that time something similar to the payment now of a *wife's dowry* when she is divorced, I mean that it was one of the rights of the woman with regard to which the man had to discharge his obligation. Accordingly *Judah's* saying, *Lest we be put to shame,* teaches us that to speak of any matters pertaining to sexual intercourse — even of those that are permitted — is shameful for us and that it is proper to be silent about them and to conceal them, even if this should lead to loss of money. This is just as you see *Judah* doing, in saying: It is better that we should suffer a loss and that she should keep what she has taken than that we should give publicity to our search and bring shame upon us. This is the excellent moral habit that we learn from this story. As for the precept of justice by which we profit, it is to be found in the word in which he answers that he is innocent of all violence with regard to the woman, that he does not go back on his word, and that he does not diminish the price agreed upon with her: *Behold, I sent this kid, and so on.* That kid was indubitably one that among those of its species was possessed of the highest excellence; therefore in referring to it he employs [the demonstrative pronoun] *this.* This is the justice that they had taken over from *Jacob, Isaac, and Abraham:* namely, that one must not make changes in one's given word or break one's promise; that all obligations must be discharged fully and integrally; that there is no difference between what has been given to one as a loan or a deposit and what you owe him in any way whatever as wages or something else. The dowry of all wives has the same status as the wages of all hired men, and there is no difference between *one who withholds the wages of a hired man* and one who does this to his wife. Again there is no difference between one who persecutes a hired man and devises ruses in order to send him away without | paying his wages and one who does the same thing to his wife with a view to sending her away without paying her dowry. Do you not behold how great is the justice of these *righteous statutes and judgments,*[19] as shown in what is ordained with regard to a man who *gives [his wife] a bad reputation.*[20] There is no doubt that a wicked man of this kind did not find his wife, *to whom he gave a bad reputation,* to his taste and thought her ugly. If he had wished to divorce her in the way this is done by everyone who divorces his wife, there would have been no impediment. But if he had divorced her, he would have been obliged to give her what was due to her. Accordingly he laid *wanton charges*[21] against her, in order to get rid

19. Deut. 4:8.   20. Cf. Deut. 22:13–19.   21. Cf. Deut. 22:14.

of her without payment, and slandered her and defamed her by accusing her of things that it was impossible for her to have committed, in order to withhold from her the sum that she had the right to demand from him, namely, *fifty shekels of silver* — this being *the dowry for virgins* fixed in the *Torah.* He, may He be exalted, has commanded that he pay *a hundred shekels of silver*, this being based upon the principle that *whom the judges shall condemn he shall pay double unto his neighbor*[22] and conforming to the *law concerning false witnesses*, as we have already explained.[23] For in a similar way he who *gave [his wife] a bad reputation* wanted to make her lose the fifty shekels that she had the right to receive from him and instead is forced to pay one hundred. This is the punishment for his having wanted to withhold the sum that he had the obligation to pay and for his having desired to appropriate it. The punishment for his having sullied her honor by accusing her of adultery is to have his own honor sullied through being flogged with a whip: *And they shall chastise him.*[24] His punishment for his preferring his concupiscence and his seeking nothing but pleasure is to have her tied to him forever: *He may not put her away all his days.*[25] For the cause that brought everything about was his thinking her ugly. In this way bad moral habits are cured, when the divine command is the physician. You will never cease discovering the clear and evident manifestation of justice in all the commandments of this Law, if you consider them carefully. Consider how the sentence of a man who *gives [his wife] a | bad reputation*, wishing to withhold the sum that he had the obligation to pay, is made to be equal to that of the *thief* who has taken property belonging to someone else; and how the sentence of a *false witness* who wished to do harm is made like the sentence, even if he did not succeed, of those who actually did harm and injury — I refer to the *thief* and the man who *gives [his wife] a bad reputation.* The sentence to be passed on all three is determined by *one Law and one judgment.*[26] Marvel exceedingly at the wisdom of His commandments, may He be exalted, just as you should marvel at the wisdom manifested in the things He had made. It says: *The Rock, His work is perfect; for all His ways are judgment.*[27] It says that just as the things made by Him are consummately perfect, so are His commandments consummately just. However, our intellects are incapable of apprehending the perfection of everything that He has made and the justice of everything He has commanded. We only apprehend the justice of some of His commandments just as we only apprehend some of the marvels in the things He has

22. Exod. 22:8.   23. Cf. III 41.   24. Deut. 22:18.   25. Deut. 22:19.
26. Num. 15:16.   27. Deut. 32:4.

made, in the parts of the body of animals and in the motions of the spheres. What is hidden from us in both these classes[28] of things is much more considerable than what is manifest. Now we shall return to the subject of the chapter.

As for the prohibitions against *illicit unions*,[29] all of them are directed to making sexual intercourse rarer and to instilling disgust for it so that it should be sought only very seldom. The reason for the prohibition against *homosexuality* and against intercourse with *beasts* is very clear. For if the thing that is natural should be abhorred except for necessity, all the more should deviations from the natural way and the quest for pleasure alone be eschewed. All *illicit unions* with females have one thing in common: namely, that in the majority of cases these females are constantly in the company of the male[30] in his house and that they are easy of access for him and can be easily controlled by him — there being no difficulty in making them come into his presence; and no judge could blame the male | for their being with him. Consequently if the status of the women with whom *union* is *illicit* were that of any *unmarried woman*, I mean to say that if it were possible to marry them and that the prohibition with regard to them were only due to their not being the man's wives, most people would have constantly succumbed and fornicated with them. However, as it is absolutely forbidden to have intercourse with them, the strongest deterrents making us avoid this — I mean by this a sentence of *death by order of a court of law* and the threat of *being cut off*[31] — so that there is no way to have intercourse with these women, men are safe from seeking to approach them and their thoughts are turned away from them.

It is very clear that relations are easy with all women included in the prohibitions concerning *illicit unions*. For it is very general that if a man has a wife, her mother, her grandmother, her daughter, her granddaughter, and her sister will be in his house most of the time, so that the husband will constantly meet them whenever he enters, goes out, and is engaged upon his business. A wife also is often in contact with her husband's brother, his father, and his son. It is likewise manifest that in most cases a man is often in the company of his sisters, maternal and paternal aunts, and the wife of his paternal uncle, and is brought up together with them. Now these are the women with whom *union* is *illicit* because of their being *relatives*. Consider this, this being one of the reasons why intercourse with *relatives* is prohibited.

28. Literally: species.　　29. Literally: nudities.　　30. Literally: of the individual.
31. Cf. III 41.

The second reason derives, in my opinion, from the wish to respect the sentiment of shame. For it would be a most shameless thing if this act could take place between the root and the branch, I refer to sexual intercourse[32] with the mother or the daughter. On the ground of the root and the branch, sexual intercourse of one of the two with the other has been forbidden. There is no difference between a root having intercourse with a branch or a branch with a root; or the root and the branch joining in having intercourse with a third individual, I mean that one individual reveals his nakedness in intercourse both with a root and a branch. Therefore it is forbidden to take together | a woman and her mother and to have intercourse with the wife of one's father and the wife of one's son, for all this is revealing one's nakedness before the nakedness of both a root and a branch. Being brother or sister is like being root and branch. But once the sister was forbidden, also the sister of the wife and the wife of the brother are forbidden. For this would constitute the joining of two individuals who are like root and branch in sexual intercourse with a third individual.

As union between a brother and a sister is strictly forbidden and as they are to have the same relation as a root and a branch or even are considered to be one and the same individual, sexual intercourse with one's maternal aunt is also forbidden, for she has the same status as one's mother, and also intercourse with one's paternal aunt, as she has the same status as one's father. And just as the daughter of one's paternal uncle and the daughter of one's paternal aunt are not forbidden, the daughter of one's brother and the daughter of one's sister are likewise not forbidden because of the analogy. The fact that the wife of a brother's son is permitted to the paternal uncle, whereas the wife of the paternal uncle is forbidden to the son of a brother, may be explained by the first reason. For a brother's son is in most cases to be found in his paternal uncle's house and approaches his paternal uncle's wife just as he approaches his brother's wife; whereas a paternal uncle is not to be found in this way in the house of his brother's son and does not approach the latter's wife. Do you not see that in view of the fact that a father has the same opportunity to approach a wife of his son as the son has to approach a wife of his father, the prohibition is equally strict in both cases, its transgression being punished by *one capital punishment.*

The reason for the prohibition against having sexual intercourse with a *menstruating woman* and with a *married woman* is too clear to be in need

32. Or: marriage. In the following passage likewise, the word translated as "sexual intercourse" may also mean "marriage."

of a search for a reason. You know that we are forbidden to take pleasure in any way *in a woman who is prohibited to us,*[33] even to look at such a woman with a view to pleasure, as we have explained in *Laws concerning Prohibited Sexual Relations.*[34] We have explained there[35] that in our Law it is not permitted in any way to let our thought range freely with regard to the subject of sexual union or in any way whatever to provoke sexual excitement. If a man becomes sexually excited without having intended it, he is obliged to | direct his mind to some other thought and to reflect on something else until this sexual excitement passes away. The *Sages, may their memory be blessed,* say in their precepts, which perfect the virtuous:[36] *My son, if this abominable one affects you, drag him to the house of study. If he is of iron, he will melt. If he is of stone, he will break into pieces. For it is said: Is not my word like as fire? saith the Lord; and like a hammer that breaketh the rock in pieces?*[37] [The Sage] says to his son with a view to giving him a rule of conduct: If you feel sexual excitement and suffer because of it, go *to the house of study,* read, take part in discussions, put questions, and be asked in your turn, for then this suffering will indubitably pass away. Marvel at his expression, *this abominable one,* and what an *abomination* this is! This precept is not only valid from the point of view of the Law, for the philosophers consider this matter in the same way. I have already made known to you[38] the text of Aristotle's saying that this sense is a disgrace to us, he means the sense of touch, which leads us to give preference to eating and sexual intercourse. In his writings he designates the people who give preference to sexual intercourse and to eating all kinds of dishes as abject, and expresses at length his blame of them and his mockery of them. You will find this in his book on Ethics and in his book on Rhetoric.[39] With a view to this excellent moral habit, which one ought to have the firm purpose to seek and to acquire, the *Sages, may their memory be blessed,* have forbidden the contemplation of *beasts and birds when they copulate.*[40] In my opinion this is also the reason why *the interbreeding of beasts* is prohibited. For it is well known that in most cases an individual of one species is not moved to copulate with an individual of another species unless it be brought to it by hand, as is constantly done, as you may see, by those loose men who are engaged in bringing about the procreation of mules. The Law did not wish that an individual of *Israel* should be so low as to engage in this

33. Literally: *in a nakedness.*   34. Cf. *Mishneh Torah,* Issurei Biʾah, XXI 1–2.
35. Cf. Issurei Biʾah, XXI 19.   36. B.T., Qiddushin, 30b.   37. Jer. 23:29.
38. Cf. II 36, 40, III 8.
39. Cf. *Nicomachean Ethics* iii.10.1118b2 ff.; *Rhetoric* i.11.1370a18 ff.
40. B.T., Abodah Zarah, 20b.

activity because of its abjectness and shamelessness and because he would thereby be engaged | in things the very mention of which— and, all the more, contact with which—is repugnant to the Law unless there be necessity. Such interbreeding, however, is not necessary. It also seems to me that the reason for the prohibition against bringing together two species for any kind of work may also be found in the wish to render more difficult the interbreeding of two species. I mean to say that its dictum, *Thou shalt not plow with an ox and an ass together*,[41] is due to the possibility that if the two are brought together they might sometimes copulate. A proof for this may be found in the fact that this commandment is general and applies not only to *oxen* and *asses: It is indifferent whether they are an ox and an ass or any other two species. But Scripture speaks about what is usual.*[42]

Similarly with regard to *circumcision*, one of the reasons for it is, in my opinion, the wish to bring about a decrease in sexual intercourse and a weakening of the organ in question, so that this activity be diminished and the organ be in as quiet a state as possible. It has been thought that circumcision perfects what is defective congenitally. This gave the possibility to everyone to raise an objection and to say: How can natural things be defective so that they need to be perfected from outside, all the more because we know how useful the foreskin is for that member? In fact this *commandment* has not been prescribed with a view to perfecting what is defective congenitally, but to perfecting what is defective morally. The bodily pain caused to that member is the real purpose of circumcision. None of the activities necessary for the preservation of the individual is harmed thereby, nor is procreation rendered impossible, but violent concupiscence and lust that goes beyond what is needed are diminished. The fact that circumcision weakens the faculty of sexual excitement and sometimes perhaps diminishes the pleasure is indubitable. For if at birth this member has been made to bleed and has had its covering taken away from it, it must indubitably be weakened. The *Sages, may their memory be blessed*, have explicitly stated: *It is hard for a woman with whom an uncircumcised man has had sexual intercourse to separate from him.*[43] In my opinion this is the strongest of the reasons for *circumcision*. Who | first began to perform this act, if not *Abraham* who was celebrated for his chastity—as has been mentioned by the *Sages*,[44] *may their memory be blessed*, with reference to his dictum: *Behold now, I know that thou art a fair woman to look upon.*[45]

According to me *circumcision* has another very important meaning,

41. Deut. 22:10.   42. Mishnah, Baba Qamma, V 7.   43. Genesis Rabbah, LXXX.
44. Cf. B.T., Baba Bathra, 16a.   45. Gen. 12:11.

namely, that all people professing this opinion — that is, those who believe in the *unity of God* — should have a bodily sign uniting them so that one who does not belong to them should not be able to claim that he was one of them, while being a stranger. For he would do this in order to profit by them or to deceive the people who profess this religion. Now a man does not perform this act[46] upon himself or upon a son of his unless it be in consequence of a genuine belief. For it is not like an incision in the leg or a burn in the arm, but is a very, very hard thing.

It is also well known what degree of mutual love and mutual help exists between people who all bear the same sign, which forms for them a sort of covenant and alliance. *Circumcision* is a covenant made by *Abraham our Father* with a view to the belief in the *unity of God*. Thus everyone who is circumcised joins *Abraham's covenant*. This covenant imposes the obligation to believe in the unity of God: *To be a God unto thee and to thy seed after thee.*[47] This also is a strong reason, as strong as the first, which may be adduced to account for *circumcision*; perhaps it is even stronger than the first.

The perfection and perpetuation of this Law can only be achieved if circumcision is performed in childhood. For this there are three wise reasons. The first is that if the child were let alone until he grew up, he would sometimes not perform it. The second is that a child does not suffer as much pain as a grown-up man because his membrane is still soft and his imagination weak; for a grown-up man would regard the thing, which he would imagine before it occurred, as terrible and hard. The third is that the parents of a child | that is just born take lightly matters concerning it, for up to that time the imaginative form that compels the parents to love it is not yet consolidated. For this imaginative form increases through habitual contact and grows with the growth of the child. Then it begins to decrease and to disappear, I refer to this imaginative form. For the love of the father and of the mother for the child when it has just been born is not like their love for it when it is one year old, and their love for it when it is one year old is not like their love when it is six years old. Consequently if it were left uncircumcised for two or three years, this would necessitate the abandonment of circumcision because of the father's love and affection for it. At the time of its birth, on the other hand, this imaginative form is very weak, especially as far as concerns the father upon whom this *commandment* is imposed.[48]

46. I.e., circumcision.   47. Gen. 17:7.   48. Cf. B.T., Qiddushin, 29a.

The fact that *circumcision* is performed on the eighth day is due to the circumstance that all living beings are very weak and exceedingly tender when they are born, as if they were still in the womb. This is so until seven days are past. It is only then that they are counted among those who have contact with the air. Do you not see that this point is also taken into account with regard to beasts? — *Seven days shall it be with its dam, and so on.*[49] It is as if before that period it were an abortion. Similarly with regard to man; he is circumcised after seven days have passed. In this way the matter is fixed: *You do not make out of it something that varies.*

This class of commandments also includes the prohibition against mutilating the sexual organs of all the males of animals,[50] which is based on the principle of *righteous statutes and judgments,*[51] I mean the principle of keeping the mean in all matters; sexual intercourse should neither be excessively indulged, as we have mentioned, nor wholly abolished. Did He[52] not command and say: *Be fruitful and multiply?*[53] Accordingly this organ is weakened by means of circumcision, but not extirpated through excision.[54] | What is natural is left according to nature, but measures are taken against excess. *He that is wounded in the stones or hath his privy member cut off*[55] is forbidden to marry a *woman of Israel*, for such cohabitation would be perverted and aimless. Such a marriage would likewise be a *stumbling-block* for the woman and for him who seeks her out. This is very clear.

In order to deter people from *illicit unions*, a *bastard* is forbidden to marry a *daughter of Israel;*[56] so that the adulterous man and adulterous woman should know that by committing their act they attach to their descendants a stigma that can never be effaced. The children born of adultery being, moreover, always despised to every way of life and in every nation,[57] the *seed of Israel* is regarded as too noble to mix with *bastards*.

Because of the nobility of *Priests* they are forbidden to marry a *prostitute*, a *divorced woman*, and a *woman born of the illicit marriage* [*of a Priest*].[58] The *High Priest*, who is the noblest among the *Priests*, is even forbidden to marry a *widow* and a *woman that is not a virgin.*[59] The reason for all this is clear. Mingling of *bastards* with the *congregation of the Lord*[60] being forbidden, that of *male and female slaves* with it is prohibited all the more.

The reason for the prohibition of intermarriage with the *Gentiles* is

---

49. Exod. 22:29.   50. Cf. Lev. 22:24.   51. Deut. 4:8.
52. Or: it (i.e., Scripture).   53. Gen. 1:22.   54. Or: entirely extirpated.
55. Cf. Deut. 23:2.   56. Cf. Deut. 23:3.   57. Or: religious community.
58. Literally: *profaned woman*. Cf. Lev. 21:7; B.T., Qiddushin, 77a.
59. Cf. Lev. 21:13–14.   60. Deut. 23:3.

explained in the text of the *Torah: And thou take of their daughters unto thy sons, and so on.*[61]

In the case of most of the *statutes* whose reason is hidden from us, everything serves to keep people away from *idolatry*. The fact that there are particulars the reason for which is hidden from me and the utility of which I do not understand, is due to the circumstance that things known by hearsay are not like things that one has seen. Hence the extent of my knowledge of the ways of the Sabians drawn from books[62] is not comparable to the knowledge of one who saw their practices with his eyes; this is even more the case since these opinions have disappeared two thousand years ago or even before that. If we knew the particulars of those practices and heard details concerning those opinions, we would become clear regarding the wisdom manifested in the details of the practices prescribed in the commandments concerning | the *sacrifices* and the forms of *uncleanness* and other matters whose reason cannot, to my mind, be easily grasped. For I for one do not doubt that all this was intended to efface those untrue opinions from the mind and to abolish those useless practices, which brought about a waste of lives *in vain and futile things.*[63] Those opinions turned away human thought from concern with the conception of an intelligible and from useful actions, as our prophets have explained to us, and have said: *They walked after vain things that do not profit.*[64] Jeremiah says: *Surely our fathers have inherited lies, vanity, and things wherein there is no profit.*[65] Consider how great was the extent of this corruption and whether or not it was fitting to spend one's efforts on putting an end to this. Most of the *commandments* serve, therefore, as we have made clear, to put an end to these opinions and to lighten the great and oppressive burdens, the toil and the fatigue, that those people imposed upon themselves in their cult. Accordingly every commandment or prohibition of the Law whose reason is hidden from you constitutes a cure for one of those diseases, which today — thank God — we do not know any more. This is what should be believed by one who is endowed with perfection and knows the true meaning of His dictum, may He be exalted: *I said not unto the seed of Jacob, Seek ye Me for nothing.*[66]

61. Exod. 34:16.   62. Literally: which I have heard from books.
63. Cf. Isa. 49:4.
64. Jer. 2:8. The text of Jeremiah reads: *They walked after things that do not profit.*
   Maimonides may also have had in mind the passage in I Sam. 12:21. Cf. III 29, n. 23.
65. Jer. 16:19.   6.6 Isa. 45:19.

I have now dealt one by one with all the *commandments* included in these classes and we have drawn attention to the reasons for them. There are only a few and some slight details for which I have not given reasons, even though in truth we have virtually given reasons also for these to him who is attentive and comprehending. |

CHAPTER 50

There are also things that belong to the *mysteries of the Torah*, which have caused many people to stumble. Accordingly they ought to be explained. These are the stories recounted in the *Torah* the telling of which is thought to be useless, as for instance the account of the branching out of tribes from *Noah* and of their names and dwelling places,[1] likewise the *sons of Secir the Horite*[2] and the account of *the kings that reigned in the land of Edom*[3] and the like. You know the saying of [the Sages] that *the impious Manasseh* occupied his vile council with nothing but criticism of such passages. They say:[4] *He used to sit there and interpret Scripture by means of blasphemous haggadoth. Thus he said: Moses did not have to write: And the sister of Lotan was Timna, and so on.*[5] As for me I shall inform you of a general principle, and then I shall come back to the details as I did with regard to the reasons for the *commandments*.

Know that all the stories that you will find mentioned in the *Torah* occur there for a necessary utility for the Law; either they give a correct notion of an opinion that is a pillar of the Law, or they rectify some action so that mutual wrongdoing and aggression should not occur between men. I shall set this forth to you in an orderly fashion.

As it is a pillar of the Law that the world was produced in time, that at first a single individual of the human species, namely, *Adam*, was created, and that approximately two thousand five hundred years elapsed between *Adam* and *Moses our Master*, men, if they were given this information only, would rapidly have begun to have doubts in those times. For people were to be found scattered up to the ends of the whole earth; there were | different tribes and different and very dissimilar languages. These doubts were put to an end through an exposition of the genealogy of all of them

1. Cf. Gen. 10.   2. Gen. 36:20.   3. Gen. 36:31.   4. B.T., Sanhedrin, 99b.
5. Gen. 36:22.

and of their branching by mentioning the names of the famous men among them — such and such, the son of such and such — and their ages and by giving the facts regarding their habitats and the reason that necessitated their being scattered up to the ends of the earth and their languages being different in spite of their having at first dwelt in one place and having had all of them one language, a fact that was a necessary consequence of their being the children of a single individual.

In the same way the story of the *Flood* and the story of *Sodom and Gomorrah* were recounted in order to bring proof for the following correct opinion: *Verily there is a reward for the righteous; verily there is a God that judgeth on the earth.*[6] In the same way the relation of that *war* of the nine kings is made with a view to making known to us the miracle consisting in the victory of *Abraham*, accompanied by a small number of men having no king with them, over four great kings. It also gives us knowledge of his defense of his relative because of the latter's sharing his belief, and of his exposing himself to the dangers of war until he saved him. It also gives us knowledge of how moderate and easily satisfied he was, of his contempt for acquisition, and of his striving for moral nobility. This is expressed by his saying: *From a thread even to a shoe-latchet, and so on.*[7]

The enumeration of the tribes of the *children of Se^cir* and of their individual genealogy[8] is made with a view to *one single commandment*; for He, may He be exalted, has commanded exterminating only the *seed of ^cAmaleq.* Now *^cAmaleq was the son of Eliphaz* and *Timna the sister of Lotan.*[9] He did not command killing the other *children of Esau.* Now *Esau* was connected by marriage with the *children of Se^cir*, as is set forth in the text;[10] he had issue from them and reigned over them, and his descendants mingled with theirs. Consequently the whole land of *Se^cir* and those tribes were called after the predominant tribe — namely, the *children of Esau* — and particularly the descendants of | *^cAmaleq*, for they were the bravest among them. Accordingly if there had been no explanation concerning these genealogies and their particulars, all of them would have been killed through neglectfulness. Consequently Scripture explained their tribes and said that those whom you see today in *Se^cir* and the kingdom of *^cAmaleq* are not all of them *children of ^cAmaleq*, but some of them are descendants of this or that individual and are only called after *^cAmaleq* because the latter's mother belonged to them. All this was an act of justice on the part of God lest a tribe be killed indiscriminately in the course of the extermination of another

6. Ps. 58:12.   7. Gen. 14:23.   8. Cf. Gen. 36:20-30.
9. Cf. Gen. 36:12 and 22.   10. Cf. Gen. 36:25.

tribe. For the *Decree* was only directed against the descendants of *ʿAmaleq*, and we have already explained in what way wisdom is manifested therein.[11]

The reason for [Scripture's] enumeration of *the kings that reigned in the land of Edom*[12] is the fact that according to one of the *commandments: Thou mayest not set a foreigner over thee, who is not thy brother.*[13] Now not one of the kings that are enumerated is from *Edom.* Do you not see that it sets forth their genealogy and their country? — this one was from this place and that one from that place. In my opinion it is probable that their conduct and their histories were generally known — I mean the conduct of those *kings of Edom*, and that they tyrannized over the *children of Esau* and humiliated them. Accordingly in mentioning them, it says as it were: Consider your brethren, the *children of Esau*, whose kings were this one and that one — whose actions were generally known. For no individual has ever been the chief of a religious community to whose race he did not belong, without doing it great or small injury.

To sum up: Just as, according to what I have told you, the doctrines of the Sabians are remote from us today,[14] the chronicles of those times are likewise hidden from us today. Hence if we knew them and were cognizant of the events that happened in those days, we would know in detail the reasons of many things mentioned in the *Torah*.

You should also understand that the status | of things that are set down in writing is not the same as the status of happenings that one sees. For in happenings that one sees, there are particulars that bring about necessary consequences of great importance, which cannot be mentioned except in a prolix manner. Accordingly, when narrations concerning these happenings are considered, the individual who reflects thinks that such narrations are too long or repetitious. If, however, he had seen what is narrated, he would know the necessity of what is recounted. Hence when you see narrations in the *Torah* that do not belong to the Law and think that it was not necessary to set down such and such a narration or that it is too long or repetitious, the reason for this is that you have not seen the particulars that necessitated that the story be told in the manner it is.

Of this kind is the enumeration of the *stations* [of the Children of Israel in the desert]. Apparently this is an enumeration that is quite useless. Because of this false fancy, which first comes to the mind, it says: *And Moses wrote their goings forth, according to their stations, by the commandment of the Lord.*[15] Now the need for this was very great. For all miracles are certain

---

11. Cf. III 41.   12. Gen. 36:31.   13. Deut. 17:15.   14. Cf. III 49.
15. Num. 33:2.

in the opinion of one who has seen them; however, at a future time their story becomes a mere traditional narrative, and there is a possibility for the hearer to consider it untrue. It is well known that it is impossible and inconceivable that a miracle lasts permanently throughout the succession of generations so that all men can see it. Now one of the miracles of the Law, and one of the greatest among them, is the sojourn of *Israel* for forty years in the *desert* and the finding of the *manna* there every day. For that *desert* was, as is stated in Scripture, a place *wherein were serpents, fiery serpents, and scorpions, and thirsty ground where there was no water.*[16] Those are places that are very remote from cultivated land and unnatural for man; *it is no place of seed or of figs or of vines or of pomegranates, and so on.*[17] It is also said of it that it is *a land that no man passed through, and so on.*[18] The text of the *Torah* states: *Ye have not eaten bread,* | *neither have ye drunk wine or strong drink, and so on.*[19] All these are manifest visible miracles. Now God, may He be exalted, knew that in the future what happens to traditional narratives would happen to those miracles: People would think that [the Children of Israel] sojourned in a desert that was near to cultivated land and in which man can live, like the deserts inhabited at present by the Arabs, or that it consisted of places in which it was possible to till and to reap or to feed on plants that were to be found there, or that it was natural for the *manna* always to come down in those places, or that there were wells of water in those places. Therefore all these fancies are rebutted and the traditional relation of all these miracles is confirmed through the enumeration of those stations, so that men to come could see them and thus know how great was the miracle constituted by the sojourn of the human species in those places for forty years. For the same reason *Joshua* cursed him who would *ever* build up *Jericho*,[20] so that this miracle should subsist permanently. For whoever would see the wall sunk in the ground, would clearly understand that such cannot be the aspect of a demolished building, but that this building sank through a miracle.

Similarly also its dictum, *At the commandment of the Lord they pitched and at the commandment of the Lord they journeyed,*[21] might suffice for the narrative; and it might appear, when one thinks about it at first, that everything dealing with this subject that comes afterwards is needless expatiation on the matter — I refer to its saying: *And when the cloud tarried long, and so on.*[22] *And so it was when the cloud was, and so on.*[23] *Or whether it were two*

16. Deut. 8:15.   17. Num. 20:5.   18. Jer. 2:6.   19. Deut. 29:5.
20. Cf. Josh. 6:26.   21. Num. 9:20.   22. Num. 9:19.   23. Num. 9:21.

days, and so on.[24] I shall inform you of the reason for all those particulars being given. The reason is that this story was to be confirmed with a view to the destruction of the opinion held at that time and even up to now by the religious communities, that [the Children of] *Israel* lost their way and did not know where they were going — just as it is said [in Scripture:] *They are perplexed | in the land.*[25] Thus the Arabs at present designate it — I mean the *desert* — as al-Tīh, thinking that [the Children of] *Israel* lost their way [tāhū] and did not know the road. Scripture accordingly is engaged in expounding and corroborating the fact that those irregular stations, the return to some of them, and the difference between the lengths of their staying at every station — so that they stayed at one station eighteen years,[26] at another one day, and at a third one night[27] — were all of them determined by divine decree and that this was not due to their having lost their way, but depended on the rising of the *pillar of cloud*. Therefore all these particulars are given. The *Torah* has already made it clear that that stretch of road was short, known, much frequented, that it was by no means unknown; I refer to the stretch between *Horeb* — where they betook themselves with a certain purpose according to what He, may He be exalted, has commanded: *Ye shall serve God upon this mountain*[28] — and *Kadesh-Barnea* — where the cultivated land begins according to the text: *Behold we are now in Kadesh, a city in the uttermost of thy border.*[29] The length of this stretch is an eleven days' march, according to what it says: *Eleven days' journey from Horeb by the way of Mount Seᶜir unto Kadesh-Barnea.*[30] This is not a road in which one may err for forty years. The reason for their tarrying are the causes literally stated in the *Torah*.

In a similar way whenever the cause for a story's being narrated is hidden from thee, there is a strong reason for that story. Apply to the whole matter the principle to which [the Sages], *may their memory be blessed*, have drawn our attention: *For it is no vain thing from you*[31] — *And if it is vain, it is so because of you.*[32] |

24. Num. 9:22.   25. Exod. 14:3.   26. Cf. Seder ᶜOlam Rabbah, VIII.
27. Cf. Num. 9:21.   28. Exod. 3:12.   29. Num. 20:16.   30. Deut. 1:2.
31. Deut. 32:47.   32. J.T., Peˀah, I. Cf. III 26.

This chapter that we bring now does not include additional matter over and above what is comprised in the other chapters of this Treatise. It is only a kind of a conclusion, at the same time explaining the worship as practiced by one who has apprehended the true realities peculiar only to Him after he has obtained an apprehension of what He is; and it also guides him toward achieving this worship, which is the end of man, and makes known to him how providence watches over him in this habitation until he is brought over to the *bundle of life*.[1]

I shall begin the discourse in this chapter with a parable that I shall compose for you. I say then: The ruler is in his palace, and all his subjects are partly within the city and partly outside the city. Of those who are within the city, some have turned their backs upon the ruler's habitation, their faces being turned another way. Others seek to reach the ruler's habitation, turn toward it, and desire to enter it and to stand before him, but up to now they have not yet seen the wall of the habitation. Some of those who seek to reach it have come up to the habitation and walk around it searching for its gate. Some of them have entered the gate and walk about in the antechambers. Some of them have entered the inner court of the habitation and have come to be with the king, in one and the same place with him, namely, in the ruler's habitation. But their having come into the inner part of the habitation does not mean that they see the ruler or speak to him. For after their coming into the inner part of the habitation, it is indispensable that they should make another effort; then they will be in the presence of the ruler, see him from afar or from nearby, or | hear the ruler's speech or speak to him.

Now I shall interpret to you this parable that I have invented. I say then: Those who are outside the city are all human individuals who have no doctrinal belief, neither one based on speculation nor one that accepts the authority of tradition: such individuals as the furthermost Turks found in the remote North, the Negroes found in the remote South, and those who resemble them from among them that are with us in these climes. The status of those is like that of irrational animals. To my mind they do not have the rank of men, but have among the beings a rank lower than the rank of man but higher than the rank of the apes. For they have the external shape

1. Cf. I Sam. 25:29. According to the commentators, these words refer to eternal life.

and lineaments of a man and a faculty of discernment that is superior to that of the apes.

Those who are within the city, but have turned their backs upon the ruler's habitation, are people who have opinions and are engaged in speculation, but who have adopted incorrect opinions either because of some great error that befell them in the course of their speculation or because of their following the traditional authority of one who had fallen into error. Accordingly because of these opinions, the more these people walk, the greater is their distance from the ruler's habitation. And they are far worse than the first. They are those concerning whom necessity at certain times impels killing them and blotting out the traces of their opinions lest they should lead astray the ways of others.

Those who seek to reach the ruler's habitation and to enter it, but never see the ruler's habitation, are the multitude of the adherents of the Law, I refer to *the ignoramuses who observe the commandments.*

Those who have come up to the habitation and walk around it are the jurists who believe true opinions on the basis of traditional authority and study the law concerning the practices of divine service, but do not engage in speculation concerning the fundamental principles of religion and make no inquiry whatever regarding | the rectification of belief.

Those who have plunged into speculation concerning the fundamental principles of religion, have entered the antechambers. People there indubitably have different ranks. He, however, who has achieved demonstration, to the extent that that is possible, of everything that may be demonstrated; and who has ascertained in divine matters, to the extent that that is possible, everything that may be ascertained; and who has come close to certainty in those matters in which one can only come close to it — has come to be with the ruler in the inner part of the habitation.

Know, my son, that as long as you are engaged in studying the mathematical sciences and the art of logic, you are one of those who walk around the house searching for its gate, as [the Sages], *may their memory be blessed,* have said resorting to a parable: *Ben Zoma is still outside.*[2] If, however, you have understood the natural things, you have entered the habitation and are walking in the antechambers. If, however, you have achieved perfection in the natural things and have understood divine science, you have entered in the ruler's place *into the inner court* and are with him in one habitation. This is the rank of the men of science; they, however, are of different grades of perfection.

2. B.T., Ḥagigah, 15a.

There are those who set their thought to work after having attained perfection in the divine science, turn wholly toward God, may He be cherished and held sublime, renounce what is other than He, and direct all the acts of their intellect toward an examination of the beings with a view to drawing from them proof with regard to Him, so as to know His governance of them in whatever way it is possible. These people are those who are present in the ruler's council. This is the rank of the prophets. Among them there is he[3] who because of the greatness of his apprehension and his renouncing everything that is other than God, may He be exalted, has attained such a degree that it is said of him, *And he was there with the Lord,*[4] putting questions and receiving answers, speaking and being spoken to, in that holy place. And because of his great joy | in that which he apprehended, *he did neither eat bread nor drink water.*[5] For his intellect attained such strength that all the gross faculties in the body ceased to function. I refer to the various kinds of the sense of touch. Some prophets could only see, some of them from close by and some from afar, as [a prophet] says: *From afar the Lord appeared unto me.*[6] The various degrees of prophecy have already been discussed by us.[7] Let us now return to the subject of this chapter, which is to confirm men in the intention to set their thought to work on God alone after they have achieved knowledge of Him, as we have explained. This is the worship peculiar to those who have apprehended the true realities; the more they think of Him and of being with Him, the more their worship increases.

As for someone who thinks and frequently mentions God, without knowledge, following a mere imagining or following a belief adopted because of his reliance on the authority of somebody else, he is to my mind outside the habitation and far away from it and does not in true reality mention or think about God. For that thing which is in his imagination and which he mentions in his speech[8] does not correspond to any being at all and has merely been invented by his imagination, as we have explained in our discourse concerning the attributes.[9] This kind of worship ought only to be engaged in after intellectual conception has been achieved. If, however, you have apprehended God and His acts in accordance with what is required by the intellect, you should afterwards engage in totally devoting yourself to Him, endeavor to come closer to Him, and strengthen the bond between you and Him — that is, the intellect. Thus it says: *Unto thee it was shown, that thou mightest know that the Lord, and so on;*[10] and it says: *Know this day,*

3. Or: there are those.   4. Exod. 34:28.   5. Exod. 34:28.   6. Jer. 31:3.
7. Cf. II 45.   8. Literally: in his mouth.   9. Cf. I 50.   10. Deut. 4:35.

and lay it to thy heart, and so on;[11] and it says: *Know ye that the Lord He is God.*[12] The *Torah* has made it clear that this last worship to which we have drawn attention in this chapter can only be engaged in after apprehension has been achieved; | it says: *To love the Lord your God, and to serve Him with all your heart and with all your soul.*[13] Now we have made it clear several times[14] that love is proportionate to apprehension. After *love* comes this worship to which attention has also been drawn by [the Sages], *may their memory be blessed*, who said: *This is the worship in the heart.*[15] In my opinion it consists in setting thought to work on the first intelligible and in devoting oneself exclusively to this as far as this is within one's capacity. Therefore you will find that *David* exhorted *Solomon* and fortified him in these two things, I mean his endeavor to apprehend Him and his endeavor to worship Him after apprehension has been achieved. He said: *And thou, Solomon my son, know thou the God of thy father and serve Him, and so on. If thou seek Him, He will be found of thee, and so on.*[16] The exhortation always refers to intellectual apprehensions, not to imagination; for thought concerning imaginings is not called *knowledge* but *that which cometh into your mind.*[17] Thus it is clear that after apprehension, total devotion to Him and the employment of intellectual thought in constantly loving Him should be aimed at. Mostly this is achieved in solitude and isolation. Hence every excellent man stays frequently in solitude and does not meet anyone unless it is necessary.

A call to attention. We have already made it clear to you[18] that that intellect which overflowed from Him, may He be exalted, toward us is the bond between us and Him. You have the choice: if you wish to strengthen and to fortify this bond,[19] you can do so; if, however, you wish gradually to make it weaker and feebler until you cut it, you can also do that. You can only strengthen this bond by employing it in loving Him and in progressing toward this, just as we have explained. And it is made weaker and feebler if you busy your thought with what is other than He. Know that even if you were the man who knew most the true reality of the divine science, you would cut that bond existing between you and God if you would empty your thought | of God and busy yourself totally in eating the necessary or in occupying yourselves with the necessary. You would not be with Him then, nor He with you. For that relation between you and Him is actually broken off at that time. It is for this reason that excellent men begrudge the

11. Deut. 4:39.   12. Ps. 100:3.   13. Deut. 11:13.   14. Cf. I 39 and III 28.
15. B.T., Ta°anith, 2a; J.T., Berakhoth, IV.   16. I Chron. 28:9.   17. Ezek. 20:32.
18. Cf. II 12 and 37.   19. I.e., the intellect.

times in which they are turned away from Him by other occupations and warn against this, saying: *Do not let God be absent from your thought.*[20] And *David* says: *I have set the Lord always before me; because He is at my right hand, I shall not bend down;*[21] he means to say: I do not empty my thought of Him, and it is as if He were my right hand from which, because of the rapidity of its motion, my attention is not distracted even for an instant, and therefore I do not bend down — that is, I do not fall.

Know that all the practices of the worship, such as reading the *Torah*, prayer, and the performance of the other *commandments*, have only the end of training you to occupy yourself with His commandments, may He be exalted, rather than with matters pertaining to this world; you should act as if you were occupied with Him, may He be exalted, and not with that which is other than He. If, however, you pray merely by moving your lips while facing a wall, and at the same time think about your buying and selling; or if you read the *Torah* with your tongue while your heart is set upon the building of your habitation and does not consider what you read; and similarly in all cases in which you perform a *commandment* merely with your limbs — as if you were digging a hole in the ground or hewing wood in the forest — without reflecting either upon the meaning of that action or upon Him from whom the commandment proceeds or upon the end of the action, you should not think that you have achieved the end. Rather you will then be similar to those of whom it is said: *Thou art near in their mouth, and far from their reins.*[22]

From here on I will begin to give you guidance with regard to the form of this training so that you should achieve this great end. The first thing that you should cause your soul to hold fast onto is | that, while *reciting* the *Shema*[c] prayer, you should empty your mind of everything and pray thus. You should not content yourself with *being intent* while *reciting the first verse of Shema*[c] and saying *the first benediction.* When this has been carried out correctly and has been practiced consistently for years, cause your soul, whenever you read or listen to the *Torah*, to be constantly directed — the whole of you and your thought — toward reflection on what you are listening to or reading. When this too has been practiced consistently for a certain time, cause your soul to be in such a way that your thought is always quite free of distraction and gives heed to all that you are reading of the other discourses of the prophets[23] and even when you read all the *benedictions*, so that you aim at meditating on what you are uttering and at considering its meaning. If, however, while performing these acts of worship, you are free

20. B.T., Shabbath, 149a.   21. Ps. 16:8.   22. Jer. 12:2.   23. I.e., not only of the Torah.

from distraction and not engaged in thinking upon any of the things pertaining to this world, cause your soul — after this has been achieved — to occupy your thought with things necessary for you or superfluous in your life, and in general with *worldly things*, while you eat or drink or bathe or talk with your wife and your small children, or while you talk with the common run of people. Thus I have provided you with many and long stretches of time in which you can think all that needs thinking regarding property, the governance of the household, and the welfare of the body. On the other hand, while performing the actions imposed by the Law, you should occupy your thought only with what you are doing, just as we have explained. When, however, you are alone with yourself and no one else is there and while you lie awake upon your bed, you should take great care during these precious times not to set your thought to work on anything other than that intellectual worship | consisting in nearness to God and being in His presence in that true reality that I have made known to you and not by way of affections of the imagination. In my opinion this end can be achieved by those of the men of knowledge who have rendered their souls worthy of it by training of this kind.

And there may be a human individual who, through his apprehension of the true realities and his joy in what he has apprehended, achieves a state in which he talks with people and is occupied with his bodily necessities while his intellect is wholly turned toward Him, may He be exalted, so that in his heart he is always in His presence, may He be exalted, while outwardly he is with people, in the sort of way described by the poetical parables that have been invented for these notions: *I sleep, but my heart waketh; it is the voice of my beloved that knocketh, and so on.*[24] I do not say that this rank is that of all the prophets; but I do say that this is the rank of *Moses our Master*, of whom it is said: *And Moses alone shall come near unto the Lord; but they shall not come near;*[25] and of whom it is said: *And he was there with the Lord;*[26] and to whom it was said: *But as for thee, stand thou here by Me.*[27] All this according to what we have explained regarding the meaning of these *verses.*[28] This was also the rank of the *Patriarchs*, the result of whose nearness to Him, may He be exalted, was that His name became known to the world through them: *The God of Abraham, the God of Isaac, and the God of Jacob . . .; this is My name for ever.*[29] Because of the union of their intellects through apprehension of Him, it came about

---

24. Song of Songs 5:2.   25. Exod. 24:2.   26. Exod. 34:28.   27. Deut. 5:28.
28. Cf. I 13, II 32, III 51 above.
29. Exod. 3:15. The Hebrew expression translated: *for ever*, may also mean: *for the world.*

that He made a lasting *covenant* with each of them: *Then I will remember My covenant with Jacob, and so on.*[30] For in those four, I mean the *Patriarchs* and *Moses our Master*, union with God — I mean apprehension of Him and love of Him — became manifest, as the texts testify. Also the providence of God watching over them and over their posterity was great. Withal they were occupied with governing people, increasing their fortune, | and endeavoring to acquire property. Now this is to my mind a proof that they performed these actions with their limbs only, while their intellects were constantly in His presence, may He be exalted. It also seems to me that the fact that these four were in a permanent state of extreme perfection in the eyes of God, and that His providence watched over them continually even while they were engaged in increasing their fortune — I mean while they tended their cattle, did agricultural work, and governed their household — was necessarily brought about by the circumstance that in all these actions their end was to come near to Him, may He be exalted; and how near! For the end of their efforts during their life was to bring into being a religious community that would know and worship God. *For I have known him, to the end that he may command, and so on.*[31] Thus it has become clear to you that the end of all their efforts was to spread the doctrine of *the unity of the Name in the world* and to guide people to love Him, may He be exalted. Therefore this rank befitted them, for these actions were pure worship of great import. This rank is not a rank that, with a view to the attainment of which, someone like myself may aspire for guidance.[32] But one may aspire to attain that rank which was mentioned before this one through the training that we described. One must beseech God that He remove the obstructions that separate us from Him, even though most of them come from us, as we have explained in certain chapters of this Treatise:[33] *Your iniquities have separated between you and your God.*[34]

A most extraordinary speculation has occurred to me just now through which doubts may be dispelled and divine secrets revealed. We have already explained in the chapters concerning providence that providence watches over everyone endowed with intellect proportionately to the measure of his intellect. Thus providence always watches over an individual endowed with perfect apprehension, whose intellect | never ceases from being occupied with God. On the other hand, an individual endowed with

---

30. Lev. 26:42.   31. Gen. 18:19.

32. The Arabic phrase can have two meanings: (*a*) Someone like myself cannot aspire to be guided with a view to achieving this rank; (*b*) Someone like myself cannot aspire to guide others with a view to their achieving this rank.

33. Cf., e.g., III 12.   34. Isa. 59:2.

perfect apprehension, whose thought sometimes for a certain time is emptied of God, is watched over by providence only during the time when he thinks of God; providence withdraws from him during the time when he is occupied with something else. However, its withdrawal then is not like its withdrawal from those who have never had intellectual cognition. But in his case that providence merely decreases because that man of perfect apprehension has, while being occupied, no intellect in actu; but that perfect man is at such times only apprehending potentially, though close to actuality. At such times he is like a skillful scribe at the time when he is not writing. On the other hand, he who has no intellectual cognition at all of God is like one who is in darkness and has never seen light, just as we have explained[35] with regard to its dictum: *The wicked shall be put to silence in darkness.*[36] He who apprehends and advances with his whole being toward the object of his apprehension, is like one who is in the pure light of the sun. He who has had apprehension, but is occupied, is while he is occupied in this state like one who has a cloudy day in which the sun does not shine because of the clouds that separate it and him. Hence it seems to me that all prophets or excellent and perfect men whom one of the evils of this world befell, had this evil happen to them during such a time of distraction, the greatness of the calamity being proportionate to the duration of the period of distraction or to the vileness of the matter with which he was occupied. If this is so, the great doubt that induced the philosophers to deny that divine providence watches over all human individuals and to assert equality between them and the individuals of the other kinds of animals is dispelled. For their proof for this opinion was the fact that excellent and good men experienced great misfortunes. Thus | the secret with regard to this has been explained even according to the requirements of their opinions: The providence of God, may He be exalted, is constantly watching over those who have obtained this overflow, which is permitted to everyone who makes efforts with a view to obtaining it. If a man's thought is free from distraction, if he apprehends Him, may He be exalted, in the right way and rejoices in what he apprehends, that individual can never be afflicted with evil of any kind. For he is with God and God is with him. When, however, he abandons Him, may He be exalted, and is thus separated from God and God separated from him, he becomes in consequence of this a target for every evil that may happen to befall him. For the thing that necessarily brings about providence and deliverance from the sea of chance consists in that intellectual overflow. Yet an impediment may

35. Cf. III 18.   36. I Sam. 2:9.

prevent for some time its reaching the excellent and good man in question, or again it was not obtained at all by such and such imperfect and wicked man, and therefore the chance occurrences that befell them happened. To my mind this belief is also shown as true by a text of the *Torah*; He, may He be exalted, says: *And I will hide My face from them, and they shall be devoured, and many evils and troubles shall come upon them; so that they will say in that day: Are not these evils come upon us because our God is not among us?*[37] It is clear that we are the cause of this *hiding of the face*, and we are the agents who produce this separation. This is the meaning of His saying: *And I will surely hide My face in that day for all the evil which they shall have wrought.*[38] There is no doubt that what is true of one is true of a community. Thus it has become clear to you that the reason for a human individual's being abandoned to chance so that he is permitted to be devoured like the beasts is his being separated from God. If, however, *his God is within him*, no evil at all will befall him. For He, may He be exalted, says: *Fear thou not, for I am with thee; be not dismayed, for I am thy God, and so on.*[39] He says: *When thou passest through the waters, I will be with thee, and through the rivers,* | *they shall not overflow thee, and so on.*[40] The determination that *when thou passest through the waters and I will be with thee, the rivers shall not overflow thee,* is accounted for by the fact that everyone who has rendered himself so worthy that the intellect in question overflows toward him, has providence attached to him, while all evils are prevented from befalling him. It says: *The Lord is for me, I will not fear; what can man do unto me?*[41] And it says, *Acquaint now thyself with Him, and be at peace,*[42] meaning to say: turn toward Him and you will be safe from all ill.

Consider the *song on mishaps:* You will find that it describes this great providence and the safeguard and the protection from all bodily ills, both the general ones and those that concern one individual rather than another, so that neither those that are consequent upon the nature of being nor those that are due to the plotting of man would occur. It says: *That He will deliver thee from the snare of the fowler, and from the noisome pestilence. He shall cover thee with His pinions, and under His wings shalt thou take refuge; His truth is a shield and a buckler. Thou shalt not be afraid of the terror by night, nor of the arrow that flieth by day; of the pestilence that walketh in darkness, nor of the destruction that wasteth at noonday.*[43] He then goes on to describe the protection against the plotting of men, saying: If you should happen to

37. Deut. 31:17.   38. Deut. 31:18.   39. Isa. 41:10.   40. Isa. 43:2.
41. Ps. 118:6.   42. Job 22:21.   43. Ps. 91:3–6.

pass on your way a widely extended field of battle and even if one thousand were killed to your left and ten thousand to your right, no evil at all would befall you. Do you not perceive and see with your eye God's judgment and retribution directed against the wicked that are killed while you are safe? These are its words: *A thousand may fall at thy side, and ten thousand at thy right hand; it shall not come nigh thee. Only with thine eyes shalt thou behold, and see the recompense of the wicked.*[44] This is followed by what is said about divine safeguard; then it gives the reason for this great protection, saying that the reason for this great providence being effective with regard to the individual in question is this: *Because he hath set his passionate love upon Me, therefore I will deliver him; I will set him on high, because he hath known My Name.*[45] We have already explained in preceding chapters that the meaning of *knowledge of the Name* | is: apprehension of Him. It is as if [the psalm] said that this individual is protected because he hath known Me and then passionately loved Me.[46] You know the difference between the terms *one who loves* [oheb] and *one who loves passionately* [hosheq]; an excess of love [mahabbah], so that no thought remains that is directed toward a thing other than the Beloved, is passionate love [ʿishq].

The philosophers have already explained that the bodily faculties impede in youth the attainment of most of the moral virtues, and all the more that of pure thought, which is achieved through the perfection of the intelligibles that lead to passionate love of Him, may He be exalted. For it is impossible that it should be achieved while the bodily humors are in effervescence. Yet in the measure in which the faculties of the body are weakened and the fire of the desires is quenched, the intellect is strengthened, its lights achieve a wider extension, its apprehension is purified, and it rejoices in what it apprehends. The result is that when a perfect man is stricken with years and approaches death, this apprehension increases very powerfully, joy over this apprehension and a great love for the object of apprehension become stronger, until the soul is separated from the body at that moment in this state of pleasure. Because of this the *Sages* have indicated with reference to the deaths of *Moses, Aaron, and Miriam* that

44. Ps. 91:7–8.   45. Ps. 91:14.
46. ʿashiqani. The meaning of the Arabic verb ʿashiqa corresponds to that of the Hebrew verb hashoq (from which the participle hosheq, mentioned by Maimonides in this passage, is derived). Both may signify: "to love passionately." On the other hand, the Arabic verbal form ahabba (from which the word mahabbah, likewise mentioned by Maimonides in this passage, is derived), corresponds to the Hebrew word ahob, from which the participle oheb is derived. Both the Hebrew and the Arabic verb mean: "to love."

the three of them died by a kiss. They said[47] that the dictum [of Scripture], *And Moses the servant of the Lord died there in the land of Moab by the mouth of the Lord,*[48] indicates that he died by a kiss. Similarly it is said of Aaron: *By the mouth of the Lord, and died there.*[49] And they said of *Miriam* in the same way: *She also died by a kiss.* But with regard to her it is not said, *by the mouth of the Lord;* because she was a woman, the use of the figurative expression was not suitable with regard to her. Their purpose was to indicate that the three of them died in the pleasure of this apprehension due to the intensity of passionate love. In this dictum the *Sages, may their memory be blessed,* followed the generally accepted poetical way of expression that calls the apprehension | that is achieved in a state of intense and passionate love for Him, may He be exalted, *a kiss,* in accordance with its dictum: *Let him kiss me with the kisses of his mouth, and so on.*[50] [The Sages], *may their memory be blessed,* mention the occurrence of this kind of death, which in true reality is salvation from death, only with regard to *Moses, Aaron, and Miriam.* The other prophets and excellent men are beneath this degree; but it holds good for all of them that the apprehension of their intellects becomes stronger at the separation, just as it is said: *And thy righteousness shall go before thee; the glory of the Lord shall be at thy rear.*[51] After having reached this condition of enduring permanence, that intellect remains in one and the same state, the impediment that sometimes screened him off having been removed. And he will remain permanently in that state of intense pleasure, which does not belong to the genus of bodily pleasures, as we have explained in our compilations and as others have explained before us.

Bring your soul to understand this chapter, and direct your efforts to the multiplying of those times[52] in which you are with God or endeavoring to approach Him and to decreasing those times in which you are with other than He and in which you make no efforts to approach Him. This guidance is sufficient in view of the purpose of this Treatise.

47. B.T., Baba Bathra, 17a.   48. Deut. 34:5.   49. Num. 33:38.
50. Song of Songs 1:2.   51. Isa. 58:8.   52. Or: moments.

CHAPTER 52

Man does not sit, move, and occupy himself when he is alone in his house, as he sits, moves, and occupies himself when he is in the presence of a great king; nor does he speak and rejoice while he is with his family and relatives, as he speaks in the king's council. Therefore he who chooses to achieve human perfection and to be in true reality *a man of God* must give heed and know | that the great king who always accompanies him and cleaves to him is greater than any human individual, even if the latter be *David* and *Solomon*. This king who cleaves to him and accompanies him is the intellect that overflows toward us and is the bond between us and Him, may He be exalted. Just as we apprehend Him by means of that light which He caused to overflow toward us — as it says, *In Thy light do we see light*[1] — so does He by means of this selfsame light examine us; and because of it, He, may He be exalted, is constantly with us, examining from on high: *Can any hide himself in secret places that I shall not see him?*[2] Understand this well. Know that when perfect men understand this, they achieve such humility, such awe and fear of God, such reverence and such shame before Him, may He be exalted — and this in ways that pertain to true reality, not to imagination — that their secret conduct with their wives and in latrines is like their public conduct with other people. This, as you will find, was the way of our most renowned Sages with their wives: *One uncovers a handbreadth and covers up a handbreadth*.[3] They also said: *Who is modest? Whoever behaves by night as he behaves by day*.[4] You know already that they forbade[5] *walking about with an erect carriage because* [of the biblical dictum,] *The whole earth is full of His glory;*[6] all this being intended firmly to establish the notion that I have mentioned to you, that we are always before Him, may He be exalted, and walk about to and fro while His Indwelling is with us. And the greatest among the *Sages, may their memory be blessed*, avoided uncovering their heads, because man is covered about by the *Indwelling*. They also spoke little for this reason. We have already given in [the Commentary on] *Aboth*[7] the explanation that was needed concerning the habit of speaking but little: *For God is in heaven and thou upon the earth; therefore let thy words be few*.[8]

This purpose to which I have drawn your attention is the purpose of all the actions prescribed by the Law. | For it is by all the particulars of the

1. Ps. 36:10.   2. Jer. 23:24.   3. B.T., Nedarim, 20a–b.
4. B.T., Berakhoth, 62a.   5. B.T., Qiddushin, 31a.   6. Isa. 6:3.
7. *Commentary on the Mishnah*, Aboth, I 17.   8. Eccles. 5:1.

25

actions and through their repetition that some excellent men obtain such training that they achieve human perfection, so that they fear, and are in dread and in awe of, God, may He be exalted, and know who it is that is with them and as a result act subsequently as they ought to. He, may He be exalted, has explained that the end of the actions prescribed by the whole Law is to bring about the passion of which it is correct that it be brought about, as we have demonstrated in this chapter for the benefit of those who know the true realities. I refer to the fear of Him, may He be exalted, and the awe before His command. It says: *If thou wilt not take care to observe all the words of this Law that are written in this book, that thou mayest fear this glorious and fearful Name, the Lord thy God.*[9] Consider how it is explicitly stated for your benefit that the intention of *all the words of this Law* is one end, namely, *that thou mayest fear the Name, and so on.* The fact that this end is achieved through actions, you can learn from its dictum in this *verse: If thou wilt not take care to observe.* For it has already been made clear that this refers to actions prescribed by *commandments and prohibitions.* As for the opinions that the *Torah* teaches us—namely, the apprehension of His being and His unity, may He be exalted—these opinions teach us *love*, as we have explained several times. You know to what extent the *Torah* lays stress upon *love: With all thy heart, and with all thy soul, and with all thy might.*[10] For these two ends, namely, *love* and *fear*, are achieved through two things: *love* through the opinions taught by the Law, which include the apprehension of His being as He, may He be exalted, is in truth; while *fear* is achieved by means of all actions prescribed by the Law, as we have explained. Understand this summary. |

CHAPTER 53

This chapter includes an interpretation of the meaning of three terms that we have need of interpreting: namely, *ḥesed [loving-kindness]*, *mishpat [judgment]*, and *ṣedaqah [righteousness]*.

We have already explained in the Commentary on *Aboth*[1] that the meaning of *ḥesed* is excess in whatever matter excess is practiced. In most cases, however, it is applied to excess in beneficence. Now it is known that

9. Deut. 28:58.   10. Deut. 6:5.
1 *Commentary on the Mishnah*, Aboth, V 6, and II 10.

beneficence includes two notions, one of them consisting in the exercise of beneficence toward one who has no right at all to claim this from you, and the other consisting in the exercise of beneficence toward one who deserves it, but in a greater measure than he deserves it. In most cases the prophetic books use the word *hesed* in the sense of practicing beneficence toward one who has no right at all to claim this from you. Therefore every benefit that comes from Him, may He be exalted, is called *hesed*. Thus it says: *I will make mention of the loving-kindnesses [hasdei] of the Lord.*[2] Hence this reality as a whole — I mean that He, may He be exalted, has brought it into being — is *hesed*. Thus it says: *The world is built up in loving-kindness [hesed];*[3] the meaning of which is: *the building-up of the world is loving-kindness.* And He, may He be exalted, says in an enumeration of *His attributes: And abundant in loving-kindness.*[4]

The word *sedaqah* is derived from *sedeq*, which means justice; justice being the granting to everyone who has a right to something, that which he has a right to and giving to every being that which corresponds to his merits. But in the books of the prophets, fulfilling the duties imposed upon you with regard to others is not called *sedaqah* in conformity with the first sense. For if you give a hired man his wages or pay a debt, this is not called *sedaqah*. On the other hand, the fulfilling of duties with regard to others imposed upon you on account of moral virtue, such as remedying the injuries of all those who are injured, is called *sedaqah*. Therefore it says with reference to the returning | of a pledge:[5] *And it shall be sedaqah unto you.*[6] For when you walk in the way of the moral virtues, you do justice unto your rational soul, giving her the due that is her right. And because every moral virtue is called *sedaqah*, it says: *And he believed in the Lord, and it was accounted to him as sedaqah.*[7] I refer to the virtue of faith. This applies likewise to his dictum, may he be exalted: *And it shall be sedaqah unto us if we take care to observe, and so on.*[8]

As for the word *mishpat*, it means judgment concerning what ought to be done to one who is judged, whether in the way of conferring a benefit or of punishment.

Thus it has been summarized that *hesed* is applied to beneficence taken absolutely; *sedaqah*, to every good action performed by you because of a moral virtue with which you perfect your soul; and *mishpat* sometimes has as its consequence punishment and sometimes the conferring of a benefit.

2. Isa. 63:7.   3. Ps. 89:3. In the English Bible: *For ever is mercy built.*
4. Exod. 34:6.   5. To the poor.   6. Deut. 24:13.   7. Gen. 15:6.
8. Deut. 6:25.

When refuting the doctrine of divine attributes, we have already explained that every attribute by which God is described in the books of the prophets is an attribute of action.[9] Accordingly He is described as *ḥasid* [*one possessing loving-kindness*][10] because He has brought the all into being; as *ṣaddiq* [*righteous*][11] because of His mercy toward the weak — I refer to the governance of the living being by means of its forces; and as *Judge*[12] because of the occurrence in the world of relative good things and of relative great calamities, necessitated by judgment that is consequent upon wisdom.[13] The *Torah* uses all three terms: *Shall the Judge of all the earth;*[14] *Ṣaddiq* [*righteous*] *and upright is He;*[15] *And abundant in ḥesed* [*loving-kindness*].[16] In interpreting the meaning of these terms, it was our purpose to prepare the way for the chapter that we shall bring after this one.

CHAPTER 54

The term *wisdom* [*hokhmah*] is applied in Hebrew in four senses. | It is applied to the apprehension of true realities, which have for their end the apprehension of Him, may He be exalted. It says: *But wisdom, where shall it be found? and so on.*[1] It says: *If thou seek her as silver, and so on.*[2] This usage is frequent. The term is applied to acquiring arts, whatever the art might be: *And every wise-hearted among you;*[3] *And all the women that were wise-hearted.*[4] It is applied to acquiring moral virtues: *And teach his elders wisdom;*[5] *Is wisdom with aged men?*[6] — for the thing that is acquired through mere old age is a disposition to achieve moral virtues. It is applied to the aptitude for stratagems and ruses: *Come, let us deal wisely with them.*[7] According to this meaning it says: *And fetched thence a wise woman,*[8] meaning thereby that she had an aptitude for stratagems and ruses. In this sense it is said: *They are wise to do evil.*[9] It is possible that the

9. Cf. I 53 and 54.
10. A word deriving from the same verbal root as *ḥesed.*
11. A word deriving from the same verbal root as *ṣedaqah.*
12. *Shophet,* a word deriving from the same verbal root as *misphat.*
13. The Arabic word for "judgment" (*ḥukm*) derives from the same verbal root as the Arabic word for "wisdom" (*ḥikma*).
14. Gen. 18:25.   15. Deut. 32:4.   16. Exod. 34:6.
1. Job 28:12.   2. Prov. 2:4.   3. Exod. 35:10.   4. Exod. 35:25.
5. Ps. 105:22.   6. Job 12:12.   7. Exod. 1:10.   8. II Sam. 14:2.
9. Jer. 4:22.

meaning of *wisdom* in Hebrew indicates aptitude for stratagems and the application of thought in such a way that the stratagems and ruses may be used in achieving either rational or moral virtues, or in achieving skill in a practical art, or in working evil and wickedness. It has accordingly become plain that the term *wise* can be applied to one possessing the rational virtues, to one possessing the moral virtues, to everyone skilled in a practical art, and to one possessing ruses in working evil and wickedness. According to this explanation, one who knows the whole of the Law in its true reality is called *wise* in two respects: in respect of the rational virtues comprised in the Law and in respect of the moral virtues included in it. But since the rational matter in the Law is received through tradition and is not demonstrated by the methods of speculation, the knowledge of the Law came to be set up in the books of the prophets and the sayings of the *Sages* as one separate species and wisdom,[10] in an unrestricted sense, as another species. It is through this wisdom, in an unrestricted sense, that | the rational matter that we receive from the Law through tradition, is demonstrated. All the texts that you find in the [scriptural] books that extol wisdom and speak of its wonder[11] and of the rarity of those who acquire it — *Not many are wise;*[12] *But wisdom, where shall it be found? and so on;*[13] and many other texts of this kind — treat of that wisdom which teaches us to demonstrate the opinions of the *Torah*. This is also frequent in the sayings of the *Sages, may their memory be blessed;* I mean that they set up the knowledge of the *Torah* as one separate species and wisdom as another species. They, *may their memory be blessed,* say of *Moses our Master: He was father in wisdom, father in the Torah, father among the prophets.*[14] And with reference to its dictum concerning *Solomon, And he was wiser than all men,*[15] they say: *Not [wiser] than Moses;*[16] for the dictum, *than all men,* means: than his contemporaries. Therefore you will find that it mentions *Heman and Khalkol and Darda, the sons of Mahol,*[17] who were celebrated then as wise men. The *Sages, may their memory be blessed,* mention likewise that man is required first to obtain knowledge of the *Torah,* then to obtain wisdom, then to know what is incumbent upon him with regard to the legal science of the Law — I mean the drawing of inferences concerning what one ought to do. And this should be the order observed: The opinions in question should first be known as

10. It is not quite clear whether Maimonides uses here the Hebrew word *ḥokhmah* or the Arabic word *ḥikma,* spelled in the same way. The Arabic word also connotes "philosophy." The Hebrew word may also have this connotation, and if Maimonides used it here, he undoubtedly had this connotation in mind.
11. Or: its strangeness.   12. Job 32:9.   13. Job 28:12.   14. B.T., Megillah, 13a.
15. I Kings 5:11.   16. B.T., Rosh Hashanah, 21b.   17. I Kings 5:11.

being received through tradition; then they should be demonstrated; then the actions through which one's way of life may be ennobled, should be precisely defined. This is what they, *may their memory be blessed*, literally say regarding man's being required to give an account with respect to these three matters in this order. They say: *When man comes to judgment, he is first asked: Have you fixed certain seasons for the study of the Torah? Have you ratiocinated concerning wisdom? Have you inferred one thing from another?*[18] It has thus become clear to you that, according to them, the science of the *Torah* is one species and wisdom is a different species, being the verification of the opinions of the *Torah* through correct speculation. After we have made all these preliminary remarks, hear what we shall say:

The ancient | and the modern philosophers have made it clear that the perfections to be found in man consist of four species. The first and the most defective, but with a view to which the people of the earth spend their lives,[19] is the perfection of possessions — that is, of what belongs to the individual in the manner of money, garments, tools, slaves, land, and other things of this kind. A man's being a great king also belongs to this species of perfection. Between this perfection and the individual himself there is no union whatever; there is only a certain relation, and most of the pleasure taken in the relation is purely imaginary. I refer to one's saying: This is my house; this is my slave; this money is mine; these are my soldiers. For if he considers his own individual self, he will find that all this is outside his self and that each of these possessions subsists as it is by itself. Therefore when the relation referred to has been abolished, there is no difference between an individual who has been a great king and the most contemptible of men, though nothing may have changed in any of the things that were attributed to him. The philosophers have explained that the endeavor and the efforts directed by man toward this kind of perfection are nothing but an effort with a view to something purely imaginary, to a thing that has no permanence. And even if these possessions should remain with him permanently during the whole of his life, he would by no means thereby achieve perfection in his self.

The second species has a greater connection than the first with the individual's self, being the perfection of the bodily constitution and shape — I refer to that individual's temperament being most harmonious, his limbs well proportioned and strong as they ought to be. Neither should this species of perfection be taken as an end, for it is a corporeal perfection and does not belong to man qua man, but qua animal; for man has this in common with

18. B.T., Shabbath, 31a.   19. Or: mutually destroy each other.

the lowest animals. Moreover even if the strength of a human individual reached its greatest | maximum,[20] it would not attain the strength of a strong mule, and still less the strength of a lion or an elephant. The end of this perfection consists, as we have mentioned, in man's transporting a heavy burden or breaking a thick bone and in other things of this kind, from which no great utility for the body may be derived. Utility for the soul is absent from this species of perfection.

The third species is a perfection that to a greater extent than the second species subsists in the individual's self. This is the perfection of the moral virtues. It consists in the individual's moral habits having attained their ultimate excellence.[21] Most of the *commandments* serve no other end than the attainment of this species of perfection. But this species of perfection is likewise a preparation for something else and not an end in itself. For all moral habits are concerned with what occurs between a human individual and someone else. This perfection regarding moral habits is, as it were, only the disposition to be useful to people; consequently it is an instrument for someone else. For if you suppose a human individual is alone, acting on no one, you will find that all his moral virtues are in vain and without employment and unneeded, and that they do not perfect the individual in anything; for he only needs them and they again become useful to him in regard to someone else.

The fourth species is the true human perfection; it consists in the acquisition of the rational virtues — I refer to the conception of intelligibles, which teach true opinions concerning the divine things. This is in true reality the ultimate end; this is what gives the individual true perfection, a perfection belonging to him alone; and it gives him permanent perdurance; through it man is man. If you consider each of the three perfections mentioned before, you will find that they pertain to others than you, not to you, even though, according to the generally accepted opinion, they inevitably | pertain both to you and to others. This ultimate perfection, however, pertains to you alone, no one else being associated in it with you in any way: *They shall be only thine own, and so on.*[22] Therefore you ought to desire to achieve this thing, which will remain permanently with you, and not weary and trouble yourself for the sake of others, O you who neglect your own soul so that its whiteness has turned into blackness through the

20. Literally: finality and end.
21. The Arabic word *faḍīla*, translated "excellence," is the singular of the word translated in the preceding sentence as "virtues."
22. Prov. 5:17.

corporeal faculties having gained dominion over it—as is said in the beginning of the poetical parables that have been coined for these notions; it says: *My mother's sons were incensed against me; they made me keeper of the vineyards; but mine own vineyard have I not kept.*[23] It says on this very same subject: *Lest thou give thy splendor unto others, and thy years unto the cruel.*[24]

The prophets too have explained to us and interpreted to us the self-same notions—just as the philosophers have interpreted them—clearly stating to us that neither the perfection of possession nor the perfection of health nor the perfection of moral habits is a perfection of which one should be proud or that one should desire; the perfection of which one should be proud and that one should desire is knowledge of Him, may He be exalted, which is the true science. *Jeremiah* says concerning these four perfections: *Thus saith the Lord: Let not the wise man glory in his wisdom, neither let the mighty man glory in his might, let not the rich man glory in his riches; but let him that glorieth glory in this, that he understandeth and knoweth Me.*[25] Consider how he mentioned them according to the order given them in the opinion of the multitude. For the greatest perfection in their opinion is that of *the rich man in his riches,* below him *the mighty man in his might,* and below him *the wise man in his wisdom.* [By the expression, "the wise man in his wisdom,"] he means him who possesses the moral virtues; for such an individual is also held in high esteem by the multitude, to whom the discourse in question is addressed. Therefore these perfections are arranged in this order. The *Sages, may their memory be blessed,* apprehended from this *verse* the | very notions we have mentioned and have explicitly stated that which I have explained to you in this chapter: namely, that the term *wisdom* [*hokhmah*], used in an unrestricted sense and regarded as the end, means in every place the apprehension of Him, may He be exalted; that the possession of the treasures acquired, and competed for, by man and thought to be perfection are not a perfection; and that similarly all the actions prescribed by the Law—I refer to the various species of worship and also the moral habits that are useful to all people in their mutual dealings—that all this is not to be compared with this ultimate end and does not equal it, being but preparations made for the sake of this end. Hear verbatim a text of theirs dealing with all these notions; it is a text in *Bereshith Rabbah.* It is said there: *One scriptural dictum says: And all things desirable are not to be compared unto her.*[26] *Another scriptural dictum says: And all things thou canst desire are not to be compared unto her.*[27] The

23. Song of Songs 1:6.   24. Prov. 5:9.   25. Jer. 9:22–23.   26. Prov. 8:11.
27. Prov. 3:15.

expression, things desirable, refers to commandments and good actions; while,
things thou canst desire, refers to precious stone and pearls. Neither things
desirable nor things thou canst desire are to be compared unto her, but let him
that glorieth glory in this, that he understandeth and knoweth Me.[28] Consider
how concise is this saying, how perfect is he who said it, and how he left
out nothing of all that we have mentioned and that we have interpreted and
led up to at length.

As we have mentioned this *verse* and the wondrous notions contained
in it, and as we have mentioned the saying of the *Sages, may their memory*
be blessed, about it, we will complete the exposition of what it includes. For
when explaining in this *verse* the noblest ends, he does not limit them only
to the apprehension of Him, may He be exalted. For if this were his purpose,
he would have said: *But let him that glorieth glory in this, that he under-*
standeth and knoweth Me, and have stopped there; or he would have said:
that he understandeth and knoweth Me that I am One; or he would have
said: *that I have no figure,* or *that | there is none like Me,* or something
similar. But he says that one should glory in the apprehension of Myself
and in the knowledge of My attributes, by which he means His actions, as
we have made clear[29] with reference to its dictum: *Show me now Thy ways,*
and so on.[30] In this *verse*[31] he makes it clear to us that those actions that
ought to be known and imitated are *loving-kindness, judgment,* and *righteous-*
ness. He adds another corroborative notion through saying, *in the earth*[32] —
this being a pivot of the Law. For matters are not as the overbold opine who
think that His providence, may He be exalted, terminates at the sphere of
the moon and that the earth and that which is in it are neglected: *The Lord*
hath forsaken the earth.[33] Rather is it as has been made clear to us by the
Master of those who know: *That the earth is the Lord's.*[34] He means to say
that His providence also extends over the earth in the way that corresponds
to what the latter is, just as His providence extends over the heavens[35] in
the way that corresponds to what they are. This is what he says: *That I am*
the Lord who exercise loving-kindness, judgment, and righteousness, in the
earth.[36] Then he completes the notion by saying: *For in these things I delight,*
saith the Lord.[37] He means that it is My purpose that there should come
from you *loving-kindness, righteousness, and judgment in the earth* in the
way we have explained[38] with regard to the *thirteen attributes:* namely, that
the purpose should be assimilation to them and that this should be our way
of life. Thus the end that he sets forth in this *verse* may be stated as follows:

28. Genesis Rabbah, XXXV *in fine.*   29. Cf. I 54.   30. Exod. 33:13.
31. Jer. 9:23 is referred to.   32. Jer. 9:23.   33. Ezek. 9:9.   34. Exod. 9:29.
35. In the singular in Arabic.   36. Jer. 9:23.   37. Jer. 9:23.   38. Cf. I 54.

It is clear that the perfection of man that may truly be gloried in is the one acquired by him who has achieved, in a measure corresponding to his capacity, apprehension of Him, may He be exalted, and who knows His providence extending over His creatures as manifested in the act of bringing them into being and in their governance as it is. The way of life of such an individual, after he has achieved this apprehension, will always have in view *loving-kindness, righteousness,* and *judgment,* through assimilation to His actions, may He be exalted, just as we have explained several times in this Treatise. |

This is the extent of what I thought fit that we should set down in this Treatise; it is a part of what I consider very useful to those like you. I hope for you that through sufficient reflection you will grasp all the intentions I have included therein, with the help of God, may He be exalted; and that He will grant us *and all [the people of] Israel, being fellows,* that which He has promised us: *Then the eyes of the blind shall be opened, and the ears of the deaf shall be unstopped.*[39] *The people that walked in darkness have seen a great light; they that dwelt in the land of the shadow of death, upon them hath the light shined.*[40]

AMEN

God is very near to everyone who calls,
If he calls truly and has no distractions;
He is found by every seeker who searches for Him,
If he marches toward Him and goes not astray.

*

The Third Part

HAS BEEN COMPLETED WITH THE HELP OF GOD

AND WITH ITS COMPLETION THERE HAS BEEN COMPLETED

THE GUIDE OF THE PERPLEXED

---

9. Isa. 35:5.   40. Isa. 9:1.

GLOSSARY

*

ABILITY TO ACT *istiṭāʿa*

ACCIDENT *ʿaraḍ*

ACT, ACTUALITY *fiʿl*

ADMISSIBILITY *tajwīz*

AFFECTION *infiʿāl*

AFFIRMATION (*see* AVER) *taṣdīq; ījāb*

AGENT (*see* EFFICIENT CAUSE; MAKER) *fāʿil*

AMPHIBOLOUS *mushakkak*

ANALOGY (*see* REASONING; SYLLOGISM) *qiyās*

APTITUDE (*see* DISPOSITION) *hayʾa*

APPREHEND (*see* GRASP) *adraka*

APPREHENSION *idrāk*

ARTIFICER *ṣāniʿ*

ASSERT (*see* ESTABLISH) *athbata*

ATOM (*see* SUBSTANCE) *jawhar, jawhar fard; juzʾ* (literal meaning "part") *juzʾ lā yatajazzaʾu*

ATTRIBUTE *ṣifa*

ATTRIBUTE, AFFIRMATIVE; ATTRIBUTE OF AFFIRMATION *ṣifat al-ījāb*

ATTRIBUTE, ESSENTIAL *ṣifa dhātiyya*

ATTRIBUTE OF NEGATION *ṣifat al-salb*

ATTRIBUTE, NEGATIVE *ṣifa salbiyya*

AVER (*see* AFFIRMATION) *ṣaddaqa*

BEGINNING (*see* PRINCIPLE) *mabdaʾ*

BEING (*see* EXISTENCE) *wujūd*

BELIEF *iʿtiqād*

BRINGER OF THE NOMOS (*see* LEGISLATOR) *wāḍiʿ al-nāmūs*

CENTER *markaz*

CERTAINTY; CERTAIN KNOWLEDGE *yaqīn*

CHAPTER *faṣl*

CHARACTER (*see* MORAL QUALITIES) *khulq*

CHARACTERISTIC (*see* MEANING; NOTION) *maʿnā*

CITY *madīna*

COMING-INTO-BEING (*see* CREATION IN TIME; GENERATION) *kawn; ḥudūth*

COMMAND (*see* MATTER; ORDER) *amr*

COMMUNITY; RELIGIOUS COMMUNITY *milla*

COMPOSITION *tarkīb*

CORPOREALITY (DOCTRINE OF) *jismāniyya; tajsīm*

CORRELATION *iḍāfa*

CORRUPTION (*see* PASSING-AWAY) *fasād*

CREATED IN TIME *muḥdath*

CREATION IN TIME (*see* COMING-INTO-BEING) *ḥudūth*

DEFINITION *ḥadd*

DEITY *ilāh*

DEMONSTRATION *burhān*

DERIVATIVE (*see* FIGURATIVE MEANING) *mustaʿār*

DISPOSITION *hay⁾a; istiᶜdād*

DISPOSITION, NATURAL *jibilla*

DISTANCE *masāfa*

DIVINE (*see* METAPHYSICAL) *ilāhī*

DIVINE SCIENCE *ᶜilm ilāhī*

ECCENTRIC SPHERE *falak khārij al-markaz*

EFFICIENT CAUSE (*see* AGENT; MAKER) *fāᶜil*

ELITE (*see* PROPERTY) *khāṣṣa*

END (FINAL) (*see* FINALITY) *ghāya*

EPICYCLE *falak tadwīr*

EQUIVOCAL *mushtarik*

ESSENCE (*see* QUIDDITY) *dhāt; māhiyya*

ESTABLISH; ESTABLISH THE TRUTH OF (*see* ASSERT) *athbata*

ETERNAL (*see* PRE-ETERNAL) *qadīm*

EXISTENCE; THAT WHICH EXISTS (*see* BEING) *wujūd*

FACULTY (*see* FORCE; POTENTIALITY) *quwwa*

FACULTY, RATIONAL *quwwa nāṭiqa*

FANTASY *wahm*

PRODUCE THE FANTASY (*see* SUGGEST TO THE ESTIMATIVE FACULTY) *awhama*

FIGURATIVE MEANING (*see* DERIVATIVE) *istiᶜāra*

FINALITY (*see* END) *ghāya*

FORCE (*see* FACULTY; POTENTIALITY) *quwwa*

GENERATION (*see* COMING-INTO-BEING) *kawn*

GENUS *jins*

GOD *allāh*

GOVERNANCE *tadbīr*

GRACE *luṭf*

GRACIOUSNESS, WILY *talaṭṭuf*

GRASP (*see* APPREHEND) *adraka*

GUIDE *dalāla*

HABIT; HABITUS *malaka*

HABIT (with reference to the doctrines held by the Mutakallimūn) *ᶜāda*

HIDDEN (*see* INNER; INTERNAL) *bāṭin*

IMAGINATION *khayāl; takhayyul*

IMAGINING, VAIN *khayāl*

INDIVIDUAL *shakhṣ*

INDWELLING *sakīna*

INFIDELITY *kufr*

INFINITE *mā lā nihāya lahu*

INNER CONTENT (*see* HIDDEN; INTERNAL MEANING) *bāṭin*

INSTANT ("NOW") *ān*

INTELLECT *ᶜaql*

INTELLECT, ACQUIRED *ᶜaql mustafād*

INTELLECT, ACTIVE *ᶜaql faᶜᶜāl*

INTELLECTUALLY COGNIZED OBJECT (*see* INTELLIGIBLE) *maᶜqūl*

INTELLECTUALLY COGNIZING SUBJECT *ᶜāqil*

INTELLIGIBLE (*see* INTELLECTUALLY COGNIZED OBJECT) *maᶜqūl*

INTERNAL MEANING (*see* HIDDEN; INNER CONTENT) *bāṭin*

LAW *sharīᶜa*

LEGAL COMPILATION *ta⁾līf fiqh*

LEGAL SCIENCE; LEGALISTIC STUDY *fiqh*

LEGISLATOR (*see* BRINGER OF THE NOMOS) *wāḍiᶜ al-nāmūs*

MAKER (*see* AGENT; EFFICIENT CAUSE) *fāᶜil*

MATTER (1) *shay⁾; amr*

MATTER (2) *mādda*

MEANING (*see* CHARACTERISTIC; NOTION; THING) *maᶜnā*

METAPHYSICAL (*see* DIVINE) *ilāhī*

MIND *dhihn*

MODE *ḥāl*

MORAL QUALITIES (*see* CHARACTER) *akhlāq*

MULTITUDE *jumhūr*

NATION *umma*

NOMOS   *nāmūs; sharī͑a nāmūsiyya*
NONBEING; NONEXISTENCE (*see* PRIVA-
    TION) *͑adam*
NOTION (*see* CHARACTERISTIC; MEAN-
    ING; THING) *ma͑nā*
ONENESS   *waḥda; waḥdāniyya*
ORDER (*see* COMMAND; MATTER) *amr*
OVERFLOW   *fayḍ*
PARABLE   *mathal*
PART; PARTICLE (*see* ATOM) *juz͗*
PART OF THE BODY   *͑aḍw*
PARTICULARIZATION   *takhṣīṣ*
PARTICULARIZE (*see* PROPRIUM; PRO-
    VIDE) *khaṣṣaṣa*
PASSING-AWAY   (*see*   CORRUPTION)
    fasād, fanā͗
PERPLEXED   *ḥā͗ir*
PLACE (*see* SPACE) *makān*
PLACE, NATURAL   *mawḍi͑ ṭabī͑ī*
POTENTIALITY (*see* FACULTY; FORCE)
    quwwa
PRE-ETERNAL   *qadīm*
PREMISE; PRIMARY PROPOSITION   *mu-
    qaddima*
PRINCIPLE (*see* BEGINNING)   *mabda͗*
PRIVATION (*see* NONBEING) *͑adam*
PROPERTY (*see* ELITE) *khāṣṣa*
PROPHET   *nabiyy*
PROPRIUM, PROVIDE WITH   *khaṣṣaṣa*
PROVIDENCE   *͑ināya*

QUIDDITY (*see* ESSENCE) *māhiyya*
REASONING (*see* ANALOGY; SYLLOGISM)
    qiyās
RELATION   *nisba*
RELIGION   *dīn*
REPRESENTATION   *taṣawwur*
RIDDLE   *laghz*
SOVEREIGN   *sulṭān*
SPACE (*see* PLACE)   *makān; bu͑d*
SPECIES   *naw͑*
SPECULATION   *naẓar*
SPHERE   *falak; kurra*
SUBSTANCE   *jawhar*
SUBSTRATUM   *maḥall; mawḍū͑*
SUBSTRATUM, SERVE AS A   *ḥamala*
SUGGEST TO THE ESTIMATIVE FACULTY
    (*see* PRODUCE THE FANTASY)
    awhama
SYLLOGISM (*see* ANALOGY; REASONING)
    qiyās
TEMPERAMENT   *mizāj*
THING (*see* CHARACTERISTIC; MEANING;
    NOTION) *shay͗; amr; ma͑nā*
TIME   *zamān*
TREATISE   *maqāla*
TRUE REALITY   *ḥaqīqa*
UNIVERSALS (*see* MEANING; NOTION)
    ma͑ānī kulliyya
VACUUM   *khalā͗*

INDEXES

BIBLICAL PASSAGES APPEARING IN THE TEXT

*

GENESIS

1:1, *349, 350, 352, 358, 438*
1:2, *90, 260, 350, 351, 352*
1:4, *352*
1:5, *349, 351*
1:7, *352*
1:8, *349, 352*
1:10, *28, 351, 352*
1:11, *354*
1:17, *352, 454*
1:18, *261, 454*
1:20, *352*
1:22, *611*
1:26, *21, 22, 262*
1:27, *22, 355*
1:28, *454*
1:30, *91*
1:31, *124, 440, 453, 503, 506*
2:1, *355*
2:2, *161*
2:4, *358*
2:5, *354*
2:6, *354*
2:7, *358*
2:15, *357*
2:16, *24*
2:19, *358*
2:20, *357*
2:21, *355*
2:23, *356*
2:24, *356*
3:2, *265*
3:5, *23, 25*
3:6, *25*
3:7, *25*
3:8, *54*
3:16, *62, 433*

GENESIS

3:18, *26*
3:19, *26*
3:23, *26*
3:24, *7, 108*
4:7, *489*
4:8, *357*
4:25, *357*
5:3, *32*
6:2, *40*
6:3, *40*
6:5, *108*
6:6, *62*
6:12, *108*
6:13, *386*
7:2, *31*
7:15, *90*
7:17, *46*
8:5, *53*
8:15, *386*
8:21, *62, 489*
8:22, *334*
9:3, *92*
11:5, *37*
11:7, *37, 262*
12:1, *386*
12:3, *515*
12:5, *154*
12:11, *609*
12:17, *147*
14:13, *55*
14:19, *358*
14:22, *282, 358*
14:23, *614*
15:1, *28, 87, 385, 386, 399, 405, 475*
15:4, *401*
15:5, *28, 404, 405*

GENESIS

15:6, *631*
15:12, *48, 385, 402*
15:13, *385*
15:17, *48, 51*
16:7, *95, 390*
16:9, *576*
16:10, *576*
16:11, *576*
17:7, *610*
17:22, *37*
18:1, *28, 389*
18:2, *265*
18:3, *147, 389*
18:8, *39*
18:19, *379, 502, 624*
18:21, *37, 57*
18:22, *86*
18:23, *44*
18:25, *632*
19:17, *28*
19:21, *266*
19:22, *266*
19:23, *52*
19:26, *28*
20:3, *387*
20:11, *387*
21:19, *25*
21:33, *3, 235, 282, 358, 415, 516*
22:1, *471*
22:8, *108*
22:11, *386*
22:12, *498, 501*
22:15, *386, 576*
22:21, *486*
23:8, *91*
23:17, *38*

DEUTERONOMY

28:9, 54
28:12, 408
28:30, 436
28:32, 373
28:39, 543
28:40, 543
28:42, 543
28:43, 36, 273
28:49, 96, 111
28:56, 499
28:58, 501, 630
28:69, 523
29:3, 89
29:5, 616
29:17, 88, 521
29:28, 380
30:6, 512
30:12, 380
30:15, 93
30:16, 512
30:20, 512
31:12, 592
31:17, 53, 626
31:18, 54, 626
31:29, 82
32:4, 42, 336, 448, 469,
    471, 498, 506, 605,
    632
32:5, 443
32:6, 236
32:13, 171
32:14, 408
32:15, 552
32:17, 587
32:18, 42
32:19, 82, 107
32:21, 82
32:22, 82
32:24, 543
32:30, 42
32:36, 107
32:47, 507, 508, 617
33:10, 551
33:16, 55
33:23, 46
33:26, 171, 175, 311
33:27, 172
33:29, 343
34:5, 628
34:10, 368
34:11, 368
34:12, 368

JOSHUA

1:5, 475
1:18, 96
3:7, 387
3:11, 358
3:13, 358
5:2, 42
5:8, 92
5:13, 389
5:14, 389
10:12, 368
10:13, 368
22:12, 565
22:16, 566
22:22, 566
24:2, 518
24:27, 160

JUDGES

2:1, 41, 262, 389
2:2, 517
2:4, 389
2:18, 397
5:4, 344, 437
7:2, 387
8:18, 21
10:16, 91
11:29, 397
13:6, 265
13:14, 601
13:17, 52
14:19, 397
21:22, 125

I SAMUEL

1:9, 37
1:18, 85
1:23, 38
2:2, 42
2:9, 476, 625
2:24, 48
2:35, 89, 91
3:7, 395
6:5, 22
11:6, 397
12:21, 518, 612
15:22, 530
16:13, 397
20:22, 411
20:34, 62
20:36, 48

I SAMUEL

22:8, 39
24:21, 39
25:9, 161
25:29, 91
25:37, 92
28:14, 21

II SAMUEL

2:23, 87
2:26, 63
14:2, 632
16:10, 411
16:12, 421
18:14, 88
21:10, 162
21:16, 158
23:1, 396
23:2, 90, 398
23:3, 399
24:11, 387

I KINGS

1:6, 62
3:5, 399
3:15, 399
5:11, 633
7:14, 46
9:2, 399
9:3, 89, 95
10:29, 174
11:11, 399
13:4, 361
13:33, 529
14:7, 46
16:2, 46
17:9, 411
17:17, 92
18:1, 387
18:26, 517
19:9, 387
22:19, 28, 401

II KINGS

5:26, 88
6:18, 361
8:4, 368
8:5, 368
10:15, 89
14:8, 86

RABBINIC PASSAGES APPEARING IN THE TEXT

*

TALMUD

MISHNAH

Aboth: I 1, *563*; II 1, *105*; II 17, *16*; III
    13, *600*; V 6, *161*; V 13–14, *124*
Baba Qamma: V 7, *609*
Bekhoroth: I 7, *553*
Berakhoth: V 3, *600*; IX 5, *489*
Ḥullin: IV 7, *549*
Middoth: III 4, *578*
Sota: I 7, *470*
Tamid: III 8, *580*
Yoma: III 3, *594*
Zebaḥim: V 8, *585*; XII 5, *597*

BABYLONIAN TALMUD

ᶜAbodah Zarah: 3a, *470*; 3b, *473*; 20b,
    608; 54b, *345*
Baba Bathra: 15a, *486*; 16a, *489*, *492*; 16b,
    492; 17a, *628*; 22a, *64*; 25a, *575*;
    116a, *322*
Baba Meṣiᶜa: 31b, *56, 62, 71, 100, 120, 140,
    453*; 32b, *473*
Baba Qamma: 38b, *470*; 50a, *470*; 87a,
    470
Berakhoth: 5a, *471*; 7a, *29*; 10b, *548*;
    18a–b, *93*; 22a, *549*; 25a, *598*; 33b,
    140, 141; 55b, *391*; 57b, *370*; 62a,
    629
ᶜErubin: 18b, *33*
Gittin: 60b, *176*
Ḥagigah: 11b, *6, 7, 70, 72*; 12a, *350*; 12b,
    172, 173, 268; 13a, *6, 69, 72, 78, 426,
    429, 486*; 13b, *427, 429*; 14a, *78, 176*;
    14b, *68, 353*; 15a, *39, 619*
Horayoth: 8a, *522*
Ḥullin: 13a, *85*; 60a, *355*; 77a, *544*; 82b,
    549; 90a, *407*; 136b, *549*; 142a, *512*

Kethuboth: 4b, *595*; 15a, *573*; 61a, *595*
Makkoth: 24a, *364*
Megillah: 7a, *398*; 13a, *633*
Menaḥoth: 109b, *151*
Nedarim: 20a, *629*; 20b, *629*; 38a, *362*
Pesaḥim: 49a, *434*; 56a, *548*; 94b, *267*;
    118a, *470*; 119a, *415*
Qiddushin: 21b, *567*; 30b, *608*; 31a, *470,
    629*; 39a, *548, 549*; 39b, *512*; 40a,
    522; 71a, *150, 151, 152*
Rosh Hashanah: 11a, *355*; 21b, *633*; 25a,
    406; 25b, *406*; 31a, *344*
Sanhedrin: 38b, *263*; 43b, *73*; 56b, *531*;
    97a, *344*; 99b, *613*
Shabbath: 30a, *19*; 30b, *372*; 31a, *634*;
    55a, *470, 498*; 67a, *543, 544*; 87b,
    531; 88b, *497*; 92a, *362*; 107b, *473*;
    119b, *490*; 146a, *357*; 149a, *622*;
    151b, *424*
Sota: 38a, *149*
Sukkah: 42b, *73*
Taᶜanith: 2a, *621*; 30b, *373*
Tamid: 2a, *407*
Yebamoth: 62b, *569*; 71a, *56, 62, 71, 100,
    120, 140, 453*; 103b, *357*; 104a, *103*
Yoma: 29a, *434*; 39b, *151*; 67b, *507*; 73b,
    398

JERUSALEM TALMUD

Berakhoth: IV, *416, 621*; XI, *357*
Kethuboth: VIII, *507*
Peᵓah: I, *507, 617*
Sanhedrin: I, *263*

MIDRASHIM

Genesis Rabbah: I, *344*; II, *260*; III, *349*;
    IV, *352, 353*; V, *345*; IX, *347, 440*;
    X, *162, 269, 270, 273, 332*; XII, *263*;
    XIII, *354*; XV, *357*; XVI, *357*; XVII,

SECTS, COMMUNITIES, AND NONBIBLICAL
WRITERS AND WRITINGS

*

DATE DUE